W9-BNB-620

DATE DUE

Chicago Public Library

Chicago Public Library
Oriole Park Branch
7454 W. Balmoral Ave.
Chicago, IL 60656

THE CHICAGO PUBLIC LIBRARY

ORIOLE PARK BRANCH
7454 W. BALMORAL
CHICAGO, IL 60656

DISCARD

VISUAL
dictionary

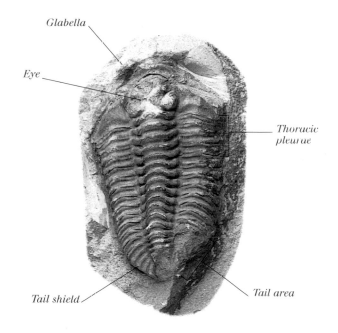

Glabella

Eye

Thoracic
pleurae

Tail shield

Tail area

PREHISTORIC TRILOBITE

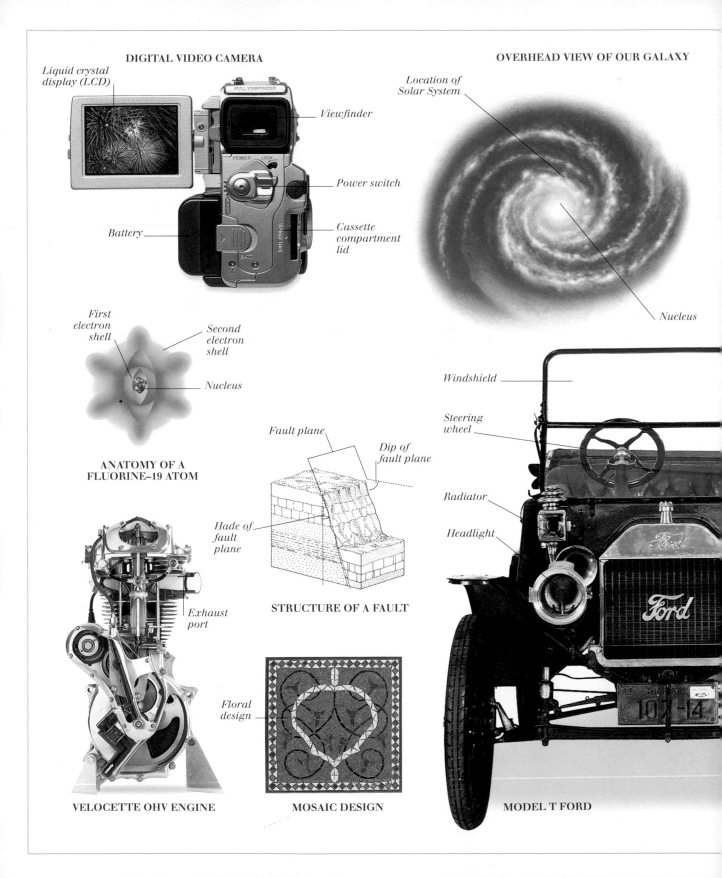

DIGITAL VIDEO CAMERA

Liquid crystal display (LCD)

Viewfinder

Power switch

Battery

Cassette compartment lid

OVERHEAD VIEW OF OUR GALAXY

Location of Solar System

Nucleus

First electron shell

Second electron shell

Nucleus

ANATOMY OF A FLUORINE–19 ATOM

Fault plane

Dip of fault plane

Hade of fault plane

STRUCTURE OF A FAULT

Windshield

Steering wheel

Radiator

Headlight

Exhaust port

VELOCETTE OHV ENGINE

Floral design

MOSAIC DESIGN

MODEL T FORD

VISUAL
dictionary

Pedicel (flower
stalk)

Sepal

Achene
(one-seeded
dry fruit)

Remains
of stigma
and style

STRAWBERRY

DK PUBLISHING

LONDON, NEW YORK, MUNICH, MELBOURNE, AND DELHI

Original Edition (*Ultimate Visual Dictionary*)
Project Art Editors Heather McCarry, Johnny Pau, Chris Walker, Kevin Williams
Designer Simon Murrell

Project Editors Luisa Caruso, Peter Jones, Jane Mason, Geoffrey Stalker
Editor Jo Evans

DTP Designer Zirrinia Austin
Picture Researcher Charlotte Bush

Managing Art Editor Toni Kay
Senior Editor Roger Tritton
Managing Editor Sean Moore

Production Manager Hilary Stephens

Anatomical And Botanical Models Supplied By Somso Modelle, Coburg, Germany

Revised Edition
Art Editor Hugh Schermuly
Designers Phil Gamble, Simon Oon, Pamela Shiels
Jacket Designer John Dinsdale
Project Editor Cathy Meeus
Editor Paul Docherty
Jacket Editor Beth Apple
Editorial Consultant Sarah Angliss
Senior Art Editor Ina Stradins
Senior Editor Angeles Gavira
Production Manager Elizabeth Cherry
Managing Art Editor Phil Ormerod
Category Publisher Jonathan Metcalf

First American edition published under the title
Ultimate Visual Dictionary, 1994
00 01 02 03 04 05 10 9 8 7 6 5 4 3 2 1

Revised edition published 2002 by
DK Publishing, Inc.
375 Hudson Street
New York, New York 10014

Copyright © 1994, 1996, 1999, 2000, 2002 Dorling Kindersley Limited

All rights reserved under International and Pan-American Copyright Conventions. No part of this publication may be reproduced, stored in a retrieval system, or transmitted in any form or by any means, electronic, mechanical, photocopying, recording, or otherwise, without the prior written permission of the copyright owner. Published in Great Britain by Dorling Kindersley Limited.

A Cataloging in Publication Record is available from the Library of Congress

ISBN 0-7894-8948-1

Reproduced by Colourscan, Singapore
Printed and bound by AGT, Spain
D.L. TO: 727 - 2002
See our complete product line at www.dk.com

RO3000 34492

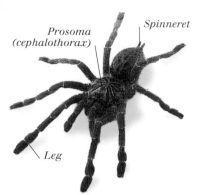

Prosoma (cephalothorax) — *Spinneret*

Leg

EXTERNAL FEATURES OF A SPIDER

Canopy — *Fin*

Super 2 · G-BNHB

Main landing gear

SIDE VIEW OF ARV SUPER 2 AIRPLANE

Barrel

Permanent black ink

FOUNTAIN PEN AND INK

Heat shield

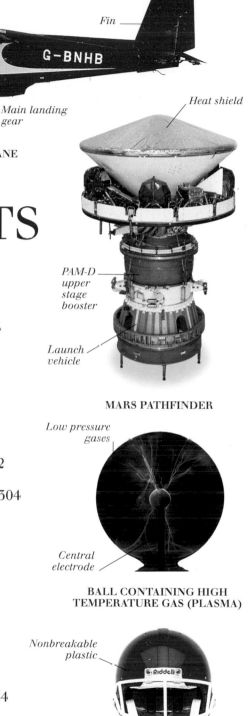

PAM-D upper stage booster

Launch vehicle

MARS PATHFINDER

CONTENTS

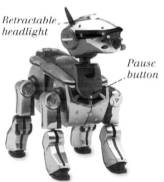

Retractable headlight

Pause button

SONY AIBO ROBOT DOG

Low pressure gases

BALL CONTAINING HIGH TEMPERATURE GAS (PLASMA)

Central electrode

Parallel bands

ONYX

Nonbreakable plastic

Riddell

Shock absorber

FOOTBALL HELMET

Oriole Park Branch
7454 W. Balmoral Ave.
Chicago, IL 60656

Introduction

THE VISUAL DICTIONARY is a completely new kind of reference book. It provides a link between pictures and words in a way that no ordinary dictionary ever has. Most dictionaries simply tell you what a word means, but the *VISUAL DICTIONARY* shows you—through a combination of detailed annotations, explicit photographs, and illustrations. In the *VISUAL DICTIONARY*, pictures define the annotations around them. You do not read definitions of the annotated words, you see them. The highly accessible format of the *VISUAL DICTIONARY*, the thoroughness of its annotations, and the range of its subject matter make it a unique and helpful reference tool.

How to use the VISUAL DICTIONARY

You will find the *VISUAL DICTIONARY* simple to use. Instead of being organized alphabetically, it is divided by subject into 14 sections—THE UNIVERSE, PREHISTORIC EARTH, PLANTS, ANIMALS, THE HUMAN BODY, etc. Each section begins with a table of contents listing the major entries within that section. For example, The Visual Arts section has entries on *Drawing, Tempera, Fresco, Oils, Watercolor, Pastels, Acrylics, Calligraphy, Printmaking, Mosaic,* and *Sculpture.* Every entry has a short introduction explaining the purpose of the photographs and illustrations, and the significance of the annotations.

If you know what something looks like, but don't know its name, find the term you need by turning to the annotations surrounding the pictures; if you know a word, but don't know what it refers to, use the comprehensive index to direct you to the appropriate page.

Suppose that you want to know what the bone at the end of your little finger is called. With a standard dictionary, you wouldn't know where to begin. But with the *VISUAL DICTIONARY* you simply turn to the entry called *Hands*—within THE HUMAN BODY section—where you will find four fully annotated, color photographs showing the skin, muscles, and bones of the human hand. In this entry you will quickly find that the bone you are searching for is called the distal phalanx, and for good measure you will discover that it is attached to the middle phalanx by the distal interphalangeal joint.

Perhaps you want to know what a catalytic converter looks like. If you look up "catalytic converter" in an ordinary dictionary, you will be told what it is and possibly what it does—but you will not be able to tell what shape it is or what it is made of. However, if you look up "catalytic converter" in the index of the *VISUAL DICTIONARY*, you will be directed to the *Modern engines* entry on page 344—where the introduction gives you basic information about what a catalytic converter is—and to page 350—where there is a spectacular exploded-view photograph of the mechanics of a Renault Clio. From these pages you will find out not only what a catalytic converter looks like, but also that it is attached at one end to an exhaust downpipe and at the other to a silencer.

Whatever it is that you want to find a name for, or whatever name you want to find a picture for, you will find it quickly and easily in the *VISUAL DICTIONARY*. Perhaps you need to know where the vamp on a shoe is; or how to tell obovate and lanceolate leaves apart; or what a spiral galaxy looks like; or whether birds have nostrils. With the *VISUAL DICTIONARY* at hand, the answers to each of these questions, and thousands more, are readily available.

The *VISUAL DICTIONARY* does not just tell you what the names of the different parts of an object are. The photographs, illustrations, and annotations are all specially arranged to help you understand which parts relate to one another and how objects function.

With the *VISUAL DICTIONARY* you can find in seconds the words or pictures that you are looking for; or you can simply browse through the pages of the book for your own pleasure. The *VISUAL DICTIONARY* is not intended to replace a standard dictionary or conventional encyclopedia, but is instead a stimulating and valuable companion to ordinary reference volumes. Giving you instant access to the language that is used by astronomers and architects, musicians and mechanics, scientists and sportspeople, it is the ideal reference book for specialists and generalists of all ages.

Sections of the VISUAL DICTIONARY

The 14 sections of the *VISUAL DICTIONARY* contain a total of more than 30,000 terms, encompassing a wide range of topics:

- In the first section, THE UNIVERSE, spectacular photographs and illustrations are used to show the names of the stars and planets and to explain the structure of solar systems, galaxies, nebulae, comets, and black holes.

- PREHISTORIC EARTH tells the story in annotations of how our own planet has evolved since its formation. It includes examples of prehistoric flora and fauna, and fascinating dinosaur models—some with parts of the body stripped away to show anatomical sections.

- PLANTS covers a huge range of species—from the familiar to the exotic. In addition to the color photographs of plants included in this section, there is a series of micrographic photographs illustrating plant details—such as pollen grains, spores, and cross-sections of stems and roots—in close-up.

- In the ANIMALS section, skeletons, anatomical diagrams, and different parts of animals' bodies have been meticulously annotated. This section provides a comprehensive guide to the vocabulary of zoological classification and animal physiology.

- The structure of the human body, its parts, and its systems are presented in THE HUMAN BODY. The section includes lifelike, three-dimensional models and the latest false-color images. Clear and authoritative annotations indicate the correct anatomical terms.

- GEOLOGY, GEOGRAPHY, AND METEOROLOGY describes the structure of the Earth—from the inner core to the exosphere—and the physical phenomena—such as volcanoes, rivers, glaciers, and climate—that shape its surface.

- PHYSICS AND CHEMISTRY is a visual journey through the fundamental principles underlying the physical universe, and provides the essential vocabulary of these sciences.

- In RAIL AND ROAD, a wide range of trains, trams and buses, cars, bicycles, and motorcycles are described. Exploded-view photographs show mechanical details with striking clarity.

- SEA AND AIR gives the names for hundreds of parts of ships and airplanes. The section includes civil and fighting craft, both historical and modern.

- THE VISUAL ARTS shows the equipment and materials used by painters, sculptors, printers, and other artists. Well-known compositions have been chosen to illustrate specific artistic techniques and effects.

- ARCHITECTURE includes photographs of exemplary architectural models and illustrates dozens of additional features such as columns, domes, and arches.

- MUSIC provides a visual introduction to the special language of music and musical instruments. It includes clearly annotated photographs of each of the major groups of traditional instruments—brass, woodwind, strings, and percussion—together with modern electronic instruments.

- The SPORTS section is a guide to the playing areas, formations, equipment, and techniques needed for many of today's most popular sports.

- In THE MODERN WORLD, items that are a familiar part of our daily lives are taken apart to reveal their inner workings and give access to the language used by their manufacturers. It also includes systems and concepts, such as the internet, that increasingly influence our 21st century world.

THE UNIVERSE

Anatomy of the Universe

Fireball of rapidly expanding, extremely hot gas lasting about one million years

THE UNIVERSE CONTAINS EVERYTHING that exists, from the tiniest subatomic particles to galactic superclusters (the largest structures known). Nobody knows how big the Universe is, but astronomers estimate that it contains about 100 billion galaxies, each comprising an average of 100 billion stars. The most widely accepted theory about the origin of the Universe is the Big Bang theory, which states that the Universe came into being in a huge explosion—the Big Bang—that took place between 10 and 20 billion years ago. The Universe initially consisted of a very hot, dense fireball of expanding, cooling gas. After about one million years, the gas probably began to condense into localized clumps called protogalaxies. During the next five billion years, the protogalaxies continued condensing, forming galaxies in which stars were being born. Today, billions of years later, the Universe as a whole is still expanding, although there are localized areas in which objects are held together by gravity; for example, many galaxies are found in clusters. The Big Bang theory is supported by the discovery of faint, cool background radiation coming evenly from all directions. This radiation is believed to be the remnant of the radiation produced by the Big Bang. Small "ripples" in the temperature of the cosmic background radiation are thought to be evidence of slight fluctuations in the density of the early Universe, which resulted in the formation of galaxies. Astronomers do not yet know if the Universe is "closed," which means it will eventually stop expanding and begin to contract, or if it is "open," which means it will continue expanding forever.

COMPUTER-ENHANCED MICROWAVE MAP OF COSMIC BACKGROUND RADIATION

Pink indicates "warm ripples" in background radiation

Pale blue indicates "cool ripples" in background radiation

Deep blue indicates background radiation corresponding to -454.5°F (remnant of the Big Bang)

Low-energy microwave radiation corresponding to about -454°F

Red and pink band indicates radiation from our galaxy

High-energy gamma radiation corresponding to about 5,400°F

ORIGIN AND EXPANSION OF THE UNIVERSE

Quasar (probably the center of a galaxy containing a massive black hole)

Universe one to five billion years after Big Bang

Protogalaxy (condensing gas cloud)

Galaxy spinning and flattening to become spiral shaped

Dark cloud (dust and gas condensing to form a protogalaxy)

Elliptical galaxy in which stars form rapidly

Universe today (10–20 billion years after Big Bang)

Cluster of galaxies held together by gravity

Elliptical galaxy containing old stars and little gas and dust

Irregular galaxy

Spiral galaxy containing gas, dust, and young stars

OBJECTS IN THE UNIVERSE

CLUSTER OF GALAXIES IN VIRGO

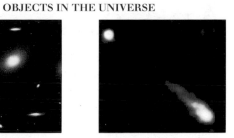

COLOR-ENHANCED IMAGE OF 3C273 (QUASAR)

NGC 4406 (ELLIPTICAL GALAXY)

NGC 5236 (SPIRAL GALAXY)

NGC 0822 (IRREGULAR GALAXY)

THE ROSETTE NEBULA (EMISSION NEBULA)

THE JEWEL BOX (STAR CLUSTER)

THE SUN (MAIN SEQUENCE STAR)

EARTH

THE MOON

Galaxies

SOMBRERO,
A SPIRAL GALAXY

A GALAXY IS A HUGE MASS OF STARS, nebulae, and interstellar material. The smallest galaxies contain about 100,000 stars, while the largest contain up to 3,000 billion stars. There are three main types of galaxy, classified according to their shape: elliptical, which are oval shaped; spiral, which have arms spiraling outward from a central bulge; and irregular, which have no obvious shape. Sometimes, the shape of a galaxy is distorted by a collision with another galaxy. Quasars (quasi-stellar objects) are thought to be galactic nuclei but are so far away that their exact nature is still uncertain. They are compact, highly luminous objects in the outer reaches of the known Universe; while the farthest known "ordinary" galaxies are about 10 billion light-years away, the farthest known quasar is about 15 billion light-years away. Active galaxies, such as Seyfert galaxies and radio galaxies, emit intense radiation. In a Seyfert galaxy, this radiation comes from the galactic nucleus; in a radio galaxy, it also comes from huge lobes on either side of the galaxy. The radiation from active galaxies and quasars is thought to be caused by black holes (see pp. 28-29).

OPTICAL IMAGE OF NGC 4486 (ELLIPTICAL GALAXY)

Globular cluster containing very old red giants

Central region containing old red giants

Less densely populated region

Neighboring galaxy

OPTICAL IMAGE OF LARGE MAGELLANIC CLOUD (IRREGULAR GALAXY)

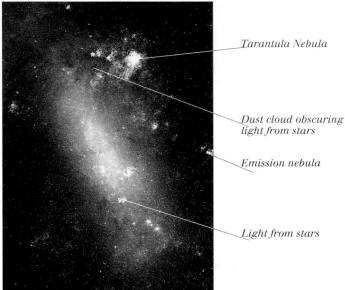

Tarantula Nebula

Dust cloud obscuring light from stars

Emission nebula

Light from stars

OPTICAL IMAGE OF NGC 2997 (SPIRAL GALAXY)

Glowing nebula in spiral arm

Spiral arm containing young stars

Galactic nucleus containing old stars

Dust in spiral arm reflecting blue light from hot young stars

Hot, ionized hydrogen gas emitting red light

Dust lane

OPTICAL IMAGE OF CENTAURUS A (RADIO GALAXY)

Dust lane crossing elliptical galaxy

Galactic nucleus containing powerful source of radiation

Light from old stars

COLOR-ENHANCED RADIO IMAGE OF CENTAURUS A

Radio lobe

Red indicates high-intensity radio waves

Blue indicates low-intensity radio waves

Radiation from galactic nucleus

Outline of optical image of Centaurus A

Radio lobe

Yellow indicates medium-intensity radio waves

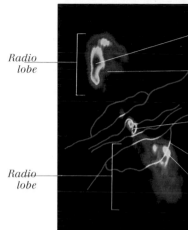

COLOR-ENHANCED RADIO IMAGE OF 3C273 (QUASAR)

Radiation from jet of high-energy particles moving away from quasar

Blue indicates low-intensity radio waves

Quasar nucleus

White indicates high-intensity radio waves

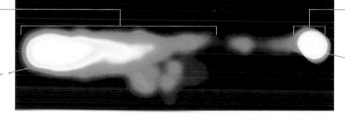

OPTICAL IMAGE OF NGC 1566 (SEYFERT GALAXY)

Nebula in spiral arm

Compact nucleus emitting intense radiation

Spiral arm

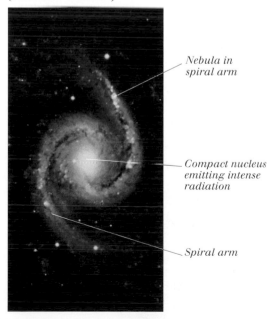

COLOR-ENHANCED OPTICAL IMAGE OF NGC 5754 (TWO COLLIDING GALAXIES)

Blue indicates low-intensity radiation

Red indicates medium-intensity radiation

Spiral arm distorted by gravitational influence of smaller galaxy

Large spiral galaxy

Smaller galaxy colliding with larger galaxy

Yellow indicates high-intensity radiation

The Milky Way

**VIEW TOWARD
GALACTIC CENTER**

THE MILKY WAY IS THE NAME GIVEN TO THE FAINT BAND OF LIGHT that stretches across the night sky. This light comes from stars and nebulae in our galaxy, known as the Milky Way Galaxy or simply as "the Galaxy." The Galaxy is shaped like a spiral, with a dense central bulge that is encircled by four arms spiraling outward and surrounded by a less dense halo. We cannot see the spiral shape because our Solar System is in one of the spiral arms, the Orion Arm (also called the Local Arm). From our position, the center of the Galaxy is completely obscured by dust clouds; as a result, optical maps give only a limited view of the Galaxy. However, a more complete picture can be obtained by studying radio, infrared, and other radiation. The central bulge of the Galaxy is a relatively small, dense sphere that contains mainly older red and yellow stars. The halo is a less dense region in which the oldest stars are situated; some of these stars may be as old as the Galaxy itself (possibly 15 billion years). The spiral arms contain mainly hot, young, blue stars, as well as nebulae (clouds of dust and gas, inside which stars are born). The Galaxy is vast—about 100,000 light-years across (a light-year is about 5,879 billion miles); in comparison, the Solar System seems small, at about 12 light-hours across (about 8 billion miles). The entire Galaxy is rotating in space, although the inner stars travel faster than those further out. The Sun, which is about two-thirds out from the center, completes one lap of the Galaxy about every 220 million years.

**PANORAMIC OPTICAL MAP OF OUR
GALAXY AND NEARBY GALAXIES**

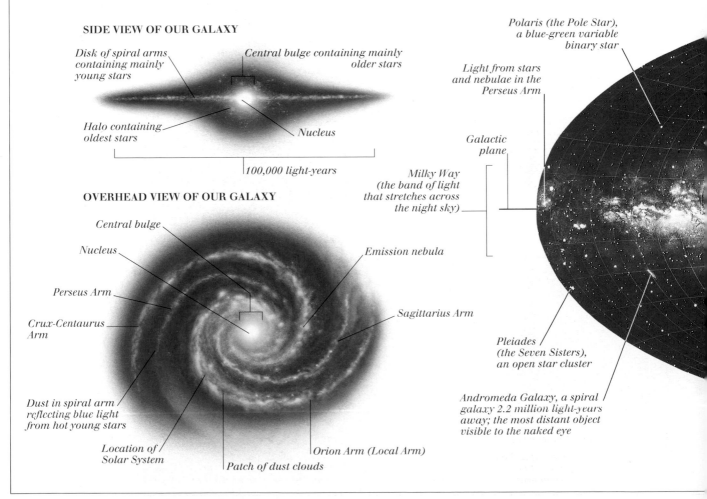

SIDE VIEW OF OUR GALAXY

Disk of spiral arms containing mainly young stars

Central bulge containing mainly older stars

Halo containing oldest stars

Nucleus

100,000 light-years

OVERHEAD VIEW OF OUR GALAXY

Central bulge

Nucleus

Perseus Arm

Crux-Centaurus Arm

Emission nebula

Sagittarius Arm

Dust in spiral arm reflecting blue light from hot young stars

Location of Solar System

Patch of dust clouds

Orion Arm (Local Arm)

Polaris (the Pole Star), a blue-green variable binary star

Light from stars and nebulae in the Perseus Arm

Galactic plane

Milky Way (the band of light that stretches across the night sky)

Pleiades (the Seven Sisters), an open star cluster

Andromeda Galaxy, a spiral galaxy 2.2 million light-years away; the most distant object visible to the naked eye

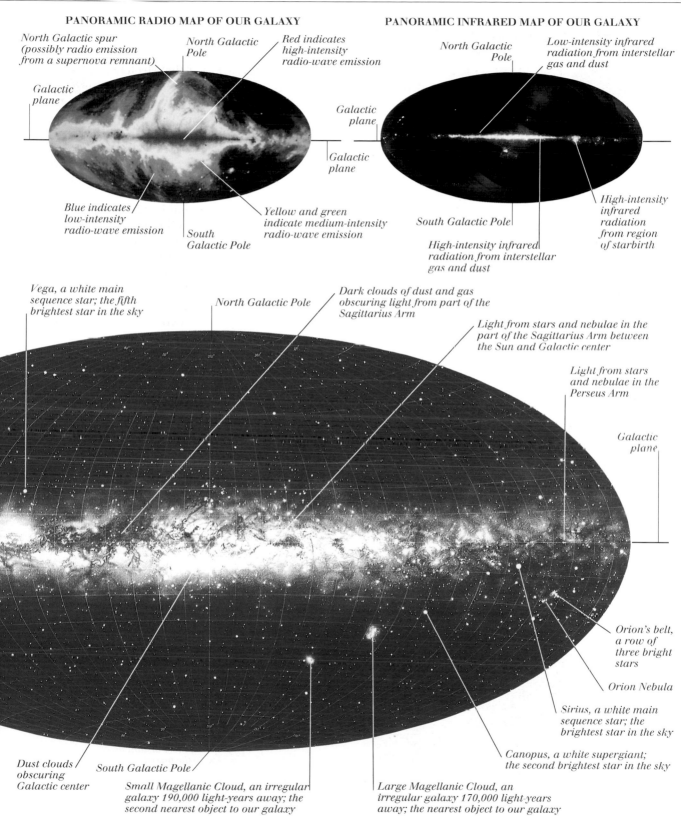

PANORAMIC RADIO MAP OF OUR GALAXY

North Galactic spur
(possibly radio emission
from a supernova remnant)

North Galactic
Pole

Red indicates
high-intensity
radio-wave emission

Galactic
plane

Blue indicates
low-intensity
radio-wave emission

South
Galactic Pole

Yellow and green
indicate medium-intensity
radio-wave emission

PANORAMIC INFRARED MAP OF OUR GALAXY

North Galactic
Pole

Low-intensity infrared
radiation from interstellar
gas and dust

Galactic
plane

Galactic
plane

South Galactic Pole

High-intensity infrared
radiation from interstellar
gas and dust

High-intensity
infrared
radiation
from region
of starbirth

Vega, a white main
sequence star; the fifth
brightest star in the sky

North Galactic Pole

Dark clouds of dust and gas
obscuring light from part of the
Sagittarius Arm

Light from stars and nebulae in the
part of the Sagittarius Arm between
the Sun and Galactic center

Light from stars
and nebulae in the
Perseus Arm

Galactic
plane

Orion's belt,
a row of
three bright
stars

Orion Nebula

Sirius, a white main
sequence star; the
brightest star in the sky

Canopus, a white supergiant;
the second brightest star in the sky

Dust clouds
obscuring
Galactic center

South Galactic Pole

Small Magellanic Cloud, an irregular
galaxy 190,000 light-years away; the
second nearest object to our galaxy

Large Magellanic Cloud, an
irregular galaxy 170,000 light-years
away; the nearest object to our galaxy

Nebulae and star clusters

A NEBULA IS A CLOUD OF DUST AND GAS inside a galaxy. Nebulae become visible if the gas glows or if the cloud reflects starlight or obscures light from more distant objects. Emission nebulae shine because their gas emits light when it is stimulated by radiation from hot young stars. Reflection nebulae shine because their dust reflects light from stars in or around the nebula. Dark nebulae appear as silhouettes because they block light from shining nebulae or stars behind them. Two types of nebula are associated with dying stars: planetary nebulae and supernova remnants. Both consist of expanding shells of gas that were once the outer layers of a star. A planetary nebula is a gas shell drifting away from a dying stellar core. A supernova remnant is a gas shell moving away from a stellar core at great speed following a violent explosion called a supernova (see pp. 26-27). Stars are often found in groups known as clusters. Open clusters are loose groups of a few thousand young stars that were born in the same cloud and are drifting apart. Globular clusters are densely packed, roughly spherical groups of hundreds of thousands of older stars.

HODGE 11, A
GLOBULAR CLUSTER

TRIFID NEBULA (EMISSION NEBULA)

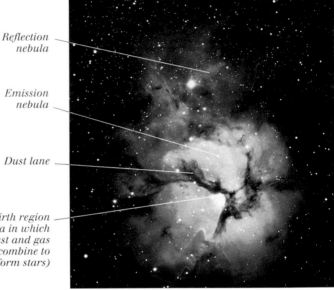

Reflection nebula

Emission nebula

Dust lane

Starbirth region (area in which dust and gas combine to form stars)

PLEIADES (OPEN STAR CLUSTER)
WITH A REFLECTION NEBULA

Wisps of dust and hydrogen gas remaining from cloud in which stars formed

Young star in an open cluster of 300–500 stars

Reflection nebula

HORSEHEAD NEBULA (DARK NEBULA)

Glowing filament of hot, ionized hydrogen gas

Alnitak (star in Orion's belt)

Dust lane

Emission nebula

Star near southern end of Orion's belt

Emission nebula

Horsehead Nebula

Reflection nebula

Dark nebula obscuring light from distant stars

ORION NEBULA (DIFFUSE EMISSION NEBULA)

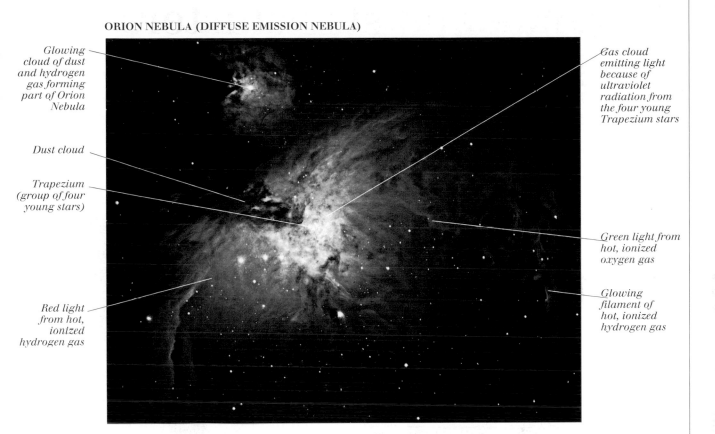

Glowing cloud of dust and hydrogen gas forming part of Orion Nebula

Dust cloud

Trapezium (group of four young stars)

Red light from hot, ionized hydrogen gas

Gas cloud emitting light because of ultraviolet radiation from the four young Trapezium stars

Green light from hot, ionized oxygen gas

Glowing filament of hot, ionized hydrogen gas

VELA SUPERNOVA REMNANT

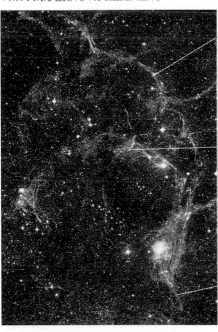

Supernova remnant (gas shell consisting of outer layers of star thrown off in supernova explosion)

Hydrogen gas emitting red light due to being heated by supernova explosion

Glowing filament of hot, ionized hydrogen gas

HELIX NEBULA (PLANETARY NEBULA)

Planetary nebula (gas shell expanding outward from dying stellar core)

Stellar core at a temperature of about 180,000°F

Red light from hot, ionized hydrogen gas

Blue-green light from hot, ionized oxygen and nitrogen gases

Stars of northern skies

WHEN YOU LOOK AT THE NORTHERN SKY, you look away from the densely populated Galactic center, so the northern sky generally appears less bright than the southern sky (see pp. 20-21). Among the best-known sights in the northern sky are the constellations Ursa Major (the Great Bear) and Orion. Some ancient civilizations believed that the stars were fixed to a celestial sphere surrounding the Earth, and modern maps of the sky are based on a similar idea. The North and South Poles of this imaginary celestial sphere are directly above the North and South Poles of the Earth, at the points where the Earth's axis of rotation intersects the sphere. The celestial North Pole is at the center of the map shown here, and Polaris (the Pole Star) lies very close to it. The celestial equator marks a projection of the Earth's equator on the sphere. The ecliptic marks the path of the Sun across the sky as the Earth orbits the Sun. The Moon and planets move against the background of the stars because the stars are much more distant; the nearest star outside the Solar System (Proxima Centauri) is more than 50,000 times farther away than the planet Jupiter.

ORION

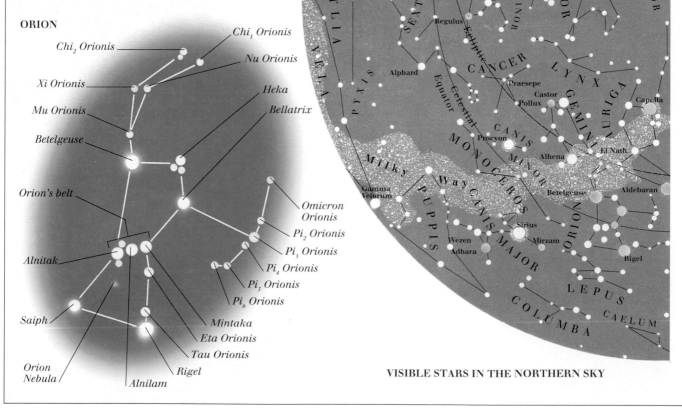

Chi₁ Orionis
Chi₂ Orionis
Nu Orionis
Xi Orionis
Heka
Mu Orionis
Bellatrix
Betelgeuse
Orion's belt
Omicron Orionis
Pi₂ Orionis
Pi₃ Orionis
Pi₄ Orionis
Alnitak
Pi₅ Orionis
Pi₆ Orionis
Mintaka
Eta Orionis
Saiph
Tau Orionis
Orion Nebula
Rigel
Alnilam

VISIBLE STARS IN THE NORTHERN SKY

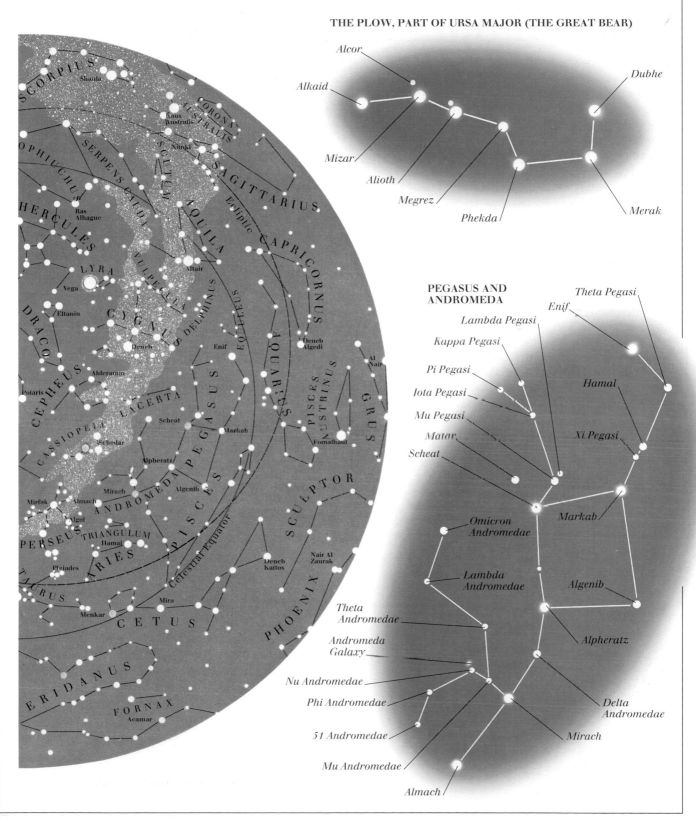

THE PLOW, PART OF URSA MAJOR (THE GREAT BEAR)

Alcor
Alkaid
Dubhe
Mizar
Alioth
Megrez
Phekda
Merak

PEGASUS AND ANDROMEDA

Theta Pegasi
Enif
Lambda Pegasi
Kappa Pegasi
Pi Pegasi
Hamal
Iota Pegasi
Mu Pegasi
Xi Pegasi
Matar
Scheat
Markab
Omicron Andromedae
Lambda Andromedae
Algenib
Alpheratz
Theta Andromedae
Andromeda Galaxy
Mirach
Nu Andromedae
Delta Andromedae
Phi Andromedae
51 Andromedae
Mu Andromedae
Almach

Star map labels (left hemisphere):

SCORPIUS
Shaula
CORONA AUSTRALIS
Kaus Australis
OPHIUCHUS
SERPENS CAUDA
Nunki
SCUTUM
SAGITTARIUS
Ecliptic
CAPRICORNUS
HERCULES
Ras Alhague
AQUILA
Altair
LYRA
Vega
VULPECULA
DELPHINUS
Deneb Algedi
Eltanin
CYGNUS
Deneb
AQUARIUS
Al Nair
DRACO
Alderamin
PISCES AUSTRINUS
GRUS
CEPHEUS
Polaris
LACERTA
Scheat
PEGASUS
Markab
Fomalhaut
CASSIOPEIA
Schedar
Enif
Alpheratz
SCULPTOR
Mirach
ANDROMEDA
Algenib
Mirfak
Almach
PERSEUS
Algol
Nair Al Zaurak
TRIANGULUM
Hamal
PISCES
ARIES
Celestial Equator
Deneb Kaitos
Pleiades
Menkar
Mira
CETUS
PHOENIX
TAURUS
ERIDANUS
FORNAX
Acamar

19

Stars of southern skies

WHEN YOU LOOK AT THE SOUTHERN SKY, you look toward the Galactic center, which has a huge population of stars. As a result, the Milky Way appears brighter in the southern sky than in the northern sky (see pp. 18-19). The southern sky is rich in nebulae and star clusters. It contains the Large and Small Magellanic Clouds, which are the two nearest galaxies to our own. Stars make fixed patterns in the sky called constellations. The constellations, however, are only apparent groupings of stars, because the distances to the stars in a constellation may vary enormously. The shapes of constellations may change over many thousands of years because of the relative motions of stars. The apparent movement of entire constellations across the sky is due to the Earth's motion in space. The daily rotation of the Earth causes the constellations to move across the sky from east to west, and the orbit of the Earth around the Sun causes different areas of sky to be visible in different seasons. The visibility of areas of sky also depends on the location of the observer. For instance, stars near the celestial equator may be seen from either hemisphere at some time during the year, while stars close to the celestial poles (the celestial South Pole is at the center of the map shown here) can never be seen from the opposite hemisphere.

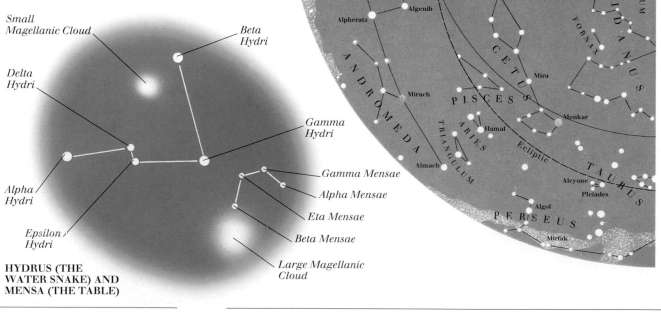

Small Magellanic Cloud

Beta Hydri

Delta Hydri

Gamma Hydri

Gamma Mensae

Alpha Mensae

Eta Mensae

Alpha Hydri

Beta Mensae

Epsilon Hydri

Large Magellanic Cloud

HYDRUS (THE WATER SNAKE) AND MENSA (THE TABLE)

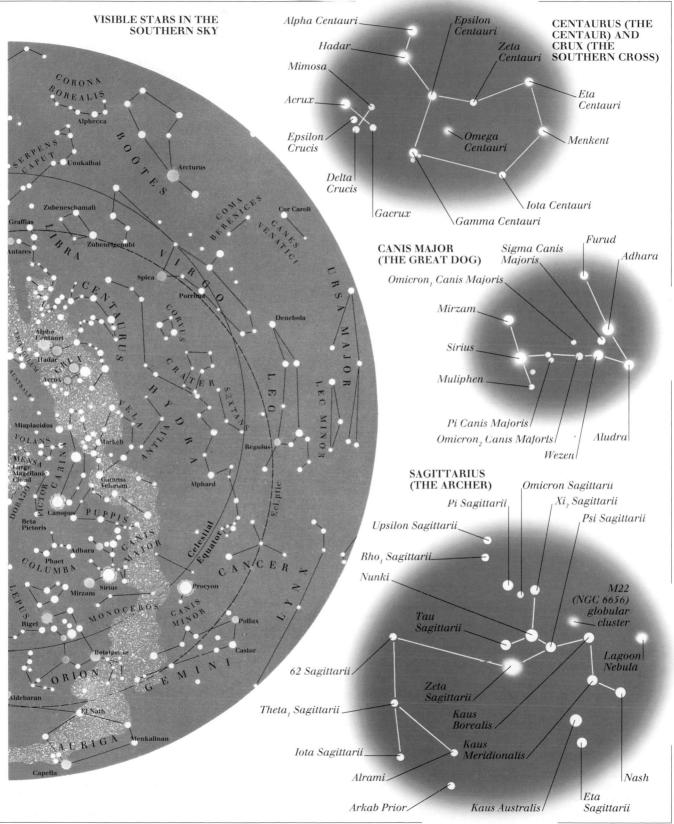

VISIBLE STARS IN THE SOUTHERN SKY

CORONA BOREALIS
Alphecca
SERPENS CAPUT
Unukalhai
BOÖTES
Arcturus
Zubeneschamali
Graffias
LIBRA
Antares
Zubenelgenubi
COMA BERENICES
CANES VENATICI
Cor Caroli
VIRGO
Spica
Porrima
CENTAURUS
Alpha Centauri
Hadar
CRUX
Acrux
TRIANGULUM
AUSTRALE
VELA
HYDRA
CORVUS
CRATER
SEXTANS
Denebola
URSA MAJOR
LEO
LEO MINOR
Regulus
Alphard
ANTLIA
Miaplacidus
VOLANS
CARINA
Markeb
Gamma Velorum
MENSA
Large Magellanic Cloud
DORADO
PICTOR
Canopus
PUPPIS
Beta Pictoris
Ecliptic
Celestial Equator
CANCER
LYNX
Procyon
CANIS MINOR
Pollux
Castor
GEMINI
Adhara
CANIS MAJOR
Phaet
COLUMBA
Mirzam
Sirius
MONOCEROS
LEPUS
Rigel
Betelgeuse
ORION
Aldebaran
El Nath
AURIGA
Menkalinan
Capella

CENTAURUS (THE CENTAUR) AND CRUX (THE SOUTHERN CROSS)

Alpha Centauri
Epsilon Centauri
Hadar
Zeta Centauri
Mimosa
Eta Centauri
Acrux
Menkent
Epsilon Crucis
Omega Centauri
Delta Crucis
Iota Centauri
Gacrux
Gamma Centauri

CANIS MAJOR (THE GREAT DOG)

Furud
Sigma Canis Majoris
Adhara
Omicron₁ Canis Majoris
Mirzam
Sirius
Muliphen
Pi Canis Majoris
Omicron₂ Canis Majoris
Aludra
Wezen

SAGITTARIUS (THE ARCHER)

Omicron Sagittarii
Pi Sagittarii
Xi₂ Sagittarii
Upsilon Sagittarii
Psi Sagittarii
Rho₁ Sagittarii
M22 (NGC 6656) globular cluster
Nunki
Tau Sagittarii
Lagoon Nebula
62 Sagittarii
Zeta Sagittarii
Theta₁ Sagittarii
Kaus Borealis
Iota Sagittarii
Kaus Meridionalis
Alrami
Nash
Arkab Prior
Kaus Australis
Eta Sagittarii

Stars

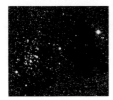

OPEN STAR CLUSTER AND DUST CLOUD

STARS ARE BODIES of hot glowing gas that are born in nebulae (see pp. 24-27). They vary enormously in size, mass, and temperature: diameters range from about 450 times smaller to over 1,000 times bigger than that of the Sun; masses range from about a twentieth to over 50 solar masses; and surface temperatures range from about 5,500°F to over 90,000°F. The color of a star is determined by its temperature: the hottest stars are blue and the coolest are red. The Sun, with a surface temperature of 10,000°F, is between these extremes and appears yellow. The energy emitted by a shining star is produced by nuclear fusion in the star's core. The brightness of a star is measured in magnitudes—the brighter the star, the lower its magnitude. There are two types of magnitude: apparent magnitude, which is the brightness seen from Earth, and absolute magnitude, which is the brightness that would be seen from a standard distance of 10 parsecs (32.6 light-years). The light emitted by a star may be split to form a spectrum containing a series of dark lines (absorption lines). The patterns of lines indicate the presence of particular chemical elements, enabling astronomers to deduce the composition of the star's atmosphere. The magnitude and spectral type (color) of stars may be plotted on a graph called a Hertzsprung-Russell diagram, which shows that stars tend to fall into several well-defined groups. The principal groups are main sequence stars (those which are fusing hydrogen to form helium), giants, supergiants, and white dwarfs.

STAR SIZES

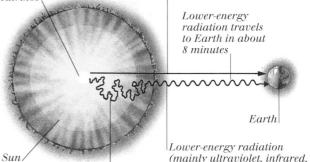

Red giant (diameters between about 10 million and 100 million miles)

The Sun (main sequence star with diameter about 870,000 miles)

White dwarf (diameters between about 2,000 and 30,000 miles)

ENERGY EMISSION FROM THE SUN

Nuclear fusion in core produces gamma rays and neutrinos

Neutrinos travel to Earth directly from Sun's core in about 8 minutes

Lower-energy radiation travels to Earth in about 8 minutes

Earth

Sun

Lower-energy radiation (mainly ultraviolet, infrared, and light rays) leaves surface

High-energy radiation (gamma rays) loses energy while traveling to surface over 2 million years

STAR MAGNITUDES

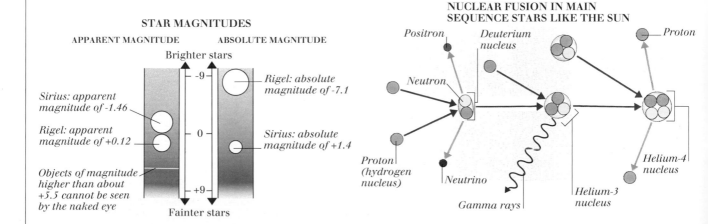

APPARENT MAGNITUDE

ABSOLUTE MAGNITUDE

Brighter stars

-9

0

+9

Fainter stars

Sirius: apparent magnitude of -1.46

Rigel: apparent magnitude of +0.12

Objects of magnitude higher than about +5.5 cannot be seen by the naked eye

Rigel: absolute magnitude of -7.1

Sirius: absolute magnitude of +1.4

NUCLEAR FUSION IN MAIN SEQUENCE STARS LIKE THE SUN

Positron

Deuterium nucleus

Proton

Neutron

Proton (hydrogen nucleus)

Neutrino

Gamma rays

Helium-3 nucleus

Helium-4 nucleus

HERTZSPRUNG-RUSSELL DIAGRAM

Hotter stars   TEMPERATURE (°F)   Cooler stars

65,000   18,000   9,000   6,500   4,500

Brighter stars -7
                -6
                -5
Deneb (blue supergiant) -4   SUPERGIANTS   Betelgeuse (red supergiant)
                -3
                -2
                -1
                 0   GIANTS
Sirius A (massive +1   Arcturus (red giant)
main sequence star) +2   MAIN SEQUENCE STARS
                +3
                +4
ABSOLUTE   +5   The Sun (yellow main
VISUAL   +6   sequence dwarf)
MAGNITUDE   +7
                +8
                +9
                +10
Sirius B (white dwarf) +11
                +12
                +13   WHITE DWARFS
                +14   Barnard's Star (main
                +15   sequence red dwarf)
Fainter stars   +16

        O5   B0   A0   F0   G0   K0   M0 M5

                        SPECTRAL TYPE

STELLAR SPECTRAL ABSORPTION LINES

Calcium line   Hydrogen   Hydrogen   Helium line   Sodium   Hydrogen
               gamma line   beta line   lines   alpha line

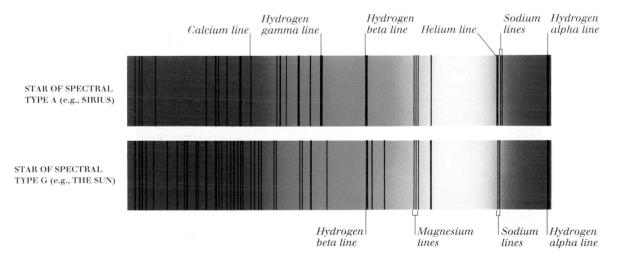

STAR OF SPECTRAL
TYPE A (e.g., SIRIUS)

STAR OF SPECTRAL
TYPE G (e.g., THE SUN)

                    Hydrogen   Magnesium   Sodium   Hydrogen
                    beta line   lines   lines   alpha line

Small stars

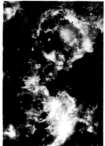

REGION OF STAR FORMATION IN ORION

SMALL STARS HAVE A MASS of up to about one and a half times that of the Sun. They begin to form when a region of higher density in a nebula condenses into a huge globule of gas and dust that contracts under its own gravity. Within a globule, regions of condensing matter heat up and begin to glow, forming protostars. If a protostar contains enough matter, the central temperature reaches about 27 million °F. At this temperature, nuclear reactions in which hydrogen fuses to form helium can start. This process releases energy, which prevents the star from contracting further, and also causes it to shine; it is now a main sequence star. A star of about one solar mass remains in the main sequence for about 10 billion years, until the hydrogen in the star's core has been converted into helium. The helium core then contracts again, and nuclear reactions continue in a shell around the core. The core becomes hot enough for helium to fuse to form carbon, while the outer layers of the star expand, cool, and shine less brightly. The expanding star is known as a red giant. When the helium in the core runs out, the outer layers of the star may drift off as an expanding gas shell called a planetary nebula. The remaining core (about 80 percent of the original star) is now in its final stages. It becomes a white dwarf star that gradually cools and dims. When it finally stops shining altogether, the dead star will become a black dwarf.

STRUCTURE OF A MAIN SEQUENCE STAR

Core containing hydrogen fusing to form helium

Radiative zone

Convective zone

Surface temperature about 10,000°F

Core temperature about 27 million °F

STRUCTURE OF A NEBULA

Young main sequence star

Dense region of dust and gas (mainly hydrogen) condensing under gravity to form globules

Hot, ionized hydrogen gas emitting red light due to stimulation by radiation from hot young stars

Dark globule of dust and gas (mainly hydrogen) contracting to form protostars

LIFE OF A SMALL STAR OF ABOUT ONE SOLAR MASS

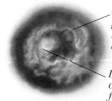

Cool cloud of gas (mainly hydrogen) and dust

Dense globule condensing to form protostars

NEBULA

Glowing ball of gas (mainly hydrogen)

Natal cocoon (shell of dust blown away by radiation from protostar)

PROTOSTAR
Duration: 50 million years

About 870,000 miles

Star producing energy by nuclear fusion in core

MAIN SEQUENCE STAR
Duration: 10 billion years

STRUCTURE OF A RED GIANT

Outer envelope consisting mainly of hydrogen

Shell where hydrogen is fusing to form helium

Cooling, expanding outer layers glow red

Intermediate layer consisting mainly of helium

Shell where helium is fusing to form carbon

Surface temperature about 6,300°F

Carbon core temperature about 180 million °F

At least 40 million miles

Outer layers form expanding gas shell

Very dense core (one teaspoonful weighs about five tons)

Cooling core glows red

Dense, contracting core

Cooling, expanding outer layers

About 8,000 miles

Cold, dead core

RED GIANT
Duration: 100 million years

PLANETARY NEBULA
Duration: 35,000 years

WHITE DWARF

COOLING WHITE DWARF

BLACK DWARF

Massive stars

MASSIVE STARS HAVE A MASS AT LEAST THREE TIMES that of the Sun, and some stars are as massive as about 50 Suns. A massive star evolves in a similar way to a small star until it reaches the main sequence stage (see pp. 24-25). During the main sequence, a star shines steadily until the hydrogen in its core has fused to form helium. This process takes billions of years in a small star, but only millions of years in a massive star. A massive star then becomes a red supergiant, which initially consists of a helium core surrounded by outer layers of cooling, expanding gas. Over the next few million years, a series of nuclear reactions form different elements in shells around an iron core. The core eventually collapses in less than a second, causing a massive explosion called a supernova, in which a shock wave blows away the outer layers of the star. Supernovae shine brighter than an entire galaxy for a short time. Sometimes, the core survives the supernova explosion. If the surviving core is between about one and a half and three solar masses, it contracts to become a tiny, dense neutron star. If the core is considerably greater than three solar masses, it contracts to become a black hole (see pp. 28-29).

(see pp. 24-25)
(see pp. 28-29)

SUPERNOVA

TARANTULA NEBULA BEFORE SUPERNOVA

STRUCTURE OF A RED SUPERGIANT

Outer envelope consisting mainly of hydrogen

Layer consisting mainly of helium

Layer consisting mainly of carbon

Layer consisting mainly of oxygen

Layer consisting mainly of silicon

Shell of hydrogen fusing to form helium

Shell of helium fusing to form carbon

Shell of carbon fusing to form oxygen

Shell of oxygen fusing to form silicon

Shell of silicon fusing to form iron core

Surface temperature about 5,500°F

Cooling, expanding outer layers glow red

Core of mainly iron at a temperature of 5.4–9 billion °F

LIFE OF A MASSIVE STAR OF ABOUT 10 SOLAR MASSES

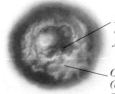

Dense globule condensing to form protostars

Cool cloud of gas (mainly hydrogen) and dust

NEBULA

Glowing ball of gas (mainly hydrogen)

Natal cocoon (shell of dust blown away by radiation from protostar)

PROTOSTAR
Duration: a few hundred thousand years

About 2 million miles

Star producing energy by nuclear fusion in core

MAIN SEQUENCE STAR
Duration: 10 million years

FEATURES OF A SUPERNOVA

**TARANTULA NEBULA SHOWING
SUPERNOVA IN 1987**

*Ejecta (outer layers of star
thrown off during explosion)
travels at speeds of up to
6,000 miles/sec*

*Shock wave travels outward
from core at speeds of up to
20,000 miles/sec*

*Reverse shock wave
moves inward and
heats ejecta, causing
it to shine*

*Heavy chemical
elements are
scattered through
space by explosion*

*Central
temperature
more than
18 billion °F*

*Contracting
core consisting
mainly of neutrons
remains after explosion*

*Light energy
of a billion Suns
emitted during explosion*

*Extremely dense core
(one teaspoonful
weighs about a
billion tons)*

About 6 miles

*Core mass of
less than three
solar masses*

NEUTRON STAR

About 60 million miles

*Outer layers of
star blown off
in explosion*

*Contracting
stellar core may
remain after
supernova*

*Core of mass greater
than three solar masses
continues contracting
to become black hole*

*Cooling,
expanding
outer layers*

*Accretion
disk*

RED SUPERGIANT
Duration: 4 million years

SUPERNOVA
Duration of
visibility: 1–2 years

BLACK HOLE

Neutron stars and black holes

NEUTRON STARS AND BLACK HOLES form from the stellar cores that remain after stars have exploded as supernovae (see pp. 26-27). If the remaining core is between about one and a half and three solar masses, it contracts to form a neutron star. If the remaining core is considerably greater than about three solar masses, it contracts to form a black hole. Neutron stars are typically only about six miles in diameter and consist almost entirely of subatomic particles called neutrons. These stars are so dense that a teaspoonful would weigh about a billion tons. Neutron stars are observed as pulsars, so-called because they rotate rapidly and emit two beams of radio waves, which sweep across the sky and are detected as short pulses. Black holes are characterized by their extremely strong gravity, which is so powerful that not even light can escape; as a result, black holes are invisible. However, they may be detected if they have a close companion star. The gravity of the black hole pulls gas from the other star, forming an accretion disk that spirals around the black hole at high speed, heating up and emitting radiation. Eventually, the matter spirals in to cross the event horizon (the boundary of the black hole), finally disappearing from the visible Universe.

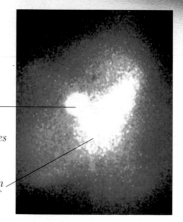

X-ray emission from pulsar (neutron star rotating 30 times each second)

X-ray emission from center of nebula

X-RAY IMAGE OF THE CRAB NEBULA (SUPERNOVA REMNANT)

PULSAR (ROTATING NEUTRON STAR)

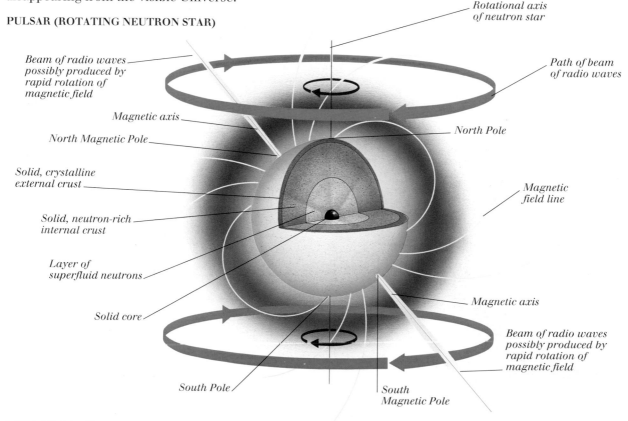

Rotational axis of neutron star

Beam of radio waves possibly produced by rapid rotation of magnetic field

Path of beam of radio waves

Magnetic axis

North Magnetic Pole

North Pole

Solid, crystalline external crust

Magnetic field line

Solid, neutron-rich internal crust

Layer of superfluid neutrons

Magnetic axis

Solid core

Beam of radio waves possibly produced by rapid rotation of magnetic field

South Pole

South Magnetic Pole

STELLAR BLACK HOLE

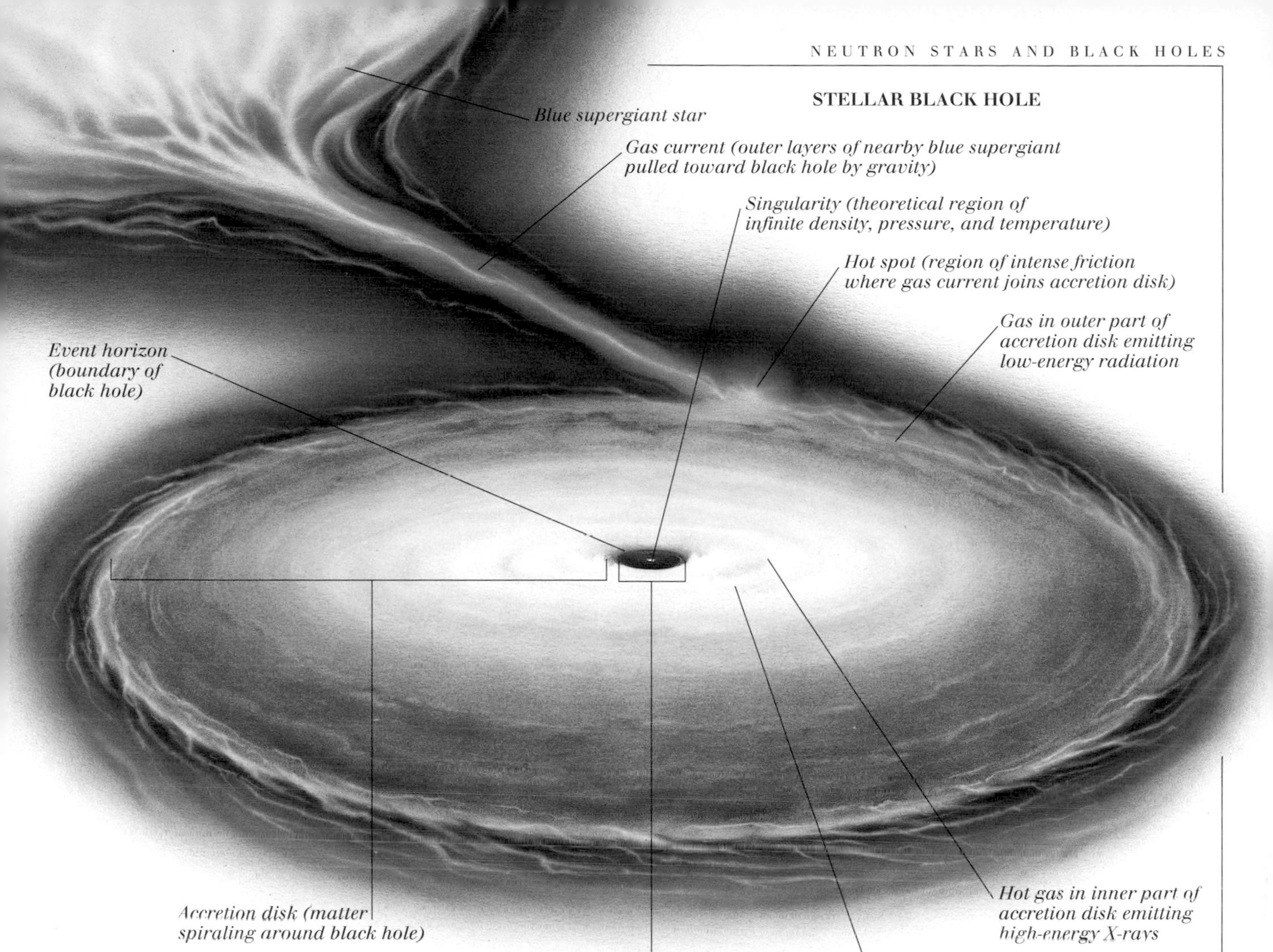

Blue supergiant star

Gas current (outer layers of nearby blue supergiant pulled toward black hole by gravity)

Singularity (theoretical region of infinite density, pressure, and temperature)

Hot spot (region of intense friction where gas current joins accretion disk)

Gas in outer part of accretion disk emitting low-energy radiation

Event horizon (boundary of black hole)

Hot gas in inner part of accretion disk emitting high-energy X-rays

Accretion disk (matter spiraling around black hole)

Black hole

Gas at temperatures of millions °F spiraling at close to the speed of light

FORMATION OF A BLACK HOLE

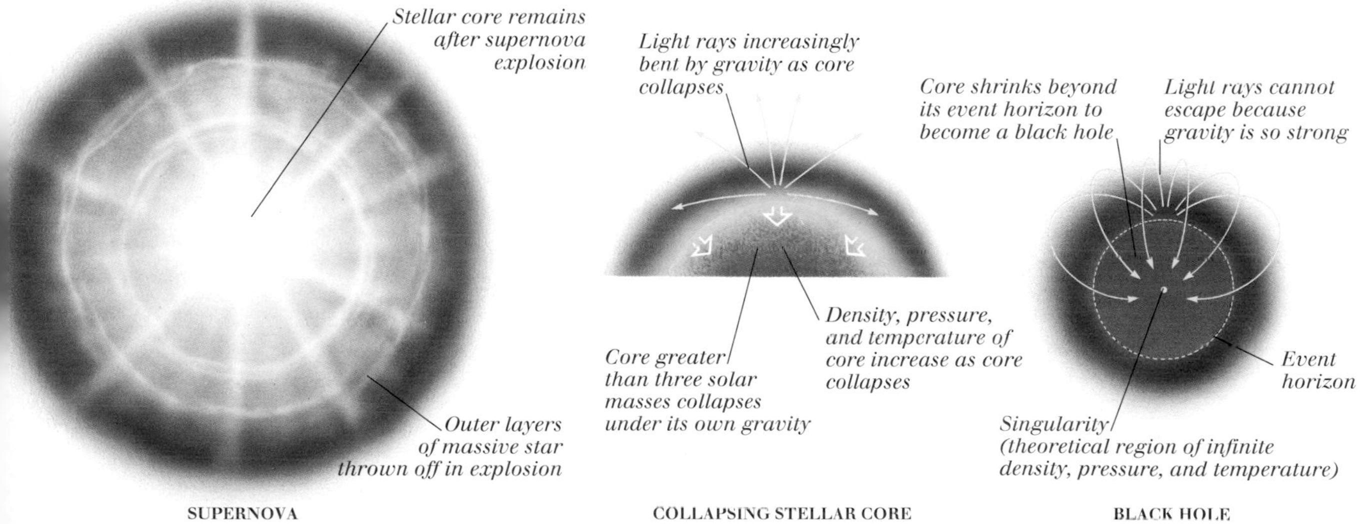

Stellar core remains after supernova explosion

Light rays increasingly bent by gravity as core collapses

Core shrinks beyond its event horizon to become a black hole

Light rays cannot escape because gravity is so strong

Outer layers of massive star thrown off in explosion

Core greater than three solar masses collapses under its own gravity

Density, pressure, and temperature of core increase as core collapses

Event horizon

Singularity (theoretical region of infinite density, pressure, and temperature)

SUPERNOVA

COLLAPSING STELLAR CORE

BLACK HOLE

The Solar System

THE SUN

THE SOLAR SYSTEM consists of a central star (the Sun) and the bodies that orbit it. These bodies include nine planets and their 61 known moons, asteroids, comets, and meteoroids. The Solar System also contains interplanetary gas and dust. Most of the planets fall into two groups: four small rocky planets near the Sun (Mercury, Venus, Earth, and Mars), and four planets farther out, the gas giants (Jupiter, Saturn, Uranus, and Neptune). Pluto belongs to neither group—it is very small, solid, and icy. Pluto is the outermost planet, except when it passes briefly inside Neptune's orbit. Between the rocky planets and gas giants is the asteroid belt, which contains thousands of chunks of rock orbiting the Sun. Most of the bodies in the Solar System move around the Sun in elliptical orbits located in a thin disk around the Sun's equator. All the planets orbit the Sun in the same direction (counterclockwise when viewed from above) and all but Venus, Uranus, and Pluto also spin around their axes in this direction. Moons also spin as they, in turn, orbit their planets. The entire Solar System orbits the center of our galaxy, the Milky Way (see pp. 14-15).

PLANETARY ORBIT

Perihelion (orbital point closest to Sun)

Sun

Elliptical orbit

Planet orbiting Sun

Direction of planetary rotation

Aphelion (orbital point farthest from Sun)

Aphelion of Neptune: 2,819 million miles

ORBITS OF INNER PLANETS

Average orbital speed of Venus: 21.8 miles/sec

Average orbital speed of Mercury: 29.8 miles/sec

Average orbital speed of Earth: 18.5 miles/sec

Average orbital speed of Mars: 15 miles/sec

Mercury

Perihelion of Mercury: 28.5 million miles

Perihelion of Venus: 66.7 million miles

Perihelion of Earth: 91.4 million miles

Mars

Perihelion of Mars: 128.4 million miles

Earth

Venus

Sun

Aphelion of Mercury: 43.3 million miles

Asteroid belt

Aphelion of Venus: 67.7 million miles

Aphelion of Earth: 94.5 million miles

Aphelion of Mars: 154.8 million miles

Aphelion of Pluto: 4,583 million miles

MERCURY
Year: 87.97 Earth days
Mass: 0.055 Earth masses
Diameter: 3,031 miles

VENUS
Year: 224.7 Earth days
Mass: 0.81 Earth masses
Diameter: 7,521 miles

EARTH
Year: 365.26 days
Mass: 1 Earth mass
Diameter: 7,926 miles

MARS
Year: 1.88 Earth years
Mass: 0.11 Earth masses
Diameter: 4,217 miles

JUPITER
Year: 11.86 Earth years
Mass: 318 Earth masses
Diameter: 88,850 miles

ORBITS OF OUTER PLANETS

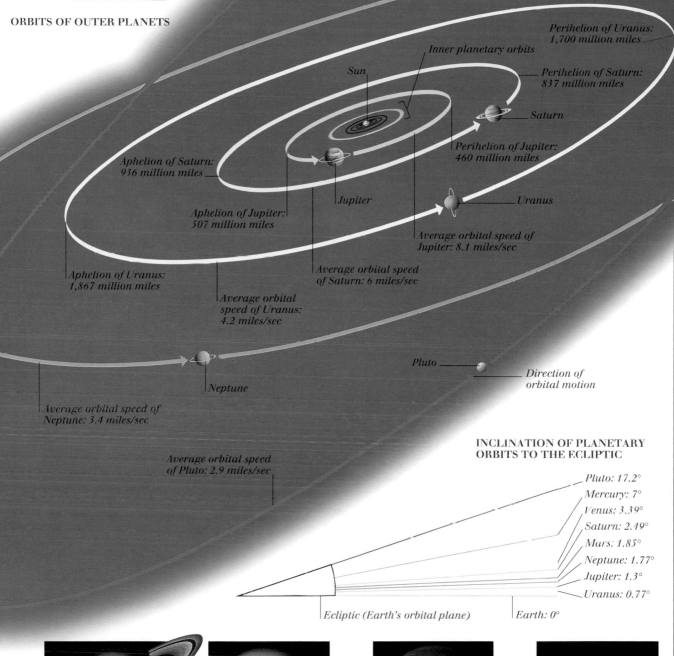

Perihelion of Uranus:
1,700 million miles

Inner planetary orbits

Perihelion of Saturn:
837 million miles

Sun

Saturn

Perihelion of Jupiter:
460 million miles

Aphelion of Saturn:
936 million miles

Jupiter

Uranus

Aphelion of Jupiter:
507 million miles

Average orbital speed of
Jupiter: 8.1 miles/sec

Aphelion of Uranus:
1,867 million miles

Average orbital speed
of Saturn: 6 miles/sec

Average orbital
speed of Uranus:
4.2 miles/sec

Pluto

Neptune

Direction of
orbital motion

Average orbital speed of
Neptune: 3.4 miles/sec

Average orbital speed
of Pluto: 2.9 miles/sec

INCLINATION OF PLANETARY ORBITS TO THE ECLIPTIC

Pluto: 17.2°

Mercury: 7°

Venus: 3.39°

Saturn: 2.49°

Mars: 1.85°

Neptune: 1.77°

Jupiter: 1.3°

Uranus: 0.77°

Ecliptic (Earth's orbital plane)

Earth: 0°

SATURN
Year: 29.46 Earth years
Mass: 95.18 Earth masses
Diameter: 74,901 miles

URANUS
Year: 84.01 Earth years
Mass: 14.5 Earth masses
Diameter: 31,765 miles

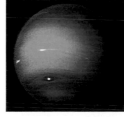

NEPTUNE
Year: 164.79 Earth years
Mass: 17.14 Earth masses
Diameter: 30,777 miles

PLUTO
Year: 248.54 Earth years
Mass: 0.0022 Earth masses
Diameter: 1,429 miles

The Sun

SOLAR PHOTOSPHERE

THE SUN IS THE STAR AT THE CENTER of our Solar System. It is about five billion years old and will probably continue to shine as it does now for about another five billion years. The Sun is a yellow main sequence star (see pp. 22-23) about 870,000 miles in diameter. It consists almost entirely of hydrogen and helium. In the Sun's core, hydrogen is converted to helium by nuclear fusion, releasing energy in the process. The energy travels from the core through the radiative and convective zones to the photosphere (visible surface), where it leaves the Sun in the form of heat and light. On the photosphere there are often dark, relatively cool areas called sunspots. These usually appear in pairs or groups and are thought to be caused by magnetic fields. Other types of solar activity are flares, which are usually associated with sunspots, and prominences. Flares are sudden discharges of high-energy radiation and atomic particles. Prominences are huge loops or filaments of gas extending into the solar atmosphere; some last for hours, others for months. Beyond the photosphere is the chromosphere (inner atmosphere) and the extremely rarified corona (outer atmosphere), which extends millions of miles into space. Tiny particles that escape from the corona give rise to the solar wind, which streams through space at hundreds of miles per second. The chromosphere and corona can be seen from Earth when the Sun is totally eclipsed by the Moon.

HOW A SOLAR ECLIPSE OCCURS

Sun

Moon passes between Sun and Earth

Umbra (inner, total shadow) of Moon

Region of Earth from which total eclipse is visible

Penumbra (outer, partial shadow) of Moon

Region of Earth from which partial eclipse is visible

Earth

Umbra (inner, total shadow) of Earth

Penumbra (outer, partial shadow) of Earth

SURFACE FEATURES

Gas loop (looped prominence)

Prominence (jet of gas at edge of Sun's disk up to hundreds of thousands of miles high)

Spicule (vertical jet of gas)

Photosphere (visible surface)

Chromosphere (inner atmosphere)

TOTAL SOLAR ECLIPSE

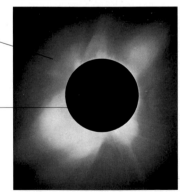

Corona (outer atmosphere of extremely hot diffuse gas)

Moon covers Sun's disk

SUNSPOTS

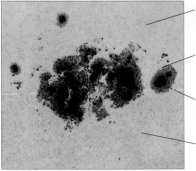

Granulated surface of Sun

Penumbra (lighter, outer region) containing radial fibrils

Umbra (darker, inner region) temperature about 7,200°F

Photosphere temperature about 9,900°F

EXTERNAL FEATURES AND
INTERNAL STRUCTURE OF THE SUN

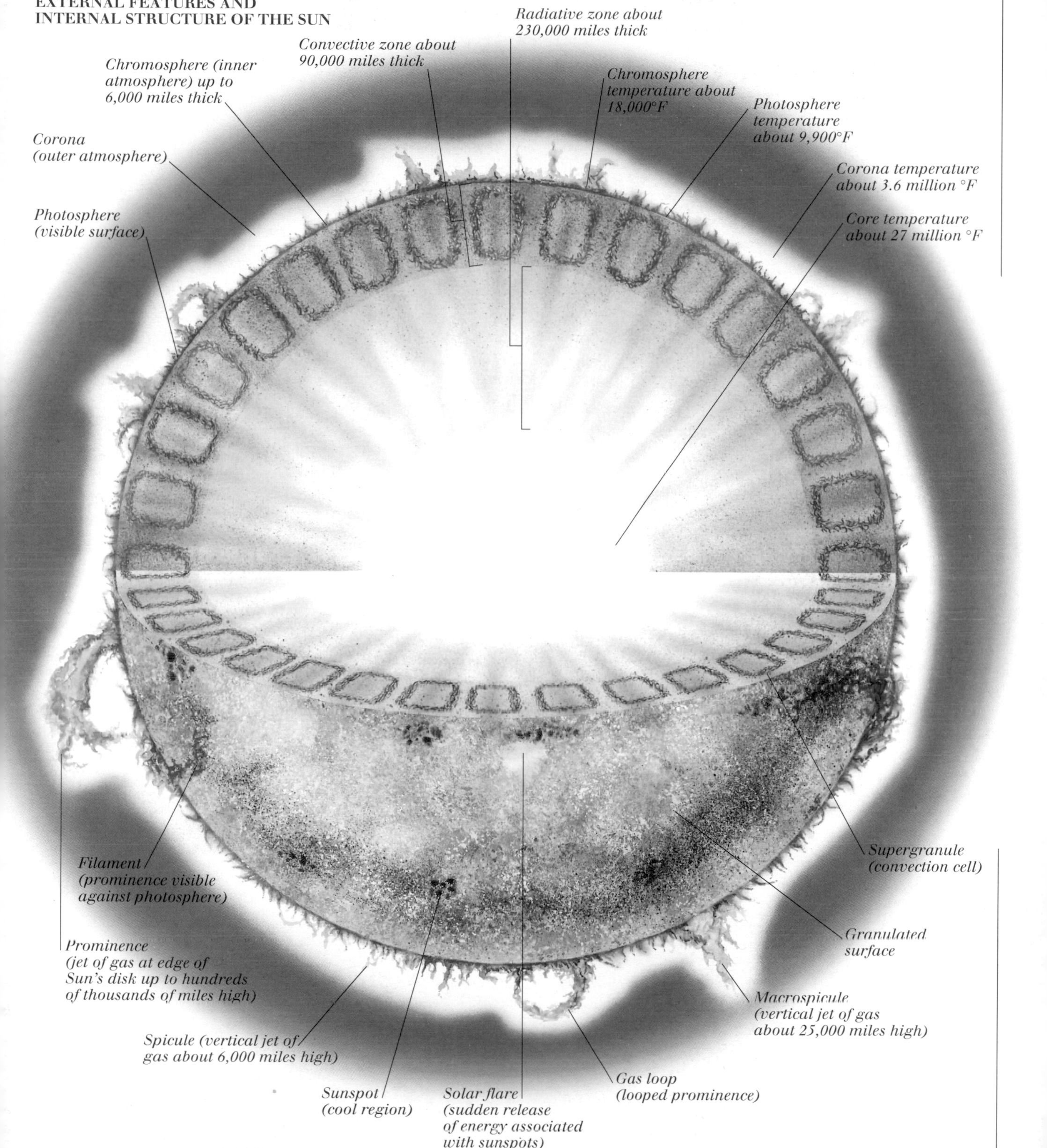

Chromosphere (inner
atmosphere) up to
6,000 miles thick

Convective zone about
90,000 miles thick

Radiative zone about
230,000 miles thick

Chromosphere
temperature about
18,000°F

Photosphere
temperature
about 9,900°F

Corona
(outer atmosphere)

Corona temperature
about 3.6 million °F

Photosphere
(visible surface)

Core temperature
about 27 million °F

Filament
(prominence visible
against photosphere)

Supergranule
(convection cell)

Granulated
surface

Prominence
(jet of gas at edge of
Sun's disk up to hundreds
of thousands of miles high)

Macrospicule
(vertical jet of gas
about 25,000 miles high)

Spicule (vertical jet of
gas about 6,000 miles high)

Sunspot
(cool region)

Solar flare
(sudden release
of energy associated
with sunspots)

Gas loop
(looped prominence)

Mercury

MERCURY

MERCURY IS THE NEAREST PLANET to the Sun, orbiting at an average distance of about 36 million miles. Because Mercury is the closest planet to the Sun, it moves faster than any other planet, traveling at an average speed of nearly 30 miles per second and completing an orbit in just under 88 days. Mercury is very small (only Pluto is smaller) and rocky. Most of the surface has been heavily cratered by the impact of meteorites, although there are also smooth, sparsely cratered plains. The Caloris Basin is the largest crater, measuring about 800 miles across. It is thought to have been formed when a rock the size of an asteroid hit the planet and is surrounded by concentric rings of mountains thrown up by the impact. The surface also has many ridges, called rupes, that are thought to have been formed when the hot core of the young planet cooled and shrank about four billion years ago, buckling the planet's surface in the process. The planet rotates about its axis very slowly, taking nearly 59 Earth days to complete one rotation. As a result, a solar day (sunrise to sunrise) on Mercury is about 176 Earth days—twice as long as the 88-day Mercurian year. Mercury has extreme surface temperatures, ranging from a maximum of 800°F on the sunlit side to -270°F on the dark side. At nightfall, the temperature drops very quickly because the planet's atmosphere is almost nonexistent. It consists only of minute amounts of helium and hydrogen captured from the solar wind, plus traces of other gases.

TILT AND ROTATION OF MERCURY

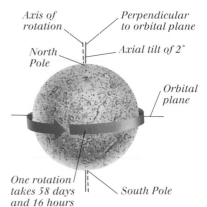

Axis of rotation

Perpendicular to orbital plane

North Pole

Axial tilt of 2°

Orbital plane

One rotation takes 58 days and 16 hours

South Pole

DEGAS AND BRONTË (RAY CRATERS)

Bright ray of ejecta (ejected material)

Brontë

Unmapped region

Degas with central peak

FORMATION OF A RAY CRATER

Debris thrown out by impact

Path of meteorite colliding with planet

Wall of rock thrown up around crater

Impact forms saucer-shaped crater

Fractured rock

METEORITE IMPACT

Path of rocky ejecta (ejected material)

Ejecta forms secondary craters

Loose debris on crater floor

SECONDARY CRATERING

Wall of rock forms ring of mountains

Ray of ejecta (ejected material)

Small secondary crater

Loose ejected rock

Central mountain rings form if floor of large crater recoils from meteorite impact

Falling debris forms ridges on side of wall

RAY CRATER

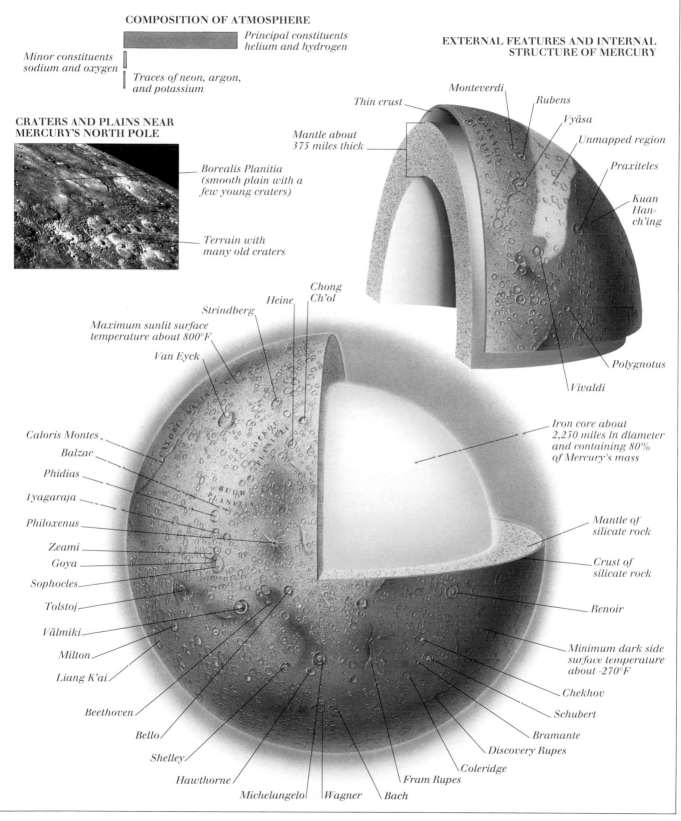

COMPOSITION OF ATMOSPHERE

Principal constituents helium and hydrogen

Minor constituents sodium and oxygen

Traces of neon, argon, and potassium

CRATERS AND PLAINS NEAR MERCURY'S NORTH POLE

Borealis Planitia (smooth plain with a few young craters)

Terrain with many old craters

EXTERNAL FEATURES AND INTERNAL STRUCTURE OF MERCURY

Thin crust

Mantle about 375 miles thick

Monteverdi

Rubens

Vyāsa

Unmapped region

Praxiteles

Kuan Han-ch'ing

Polygnotus

Vivaldi

Maximum sunlit surface temperature about 800°F

Van Eyck

Strindberg

Heine

Chong Ch'ol

Caloris Montes

Balzac

Phidias

Tyagaraja

Philoxenus

Zeami

Goya

Sophocles

Tolstoj

Vālmiki

Milton

Liang K'ai

Beethoven

Bello

Shelley

Hawthorne

Michelangelo

Wagner

Bach

Fram Rupes

Coleridge

Discovery Rupes

Bramante

Schubert

Chekhov

Minimum dark side surface temperature about -270°F

Renoir

Crust of silicate rock

Mantle of silicate rock

Iron core about 2,250 miles in diameter and containing 80% of Mercury's mass

35

Venus

RADAR IMAGE OF VENUS

VENUS IS A ROCKY PLANET and the second planet from the Sun. Venus spins slowly backward as it orbits the Sun, causing its rotational period to be the longest in the Solar System, at about 243 Earth days. It is slightly smaller than Earth and probably has a similar internal structure, consisting of a semisolid metal core surrounded by a rocky mantle and crust. Venus is the brightest object in the sky after the Sun and Moon because its atmosphere reflects sunlight strongly. The main component of the atmosphere is carbon dioxide, which traps heat in a greenhouse effect far stronger than that on Earth. As a result, Venus is the hottest planet, with a maximum surface temperature of about 900°F. The thick cloud layers contain droplets of sulfuric acid and are driven around the planet by winds at speeds of up to 220 miles per hour. Although the planet takes 243 Earth days to rotate once, the high-speed winds cause the clouds to circle the planet in only four Earth days. The high temperature, acidic clouds, and enormous atmospheric pressure (about 90 times greater at the surface than that on Earth) make the environment extremely hostile. However, orbiting satellites have managed to land on Venus and photograph its dry, dusty surface. The Venusian surface has also been mapped by probes with radar equipment that can "see" through the cloud layers. Such radar maps reveal a terrain with craters, mountains, volcanoes, and areas where craters have been covered by plains of solidified volcanic lava. There are two large highland regions called Aphrodite Terra and Ishtar Terra.

TILT AND ROTATION OF VENUS

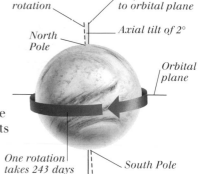

Axis of rotation
Perpendicular to orbital plane
North Pole
Axial tilt of 2°
Orbital plane
One rotation takes 243 days and 14 minutes
South Pole

CLOUD FEATURES

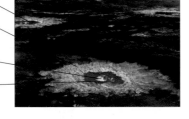

Polar hood
Dark, mid-latitude band
Cloud features swept around planet by winds of up to 220 mph
Dirty yellow hue due to sulfuric acid in atmosphere
Bright polar band

VENUSIAN CRATERS

Danilova
Ejecta (ejected material)
Central peak
Howe

COMPUTER-ENHANCED RADAR MAP OF THE SURFACE OF VENUS

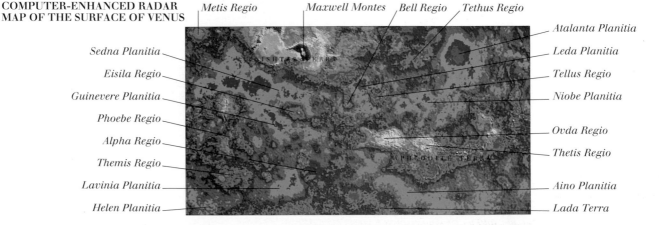

Metis Regio
Maxwell Montes
Bell Regio
Tethus Regio
Atalanta Planitia
Sedna Planitia
Leda Planitia
Eisila Regio
Tellus Regio
Guinevere Planitia
Niobe Planitia
Phoebe Regio
Alpha Regio
Ovda Regio
Themis Regio
Thetis Regio
Lavinia Planitia
Aino Planitia
Helen Planitia
Lada Terra

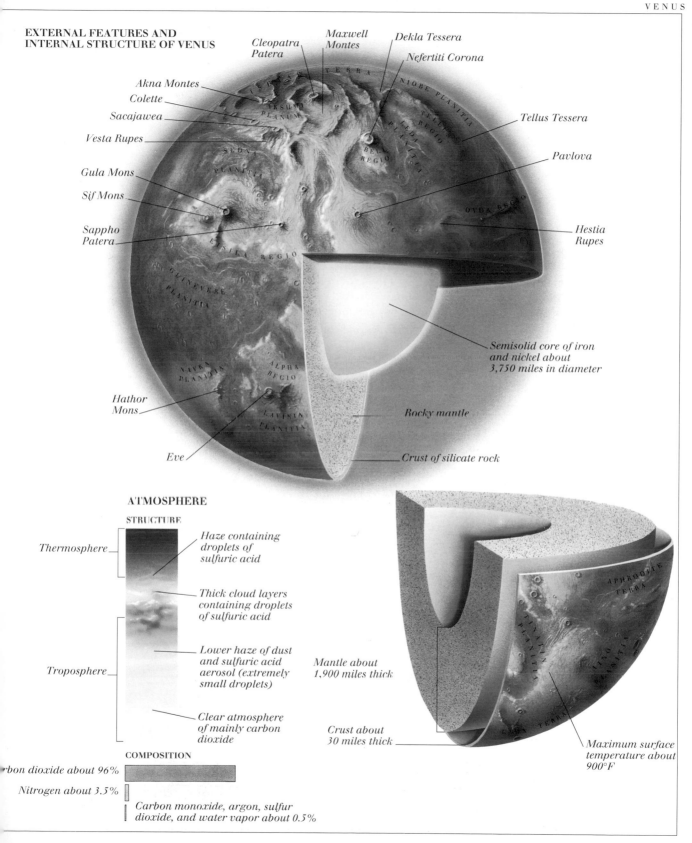

**EXTERNAL FEATURES AND
INTERNAL STRUCTURE OF VENUS**

Cleopatra Patera

Maxwell Montes

Dekla Tessera

Nefertiti Corona

Akna Montes

Colette

Sacajawea

Vesta Rupes

Gula Mons

Sif Mons

Sappho Patera

Tellus Tessera

Pavlova

Hestia Rupes

Semisolid core of iron and nickel about 3,750 miles in diameter

Rocky mantle

Crust of silicate rock

Hathor Mons

Eve

ATMOSPHERE

STRUCTURE

Thermosphere

Haze containing droplets of sulfuric acid

Thick cloud layers containing droplets of sulfuric acid

Lower haze of dust and sulfuric acid aerosol (extremely small droplets)

Troposphere

Clear atmosphere of mainly carbon dioxide

Mantle about 1,900 miles thick

Crust about 30 miles thick

Maximum surface temperature about 900°F

COMPOSITION

Carbon dioxide about 96%

Nitrogen about 3.5%

Carbon monoxide, argon, sulfur dioxide, and water vapor about 0.5%

The Earth

THE EARTH

THE EARTH IS THE THIRD of the nine planets that orbit the Sun. It is the largest and densest rocky planet, and the only one known to support life. About 70 percent of the Earth's surface is covered by water, which is not found in liquid form on the surface of any other planet. There are four main layers: the inner core, the outer core, the mantle, and the crust. At the heart of the planet the solid inner core has a temperature of about 7,230°F. The heat from this inner core causes material in the molten outer core and mantle to circulate in convection currents. It is thought that these convection currents generate the Earth's magnetic field, which extends into space as the magnetosphere. The Earth's atmosphere helps screen out some of the harmful radiation from the Sun, stops meteorites from reaching the planet's surface, and traps enough heat to prevent extremes of cold. The Earth has one natural satellite, the Moon, which is large enough for both bodies to be considered a double-planet system.

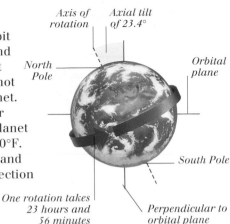

TILT AND ROTATION OF THE EARTH

Axis of rotation

Axial tilt of 23.4°

North Pole

Orbital plane

South Pole

One rotation takes 23 hours and 56 minutes

Perpendicular to orbital plane

THE FORMATION OF THE EARTH

The heat of the collisions caused the planet to glow red

The cloud broke up into particles of ice and rock, which stuck together to form planets

Microorganisms began to photosynthesize, creating a supply of oxygen

4,600 YEARS AGO, THE SOLAR SYSTEM FORMED FROM A CLOUD OF GAS AND DUST

THE EARTH WAS FORMED FROM COLLIDING ROCKS

4,500 YEARS AGO THE SURFACE COOLED TO FORM THE CRUST

THE CONTINENTS BROKE UP AND REFORMED, GRADUALLY TAKING THEIR PRESENT POSITIONS

Solar wind enters atmosphere and produces aurora

Magnetosphere (magnetic field)

Solar wind (stream of electrically charged particles)

THE EARTH'S MAGNETOSPHERE

Van Allen radiation belt

Earth

Axis of geographic poles

Axis of magnetic poles

EXTERNAL FEATURES AND INTERNAL STRUCTURE OF THE EARTH

COMPOSITION OF THE EARTH

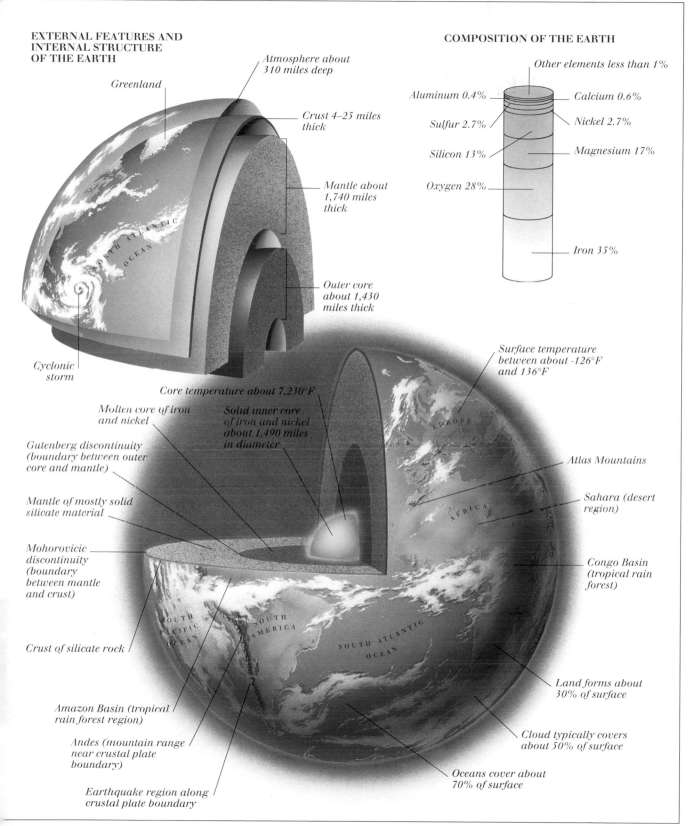

Greenland

Atmosphere about 310 miles deep

Crust 4–25 miles thick

Mantle about 1,740 miles thick

Outer core about 1,430 miles thick

Cyclonic storm

Other elements less than 1%

Aluminum 0.4%

Calcium 0.6%

Sulfur 2.7%

Nickel 2.7%

Silicon 13%

Magnesium 17%

Oxygen 28%

Iron 35%

Core temperature about 7,230°F

Molten core of iron and nickel

Solid inner core of iron and nickel about 1,490 miles in diameter

Gutenberg discontinuity (boundary between outer core and mantle)

Mantle of mostly solid silicate material

Mohorovicic discontinuity (boundary between mantle and crust)

Crust of silicate rock

Amazon Basin (tropical rain forest region)

Andes (mountain range near crustal plate boundary)

Earthquake region along crustal plate boundary

Surface temperature between about -126°F and 136°F

Atlas Mountains

Sahara (desert region)

Congo Basin (tropical rain forest)

Land forms about 30% of surface

Cloud typically covers about 50% of surface

Oceans cover about 70% of surface

The Moon

THE MOON FROM EARTH

THE MOON IS THE EARTH'S only natural satellite. It is relatively large for a moon, with a diameter of about 2,155 miles—just over a quarter that of the Earth. The Moon takes the same time to rotate on its axis as it takes to orbit the Earth (27.3 days), and so the same side (the near side) always faces us. However, the amount of the surface we can see—the phase of the Moon—depends on how much of the near side is in sunlight. The Moon is dry and barren, with no atmosphere or water. It consists mainly of solid rock, although its core may contain molten rock or iron. The surface is dusty, with highlands covered in craters caused by meteorite impacts, and lowlands in which large craters have been filled by solidified lava to form dark areas called maria or "seas." Maria occur mainly on the near side, which has a thinner crust than the far side. Many of the craters are rimmed by mountain ranges that form the crater walls and can be thousands of feet high.

TILT AND ROTATION OF THE MOON

Axis of rotation
Perpendicular to orbital plane
Axial tilt of 6.7°
North Pole
Orbital plane
One rotation takes 27 Earth days and 8 hours
South Pole

CRATERS ON OCEANUS PROCELLARUM

Aristarchus
Cobra Head (head of Schröter's Valley)
Herodotus

NEAR SIDE OF THE MOON

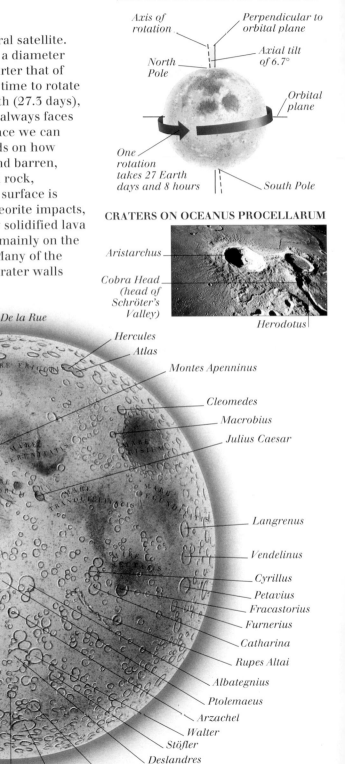

Aristoteles
De la Rue
Hercules
Atlas
Aristillus
Montes Apenninus
Plato
Archimedes
Cleomedes
Montes Jura
Macrobius
Sinus Iridum
Julius Caesar
Bright rays of ejected material
Copernicus
Aristarchus
Langrenus
Kepler
Vendelinus
Encke
Cyrillus
Flamsteed
Petavius
Fra Mauro
Fracastorius
Grimaldi
Furnerius
Letronne
Catharina
Gassendi
Rupes Altai
Mersenius
Albategnius
Ptolemaeus
Arzachel
Walter
Stöfler
Deslandres
Pitatus
Schickard
Alphonsus
Bailly
Tycho
Clavius
Maginus

MARE FRIGORIS
MARE IMBRIUM
MARE SERENITATIS
MARE CRISIUM
MARE VAPORUM
MARE TRANQUILLITATIS
MARE FECUNDITATIS
OCEANUS PROCELLARUM
MARE NECTARIS
MARE HUMORUM
MARE NUBIUM

PHASES OF THE MOON

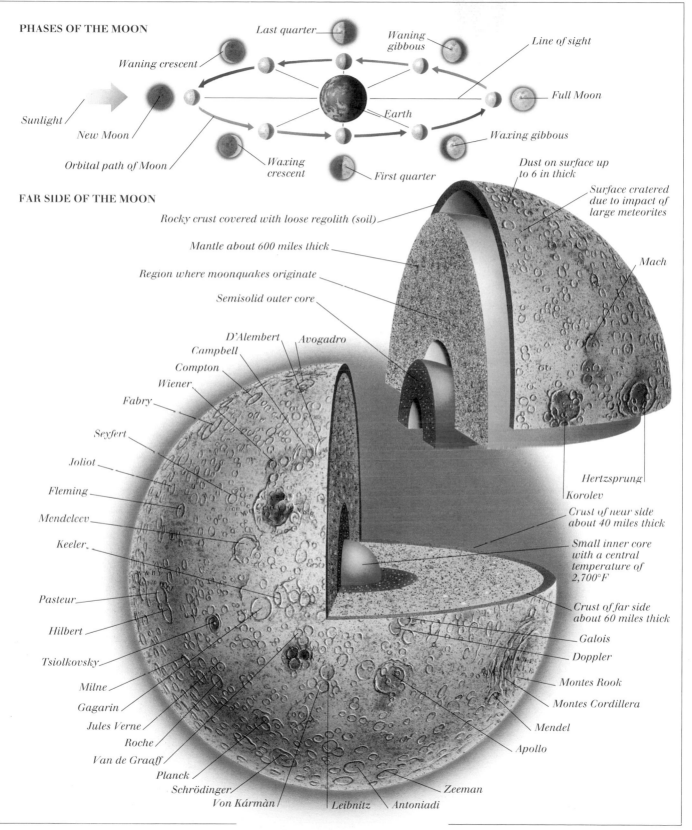

Last quarter

Waning crescent

Waning gibbous

Line of sight

Sunlight

New Moon

Orbital path of Moon

Waxing crescent

First quarter

Earth

Full Moon

Waxing gibbous

FAR SIDE OF THE MOON

Dust on surface up to 6 in thick

Surface cratered due to impact of large meteorites

Rocky crust covered with loose regolith (soil)

Mantle about 600 miles thick

Region where moonquakes originate

Semisolid outer core

Mach

D'Alembert

Avogadro

Campbell

Compton

Wiener

Fabry

Seyfert

Joliot

Fleming

Mendeleev

Keeler

Pasteur

Hilbert

Tsiolkovsky

Milne

Gagarin

Jules Verne

Roche

Van de Graaff

Planck

Schrödinger

Von Kármàn

Leibnitz

Antoniadi

Zeeman

Apollo

Mendel

Montes Cordillera

Montes Rook

Doppler

Galois

Crust of far side about 60 miles thick

Small inner core with a central temperature of 2,700°F

Crust of near side about 40 miles thick

Korolev

Hertzsprung

Mars

MARS

MARS, KNOWN AS THE RED PLANET, is the fourth planet from the Sun and the outermost rocky planet. In the 19th century, astronomers first observed what were thought to be signs of life on Mars. These signs included apparent canal-like markings on the surface, and dark patches that were thought to be vegetation. It is now known that the canals are an optical illusion and the dark patches are areas where the red dust that covers most of the planet has blown away. The fine dust particles are often whipped up by winds into dust storms that occasionally obscure almost all Mars's surface. Residual dust in the atmosphere gives the Martian sky a pinkish hue. The northern hemisphere of Mars has many large plains formed of solidified volcanic lava, while the southern hemisphere has many craters and large impact basins. There are also several huge, extinct volcanoes, including Olympus Mons, which at 370 miles wide and 15 miles high is the largest known volcano in the Solar System. The surface also has many canyons and branching channels. The canyons were formed by movements of the surface crust, but the channels are thought to have been formed by flowing water that has now vaporized almost completely and escaped from the atmosphere. The Martian atmosphere is much thinner than Earth's, with only a few clouds and morning mists. Mars has two tiny irregularly shaped moons, Phobos and Deimos. Their small size indicates that they may be asteroids that have been captured by the gravity of Mars.

TILT AND ROTATION OF MARS

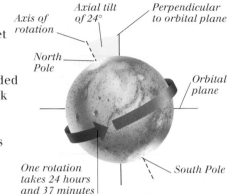

Axis of rotation

Axial tilt of 24°

Perpendicular to orbital plane

North Pole

Orbital plane

One rotation takes 24 hours and 37 minutes

South Pole

SURFACE FEATURES OF MARS

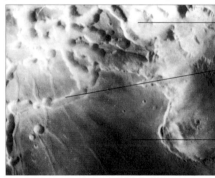

Bright water-ice fog

Fog in canyon about 12 miles wide at end of Valles Marineris

Syria Planum

NOCTIS LABYRINTHUS (CANYON SYSTEM)

Summit caldera consisting of overlapping collapsed volcanic craters

Crater

Gentle slope produced by lava flow

Cloud formation

OLYMPUS MONS (EXTINCT SHIELD VOLCANO)

THE SURFACE OF MARS

Dark area where dust has been blown away by wind

South polar ice cap

Surface covered with red-colored iron oxide dust

MOONS OF MARS

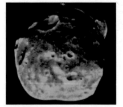

PHOBOS
Average diameter: 14 miles
Average distance from planet: 5,800 miles

DEIMOS
Average diameter: 8 miles
Average distance from planet: 14,600 miles

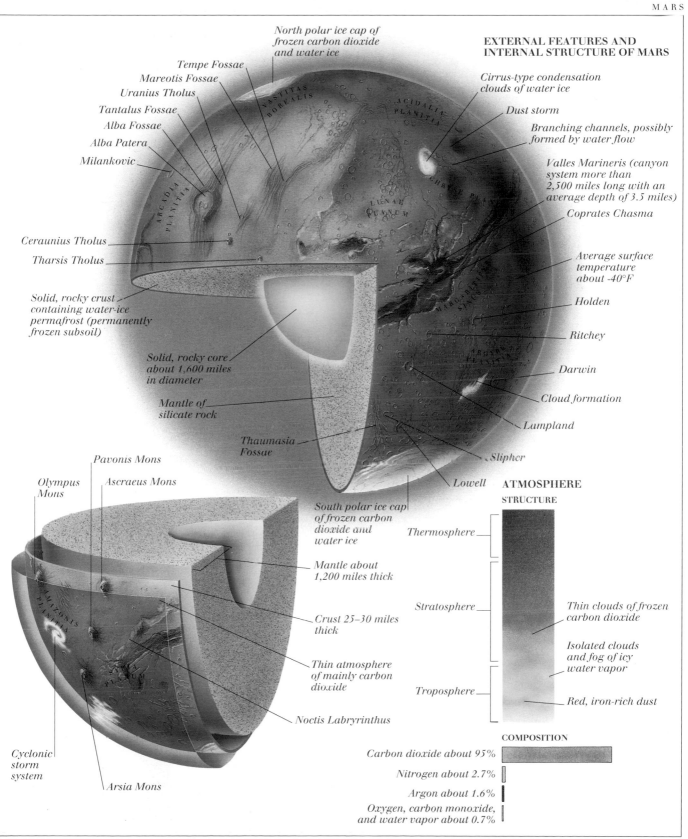

EXTERNAL FEATURES AND
INTERNAL STRUCTURE OF MARS

North polar ice cap of
frozen carbon dioxide
and water ice

Tempe Fossae

Mareotis Fossae

Uranius Tholus

Tantalus Fossae

Alba Fossae

Alba Patera

Milankovic

Ceraunius Tholus

Tharsis Tholus

Solid, rocky crust
containing water-ice
permafrost (permanently
frozen subsoil)

Solid, rocky core
about 1,600 miles
in diameter

Mantle of
silicate rock

Thaumasia
Fossae

Cirrus-type condensation
clouds of water ice

Dust storm

Branching channels, possibly
formed by water flow

Valles Marineris (canyon
system more than
2,500 miles long with an
average depth of 3.5 miles)

Coprates Chasma

Average surface
temperature
about -40°F

Holden

Ritchey

Darwin

Cloud formation

Lumpland

Slipher

Lowell

South polar ice cap
of frozen carbon
dioxide and
water ice

ATMOSPHERE

STRUCTURE

Thermosphere

Stratosphere

Troposphere

Thin clouds of frozen
carbon dioxide

Isolated clouds
and fog of icy
water vapor

Red, iron-rich dust

Olympus
Mons

Pavonis Mons

Ascraeus Mons

Mantle about
1,200 miles thick

Crust 25–30 miles
thick

Thin atmosphere
of mainly carbon
dioxide

Noctis Labryrinthus

Cyclonic
storm
system

Arsia Mons

COMPOSITION

Carbon dioxide about 95%

Nitrogen about 2.7%

Argon about 1.6%

Oxygen, carbon monoxide,
and water vapor about 0.7%

Jupiter

JUPITER

JUPITER IS THE FIFTH PLANET from the Sun and the first of the four gas giants. It is the largest and the most massive planet, with a diameter about 11 times that of the Earth and a mass about 2.5 times the combined mass of the eight other planets. Jupiter is thought to have a small rocky core surrounded by an inner mantle of metallic hydrogen (liquid hydrogen that acts like a metal). Outside the inner mantle is an outer mantle of liquid hydrogen and helium that merges into the gaseous atmosphere. Jupiter's rapid rate of rotation causes the clouds in its atmosphere to form belts and zones that encircle the planet parallel to the equator. Belts are dark, low-lying, relatively warm cloud layers. Zones are bright, high-altitude, cooler cloud layers. Within the belts and zones, turbulence causes the formation of cloud features such as white ovals and red spots, both of which are huge storm systems. The most prominent cloud feature is a storm called the Great Red Spot, which consists of a spiraling column of clouds three times wider than the Earth that rises about five miles above the upper cloud layer. Jupiter has one thin, faint, main ring, inside of which is a halo ring of tiny particles extending toward the planet. There are 16 known Jovian moons. The four largest moons (called the Galileans) are Ganymede, Callisto, Io, and Europa. Ganymede and Callisto are cratered and probably icy. Europa is smooth and icy and may contain water. Io is covered in bright red, orange, and yellow splotches. This coloring is caused by sulfurous material from active volcanoes that shoot plumes of lava hundreds of miles above the surface.

TILT AND ROTATION OF JUPITER

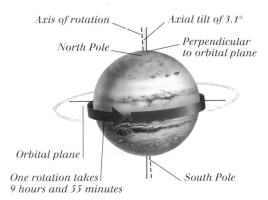

Axis of rotation

Axial tilt of 3.1°

North Pole

Perpendicular to orbital plane

Orbital plane

One rotation takes 9 hours and 55 minutes

South Pole

GREAT RED SPOT AND WHITE OVAL

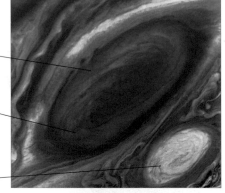

Great Red Spot (anticyclonic storm system)

Red color probably due to phosphorus

White oval (temporary anticyclonic storm system)

GALILEAN MOONS OF JUPITER

EUROPA
Diameter: 1,950 miles
Average distance from planet: 416,900 miles

CALLISTO
Diameter: 2,983 miles
Average distance from planet: 1,168,200 miles

GANYMEDE
Diameter: 3,270 miles
Average distance from planet: 664,900 miles

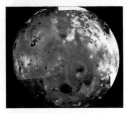

IO
Diameter: 2,263 miles
Average distance from planet: 262,100 miles

RINGS OF JUPITER

Main ring

Halo ring

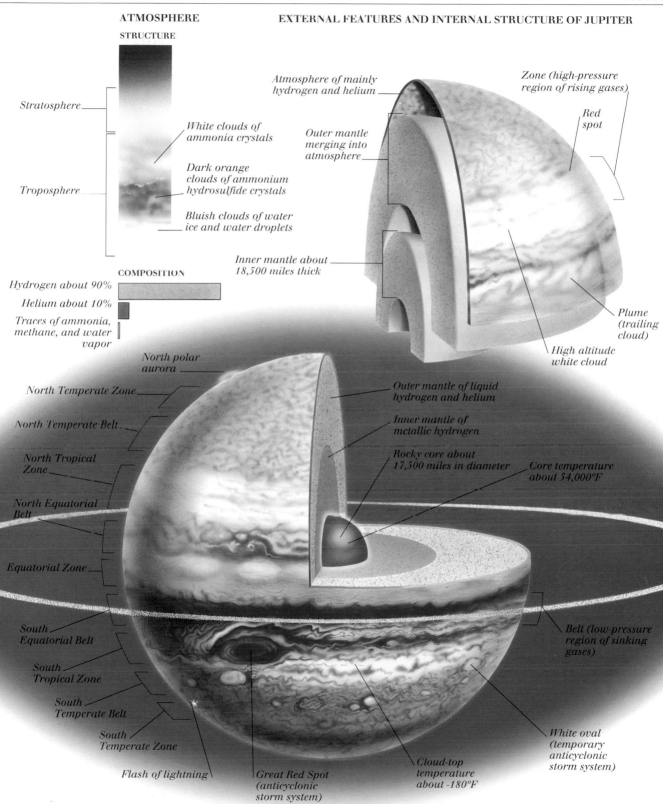

ATMOSPHERE

STRUCTURE

EXTERNAL FEATURES AND INTERNAL STRUCTURE OF JUPITER

Stratosphere

Troposphere

White clouds of ammonia crystals

Dark orange clouds of ammonium hydrosulfide crystals

Bluish clouds of water ice and water droplets

Atmosphere of mainly hydrogen and helium

Outer mantle merging into atmosphere

Inner mantle about 18,500 miles thick

Zone (high-pressure region of rising gases)

Red spot

Plume (trailing cloud)

High altitude white cloud

COMPOSITION

Hydrogen about 90%

Helium about 10%

Traces of ammonia, methane, and water vapor

North polar aurora

North Temperate Zone

North Temperate Belt

North Tropical Zone

North Equatorial Belt

Equatorial Zone

South Equatorial Belt

South Tropical Zone

South Temperate Belt

South Temperate Zone

Flash of lightning

Great Red Spot (anticyclonic storm system)

Outer mantle of liquid hydrogen and helium

Inner mantle of metallic hydrogen

Rocky core about 17,500 miles in diameter

Core temperature about 54,000°F

Belt (low-pressure region of sinking gases)

White oval (temporary anticyclonic storm system)

Cloud-top temperature about -180°F

Saturn

COLOR-ENHANCED
IMAGE OF SATURN

SATURN IS THE SIXTH PLANET from the Sun. It is a gas giant almost as big as Jupiter, with an equatorial diameter of about 74,900 miles. Saturn is thought to consist of a small core of rock and ice surrounded by an inner mantle of metallic hydrogen (liquid hydrogen that acts like a metal). Outside the inner mantle is an outer mantle of liquid hydrogen that merges into a gaseous atmosphere. Saturn's clouds form belts and zones similar to those on Jupiter, but obscured by overlying haze. Storms and eddies, seen as red or white ovals, occur in the clouds. Saturn has an extremely thin but wide system of rings that is less than one mile thick but extends outward to about 260,000 miles from the planet's surface. The main rings comprise thousands of narrow ringlets, each made of icy lumps that range in size from tiny particles to chunks several yards across. The D, E, and G rings are very faint, the F ring is brighter, and the A, B, and C rings are bright enough to be seen from Earth with binoculars. Saturn has 18 known moons, some of which orbit inside the rings and are thought to exert a gravitational influence on the shapes of the rings. Unusually, seven of the moons are co-orbital—they share an orbit with another moon. Astronomers believe that such co-orbital moons may have originated from a single satellite that broke up.

TILT AND ROTATION OF SATURN

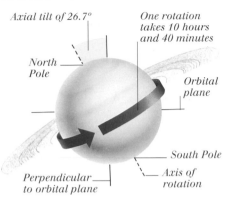

Axial tilt of 26.7°

One rotation takes 10 hours and 40 minutes

North Pole

Orbital plane

South Pole

Axis of rotation

Perpendicular to orbital plane

COLOR-ENHANCED IMAGE OF SATURN'S CLOUD FEATURES

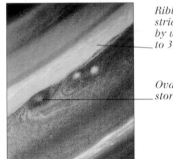

Ribbon-shaped striation caused by winds of up to 335 mph

Oval (rotating storm system)

INNER RINGS OF SATURN

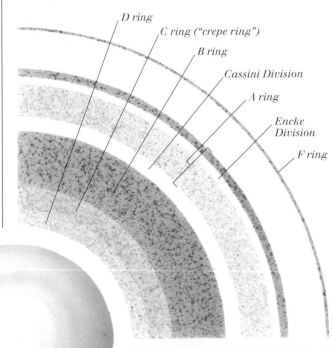

D ring

C ring ("crepe ring")

B ring

Cassini Division

A ring

Encke Division

F ring

MOONS OF SATURN

ENCELADUS
Diameter: 309 miles
Average distance from
planet: 148,000 miles

TETHYS
Diameter: 652 miles
Average distance from
planet: 183,000 miles

DIONE
Diameter: 695 miles
Average distance from
planet: 234,000 miles

MIMAS
Diameter: 247 miles
Average distance from
planet: 115,600 miles

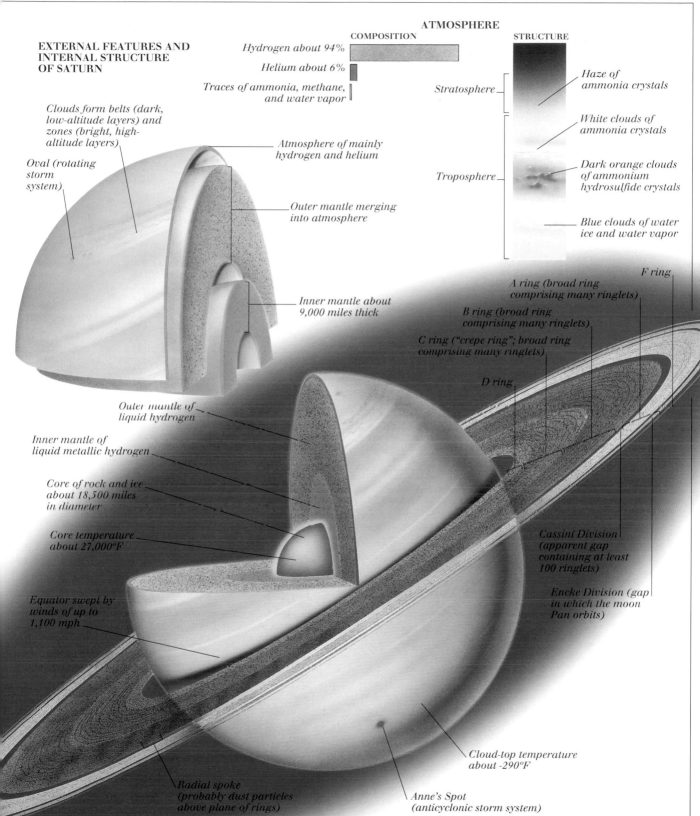

EXTERNAL FEATURES AND
INTERNAL STRUCTURE
OF SATURN

ATMOSPHERE

COMPOSITION

Hydrogen about 94%

Helium about 6%

Traces of ammonia, methane,
and water vapor

STRUCTURE

Stratosphere

Troposphere

Haze of
ammonia crystals

White clouds of
ammonia crystals

Dark orange clouds
of ammonium
hydrosulfide crystals

Blue clouds of water
ice and water vapor

Clouds form belts (dark,
low-altitude layers) and
zones (bright, high-
altitude layers)

Oval (rotating
storm
system)

Atmosphere of mainly
hydrogen and helium

Outer mantle merging
into atmosphere

Inner mantle about
9,000 miles thick

Outer mantle of
liquid hydrogen

Inner mantle of
liquid metallic hydrogen

Core of rock and ice
about 18,500 miles
in diameter

Core temperature
about 27,000°F

Equator swept by
winds of up to
1,100 mph

F ring

A ring (broad ring
comprising many ringlets)

B ring (broad ring
comprising many ringlets)

C ring ("crepe ring"; broad ring
comprising many ringlets)

D ring

Cassini Division
(apparent gap
containing at least
100 ringlets)

Encke Division (gap
in which the moon
Pan orbits)

Cloud-top temperature
about -290°F

Radial spoke
(probably dust particles
above plane of rings)

Anne's Spot
(anticyclonic storm system)

Uranus

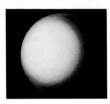

**COLOR-ENHANCED
IMAGE OF URANUS**

URANUS IS THE SEVENTH PLANET from the Sun and the third largest, with a diameter of about 32,000 miles. It is thought to consist of a dense mixture of different types of ice and gas around a solid core. Its atmosphere contains traces of methane, giving the planet a blue-green hue, and the temperature at the cloud tops is about -350°F. Uranus is the most featureless planet to have been closely observed: only a few icy clouds of methane have been seen so far. Uranus is unique among the planets in that its axis of rotation lies close to its orbital plane. As a result of its strongly tilted rotational axis, Uranus rolls on its side along its orbital path around the Sun, while other planets spin more or less upright. Uranus is encircled by 11 rings that consist of rocks interspersed with dust lanes. The rings contain some of the darkest matter in the Solar System. They are extremely narrow, making them difficult to detect: nine of them are less than six miles wide, whereas most of Saturn's rings are thousands of miles in width. There are 15 known Uranian moons, all of which are icy and most of which are farther out than the rings. The 10 inner moons are small and dark, with diameters of less than 100 miles, and the five outer moons are between about 290 and 1,000 miles in diameter. The outer moons have a wide variety of surface features. Miranda has the most varied surface, with cratered areas broken up by huge ridges and cliffs 12 miles high.

TILT AND ROTATION OF URANUS

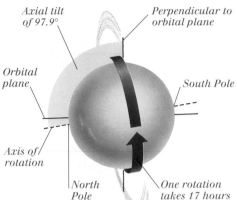

Axial tilt of 97.9°

Perpendicular to orbital plane

Orbital plane

South Pole

Axis of rotation

North Pole

One rotation takes 17 hours and 14 minutes

OUTER MOONS

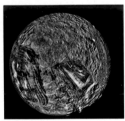

MIRANDA
Diameter: 293 miles
Average distance from planet: 80,700 miles

RINGS OF URANUS

Epsilon ring

Ring 1986 U1R

Delta ring

Gamma ring

Eta ring

Beta ring

Alpha ring

Rings 4 and 5

Ring 6

Ring 1986 U2R

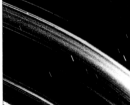

RINGS AND DUST LANES

ARIEL
Diameter: 720 miles
Average distance from planet: 118,800 miles

TITANIA
Diameter: 981 miles
Average distance from planet: 270,900 miles

UMBRIEL
Diameter: 726 miles
Average distance from planet: 165,300 miles

OBERON
Diameter: 946 miles
Average distance from planet: 362,000 miles

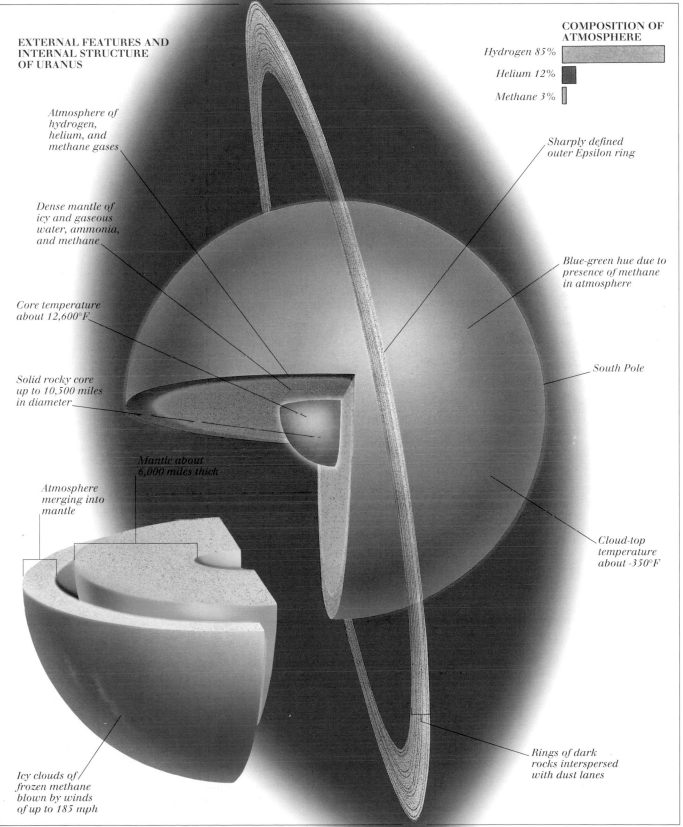

**EXTERNAL FEATURES AND
INTERNAL STRUCTURE
OF URANUS**

**COMPOSITION OF
ATMOSPHERE**

Hydrogen 85%

Helium 12%

Methane 3%

Atmosphere of
hydrogen,
helium, and
methane gases

Dense mantle of
icy and gaseous
water, ammonia,
and methane

Core temperature
about 12,600°F

Solid rocky core
up to 10,500 miles
in diameter

Mantle about
6,000 miles thick

Atmosphere
merging into
mantle

Icy clouds of
frozen methane
blown by winds
of up to 185 mph

Sharply defined
outer Epsilon ring

Blue-green hue due to
presence of methane
in atmosphere

South Pole

Cloud-top
temperature
about -350°F

Rings of dark
rocks interspersed
with dust lanes

49

Neptune and Pluto

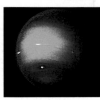

COLOR-ENHANCED
IMAGE OF NEPTUNE

NEPTUNE AND PLUTO are the two farthest planets from the Sun, at an average distance of about 2,800 million miles and 3,700 million miles, respectively. Neptune is a gas giant and is thought to consist of a small rocky core surrounded by a mixture of liquids and gases. The atmosphere contains several prominent cloud features. The largest of these are the Great Dark Spot, which is as wide as the Earth, the Small Dark Spot, and the Scooter. The Great and Small Dark Spots are huge storms that are swept around the planet by winds of about 1,200 miles per hour. The Scooter is a large area of cirrus cloud. Neptune has four tenuous rings and eight known moons. Triton is the largest Neptunian moon and the coldest object in the Solar System, with a temperature of -391°F. Unlike most moons in the Solar System, Triton orbits its mother planet in the opposite direction to the planet's rotation. Pluto is usually the outermost planet, but its elliptical orbit causes it to pass inside the orbit of Neptune for 20 years of its 248-year orbit. Pluto is so small and distant that little is known about it. It is a rocky planet, probably covered with ice and frozen methane. Pluto's only known moon, Charon, is large for a moon, at half the size of its parent planet. Because of the small difference in their sizes, Pluto and Charon are sometimes considered to be a double-planet system.

TILT AND ROTATION OF NEPTUNE

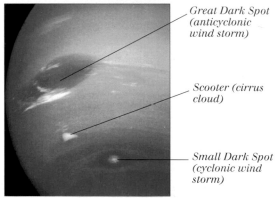

Axial tilt of 28.8°
Perpendicular to orbital plane
Axis of rotation
North Pole
Orbital plane
South Pole
One rotation takes 16 hours and 7 minutes

CLOUD FEATURES OF NEPTUNE

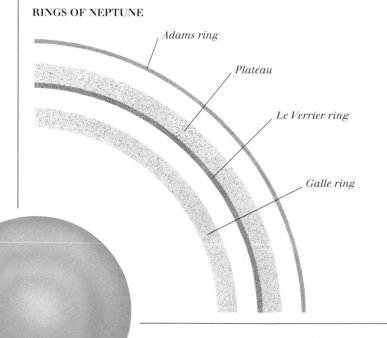

Great Dark Spot (anticyclonic wind storm)

Scooter (cirrus cloud)

Small Dark Spot (cyclonic wind storm)

HIGH-ALTITUDE CLOUDS

Methane cirrus clouds 25 miles above main cloud deck

Cloud shadow

Main cloud deck blown by winds at speeds of about 1,200 mph

RINGS OF NEPTUNE

Adams ring

Plateau

Le Verrier ring

Galle ring

MOONS OF NEPTUNE

TRITON
Diameter: 1,681 miles
Average distance from planet: 220,500 miles

PROTEUS
Diameter: 259 miles
Average distance from planet: 73,100 miles

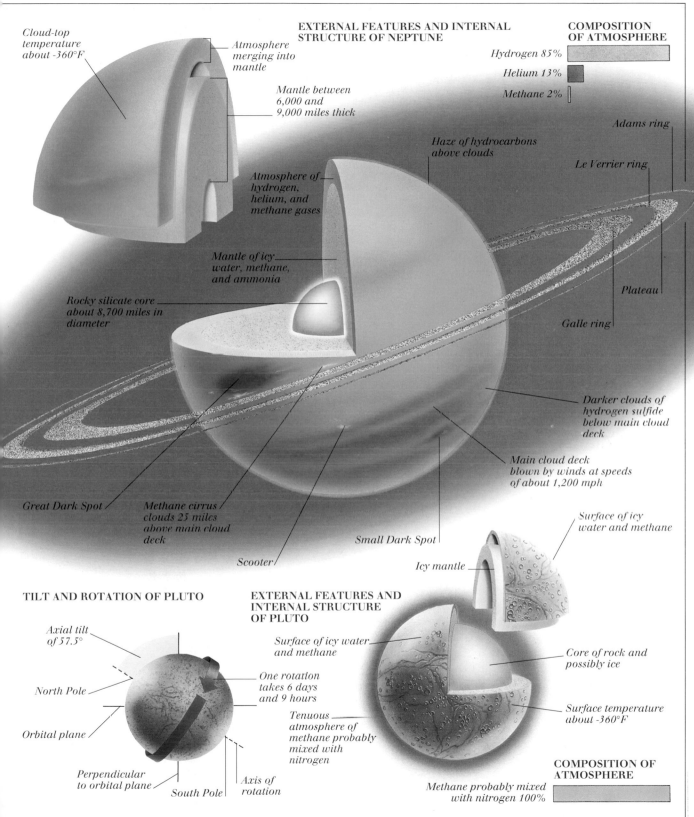

EXTERNAL FEATURES AND INTERNAL STRUCTURE OF NEPTUNE

COMPOSITION OF ATMOSPHERE

Hydrogen 85%

Helium 13%

Methane 2%

Cloud-top temperature about -360°F

Atmosphere merging into mantle

Mantle between 6,000 and 9,000 miles thick

Haze of hydrocarbons above clouds

Adams ring

Le Verrier ring

Atmosphere of hydrogen, helium, and methane gases

Mantle of icy water, methane, and ammonia

Rocky silicate core about 8,700 miles in diameter

Plateau

Galle ring

Darker clouds of hydrogen sulfide below main cloud deck

Main cloud deck blown by winds at speeds of about 1,200 mph

Great Dark Spot

Methane cirrus clouds 25 miles above main cloud deck

Scooter

Small Dark Spot

Surface of icy water and methane

Icy mantle

TILT AND ROTATION OF PLUTO

EXTERNAL FEATURES AND INTERNAL STRUCTURE OF PLUTO

Surface of icy water and methane

Core of rock and possibly ice

Axial tilt of 57.5°

North Pole

Orbital plane

One rotation takes 6 days and 9 hours

Tenuous atmosphere of methane probably mixed with nitrogen

Surface temperature about -360°F

Perpendicular to orbital plane

South Pole

Axis of rotation

COMPOSITION OF ATMOSPHERE

Methane probably mixed with nitrogen 100%

Asteroids, comets, and meteoroids

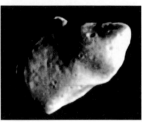

ASTEROID 951 GASPRA

ASTEROIDS, COMETS, AND METEOROIDS are all debris remaining from the nebula in which the Solar System formed 4.6 billion years ago. Asteroids are rocky bodies up to several hundred miles in diameter, although most are much smaller. Most of them orbit the Sun in the asteroid belt, which lies between the orbits of Mars and Jupiter. Comets may originate in a huge cloud, called the Oort Cloud, that is thought to surround the Solar System. They are made of frozen gases and dust, and are a few miles in diameter. Occasionally, a comet is deflected from the Oort Cloud to orbit the Sun in a long, elliptical path. As the comet approaches the Sun, the comet's surface starts to vaporize in the heat, producing a brightly shining coma (a huge sphere of gas and dust around the nucleus), a gas tail, and a dust tail. Meteoroids are small chunks of stone or stone and iron, some of which are fragments of asteroids or comets. Meteoroids range in size from tiny dust particles to objects tens of yards across. If a meteoroid enters the Earth's atmosphere, it is heated by friction and appears as a glowing streak of light called a meteor (also known as a shooting star). Meteor showers occur when the Earth passes through the trail of dust particles left by a comet. Most meteors burn up in the atmosphere. The few that are large enough to reach the Earth's surface are termed meteorites.

COLOR-ENHANCED IMAGE
OF HALLEY'S COMET

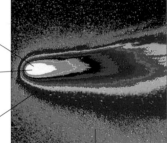

High-intensity
light emission

Nucleus

Medium-intensity
light emission

Low-intensity
light emission

COLOR-ENHANCED IMAGE OF
A LEONID METEOR SHOWER

METEORITES

DEVELOPMENT OF COMET TAILS

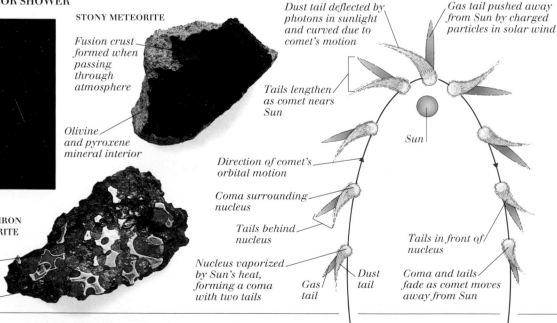

STONY METEORITE

Fusion crust
formed when
passing
through
atmosphere

Olivine
and pyroxene
mineral interior

STONY-IRON
METEORITE

Iron

Stone (olivine)

Dust tail deflected by
photons in sunlight
and curved due to
comet's motion

Gas tail pushed away
from Sun by charged
particles in solar wind

Tails lengthen
as comet nears
Sun

Sun

Direction of comet's
orbital motion

Coma surrounding
nucleus

Tails behind
nucleus

Tails in front of
nucleus

Nucleus vaporized
by Sun's heat,
forming a coma
with two tails

Gas
tail

Dust
tail

Coma and tails
fade as comet moves
away from Sun

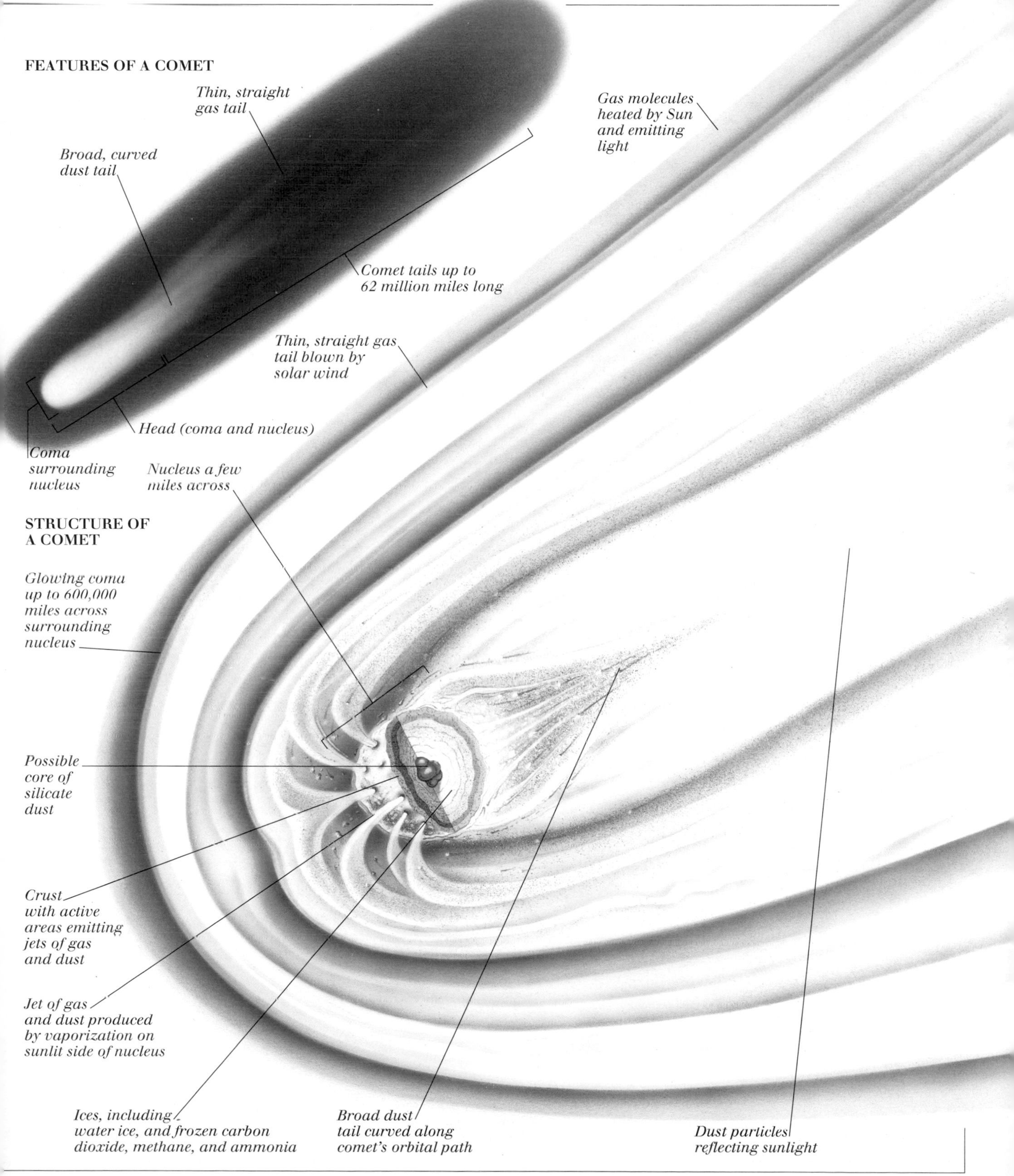

FEATURES OF A COMET

Thin, straight gas tail

Broad, curved dust tail

Gas molecules heated by Sun and emitting light

Comet tails up to 62 million miles long

Thin, straight gas tail blown by solar wind

Head (coma and nucleus)

Coma surrounding nucleus

Nucleus a few miles across

STRUCTURE OF A COMET

Glowing coma up to 600,000 miles across surrounding nucleus

Possible core of silicate dust

Crust with active areas emitting jets of gas and dust

Jet of gas and dust produced by vaporization on sunlit side of nucleus

Ices, including water ice, and frozen carbon dioxide, methane, and ammonia

Broad dust tail curved along comet's orbital path

Dust particles reflecting sunlight

PREHISTORIC EARTH

The changing Earth

THE EARTH FORMED FROM A CLOUD OF DUST and gas drifting through space about 4,600 million years ago. Dense minerals sank to the center while lighter ones formed a thin rocky crust. However, the first known life forms—bacteria and blue-green algae—did not appear until about 3,400 million years ago, and it was only about 700 million years ago that more complex plants and animals began to develop. Since then, thousands of animal and plant species have evolved. Some, such as the dinosaurs, survived for millions of years, while others died out quickly. The Earth itself is continually changing. Although continents neared their present locations about 50 million years ago, they are still drifting slowly over the planet's surface, and mountain ranges such as the Himalayas—which began to form 40 million years ago—are continually being built up and worn away. Climate is also subject to change: the Earth has undergone a series of ice ages interspersed with warmer periods (the most recent ice age was at its height about 20,000 years ago).

Small mammals appeared (e.g., Crusafontia)

Dinosaurs became extinct

Global mountain building occurred

Multicellular soft-bodied animals appeared (e.g., worms and jellyfish)

Shelled invertebrates appeared (e.g., trilobites)

Marine plants flourished

Land plants appeared (e.g., Cooksonia)

Unicellular organisms appeared (e.g., blue-green algae)

Earth formed

Coral reefs appeared

Vertebrates appeared (e.g., Hemicyclaspis)

More complex types of algae appeared

Amphibians appeared (e.g., Ichthyostega)

CRETACEO

ORDOVICIAN   CAMBRIAN   PRECAMBRIAN TIME

SILURIAN   DEVONIAN

GEOLOGICAL TIMESCALE

MILLIONS OF
YEARS AGO (MYA)

| 4,600 | 570 | 510 | 439 | 409 | 363 | 323 | 29 |

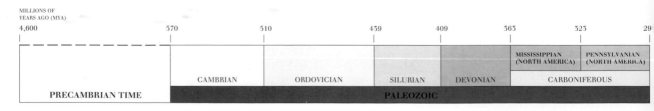

					MISSISSIPPIAN (NORTH AMERICA)	PENNSYLVANIAN (NORTH AMERICA)	
	CAMBRIAN	ORDOVICIAN	SILURIAN	DEVONIAN	CARBONIFEROUS		
PRECAMBRIAN TIME	PALEOZOIC						

EVOLUTION OF THE EARTH

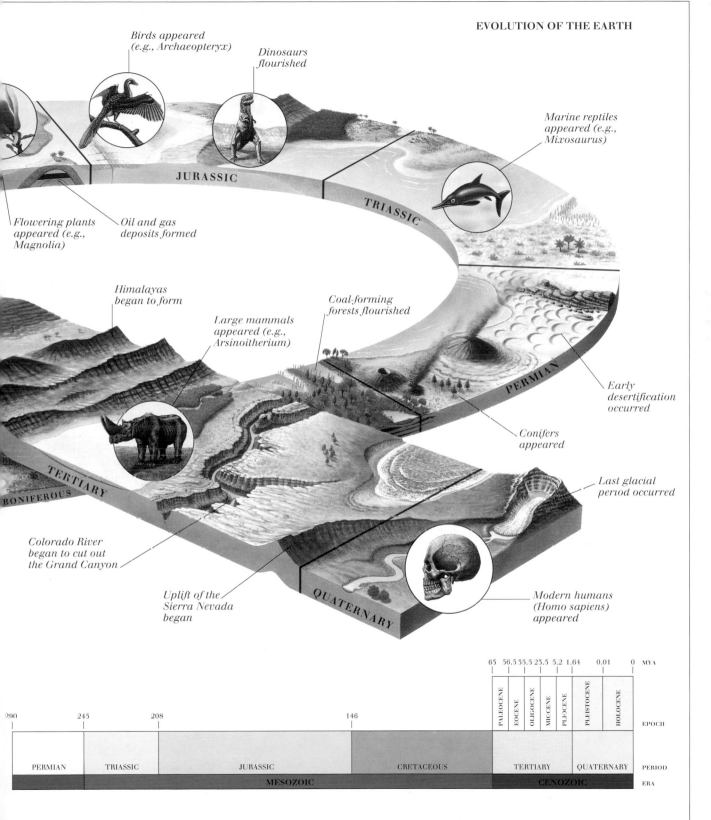

Birds appeared
(e.g., Archaeopteryx)

Dinosaurs
flourished

Marine reptiles
appeared (e.g.,
Mixosaurus)

JURASSIC

TRIASSIC

Flowering plants
appeared (e.g.,
Magnolia)

Oil and gas
deposits formed

Himalayas
began to form

Large mammals
appeared (e.g.,
Arsinoitherium)

Coal-forming
forests flourished

PERMIAN

Early
desertification
occurred

Conifers
appeared

TERTIARY

BONIFEROUS

Last glacial
period occurred

Colorado River
began to cut out
the Grand Canyon

Uplift of the
Sierra Nevada
began

QUATERNARY

Modern humans
(Homo sapiens)
appeared

					65	56.5	35.5	23.5	5.2	1.64		0.01		0 MYA
					PALEOCENE	EOCENE	OLIGOCENE	MIOCENE	PLIOCENE		PLEISTOCENE		HOLOCENE	EPOCH
290	245	208		146										
PERMIAN	TRIASSIC	JURASSIC		CRETACEOUS				TERTIARY			QUATERNARY			PERIOD
		MESOZOIC						CENOZOIC						ERA

57

The Earth's crust

THE EARTH'S CRUST IS THE SOLID outer shell of the Earth. It includes continental crust (about 25 miles thick) and oceanic crust (about four miles thick). The crust and the topmost layer of the mantle form the lithosphere. The lithosphere consists of semi-rigid plates that move relative to each other on the underlying asthenosphere (a partly molten layer of the mantle). This movement is known as plate tectonics and helps explain continental drift. Where two plates move apart, there are rifts in the crust. In mid-ocean, this movement results in seafloor spreading and the formation of ocean ridges; on continents, crustal spreading can form rift valleys. When plates move toward each other, one may be subducted beneath (forced under) the other. In mid-ocean, this causes ocean trenches, seismic activity, and arcs of volcanic islands. Where oceanic crust is subducted beneath continental crust or where continents collide, land may be uplifted and mountains formed (see pp. 62–63). Plates may also slide past each other—along the San Andreas fault, for example. Crustal movement on continents may result in earthquakes, while movement under the seabed can lead to tidal waves.

ELEMENTS IN THE EARTH'S CRUST

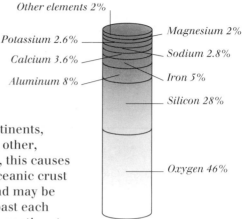

Other elements 2%

Potassium 2.6%

Calcium 3.6%

Aluminum 8%

Magnesium 2%

Sodium 2.8%

Iron 5%

Silicon 28%

Oxygen 46%

FEATURES OF PLATE MOVEMENTS

Ocean trench formed where oceanic crust is forced under continental crust

Subduction zone

Ridge where magma is rising to form new oceanic crust

Region of seafloor spreading

Rift formed where two plates are moving apart

Magma rises to form a hot spot

Magma (molten rock) erupts at rift

Volcano develops over hot spot and builds up to form an island

Volcanic island that originally formed over hot spot

Oceanic crust melts

Magma rises to form a volcano

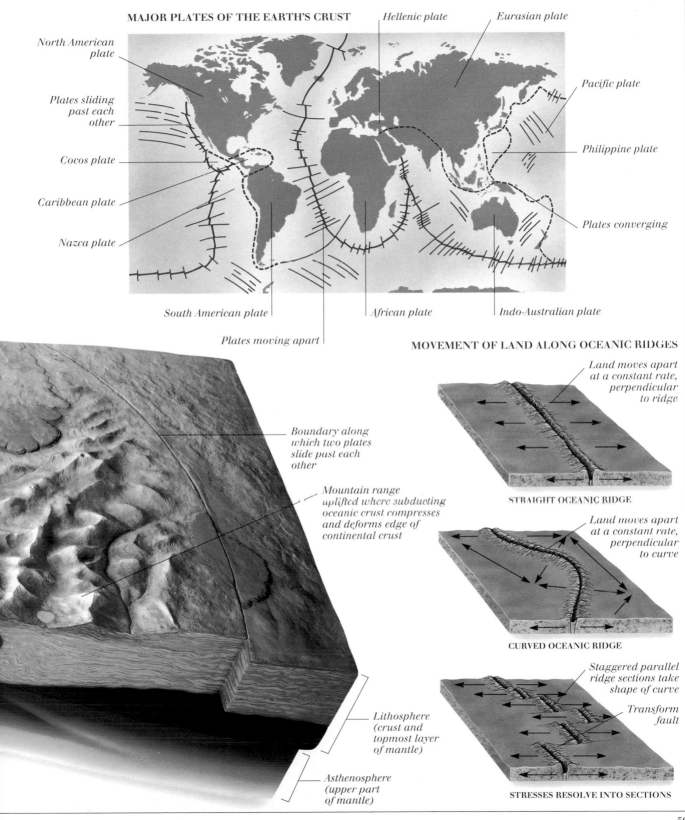

MAJOR PLATES OF THE EARTH'S CRUST

North American plate

Plates sliding past each other

Cocos plate

Caribbean plate

Nazca plate

Hellenic plate

Eurasian plate

Pacific plate

Philippine plate

Plates converging

South American plate

Plates moving apart

African plate

Indo-Australian plate

Boundary along which two plates slide past each other

Mountain range uplifted where subducting oceanic crust compresses and deforms edge of continental crust

Lithosphere (crust and topmost layer of mantle)

Asthenosphere (upper part of mantle)

MOVEMENT OF LAND ALONG OCEANIC RIDGES

Land moves apart at a constant rate, perpendicular to ridge

STRAIGHT OCEANIC RIDGE

Land moves apart at a constant rate, perpendicular to curve

CURVED OCEANIC RIDGE

Staggered parallel ridge sections take shape of curve

Transform fault

STRESSES RESOLVE INTO SECTIONS

Faults and folds

THE CONTINUOUS MOVEMENT of the Earth's crustal plates (see pp. 58–59) can squeeze, stretch, or break rock strata, deforming them and producing faults and folds. A fault is a fracture in a rock along which there is movement of one side relative to the other. The movement can be vertical, horizontal, or oblique (vertical and horizontal). Faults develop when rocks are subjected to compression or tension. They tend to occur in hard, rigid rocks, which are more likely to break than bend. The smallest faults occur in single mineral crystals and are microscopically small, while the largest —the Great Rift Valley in Africa, which formed between 5 million and 100,000 years ago—is more than 6,000 miles long. A fold is a bend in a rock layer caused by compression. Folds occur in elastic rocks, which tend to bend rather than break. The two main types of fold are anticlines (upfolds) and synclines (downfolds). Folds vary in size from a few millimeters long to folded mountain ranges hundreds of miles long, such as the Himalayas (see pp. 62–63) and the Alps, which are repeatedly folding. In addition to faults and folds, other features associated with rock deformations include boudins, mullions, and *en échelon* fractures.

STRUCTURE OF A FOLD

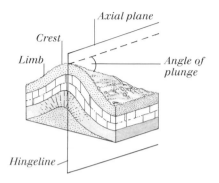

Axial plane
Crest
Limb
Angle of plunge
Hingeline

STRUCTURE OF A FAULT

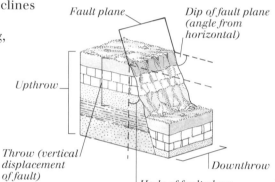

Fault plane
Dip of fault plane (angle from horizontal)
Upthrow
Throw (vertical displacement of fault)
Downthrow
Hade of fault plane (angle from vertical)

STRUCTURE OF A SLOPE

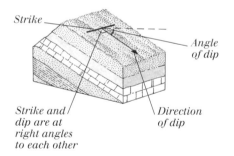

Strike
Angle of dip
Strike and dip are at right angles to each other
Direction of dip

FOLDED ROCK

Steeply dipping limbs
Crest of anticline
Plunge

SECTION THROUGH FOLDED ROCK STRATA THAT HAVE BEEN ERODED

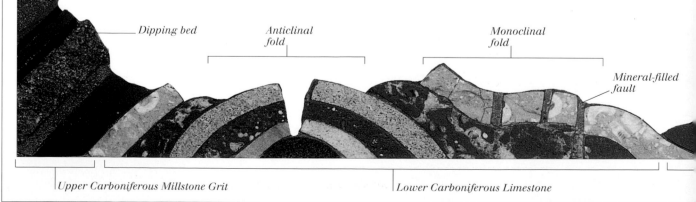

Dipping bed
Anticlinal fold
Monoclinal fold
Mineral-filled fault

Upper Carboniferous Millstone Grit
Lower Carboniferous Limestone

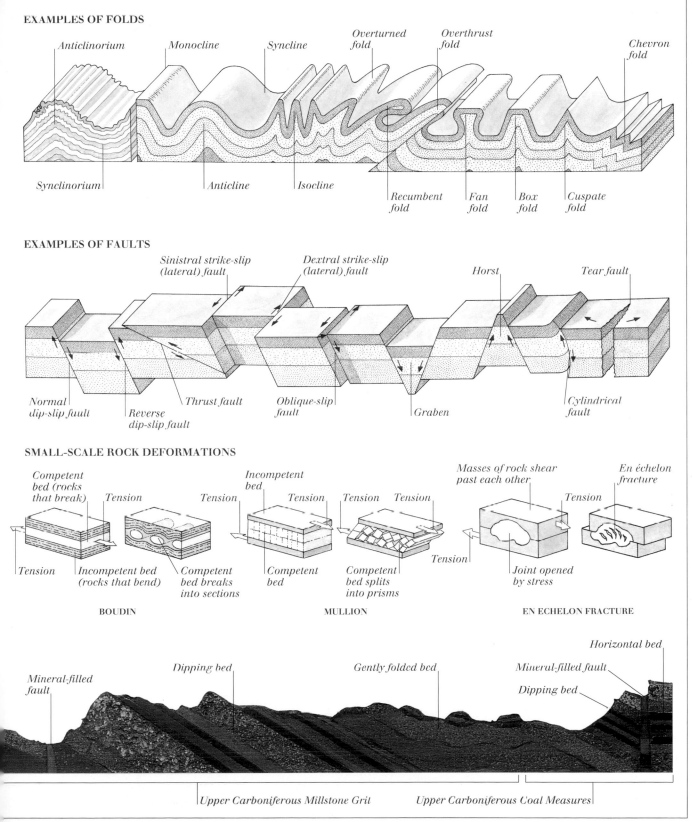

EXAMPLES OF FOLDS

Anticlinorium

Monocline

Syncline

Overturned fold

Overthrust fold

Chevron fold

Synclinorium

Anticline

Isocline

Recumbent fold

Fan fold

Box fold

Cuspate fold

EXAMPLES OF FAULTS

Sinistral strike-slip (lateral) fault

Dextral strike-slip (lateral) fault

Horst

Tear fault

Normal dip-slip fault

Reverse dip-slip fault

Thrust fault

Oblique-slip fault

Graben

Cylindrical fault

SMALL-SCALE ROCK DEFORMATIONS

Competent bed (rocks that break)

Tension

Incompetent bed

Tension

Tension

Tension

Masses of rock shear past each other

En échelon fracture

Tension

Tension

Incompetent bed (rocks that bend)

Competent bed breaks into sections

Competent bed

Competent bed splits into prisms

Tension

Joint opened by stress

BOUDIN

MULLION

EN ECHELON FRACTURE

Mineral-filled fault

Dipping bed

Gently folded bed

Horizontal bed

Mineral-filled fault

Dipping bed

Upper Carboniferous Millstone Grit

Upper Carboniferous Coal Measures

Mountain building

THE PROCESSES INVOLVED in mountain building—termed orogenesis—occur as a result of the movement of the Earth's crustal plates (see pp. 58-59). There are three main types of mountains: volcanic mountains, fold mountains, and block mountains. Most volcanic mountains have been formed along plate boundaries where plates have come together or moved apart and lava and other debris have been ejected onto the Earth's surface. The lava and debris may have built up to form a dome around the vent of a volcano. Fold mountains are formed where plates push together and cause the rock to buckle upward. Where oceanic crust meets less dense continental crust, the oceanic crust is forced under the continental crust. The continental crust is buckled by the impact. This is how folded mountain ranges, such as the Appalachian Mountains in North America, were formed. Fold mountains are also formed where two areas of continental crust meet. The Himalayas, for example, began to form when India collided with Asia, buckling the sediments and parts of the oceanic crust between them. Block mountains are formed when a block of land is uplifted between two faults as a result of compression or tension in the Earth's crust (see pp. 60-61). Often, the movement along faults has taken place gradually over millions of years. However, two plates may cause an earthquake by suddenly sliding past each other along a faultline.

BHAGIRATHI PARBAT, HIMALAYAS

FORMATION OF THE HIMALAYAS

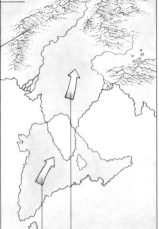

Asia

Himalayas formed by buckling of sediment and part of the oceanic crust between two colliding continents

India moves north

India collides with Asia about 40 million years ago

EXAMPLES OF MOUNTAINS

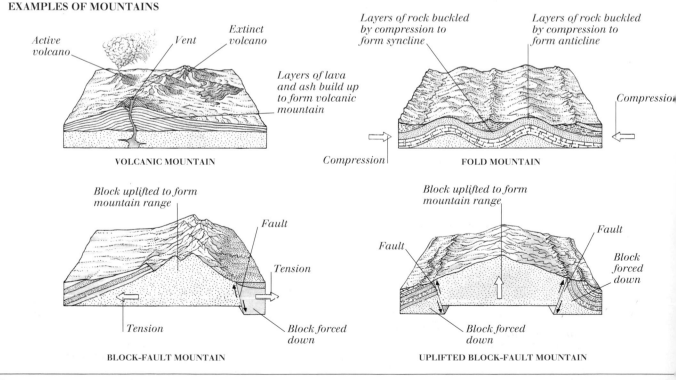

Active volcano

Vent

Extinct volcano

Layers of lava and ash build up to form volcanic mountain

VOLCANIC MOUNTAIN

Layers of rock buckled by compression to form syncline

Layers of rock buckled by compression to form anticline

Compression

Compression

FOLD MOUNTAIN

Block uplifted to form mountain range

Fault

Tension

Tension

Block forced down

BLOCK-FAULT MOUNTAIN

Block uplifted to form mountain range

Fault

Fault

Block forced down

Block forced down

UPLIFTED BLOCK-FAULT MOUNTAIN

STAGES IN THE FORMATION OF THE HIMALAYAS

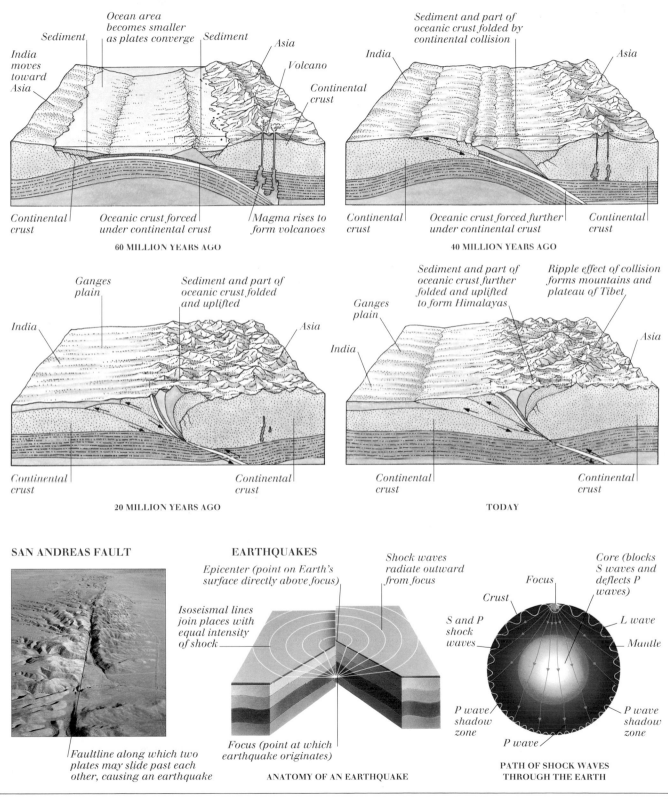

Ocean area
becomes smaller
as plates converge

India
moves
toward
Asia

Sediment

Sediment

Asia

Volcano

Continental
crust

Continental
crust

Oceanic crust forced
under continental crust

Magma rises to
form volcanoes

60 MILLION YEARS AGO

Sediment and part of
oceanic crust folded by
continental collision

India

Asia

Continental
crust

Oceanic crust forced further
under continental crust

Continental
crust

40 MILLION YEARS AGO

Ganges
plain

India

Sediment and part of
oceanic crust folded
and uplifted

Asia

Continental
crust

Continental
crust

20 MILLION YEARS AGO

Sediment and part of
oceanic crust further
folded and uplifted
to form Himalayas

Ripple effect of collision
forms mountains and
plateau of Tibet

Ganges
plain

India

Asia

Continental
crust

Continental
crust

TODAY

SAN ANDREAS FAULT

Faultline along which two
plates may slide past each
other, causing an earthquake

EARTHQUAKES

Epicenter (point on Earth's
surface directly above focus)

Isoseismal lines
join places with
equal intensity
of shock

Shock waves
radiate outward
from focus

Focus (point at which
earthquake originates)

ANATOMY OF AN EARTHQUAKE

Focus

Crust

S and P
shock
waves

Core (blocks
S waves and
deflects P
waves)

L wave

Mantle

P wave
shadow
zone

P wave
shadow
zone

P wave

**PATH OF SHOCK WAVES
THROUGH THE EARTH**

Precambrian to Devonian periods

WHEN THE EARTH FORMED about 4,600 million years ago,
its atmosphere consisted of volcanic gases with little oxygen,
making it hostile to most forms of life. One large supercontinent,
Gondwanaland, was situated over the southern polar region,
while other smaller continents were spread over the rest of the
world. Constant movement of the earth's crustal plates carried
continents across the earth's surface. The first primitive life-forms
emerged around 3,400 million years ago in shallow, warm seas.
The build up of oxygen began to form a shield of ozone
around the earth, protecting living organisms from the
sun's harmful rays and helping to establish an atmosphere
in which life could sustain itself. The first vertebrates appeared
about 470 million years ago, during the Ordovician period (510–439 million
years ago), the first land plants appeared around 400 million years ago during the
Devonian period (409–363 million years ago), and the first land animals about 30 million years later.

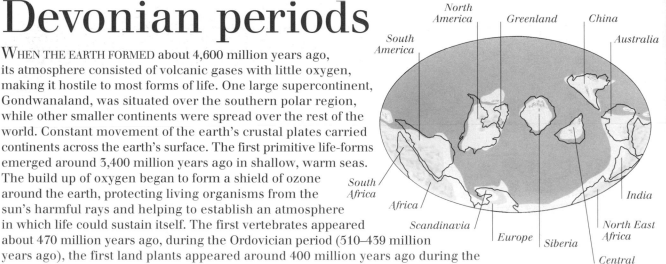

**MIDDLE ORDOVICIAN POSITIONS
OF PRESENT-DAY LANDMASSES**

North America · South America · Greenland · China · Australia · South Africa · Africa · Scandinavia · Europe · Siberia · India · North East Africa · Central Asia

EXAMPLES OF PRECAMBRIAN TO DEVONIAN PLANT GROUPS

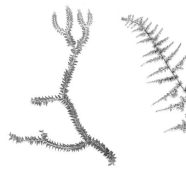

A PRESENT-DAY CLUBMOSS
(*Lycopodium sp.*)

**A PRESENT-DAY
LAND PLANT**
(*Asparagus setaceous*)

FOSSIL OF AN EXTINCT LAND PLANT
(*Cooksonia hemisphaerica*)

FOSSIL OF AN EXTINCT SWAMP PLANT
(*Zosterophyllum llanoveranum*)

EXAMPLES OF PRECAMBRIAN
TO DEVONIAN TRILOBITES

ACADAGNOSTUS
Family: Agnostidae
Length: $^1/_3$ in (8 mm)

PHACOPS
Family: Phacopidae
Length: $1^3/_4$ in (4.5 cm)

OLENELLUS
Family: Olenellidae
Length: $2^1/_2$ in (6 cm)

ELRATHIA
Family: Ptychopariidae
Length: $^3/_4$ in (2 cm)

THE EARTH DURING THE MIDDLE ORDOVICIAN PERIOD

EXAMPLES OF EARLY MARINE INVERTEBRATES

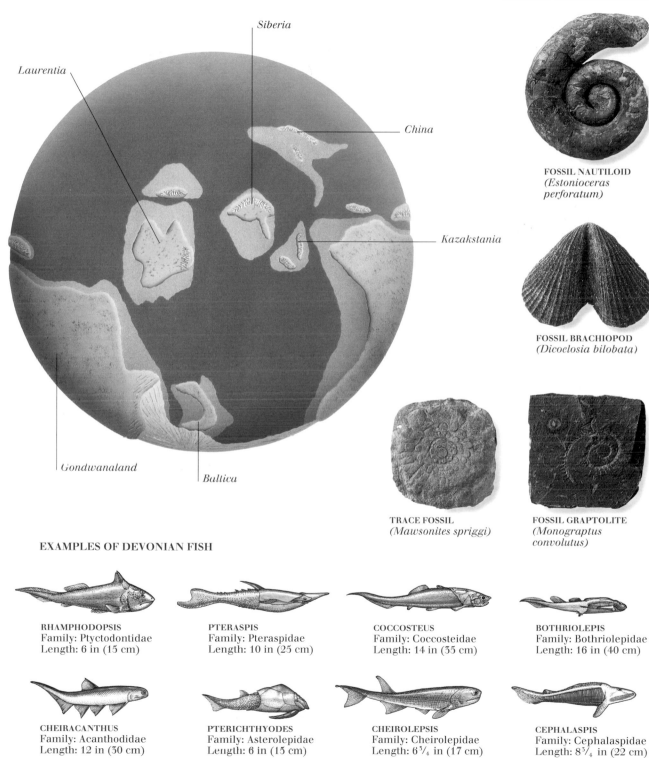

Siberia

Laurentia

China

Kazakstania

Gondwanaland

Baltica

FOSSIL NAUTILOID
(*Estonioceras perforatum*)

FOSSIL BRACHIOPOD
(*Dicoelosia bilobata*)

TRACE FOSSIL
(*Mawsonites spriggi*)

FOSSIL GRAPTOLITE
(*Monograptus convolutus*)

EXAMPLES OF DEVONIAN FISH

RHAMPHODOPSIS
Family: Ptyctodontidae
Length: 6 in (15 cm)

PTERASPIS
Family: Pteraspidae
Length: 10 in (25 cm)

COCCOSTEUS
Family: Coccosteidae
Length: 14 in (35 cm)

BOTHRIOLEPIS
Family: Bothriolepidae
Length: 16 in (40 cm)

CHEIRACANTHUS
Family: Acanthodidae
Length: 12 in (30 cm)

PTERICHTHYODES
Family: Asterolepidae
Length: 6 in (15 cm)

CHEIROLEPIS
Family: Cheirolepidae
Length: $6^{3}/_{4}$ in (17 cm)

CEPHALASPIS
Family: Cephalaspidae
Length: $8^{3}/_{4}$ in (22 cm)

Carboniferous to Permian periods

North America · Greenland · Siberia · China · South America · Antarctica · Africa · India · Australia · Antarctica

THE CARBONIFEROUS PERIOD (363–290 million years ago) takes its name from the thick, carbon-rich layers—now coal—that were produced during this period when swampy tropical forests were repeatedly drowned by shallow seas. The humid climate across northern and equatorial continents throughout Carboniferous times produced the first dense plant cover on Earth. During the early part of this period, the first reptiles appeared. Their development of a waterproof egg with a protective internal structure ended animal life's dependence on an aquatic environment. Toward the end of Carboniferous times, the earth's continents Laurussia and Gondwanaland collided, resulting in the huge landmass of Pangaea. Glaciers smothered much of the southern hemisphere during the Permian period (290–245 million years ago), covering Antarctica, parts of Australia, and much of South America, Africa, and India. Ice locked up much of the world's water and large areas of the northern hemisphere experienced a drop in sea-level. Away from the poles, deserts and a hot dry climate predominated. As a result of these conditions, the Permian period ended with the greatest mass extinction of life on earth ever.

EXAMPLES OF CARBONIFEROUS AND PERMIAN PLANT GROUPS

A PRESENT-DAY FIR
(Abies concolor)

FOSSIL OF AN EXTINCT FERN
(Zeilleria frenzlii)

**FOSSIL OF AN
EXTINCT HORSETAIL**
(Equisetites sp.)

**FOSSIL OF AN
EXTINCT CLUBMOSS**
(Lepidodendron sp.)

EXAMPLES OF CARBONIFEROUS AND PERMIAN TREES

PECOPTERIS
Family: Marattiaceae
Height: 13 ft (4 m)

PARIPTERIS
Family: Medullosaceae
Height: 16 ft 6 in (5 m)

MARIOPTERIS
Family: Unclassified
Height: 16 ft 6 in (5 m)

MEDULLOSA
Family: Medullosaceae
Height: 16 ft 6 in (5 m)

THE EARTH DURING THE LATE CARBONIFEROUS PERIOD

EXAMPLES OF CARBONIFEROUS AND PERMIAN ANIMALS

Siberia

Laurussia

China

Ural Mountains

Caledonian Mountains

Appalachian Mountains

Gondwanaland

SKULL OF AN EXTINCT SYNAPSID REPTILE
(*Dimetrodon loomisi*)

FOSSIL TEETH OF
AN EXTINCT SHARK
(*Helicoprion bessonowi*)

MODEL OF AN EXTINCT
CARBONIFEROUS REPTILE
(*Westlothiana lizziae*)

LEPIDODENDRON
Family: Lepidodendraceae
Height: 100 ft (30 m)

CORDAITES
Family: Cordaitacea
Height: 33 ft (10 m)

GLOSSOPTERIS
Family: Glossopteridaceae
Height: 26 ft (8 m)

ALETHOPTERIS
Family Medullosaceae
Height: 16 ft 6 in (5 m)

Triassic period

THE TRIASSIC PERIOD (245–208 million years ago) marked the beginning of what is known as the Age of the Dinosaurs (the Mesozoic era). During this period, the present-day continents were massed together, forming one huge continent known as Pangaea. This landmass experienced extremes of climate, with lush green areas around the coast or by lakes and rivers, and arid deserts in the interior. The only forms of plant life were nonflowering plants, such as conifers, ferns, cycads, and ginkgos; flowering plants had not yet evolved. The principal forms of animal life included primitive amphibians, rhynchosaurs ("beaked lizards"), and primitive crocodilians. Dinosaurs first appeared about 230 million years ago, at the beginning of the Late Triassic period. The earliest known dinosaurs were the carnivorous (flesh-eating) herrerasaurids and staurikosaurids, such as *Herrerasaurus* and *Staurikosaurus*. Early herbivorous (plant-eating) dinosaurs first appeared in Late Triassic times and included *Plateosaurus* and *Technosaurus*. By the end of the Triassic period, dinosaurs dominated Pangaea, possibly contributing to the extinction of many other reptiles.

TRIASSIC POSITIONS OF PRESENT-DAY LANDMASSES

North America
Europe
Asia
South America
Africa
Antarctica
India
Australia

EXAMPLES OF TRIASSIC PLANT GROUPS

A PRESENT-DAY CYCAD
(*Cycas revoluta*)

A PRESENT-DAY GINKGO
(*Ginkgo biloba*)

A PRESENT-DAY CONIFER
(*Araucaria araucana*)

FOSSIL OF AN EXTINCT FERN
(*Pachypteris* sp.)

FOSSIL LEAF OF AN EXTINCT CYCAD
(*Cycas* sp.)

EXAMPLES OF TRIASSIC DINOSAURS

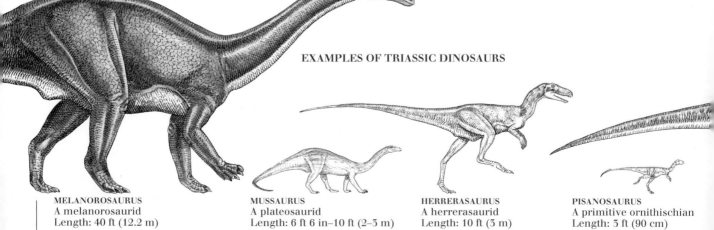

MELANOROSAURUS
A melanorosaurid
Length: 40 ft (12.2 m)

MUSSAURUS
A plateosaurid
Length: 6 ft 6 in–10 ft (2–3 m)

HERRERASAURUS
A herrerasaurid
Length: 10 ft (3 m)

PISANOSAURUS
A primitive ornithischian
Length: 3 ft (90 cm)

THE EARTH DURING THE TRIASSIC PERIOD

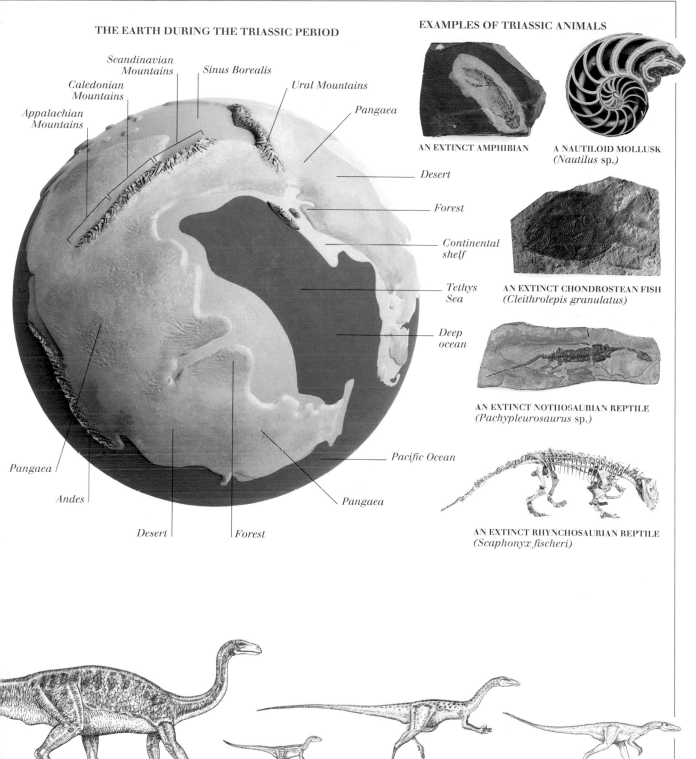

Scandinavian
Mountains

Caledonian
Mountains

Sinus Borealis

Ural Mountains

Appalachian
Mountains

Pangaea

Desert

Forest

Continental
shelf

Tethys
Sea

Deep
ocean

Pangaea

Andes

Pacific Ocean

Desert

Forest

Pangaea

EXAMPLES OF TRIASSIC ANIMALS

AN EXTINCT AMPHIBIAN

A NAUTILOID MOLLUSK
(*Nautilus* sp.)

AN EXTINCT CHONDROSTEAN FISH
(*Cleithrolepis granulatus*)

AN EXTINCT NOTHOSAURIAN REPTILE
(*Pachypleurosaurus* sp.)

AN EXTINCT RHYNCHOSAURIAN REPTILE
(*Scaphonyx fischeri*)

PLATEOSAURUS
A plateosaurid
Length: 26 ft (7.9 m)

TECHNOSAURUS
A primitive ornithischian
Length: 3 ft 3 in (1 m)

COELOPHYSIS
A coelophysid
Length: 10 ft (3 m)

STAURIKOSAURUS
A staurikosaurid
Length: 6 ft 6 in (2 m)

Jurassic period

THE JURASSIC PERIOD, the middle part of the Mesozoic era, lasted from 208 to 146 million years ago. During the Jurassic period, the landmass of Pangaea broke up into the continents of Gondwanaland and Laurasia, and sea-levels rose, flooding areas of lower land. The Jurassic climate was warm and moist. Plants such as ginkgos, horsetails, and conifers thrived, and giant redwood trees appeared, as did the first flowering plants. The abundance of plant food coincided with the proliferation of herbivorous (plant-eating) dinosaurs, such as the large sauropods (e.g., *Diplodocus*) and stegosaurs (e.g., *Stegosaurus*). Carnivorous (flesh-eating) dinosaurs, such as *Compsognathus* and *Allosaurus*, also flourished by hunting the many animals that existed—among them other dinosaurs. Further Jurassic animals included shrewlike mammals, and pterosaurs (flying reptiles), as well as plesiosaurs and ichthyosaurs (both marine reptiles).

JURASSIC POSITIONS OF PRESENT-DAY LANDMASSES

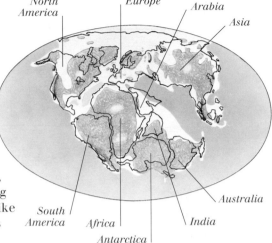

North America

Europe

Arabia

Asia

South America

Africa

Antarctica

India

Australia

EXAMPLES OF JURASSIC PLANT GROUPS

A PRESENT-DAY FERN
(*Dicksonia antarctica*)

A PRESENT-DAY HORSETAIL
(*Equisetum arvense*)

A PRESENT-DAY CONIFER
(*Taxus baccata*)

FOSSIL LEAF OF AN EXTINCT CONIFER
(*Taxus sp.*)

FOSSIL LEAF OF AN EXTINCT REDWOOD
(*Sequoiadendron affinis*)

EXAMPLES OF JURASSIC DINOSAURS

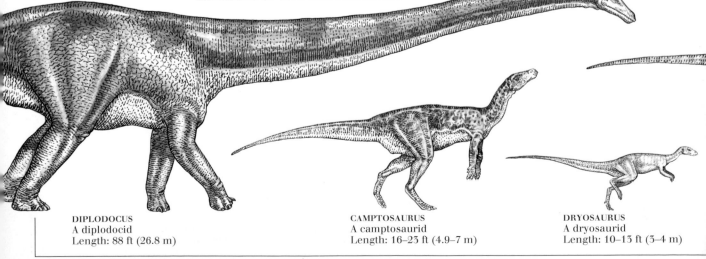

DIPLODOCUS
A diplodocid
Length: 88 ft (26.8 m)

CAMPTOSAURUS
A camptosaurid
Length: 16–23 ft (4.9–7 m)

DRYOSAURUS
A dryosaurid
Length: 10–15 ft (3–4 m)

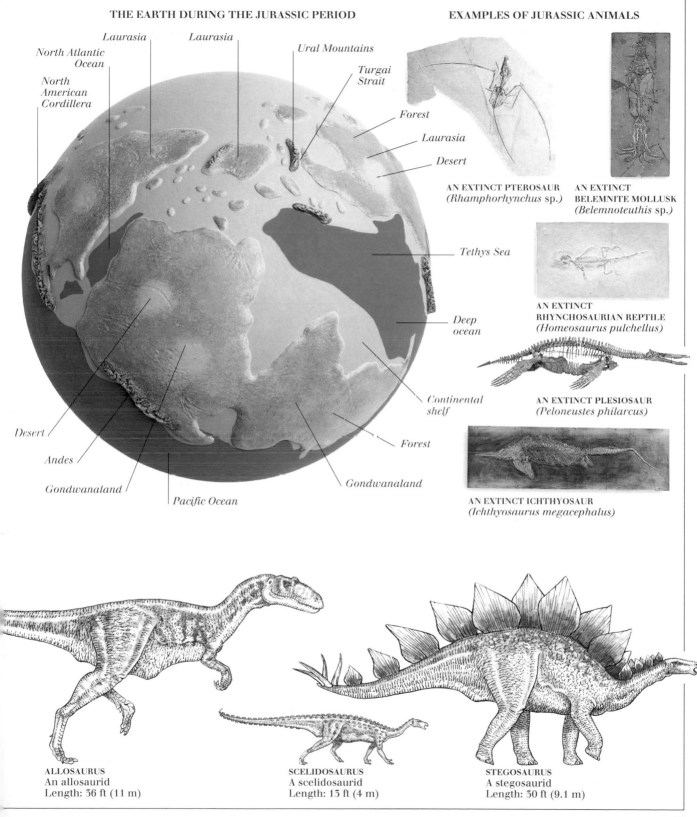

THE EARTH DURING THE JURASSIC PERIOD

North American Cordillera

North Atlantic Ocean

Laurasia

Laurasia

Ural Mountains

Turgai Strait

Forest

Laurasia

Desert

Tethys Sea

Deep ocean

Continental shelf

Forest

Gondwanaland

Gondwanaland

Pacific Ocean

Andes

Desert

EXAMPLES OF JURASSIC ANIMALS

AN EXTINCT PTEROSAUR
(*Rhamphorhynchus* sp.)

AN EXTINCT BELEMNITE MOLLUSK
(*Belemnoteuthis* sp.)

AN EXTINCT RHYNCHOSAURIAN REPTILE
(*Homeosaurus pulchellus*)

AN EXTINCT PLESIOSAUR
(*Peloneustes philarcus*)

AN EXTINCT ICHTHYOSAUR
(*Ichthyosaurus megacephalus*)

ALLOSAURUS
An allosaurid
Length: 36 ft (11 m)

SCELIDOSAURUS
A scelidosaurid
Length: 13 ft (4 m)

STEGOSAURUS
A stegosaurid
Length: 30 ft (9.1 m)

Cretaceous period

THE MESOZOIC ERA ENDED WITH the Cretaceous period, which lasted from 146 to 65 million years ago. During this period, Gondwanaland and Laurasia were breaking up into smaller landmasses that more closely resembled those of the modern continents. The climate remained mild and moist, but the seasons became more marked. Flowering plants, including deciduous trees, replaced many cycads, seed ferns, and conifers. Animal species became more varied, with the evolution of new mammals, insects, fish, crustaceans, and turtles. Dinosaurs evolved into a wide variety of species during Cretaceous times; more than half of all known dinosaurs—including *Iguanodon*, *Deinonychus*, *Tyrannosaurus*, and *Hypsilophodon* —lived during this period. At the end of the Cretaceous period, however, large dinosaurs became extinct. The reason for this mass extinction is unknown but it is thought to have been caused by climatic changes due to either a catastrophic meteor impact with the Earth or extensive volcanic eruptions.

CRETACEOUS POSITIONS OF PRESENT-DAY LANDMASSES

North America
Europe
Arabia
Asia
South America
Africa
India
Antarctica
Australia

EXAMPLES OF CRETACEOUS PLANT GROUPS

A PRESENT-DAY CONIFER
(Pinus muricata)

A PRESENT-DAY DECIDUOUS TREE
(Magnolia sp.)

FOSSIL OF AN EXTINCT FERN
(Sphenopteris latiloba)

FOSSIL OF AN EXTINCT GINKGO
(Ginkgo pluripartita)

FOSSIL LEAVES OF AN EXTINCT DECIDUOUS TREE
(Cercidyphyllum sp.)

EXAMPLES OF CRETACEOUS DINOSAURS

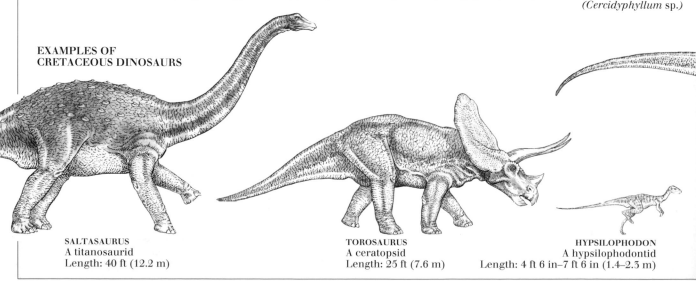

SALTASAURUS
A titanosaurid
Length: 40 ft (12.2 m)

TOROSAURUS
A ceratopsid
Length: 25 ft (7.6 m)

HYPSILOPHODON
A hypsilophodontid
Length: 4 ft 6 in–7 ft 6 in (1.4–2.3 m)

THE EARTH DURING THE CRETACEOUS PERIOD

EXAMPLES OF CRETACEOUS ANIMALS

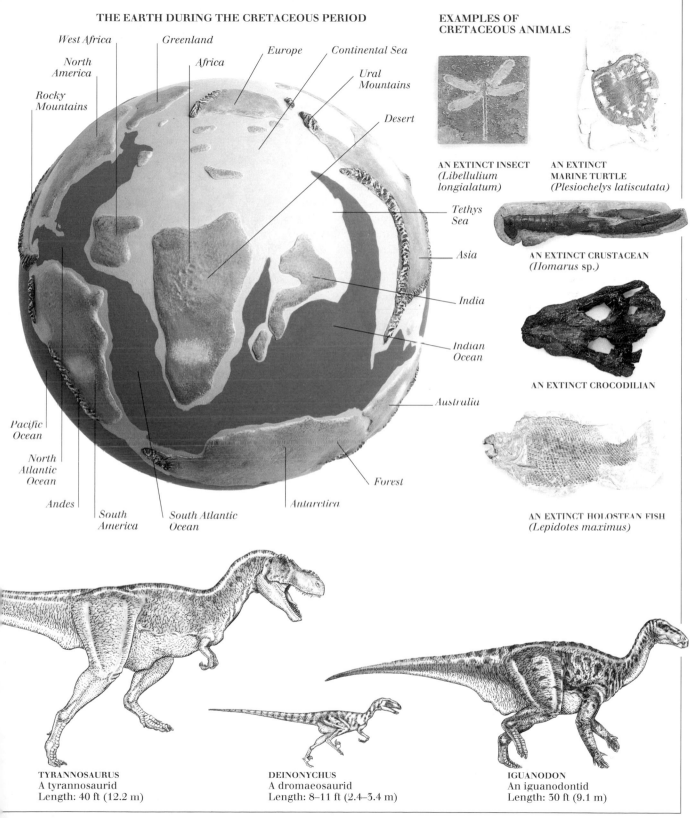

West Africa

North America

Rocky Mountains

Greenland

Africa

Europe

Continental Sea

Ural Mountains

Desert

Tethys Sea

Asia

India

Indian Ocean

Australia

Pacific Ocean

North Atlantic Ocean

Andes

South America

South Atlantic Ocean

Antarctica

Forest

AN EXTINCT INSECT
(*Libellulium longialatum*)

AN EXTINCT MARINE TURTLE
(*Plesiochelys latiscutata*)

AN EXTINCT CRUSTACEAN
(*Homarus* sp.)

AN EXTINCT CROCODILIAN

AN EXTINCT HOLOSTEAN FISH
(*Lepidotes maximus*)

TYRANNOSAURUS
A tyrannosaurid
Length: 40 ft (12.2 m)

DEINONYCHUS
A dromaeosaurid
Length: 8–11 ft (2.4–3.4 m)

IGUANODON
An iguanodontid
Length: 30 ft (9.1 m)

Tertiary period

FOLLOWING THE DEMISE OF THE DINOSAURS at the end of the Cretaceous period, the Tertiary period (65–1.6 million years ago), which formed the first part of the Cenozoic era (65 million years ago–present), was characterized by a huge expansion of mammal life. Placental mammals nourish and maintain their young in the mother's uterus; only three orders of placental mammals existed during Cretaceous times, compared with 25 orders during the Tertiary period. One of these 25 included the first hominid (see pp.108–109), *Australopithecus*, which appeared in Africa. By the beginning of the Tertiary period, the continents had almost reached their present position. The Tethys Sea, which had separated the northern continents from Africa and India, began to close up, forming the Mediterranean Sea and allowing the migration of terrestrial animals between Africa and western Europe. India's collision with Asia led to the formation of the Himalayas. During the middle part of the Tertiary period, the forest-dwelling and browsing mammals were replaced by mammals such as the horse, better suited to grazing the open savannahs that began to dominate. Repeated cool periods throughout the Tertiary period established the Antarctic as an icy island continent.

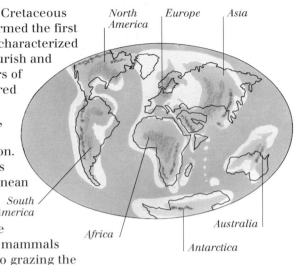

North America
Europe
Asia
South America
Africa
Antarctica
Australia

EXAMPLES OF TERTIARY PLANT GROUPS

A PRESENT-DAY OAK
(*Quercus palustris*)

A PRESENT-DAY BIRCH
(*Betula grossa*)

**FOSSIL LEAF OF AN
EXTINCT BIRCH**
(*Betulites sp.*)

**FOSSIL STEM OF AN
EXTINCT PALM**
(*Palmoxylon*)

EXAMPLES OF TERTIARY
ANIMAL GROUPS

HYAENODON
An hyaenodontid
Length: 6 ft 6 in (2 m)

TITANOHYRAX
A pliohyracid
Length: 6 ft 6 in (2 m)

PHORUSRHACUS
A phorusrhacid
Length: 5 ft (1.5 m)

SAMOTHERIUM
A giraffid
Length: 10 ft (3 m)

THE EARTH DURING THE TERTIARY PERIOD

EXAMPLES OF TERTIARY ANIMALS

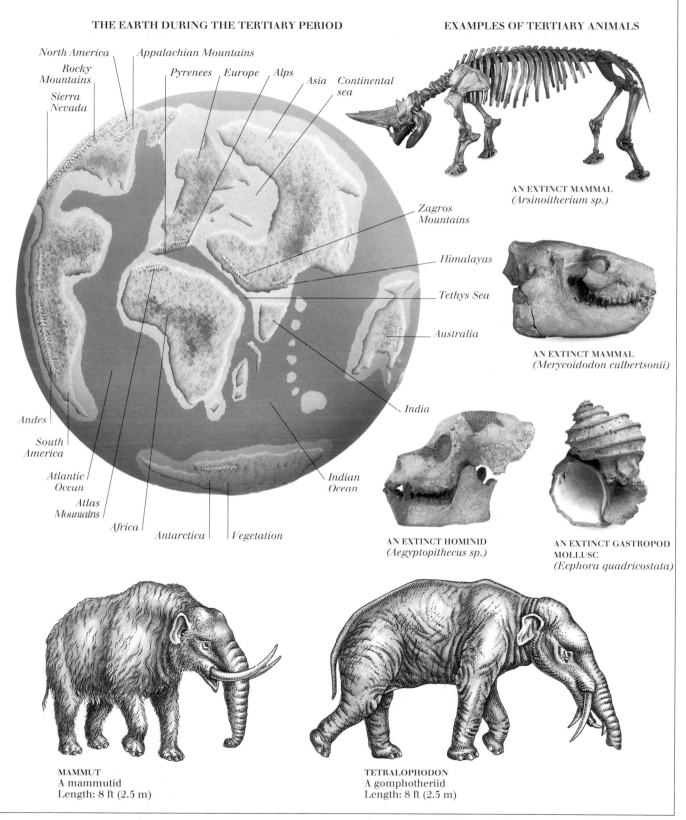

North America

Rocky
Mountains

Sierra
Nevada

Appalachian Mountains

Pyrenees   Europe   Alps

Asia   Continental
sea

Zagros
Mountains

Himalayas

Tethys Sea

Australia

India

Andes

South
America

Atlantic
Ocean

Atlas
Mountains

Africa   Antarctica   Vegetation

Indian
Ocean

AN EXTINCT MAMMAL
(*Arsinoitherium sp.*)

AN EXTINCT MAMMAL
(*Merycoidodon culbertsonii*)

AN EXTINCT HOMINID
(*Aegyptopithecus sp.*)

**AN EXTINCT GASTROPOD
MOLLUSC**
(*Ecphora quadricostata*)

MAMMUT
A mammutid
Length: 8 ft (2.5 m)

TETRALOPHODON
A gomphotheriid
Length: 8 ft (2.5 m)

Quaternary period

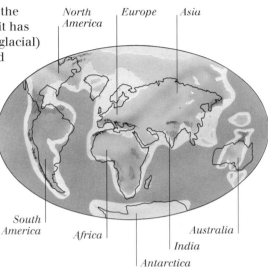

North America · Europe · Asia · South America · Africa · India · Antarctica · Australia

THE QUATERNARY PERIOD (1.6 million years ago–present) forms the second part of the Cenozoic era (65 million years ago–present): it has been characterized by alternating cold (glacial) and warm (interglacial) periods. During cold periods, ice sheets and glaciers have formed repeatedly on northern and southern continents. The cold environments in North America and Eurasia, and to a lesser extent in southern South America and parts of Australia, have caused the migration of many life forms toward the Equator. Only the specialized ice-age mammals such as *Mammuthus* and *Coelodonta*, with their thick wool and fat insulation, were suited to life in very cold climates. Humans developed throughout the Pleistocene period (1.6 million–10,000 years ago) in Africa and migrated northward into Europe and Asia. Modern humans, *Homo sapiens*, lived on the cold European continent 30,000 years ago and hunted mammals. The end of the last ice age and the climatic changes that occurred about 10,000 years ago brought extinction to many Pleistocene mammals, but enabled humans to flourish.

EXAMPLES OF QUATERNARY PLANT GROUPS

A PRESENT-DAY BIRCH
(Betula lenta)

A PRESENT-DAY SWEEETGUM
(Liquidambar styraciflua)

FOSSIL LEAF OF A SWEETGUM
(Liquidambar europeanum)

FOSSIL LEAF OF A BIRCH
(Betula sp.)

EXAMPLES OF QUATERNARY ANIMAL GROUPS

PROCOPTODON
A macropodid
Length: 10 ft (3 m)

DIPROTODON
A diprotodontid
Length: 10 ft (3 m)

TOXODON
A toxodontid
Length: 10 ft (3 m)

MAMMUTHUS
An elephantid
Length: 10 ft (3 m)

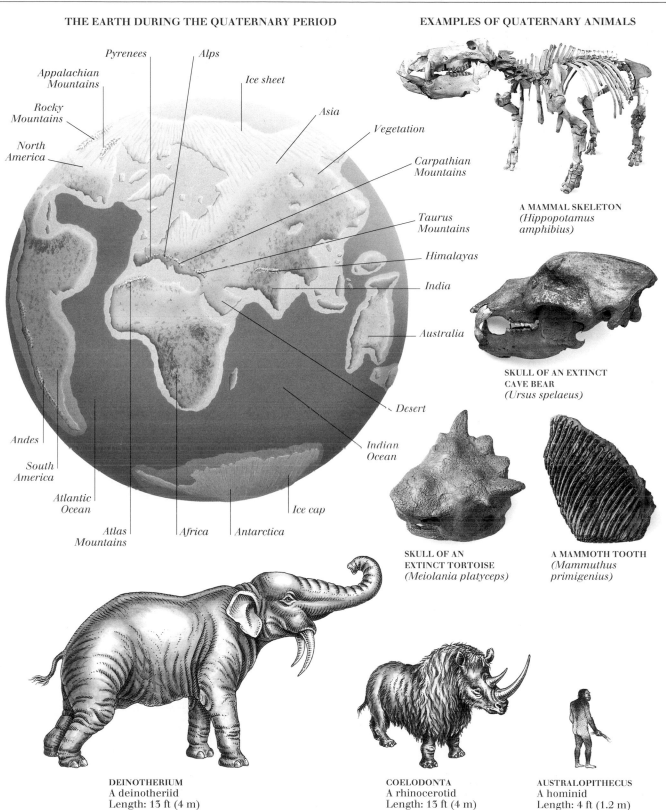

THE EARTH DURING THE QUATERNARY PERIOD

Pyrenees
Alps
Appalachian Mountains
Ice sheet
Rocky Mountains
Asia
North America
Vegetation
Carpathian Mountains
Taurus Mountains
Himalayas
India
Australia
Desert
Andes
Indian Ocean
South America
Atlantic Ocean
Atlas Mountains
Africa
Antarctica
Ice cap

EXAMPLES OF QUATERNARY ANIMALS

A MAMMAL SKELETON
(*Hippopotamus amphibius*)

SKULL OF AN EXTINCT CAVE BEAR
(*Ursus spelaeus*)

SKULL OF AN EXTINCT TORTOISE
(*Meiolania platyceps*)

A MAMMOTH TOOTH
(*Mammuthus primigenius*)

DEINOTHERIUM
A deinotheriid
Length: 13 ft (4 m)

COELODONTA
A rhinocerotid
Length: 13 ft (4 m)

AUSTRALOPITHECUS
A hominid
Length: 4 ft (1.2 m)

Early signs of life

FOR ALMOST A THOUSAND MILLION YEARS after its formation, there was no known life on Earth. The first simple, sea-dwelling organic structures appeared about 3,500 million years ago; they may have formed when certain chemical molecules joined together. Prokaryotes, single-celled micro-organisms such as blue-green algae, were able to photosynthesize (see pp. 138–139), and thus produce oxygen. A thousand million years later, sufficient oxygen had built up in the earth's atmosphere to allow multicellular organisms to proliferate in the Precambrian seas (before 570 million years ago). Soft-bodied jellyfish, corals, and seaworms flourished about 700 million years ago. Trilobites, the first animals with hard body frames, developed during the Cambrian period (570–510 million years ago). However, it was not until the beginning of the Devonian period (409–363 million years ago) that early land plants, such as *Asteroxylon*, formed a water-retaining cuticle, which ended their dependence on an aquatic environment. About 360 million years ago, the first amphibians (see pp. 80–81) crawled onto the land, although they still returned to the water to lay their soft eggs. Not until the emergence of the first reptiles would animals with backbones appear that were not dependent on water in this way.

STROMATOLITIC LIMESTONE

Alternate layers of mud and sand

Layers bound by algae

Layered structure

Limestone

Long, beaklike snout

Growth line

Dorsal plate

Dorsal spine base

Fixed lateral plate

Bony dorsal shield

FOSSILIZED JAWLESS FISH

Glabella

Eye

Thoracic pleurae

Tail shield

Tail area

FOSSILIZED TRILOBITE

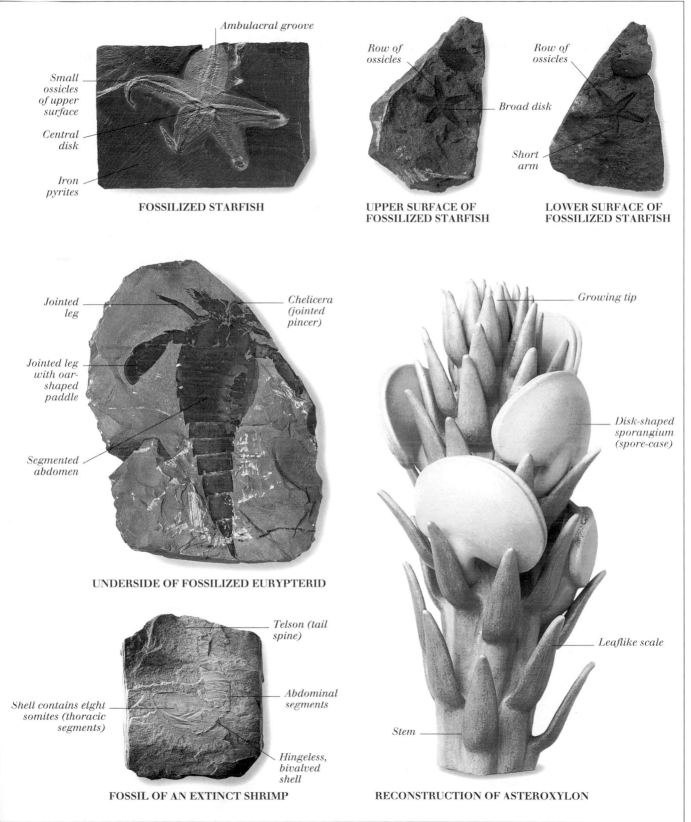

Ambulacral groove

Small
ossicles
of upper
surface

Central
disk

Iron
pyrites

FOSSILIZED STARFISH

Row of
ossicles

Broad disk

**UPPER SURFACE OF
FOSSILIZED STARFISH**

Row of
ossicles

Short
arm

**LOWER SURFACE OF
FOSSILIZED STARFISH**

Jointed
leg

Chelicera
(jointed
pincer)

Jointed leg
with oar-
shaped
paddle

Segmented
abdomen

UNDERSIDE OF FOSSILIZED EURYPTERID

Growing tip

Disk-shaped
sporangium
(spore-case)

Telson (tail
spine)

Abdominal
segments

Shell contains eight
somites (thoracic
segments)

Hingeless,
bivalved
shell

FOSSIL OF AN EXTINCT SHRIMP

Leaflike scale

Stem

RECONSTRUCTION OF ASTEROXYLON

79

Amphibians and reptiles

THE EARLIEST KNOWN AMPHIBIANS, such as *Acanthostega* and *Ichthyostega*, lived about 363 million years ago at the end of the Devonian period (409–363 million years ago). Their limbs may have evolved from the muscular fins of lungfish-like creatures. These fish can use their fins to push themselves along the bottom of lakes and some can breathe at the water's surface. While amphibians (see pp. 182–183) can exist on land, they are dependent on a wet environment because their skin does not retain moisture and they must return to the water to lay their eggs. Evolving from amphibians, reptiles (see pp. 184–187) first appeared during the Carboniferous period (363–290 million years ago): *Westlothiana*, a possible early reptile, lived on land 338 million years ago. The development of the amniotic egg, with an embryo enclosed in its own wet environment (the amnion) and protected by a waterproof shell, freed reptiles from the amphibian's dependence on a wet habitat. A scaly skin protected the reptile from desiccation on land and enabled it to exploit ways of life closed to its amphibian ancestors. Reptiles include the dinosaurs, which came to dominate life on land during the Mesozoic era (245–65 million years ago).

Orbit

Pocket enclosing nostril

Sculpted or pitted bone surface

Spiracle to draw in water

Mandible

Small tooth

FOSSIL SKULL OF ACANTHOSTEGA

Muscular back

Shoulder girdle

Scaly skin

Finned tail

Hip girdle

MODEL OF ICHTHYOSTEGA

Dorsal vertebra

Scapula

Cleithrum

Cervical vertebra

Cranium

Orbit

Maxilla

Naris

Rib

Glenoid cavity

Humerus

Elbow joint

Mandible

Clavicle

Radius

Ulna

Sharp tooth

Phalanges

Metacarpals

SKELETON OF ERYOPS

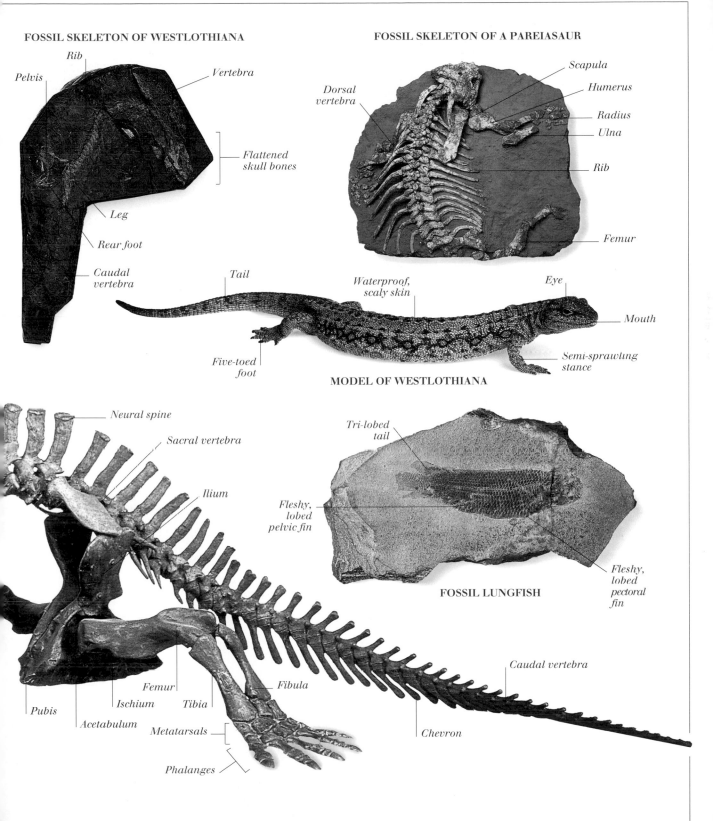

FOSSIL SKELETON OF WESTLOTHIANA

Rib

Vertebra

Pelvis

Flattened
skull bones

Leg

Rear foot

Caudal
vertebra

FOSSIL SKELETON OF A PAREIASAUR

Scapula

Humerus

Dorsal
vertebra

Radius

Ulna

Rib

Femur

Tail

Waterproof,
scaly skin

Eye

Mouth

Five-toed
foot

Semi-sprawling
stance

MODEL OF WESTLOTHIANA

Neural spine

Sacral vertebra

Ilium

Tri-lobed
tail

Fleshy,
lobed
pelvic fin

Fleshy,
lobed
pectoral
fin

FOSSIL LUNGFISH

Caudal vertebra

Femur

Fibula

Pubis

Ischium

Tibia

Acetabulum

Metatarsals

Chevron

Phalanges

The dinosaurs

THE DINOSAURS WERE A LARGE GROUP of reptiles that were the dominant land vertebrates (animals with backbones) for most of the Mesozoic era (245–65 million years ago). They appeared some 230 million years ago and were distinguished from other scaly, egg-laying reptiles by an important feature: dinosaurs had an erect limb stance. This enabled them to keep their bodies well above the ground, unlike the sprawling and semi-sprawling stance of other reptiles. The head of the dinosaur's femur (thighbone) fits into a socket in its pelvis (hipbone), producing efficient and mobile locomotion. Dinosaurs are categorized into two groups according to the structure of their pelvis: saurischian (lizard-hipped) and ornithischian (bird-hipped) dinosaurs. In the case of most saurischians, the pubis (part of the pelvis) jutted forward, while in ornithischians it slanted back, parallel to the ischium (another part of the pelvis). Dinosaurs ranged in size from smaller than a domestic cat to the biggest land animals ever known. The Dinosauria were the most successful land vertebrates ever, and survived for 165 million years, until their extinction 65 million years ago.

STRUCTURE OF SAURISCHIAN PELVIS

Ilium

Hook of preacetabular process

Postacetabular process

Ilio-pubic joint

Acetabulum

Ilio-ischial joint

Pubis

Ischium

Pubic foot

GALLIMIMUS
A saurischian dinosaur

POSITION OF PELVIS IN A SAURISCHIAN DINOSAUR

STRUCTURE OF ORNITHISCHIAN PELVIS

Ilium

Preacetabular process

Postacetabular process

Ilio-pubic joint

Ilio-ischial joint

Prepubis

Acetabulum

Pubis

Ischium

HYPSILOPHODON
An ornithischian dinosaur

POSITION OF PELVIS IN AN ORNITHISCHIAN DINOSAUR

BAROSAURUS
A saurischian dinosaur

COMPARISON OF ANIMAL STANCES

SPRAWLING STANCE
The thighs and upper arms project straight out from the body so that the knees and elbows are bent at right angles.

COMMON IGUANA
(*Iguana iguana*)
A present-day reptile

ERECT STANCE
The thighs and upper arms project straight down from the body so that the knees and elbows are straight.

SEMI-SPRAWLING STANCE
The thighs and upper arms project downward and outward so that the knees and elbows are slightly bent.

DWARF CROCODILE
(*Osteolaemus tetraspis*)
A present-day reptile

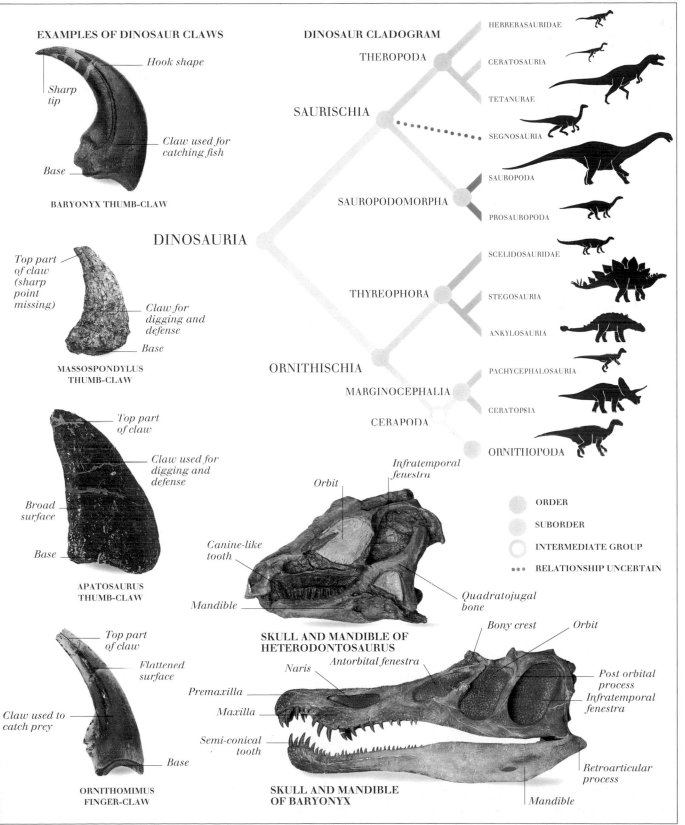

EXAMPLES OF DINOSAUR CLAWS

Hook shape

Sharp tip

Claw used for catching fish

Base

BARYONYX THUMB-CLAW

Top part of claw (sharp point missing)

Claw for digging and defense

Base

MASSOSPONDYLUS THUMB-CLAW

Top part of claw

Claw used for digging and defense

Broad surface

Base

APATOSAURUS THUMB-CLAW

Top part of claw

Flattened surface

Claw used to catch prey

Base

ORNITHOMIMUS FINGER-CLAW

DINOSAUR CLADOGRAM

HERRERASAURIDAE

THEROPODA

CERATOSAURIA

SAURISCHIA

TETANURAE

SEGNOSAURIA

SAUROPODA

SAUROPODOMORPHA

PROSAUROPODA

DINOSAURIA

SCELIDOSAURIDAE

THYREOPHORA

STEGOSAURIA

ANKYLOSAURIA

ORNITHISCHIA

PACHYCEPHALOSAURIA

MARGINOCEPHALIA

CERATOPSIA

CERAPODA

ORNITHOPODA

⬤ ORDER

⬤ SUBORDER

◯ INTERMEDIATE GROUP

••• RELATIONSHIP UNCERTAIN

Infratemporal fenestra

Orbit

Canine-like tooth

Quadratojugal bone

Mandible

SKULL AND MANDIBLE OF HETERODONTOSAURUS

Bony crest

Orbit

Antorbital fenestra

Naris

Post orbital process

Premaxilla

Infratemporal fenestra

Maxilla

Semi-conical tooth

Retroarticular process

SKULL AND MANDIBLE OF BARYONYX

Mandible

Theropods 1

AN ENORMOUSLY SUCCESSFUL SUBORDER of the Saurischia, the bipedal (two-footed) theropods ("beast feet") emerged 230 million years ago in Late Triassic times; the oldest known example comes from South America. Theropods spanned the whole of the Age of the Dinosaurs (230–65 million years ago) and included most of the known predatory dinosaurs. The typical theropod had small arms with sharp, clawed fingers; powerful jaws lined with sharp teeth; an S-shaped neck; long, muscular hind limbs; and clawed, usually four-toed feet. Many theropods may have been warm-blooded; most were exclusively carnivorous. Theropods ranged from animals no larger than a chicken to huge creatures, such as Tyrannosaurus and Baryonyx. The group also included ostrich-like omnivores and herbivores with toothless beaks, such as Struthiomimus and Gallimimus. Many scientists believe that birds are the closest living relatives to the dinosaurs, and share a common ancestor with the theropods. Archaeopteryx, small and feathered, was the first known bird and lived alongside its dinosaur relatives.

INTERNAL ANATOMY OF
ALBERTOSAURUS LEG

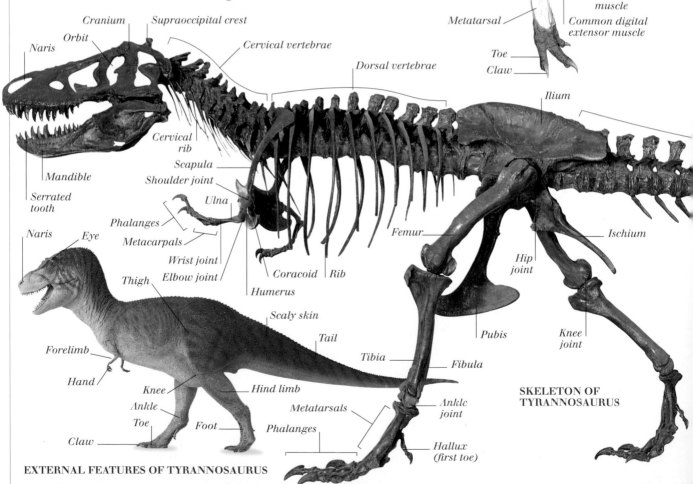

Ilio-tibial muscle

Ilio-femoral muscle

Femoro-tibial muscle

Internal tibial flexor muscle

Femur

Ilio-fibular muscle

Gastrocnemius muscle

Digital flexor muscle

Fibula

Tarsal

Metatarsal

Ambiens muscle

Femoro-tibial muscle

Anterior tibial muscle

Common digital extensor muscle

Toe

Claw

Cranium　*Supraoccipital crest*

Orbit

Naris

Cervical vertebrae

Dorsal vertebrae

Ilium

Cervical rib

Scapula

Shoulder joint

Ulna

Phalanges

Metacarpals

Wrist joint

Elbow joint

Coracoid　*Rib*

Humerus

Femur

Ischium

Hip joint

Mandible

Serrated tooth

Naris　*Eye*

Thigh

Scaly skin

Tail

Tibia

Fibula

Pubis

Knee joint

Forelimb

Hand

Knee

Hind limb

Ankle

Toe

Foot

Claw

Metatarsals

Phalanges

Ankle joint

Hallux (first toe)

SKELETON OF
TYRANNOSAURUS

EXTERNAL FEATURES OF TYRANNOSAURUS

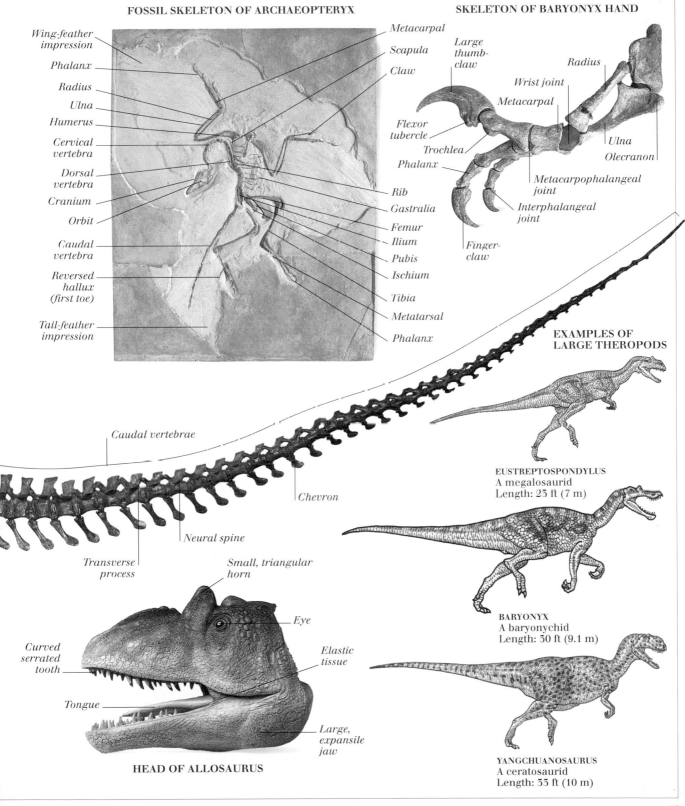

FOSSIL SKELETON OF ARCHAEOPTERYX

Wing-feather impression
Phalanx
Radius
Ulna
Humerus
Cervical vertebra
Dorsal vertebra
Cranium
Orbit
Caudal vertebra
Reversed hallux (first toe)
Tail-feather impression

Metacarpal
Scapula
Claw

Rib
Gastralia
Femur
Ilium
Pubis
Ischium
Tibia
Metatarsal
Phalanx

SKELETON OF BARYONYX HAND

Large thumb-claw
Flexor tubercle
Trochlea
Phalanx
Finger-claw

Radius
Wrist joint
Metacarpal
Ulna
Olecranon
Metacarpophalangeal joint
Interphalangeal joint

Caudal vertebrae
Chevron
Neural spine
Transverse process

EXAMPLES OF LARGE THEROPODS

EUSTREPTOSPONDYLUS
A megalosaurid
Length: 23 ft (7 m)

BARYONYX
A baryonychid
Length: 30 ft (9.1 m)

YANGCHUANOSAURUS
A ceratosaurid
Length: 33 ft (10 m)

Small, triangular horn
Eye
Curved serrated tooth
Elastic tissue
Tongue
Large, expansile jaw

HEAD OF ALLOSAURUS

Theropods 2

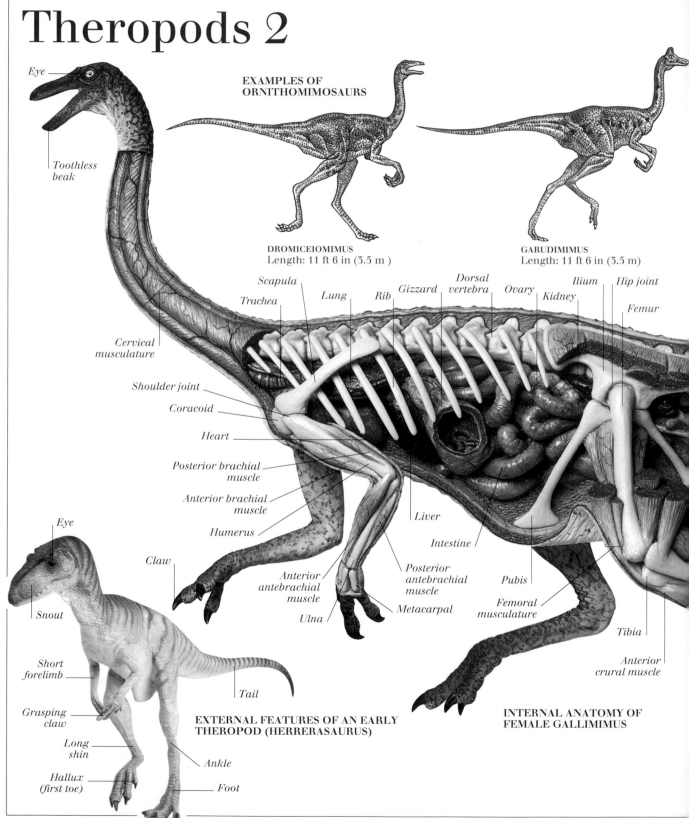

Eye

Toothless beak

EXAMPLES OF ORNITHOMIMOSAURS

DROMICEIOMIMUS
Length: 11 ft 6 in (3.5 m)

GARUDIMIMUS
Length: 11 ft 6 in (3.5 m)

Cervical musculature

Scapula

Trachea

Lung

Rib

Gizzard

Dorsal vertebra

Ovary

Kidney

Ilium

Hip joint

Femur

Shoulder joint

Coracoid

Heart

Posterior brachial muscle

Anterior brachial muscle

Humerus

Liver

Intestine

Posterior antebrachial muscle

Pubis

Femoral musculature

Tibia

Anterior crural muscle

Eye

Claw

Anterior antebrachial muscle

Ulna

Metacarpal

Snout

Short forelimb

Grasping claw

Long shin

Hallux (first toe)

Ankle

Foot

Tail

EXTERNAL FEATURES OF AN EARLY THEROPOD (HERRERASAURUS)

INTERNAL ANATOMY OF FEMALE GALLIMIMUS

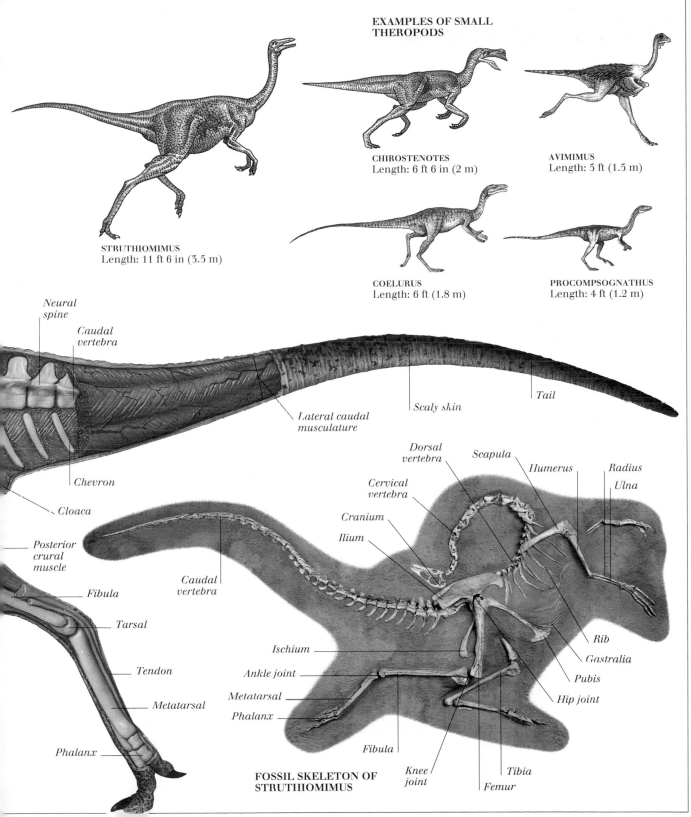

EXAMPLES OF SMALL THEROPODS

CHIROSTENOTES
Length: 6 ft 6 in (2 m)

AVIMIMUS
Length: 5 ft (1.5 m)

STRUTHIOMIMUS
Length: 11 ft 6 in (3.5 m)

COELURUS
Length: 6 ft (1.8 m)

PROCOMPSOGNATHUS
Length: 4 ft (1.2 m)

Neural spine

Caudal vertebra

Lateral caudal musculature

Scaly skin

Tail

Chevron

Cloaca

Dorsal vertebra

Scapula

Humerus

Radius

Ulna

Cervical vertebra

Cranium

Ilium

Posterior crural muscle

Caudal vertebra

Fibula

Tarsal

Rib

Gastralia

Tendon

Pubis

Ischium

Hip joint

Ankle joint

Metatarsal

Metatarsal

Phalanx

Phalanx

Fibula

Knee joint

Femur

Tibia

FOSSIL SKELETON OF STRUTHIOMIMUS

Sauropodomorphs 1

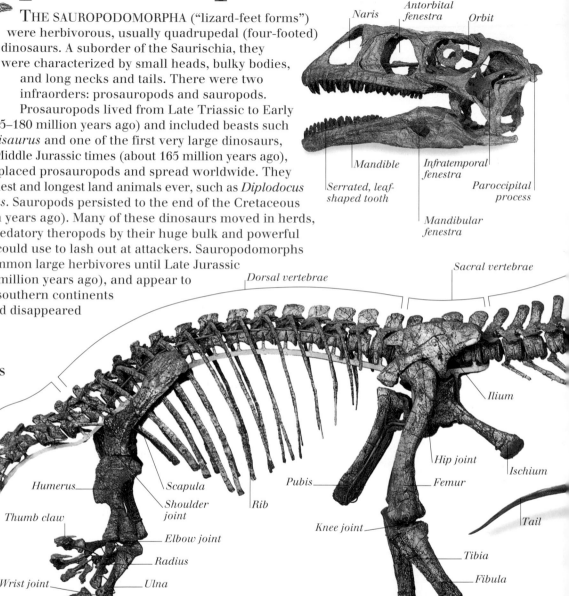

THE SAUROPODOMORPHA ("lizard-feet forms") were herbivorous, usually quadrupedal (four-footed) dinosaurs. A suborder of the Saurischia, they were characterized by small heads, bulky bodies, and long necks and tails. There were two infraorders: prosauropods and sauropods. Prosauropods lived from Late Triassic to Early Jurassic times (225–180 million years ago) and included beasts such as the small *Anchisaurus* and one of the first very large dinosaurs, *Plateosaurus*. By Middle Jurassic times (about 165 million years ago), sauropods had replaced prosauropods and spread worldwide. They included the heaviest and longest land animals ever, such as *Diplodocus* and *Brachiosaurus*. Sauropods persisted to the end of the Cretaceous period (65 million years ago). Many of these dinosaurs moved in herds, protected from predatory theropods by their huge bulk and powerful tails, which they could use to lash out at attackers. Sauropodomorphs were the most common large herbivores until Late Jurassic times (about 145 million years ago), and appear to have survived in southern continents long after they had disappeared from the north.

THECODONTOSAURUS

SKULL AND MANDIBLE OF PLATEOSAURUS

Naris

Antorbital fenestra

Orbit

Mandible

Infratemporal fenestra

Paroccipital process

Serrated, leaf-shaped tooth

Mandibular fenestra

SKELETON OF PLATEOSAURUS

Dorsal vertebrae

Sacral vertebrae

Ilium

Hip joint

Ischium

Cervical vertebrae

Humerus

Scapula

Shoulder joint

Pubis

Femur

Tail

Thumb claw

Rib

Knee joint

Elbow joint

Tibia

Radius

Fibula

Wrist joint

Ulna

Metacarpal

Ankle joint

Metatarsals

Cranium

Phalanx

Orbit

Mandible

Phalanges

Naris

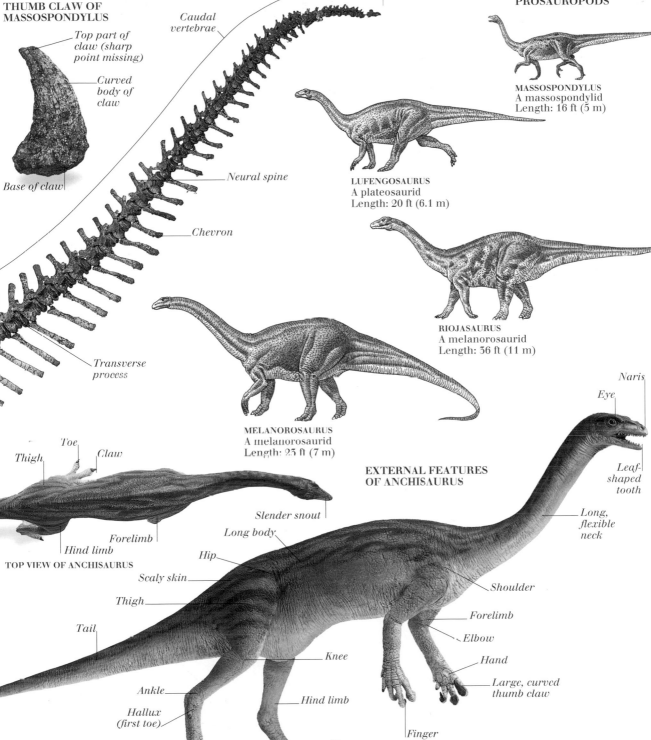

THUMB CLAW OF MASSOSPONDYLUS

Top part of claw (sharp point missing)

Curved body of claw

Base of claw

Caudal vertebrae

Neural spine

Chevron

Transverse process

EXAMPLES OF PROSAUROPODS

MASSOSPONDYLUS
A massospondylid
Length: 16 ft (5 m)

LUFENGOSAURUS
A plateosaurid
Length: 20 ft (6.1 m)

RIOJASAURUS
A melanorosaurid
Length: 36 ft (11 m)

MELANOROSAURUS
A melanorosaurid
Length: 23 ft (7 m)

EXTERNAL FEATURES OF ANCHISAURUS

Thigh

Toe

Claw

Forelimb

Hind limb

TOP VIEW OF ANCHISAURUS

Slender snout

Long body

Hip

Scaly skin

Thigh

Tail

Knee

Ankle

Hallux (first toe)

Foot

Hind limb

Toe

Claw

Naris

Eye

Leaf-shaped tooth

Long, flexible neck

Shoulder

Forelimb

Elbow

Hand

Large, curved thumb claw

Finger

SIDE VIEW OF ANCHISAURUS

Sauropodomorphs 2

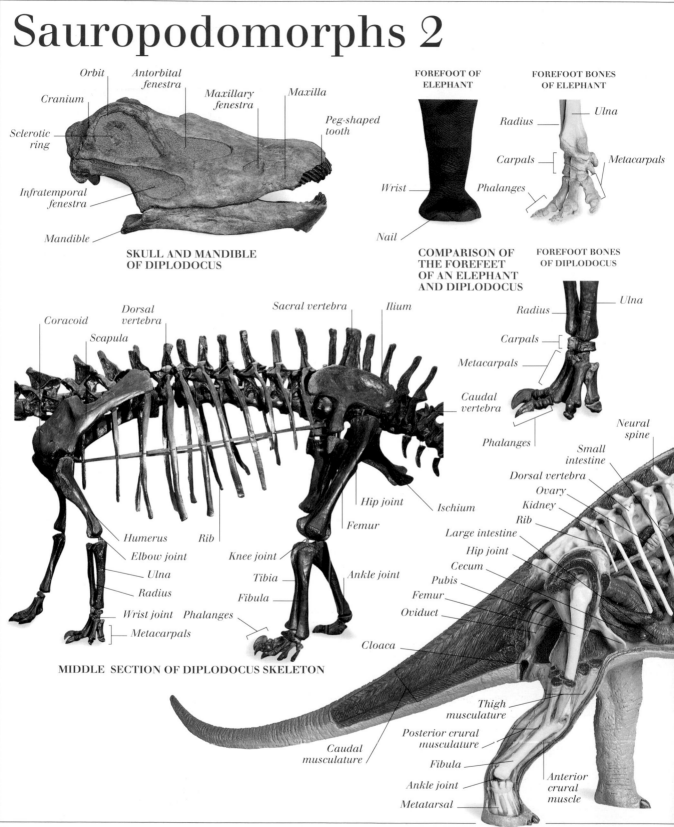

SKULL AND MANDIBLE OF DIPLODOCUS

Orbit

Antorbital fenestra

Maxillary fenestra

Maxilla

Cranium

Peg-shaped tooth

Sclerotic ring

Infratemporal fenestra

Mandible

FOREFOOT OF ELEPHANT

Wrist

Nail

FOREFOOT BONES OF ELEPHANT

Radius

Ulna

Carpals

Metacarpals

Phalanges

COMPARISON OF THE FOREFEET OF AN ELEPHANT AND DIPLODOCUS

FOREFOOT BONES OF DIPLODOCUS

Radius

Ulna

Carpals

Metacarpals

Phalanges

MIDDLE SECTION OF DIPLODOCUS SKELETON

Coracoid

Dorsal vertebra

Sacral vertebra

Ilium

Scapula

Humerus

Rib

Elbow joint

Ulna

Radius

Wrist joint

Phalanges

Metacarpals

Knee joint

Tibia

Fibula

Hip joint

Femur

Ankle joint

Ischium

Caudal vertebra

Caudal musculature

Neural spine

Small intestine

Dorsal vertebra

Ovary

Kidney

Rib

Large intestine

Hip joint

Cecum

Pubis

Femur

Oviduct

Cloaca

Thigh musculature

Posterior crural musculature

Fibula

Ankle joint

Metatarsal

Anterior crural muscle

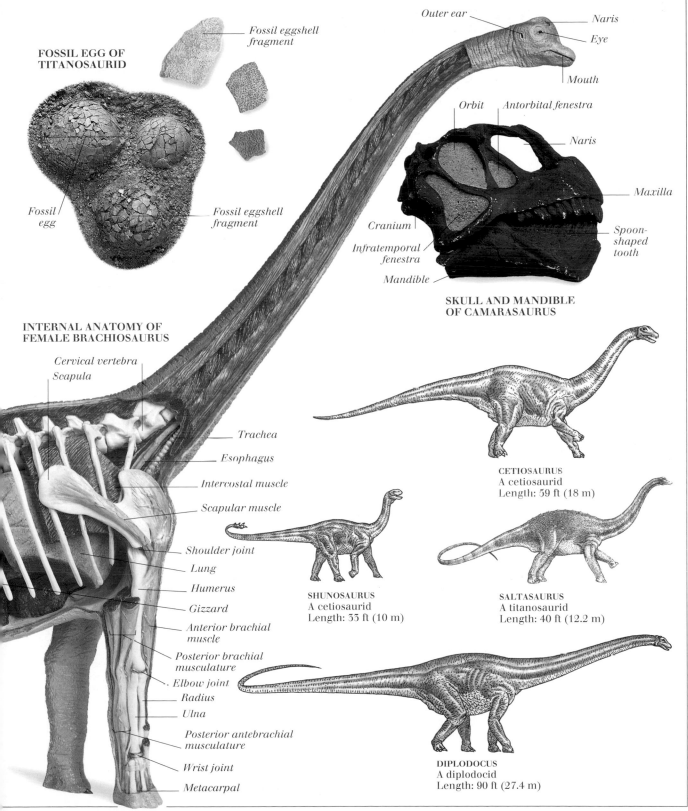

FOSSIL EGG OF TITANOSAURID

Fossil eggshell fragment

Fossil egg

Fossil eggshell fragment

Outer ear

Naris

Eye

Mouth

Orbit

Antorbital fenestra

Naris

Cranium

Maxilla

Infratemporal fenestra

Spoon-shaped tooth

Mandible

SKULL AND MANDIBLE OF CAMARASAURUS

INTERNAL ANATOMY OF FEMALE BRACHIOSAURUS

Cervical vertebra

Scapula

Trachea

Esophagus

Intercostal muscle

Scapular muscle

Shoulder joint

Lung

Humerus

Gizzard

Anterior brachial muscle

Posterior brachial musculature

Elbow joint

Radius

Ulna

Posterior antebrachial musculature

Wrist joint

Metacarpal

CETIOSAURUS
A cetiosaurid
Length: 59 ft (18 m)

SHUNOSAURUS
A cetiosaurid
Length: 33 ft (10 m)

SALTASAURUS
A titanosaurid
Length: 40 ft (12.2 m)

DIPLODOCUS
A diplodocid
Length: 90 ft (27.4 m)

Thyreophorans 1

THYREOPHORANS ("SHIELD BEARERS") were a group of quadrupedal armoured dinosaurs. A sub-order of the Ornithischia (bird-hipped dinosaurs), they were characterized by rows of bony studs, plates, or spikes along the back, which protected some from predators and may have helped others regulate body temperature. Up to 30ft (9m) long, with a small head and small cheek teeth, Thyreophorans had shorter forelimbs than hind limbs and probably browsed on low-level vegetation. The earliest thyreophorans were small and lived in Early Jurassic times (about 200 million years ago) in Europe, North America, and China. Stegosaurs, such as Stegosaurus and Kentrosaurus, replaced these older forms. The earliest stegosaur remains come mainly from China. Several genera of stegosaurs survived into the Early Cretaceous period (146–100 million years ago), but only in India did they persist into Late Cretaceous times (97–65 million years ago). Ankylosaurs, with their toothless beaks and cheek teeth adapted for cropping vegetation, appeared later than stegosaurs. They originated in the Late Jurassic period (155 million years ago) and in North America survived until 65 million years ago.

TUOJIANGOSAURUS
A stegosaurid
Length: 23 ft (7 m)

Dorsal plate

Hip

Thigh

Cervical plate

Eye

Naris

Beak

Cheek

Neck

Outer ear

Knee

Shoulder

Short forelimb

Long hind limb

Elbow

Ankle

Nail

Wrist

Nail

Forefoot

Hind foot

EXTERNAL FEATURES OF STEGOSAURUS

EXAMPLES OF STEGOSAURS

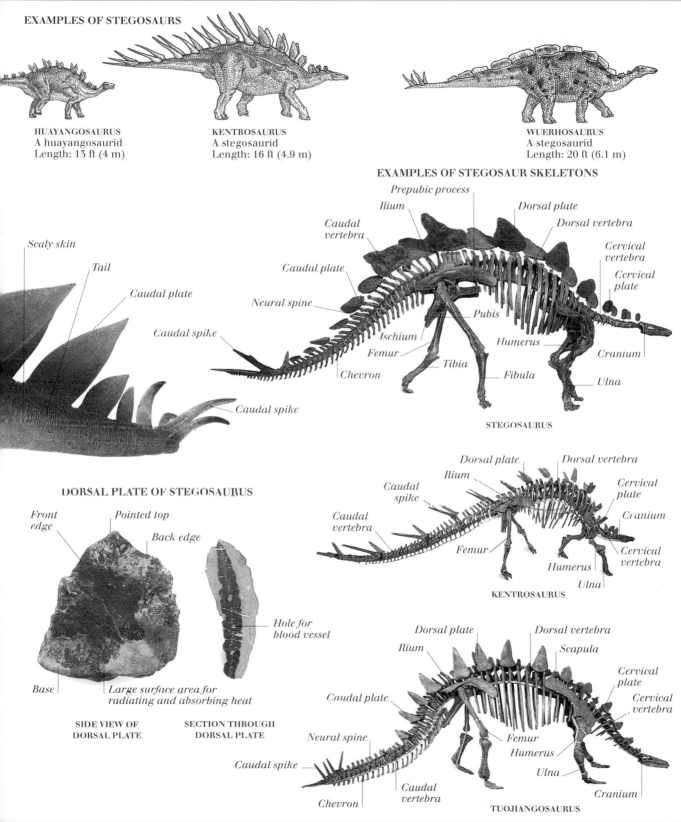

HUAYANGOSAURUS
A huayangosaurid
Length: 13 ft (4 m)

KENTROSAURUS
A stegosaurid
Length: 16 ft (4.9 m)

WUERHOSAURUS
A stegosaurid
Length: 20 ft (6.1 m)

EXAMPLES OF STEGOSAUR SKELETONS

Scaly skin

Tail

Caudal plate

Caudal spike

Caudal spike

Prepubic process

Ilium

Caudal vertebra

Caudal plate

Neural spine

Dorsal plate

Dorsal vertebra

Cervical vertebra

Cervical plate

Pubis

Ischium

Femur

Chevron

Tibia

Humerus

Fibula

Cranium

Ulna

STEGOSAURUS

DORSAL PLATE OF STEGOSAURUS

Front edge

Pointed top

Back edge

Hole for blood vessel

Base

Large surface area for radiating and absorbing heat

SIDE VIEW OF DORSAL PLATE

SECTION THROUGH DORSAL PLATE

Dorsal plate

Ilium

Caudal spike

Caudal vertebra

Dorsal vertebra

Cervical plate

Cranium

Femur

Humerus

Ulna

Cervical vertebra

KENTROSAURUS

Dorsal plate

Ilium

Caudal plate

Neural spine

Caudal spike

Chevron

Caudal vertebra

Dorsal vertebra

Scapula

Cervical plate

Cervical vertebra

Femur

Humerus

Ulna

Cranium

TUOJIANGOSAURUS

Thyreophorans 2

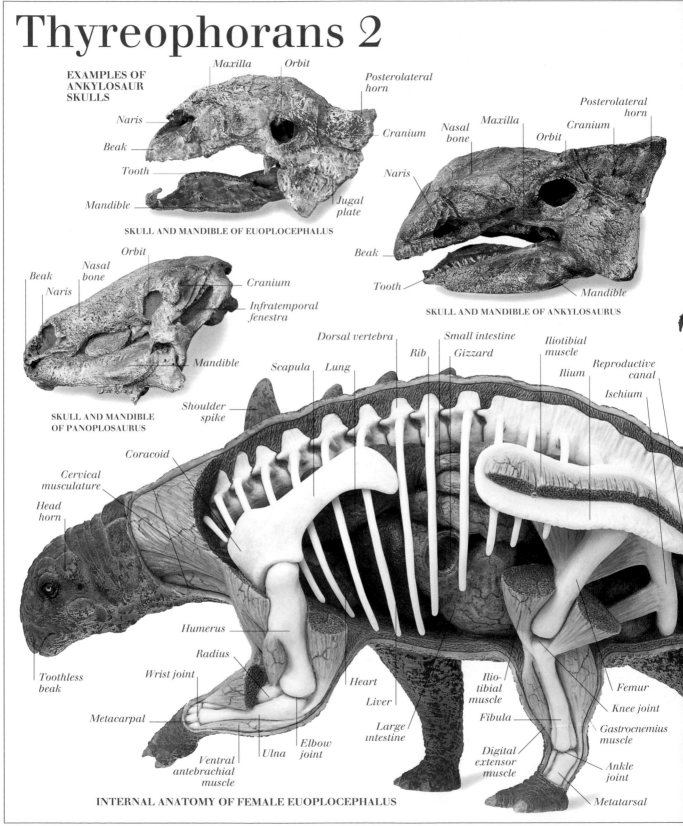

**EXAMPLES OF
ANKYLOSAUR
SKULLS**

Maxilla

Orbit

Posterolateral
horn

Naris

Cranium

Beak

Tooth

Mandible

Jugal
plate

SKULL AND MANDIBLE OF EUOPLOCEPHALUS

Posterolateral
horn

Nasal
bone

Maxilla

Cranium

Orbit

Naris

Beak

Tooth

Mandible

SKULL AND MANDIBLE OF ANKYLOSAURUS

Beak

Orbit

Nasal
bone

Naris

Cranium

Infratemporal
fenestra

Mandible

**SKULL AND MANDIBLE
OF PANOPLOSAURUS**

Dorsal vertebra

Rib

Small intestine

Gizzard

Iliotibial
muscle

Ilium

Reproductive
canal

Scapula

Lung

Ischium

Shoulder
spike

Coracoid

Cervical
musculature

Head
horn

Humerus

Radius

Wrist joint

Heart

Ilio-
tibial
muscle

Femur

Knee joint

Toothless
beak

Liver

Metacarpal

Fibula

Gastrocnemius
muscle

Large
intestine

Ventral
antebrachial
muscle

Ulna

Elbow
joint

Digital
extensor
muscle

Ankle
joint

Metatarsal

INTERNAL ANATOMY OF FEMALE EUOPLOCEPHALUS

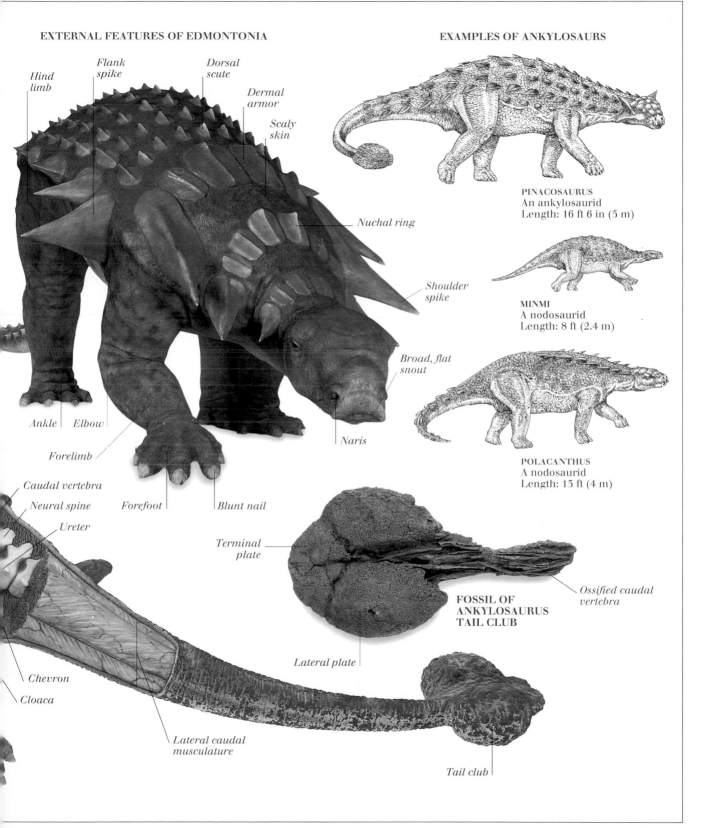

EXTERNAL FEATURES OF EDMONTONIA

Hind limb

Flank spike

Dorsal scute

Dermal armor

Scaly skin

Nuchal ring

Shoulder spike

Broad, flat snout

Ankle

Elbow

Forelimb

Caudal vertebra

Neural spine

Ureter

Forefoot

Blunt nail

Naris

Chevron

Cloaca

Lateral caudal musculature

Terminal plate

Lateral plate

EXAMPLES OF ANKYLOSAURS

PINACOSAURUS
An ankylosaurid
Length: 16 ft 6 in (5 m)

MINMI
A nodosaurid
Length: 8 ft (2.4 m)

POLACANTHUS
A nodosaurid
Length: 13 ft (4 m)

FOSSIL OF ANKYLOSAURUS TAIL CLUB

Ossified caudal vertebra

Tail club

Ornithopods 1

IGUANODON TOOTH

ORNITHOPODS ("BIRD FEET") were a group of ornithischian ("bird-hipped") dinosaurs. These bipedal and quadrupedal herbivores had a horny beak, plant-cutting or grinding cheek teeth, and a pelvic and tail region stiffened by bony tendons. They evolved teeth and jaws adapted to pulping vegetation and flourished from the Middle Jurassic to the Late Cretaceous period (165–65 million years ago) in North America, Europe, Africa, China, Australia, and Antarctica. Some ornithopods were no larger than a dog, while others were immense creatures up to 49 ft (15 m) long. Iguanodonts, an ornithopod group, had a broad, toothless beak at the end of a long snout, large jaws with long rows of ridged, closely packed teeth for grinding vegetation, a bulky body, and a heavy tail. *Iguanodon* and some other iguanodonts had large thumb-spikes that were strong enough to stab attackers. Another group, the hadrosaurs, such as *Gryposaurus* and *Hadrosaurus,* lived in Late Cretaceous times (97–65 million years ago) and with their broad beaks are sometimes known as "duckbills." They were characterized by their deep skulls and closely packed rows of teeth, while some, such as *Corythosaurus* and *Lambeosaurus,* had tall, hollow, bony head crests.

SKELETON OF IGUANODON

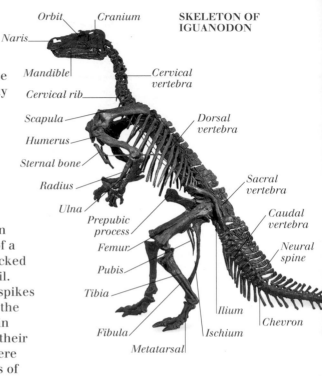

- Orbit
- Cranium
- Naris
- Mandible
- Cervical rib
- Scapula
- Humerus
- Sternal bone
- Radius
- Ulna
- Prepubic process
- Femur
- Pubis
- Tibia
- Fibula
- Metatarsal
- Cervical vertebra
- Dorsal vertebra
- Sacral vertebra
- Caudal vertebra
- Neural spine
- Ilium
- Ischium
- Chevron

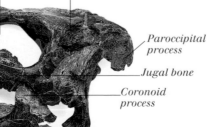

- Thigh
- Heavy, stiff tail
- Knee
- Hind limb
- Ankle
- Toe
- Foot
- Hooflike nail

SKULL AND MANDIBLE OF YOUNG IGUANODON

- Premaxilla
- Maxilla
- Cheek tooth
- Orbit
- Cranium
- Paroccipital process
- Jugal bone
- Coronoid process
- Predentary bone
- Dentary bone
- Mandible

EXAMPLES OF IGUANODONTS

OURANOSAURUS
An iguanodontid
Length: 23 ft (7 m)

CAMPTOSAURUS
A camptosaurid
Length: 16–23 ft (4.9–7 m)

MUTTABURRASAURUS
A camptosaurid
Length: 23 ft (7 m)

PROBACTROSAURUS
An iguanodontid
Length: 20 ft (6.1 m)

EXTERNAL FEATURES OF IGUANODON

Eye

Naris

Shoulder

Neck

Ambiens
muscle

Tongue

Beak

Scaly skin

External pubo-ischio-
femoral muscle

Forelimb

Elbow

Wrist

Hand

Thumb-spike

Finger

Hooflike nail

**INTERNAL ANATOMY OF
HIND LEG OF IGUANODON**

Iliofemoral
muscle

Ilium

Iliotibial
muscle

Short
caudo-
femoral
muscle

Tibial flexor
muscle

Femur

Iliofibular
muscle

Gastrocnemius
muscle

Common digital
extensor muscle

Anterior tibial
muscle

Tibia

Fibula

Tarsal

Metatarsal

Toe

Hooflike nail

Ornithopods 2

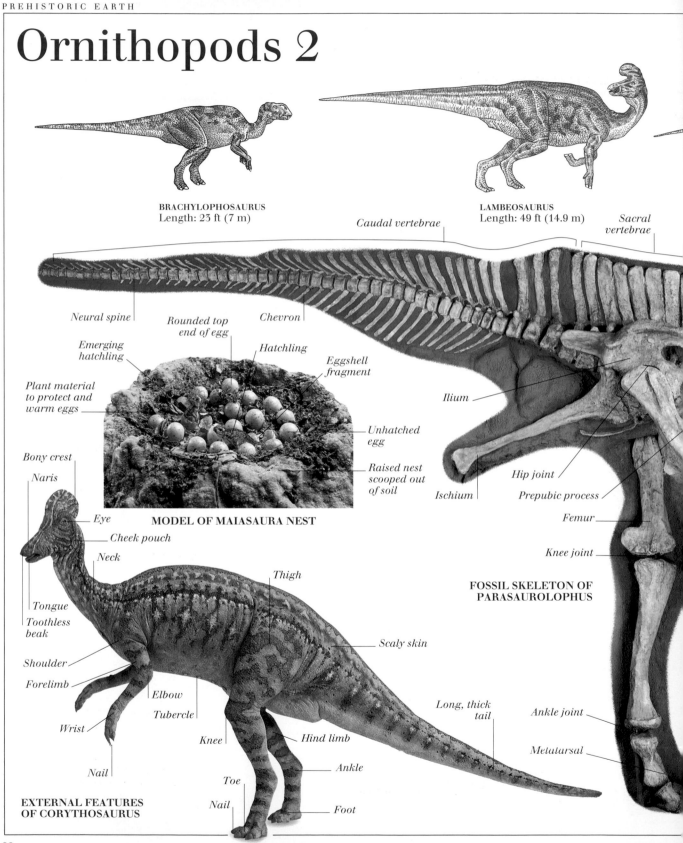

BRACHYLOPHOSAURUS
Length: 23 ft (7 m)

LAMBEOSAURUS
Length: 49 ft (14.9 m)

Caudal vertebrae

Sacral
vertebrae

Neural spine

Chevron

Rounded top
end of egg

Emerging
hatchling

Hatchling

Eggshell
fragment

Plant material
to protect and
warm eggs

Ilium

Unhatched
egg

Raised nest
scooped out
of soil

Hip joint

Ischium

Prepubic process

Femur

Knee joint

MODEL OF MAIASAURA NEST

Bony crest

Naris

Eye

**FOSSIL SKELETON OF
PARASAUROLOPHUS**

Cheek pouch

Neck

Thigh

Tongue

Toothless
beak

Scaly skin

Shoulder

Forelimb

Elbow

Tubercle

Long, thick
tail

Ankle joint

Wrist

Knee

Hind limb

Metatarsal

Nail

Ankle

Toe

**EXTERNAL FEATURES
OF CORYTHOSAURUS**

Nail

Foot

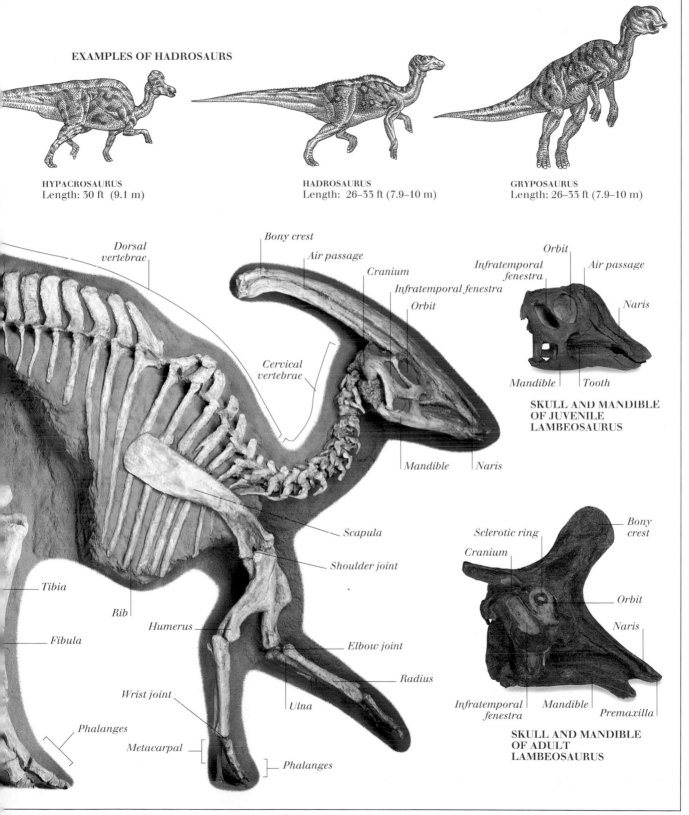

EXAMPLES OF HADROSAURS

HYPACROSAURUS
Length: 30 ft (9.1 m)

HADROSAURUS
Length: 26–33 ft (7.9–10 m)

GRYPOSAURUS
Length: 26–33 ft (7.9–10 m)

Dorsal vertebrae

Bony crest

Air passage

Cranium

Infratemporal fenestra

Orbit

Orbit

Infratemporal fenestra

Air passage

Naris

Cervical vertebrae

Mandible

Naris

Mandible

Tooth

**SKULL AND MANDIBLE
OF JUVENILE
LAMBEOSAURUS**

Scapula

Shoulder joint

Tibia

Rib

Humerus

Fibula

Elbow joint

Radius

Wrist joint

Ulna

Phalanges

Metacarpal

Phalanges

Sclerotic ring

Cranium

Bony crest

Orbit

Naris

Infratemporal fenestra

Mandible

Premaxilla

**SKULL AND MANDIBLE
OF ADULT
LAMBEOSAURUS**

Marginocephalians 1

HEAD-BUTTING PRENOCEPHALES

MARGINOCEPHALIA ("margined heads") were a group of bipedal and quadrupedal ornithischian dinosaurs with a narrow shelf or deep, bony frill at the back of the skull. Marginocephalians were probably descended from the same ancestor as the ornithopods and lived in what are now North America, Africa, Asia, and Europe during the Cretaceous period (146–65 million years ago). They were divided into two infraorders: Pachycephalosauria ("thick-headed lizards"), such as *Pachycephalosaurus* and *Stegoceras*, and Ceratopsia ("horned faces"), such as *Triceratops* and *Psittacosaurus*. The thick skulls of Pachycephalosauria protected their brains during head-butting contests fought to win territory and mates; their hips and spines were also strengthened to withstand the shock. The bony frill of Ceratopsia would have added to their frightening appearance when charging; the neck was strengthened for impact and to support the huge head, with its snipping beak and powerful slicing toothed jaws. A charging ceratops would have been a formidable opponent for even the largest predators. Ceratopsia were among the most abundant herbivorous dinosaurs of the Late Cretaceous period (97–65 million years ago).

Thick, high-domed cranium
Supraorbital ridge
Orbit
Naris
Mandible
Neural spine
Cervical rib
Humerus
Ulna
Radius
Prepubis
Wrist joint
Metacarpal
Phalanx
Ilium
Ischium
Metatarsals
Phalanges

EXAMPLES OF SKULLS OF PACHYCEPHALOSAURS

Orbit
Thickened dome of cranium
Maxilla
Bony ridge
Tooth
Mandible
SKULL AND MANDIBLE OF STEGOCERAS

Thickened dome of cranium
Orbit
Maxilla
Bony nodule
SKULL OF PRENOCEPHALE

Thickened dome of cranium
Bony spike
Maxilla
Orbit
Bony nodule
SKULL OF PACHYCEPHALOSAURUS

EXTERNAL FEATURES OF PACHYCEPHALOSAURUS

Scaly skin
Bony nodule
Domed head
Eye
Bony spike
Neck
Snout
Tail
Knee
Forelimb
Finger
Hind limb
Hand
Ankle
Claw
Foot
Toe

Thickened dome of cranium
Bony nodule
Buccal cavity
Brain cavity
SECTION THROUGH SKULL OF PACHYCEPHALOSAURUS

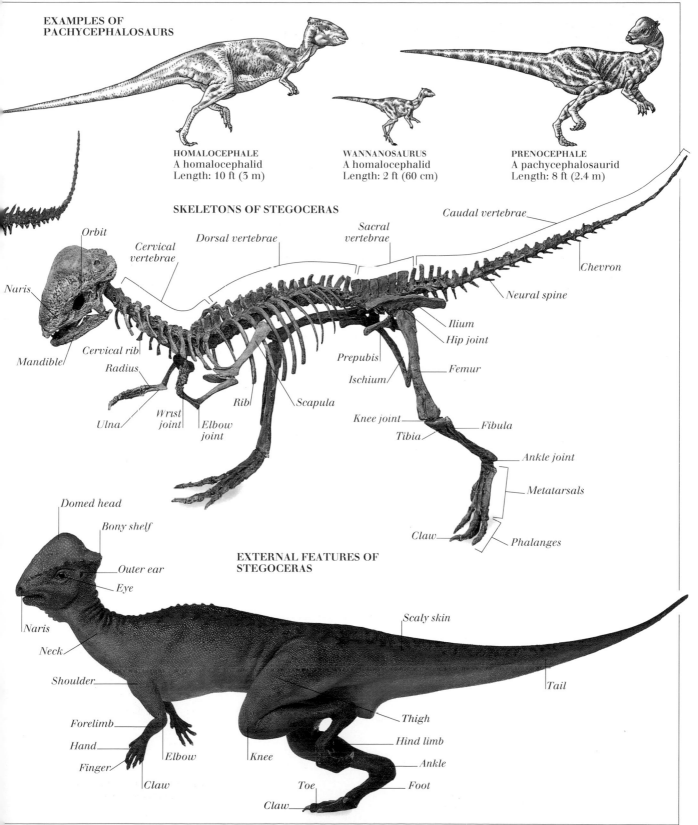

**EXAMPLES OF
PACHYCEPHALOSAURS**

HOMALOCEPHALE
A homalocephalid
Length: 10 ft (3 m)

WANNANOSAURUS
A homalocephalid
Length: 2 ft (60 cm)

PRENOCEPHALE
A pachycephalosaurid
Length: 8 ft (2.4 m)

SKELETONS OF STEGOCERAS

Orbit

*Cervical
vertebrae*

Dorsal vertebrae

*Sacral
vertebrae*

Caudal vertebrae

Chevron

Naris

Neural spine

Ilium

Hip joint

Mandible

Cervical rib

Prepubis

Femur

Radius

Ischium

*Wrist
joint*

Rib

Scapula

Ulna

*Elbow
joint*

Knee joint

Fibula

Tibia

Ankle joint

Metatarsals

Claw

Phalanges

Domed head

Bony shelf

**EXTERNAL FEATURES OF
STEGOCERAS**

Outer ear

Eye

Scaly skin

Naris

Neck

Shoulder

Tail

Forelimb

Thigh

Hand

Hind limb

Finger

Elbow

Knee

Ankle

Claw

Toe

Foot

Claw

Marginocephalians 2

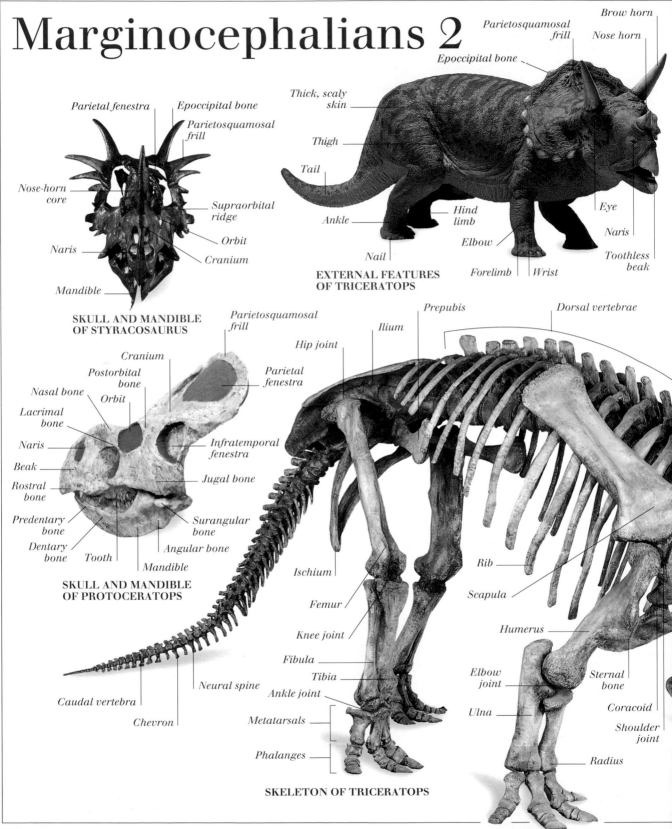

SKULL AND MANDIBLE OF STYRACOSAURUS

Parietal fenestra

Epoccipital bone

Parietosquamosal frill

Nose-horn core

Supraorbital ridge

Naris

Orbit

Cranium

Mandible

EXTERNAL FEATURES OF TRICERATOPS

Brow horn

Parietosquamosal frill

Nose horn

Epoccipital bone

Thick, scaly skin

Thigh

Tail

Hind limb

Ankle

Elbow

Eye

Naris

Nail

Toothless beak

Forelimb

Wrist

SKULL AND MANDIBLE OF PROTOCERATOPS

Cranium

Postorbital bone

Nasal bone

Orbit

Lacrimal bone

Naris

Beak

Rostral bone

Predentary bone

Dentary bone

Tooth

Mandible

Surangular bone

Angular bone

Jugal bone

Infratemporal fenestra

Parietosquamosal frill

Parietal fenestra

SKELETON OF TRICERATOPS

Hip joint

Ilium

Prepubis

Dorsal vertebrae

Caudal vertebra

Chevron

Neural spine

Ischium

Femur

Knee joint

Fibula

Tibia

Ankle joint

Metatarsals

Phalanges

Rib

Scapula

Humerus

Elbow joint

Sternal bone

Ulna

Coracoid

Shoulder joint

Radius

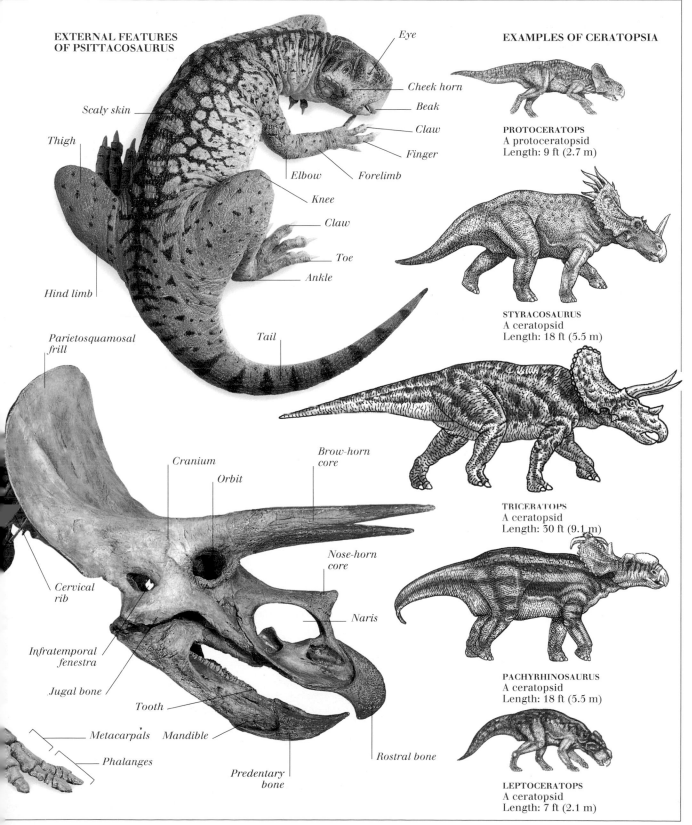

EXTERNAL FEATURES OF PSITTACOSAURUS

Eye

Cheek horn

Beak

Claw

Finger

Elbow

Forelimb

Knee

Claw

Toe

Ankle

Scaly skin

Thigh

Hind limb

Parietosquamosal frill

Tail

Cranium

Orbit

Brow-horn core

Nose-horn core

Naris

Cervical rib

Infratemporal fenestra

Jugal bone

Tooth

Mandible

Metacarpals

Phalanges

Predentary bone

Rostral bone

EXAMPLES OF CERATOPSIA

PROTOCERATOPS
A protoceratopsid
Length: 9 ft (2.7 m)

STYRACOSAURUS
A ceratopsid
Length: 18 ft (5.5 m)

TRICERATOPS
A ceratopsid
Length: 30 ft (9.1 m)

PACHYRHINOSAURUS
A ceratopsid
Length: 18 ft (5.5 m)

LEPTOCERATOPS
A ceratopsid
Length: 7 ft (2.1 m)

Mammals 1

TETRALOPHODON CHEEK TEETH

MODEL OF A MEGAZOSTRODON

SINCE THE EXTINCTION of the dinosaurs 65 million years ago, mammals have been the dominant vertebrates on land. This class includes terrestrial, aerial, and aquatic forms. Having developed from the reptilian Therapsids, the first true mammals—small, nocturnal, shrewlike creatures, such as *Megazostrodon*—appeared over 200 million years ago during the Triassic period (245–208 million years ago). Mammals had several features that improved on those of their reptilian ancestors: an efficient four-chambered heart allowed these warm-blooded animals to sustain high levels of activity; a covering of hair helped them maintain a constant body temperature; an improved limb structure gave them more efficient locomotion; and the birth of live young and the immediate supply of food from the mother's milk aided their rapid growth. Since the end of the Mesozoic era (65 million years ago), the number of different mammal orders and the abundance of species in each order have varied dramatically. For example, the Perissodactyla (the order that includes *Coelodonta* and modern horses) was a common group during the Early Tertiary period (about 54 million years ago). Today, the mammalian orders with the most populous species are the Rodentia (rats and mice), the Chiroptera (bats), the Primates (monkeys and apes), the Carnivora (bears, cats, and dogs), and the Artiodactyla (cattle, deer, and pigs), while the Proboscidea order, which formerly included many genera, such as *Phiomia*, *Moeritherium*, *Tetralophodon*, and *Mammuthus*, now has only three species of elephant. In Australia and South America, millions of years of continental isolation led to increased diversity of the marsupials, a group of mammals distinct from the placentals (see p. 74) that existed elsewhere.

Long tail aids balance

Insulating hair

Neural spine

Scapula

Cervical vertebra

Nasal horn

Naris

Predentary bone

Chisel-edged molar

Orbit

Mandible

Humerus

Radius

Ulna

Metacarpal

Phalanx

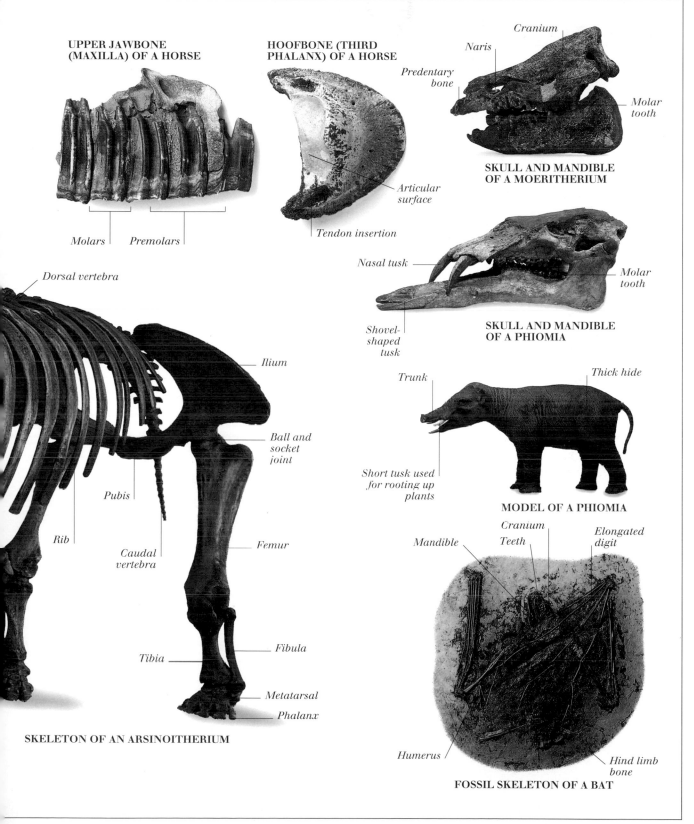

UPPER JAWBONE (MAXILLA) OF A HORSE

Molars Premolars

HOOFBONE (THIRD PHALANX) OF A HORSE

Articular surface

Tendon insertion

Cranium

Naris

Predentary bone

Molar tooth

SKULL AND MANDIBLE OF A MOERITHERIUM

Nasal tusk

Molar tooth

Shovel-shaped tusk

SKULL AND MANDIBLE OF A PHIOMIA

Dorsal vertebra

Ilium

Ball and socket joint

Pubis

Rib

Caudal vertebra

Femur

Tibia

Fibula

Metatarsal

Phalanx

SKELETON OF AN ARSINOITHERIUM

Trunk

Thick hide

Short tusk used for rooting up plants

MODEL OF A PHIOMIA

Mandible

Cranium

Teeth

Elongated digit

Humerus

Hind limb bone

FOSSIL SKELETON OF A BAT

Mammals 2

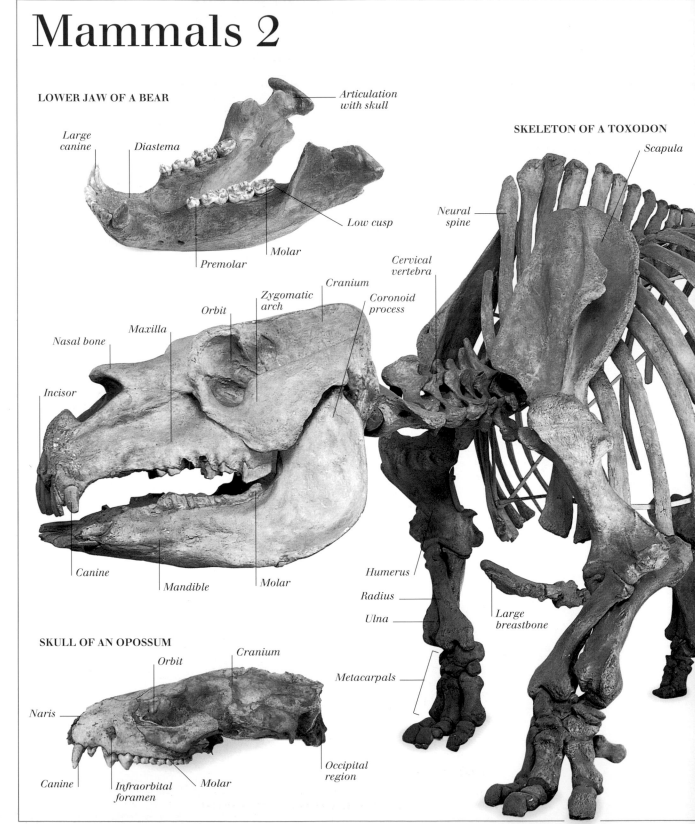

LOWER JAW OF A BEAR

Articulation
with skull

Large
canine

Diastema

Low cusp

Molar

Premolar

Orbit

Maxilla

Zygomatic
arch

Cranium

Coronoid
process

Nasal bone

Incisor

Canine

Mandible

Molar

SKULL OF AN OPOSSUM

Orbit

Cranium

Naris

Canine

Infraorbital
foramen

Molar

Occipital
region

SKELETON OF A TOXODON

Scapula

Neural
spine

Cervical
vertebra

Humerus

Radius

Ulna

Large
breastbone

Metacarpals

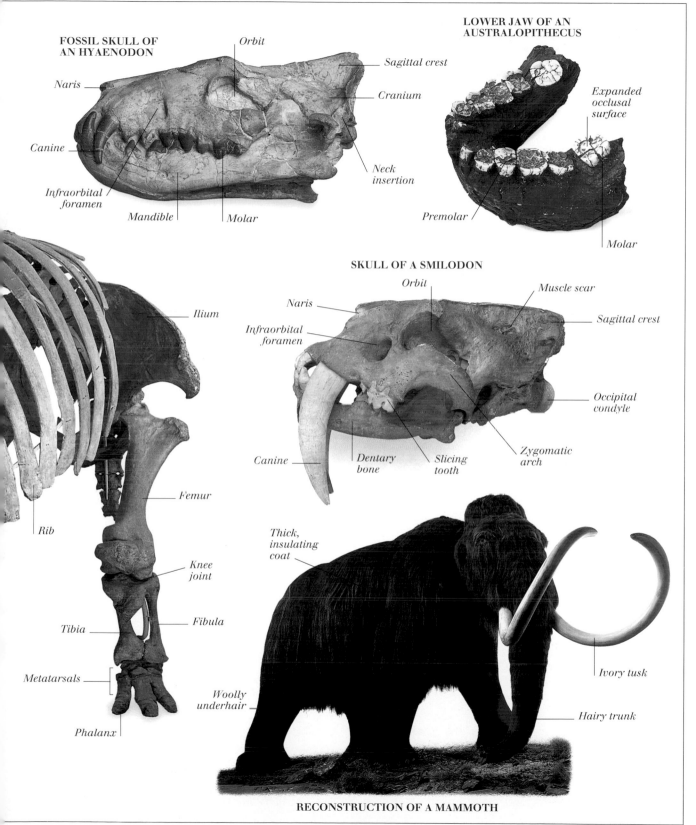

**FOSSIL SKULL OF
AN HYAENODON**

Orbit

Sagittal crest

Cranium

Naris

Neck
insertion

Canine

Infraorbital
foramen

Mandible

Molar

**LOWER JAW OF AN
AUSTRALOPITHECUS**

Expanded
occlusal
surface

Premolar

Molar

SKULL OF A SMILODON

Orbit

Muscle scar

Naris

Sagittal crest

Infraorbital
foramen

Occipital
condyle

Canine

Dentary
bone

Slicing
tooth

Zygomatic
arch

Ilium

Femur

Rib

Knee
joint

Tibia

Fibula

Metatarsals

Phalanx

Thick,
insulating
coat

Ivory tusk

Hairy trunk

Woolly
underhair

RECONSTRUCTION OF A MAMMOTH

The first hominids

MODERN HUMANS BELONG TO THE MAMMALIAN order of primates (see pp. 202–203), which originated about 55 million years ago; they comprise the only extant hominid species. The earliest hominid was *Australopithecus* ("southern ape"), a small-brained intermediate between apes and humans that was capable of standing and walking upright. *Homo habilis*, the first known human appeared at least 2 million years ago. This larger-brained "handy man" began making tools for hunting. *Homo erectus* first appeared in Africa about 1.8 million years ago and spread into Asia about 800,000 years later. Smaller toothed than *Homo habilis*, it developed fire as a tool, which enabled it to cook food. Neanderthals, a near relative of modern humans, originated about 200,000 years ago, and *Homo sapiens* (modern humans) appeared in Africa about 100,000 years later. The two coexisted for thousands of years, but by 30,000 years ago, *Homo sapiens* had become dominant and the Neanderthals had died out. Classification of *Homo sapiens* in relation to its ancestors is enormously problematic: modern humans must be classified not only by bone structure, but also by specific behavior—the ability to plan future action; to follow traditions; and to use symbolic communication, including complex language and the ability to use and recognize symbols.

JAWBONE OF AUSTRALOPITHECUS (SOUTHERN APE)

Larger jawbone than modern human

Large back tooth

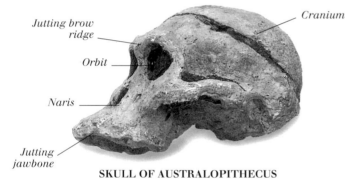

Jutting brow ridge

Cranium

Orbit

Naris

Jutting jawbone

SKULL OF AUSTRALOPITHECUS (SOUTHERN APE)

Orbit

Naris

SKULL OF HOMO HABILIS (FIRST KNOWN HUMAN)

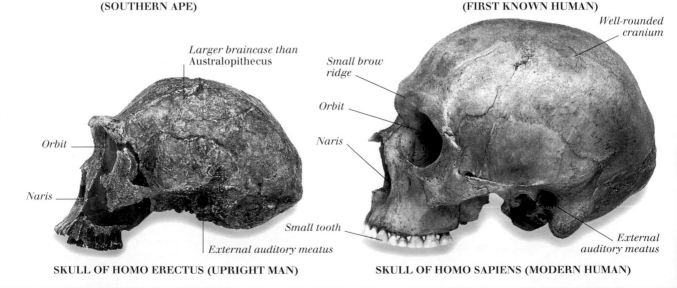

Larger braincase than Australopithecus

Orbit

Naris

External auditory meatus

SKULL OF HOMO ERECTUS (UPRIGHT MAN)

Well-rounded cranium

Small brow ridge

Orbit

Naris

Small tooth

External auditory meatus

SKULL OF HOMO SAPIENS (MODERN HUMAN)

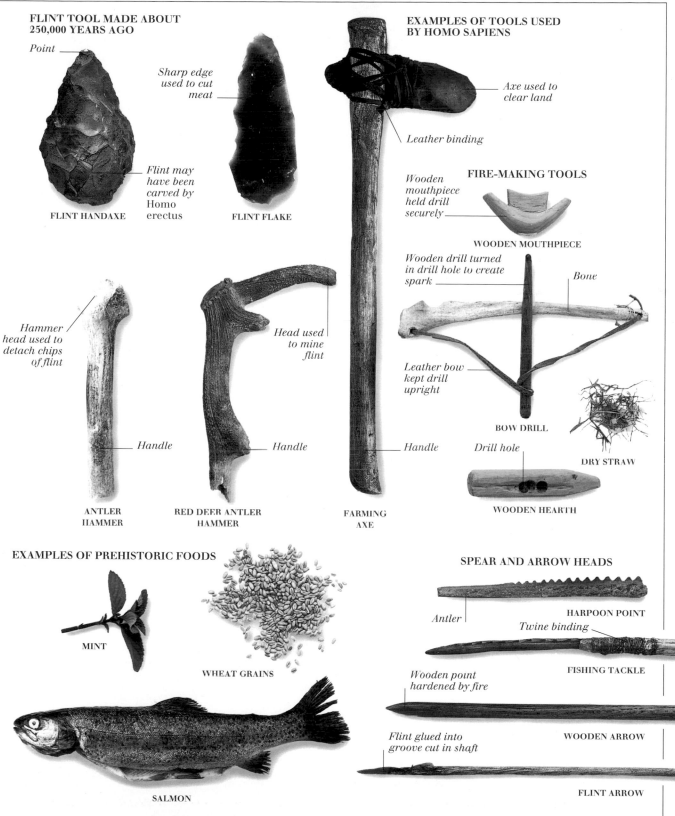

FLINT TOOL MADE ABOUT 250,000 YEARS AGO

Point

Sharp edge used to cut meat

Flint may have been carved by Homo erectus

FLINT HANDAXE

FLINT FLAKE

EXAMPLES OF TOOLS USED BY HOMO SAPIENS

Axe used to clear land

Leather binding

FIRE-MAKING TOOLS

Wooden mouthpiece held drill securely

WOODEN MOUTHPIECE

Wooden drill turned in drill hole to create spark

Bone

Leather bow kept drill upright

BOW DRILL

Drill hole

DRY STRAW

Hammer head used to detach chips of flint

Head used to mine flint

Handle

Handle

Handle

ANTLER HAMMER

RED DEER ANTLER HAMMER

FARMING AXE

WOODEN HEARTH

EXAMPLES OF PREHISTORIC FOODS

MINT

WHEAT GRAINS

SALMON

SPEAR AND ARROW HEADS

Antler

HARPOON POINT

Twine binding

FISHING TACKLE

Wooden point hardened by fire

WOODEN ARROW

Flint glued into groove cut in shaft

FLINT ARROW

PLANTS

Plant varieties

THERE ARE MORE THAN 300,000 SPECIES of plants. They
show a wide diversity of forms, ranging from delicate liverworts, adapted for life
in a damp habitat, to cacti, capable of surviving in the desert. The plant kingdom includes
herbaceous plants, such as corn, which completes its life cycle in one year, to the giant redwood tree, which
can live for thousands of years. This diversity reflects the adaptations of plants to survive in a wide range of
habitats. This is seen most clearly in the flowering plants (phylum Angiospermophyta), which are the most
numerous, with over 250,000 species. They are also the most widespread, being found from the tropics to the
arctic. Despite their diversity, plants share certain characteristics. Typically, plants are green, and make their
food by photosynthesis. Most plants live in or on a substrate, such as soil, and do not actively move. Algae
(kingdom Protista) and fungi (kingdom Fungi) have some plantlike characteristics and are
often studied alongside plants, although they are not true plants.

GREEN ALGA
Micrograph of desmid
(*Micrasterias sp.*)

*Pyrenoid
(small protein
body)*

Chloroplast

*Sinus
(division between
two halves of cell)*

Cell wall

FERN
Tree fern
(*Dicksonia antarctica*)

*Rachis
(main axis
of pinnate leaf)*

*Petiole
(leaf stalk)*

*Ramentum
(brown scale)*

*Base of dead
frond (leaf)*

Trunk

*Adventitious
root*

*Epiphytic
fern growing
at base*

BRYOPHYTE
Moss
(*Bryum sp.*)

*Seta
(stalk)*

Immature capsule

*Sporophyte
(spore-
producing
plant)*

*Capsule
(site of spore
production)*

"Leaf"

*Gametophyte
(gamete-producing
plant)*

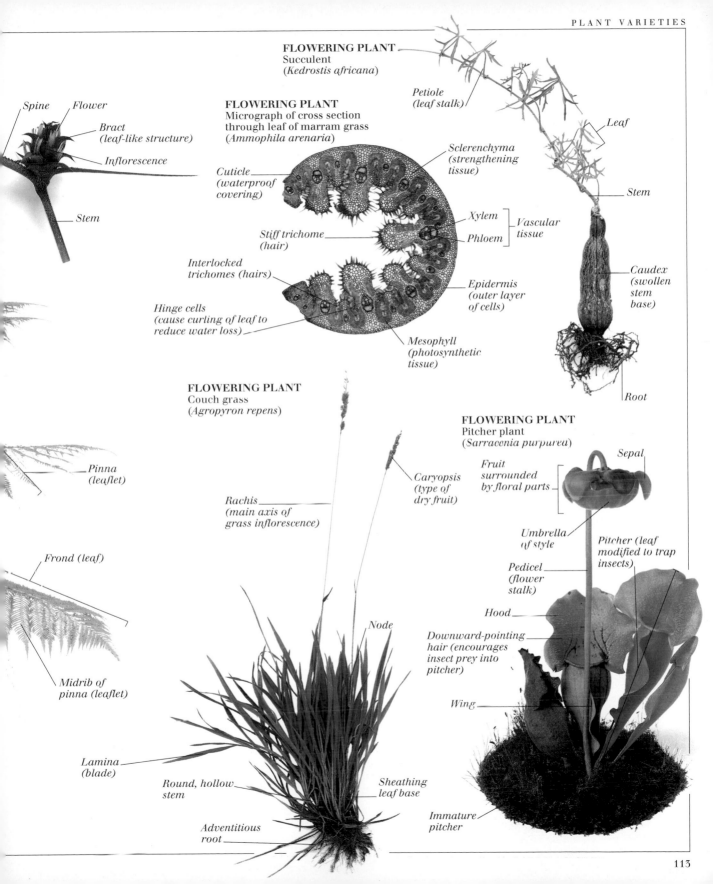

FLOWERING PLANT
Succulent
(*Kedrostis africana*)

*Petiole
(leaf stalk)*

Leaf

Stem

*Caudex
(swollen
stem
base)*

Root

FLOWERING PLANT
Micrograph of cross section
through leaf of marram grass
(*Ammophila arenaria*)

*Cuticle
(waterproof
covering)*

*Sclerenchyma
(strengthening
tissue)*

Xylem

Phloem

*Vascular
tissue*

*Stiff trichome
(hair)*

*Interlocked
trichomes (hairs)*

*Hinge cells
(cause curling of leaf to
reduce water loss)*

*Epidermis
(outer layer
of cells)*

*Mesophyll
(photosynthetic
tissue)*

Spine

Flower

*Bract
(leaf-like structure)*

Inflorescence

Stem

*Pinna
(leaflet)*

Frond (leaf)

*Midrib of
pinna (leaflet)*

FLOWERING PLANT
Couch grass
(*Agropyron repens*)

*Rachis
(main axis of
grass inflorescence)*

*Caryopsis
(type of
dry fruit)*

Node

*Lamina
(blade)*

*Round, hollow
stem*

*Sheathing
leaf base*

*Adventitious
root*

FLOWERING PLANT
Pitcher plant
(*Sarracenia purpurea*)

Sepal

*Fruit
surrounded
by floral parts*

*Umbrella
of style*

*Pitcher (leaf
modified to trap
insects)*

*Pedicel
(flower
stalk)*

Hood

*Downward-pointing
hair (encourages
insect prey into
pitcher)*

Wing

*Immature
pitcher*

Fungi and lichens

FUNGI WERE ONCE THOUGHT OF AS PLANTS but are now classified as a separate kingdom. This kingdom includes not only the familiar mushrooms, puffballs, stinkhorns, and molds, but also yeasts, smuts, rusts, and lichens. Most fungi are multicellular, consisting of a mass of thread-like hyphae that together form a mycelium. However, the simpler fungi, like yeasts, are microscopic, single-celled organisms. Typically, fungi reproduce by means of spores. Most fungi feed on dead or decaying matter or on living organisms. A few fungi obtain their food from plants or algae, with which they have a symbiotic (mutually advantageous) relationship. Lichens are a symbiotic partnership between algae and fungi. Of the six types of lichens the three most common are crustose (flat and crusty), foliose (leafy), and fruticose (shrub-like). Some lichens (such as *Cladonia floerkeana*) are a combination of types. Lichens reproduce by means of spores or soredia (powdery vegetative fragments).

EXAMPLES OF FUNGI

Emerging sporophore (spore-bearing structure)

Pileus (cap) continuous with stipe (stalk)

Bark of dead beech tree

Inrolled margin of pileus (cap)

Gill (site of spore production)

Sporophore (spore-bearing structure)

Stipe (stalk)

Hyphae (fungal filaments)

OYSTER FUNGUS
(*Pleurotus pulmonarius*)

EXAMPLES OF LICHENS

Secondary fruticose thallus

Branched, hollow stem

Apothecium (spore-producing body)

FRUTICOSE
Cladonia portentosa

Soredia (powdery vegetative fragments) produced at end of lobe

Tree bark

Foliose thallus

FOLIOSE
Hypogymnia physodes

Soredia (powdery vegetative fragments) released onto surface of squamulose thallus

Apothecium (spore-producing body)

Basal scale of primary squamulose thallus

Podetium (granular stalk) of secondary fruticose thallus

Moss

SQUAMULOSE (SCALY) AND FRUTICOSE THALLUS
Cladonia floerkeana

Gleba (spore-producing tissue found in this type of fungus)

Sporophore (spore-bearing structure)

Porous stipe (stalk)

Volva (remains of universal veil)

STINKHORN
(*Phallus impudicus*)

Toothed branchlet

Branch

Sporophore (spore-bearing structure)

Stipe (stalk)

RAMARIA FORMOSA

SECTION THROUGH FOLIOSE LICHEN SHOWING REPRODUCTION BY SOREDIA

Soredium (powdery vegetative fragment involved in propagation) released from lichen

Algal cell

Fungal hypha

Upper cortex

Algal layer

Medulla of fungal hyphae (mycelium)

Lower cortex

Rhizine (bundle of absorptive hyphae)

Soralium (pore in upper surface of thallus)

Upper surface of thallus

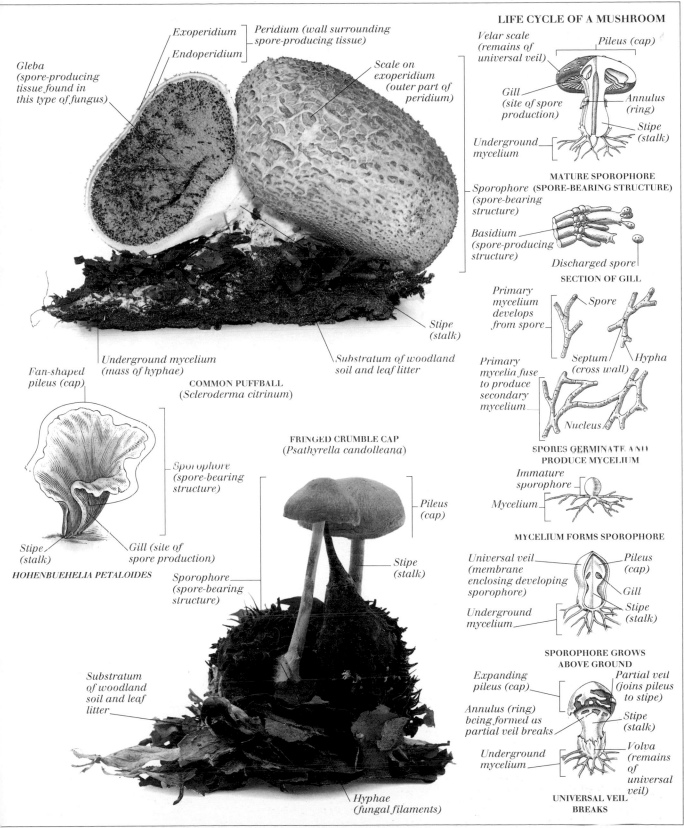

Gleba
(spore-producing
tissue found in
this type of fungus)

Exoperidium

Endoperidium

Peridium (wall surrounding
spore-producing tissue)

Scale on
exoperidium (outer part of
peridium)

LIFE CYCLE OF A MUSHROOM

Velar scale
(remains of
universal veil)

Pileus (cap)

Gill
(site of spore
production)

Annulus
(ring)

Underground
mycelium

Stipe
(stalk)

MATURE SPOROPHORE (SPORE-BEARING STRUCTURE)

Sporophore
(spore-bearing
structure)

Basidium
(spore-producing
structure)

Discharged spore

SECTION OF GILL

Primary
mycelium
develops
from spore

Spore

Primary
mycelia fuse
to produce
secondary
mycelium

Septum
(cross wall)

Hypha

Nucleus

SPORES GERMINATE AND PRODUCE MYCELIUM

Immature
sporophore

Mycelium

MYCELIUM FORMS SPOROPHORE

Universal veil
(membrane
enclosing developing
sporophore)

Pileus
(cap)

Gill

Underground
mycelium

Stipe
(stalk)

SPOROPHORE GROWS ABOVE GROUND

Expanding
pileus (cap)

Partial veil
(joins pileus
to stipe)

Annulus (ring)
being formed as
partial veil breaks

Stipe
(stalk)

Underground
mycelium

Volva
(remains
of
universal
veil)

UNIVERSAL VEIL BREAKS

Stipe
(stalk)

Substratum of woodland
soil and leaf litter

Underground mycelium
(mass of hyphae)

COMMON PUFFBALL
(Scleroderma citrinum)

Fan-shaped
pileus (cap)

Sporophore
(spore-bearing
structure)

Stipe
(stalk)

Gill (site of
spore production)

HOHENBUEHELIA PETALOIDES

FRINGED CRUMBLE CAP
(Psathyrella candolleana)

Pileus
(cap)

Sporophore
(spore-bearing
structure)

Stipe
(stalk)

Substratum
of woodland
soil and leaf
litter

Hyphae
(fungal filaments)

Algae and seaweed

ALGAE ARE NOT TRUE PLANTS. They form a diverse group of plantlike organisms that belong to the kingdom Protista. Like plants, algae possess the green pigment chlorophyll and make their own food by photosynthesis (see pp. 138-139). Many algae also possess other pigments by which they can be classified. For example, the brown pigment fucoxanthin is found in brown algae. Some of the ten phyla of algae are exclusively unicellular (single-celled); others also contain aggregates of cells in filaments or colonies. Three phyla— the Chlorophyta (green algae), Rhodophyta (red algae), and Phaeophyta (brown algae)—contain larger, multicellular, thalloid (flat), marine organisms commonly known as seaweed. Most algae can reproduce sexually. For example, in brown seaweed *Fucus vesiculosus*, gametes (sex cells) are produced in conceptacles (chambers) in the receptacles (fertile tips of fronds); after their release into the sea, antherozoids (male gametes) and oospheres (female gametes) fuse. The resulting zygote settles on a rock and develops into a new seaweed.

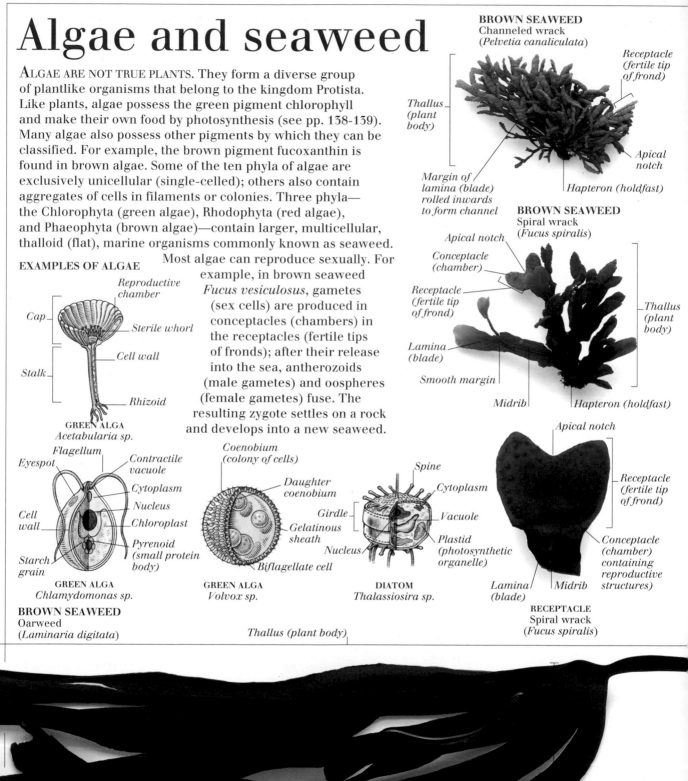

EXAMPLES OF ALGAE

GREEN ALGA
Acetabularia sp.

- Cap
- Reproductive chamber
- Sterile whorl
- Cell wall
- Stalk
- Rhizoid

GREEN ALGA
Chlamydomonas sp.

- Flagellum
- Eyespot
- Contractile vacuole
- Cytoplasm
- Nucleus
- Cell wall
- Chloroplast
- Pyrenoid (small protein body)
- Starch grain

GREEN ALGA
Volvox sp.

- Coenobium (colony of cells)
- Daughter coenobium
- Gelatinous sheath
- Biflagellate cell

DIATOM
Thalassiosira sp.

- Spine
- Cytoplasm
- Girdle
- Vacuole
- Nucleus
- Plastid (photosynthetic organelle)

BROWN SEAWEED
Channeled wrack
(*Pelvetia canaliculata*)

- Thallus (plant body)
- Receptacle (fertile tip of frond)
- Apical notch
- Margin of lamina (blade) rolled inwards to form channel
- Hapteron (holdfast)

BROWN SEAWEED
Spiral wrack
(*Fucus spiralis*)

- Apical notch
- Conceptacle (chamber)
- Receptacle (fertile tip of frond)
- Lamina (blade)
- Smooth margin
- Midrib
- Thallus (plant body)
- Hapteron (holdfast)

RECEPTACLE
Spiral wrack
(*Fucus spiralis*)

- Apical notch
- Receptacle (fertile tip of frond)
- Conceptacle (chamber) containing reproductive structures
- Lamina (blade)
- Midrib

BROWN SEAWEED
Oarweed
(*Laminaria digitata*)

Thallus (plant body)

Lamina (blade) palmately divided

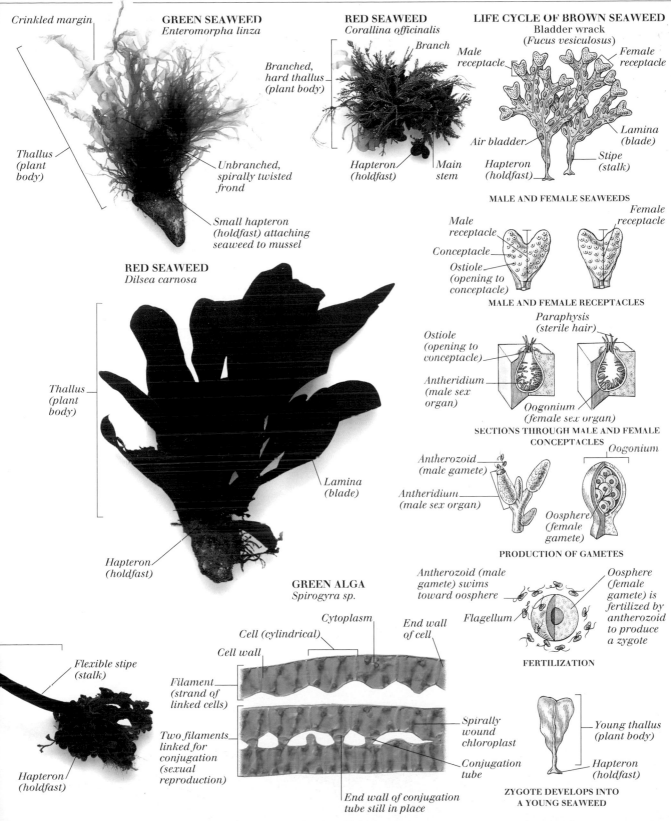

GREEN SEAWEED
Enteromorpha linza

Crinkled margin

Thallus (plant body)

Unbranched, spirally twisted frond

Small hapteron (holdfast) attaching seaweed to mussel

RED SEAWEED
Corallina officinalis

Branch

Branched, hard thallus (plant body)

Hapteron (holdfast)

Main stem

LIFE CYCLE OF BROWN SEAWEED
Bladder wrack
(*Fucus vesiculosus*)

Male receptacle

Female receptacle

Air bladder

Lamina (blade)

Hapteron (holdfast)

Stipe (stalk)

MALE AND FEMALE SEAWEEDS

Male receptacle

Female receptacle

Conceptacle

Ostiole (opening to conceptacle)

MALE AND FEMALE RECEPTACLES

Paraphysis (sterile hair)

Ostiole (opening to conceptacle)

Antheridium (male sex organ)

Oogonium (female sex organ)

SECTIONS THROUGH MALE AND FEMALE CONCEPTACLES

Antherozoid (male gamete)

Oogonium

Antheridium (male sex organ)

Oosphere (female gamete)

PRODUCTION OF GAMETES

RED SEAWEED
Dilsea carnosa

Thallus (plant body)

Lamina (blade)

Hapteron (holdfast)

Antherozoid (male gamete) swims toward oosphere

Oosphere (female gamete) is fertilized by antherozoid to produce a zygote

Flagellum

FERTILIZATION

GREEN ALGA
Spirogyra sp.

Cytoplasm

Cell (cylindrical)

End wall of cell

Cell wall

Filament (strand of linked cells)

Two filaments linked for conjugation (sexual reproduction)

Spirally wound chloroplast

Conjugation tube

End wall of conjugation tube still in place

Young thallus (plant body)

Hapteron (holdfast)

ZYGOTE DEVELOPS INTO A YOUNG SEAWEED

Flexible stipe (stalk)

Hapteron (holdfast)

Liverworts and mosses

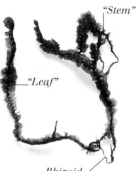

"Stem"

"Leaf"

Rhizoid

LIVERWORTS AND MOSSES ARE SMALL, LOW-GROWING PLANTS that belong to the phylum Bryophyta. Bryophytes do not have true stems, leaves, or roots (they are anchored to the ground by rhizoids), nor do they have the vascular tissues (xylem and phloem) that transport water and nutrients in higher plants. With no outer, waterproof cuticle, bryophytes are susceptible to dehydration, and most grow in moist habitats. The bryophyte life cycle has two stages. In stage one, the green plant (gametophyte) produces male and female gametes (sex cells), which fuse to form a zygote. In stage two, the zygote develops into a sporophyte that remains attached to the gametophyte. The sporophyte produces spores, which are released and germinate into new green plants. Liverworts (class Hepaticae) grow horizontally and may be thalloid (flat and ribbon-like) or "leafy." Mosses (class Musci) typically have an upright "stem" with spirally arranged "leaves."

A THALLOID LIVERWORT
Marchantia polymorpha

Gemma cup

Gemma (detachable tissue that produces new plants)

Thallus (plant body)

Toothed margin of cup

DETAIL OF GEMMA CUP

Archegoniophore (stalked structure carrying archegonia)

Disk

Lobe

Stalk

Thallus (plant body)

Apical notch

Rhizoid

FEMALE GAMETOPHYTE

Disk

Lobe

Stalk

SIDE VIEW OF ARCHEGONIOPHORE

Lobe

Disk

Ray (radial groove)

Stalk

ARCHEGONIOPHORE FROM BELOW

Pore

Ray (radial groove)

MICROGRAPH OF LOBE

Gemma cup

Thallus (plant body)

Midrib

Archegoniophore (stalked structure carrying archegonia)

MICROGRAPH OF THALLUS
Conocephalum conicum

Position of air chamber

Pore for exchange of gases

Upper surface

Rhizoid

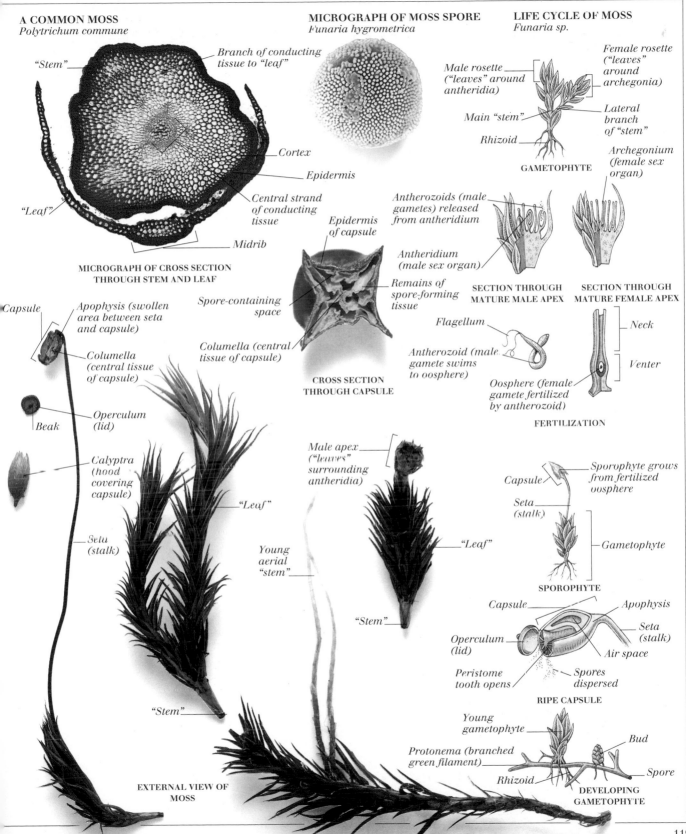

A COMMON MOSS
Polytrichum commune

"Stem"

Branch of conducting tissue to "leaf"

"Leaf"

Cortex

Epidermis

Central strand of conducting tissue

Midrib

MICROGRAPH OF CROSS SECTION THROUGH STEM AND LEAF

MICROGRAPH OF MOSS SPORE
Funaria hygrometrica

LIFE CYCLE OF MOSS
Funaria sp.

Male rosette ("leaves" around antheridia)

Female rosette ("leaves" around archegonia)

Main "stem"

Lateral branch of "stem"

Rhizoid

GAMETOPHYTE

Archegonium (female sex organ)

Epidermis of capsule

Spore-containing space

Columella (central tissue of capsule)

Remains of spore-forming tissue

CROSS SECTION THROUGH CAPSULE

Antherozoids (male gametes) released from antheridium

Antheridium (male sex organ)

SECTION THROUGH MATURE MALE APEX

SECTION THROUGH MATURE FEMALE APEX

Flagellum

Antherozoid (male gamete swims to oosphere)

Oosphere (female gamete fertilized by antherozoid)

Neck

Venter

FERTILIZATION

Capsule

Apophysis (swollen area between seta and capsule)

Columella (central tissue of capsule)

Operculum (lid)

Beak

Calyptra (hood covering capsule)

Seta (stalk)

Male apex ("leaves" surrounding antheridia)

"Leaf"

Young aerial "stem"

"Stem"

"Leaf"

"Stem"

Capsule

Seta (stalk)

Sporophyte grows from fertilized oosphere

Gametophyte

SPOROPHYTE

Capsule

Operculum (lid)

Peristome tooth opens

Apophysis

Seta (stalk)

Air space

Spores dispersed

RIPE CAPSULE

Young gametophyte

Protonema (branched green filament)

Rhizoid

Bud

Spore

DEVELOPING GAMETOPHYTE

"Leaf"

"Stem"

EXTERNAL VIEW OF MOSS

Horsetails, club mosses, and ferns

HORSETAILS, CLUB MOSSES, AND FERNS are primitive land plants, which, like higher plants, have stems, roots, leaves, and vascular systems that transport water, minerals, and food. Unlike higher plants, however, they do not produce seeds when reproducing. Their life cycles involve two stages. In stage one, the sporophyte (green plant) produces spores in sporangia. In stage two, the spores germinate, developing into small, short-lived gametophyte plants that produce male and female gametes (sex cells). The gametes fuse to form a zygote from which a new sporophyte plant develops. Horsetails (phylum Sphenophyta) have erect green stems with branches arranged in whorls. Some stems are fertile and have a single spore-producing strobilus (group of sporangia) at the tip. Club mosses (phylum Lycopodophyta) typically have small leaves arranged spirally around the stem, with spore-producing strobili at the tip of some stems. Ferns (phylum Filicinophyta) usually have large, pinnate leaves called fronds. Sporangia, grouped together in sori, develop on the underside of fertile fronds.

FROND
Male fern
(*Dryopteris filix-mas*)

CLUB MOSS
Lycopodium sp.

Stem with spirally arranged leaves

Branch

Strobilus (group of sporangia)

CLUB MOSS
Selaginella sp.

Epidermis (outer layer of cells)

Cortex (layer between epidermis and vascular tissue)

Vascular tissue — Phloem / Xylem

Lacuna (air space)

Root

MICROGRAPH OF CROSS SECTION THROUGH CLUB MOSS STEM

Shoot apex

Branch

Rhizophore (leafless branch)

Creeping stem with spirally arranged leaves

HORSETAIL
Common horsetail
(*Equisetum arvense*)

Apex of sterile shoot

Sporangiophore (structure carrying sporangia)

Strobilus (group of sporangia)

Non-photosynthetic fertile stem

Collar of small brown leaves

Young shoot

Lateral branch

Photosynthetic sterile stem

Node

Internode

Node

Tuber

Rhizome

Adventitious root

Endodermis (inner layer of cortex)

Vascular tissue

Sclerenchyma (strengthening tissue)

Epidermis (outer layer of cells)

Chlorenchyma (photosynthetic tissue)

Cortex (layer between epidermis and vascular tissue)

Parenchyma (packing tissue)

Hollow pith cavity

Vallecular canal (longitudinal channel)

Carinal canal (longitudinal channel)

MICROGRAPH OF CROSS SECTION THROUGH HORSETAIL STEM

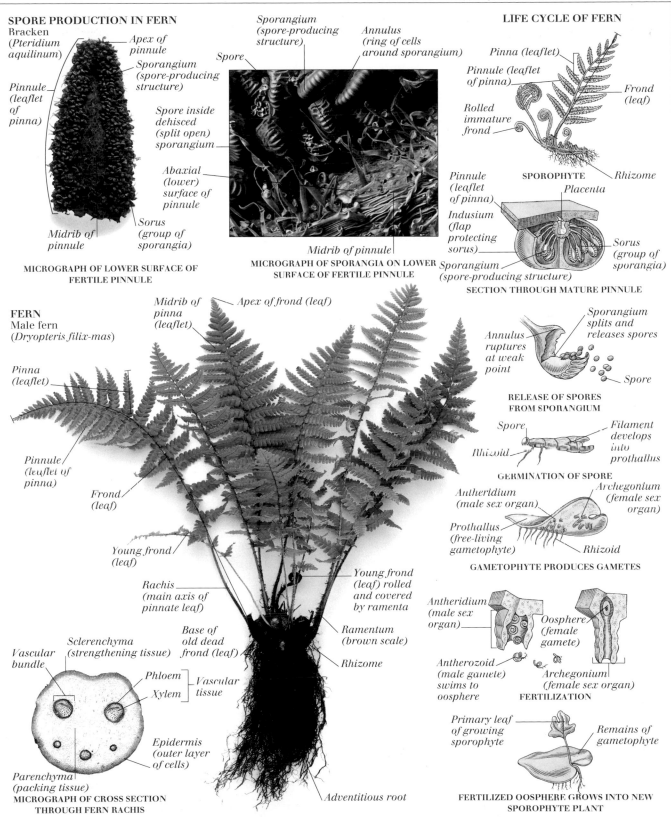

SPORE PRODUCTION IN FERN
Bracken
(*Pteridium aquilinum*)

Apex of pinnule

Sporangium (spore-producing structure)

Pinnule (leaflet of pinna)

Spore inside dehisced (split open) sporangium

Abaxial (lower) surface of pinnule

Midrib of pinnule

Sorus (group of sporangia)

MICROGRAPH OF LOWER SURFACE OF FERTILE PINNULE

Sporangium (spore-producing structure)

Spore

Annulus (ring of cells around sporangium)

Abaxial (lower) surface of pinnule

Midrib of pinnule

MICROGRAPH OF SPORANGIA ON LOWER SURFACE OF FERTILE PINNULE

LIFE CYCLE OF FERN

Pinna (leaflet)

Pinnule (leaflet of pinna)

Frond (leaf)

Rolled immature frond

SPOROPHYTE

Rhizome

Pinnule (leaflet of pinna)

Placenta

Indusium (flap protecting sorus)

Sorus (group of sporangia)

Sporangium (spore-producing structure)

SECTION THROUGH MATURE PINNULE

Sporangium splits and releases spores

Annulus ruptures at weak point

Spore

RELEASE OF SPORES FROM SPORANGIUM

Spore

Filament develops into prothallus

Rhizoid

GERMINATION OF SPORE

Antheridium (male sex organ)

Archegonium (female sex organ)

Prothallus (free-living gametophyte)

Rhizoid

GAMETOPHYTE PRODUCES GAMETES

FERN
Male fern
(*Dryopteris filix-mas*)

Midrib of pinna (leaflet)

Apex of frond (leaf)

Pinna (leaflet)

Pinnule (leaflet of pinna)

Frond (leaf)

Young frond (leaf)

Rachis (main axis of pinnate leaf)

Base of old dead frond (leaf)

Young frond (leaf) rolled and covered by ramenta

Ramentum (brown scale)

Rhizome

Antheridium (male sex organ)

Oosphere (female gamete)

Antherozoid (male gamete) swims to oosphere

Archegonium (female sex organ)

FERTILIZATION

Primary leaf of growing sporophyte

Remains of gametophyte

FERTILIZED OOSPHERE GROWS INTO NEW SPOROPHYTE PLANT

Vascular bundle

Sclerenchyma (strengthening tissue)

Phloem

Xylem

Vascular tissue

Epidermis (outer layer of cells)

Parenchyma (packing tissue)

Adventitious root

MICROGRAPH OF CROSS SECTION THROUGH FERN RACHIS

Gymnosperms 1

THE GYMNOSPERMS ARE FOUR RELATED PHYLA of seed-producing plants: Their seeds, however, lack the protective outer covering which surrounds the seeds of flowering plants. Typically, gymnosperms are woody, perennial shrubs or trees, with stems, leaves, roots, and a well-developed vascular (transport) system. The reproductive structures in most gymnosperms are cones. Male cones produce microspores in which male gametes (sex cells) develop; female cones produce megaspores in which female gametes develop. Microspores are blown by the wind to female cones, male and female gametes fuse during fertilization, and a seed develops. The four gymnosperm phyla are the conifers (phylum Coniferophyta), mostly tall trees; cycads (phylum Cycadophyta), small palm-like trees; the ginkgo or maidenhair tree (phylum Ginkgophyta), a tall tree with bilobed leaves; and gnetophytes (phylum Gnetophyta), a diverse group of plants, mainly shrubs, but also including the horizontally growing welwitschia.

LIFE CYCLE OF SCOTS PINE
(*Pinus sylvestris*)

Needle (foliage leaf)

Cone

Ovuliferous scale (ovule-/seed-bearing structure)

MALE CONES

YOUNG FEMALE CONE

Pollen grain in micropyle (entrance to ovule)

Ovuliferous scale

Pollen grain

Nucleus

Air sac

Ovule (contains female gamete)

POLLINATION

Integument (outer part of ovule)

Archegonium (containing female gamete)

Pollen tube (carries male gamete from pollen grain to ovum)

FERTILIZATION

SCALE AND SEEDS
Pine (*Pinus sp.*)

Ovuliferous scale (ovule-/seed-bearing structure)

Wing scar

Wing of seed derived from ovuliferous scale

Seed

Seed

Point of attachment to axis of cone

Seed scar

OVULIFEROUS SCALE FROM THIRD-YEAR FEMALE CONE

Ovuliferous scale (ovule-/seed-bearing structure)

Seed

Seed

Wing

MATURE FEMALE CONE AND WINGED SEED

Plumule (embryonic shoot)

Cotyledon (seed leaf)

Root

GERMINATION OF PINE SEEDLING

Microsporangium (structure in which pollen grains are formed)

Microsporophyll (modified leaf carrying microsporangia)

Ovule (contains female gametes)

Bract scale

Scale leaf

Axis of cone

Ovuliferous scale (ovule-/seed-bearing structure)

Axis of cone

MICROGRAPH OF LONGITUDINAL SECTION THROUGH YOUNG MALE CONE

MICROGRAPH OF LONGITUDINAL SECTION THROUGH SECOND-YEAR FEMALE CONE

WELWITSCHIA
(*Welwitschia mirabilis*)

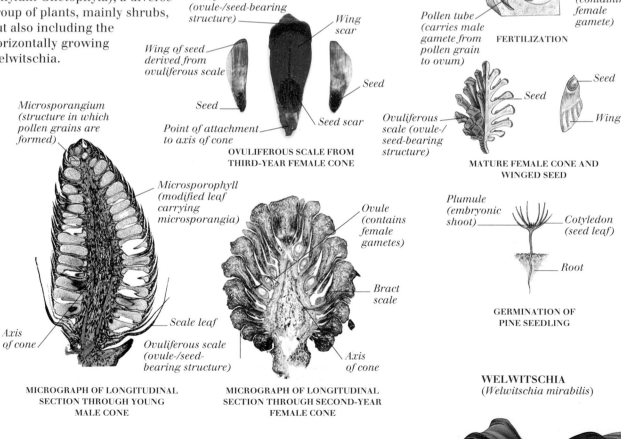

Frayed end of leaf

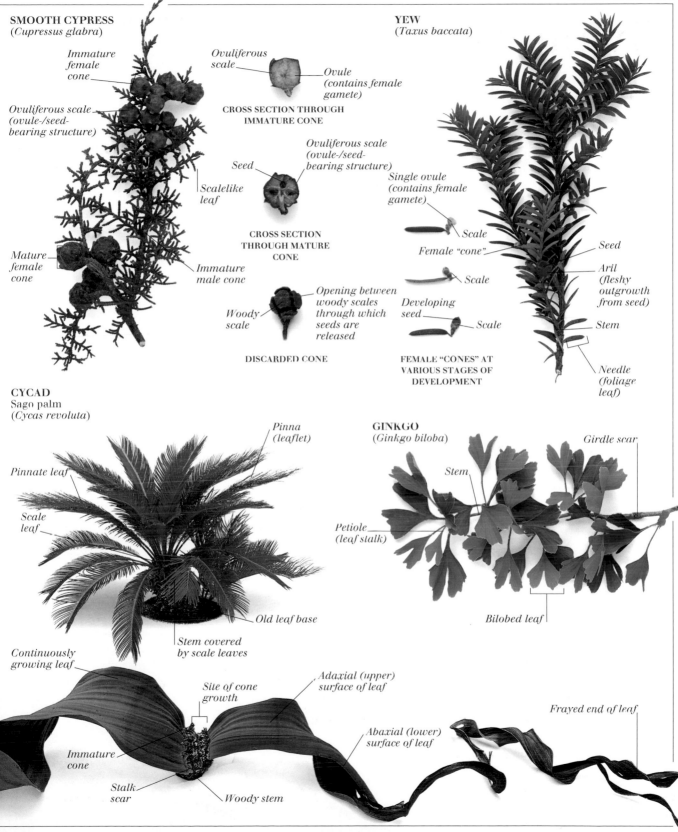

SMOOTH CYPRESS
(*Cupressus glabra*)

Immature female cone

Ovuliferous scale (ovule-/seed-bearing structure)

Scalelike leaf

Mature female cone

Immature male cone

YEW
(*Taxus baccata*)

Ovuliferous scale

Ovule (contains female gamete)

CROSS SECTION THROUGH IMMATURE CONE

Ovuliferous scale (ovule-/seed-bearing structure)

Seed

CROSS SECTION THROUGH MATURE CONE

Woody scale

Opening between woody scales through which seeds are released

DISCARDED CONE

Single ovule (contains female gamete)

Scale

Female "cone"

Scale

Developing seed

Scale

FEMALE "CONES" AT VARIOUS STAGES OF DEVELOPMENT

Seed

Aril (fleshy outgrowth from seed)

Stem

Needle (foliage leaf)

CYCAD
Sago palm
(*Cycas revoluta*)

Pinna (leaflet)

Pinnate leaf

Scale leaf

Old leaf base

Stem covered by scale leaves

GINKGO
(*Ginkgo biloba*)

Girdle scar

Stem

Petiole (leaf stalk)

Bilobed leaf

Continuously growing leaf

Site of cone growth

Adaxial (upper) surface of leaf

Abaxial (lower) surface of leaf

Frayed end of leaf

Immature cone

Stalk scar

Woody stem

Gymnosperms 2

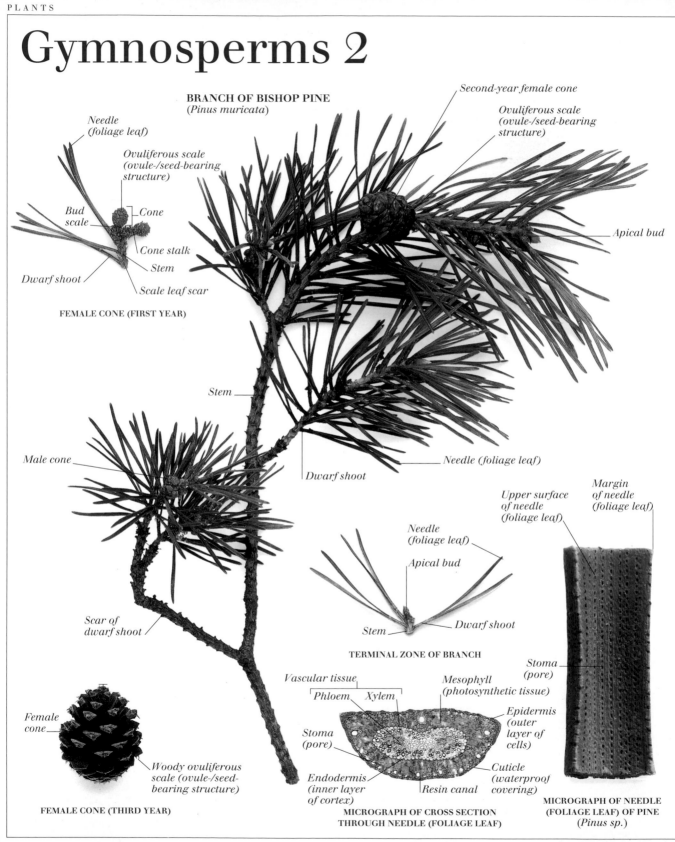

BRANCH OF BISHOP PINE
(*Pinus muricata*)

*Needle
(foliage leaf)*

*Ovuliferous scale
(ovule-/seed-bearing
structure)*

*Bud
scale*

Cone

Cone stalk

Stem

Dwarf shoot

Scale leaf scar

FEMALE CONE (FIRST YEAR)

Second-year female cone

*Ovuliferous scale
(ovule-/seed-bearing
structure)*

Apical bud

Stem

Male cone

Needle (foliage leaf)

Dwarf shoot

*Scar of
dwarf shoot*

*Upper surface
of needle
(foliage leaf)*

*Margin
of needle
(foliage leaf)*

*Needle
(foliage leaf)*

Apical bud

Stem

Dwarf shoot

TERMINAL ZONE OF BRANCH

*Stoma
(pore)*

*Female
cone*

*Woody ovuliferous
scale (ovule-/seed-
bearing structure)*

FEMALE CONE (THIRD YEAR)

Vascular tissue

Phloem   *Xylem*

*Mesophyll
(photosynthetic tissue)*

*Stoma
(pore)*

*Epidermis
(outer
layer of
cells)*

*Endodermis
(inner layer
of cortex)*

Resin canal

*Cuticle
(waterproof
covering)*

**MICROGRAPH OF CROSS SECTION
THROUGH NEEDLE (FOLIAGE LEAF)**

**MICROGRAPH OF NEEDLE
(FOLIAGE LEAF) OF PINE**
(*Pinus sp.*)

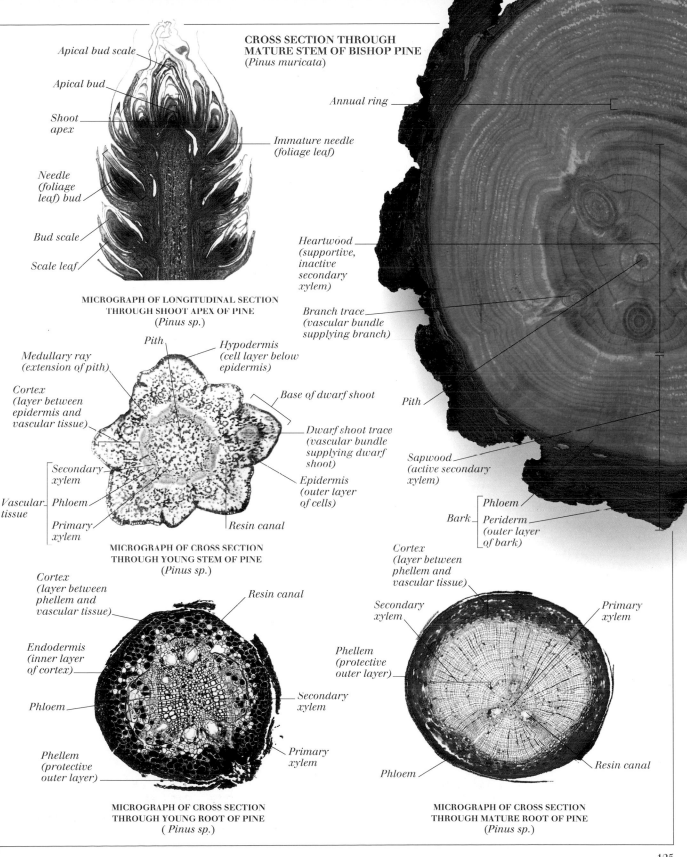

CROSS SECTION THROUGH
MATURE STEM OF BISHOP PINE
(*Pinus muricata*)

Apical bud scale

Apical bud

Shoot apex

Immature needle (foliage leaf)

Needle (foliage leaf) bud

Bud scale

Scale leaf

Annual ring

Heartwood (supportive, inactive secondary xylem)

Branch trace (vascular bundle supplying branch)

Pith

Sapwood (active secondary xylem)

Phloem

Bark

Periderm (outer layer of bark)

MICROGRAPH OF LONGITUDINAL SECTION THROUGH SHOOT APEX OF PINE
(*Pinus sp.*)

Pith

Hypodermis (cell layer below epidermis)

Medullary ray (extension of pith)

Cortex (layer between epidermis and vascular tissue)

Base of dwarf shoot

Dwarf shoot trace (vascular bundle supplying dwarf shoot)

Secondary xylem

Epidermis (outer layer of cells)

Vascular tissue

Phloem

Primary xylem

Resin canal

MICROGRAPH OF CROSS SECTION THROUGH YOUNG STEM OF PINE
(*Pinus sp.*)

Cortex (layer between phellem and vascular tissue)

Resin canal

Endodermis (inner layer of cortex)

Secondary xylem

Phloem

Primary xylem

Phellem (protective outer layer)

MICROGRAPH OF CROSS SECTION THROUGH YOUNG ROOT OF PINE
(*Pinus sp.*)

Cortex (layer between phellem and vascular tissue)

Secondary xylem

Primary xylem

Phellem (protective outer layer)

Phloem

Resin canal

MICROGRAPH OF CROSS SECTION THROUGH MATURE ROOT OF PINE
(*Pinus sp.*)

125

Monocotyledons and dicotyledons

FLOWERING PLANTS (PHYLUM ANGIOSPERMOPHYTA) are divided into two classes: monocotyledons (class Monocotyledoneae) and dicotyledons (class Dicotyledoneae). Typically, monocotyledons have seeds with one cotyledon (seed leaf); their foliage leaves are narrow with parallel veins; the flower components occur in multiples of three; sepals and petals are indistinguishable and are known as tepals; vascular (transport) tissues are scattered in random bundles throughout the stem; and, because they lack stem cambium (actively dividing cells that produce wood), most monocotyledons are herbaceous (see pp. 128-129). Dicotyledons have seeds with two cotyledons; leaves are broad with a central midrib and branched veins; flower parts occur in multiples of four or five; sepals are generally small and green; petals are large and colorful; vascular bundles are arranged in a ring around the edge of the stem; and, because many dicotyledons possess wood-producing stem cambium, there are woody forms (see pp. 130-131) as well as herbaceous ones.

CROSS SECTION THROUGH MONOCOTYLEDONOUS LEAF BASES

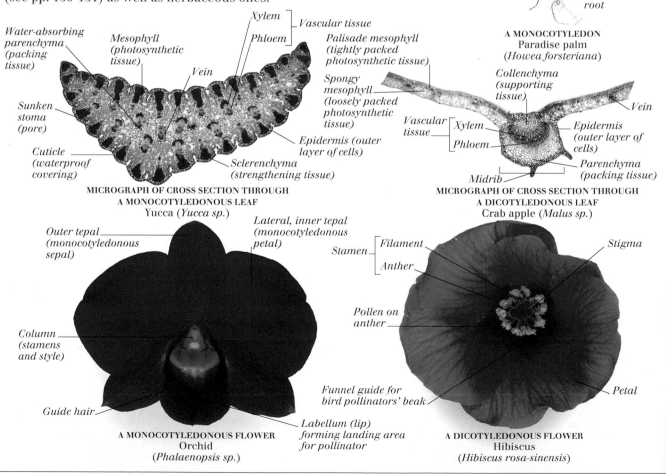

Vein (parallel venation)

Leaflet

Petiole (leaf stalk)

Emerging leaf

Leaf base

Adventitious root

A MONOCOTYLEDON
Paradise palm
(*Howea forsteriana*)

Water-absorbing parenchyma (packing tissue)

Mesophyll (photosynthetic tissue)

Xylem

Phloem

Vascular tissue

Vein

Sunken stoma (pore)

Cuticle (waterproof covering)

Sclerenchyma (strengthening tissue)

Epidermis (outer layer of cells)

MICROGRAPH OF CROSS SECTION THROUGH A MONOCOTYLEDONOUS LEAF
Yucca (*Yucca sp.*)

Palisade mesophyll (tightly packed photosynthetic tissue)

Spongy mesophyll (loosely packed photosynthetic tissue)

Collenchyma (supporting tissue)

Vein

Vascular tissue

Xylem

Phloem

Epidermis (outer layer of cells)

Parenchyma (packing tissue)

Midrib

MICROGRAPH OF CROSS SECTION THROUGH A DICOTYLEDONOUS LEAF
Crab apple (*Malus sp.*)

Outer tepal (monocotyledonous sepal)

Lateral, inner tepal (monocotyledonous petal)

Column (stamens and style)

Guide hair

Labellum (lip) forming landing area for pollinator

A MONOCOTYLEDONOUS FLOWER
Orchid
(*Phalaenopsis sp.*)

Stamen

Filament

Anther

Stigma

Pollen on anther

Funnel guide for bird pollinators' beak

Petal

A DICOTYLEDONOUS FLOWER
Hibiscus
(*Hibiscus rosa-sinensis*)

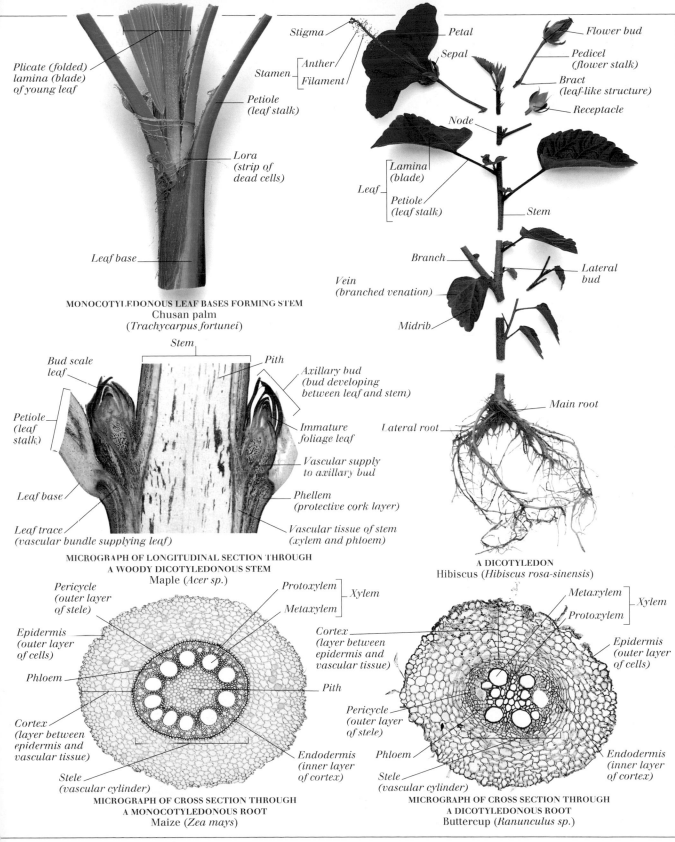

Plicate (folded) lamina (blade) of young leaf

Petiole (leaf stalk)

Lora (strip of dead cells)

Leaf base

MONOCOTYLEDONOUS LEAF BASES FORMING STEM
Chusan palm
(*Trachycarpus fortunei*)

Stigma

Anther
Stamen
Filament

Petal

Sepal

Flower bud

Pedicel (flower stalk)

Bract (leaf-like structure)

Receptacle

Node

Lamina (blade)

Leaf

Petiole (leaf stalk)

Stem

Branch

Vein (branched venation)

Midrib

Lateral bud

Bud scale leaf

Stem

Pith

Axillary bud (bud developing between leaf and stem)

Petiole (leaf stalk)

Immature foliage leaf

Vascular supply to axillary bud

Leaf base

Leaf trace (vascular bundle supplying leaf)

Phellem (protective cork layer)

Vascular tissue of stem (xylem and phloem)

MICROGRAPH OF LONGITUDINAL SECTION THROUGH
A WOODY DICOTYLEDONOUS STEM
Maple (*Acer sp.*)

Main root

Lateral root

A DICOTYLEDON
Hibiscus (*Hibiscus rosa-sinensis*)

Pericycle (outer layer of stele)

Epidermis (outer layer of cells)

Phloem

Cortex (layer between epidermis and vascular tissue)

Stele (vascular cylinder)

Protoxylem
Xylem
Metaxylem

Pith

Endodermis (inner layer of cortex)

MICROGRAPH OF CROSS SECTION THROUGH
A MONOCOTYLEDONOUS ROOT
Maize (*Zea mays*)

Metaxylem
Xylem
Protoxylem

Cortex (layer between epidermis and vascular tissue)

Epidermis (outer layer of cells)

Pericycle (outer layer of stele)

Phloem

Stele (vascular cylinder)

Endodermis (inner layer of cortex)

MICROGRAPH OF CROSS SECTION THROUGH
A DICOTYLEDONOUS ROOT
Buttercup (*Ranunculus sp.*)

127

Herbaceous flowering plants

HERBACEOUS FLOWERING PLANTS TYPICALLY HAVE GREEN NON-WOODY STEMS, and tend to be relatively short-lived. Many herbaceous plants live for only one or two years. Annuals (such as sweet peas) grow from seed, produce flowers and then seeds, and die within a single year. Biennials (like carrots) have a two-year life cycle. In the first year, seeds grow into plants, which produce leaves and store food in underground storage organs; the stems and foliage then die in winter. In the second year, new stems grow from the storage organs, produce leaves, flowers, and seeds, and then die. Some herbaceous plants (such as potatoes) are perennial. They grow back year after year, producing shoots and flowers in spring, storing food in underground tubers or rhizomes during summer, dying in autumn, and surviving underground during winter.

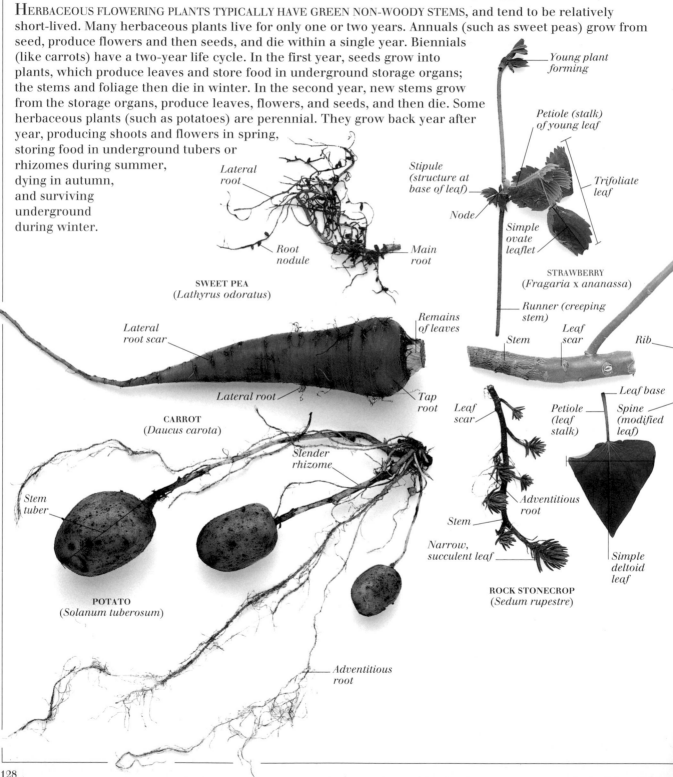

Young plant
forming

Petiole (stalk)
of young leaf

Lateral
root

Stipule
(structure at
base of leaf)

Trifoliate
leaf

Node

Simple
ovate
leaflet

Root
nodule

Main
root

SWEET PEA
(*Lathyrus odoratus*)

STRAWBERRY
(*Fragaria* x *ananassa*)

Runner (creeping
stem)

Remains
of leaves

Leaf
scar

Rib

Lateral
root scar

Stem

Leaf base

Lateral root

Tap
root

Leaf
scar

Petiole
(leaf
stalk)

Spine
(modified
leaf)

CARROT
(*Daucus carota*)

Slender
rhizome

Stem
tuber

Adventitious
root

Stem

Narrow,
succulent leaf

Simple
deltoid
leaf

POTATO
(*Solanum tuberosum*)

ROCK STONECROP
(*Sedum rupestre*)

Adventitious
root

PARTS OF HERBACEOUS FLOWERING PLANTS

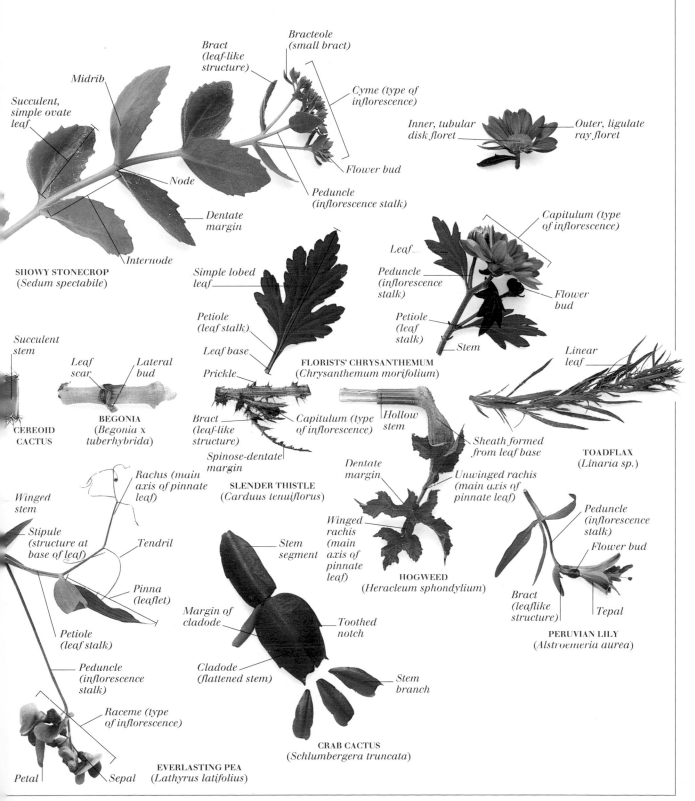

Bract (leaf-like structure)

Bracteole (small bract)

Midrib

Cyme (type of inflorescence)

Succulent, simple ovate leaf

Inner, tubular disk floret

Outer, ligulate ray floret

Node

Flower bud

Dentate margin

Peduncle (inflorescence stalk)

Internode

SHOWY STONECROP
(Sedum spectabile)

Capitulum (type of inflorescence)

Leaf

Simple lobed leaf

Peduncle (inflorescence stalk)

Flower bud

Succulent stem

Leaf scar

Lateral bud

Petiole (leaf stalk)

Petiole (leaf stalk)

Stem

Linear leaf

Leaf base

Prickle

FLORISTS' CHRYSANTHEMUM
(Chrysanthemum morifolium)

CEREOID CACTUS

BEGONIA
(Begonia x tuberhybrida)

Bract (leaf-like structure)

Capitulum (type of inflorescence)

Hollow stem

Sheath formed from leaf base

TOADFLAX
(Linaria sp.)

Spinose-dentate margin

Dentate margin

Unwinged rachis (main axis of pinnate leaf)

Rachis (main axis of pinnate leaf)

SLENDER THISTLE
(Carduus tenuiflorus)

Winged stem

Stipule (structure at base of leaf)

Tendril

Stem segment

Winged rachis (main axis of pinnate leaf)

Peduncle (inflorescence stalk)

Flower bud

Pinna (leaflet)

Margin of cladode

Toothed notch

HOGWEED
(Heracleum sphondylium)

Bract (leaflike structure)

Tepal

Petiole (leaf stalk)

Cladode (flattened stem)

Stem branch

PERUVIAN LILY
(Alstroemeria aurea)

Peduncle (inflorescence stalk)

Raceme (type of inflorescence)

Petal

Sepal

EVERLASTING PEA
(Lathyrus latifolius)

CRAB CACTUS
(Schlumbergera truncata)

Woody flowering plants

WOODY FLOWERING PLANTS ARE PERENNIAL: They continue to grow and reproduce for many years. They have one or more permanent stems above ground and numerous smaller branches. The stems and branches have a strong woody core that supports the plant and contains vascular tissue for transporting water and nutrients. Outside the woody core is a layer of tough, protective bark, which has lenticels (tiny pores) to allow gases to pass through. Woody flowering plants may be shrubs, which have several stems rising from the soil; bushes, which are shrubs with dense branching and foliage; or trees, which typically have a single upright stem (the trunk) that bears branches. Deciduous woody plants (like roses) shed all their leaves once a year and remain leafless during winter. Evergreen woody plants (such as holly) shed their leaves gradually, so they retain full leaf cover throughout the year.

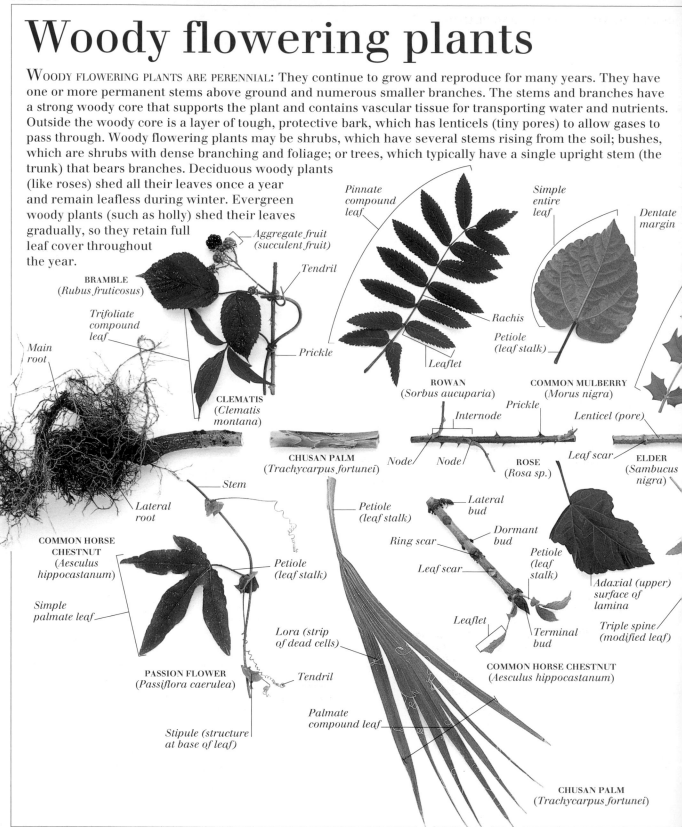

Aggregate fruit (succulent fruit)

Tendril

BRAMBLE
(*Rubus fruticosus*)

Trifoliate compound leaf

Prickle

CLEMATIS
(*Clematis montana*)

Pinnate compound leaf

Simple entire leaf

Dentate margin

Rachis

Petiole (leaf stalk)

Leaflet

ROWAN
(*Sorbus aucuparia*)

COMMON MULBERRY
(*Morus nigra*)

Main root

Lateral root

Stem

COMMON HORSE CHESTNUT
(*Aesculus hippocastanum*)

Simple palmate leaf

PASSION FLOWER
(*Passiflora caerulea*)

Petiole (leaf stalk)

Tendril

Stipule (structure at base of leaf)

CHUSAN PALM
(*Trachycarpus fortunei*)

Node *Node*

Internode

Prickle

Lenticel (pore)

Leaf scar

ROSE
(*Rosa sp.*)

ELDER
(*Sambucus nigra*)

Petiole (leaf stalk)

Lora (strip of dead cells)

Palmate compound leaf

Lateral bud

Ring scar

Leaf scar

Dormant bud

Leaflet

Terminal bud

Petiole (leaf stalk)

Adaxial (upper) surface of lamina

Triple spine (modified leaf)

COMMON HORSE CHESTNUT
(*Aesculus hippocastanum*)

CHUSAN PALM
(*Trachycarpus fortunei*)

PARTS OF WOODY FLOWERING PLANTS

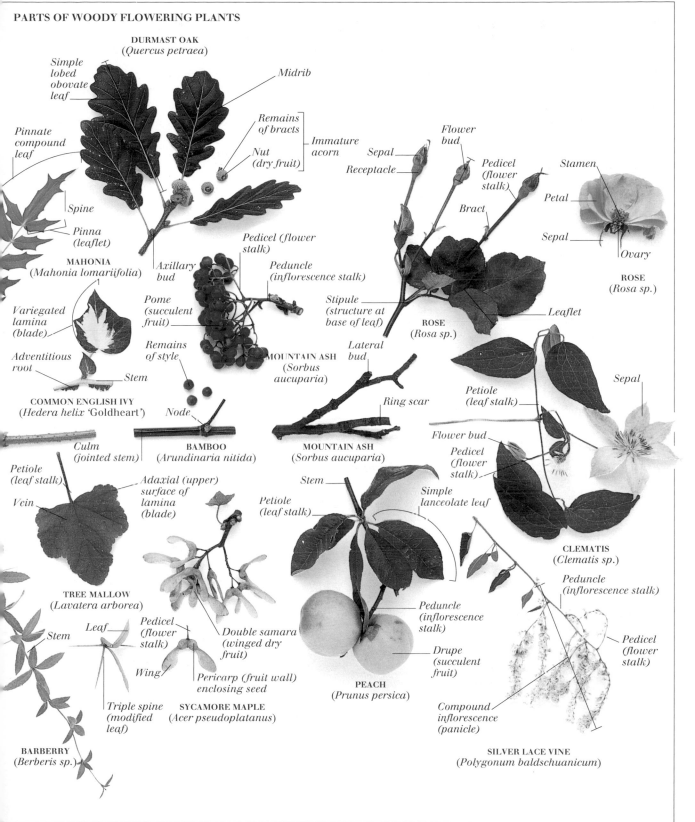

DURMAST OAK
(*Quercus petraea*)

Simple lobed obovate leaf

Midrib

Pinnate compound leaf

Remains of bracts

Nut (dry fruit)

Immature acorn

Spine

Pinna (leaflet)

MAHONIA
(*Mahonia lomariifolia*)

Axillary bud

Pedicel (flower stalk)

Peduncle (inflorescence stalk)

Flower bud

Sepal

Receptacle

Pedicel (flower stalk)

Stamen

Petal

Sepal

Bract

Ovary

ROSE
(*Rosa sp.*)

Pome (succulent fruit)

Variegated lamina (blade)

Adventitious root

Stem

Remains of style

COMMON ENGLISH IVY
(*Hedera helix* 'Goldheart')

Node

MOUNTAIN ASH
(*Sorbus aucuparia*)

Stipule (structure at base of leaf)

Leaflet

ROSE
(*Rosa sp.*)

Lateral bud

Ring scar

Sepal

Petiole (leaf stalk)

Culm (jointed stem)

BAMBOO
(*Arundinaria nitida*)

MOUNTAIN ASH
(*Sorbus aucuparia*)

Flower bud

Pedicel (flower stalk)

CLEMATIS
(*Clematis sp.*)

Petiole (leaf stalk)

Vein

Adaxial (upper) surface of lamina (blade)

Stem

Petiole (leaf stalk)

Simple lanceolate leaf

Peduncle (inflorescence stalk)

Pedicel (flower stalk)

TREE MALLOW
(*Lavatera arborea*)

Stem

Leaf

Pedicel (flower stalk)

Double samara (winged dry fruit)

Wing

Pericarp (fruit wall) enclosing seed

Triple spine (modified leaf)

SYCAMORE MAPLE
(*Acer pseudoplatanus*)

Peduncle (inflorescence stalk)

Drupe (succulent fruit)

PEACH
(*Prunus persica*)

Compound inflorescence (panicle)

SILVER LACE VINE
(*Polygonum baldschuanicum*)

BARBERRY
(*Berberis sp.*)

Roots

ROOTS ARE THE UNDERGROUND PARTS OF PLANTS. They have three main functions. First, they anchor the plant in the soil. Second, they absorb water and minerals from the spaces between soil particles. The roots' absorptive properties are increased by root hairs, which grow behind the root tip, allowing maximum absorption of vital substances. Third, the root is part of the plant's transport system. Xylem carries water and minerals from the roots to the stem and leaves, and phloem carries nutrients from the leaves to all parts of the root system. In addition, some roots (like carrots) are food stores. Roots have an outer epidermis covering a cortex of parenchyma (packing tissue), and a central cylinder of vascular tissue. This arrangement helps the roots resist the forces of compression as they grow through the soil.

MICROGRAPH OF PRIMARY ROOT DEVELOPMENT
Cabbage (*Brassica sp.*)

Split in testa as seed germinates

Cotyledon (seed leaf)

Primary root

Testa (seed coat)

Root hair

Root tip (region of cell division)

CARROT (*Daucus carota*)

FEATURES OF A TYPICAL ROOT
Buttercup (*Ranunculus sp.*)

Pericycle (outer layer of stele)

Root hair

Air space (allowing gas diffusion in the root)

Stele (vascular cylinder)

Phloem sieve tube (through which nutrients are transported)

Companion cell (cell associated with phloem sieve tube)

Cortex (layer between epidermis and vascular tissue)

Root hair

Epidermis (outer layer of cells)

Xylem vessel (through which water and minerals are transported)

Endodermis (inner layer of cortex)

Cell wall

Nucleus

Cytoplasm

Parenchyma (packing) cell

PRIMARY ROOT AND MICROGRAPHS OF SECTIONS THROUGH ROOTS

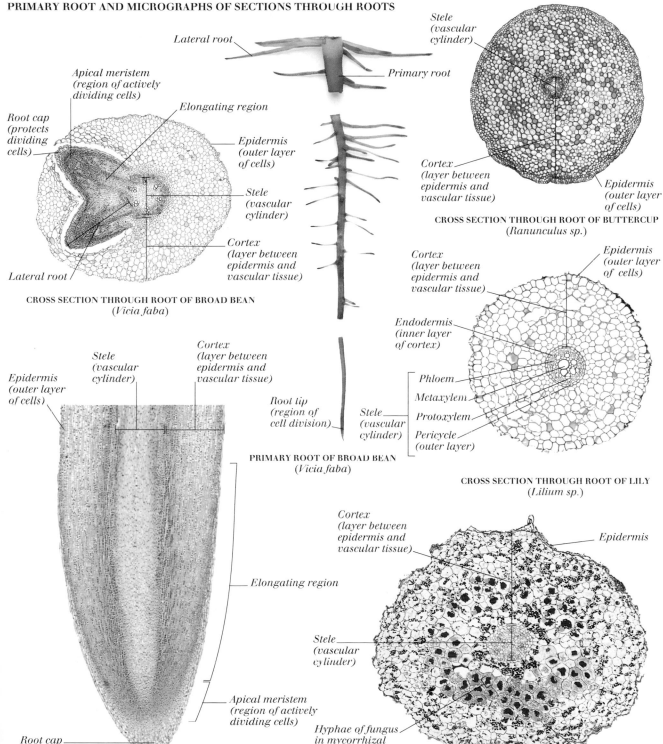

Lateral root

Primary root

Stele (vascular cylinder)

Apical meristem (region of actively dividing cells)

Elongating region

Root cap (protects dividing cells)

Epidermis (outer layer of cells)

Stele (vascular cylinder)

Cortex (layer between epidermis and vascular tissue)

Lateral root

CROSS SECTION THROUGH ROOT OF BROAD BEAN
(*Vicia faba*)

Cortex (layer between epidermis and vascular tissue)

Epidermis (outer layer of cells)

CROSS SECTION THROUGH ROOT OF BUTTERCUP
(*Ranunculus sp.*)

Stele (vascular cylinder)

Cortex (layer between epidermis and cortex)

Epidermis (outer layer of cells)

Cortex (layer between epidermis and vascular tissue)

Epidermis (outer layer of cells)

Root tip (region of cell division)

Stele (vascular cylinder)

Endodermis (inner layer of cortex)

Phloem

Metaxylem

Protoxylem

Pericycle (outer layer)

PRIMARY ROOT OF BROAD BEAN
(*Vicia faba*)

CROSS SECTION THROUGH ROOT OF LILY
(*Lilium sp.*)

Elongating region

Apical meristem (region of actively dividing cells)

Root cap (protects dividing cells)

**LONGITUDINAL SECTION
THROUGH ROOT TIP OF BROAD BEAN**
(*Vicia faba*)

Cortex (layer between epidermis and vascular tissue)

Epidermis

Stele (vascular cylinder)

Hyphae of fungus in mycorrhizal (symbiotic) association with orchid

Starch grain

**CROSS SECTION THROUGH ROOT OF ORCHID IN
MYCORRHIZAL ASSOCIATION WITH FUNGUS**

Stems

THE STEM IS THE MAIN SUPPORTIVE PART OF A PLANT that grows above ground. Stems bear leaves (organs of photosynthesis), which grow at nodes; buds (shoots covered by protective scales), which grow at the stem tip (apical or terminal buds) and in the angle between a leaf and the stem (axillary or lateral buds); and flowers (reproductive structures). The stem forms part of the plant's transport system. Xylem tissue in the stem transports water and minerals from the roots to the aerial parts of the plant, and phloem tissue transports nutrients manufactured in the leaves to other parts of the plant. Stem tissues are also used for storing water and food. Herbaceous (nonwoody) stems have an outer protective epidermis covering a cortex that consists mainly of parenchyma (packing tissue) but also has some collenchyma (supporting tissue). The vascular tissue of such stems is arranged in bundles, each of which consists of xylem, phloem, and sclerenchyma (strengthening tissue). Woody stems have an outer protective layer of tough bark, which is perforated with lenticels (pores) to allow gas exchange. Inside the bark is a ring of secondary phloem, which surrounds an inner core of secondary xylem.

MICROGRAPH OF LONGITUDINAL SECTION THROUGH APEX OF STEM
Coleus sp.

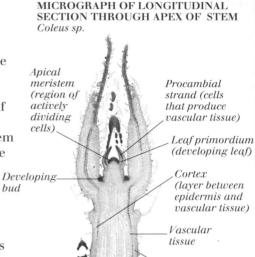

Apical meristem (region of actively dividing cells)

Procambial strand (cells that produce vascular tissue)

Leaf primordium (developing leaf)

Developing bud

Cortex (layer between epidermis and vascular tissue)

Vascular tissue

Epidermis (outer layer of cells)

Pith

YOUNG WOODY STEM
Linden
(*Tilia sp.*)

EMERGENT BUDS
Maple
(*Acer*)

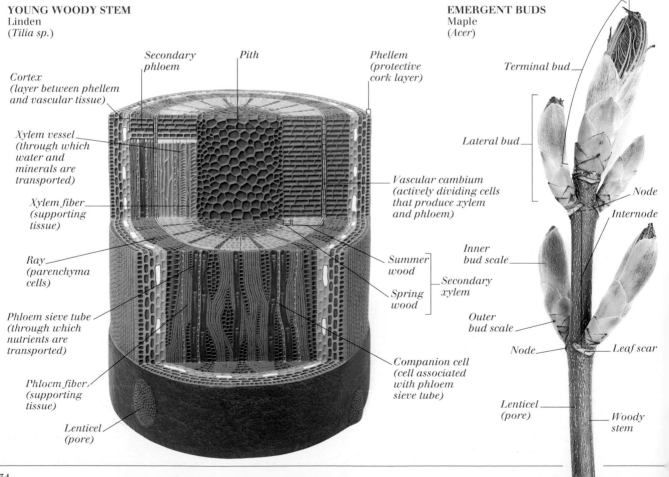

Secondary phloem

Pith

Phellem (protective cork layer)

Cortex (layer between phellem and vascular tissue)

Xylem vessel (through which water and minerals are transported)

Xylem fiber (supporting tissue)

Ray (parenchyma cells)

Phloem sieve tube (through which nutrients are transported)

Phloem fiber (supporting tissue)

Lenticel (pore)

Vascular cambium (actively dividing cells that produce xylem and phloem)

Summer wood

Spring wood

Secondary xylem

Companion cell (cell associated with phloem sieve tube)

Young leaves emergi...

Terminal bud

Lateral bud

Node

Internode

Inner bud scale

Outer bud scale

Node

Leaf scar

Lenticel (pore)

Woody stem

MICROGRAPHS OF CROSS SECTIONS THROUGH VARIOUS STEMS

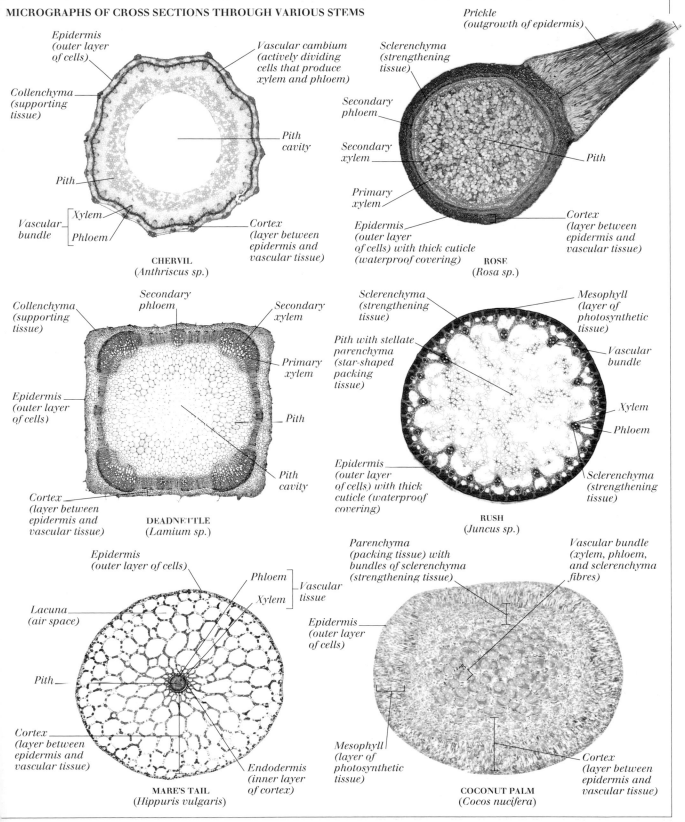

Epidermis (outer layer of cells)

Collenchyma (supporting tissue)

Pith

Vascular bundle

Xylem

Phloem

Vascular cambium (actively dividing cells that produce xylem and phloem)

Pith cavity

Cortex (layer between epidermis and vascular tissue)

CHERVIL (Anthriscus sp.)

Prickle (outgrowth of epidermis)

Sclerenchyma (strengthening tissue)

Secondary phloem

Secondary xylem

Primary xylem

Epidermis (outer layer of cells) with thick cuticle (waterproof covering)

Pith

Cortex (layer between epidermis and vascular tissue)

ROSE (Rosa sp.)

Collenchyma (supporting tissue)

Secondary phloem

Secondary xylem

Primary xylem

Epidermis (outer layer of cells)

Pith

Pith cavity

Cortex (layer between epidermis and vascular tissue)

DEADNETTLE (Lamium sp.)

Sclerenchyma (strengthening tissue)

Pith with stellate parenchyma (star-shaped packing tissue)

Epidermis (outer layer of cells) with thick cuticle (waterproof covering)

Mesophyll (layer of photosynthetic tissue)

Vascular bundle

Xylem

Phloem

Sclerenchyma (strengthening tissue)

RUSH (Juncus sp.)

Epidermis (outer layer of cells)

Lacuna (air space)

Pith

Cortex (layer between epidermis and vascular tissue)

Phloem

Xylem

Vascular tissue

Endodermis (inner layer of cortex)

MARE'S TAIL (Hippuris vulgaris)

Parenchyma (packing tissue) with bundles of sclerenchyma (strengthening tissue)

Epidermis (outer layer of cells)

Mesophyll (layer of photosynthetic tissue)

Vascular bundle (xylem, phloem, and sclerenchyma fibres)

Cortex (layer between epidermis and vascular tissue)

COCONUT PALM (Cocos nucifera)

Leaves

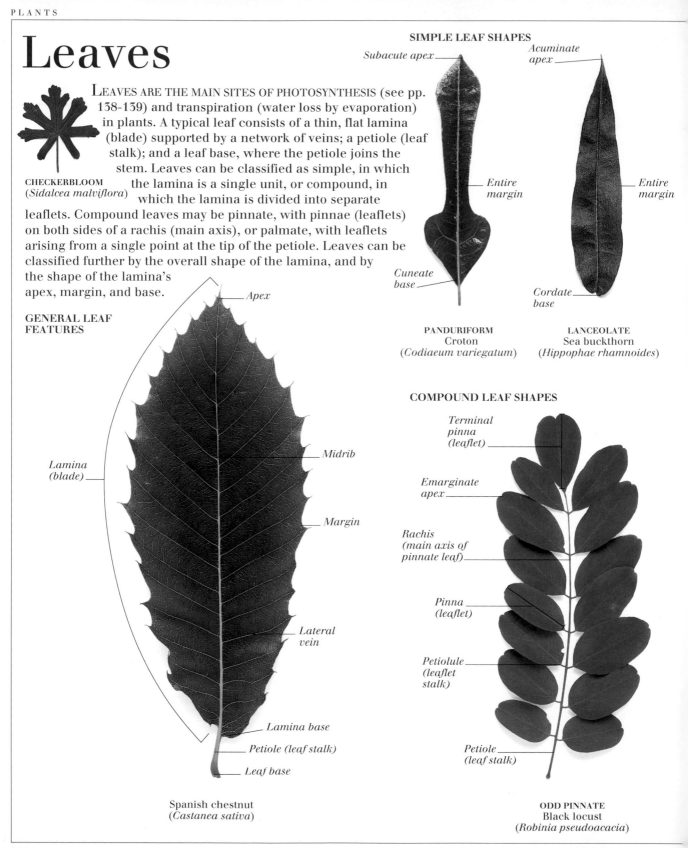

LEAVES ARE THE MAIN SITES OF PHOTOSYNTHESIS (see pp. 138-139) and transpiration (water loss by evaporation) in plants. A typical leaf consists of a thin, flat lamina (blade) supported by a network of veins; a petiole (leaf stalk); and a leaf base, where the petiole joins the stem. Leaves can be classified as simple, in which the lamina is a single unit, or compound, in which the lamina is divided into separate leaflets. Compound leaves may be pinnate, with pinnae (leaflets) on both sides of a rachis (main axis), or palmate, with leaflets arising from a single point at the tip of the petiole. Leaves can be classified further by the overall shape of the lamina, and by the shape of the lamina's apex, margin, and base.

CHECKERBLOOM
(*Sidalcea malviflora*)

SIMPLE LEAF SHAPES

Subacute apex

Acuminate apex

Entire margin

Entire margin

Cuneate base

Cordate base

PANDURIFORM
Croton
(*Codiaeum variegatum*)

LANCEOLATE
Sea buckthorn
(*Hippophae rhamnoides*)

GENERAL LEAF FEATURES

Apex

Midrib

Lamina (blade)

Margin

Lateral vein

Lamina base

Petiole (leaf stalk)

Leaf base

Spanish chestnut
(*Castanea sativa*)

COMPOUND LEAF SHAPES

Terminal pinna (leaflet)

Emarginate apex

Rachis (main axis of pinnate leaf)

Pinna (leaflet)

Petiolule (leaflet stalk)

Petiole (leaf stalk)

ODD PINNATE
Black locust
(*Robinia pseudoacacia*)

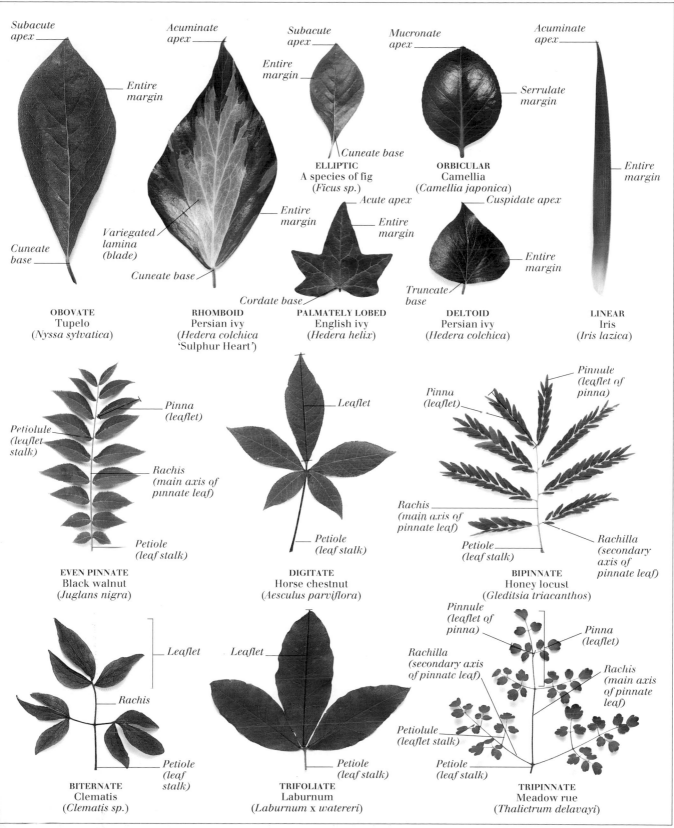

Subacute apex

Acuminate apex

Subacute apex

Entire margin

Mucronate apex

Serrulate margin

Acuminate apex

Entire margin

Cuneate base

ELLIPTIC
A species of fig
(*Ficus sp.*)

ORBICULAR
Camellia
(*Camellia japonica*)

Entire margin

Variegated lamina (blade)

Entire margin

Acute apex

Entire margin

Cuspidate apex

Entire margin

Cuneate base

Cuneate base

Entire margin

Cordate base

Truncate base

OBOVATE
Tupelo
(*Nyssa sylvatica*)

RHOMBOID
Persian ivy
(*Hedera colchica* 'Sulphur Heart')

PALMATELY LOBED
English ivy
(*Hedera helix*)

DELTOID
Persian ivy
(*Hedera colchica*)

LINEAR
Iris
(*Iris lazica*)

Pinna (leaflet)

Petiolule (leaflet stalk)

Rachis (main axis of pinnate leaf)

Petiole (leaf stalk)

Leaflet

Petiole (leaf stalk)

Pinnule (leaflet of pinna)

Pinna (leaflet)

Rachis (main axis of pinnate leaf)

Petiole (leaf stalk)

Rachilla (secondary axis of pinnate leaf)

EVEN PINNATE
Black walnut
(*Juglans nigra*)

DIGITATE
Horse chestnut
(*Aesculus parviflora*)

BIPINNATE
Honey locust
(*Gleditsia triacanthos*)

Leaflet

Rachis

Petiole (leaf stalk)

Leaflet

Petiole (leaf stalk)

Pinnule (leaflet of pinna)

Pinna (leaflet)

Rachilla (secondary axis of pinnate leaf)

Rachis (main axis of pinnate leaf)

Petiolule (leaflet stalk)

Petiole (leaf stalk)

BITERNATE
Clematis
(*Clematis sp.*)

TRIFOLIATE
Laburnum
(*Laburnum x watereri*)

TRIPINNATE
Meadow rue
(*Thalictrum delavayi*)

Photosynthesis

PHOTOSYNTHESIS IS THE PROCESS by which plants make their food using sunlight, water, and carbon dioxide. It takes place inside special structures in leaf cells called chloroplasts. The chloroplasts contain chlorophyll, a green pigment that absorbs energy from sunlight. During photosynthesis, the absorbed energy is used to join together carbon dioxide and water to form the sugar glucose, which is the energy source for the whole plant. Oxygen, a waste product, is released into the air. Leaves are the main sites of photosynthesis and have various adaptations for that purpose. Flat laminae (blades) provide a large surface for absorbing sunlight; stomata (pores) in the lower surface of the laminae allow gases (carbon dioxide and oxygen) to pass into and out of the leaves; and an extensive network of veins brings water into the leaves and transports the glucose produced by photosynthesis to the rest of the plant.

MICROGRAPH OF LEAF
Lily (*Lilium sp.*)

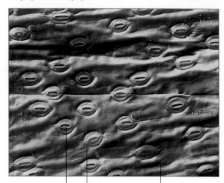

Stoma (pore)

Guard cell (controls opening and closing of stoma)

Lower surface of lamina (blade)

THE PROCESS OF PHOTOSYNTHESIS

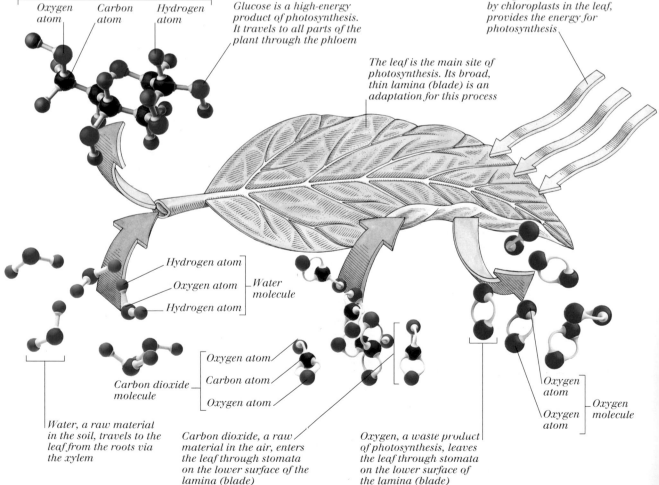

Glucose molecule

Oxygen atom

Carbon atom

Hydrogen atom

Glucose is a high-energy product of photosynthesis. It travels to all parts of the plant through the phloem

Sunlight, which is absorbed by chloroplasts in the leaf, provides the energy for photosynthesis

The leaf is the main site of photosynthesis. Its broad, thin lamina (blade) is an adaptation for this process

Hydrogen atom

Oxygen atom — Water molecule

Hydrogen atom

Oxygen atom

Carbon atom

Oxygen atom

Carbon dioxide molecule

Oxygen atom

Oxygen molecule

Oxygen atom

Water, a raw material in the soil, travels to the leaf from the roots via the xylem

Carbon dioxide, a raw material in the air, enters the leaf through stomata on the lower surface of the lamina (blade)

Oxygen, a waste product of photosynthesis, leaves the leaf through stomata on the lower surface of the lamina (blade)

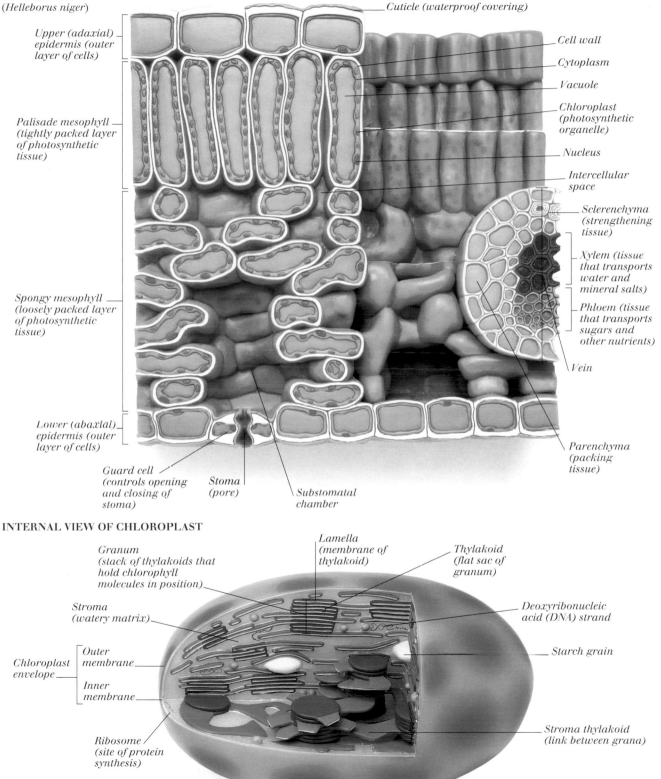

CROSS SECTION THROUGH LEAF
Christmas rose
(*Helleborus niger*)

Cuticle (waterproof covering)

Upper (adaxial) epidermis (outer layer of cells)

Cell wall

Cytoplasm

Vacuole

Chloroplast (photosynthetic organelle)

Palisade mesophyll (tightly packed layer of photosynthetic tissue)

Nucleus

Intercellular space

Sclerenchyma (strengthening tissue)

Xylem (tissue that transports water and mineral salts)

Phloem (tissue that transports sugars and other nutrients)

Spongy mesophyll (loosely packed layer of photosynthetic tissue)

Vein

Lower (abaxial) epidermis (outer layer of cells)

Parenchyma (packing tissue)

Guard cell (controls opening and closing of stoma)

Stoma (pore)

Substomatal chamber

INTERNAL VIEW OF CHLOROPLAST

Lamella (membrane of thylakoid)

Granum (stack of thylakoids that hold chlorophyll molecules in position)

Thylakoid (flat sac of granum)

Stroma (watery matrix)

Deoxyribonucleic acid (DNA) strand

Chloroplast envelope

Outer membrane

Inner membrane

Starch grain

Ribosome (site of protein synthesis)

Stroma thylakoid (link between grana)

Flowers 1

FLOWERS ARE THE SITES OF SEXUAL REPRODUCTION in flowering plants. Their component parts are arranged in whorls around the receptacle (tip of the flower stalk). The sepals (collectively called the calyx) are outermost; typically small and green, they protect the developing flower. The petals (collectively called the corolla) are typically large and brightly colored; they are found inside the sepals. In monocotyledonous flowers (see pp. 126-127), sepals and petals are indistinguishable; individually they are called tepals (collectively called the perianth). The petals surround the male and female reproductive structures (androecium and gynoecium). The androecium consists of stamens (male organs); each stamen is made up of a filament (stalk) and anther. The gynoecium has one or more carpels (female organs); each carpel consists of an ovary, style, and stigma. Some flowers (like the lily) occur singly on a pedicel (flower stalk); others (such as elder, sunflower) are arranged in a group (inflorescence) on a peduncle (inflorescence stalk).

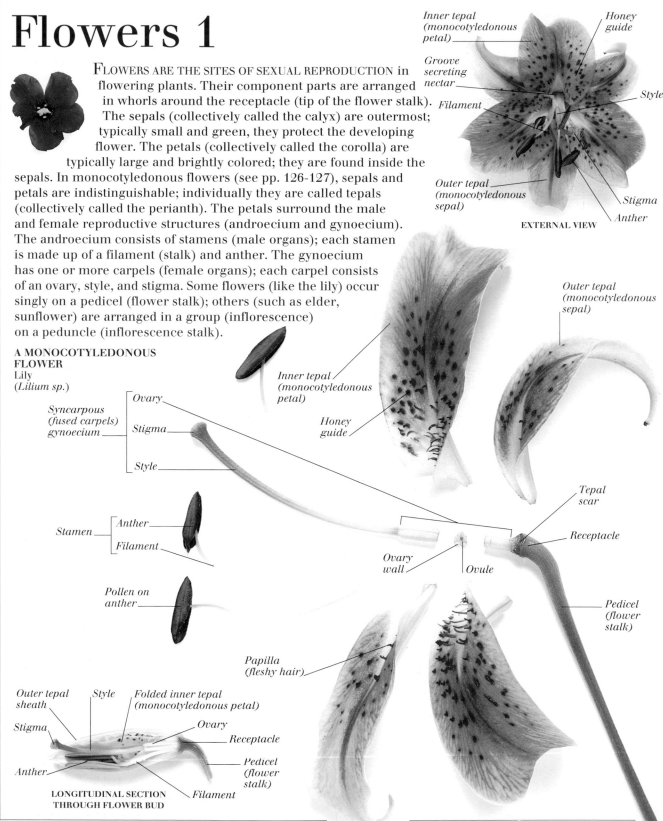

EXTERNAL VIEW

Inner tepal (monocotyledonous petal)
Honey guide
Groove secreting nectar
Filament
Style
Stigma
Anther
Outer tepal (monocotyledonous sepal)

A MONOCOTYLEDONOUS FLOWER
Lily
(*Lilium sp.*)

Syncarpous (fused carpels) gynoecium
Ovary
Stigma
Style

Stamen
Anther
Filament

Pollen on anther

Inner tepal (monocotyledonous petal)
Honey guide

Outer tepal (monocotyledonous sepal)

Tepal scar
Receptacle

Ovary wall
Ovule

Pedicel (flower stalk)

Papilla (fleshy hair)

Outer tepal sheath
Style
Folded inner tepal (monocotyledonous petal)
Stigma
Ovary
Receptacle
Anther
Pedicel (flower stalk)
Filament

LONGITUDINAL SECTION THROUGH FLOWER BUD

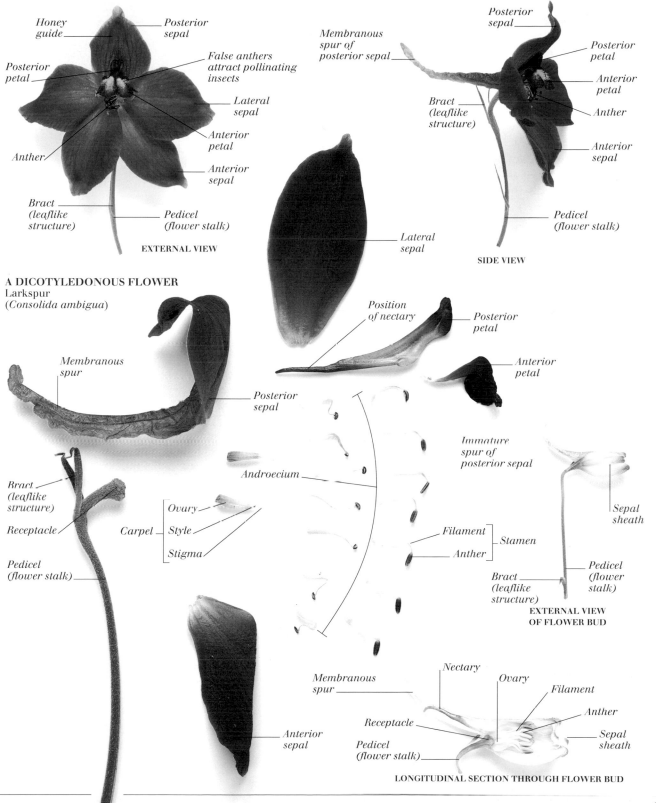

EXTERNAL VIEW

Honey guide

Posterior sepal

False anthers attract pollinating insects

Posterior petal

Lateral sepal

Anterior petal

Anterior sepal

Anther

Bract (leaflike structure)

Pedicel (flower stalk)

SIDE VIEW

Membranous spur of posterior sepal

Posterior sepal

Posterior petal

Anterior petal

Anther

Bract (leaflike structure)

Anterior sepal

Pedicel (flower stalk)

Lateral sepal

A DICOTYLEDONOUS FLOWER
Larkspur
(*Consolida ambigua*)

Membranous spur

Posterior sepal

Position of nectary

Posterior petal

Anterior petal

Immature spur of posterior sepal

Androecium

Bract (leaflike structure)

Receptacle

Carpel

Ovary

Style

Stigma

Filament

Anther

Stamen

Bract (leaflike structure)

Sepal sheath

Pedicel (flower stalk)

EXTERNAL VIEW OF FLOWER BUD

Pedicel (flower stalk)

Membranous spur

Anterior sepal

Nectary

Ovary

Filament

Anther

Receptacle

Pedicel (flower stalk)

Sepal sheath

LONGITUDINAL SECTION THROUGH FLOWER BUD

Flowers 2

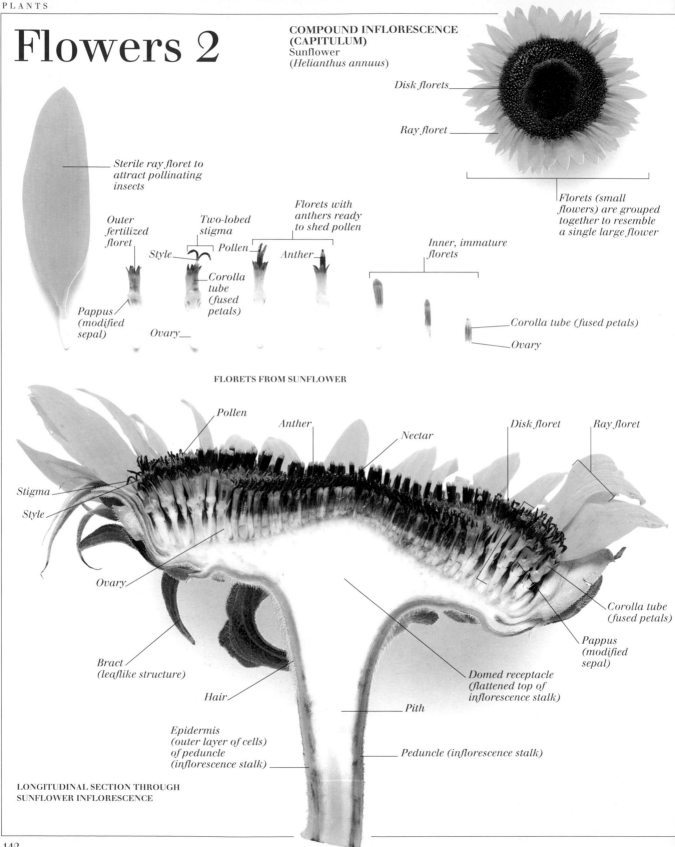

COMPOUND INFLORESCENCE (CAPITULUM)
Sunflower
(*Helianthus annuus*)

Disk florets

Ray floret

Florets (small flowers) are grouped together to resemble a single large flower

Sterile ray floret to attract pollinating insects

Outer fertilized floret

Two-lobed stigma

Style

Pollen

Florets with anthers ready to shed pollen

Anther

Inner, immature florets

Corolla tube (fused petals)

Ovary

Corolla tube (fused petals)

Pappus (modified sepal)

Ovary

FLORETS FROM SUNFLOWER

Pollen

Anther

Nectar

Disk floret

Ray floret

Stigma

Style

Ovary

Corolla tube (fused petals)

Pappus (modified sepal)

Bract (leaflike structure)

Hair

Domed receptacle (flattened top of inflorescence stalk)

Pith

Epidermis (outer layer of cells) of peduncle (inflorescence stalk)

Peduncle (inflorescence stalk)

LONGITUDINAL SECTION THROUGH SUNFLOWER INFLORESCENCE

ARRANGEMENT OF FLOWERS ON STEM

Bract
(leaflike
structure)

Flower

Ovary

Peduncle
(inflorescence
stalk)

Remains of tepals
(monocotyledonous
petals and sepals)

INFLORESCENCE (SPIKE)
Heliconia peruviana

Flower

Petal

Peduncle
(inflorescence
stalk)

Pedicel
(flower
stalk)

**INFLORESCENCE
(COMPOUND UMBEL)**
European elder
(*Sambucus nigra*)

Spathe
(large bract) to
attract pollinating
insects

Spadix (fleshy
axis) carrying
male and female
flowers

Peduncle
(inflorescence
stalk)

INFLORESCENCE (SPADIX)
Flamingo Flower
(*Anthurium andreanum*)

Stigma

Style

Anther

Filament

Stamen

Flower
bud

Pedicel
(flower
stalk)

Bract
(leaflike
structure)

Peduncle
(inflorescence
stalk) fused
to bract

**INFLORESCENCE
(DICHASIAL CYME)**
Common linden
(*Tilia* x *europaea*)

Three-lobed
stigma

Inner tepal
(monocotyledonous
petal)

Style

Ovary

Filament

Anther

Stamen

Outer tepal
(monocotyledonous
sepal)

Pedicel
(flower stalk)

SINGLE FLOWER
Glory lily
(*Gloriosa superba*)

Flower

Peduncle
(inflorescence
stalk)

Corolla

Calyx

Bract
(leaflike
structure)

**SINGLE
FLOWER**

**INFLORESCENCE
(SPHERICAL UMBEL)**
Echinops sp.

Pollination

POLLINATION IS THE TRANSFER OF POLLEN (which contains the male sex cells) from an anther (part of the male reproductive organ) to a stigma (part of the female reproductive organ). This process precedes fertilization (see pp. 146-147). Pollination may occur within the same flower (self-pollination), or between flowers on separate plants of the same species (cross-pollination). In most plants, pollination is carried out either by insects (entomophilous pollination) or by the wind (anemophilous pollination). Less commonly, birds, bats, or water are the agents of pollination. Insect-pollinated flowers are typically scented and brightly colored. They also produce nectar, on which insects feed. Such flowers also tend to have patterns that are visible only in ultraviolet light, which many insects can see but which humans cannot. These features attract insects, which become covered with the sticky pollen grains when they visit one flower, and then transfer the pollen to the next flower they visit. Wind-pollinated flowers are generally small, relatively inconspicuous, and unscented. They produce large quantities of light pollen grains that are easily blown by the wind to other flowers.

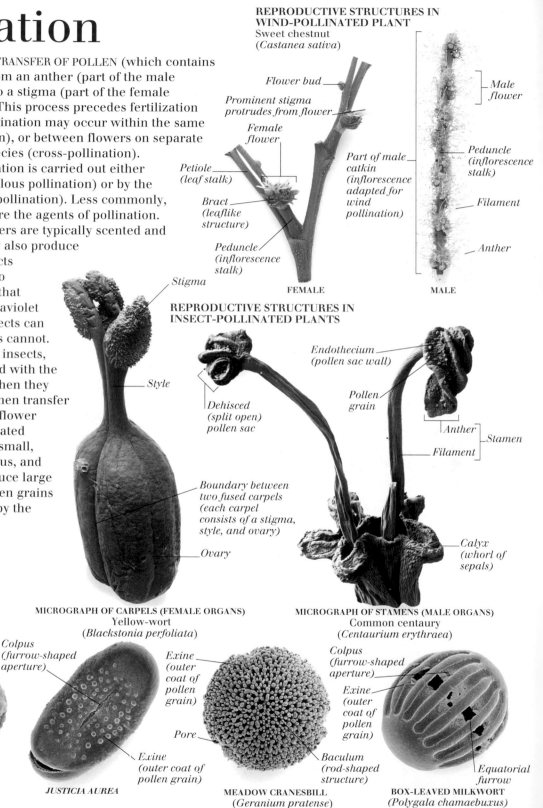

REPRODUCTIVE STRUCTURES IN WIND-POLLINATED PLANT
Sweet chestnut
(*Castanea sativa*)

Flower bud

Prominent stigma protrudes from flower

Female flower

Petiole (leaf stalk)

Bract (leaflike structure)

Peduncle (inflorescence stalk)

Part of male catkin (inflorescence adapted for wind pollination)

Male flower

Peduncle (inflorescence stalk)

Filament

Anther

FEMALE

MALE

REPRODUCTIVE STRUCTURES IN INSECT-POLLINATED PLANTS

Stigma

Style

Dehisced (split open) pollen sac

Boundary between two fused carpels (each carpel consists of a stigma, style, and ovary)

Ovary

Endothecium (pollen sac wall)

Pollen grain

Anther

Filament

Stamen

Calyx (whorl of sepals)

MICROGRAPHS OF POLLEN GRAINS

Exine (outer coat of pollen grain)

Pore

EUROPEAN FIELD ELM
(*Ulmus minor*)

Colpus (furrow-shaped aperture)

Exine (outer coat of pollen grain)

JUSTICIA AUREA

MICROGRAPH OF CARPELS (FEMALE ORGANS)
Yellow-wort
(*Blackstonia perfoliata*)

Exine (outer coat of pollen grain)

Pore

Baculum (rod-shaped structure)

MEADOW CRANESBILL
(*Geranium pratense*)

MICROGRAPH OF STAMENS (MALE ORGANS)
Common centaury
(*Centaurium erythraea*)

Colpus (furrow-shaped aperture)

Exine (outer coat of pollen grain)

Equatorial furrow

BOX-LEAVED MILKWORT
(*Polygala chamaebuxus*)

INSECT POLLINATION OF MEADOW SAGE

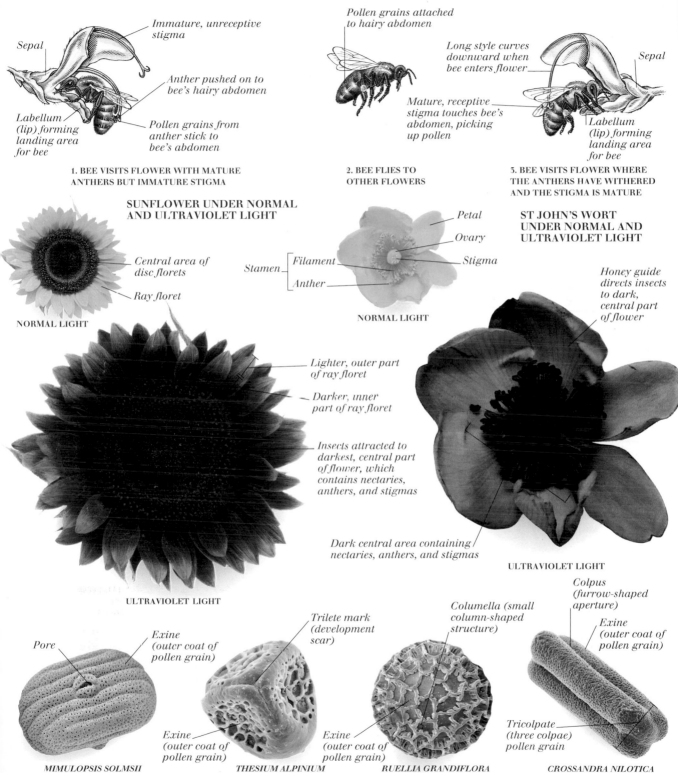

Sepal

Immature, unreceptive stigma

Anther pushed on to bee's hairy abdomen

Labellum (lip) forming landing area for bee

Pollen grains from anther stick to bee's abdomen

1. BEE VISITS FLOWER WITH MATURE ANTHERS BUT IMMATURE STIGMA

Pollen grains attached to hairy abdomen

2. BEE FLIES TO OTHER FLOWERS

Long style curves downward when bee enters flower

Sepal

Mature, receptive stigma touches bee's abdomen, picking up pollen

Labellum (lip) forming landing area for bee

3. BEE VISITS FLOWER WHERE THE ANTHERS HAVE WITHERED AND THE STIGMA IS MATURE

SUNFLOWER UNDER NORMAL AND ULTRAVIOLET LIGHT

Central area of disc florets

Ray floret

NORMAL LIGHT

Petal

Ovary

Stamen { Filament / Anther }

Stigma

NORMAL LIGHT

ST JOHN'S WORT UNDER NORMAL AND ULTRAVIOLET LIGHT

Honey guide directs insects to dark, central part of flower

Lighter, outer part of ray floret

Darker, inner part of ray floret

Insects attracted to darkest, central part of flower, which contains nectaries, anthers, and stigmas

Dark central area containing nectaries, anthers, and stigmas

ULTRAVIOLET LIGHT

ULTRAVIOLET LIGHT

Pore

Exine (outer coat of pollen grain)

Trilete mark (development scar)

Exine (outer coat of pollen grain)

Columella (small column-shaped structure)

Exine (outer coat of pollen grain)

Colpus (furrow-shaped aperture)

Exine (outer coat of pollen grain)

Tricolpate (three colpae) pollen grain

MIMULOPSIS SOLMSII

THESIUM ALPINIUM

RUELLIA GRANDIFLORA

CROSSANDRA NILOTICA

Fertilization

FERTILIZATION IS THE FUSION of male and female gametes (sex cells) to produce a zygote (embryo). Following pollination (see pp. 144-145), the pollen grains that contain the male gametes are on the stigma, some distance from the female gamete (ovum) inside the ovule. To enable the gametes to meet, the pollen grain germinates and produces a pollen tube, which grows down and enters the embryo sac (the inner part of the ovule that contains the ovum). Two male gametes, traveling at the tip of the pollen tube, enter the embryo sac. One gamete fuses with the ovum to produce a zygote that will develop into an embryo plant. The other male gamete fuses with two polar nuclei to produce the endosperm, which acts as a food supply for the developing embryo. Fertilization also initiates other changes: the integument (outer part of ovule) forms a testa (seed coat) around the embryo and endosperm; the petals fall off; the stigma and style wither; and the ovary wall forms a layer (called the pericarp) around the seed. Together, the pericarp and seed form the fruit, which may be succulent (see pp. 148-149) or dry (see pp. 150-151). In some species (such as blackberry), apomixis can occur: The seed develops without fertilization of the ovum by a male gamete, but endosperm formation and fruit development take place as in other species.

BANANA
(*Musa 'Lacatan'*)

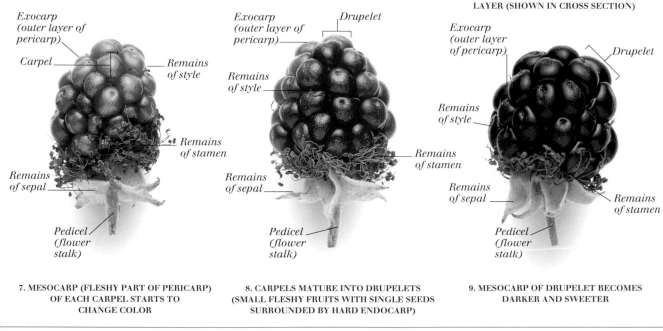

DEVELOPMENT OF A SUCCULENT FRUIT
Blackberry
(*Rubus fruticosus*)

Petal

Stamen { Filament
Anther

Carpel { Ovary
Stigma
Style

1. FLOWER IN FULL BLOOM ATTRACTS POLLINATORS

Endocarp (inner layer of pericarp)
Mesocarp (middle layer of pericarp)
Exocarp (outer layer of pericarp)
Sepal
Abortive seed
Remains of style
Carpel
Receptacle
Remains of stamen
Pedicel (flower stalk)

4. PERICARP FORMS FLESH, SKIN, AND A HARD INNER LAYER (SHOWN IN CROSS SECTION)

Exocarp (outer layer of pericarp)
Carpel
Remains of style
Remains of stamen
Remains of sepal
Pedicel (flower stalk)

7. MESOCARP (FLESHY PART OF PERICARP) OF EACH CARPEL STARTS TO CHANGE COLOR

Exocarp (outer layer of pericarp)
Drupelet
Remains of style
Remains of stamen
Remains of sepal
Pedicel (flower stalk)

8. CARPELS MATURE INTO DRUPELETS (SMALL FLESHY FRUITS WITH SINGLE SEEDS SURROUNDED BY HARD ENDOCARP)

Exocarp (outer layer of pericarp)
Drupelet
Remains of style
Remains of stamen
Remains of sepal
Pedicel (flower stalk)

9. MESOCARP OF DRUPELET BECOMES DARKER AND SWEETER

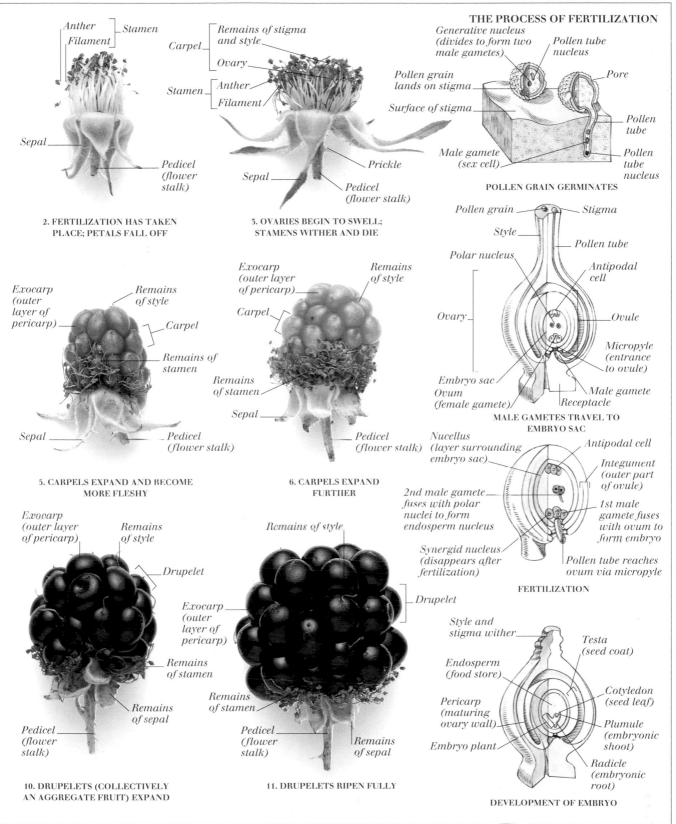

THE PROCESS OF FERTILIZATION

2. FERTILIZATION HAS TAKEN PLACE; PETALS FALL OFF

Anther — Stamen
Filament
Sepal
Pedicel (flower stalk)

5. OVARIES BEGIN TO SWELL; STAMENS WITHER AND DIE

Remains of stigma and style — Carpel
Ovary
Stamen — Anther
Filament
Sepal
Prickle
Pedicel (flower stalk)

POLLEN GRAIN GERMINATES

Generative nucleus (divides to form two male gametes)
Pollen tube nucleus
Pore
Pollen grain lands on stigma
Surface of stigma
Pollen tube
Pollen tube nucleus
Male gamete (sex cell)

5. CARPELS EXPAND AND BECOME MORE FLESHY

Exocarp (outer layer of pericarp)
Remains of style
Carpel
Remains of stamen
Sepal
Pedicel (flower stalk)

6. CARPELS EXPAND FURTHER

Exocarp (outer layer of pericarp)
Remains of style
Carpel
Remains of stamen
Sepal
Pedicel (flower stalk)

MALE GAMETES TRAVEL TO EMBRYO SAC

Pollen grain
Stigma
Style
Pollen tube
Polar nucleus
Antipodal cell
Ovary
Ovule
Micropyle (entrance to ovule)
Embryo sac
Ovum (female gamete)
Male gamete
Receptacle

10. DRUPELETS (COLLECTIVELY AN AGGREGATE FRUIT) EXPAND

Exocarp (outer layer of pericarp)
Remains of style
Drupelet
Remains of stamen
Remains of sepal
Pedicel (flower stalk)

11. DRUPELETS RIPEN FULLY

Remains of style
Exocarp (outer layer of pericarp)
Drupelet
Remains of stamen
Pedicel (flower stalk)
Remains of sepal

FERTILIZATION

Nucellus (layer surrounding embryo sac)
Antipodal cell
Integument (outer part of ovule)
2nd male gamete fuses with polar nuclei to form endosperm nucleus
1st male gamete fuses with ovum to form embryo
Synergid nucleus (disappears after fertilization)
Pollen tube reaches ovum via micropyle

DEVELOPMENT OF EMBRYO

Style and stigma wither
Testa (seed coat)
Endosperm (food store)
Cotyledon (seed leaf)
Pericarp (maturing ovary wall)
Plumule (embryonic shoot)
Embryo plant
Radicle (embryonic root)

Succulent fruits

A FRUIT IS A FULLY DEVELOPED and ripened ovary—the seed-producing part of a plant's female reproductive organs. Fruits may be succulent or dry (see pp. 150-151). Succulent fruits are fleshy and brightly colored, making them attractive to animals, which eat them and disperse the seeds away from the parent plant. The wall (pericarp) of a succulent fruit has three layers: an outer exocarp, a middle mesocarp, and an inner endocarp. These three layers vary in thickness and texture in different types of fruits and may blend into each other. Succulent fruits can be classed as simple (derived from one ovary) or compound (derived from several ovaries). Simple succulent fruits include berries, which typically have many seeds, and drupes, which typically have a single stone or pit (such as cherry and peach). Compound succulent fruits include aggregate fruits, which are formed from many ovaries in one flower, and multiple fruits, which develop from the ovaries of many flowers. Some fruits, known as false fruits or pseudocarps, develop from parts of the flower in addition to the ovaries. For example, the flesh of the apple is formed from the receptacle (the upper end of the flower stalk).

BERRY
Cocoa
(*Theobroma cacao*)

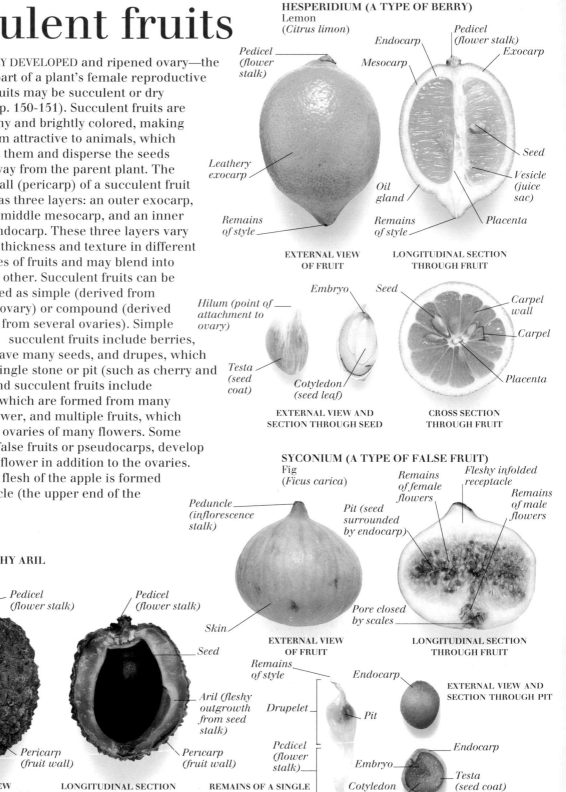

HESPERIDIUM (A TYPE OF BERRY)
Lemon
(*Citrus limon*)

Pedicel (flower stalk)

Endocarp

Mesocarp

Pedicel (flower stalk)

Exocarp

Leathery exocarp

Seed

Oil gland

Vesicle (juice sac)

Remains of style

Remains of style

Placenta

EXTERNAL VIEW OF FRUIT

LONGITUDINAL SECTION THROUGH FRUIT

Hilum (point of attachment to ovary)

Embryo

Seed

Carpel wall

Testa (seed coat)

Cotyledon (seed leaf)

Carpel

Placenta

EXTERNAL VIEW AND SECTION THROUGH SEED

CROSS SECTION THROUGH FRUIT

SYCONIUM (A TYPE OF FALSE FRUIT)
Fig
(*Ficus carica*)

Remains of female flowers

Fleshy infolded receptacle

Remains of male flowers

Peduncle (inflorescence stalk)

Pit (seed surrounded by endocarp)

Skin

Pore closed by scales

EXTERNAL VIEW OF FRUIT

LONGITUDINAL SECTION THROUGH FRUIT

FRUIT WITH FLESHY ARIL
Lychee
(*Litchi chinensis*)

Pedicel (flower stalk)

Pedicel (flower stalk)

Seed

Aril (fleshy outgrowth from seed stalk)

Pericarp (fruit wall)

Pericarp (fruit wall)

EXTERNAL VIEW OF FRUIT

LONGITUDINAL SECTION THROUGH FRUIT

Remains of style

Endocarp

EXTERNAL VIEW AND SECTION THROUGH PIT

Drupelet

Pit

Pedicel (flower stalk)

Embryo

Endocarp

Cotyledon (seed leaf)

Testa (seed coat)

REMAINS OF A SINGLE FEMALE FLOWER

BERRY
Cape gooseberry
(*Physalis peruviana*)

Calyx (whorl of sepals)

Calyx (whorl of sepals) surrounding berry

Exocarp of berry

Pedicel (flower stalk)

Pedicel (flower stalk)

EXTERNAL VIEW
OF FRUIT

INTERNAL VIEW
OF FRUIT

Seed

Placenta

Pericarp

Testa (seed coat)

CROSS SECTION
THROUGH FRUIT

EXTERNAL
VIEW OF SEED

AGGREGATE FRUIT
Raspberry
(*Rubus idaeus*)

Remains of stamen

Drupelet

Remains of style

Pedicel (flower stalk)

Mesocarp and exocarp

Pit (seed surrounded by endocarp)

Receptacle

Drupelet

EXTERNAL VIEW
OF FRUIT

LONGITUDINAL SECTION
THROUGH FRUIT

Hard endocarp

Pit

Hard endocarp

Cotyledon (seed leaf)

Testa (seed coat)

Seed

EXTERNAL VIEW AND
SECTION THROUGH PIT

POME (A TYPE OF FALSE FRUIT)
Apple
(*Malus sylvestris*)

Pedicel (flower stalk)

Seed

Mesocarp and exocarp

Swollen receptacle

Vascular strand

Waxy skin

Endocarp

EXTERNAL
VIEW OF FRUIT

CROSS SECTION
THROUGH FRUIT

Hilum (point of attachment to ovary)

Testa (seed coat)

Embryo

Cotyledon (seed leaf)

Testa (seed coat)

EXTERNAL VIEW AND
SECTION THROUGH SEED

PEPO (A TYPE OF BERRY)
Charentais melon
(*Cucumis melo*)

Rind (fused receptacle and exocarp)

Pedicel (flower stalk)

Seed

Rind (fused receptacle and exocarp)

Mesocarp and endocarp

EXTERNAL VIEW
OF FRUIT

CROSS SECTION
THROUGH FRUIT

Testa (seed coat)

Embryo

Testa (seed coat)

Cotyledon (seed leaf)

EXTERNAL VIEW AND
SECTION THROUGH SEED

Dry fruits

DRY FRUITS HAVE A HARD, DRY PERICARP (fruit wall) around their seeds, unlike succulent fruits, which have fleshy pericarps (see pp. 148-149). Dry fruits are divided into three types: dehiscent, in which the pericarp splits open to release the seeds; indehiscent, which do not split open; and schizocarpic, in which the fruit splits but the seeds are not exposed. Dehiscent dry fruits include capsules (for example, love-in-a-mist), follicles (delphinium), legumes (pea), and silicles (honesty). Typically, the seeds of dehiscent fruits are dispersed by the wind. Indehiscent dry fruits include nuts (sweet chestnut), nutlets (goose grass), achenes (strawberry), caryopses (wheat), samaras (elm), and cypselas (dandelion). Some indehiscent dry fruits are dispersed by the wind, assisted by "wings" (elm) or "parachutes" (dandelion); others (goose grass) have hooked pericarps to aid dispersal on animals' fur. Schizocarpic dry fruits include cremocarps (hogweed), and double samaras (sycamore maple); these are dispersed by the wind.

NUTLET
Goose grass
(*Galium aparine*)

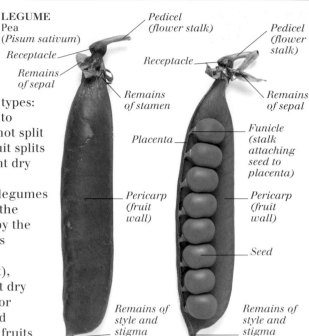

LEGUME
Pea
(*Pisum sativum*)

- *Pedicel (flower stalk)*
- *Receptacle*
- *Remains of sepal*
- *Remains of stamen*
- *Placenta*
- *Pericarp (fruit wall)*
- *Remains of style and stigma*

- *Pedicel (flower stalk)*
- *Receptacle*
- *Remains of sepal*
- *Funicle (stalk attaching seed to placenta)*
- *Pericarp (fruit wall)*
- *Seed*
- *Remains of style and stigma*

EXTERNAL VIEW OF FRUIT

INTERNAL VIEW OF FRUIT

- *Funicle (stalk attaching seed to placenta)*
- *Micropyle (pore for water absorption)*
- *Testa (seed coat)*

- *Cotyledon (seed leaf)*
- *Radicle (embryonic root)*
- *Testa (seed coat)*
- *Plumule (embryonic shoot)*

EXTERIOR VIEW AND SECTION THROUGH SEED

NUT
Spanish chestnut
(*Castanea sativa*)

- *Line of splitting between valves of cupule*
- *Peduncle (inflorescence stalk)*
- *Remains of male inflorescence*
- *Nut (indehiscent fruit)*
- *Spiky cupule (husk around fruit formed from bracts)*

EXTERNAL VIEW OF FRUIT WITH SURROUNDING CUPULE

- *Remains of stigma*
- *Remains of style*
- *Nut (indehiscent fruit)*
- *Woody pericarp (fruit wall)*

- *Remains of stigma*
- *Remains of style*
- *Embryo*
- *Cotyledon (seed leaf)*
- *Testa (seed coat)*
- *Woody pericarp (fruit wall)*

EXTERNAL VIEW AND SECTION THROUGH FRUIT

ACHENE
Strawberry
(*Fragaria* x *ananassa*)

- *Sepal*
- *Pedicel (flower stalk)*
- *Swollen receptacle*
- *Remains of stigma and style*
- *Achene (one-seeded dry fruit)*

- *Sepal*
- *Pedicel (flower stalk)*
- *Swollen fleshy tissues of receptacle*

EXTERNAL VIEW OF FRUIT

LONGITUDINAL SECTION THROUGH FRUIT

- *Pericarp (fruit wall)*
- *Pericarp (fruit wall)*
- *Cotyledon (seed leaf)*
- *Testa (seed coat)*

EXTERNAL VIEW AND SECTION THROUGH SEED

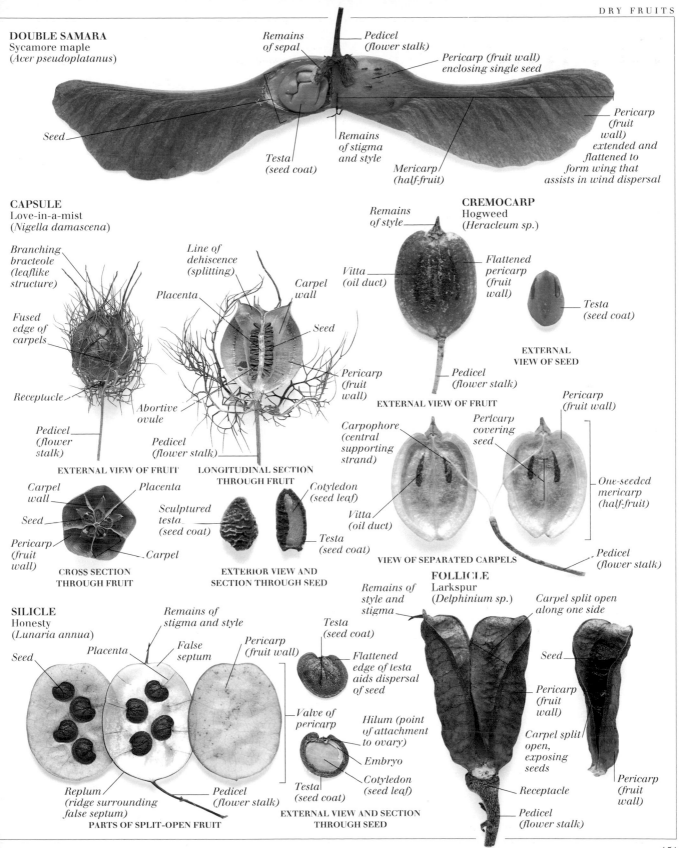

DOUBLE SAMARA
Sycamore maple
(*Acer pseudoplatanus*)

Remains of sepal

Pedicel (flower stalk)

Pericarp (fruit wall) enclosing single seed

Pericarp (fruit wall) extended and flattened to form wing that assists in wind dispersal

Seed

Testa (seed coat)

Remains of stigma and style

Mericarp (half-fruit)

CAPSULE
Love-in-a-mist
(*Nigella damascena*)

Branching bracteole (leaflike structure)

Line of dehiscence (splitting)

Carpel wall

Placenta

Seed

Fused edge of carpels

Pericarp (fruit wall)

Receptacle

Pedicel (flower stalk)

Pedicel (flower stalk)

Abortive ovule

EXTERNAL VIEW OF FRUIT

LONGITUDINAL SECTION THROUGH FRUIT

CREMOCARP
Hogweed
(*Heracleum sp.*)

Remains of style

Vitta (oil duct)

Flattened pericarp (fruit wall)

Testa (seed coat)

EXTERNAL VIEW OF SEED

Pedicel (flower stalk)

EXTERNAL VIEW OF FRUIT

Carpophore (central supporting strand)

Pericarp covering seed

Pericarp (fruit wall)

Vitta (oil duct)

One-seeded mericarp (half-fruit)

Pedicel (flower stalk)

VIEW OF SEPARATED CARPELS

Carpel wall

Placenta

Seed

Pericarp (fruit wall)

Carpel

CROSS SECTION THROUGH FRUIT

Sculptured testa (seed coat)

Cotyledon (seed leaf)

Testa (seed coat)

EXTERIOR VIEW AND SECTION THROUGH SEED

SILICLE
Honesty
(*Lunaria annua*)

Remains of stigma and style

False septum

Pericarp (fruit wall)

Seed

Placenta

Valve of pericarp

Replum (ridge surrounding false septum)

Pedicel (flower stalk)

PARTS OF SPLIT-OPEN FRUIT

Testa (seed coat)

Flattened edge of testa aids dispersal of seed

Hilum (point of attachment to ovary)

Embryo

Testa (seed coat)

Cotyledon (seed leaf)

EXTERNAL VIEW AND SECTION THROUGH SEED

FOLLICLE
Larkspur
(*Delphinium sp.*)

Remains of style and stigma

Carpel split open along one side

Seed

Pericarp (fruit wall)

Carpel split open, exposing seeds

Receptacle

Pericarp (fruit wall)

Pedicel (flower stalk)

Germination

GERMINATION IS THE GROWTH OF SEEDS INTO SEEDLINGS. It starts when seeds become active below ground, and ends when the first foliage leaves appear above ground. A seed consists of an embryo and its food supply, surrounded by a testa (seed coat). The embryo is made up of one or two cotyledons (seed leaves) attached to a central axis. The upper part of the axis consists of an epicotyl, which has a plumule (embryonic shoot) at its tip. The lower part of the axis consists of a hypocotyl and a radicle (embryonic root). After dispersal from the parent plant, the seeds dehydrate and enter a period of dormancy. Germination begins, following this dormant period, as long as the seeds have enough water, oxygen, warmth, and, in some cases, light. In the first stages of germination, the seed takes in water; the embryo starts to use its food store; and the radicle swells, breaks through the testa, and grows downward. Germination then proceeds in one of two ways, depending on the type of seed. In epigeal germination, the hypocotyl lengthens, pulling the plumule and its protective cotyledons out of the soil. In hypogeal germination, the cotyledons remain below ground and the epicotyl lengthens, pushing the plumule upward.

HYPOGEAL GERMINATION
Broad bean
(*Vicia faba*)

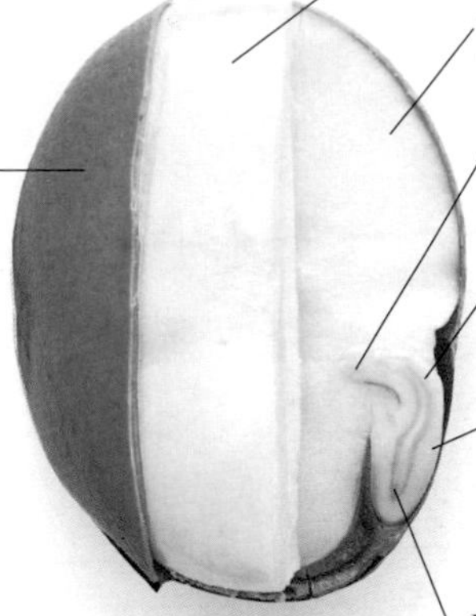

Cotyledon
(seed leaf)

Cotyledon
(seed leaf)

Plumule
(embryonic
shoot)

Testa
(seed
coat)

Epicotyl
(upper part
of axis)

Hypocotyl
(region
between
epicotyl and
radicle)

Radicle
(embryonic
root)

**SEED AT START OF
GERMINATION**

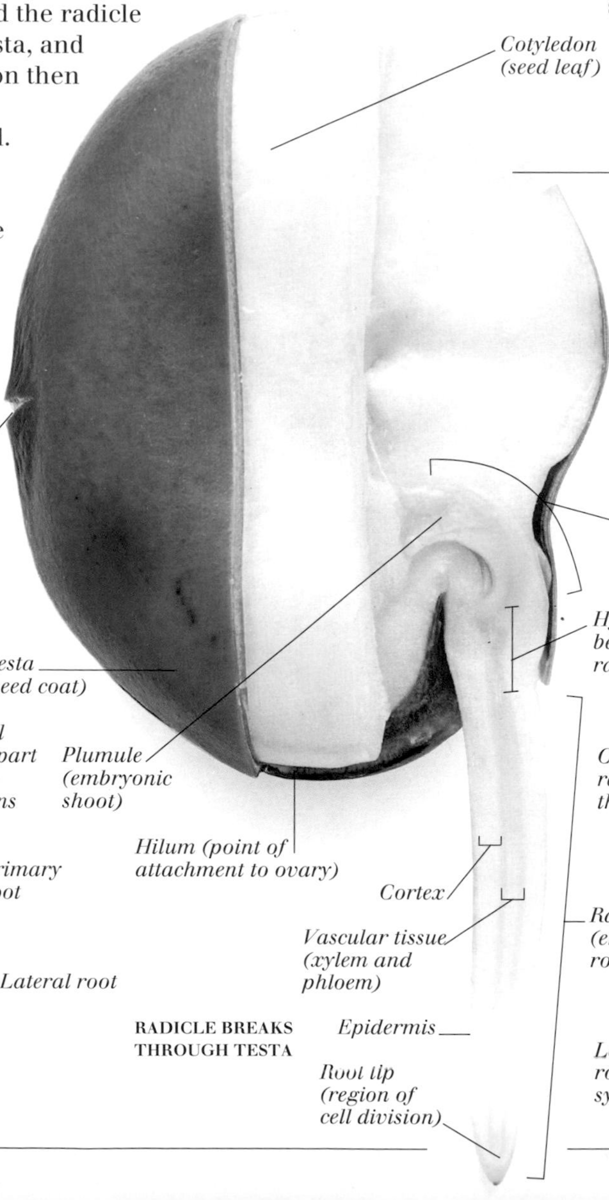

Cotyledon
(seed leaf)

Foliage leaf

Cotyledon
(seed leaf)

Stipule
(structure at
base of leaf)

Epicotyl
increases in
length and
turns green

Cataphyll
(scale leaf
of plumule)

Epicotyl
(upper part
of axis)

Hypocotyl (region
between epicotyl and
radicle)

**FOLIAGE LEAVES
APPEAR**

Split in testa
(seed coat) due
to expanding
cotyledons

Young
shoot

Cataphyll
(scale leaf of
plumule)

Testa
(seed coat)

Epicotyl
(upper part
of axis)
lengthens

Plumule
(embryonic
shoot)

Hilum (point of
attachment to ovary)

Cortex

Vascular tissue
(xylem and
phloem)

Cotyledons
(seed leaves)
remain within
testa (seed
coat) below
soil's surface

Cotyledons (seed leaves)
remain food source for
the seedling

Primary
root

Radicle
(embryonic
root)

Primary
root

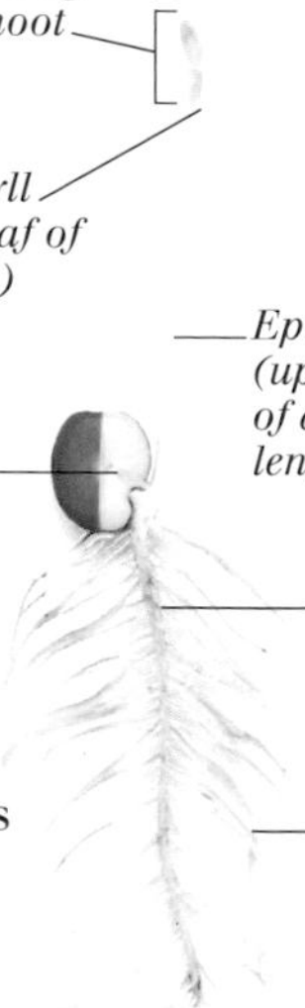

**SHOOT APPEARS
ABOVE SOIL**

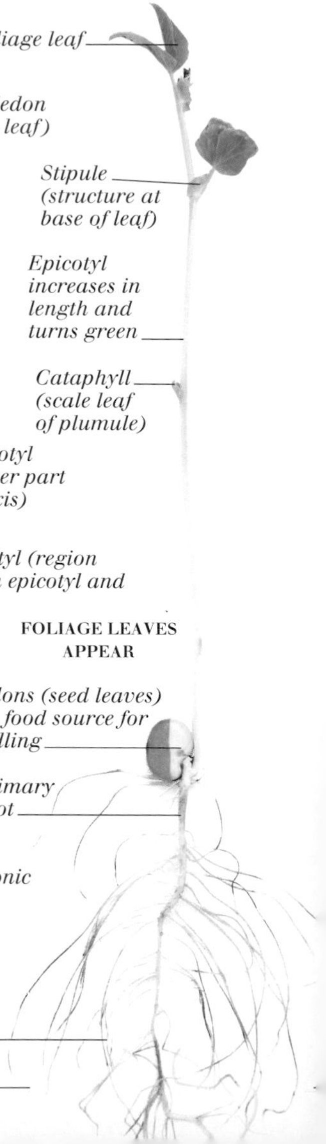

Lateral root

**RADICLE BREAKS
THROUGH TESTA**

Epidermis

Root tip
(region of
cell division)

Lateral
root
system

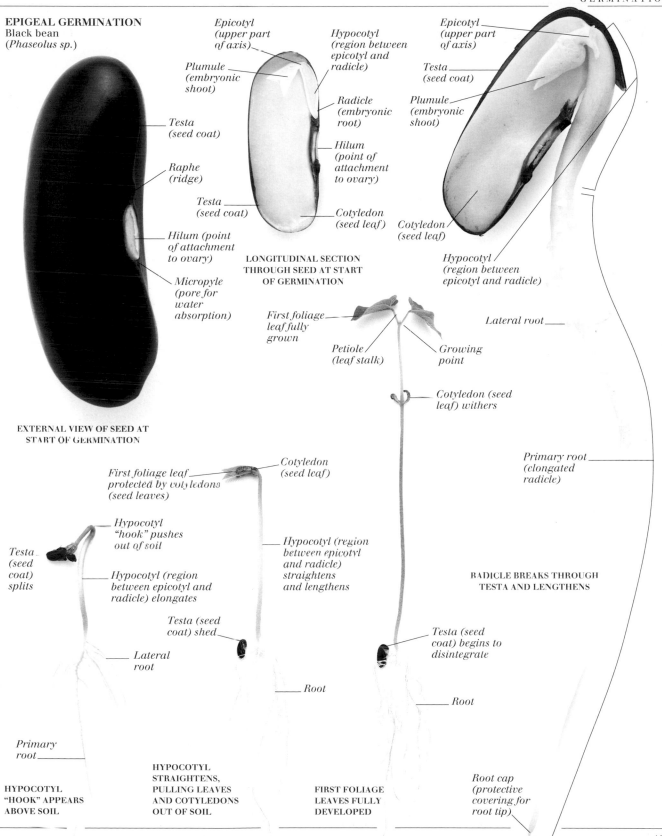

EPIGEAL GERMINATION
Black bean
(*Phaseolus sp.*)

*Testa
(seed coat)*

*Raphe
(ridge)*

*Hilum (point
of attachment
to ovary)*

*Micropyle
(pore for
water
absorption)*

**EXTERNAL VIEW OF SEED AT
START OF GERMINATION**

*Epicotyl
(upper part
of axis)*

*Plumule
(embryonic
shoot)*

*Hypocotyl
(region between
epicotyl and
radicle)*

*Radicle
(embryonic
root)*

*Hilum
(point of
attachment
to ovary)*

*Testa
(seed coat)*

*Cotyledon
(seed leaf)*

**LONGITUDINAL SECTION
THROUGH SEED AT START
OF GERMINATION**

*Epicotyl
(upper part
of axis)*

*Testa
(seed coat)*

*Plumule
(embryonic
shoot)*

*Cotyledon
(seed leaf)*

*Hypocotyl
(region between
epicotyl and radicle)*

*First foliage
leaf fully
grown*

*Petiole
(leaf stalk)*

*Growing
point*

Lateral root

*Cotyledon (seed
leaf) withers*

*Primary root
(elongated
radicle)*

*First foliage leaf
protected by cotyledons
(seed leaves)*

*Cotyledon
(seed leaf)*

*Hypocotyl
"hook" pushes
out of soil*

*Testa
(seed
coat)
splits*

*Hypocotyl (region
between epicotyl and
radicle) elongates*

*Testa (seed
coat) shed*

*Lateral
root*

*Hypocotyl (region
between epicotyl
and radicle)
straightens
and lengthens*

Root

**RADICLE BREAKS THROUGH
TESTA AND LENGTHENS**

*Testa (seed
coat) begins to
disintegrate*

Root

*Primary
root*

**HYPOCOTYL
"HOOK" APPEARS
ABOVE SOIL**

**HYPOCOTYL
STRAIGHTENS,
PULLING LEAVES
AND COTYLEDONS
OUT OF SOIL**

**FIRST FOLIAGE
LEAVES FULLY
DEVELOPED**

*Root cap
(protective
covering for
root tip)*

Vegetative reproduction

MANY PLANTS CAN PROPAGATE THEMSELVES by vegetative reproduction. In this process, part of a plant separates, takes root, and grows into a new plant. Vegetative reproduction is a type of asexual reproduction; it involves only one parent and there is no fusion of gametes (sex cells). Plants use various structures to reproduce vegetatively. Some plants use underground storage organs. Such organs include rhizomes (horizontal, underground stems), the branches of which produce new plants; bulbs (swollen leaf bases) and corms (swollen stems), which produce daughter bulbs or corms that separate from the parent; and stem tubers (thickened underground stems) and root tubers (swollen adventitious roots), which also separate from the parent. Other propagative structures include runners and stolons, creeping horizontal stems that take root and produce new plants; bulbils, small bulbs that develop on the stem or in the place of flowers, and then drop off and grow into new plants; and adventitious buds, miniature plants that form on leaf margins before dropping to the ground and growing into mature plants.

CORM
Gladiolus
(*Gladiolus sp.*)

ADVENTITIOUS BUD
Mexican hat plant
(*Kalanchoe daigremontiana*)

Apex of leaf

Lamina (blade) of leaf

Leaf margin

Notch in leaf margin containing meristematic (actively dividing) cells

Adventitious bud (detachable bud with adventitious roots) drops from leaf

Petiole (leaf stalk)

BULBIL IN PLACE OF FLOWER
Orange lily
(*Lilium bulbiferum*)

Scar left by flower

Leaf

Pedicel (flower stalk)

Detachable bulbil formed in place of flower

Peduncle (inflorescence stalk)

STOLON
Ground ivy
(*Glechoma hederacea*)

Terminal bud

Internode

Node

Node

Parent plant

Stolon (creeping stem)

Adventitious root of daughter plant

Daughter plant developed from lateral bud

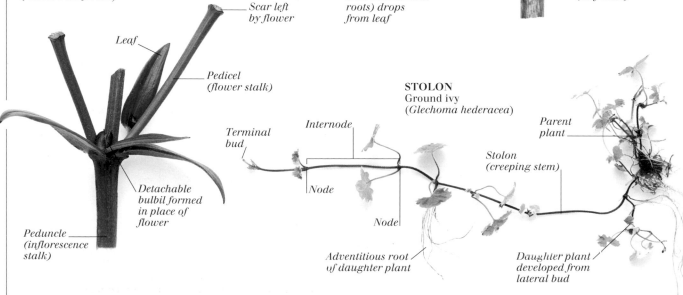

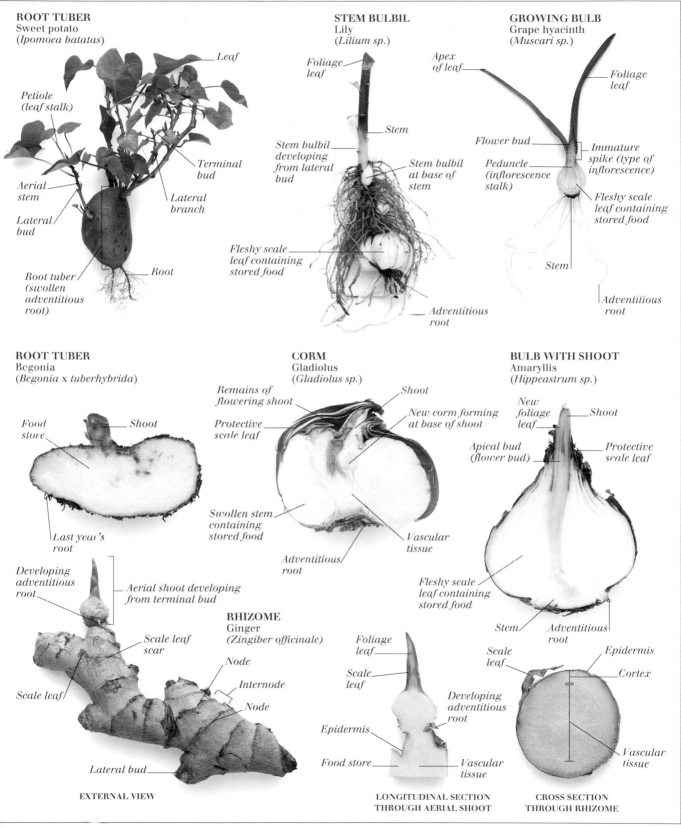

ROOT TUBER
Sweet potato
(*Ipomoea batatas*)

Leaf

Petiole
(leaf stalk)

Terminal
bud

Aerial
stem

Lateral
branch

Lateral
bud

Root tuber
(swollen
adventitious
root)

Root

STEM BULBIL
Lily
(*Lilium sp.*)

Foliage
leaf

Stem

Stem bulbil
developing
from lateral
bud

Stem bulbil
at base of
stem

Fleshy scale
leaf containing
stored food

Adventitious
root

GROWING BULB
Grape hyacinth
(*Muscari sp.*)

Apex
of leaf

Foliage
leaf

Flower bud

Immature
spike (type of
inflorescence)

Peduncle
(inflorescence
stalk)

Fleshy scale
leaf containing
stored food

Stem

Adventitious
root

ROOT TUBER
Begonia
(*Begonia* x *tuberhybrida*)

Food
store

Shoot

Last year's
root

CORM
Gladiolus
(*Gladiolus sp.*)

Remains of
flowering shoot

Shoot

Protective
scale leaf

New corm forming
at base of shoot

Swollen stem
containing
stored food

Vascular
tissue

Adventitious
root

BULB WITH SHOOT
Amaryllis
(*Hippeastrum sp.*)

New
foliage
leaf

Shoot

Apical bud
(flower bud)

Protective
scale leaf

Fleshy scale
leaf containing
stored food

Stem

Adventitious
root

Developing
adventitious
root

Aerial shoot developing
from terminal bud

Scale leaf
scar

Node

Internode

Node

Scale leaf

RHIZOME
Ginger
(*Zingiber officinale*)

Foliage
leaf

Scale
leaf

Developing
adventitious
root

Epidermis

Food store

Vascular
tissue

Scale
leaf

Epidermis

Cortex

Vascular
tissue

Lateral bud

EXTERNAL VIEW

**LONGITUDINAL SECTION
THROUGH AERIAL SHOOT**

**CROSS SECTION
THROUGH RHIZOME**

Dryland plants

DRYLAND PLANTS (XEROPHYTES) are able to survive in unfavorable habitats. All are found in places where little water is available; some live in high temperatures that cause excessive loss of water from the leaves. Xerophytes show a number of adaptations to dry conditions. These include reduced leaf area, rolled leaves, sunken stomata, hairs, spines, and thick cuticles. One group, succulent plants, stores water in specially enlarged spongy tissues found in leaves, roots, or stems. Leaf succulents have enlarged, fleshy, water-storing leaves. Root succulents have a large underground water-storage organ with short-lived stems and leaves above ground. Stem succulents are represented by the cacti (family Cactaceae). Cacti stems are fleshy, green, and photosynthetic. They are typically ribbed or covered by tubercles in rows, with leaves being reduced to spines or entirely absent.

LEAF SUCCULENT
Lithops sp.

STEM SUCCULENT
Golden barrel cactus
(*Echinocactus grusonii*)

Areole (modified lateral shoot)

Trichome (hair)

Spine (modified leaf)

Spine (modified leaf)

Tubercle (projection from stem surface)

Root

Waxy cuticle (waterproof covering)

Water-storing parenchyma (packing tissue)

Sinuous (wavy) cell wall

Stoma (pore) controlling exchange of gases

Tubercle (projection from stem surface)

Vascular cylinder (transport tissue)

EXTERNAL VIEW

MICROGRAPH OF STEM SURFACE

Root

Spine (modified leaf)

Areole (modified lateral shoot)

Tubercle (projection from stem surface)

Waxy cuticle (waterproof covering)

DETAIL OF STEM SURFACE

LONGITUDINAL SECTION THROUGH STEM

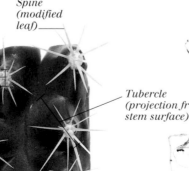

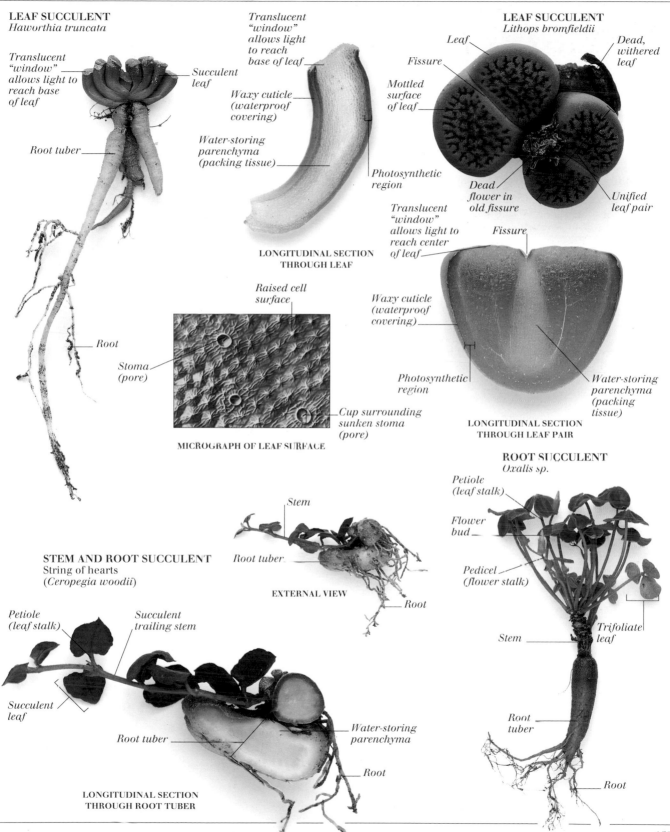

LEAF SUCCULENT
Haworthia truncata

Translucent "window" allows light to reach base of leaf

Succulent leaf

Root tuber

Root

Translucent "window" allows light to reach base of leaf

Waxy cuticle (waterproof covering)

Water-storing parenchyma (packing tissue)

Photosynthetic region

LONGITUDINAL SECTION THROUGH LEAF

Raised cell surface

Stoma (pore)

Cup surrounding sunken stoma (pore)

MICROGRAPH OF LEAF SURFACE

LEAF SUCCULENT
Lithops bromfieldii

Leaf

Fissure

Mottled surface of leaf

Dead, withered leaf

Dead flower in old fissure

Unified leaf pair

Translucent "window" allows light to reach center of leaf

Fissure

Waxy cuticle (waterproof covering)

Photosynthetic region

Water-storing parenchyma (packing tissue)

LONGITUDINAL SECTION THROUGH LEAF PAIR

STEM AND ROOT SUCCULENT
String of hearts
(*Ceropegia woodii*)

Petiole (leaf stalk)

Succulent trailing stem

Succulent leaf

Root tuber

Water-storing parenchyma

Root

LONGITUDINAL SECTION THROUGH ROOT TUBER

Stem

Root tuber

Root

EXTERNAL VIEW

ROOT SUCCULENT
Oxalis sp.

Petiole (leaf stalk)

Flower bud

Pedicel (flower stalk)

Stem

Trifoliate leaf

Root tuber

Root

Wetland plants

WETLAND PLANTS GROW SUBMERGED IN WATER, either partially, like the water hyacinth, or completely, like the pondweeds, and show various adaptations to this habitat. Typically, there are numerous air spaces inside the stems, leaves, and roots; these aid gas exchange and buoyancy. Submerged parts generally have no cuticle (waterproof covering), allowing the plants to absorb minerals and gases directly from the water. Also, because they are supported by the water, wetland plants need little of the supportive tissue found in land plants. Stomata, the gas exchange pores, are absent from plants that are completely submerged. In partially submerged plants with floating leaves, such as water lilies, stomata are found on the upper leaf surfaces, where they cannot be flooded.

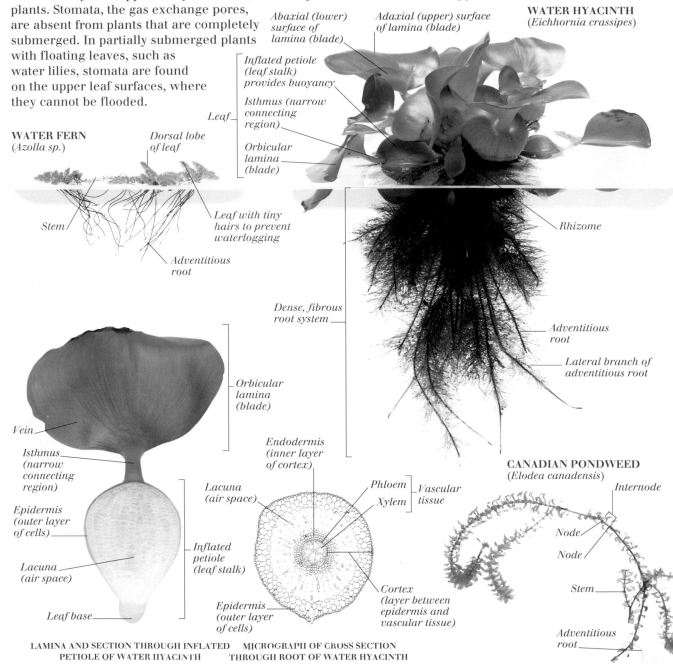

WATER HYACINTH
(*Eichhornia crassipes*)

Abaxial (lower) surface of lamina (blade)

Adaxial (upper) surface of lamina (blade)

Inflated petiole (leaf stalk) provides buoyancy

Isthmus (narrow connecting region)

Leaf

Orbicular lamina (blade)

WATER FERN
(*Azolla sp.*)

Dorsal lobe of leaf

Stem

Leaf with tiny hairs to prevent waterlogging

Adventitious root

Rhizome

Dense, fibrous root system

Adventitious root

Lateral branch of adventitious root

Orbicular lamina (blade)

Vein

Isthmus (narrow connecting region)

Epidermis (outer layer of cells)

Lacuna (air space)

Leaf base

Endodermis (inner layer of cortex)

Lacuna (air space)

Phloem
Xylem

Vascular tissue

Inflated petiole (leaf stalk)

Epidermis (outer layer of cells)

Cortex (layer between epidermis and vascular tissue)

CANADIAN PONDWEED
(*Elodea canadensis*)

Internode

Node

Node

Stem

Adventitious root

LAMINA AND SECTION THROUGH INFLATED PETIOLE OF WATER HYACINTH

MICROGRAPH OF CROSS SECTION THROUGH ROOT OF WATER HYACINTH

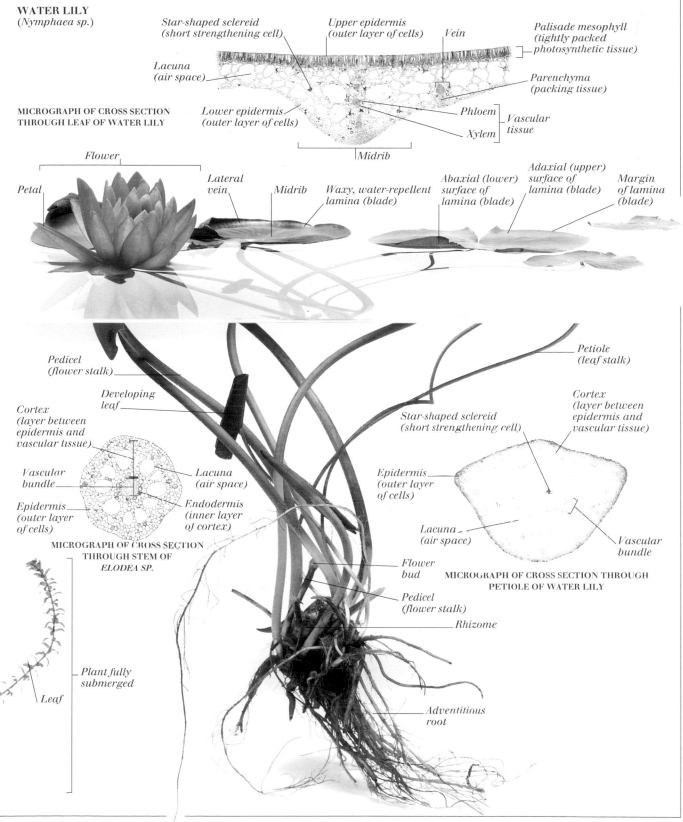

WATER LILY
(Nymphaea sp.)

*Star-shaped sclereid
(short strengthening cell)*

*Upper epidermis
(outer layer of cells)*

Vein

*Palisade mesophyll
(tightly packed
photosynthetic tissue)*

*Lacuna
(air space)*

*Parenchyma
(packing tissue)*

MICROGRAPH OF CROSS SECTION
THROUGH LEAF OF WATER LILY

*Lower epidermis
(outer layer of cells)*

Phloem

Xylem

*Vascular
tissue*

Midrib

Flower

Petal

*Lateral
vein*

Midrib

*Waxy, water-repellent
lamina (blade)*

*Abaxial (lower)
surface of
lamina (blade)*

*Adaxial (upper)
surface of
lamina (blade)*

*Margin
of lamina
(blade)*

*Pedicel
(flower stalk)*

*Petiole
(leaf stalk)*

*Developing
leaf*

*Cortex
(layer between
epidermis and
vascular tissue)*

*Star-shaped sclereid
(short strengthening cell)*

*Cortex
(layer between
epidermis and
vascular tissue)*

*Vascular
bundle*

*Lacuna
(air space)*

*Epidermis
(outer layer
of cells)*

*Epidermis
(outer layer
of cells)*

*Endodermis
(inner layer
of cortex)*

MICROGRAPH OF CROSS SECTION
THROUGH STEM OF
ELODEA SP.

*Lacuna
(air space)*

*Vascular
bundle*

MICROGRAPH OF CROSS SECTION THROUGH
PETIOLE OF WATER LILY

*Flower
bud*

*Pedicel
(flower stalk)*

Rhizome

*Plant fully
submerged*

Leaf

*Adventitious
root*

Carnivorous plants

CARNIVOROUS (INSECTIVOROUS) PLANTS FEED ON INSECTS and other small animals in addition to producing food in their leaves by photosynthesis. The nutrients absorbed from trapped insects allow carnivorous plants to thrive in acid, boggy soils that lack essential minerals, especially nitrates, where most other plants could not survive. All carnivorous plants have some leaves modified as traps. Many use bright colors and scented nectar to attract prey, and most use enzymes to digest the prey. There are three types of traps. Pitcher plants, such as the monkey cup and cobra lily, have leaves modified as pitcher-shaped pitfall traps, half-filled with water. Once lured inside the mouth of the trap, insects lose their footing on the slippery surface, fall into the liquid, and either decompose or are digested. Venus flytraps use a spring-trap mechanism; when an insect touches trigger hairs on the inner surfaces of the leaves, the two lobes of the trap snap shut. Butterworts and sundews entangle prey by sticky droplets on the leaf surface, while the edges of the leaves slowly curl over to envelop and digest the prey.

A PITCHER PLANT
Cobra lily (*Darlingtonia californica*)

Areola ("window" of transparent tissue)

Fishtail nectary

Wing

Hood

Pitcher

Tubular petiole (leaf stalk)

Areola ("window" of transparent tissue)

Dome-shaped hood develops

Fishtail nectary appears

Immature pitcher

Smooth surface

Nectar roll

Mouth

Wing

Downward-pointing hair

DEVELOPMENT OF MODIFIED LEAF IN COBRA LILY

Immature trap

Interlocked teeth

Closed trap

Red color of trap attracts insects

VENUS FLYTRAP
(*Dionaea muscipula*)

Phyllode (flattened petiole)

Summer petiole (leaf stalk)

Nectary zone (glands secrete nectar)

Digestive zone (glands secrete digestive enzymes)

Tooth

Lobe of trap

Midrib (hinge of trap)

Trigger hair

Spring petiole (leaf stalk)

Trap (twin-lobed leaf blade)

Sensory hinge

Trigger hair

Inner surface of trap

Digestive gland

MICROGRAPH OF LOBE OF VENUS FLYTRAP

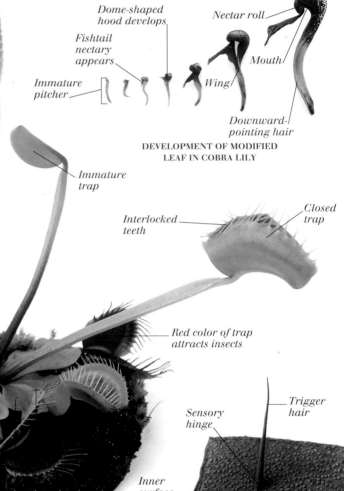

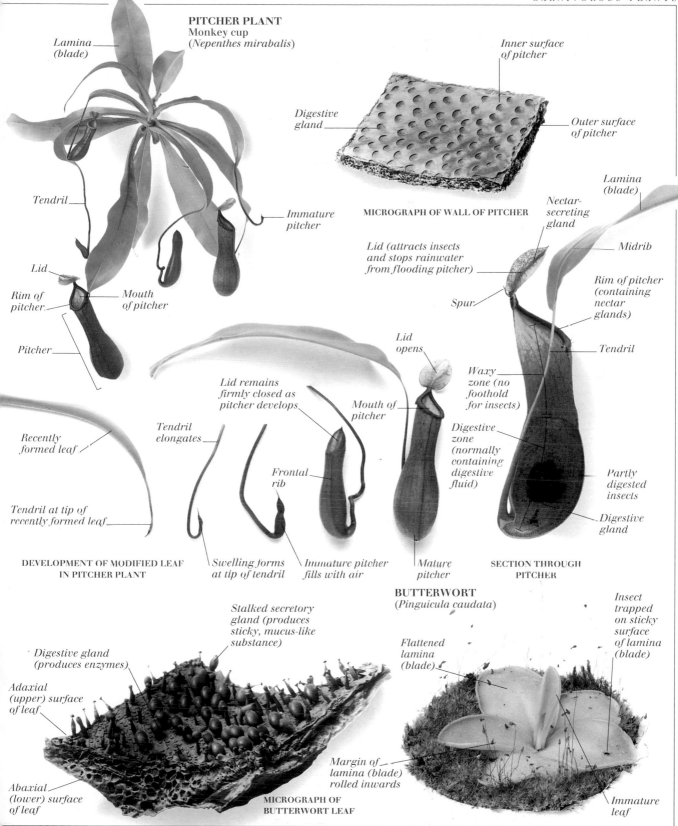

PITCHER PLANT
Monkey cup
(*Nepenthes mirabalis*)

Lamina (blade)

Tendril

Lid

Rim of pitcher

Mouth of pitcher

Pitcher

Immature pitcher

Digestive gland

Inner surface of pitcher

Outer surface of pitcher

MICROGRAPH OF WALL OF PITCHER

Lamina (blade)

Nectar-secreting gland

Midrib

Lid (attracts insects and stops rainwater from flooding pitcher)

Spur

Rim of pitcher (containing nectar glands)

Tendril

Waxy zone (no foothold for insects)

Digestive zone (normally containing digestive fluid)

Partly digested insects

Digestive gland

Recently formed leaf

Tendril at tip of recently formed leaf

Lid remains firmly closed as pitcher develops

Tendril elongates

Frontal rib

Lid opens

Mouth of pitcher

DEVELOPMENT OF MODIFIED LEAF IN PITCHER PLANT

Swelling forms at tip of tendril

Immature pitcher fills with air

Mature pitcher

SECTION THROUGH PITCHER

BUTTERWORT
(*Pinguicula caudata*)

Stalked secretory gland (produces sticky, mucus-like substance)

Digestive gland (produces enzymes)

Adaxial (upper) surface of leaf

Abaxial (lower) surface of leaf

MICROGRAPH OF BUTTERWORT LEAF

Flattened lamina (blade)

Margin of lamina (blade) rolled inwards

Insect trapped on sticky surface of lamina (blade)

Immature leaf

Epiphytic and parasitic plants

EPIPHYTIC AND PARASITIC PLANTS GROW ON OTHER LIVING PLANTS. Typically, epiphytic plants are not rooted in the soil. Instead, they live above ground level on the stems and branches of other plants. Epiphytes obtain water from trapped rainwater and from moisture in the air. They obtain minerals from organic matter that has accumulated on the surface of the plant on which they are growing. Like other green plants, epiphytes produce their food by photosynthesis. Epiphytes include tropical orchids and bromeliads (air plants) and some mosses that live in temperate regions. Parasitic plants obtain all their nutrient requirements from the host plants on which they grow. The parasites produce haustoria, root-like organs that penetrate the stem or roots of the host and grow inward to merge with the host's vascular tissue. These extract water, minerals, and manufactured nutrients. Because they have no need to produce their own food, parasitic plants lack chlorophyll, the green photosynthetic pigment, and they have no foliage leaves. Partial parasitic plants, like mistletoe, obtain water and minerals from the host plant but have green leaves and stems and are therefore able to produce their own food by photosynthesis.

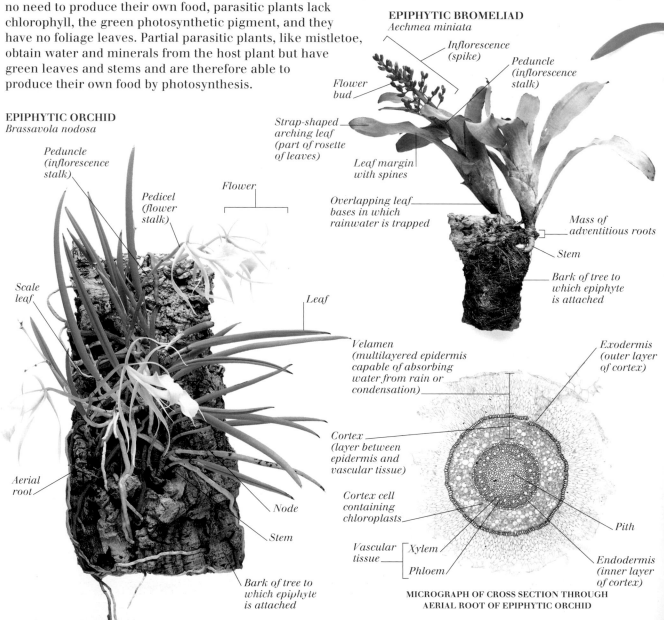

EPIPHYTIC BROMELIAD
Aechmea miniata

Inflorescence (spike)

Peduncle (inflorescence stalk)

Flower bud

Strap-shaped arching leaf (part of rosette of leaves)

Leaf margin with spines

Overlapping leaf bases in which rainwater is trapped

Mass of adventitious roots

Stem

Bark of tree to which epiphyte is attached

EPIPHYTIC ORCHID
Brassavola nodosa

Peduncle (inflorescence stalk)

Pedicel (flower stalk)

Flower

Scale leaf

Leaf

Velamen (multilayered epidermis capable of absorbing water from rain or condensation)

Cortex (layer between epidermis and vascular tissue)

Exodermis (outer layer of cortex)

Cortex cell containing chloroplasts

Pith

Aerial root

Node

Stem

Vascular tissue — Xylem / Phloem

Endodermis (inner layer of cortex)

Bark of tree to which epiphyte is attached

MICROGRAPH OF CROSS SECTION THROUGH AERIAL ROOT OF EPIPHYTIC ORCHID

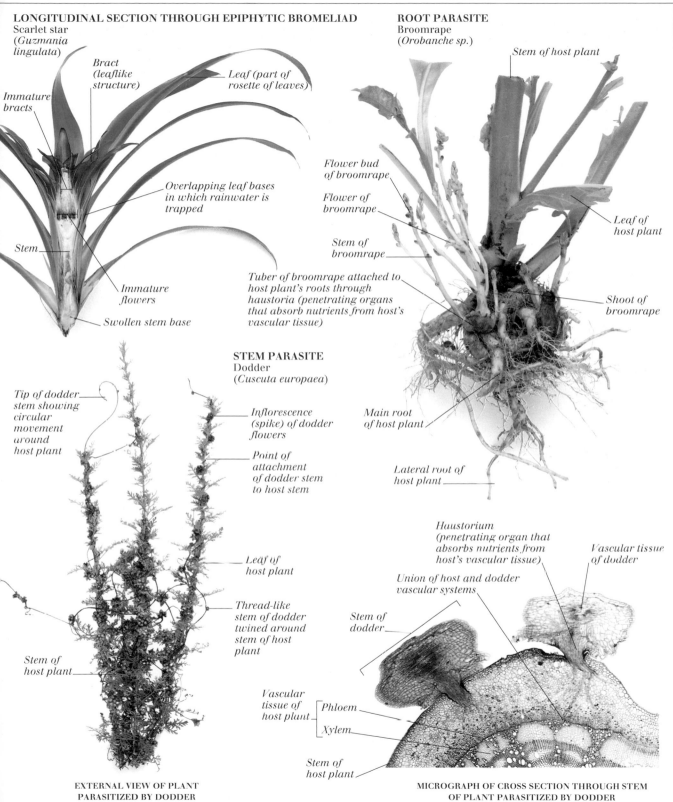

LONGITUDINAL SECTION THROUGH EPIPHYTIC BROMELIAD
Scarlet star
(*Guzmania lingulata*)

Immature bracts

Bract (leaflike structure)

Leaf (part of rosette of leaves)

Overlapping leaf bases in which rainwater is trapped

Stem

Immature flowers

Swollen stem base

ROOT PARASITE
Broomrape
(*Orobanche sp.*)

Stem of host plant

Flower bud of broomrape

Flower of broomrape

Stem of broomrape

Tuber of broomrape attached to host plant's roots through haustoria (penetrating organs that absorb nutrients from host's vascular tissue)

Leaf of host plant

Shoot of broomrape

Main root of host plant

Lateral root of host plant

STEM PARASITE
Dodder
(*Cuscuta europaea*)

Tip of dodder stem showing circular movement around host plant

Inflorescence (spike) of dodder flowers

Point of attachment of dodder stem to host stem

Leaf of host plant

Thread-like stem of dodder twined around stem of host plant

Stem of host plant

EXTERNAL VIEW OF PLANT PARASITIZED BY DODDER

Haustorium (penetrating organ that absorbs nutrients from host's vascular tissue)

Vascular tissue of dodder

Union of host and dodder vascular systems

Stem of dodder

Vascular tissue of host plant
- Phloem
- Xylem

Stem of host plant

MICROGRAPH OF CROSS SECTION THROUGH STEM OF PLANT PARASITIZED BY DODDER

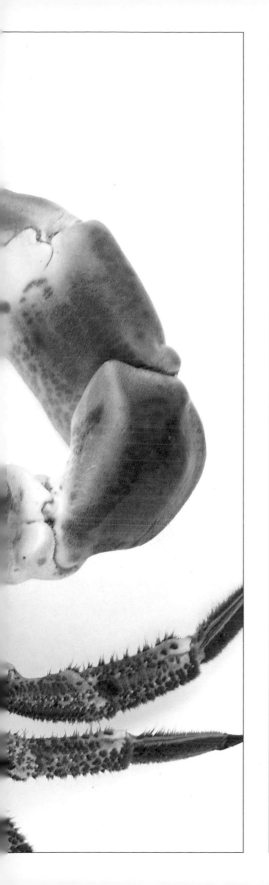

ANIMALS

Sponges, jellyfish, and sea anemones

SPONGES ARE MAINLY MARINE animals that make up the phylum Porifera. They are among the simplest of all animals, having no tissues or organs. Their bodies consist of two layers of cells separated by a jelly-like layer (mesohyal) that is strengthened by mineral spicules or protein fibers. The body is perforated by a system of pores and water channels called the aquiferous system. Special cells (choanocytes) with whip-like structures (flagella) draw water through the aquiferous system, thereby bringing tiny food particles to the sponge's cells. Jellyfish (class Scyphozoa), sea anemones (class Anthozoa), and corals (also class Anthozoa) belong to the phylum Cnidaria, also known as Coelenterata. More complex than sponges, coelenterates have simple tissues, such as nervous tissue; a radially symmetrical body; and a mouth surrounded by tentacles with unique stinging cells (cnidocytes).

INTERNAL ANATOMY OF A SPONGE

Amebocyte

Osculum (excurrent pore)

Choanocyte (collar cell)

Ostium (incurrent pore)

Porocyte (pore cell)

Mesohyal

Spongocoel (atrium; paragaster)

Spicule

Pinacocyte (epidermal cell)

Ostium (incurrent pore)

SKELETON OF A SPONGE

Protein matrix

Pore

EXTERNAL FEATURES OF A SEA ANEMONE

Tentacle

EXAMPLES OF SEA ANEMONES

JEWEL ANEMONE
(Corynactis viridis)

PARASITIC ANEMONE
(Calliactis parasitica)

PLUMOSE ANEMONE
(Metridium senile)

MEDITERRANEAN SEA ANEMONE
(Condylactis sp.)

GREEN SNAKELOCK ANEMONE
(Anemonia viridis)

BEADLET ANEMONE
(Actinia equina)

GHOST ANEMONE
(Actinothoe sphyrodeta)

Sagartia elegans

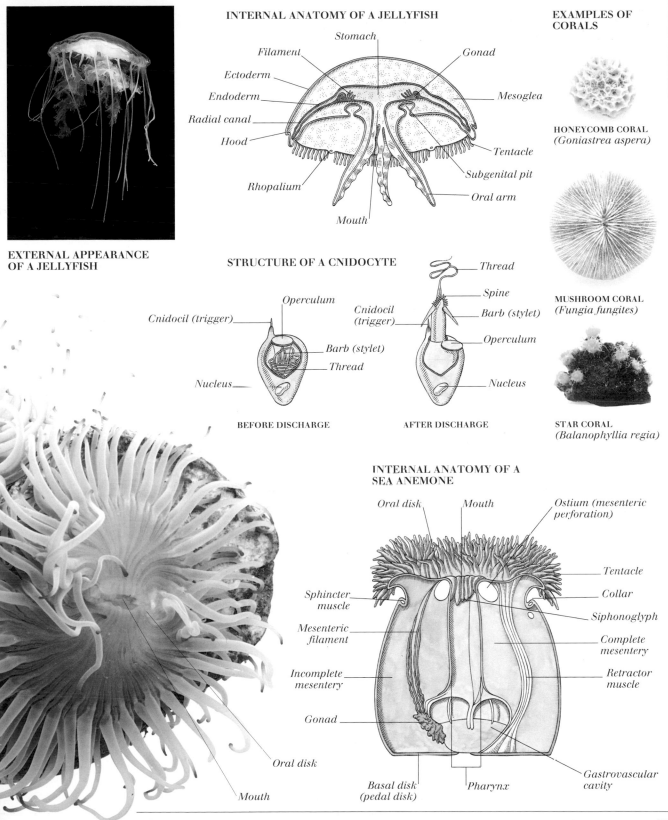

INTERNAL ANATOMY OF A JELLYFISH

Stomach

Filament

Gonad

Ectoderm

Endoderm

Mesoglea

Radial canal

Hood

Tentacle

Rhopalium

Subgenital pit

Oral arm

Mouth

**EXTERNAL APPEARANCE
OF A JELLYFISH**

**EXAMPLES OF
CORALS**

HONEYCOMB CORAL
(Goniastrea aspera)

MUSHROOM CORAL
(Fungia fungites)

STRUCTURE OF A CNIDOCYTE

Operculum

Thread

Cnidocil (trigger)

Spine

Cnidocil
(trigger)

Barb (stylet)

Barb (stylet)

Operculum

Thread

Nucleus

Nucleus

BEFORE DISCHARGE

AFTER DISCHARGE

STAR CORAL
(Balanophyllia regia)

**INTERNAL ANATOMY OF A
SEA ANEMONE**

Oral disk

Mouth

Ostium (mesenteric
perforation)

Tentacle

Sphincter
muscle

Collar

Siphonoglyph

Mesenteric
filament

Complete
mesentery

Incomplete
mesentery

Retractor
muscle

Gonad

Oral disk

Basal disk
(pedal disk)

Pharynx

Gastrovascular
cavity

Mouth

Insects

THE WORD INSECT REFERS to small invertebrate creatures, especially those with bodies divided into sections. Insects, including beetles, ants, bees, butterflies, and moths, belong to various orders in the class Insecta, which is a division of the phylum Arthropoda. Features common to all insects are an exoskeleton (external skeleton); three pairs of jointed legs; three body sections (head, thorax, and abdomen); and one pair of sensory antennae. Beetles (order Coleoptera) are the biggest group of insects, with about 300,000 species (about 30 percent of all known insects). They have a pair of hard elytra (wing cases), which are modified front wings. The principal function of the elytra is to protect the hind wings, which are used for flying. Ants, together with bees and wasps, form the order Hymenoptera, which contains about 200,000 species. This group is characterized by a marked narrowing between the thorax and abdomen. Butterflies and moths form the order Lepidoptera, which has about 150,000 species. They have wings covered with tiny scales, hence the name of their order (Lepidoptera means "scale wings"). The separation of lepidopterans into butterflies and moths is largely artificial as there are no features that categorically distinguish one group from the other. In general, however, most butterflies fly by day, whereas most moths are night flyers. Some insects, including butterflies and moths, undergo complete metamorphosis (transformation) during their life cycle. A butterfly metamorphoses from an egg to a larva (caterpillar), then to a pupa (chrysalis), and finally to an imago (adult).

PUPA (CHRYSALIS)

EXAMPLES OF INSECTS

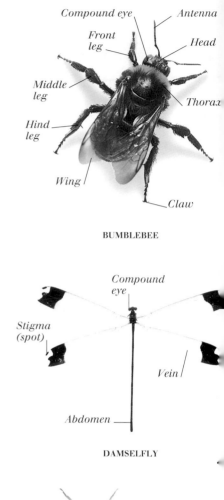

Compound eye • Antenna • Front leg • Head • Middle leg • Thorax • Hind leg • Wing • Claw

BUMBLEBEE

Compound eye • Stigma (spot) • Vein • Abdomen

DAMSELFLY

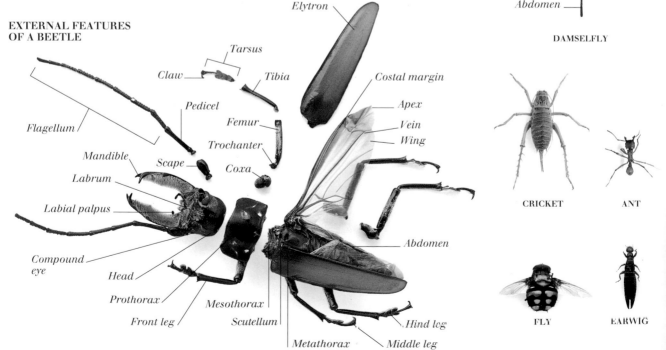

EXTERNAL FEATURES OF A BEETLE

Elytron • Tarsus • Claw • Tibia • Costal margin • Pedicel • Apex • Femur • Vein • Trochanter • Wing • Flagellum • Scape • Coxa • Mandible • Labrum • Labial palpus • Abdomen • Compound eye • Head • Prothorax • Mesothorax • Front leg • Scutellum • Hind leg • Metathorax • Middle leg

CRICKET

ANT

FLY

EARWIG

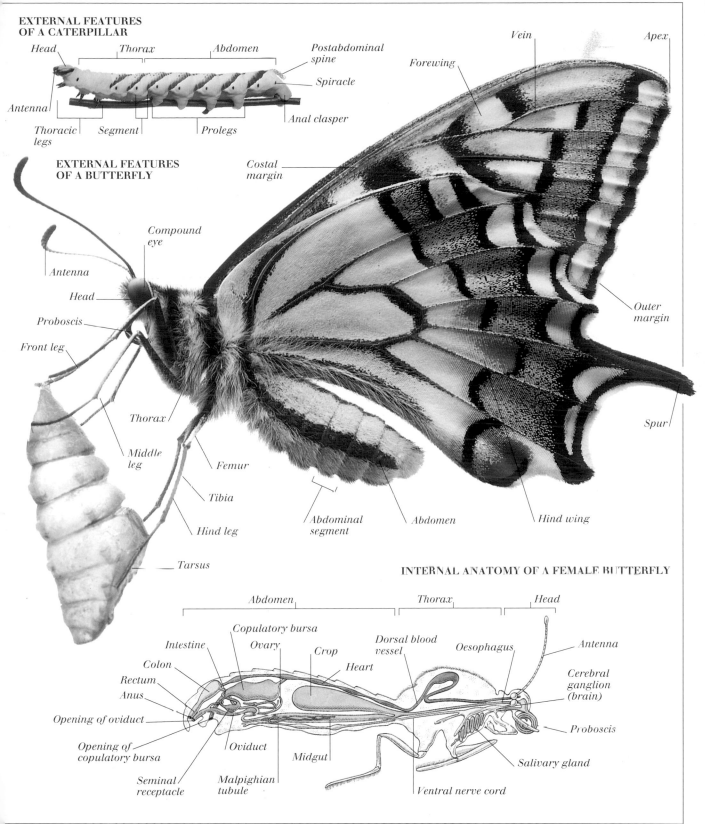

EXTERNAL FEATURES OF A CATERPILLAR

Head
Thorax
Abdomen
Postabdominal spine
Spiracle
Antenna
Thoracic legs
Segment
Prolegs
Anal clasper

EXTERNAL FEATURES OF A BUTTERFLY

Vein
Apex
Forewing
Costal margin
Outer margin
Spur
Compound eye
Antenna
Head
Proboscis
Front leg
Thorax
Middle leg
Femur
Tibia
Hind leg
Abdominal segment
Abdomen
Hind wing
Tarsus

INTERNAL ANATOMY OF A FEMALE BUTTERFLY

Abdomen
Thorax
Head
Copulatory bursa
Dorsal blood vessel
Oesophagus
Antenna
Intestine
Ovary
Crop
Heart
Cerebral ganglion (brain)
Colon
Rectum
Anus
Opening of oviduct
Opening of copulatory bursa
Seminal receptacle
Malpighian tubule
Oviduct
Midgut
Salivary gland
Ventral nerve cord
Proboscis

Arachnids

THE CLASS ARACHNIDA INCLUDES SPIDERS (order Araneae) and scorpions (order Scorpiones). The class is part of the phylum Arthropoda, which also includes insects and crustaceans.

Spiders and scorpions are characterized by having four pairs of walking legs; a pair of pincer-like mouthparts called chelicerae; another pair of frontal appendages called pedipalps, which are sensory in spiders but used for grasping in scorpions; and a body divided into two sections (a combined head and thorax called a cephalothorax, or prosoma, and an abdomen, or opisthosoma). Unlike other arthropods, spiders and scorpions lack antennae. Spiders and scorpions are carnivorous. Spiders poison prey by biting with the fanged chelicerae, scorpions by stinging with the end of the metasoma (tail).

MEXICAN TRUE RED-LEGGED TARANTULA
(Euathlus emilia)

INTERNAL ANATOMY OF A FEMALE SPIDER

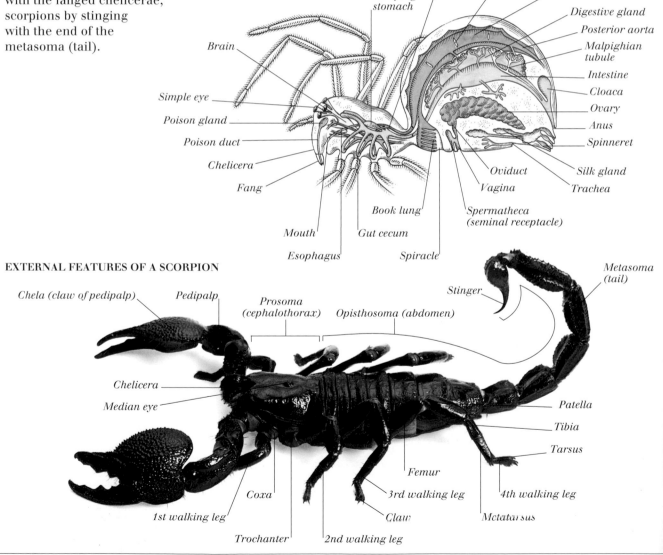

EXTERNAL FEATURES OF A SCORPION

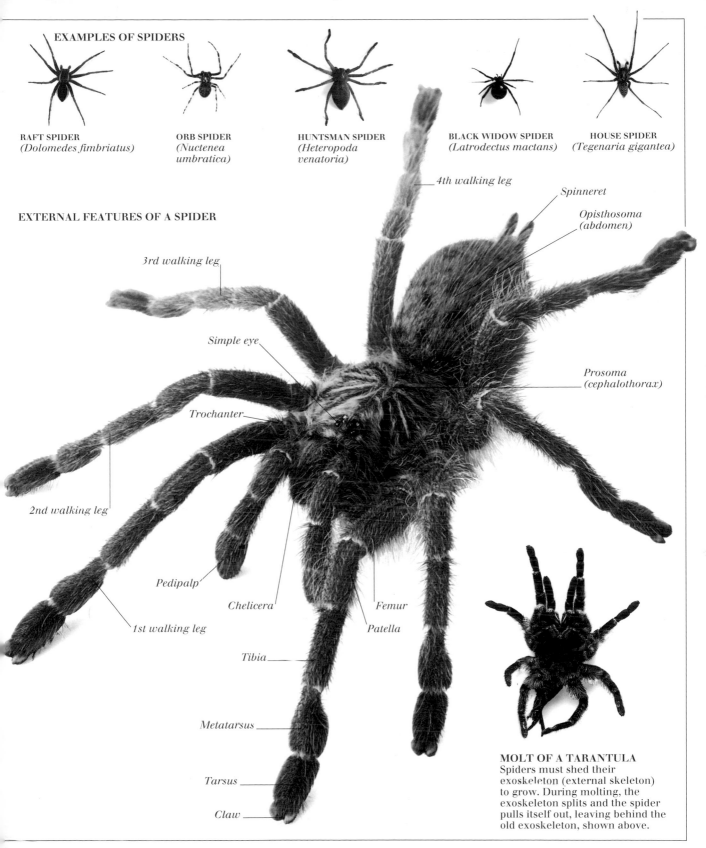

EXAMPLES OF SPIDERS

RAFT SPIDER
(Dolomedes fimbriatus)

ORB SPIDER
(Nuctenea umbratica)

HUNTSMAN SPIDER
(Heteropoda venatoria)

BLACK WIDOW SPIDER
(Latrodectus mactans)

HOUSE SPIDER
(Tegenaria gigantea)

EXTERNAL FEATURES OF A SPIDER

4th walking leg

Spinneret

Opisthosoma (abdomen)

3rd walking leg

Simple eye

Prosoma (cephalothorax)

Trochanter

2nd walking leg

Pedipalp

Chelicera

Femur

Patella

1st walking leg

Tibia

Metatarsus

Tarsus

Claw

MOLT OF A TARANTULA
Spiders must shed their exoskeleton (external skeleton) to grow. During molting, the exoskeleton splits and the spider pulls itself out, leaving behind the old exoskeleton, shown above.

Crustaceans

THE SUBPHYLUM CRUSTACEA is one of the largest groups in the phylum Arthropoda. The subphylum is divided into several classes, the most important of which are Malacostraca and Cirripedia. The class Malacostraca includes crayfish, crabs, lobsters, and shrimps. Typical features of malacostracans include a body divided into two sections (a combined head and thorax called a cephalothorax, and an abdomen); an exoskeleton (external skeleton) with a large plate (carapace) covering the cephalothorax; stalked, compound eyes; and two pairs of antennae. The class Cirripedia includes barnacles, which, unlike other crustaceans, spend their adult lives attached to a surface, such as a rock. Other characteristics of cirripedes include an exoskeleton of overlapping calcareous plates; a body consisting almost entirely of thorax (the abdomen and head are minute); and six pairs of thoracic appendages (cirri) used for filter feeding.

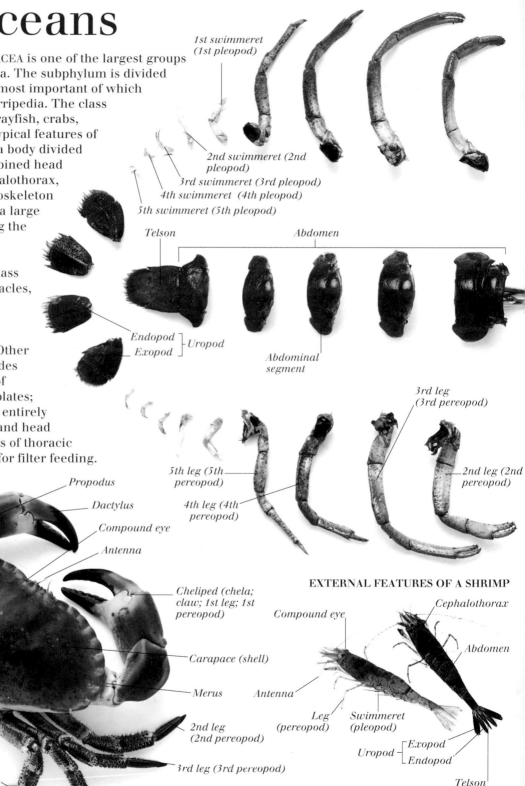

1st swimmeret (1st pleopod)

2nd swimmeret (2nd pleopod)

3rd swimmeret (3rd pleopod)

4th swimmeret (4th pleopod)

5th swimmeret (5th pleopod)

Telson

Abdomen

Endopod
Exopod
Uropod

Abdominal segment

3rd leg (3rd pereopod)

2nd leg (2nd pereopod)

4th leg (4th pereopod)

5th leg (5th pereopod)

EXTERNAL FEATURES OF A CRAB

Carpus

Propodus

Dactylus

Compound eye

Antenna

Cheliped (chela; claw; 1st leg; 1st pereopod)

Carapace (shell)

Merus

Abdomen

5th leg (5th pereopod)

2nd leg (2nd pereopod)

3rd leg (3rd pereopod)

4th leg (4th pereopod)

EXTERNAL FEATURES OF A SHRIMP

Compound eye

Cephalothorax

Abdomen

Antenna

Leg (pereopod)

Swimmeret (pleopod)

Uropod
Exopod
Endopod

Telson

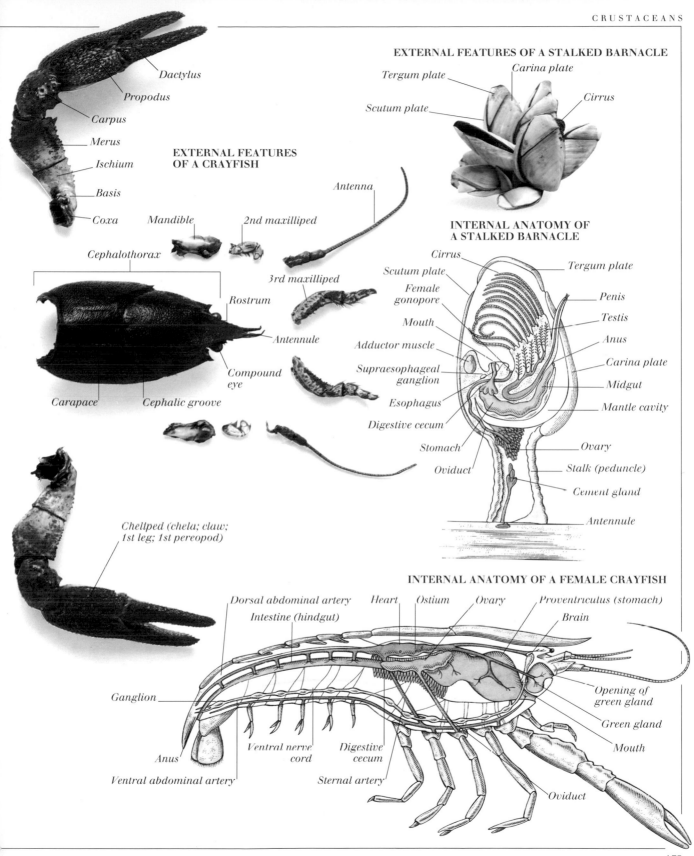

EXTERNAL FEATURES OF A STALKED BARNACLE

Tergum plate

Carina plate

Scutum plate

Cirrus

Dactylus

Propodus

Carpus

Merus

Ischium

Basis

Coxa

EXTERNAL FEATURES OF A CRAYFISH

Mandible

2nd maxilliped

Antenna

Cephalothorax

3rd maxilliped

Rostrum

Antennule

Compound eye

Carapace

Cephalic groove

INTERNAL ANATOMY OF A STALKED BARNACLE

Cirrus

Tergum plate

Scutum plate

Penis

Female gonopore

Testis

Mouth

Anus

Adductor muscle

Carina plate

Supraesophageal ganglion

Midgut

Esophagus

Mantle cavity

Digestive cecum

Stomach

Ovary

Oviduct

Stalk (peduncle)

Cement gland

Antennule

Chellped (chela; claw; 1st leg; 1st pereopod)

INTERNAL ANATOMY OF A FEMALE CRAYFISH

Dorsal abdominal artery

Heart

Ostium

Ovary

Proventriculus (stomach)

Intestine (hindgut)

Brain

Ganglion

Opening of green gland

Green gland

Mouth

Anus

Ventral nerve cord

Digestive cecum

Sternal artery

Oviduct

Ventral abdominal artery

Starfish and sea urchins

STARFISH, SEA URCHINS, AND THEIR relatives (including feather stars, brittle stars, basket stars, sea daisies, sea lilies, and sea cucumbers) make up the phylum Echinodermata. A unique feature of echinoderms is the water vascular system, which consists of a series of water-filled canals from which protrude thousands of tiny tube feet. The tube feet may be used for movement, feeding, or respiration. Other features include pentaradiate symmetry (that is, the body can be divided into five parts radiating from the center); no head; a diffuse, decentralized nervous system that lacks a brain; and no excretory organs. Typically, echinoderms also have an endoskeleton (internal skeleton) consisting of hard calcite ossicles embedded in the body wall and often bearing protruding spines or tubercles. The ossicles may fit together to form a test (as in sea urchins) or remain separate (as in sea cucumbers).

EXTERNAL FEATURES OF A STARFISH (UPPER, OR ABORAL, SURFACE)

Disk

Madreporite

Spine

Arm

INTERNAL ANATOMY OF A STARFISH

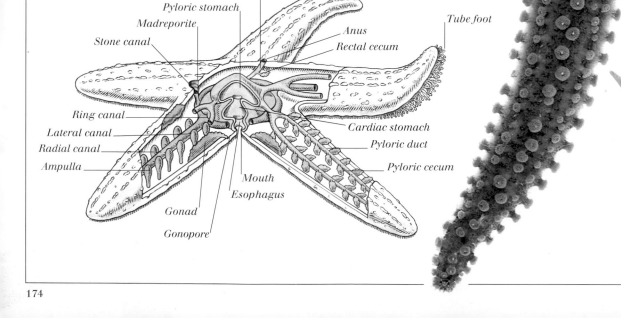

Rectum

Pyloric stomach

Madreporite

Stone canal

Anus

Rectal cecum

Tube foot

Ring canal

Lateral canal

Radial canal

Ampulla

Cardiac stomach

Pyloric duct

Pyloric cecum

Mouth

Esophagus

Gonad

Gonopore

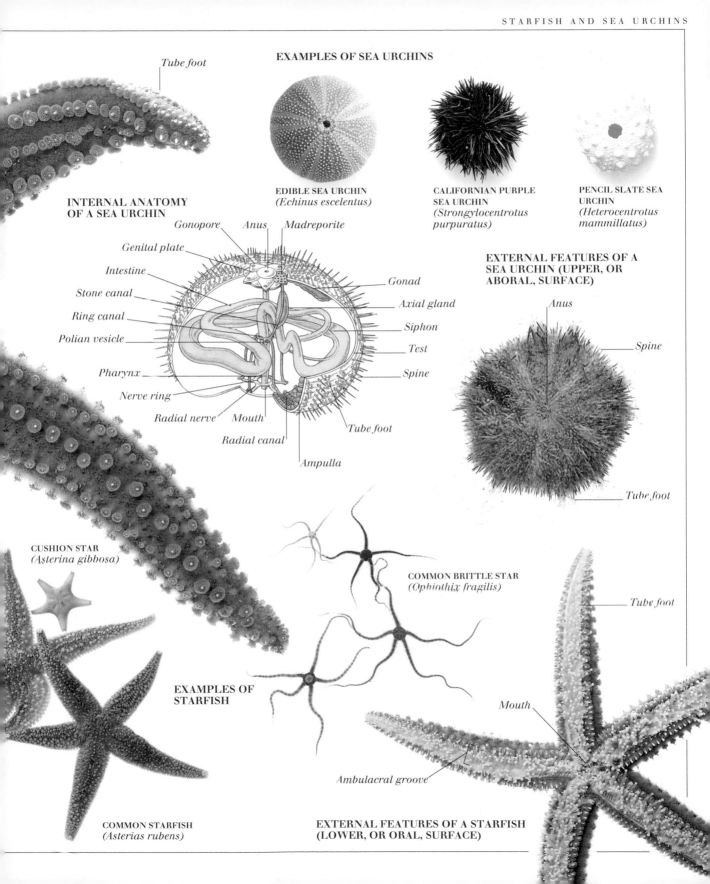

Tube foot

EXAMPLES OF SEA URCHINS

EDIBLE SEA URCHIN
(*Echinus escelentus*)

CALIFORNIAN PURPLE SEA URCHIN
(*Strongylocentrotus purpuratus*)

PENCIL SLATE SEA URCHIN
(*Heterocentrotus mammillatus*)

INTERNAL ANATOMY OF A SEA URCHIN

Gonopore

Anus

Madreporite

Genital plate

Intestine

Stone canal

Ring canal

Polian vesicle

Pharynx

Nerve ring

Radial nerve

Mouth

Radial canal

Ampulla

Gonad

Axial gland

Siphon

Test

Spine

Tube foot

EXTERNAL FEATURES OF A SEA URCHIN (UPPER, OR ABORAL, SURFACE)

Anus

Spine

Tube foot

CUSHION STAR
(*Asterina gibbosa*)

COMMON BRITTLE STAR
(*Ophiothix fragilis*)

Tube foot

EXAMPLES OF STARFISH

Mouth

Ambulacral groove

COMMON STARFISH
(*Asterias rubens*)

EXTERNAL FEATURES OF A STARFISH (LOWER, OR ORAL, SURFACE)

Mollusks

THE PHYLUM MOLLUSCA (MOLLUSKS) is a large group of animals that includes octopuses, snails, and scallops. Octopuses and their relatives —including squid and cuttlefish—form the class Cephalopoda. Cephalopods typically have a head with a radula (a file-like feeding organ) and beak; a well-developed nervous system; sucker-bearing tentacles; a muscular mantle (part of the body wall) that can expel water through the siphon, enabling movement by jet propulsion; and a small shell or no shell. Snails and their relatives—including slugs, limpets, and abalones—make up the class Gastropoda. Gastropods typically have a coiled external shell, although some, such as slugs, have a small internal shell or no shell; a flat foot; and a head with tentacles and a radula. Scallops and their relatives—including clams, mussels, and oysters—make up the class Bivalvia (also called Pelecypoda). Features of bivalves include a shell with two halves (valves); large gills that are used for breathing and filter feeding; and no radula.

EXTERNAL FEATURES OF A SCALLOP

Upper valve (shell) Mantle Ocellus (eye)

Lower valve (shell) Shell rib Sensory tentacle

Sensory tentacle Ventral margin of shell Shell rib

Anterior wing of shell

Umbo Posterior wing of shell

Dorsal margin of shell

INTERNAL ANATOMY OF AN OCTOPUS

Cephalic vein Poison gland

Skull Crop Digestive cecum

Brain Dorsal mantle cavity

Siphon (funnel) Mantle muscles

Buccal mass Shell rudiment

Beak Stomach

Cecum

Gonad

Systemic heart

Kidney

Branchial heart

Ctenidium

Anus Ink sac

Muscular septum

Sucker

Tentacle

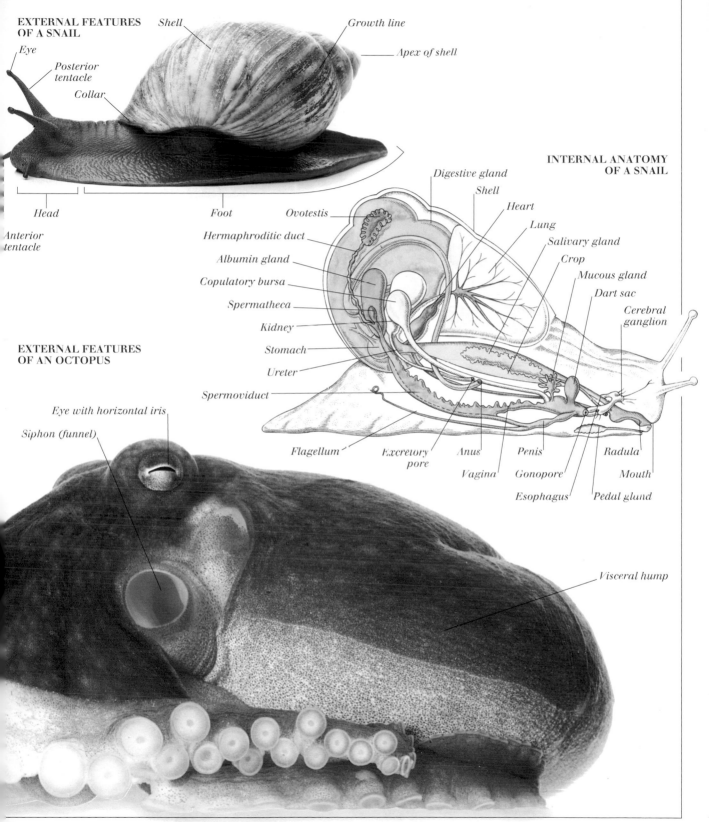

EXTERNAL FEATURES OF A SNAIL

Eye

Posterior tentacle

Collar

Shell

Growth line

Apex of shell

Head

Foot

Anterior tentacle

INTERNAL ANATOMY OF A SNAIL

Digestive gland

Ovotestis

Shell

Heart

Lung

Salivary gland

Crop

Mucous gland

Dart sac

Cerebral ganglion

Hermaphroditic duct

Albumin gland

Copulatory bursa

Spermatheca

Kidney

Stomach

Ureter

Spermoviduct

Flagellum

Excretory pore

Anus

Penis

Radula

Vagina

Gonopore

Mouth

Esophagus

Pedal glund

EXTERNAL FEATURES OF AN OCTOPUS

Eye with horizontal iris

Siphon (funnel)

Visceral hump

Sharks and jawless fish

SHARKS, DOGFISH (WHICH ARE actually small sharks), skates, and rays belong to a class of fish called Chondrichthyes, which is a division of the superclass Gnathostomata (meaning "jawed mouths"). Also sometimes known as elasmobranchs, sharks and their relatives have a skeleton made of cartilage (hence their common name, cartilaginous fish), a characteristic that distinguishes them from bony fish (see pp. 180-181). Other important features of cartilaginous fish are extremely tough, tooth-like scales, and lack of a swim bladder. Jawless fish—lampreys and hagfish—are primitive, eel-like fish that make up the order Cyclostomata (meaning "round mouths"), a division of the superclass Agnatha (meaning "without jaws"). In addition to their characteristic round, sucker-like mouths and lack of jaws, cyclostomes also have smooth, slimy skin without scales, and unpaired fins.

SHARKS' JAWS

Jaws of an adult tiger shark

Jaws of a young tiger shark

EXTERNAL FEATURES OF A DOGFISH

Snout

Eye

Gill slit

Pectoral fin

FEATURES OF A LAMPREY'S HEAD

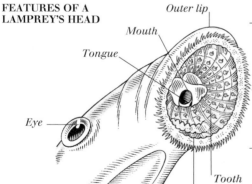

Outer lip

Mouth

Tongue

Sucker

Eye

Tooth

Fringed inner lip

EXTERNAL FEATURES OF A LAMPREY

Eye

Anterior dorsal fin

Posterior dorsal fin

Gill opening

Anal fin

Caudal fin

Sucker

EXAMPLES OF CARTILAGINOUS FISH

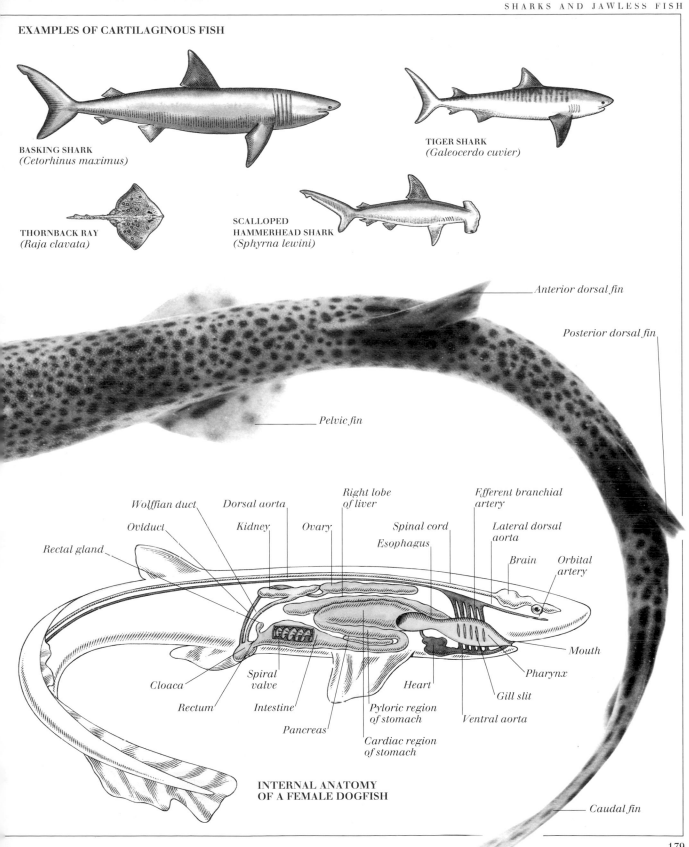

BASKING SHARK
(Cetorhinus maximus)

TIGER SHARK
(Galeocerdo cuvier)

THORNBACK RAY
(Raja clavata)

**SCALLOPED
HAMMERHEAD SHARK**
(Sphyrna lewini)

Anterior dorsal fin

Posterior dorsal fin

Pelvic fin

Right lobe
of liver

Efferent branchial
artery

Wolffian duct

Dorsal aorta

Ovary

Spinal cord

Lateral dorsal
aorta

Oviduct

Kidney

Esophagus

Brain

Orbital
artery

Rectal gland

Mouth

Cloaca

Spiral
valve

Heart

Pharynx

Rectum

Intestine

Gill slit

Pancreas

Ventral aorta

Pyloric region
of stomach

Cardiac region
of stomach

**INTERNAL ANATOMY
OF A FEMALE DOGFISH**

Caudal fin

Bony fish

BONY FISH, SUCH AS CARP, TROUT, SALMON, perch, and cod, are by far the best known and largest group of fish, with more than 20,000 species (over 95 percent of all known fish). As their name suggests, bony fish have skeletons made of bone, in contrast to the cartilaginous skeletons of sharks, jawless fish, and their relatives (see pp. 178-179). Other typical features of bony fish include a swim bladder, which functions as a variable-buoyancy organ, enabling a fish to remain effortlessly at whatever depth it is swimming; relatively thin, bone-like scales; a flap (called an operculum) covering the gills; and paired pelvic and pectoral fins. Scientifically, bony fish belong to the class Osteichthyes, which is a division of the superclass Gnathostomata (meaning "jawed mouths").

HOW FISH BREATHE

Fish "breathe" by extracting oxygen from water through their gills. Water is sucked in through the mouth; simultaneously, the opercula close to prevent the water from escaping. The mouth is then closed, and muscles in the walls of the mouth, pharynx, and opercular cavity contract to pump the water inside over the gills and out through the opercula. Some fish rely on swimming with their mouths open to keep water flowing over the gills.

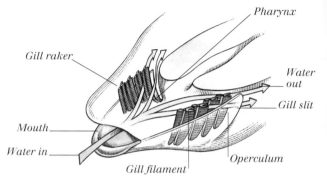

Pharynx

Gill raker

Water out

Gill slit

Mouth

Water in

Gill filament

Operculum

EXAMPLES OF BONY FISH

MANDARINFISH
(Synchiropus splendidus)

ANGLERFISH
(Caulophryne jordani)

OCEANIC SEAHORSE
(Hippocampus kuda)

LIONFISH
(Pterois volitans)

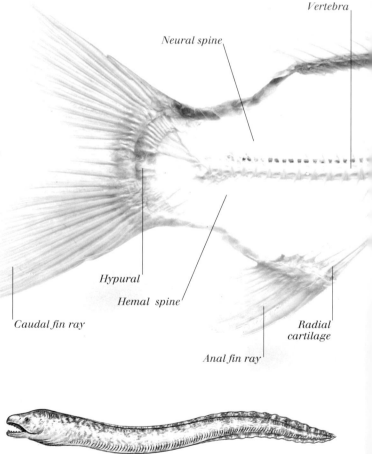

Vertebra

Neural spine

Hypural

Hemal spine

Caudal fin ray

Anal fin ray

Radial cartilage

STURGEON
(Acipenser sturio)

SNOWFLAKE MORAY EEL
(Echidna nebulosa)

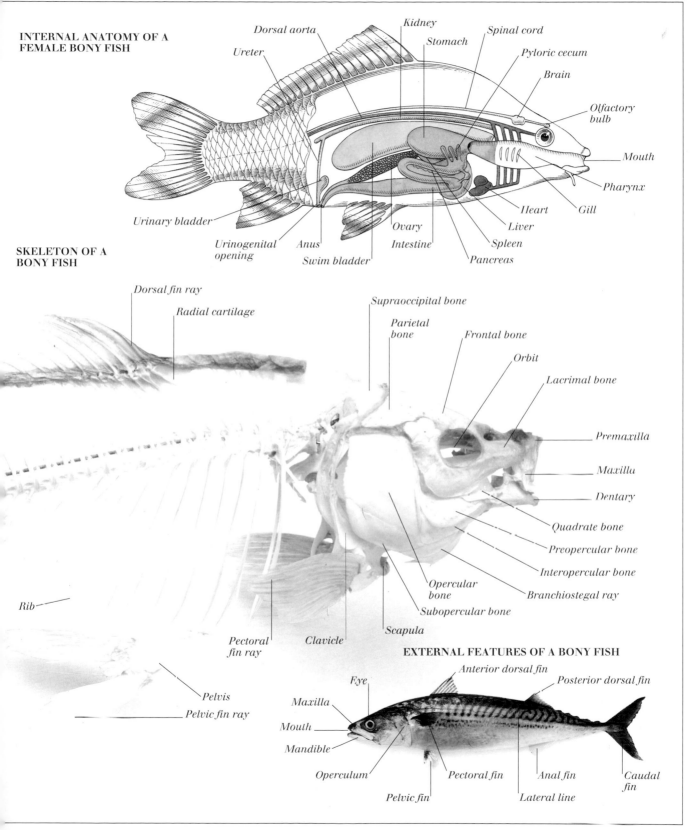

INTERNAL ANATOMY OF A FEMALE BONY FISH

Dorsal aorta

Kidney

Ureter

Stomach

Spinal cord

Pyloric cecum

Brain

Olfactory bulb

Mouth

Pharynx

Gill

Heart

Liver

Spleen

Pancreas

Intestine

Ovary

Swim bladder

Anus

Urinogenital opening

Urinary bladder

SKELETON OF A BONY FISH

Dorsal fin ray

Radial cartilage

Supraoccipital bone

Parietal bone

Frontal bone

Orbit

Lacrimal bone

Premaxilla

Maxilla

Dentary

Quadrate bone

Preopercular bone

Interopercular bone

Branchiostegal ray

Subopercular bone

Opercular bone

Scapula

Clavicle

Pectoral fin ray

Rib

Pelvis

Pelvic fin ray

EXTERNAL FEATURES OF A BONY FISH

Eye

Maxilla

Mouth

Mandible

Operculum

Pelvic fin

Pectoral fin

Anterior dorsal fin

Posterior dorsal fin

Anal fin

Lateral line

Caudal fin

Amphibians

THE CLASS AMPHIBIA INCLUDES FROGS and toads (which make up the order Anura) and newts and salamanders (which make up the order Urodela). Amphibians typically have moist, scaleless, hairless skin; lungs; and are cold-blooded. They also undergo complete metamorphosis, from eggs laid in water through various water-living larval stages (such as the tadpole stage) to land-living adults. Typical features of adult frogs and toads include a squat body with no tail; long, powerful hind legs; and large, often bulging, eyes. Adult newts and salamanders typically have a long body with a well-developed tail; and relatively short legs of equal size. However, newts and salamanders show considerable variation; for example, in some species the adults have minute legs, external gills rather than lungs, and spend their entire lives in water.

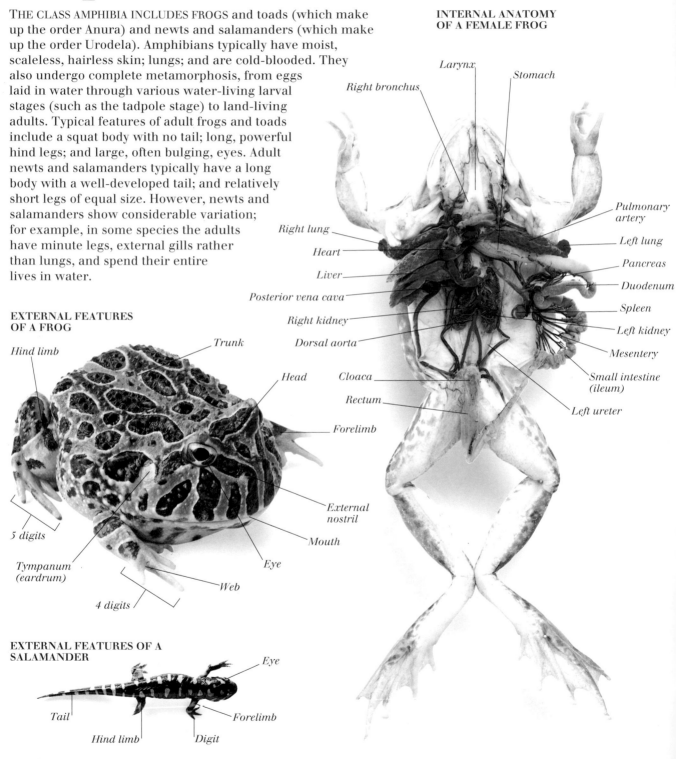

INTERNAL ANATOMY OF A FEMALE FROG

Larynx
Right bronchus
Stomach
Right lung
Heart
Liver
Posterior vena cava
Right kidney
Dorsal aorta
Cloaca
Rectum
Pulmonary artery
Left lung
Pancreas
Duodenum
Spleen
Left kidney
Mesentery
Small intestine (ileum)
Left ureter

EXTERNAL FEATURES OF A FROG

Hind limb
Trunk
Head
Forelimb
5 digits
Tympanum (eardrum)
External nostril
Mouth
Eye
Web
4 digits

EXTERNAL FEATURES OF A SALAMANDER

Eye
Tail
Forelimb
Hind limb
Digit

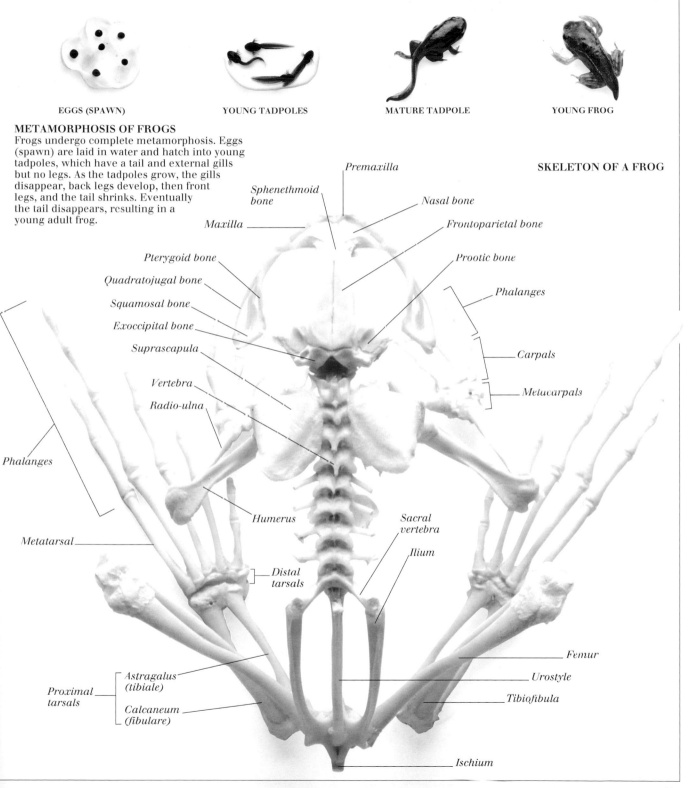

EGGS (SPAWN)

YOUNG TADPOLES

MATURE TADPOLE

YOUNG FROG

METAMORPHOSIS OF FROGS
Frogs undergo complete metamorphosis. Eggs (spawn) are laid in water and hatch into young tadpoles, which have a tail and external gills but no legs. As the tadpoles grow, the gills disappear, back legs develop, then front legs, and the tail shrinks. Eventually the tail disappears, resulting in a young adult frog.

SKELETON OF A FROG

Premaxilla

Sphenethmoid bone

Nasal bone

Maxilla

Frontoparietal bone

Pterygoid bone

Prootic bone

Quadratojugal bone

Phalanges

Squamosal bone

Exoccipital bone

Suprascapula

Carpals

Vertebra

Metacarpals

Radio-ulna

Phalanges

Humerus

Metatarsal

Sacral vertebra

Ilium

Distal tarsals

Femur

Astragalus (tibiale)

Urostyle

Proximal tarsals

Tibiofibula

Calcaneum (fibulare)

Ischium

Lizards and snakes

LIZARDS AND SNAKES BELONG to the order Squamata, a division of the class Reptilia. Characteristic reptilian features include scaly skin, lungs, and cold-bloodedness. Most reptiles lay leathery-shelled eggs, although some hatch the eggs inside their bodies and give birth to live young. Lizards belong to the suborder Lacertilia. Typically, they have long tails, and shed their skin in several pieces. Many lizards can regenerate a tail if it is lost; some can change color; and some are limbless. Snakes make up the suborder Ophidia (also called Serpentes). All snakes have long, limbless bodies; can dislocate their lower jaw to swallow large prey; and have eyelids that are joined together to form a single transparent covering over the front of the eye. Most snakes shed their skin in a single piece. Constrictor snakes kill their prey by squeezing; venomous snakes poison their prey.

EXAMPLES OF SNAKES

MEXICAN MOUNTAIN KING SNAKE (*Lampropeltis triangulum annulata*)

EXTERNAL FEATURES OF A LIZARD

BANDED MILK SNAKE (*Lampropeltis ruthveni*)

SKELETON OF A LIZARD

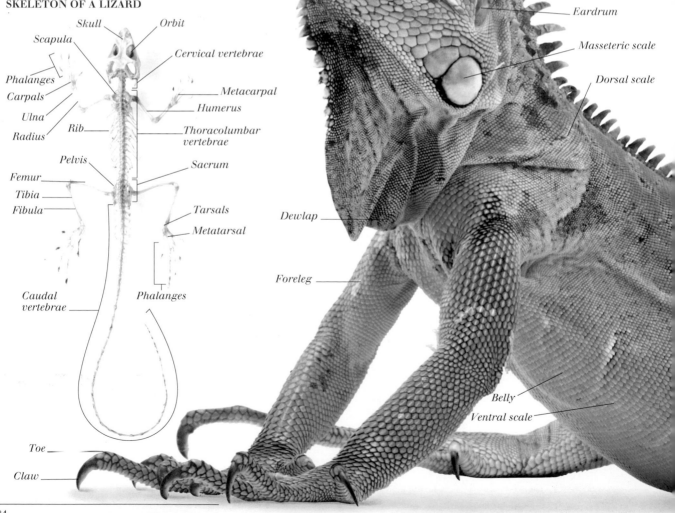

- Skull
- Orbit
- Scapula
- Cervical vertebrae
- Phalanges
- Carpals
- Metacarpal
- Ulna
- Humerus
- Radius
- Rib
- Thoracolumbar vertebrae
- Pelvis
- Sacrum
- Femur
- Tibia
- Fibula
- Tarsals
- Metatarsal
- Caudal vertebrae
- Phalanges
- Toe
- Claw

- Eye
- Mouth
- External nostril
- Crest
- Eardrum
- Masseteric scale
- Dorsal scale
- Dewlap
- Foreleg
- Belly
- Ventral scale

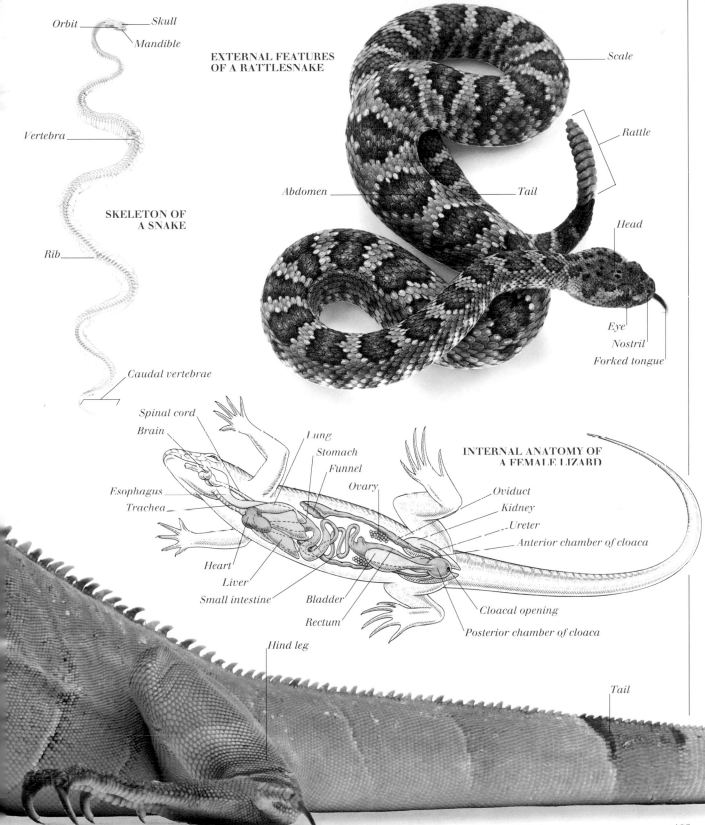

EXTERNAL FEATURES
OF A RATTLESNAKE

Orbit

Skull

Mandible

Scale

Vertebra

Rattle

SKELETON OF
A SNAKE

Abdomen

Tail

Head

Rib

Eye

Nostril

Forked tongue

Caudal vertebrae

Spinal cord

Brain

Lung

Stomach

Funnel

Ovary

INTERNAL ANATOMY OF
A FEMALE LIZARD

Esophagus

Oviduct

Trachea

Kidney

Ureter

Anterior chamber of cloaca

Heart

Liver

Small intestine

Bladder

Rectum

Cloacal opening

Posterior chamber of cloaca

Hind leg

Tail

185

Crocodilians and turtles

CROCODILIANS AND TURTLES BELONG to different orders in the class Reptilia. The order Crocodilia includes crocodiles, alligators, caimans, and gharials. Typically, crocodilians are carnivores (flesh-eaters), and have a long snout, sharp teeth for gripping prey, and hard, square scales. All crocodilians are adapted to living on land and in water: they have four strong legs for moving on land; a powerful tail for swimming; and their eyes and nostrils are high on the head so that they stay above water while the rest of the body is submerged. The order Chelonia includes marine turtles, freshwater turtles (terrapins), and land turtles (tortoises). Characteristically, chelonians have a short, broad body encased in a bony shell with an outer horny covering, into which the head and limbs can be withdrawn; and a horny beak instead of teeth.

SKULLS OF CROCODILIANS

GHARIAL
(Gavialis gangeticus)

NILE CROCODILE
(Crocodylus niloticus)

MISSISSIPPI ALLIGATOR
(Alligator mississippiensis)

SKELETON OF A CROCODILE

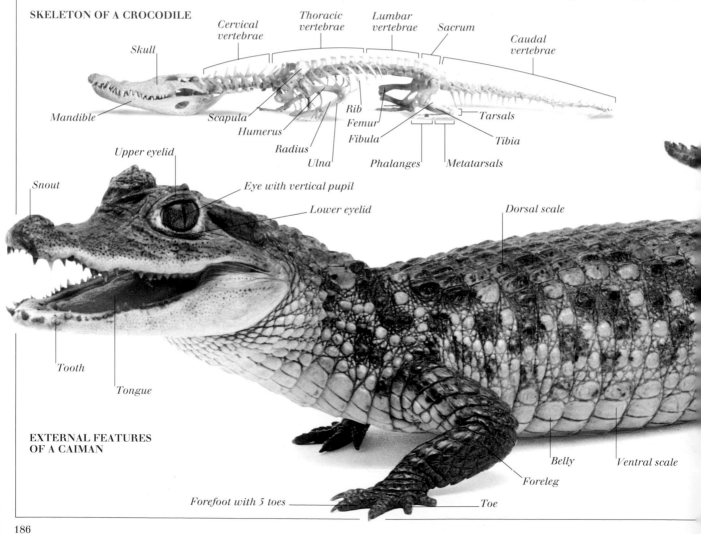

Cervical vertebrae

Thoracic vertebrae

Lumbar vertebrae

Sacrum

Caudal vertebrae

Skull

Mandible

Scapula

Humerus

Radius

Ulna

Rib

Femur

Fibula

Phalanges

Tarsals

Tibia

Metatarsals

Upper eyelid

Eye with vertical pupil

Lower eyelid

Snout

Tooth

Tongue

Dorsal scale

EXTERNAL FEATURES OF A CAIMAN

Belly

Ventral scale

Foreleg

Forefoot with 5 toes

Toe

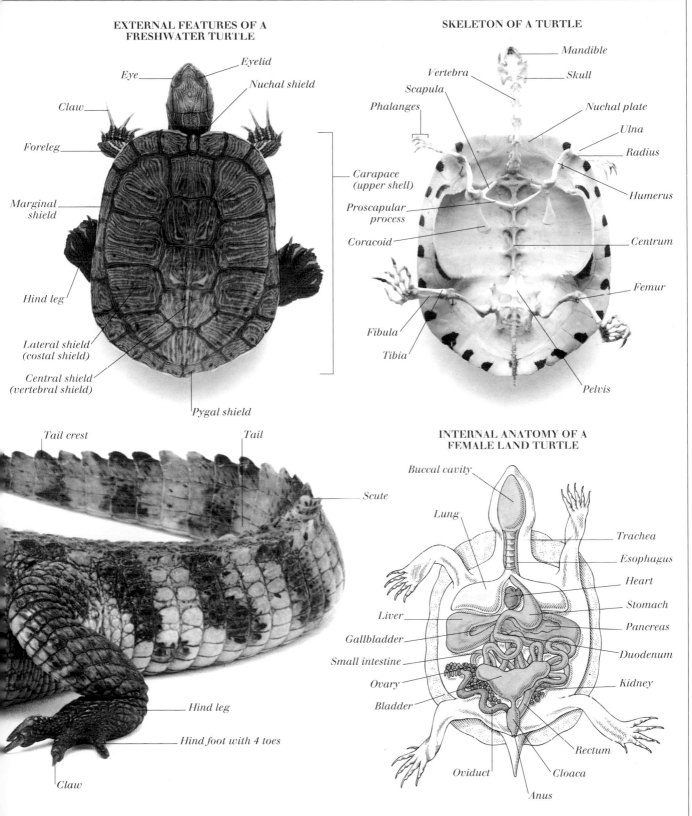

**EXTERNAL FEATURES OF A
FRESHWATER TURTLE**

Eyelid

Eye

Nuchal shield

Claw

Foreleg

Marginal
shield

Hind leg

Lateral shield
(costal shield)

Central shield
(vertebral shield)

Pygal shield

Carapace
(upper shell)

SKELETON OF A TURTLE

Mandible

Vertebra

Skull

Scapula

Phalanges

Nuchal plate

Ulna

Radius

Humerus

Proscapular
process

Coracoid

Centrum

Femur

Fibula

Tibia

Pelvis

Tail crest

Tail

Scute

**INTERNAL ANATOMY OF A
FEMALE LAND TURTLE**

Buccal cavity

Lung

Trachea

Esophagus

Heart

Stomach

Pancreas

Liver

Duodenum

Gallbladder

Small intestine

Kidney

Ovary

Bladder

Hind leg

Hind foot with 4 toes

Rectum

Claw

Oviduct

Cloaca

Anus

187

Birds 1

BIRDS MAKE UP THE CLASS AVES. There are more than 9,000 species, almost all of which can fly (the only flightless birds are penguins, ostriches, rheas, cassowaries, and kiwis). The ability to fly is reflected in the typical bird features: forelimbs modified as wings, a streamlined body, and hollow bones to reduce weight. All birds lay hard-shelled eggs, which the parents incubate. Birds' beaks and feet vary according to diet and way of life. Beaks range from general purpose types suitable for a mixed diet (those of thrushes, for example), to types specialized for particular foods (such as the large, curved, sieving beaks of flamingos). Feet range from the webbed "paddles" of ducks, to the talons of birds of prey. Plumage also varies widely, and in many species the male is brightly colored for courtship display whereas the female is drab.

EXTERNAL FEATURES OF A BIRD

Forehead

Eye

Crown

Nostril

Nape

Upper mandible

Beak

Lower mandible

Chin

Throat

EXAMPLES OF BIRDS

MALE TUFTED DUCK
(*Aythya fuligula*)

WHITE STORK
(*Ciconia ciconia*)

MALE OSTRICH
(*Struthio camelus*)

Minor coverts

Lesser wing coverts

Median wing coverts

Greater wing coverts
(major coverts)

Secondary flight feathers
(secondary remiges)

Primary flight feathers
(primary remiges)

Breast

Belly

Flank

Thigh

Under tail
coverts

Tarsus

Tail feathers (retrices)

Claw

Toe

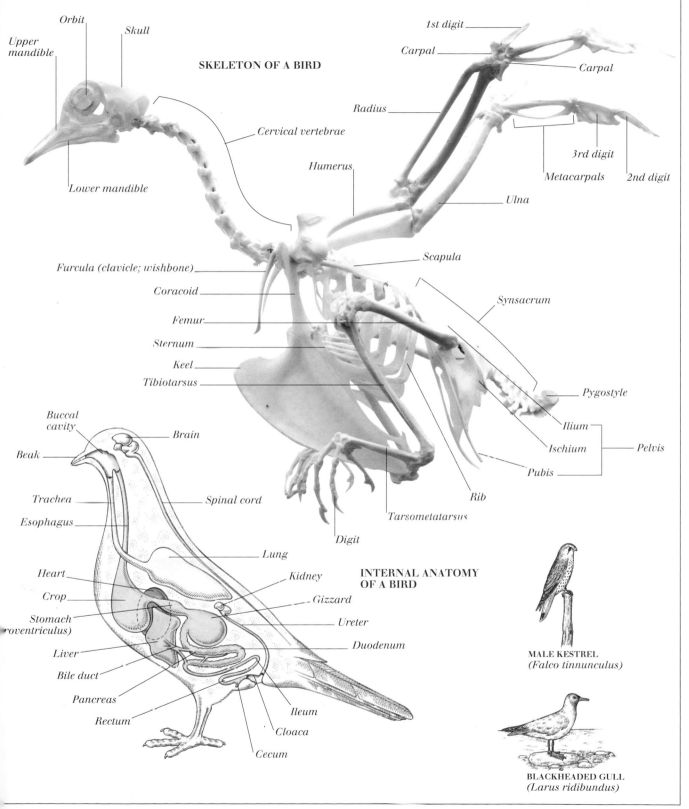

SKELETON OF A BIRD

Orbit

Skull

Upper mandible

1st digit

Carpal

Carpal

Radius

3rd digit

Metacarpals

2nd digit

Cervical vertebrae

Humerus

Ulna

Lower mandible

Scapula

Furcula (clavicle; wishbone)

Synsacrum

Coracoid

Femur

Sternum

Keel

Tibiotarsus

Pygostyle

Ilium

Ischium

Pelvis

Pubis

Rib

Buccal cavity

Brain

Beak

Spinal cord

Trachea

Esophagus

Tarsometatarsus

Digit

Lung

INTERNAL ANATOMY OF A BIRD

Heart

Kidney

Crop

Gizzard

Stomach (proventriculus)

Ureter

Liver

Duodenum

Bile duct

Pancreas

Ileum

Rectum

Cloaca

Cecum

MALE KESTREL
(Falco tinnunculus)

BLACKHEADED GULL
(Larus ridibundus)

189

Birds 2

EXAMPLES OF BIRDS' FEET

KITTIWAKE
(Rissa tridactyla)
The webbed feet are
adapted for paddling
through water.

LITTLE GREBE
(Tachybaptus ruficollis)
The lobed, flattened feet
are adapted for swimming
underwater.

TAWNY OWL
(Strix aluco)
The clawed feet are adapted
for gripping prey.

EXAMPLES OF BIRDS' BEAKS

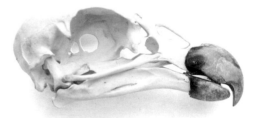

KING VULTURE
(Sarcorhamphus papa)
The hooked beak is adapted
for pulling apart flesh.

GREATER FLAMINGO
(Phoenicopterus ruber)
In the living bird, the large,
curved beak contains a
cartilaginous "sieve" for
filtering food particles
from water.

MAVIS, OR MISTLE THRUSH
(Turdus viscivorus)
The all-purpose beak is suitable
for gathering a wide range of
animal and plant foods.

BLUE-AND-YELLOW MACAW
(Ara ararauna)
The broad, powerful, hooked beak
is adapted for crushing seeds and
eating fruit.

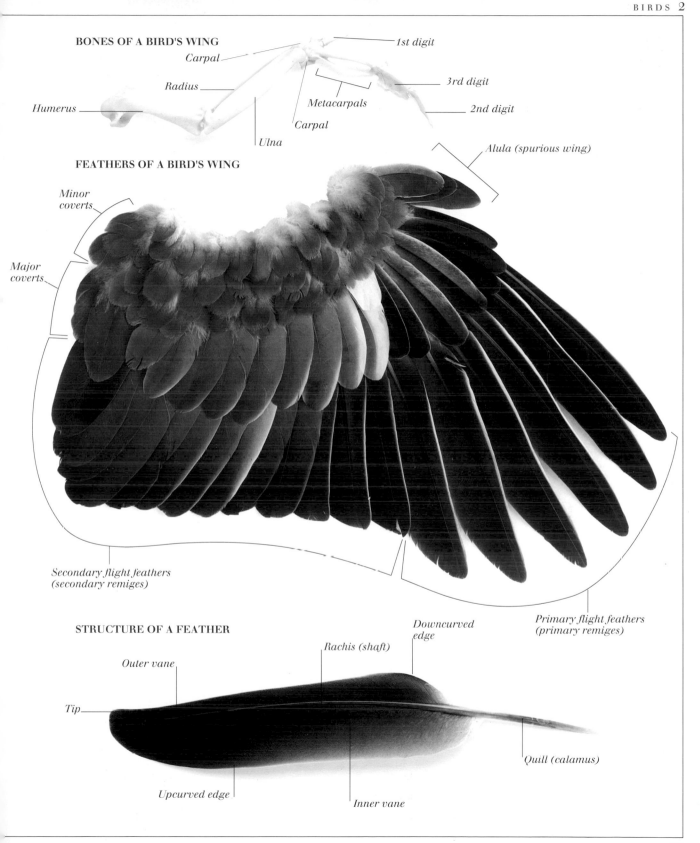

BONES OF A BIRD'S WING

Carpal

1st digit

Radius

Humerus

Metacarpals

3rd digit

Carpal

2nd digit

Ulna

Alula (spurious wing)

FEATHERS OF A BIRD'S WING

Minor coverts

Major coverts

Secondary flight feathers (secondary remiges)

Downcurved edge

Primary flight feathers (primary remiges)

STRUCTURE OF A FEATHER

Outer vane

Rachis (shaft)

Tip

Upcurved edge

Inner vane

Quill (calamus)

Eggs

AN EGG IS A SINGLE CELL, produced by the female, with the capacity to develop into a new individual. Development may take place inside the mother's body (as in most mammals) or outside, in which case the egg has a protective covering such as a shell. Egg yolk nourishes the growing young. Eggs developing inside the mother generally have little yolk, because the young are nourished from her body. Eggs developing outside may also have little yolk if they are produced by animals whose young go through a larval stage (such as a caterpillar) that feeds itself while developing into the adult form. The shelled eggs of birds and reptiles contain enough yolk to sustain the young until it hatches into a juvenile version of the adult.

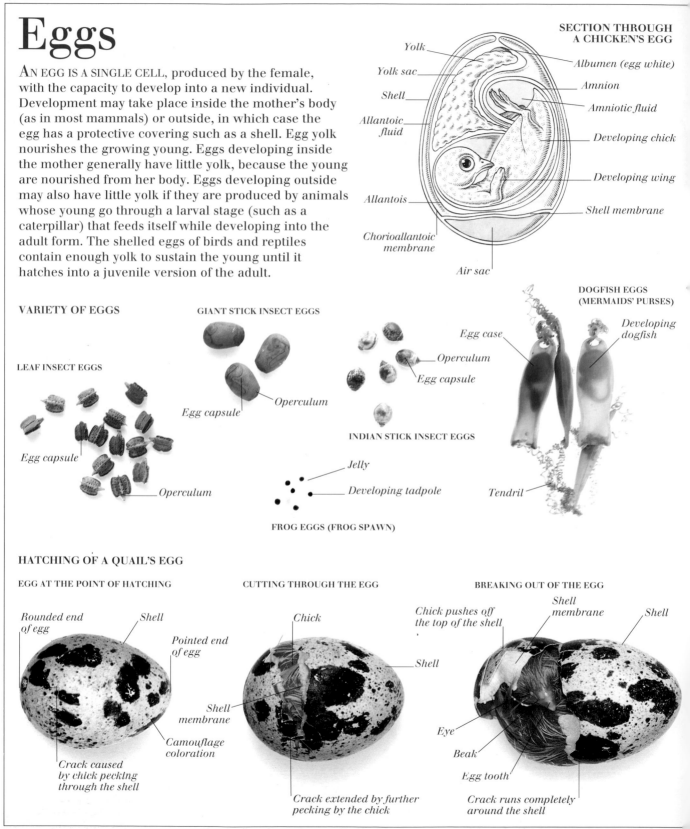

SECTION THROUGH A CHICKEN'S EGG

Yolk
Yolk sac
Shell
Allantoic fluid
Allantois
Chorioallantoic membrane
Air sac
Albumen (egg white)
Amnion
Amniotic fluid
Developing chick
Developing wing
Shell membrane

VARIETY OF EGGS

GIANT STICK INSECT EGGS

LEAF INSECT EGGS

Egg capsule
Operculum

Egg capsule
Operculum

Operculum
Egg capsule

INDIAN STICK INSECT EGGS

Jelly
Developing tadpole

FROG EGGS (FROG SPAWN)

DOGFISH EGGS (MERMAIDS' PURSES)

Egg case
Developing dogfish
Tendril

HATCHING OF A QUAIL'S EGG

EGG AT THE POINT OF HATCHING

Rounded end of egg
Shell
Pointed end of egg
Shell membrane
Camouflage coloration
Crack caused by chick pecking through the shell

CUTTING THROUGH THE EGG

Chick
Shell
Crack extended by further pecking by the chick

BREAKING OUT OF THE EGG

Chick pushes off the top of the shell
Shell membrane
Shell
Eye
Beak
Egg tooth
Crack runs completely around the shell

EXAMPLES OF BIRDS' EGGS

BEE HUMMINGBIRD
(Calypte helenae)

GREATER BLACKBACKED GULL
(Larus marinus)

BALTIMORE ORIOLE
(Icterus galbula)

WILLOW GROUSE
(Lagopus lagopus)

COMMON TERN
(Sterna hirundo)

CARRION CROW
(Corvus corone)

CHAFFINCH
(Fringilla coelebs)

OSTRICH
(Struthio camelus)

EMERGING FROM THE EGG

Eye

Beak

Egg tooth

Chick heaves itself
out of the egg

Tympanum (eardrum)

Shell

Wet down

Remains of egg membranes
(amnion and allantois)

THE NEWLY HATCHED CHICK

Eye

Beak

Egg tooth

Nostril

Tympanum
(eardrum)

Chick is dry
about an hour
after hatching

Dry down

Toe

Claw

Leg

Eggshell

193

Carnivores

THE MAMMALIAN ORDER CARNIVORA includes cats, dogs, bears, raccoons, pandas, weasels, badgers, skunks, otters, civets, mongooses, and hyenas. The order's name is derived from the fact that most of its members are carnivores (flesh-eaters). Typical carnivore features therefore reflect a hunting lifestyle: speed and agility; sharp claws and well-developed canine teeth for holding and killing prey; carnassial teeth (cheek teeth) for cutting flesh; and forward-facing eyes for good distance judgment. However, some members of the order—bears, badgers, and foxes, for example—have a more mixed diet, and a few are entirely herbivorous (plant-eating), notably pandas. Such animals have no carnassial teeth and tend to be slower-moving than pure flesh-eaters.

EXTERNAL FEATURES OF A MALE LION

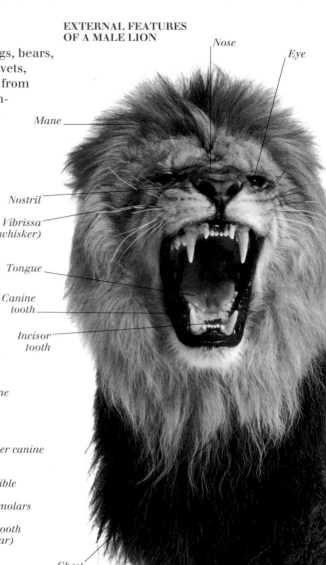

Nose

Eye

Mane

Nostril

Vibrissa (whisker)

Tongue

Canine tooth

Incisor tooth

Chest

Elbow

Lower arm

Toe

SKULL OF A LION

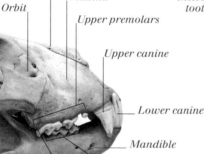

Zygomatic arch

Coronoid process

Orbit

Nasal bone

Maxilla

Upper premolars

Sagittal crest

Upper canine

Lower canine

Mandible

Lower premolars

Occipital condyle

Condyle

Upper carnassial tooth (4th upper premolar)

Tympanic bulla

Angular process

SKULL OF A BEAR

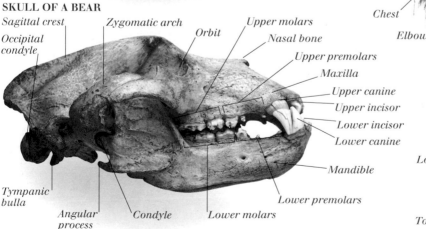

Sagittal crest

Zygomatic arch

Orbit

Upper molars

Occipital condyle

Nasal bone

Upper premolars

Maxilla

Upper canine

Upper incisor

Lower incisor

Lower canine

Mandible

Tympanic bulla

Angular process

Condyle

Lower molars

Lower premolars

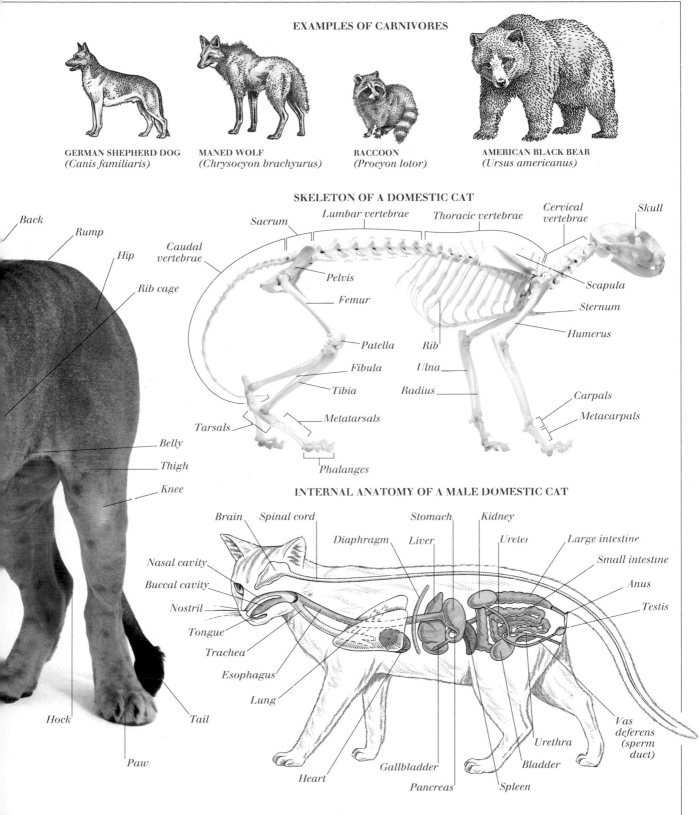

EXAMPLES OF CARNIVORES

GERMAN SHEPHERD DOG
(*Canis familiaris*)

MANED WOLF
(*Chrysocyon brachyurus*)

RACCOON
(*Procyon lotor*)

AMERICAN BLACK BEAR
(*Ursus americanus*)

SKELETON OF A DOMESTIC CAT

Back

Rump

Hip

Rib cage

Sacrum

Lumbar vertebrae

Thoracic vertebrae

Cervical vertebrae

Skull

Caudal vertebrae

Pelvis

Scapula

Femur

Sternum

Humerus

Patella

Rib

Belly

Fibula

Ulna

Thigh

Tibia

Radius

Carpals

Knee

Tarsals

Metatarsals

Metacarpals

Phalanges

INTERNAL ANATOMY OF A MALE DOMESTIC CAT

Brain

Spinal cord

Stomach

Kidney

Diaphragm

Liver

Ureter

Large intestine

Nasal cavity

Small intestine

Buccal cavity

Anus

Nostril

Testis

Tongue

Trachea

Esophagus

Lung

Vas deferens (sperm duct)

Hock

Tail

Urethra

Paw

Heart

Gallbladder

Pancreas

Spleen

Bladder

Rabbits and rodents

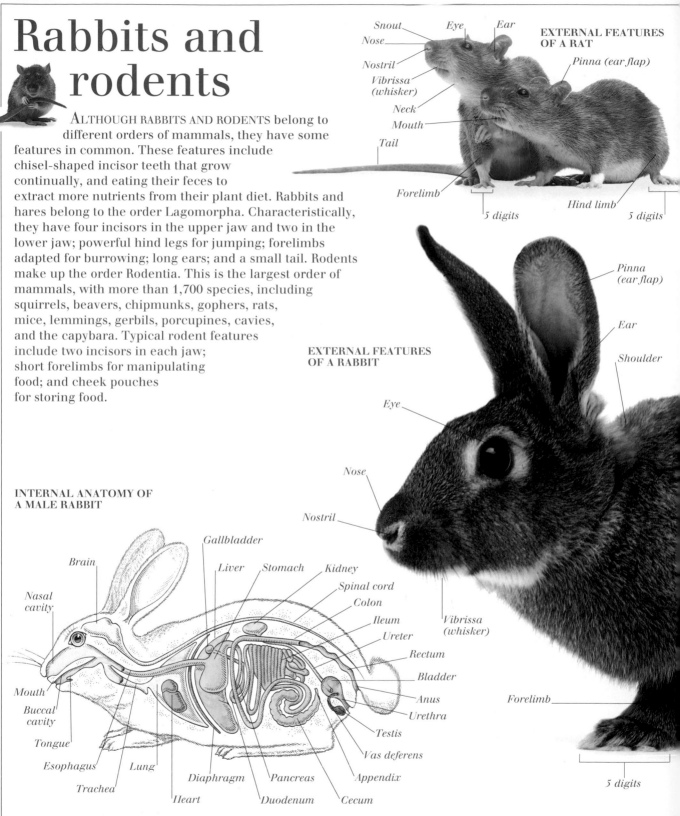

ALTHOUGH RABBITS AND RODENTS belong to different orders of mammals, they have some features in common. These features include chisel-shaped incisor teeth that grow continually, and eating their feces to extract more nutrients from their plant diet. Rabbits and hares belong to the order Lagomorpha. Characteristically, they have four incisors in the upper jaw and two in the lower jaw; powerful hind legs for jumping; forelimbs adapted for burrowing; long ears; and a small tail. Rodents make up the order Rodentia. This is the largest order of mammals, with more than 1,700 species, including squirrels, beavers, chipmunks, gophers, rats, mice, lemmings, gerbils, porcupines, cavies, and the capybara. Typical rodent features include two incisors in each jaw; short forelimbs for manipulating food; and cheek pouches for storing food.

EXTERNAL FEATURES OF A RAT

Snout
Eye
Ear
Nose
Nostril
Pinna (ear flap)
Vibrissa (whisker)
Neck
Mouth
Tail
Forelimb
Hind limb
5 digits
5 digits

EXTERNAL FEATURES OF A RABBIT

Pinna (ear flap)
Ear
Shoulder
Eye
Nose
Nostril
Vibrissa (whisker)
Forelimb
5 digits

INTERNAL ANATOMY OF A MALE RABBIT

Brain
Gallbladder
Liver
Stomach
Kidney
Spinal cord
Colon
Ileum
Ureter
Rectum
Bladder
Anus
Urethra
Testis
Vas deferens
Appendix
Nasal cavity
Mouth
Buccal cavity
Tongue
Esophagus
Lung
Trachea
Diaphragm
Pancreas
Duodenum
Cecum
Heart

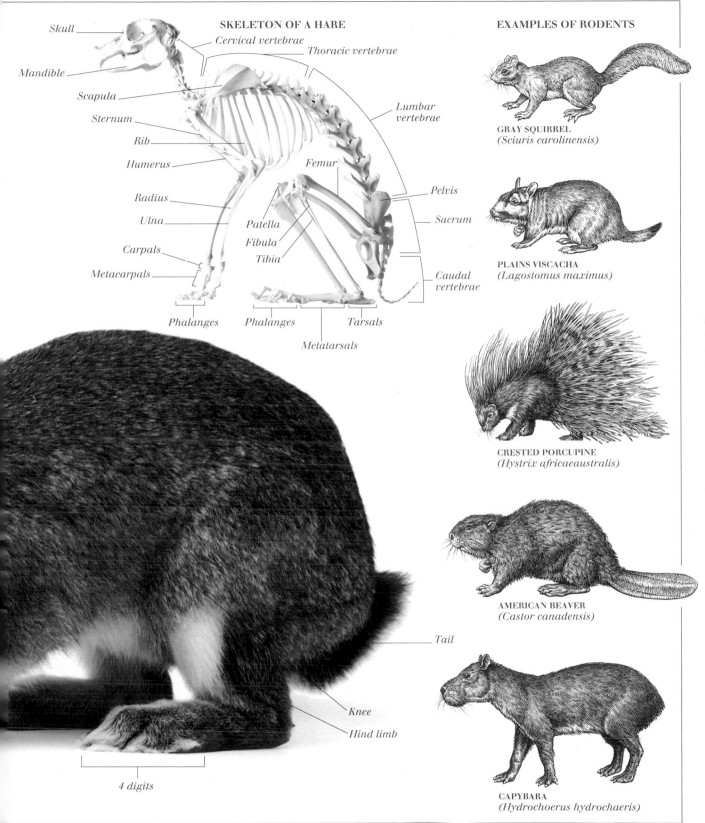

SKELETON OF A HARE

Skull

Mandible

Scapula

Sternum

Rib

Humerus

Radius

Ulna

Carpals

Metacarpals

Phalanges

Cervical vertebrae

Thoracic vertebrae

Lumbar vertebrae

Femur

Patella

Fibula

Tibia

Pelvis

Sacrum

Caudal vertebrae

Phalanges

Metatarsals

Tarsals

Tail

Knee

Hind limb

4 digits

EXAMPLES OF RODENTS

GRAY SQUIRREL
(*Sciuris carolinensis*)

PLAINS VISCACHA
(*Lagostomus maximus*)

CRESTED PORCUPINE
(*Hystrix africaeaustralis*)

AMERICAN BEAVER
(*Castor canadensis*)

CAPYBARA
(*Hydrochoerus hydrochaeris*)

Ungulates

UNGULATES IS A GENERAL TERM FOR a large, varied group of mammals that includes horses, cattle, and their relatives. The ungulates are divided into two orders on the basis of the number of toes. Members of the order Perissodactyla (odd-toed ungulates) have one or three toes. Perissodactyls include horses, asses, and zebras (all of which are one-toed), and rhinoceroses and tapirs (which are three-toed). Members of the order Artiodactyla (even-toed ungulates) have two or four toes. Most artiodactyls have two toes, which are typically encased in hooves to give the so-called cloven hoof. Two-toed, cloven-hoofed artiodactyls include cows and other cattle, sheep, goats, antelopes, deer, and giraffes. The other main two-toed artiodactyls are camels and llamas. Most two-toed artiodactyls are ruminants; that is, they have a four-chambered stomach and chew the cud. The principal four-toed artiodactyls are hogs and hippopotamuses.

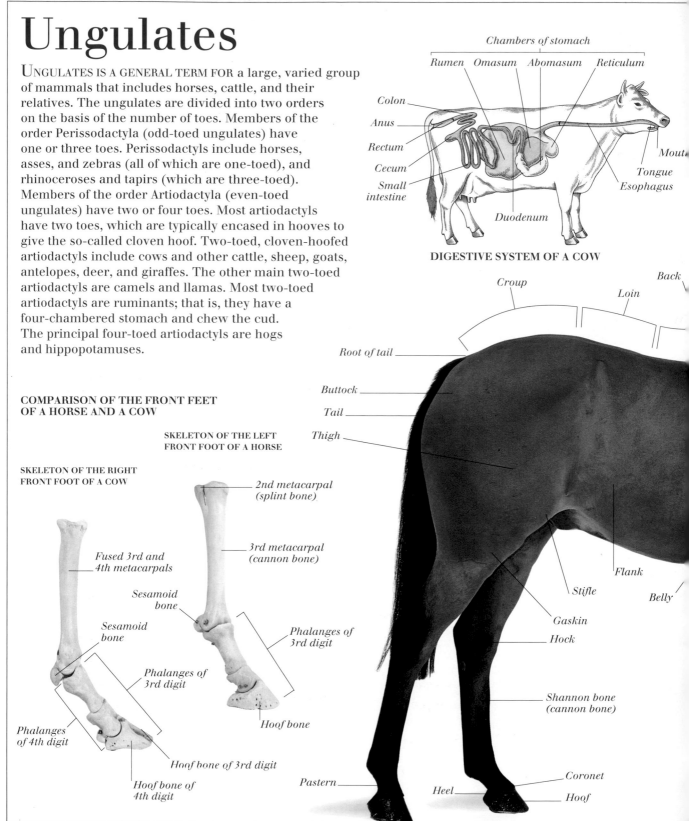

Chambers of stomach

Rumen Omasum Abomasum Reticulum

Colon

Anus

Rectum

Cecum

Small intestine

Duodenum

Mout

Tongue

Esophagus

DIGESTIVE SYSTEM OF A COW

Croup

Loin

Back

Root of tail

Buttock

Tail

Thigh

Flank

Belly

Stifle

Gaskin

Hock

Shannon bone (cannon bone)

Coronet

Pastern

Heel

Hoof

COMPARISON OF THE FRONT FEET OF A HORSE AND A COW

SKELETON OF THE LEFT FRONT FOOT OF A HORSE

SKELETON OF THE RIGHT FRONT FOOT OF A COW

2nd metacarpal (splint bone)

3rd metacarpal (cannon bone)

Fused 3rd and 4th metacarpals

Sesamoid bone

Sesamoid bone

Phalanges of 3rd digit

Phalanges of 3rd digit

Hoof bone

Phalanges of 4th digit

Hoof bone of 3rd digit

Hoof bone of 4th digit

EXAMPLES OF UNGULATES

MALE WAPITI
(Cervus elephas)
An even-toed ungulate
(order Artiodactyla)

BACTRIAN CAMEL
(Camelus ferus)
An even-toed ungulate
(order Artiodactyla)

GIRAFFE
(Giraffa camelopardalis)
An even-toed ungulate
(order Artiodactyla)

BLACK RHINOCEROS
(Diceros bicornis)
An odd-toed ungulate
(order Perissodactyla)

EXTERNAL FEATURES OF A HORSE

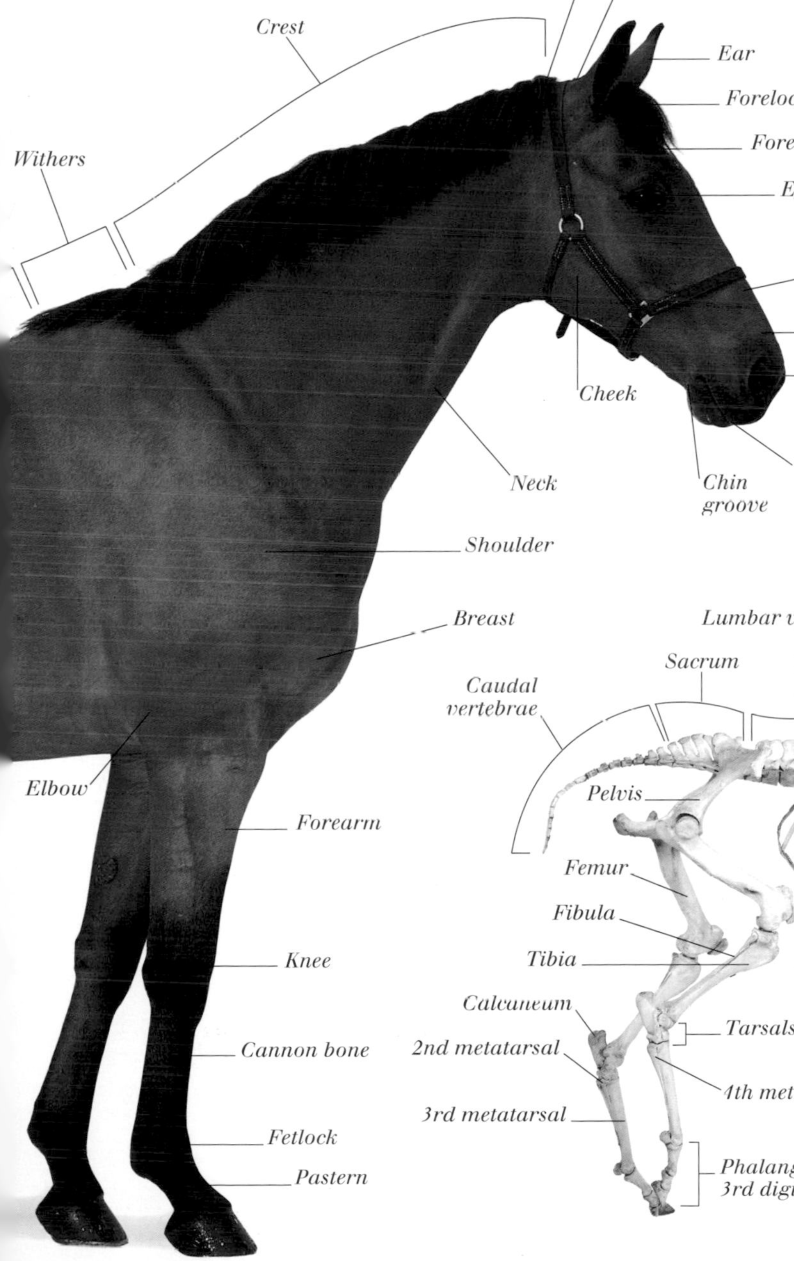

Mane
Poll
Crest
Ear
Forelock
Forehead
Withers
Eye
Muzzle
Nose
Nostril
Cheek
Mouth
Neck
Chin groove
Shoulder
Breast
Elbow
Forearm
Knee
Cannon bone
Fetlock
Pastern

SKELETON OF A HORSE

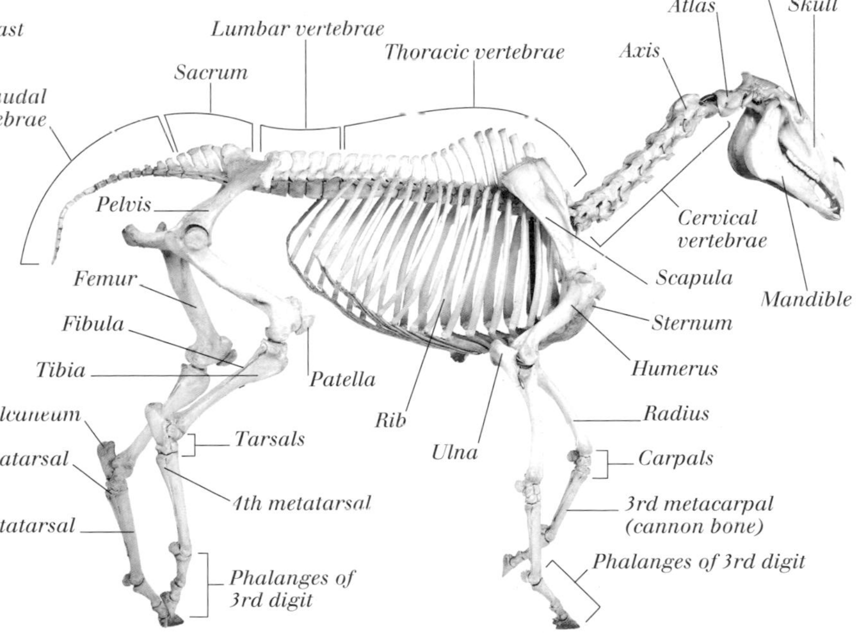

Lumbar vertebrae
Sacrum
Thoracic vertebrae
Orbit
Atlas
Skull
Axis
Caudal vertebrae
Cervical vertebrae
Pelvis
Scapula
Mandible
Femur
Sternum
Fibula
Humerus
Tibia
Patella
Calcaneum
Rib
Radius
2nd metatarsal
Tarsals
Ulna
Carpals
3rd metatarsal
4th metatarsal
3rd metacarpal (cannon bone)
Phalanges of 3rd digit
Phalanges of 3rd digit

Elephants

THE TWO SPECIES of elephants—African and Asian—are the only members of the mammalian order Proboscidea. The bigger African elephant is the largest land animal: a fully grown male may be up to 13 ft (4m) tall and weigh as much as 7.7 tons (7 tonnes). A fully grown male Asian elephant may be 11 ft (3.3 m) tall and weigh 6 tons (5.4 tonnes). The muscular trunk—an extension of the nose and upper lip—is the elephant's most obvious feature. It is used for manipulating and lifting, feeding, drinking and spraying water, smelling, touching, and producing trumpeting sounds. Other characteristic features of this mighty plant-eater include a pair of ivory tusks, used for defense and for crushing vegetation; thick, pillar-like legs and broad feet to support the massive body; and large ear flaps that act as radiators to keep the elephant cool.

DIFFERENCES BETWEEN AFRICAN AND ASIAN ELEPHANTS

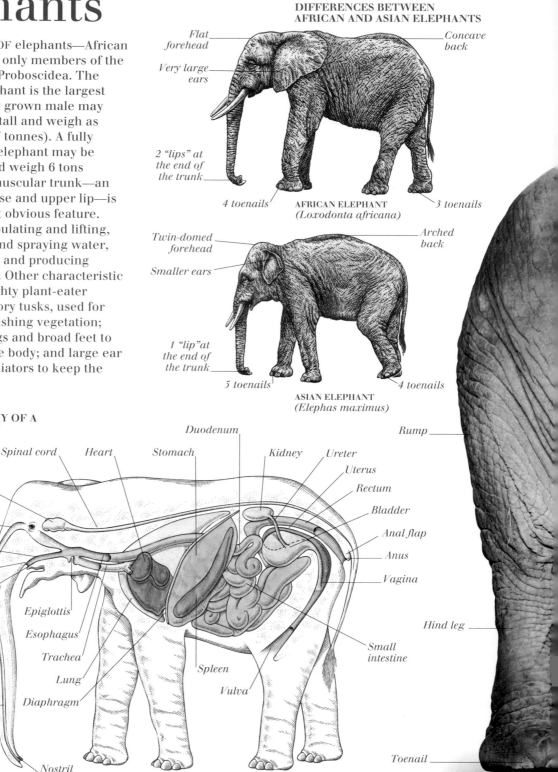

Flat forehead

Very large ears

2 "lips" at the end of the trunk

4 toenails

Concave back

3 toenails

AFRICAN ELEPHANT
(*Loxodonta africana*)

Twin-domed forehead

Smaller ears

1 "lip" at the end of the trunk

5 toenails

Arched back

4 toenails

ASIAN ELEPHANT
(*Elephas maximus*)

Rump

Hind leg

Toenail

INTERNAL ANATOMY OF A FEMALE ELEPHANT

Spinal cord

Heart

Stomach

Duodenum

Kidney

Ureter

Uterus

Brain

Rectum

Nasal cavity

Bladder

Buccal cavity

Anal flap

Anus

Mouth

Vagina

Tongue

Tusk

Epiglottis

Esophagus

Small intestine

Trachea

Lung

Spleen

Nasal passage

Diaphragm

Vulva

Nostril

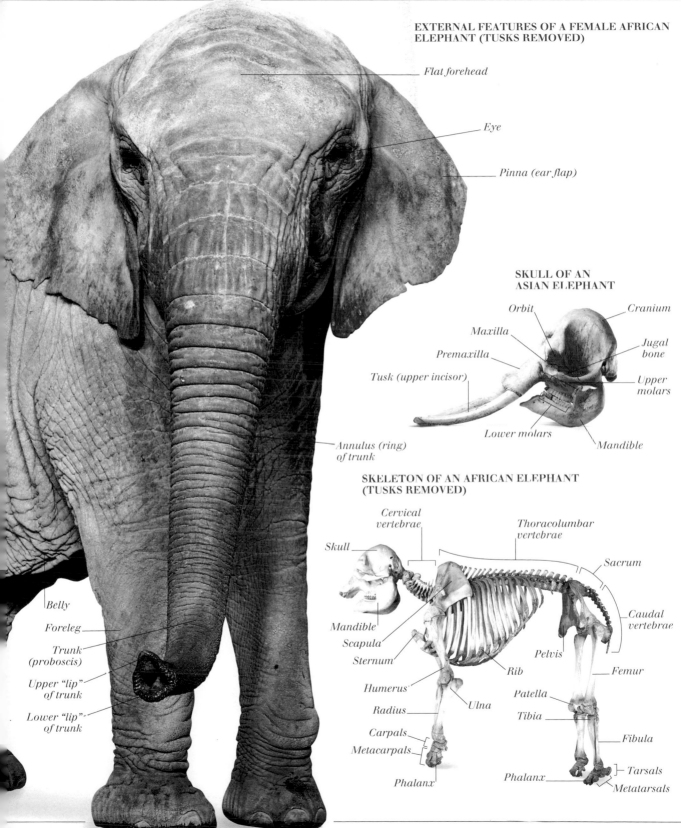

EXTERNAL FEATURES OF A FEMALE AFRICAN ELEPHANT (TUSKS REMOVED)

Flat forehead

Eye

Pinna (ear flap)

Belly

Foreleg

Trunk (proboscis)

Upper "lip" of trunk

Lower "lip" of trunk

Annulus (ring) of trunk

SKULL OF AN ASIAN ELEPHANT

Orbit

Cranium

Maxilla

Jugal bone

Premaxilla

Tusk (upper incisor)

Upper molars

Lower molars

Mandible

SKELETON OF AN AFRICAN ELEPHANT (TUSKS REMOVED)

Cervical vertebrae

Thoracolumbar vertebrae

Skull

Sacrum

Mandible

Caudal vertebrae

Scapula

Sternum

Pelvis

Rib

Femur

Humerus

Patella

Radius

Ulna

Tibia

Carpals

Fibula

Metacarpals

Phalanx

Tarsals

Phalanx

Metatarsals

Primates

THE MAMMALIAN ORDER PRIMATES consists of monkeys, apes, and their relatives (including humans). There are two suborders of primates: Prosimii, the primitive primates, which include lemurs, tarsiers, and lorises; and Anthropoidea, the advanced primates, which include monkeys, apes, and humans. The anthropoids are divided into New World monkeys, Old World monkeys, and hominids. New World monkeys typically have widespread nostrils that open to the side; and long tails, which are prehensile (grasping) in some species. This group of monkeys lives in South America, and includes marmosets, tamarins, and howler monkeys. Old World monkeys typically have close-set nostrils that open forward or downward and nonprehensile tails. This group of monkeys lives in Africa and Asia, and includes langurs, mandrills, macaques, and baboons. Hominids typically have large brains and no tail. This group includes the apes—chimpanzees, gibbons, gorillas, and orangutans—and humans.

INTERNAL ANATOMY OF A FEMALE CHIMPANZEE

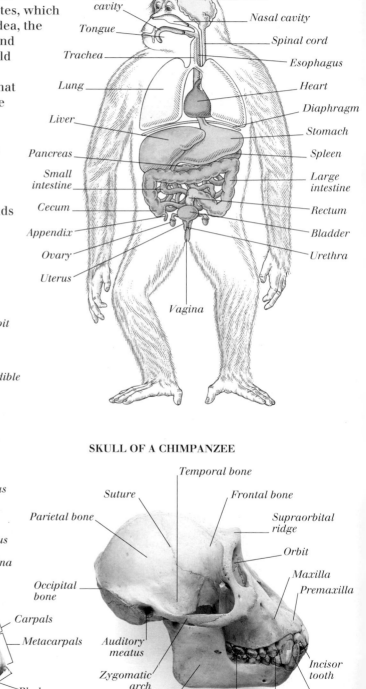

Buccal cavity · Tongue · Trachea · Lung · Liver · Pancreas · Small intestine · Cecum · Appendix · Ovary · Uterus · Vagina · Brain · Nasal cavity · Spinal cord · Esophagus · Heart · Diaphragm · Stomach · Spleen · Large intestine · Rectum · Bladder · Urethra

SKELETON OF A RHESUS MONKEY

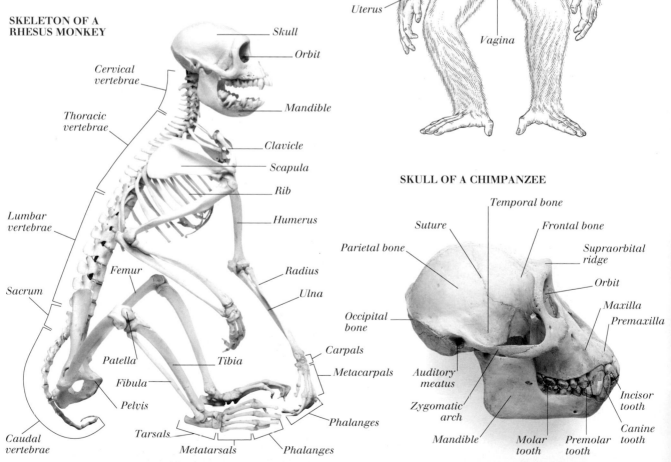

Skull · Orbit · Cervical vertebrae · Mandible · Thoracic vertebrae · Clavicle · Scapula · Rib · Humerus · Lumbar vertebrae · Radius · Ulna · Sacrum · Femur · Patella · Tibia · Carpals · Metacarpals · Fibula · Pelvis · Phalanges · Caudal vertebrae · Tarsals · Metatarsals · Phalanges

SKULL OF A CHIMPANZEE

Temporal bone · Suture · Frontal bone · Parietal bone · Supraorbital ridge · Orbit · Occipital bone · Maxilla · Premaxilla · Auditory meatus · Zygomatic arch · Mandible · Molar tooth · Premolar tooth · Canine tooth · Incisor tooth

EXAMPLES OF PRIMATES

RING-TAILED LEMUR
(*Lemur catta*)
A prosimian

MALE RED HOWLER MONKEY
(*Alouatta seniculus*)
A New World monkey

MALE MANDRILL
(*Mandrillus sphinx*)
An Old World monkey

CHIMPANZEE
(*Pan troglodytes*)
An ape

**EXTERNAL FEATURES OF
A YOUNG GORILLA**

GOLDEN LION TAMARIN
(*Leontopithecus rosalia*)
A New World monkey

Pinna (ear flap)

Shoulder

Brow ridge

Eye

Nostril

Mouth

Upper arm

Thigh

Forearm

Chest

Knee

Elbow

Lower leg

Hand

Foot

Toe

Finger

Toenail

Dolphins, whales, and seals

DOLPHINS, WHALES, AND SEALS belong to
two orders of mammals adapted to living
in water. Dolphins and whales make up the
order Cetacea. Typical cetacean features include
a streamlined, fish-like shape; forelimbs in the form
of flippers; no visible hind limbs; a horizontally flattened
tail; and thick blubber under the skin. There are two groups
of cetaceans: toothed whales, including sperm whales, white whales,
beaked whales, dolphins, and porpoises; and the larger whalebone (baleen)
whales, including rorquals, gray whales, and right whales. The blue whale—a
rorqual—is the largest living animal: an adult may be up to 100 ft (30m) long
and weigh 145 tons (130 tonnes). Seals and their relatives—sea lions and
walruses—make up the order Pinnipedia. Characteristically, they have a
streamlined, torpedo-shaped body; forelimbs and hind limbs modified as
flippers; thick blubber; and no external ears.

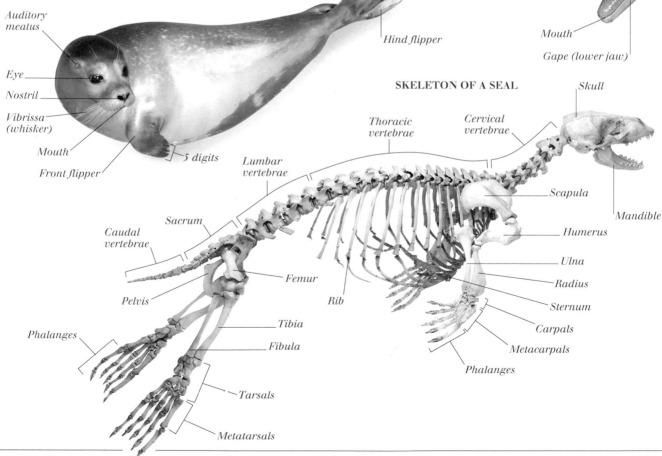

Forehead

Rostrum (beak)

Mouth

*Gape
(lower jaw)*

Eye

Flipper

Belly

Mouth

Gape (lower jaw)

EXTERNAL FEATURES OF A SEAL

*Auditory
meatus*

Eye

Nostril

*Vibrissa
(whisker)*

Mouth

Front flipper

5 digits

Hind flipper

5 digits

SKELETON OF A SEAL

Skull

*Thoracic
vertebrae*

*Cervical
vertebrae*

Mandible

*Lumbar
vertebrae*

Scapula

Humerus

Sacrum

Ulna

*Caudal
vertebrae*

Radius

Femur

Sternum

Pelvis

Rib

Carpals

Phalanges

Tibia

Metacarpals

Fibula

Phalanges

Tarsals

Metatarsals

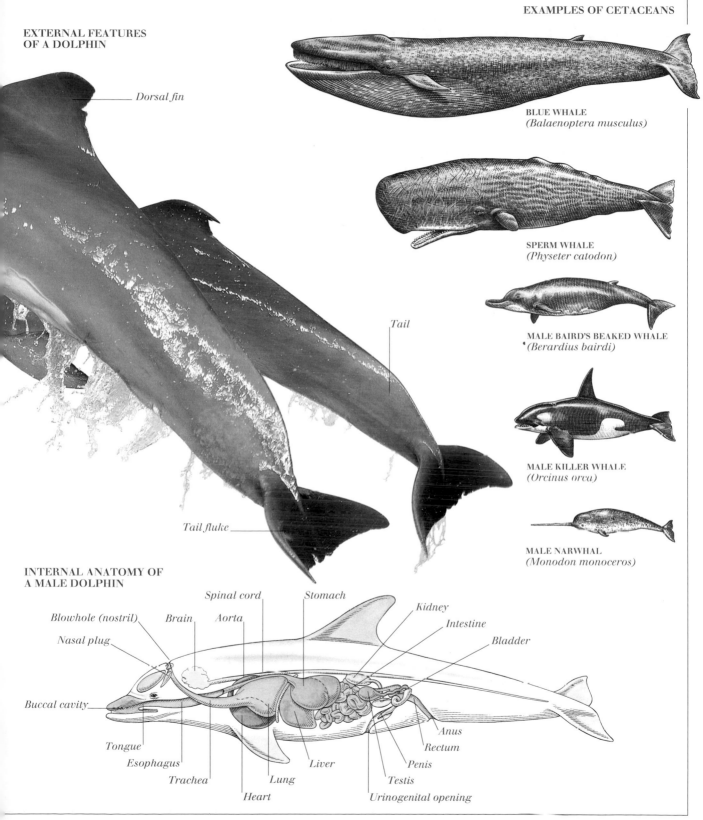

**EXTERNAL FEATURES
OF A DOLPHIN**

Dorsal fin

Tail

Tail fluke

EXAMPLES OF CETACEANS

BLUE WHALE
(*Balaenoptera musculus*)

SPERM WHALE
(*Physeter catodon*)

MALE BAIRD'S BEAKED WHALE
(*Berardius bairdi*)

MALE KILLER WHALE
(*Orcinus orca*)

MALE NARWHAL
(*Monodon monoceros*)

**INTERNAL ANATOMY OF
A MALE DOLPHIN**

Spinal cord

Stomach

Blowhole (nostril)

Brain

Aorta

Kidney

Intestine

Nasal plug

Bladder

Buccal cavity

Anus

Rectum

Tongue

Penis

Esophagus

Testis

Trachea

Liver

Urinogenital opening

Heart

Lung

Marsupials and Monotremes

MARSUPIALS AND MONOTREMES are two orders of mammals that differ from other mammalian groups in the ways that their young develop. The order Marsupalia, the pouched mammals, is made up of kangaroos and their relatives. Typically, marsupials give birth to their young at a very early stage of development. The young then crawls to the mother's pouch (which is on the outside of her abdomen), where it attaches itself to a nipple and remains until fully developed. Most marsupials live in Australia, although the opossums—which are classified as marsupials despite not having a pouch—live in the Americas. The order Monotremata is made up of the platypus and its relatives (the echidnas, or spiny anteaters). The monotremes are primitive mammals that lay eggs, which the mother incubates. The monotremes are found only in Australia and New Guinea.

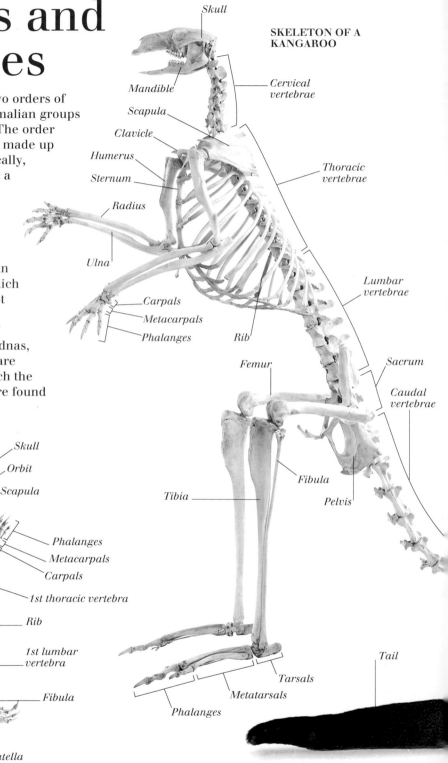

SKELETON OF A KANGAROO

Skull

Mandible

Scapula

Clavicle

Humerus

Sternum

Radius

Ulna

Cervical vertebrae

Thoracic vertebrae

Lumbar vertebrae

Carpals

Metacarpals

Phalanges

Rib

Femur

Sacrum

Caudal vertebrae

Fibula

Pelvis

Tibia

Tarsals

Metatarsals

Phalanges

Tail

SKELETON OF A PLATYPUS

Skull

Orbit

Scapula

1st cervical vertebra

Phalanges

Metacarpals

Carpals

1st thoracic vertebra

Ulna

Radius

Humerus

Rib

1st lumbar vertebra

Femur

Fibula

Tarsals

Metatarsals

Phalanges

Patella

Tibia

Pelvis

1st caudal vertebra

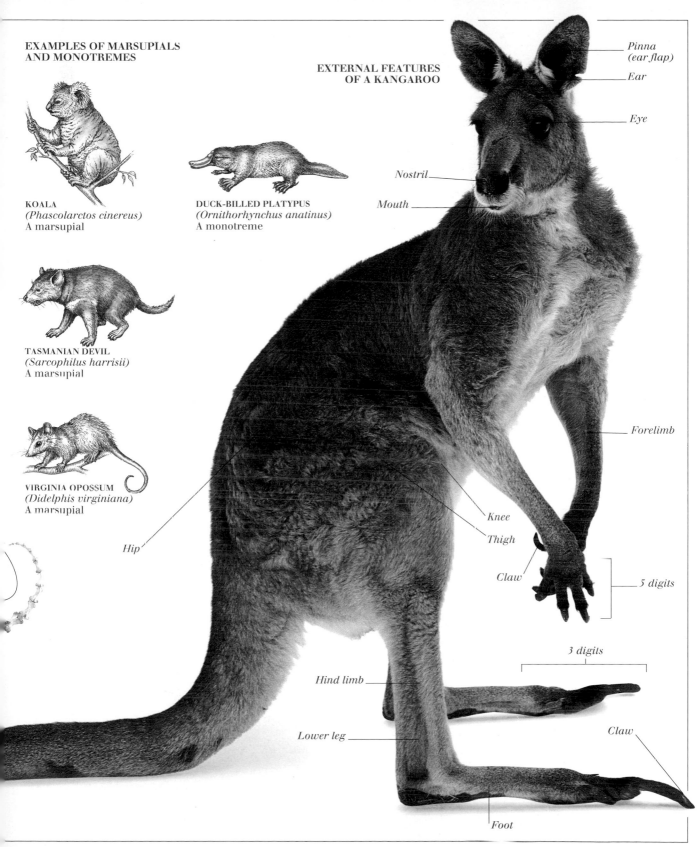

EXAMPLES OF MARSUPIALS AND MONOTREMES

KOALA
(Phascolarctos cinereus)
A marsupial

DUCK-BILLED PLATYPUS
(Ornithorhynchus anatinus)
A monotreme

TASMANIAN DEVIL
(Sarcophilus harrisii)
A marsupial

VIRGINIA OPOSSUM
(Didelphis virginiana)
A marsupial

EXTERNAL FEATURES OF A KANGAROO

Pinna
(ear flap)

Ear

Eye

Nostril

Mouth

Forelimb

Hip

Knee

Thigh

Claw

5 digits

3 digits

Hind limb

Lower leg

Claw

Foot

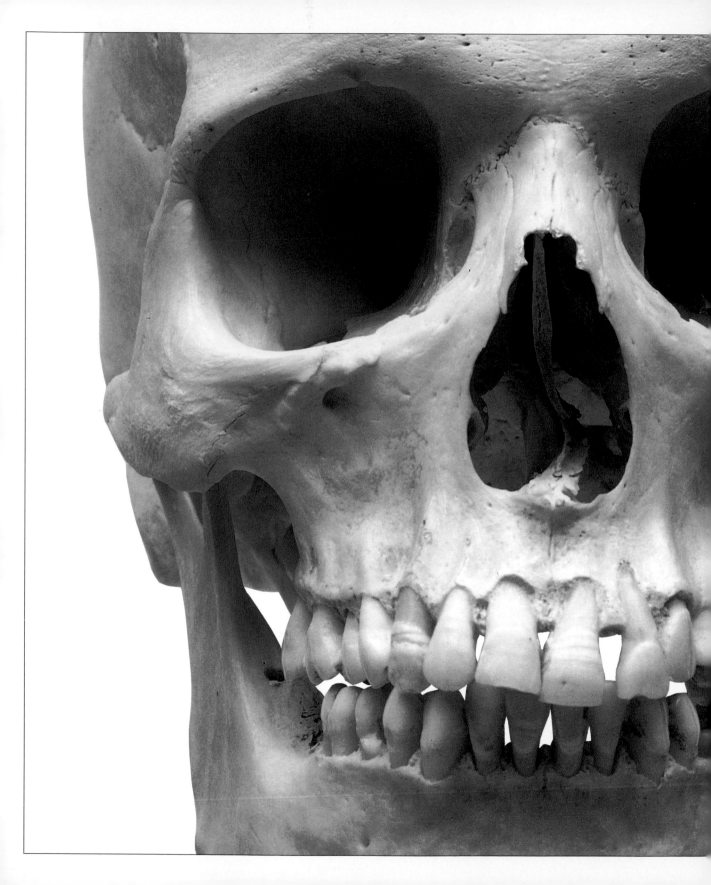

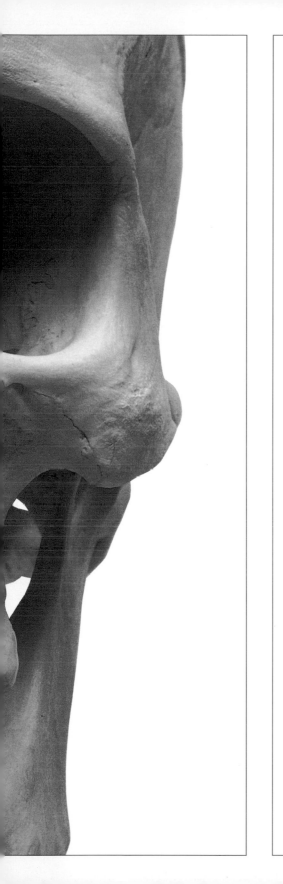

THE HUMAN BODY

Body features

ALTHOUGH THERE IS enormous variation between the external appearances of humans, all bodies contain the same basic features. The outward form of the human body depends on the size of the skeleton, the shape of the muscles, the thickness of the fat layer beneath the skin, the elasticity or sagginess of the skin, and the person's age and gender. Males tend to be taller than females, with broader shoulders, more body hair, and a different pattern of fat deposits under the skin; the female body tends to be less muscular and has a shallower and wider pelvis to allow for childbirth.

Back

Ear

Nape of neck

Shoulder

Scapula
(shoulder blade)

Upper arm

Elbow

Loin

Waist

Forearm

Natal
cleft

Buttock

Arm

Hand

Gluteal fold

Popliteal fossa

Leg

Calf

Foot

Heel

**FRONT VIEWS OF
MALE AND FEMALE**

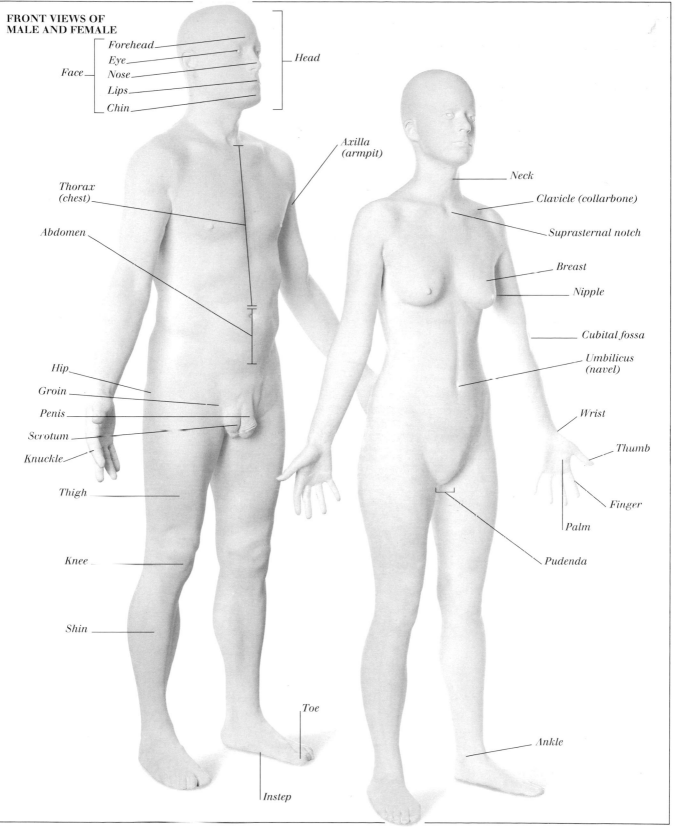

Forehead
Eye
Face
Nose
Lips
Chin

Head

Thorax
(chest)

Abdomen

Hip

Groin

Penis

Scrotum

Knuckle

Thigh

Knee

Shin

Toe

Instep

Axilla
(armpit)

Neck

Clavicle (collarbone)

Suprasternal notch

Breast

Nipple

Cubital fossa

Umbilicus
(navel)

Wrist

Thumb

Finger

Palm

Pudenda

Ankle

Head

IN A NEWBORN BABY, the head accounts for one quarter of the total body length; by adulthood, the proportion has reduced to one eighth. Contained in the head are the body's main sense organs: eyes, ears, olfactory nerves that detect smells, and the taste buds of the tongue. Signals from these organs pass to the body's great coordination center: the brain, housed in the protective, bony dome of the skull. Hair on the head insulates against heat loss, and adult males also grow thick facial hair. The face has three important openings: two nostrils through which air passes, and the mouth, which takes in nourishment and helps form speech. Although all heads are basically similar, differences in the size, shape, and color of features produce an infinite variety of appearances.

SIDE VIEW OF EXTERNAL FEATURES OF HEAD

Crown (vertex)
Forehead
Eyebrow
Eyelash
Eye
Nose
Cheek
Lip
Mouth
Chin
Jaw
Throat
Ear

SECTION THROUGH HEAD

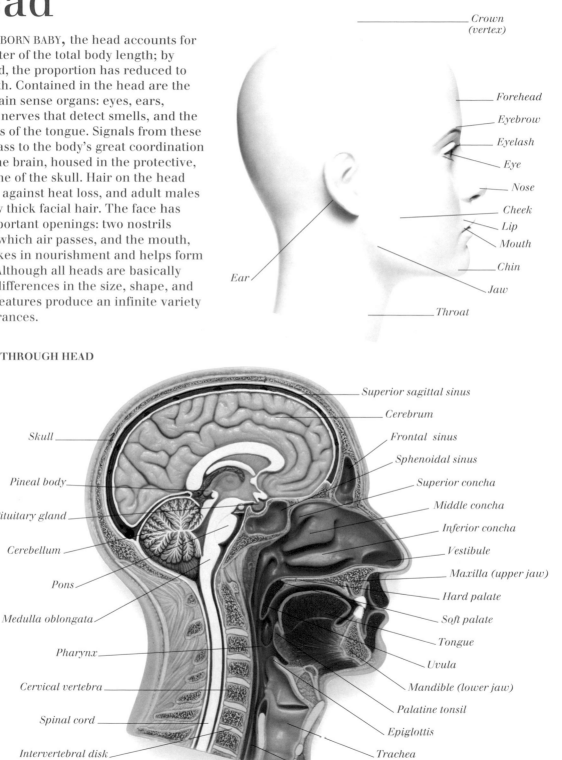

Superior sagittal sinus
Cerebrum
Frontal sinus
Sphenoidal sinus
Superior concha
Middle concha
Inferior concha
Vestibule
Maxilla (upper jaw)
Hard palate
Soft palate
Tongue
Uvula
Mandible (lower jaw)
Palatine tonsil
Epiglottis
Trachea
Esophagus

Skull
Pineal body
Pituitary gland
Cerebellum
Pons
Medulla oblongata
Pharynx
Cervical vertebra
Spinal cord
Intervertebral disk

**FRONT VIEW OF EXTERNAL
FEATURES OF HEAD**

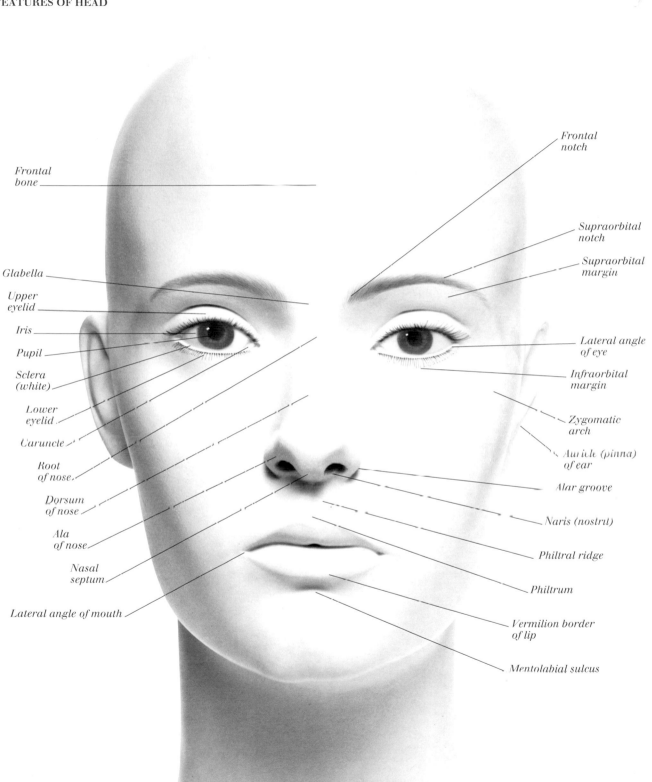

*Frontal
notch*

*Supraorbital
notch*

*Supraorbital
margin*

*Frontal
bone*

Glabella

*Upper
eyelid*

Iris

Pupil

*Sclera
(white)*

*Lower
eyelid*

Caruncle

*Root
of nose*

*Dorsum
of nose*

*Ala
of nose*

*Nasal
septum*

Lateral angle of mouth

*Lateral angle
of eye*

*Infraorbital
margin*

*Zygomatic
arch*

*Auricle (pinna)
of ear*

Alar groove

Naris (nostril)

Philtral ridge

Philtrum

*Vermilion border
of lip*

Mentolabial sulcus

215

Body organs

ALL THE VITAL BODY ORGANS except for the brain are enclosed within the trunk or torso (the body apart from the head and limbs). The trunk contains two large cavities separated by a muscular sheet called the diaphragm. The upper cavity, known as the thorax or chest cavity, contains the heart and lungs. The lower cavity, called the abdominal cavity, contains the stomach, intestines, liver, and pancreas, which all play a role in digesting food. Also within the trunk are the kidneys and bladder, which are part of the urinary system, and the reproductive organs, which hold the seeds of new human life. Modern imaging techniques, such as contrast X-rays and different types of scans, make it possible to see and study body organs without the need to cut through their protective coverings of skin, fat, muscle, and bone.

MAJOR INTERNAL STRUCTURES

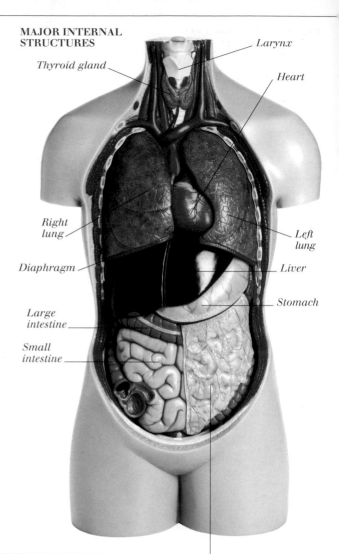

Thyroid gland

Larynx

Heart

Right lung

Left lung

Diaphragm

Liver

Large intestine

Stomach

Small intestine

Greater omentum

IMAGING THE BODY

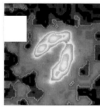

SCINTIGRAM OF HEART CHAMBERS

ANGIOGRAM OF RIGHT LUNG

CONTRAST X-RAY OF GALLBLADDER

SCINTIGRAM OF NERVOUS SYSTEM

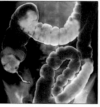

DOUBLE CONTRAST X-RAY OF COLON

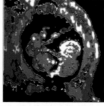

ULTRASOUND SCAN OF TWINS IN UTERUS

ANGIOGRAM OF KIDNEYS

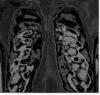

ANGIOGRAM OF ARTERIES OF HEAD

CT SCAN THROUGH FEMALE CHEST

THERMOGRAM OF CHEST REGION

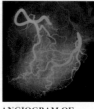

ANGIOGRAM OF ARTERIES OF HEART

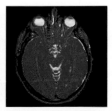

MRI SCAN THROUGH HEAD AT EYE LEVEL

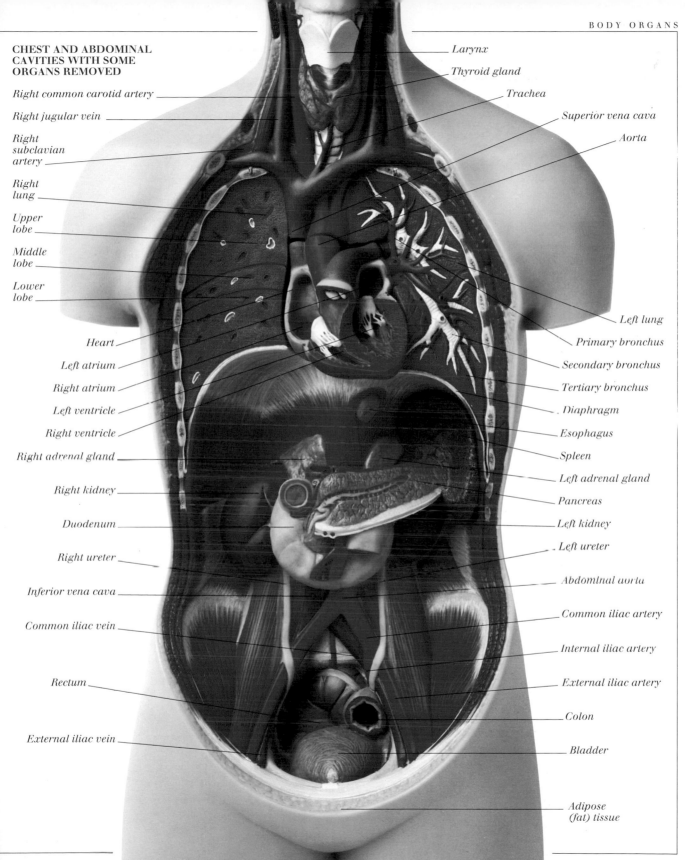

CHEST AND ABDOMINAL CAVITIES WITH SOME ORGANS REMOVED

Right common carotid artery

Right jugular vein

Right subclavian artery

Right lung

Upper lobe

Middle lobe

Lower lobe

Heart

Left atrium

Right atrium

Left ventricle

Right ventricle

Right adrenal gland

Right kidney

Duodenum

Right ureter

Inferior vena cava

Common iliac vein

Rectum

External iliac vein

Larynx

Thyroid gland

Trachea

Superior vena cava

Aorta

Left lung

Primary bronchus

Secondary bronchus

Tertiary bronchus

Diaphragm

Esophagus

Spleen

Left adrenal gland

Pancreas

Left kidney

Left ureter

Abdominal aorta

Common iliac artery

Internal iliac artery

External iliac artery

Colon

Bladder

Adipose (fat) tissue

215

Body cells

EVERYONE IS MADE UP OF BILLIONS OF CELLS, which are the basic structural units of the body. Bones, muscles, nerves, skin, blood, and all other body tissues are formed from different types of cells. Each cell has a specific function but works with other types of cells to perform the enormous number of tasks needed to sustain life. Most body cells have a similar basic structure. Each cell has an outer layer (called the cell membrane) and contains a fluid material (cytoplasm). Within the cytoplasm are many specialized structures (organelles). The most important organelle is the nucleus, which contains vital genetic material and acts as the cell's control center.

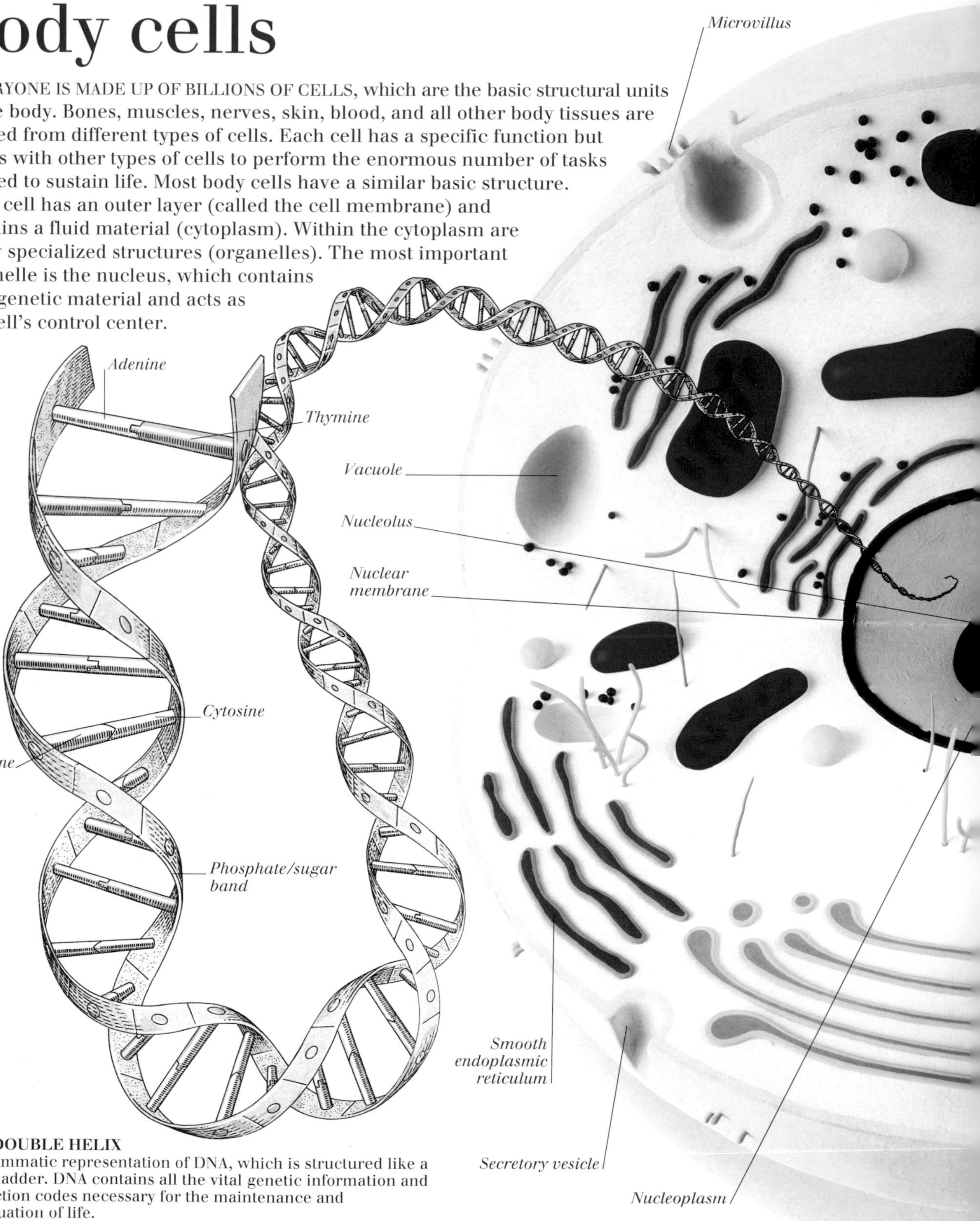

Microvillus

Adenine

Thymine

Vacuole

Nucleolus

Nuclear membrane

Cytosine

Guanine

Phosphate/sugar band

Smooth endoplasmic reticulum

Secretory vesicle

Nucleoplasm

THE DOUBLE HELIX
Diagrammatic representation of DNA, which is structured like a spiral ladder. DNA contains all the vital genetic information and instruction codes necessary for the maintenance and continuation of life.

GENERALIZED HUMAN CELL

Cytoplasm

Lysosome

Cell membrane

Mitochondrial crista

Nucleus

Rough endoplasmic reticulum

Microfilament

Pore of nuclear membrane

Ribosome

Centriole

Mitochondrion

Microtubule

Peroxisome

Pinocytotic vesicle

Golgi complex (Golgi apparatus; Golgi body)

TYPES OF CELLS

BONE-FORMING CELL

NERVE CELLS IN SPINAL CORD

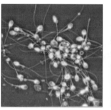

SPERM CELLS IN SEMEN

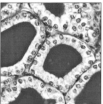

SECRETORY THYROID GLAND CELLS

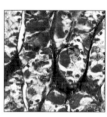

ACID-SECRETING STOMACH CELLS

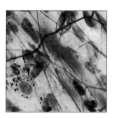

CONNECTIVE TISSUE CELLS

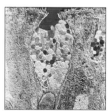

MUCUS-SECRETING DUODENAL CELLS

RED AND TWO WHITE BLOOD CELLS

FAT CELLS IN ADIPOSE TISSUE

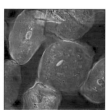

EPITHELIAL CELLS IN CHEEK

Skeleton

THE SKELETON IS A MOBILE FRAMEWORK made up of 206 bones, approximately
half of which are in the hands and feet. Although individual bones are rigid,
the skeleton as a whole is remarkably flexible and allows the human body a
huge range of movement. The skeleton serves as an anchorage for the skeletal
muscles, and as a protective cage for the body's internal organs.
Female bones are usually smaller and lighter
than male bones, and the female pelvis
is shallower and has a wider cavity.

Metacarpal

Carpus

Ulna

Radius

Humerus

Wrist joint

Shoulder joint

Elbow joint

Hip joint

Rib cage

*Intervertebral
disk*

*Sternum
(breastbone)*

*Costal
cartilage*

Coccyx

Sacrum

Pubis

*Vertebral
column
(spine)*

Ischium

Skull

*"True" ribs
(1st to 7th)*

Ilium

*Clavicle
(collarbone)*

*"False" ribs
(8th to 10th)*

*"Floating" ribs
(11th and 12th)*

*Scapula
(shoulder blade)*

Humerus

Radius

Ulna

Carpus

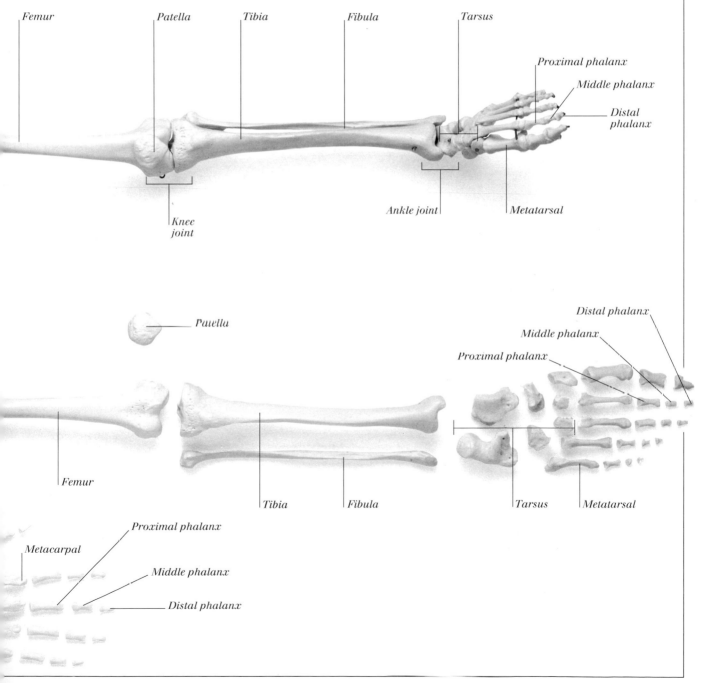

Distal phalanx

Middle phalanx

Proximal phalanx

Femur

Patella

Tibia

Fibula

Tarsus

Proximal phalanx

Middle phalanx

Distal phalanx

Knee joint

Ankle joint

Metatarsal

Patella

Distal phalanx

Middle phalanx

Proximal phalanx

Femur

Tibia

Fibula

Tarsus

Metatarsal

Metacarpal

Proximal phalanx

Middle phalanx

Distal phalanx

Skull

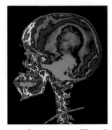

THE SKULL is the most complicated bony structure of the body—but every feature serves a purpose. Internally, the main hollow chamber of the skull has three levels that support the brain, with every bump and hollow corresponding to the shape of the brain. Underneath and toward the back of the skull is a large round hole, called the foramen magnum, through which the spinal cord passes. To the front of this are many smaller openings through which nerves, arteries, and veins pass to and from the brain. The roof of the skull is formed from four thin, curved bones that are firmly fixed together from the age of about two years. At the front of the skull are two orbits, which contain the eyeballs, and a central hole for the airway of the nose. The jawbone hinges on either side of the skull at ear level.

RIGHT SIDE VIEW OF A FETAL SKULL

Anterior fontanelle

Parietal bone

Coronal suture

Frontal bone

Nasal bone

Mental symphysis

Lambdoid suture

Occipital bone

Mastoid fontanelle

External auditory meatus

Sphenoidal fontanelle

RIGHT SIDE VIEW OF SKULL

Greater wing of sphenoid bone

Coronal suture

Frontal bone

Frontozygomatic suture

Parietal bone

Squamous suture

Supraorbital margin

Orbital cavity

Nasal bone

Anterior nasal spine

Maxilla (upper jaw)

Mandible (lower jaw)

Lambdoid suture

Occipital bone

Temporal bone

External auditory meatus

Mastoid process

Condyle

Coronoid process

Zygomatic bone

Mental foramen

VIEW OF SKULL FROM BELOW

External occipital crest

Foramen magnum

Occipital condyle

Carotid canal

Mastoid process

Pharyngeal tubercle

Pterygoid plate

Pterygoid hamulus

Greater palatine foramen

Styloid process

Zygomatic arch

Posterior border of vomer

Concha

Mandible (lower jaw)

Posterior nasal aperture

FRONT VIEW OF SKULL

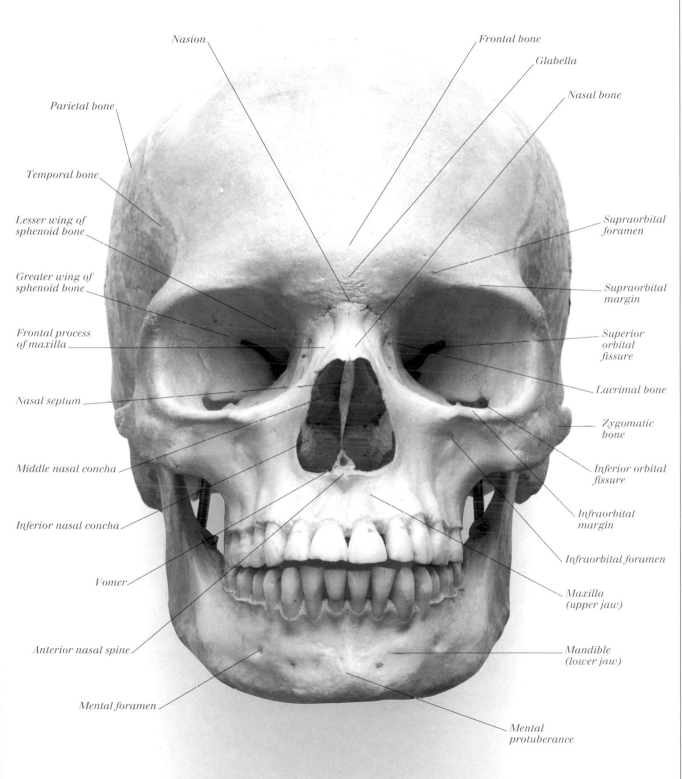

Nasion

Frontal bone

Glabella

Nasal bone

Parietal bone

Temporal bone

Lesser wing of
sphenoid bone

Greater wing of
sphenoid bone

Frontal process
of maxilla

Nasal septum

Middle nasal concha

Inferior nasal concha

Vomer

Anterior nasal spine

Mental foramen

Supraorbital
foramen

Supraorbital
margin

Superior
orbital
fissure

Lacrimal bone

Zygomatic
bone

Inferior orbital
fissure

Infraorbital
margin

Infraorbital foramen

Maxilla
(upper jaw)

Mandible
(lower jaw)

Mental
protuberance

Spine

THE SPINE (OR VERTEBRAL COLUMN) has two main functions: it serves as a protective surrounding for the delicate spinal cord and forms the supporting back bone of the skeleton. The spine consists of 24 separate differently shaped bones (vertebrae) with a curved, triangular bone (the sacrum) at the bottom. The sacrum is made up of fused vertebrae; at its lower end is a small tail-like structure made up of tiny bones collectively called the coccyx. Between each pair of vertebrae is a disc of cartilage that cushions the bones during movement. The top two vertebrae differ in appearance from the others and work as a pair: the first, called the atlas, rotates around a stout vertical peg on the second, the axis. This arrangement allows the skull to move freely up and down, and from side to side.

SPINE DIVIDED INTO VERTEBRAL SECTIONS

FRONT

Cervical vertebrae

Thoracic vertebrae

Lumbar vertebrae

Sacral vertebrae

Coccygeal vertebrae

TYPES OF VERTEBRAE (VIEWED FROM ABOVE)

ATLAS

Anterior arch
Anterior tubercle
Vertebral foramen
Transverse process
Lateral mass with superior articular facet
Posterior arch
Posterior tubercle
Transverse foramen

AXIS

Facet
Dens
Vertebral foramen
Spinous process
Lamina
Transverse process and foramen

CERVICAL VERTEBRA

Body
Anterior tubercle
Posterior tubercle
Superior articular process
Spinous process
Vertebral foramen
Transverse foramen

SKULL AND SPINE

Skull

Cervical vertebrae
1st 2nd 3rd 4th 5th 6th 7th

Thoracic vertebrae
1st 2nd 3rd 4th 5th 6th 7th

Atlas   Axis

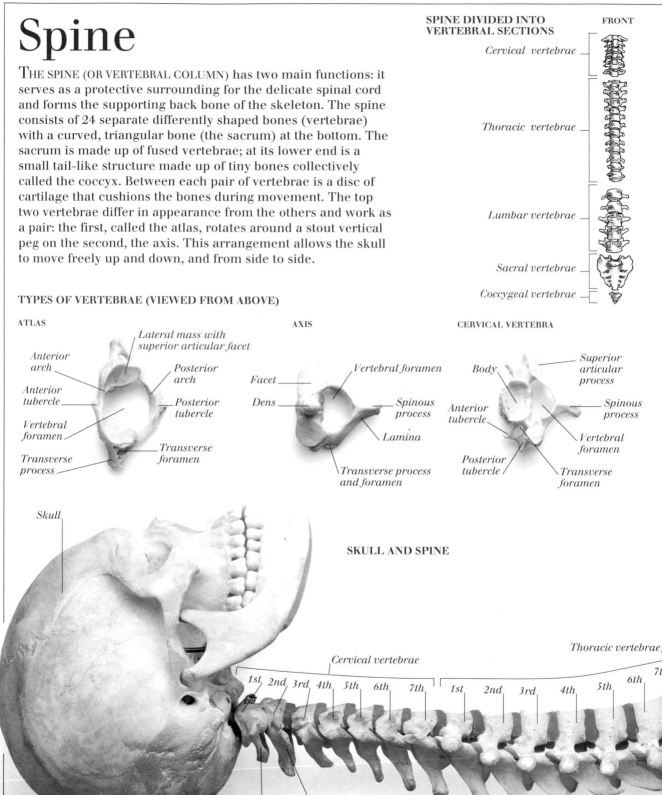

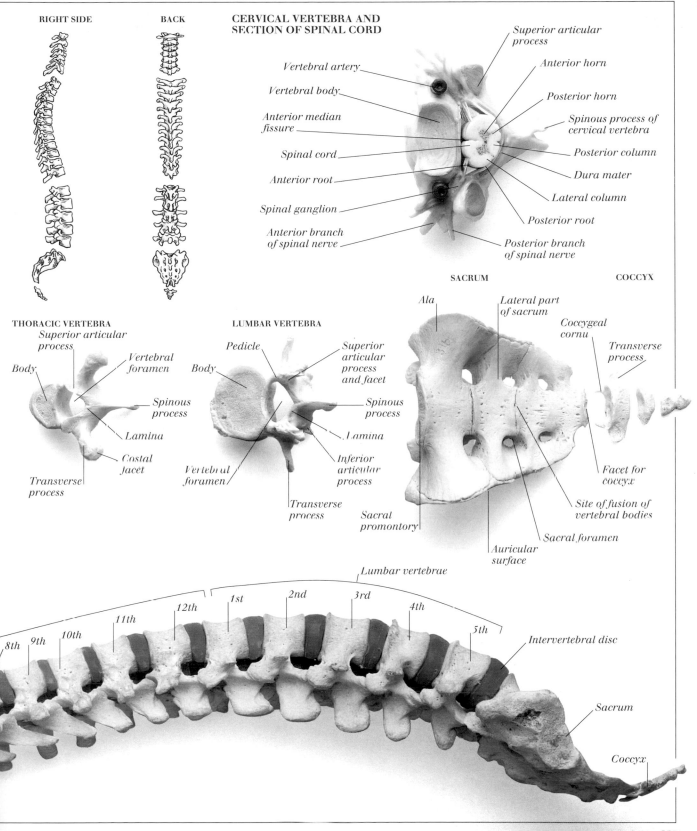

RIGHT SIDE

BACK

**CERVICAL VERTEBRA AND
SECTION OF SPINAL CORD**

Superior articular
process

Vertebral artery

Anterior horn

Vertebral body

Posterior horn

Anterior median
fissure

Spinous process of
cervical vertebra

Spinal cord

Posterior column

Anterior root

Dura mater

Spinal ganglion

Lateral column

Anterior branch
of spinal nerve

Posterior root

Posterior branch
of spinal nerve

THORACIC VERTEBRA

Superior articular
process

Vertebral
foramen

Body

Spinous
process

Lamina

Costal
facet

Transverse
process

LUMBAR VERTEBRA

Pedicle

Superior
articular
process
and facet

Body

Spinous
process

Lamina

Inferior
articular
process

Vertebral
foramen

Transverse
process

SACRUM

Ala

Lateral part
of sacrum

Sacral
promontory

Auricular
surface

Sacral foramen

Site of fusion of
vertebral bodies

COCCYX

Coccygeal
cornu

Transverse
process

Facet for
coccyx

Lumbar vertebrae

1st   2nd   3rd   4th   5th

12th

11th

10th

9th

8th

Intervertebral disc

Sacrum

Coccyx

Bones and joints

BONES FORM the body's hard, strong skeletal framework. Each bone has a hard, compact exterior surrounding a spongy, lighter interior. The long bones of the arms and legs, such as the femur (thigh bone), have a central cavity containing bone marrow. Bones are composed chiefly of calcium, phosphorus, and a fibrous substance known as collagen. Bones meet at joints, which are of several different types. For example, the hip is a ball-and-socket joint that allows the femur a wide range of movement, whereas finger joints are simple hinge joints that allow only bending and straightening. Joints are held in place by bands of tissue called ligaments. Movement of joints is facilitated by the smooth hyaline cartilage that covers the bone ends and by the synovial membrane that lines and lubricates the joint.

LIGAMENTS SURROUNDING HIP JOINT

Iliac crest

Iliac fossa

Pubofemoral ligament

Iliac spine

Obturator canal

Superior ramus of pubis

Greater trochanter of femur

Body of pubis

Iliofemoral ligament

Obturator membrane

Intertrochanteric line

Ischial tuberosity

Lesser trochanter of femur

Femur

Ischium

SECTION THROUGH LEFT FEMUR

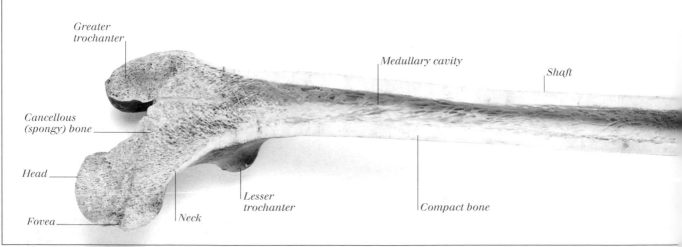

Greater trochanter

Medullary cavity

Shaft

Cancellous (spongy) bone

Head

Lesser trochanter

Compact bone

Fovea

Neck

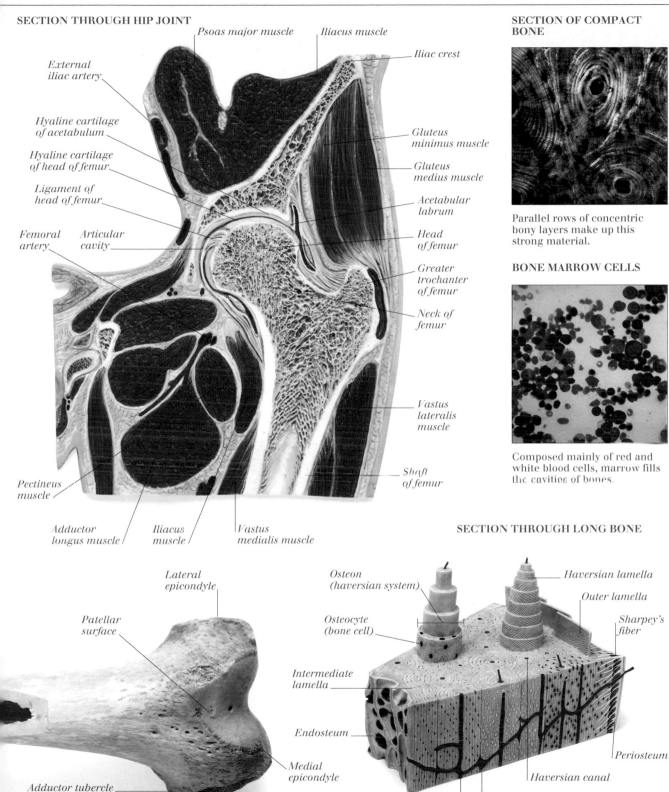

SECTION THROUGH HIP JOINT

Psoas major muscle

Iliacus muscle

Iliac crest

External
iliac artery

Hyaline cartilage
of acetabulum

Hyaline cartilage
of head of femur

Ligament of
head of femur

Gluteus
minimus muscle

Gluteus
medius muscle

Acetabular
labrum

Femoral
artery

Articular
cavity

Head
of femur

Greater
trochanter
of femur

Neck of
femur

Vastus
lateralis
muscle

Pectineus
muscle

Shaft
of femur

Adductor
longus muscle

Iliacus
muscle

Vastus
medialis muscle

SECTION OF COMPACT BONE

Parallel rows of concentric bony layers make up this strong material.

BONE MARROW CELLS

Composed mainly of red and white blood cells, marrow fills the cavities of bones.

SECTION THROUGH LONG BONE

Lateral
epicondyle

Patellar
surface

Osteon
(haversian system)

Haversian lamella

Outer lamella

Osteocyte
(bone cell)

Sharpey's
fiber

Intermediate
lamella

Endosteum

Periosteum

Adductor tubercle

Medial
epicondyle

Haversian canal

Volkmann's vessel

Lacuna

225

Muscles 1

THERE ARE THREE MAIN TYPES OF MUSCLE: skeletal muscle (also called voluntary muscle because it can be consciously controlled); smooth muscle (also called involuntary muscle because it is not under voluntary control); and the specialized muscle tissue of the heart. Humans have more than 600 skeletal muscles, which differ in size and shape according to the jobs they do. Skeletal muscles are attached either directly or indirectly (via tendons) to bones, and work in opposing pairs (one muscle in the pair contracts while the other relaxes) to produce body movements as diverse as walking, threading a needle, and an array of facial expressions. Smooth muscles occur in the walls of internal body organs and perform actions such as forcing food through the intestines, contracting the uterus (womb) in childbirth, and pumping blood through the blood vessels.

SOME OTHER MUSCLES IN THE BODY

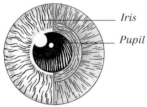

Iris

Pupil

IRIS
The muscle fibers contract and dilate (expand) to alter pupil size.

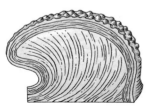

TONGUE
Interlacing layers of muscle allow great mobility.

ILEUM
Opposing muscle layers transport semidigested food.

SUPERFICIAL SKELETAL MUSCLES

FRONT VIEW

Brachioradialis

Flexors of forearm

Brachialis

Frontalis

Orbicularis oculi

Temporalis

Sternocleidomastoid

Trapezius

Pectoralis major

Deltoid

Serratus anterior

Rectus abdominis

Biceps brachii

Linea alba

External oblique

Tensor fasciae latae

Iliopsoas

Pectineus

Adductor longus

Vastus lateralis

Gracilis

Rectus femoris

Sartorius

Vastus medialis

Gastrocnemius

Tibialis anterior

BACK VIEW

Temporalis

Sternocleidomastoid

Trapezius

Deltoid

Biceps femoris

Semitendinosus

Gastrocnemius

Soleus

Peroneus
brevis

Extensors
of hand

Flexors
of hand

Triceps
brachii

Teres minor

Teres major

Infraspinatus

Rhomboideus major

Latissimus dorsi

Gluteus
maximus

Adductor
magnus

Gracilis

MOVEMENT OF THE FOREARM
Controlled movement of the limbs relies
on coordinated relaxation and contraction
of opposing muscles. To raise the forearm,
the biceps (two-rooted muscle) contracts
and shortens while the triceps (three-
rooted muscle) relaxes; the reverse occurs
when the forearm is lowered.

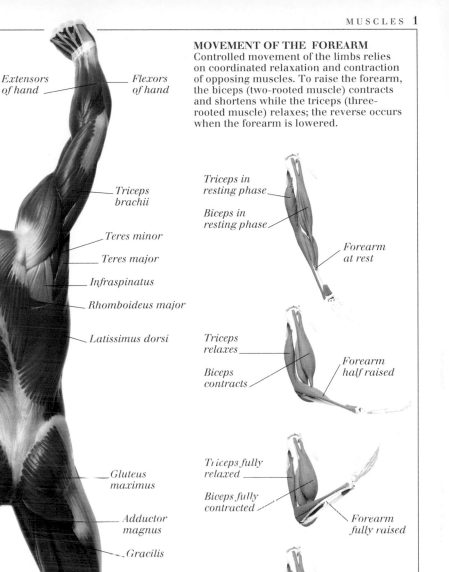

Triceps in
resting phase

Biceps in
resting phase

Forearm
at rest

Triceps
relaxes

Biceps
contracts

Forearm
half raised

Triceps fully
relaxed

Biceps fully
contracted

Forearm
fully raised

Triceps
contracts

Biceps
relaxes

Forearm
half lowered

Triceps back in
resting phase

Biceps back in
resting phase

Forearm
back at rest

Muscles 2

SKELETAL MUSCLE FIBER

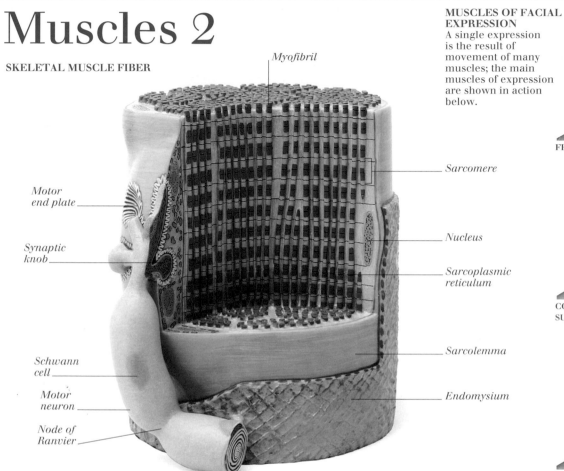

Myofibril

Sarcomere

Nucleus

Sarcoplasmic reticulum

Sarcolemma

Endomysium

Motor end plate

Synaptic knob

Schwann cell

Motor neuron

Node of Ranvier

MUSCLES OF FACIAL EXPRESSION
A single expression is the result of movement of many muscles; the main muscles of expression are shown in action below.

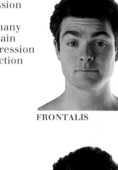

FRONTALIS

CORRUGATOR SUPERCILII

ORBICULARIS ORIS

ZYGOMATICUS MAJOR

DEPRESSOR ANGULI ORIS

TYPES OF MUSCLE

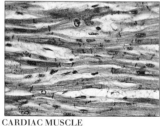

CARDIAC MUSCLE

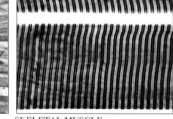

SKELETAL MUSCLE

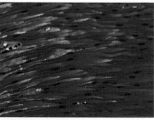

SMOOTH MUSCLE

CONTRACTION OF SKELETAL MUSCLE

RELAXED STATE

CONTRACTED STATE

**MUSCLES OF
HEAD AND NECK**

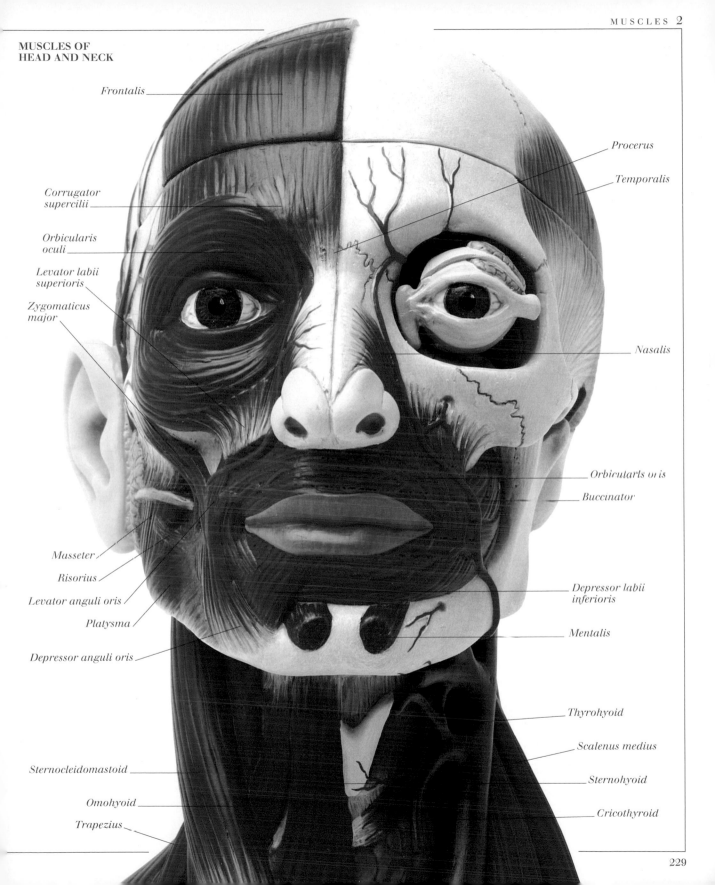

Frontalis

Procerus

Temporalis

Corrugator
supercilii

Orbicularis
oculi

Levator labii
superioris

Zygomaticus
major

Nasalis

Orbicularis oris

Buccinator

Masseter

Risorius

Levator anguli oris

Depressor labii
inferioris

Platysma

Mentalis

Depressor anguli oris

Thyrohyoid

Scalenus medius

Sternocleidomastoid

Sternohyoid

Omohyoid

Cricothyroid

Trapezius

Hands

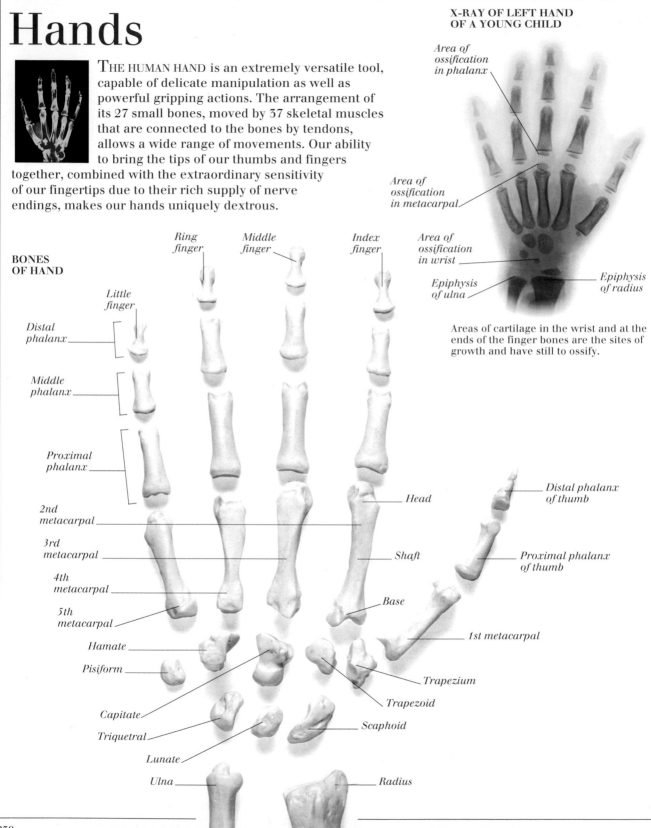

THE HUMAN HAND is an extremely versatile tool, capable of delicate manipulation as well as powerful gripping actions. The arrangement of its 27 small bones, moved by 37 skeletal muscles that are connected to the bones by tendons, allows a wide range of movements. Our ability to bring the tips of our thumbs and fingers together, combined with the extraordinary sensitivity of our fingertips due to their rich supply of nerve endings, makes our hands uniquely dextrous.

X-RAY OF LEFT HAND OF A YOUNG CHILD

Area of ossification in phalanx

Area of ossification in metacarpal

Area of ossification in wrist

Epiphysis of ulna

Epiphysis of radius

Areas of cartilage in the wrist and at the ends of the finger bones are the sites of growth and have still to ossify.

BONES OF HAND

Ring finger

Middle finger

Index finger

Little finger

Distal phalanx

Middle phalanx

Proximal phalanx

2nd metacarpal

3rd metacarpal

4th metacarpal

5th metacarpal

Hamate

Pisiform

Capitate

Triquetral

Lunate

Ulna

Head

Shaft

Base

Distal phalanx of thumb

Proximal phalanx of thumb

1st metacarpal

Trapezium

Trapezoid

Scaphoid

Radius

230

STRUCTURES UNDERLYING SKIN OF PALM OF HAND

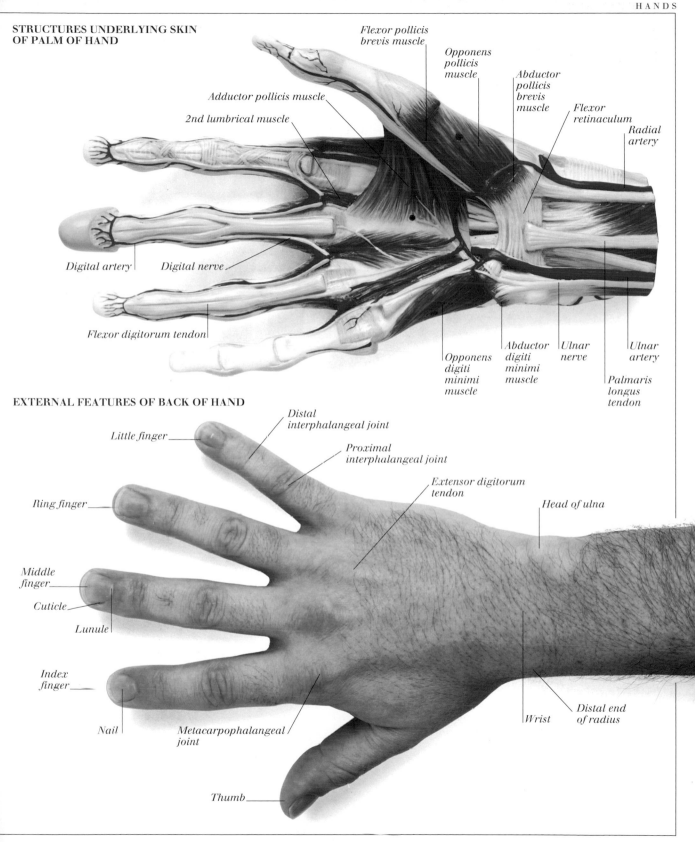

Flexor pollicis brevis muscle

Opponens pollicis muscle

Abductor pollicis brevis muscle

Flexor retinaculum

Radial artery

Adductor pollicis muscle

2nd lumbrical muscle

Digital artery

Digital nerve

Flexor digitorum tendon

Opponens digiti minimi muscle

Abductor digiti minimi muscle

Ulnar nerve

Ulnar artery

Palmaris longus tendon

EXTERNAL FEATURES OF BACK OF HAND

Distal interphalangeal joint

Little finger

Proximal interphalangeal joint

Extensor digitorum tendon

Head of ulna

Ring finger

Middle finger

Cuticle

Lunule

Index finger

Nail

Metacarpophalangeal joint

Wrist

Distal end of radius

Thumb

Feet

THE FEET AND TOES are essential elements in body movement. They bear and propel the weight of the body during walking and running, and also help to maintain balance during changes of body position. Each foot has 26 bones, more than 100 ligaments, and 33 muscles, some of which are attached to the lower leg. The heel pad and the arch of the foot act as shock absorbers, providing a cushion against the jolts that occur with every step.

BONES OF FOOT

- *2nd toe*
- *Hallux (big toe)*
- *3rd toe*
- *4th toe*
- *Distal phalanx of hallux*
- *5th (little) toe*
- *Distal phalanx*
- *Proximal phalanx of hallux*
- *Middle phalanx*
- *Proximal phalanx*
- *1st metatarsal*
- *2nd metatarsal*
- *3rd metatarsal*
- *4th metatarsal*
- *1st cuneiform*
- *5th metatarsal*
- *2nd cuneiform*
- *3rd cuneiform*
- *Cuboid*
- *Navicular*
- *Talus*
- *Calcaneus*

LIGAMENTS OF FOOT

- *Posterior cuneonavicular ligament*
- *Articular capsule of interphalangeal joint*
- *Plantar calcaneonavicular ligament*
- *Articular capsule of metatarsophalangeal joint*
- *Posterior tarsometatarsal ligament*
- *Talonavicular ligament*
- *Bifurcate ligament*
- *Deltoid ligament*
- *Fibula*
- *Tibia*
- *Calcanean (Achilles) tendon*
- *Interosseous ligament*

STRUCTURES UNDERLYING SKIN OF FOOT

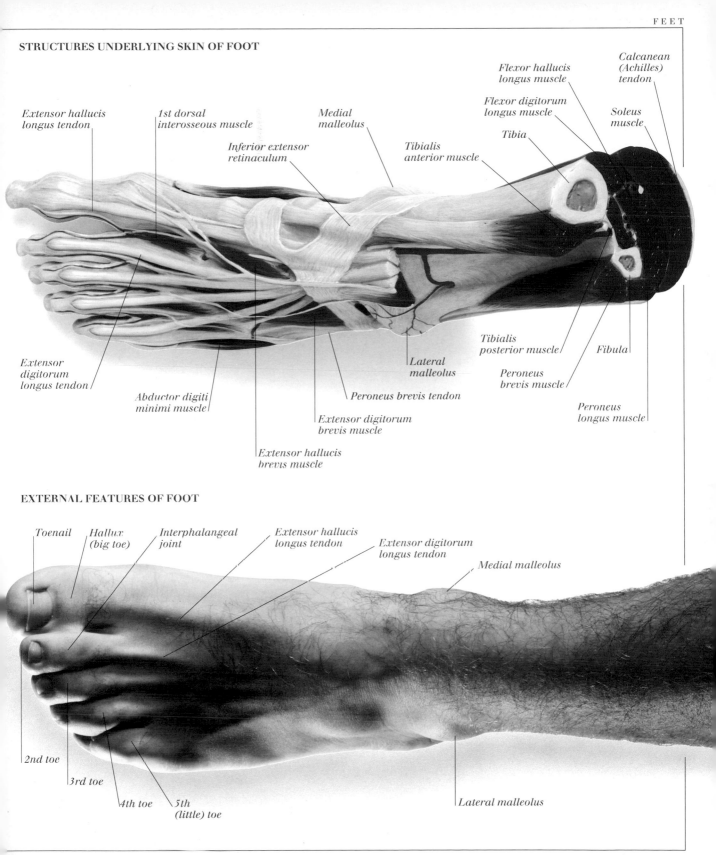

Flexor hallucis
longus muscle

Calcanean
(Achilles)
tendon

Flexor digitorum
longus muscle

Soleus
muscle

Extensor hallucis
longus tendon

1st dorsal
interosseous muscle

Medial
malleolus

Tibia

Inferior extensor
retinaculum

Tibialis
anterior muscle

Extensor
digitorum
longus tendon

Tibialis
posterior muscle

Fibula

Abductor digiti
minimi muscle

Lateral
malleolus

Peroneus
brevis muscle

Peroneus brevis tendon

Peroneus
longus muscle

Extensor digitorum
brevis muscle

Extensor hallucis
brevis muscle

EXTERNAL FEATURES OF FOOT

Toenail

Hallux
(big toe)

Interphalangeal
joint

Extensor hallucis
longus tendon

Extensor digitorum
longus tendon

Medial malleolus

2nd toe

3rd toe

4th toe

5th
(little) toe

Lateral malleolus

Skin and hair

SKIN IS THE BODY'S LARGEST ORGAN, a waterproof barrier that protects the internal organs against infection, injury, and harmful sun rays. The skin is also an important sensory organ and helps to control body temperature. The outer layer of the skin, known as the epidermis, is coated with keratin, a tough, horny protein that is also the chief constituent of hair and nails. Dead cells are shed from the skin's surface and are replaced by new cells from the base of the epidermis, the region that also produces the skin pigment, melanin. The dermis contains most of the skin's living structures, and includes nerve endings, blood vessels, elastic fibers, sweat glands that cool the skin, and sebaceous glands that produce oil to keep the skin supple. Beneath the dermis lies the subcutaneous tissue (hypodermis), which is rich in fat and blood vessels. Hair shafts grow from hair follicles situated in the dermis and subcutaneous tissue. Hair grows on every part of the skin apart from the palms of the hands and soles of the feet.

SECTION OF HAIR

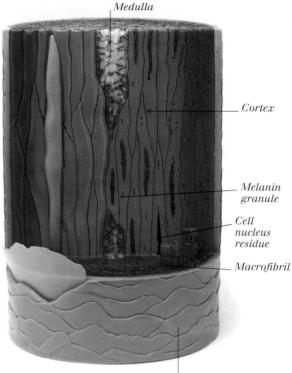

- Medulla
- Cortex
- Melanin granule
- Cell nucleus residue
- Macrofibril
- Cuticle

SECTIONS OF DIFFERENT TYPES OF SKIN

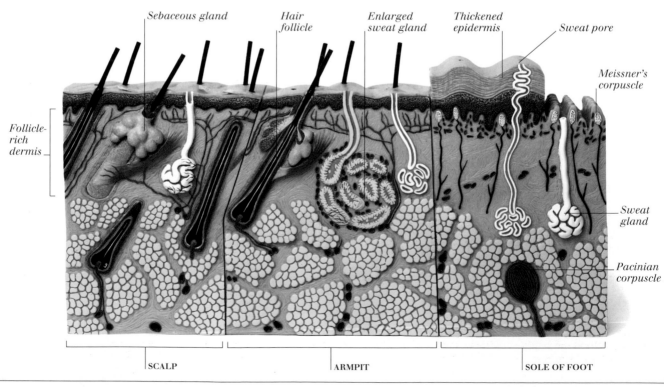

- Sebaceous gland
- Hair follicle
- Enlarged sweat gland
- Thickened epidermis
- Sweat pore
- Meissner's corpuscle
- Follicle-rich dermis
- Sweat gland
- Pacinian corpuscle

SCALP   ARMPIT   SOLE OF FOOT

SECTION OF SKIN

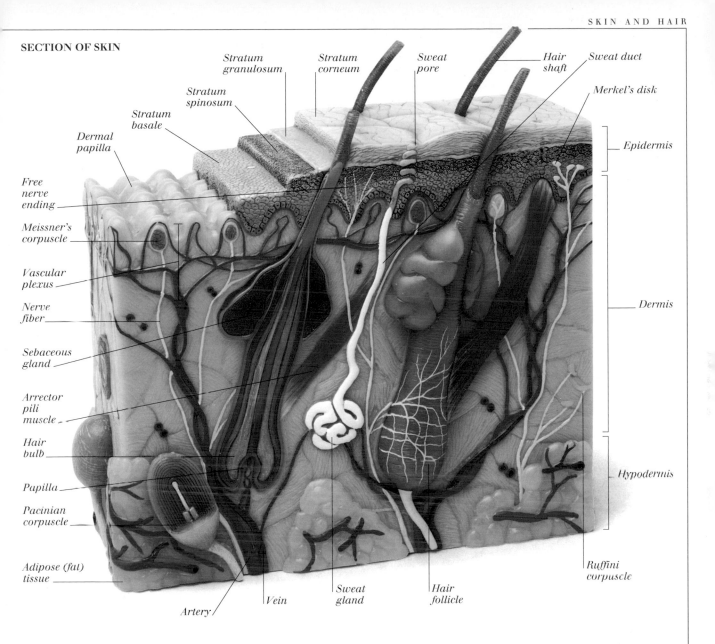

Stratum granulosum

Stratum corneum

Sweat pore

Hair shaft

Sweat duct

Stratum spinosum

Merkel's disk

Stratum basale

Epidermis

Dermal papilla

Free nerve ending

Meissner's corpuscle

Vascular plexus

Nerve fiber

Sebaceous gland

Arrector pili muscle

Hair bulb

Papilla

Pacinian corpuscle

Adipose (fat) tissue

Dermis

Hypodermis

Ruffini corpuscle

Artery

Vein

Sweat gland

Hair follicle

PHOTOMICROGRAPHS OF SKIN AND HAIR

SECTION OF SKIN
The flaky cells at the skin's surface are shed continuously.

SWEAT PORE
This allows loss of fluid as part of temperature control.

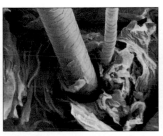

SKIN HAIR
Two hairs pushing through the outer layer of skin.

HEAD HAIR
The root and part of the shaft of a hair from the scalp.

Brain

THE BRAIN IS THE MAJOR ORGAN of the central nervous system and the control center for all the body's voluntary and involuntary activities. It is also responsible for the complexities of thought, memory, emotion, and language. In adults, this complex organ is a mere 3 lb (1.4 kg) in weight, containing over 10 thousand million nerve cells. Three distinct regions can easily be seen—the brainstem, the cerebellum, and the large cerebrum. The brainstem controls vital body functions, such as breathing and digestion. The cerebellum's main functions are the maintenance of posture and the coordination of body movements. The cerebrum, which consists of the right and left cerebral hemispheres joined by the corpus callosum, is the site of most conscious and intelligent activities.

MRI SCAN OF TRANSVERSE SECTION THROUGH BRAIN

Gray matter

White matter

Skull

Scalp

Longitudinal fissure

Lateral ventricle

Coronal section

Sagittal section

SAGITTAL SECTION THROUGH BRAIN

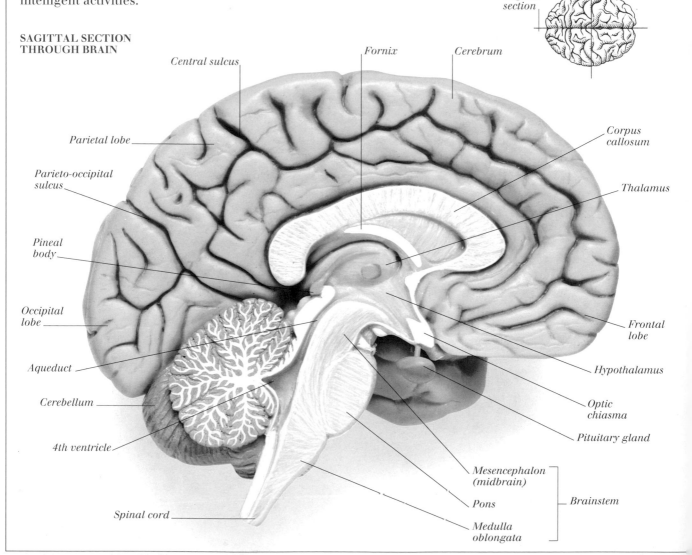

Central sulcus

Fornix

Cerebrum

Parietal lobe

Corpus callosum

Parieto-occipital sulcus

Thalamus

Pineal body

Occipital lobe

Frontal lobe

Aqueduct

Hypothalamus

Cerebellum

Optic chiasma

4th ventricle

Pituitary gland

Mesencephalon (midbrain)

Spinal cord

Pons

Brainstem

Medulla oblongata

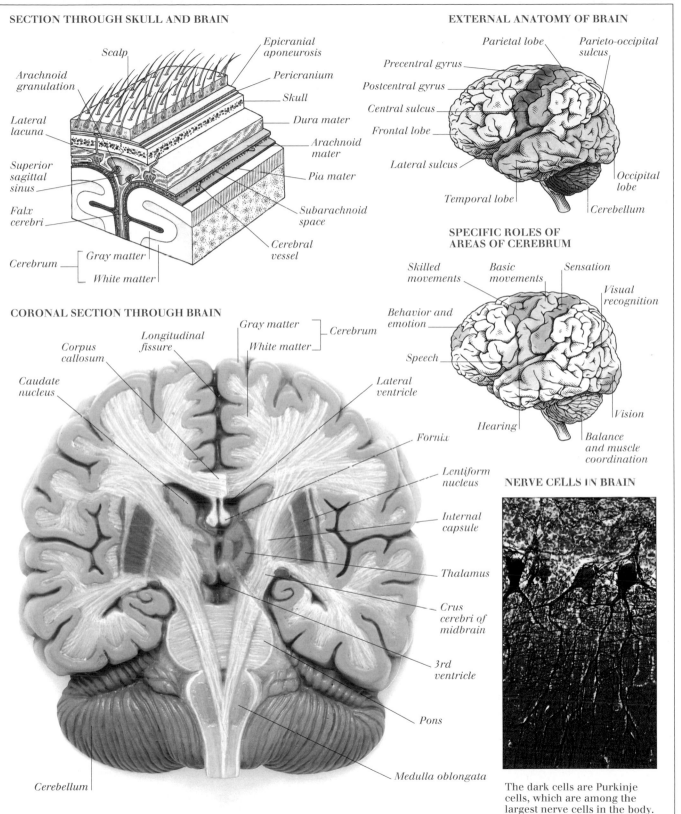

SECTION THROUGH SKULL AND BRAIN

Scalp
Epicranial aponeurosis
Arachnoid granulation
Pericranium
Skull
Lateral lacuna
Dura mater
Arachnoid mater
Superior sagittal sinus
Pia mater
Falx cerebri
Subarachnoid space
Cerebral vessel
Cerebrum
Gray matter
White matter

EXTERNAL ANATOMY OF BRAIN

Parietal lobe
Parieto-occipital sulcus
Precentral gyrus
Postcentral gyrus
Central sulcus
Frontal lobe
Lateral sulcus
Occipital lobe
Temporal lobe
Cerebellum

SPECIFIC ROLES OF AREAS OF CEREBRUM

Skilled movements
Basic movements
Sensation
Visual recognition
Behavior and emotion
Speech
Hearing
Vision
Balance and muscle coordination

CORONAL SECTION THROUGH BRAIN

Corpus callosum
Longitudinal fissure
Gray matter
White matter
Cerebrum
Caudate nucleus
Lateral ventricle
Fornix
Lentiform nucleus
Internal capsule
Thalamus
Crus cerebri of midbrain
3rd ventricle
Pons
Medulla oblongata
Cerebellum

NERVE CELLS IN BRAIN

The dark cells are Purkinje cells, which are among the largest nerve cells in the body.

Nervous system

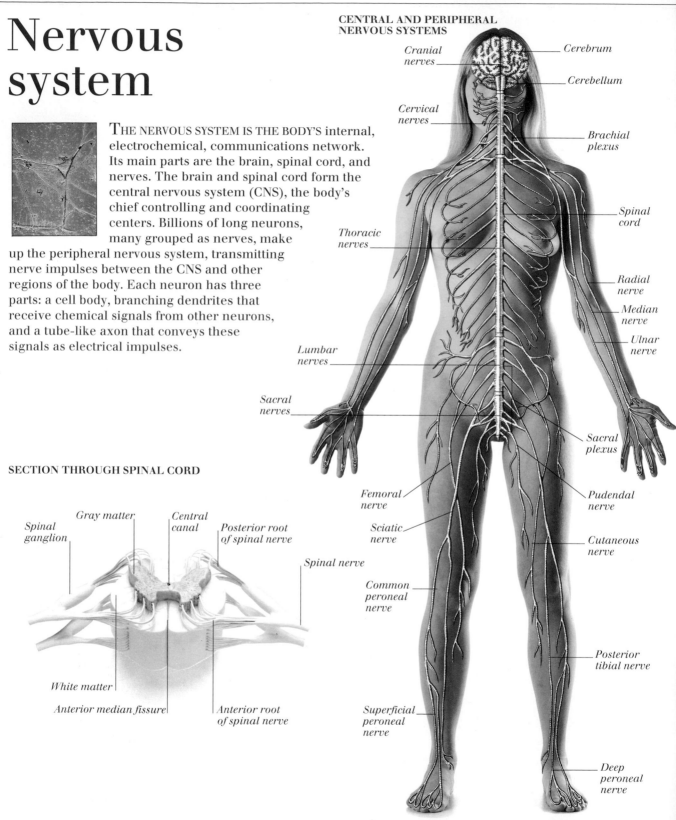

THE NERVOUS SYSTEM IS THE BODY'S internal, electrochemical, communications network. Its main parts are the brain, spinal cord, and nerves. The brain and spinal cord form the central nervous system (CNS), the body's chief controlling and coordinating centers. Billions of long neurons, many grouped as nerves, make up the peripheral nervous system, transmitting nerve impulses between the CNS and other regions of the body. Each neuron has three parts: a cell body, branching dendrites that receive chemical signals from other neurons, and a tube-like axon that conveys these signals as electrical impulses.

CENTRAL AND PERIPHERAL NERVOUS SYSTEMS

Cranial nerves

Cerebrum

Cerebellum

Cervical nerves

Brachial plexus

Thoracic nerves

Spinal cord

Radial nerve

Median nerve

Ulnar nerve

Lumbar nerves

Sacral nerves

Sacral plexus

Femoral nerve

Sciatic nerve

Pudendal nerve

Cutaneous nerve

Common peroneal nerve

Posterior tibial nerve

Superficial peroneal nerve

Deep peroneal nerve

SECTION THROUGH SPINAL CORD

Spinal ganglion

Gray matter

Central canal

Posterior root of spinal nerve

Spinal nerve

White matter

Anterior median fissure

Anterior root of spinal nerve

STRUCTURE OF A MOTOR NEURON

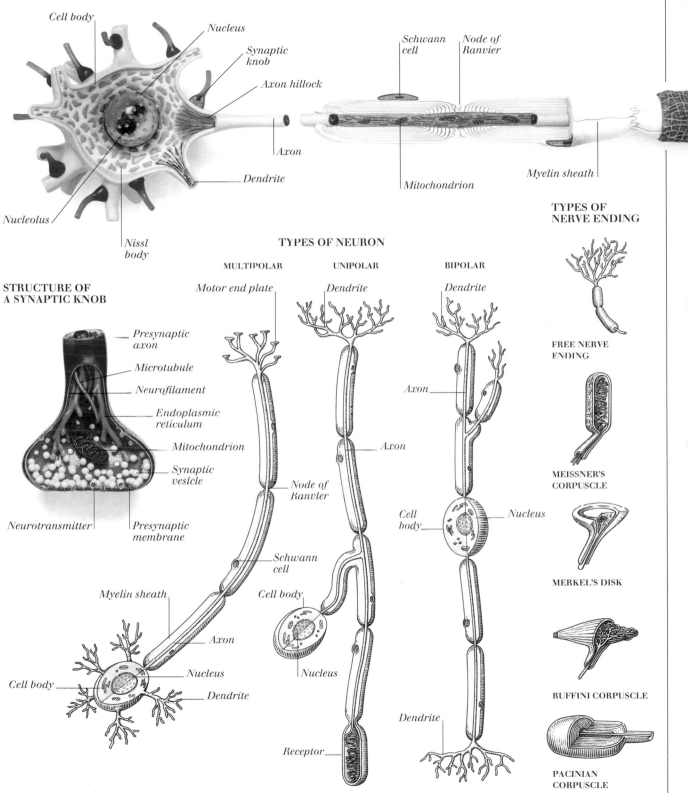

Cell body

Nucleus

Synaptic knob

Axon hillock

Axon

Dendrite

Nucleolus

Nissl body

Schwann cell

Node of Ranvier

Mitochondrion

Myelin sheath

TYPES OF NERVE ENDING

FREE NERVE ENDING

MEISSNER'S CORPUSCLE

MERKEL'S DISK

RUFFINI CORPUSCLE

PACINIAN CORPUSCLE

STRUCTURE OF A SYNAPTIC KNOB

Presynaptic axon

Microtubule

Neurofilament

Endoplasmic reticulum

Mitochondrion

Synaptic vesicle

Neurotransmitter

Presynaptic membrane

TYPES OF NEURON

MULTIPOLAR

Motor end plate

Node of Ranvier

Schwann cell

Myelin sheath

Axon

Cell body

Nucleus

Dendrite

UNIPOLAR

Dendrite

Axon

Cell body

Nucleus

Receptor

BIPOLAR

Dendrite

Axon

Cell body

Nucleus

Dendrite

Eye

THE EYE IS THE ORGAN OF SIGHT. The two eyeballs, protected within
bony sockets called orbits and on the outside by the eyelids,
eyebrows, and tear film, are directly connected to the brain
by the optic nerves. Each eye is moved by six muscles,
which are attached around the eyeball. Light rays
entering the eye through the pupil are focused by
the cornea and lens to form an image on the
retina. The retina contains millions of
light-sensitive cells, called rods and cones,
which convert the image into a pattern of
nerve impulses. These impulses are
transmitted along the optic nerve to the
brain. Information from the two optic
nerves is processed in the brain to
produce a single coordinated image.

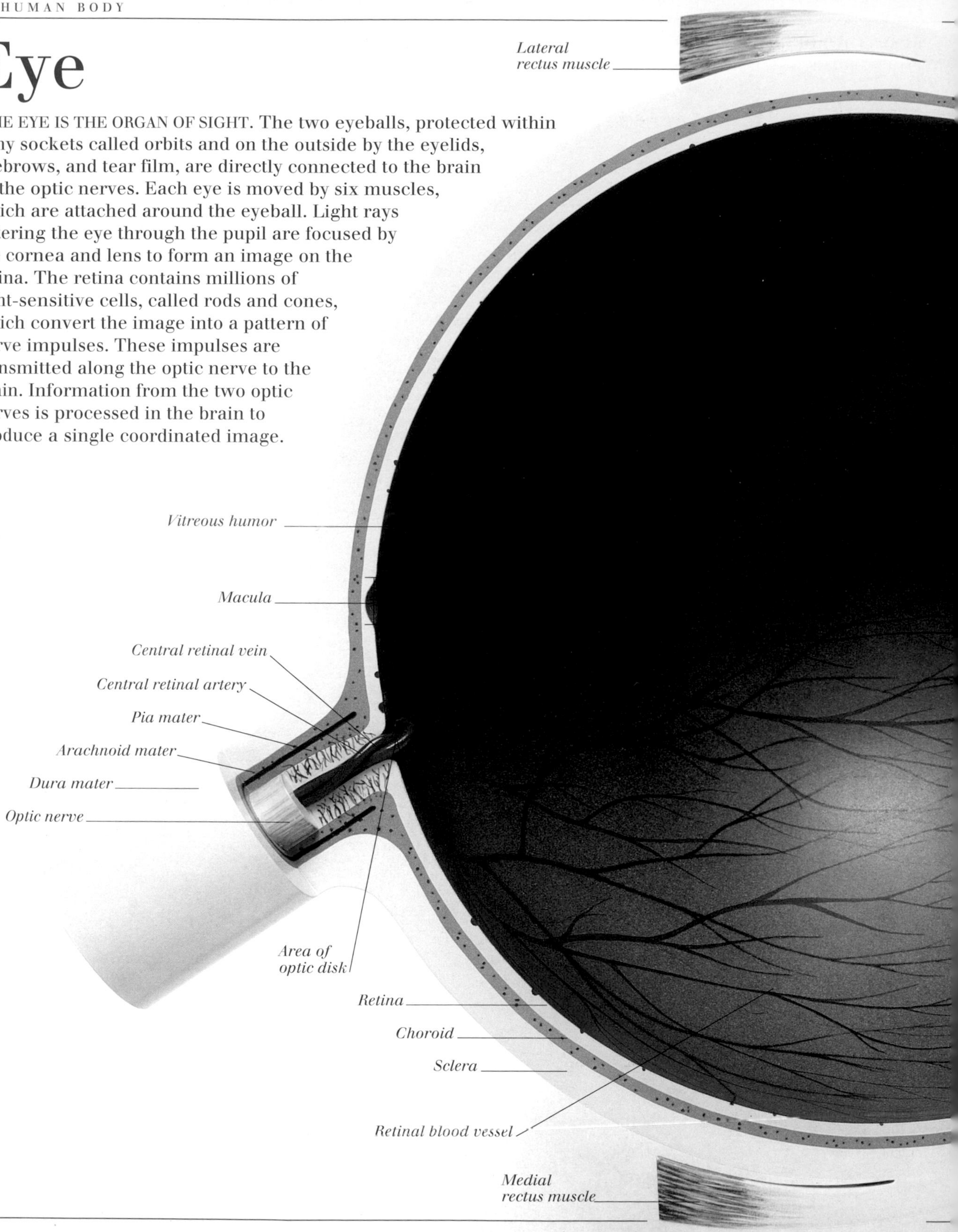

Lateral
rectus muscle

Vitreous humor

Macula

Central retinal vein

Central retinal artery

Pia mater

Arachnoid mater

Dura mater

Optic nerve

Area of
optic disk

Retina

Choroid

Sclera

Retinal blood vessel

Medial
rectus muscle

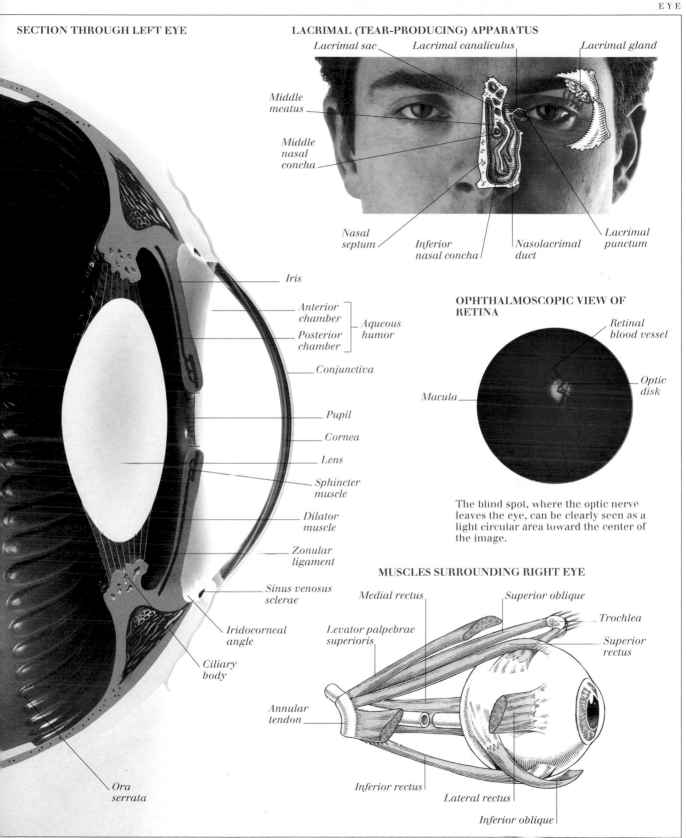

SECTION THROUGH LEFT EYE

LACRIMAL (TEAR-PRODUCING) APPARATUS

Lacrimal sac
Lacrimal canaliculus
Lacrimal gland

Middle
meatus

Middle
nasal
concha

Lacrimal
punctum

Nasal
septum

Inferior
nasal concha

Nasolacrimal
duct

Iris

Anterior
chamber

Aqueous
humor

Posterior
chamber

Conjunctiva

Pupil

Cornea

Lens

Sphincter
muscle

Dilator
muscle

Zonular
ligament

Sinus venosus
sclerae

Iridocorneal
angle

Ciliary
body

Ora
serrata

**OPHTHALMOSCOPIC VIEW OF
RETINA**

Retinal
blood vessel

Optic
disk

Macula

The blind spot, where the optic nerve
leaves the eye, can be clearly seen as a
light circular area toward the center of
the image.

MUSCLES SURROUNDING RIGHT EYE

Medial rectus
Superior oblique

Levator palpebrae
superioris

Trochlea

Superior
rectus

Annular
tendon

Inferior rectus
Lateral rectus

Inferior oblique

Ear

THE EAR IS THE ORGAN OF HEARING AND BALANCE. The outer ear consists of a flap called the auricle or pinna and the auditory canal. The main functional parts—the middle and inner ears—are enclosed within the skull. The middle ear consists of three tiny bones, known as auditory ossicles, and the eustachian tube, which links the ear to the back of the nose. The inner ear consists of the spiral-shaped cochlea, and also the semicircular canals and the vestibule, which are the organs of balance. Sound waves entering the ear travel through the auditory canal to the tympanic membrane (eardrum), where they are converted to vibrations that are transmitted via the ossicles to the cochlea. Here, the vibrations are converted by millions of microscopic hairs into electrical nerve signals to be interpreted by the brain.

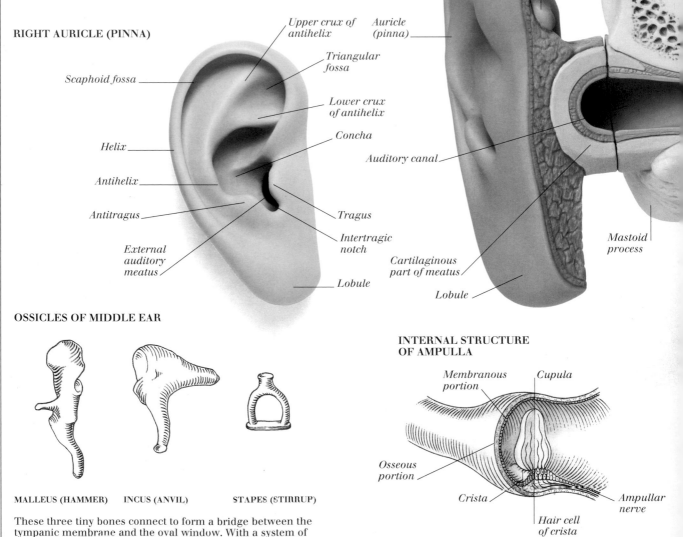

RIGHT AURICLE (PINNA)

Scaphoid fossa

Helix

Antihelix

Antitragus

External auditory meatus

Upper crux of antihelix

Triangular fossa

Lower crux of antihelix

Concha

Tragus

Intertragic notch

Lobule

Temporal bone

Cartilage of auricle

Auricle (pinna)

Auditory canal

Cartilaginous part of meatus

Lobule

Mastoid process

OSSICLES OF MIDDLE EAR

MALLEUS (HAMMER) **INCUS (ANVIL)** **STAPES (STIRRUP)**

These three tiny bones connect to form a bridge between the tympanic membrane and the oval window. With a system of membranes they convey sound vibrations to the inner ear.

INTERNAL STRUCTURE OF AMPULLA

Membranous portion

Cupula

Osseous portion

Crista

Hair cell of crista

Ampullar nerve

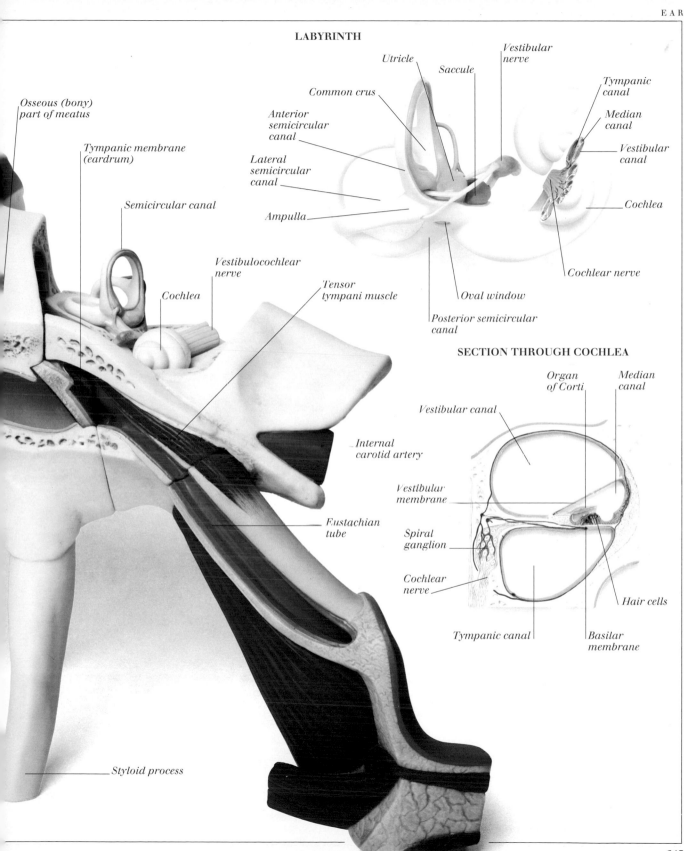

LABYRINTH

Utricle

Saccule

Vestibular nerve

Tympanic canal

Median canal

Common crus

Anterior semicircular canal

Vestibular canal

Lateral semicircular canal

Osseous (bony) part of meatus

Tympanic membrane (eardrum)

Ampulla

Cochlea

Semicircular canal

Vestibulocochlear nerve

Cochlear nerve

Tensor tympani muscle

Cochlea

Oval window

Posterior semicircular canal

Internal carotid artery

SECTION THROUGH COCHLEA

Organ of Corti

Median canal

Vestibular canal

Vestibular membrane

Spiral ganglion

Eustachian tube

Cochlear nerve

Hair cells

Tympanic canal

Basilar membrane

Styloid process

Nose, mouth, and throat

WITH EVERY BREATH, air passes through the nasal cavity down the pharynx (throat), larynx ("voice box"), and trachea (windpipe) to the lungs. The nasal cavity warms and moistens air, and the tiny layers in its lining protect the airway against damage by foreign bodies. During swallowing, the tongue moves up and back, the larynx rises, the epiglottis closes off the entrance to the trachea, and the soft palate separates the nasal cavity from the pharynx. Saliva, secreted from three pairs of salivary glands, lubricates food to make swallowing easier; it also begins the chemical breakdown of food, and helps to produce taste. The senses of taste and smell are closely linked. Both depend on the detection of dissolved molecules by sensory receptors in the olfactory nerve endings of the nose and in the taste buds of the tongue.

STRUCTURE OF TONGUE

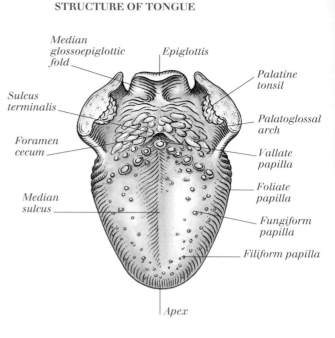

Median glossoepiglottic fold
Epiglottis
Palatine tonsil
Sulcus terminalis
Palatoglossal arch
Foramen cecum
Vallate papilla
Foliate papilla
Median sulcus
Fungiform papilla
Filiform papilla
Apex

STRUCTURES SURROUNDING PHARYNX

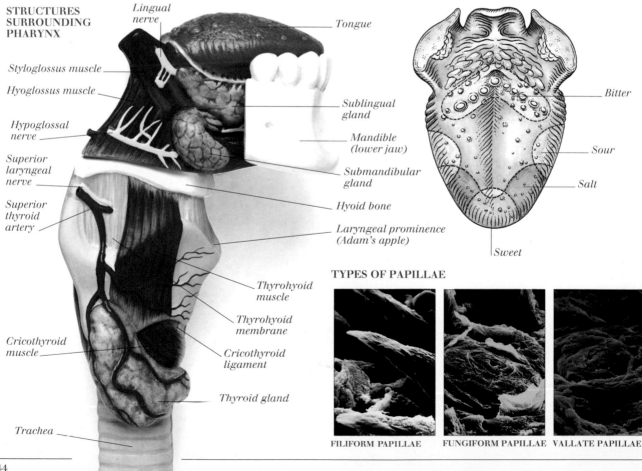

Lingual nerve
Tongue
Styloglossus muscle
Hyoglossus muscle
Sublingual gland
Hypoglossal nerve
Mandible (lower jaw)
Superior laryngeal nerve
Submandibular gland
Superior thyroid artery
Hyoid bone
Laryngeal prominence (Adam's apple)
Thyrohyoid muscle
Thyrohyoid membrane
Cricothyroid muscle
Cricothyroid ligament
Thyroid gland
Trachea

TASTE AREAS ON TONGUE

Bitter
Sour
Salt
Sweet

TYPES OF PAPILLAE

FILIFORM PAPILLAE   FUNGIFORM PAPILLAE   VALLATE PAPILLAE

SECTION THROUGH NOSE, MOUTH, AND THROAT

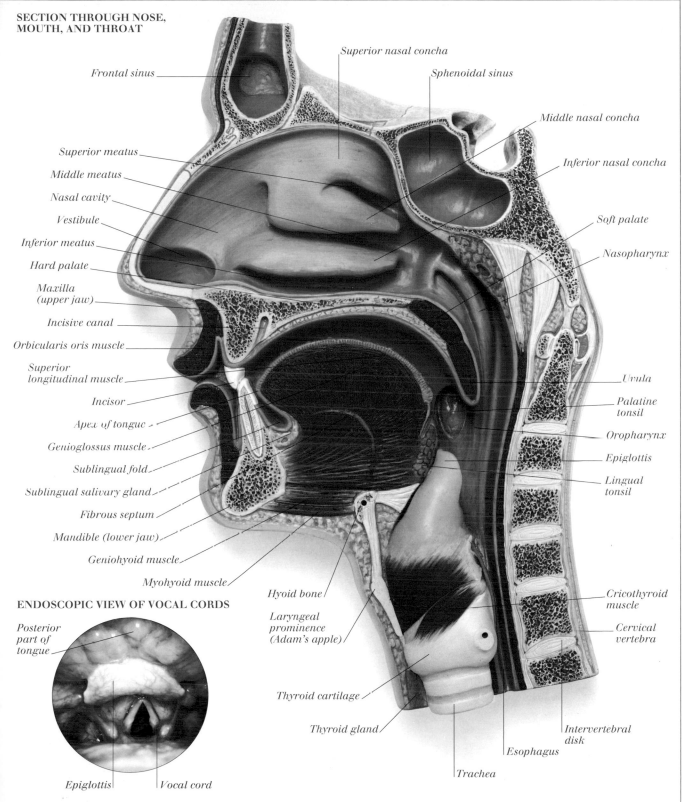

Frontal sinus

Superior nasal concha

Sphenoidal sinus

Middle nasal concha

Superior meatus

Middle meatus

Nasal cavity

Inferior nasal concha

Vestibule

Inferior meatus

Soft palate

Hard palate

Nasopharynx

Maxilla (upper jaw)

Incisive canal

Orbicularis oris muscle

Superior longitudinal muscle

Incisor

Apex of tongue

Uvula

Palatine tonsil

Oropharynx

Genioglossus muscle

Sublingual fold

Epiglottis

Lingual tonsil

Sublingual salivary gland

Fibrous septum

Mandible (lower jaw)

Geniohyoid muscle

Myohyoid muscle

Hyoid bone

Laryngeal prominence (Adam's apple)

Cricothyroid muscle

Cervical vertebra

ENDOSCOPIC VIEW OF VOCAL CORDS

Posterior part of tongue

Thyroid cartilage

Thyroid gland

Intervertebral disk

Esophagus

Epiglottis

Vocal cord

Trachea

Teeth

THE 20 PRIMARY TEETH (also called deciduous or milk teeth) usually begin to erupt when a baby is about six months old. They start to be replaced by the permanent teeth when the child is about six years old. By the age of 20, most adults have a full set of 32 teeth although the third molars (commonly called wisdom teeth) may never erupt. While teeth help people to speak clearly and give shape to the face, their main function is the chewing of food. Incisors and canines shear and tear the food into pieces; premolars and molars crush and grind it further. Although tooth enamel is the hardest substance in the body, it tends to be eroded and destroyed by acid produced in the mouth during the breakdown of food.

DEVELOPMENT OF TEETH IN A FETUS

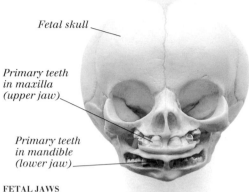

Fetal skull

Primary teeth in maxilla (upper jaw)

Primary teeth in mandible (lower jaw)

FETAL JAWS
By the sixth week of embryonic development areas of thickening occur in each jaw; these areas give rise to tooth buds. By the time the fetus is six months old, enamel has formed on the tooth buds.

DEVELOPMENT OF JAW AND TEETH

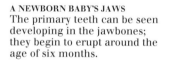

Maxilla (upper jaw)

Mandible (lower jaw)

A NEWBORN BABY'S JAWS
The primary teeth can be seen developing in the jawbones; they begin to erupt around the age of six months.

A FIVE-YEAR-OLD CHILD'S TEETH
There is a full set of 20 erupted primary teeth; the permanent teeth can be seen developing in the upper and lower jaws.

A NINE-YEAR-OLD CHILD'S TEETH
Most of the teeth are primary teeth but the permanent incisors and first molars have now emerged.

AN ADULT'S TEETH
By the age of 20, the full set of 32 permanent teeth (including the wisdom teeth) should be in position.

THE PERMANENT TEETH

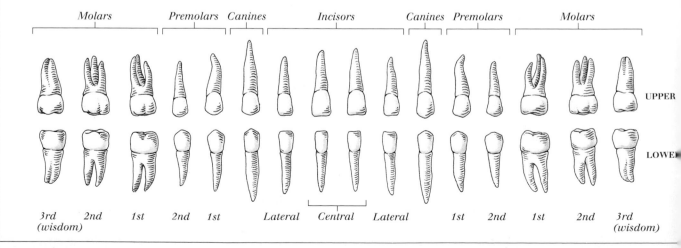

Molars — Premolars — Canines — Incisors — Canines — Premolars — Molars

UPPER

LOWER

3rd (wisdom) — 2nd — 1st — 2nd — 1st — Lateral — Central — Lateral — 1st — 2nd — 1st — 2nd — 3rd (wisdom)

STRUCTURE OF A TOOTH

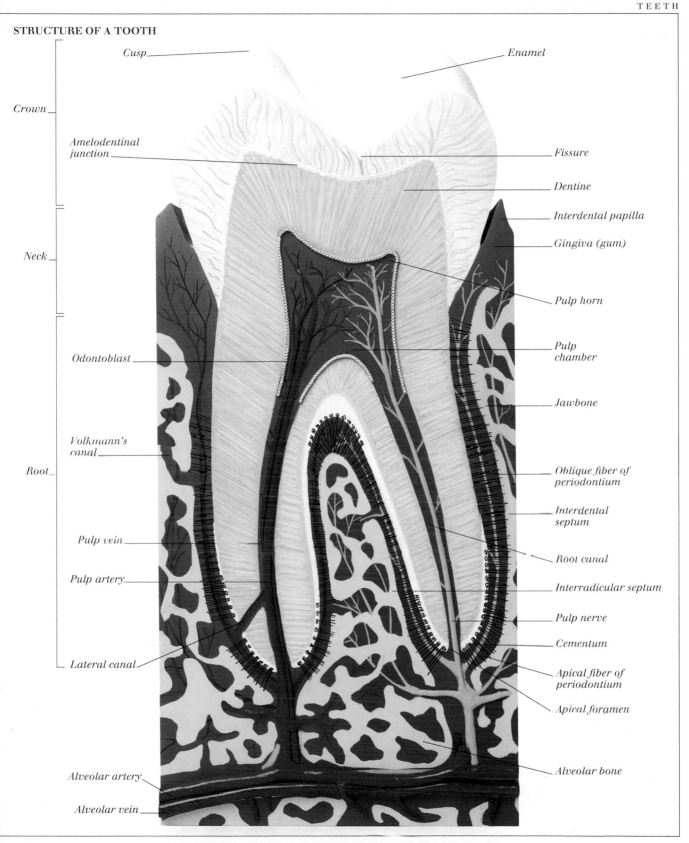

Cusp

Enamel

Crown

Amelodentinal junction

Fissure

Dentine

Interdental papilla

Neck

Gingiva (gum)

Pulp horn

Odontoblast

Pulp chamber

Jawbone

Volkmann's canal

Oblique fiber of periodontium

Root

Interdental septum

Pulp vein

Root canal

Pulp artery

Interradicular septum

Pulp nerve

Cementum

Apical fiber of periodontium

Lateral canal

Apical foramen

Alveolar bone

Alveolar artery

Alveolar vein

Digestive system

THE DIGESTIVE SYSTEM BREAKS DOWN FOOD into particles so tiny that blood can take nourishment to all parts of the body. The system's main part is a 30-foot (9 m) tube from mouth to rectum; muscles in this alimentary canal force food along. Chewed food first travels through the esophagus to the stomach, which churns and liquidizes food before it passes through the duodenum, jejunum, and ileum—the three parts of the long, convoluted small intestine. Here, digestive juices from the gallbladder and pancreas break down food particles; many filter out into the blood through tiny fingerlike villi that line the small intestine's inner wall. Undigested food in the colon forms feces that leave the body through the anus.

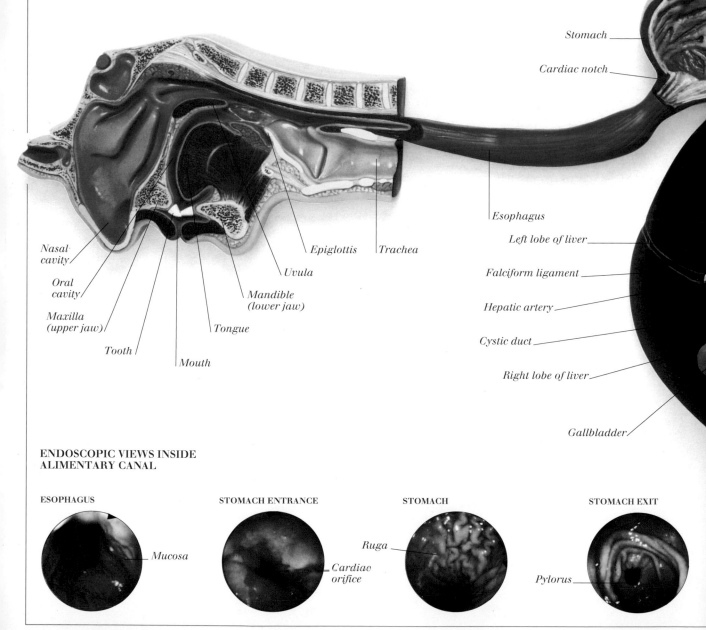

Stomach

Cardiac notch

Esophagus

Left lobe of liver

Falciform ligament

Hepatic artery

Cystic duct

Right lobe of liver

Gallbladder

Nasal cavity

Oral cavity

Maxilla (upper jaw)

Tooth

Mouth

Tongue

Mandible (lower jaw)

Uvula

Epiglottis

Trachea

ENDOSCOPIC VIEWS INSIDE ALIMENTARY CANAL

ESOPHAGUS

Mucosa

STOMACH ENTRANCE

Cardiac orifice

STOMACH

Ruga

STOMACH EXIT

Pylorus

ALIMENTARY CANAL

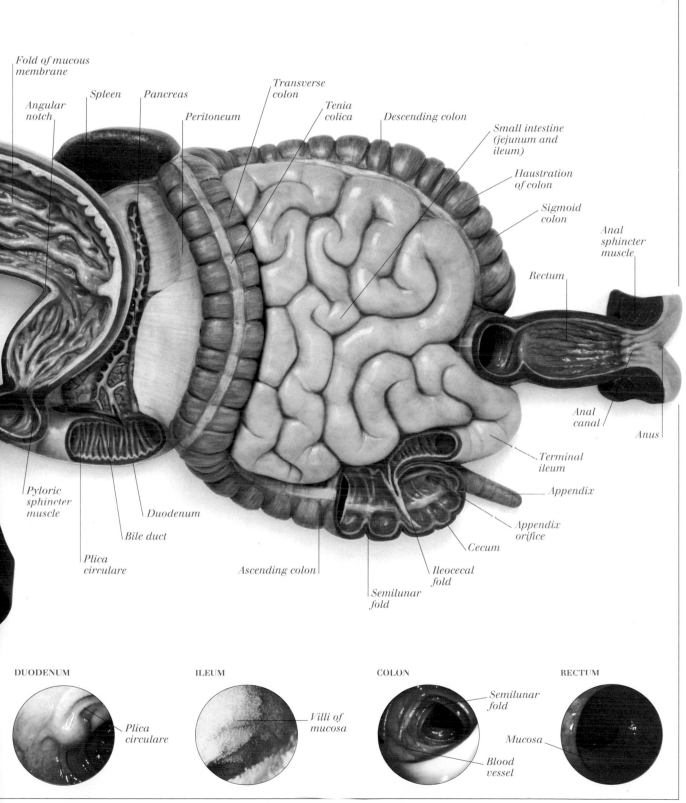

Fold of mucous membrane

Angular notch

Spleen

Pancreas

Peritoneum

Transverse colon

Tenia colica

Descending colon

Small intestine (jejunum and ileum)

Haustration of colon

Sigmoid colon

Anal sphincter muscle

Rectum

Anal canal

Anus

Terminal ileum

Appendix

Appendix orifice

Cecum

Ileocecal fold

Semilunar fold

Ascending colon

Pyloric sphincter muscle

Duodenum

Bile duct

Plica circulare

DUODENUM

Plica circulare

ILEUM

Villi of mucosa

COLON

Semilunar fold

Blood vessel

RECTUM

Mucosa

Heart

THE HEART IS A HOLLOW MUSCLE in the middle of the chest that pumps blood around the body, supplying cells with oxygen and nutrients. A muscular wall, called the septum, divides the heart lengthwise into left and right sides. A valve divides each side into two chambers: an upper atrium and a lower ventricle. When the heart muscle contracts, it squeezes blood through the atria and then through the ventricles. Oxygenated blood from the lungs flows from the pulmonary veins into the left atrium, through the left ventricle, and then out via the aorta to all parts of the body. Deoxygenated blood returning from the body flows from the vena cava into the right atrium, through the right ventricle, and then out via the pulmonary artery to the lungs for reoxygenation. At rest the heart beats between 60 and 80 times a minute; during exercise or at times of stress or excitement the rate may increase to 200 beats a minute.

ARTERIES AND VEINS SURROUNDING HEART

Aorta

Left coronary artery

Cardiac vein

Right coronary artery

Coronary sinus

Main branch of left coronary artery

SECTION THROUGH HEART WALL

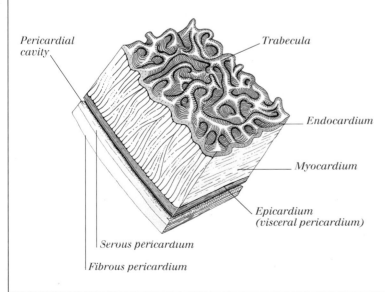

Pericardial cavity

Trabecula

Endocardium

Myocardium

Epicardium (visceral pericardium)

Serous pericardium

Fibrous pericardium

HEARTBEAT SEQUENCE

ATRIAL DIASTOLE

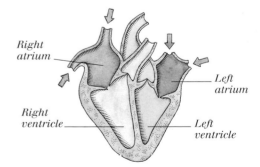

Right atrium

Left atrium

Right ventricle

Left ventricle

Deoxygenated blood enters the right atrium while the left atrium receives oxygenated blood.

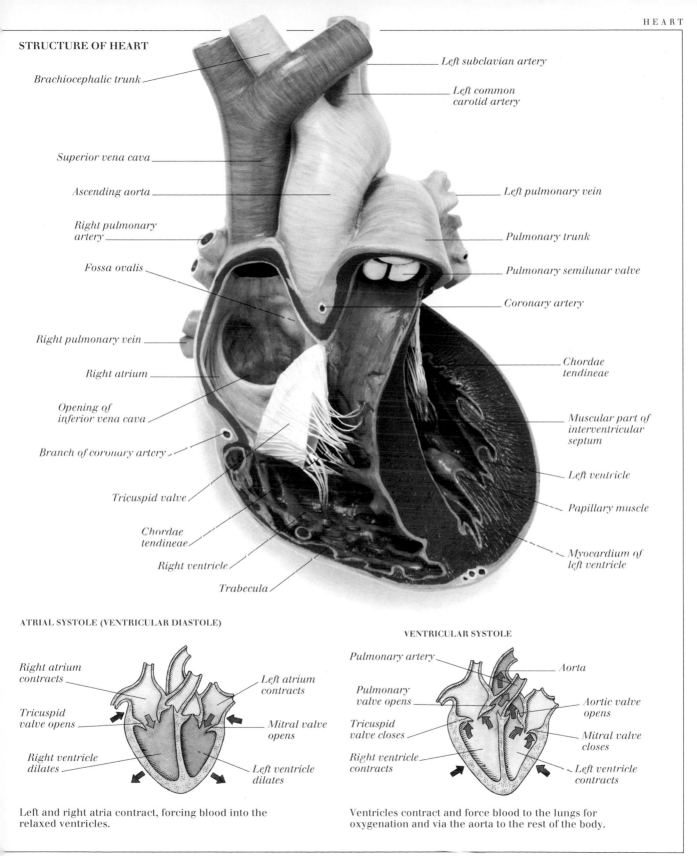

STRUCTURE OF HEART

Brachiocephalic trunk

Left subclavian artery

Left common carotid artery

Superior vena cava

Ascending aorta

Right pulmonary artery

Left pulmonary vein

Pulmonary trunk

Pulmonary semilunar valve

Fossa ovalis

Coronary artery

Right pulmonary vein

Right atrium

Chordae tendineae

Opening of inferior vena cava

Muscular part of interventricular septum

Branch of coronary artery

Left ventricle

Tricuspid valve

Papillary muscle

Chordae tendineae

Right ventricle

Myocardium of left ventricle

Trabecula

ATRIAL SYSTOLE (VENTRICULAR DIASTOLE)

Right atrium contracts

Left atrium contracts

Tricuspid valve opens

Mitral valve opens

Right ventricle dilates

Left ventricle dilates

Left and right atria contract, forcing blood into the relaxed ventricles.

VENTRICULAR SYSTOLE

Pulmonary artery

Aorta

Pulmonary valve opens

Aortic valve opens

Tricuspid valve closes

Mitral valve closes

Right ventricle contracts

Left ventricle contracts

Ventricles contract and force blood to the lungs for oxygenation and via the aorta to the rest of the body.

Circulatory system

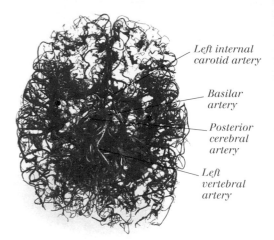

Left internal
carotid artery

Basilar
artery

Posterior
cerebral
artery

Left
vertebral
artery

THE CIRCULATORY SYSTEM consists of the heart and
blood vessels, which together maintain a continuous
flow of blood around the body. The heart pumps
oxygen-rich blood from the lungs to all parts of the
body through a network of tubes called arteries, and
smaller branches called arterioles. Blood returns to the heart via
small vessels called venules, which lead in turn into larger tubes
called veins. Arterioles and venules are linked by a network of
tiny vessels called capillaries, where the exchange of oxygen
and carbon dioxide between blood and body cells takes place.
Blood has four main components: red blood cells, white blood
cells, platelets, and liquid plasma.

CIRCULATORY SYSTEM OF HEART AND LUNGS

Superior vena cava

Aorta

CIRCULATORY SYSTEM OF LIVER

Inferior vena cava

Portal vein

Common
bile duct

Hepatic
artery

Gallbladder

Right ventricle

Left ventricle

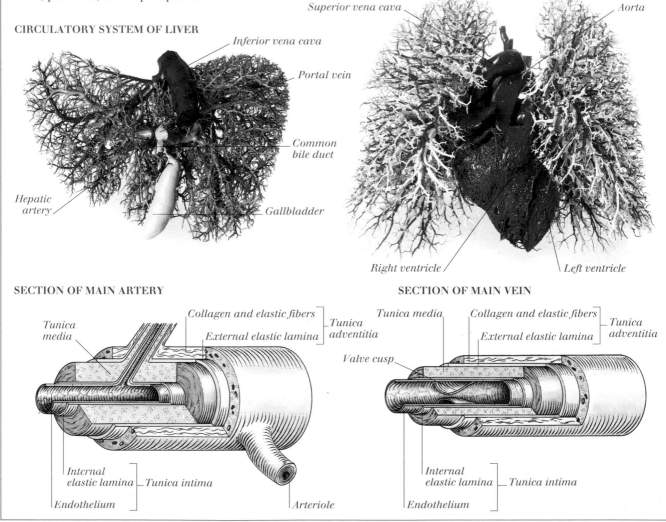

SECTION OF MAIN ARTERY

Tunica
media

Collagen and elastic fibers

External elastic lamina

Tunica
adventitia

Internal
elastic lamina — Tunica intima

Endothelium

Arteriole

SECTION OF MAIN VEIN

Tunica media

Collagen and elastic fibers

External elastic lamina

Tunica
adventitia

Valve cusp

Internal
elastic lamina — Tunica intima

Endothelium

PRINCIPAL ARTERIES AND VEINS OF CIRCULATORY SYSTEM

Common carotid artery

Subclavian artery

Arch of aorta

Axillary artery

Pulmonary artery

Coronary artery

Brachial artery

Gastric artery

Hepatic artery

Splenic artery

Superior mesenteric artery

Radial artery

Ulnar artery

Palmar arch

Digital artery

Common iliac artery

External iliac artery

Internal iliac artery

Femoral artery

Popliteal artery

Peroneal artery

Anterior tibial artery

Posterior tibial artery

Lateral plantar artery

Dorsal metatarsal artery

Internal jugular vein

Brachiocephalic vein

Subclavian vein

Axillary vein

Cephalic vein

Superior vena cava

Pulmonary vein

Basilic vein

Hepatic portal vein

Median cubital vein

Inferior vena cava

Anterior median vein

Gastroepiploic vein

Palmar vein

Digital vein

Inferior mesenteric vein

Superior mesenteric vein

Common iliac vein

External iliac vein

Internal iliac vein

Femoral vein

Great saphenous vein

Short saphenous vein

Dorsal venous arch

Digital vein

TYPES OF BLOOD CELLS

RED BLOOD CELLS
These cells are biconcave in shape to maximize their oxygen-carrying capacity.

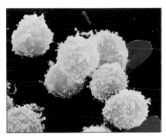

WHITE BLOOD CELLS
Lymphocytes are the smallest white blood cells; they form antibodies against disease.

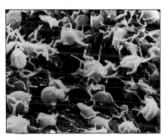

PLATELETS
Tiny cells that are activated whenever blood clotting or repair to vessels is necessary.

BLOOD CLOTTING

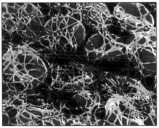

Filaments of fibrin enmesh red blood cells as part of the process of blood clotting.

Respiratory system

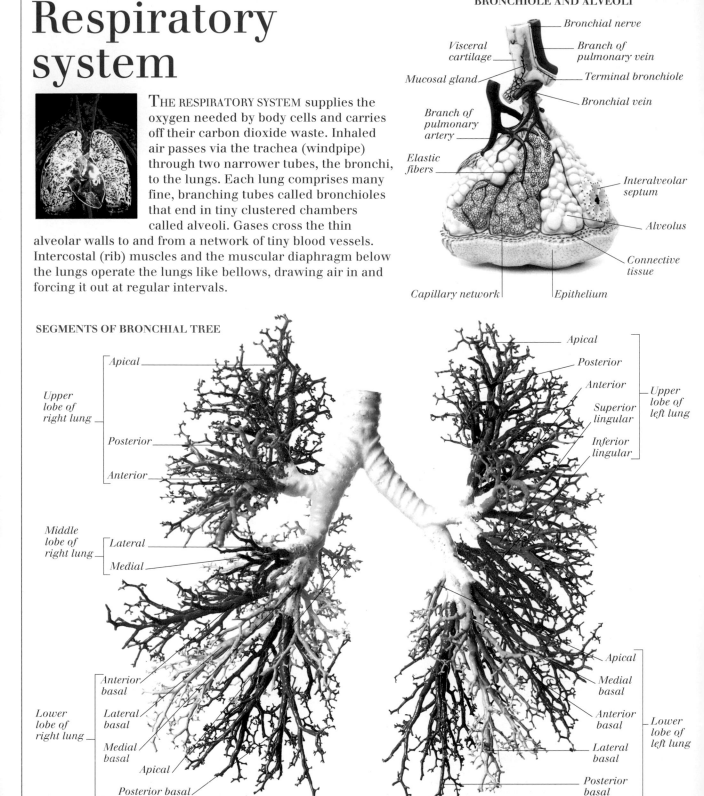

THE RESPIRATORY SYSTEM supplies the oxygen needed by body cells and carries off their carbon dioxide waste. Inhaled air passes via the trachea (windpipe) through two narrower tubes, the bronchi, to the lungs. Each lung comprises many fine, branching tubes called bronchioles that end in tiny clustered chambers called alveoli. Gases cross the thin alveolar walls to and from a network of tiny blood vessels. Intercostal (rib) muscles and the muscular diaphragm below the lungs operate the lungs like bellows, drawing air in and forcing it out at regular intervals.

BRONCHIOLE AND ALVEOLI

Bronchial nerve

Visceral cartilage

Branch of pulmonary vein

Mucosal gland

Terminal bronchiole

Bronchial vein

Branch of pulmonary artery

Elastic fibers

Interalveolar septum

Alveolus

Connective tissue

Capillary network

Epithelium

SEGMENTS OF BRONCHIAL TREE

Apical

Posterior

Anterior

Upper lobe of right lung

Apical

Posterior

Anterior

Superior lingular

Inferior lingular

Upper lobe of left lung

Middle lobe of right lung

Lateral

Medial

Apical

Medial basal

Anterior basal

Lower lobe of left lung

Lateral basal

Posterior basal

Anterior basal

Lateral basal

Medial basal

Apical

Posterior basal

Lower lobe of right lung

STRUCTURES OF THORACIC CAVITY

GASEOUS EXCHANGE IN ALVEOLUS

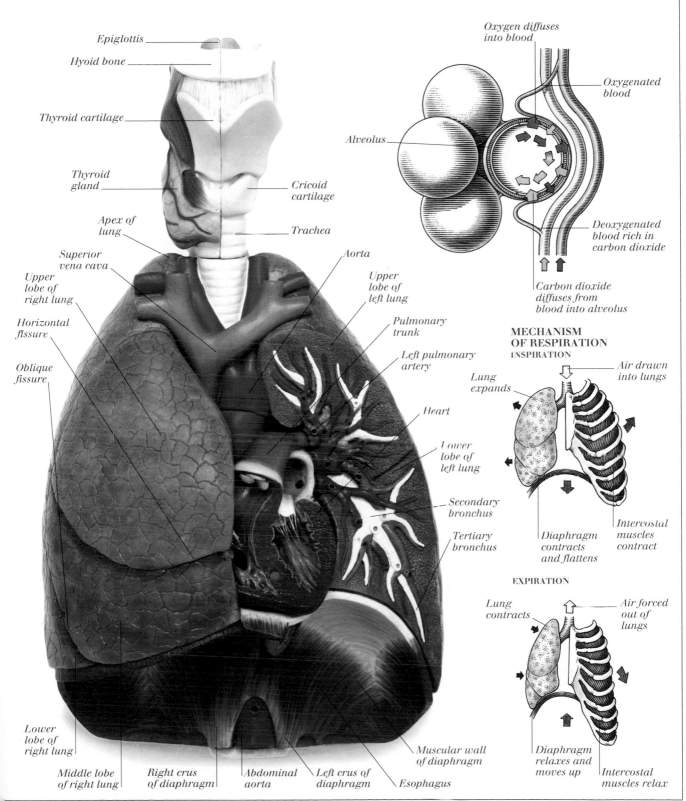

Epiglottis

Hyoid bone

Thyroid cartilage

Thyroid gland

Cricoid cartilage

Trachea

Apex of lung

Aorta

Superior vena cava

Upper lobe of left lung

Upper lobe of right lung

Pulmonary trunk

Horizontal fissure

Left pulmonary artery

Oblique fissure

Heart

Lower lobe of left lung

Secondary bronchus

Tertiary bronchus

Lower lobe of right lung

Middle lobe of right lung

Right crus of diaphragm

Abdominal aorta

Left crus of diaphragm

Esophagus

Muscular wall of diaphragm

Oxygen diffuses into blood

Oxygenated blood

Alveolus

Deoxygenated blood rich in carbon dioxide

Carbon dioxide diffuses from blood into alveolus

MECHANISM OF RESPIRATION
INSPIRATION

Lung expands

Air drawn into lungs

Diaphragm contracts and flattens

Intercostal muscles contract

EXPIRATION

Lung contracts

Air forced out of lungs

Diaphragm relaxes and moves up

Intercostal muscles relax

Urinary system

THE URINARY SYSTEM FILTERS WASTE PRODUCTS from the blood and removes them from the body via a system of tubes. Blood is filtered in the two kidneys, which are fist-sized, bean-shaped organs. The renal arteries carry blood to the kidneys; the renal veins remove blood after filtering. Each kidney contains about one million tiny units called nephrons. Each nephron is made up of a tubule and a filtering unit called a glomerulus, which consists of a collection of tiny blood vessels surrounded by the hollow Bowman's capsule. The filtering process produces a watery fluid that leaves the kidney as urine. The urine is carried via two tubes called ureters to the bladder, where it is stored until its release from the body through another tube called the urethra.

ARTERIAL SYSTEM OF KIDNEYS

Aorta

Celiac trunk

Superior mesenteric artery

Right renal artery

Left renal artery

Right ureter

Left ureter

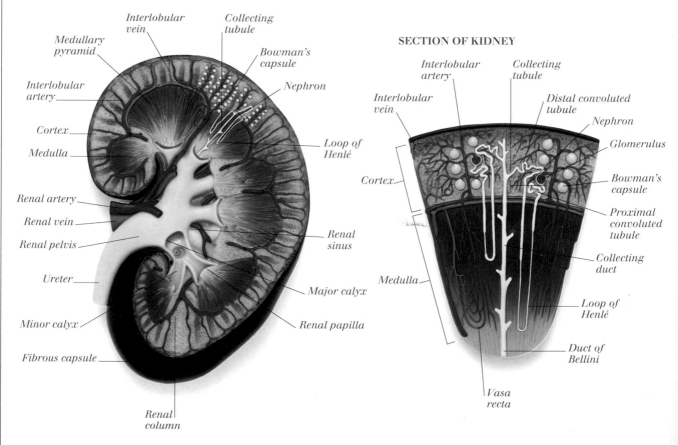

SECTION THROUGH LEFT KIDNEY

Interlobular vein

Collecting tubule

Medullary pyramid

Bowman's capsule

Interlobular artery

Nephron

Cortex

Medulla

Loop of Henlé

Renal artery

Renal vein

Renal pelvis

Renal sinus

Ureter

Major calyx

Minor calyx

Renal papilla

Fibrous capsule

Renal column

SECTION OF KIDNEY

Interlobular artery

Collecting tubule

Interlobular vein

Distal convoluted tubule

Nephron

Glomerulus

Cortex

Bowman's capsule

Proximal convoluted tubule

Medulla

Collecting duct

Loop of Henlé

Duct of Bellini

Vasa recta

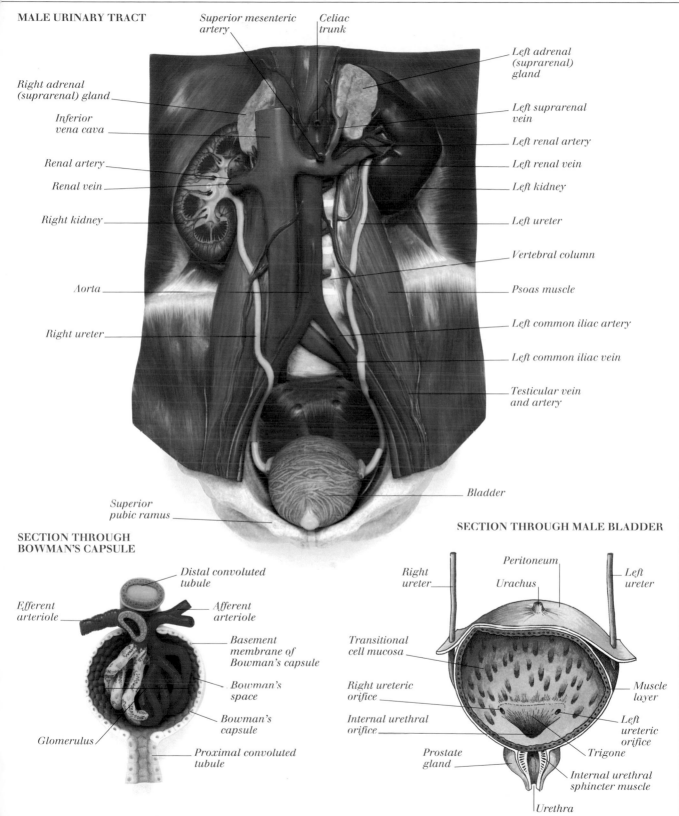

MALE URINARY TRACT

Superior mesenteric artery

Celiac trunk

Left adrenal (suprarenal) gland

Right adrenal (suprarenal) gland

Inferior vena cava

Left suprarenal vein

Left renal artery

Renal artery

Left renal vein

Renal vein

Left kidney

Right kidney

Left ureter

Vertebral column

Aorta

Psoas muscle

Right ureter

Left common iliac artery

Left common iliac vein

Testicular vein and artery

Bladder

Superior pubic ramus

SECTION THROUGH BOWMAN'S CAPSULE

Distal convoluted tubule

Efferent arteriole

Afferent arteriole

Basement membrane of Bowman's capsule

Bowman's space

Bowman's capsule

Glomerulus

Proximal convoluted tubule

SECTION THROUGH MALE BLADDER

Right ureter

Peritoneum

Urachus

Left ureter

Transitional cell mucosa

Right ureteric orifice

Muscle layer

Internal urethral orifice

Left ureteric orifice

Prostate gland

Trigone

Internal urethral sphincter muscle

Urethra

257

Reproductive system

SEX ORGANS LOCATED IN THE PELVIS create new human lives. Each month a ripe egg is released from one of the female's ovaries into a fallopian tube leading to the uterus (womb), a muscular pear-sized organ. A male produces minute tadpole-like sperm in two oval glands called testes. When the male is ready to release sperm into the female's vagina, many millions pass into his urethra and leave his body through the fleshy penis. The sperm travel up through the vagina into the uterus and fallopian tubes, and one sperm may enter and fertilize an egg. The fertilized egg becomes embedded in the uterus wall and starts to grow into a new human being.

SECTION THROUGH OVARY

Corpus albicans

Fallopian tube

Corpus luteum

Mature ruptured follicle

Primary follicle

Germinal epithelium

Graffian follicle

Oocyte (egg)

Secondary follicle

SECTION THROUGH FEMALE PELVIC REGION

Ureter

Ampulla of fallopian tube

Fimbria of fallopian tube

Isthmus of fallopian tube

Ovary

Fundus of uterus

Uterus (womb)

Cervix (neck of uterus)

Os

Rectum

Vagina

Anus

Perineum

Introitus (vaginal opening)

Bladder

Pubic symphysis

Urethra

Clitoris

External urinary meatus

Labia minora

Labia majora

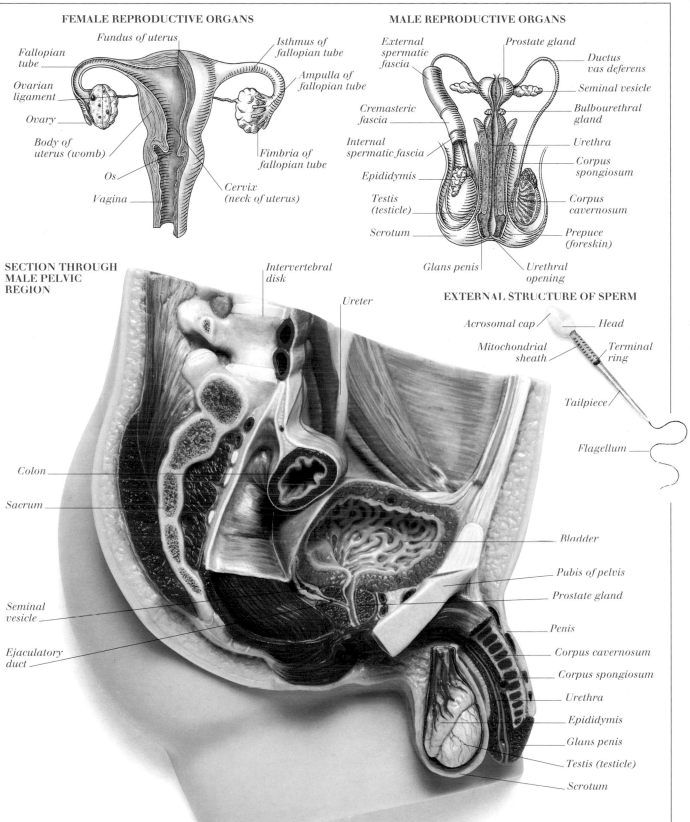

FEMALE REPRODUCTIVE ORGANS

Fundus of uterus
Fallopian tube
Ovarian ligament
Ovary
Body of uterus (womb)
Os
Vagina
Isthmus of fallopian tube
Ampulla of fallopian tube
Fimbria of fallopian tube
Cervix (neck of uterus)

MALE REPRODUCTIVE ORGANS

External spermatic fascia
Cremasteric fascia
Internal spermatic fascia
Epididymis
Testis (testicle)
Scrotum
Glans penis
Prostate gland
Ductus vas deferens
Seminal vesicle
Bulbourethral gland
Urethra
Corpus spongiosum
Corpus cavernosum
Prepuce (foreskin)
Urethral opening

SECTION THROUGH MALE PELVIC REGION

Intervertebral disk
Ureter
Colon
Sacrum
Seminal vesicle
Ejaculatory duct
Bladder
Pubis of pelvis
Prostate gland
Penis
Corpus cavernosum
Corpus spongiosum
Urethra
Epididymis
Glans penis
Testis (testicle)
Scrotum

EXTERNAL STRUCTURE OF SPERM

Acrosomal cap
Mitochondrial sheath
Head
Terminal ring
Tailpiece
Flagellum

Development of a baby

A FERTILIZED EGG IS NOURISHED AND PROTECTED as it
develops into an embryo and then a fetus during the 40
weeks of pregnancy. The placenta, a mass of blood vessels
implanted in the uterus lining, delivers nourishment and
oxygen, and removes waste through the umbilical cord.
Meanwhile, the fetus lies snugly in its amniotic sac, a bag of
fluid that protects it against any sudden jolts. In the last
weeks of the pregnancy, the rapidly growing fetus turns
head down: a baby ready to be born.

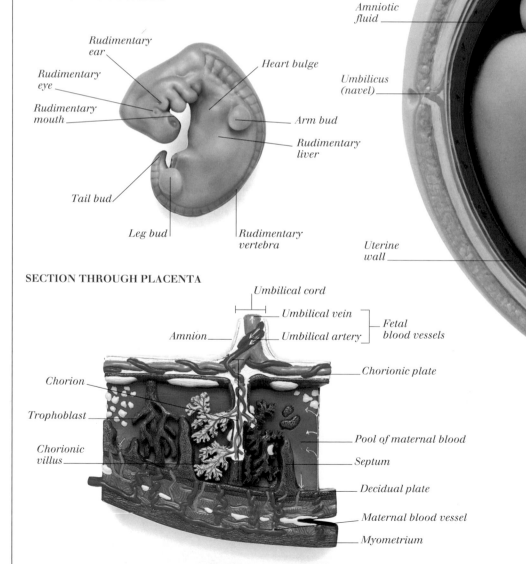

EMBRYO AT FIVE WEEKS

Rudimentary
ear

Rudimentary
eye

Rudimentary
mouth

Heart bulge

Arm bud

Rudimentary
liver

Tail bud

Leg bud

Rudimentary
vertebra

Amniotic
fluid

Umbilicus
(navel)

Uterine
wall

Fetus

SECTION THROUGH PLACENTA

Umbilical cord

Umbilical vein

Amnion

Umbilical artery

Fetal
blood vessels

Chorionic plate

Chorion

Trophoblast

Pool of maternal blood

Chorionic
villus

Septum

Decidual plate

Maternal blood vessel

Myometrium

SECTION THROUGH PELVIS IN NINTH MONTH OF PREGNANCY

THE DEVELOPING FETUS

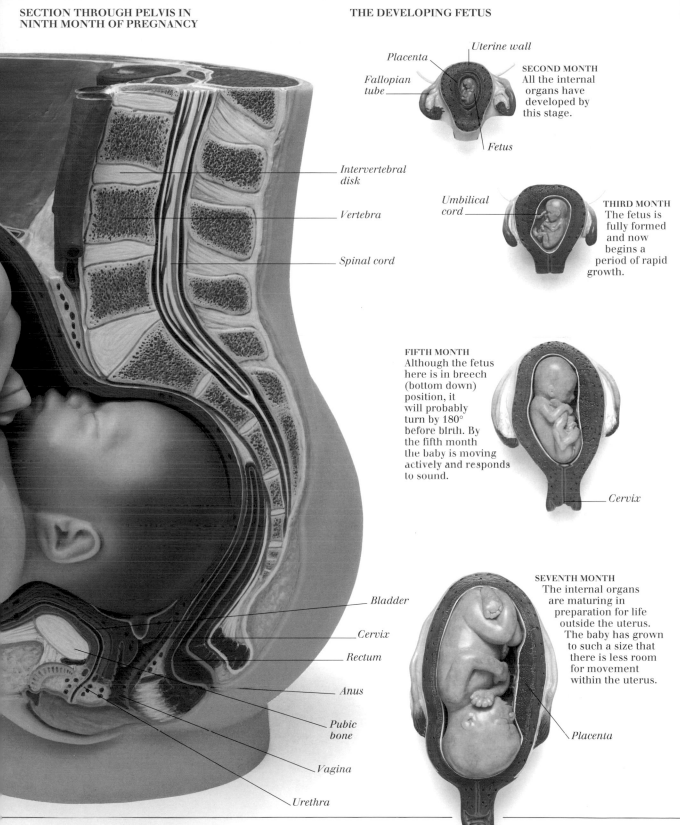

Placenta

Uterine wall

Fallopian tube

SECOND MONTH All the internal organs have developed by this stage.

Fetus

Intervertebral disk

Vertebra

Spinal cord

Umbilical cord

THIRD MONTH The fetus is fully formed and now begins a period of rapid growth.

FIFTH MONTH Although the fetus here is in breech (bottom down) position, it will probably turn by 180° before birth. By the fifth month the baby is moving actively and responds to sound.

Cervix

SEVENTH MONTH The internal organs are maturing in preparation for life outside the uterus. The baby has grown to such a size that there is less room for movement within the uterus.

Bladder

Cervix

Rectum

Anus

Pubic bone

Placenta

Vagina

Urethra

GEOLOGY, GEOGRAPHY, AND METEOROLGY

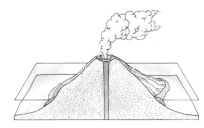

Earth's physical features

MOST OF THE EARTH'S SURFACE (about 70 percent) is covered with water. The largest single body of water, the Pacific Ocean, alone covers about 30 percent of the surface. Most of the land is distributed as seven continents; these are (from largest to smallest) Asia, Africa, North America, South America, Antarctica, Europe, and Australasia. The physical features of the land are remarkably varied. Among the most notable are mountain ranges, rivers, and deserts. The largest mountain ranges—the Himalayas in Asia and the Andes in South America—extend for thousands of miles. The Himalayas include the world's highest mountain, Mount Everest (29,029 feet). The longest rivers are the River Nile in Africa (4,160 miles) and the Amazon River in South America (4,000 miles). Deserts cover about 20 percent of the total land area. The largest is the Sahara, which covers nearly a third of Africa. The Earth's surface features can be represented in various ways. Only a globe can correctly represent areas, shapes, sizes, and directions, because there is always distortion when a spherical surface like the Earth's is projected onto the flat surface of a map. Each map projection is therefore a compromise: some aspects of global features are shown accurately by allowing others to be distorted. Even satellite mapping does not produce completely accurate maps, although they can show physical features with great clarity.

CYLINDRICAL
PROJECTION

CYLINDRICAL-
PROJECTION MAP

180° 160° 120° 80°

Great Slave
Lake

Great Bear
Lake

Lake
Superior

Greenland

Mackenzie-
Peace River

Baffin
Island

Bering
Sea

Hudson
Bay

Rocky
Mountains

NORTH
AMERICA

Mississippi-
Missouri River

Lake Huron

Lake Ontario

Lake Erie

Lake Michigan

Sonoran
Desert

Appalachian
Mountains

ATLANTIC
OCEAN

Sierra
Madre

Gulf of
Mexico

Chihuahuan
Desert

Caribbean
Sea

Guiana
Highlands

Amaz
River

Braz
Hight

PACIFIC
OCEAN

Andes

Atacama
Desert

Gran
Chaco

Parana
River

Pampas

Patagonia

Mat
Gro

180° 160° 120° 80°

WEST OF GREENW
MERIDIAN

SATELLITE MAPPING OF THE EARTH

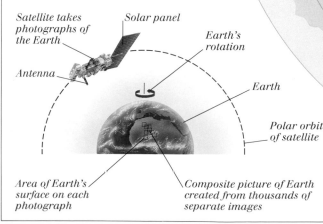

Satellite takes
photographs of
the Earth

Solar panel

Earth's
rotation

Antenna

Earth

Polar orbit
of satellite

Area of Earth's
surface on each
photograph

Composite picture of Earth
created from thousands of
separate images

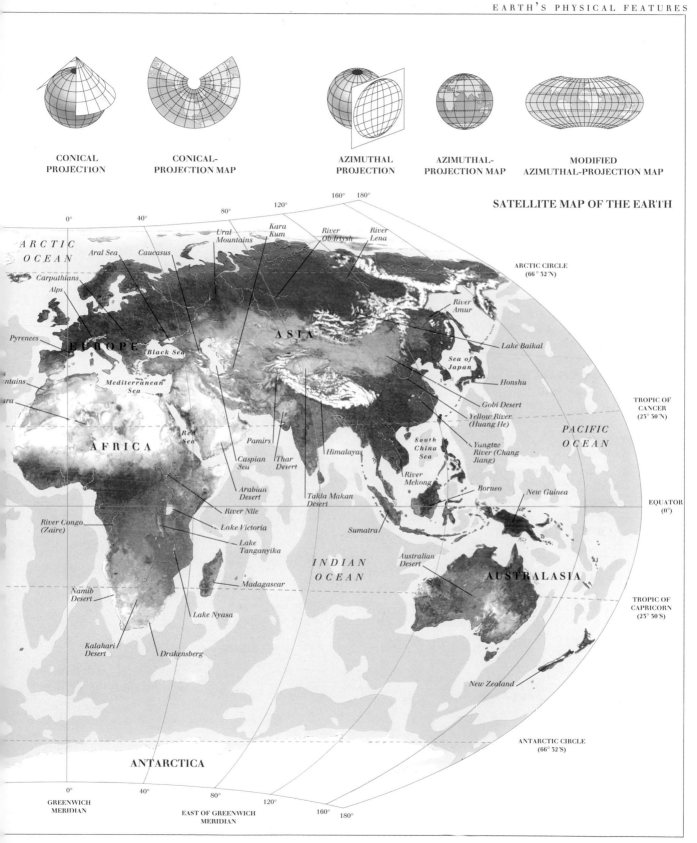

CONICAL
PROJECTION

CONICAL-
PROJECTION MAP

AZIMUTHAL
PROJECTION

AZIMUTHAL-
PROJECTION MAP

MODIFIED
AZIMUTHAL-PROJECTION MAP

SATELLITE MAP OF THE EARTH

160° 180°
120°
80°
40°
0°

*ARCTIC
OCEAN*

ARCTIC CIRCLE
(66° 52'N)

Aral Sea
Caucasus
Carpathians
Alps
Pyrenees

Ural
Mountains
Kara
Kum
River
Ob-Irtysh
River
Lena

EUROPE
Black Sea

ASIA

River
Amur

Lake Baikal

*Sea of
Japan*

Honshu

ntains
ura

*Mediterranean
Sea*

Gobi Desert

TROPIC OF
CANCER
(25° 30'N)

*Red
Sea*

AFRICA

Pamirs

*Caspian
Sea*

Thar
Desert

Himalayas

*South
China
Sea*

Yellow River
(Huang He)

Yungtse
River (Chang
Jiang)

*PACIFIC
OCEAN*

Arabian
Desert

Takla Makan
Desert

River
Mekong

Borneo

New Guinea

EQUATOR
(0°)

River Nile
Lake Victoria

*River Congo
(Zaire)*

Lake
Tanganyika

Sumatra

*INDIAN
OCEAN*

Australian
Desert

AUSTRALASIA

*Namib
Desert*

Madagascar

TROPIC OF
CAPRICORN
(25° 30'S)

Lake Nyasa

*Kalahari
Desert*

Drakensberg

New Zealand

ANTARCTIC CIRCLE
(66° 52'S)

ANTARCTICA

0°
40°
80°
120°
160° 180°

GREENWICH
MERIDIAN

EAST OF GREENWICH
MERIDIAN

The rock cycle

HEXAGONAL BASALT COLUMNS, ICELAND

THE ROCK CYCLE IS A CONTINUOUS PROCESS through which old rocks are transformed into new ones. Rocks can be divided into three main groups: igneous, sedimentary, and metamorphic. Igneous rocks are formed when magma (molten rock) from the Earth's interior cools and solidifies (see pp. 274-275). Sedimentary rocks are formed when sediment (rock particles, for example) becomes compressed and cemented together in a process known as lithification (see pp. 276-277). Metamorphic rocks are formed when igneous, sedimentary, or other metamorphic rocks are changed by heat or pressure (see pp. 274-275). Rocks are added to the Earth's surface by crustal movements and volcanic activity. Once exposed on the surface, the rocks are broken down into rock particles by weathering (see pp. 282-283). The particles are then transported by glaciers, rivers, and wind and are deposited as sediment in lakes, deltas, deserts, and on the ocean floor. Some of this sediment undergoes lithification and forms sedimentary rock. This rock may be thrust back to the surface by crustal movements or forced deeper into the Earth's interior, where heat and pressure transform it into metamorphic rock. The metamorphic rock in turn may be pushed up to the surface or may be melted to form magma. Eventually, the magma cools and solidifies—below or on the surface—forming igneous rock. When the sedimentary, igneous, and metamorphic rocks are exposed once more on the Earth's surface, the cycle begins again.

THE ROCK CYCLE

- Igneous rock
- Cooling and solidification (crystallization)
- Weathering, transport, and deposition
- Sediment
- Magma
- Heat and pressure (metamorphism)
- Weathering, transport, and deposition
- Weathering, transport, and deposition
- Compression and cementation (lithification)
- Melting
- Metamorphic rock
- Heat and pressure (metamorphism)
- Sedimentary rock

STAGES IN THE ROCK CYCLE

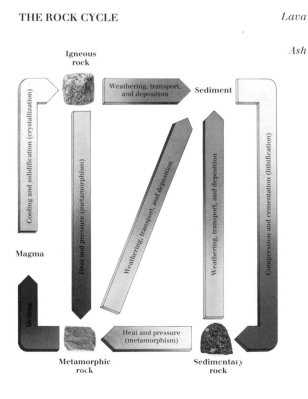

Magma extruded as lava, which solidifies to form igneous rock

Lava flow

Vent

Main conduit

Secondary conduit

Lava

Ash

Rock surrounding magma changed by heat to form metamorphic rock

Intense heat of rising magma melts some of the surrounding rock

Sedimentary rock crushed and folded to form metamorphic rock

IGNEOUS ROCK

*Pyroxene
crystal*

*Olivine
crystal*

*Coarse-
grained
texture*

*Dark
pyroxene
crystal*

*Plagioclase
feldspar*

**PHOTOMICROGRAPH
OF GABBRO**

**PIECE OF
GABBRO**

SEDIMENTARY ROCK

*Mud groundmass
(matrix)*

*Brown coloring
from iron oxides*

*Fine-
grained
texture*

*Ammonite
shell embedded
in rock*

*Ammonite
shell*

**PHOTOMICROGRAPH OF
SHELLY LIMESTONE**

**PIECE OF SHELLY
LIMESTONE**

METAMORPHIC ROCK

*Garnet crystal
(pink)*

*Red garnet
crystal*

*Wavy
foliation*

*Quartz and
feldspar crystal
(gray)*

**PHOTOMICROGRAPH OF
GARNET-MICA SCHIST**

**PIECE OF GARNET-
MICA SCHIST**

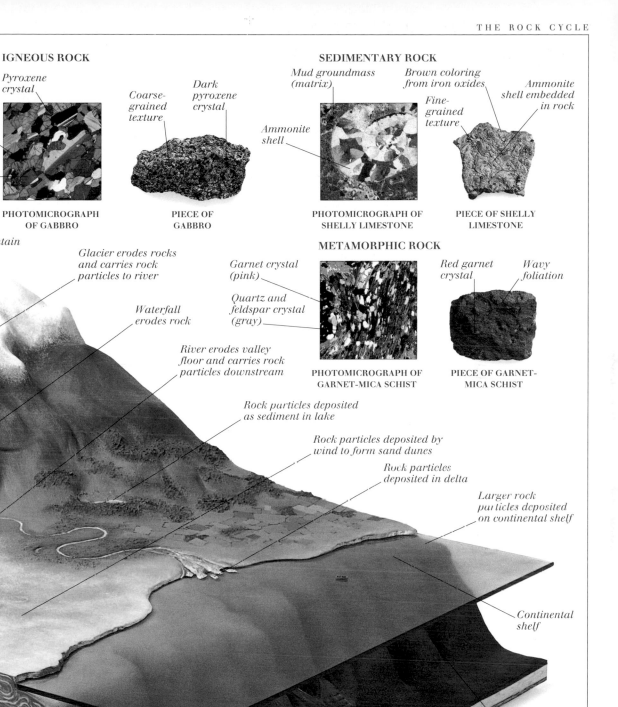

Mountain

*Glacier erodes rocks
and carries rock
particles to river*

*Waterfall
erodes rock*

*River erodes valley
floor and carries rock
particles downstream*

*Rock particles deposited
as sediment in lake*

*Rock particles deposited by
wind to form sand dunes*

*Rock particles
deposited in delta*

*Larger rock
particles deposited
on continental shelf*

*Continental
shelf*

*Continental
slope*

*Finer rock particles
collect on ocean floor to
form layers of sediment*

*Layers of sediment compressed and
cemented to form sedimentary rock*

Minerals

A MINERAL IS A NATURALLY OCCURRING SUBSTANCE that has a characteristic chemical composition and specific physical properties, such as habit and streak (see pp. 270-271). A rock, by comparison, is an aggregate of minerals and need not have a specific chemical composition. Minerals are made up of elements (substances that cannot be broken down chemically into simpler substances), each of which can be represented by a chemical symbol. Minerals can be divided into two main groups: native elements and compounds. Native elements are made up of a pure element. Examples include gold (chemical symbol Au), silver (Ag), copper (Cu), and carbon (C); carbon occurs as a native element in two forms, diamond and graphite. Compounds are combinations of two or more elements. For example, sulfides are compounds of sulfur (S) and one or more other elements, such as lead (Pb) in the mineral galena, or antimony (Sb) in the mineral stibnite.

NATIVE ELEMENTS

Dendritic (branching) copper

Limonite groundmass (matrix)

COPPER
(Cu)

SULFIDES

Cubic galena crystal

GALENA
(PbS)

Dendritic (branching) gold

Quartz vein

GOLD
(Au)

White diamond

Kimberlite groundmass (matrix)

DIAMOND
(C)

Hexagonal graphite crystal

GRAPHITE
(C)

OXIDES/HYDROXIDES

Milky quartz groundmass (matrix)

Smoky quartz crystal

SMOKY QUARTZ
(SiO_2)

Rounded bauxite grains in groundmass (matrix)

BAUXITE
($FeO(OH)$ and $Al_2O_3.2H_2O$)

Mass of specular hematite crystals

SPECULAR HEMATITE
(Fe_2O_3)

Prismatic stibnite crystal

Quartz groundmass (matrix)

STIBNITE
(Sb_2S_3)

Perfect octahedral pyrites crystal

Quartz crystal

PYRITES
(FeS_2)

Parallel bands of onyx

ONYX
(SiO_2)

Kidney ore hematite

Specular crystals of hematite

KIDNEY ORE HEMATITE
(Fe_2O_3)

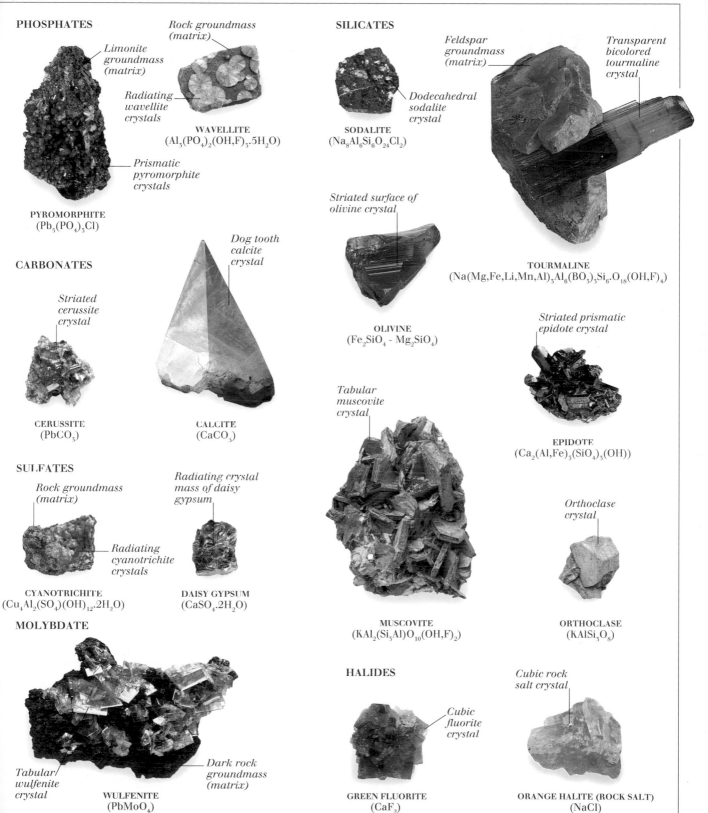

PHOSPHATES

Limonite groundmass (matrix)

Rock groundmass (matrix)

Radiating wavellite crystals

WAVELLITE
$(Al_5(PO_4)_2(OH,F)_5.5H_2O)$

Prismatic pyromorphite crystals

PYROMORPHITE
$(Pb_5(PO_4)_3Cl)$

SILICATES

Feldspar groundmass (matrix)

Dodecahedral sodalite crystal

SODALITE
$(Na_8Al_6Si_6O_{24}Cl_2)$

Transparent bicolored tourmaline crystal

Striated surface of olivine crystal

OLIVINE
$(Fe_2SiO_4 - Mg_2SiO_4)$

TOURMALINE
$(Na(Mg,Fe,Li,Mn,Al)_3Al_6(BO_3)_3Si_6.O_{18}(OH,F)_4)$

CARBONATES

Striated cerussite crystal

Dog tooth calcite crystal

CERUSSITE
$(PbCO_3)$

CALCITE
$(CaCO_3)$

Striated prismatic epidote crystal

EPIDOTE
$(Ca_2(Al,Fe)_3(SiO_4)_3(OH))$

SULFATES

Rock groundmass (matrix)

Radiating crystal mass of daisy gypsum

Radiating cyanotrichite crystals

CYANOTRICHITE
$(Cu_4Al_2(SO_4)(OH)_{12}.2H_2O)$

DAISY GYPSUM
$(CaSO_4.2H_2O)$

Tabular muscovite crystal

Orthoclase crystal

MUSCOVITE
$(KAl_2(Si_3Al)O_{10}(OH,F)_2)$

ORTHOCLASE
$(KAlSi_3O_8)$

MOLYBDATE

HALIDES

Cubic rock salt crystal

Cubic fluorite crystal

Tabular wulfenite crystal

Dark rock groundmass (matrix)

WULFENITE
$(PbMoO_4)$

GREEN FLUORITE
(CaF_2)

ORANGE HALITE (ROCK SALT)
$(NaCl)$

Mineral features

MINERALS CAN BE IDENTIFIED BY STUDYING features such as fracture, cleavage, crystal system, habit, hardness, color, and streak. Minerals can break in different ways. If a mineral breaks in an irregular way, leaving rough surfaces, it possesses fracture. If a mineral breaks along well-defined planes of weakness, it possesses cleavage. Specific minerals have distinctive patterns of cleavage. For example, mica cleaves along one plane. Most minerals form crystals that can be categorized into crystal systems according to their symmetry and number of faces. Within each system, several different but related forms of crystal are possible; for example, a cubic crystal can have six, eight, or twelve sides. A mineral's habit is the typical form taken by an aggregate of its crystals. Examples of habit include botryoidal (like a bunch of grapes) and massive (no definite form). The relative hardness of a mineral may be assessed by testing its resistance to scratching. This property is usually measured using Mohs' scale, which increases in hardness from 1 (talc) to 10 (diamond). The color of a mineral is not a dependable guide to its identity as some minerals have a range of colors. Streak (the color the powdered mineral makes when rubbed across an unglazed tile) is a more reliable indicator.

CLEAVAGE

Cleavage in one direction

CLEAVAGE ALONG ONE PLANE

Cleavage in three directions, forming a block cube

CLEAVAGE ALONG THREE PLANES

Horizontal cleavage

Vertical cleavage

CLEAVAGE ALONG TWO PLANES

Cleavage in four directions, forming a double-pyramid crystal

CLEAVAGE ALONG FOUR PLANES

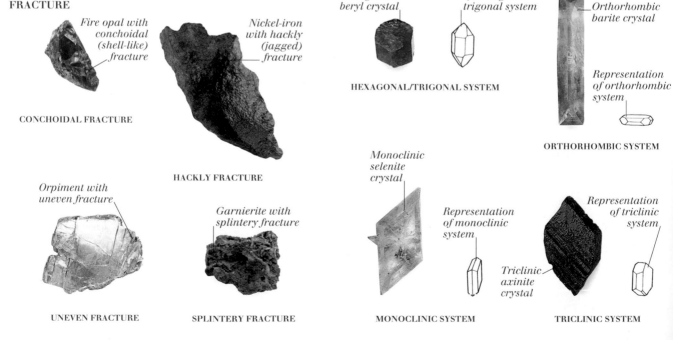

CRYSTAL SYSTEMS

Cubic iron pyrites crystal

Tetragonal idocrase crystal

Representation of tetragonal system

TETRAGONAL SYSTEM

CUBIC SYSTEM

Representation of cubic system

Hexagonal beryl crystal

Representation of hexagonal/trigonal system

Orthorhombic barite crystal

HEXAGONAL/TRIGONAL SYSTEM

Representation of orthorhombic system

ORTHORHOMBIC SYSTEM

FRACTURE

Fire opal with conchoidal (shell-like) fracture

Nickel-iron with hackly (jagged) fracture

CONCHOIDAL FRACTURE

HACKLY FRACTURE

Orpiment with uneven fracture

Garnierite with splintery fracture

UNEVEN FRACTURE

SPLINTERY FRACTURE

Monoclinic selenite crystal

Representation of monoclinic system

Triclinic axinite crystal

Representation of triclinic system

MONOCLINIC SYSTEM

TRICLINIC SYSTEM

HABIT

Kunzite with prismatic habit

Silver with twisted wire habit

TWISTED WIRE HABIT

PRISMATIC HABIT

Wollastonite with fibrous habit

Hematite with tabular habit (flattened structure)

TABULAR HABIT

FIBROUS HABIT

Chalcedony with botryoidal habit (like a bunch of grapes)

Carnallite with massive habit (no definite shape)

BOTRYOIDAL HABIT

MASSIVE HABIT

STREAK

COLOR OF MINERAL

COLOR OF STREAK

Yellow orpiment — *Golden-yellow*

Brown hematite — *Red-brown*

Red-brown crocoite — *Yellow*

Gold chalcopyrite — *Black*

Black-red cinnabar — *Red*

Silver molybdenite — *Gray*

COLOR

Rose-colored crystal of rose quartz

ROSE, PINK

Translucent white-gray crystal of milky quartz

WHITE-GRAY

Translucent crystal of orange citrine

Transparent glassy crystal of rock crystal

ORANGE

BEIGE, TRANSPARENT

MOHS' SCALE OF HARDNESS

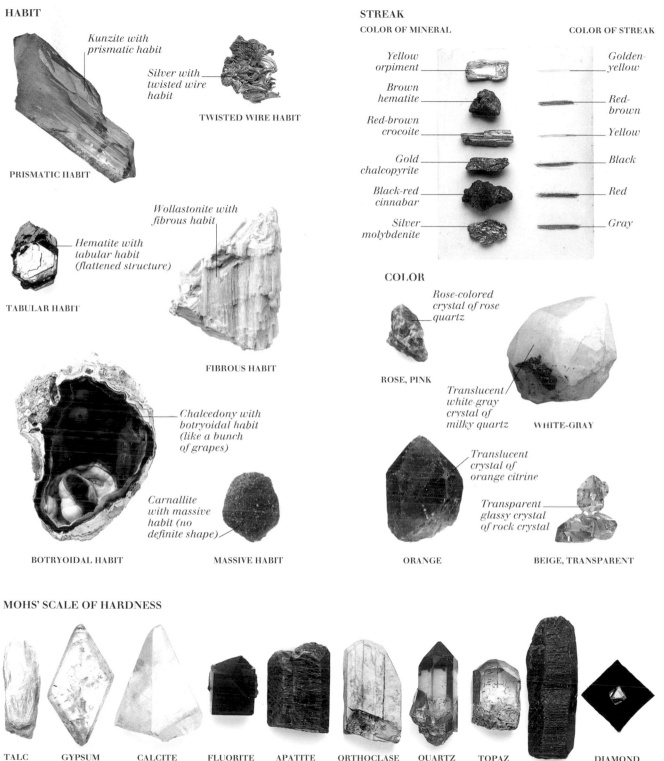

| TALC | GYPSUM | CALCITE | FLUORITE | APATITE | ORTHOCLASE | QUARTZ | TOPAZ | CORUNDUM | DIAMOND |
| 1 | 2 | 3 | 4 | 5 | 6 | 7 | 8 | 9 | 10 |

Volcanoes

VOLCANOES ARE VENTS OR FISSURES IN THE EARTH'S CRUST through which magma (molten rock that originates from deep beneath the crust) is forced onto the surface as lava. They occur most commonly along the boundaries of crustal plates; most volcanoes lie in a belt called the "Ring of Fire," which runs along the edge of the Pacific Ocean. Volcanoes can be classified according to the violence and frequency of their eruptions.

Nonexplosive volcanic eruptions generally occur where crustal plates pull apart. These eruptions produce runny basaltic lava that spreads quickly over a wide area to form relatively flat cones. The most violent eruptions take place where plates collide. Such eruptions produce thick rhyolitic lava and may also blast out clouds of dust and pyroclasts (lava fragments). The lava does not flow far before cooling and therefore builds up steep-sided, conical volcanoes. Some volcanoes produce lava and ash eruptions, which build up composite volcanic cones. Volcanoes that erupt frequently are described as active, those that erupt rarely are termed dormant, and those that have stopped erupting altogether are termed extinct. Besides the volcanoes themselves, other features associated with volcanic regions include geysers, hot mineral springs, solfataras, fumaroles, and bubbling mud pools.

Folded, rope-like surface

PAHOEHOE (ROPY LAVA)

HORU GEYSER, NEW ZEALAND

VOLCANO TYPES

Basaltic lava plateau   *Fissure created by plates moving apart*   *Gentle slope*

FISSURE VOLCANO

Gentle slope built up by numerous basaltic lava flows   *Vent*

BASIC SHIELD VOLCANO

Vent   *Steep, convex sides caused by thick lava cooling quickly*

DOME VOLCANO

Slightly concave sides   *Vent*   *Cinder*   *Fine ash*

ASH-CINDER VOLCANO

Vent   *Steep conical shape*   *Lava*   *Ash*   *Secondary conduit*

COMPOSITE VOLCANO

Caldera (volcanic crater)   *New cone*   *Old cone*   *Ash*

CALDERA VOLCANO

Layers of sedimentary rocks

Metamorphic rocks (rocks altered by heat and pressure)

HOW VOLCANIC PLUGS BECOME EXPOSED

Extinct volcano   *Solidified lava forms plug*

PLUG FORMATION

Plug exposed   *Volcanic cone slowly eroded away*

INITIAL EROSION AROUND PLUG

Resistant lava plug remains   *Volcanic cone completely eroded away*

COMPLETE DENUDATION OF PLUG

LAPILLI (LAVA FRAGMENTS)

Small piece of solidified lava

TYPES OF LAVA

Scoria (sharp, angular chunks)

Driblets of lava from roof of tunnel

AA (BLOCKY LAVA)

REMELTED LAVA

LOCATION OF VOLCANOES

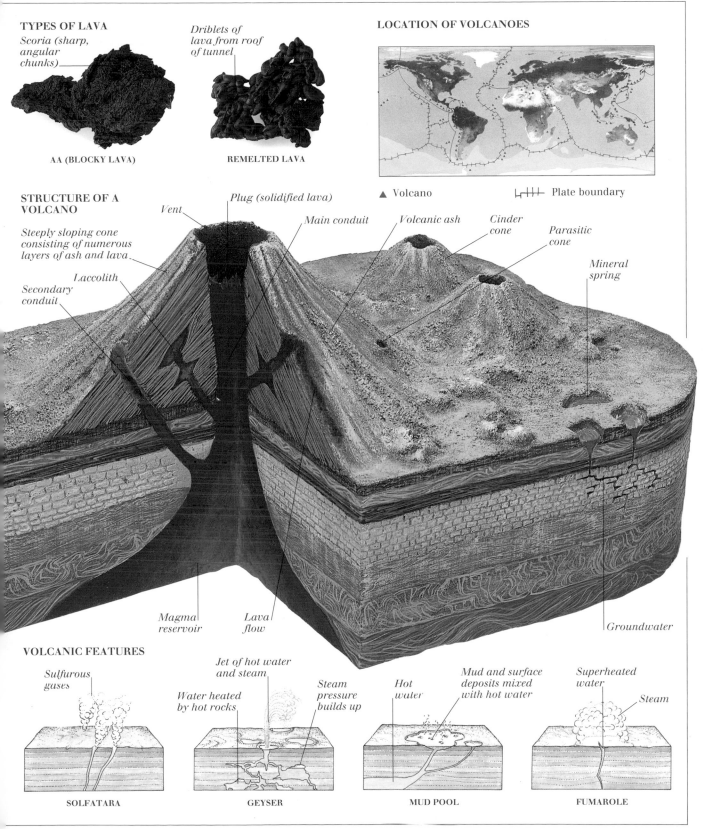

▲ Volcano   ⊢╫┼ Plate boundary

STRUCTURE OF A VOLCANO

Steeply sloping cone consisting of numerous layers of ash and lava

Laccolith

Secondary conduit

Vent

Plug (solidified lava)

Main conduit

Volcanic ash

Cinder cone

Parasitic cone

Mineral spring

Magma reservoir

Lava flow

Groundwater

VOLCANIC FEATURES

Sulfurous gases

Jet of hot water and steam

Water heated by hot rocks

Steam pressure builds up

Hot water

Mud and surface deposits mixed with hot water

Superheated water

Steam

SOLFATARA

GEYSER

MUD POOL

FUMAROLE

Igneous and metamorphic rocks

IGNEOUS ROCKS ARE FORMED WHEN MAGMA (molten rock that originates from deep beneath the Earth's crust) cools and solidifies. There are two main types of igneous rock: intrusive and extrusive. Intrusive rocks are formed deep underground, where magma is forced into cracks or between rock layers to form structures including sills, dikes, and batholiths. The magma cools slowly to form coarse-grained rocks such as gabbro and pegmatite. Extrusive rocks are formed above the Earth's surface from lava (magma that has been ejected in a volcanic eruption). The molten lava cools quickly, producing fine-grained rocks such as rhyolite and basalt. Metamorphic rocks are those that have been altered by intense heat (contact metamorphism) or extreme pressure (regional metamorphism). Contact metamorphism occurs when rocks are changed by heat from, for example, an igneous intrusion or lava flow. Regional metamorphism occurs when rock is crushed in the middle of a folding mountain range. Metamorphic rocks can be formed from igneous rocks, sedimentary rocks, or even other metamorphic rocks.

BASALT COLUMNS

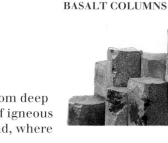

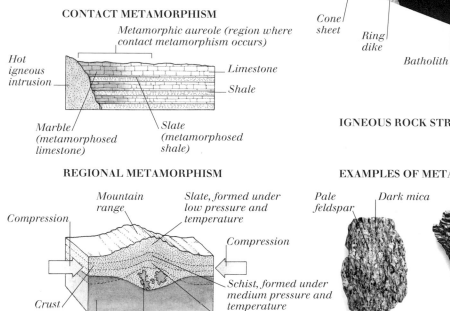

Butte

Plug

Cedar tree laccolith

Cinder cone

Large eroded lava flow

Cone sheet

Ring dike

Batholith

Dike

Sill

Dike swarm

Lopolith

IGNEOUS ROCK STRUCTURES

CONTACT METAMORPHISM

Metamorphic aureole (region where contact metamorphism occurs)

Hot igneous intrusion

Limestone

Shale

Marble (metamorphosed limestone)

Slate (metamorphosed shale)

REGIONAL METAMORPHISM

Mountain range

Slate, formed under low pressure and temperature

Compression

Compression

Crust

Mantle

Magma

Schist, formed under medium pressure and temperature

Gneiss, formed under high pressure and temperature

EXAMPLES OF METAMORPHIC ROCKS

Pale feldspar

Dark mica

Dark mineral band

Pale calcite

GNEISS

FOLDED SCHIST

SKARN

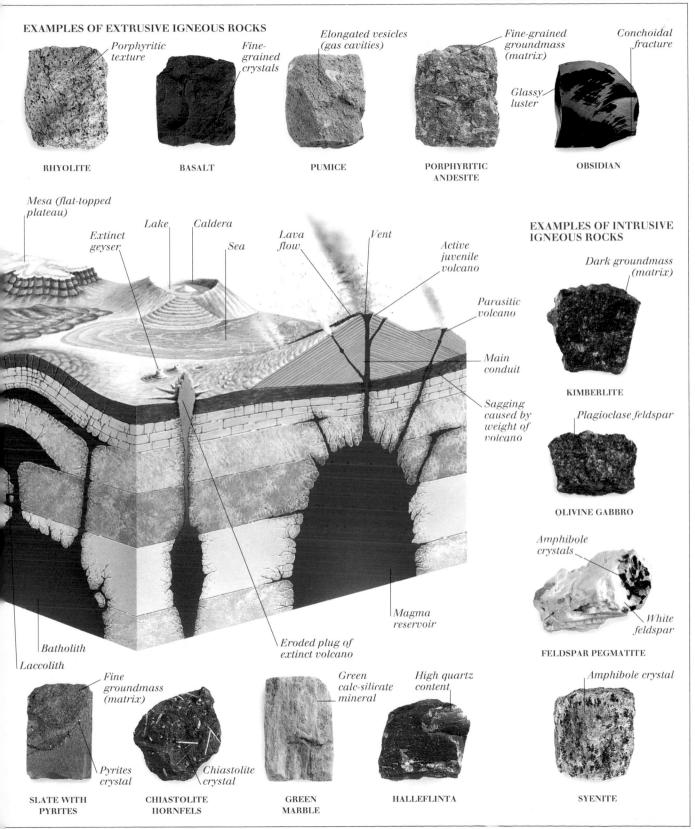

EXAMPLES OF EXTRUSIVE IGNEOUS ROCKS

Porphyritic texture

Fine-grained crystals

Elongated vesicles (gas cavities)

Fine-grained groundmass (matrix)

Conchoidal fracture

Glassy luster

RHYOLITE

BASALT

PUMICE

PORPHYRITIC ANDESITE

OBSIDIAN

Mesa (flat-topped plateau)

Extinct geyser

Lake

Caldera

Sea

Lava flow

Vent

Active juvenile volcano

Parasitic volcano

Main conduit

Sagging caused by weight of volcano

Magma reservoir

Eroded plug of extinct volcano

Batholith

Laccolith

EXAMPLES OF INTRUSIVE IGNEOUS ROCKS

Dark groundmass (matrix)

KIMBERLITE

Plagioclase feldspar

OLIVINE GABBRO

Amphibole crystals

White feldspar

FELDSPAR PEGMATITE

Amphibole crystal

SYENITE

Fine groundmass (matrix)

Pyrites crystal

SLATE WITH PYRITES

Chiastolite crystal

CHIASTOLITE HORNFELS

Green calc-silicate mineral

GREEN MARBLE

High quartz content

HALLEFLINTA

Sedimentary rocks

SEDIMENTARY ROCKS ARE FORMED BY THE ACCUMULATION and consolidation of sediments (see pp. 266-267). There are three main types of sedimentary rock: clastic sedimentary rocks, such as breccia or sandstone, are formed from other rocks that have been broken down into fragments by weathering (see pp. 282-283), which have then been transported and deposited elsewhere; organic sedimentary rocks, such as coal (see pp. 280-281), are derived from plant and animal remains; and chemical sedimentary rocks are formed by chemical processes. For example, rock salt is formed when salt dissolved in water is deposited as the water evaporates. Sedimentary rocks are laid down in layers called beds, or strata. Each new layer is laid down horizontally over older ones. There are usually some gaps in the sequence, called unconformities. These represent periods in which no new sediments were being laid down, or when earlier sedimentary layers were raised above sea level and eroded away.

THE GRAND CANYON, U.S.A.

EXAMPLES OF UNCONFORMITIES

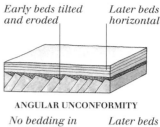

Early beds tilted and eroded *Later beds horizontal*

ANGULAR UNCONFORMITY

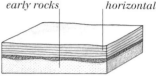

No bedding in early rocks *Later beds horizontal*

NONCONFORMITY

Early beds folded and eroded *Later beds horizontal*

DISCONFORMITY

SEDIMENTARY LAYERS OF THE GRAND CANYON REGION

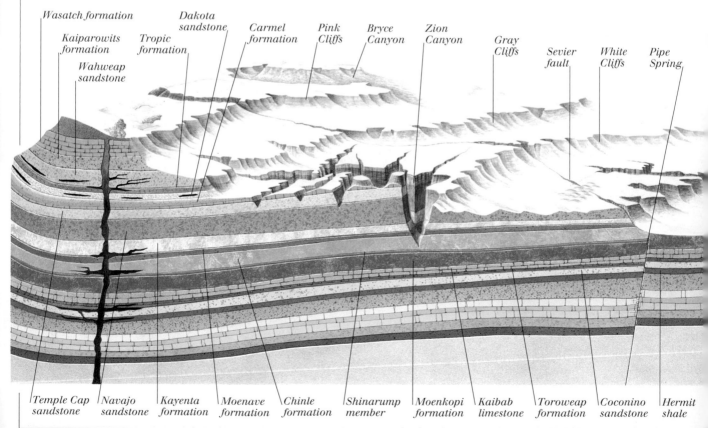

Wasatch formation · Kaiparowits formation · Wahweap sandstone · Tropic formation · Dakota sandstone · Carmel formation · Pink Cliffs · Bryce Canyon · Zion Canyon · Gray Cliffs · Sevier fault · White Cliffs · Pipe Spring

Temple Cap sandstone · Navajo sandstone · Kayenta formation · Moenave formation · Chinle formation · Shinarump member · Moenkopi formation · Kaibab limestone · Toroweap formation · Coconino sandstone · Hermit shale

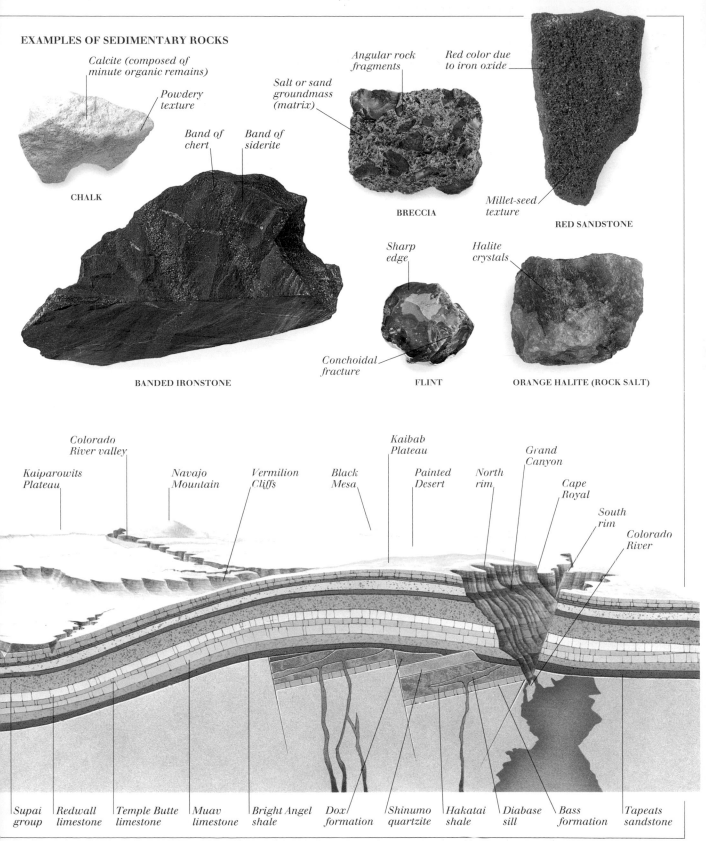

EXAMPLES OF SEDIMENTARY ROCKS

Calcite (composed of minute organic remains)

Powdery texture

CHALK

Band of chert

Band of siderite

BANDED IRONSTONE

Angular rock fragments

Salt or sand groundmass (matrix)

BRECCIA

Red color due to iron oxide

Millet-seed texture

RED SANDSTONE

Sharp edge

Conchoidal fracture

FLINT

Halite crystals

ORANGE HALITE (ROCK SALT)

Colorado River valley

Kaibab Plateau

Grand Canyon

Kaiparowits Plateau

Navajo Mountain

Vermilion Cliffs

Black Mesa

Painted Desert

North rim

Cape Royal

South rim

Colorado River

Supai group

Redwall limestone

Temple Butte limestone

Muav limestone

Bright Angel shale

Dox formation

Shinumo quartzite

Hakatai shale

Diabase sill

Bass formation

Tapeats sandstone

Fossils

FOSSILS ARE THE REMAINS of plants and animals that have been preserved in rock. A fossil may be the preserved remains of an organism itself, an impression of it in rock, or preserved traces (known as trace fossils) left by an organism while it was alive, such as organic carbon outlines, fossilized footprints, or droppings. Most dead organisms soon rot away or are eaten by scavengers. For fossilization to occur, rapid burial by sediment is necessary. The organism decays, but the harder parts—bones, teeth, and shells, for example—may be preserved and hardened by minerals from the surrounding sediment. Fossilization may also occur even when the hard parts of an organism are dissolved away to leave an impression called a mold. The mold is filled by minerals, thereby creating a cast of the organism. The study of fossils (paleontology) not only can show how living things have evolved, but can also help reveal the Earth's geological history—for example, by aiding in the dating of rock strata.

PROCESS OF FOSSILIZATION

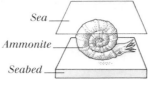

Sea
Ammonite
Seabed

ANIMAL DIES

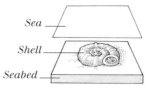

Sea
Shell
Seabed

SOFT PARTS ROT

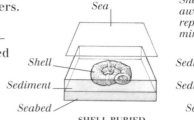

Sea
Shell
Sediment
Seabed

SHELL BURIED

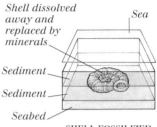

Shell dissolved away and replaced by minerals
Sea
Sediment
Sediment
Seabed

SHELL FOSSILIZED

EXAMPLES OF FOSSILS

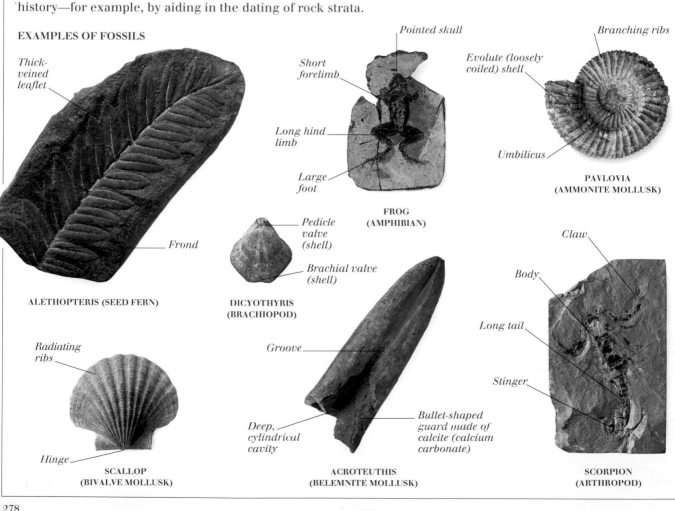

Thick-veined leaflet

Frond

ALETHOPTERIS (SEED FERN)

Radiating ribs

Hinge

SCALLOP (BIVALVE MOLLUSK)

Pointed skull

Short forelimb

Long hind limb

Large foot

FROG (AMPHIBIAN)

Pedicle valve (shell)

Brachial valve (shell)

DICYOTHYRIS (BRACHIOPOD)

Groove

Deep, cylindrical cavity

Bullet-shaped guard made of calcite (calcium carbonate)

ACROTEUTHIS (BELEMNITE MOLLUSK)

Evolute (loosely coiled) shell

Branching ribs

Umbilicus

PAVLOVIA (AMMONITE MOLLUSK)

Claw

Body

Long tail

Stinger

SCORPION (ARTHROPOD)

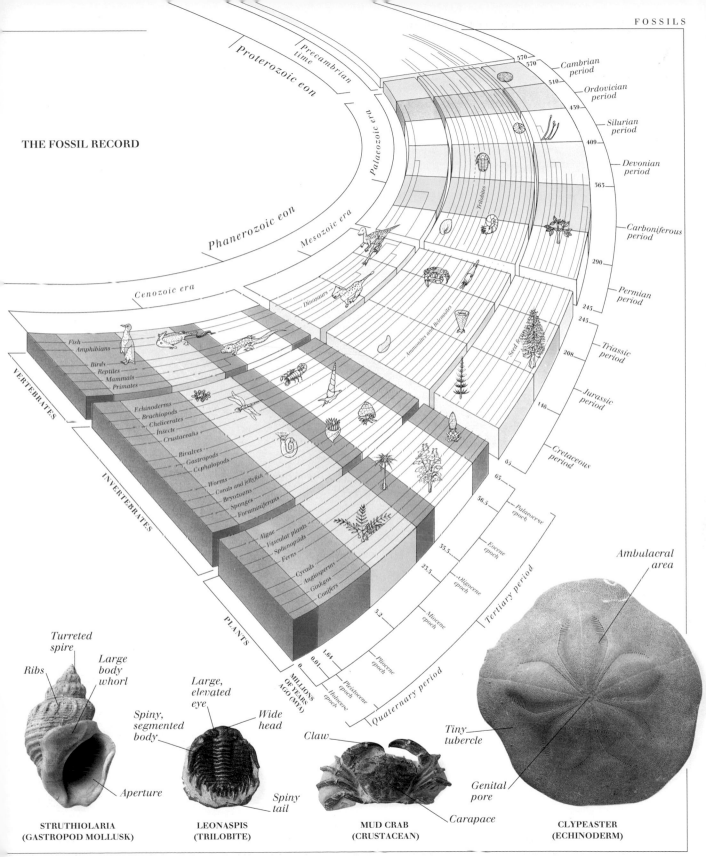

THE FOSSIL RECORD

Precambrian time

Proterozoic eon

Palaeozoic era

Phanerozoic eon

Mesozoic era

Cenozoic era

570 Cambrian period
510 Ordovician period
459 Silurian period
409 Devonian period
363 Carboniferous period
290 Permian period
245 Triassic period
208 Jurassic period
140 Cretaceous period
65 Tertiary period
56.5 Palaeocene epoch
35.5 Eocene epoch
23.5 Oligocene epoch
5.2 Miocene epoch
1.64 Pliocene epoch
0.01 Pleistocene epoch
0 Holocene epoch
Quaternary period

Trilobites

Dinosaurs

Ammonites and Belemnites

Seed fern

570
510
459
409
363
290
245
245
208
140
65
65
56.5
35.5
23.5
5.2
1.64
0.01
0

MILLIONS OF YEARS AGO (MYA)

VERTEBRATES
INVERTEBRATES
PLANTS

Fish
Amphibians
Birds
Reptiles
Mammals
Primates

Echinoderms
Brachiopods
Chelicerates
Insects
Crustaceans
Bivalves
Gastropods
Cephalopods
Worms
Corals and jellyfish
Bryozoans
Sponges
Foraminiferans

Algae
Vascular plants
Sphenopsids
Ferns
Cycads
Angiosperms
Ginkgos
Conifers

Ambulacral area

Turreted spire
Ribs
Large body whorl
Aperture

STRUTHIOLARIA
(GASTROPOD MOLLUSK)

Large, elevated eye
Spiny, segmented body
Wide head
Spiny tail

LEONASPIS
(TRILOBITE)

Claw
Carapace

MUD CRAB
(CRUSTACEAN)

Tiny tubercle
Genital pore

CLYPEASTER
(ECHINODERM)

279

Mineral resources

MINERAL RESOURCES CAN BE DEFINED AS naturally occurring substances that can be extracted from the Earth and are useful as fuels and raw materials. Coal, oil, and gas—collectively called fossil fuels—are commonly included in this group, but are not strictly minerals, because they are of organic origin. Coal formation begins when vegetation is buried and partly decomposed to form peat. Overlying sediments compress the peat and transform it into lignite (soft brown coal). As the overlying sediments accumulate, increasing pressure and temperature eventually transform the lignite into bituminous and hard anthracite coals. Oil and gas are usually formed from organic molecules that were deposited in marine sediments. Under the effects of heat and pressure, the compressed organic molecules undergo complex chemical changes to form oil and gas. The oil and gas percolate upward through water-saturated permeable rocks. They may rise to the Earth's surface, or accumulate below an impermeable layer of rock that has been folded or faulted to form a trap—an anticline (upfold) trap, for example. Minerals are inorganic substances that may consist of a single chemical element, such as gold, silver, or copper, or combinations of elements (see pp. 268-269). Some minerals are concentrated in mineralization zones in rock associated with crustal movements or volcanic activity. Others may be found in sediments as placer deposits— accumulations of high-density minerals that have been weathered out of rocks, transported, and deposited (on riverbeds, for example).

OIL RIG, NORTH SEA

Stalk   Leaf

PLANT MATTER

Decayed
plant matter

About 60%   PEAT
carbon

About 70%
carbon

Crumbly   LIGNITE (BROWN COAL)   Powdery
texture   texture

About 80%
carbon

Shiny   BITUMINOUS COAL   About 95%
surface   carbon

ANTHRACITE COAL

HOW COAL IS FORMED

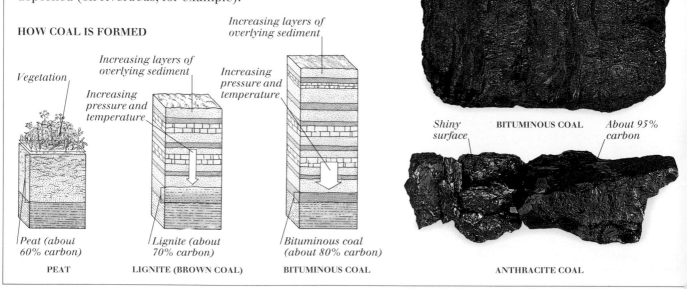

Increasing layers of
overlying sediment

Vegetation

Increasing layers of
overlying sediment

Increasing
pressure and
temperature

Increasing
pressure and
temperature

Increasing
pressure and
temperature

Peat (about   Lignite (about   Bituminous coal
60% carbon)   70% carbon)   (about 80% carbon)

PEAT   LIGNITE (BROWN COAL)   BITUMINOUS COAL

EXAMPLES OF OIL AND GAS TRAPS

MAJOR COAL, OIL, AND GAS DEPOSITS

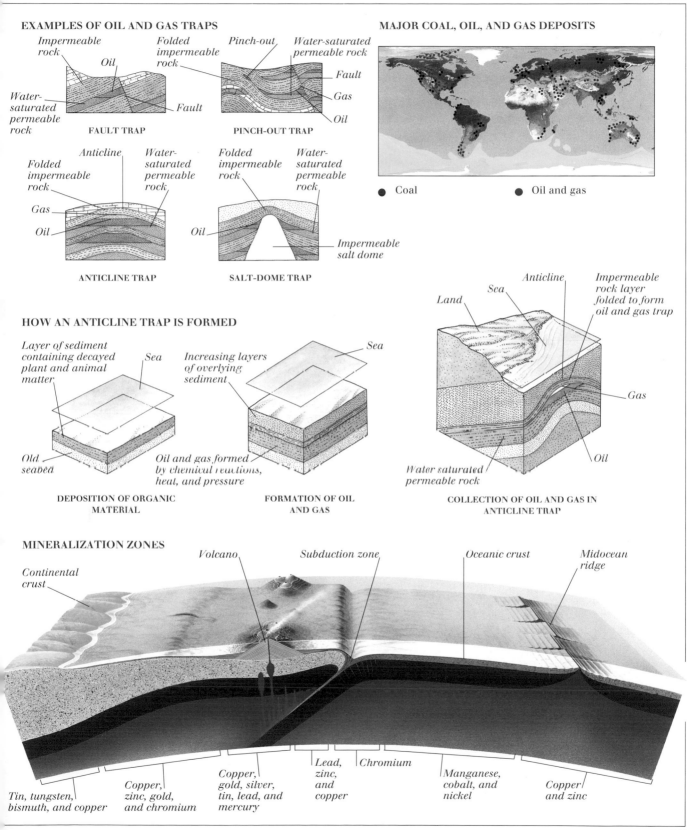

Impermeable rock
Oil
Water-saturated permeable rock
Fault
FAULT TRAP

Pinch-out
Water-saturated permeable rock
Fault
Gas
Oil
PINCH-OUT TRAP

Anticline
Water-saturated permeable rock
Folded impermeable rock
Gas
Oil
ANTICLINE TRAP

Folded impermeable rock
Water-saturated permeable rock
Oil
Impermeable salt dome
SALT-DOME TRAP

● Coal   ● Oil and gas

HOW AN ANTICLINE TRAP IS FORMED

Layer of sediment containing decayed plant and animal matter
Sea
Old seabed
DEPOSITION OF ORGANIC MATERIAL

Increasing layers of overlying sediment
Sea
Oil and gas formed by chemical reactions, heat, and pressure
FORMATION OF OIL AND GAS

Land
Sea
Anticline
Impermeable rock layer folded to form oil and gas trap
Gas
Oil
Water saturated permeable rock
COLLECTION OF OIL AND GAS IN ANTICLINE TRAP

MINERALIZATION ZONES

Continental crust
Volcano
Subduction zone
Oceanic crust
Midocean ridge

Tin, tungsten, bismuth, and copper
Copper, zinc, gold, and chromium
Copper, gold, silver, tin, lead, and mercury
Lead, zinc, and copper
Chromium
Manganese, cobalt, and nickel
Copper and zinc

Weathering and erosion

WEATHERING IS THE BREAKING DOWN of rocks on the Earth's surface. There are two main types: physical (or mechanical), and chemical. Physical weathering may be caused by temperature changes, such as freezing and thawing, or by abrasion from material carried by winds, rivers, or glaciers. Rocks may also be broken down by the actions of animals and plants, such as the burrowing of animals and the growth of roots. Chemical weathering causes rocks to decompose by changing their chemical composition. For example, rainwater may dissolve certain minerals in a rock. Erosion is the wearing away and removal of land surfaces by water, wind, or ice. It is greatest in areas of little or no surface vegetation, such as deserts, where sand dunes may form.

FORMATION OF A ROCK PAVEMENT (HAMADA)

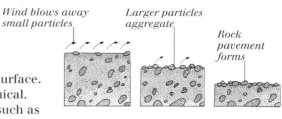

Wind blows away small particles

Larger particles aggregate

Rock pavement forms

FIRST STAGE **SECOND STAGE** **FINAL STAGE**

FEATURES OF WEATHERING AND EROSION

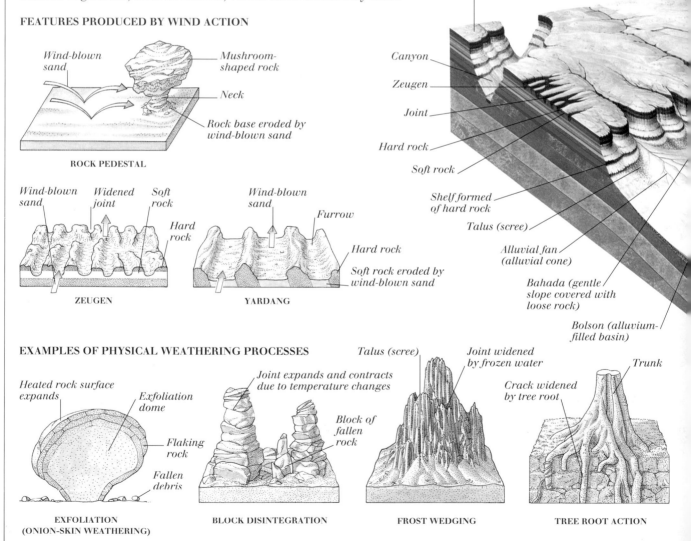

FEATURES PRODUCED BY WIND ACTION

Wind-blown sand

Mushroom-shaped rock

Neck

Rock base eroded by wind-blown sand

ROCK PEDESTAL

Wind-blown sand

Widened joint

Soft rock

Hard rock

ZEUGEN

Wind-blown sand

Furrow

Hard rock

Soft rock eroded by wind-blown sand

YARDANG

Mesa (flat-topped plateau)

Canyon

Zeugen

Joint

Hard rock

Soft rock

Shelf formed of hard rock

Talus (scree)

Alluvial fan (alluvial cone)

Bahada (gentle slope covered with loose rock)

Bolson (alluvium-filled basin)

EXAMPLES OF PHYSICAL WEATHERING PROCESSES

Heated rock surface expands

Exfoliation dome

Flaking rock

Fallen debris

EXFOLIATION (ONION-SKIN WEATHERING)

Joint expands and contracts due to temperature changes

Block of fallen rock

BLOCK DISINTEGRATION

Talus (scree)

Joint widened by frozen water

FROST WEDGING

Crack widened by tree root

Trunk

TREE ROOT ACTION

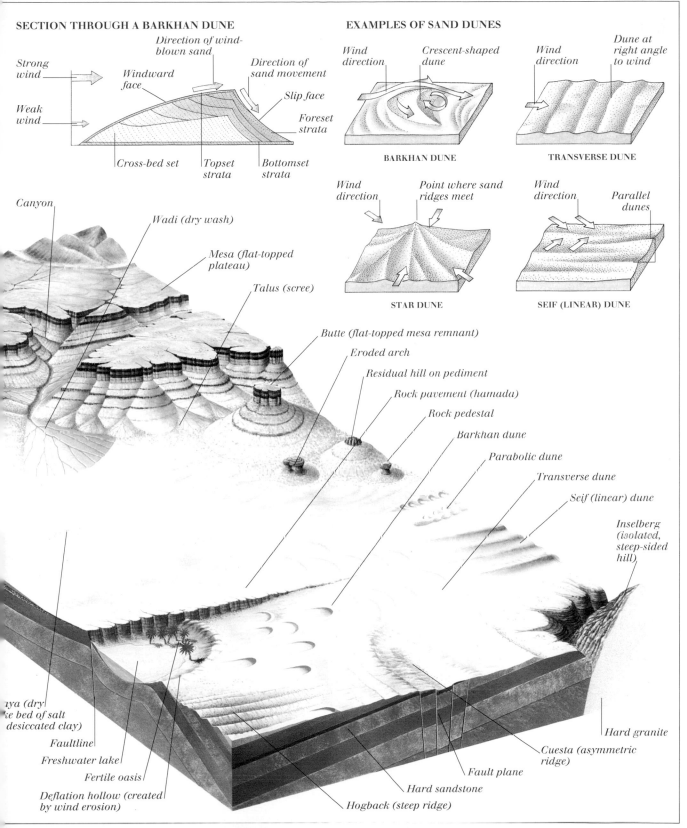

SECTION THROUGH A BARKHAN DUNE

Strong wind

Weak wind

Direction of wind-blown sand

Windward face

Direction of sand movement

Slip face

Foreset strata

Cross-bed set

Topset strata

Bottomset strata

EXAMPLES OF SAND DUNES

Wind direction

Crescent-shaped dune

BARKHAN DUNE

Wind direction

Dune at right angle to wind

TRANSVERSE DUNE

Wind direction

Point where sand ridges meet

STAR DUNE

Wind direction

Parallel dunes

SEIF (LINEAR) DUNE

Canyon

Wadi (dry wash)

Mesa (flat-topped plateau)

Talus (scree)

Butte (flat-topped mesa remnant)

Eroded arch

Residual hill on pediment

Rock pavement (hamada)

Rock pedestal

Barkhan dune

Parabolic dune

Transverse dune

Seif (linear) dune

Inselberg (isolated, steep-sided hill)

Hard granite

Cuesta (asymmetric ridge)

Fault plane

Hard sandstone

Hogback (steep ridge)

Deflation hollow (created by wind erosion)

Fertile oasis

Freshwater lake

Faultline

ıya (dry e bed of salt desiccated clay)

Caves

CAVES COMMONLY FORM in areas of limestone, although on coastlines they also occur in other rocks. Limestone is made of calcite (calcium carbonate), which dissolves in the carbonic acid naturally present in rainwater, and in humic acids from the decay of vegetation. The acidic water trickles down through cracks and joints in the limestone and between rock layers, breaking up the surface terrain into clints (blocks of rock), separated by grikes (deep cracks), and punctuated by sinkholes (also called swallow holes or potholes) into which surface streams may disappear. Underground, the acidic water dissolves the rock around crevices, opening up a network of passages and caves, which can become large caverns if the roofs collapse. Various features are formed when the dissolved calcite is redeposited. For example, it may be redeposited along an underground stream to form a gour (series of calcite ridges), or in caves and passages to form stalactites and stalagmites. Stalactites develop where calcite is left behind as water drips from the roof; where the drops land, stalagmites build up.

STALACTITE WITH RING MARKS

Ring mark

MERGED STALACTITE

SURFACE TOPOGRAPHY OF A CAVE SYSTEM

Doline (depression caused by collapse of cave roof)

Sinkhole

Porous limestone

Gorge where cave roof has fallen in

Resurgence

Limestone terrain with clints and grikes

Impermeable rock

STALAGMITE FORMATIONS

Calcite (calcium carbonate) crystalized under water

Thin encrustations of calcite (calcium carbonate)

CRYSTALLINE STALAGMITIC FLOOR

CALCAREOUS TUFA

Encrustations on dead stems of small plants

Calcite (calcium carbonate)

Calcite (calcium carbonate)

STALAGMITIC FLOOR

Encrustations with fungoid structure

STALAGMITIC BOSS

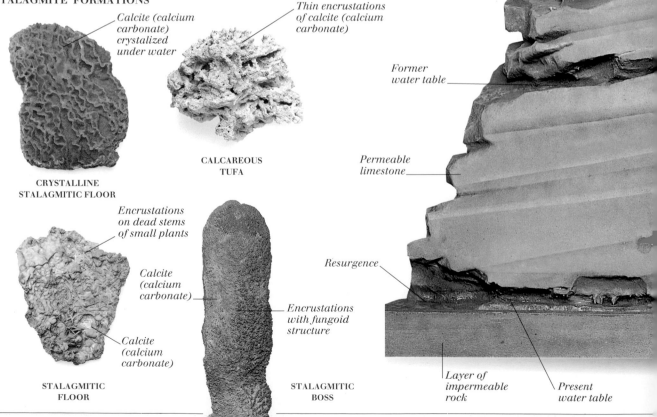

Scar of bare rock

Former water table

Permeable limestone

Resurgence

Layer of impermeable rock

Present water table

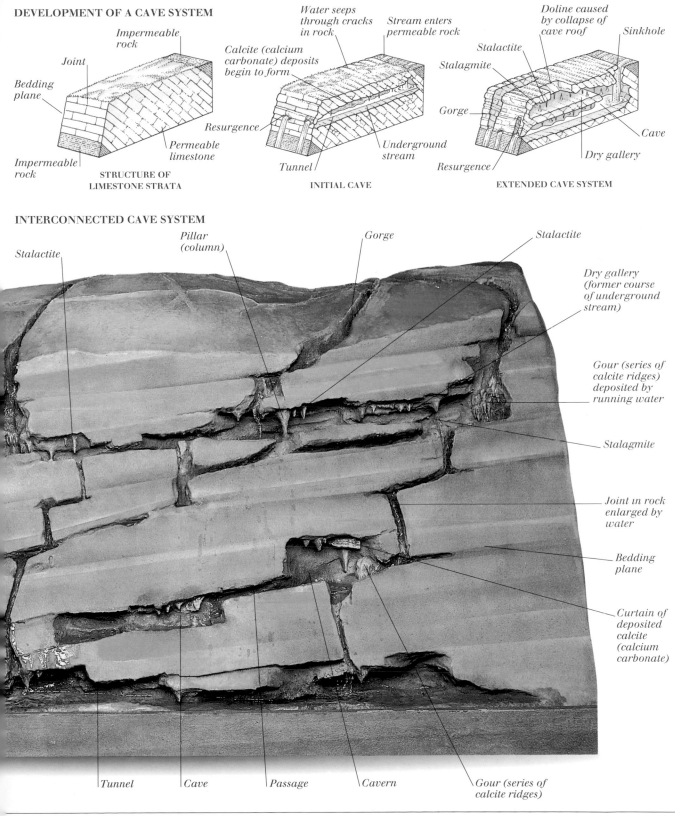

DEVELOPMENT OF A CAVE SYSTEM

STRUCTURE OF LIMESTONE STRATA

Impermeable rock
Joint
Bedding plane
Impermeable rock
Permeable limestone

INITIAL CAVE

Water seeps through cracks in rock
Stream enters permeable rock
Calcite (calcium carbonate) deposits begin to form
Resurgence
Underground stream
Tunnel

EXTENDED CAVE SYSTEM

Doline caused by collapse of cave roof
Sinkhole
Stalactite
Stalagmite
Gorge
Resurgence
Cave
Dry gallery

INTERCONNECTED CAVE SYSTEM

Stalactite
Pillar (column)
Gorge
Stalactite
Dry gallery (former course of underground stream)
Gour (series of calcite ridges) deposited by running water
Stalagmite
Joint in rock enlarged by water
Bedding plane
Curtain of deposited calcite (calcium carbonate)
Tunnel
Cave
Passage
Cavern
Gour (series of calcite ridges)

Glaciers

GLACIER BAY, ALASKA

A VALLEY GLACIER IS A LARGE MASS OF ICE that forms on land and moves slowly downhill under its own weight. It is formed from snow that collects in cirques (mountain hollows also known as corries), compressing into ice as more and more snow accumulates. The cirque is deepened by frost wedging and abrasion (see pp. 282-283), and arêtes (sharp ridges) develop between adjacent cirques. Eventually, so much ice builds up that the glacier begins to flow. As the glacier moves it collects moraine (debris), which may range in size from particles of dust to large boulders. The rocks at the base of the glacier erode the glacial valley, giving it a U-shaped cross section. Under the glacier, *roches moutonnées* (eroded outcrops of hard rock) and drumlins (rounded mounds of rock and clay) are left behind on the valley floor. The glacier ends at a terminus (the snout), where the ice melts as fast as it arrives. If the temperature increases, the ice melts faster than it arrives, and the glacier retreats. The retreating glacier leaves behind its moraine and also erratics (isolated single boulders). Glacial streams from the melting glacier deposit eskers and kames (ridges and mounds of sand and gravel) but carry away the finer sediment to form a stratified outwash plain. Lumps of ice carried on to this plain melt, creating holes called kettles.

VALLEY GLACIER

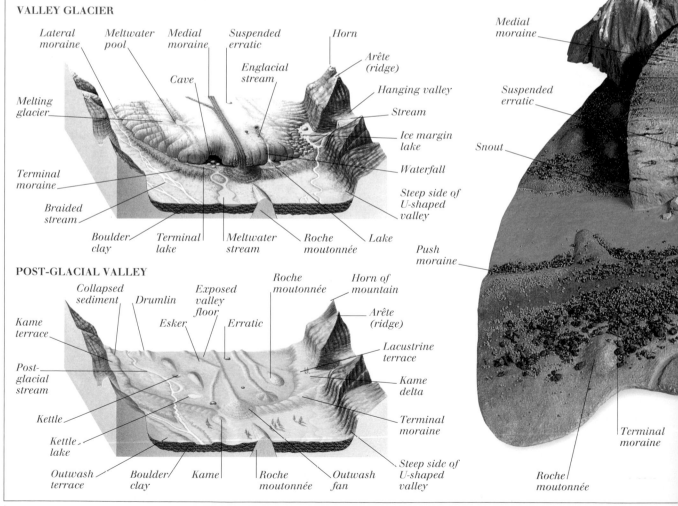

Lateral moraine
Meltwater pool
Medial moraine
Suspended erratic
Horn
Arête (ridge)
Medial moraine
Cave
Englacial stream
Hanging valley
Suspended erratic
Melting glacier
Stream
Ice margin lake
Snout
Waterfall
Terminal moraine
Steep side of U-shaped valley
Braided stream
Boulder clay
Terminal lake
Meltwater stream
Roche moutonnée
Lake
Push moraine

POST-GLACIAL VALLEY

Collapsed sediment
Drumlin
Exposed valley floor
Roche moutonnée
Horn of mountain
Kame terrace
Esker
Erratic
Arête (ridge)
Post-glacial stream
Lacustrine terrace
Kame delta
Kettle
Terminal moraine
Kettle lake
Outwash terrace
Boulder clay
Kame
Roche moutonnée
Outwash fan
Steep side of U-shaped valley
Terminal moraine
Roche moutonnée

286

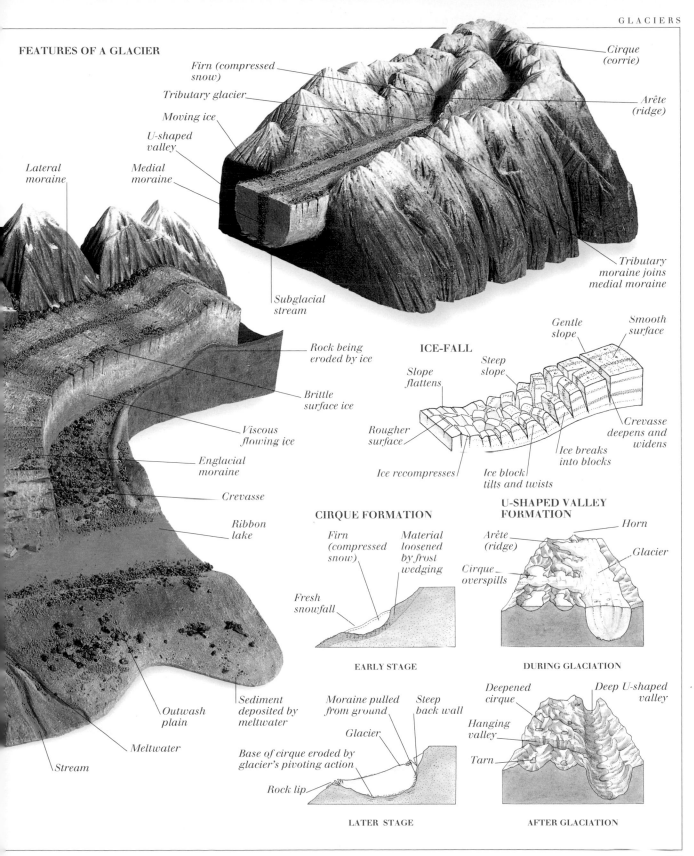

FEATURES OF A GLACIER

Firn (compressed snow)

Tributary glacier

Moving ice

U-shaped valley

Medial moraine

Lateral moraine

Cirque (corrie)

Arête (ridge)

Tributary moraine joins medial moraine

Subglacial stream

Rock being eroded by ice

Brittle surface ice

Viscous flowing ice

Englacial moraine

Crevasse

Ribbon lake

Sediment deposited by meltwater

Outwash plain

Meltwater

Stream

ICE-FALL

Gentle slope

Smooth surface

Slope flattens

Steep slope

Rougher surface

Crevasse deepens and widens

Ice recompresses

Ice block tilts and twists

Ice breaks into blocks

CIRQUE FORMATION

Firn (compressed snow)

Material loosened by frost wedging

Fresh snowfall

EARLY STAGE

Moraine pulled from ground

Steep back wall

Glacier

Base of cirque eroded by glacier's pivoting action

Rock lip

LATER STAGE

U-SHAPED VALLEY FORMATION

Arête (ridge)

Horn

Glacier

Cirque overspills

DURING GLACIATION

Deepened cirque

Deep U-shaped valley

Hanging valley

Tarn

AFTER GLACIATION

287

Rivers

RIVERS FORM PART of the water cycle—the continuous circulation of water between the land, sea, and atmosphere. The source of a river may be a mountain spring, or lake, or a melting glacier. The course that the river subsequently takes depends on the slope of the terrain and on the rock types and formations over which it flows. In its early, upland stages, a river tumbles steeply over rocks and boulders and cuts a steep-sided V-shaped valley. Farther downstream, it flows smoothly over sediments and forms winding meanders, eroding sideways to create broad valleys and plains. On reaching the coast, the river may deposit sediment, forming an estuary or delta (see pp. 290-291).

RIVER CAPTURE

River

Tributary erodes headward

River

EARLY STAGE

Dry valley

River captured by tributary

River flow decreases

River flow increases

LATER STAGE

THE WATER CYCLE

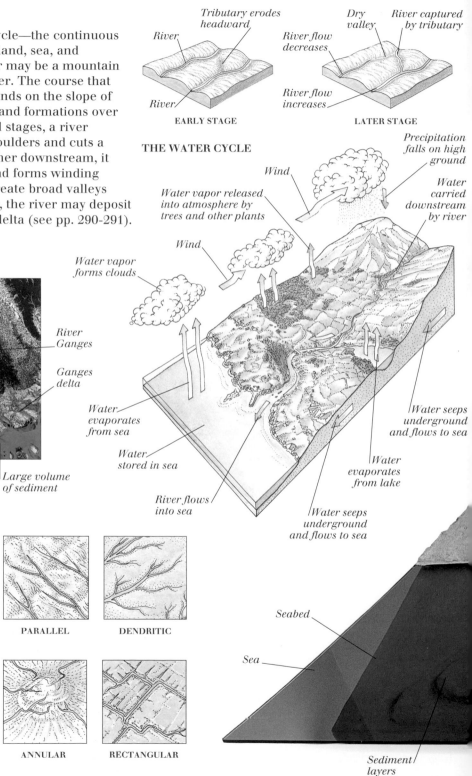

Wind

Precipitation falls on high ground

Water carried downstream by river

Water vapor released into atmosphere by trees and other plants

Wind

Water vapor forms clouds

Water evaporates from sea

Water stored in sea

River flows into sea

Water seeps underground and flows to sea

Water evaporates from lake

Water seeps underground and flows to sea

Seabed

Sea

Sediment layers

SATELLITE IMAGE OF GANGES RIVER DELTA, BANGLADESH

River Ganges

Ganges delta

Infertile swampland

Distributary

Large volume of sediment

RIVER DRAINAGE PATTERNS

RADIAL

CENTRIPETAL

PARALLEL

DENDRITIC

DERANGED

TRELLISED

ANNULAR

RECTANGULAR

STAGES IN A RIVER'S DEVELOPMENT

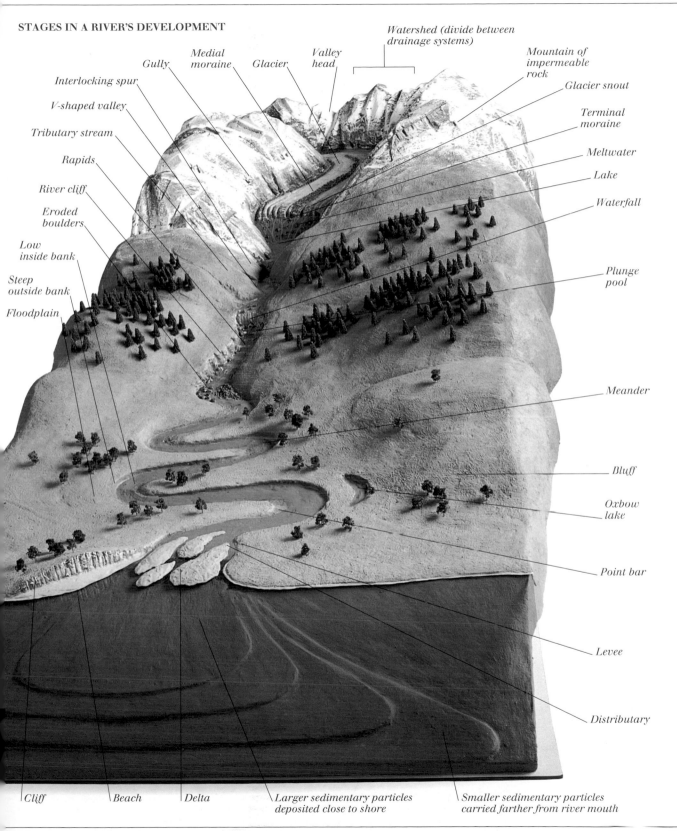

Medial moraine

Gully

Interlocking spur

V-shaped valley

Tributary stream

Rapids

River cliff

Eroded boulders

Low inside bank

Steep outside bank

Floodplain

Glacier

Valley head

Watershed (divide between drainage systems)

Mountain of impermeable rock

Glacier snout

Terminal moraine

Meltwater

Lake

Waterfall

Plunge pool

Meander

Bluff

Oxbow lake

Point bar

Levee

Distributary

Cliff

Beach

Delta

Larger sedimentary particles deposited close to shore

Smaller sedimentary particles carried farther from river mouth

River features

RIVERS ARE ONE OF THE MAJOR FORCES that shape the landscape. Near its source, a river is steep (see pp. 288-289). It erodes downward, carving out V-shaped valleys and deep gorges. Waterfalls and rapids are formed where the river flows from hard rock to softer, more easily eroded rock. Farther downstream, meanders may form and there is greater sideways erosion, resulting in a broad river valley. The river sometimes erodes through the neck of a meander to form an oxbow lake. Sediment deposited on the valley floor by meandering rivers and during floods helps to create a floodplain. Floods may also deposit sediment on the banks of the river to form levees. As a river spills into the sea or a lake, it deposits large amounts of sediment, and may form a delta. A delta is an area of sand bars, swamps and lagoons through which the river flows in several channels called distributaries—the Mississippi delta, for example. Often, a rise in sea level may have flooded the river mouth to form a broad estuary, a tidal section where seawater mixes with fresh water.

HOW WATERFALLS AND RAPIDS ARE FORMED

Plunge pool

Hard rock

Softer rock

WATERFALL

Hard rock

Softer rock

River erodes softer rocks to form rapids

Gently sloping rock strata

RAPIDS

A RIVER VALLEY DRAINAGE SYSTEM

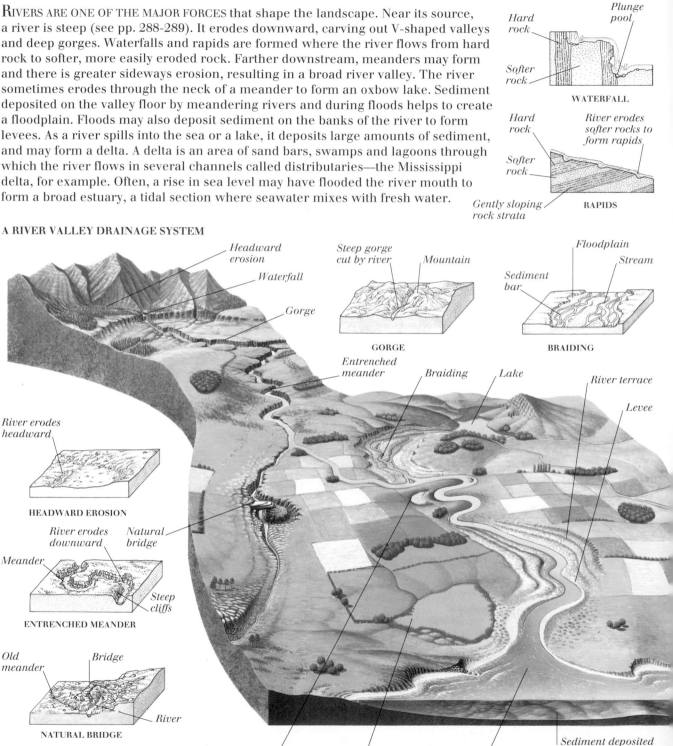

Headward erosion

Waterfall

Gorge

Steep gorge cut by river

Mountain

GORGE

Floodplain

Stream

Sediment bar

BRAIDING

Entrenched meander

Braiding

Lake

River terrace

Levee

River erodes headward

HEADWARD EROSION

River erodes downward

Meander

Natural bridge

Steep cliffs

ENTRENCHED MEANDER

Old meander

Bridge

River

NATURAL BRIDGE

Oxbow lake

Lake

River mouth

Sediment deposited on seabed

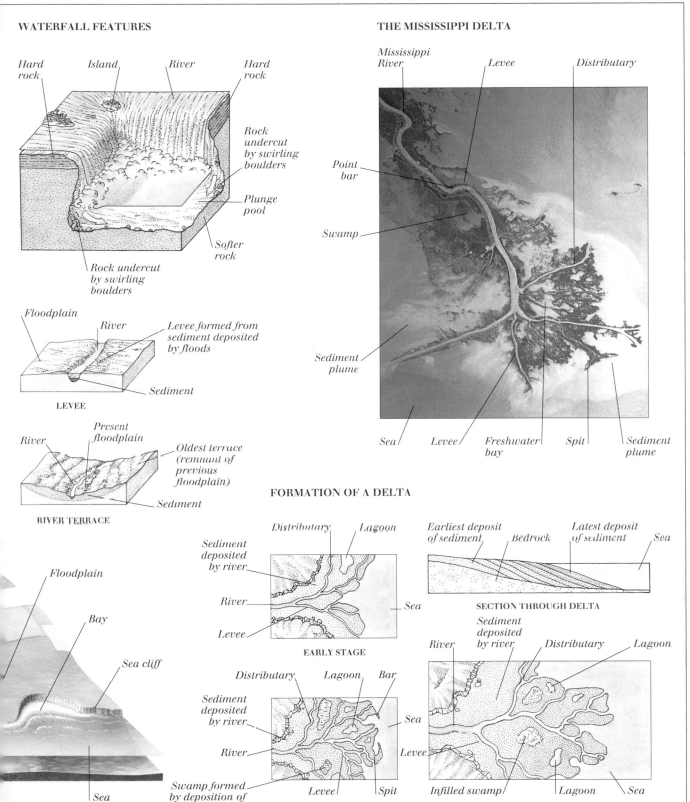

WATERFALL FEATURES

Hard rock

Island

River

Hard rock

Rock undercut by swirling boulders

Plunge pool

Softer rock

Rock undercut by swirling boulders

Floodplain

River

Levee formed from sediment deposited by floods

Sediment

LEVEE

River

Present floodplain

Oldest terrace (remnant of previous floodplain)

Sediment

RIVER TERRACE

Floodplain

Bay

Sea cliff

Sea

THE MISSISSIPPI DELTA

Mississippi River

Levee

Distributary

Point bar

Swamp

Sediment plume

Sea

Levee

Freshwater bay

Spit

Sediment plume

FORMATION OF A DELTA

Distributary

Lagoon

Sediment deposited by river

River

Levee

EARLY STAGE

Earliest deposit of sediment

Bedrock

Latest deposit of sediment

Sea

SECTION THROUGH DELTA

Distributary

Lagoon

Bar

Sediment deposited by river

River

Levee

Spit

Sea

Swamp formed by deposition of sediment in lagoon

MIDDLE STAGE

Sediment deposited by river

River

Distributary

Lagoon

Levee

Infilled swamp

Lagoon

Sea

LATE STAGE

Lakes and groundwater

NATURAL LAKES OCCUR WHERE a large quantity of water collects in a hollow in impermeable rock or is prevented from draining away by a barrier, such as moraine (glacial deposits) or solidified lava. Lakes are often relatively short-lived landscape features, because they tend to become silted up by sediment from the streams and rivers that feed them. Some of the more long-lasting lakes are found in deep rift valleys formed by vertical movements of the Earth's crust (see pp. 58-59)—for example, Lake Baikal in Russia, the world's largest freshwater lake, and the Dead Sea in the Middle East, one of the world's saltiest lakes. Where water is able to drain away, it sinks into the ground until it reaches a layer of impermeable rock, then accumulates in the permeable rock above it. This water-saturated permeable rock is called an aquifer. The saturated zone varies in depth according to seasonal and climatic changes. In wet conditions, the water stored underground builds up, while in dry periods it becomes depleted. Where the upper edge of the saturated zone—the water table—meets the ground surface, water emerges as springs. In an artesian basin, where the aquifer is below an aquiclude (layer of impermeable rock), the water table throughout the basin is determined by its height at the rim. At the center of such a basin, the water table is above ground level. The water in the basin is thus trapped below the water table and can rise under its own pressure along fault lines or well shafts.

LAKE BAIKAL, RUSSIA

(see pp. 58-59)

EXAMPLES OF SPRINGS

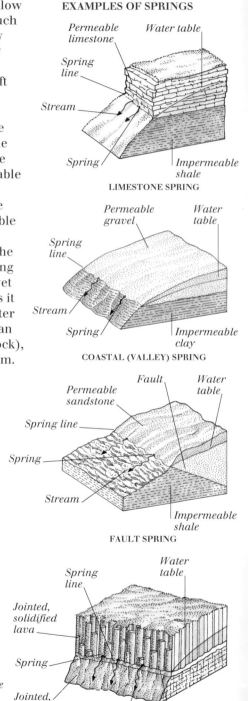

LIMESTONE SPRING

COASTAL (VALLEY) SPRING

FAULT SPRING

LAVA SPRING

STRUCTURE OF AN ARTESIAN BASIN

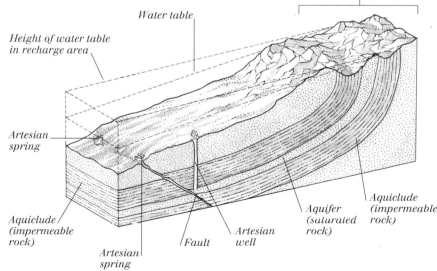

FEATURES OF A GROUNDWATER SYSTEM

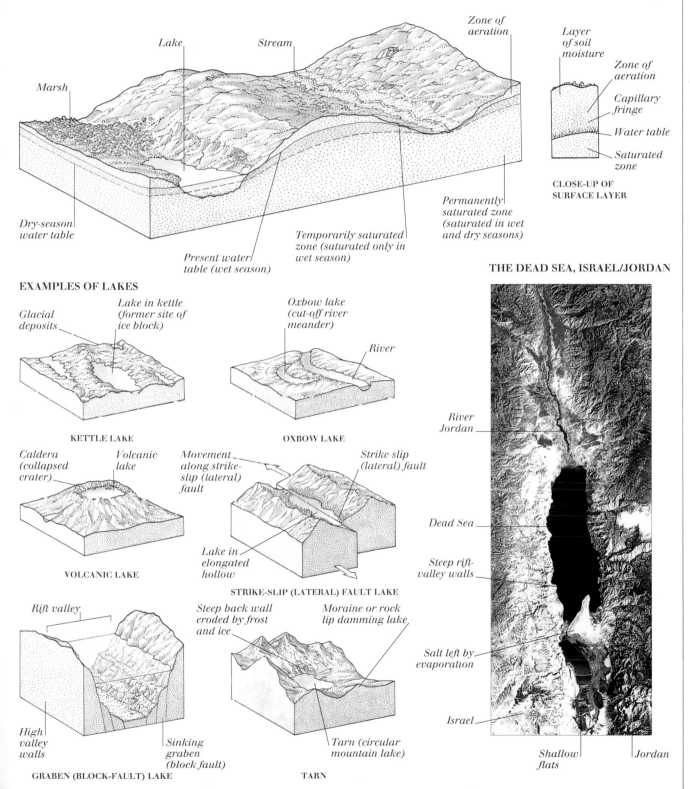

Marsh

Lake

Stream

Zone of aeration

Layer of soil moisture

Zone of aeration

Capillary fringe

Water table

Saturated zone

CLOSE-UP OF SURFACE LAYER

Dry-season water table

Present water table (wet season)

Temporarily saturated zone (saturated only in wet season)

Permanently saturated zone (saturated in wet and dry seasons)

EXAMPLES OF LAKES

Glacial deposits

Lake in kettle (former site of ice block)

Oxbow lake (cut-off river meander)

River

KETTLE LAKE

OXBOW LAKE

Caldera (collapsed crater)

Volcanic lake

Movement along strike-slip (lateral) fault

Strike slip (lateral) fault

Lake in elongated hollow

VOLCANIC LAKE

STRIKE-SLIP (LATERAL) FAULT LAKE

Rift valley

Steep back wall eroded by frost and ice

Moraine or rock lip damming lake

High valley walls

Sinking graben (block fault)

Tarn (circular mountain lake)

GRABEN (BLOCK-FAULT) LAKE

TARN

THE DEAD SEA, ISRAEL/JORDAN

River Jordan

Dead Sea

Steep rift-valley walls

Salt left by evaporation

Israel

Shallow flats

Jordan

Coastlines

COASTLINES ARE AMONG THE MOST RAPIDLY changing landscape features. Some are eroded by waves, wind, and rain, causing cliffs to be undercut and caves to be hollowed out of solid rock. Others are built up by waves transporting sand and small rocks in a process known as longshore drift and by rivers depositing sediment in deltas. Additional influences include the activities of living organisms such as coral, crustal movements, and sea-level variations due to climatic changes. Rising land or a drop in sea level creates an emergent coastline, with cliffs and beaches standing above the new shoreline. Sinking land or a rise in sea level produces a drowned coastline, typified by fjords (submerged glacial valleys) or submerged river valleys.

FEATURES OF A SEA CLIFF

Cliff top

Cliff face

High tide level

Low tide level

Offshore deposits

Wave-cut platform

Undercut area of cliff

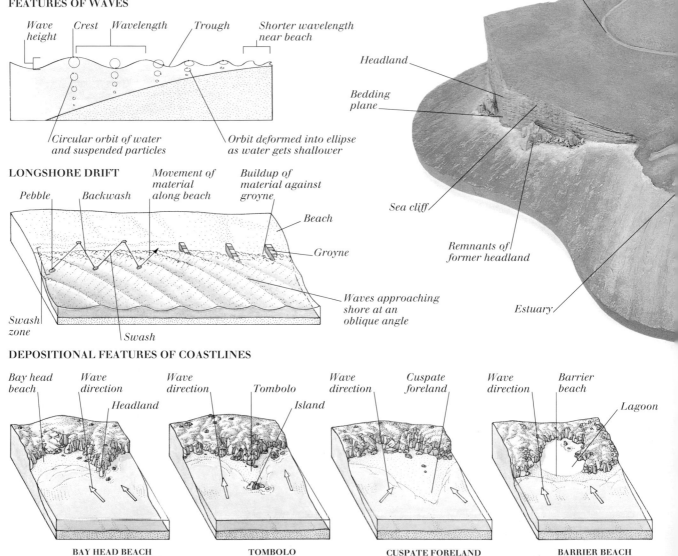

FEATURES OF WAVES

Wave height

Crest

Wavelength

Trough

Shorter wavelength near beach

Circular orbit of water and suspended particles

Orbit deformed into ellipse as water gets shallower

Mature river

Headland

Bedding plane

Sea cliff

Remnants of former headland

Estuary

LONGSHORE DRIFT

Pebble

Backwash

Movement of material along beach

Buildup of material against groyne

Beach

Groyne

Waves approaching shore at an oblique angle

Swash zone

Swash

DEPOSITIONAL FEATURES OF COASTLINES

Bay head beach

Wave direction

Headland

Wave direction

Tombolo

Island

Wave direction

Cuspate foreland

Wave direction

Barrier beach

Lagoon

BAY HEAD BEACH

TOMBOLO

CUSPATE FORELAND

BARRIER BEACH

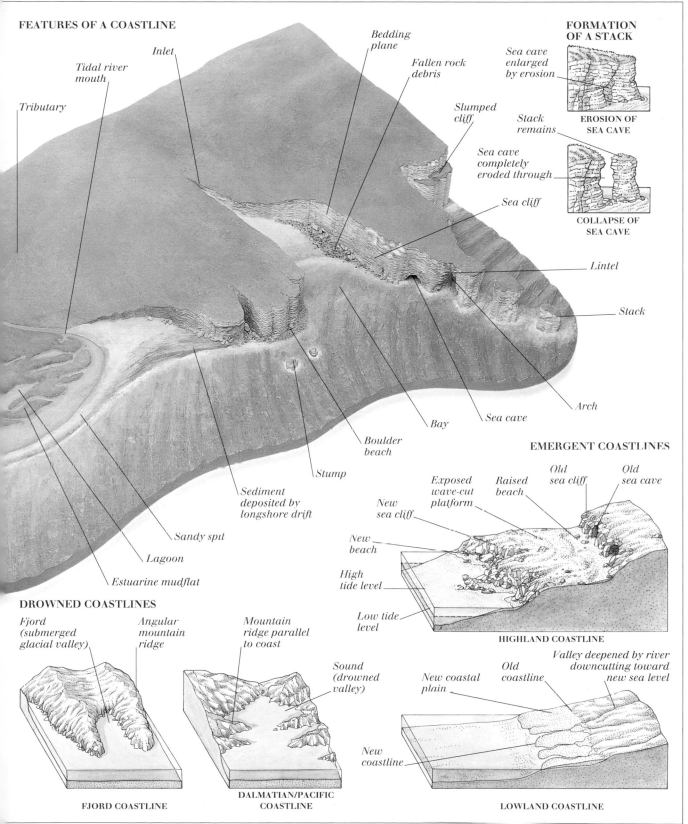

FEATURES OF A COASTLINE

Tributary

Tidal river mouth

Inlet

Bedding plane

Fallen rock debris

Slumped cliff

FORMATION OF A STACK

Sea cave enlarged by erosion

EROSION OF SEA CAVE

Stack remains

Sea cave completely eroded through

COLLAPSE OF SEA CAVE

Sea cliff

Lintel

Stack

Arch

Sea cave

Bay

Boulder beach

Stump

Sediment deposited by longshore drift

Sandy spit

Lagoon

Estuarine mudflat

EMERGENT COASTLINES

Exposed wave-cut platform

New sea cliff

New beach

High tide level

Low tide level

Raised beach

Old sea cliff

Old sea cave

HIGHLAND COASTLINE

DROWNED COASTLINES

Fjord (submerged glacial valley)

Angular mountain ridge

Mountain ridge parallel to coast

Sound (drowned valley)

FJORD COASTLINE

DALMATIAN/PACIFIC COASTLINE

New coastal plain

Old coastline

Valley deepened by river downcutting toward new sea level

New coastline

LOWLAND COASTLINE

Oceans and seas

OCEANS AND SEAS COVER ABOUT 70 PERCENT of the Earth's surface and account for about 97 percent of its total water. These oceans and seas play a crucial role in regulating temperature variations and determining climate. Their waters absorb heat from the Sun, especially in tropical regions, and the surface currents distribute it around the Earth, warming overlying air masses and neighboring land in winter and cooling them in summer. The oceans are never still. Differences in temperature and salinity drive deep current systems, while surface currents are generated by winds blowing over the oceans. All currents are deflected—to the right in the Northern Hemisphere, to the left in the Southern Hemisphere—as a result of the Earth's rotation. This deflective factor is known as the Coriolis force. A current that begins on the surface is immediately deflected. This current in turn generates a current in the layer of water beneath, which is also deflected. As the movement is transmitted downward, the deflections form an Ekman spiral. The waters of the oceans and seas are also moved by the constant ebb and flow of tides. These are caused by the gravitational pull of the Moon and Sun. The highest tides (Spring tides) occur at full and new Moon; the lowest tides (neap tides) occur at first and last quarter.

SURFACE CURRENTS

OFFSHORE CURRENTS

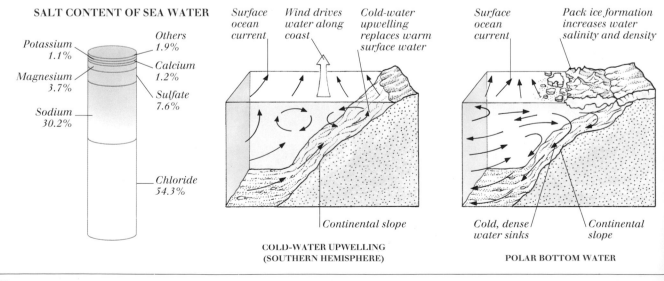

SALT CONTENT OF SEA WATER

Potassium 1.1%

Magnesium 3.7%

Sodium 30.2%

Others 1.9%

Calcium 1.2%

Sulfate 7.6%

Chloride 54.3%

Surface ocean current

Wind drives water along coast

Cold-water upwelling replaces warm surface water

Continental slope

COLD-WATER UPWELLING (SOUTHERN HEMISPHERE)

Surface ocean current

Pack ice formation increases water salinity and density

Cold, dense water sinks

Continental slope

POLAR BOTTOM WATER

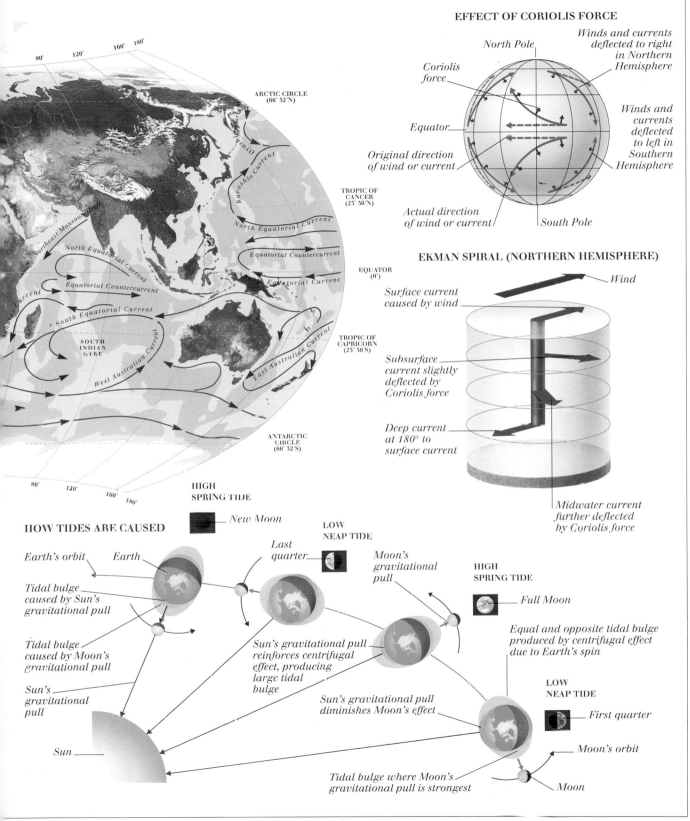

EFFECT OF CORIOLIS FORCE

North Pole

Coriolis force

Winds and currents deflected to right in Northern Hemisphere

Equator

Winds and currents deflected to left in Southern Hemisphere

Original direction of wind or current

South Pole

Actual direction of wind or current

EKMAN SPIRAL (NORTHERN HEMISPHERE)

Wind

Surface current caused by wind

Subsurface current slightly deflected by Coriolis force

Deep current at 180° to surface current

Midwater current further deflected by Coriolis force

ARCTIC CIRCLE
(66° 52'N)

Oyashio Current

Kuroshio Current

Northeast Monsoon Drift

North Equatorial Current

TROPIC OF CANCER
(23° 30'N)

North Equatorial Current

Equatorial Countercurrent

North Equatorial Current

Equatorial Countercurrent

EQUATOR
(0°)

South Equatorial Current

Agulhas Current

Equatorial Countercurrent

South Equatorial Current

SOUTH INDIAN GYRE

West Australian Current

East Australian Current

TROPIC OF CAPRICORN
(23° 30'S)

ANTARCTIC CIRCLE
(66° 52'S)

80°   120°   160°   180°

80°   120°   160°   180°

HOW TIDES ARE CAUSED

HIGH SPRING TIDE

New Moon

LOW NEAP TIDE

Last quarter

Moon's gravitational pull

HIGH SPRING TIDE

Full Moon

Earth's orbit

Earth

Tidal bulge caused by Sun's gravitational pull

Tidal bulge caused by Moon's gravitational pull

Sun's gravitational pull

Sun's gravitational pull reinforces centrifugal effect, producing large tidal bulge

Sun's gravitational pull diminishes Moon's effect

Equal and opposite tidal bulge produced by centrifugal effect due to Earth's spin

LOW NEAP TIDE

First quarter

Moon's orbit

Sun

Tidal bulge where Moon's gravitational pull is strongest

Moon

The ocean floor

THE OCEAN FLOOR INCLUDES TWO SECTIONS: the continental shelf and slope, and the deep-ocean floor. The continental shelf and slope are part of the continental crust, but may extend far into the ocean. Sloping quite gently to a depth of about 460 feet, the continental shelf is covered in sandy deposits shaped by waves and tidal currents. At the edge of the continental shelf, the seabed slopes down to the abyssal plain, which lies at an average depth of about 12,500 feet. On this deep-ocean floor is a layer of sediment made up of clays, fine oozes formed from the remains of tiny sea creatures, and occasional mineral-rich deposits. Echo-sounding and remote sensing from satellites has revealed that the abyssal plain is divided by a world-circling system of mountain ranges, far bigger than any on land—the midocean ridge. Here, magma (molten rock) wells up from the Earth's interior and solidifies, widening the ocean floor (see pp. 58-59). As the ocean floor spreads, volcanoes that have formed over hot spots in the crust move away from their magma source; they become extinct and are increasingly submerged and eroded. Volcanoes eroded below sea level remain as seamounts (underwater mountains). In warm waters, a volcano that projects above the ocean surface often acquires a fringing coral reef, which may develop into an atoll as the volcano becomes submerged.

CONTINENTAL-SHELF FLOOR

Bedrock exposed by tidal scour

Shoreline

Parallel strips of coarse material left by strong tidal currents

Sand deposited in wavy pattern by weaker currents

Irregular patches of fine sand deposited by weakest currents

FEATURES OF THE OCEAN FLOOR

Sediment

Submarine canyon

Continental shelf

Course of mud river

Continental rise

Continental slope

Continental crust

Ooze (sediment consisting of remains of tiny sea creatures)

Layer of volcanic rock

Pillow lava

Volcanic crystalline rock

Oceanic crust

Guyot (flat-topped seamount)

Seamount (underwater mountain)

Abyssal plain

DEEP-OCEAN FLOOR SEDIMENTS

KEY

Calcareous ooze

Pelagic clay

Glacial sediments

Siliceous ooze

Terrigenous sediments

Continental margin sediments

Metalliferous muds

Major nodule fields

ECHO-SOUND PROFILE OF OCEAN FLOOR

Sand wave

Event mark indicates synchronization of survey equipment

Sand wave

Seabed profile

Minor oscillations caused by ship's movement

22 149.3 22

Midocean ridge

Velocity of sound in water (1,493 m/sec; 4,898 ft/sec)

Reference code

Ocean trench

Magma (molten rock)

Sediment

DEVELOPMENT OF AN ATOLL

Volcanic island

Coral grows on shoreline

Sea level

FRINGING REEF

Lagoon

Coral continues to grow, forming barrier reef

Eroded volcanic island subsides

BARRIER REEF

Coral continues to grow where waves bring food

Lagoon

Dead coral

Volcanic island becomes submerged

ATOLL

Coral submerged too deeply to grow

Volcanic island is submerged further

SUBMERGED ATOLL

299

The atmosphere

JET STREAM

THE EARTH IS SURROUNDED BY ITS ATMOSPHERE, a blanket of gases that enables life to exist on the planet. This layer has no definite outer edge, gradually becoming thinner until it merges into space, but over 80 percent of atmospheric gases are held by gravity within about 10 miles of the Earth's surface. The atmosphere blocks out much harmful ultraviolet solar radiation, and insulates the Earth against extremes of temperature by limiting both incoming solar radiation and the escape of re-radiated heat into space. This natural balance may be distorted by the greenhouse effect, as gases such as carbon dioxide have built up in the atmosphere, trapping more heat. Close to the Earth's surface, differences in air temperature and pressure cause air to circulate between the equator and poles. This circulation, together with the Coriolis force, gives rise to the prevailing surface winds and the high-level jet streams.

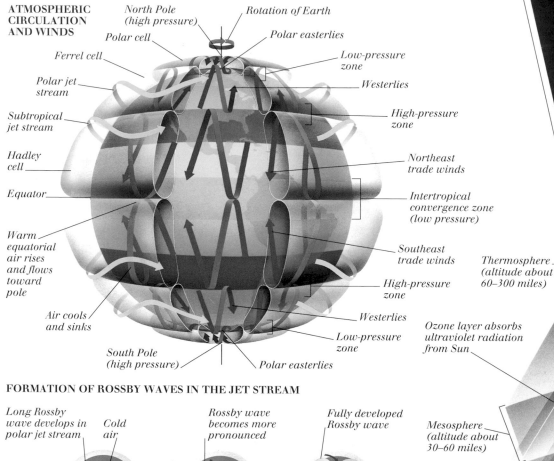

ATMOSPHERIC CIRCULATION AND WINDS

North Pole (high pressure)
Rotation of Earth
Polar cell
Polar easterlies
Ferrel cell
Low-pressure zone
Polar jet stream
Westerlies
Subtropical jet stream
High-pressure zone
Hadley cell
Northeast trade winds
Equator
Intertropical convergence zone (low pressure)
Warm equatorial air rises and flows toward pole
Southeast trade winds
High-pressure zone
Air cools and sinks
Westerlies
Low-pressure zone
South Pole (high pressure)
Polar easterlies

Exosphere (altitude above about 300 miles)
Corona
Thermosphere (altitude about 60–300 miles)
Ozone layer absorbs ultraviolet radiation from Sun
Mesosphere (altitude about 30–60 miles)
Stratosphere (altitude about 6–30 miles)
Troposphere (altitude up to about 6 miles)

FORMATION OF ROSSBY WAVES IN THE JET STREAM

Long Rossby wave develops in polar jet stream
Cold air
Rossby wave becomes more pronounced
Fully developed Rossby wave
Warm air

INITIAL UNDULATION

DEEPENING WAVE

DEVELOPED WAVE

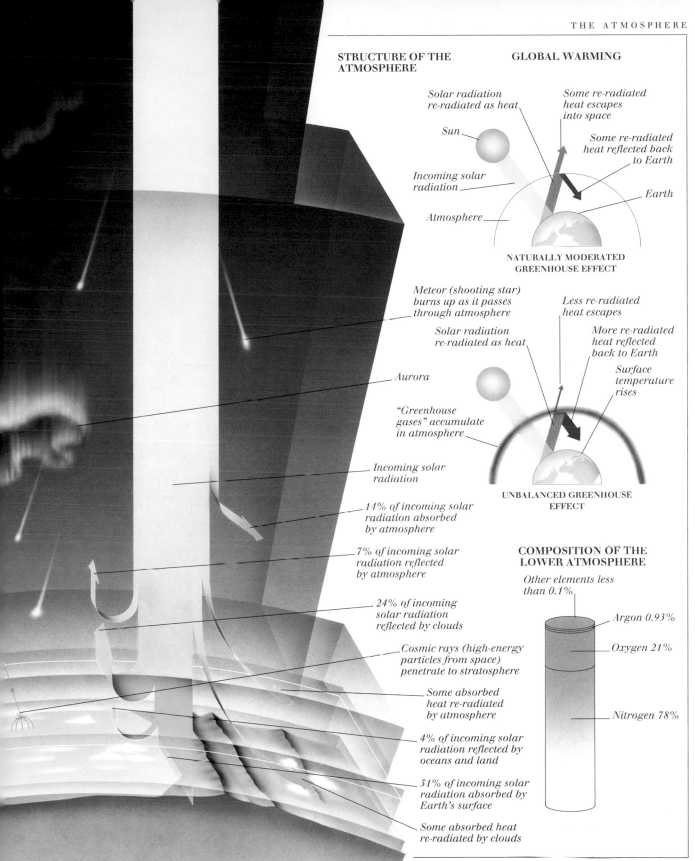

STRUCTURE OF THE ATMOSPHERE

GLOBAL WARMING

Solar radiation re-radiated as heat

Some re-radiated heat escapes into space

Sun

Some re-radiated heat reflected back to Earth

Incoming solar radiation

Earth

Atmosphere

NATURALLY MODERATED GREENHOUSE EFFECT

Meteor (shooting star) burns up as it passes through atmosphere

Less re-radiated heat escapes

Solar radiation re-radiated as heat

More re-radiated heat reflected back to Earth

Aurora

Surface temperature rises

"Greenhouse gases" accumulate in atmosphere

Incoming solar radiation

UNBALANCED GREENHOUSE EFFECT

14% of incoming solar radiation absorbed by atmosphere

7% of incoming solar radiation reflected by atmosphere

COMPOSITION OF THE LOWER ATMOSPHERE

24% of incoming solar radiation reflected by clouds

Other elements less than 0.1%

Argon 0.93%

Cosmic rays (high-energy particles from space) penetrate to stratosphere

Oxygen 21%

Some absorbed heat re-radiated by atmosphere

4% of incoming solar radiation reflected by oceans and land

Nitrogen 78%

51% of incoming solar radiation absorbed by Earth's surface

Some absorbed heat re-radiated by clouds

Weather

WEATHER IS DEFINED AS THE ATMOSPHERIC CONDITIONS at a particular time and place; climate is the average weather conditions for a given region over time. Weather conditions include temperature, wind, cloud cover, and precipitation, such as rain or snow. Good weather is associated with high-pressure areas, where air is sinking. Cloudy, wet, changeable weather is common in low-pressure zones with rising, unstable air. Such conditions occur at temperate latitudes, where warm air meets cool air along the polar fronts. Here, spiraling low-pressure cells known as depressions (mid-latitude cyclones) often form. A depression usually contains a sector of warmer air, beginning at a warm front and ending at a cold front. If the two fronts merge, forming an occluded front, the warm air is pushed upward. An extreme form of low-pressure cell is a hurricane (also called a typhoon or tropical cyclone), which brings torrential rain, and exceptionally strong winds.

TYPES OF CLOUD

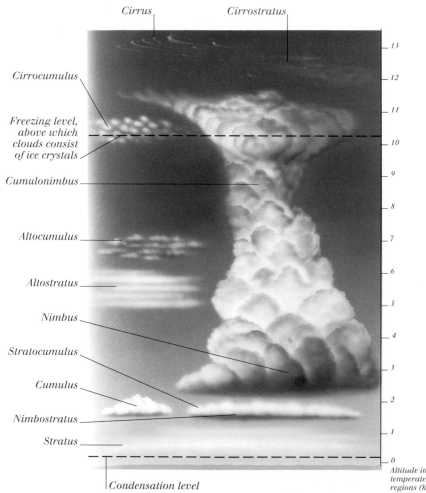

Cirrus

Cirrostratus

Cirrocumulus

Freezing level, above which clouds consist of ice crystals

Cumulonimbus

Altocumulus

Altostratus

Nimbus

Stratocumulus

Cumulus

Nimbostratus

Stratus

Condensation level

13
12
11
10
9
8
7
6
5
4
3
2
1
0

Altitude in temperate regions (km)

TYPES OF OCCLUDED FRONT

Advancing cold front rises up over warm front

Warm air

Warm front

Cool air

Cold air

WARM OCCLUSION

Cold air

Warm air

Warm front

Cold front undercuts warm front

Cool air

COLD OCCLUSION

FORMS OF PRECIPITATION

Water droplets less than 0.5 mm in diameter fall as drizzle

Water droplets coalesce to form raindrops 0.5–5.0 mm in diameter

Rising air

RAIN FROM CLOUDS NOT REACHING FREEZING LEVEL

Coalesced water droplets fall as rain

Ice crystal

Snowflakes grown from ice crystals fall as snow

Rising air

Snowflakes melt to fall as rain

RAIN AND SNOW FROM CLOUDS REACHING FREEZING LEVEL

Vertical air currents toss frozen water droplets up and down

Alternate freezing and melting builds up layers of ice

Rising air

Ice falls as hailstones

HAIL

STRUCTURE OF A HURRICANE

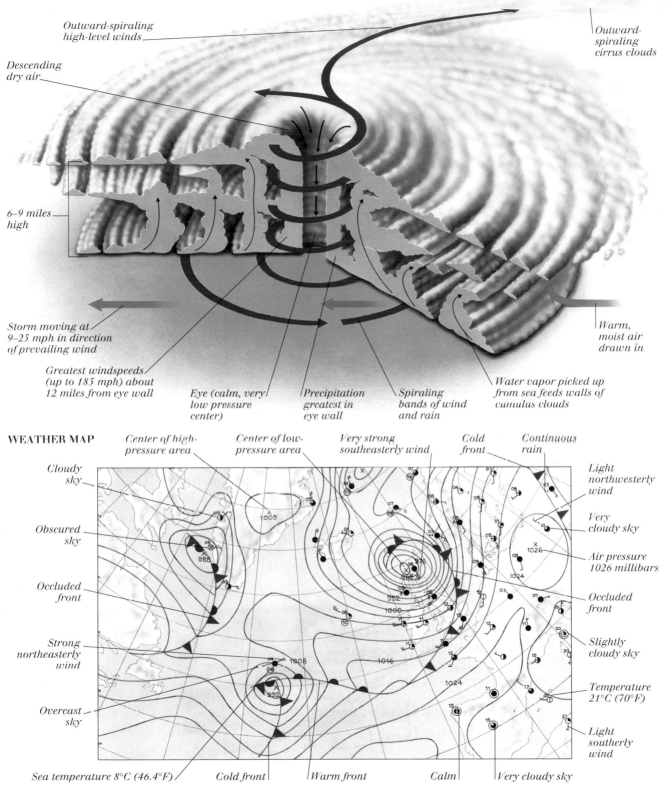

Outward-spiraling
high-level winds

Outward-
spiraling
cirrus clouds

Descending
dry air

6–9 miles
high

Storm moving at
9–25 mph in direction
of prevailing wind

Warm,
moist air
drawn in

Greatest windspeeds
(up to 185 mph) about
12 miles from eye wall

Eye (calm, very
low pressure
center)

Precipitation
greatest in
eye wall

Spiraling
bands of wind
and rain

Water vapor picked up
from sea feeds walls of
cumulus clouds

WEATHER MAP

Center of high-
pressure area

Center of low-
pressure area

Very strong
southeasterly wind

Cold
front

Continuous
rain

Cloudy
sky

Light
northwesterly
wind

Obscured
sky

Very
cloudy sky

Air pressure
1026 millibars

Occluded
front

Occluded
front

Strong
northeasterly
wind

Slightly
cloudy sky

Temperature
21°C (70°F)

Overcast
sky

Light
southerly
wind

Sea temperature 8°C (46.4°F)

Cold front

Warm front

Calm

Very cloudy sky

PHYSICS AND CHEMISTRY

The variety of matter

**PLANT AND INSECT
(LIVING MATTER)**

MATTER IS ANYTHING THAT HAS A MASS. It includes everything from natural substances, such as minerals or living organisms, to synthetic materials. Matter can exist in three distinct states—solid, liquid, and gas. A solid is rigid and retains its shape. A liquid is fluid, has a definite volume, and will take the shape of its container. A gas (also fluid) fills a space, so its volume will be the same as the volume of its container. Most substances can exist as a solid, a liquid, or a gas: the state is determined by temperature. At very high temperatures, matter becomes plasma, often considered to be a fourth state of matter. All matter is composed of microscopic particles, such as atoms and molecules (see pp. 308-309). The arrangement and interactions of these particles give a substance its physical and chemical properties, by which matter can be identified. There is a huge variety of matter because particles can arrange themselves in countless ways, in one substance or by mixing with others. Natural glass, for example, seems to be a solid but is, in fact, a supercool liquid: the atoms are not locked into a pattern and can flow. Pure substances known as elements (see p. 310) combine to form compounds or mixtures. Mixtures called colloids are made up of larger particles of matter suspended in a solid, liquid, or gas, while a solution is one substance dissolved in another.

TYPES OF COLLOID

HAIR GEL (SOLID IN LIQUID)

**SHAVING CREAM
(AIR IN LIQUID)**

**MIST
(LIQUID IN GAS)**

EXAMPLES OF MATTER

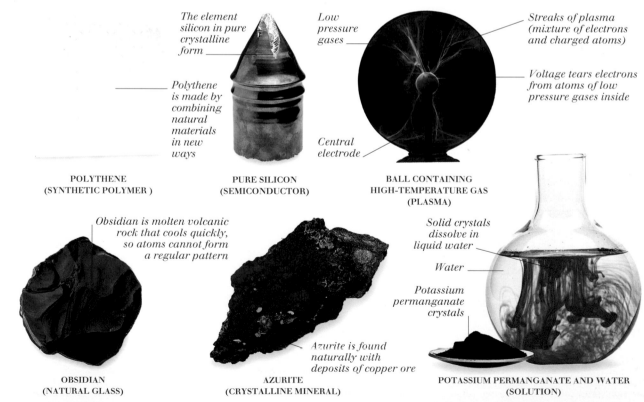

The element silicon in pure crystalline form

Polythene is made by combining natural materials in new ways

Low pressure gases

Streaks of plasma (mixture of electrons and charged atoms)

Voltage tears electrons from atoms of low pressure gases inside

Central electrode

**POLYTHENE
(SYNTHETIC POLYMER)**

**PURE SILICON
(SEMICONDUCTOR)**

**BALL CONTAINING
HIGH-TEMPERATURE GAS
(PLASMA)**

Obsidian is molten volcanic rock that cools quickly, so atoms cannot form a regular pattern

Solid crystals dissolve in liquid water

Water

Potassium permanganate crystals

Azurite is found naturally with deposits of copper ore

**OBSIDIAN
(NATURAL GLASS)**

**AZURITE
(CRYSTALLINE MINERAL)**

**POTASSIUM PERMANGANATE AND WATER
(SOLUTION)**

STATES OF MATTER

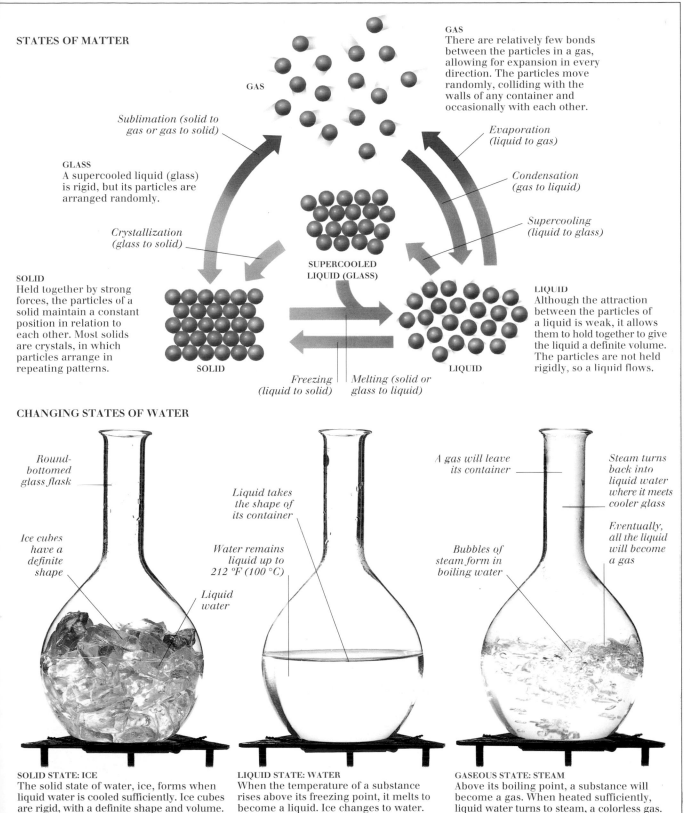

GAS
There are relatively few bonds between the particles in a gas, allowing for expansion in every direction. The particles move randomly, colliding with the walls of any container and occasionally with each other.

GAS

Sublimation (solid to gas or gas to solid)

Evaporation (liquid to gas)

GLASS
A supercooled liquid (glass) is rigid, but its particles are arranged randomly.

Condensation (gas to liquid)

Crystallization (glass to solid)

Supercooling (liquid to glass)

SUPERCOOLED LIQUID (GLASS)

SOLID
Held together by strong forces, the particles of a solid maintain a constant position in relation to each other. Most solids are crystals, in which particles arrange in repeating patterns.

LIQUID
Although the attraction between the particles of a liquid is weak, it allows them to hold together to give the liquid a definite volume. The particles are not held rigidly, so a liquid flows.

SOLID

LIQUID

Freezing (liquid to solid)

Melting (solid or glass to liquid)

CHANGING STATES OF WATER

Round-bottomed glass flask

Ice cubes have a definite shape

Liquid water

Liquid takes the shape of its container

Water remains liquid up to 212 °F (100 °C)

A gas will leave its container

Bubbles of steam form in boiling water

Steam turns back into liquid water where it meets cooler glass

Eventually, all the liquid will become a gas

SOLID STATE: ICE
The solid state of water, ice, forms when liquid water is cooled sufficiently. Ice cubes are rigid, with a definite shape and volume.

LIQUID STATE: WATER
When the temperature of a substance rises above its freezing point, it melts to become a liquid. Ice changes to water.

GASEOUS STATE: STEAM
Above its boiling point, a substance will become a gas. When heated sufficiently, liquid water turns to steam, a colorless gas.

Atoms and molecules

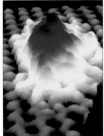

FALSE-COLOR IMAGE OF ACTUAL GOLD ATOMS

ATOMS ARE THE smallest individual parts of an element (see pp. 310-311). They are tiny, with diameters in the order of one ten-thousand-millionth of a meter (10^{-10} m). Two or more atoms join together (bond) to form a molecule of a substance known as a compound. For example, when atoms of the elements hydrogen and fluorine join together, they form a molecule of the compound hydrogen fluoride. So molecules are the smallest individual parts of a compound. Atoms themselves are not indivisible —they possess an internal structure. At their center is a dense nucleus consisting of protons, which have a positive electric charge (see p. 316), and neutrons, which are uncharged. Around the nucleus are negatively charged electrons. It is the electrons that give a substance most of its physical and chemical properties. They do not follow definite paths around the nucleus. Instead, electrons are said to be found within certain regions, called orbitals. These are arranged around the nucleus in "shells," each containing electrons of a particular energy. For example, the first shell (1) can hold up to two electrons, in a so-called s-orbital (1s). The second shell (2) can hold up to eight electrons in s-orbitals (2s) and p-orbitals (2p). If an atom loses an electron, it becomes a positive ion (cation). If an electron is gained, an atom becomes a negative ion (anion). Ions of opposite charges will attract and join together in a type of bonding known as ionic bonding. In covalent bonding, the atoms bond by sharing their electrons in what become molecular orbitals.

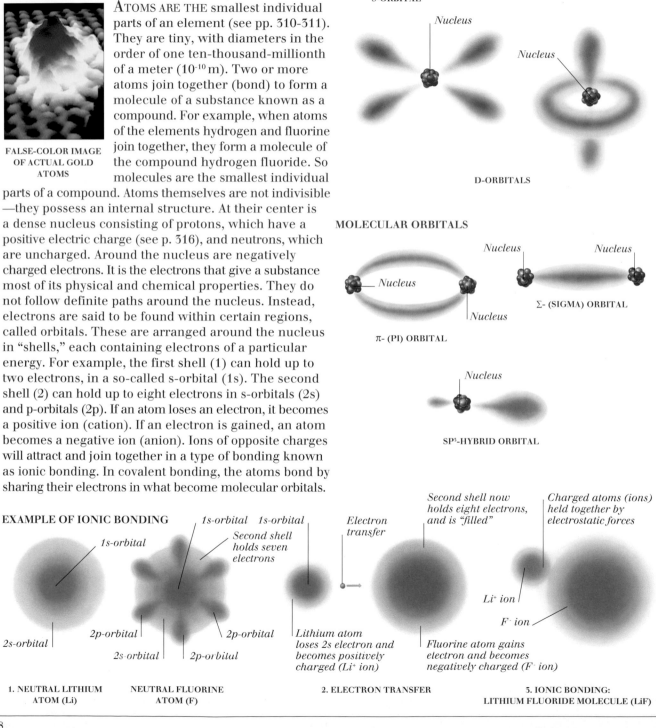

ATOMIC ORBITALS

Nucleus

S-ORBITAL

P-ORBITAL

Nucleus

Nucleus

D-ORBITALS

MOLECULAR ORBITALS

Nucleus

Nucleus

Nucleus

Nucleus

π- (PI) ORBITAL

Σ- (SIGMA) ORBITAL

Nucleus

SP⁵-HYBRID ORBITAL

EXAMPLE OF IONIC BONDING

1s-orbital

1s-orbital   *1s-orbital*

Second shell holds seven electrons

Electron transfer

Second shell now holds eight electrons, and is "filled"

Charged atoms (ions) held together by electrostatic forces

2s-orbital

2p-orbital

2s-orbital   *2p-orbital*

2p-orbital

Lithium atom loses 2s electron and becomes positively charged (Li⁺ ion)

Fluorine atom gains electron and becomes negatively charged (F⁻ ion)

Li⁺ ion

F⁻ ion

1. NEUTRAL LITHIUM ATOM (Li)

NEUTRAL FLUORINE ATOM (F)

2. ELECTRON TRANSFER

3. IONIC BONDING: LITHIUM FLUORIDE MOLECULE (LiF)

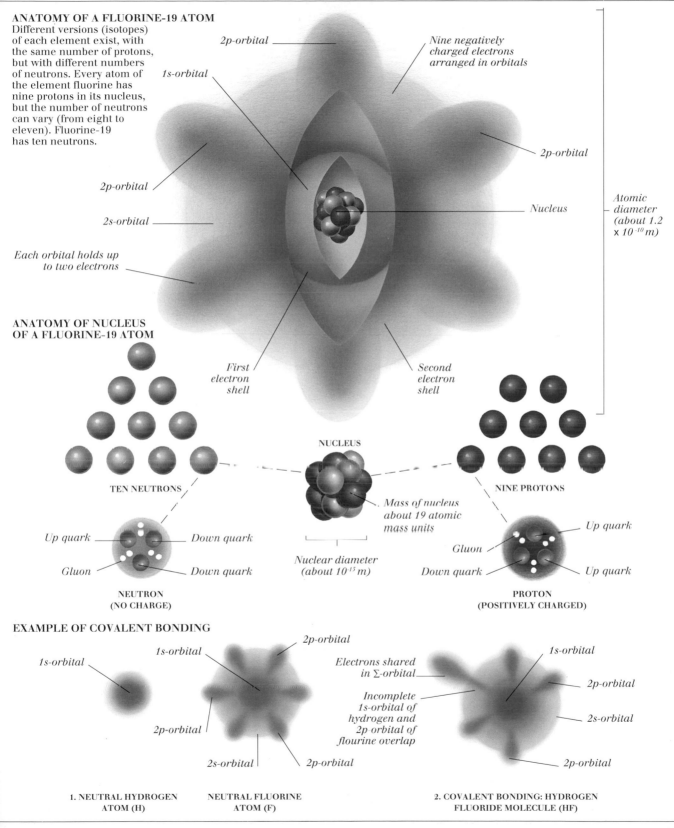

ANATOMY OF A FLUORINE-19 ATOM
Different versions (isotopes) of each element exist, with the same number of protons, but with different numbers of neutrons. Every atom of the element fluorine has nine protons in its nucleus, but the number of neutrons can vary (from eight to eleven). Fluorine-19 has ten neutrons.

2p-orbital

Nine negatively charged electrons arranged in orbitals

1s-orbital

2p-orbital

2p-orbital

Nucleus

2s-orbital

Atomic diameter (about 1.2 × 10^{-10} m)

Each orbital holds up to two electrons

First electron shell

Second electron shell

ANATOMY OF NUCLEUS OF A FLUORINE-19 ATOM

NUCLEUS

TEN NEUTRONS

NINE PROTONS

Mass of nucleus about 19 atomic mass units

Up quark — *Down quark*

Up quark

Gluon

Gluon — *Down quark*

Down quark

Up quark

Nuclear diameter (about 10^{-15} m)

NEUTRON (NO CHARGE)

PROTON (POSITIVELY CHARGED)

EXAMPLE OF COVALENT BONDING

2p-orbital

1s-orbital

1s-orbital

1s-orbital

2p-orbital

Electrons shared in Σ-orbital

2p-orbital

Incomplete 1s-orbital of hydrogen and 2p orbital of flourine overlap

2s-orbital

2p-orbital

2s-orbital

2p-orbital

2p-orbital

1. NEUTRAL HYDROGEN ATOM (H)

NEUTRAL FLUORINE ATOM (F)

2. COVALENT BONDING: HYDROGEN FLUORIDE MOLECULE (HF)

The periodic table

An ELEMENT is a substance that consists of atoms of one type only. The 92 elements that occur naturally, and the 17 elements created artificially, are often arranged into a chart called the periodic table. Each element is defined by its atomic number—the number of protons in the nucleus of each of its atoms (it is also the number of electrons present). Atomic numbers increase along each row (period) and down each column (group). The shape of the table is determined by the way in which electrons arrange themselves around the nucleus: the positioning of elements in order of increasing atomic number brings together atoms with a similar pattern of orbiting electrons (orbitals). These appear in blocks. Electrons occupy shells of a certain energy (see pp. 308-309). Periods are ordered according to the filling of successive shells with electrons, while groups reflect the number of electrons in the outer shell (valency electrons). These outer electrons are important—they decide the chemical properties of the atom. Elements that appear in the same group have similar properties because they have the same number of electrons in their outer shell. Elements in Group 0 have filled shells, where the outer shell holds its maximum number of electrons, and are stable. Atoms of Group I elements have just one electron in their outer shell. This makes them unstable—and ready to react with other substances.

METALS AND NON-METALS
Elements at the left-hand side of each period are metals. Metals easily lose electrons and form positive ions. Non-metals, on the right of a period, tend to become negative ions. Semi-metals, which have properties of both metals and non-metals, are between the two.

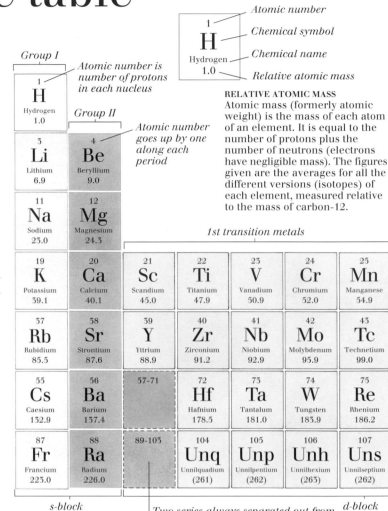

Atomic number is number of protons in each nucleus

Group I

Group II

Atomic number goes up by one along each period

Atomic number
H
Hydrogen
1.0

Atomic number — Chemical symbol — Chemical name — Relative atomic mass

RELATIVE ATOMIC MASS
Atomic mass (formerly atomic weight) is the mass of each atom of an element. It is equal to the number of protons plus the number of neutrons (electrons have negligible mass). The figures given are the averages for all the different versions (isotopes) of each element, measured relative to the mass of carbon-12.

1st transition metals

Group I	Group II					
1 **H** Hydrogen 1.0						
3 **Li** Lithium 6.9	4 **Be** Beryllium 9.0					
11 **Na** Sodium 23.0	12 **Mg** Magnesium 24.3					
19 **K** Potassium 39.1	20 **Ca** Calcium 40.1	21 **Sc** Scandium 45.0	22 **Ti** Titanium 47.9	23 **V** Vanadium 50.9	24 **Cr** Chromium 52.0	25 **Mn** Manganese 54.9
37 **Rb** Rubidium 85.5	38 **Sr** Strontium 87.6	39 **Y** Yttrium 88.9	40 **Zr** Zirconium 91.2	41 **Nb** Niobium 92.9	42 **Mo** Molybdenum 95.9	43 **Tc** Technetium 99.0
55 **Cs** Caesium 132.9	56 **Ba** Barium 137.4	57-71	72 **Hf** Hafnium 178.5	73 **Ta** Tantalum 181.0	74 **W** Tungsten 183.9	75 **Re** Rhenium 186.2
87 **Fr** Francium 225.0	88 **Ra** Radium 226.0	89-103	104 **Unq** Unnilquadium (261)	105 **Unp** Unnilpentium (262)	106 **Unh** Unnilhexium (263)	107 **Uns** Unnilseptium (262)

s-block

d-block

Two series always separated out from the table to give it a coherent shape

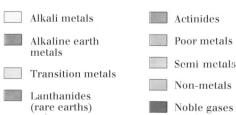

Soft, silvery, and highly reactive metal

SODIUM: GROUP 1 METAL

Silvery, reactive metal

MAGNESIUM: GROUP 2 METAL

Hard, silvery metal

CHROMIUM: 1ST TRANSITION METAL

Radioactive metal

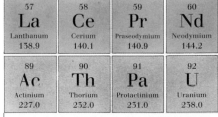

PLUTONIUM: ACTINIDE SERIES METAL

57 **La** Lanthanum 138.9	58 **Ce** Cerium 140.1	59 **Pr** Praseodymium 140.9	60 **Nd** Neodymium 144.2
89 **Ac** Actinium 227.0	90 **Th** Thorium 232.0	91 **Pa** Protactinium 231.0	92 **U** Uranium 238.0

TYPES OF ELEMENT KEY:
- ☐ Alkali metals
- ☐ Alkaline earth metals
- ☐ Transition metals
- ☐ Lanthanides (rare earths)
- ☐ Actinides
- ☐ Poor metals
- ☐ Semi metals
- ☐ Non-metals
- ☐ Noble gases

ALLOTROPES OF CARBON
Some elements exist in more than one form —these are known as allotropes. Carbon powder, graphite, and diamond are allotropes of carbon. They all consist of carbon atoms, but have very different physical properties.

DIAMOND

GRAPHITE

CARBON POWDER

Bright yellow crystal

SULFUR:
GROUP 6 SOLID NON-METAL

IODINE:
GROUP 7
SOLID NON-METAL

Purple-black solid turns to gas easily

Group 0

	Boron and carbon groups		Nitrogen and oxygen groups		Halogens	2 He Helium 4.0	Period
	Group III	*Group IV*	*Group V*	*Group VI*	*Group VII*		

2nd transition metals			3rd transition metals							
					5 B Boron 10.8	6 C Carbon 12.0	7 N Nitrogen 14.0	8 O Oxygen 16.0	9 F Fluorine 19.0	10 Ne Neon 20.2
					13 Al Aluminum 27.0	14 Si Silicon 28.1	15 P Phosphorus 31.0	16 S Sulfur 32.1	17 Cl Chlorine 35.5	18 Ar Argon 40.0
26 Fe Iron 55.9	27 Co Cobalt 58.9	28 Ni Nickel 58.7	29 Cu Copper 63.5	30 Zn Zinc 65.4	31 Ga Gallium 69.7	32 Ge Germanium 72.6	33 As Arsenic 74.9	34 Se Selenium 79.0	35 Br Bromine 83.9	36 Kr Krypton 83.8
44 Ru Ruthenium 101.0	45 Rh Rhodium 102.9	46 Pd Palladium 106.4	47 Ag Silver 107.9	48 Cd Cadmium 112.4	49 In Indium 114.8	50 Sn Tin 118.7	51 Sb Antimony 121.8	52 Te Tellurium 127.6	53 I Iodine 126.9	54 Xe Xenon 151.3
76 Os Osmium 190.2	77 Ir Iridium 192.2	78 Pt Platinum 195.1	79 Au Gold 197.0	80 Hg Mercury 200.6	81 Tl Thallium 204.4	82 Pb Lead 207.2	83 Bi Bismuth 209.0	84 Po Polonium 210.0	85 At Astatine 210.0	86 Rn Radon 222.0
108 Uno Unniloctium (265)	109 Une Unnilennium (266)									

Short period
Long period

d block
p-block

Atomic mass is estimated, as element exists fleetingly

Shiny semi-metal

Unreactive, colorless gas glows red in discharge tube

NOBLE GASES
Group 0 contains elements that have a filled (complete) outer shell of electrons, which means the atoms do not need to lose or gain electrons by bonding with other atoms. This makes them stable and they do not easily form ions or react with other elements. Noble gases are also called rare or inert gases.

Yellow, unreactive precious metal

Soft, shiny, reactive metal

GOLD:
3RD TRANSITION METAL

TIN:
GROUP 4 POOR METAL

ANTIMONY:
GROUP 5 SEMI-METAL

NEON:
GROUP 0
COLORLESS GAS

61 Pm Promethium 147.0	62 Sm Samarium 150.4	63 Eu Europium 152.0	64 Gd Gadolinium 157.3	65 Tb Terbium 158.9	66 Dy Dysprosium 162.5	67 Ho Holmium 164.9	68 Er Erbium 167.3	69 Tm Thulium 168.9	70 Yb Ytterbium 175.0	71 Lu Lutetium 175.0
93 Np Neptunium 237.0	94 Pu Plutonium 242.0	95 Am Americium 243.0	96 Cm Curium 247.0	97 Bk Berkelium 247.0	98 Cf Californium 251.0	99 Es Einsteinium 254.0	100 Fm Fermium 253.0	101 Md Mendelevium 256.0	102 No Nobelium 254.0	103 Lr Lawrencium 257.0

f-block

Chemical reactions

A CHEMICAL REACTION TAKES PLACE whenever bonds between atoms are broken or made. In each case, atoms or groups of atoms rearrange, making new substances (products) from the original ones (reactants). Reactions happen naturally, or can be made to happen; they may take years, or only an instant. Some of the main types are shown here. A reaction usually involves a change in energy (see pp. 314-315). In a burning reaction, for example, the making of new bonds between atoms releases energy as heat and light. This type of reaction, in which heat is given off, is an exothermic reaction. Many reactions, like burning, are irreversible, but some can take place in either direction, and are said to be reversible. Reactions can be used to form solids from solutions: in a double decomposition reaction, two compounds in solution break down and re-form into two new substances, often creating a precipitate (insoluble solid); in displacement, an element (eg. copper) displaces another element (eg. silver) from a solution. The rate (speed) of a reaction is determined by many different factors, such as temperature, and the size and shape of the reactants. To describe and keep track of reactions, internationally recognized chemical symbols and equations are used. Reactions are also used in the laboratory to identify matter. An experiment with candle wax, for example, demonstrates that it contains carbon and hydrogen.

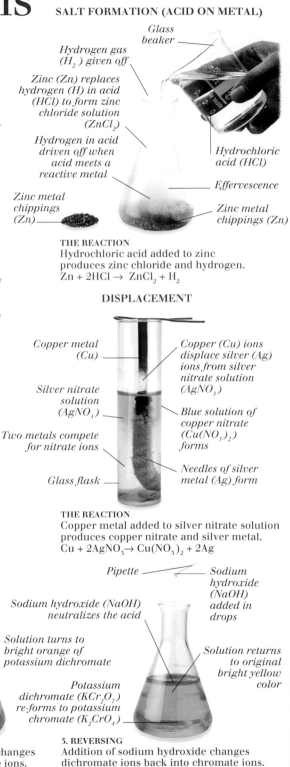

SALT FORMATION (ACID ON METAL)

Glass beaker

Hydrogen gas (H_2) given off

Zinc (Zn) replaces hydrogen (H) in acid (HCl) to form zinc chloride solution ($ZnCl_2$)

Hydrogen in acid driven off when acid meets a reactive metal

Hydrochloric acid (HCl)

Effervescence

Zinc metal chippings (Zn)

Zinc metal chippings (Zn)

THE REACTION
Hydrochloric acid added to zinc produces zinc chloride and hydrogen.
$Zn + 2HCl \rightarrow ZnCl_2 + H_2$

DISPLACEMENT

Copper metal (Cu)

Copper (Cu) ions displace silver (Ag) ions from silver nitrate solution ($AgNO_3$)

Silver nitrate solution ($AgNO_3$)

Blue solution of copper nitrate ($Cu(NO_3)_2$) forms

Two metals compete for nitrate ions

Needles of silver metal (Ag) form

Glass flask

THE REACTION
Copper metal added to silver nitrate solution produces copper nitrate and silver metal.
$Cu + 2AgNO_3 \rightarrow Cu(NO_3)_2 + 2Ag$

BURNING MATTER

Ammonium dichromate ((NH_4)$_2Cr_2O_7$)

Flame

In this burning reaction, atoms form simpler substances and give off heat and light

Ammonium dichromate ((NH_4)$_2Cr_2O_7$) converts to chromium oxide (Cr_2O_3)

Nitrogen monoxide (NO) and water vapor (H_2O) given off as colorless gases

THE REACTION
When lit, ammonium dichromate combines with oxygen from air.
$(NH_4)_2Cr_2O_7 + O_2 \rightarrow Cr_2O_3 + 4H_2O + 2NO$

A REVERSIBLE REACTION

Flat-bottomed glass flask

Potassium chromate solution (K_2CrO_4)

Bright yellow solution contains potassium and chromate ions

1. THE REACTANT
Potassium chromate dissolves in water to form potassium ions and chromate ions.
$K_2CrO_4 \rightarrow 2K^+ + CrO_4^{2-}$

Pipette

Hydrochloric acid (HCl) added in drops

Acid causes reaction to take place

Chromate ions converted to orange dichromate ions

Potassium dichromate (KCr_2O_7) forms

2. THE REACTION
Addition of hydrochloric acid changes chromate ions into dichromate ions.
$2CrO_4^{2-} \rightarrow Cr_2O_7^{2-}$

Pipette

Sodium hydroxide (NaOH) added in drops

Sodium hydroxide (NaOH) neutralizes the acid

Solution turns to bright orange of potassium dichromate

Potassium dichromate (KCr_2O_7) re-forms to potassium chromate (K_2CrO_4)

Solution returns to original bright yellow color

3. REVERSING
Addition of sodium hydroxide changes dichromate ions back into chromate ions.
$Cr_2O_7^{2-} \rightarrow 2CrO_4^{2-}$

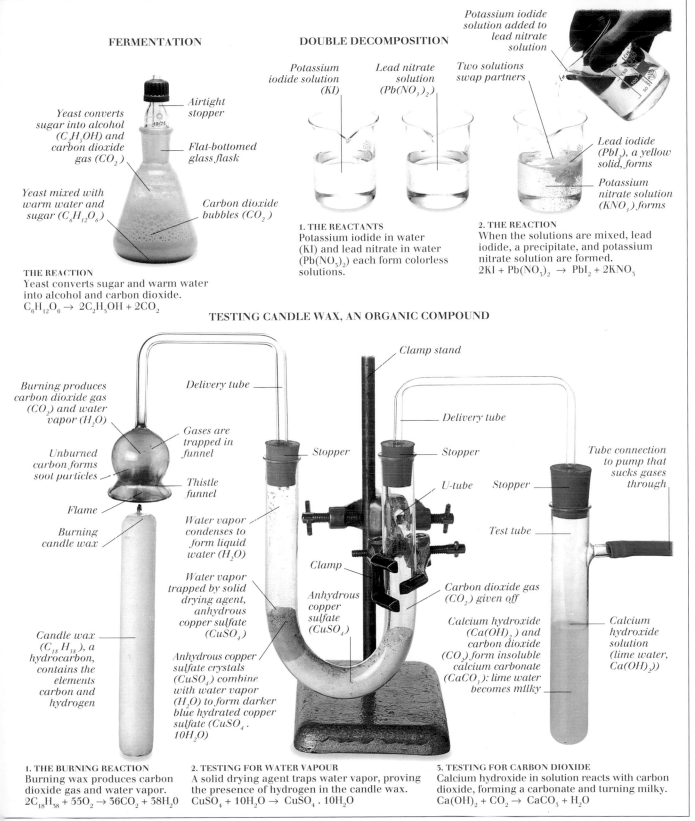

FERMENTATION

Yeast converts sugar into alcohol (C_2H_5OH) and carbon dioxide gas (CO_2)

Airtight stopper

Flat-bottomed glass flask

Yeast mixed with warm water and sugar ($C_6H_{12}O_6$)

Carbon dioxide bubbles (CO_2)

THE REACTION
Yeast converts sugar and warm water into alcohol and carbon dioxide.
$C_6H_{12}O_6 \rightarrow 2C_2H_5OH + 2CO_2$

DOUBLE DECOMPOSITION

Potassium iodide solution (KI)

Lead nitrate solution ($Pb(NO_3)_2$)

Potassium iodide solution added to lead nitrate solution

Two solutions swap partners

Lead iodide (PbI_2), a yellow solid, forms

Potassium nitrate solution (KNO_3) forms

1. THE REACTANTS
Potassium iodide in water (KI) and lead nitrate in water ($Pb(NO_5)_2$) each form colorless solutions.

2. THE REACTION
When the solutions are mixed, lead iodide, a precipitate, and potassium nitrate solution are formed.
$2KI + Pb(NO_3)_2 \rightarrow PbI_2 + 2KNO_3$

TESTING CANDLE WAX, AN ORGANIC COMPOUND

Burning produces carbon dioxide gas (CO_2) and water vapor (H_2O)

Delivery tube

Clamp stand

Delivery tube

Gases are trapped in funnel

Stopper

Stopper

Tube connection to pump that sucks gases through

Unburned carbon forms soot particles

Thistle funnel

U-tube

Stopper

Flame

Test tube

Burning candle wax

Water vapor condenses to form liquid water (H_2O)

Clamp

Carbon dioxide gas (CO_2) given off

Water vapor trapped by solid drying agent, anhydrous copper sulfate ($CuSO_4$)

Anhydrous copper sulfate ($CuSO_4$)

Calcium hydroxide ($Ca(OH)_2$) and carbon dioxide (CO_2) form insoluble calcium carbonate ($CaCO_3$): lime water becomes milky

Calcium hydroxide solution (lime water, $Ca(OH)_2$)

Candle wax ($C_{18}H_{38}$), a hydrocarbon, contains the elements carbon and hydrogen

Anhydrous copper sulfate crystals ($CuSO_4$) combine with water vapor (H_2O) to form darker blue hydrated copper sulfate ($CuSO_4 . 10H_2O$)

1. THE BURNING REACTION
Burning wax produces carbon dioxide gas and water vapor.
$2C_{18}H_{38} + 55O_2 \rightarrow 36CO_2 + 38H_2O$

2. TESTING FOR WATER VAPOUR
A solid drying agent traps water vapor, proving the presence of hydrogen in the candle wax.
$CuSO_4 + 10H_2O \rightarrow CuSO_4 . 10H_2O$

3. TESTING FOR CARBON DIOXIDE
Calcium hydroxide in solution reacts with carbon dioxide, forming a carbonate and turning milky.
$Ca(OH)_2 + CO_2 \rightarrow CaCO_3 + H_2O$

Energy

ANYTHING THAT HAPPENS—from a pin drop to an explosion —requires energy. Energy is the capacity for doing work (making something happen). Various forms of energy exist, including light, heat, sound, electrical, chemical, nuclear, kinetic, and potential energies. The Law of Conservation of Energy states that the total amount of energy in the Universe is fixed—energy cannot be created or destroyed, it can only change from one form to another (energy transfer). For example, potential energy is energy that is stored, and can be used in the future. An object gains potential energy when it is lifted; as the object is released, potential energy changes into the energy of motion (kinetic energy). During transference, some of the energy converts into heat. A combined heat and power station can put some of the "waste" heat to useful effect in local schools and housing. Most of the Earth's energy is provided by the Sun, in the form of electromagnetic radiation (see pp. 316-317). Some of this energy transfers to plant and animal life, and ultimately to fossil fuels, where it is stored in chemical form. Our bodies obtain energy from the food we eat, while energy needed for other tasks, such as heating and transportation, can be obtained by burning fossil fuels —or by harnessing natural forces like wind or moving water—to generate electricity. Another source is nuclear power, where energy is released by reactions in the nucleus of an atom. All energy is measured by the international unit, the joule (J). As a guide, one joule is about equal to the amount of energy needed to lift an apple one yard.

SANKEY DIAGRAM SHOWING ENERGY FLOW IN A COAL-FIRED COMBINED HEAT AND POWER STATION

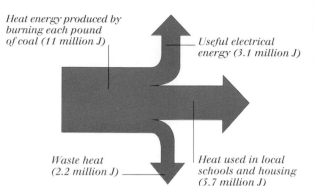

Heat energy produced by burning each pound of coal (11 million J)

Useful electrical energy (3.1 million J)

Waste heat (2.2 million J)

Heat used in local schools and housing (5.7 million J)

CROSS-SECTION OF HYDROELECTRIC POWER STATION WITH FRANCIS TURBINE

Transformer
Insulator
High voltage cable
Switch gear including circuit braker
Bushing
Rotor house
Generator unit
Gate
Generator rotor turned by turbine
Shaft
Francis turbine
Curved blade
Gate
Afterbay
Screen
Water in reservoir
Potential energy of water intake turns turbine
Penstock
Draft tube
Tailrace
Water that flows out has lost some energy

CROSS-SECTION OF NUCLEAR POWER STATION WITH PRESSURIZED WATER REACTOR

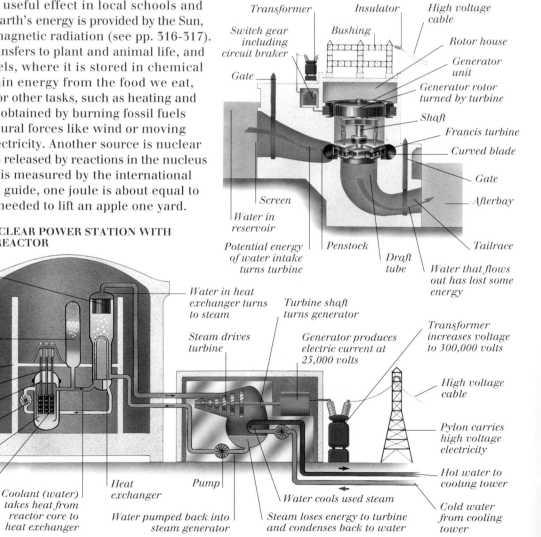

Steam generator
Concrete shielding
Water pressurizer
Steel girder framework
Control rod
Reactor core
Pump
Moderator (water)
Enriched uranium fuel
Coolant (water) takes heat from reactor core to heat exchanger
Heat exchanger
Water pumped back into steam generator
Water in heat exchanger turns to steam
Steam drives turbine
Pump
Water cools used steam
Steam loses energy to turbine and condenses back to water
Turbine shaft turns generator
Generator produces electric current at 25,000 volts
Transformer increases voltage to 300,000 volts
High voltage cable
Pylon carries high voltage electricity
Hot water to cooling tower
Cold water from cooling tower

ENERGY SYSTEMS

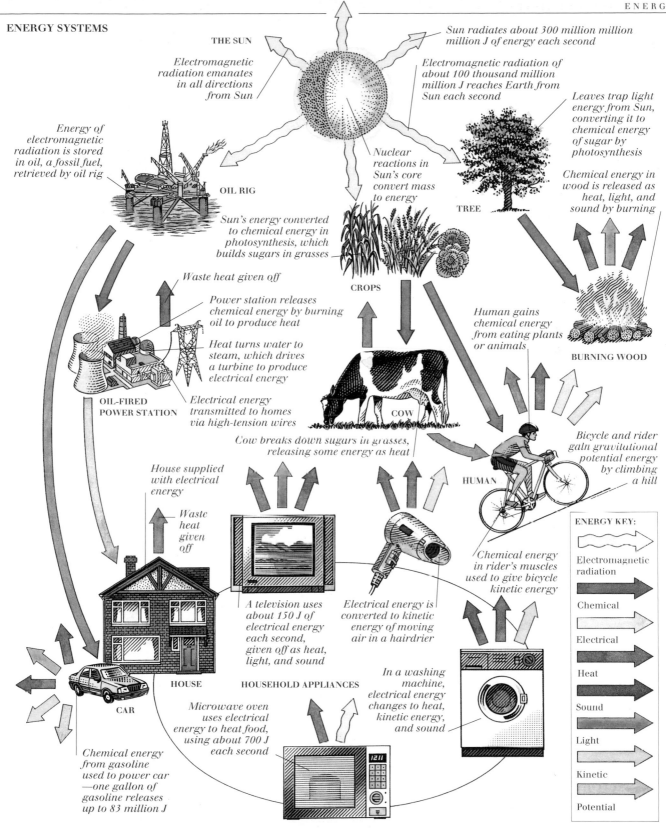

Sun radiates about 300 million million million J of energy each second

THE SUN

Electromagnetic radiation emanates in all directions from Sun

Electromagnetic radiation of about 100 thousand million million J reaches Earth from Sun each second

Leaves trap light energy from Sun, converting it to chemical energy of sugar by photosynthesis

Energy of electromagnetic radiation is stored in oil, a fossil fuel, retrieved by oil rig

OIL RIG

Nuclear reactions in Sun's core convert mass to energy

TREE

Chemical energy in wood is released as heat, light, and sound by burning

Sun's energy converted to chemical energy in photosynthesis, which builds sugars in grasses

Waste heat given off

Power station releases chemical energy by burning oil to produce heat

Heat turns water to steam, which drives a turbine to produce electrical energy

CROPS

Human gains chemical energy from eating plants or animals

BURNING WOOD

OIL-FIRED POWER STATION

Electrical energy transmitted to homes via high-tension wires

COW

Cow breaks down sugars in grasses, releasing some energy as heat

Bicycle and rider gain gravitational potential energy by climbing a hill

HUMAN

House supplied with electrical energy

Waste heat given off

Chemical energy in rider's muscles used to give bicycle kinetic energy

A television uses about 150 J of electrical energy each second, given off as heat, light, and sound

Electrical energy is converted to kinetic energy of moving air in a hairdrier

HOUSE

HOUSEHOLD APPLIANCES

In a washing machine, electrical energy changes to heat, kinetic energy, and sound

CAR

Chemical energy from gasoline used to power car —one gallon of gasoline releases up to 83 million J

Microwave oven uses electrical energy to heat food, using about 700 J each second

ENERGY KEY:

Electromagnetic radiation

Chemical

Electrical

Heat

Sound

Light

Kinetic

Potential

Electricity and magnetism

ELECTRICAL EFFECTS result from an imbalance of electric charge. There are two types of electric charge: positive (carried by protons) and negative (carried by electrons). If charges are opposite (unlike), they attract one another, while like charges repel. These forces of attraction and repulsion (electrostatic forces) exist between any two charged particles. Matter is normally uncharged, but if electrons are gained, an object will gain an overall negative charge; if they are removed, it becomes positive. Objects with an overall negative or positive charge are said to have an imbalance of charge, and exert the same forces as individual negative and positive charges. On this larger scale, the forces will always act to regain the balance of charge. This causes static electricity. Lightning, for example, is produced by clouds discharging a huge excess of negative electrons. If charges are free—in a wire or material that allows electrons to pass through it—the forces cause a flow of charge called an electric current. Some substances exhibit the strange phenomenon of magnetism—which also produces attractive and repulsive forces. Magnetic substances consist of small regions called domains. Normally unmagnetized, they can be magnetized by being placed in a magnetic field. Magnetism and electricity are inextricably linked, a fact put to use in motors and generators.

LIGHTNING

VAN DE GRAAFF (ELECTROSTATIC) GENERATOR

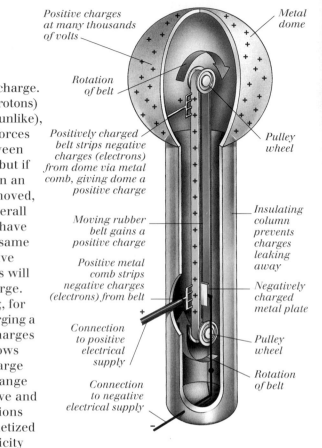

Positive charges at many thousands of volts

Metal dome

Rotation of belt

Positively charged belt strips negative charges (electrons) from dome via metal comb, giving dome a positive charge

Pulley wheel

Moving rubber belt gains a positive charge

Insulating column prevents charges leaking away

Positive metal comb strips negative charges (electrons) from belt

Negatively charged metal plate

Connection to positive electrical supply

Pulley wheel

Connection to negative electrical supply

Rotation of belt

CURRENT ELECTRICITY

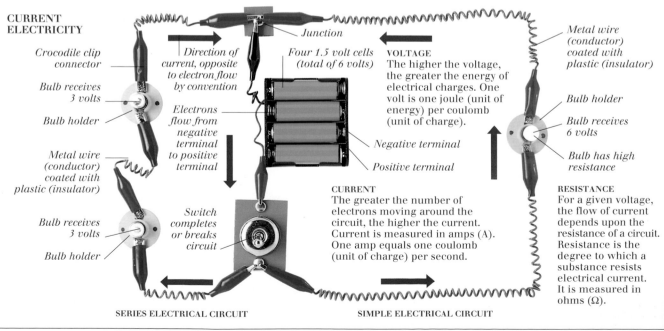

Crocodile clip connector

Bulb receives 3 volts

Bulb holder

Metal wire (conductor) coated with plastic (insulator)

Bulb receives 3 volts

Bulb holder

Direction of current, opposite to electron flow by convention

Electrons flow from negative terminal to positive terminal

Switch completes or breaks circuit

Junction

Four 1.5 volt cells (total of 6 volts)

Negative terminal

Positive terminal

VOLTAGE
The higher the voltage, the greater the energy of electrical charges. One volt is one joule (unit of energy) per coulomb (unit of charge).

CURRENT
The greater the number of electrons moving around the circuit, the higher the current. Current is measured in amps (A). One amp equals one coulomb (unit of charge) per second.

Metal wire (conductor) coated with plastic (insulator)

Bulb holder

Bulb receives 6 volts

Bulb has high resistance

RESISTANCE
For a given voltage, the flow of current depends upon the resistance of a circuit. Resistance is the degree to which a substance resists electrical current. It is measured in ohms (Ω).

SERIES ELECTRICAL CIRCUIT   **SIMPLE ELECTRICAL CIRCUIT**

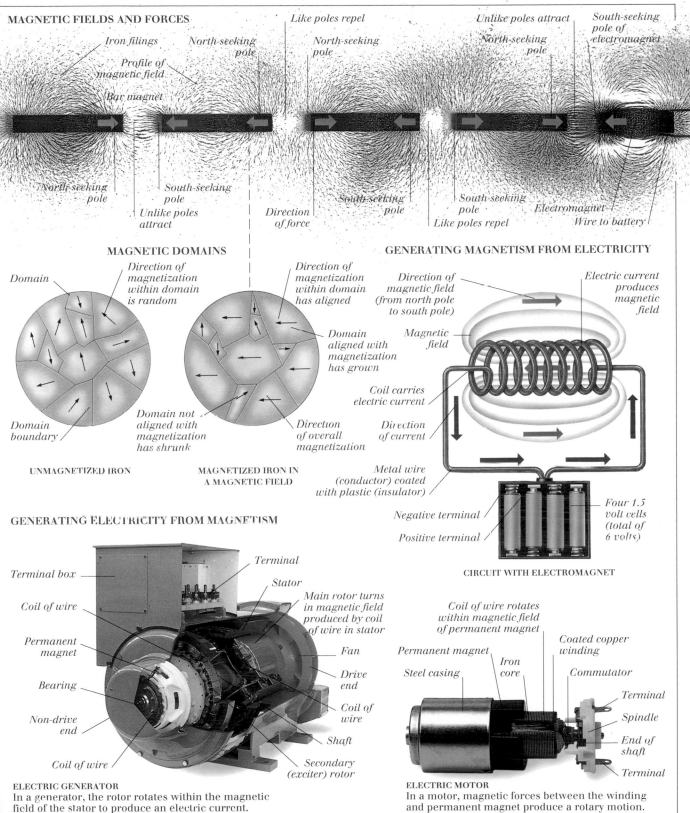

MAGNETIC FIELDS AND FORCES

Iron filings

Profile of magnetic field

Bar magnet

North-seeking pole

North-seeking pole

Like poles repel

North-seeking pole

Unlike poles attract

North-seeking pole

South-seeking pole of electromagnet

North-seeking pole

South-seeking pole

Unlike poles attract

Direction of force

South-seeking pole

South-seeking pole

Like poles repel

Electromagnet

Wire to battery

MAGNETIC DOMAINS

Domain

Direction of magnetization within domain is random

Domain boundary

Direction of magnetization within domain has aligned

Domain aligned with magnetization has grown

Domain not aligned with magnetization has shrunk

Direction of overall magnetization

UNMAGNETIZED IRON

MAGNETIZED IRON IN A MAGNETIC FIELD

GENERATING MAGNETISM FROM ELECTRICITY

Direction of magnetic field (from north pole to south pole)

Magnetic field

Coil carries electric current

Metal wire (conductor) coated with plastic (insulator)

Electric current produces magnetic field

Direction of current

Negative terminal

Positive terminal

Four 1.5 volt cells (total of 6 volts)

CIRCUIT WITH ELECTROMAGNET

GENERATING ELECTRICITY FROM MAGNETISM

Terminal box

Coil of wire

Permanent magnet

Bearing

Non-drive end

Coil of wire

Terminal

Stator

Main rotor turns in magnetic field produced by coil of wire in stator

Fan

Drive end

Coil of wire

Shaft

Secondary (exciter) rotor

ELECTRIC GENERATOR
In a generator, the rotor rotates within the magnetic field of the stator to produce an electric current.

Coil of wire rotates within magnetic field of permanent magnet

Permanent magnet

Steel casing

Iron core

Coated copper winding

Commutator

Terminal

Spindle

End of shaft

Terminal

ELECTRIC MOTOR
In a motor, magnetic forces between the winding and permanent magnet produce a rotary motion.

Light

INFRARED IMAGE
OF A HOUSE

LIGHT IS A FORM OF ENERGY. It is a type of electromagnetic radiation, like X rays or radio waves. All electromagnetic radiation is produced by electric charges (see pp. 316-317): it is caused by the effects of oscillating electric and magnetic fields as they travel through space. Electromagnetic radiation is considered to have both wave and particle properties. It can be thought of as a wave of electricity and magnetism. In that case, the difference between the various forms of radiation is their wavelength. Radiation can also be said to consist of particles, or packets of energy, called photons. The difference between light and X rays, for instance, is the amount of energy that each photon carries. The complete range of radiation is referred to as the electromagnetic spectrum, extending from low energy, long wavelength radio waves to high energy, short wavelength gamma rays. Light is the only part of the electromagnetic spectrum that is visible. White light from the Sun is made up of all the visible wavelengths of radiation, which can be seen when it is separated by using a prism. Light, like all forms of electromagnetic radiation, can be reflected (bounced back) and refracted (bent). Different parts of the electromagnetic spectrum are produced in different ways. Sometimes visible light—and infrared radiation—is generated by the vibrating particles of warm or hot objects. The emission of light in this way is called incandescence. Light can also be produced by fluorescence, a phenomenon in which electrons gain and lose energy within atoms.

MAXWELLIAN DIAGRAM OF ELECTROMAGNETIC RADIATION AS WAVES

Oscillating electric field

Wavelength

Oscillating magnetic field

Two fields at right angles

Direction of travel

ELECTROMAGNETIC RADIATION AS PARTICLES

Photon thought of as wave packet of energy

Blue light has about twice the energy of red light

Red light has long wavelength

Blue light has shorter wavelength: waves are more tightly packed

PHOTON OF RED LIGHT

PHOTON OF BLUE LIGHT

SPLITTING WHITE LIGHT INTO THE SPECTRUM

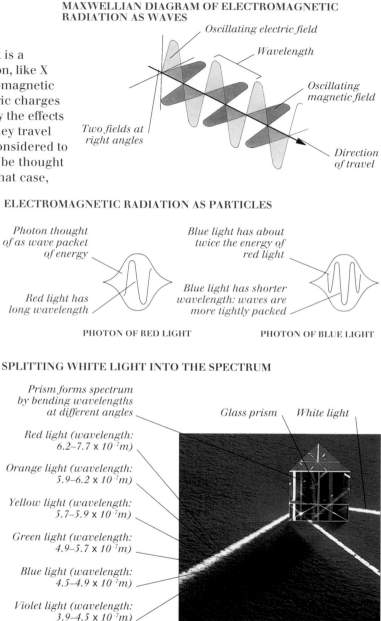

Prism forms spectrum by bending wavelengths at different angles

Glass prism   White light

Red light (wavelength: 6.2–$7.7 \times 10^{-7}m$)

Orange light (wavelength: 5.9–$6.2 \times 10^{-7}m$)

Yellow light (wavelength: 5.7–$5.9 \times 10^{-7}m$)

Green light (wavelength: 4.9–$5.7 \times 10^{-7}m$)

Blue light (wavelength: 4.5–$4.9 \times 10^{-7}m$)

Violet light (wavelength: 3.9–$4.5 \times 10^{-7}m$)

THE ELECTROMAGNETIC SPECTRUM

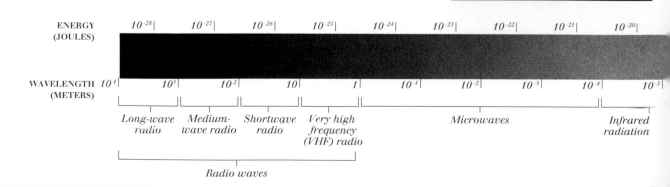

ENERGY (JOULES)	10^{-28}	10^{-27}	10^{-26}	10^{-25}	10^{-24}	10^{-23}	10^{-22}	10^{-21}	10^{-20}

WAVELENGTH (METERS)	10^4	10^3	10^2	10	1	10^{-1}	10^{-2}	10^{-3}	10^{-4}	10^{-5}

Long-wave radio   Medium-wave radio   Shortwave radio   Very high frequency (VHF) radio   Microwaves   Infrared radiation

Radio waves

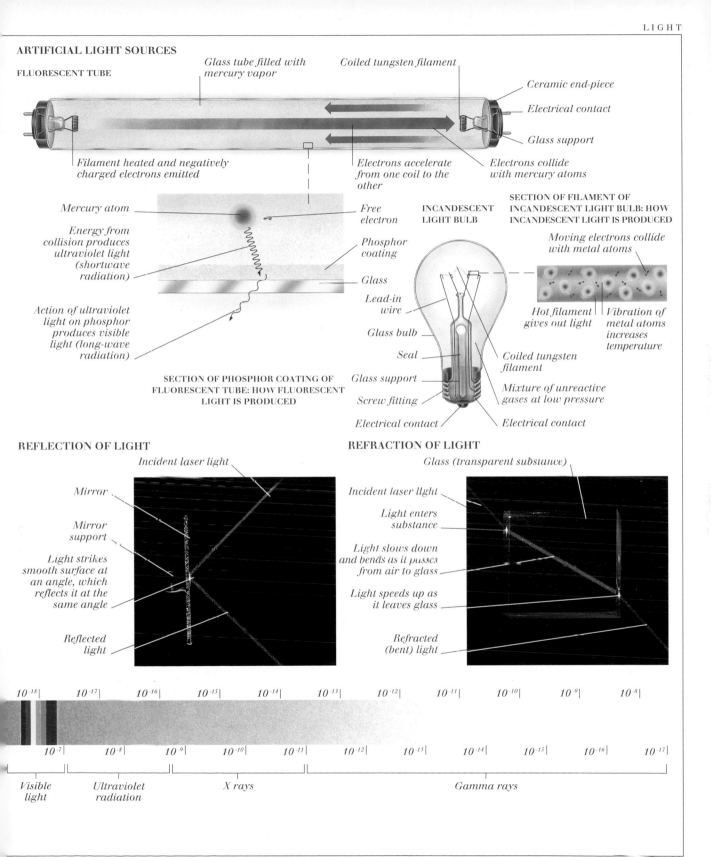

ARTIFICIAL LIGHT SOURCES

FLUORESCENT TUBE

Glass tube filled with mercury vapor

Coiled tungsten filament

Ceramic end-piece

Electrical contact

Glass support

Filament heated and negatively charged electrons emitted

Electrons accelerate from one coil to the other

Electrons collide with mercury atoms

Mercury atom

Free electron

Energy from collision produces ultraviolet light (shortwave radiation)

Phosphor coating

Glass

Action of ultraviolet light on phosphor produces visible light (long-wave radiation)

SECTION OF PHOSPHOR COATING OF FLUORESCENT TUBE: HOW FLUORESCENT LIGHT IS PRODUCED

INCANDESCENT LIGHT BULB

SECTION OF FILAMENT OF INCANDESCENT LIGHT BULB: HOW INCANDESCENT LIGHT IS PRODUCED

Moving electrons collide with metal atoms

Hot filament gives out light

Vibration of metal atoms increases temperature

Lead-in wire

Glass bulb

Seal

Coiled tungsten filament

Glass support

Mixture of unreactive gases at low pressure

Screw fitting

Electrical contact

Electrical contact

REFLECTION OF LIGHT

Incident laser light

Mirror

Mirror support

Light strikes smooth surface at an angle, which reflects it at the same angle

Reflected light

REFRACTION OF LIGHT

Glass (transparent substance)

Incident laser light

Light enters substance

Light slows down and bends as it passes from air to glass

Light speeds up as it leaves glass

Refracted (bent) light

10^{-18} | 10^{-17} | 10^{-16} | 10^{-15} | 10^{-14} | 10^{-13} | 10^{-12} | 10^{-11} | 10^{-10} | 10^{-9} | 10^{-8} |

10^{-7} | 10^{-8} | 10^{-9} | 10^{-10} | 10^{-11} | 10^{-12} | 10^{-13} | 10^{-14} | 10^{-15} | 10^{-16} | 10^{-17} |

Visible light

Ultraviolet radiation

X rays

Gamma rays

Force and motion

FORCES ARE PUSHES OR PULLS that change the motion of objects. To make a stationary object move, or a moving object stop, a force is needed. A force is also required to change the speed or direction of an object. This change in speed or direction is known as acceleration. Acceleration depends on the size (magnitude) of the force, and on the mass of the object. The effects of forces were first summarized by Isaac Newton in his three laws of motion. The international unit of force, named after him, is the newton (N), which is approximately equal to the weight of one apple. Gravity—the force of attraction between any two masses—can be measured using a newton meter (spring balance). Forces are put to useful effect in machines. A simple machine, such as a wheel and axle, is a device that changes the size or direction of an applied force. It allows an applied force (the effort) to produce another force (the load). A lever uses a bar that turns on a fulcrum to exert force. In all simple machines, there is a relationship between force and distance. A small force (in a compound pulley, for instance) moves through a large distance to lift a heavy object a small distance. This is called the Law of Simple Machines.

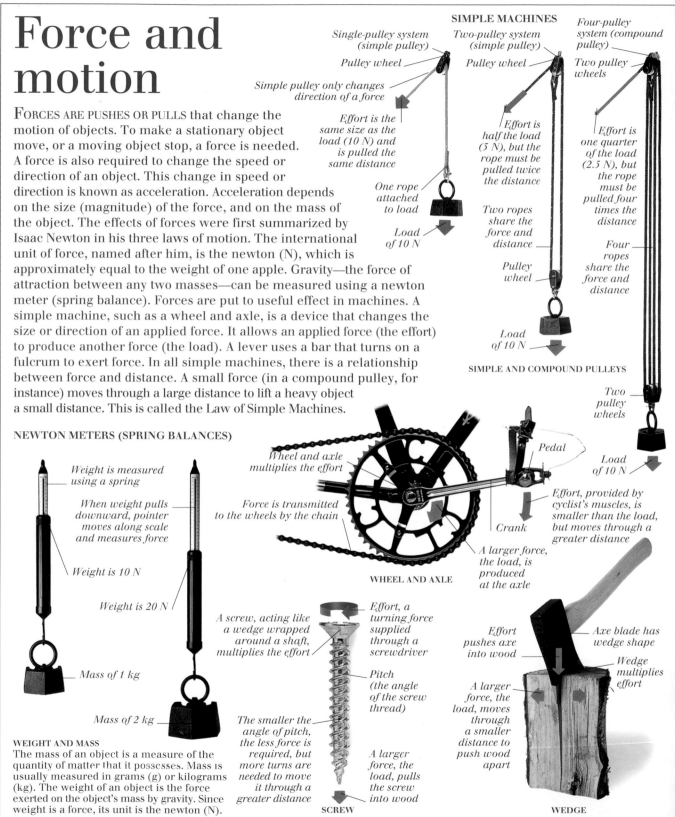

SIMPLE MACHINES

Single-pulley system (simple pulley)
Pulley wheel
Simple pulley only changes direction of a force
Effort is the same size as the load (10 N) and is pulled the same distance
One rope attached to load
Load of 10 N

Two-pulley system (simple pulley)
Pulley wheel
Effort is half the load (5 N), but the rope must be pulled twice the distance
Two ropes share the force and distance
Pulley wheel
Load of 10 N

Four-pulley system (compound pulley)
Two pulley wheels
Effort is one quarter of the load (2.5 N), but the rope must be pulled four times the distance
Four ropes share the force and distance
Two pulley wheels
Load of 10 N

SIMPLE AND COMPOUND PULLEYS

NEWTON METERS (SPRING BALANCES)

Weight is measured using a spring
When weight pulls downward, pointer moves along scale and measures force
Weight is 10 N
Weight is 20 N
Mass of 1 kg
Mass of 2 kg

WEIGHT AND MASS
The mass of an object is a measure of the quantity of matter that it possesses. Mass is usually measured in grams (g) or kilograms (kg). The weight of an object is the force exerted on the object's mass by gravity. Since weight is a force, its unit is the newton (N).

Wheel and axle multiplies the effort
Force is transmitted to the wheels by the chain
Pedal
Crank
Effort, provided by cyclist's muscles, is smaller than the load, but moves through a greater distance
A larger force, the load, is produced at the axle

WHEEL AND AXLE

A screw, acting like a wedge wrapped around a shaft, multiplies the effort
Effort, a turning force supplied through a screwdriver
Pitch (the angle of the screw thread)
The smaller the angle of pitch, the less force is required, but more turns are needed to move it through a greater distance
A larger force, the load, pulls the screw into wood
SCREW

Effort pushes axe into wood
Axe blade has wedge shape
Wedge multiplies effort
A larger force, the load, moves through a smaller distance to push wood apart
WEDGE

NEWTON'S THREE LAWS OF MOTION

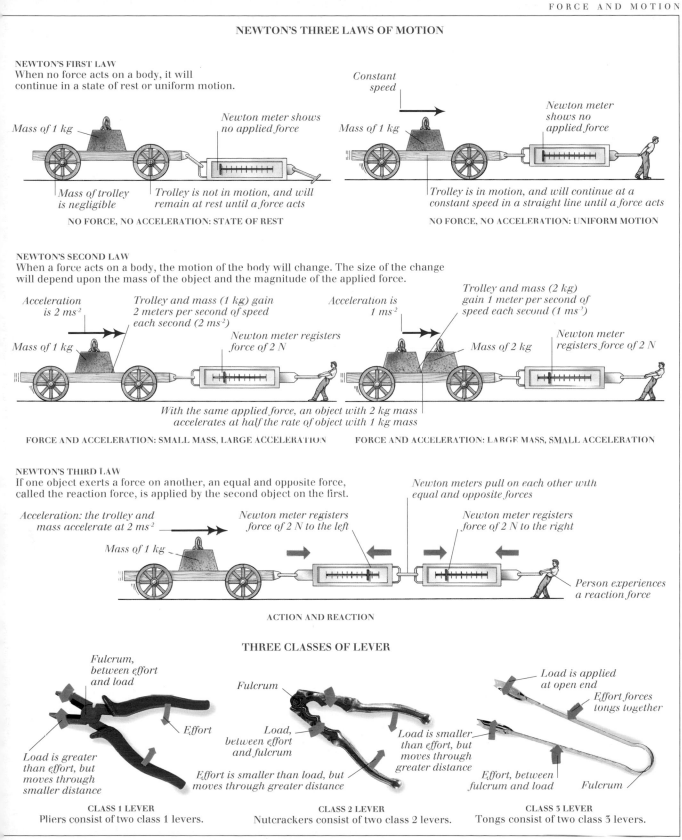

NEWTON'S FIRST LAW
When no force acts on a body, it will continue in a state of rest or uniform motion.

Newton meter shows no applied force

Mass of 1 kg

Mass of trolley is negligible

Trolley is not in motion, and will remain at rest until a force acts

NO FORCE, NO ACCELERATION: STATE OF REST

Constant speed

Mass of 1 kg

Newton meter shows no applied force

Trolley is in motion, and will continue at a constant speed in a straight line until a force acts

NO FORCE, NO ACCELERATION: UNIFORM MOTION

NEWTON'S SECOND LAW
When a force acts on a body, the motion of the body will change. The size of the change will depend upon the mass of the object and the magnitude of the applied force.

Acceleration is 2 ms⁻²

Trolley and mass (1 kg) gain 2 meters per second of speed each second (2 ms⁻²)

Mass of 1 kg

Newton meter registers force of 2 N

With the same applied force, an object with 2 kg mass accelerates at half the rate of object with 1 kg mass

FORCE AND ACCELERATION: SMALL MASS, LARGE ACCELERATION

Acceleration is 1 ms⁻²

Trolley and mass (2 kg) gain 1 meter per second of speed each second (1 ms⁻²)

Mass of 2 kg

Newton meter registers force of 2 N

FORCE AND ACCELERATION: LARGE MASS, SMALL ACCELERATION

NEWTON'S THIRD LAW
If one object exerts a force on another, an equal and opposite force, called the reaction force, is applied by the second object on the first.

Acceleration: the trolley and mass accelerate at 2 ms⁻²

Mass of 1 kg

Newton meter registers force of 2 N to the left

Newton meters pull on each other with equal and opposite forces

Newton meter registers force of 2 N to the right

Person experiences a reaction force

ACTION AND REACTION

THREE CLASSES OF LEVER

Fulcrum, between effort and load

Effort

Load is greater than effort, but moves through smaller distance

CLASS 1 LEVER
Pliers consist of two class 1 levers.

Fulcrum

Load, between effort and fulcrum

Effort is smaller than load, but moves through greater distance

CLASS 2 LEVER
Nutcrackers consist of two class 2 levers.

Load is applied at open end

Effort forces tongs together

Load is smaller than effort, but moves through greater distance

Effort, between fulcrum and load

Fulcrum

CLASS 3 LEVER
Tongs consist of two class 3 levers.

Rail and Road

Steam locomotives

WAGONS THAT ARE PULLED along tracks have been used to transport material since the 16th century, but these trains were drawn by men or horses until the invention of the steam locomotive. Steam locomotives enabled the basic railroad system to realize its true potential. In 1804, Richard Trevithick built the world's first working steam locomotive in South Wales. It was not entirely successful, but it encouraged others to develop new designs. By 1829, the British engineer Robert Stephenson had built the Rocket, considered to be the forerunner of the modern locomotive. The Rocket was a self-sufficient unit, carrying coal to heat the boiler and a water supply for generating steam. Steam passed from the boiler to force the pistons back and forth, and this movement turned the driving wheels, propelling the train forward. Used steam was then expelled in characteristic puffs. Later steam locomotives, like Ellerman Lines and the Mallard, worked in a similar way, but on a much larger scale. The simple design and reliability of steam locomotives ensured that they changed very little in 120 years of use, before being replaced in the 1950s by more efficient diesel and electric power (see pp. 326-329).

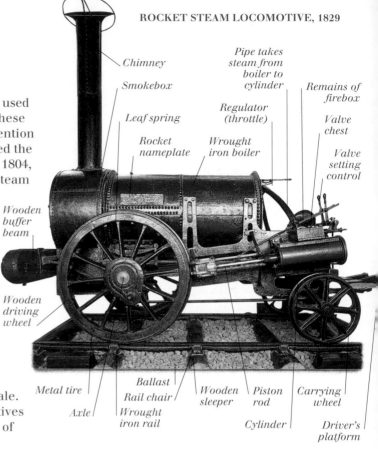

ROCKET STEAM LOCOMOTIVE, 1829

Chimney

Smokebox

Leaf spring

Rocket nameplate

Pipe takes steam from boiler to cylinder

Regulator (throttle)

Wrought iron boiler

Remains of firebox

Valve chest

Valve setting control

Wooden buffer beam

Wooden driving wheel

Metal tire

Axle

Ballast

Rail chair

Wrought iron rail

Wooden sleeper

Piston rod

Cylinder

Carrying wheel

Driver's platform

ELLERMAN LINES, 1949 (CUTAWAY VIEW)

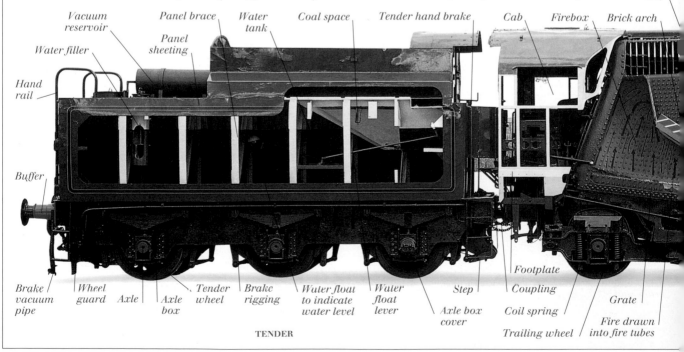

Vacuum reservoir

Panel brace

Panel sheeting

Water tank

Coal space

Tender hand brake

Cab

Firebox

Brick arch

Stay

Water filler

Hand rail

Buffer

Brake vacuum pipe

Wheel guard

Axle

Axle box

Tender wheel

Brake rigging

Water float to indicate water level

Water float lever

Axle box cover

Step

Footplate

Coupling

Coil spring

Trailing wheel

Grate

Fire drawn into fire tubes

TENDER

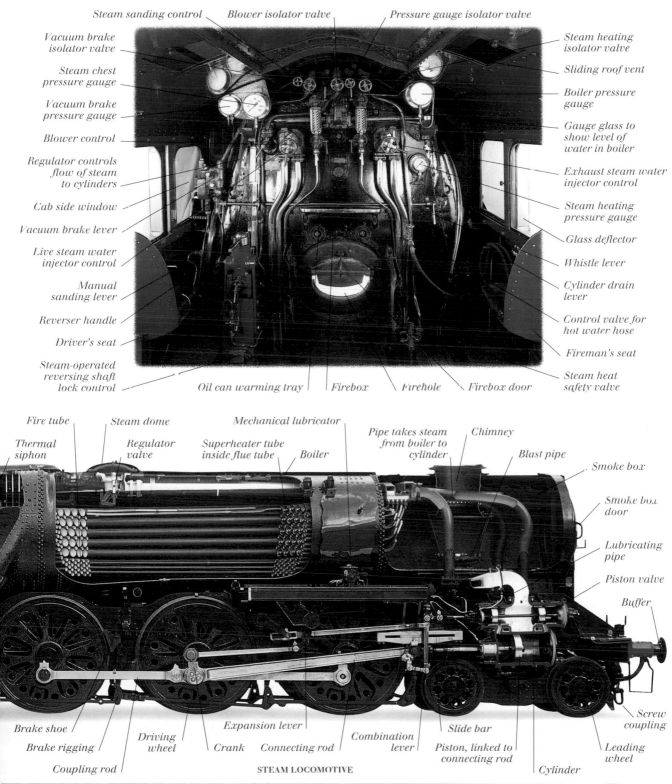

CAB INTERIOR OF MALLARD EXPRESS STEAM LOCOMOTIVE, 1938

Steam sanding control

Blower isolator valve

Pressure gauge isolator valve

Vacuum brake isolator valve

Steam heating isolator valve

Steam chest pressure gauge

Sliding roof vent

Vacuum brake pressure gauge

Boiler pressure gauge

Blower control

Gauge glass to show level of water in boiler

Regulator controls flow of steam to cylinders

Exhaust steam water injector control

Cab side window

Steam heating pressure gauge

Vacuum brake lever

Glass deflector

Live steam water injector control

Whistle lever

Manual sanding lever

Cylinder drain lever

Reverser handle

Control valve for hot water hose

Driver's seat

Steam-operated reversing shaft lock control

Fireman's seat

Oil can warming tray

Firebox

Firehole

Firebox door

Steam heat safety valve

Fire tube

Steam dome

Mechanical lubricator

Pipe takes steam from boiler to cylinder

Chimney

Thermal siphon

Regulator valve

Superheater tube inside flue tube

Boiler

Blast pipe

Smoke box

Smoke box door

Lubricating pipe

Piston valve

Buffer

Brake shoe

Expansion lever

Slide bar

Screw coupling

Brake rigging

Driving wheel

Combination lever

Crank

Connecting rod

Piston, linked to connecting rod

Leading wheel

Coupling rod

Cylinder

STEAM LOCOMOTIVE

Diesel trains

RUDOLF DIESEL FIRST DEMONSTRATED the diesel engine in
Germany in 1898, but it was not until the 1940s that diesel
locomotives were successfully established on both passenger
and freight services in the U.S. Early diesel locomotives like
the Union Pacific were more expensive to build than steam
locomotives, but were more efficient and cheaper to operate,
especially where oil was plentiful. One feature of diesel engines
is that the power output cannot be coupled directly to the wheels.
To convert the mechanical energy produced by diesel engines,
a transmission system is needed. Almost all diesel locomotives
have electric transmissions, and are known as diesel-electric
locomotives. The diesel engine works by drawing air into the
cylinders and compressing it to increase its temperature; a small
quantity of diesel fuel is then injected into it. The resulting
combustion drives the generator (more recently an alternator)
to produce electricity, which is fed to electric motors connected
to the wheels. Diesel-electric locomotives are essentially
electric locomotives that carry their own power plants, and
are used worldwide today. The Deltic diesel-electric
locomotive, similar to the one shown here, replaced
classic express steam locomotives, and ran
at speeds up to 100 mph.

FRONT VIEW OF UNION PACIFIC DIESEL-ELECTRIC LOCOMOTIVE, 1950s

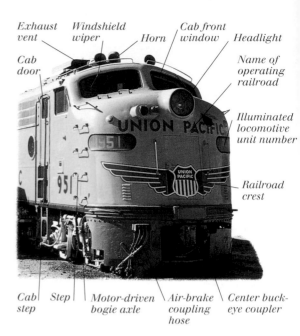

Exhaust vent
Windshield wiper
Horn
Cab front window
Headlight
Cab door
Name of operating railroad
Illuminated locomotive unit number
Railroad crest
Cab step
Step
Motor-driven bogie axle
Air-brake coupling hose
Center buck-eye coupler

PROTOTYPE DELTIC DIESEL-ELECTRIC LOCOMOTIVE, 1956

Engine room vent
Inspection hatch
Engine exhaust port
Radiator fan
Engine room window
Engine room vent

DELTIC

Fuel tank
Water for heating boiler
Inspection socket
Folding step
Drain for radiator coolant
Radiator coolant
Sand box
Telescopic damper
Drain for control reservoir

DIESEL ENGINE OF BRITISH RAIL CLASS 20 DIESEL-ELECTRIC LOCOMOTIVE

EXAMPLES OF FREIGHT CARS

Exhaust vent

Cylinder head
(V-four configuration)

Turbo-charged diesel
engine drives generator

Generator
cooling fan

Generator
compartment
vent

Auxiliary
generator

Main generator
produces
electricity that
drives wheels

Main chassis
member

Innermost
wheel set on
cab-end bogie

Brake
rigging

Battery
box

Engine crankcase

Air reservoir and
isolator valves

Lubricating oil
primary pump and
fuel supply pump

Air brake pipe

BOX CAR

HOPPER CAR

REFRIGERATOR CAR

LIVESTOCK CAR

FLAT CAR WITH BULKHEADS

AUTOMOBILE CAR

Cab door

Driver's seat

Cab

Warning horn

Windshield

Windshield wiper

Cab window

Manufacturer's
logo

Cab vent

Indicator
light

Sand box

Buffer

Brake cylinder

Roller-bearing
axle box

Brake
shoe

Brake
actuating chain

Transverse leaf spring
secondary suspension

Coil spring primary
suspension

Electric and high-speed trains

THE FIRST ELECTRIC LOCOMOTIVE ran in 1879 in Berlin, Germany. In Europe, electric trains developed as a more efficient alternative to the steam locomotive and diesel-electric power. Like diesels, electric trains employ electric motors to drive the wheels but, unlike diesels, the electricity is generated externally at a power station. Electric current is picked up either from a catenary (overhead cable) via a pantograph, or from a third rail. Since it does not carry its own power-generating equipment, an electric locomotive has a better power-to-weight ratio and greater acceleration than its diesel-electric equivalent. This makes electric trains highly suitable for urban routes with many stops. They are also faster, quieter, and cause less pollution. The latest electric French TGV (Train à Grande Vitesse) reaches 186 mph; other trains, like the London to Paris and Brussels Eurostar, can run at several voltages and operate between different countries. Simpler electric trains perform special duties—the "People Mover" at Gatwick Airport, London, runs between terminals.

HOW ALTERNATING CURRENT (AC) ELECTRIC TRAINS WORK

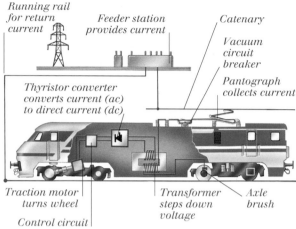

Running rail for return current

Feeder station provides current

Catenary

Vacuum circuit breaker

Pantograph collects current

Thyristor converter converts current (ac) to direct current (dc)

Traction motor turns wheel

Control circuit

Transformer steps down voltage

Axle brush

FRONT VIEW OF PARIS METRO

Route number

Windshield wiper

Unit number

Operator's initials (Régie Autonome des Transports Parisien)

Rubber running wheel

Guard for rubber wheel

Door open/shut indicator light

Driver's seat

Handle

Front light (white)

Rear light (red)

Buffing pad

Rubber guide wheel

FRONT VIEW OF ITALIAN STATE RAILWAYS CLASS 402 ELECTRIC LOCOMOTIVE

Collector strip for electric current

Double-arm pantograph

Headlight

Windshield wiper

Italian State Railways crest

Number of electric (E) locomotive (class 402 No. 5)

Buffer

Jumper cable

Conventional hook-screw coupling

Front light (white)

Rear light (red)

SIDE VIEW OF GATWICK EXPRESS "PEOPLE MOVER"

Pneumatic rubber wheel

Concrete track

Automatic door

No driver (train controlled by central computer)

EUROSTAR MULTI-VOLTAGE ELECTRIC TRAIN

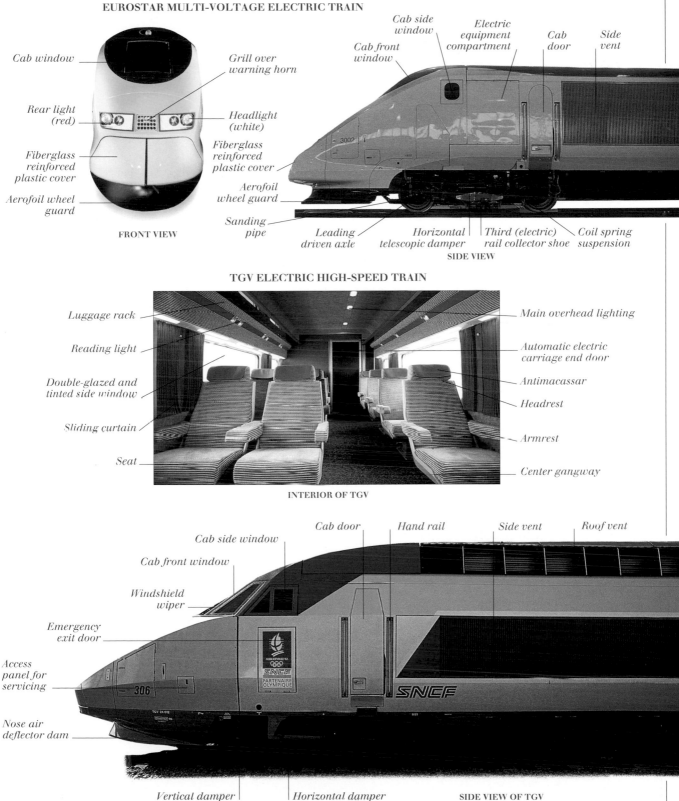

Cab window

Rear light (red)

Fiberglass reinforced plastic cover

Aerofoil wheel guard

Grill over warning horn

Headlight (white)

Fiberglass reinforced plastic cover

Aerofoil wheel guard

Sanding pipe

FRONT VIEW

Cab side window

Cab front window

Electric equipment compartment

Cab door

Side vent

3002

Leading driven axle

Horizontal telescopic damper

Third (electric) rail collector shoe

Coil spring suspension

SIDE VIEW

TGV ELECTRIC HIGH-SPEED TRAIN

Luggage rack

Reading light

Double-glazed and tinted side window

Sliding curtain

Seat

Main overhead lighting

Automatic electric carriage end door

Antimacassar

Headrest

Armrest

Center gangway

INTERIOR OF TGV

Cab side window

Cab front window

Windshield wiper

Emergency exit door

Access panel for servicing

Nose air deflector dam

Cab door

Hand rail

Side vent

Roof vent

306

SNCF

SNCF PARTENAIRE OLYMPIQUE

Vertical damper

Horizontal damper

SIDE VIEW OF TGV

Train equipment

MODERN RAILROAD TRACK consists of two parallel steel rails clipped onto a support called a sleeper. Sleepers are usually made of reinforced concrete, although wood and steel are still used. The distance between the inside edges of the rails is the track gauge. It evolved in Britain, which uses a gauge of 4 ft 8½ in (1,435 mm), known as the standard gauge. As engineering grew more sophisticated, narrower gauges were adopted because they cost less to build. The loading gauge, which is equally important, determines the size of the largest loaded vehicle that may pass through tunnels and under bridges with adequate clearance. Safe train operation relies on following a signaling system. At first, signaling was based on a simple time interval between trains, but it now depends on maintaining a safe distance between successive trains traveling in the same direction. Most modern signals are colored lights, but older mechanical semaphore signals are still used. On the latest high-speed lines, train drivers receive control instructions by electronic means. Signaling depends on reliable control of the train by effective braking. For fast, modern trains, which have considerable momentum, it is essential that each vehicle in the train can be braked by the driver or by a train control system, such as Automatic Train Protection (ATP). Braking is achieved by the brake shoe acting on the wheel rim (rim brakes), by disc brakes, or, increasingly, by electrical braking.

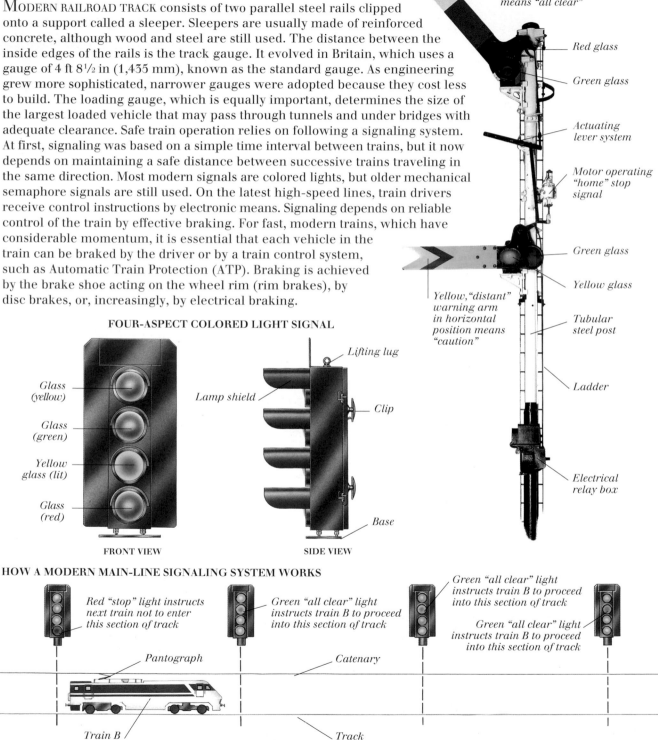

MECHANICAL SEMAPHORE SIGNAL

Red, square-ended arm in raised position means "all clear"

Red glass

Green glass

Actuating lever system

Motor operating "home" stop signal

Green glass

Yellow glass

Yellow, "distant" warning arm in horizontal position means "caution"

Tubular steel post

Ladder

Electrical relay box

FOUR-ASPECT COLORED LIGHT SIGNAL

Glass (yellow)

Glass (green)

Yellow glass (lit)

Glass (red)

FRONT VIEW

Lifting lug

Lamp shield

Clip

Base

SIDE VIEW

HOW A MODERN MAIN-LINE SIGNALING SYSTEM WORKS

Green "all clear" light instructs train B to proceed into this section of track

Red "stop" light instructs next train not to enter this section of track

Green "all clear" light instructs train B to proceed into this section of track

Green "all clear" light instructs train B to proceed into this section of track

Green "all clear" light instructs train B to proceed into this section of track

Pantograph

Catenary

Train B

Track

EXAMPLES OF INTERNATIONAL TRACK GAUGES

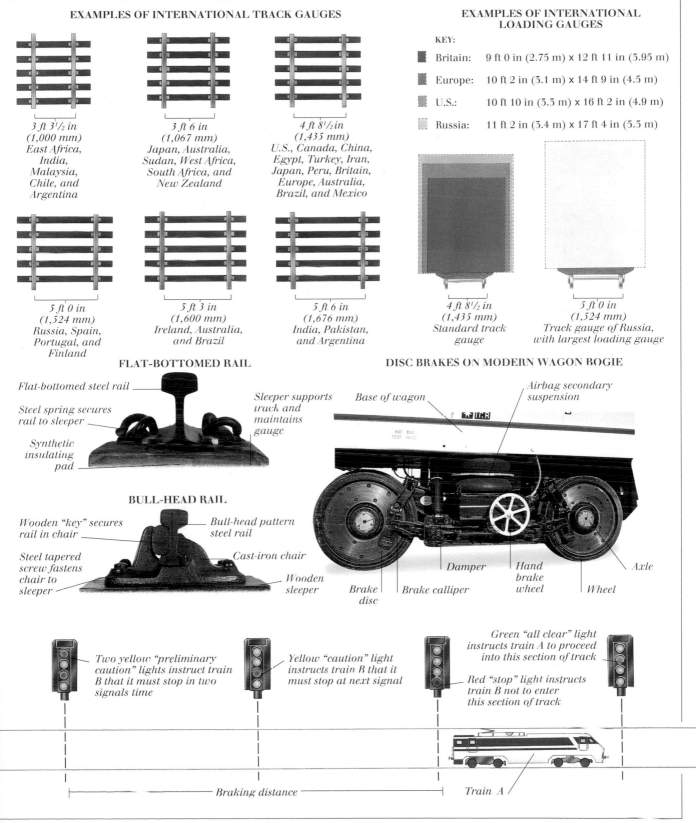

3 ft 3½ in
(1,000 mm)
*East Africa,
India,
Malaysia,
Chile, and
Argentina*

3 ft 6 in
(1,067 mm)
*Japan, Australia,
Sudan, West Africa,
South Africa, and
New Zealand*

4 ft 8½ in
(1,435 mm)
*U.S., Canada, China,
Egypt, Turkey, Iran,
Japan, Peru, Britain,
Europe, Australia,
Brazil, and Mexico*

5 ft 0 in
(1,524 mm)
*Russia, Spain,
Portugal, and
Finland*

5 ft 3 in
(1,600 mm)
*Ireland, Australia,
and Brazil*

5 ft 6 in
(1,676 mm)
*India, Pakistan,
and Argentina*

EXAMPLES OF INTERNATIONAL LOADING GAUGES

KEY:

- Britain: 9 ft 0 in (2.75 m) x 12 ft 11 in (3.95 m)
- Europe: 10 ft 2 in (3.1 m) x 14 ft 9 in (4.5 m)
- U.S.: 10 ft 10 in (3.3 m) x 16 ft 2 in (4.9 m)
- Russia: 11 ft 2 in (3.4 m) x 17 ft 4 in (5.3 m)

4 ft 8½ in
(1,435 mm)
*Standard track
gauge*

5 ft 0 in
(1,524 mm)
*Track gauge of Russia,
with largest loading gauge*

FLAT-BOTTOMED RAIL

Flat-bottomed steel rail

Steel spring secures
rail to sleeper

Synthetic
insulating
pad

Sleeper supports
track and
maintains
gauge

BULL-HEAD RAIL

Wooden "key" secures
rail in chair

Bull-head pattern
steel rail

Steel tapered
screw fastens
chair to
sleeper

Cast-iron chair

Wooden
sleeper

DISC BRAKES ON MODERN WAGON BOGIE

Base of wagon

Airbag secondary
suspension

Damper

Hand
brake
wheel

Axle

Brake
disc

Brake calliper

Wheel

Green "all clear" light
instructs train A to proceed
into this section of track

Two yellow "preliminary
caution" lights instruct train
B that it must stop in two
signals time

Yellow "caution" light
instructs train B that it
must stop at next signal

Red "stop" light instructs
train B not to enter
this section of track

Braking distance

Train A

Trolleys and buses

METROLINK TROLLEY, MANCHESTER, BRITAIN

WHEN CITY POPULATIONS exploded in the 1800s, there was an urgent need for mass transportation. Trolleys were an early solution. The first trolleys, like buses, were horse-drawn, but in 1881, electric streetcars appeared in Berlin, Germany. Electric trolleys soon became widespread throughout Europe and North America. Trolleys run on rails along a fixed route, using electric motors that receive power from overhead cables. As road networks developed, motorized buses offered a flexible alternative to trolleys. By the 1930s, they had replaced trolley systems in many cities. City buses typically have doors at both the front and rear to make loading and unloading easier. Double-decker designs are popular, occupying the same amount of street space as single-decker buses but able to transport twice the number of people. Buses are also commonly used for inter-city travel and touring. Tour buses have reclining seats, large windows, luggage space, and toilets. Recently, as city traffic has become increasingly congested, many city planners have designed new electric streetcar routes to run alongside bus routes as part of an integrated transport system.

EARLY TROLLEY, c.1900

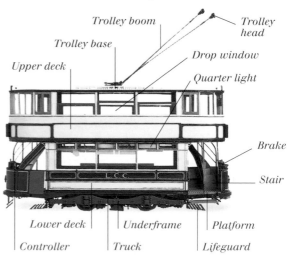

Trolley boom
Trolley head
Trolley base
Drop window
Upper deck
Quarter light
Brake
Stair
Lower deck
Underframe
Platform
Controller
Truck
Lifeguard

MCW METROBUS, LONDON, ENGLAND

Window vent
Upper deck windshield
Route information
Destination screen
Side mirror
Asymmetric windshield
Windshield wiper
Sidelight
Headlight
Grill
Fog light
License plate
Manufacturer's logo

Upper deck air intake
Route number
Side mirror
Permit holder
Turning indicator

LONDON NORTHERN

Hornsey Rise   Crouch End
Turnpike Lane
West Green Road

41

ARCHWAY STN.

PAY DRIVER

MCW

KYV 739X

FRONT VIEW

Square roof dome
Mirror for driver to see upstairs
Operator's logo
Destination screen
Side mirror
Front bumper
Entrance door
Emergency door control
Turning indicator

LONDON NORTHERN

SINGLE-DECKER BUS, NEW YORK CITY, NEW YORK

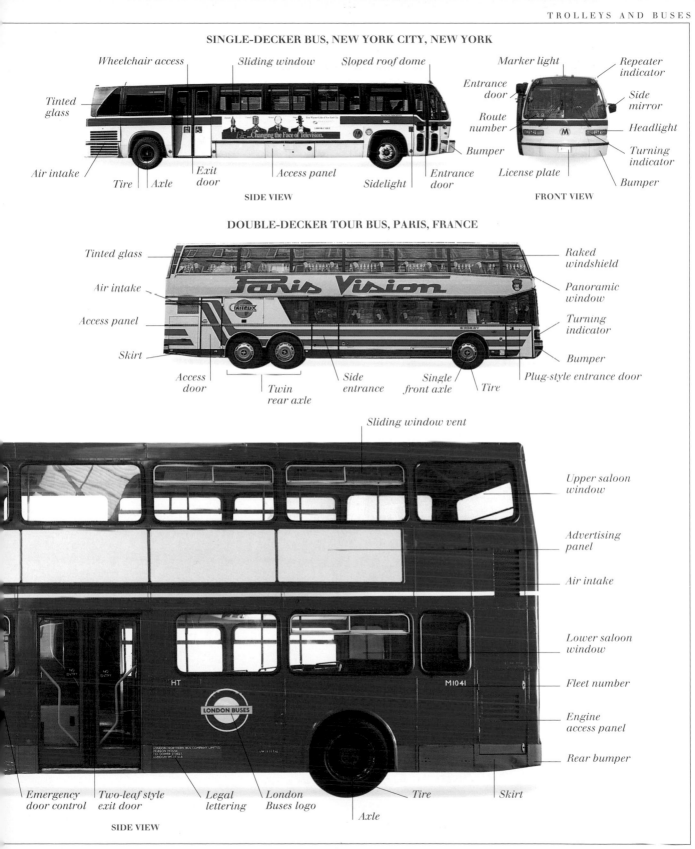

Wheelchair access

Sliding window

Sloped roof dome

Tinted glass

Air intake

Tire

Axle

Exit door

Access panel

Sidelight

Entrance door

SIDE VIEW

Marker light

Repeater indicator

Entrance door

Side mirror

Route number

Headlight

Bumper

Turning indicator

License plate

Bumper

FRONT VIEW

DOUBLE-DECKER TOUR BUS, PARIS, FRANCE

Tinted glass

Air intake

Access panel

Skirt

Access door

Twin rear axle

Side entrance

Single front axle

Tire

Paris Vision

Raked windshield

Panoramic window

Turning indicator

Bumper

Plug-style entrance door

Sliding window vent

Upper saloon window

Advertising panel

Air intake

Lower saloon window

Fleet number

M1041

Engine access panel

Rear bumper

LONDON BUSES

Emergency door control

Two-leaf style exit door

Legal lettering

London Buses logo

Axle

Tire

Skirt

SIDE VIEW

The first cars

THE EARLIEST ROAD VEHICLE powered by an engine, the Cugnot steam traction engine, was built in 1770. More practical steam carriages, such as the Bordino, were available in the early 19th century, but they were heavy and cumbersome. Restrictive laws and the introduction of railways, faster and able to carry more passengers, saw the decline of "cars" powered by steam. It was not until 1860 that the first practical power unit for road vehicles was developed with the invention of the internal combustion engine by the Belgian Étienne Lenoir. By around 1890, Karl Benz and Gottlieb Daimler in Germany and Albert de Dion and Armand Peugeot in France were building cars for sale to the public. These early cars, despite being primitive, expensive, and produced in limited numbers, heralded the age of the automobile.

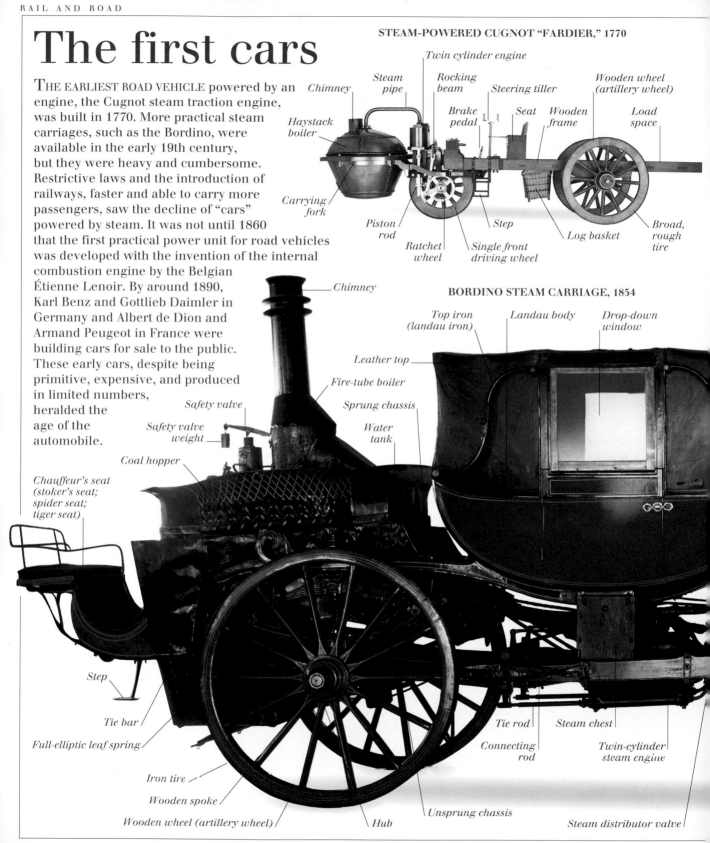

STEAM-POWERED CUGNOT "FARDIER," 1770

Twin cylinder engine
Steam pipe
Chimney
Rocking beam
Steering tiller
Wooden wheel (artillery wheel)
Haystack boiler
Brake pedal
Seat
Wooden frame
Load space
Carrying fork
Piston rod
Ratchet wheel
Single front driving wheel
Step
Log basket
Broad, rough tire

BORDINO STEAM CARRIAGE, 1854

Chimney
Top iron (landau iron)
Landau body
Drop-down window
Safety valve
Leather top
Fire-tube boiler
Safety valve weight
Sprung chassis
Coal hopper
Water tank
Chauffeur's seat (stoker's seat; spider seat; tiger seat)
Step
Tie bar
Full-elliptic leaf spring
Iron tire
Wooden spoke
Wooden wheel (artillery wheel)
Hub
Unsprung chassis
Tie rod
Connecting rod
Steam chest
Twin-cylinder steam engine
Steam distributor valve

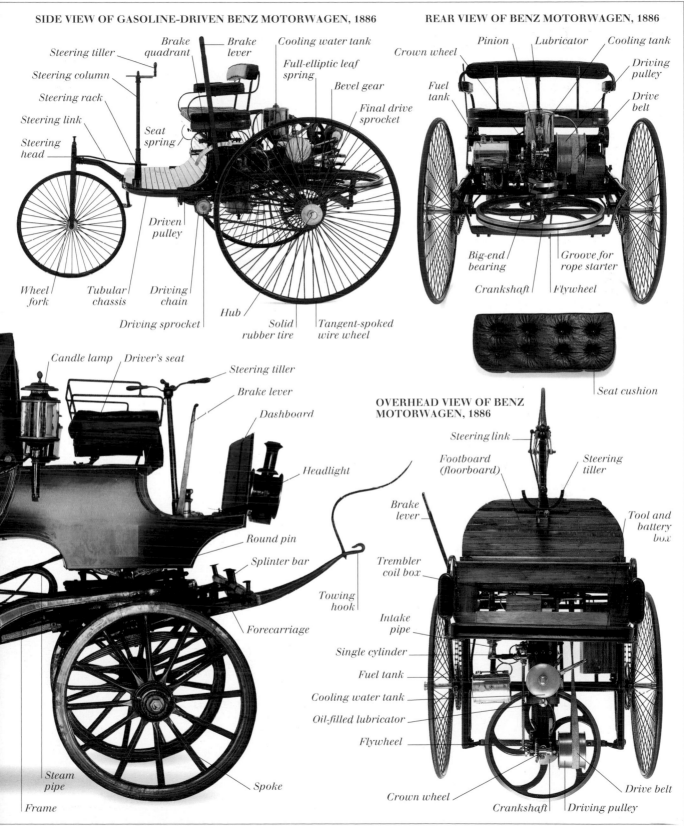

SIDE VIEW OF GASOLINE-DRIVEN BENZ MOTORWAGEN, 1886

Steering tiller
Brake quadrant
Brake lever
Cooling water tank
Full-elliptic leaf spring
Steering column
Steering rack
Bevel gear
Final drive sprocket
Steering link
Steering head
Seat spring
Driven pulley
Wheel fork
Tubular chassis
Driving chain
Driving sprocket
Hub
Solid rubber tire
Tangent-spoked wire wheel

REAR VIEW OF BENZ MOTORWAGEN, 1886

Pinion
Lubricator
Cooling tank
Crown wheel
Driving pulley
Fuel tank
Drive belt
Big-end bearing
Groove for rope starter
Crankshaft
Flywheel

Seat cushion

Candle lamp
Driver's seat
Steering tiller
Brake lever
Dashboard
Headlight
Round pin
Splinter bar
Towing hook
Forecarriage
Steam pipe
Spoke
Frame

OVERHEAD VIEW OF BENZ MOTORWAGEN, 1886

Steering link
Footboard (floorboard)
Steering tiller
Brake lever
Tool and battery box
Trembler coil box
Intake pipe
Single cylinder
Fuel tank
Cooling water tank
Oil-filled lubricator
Flywheel
Crown wheel
Crankshaft
Driving pulley
Drive belt

Elegance and utility

DURING THE FIRST DECADE OF THE 20TH CENTURY, the motorist who could afford it had a choice of some of the finest cars ever made. These handbuilt cars were powerful and luxurious, using the finest wood, leather, and cloth, and bodywork made to the customer's individual requirements. Some had six-cylinder engines as big as 15 liters. The price of such cars was several times that of an average house, and their yearly running costs were also very high. As a result, basic, utilitarian cars became popular. Costing perhaps one-tenth of the price of a luxury car, these cars had very little trim and often had only single-cylinder engines.

1904 OLDSMOBILE SINGLE-CYLINDER ENGINE

Oil bottle dripfeed
Crankcase
Starting handle bracket
Exhaust pipe
Cylinder head
Cylinder
Starter cog
Carburetor
Engine timing gear
Crankshaft
Gear band
Flywheel

FRONT VIEW OF 1906 RENAULT

Canopy
Mahogany-framed windshield
Cast aluminum wheel spider
Rear window
British Automobile Association badge
Bedford cord upholstery
British Royal Automobile Club badge
Window blind
Blind pull
Window lift strap
Broad lace trim
Rearview mirror
Lamp bracket
Oil side lamp
Windshield support
Dashboard radiator
Fender
Brass bevel
Hood catch
Access panel
Bail handle
Lifting handle
Mirror reflector
Acetylene headlight
Steering spindle
Elliott steering knuckle
Chevron-tread tire
Dumb iron
Screwdown greaser
Front axle
Starting handle
Tie rod

SIDE VIEW OF 1906 RENAULT

Luggage grid
Button-quilted upholstery
Mahogany-framed plate glass window
Round-corner single limousine coachwork
Rear oil lamp
Shock absorber
Hub
Hubcap
Beaded edge tire
Tire security bolt

1904 OLDSMOBILE TRIM AND BODYWORK

1904 OLDSMOBILE CHASSIS

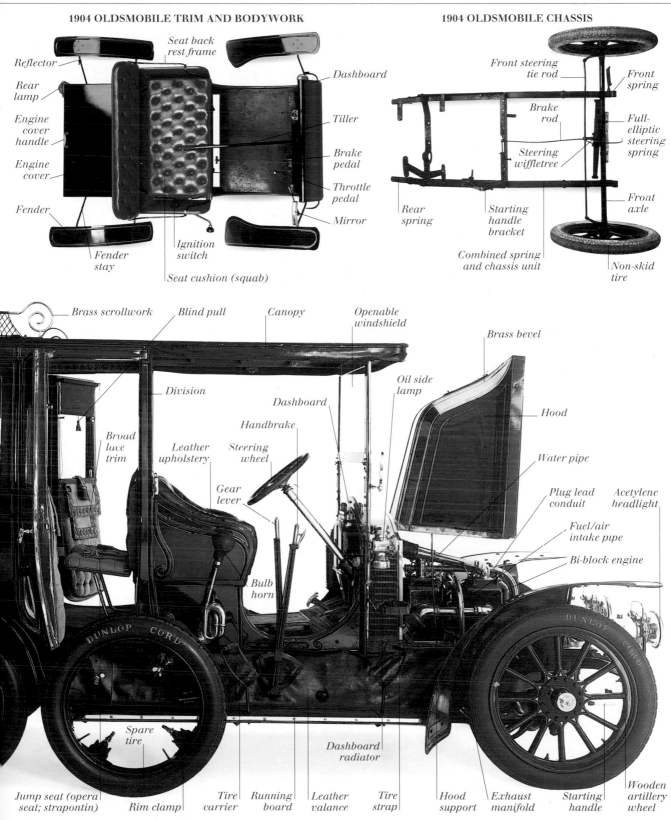

Reflector

Rear lamp

Engine cover handle

Engine cover

Fender

Fender stay

Seat back rest frame

Dashboard

Tiller

Brake pedal

Throttle pedal

Mirror

Ignition switch

Seat cushion (squab)

Front steering tie rod

Front spring

Brake rod

Full-elliptic steering spring

Steering wiffletree

Rear spring

Starting handle bracket

Front axle

Front axle

Combined spring and chassis unit

Non-skid tire

Brass scrollwork

Blind pull

Canopy

Openable windshield

Brass bevel

Division

Dashboard

Hood

Broad lace trim

Leather upholstery

Handbrake

Steering wheel

Oil side lamp

Water pipe

Gear lever

Plug lead conduit

Acetylene headlight

Fuel/air intake pipe

Bi-block engine

Bulb horn

Spare tire

Jump seat (opera seat; strapontin)

Rim clamp

Tire carrier

Running board

Leather valance

Dashboard radiator

Tire strap

Hood support

Exhaust manifold

Starting handle

Wooden artillery wheel

Mass production

THE FIRST CARS WERE HAND-ASSEMBLED from individually built parts, a time-consuming procedure that required skilled mechanics and made cars very expensive. This problem was solved, in America, by a Detroit car manufacturer named Henry Ford. He introduced mass production by using standardized parts, and later combined these with a moving production line. The work was brought to the workers, each of whom performed one simple task in the construction process as the chassis moved along the line. The first mass-produced car, the Ford Model T, was launched in 1908. At first it was available in a limited range of body styles and colors. However, when the production line was introduced in 1914, the color range was cut back; the Model T became available, as Henry Ford said, in "any color you like, so long as it's black." Ford cut the production time for a car from several days to about 12 hours, and eventually to minutes, making cars much cheaper than before. As a result, half the cars in the world were Model T Fords by 1920.

FRONT VIEW OF 1913 FORD MODEL T

Throttle lever
Openable windshield
Steering wheel
Ignition lever
Dashboard
Side lamp
Bulb horn
Fender
Headlight
Radiator
Front transverse leaf spring
Windshield stay
Spring shock absorber
Front axle
License plate
Starting handle
Steering knuckle
Steering spindle connecting-rod

STAGES OF FORD MODEL T PRODUCTION

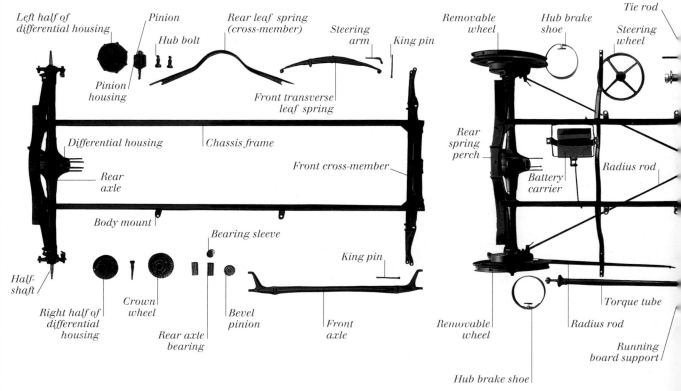

Left half of differential housing
Pinion
Hub bolt
Rear leaf spring (cross-member)
Steering arm
King pin
Removable wheel
Hub brake shoe
Steering wheel
Tie rod
Pinion housing
Front transverse leaf spring
Differential housing
Chassis frame
Front cross-member
Rear spring perch
Radius rod
Rear axle
Battery carrier
Body mount
Bearing sleeve
King pin
Half-shaft
Right half of differential housing
Crown wheel
Rear axle bearing
Bevel pinion
Front axle
Removable wheel
Hub brake shoe
Torque tube
Radius rod
Running board support

SIDE VIEW OF 1913 FORD MODEL T

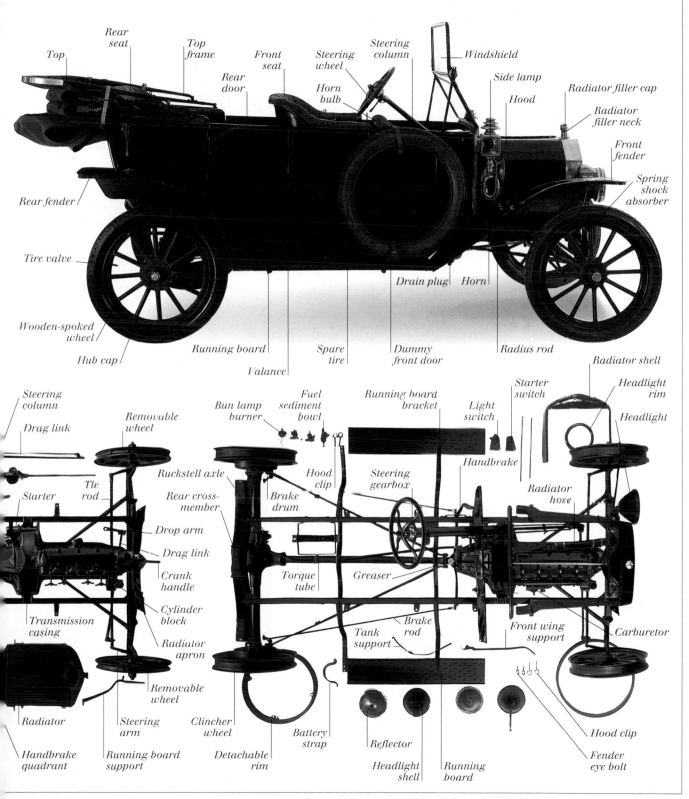

Top

Rear seat

Top frame

Rear door

Front seat

Steering wheel

Horn bulb

Steering column

Windshield

Side lamp

Hood

Radiator filler cap

Radiator filler neck

Front fender

Spring shock absorber

Rear fender

Tire valve

Drain plug

Horn

Wooden-spoked wheel

Hub cap

Running board

Valance

Spare tire

Dummy front door

Radius rod

Radiator shell

Steering column

Drag link

Removable wheel

Bun lamp burner

Fuel sediment bowl

Running board bracket

Light switch

Starter switch

Headlight rim

Headlight

Ruckstell axle

Hood clip

Steering gearbox

Handbrake

Radiator hose

Starter

Tie rod

Rear cross-member

Brake drum

Drop arm

Drag link

Crank handle

Cylinder block

Torque tube

Greaser

Brake rod

Front wing support

Carburetor

Transmission casing

Radiator apron

Tank support

Radiator

Removable wheel

Steering arm

Clincher wheel

Battery strap

Reflector

Hood clip

Fender eye bolt

Handbrake quadrant

Running board support

Detachable rim

Headlight shell

Running board

The "people's car"

THE MOST POPULAR CAR in the history of car manufacture is the Volkswagen Beetle, originally called the KdF Wagen. The car was developed in Germany in the 1930s by Dr. Ferdinand Porsche. At that time, Germany had only half the number of cars of Britain or France, and Adolf Hitler took a personal interest in the development of the Volkswagen ("people's car"). The intention was to provide a new industry, new jobs, and a car so inexpensive that anyone with a job could afford it. Dr. Porsche designed a car that was cheap to build and run; its rear-mounted, air-cooled engine cut down the number of parts needed and also reduced weight. However, few civilians managed to obtain the Beetle before the outbreak of the Second World War in 1939. After the war, the Beetle proved so popular that eventually more than 20 million were sold.

CUSTOMIZED VOLKSWAGEN BEETLE

FLAT-FOUR CYLINDER ARRANGEMENT

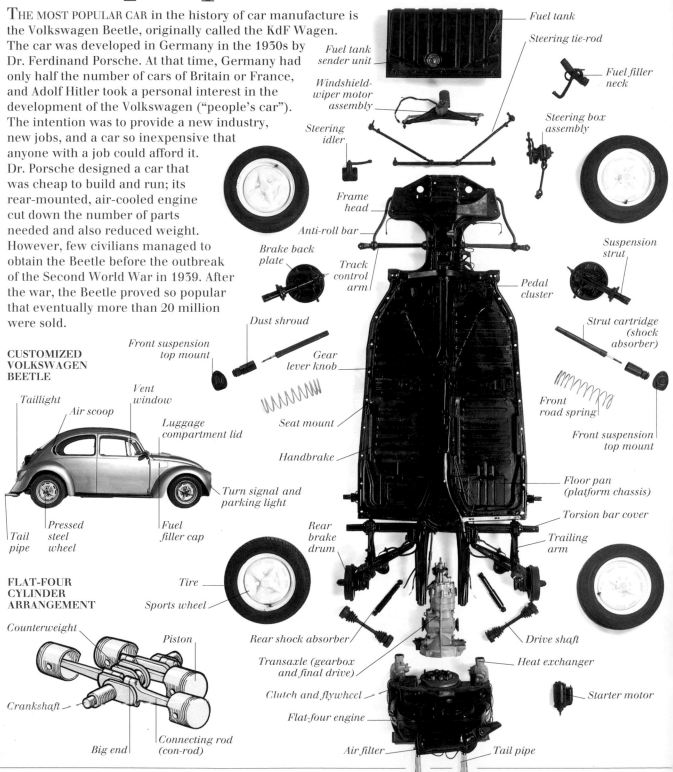

Fuel tank
Steering tie-rod
Fuel tank sender unit
Fuel filler neck
Windshield-wiper motor assembly
Steering box assembly
Steering idler
Suspension strut
Frame head
Anti-roll bar
Brake back plate
Track control arm
Pedal cluster
Dust shroud
Strut cartridge (shock absorber)
Front suspension top mount
Gear lever knob
Seat mount
Front road spring
Front suspension top mount
Handbrake
Floor pan (platform chassis)
Torsion bar cover
Trailing arm
Rear brake drum
Tire
Sports wheel
Rear shock absorber
Transaxle (gearbox and final drive)
Drive shaft
Heat exchanger
Clutch and flywheel
Starter motor
Flat-four engine
Air filter
Tail pipe

Taillight
Air scoop
Vent window
Luggage compartment lid
Turn signal and parking light
Tail pipe
Pressed steel wheel
Fuel filler cap

Counterweight
Piston
Crankshaft
Big end
Connecting rod (con-rod)

BODY SHELL OF VOLKSWAGEN BEETLE

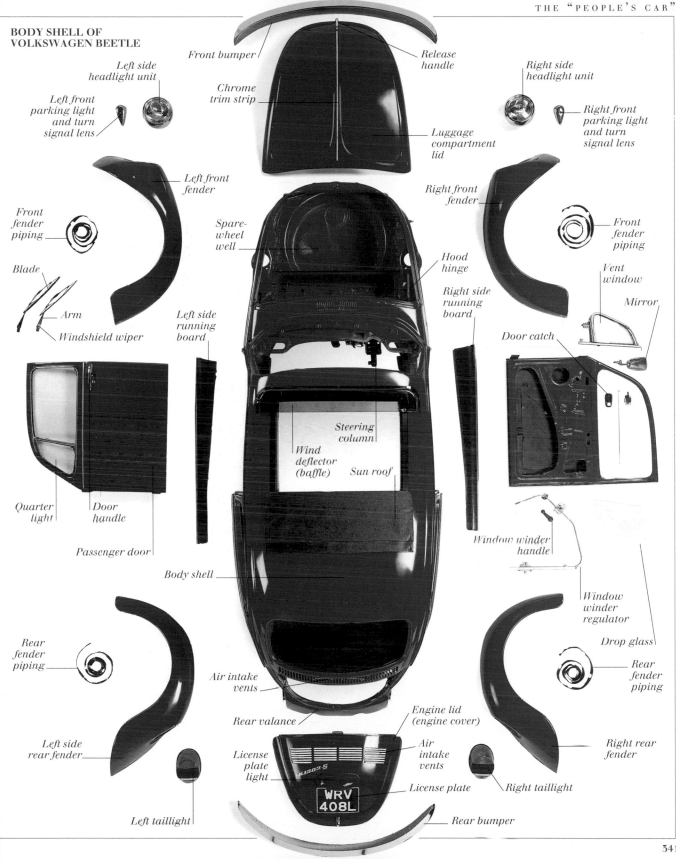

Front bumper

Release handle

Left side headlight unit

Chrome trim strip

Right side headlight unit

Left front parking light and turn signal lens

Luggage compartment lid

Right front parking light and turn signal lens

Left front fender

Right front fender

Front fender piping

Spare-wheel well

Hood hinge

Front fender piping

Vent window

Blade

Mirror

Arm

Left side running board

Right side running board

Windshield wiper

Door catch

Wind deflector (baffle)

Steering column

Sun roof

Quarter light

Door handle

Window winder handle

Passenger door

Window winder regulator

Body shell

Drop glass

Rear fender piping

Rear fender piping

Air intake vents

Engine lid (engine cover)

Air intake vents

Rear valance

Rear fender piping

Left side rear fender

License plate light

License plate

Right rear fender

Left taillight

WRV 408L

Right taillight

Rear bumper

Early engines

STEAM AND ELECTRICITY were used to power cars until early this century, but neither power source was ideal. Electric cars had to stop frequently to recharge their heavy batteries, and steam cars gave smooth power delivery but were too complicated for the average motorist to use. A rival power source, the internal combustion engine, was invented in 1860 by Étienne Lenoir (see pp. 334-335). This engine converted the force of a controlled explosion into rotary motion to turn the wheels of a vehicle. Early variations on this basic model included sleeve valves, separately cast cylinders, and the two-stroke combustion cycle. Today, many internal combustion engines, including the Wankel rotary and diesels (see pp. 346-347), use the four-stroke cycle, first demonstrated by Nikolaus Otto in 1876. The Otto cycle has proved the best method of ensuring that the engine turns over smoothly and that exhaust emissions are controllable.

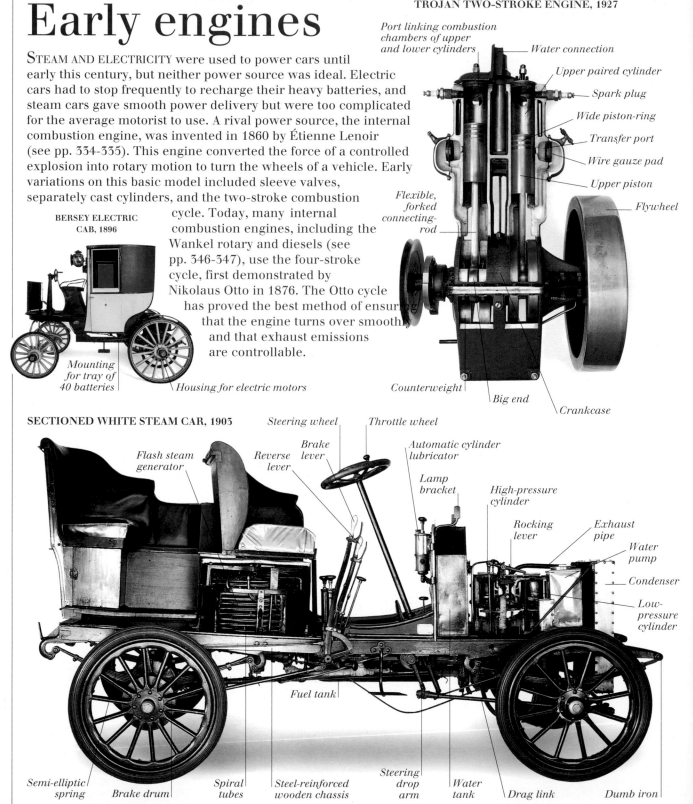

TROJAN TWO-STROKE ENGINE, 1927

Port linking combustion chambers of upper and lower cylinders

Water connection

Upper paired cylinder

Spark plug

Wide piston-ring

Transfer port

Wire gauze pad

Upper piston

Flexible, forked connecting-rod

Flywheel

Counterweight

Big end

Crankcase

BERSEY ELECTRIC CAB, 1896

Mounting for tray of 40 batteries

Housing for electric motors

SECTIONED WHITE STEAM CAR, 1903

Steering wheel

Throttle wheel

Brake lever

Reverse lever

Automatic cylinder lubricator

Flash steam generator

Lamp bracket

High-pressure cylinder

Rocking lever

Exhaust pipe

Water pump

Condenser

Low-pressure cylinder

Fuel tank

Semi-elliptic spring

Brake drum

Spiral tubes

Steel-reinforced wooden chassis

Steering drop arm

Water tank

Drag link

Dumb iron

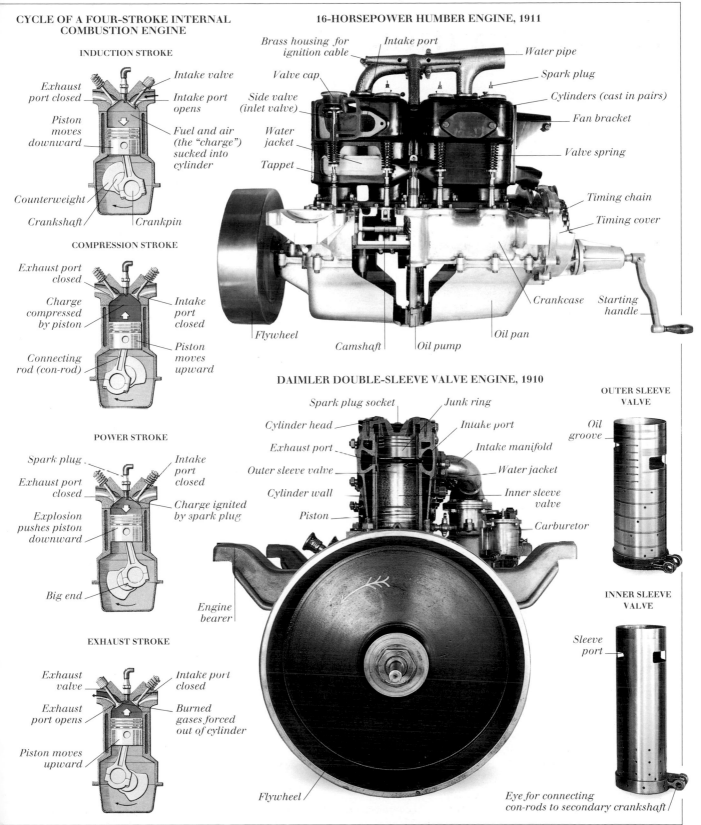

CYCLE OF A FOUR-STROKE INTERNAL COMBUSTION ENGINE

INDUCTION STROKE

Exhaust port closed
Intake valve
Intake port opens
Piston moves downward
Fuel and air (the "charge") sucked into cylinder
Counterweight
Crankshaft
Crankpin

COMPRESSION STROKE

Exhaust port closed
Charge compressed by piston
Intake port closed
Connecting rod (con-rod)
Piston moves upward

POWER STROKE

Spark plug
Intake port closed
Exhaust port closed
Charge ignited by spark plug
Explosion pushes piston downward
Big end

EXHAUST STROKE

Exhaust valve
Intake port closed
Exhaust port opens
Burned gases forced out of cylinder
Piston moves upward

16-HORSEPOWER HUMBER ENGINE, 1911

Brass housing for ignition cable
Intake port
Water pipe
Valve cap
Spark plug
Side valve (inlet valve)
Cylinders (cast in pairs)
Water jacket
Fan bracket
Tappet
Valve spring
Timing chain
Timing cover
Flywheel
Camshaft
Oil pump
Oil pan
Crankcase
Starting handle

DAIMLER DOUBLE-SLEEVE VALVE ENGINE, 1910

Spark plug socket
Junk ring
Cylinder head
Intake port
Exhaust port
Intake manifold
Outer sleeve valve
Water jacket
Cylinder wall
Inner sleeve valve
Piston
Carburetor
Engine bearer
Flywheel

OUTER SLEEVE VALVE

Oil groove

INNER SLEEVE VALVE

Sleeve port
Eye for connecting con-rods to secondary crankshaft

Modern engines

TODAY'S GASOLINE ENGINE WORKS on the same basic principles as the first car engines of a century ago, although it has been greatly refined. Modern engines, often made from special metal alloys, are much lighter than earlier engines. Computerized ignition systems, fuel injectors, and multi-valve cylinder heads achieve a more efficient combustion of the fuel/air mixture (the charge) so that less fuel is wasted. As a result of this greater efficiency, the power and performance of a modern engine are increased, and the level of pollution in the exhaust gases is reduced. Exhaust pollution levels today are also lowered by the increasing use of special filters called catalytic converters, which absorb many exhaust pollutants. The need to produce ever more efficient engines means that it can take up to seven years to develop a new engine for a family car, at a cost of many millions of dollars.

FRONT VIEW OF A FORD COSWORTH V6 12-VALVE

Idle control valve
Plenum chamber
Valve rocker
Power steering pump reservoir
Oil dipstick
High-tension ignition lead (spark plug lead)
Steering pump pulley
Cogged drive belt
Fan
Alternator
Crankshaft pulley
Viscous coupling
Oil pan

FRONT VIEW OF A FORD COSWORTH V6 24-VALVE

Idle control valve
Plenum chamber
Exhaust gas recirculation valve
Camshaft timing gear
Camshaft chain
Steering pump drive pulley
Belt tensioner
Air-conditioning compressor
Alternator cooling fan
Drive belt
Oil pan
Crankshaft pulley

SECTIONED VIEW OF A JAGUAR STRAIGHT 6

Cam follower (bucket tappet)
Valve spring
Cam lobe
Cam
Combustion chamber
Compression ring
Cam cover
Camshaft
Distributor
Cylinder head
Fan
Valve stem
Air-conditioning refrigerant pipe
Exhaust valve
Suspension self-leveling pump
Cylinder liner
Power steering pump
Water jacket
Swash plate
Piston
Drive belt
Connecting rod (con-rod)
Main bearing housing
Compressor piston
Big end
Transmission adaptor plate
Air-conditioning compressor
Crankshaft counterweight
Oil pan
Oil pick-up pipe
Anti-surge baffle
Crankcase
Oil-control ring (scraper ring)

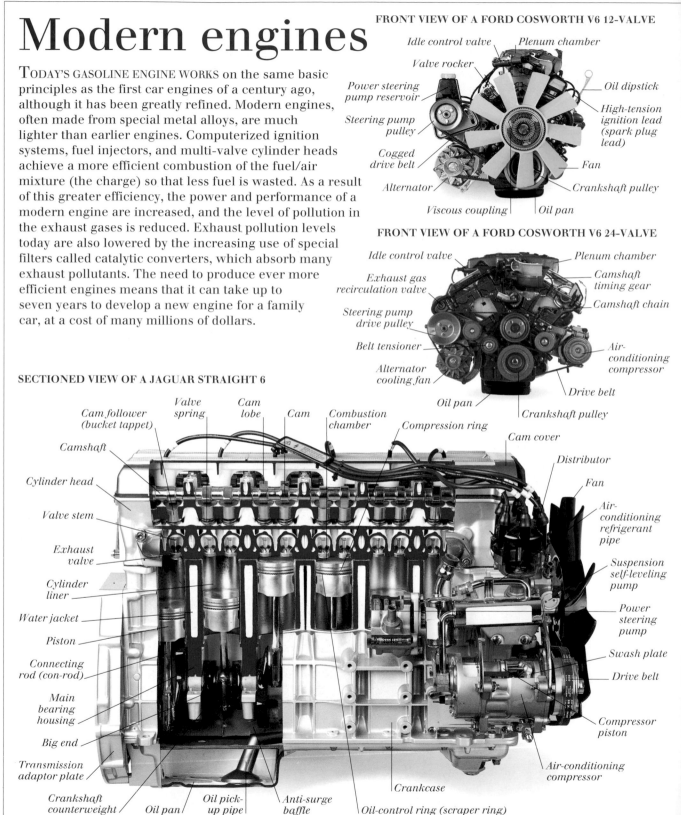

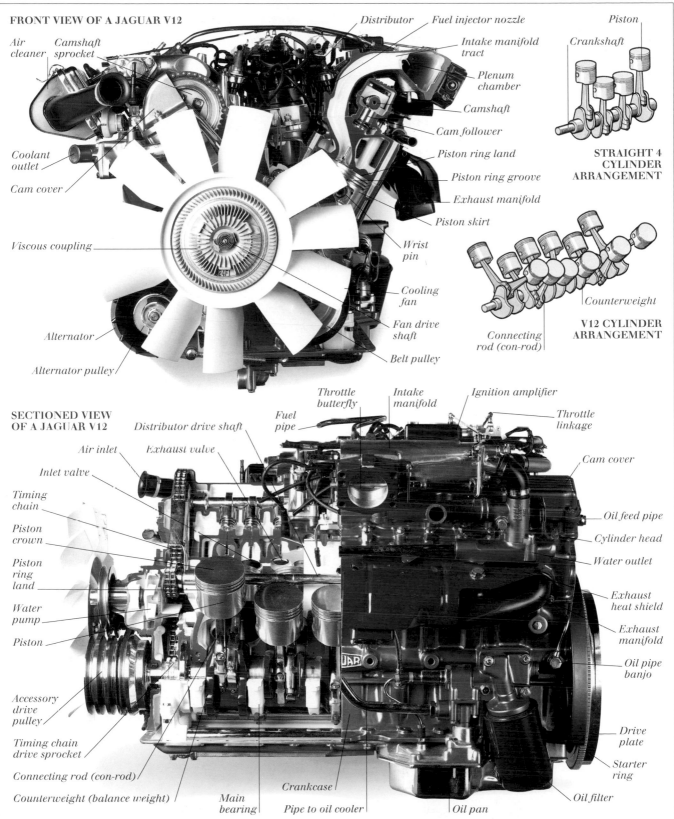

FRONT VIEW OF A JAGUAR V12

Air cleaner

Camshaft sprocket

Distributor

Fuel injector nozzle

Piston

Crankshaft

Intake manifold tract

Plenum chamber

Camshaft

Cam follower

Piston ring land

Piston ring groove

Exhaust manifold

Piston skirt

STRAIGHT 4 CYLINDER ARRANGEMENT

Coolant outlet

Cam cover

Viscous coupling

Wrist pin

Cooling fan

Fan drive shaft

Counterweight

Alternator

Alternator pulley

Belt pulley

Connecting rod (con-rod)

V12 CYLINDER ARRANGEMENT

SECTIONED VIEW OF A JAGUAR V12

Throttle butterfly

Fuel pipe

Intake manifold

Ignition amplifier

Throttle linkage

Air inlet

Distributor drive shaft

Exhaust valve

Inlet valve

Cam cover

Timing chain

Oil feed pipe

Piston crown

Cylinder head

Piston ring land

Water outlet

Water pump

Exhaust heat shield

Piston

Exhaust manifold

Oil pipe banjo

Accessory drive pulley

Timing chain drive sprocket

Connecting rod (con-rod)

Drive plate

Starter ring

Counterweight (balance weight)

Main bearing

Crankcase

Pipe to oil cooler

Oil pan

Oil filter

Alternative engines

THE MOST COMMON TYPE OF ALTERNATIVE ENGINE is the diesel engine. Instead of igniting the compressed fuel/air mixture with a spark, the diesel engine uses compression alone, which heats the mixture to the point where it explodes. A diesel engine's fuel consumption is low in comparison with similarly sized piston engines, despite its heavier, reinforced moving parts and cylinder block. Another type of engine is the rotary-combustion, first successfully developed by Felix Wankel in the 1950s. Its two trilobate (three-sided) rotors revolve in housings shaped in a fat figure eight. The four sequences of the four-stroke cycle, which occur consecutively in a piston engine, occur simultaneously in a rotary engine, producing power in a continuous stream.

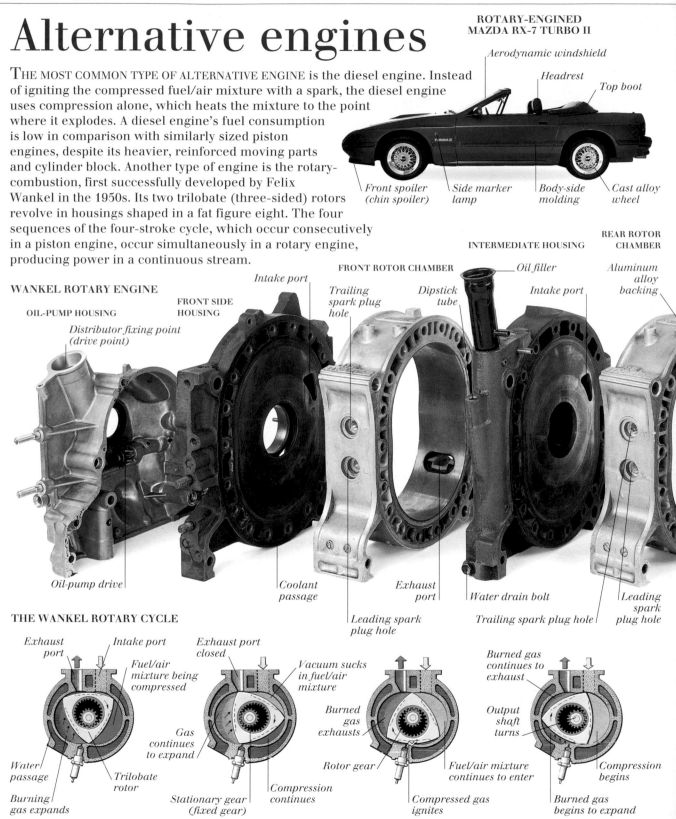

Aerodynamic windshield

Headrest

Top boot

Front spoiler (chin spoiler)

Side marker lamp

Body-side molding

Cast alloy wheel

WANKEL ROTARY ENGINE

OIL-PUMP HOUSING

FRONT SIDE HOUSING

Distributor fixing point (drive point)

Intake port

FRONT ROTOR CHAMBER

Trailing spark plug hole

Dipstick tube

Oil filler

INTERMEDIATE HOUSING

REAR ROTOR CHAMBER

Intake port

Aluminum alloy backing

Oil-pump drive

Coolant passage

Exhaust port

Leading spark plug hole

Water drain bolt

Trailing spark plug hole

Leading spark plug hole

THE WANKEL ROTARY CYCLE

Exhaust port

Intake port

Fuel/air mixture being compressed

Water passage

Burning gas expands

Trilobate rotor

Stationary gear (fixed gear)

Gas continues to expand

Compression continues

Exhaust port closed

Vacuum sucks in fuel/air mixture

Burned gas exhausts

Rotor gear

Compressed gas ignites

Fuel/air mixture continues to enter

Burned gas continues to exhaust

Output shaft turns

Compression begins

Burned gas begins to expand

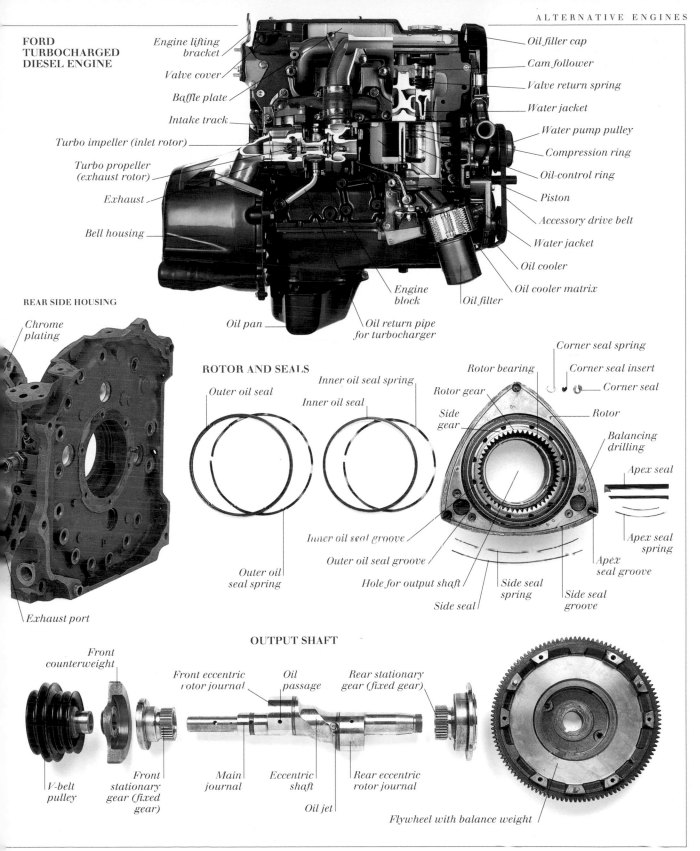

FORD TURBOCHARGED DIESEL ENGINE

Engine lifting bracket

Valve cover

Baffle plate

Intake track

Turbo impeller (inlet rotor)

Turbo propeller (exhaust rotor)

Exhaust

Bell housing

Oil filler cap

Cam follower

Valve return spring

Water jacket

Water pump pulley

Compression ring

Oil-control ring

Piston

Accessory drive belt

Water jacket

Oil cooler

Oil cooler matrix

Oil filter

Engine block

Oil pan

Oil return pipe for turbocharger

REAR SIDE HOUSING

Chrome plating

Exhaust port

ROTOR AND SEALS

Outer oil seal

Inner oil seal spring

Inner oil seal

Rotor bearing

Rotor gear

Side gear

Inner oil seal groove

Outer oil seal groove

Hole for output shaft

Side seal

Side seal spring

Corner seal spring

Corner seal insert

Corner seal

Rotor

Balancing drilling

Apex seal

Apex seal spring

Apex seal groove

Side seal groove

Outer oil seal spring

OUTPUT SHAFT

Front counterweight

V-belt pulley

Front stationary gear (fixed gear)

Front eccentric rotor journal

Main journal

Oil passage

Eccentric shaft

Oil jet

Rear stationary gear (fixed gear)

Rear eccentric rotor journal

Flywheel with balance weight

Bodywork

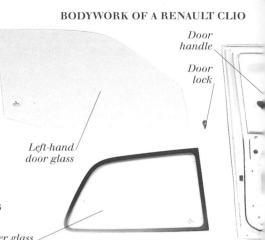

**RENAULT
LOGO**

THE BODY OF A MODERN mass-produced car is built on the monocoque (single-shell) principle, in which the roof, side panels, and floor are welded into a single integral unit. This bodyshell protects and supports the car's internal parts. Steel and glass are used to construct the bodyshell, creating a unit that is both light and strong. Its lightness helps to conserve energy, while its strength protects the occupants. Modern bodywork is designed with the aid of computers, which are used to predict factors such as aerodynamic efficiency and impact-resistance. High-technology is also employed on the production line, where robots are used to assemble, weld, and paint the body.

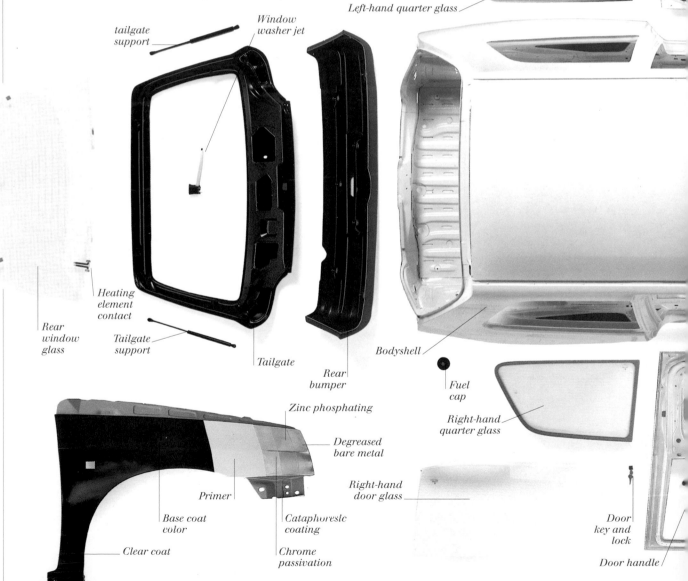

Door handle

Door lock

Left-hand door glass

Left-hand quarter glass

tailgate support

Window washer jet

Heating element contact

Rear window glass

Tailgate support

Tailgate

Rear bumper

Bodyshell

Fuel cap

Right-hand quarter glass

Zinc phosphating

Degreased bare metal

Right-hand door glass

Primer

Base coat color

Clear coat

Cataphoreslc coating

Chrome passivation

Door key and lock

Door handle

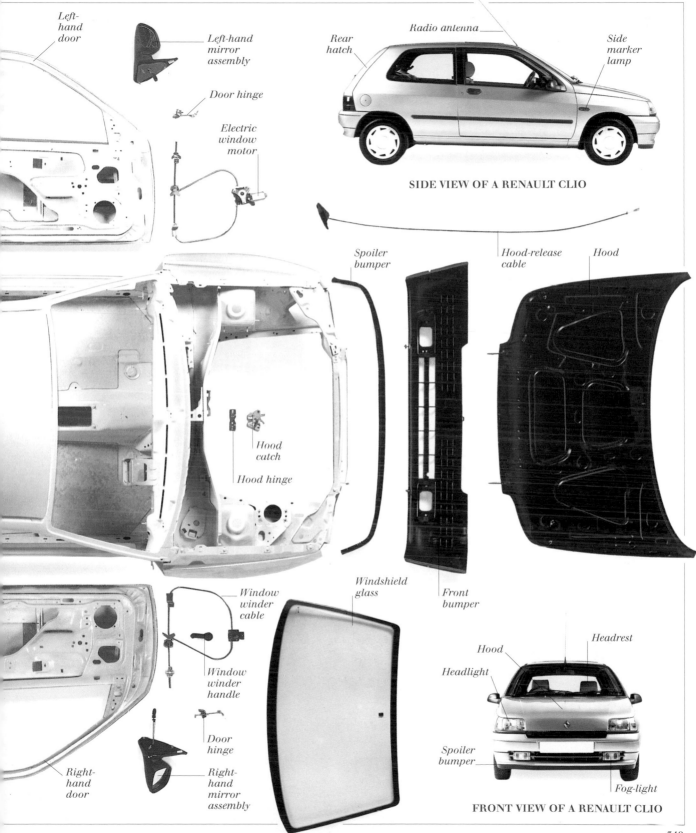

Left-hand door

Left-hand mirror assembly

Door hinge

Electric window motor

Rear hatch

Radio antenna

Side marker lamp

SIDE VIEW OF A RENAULT CLIO

Spoiler bumper

Hood-release cable

Hood

Hood catch

Hood hinge

Window winder cable

Window winder handle

Windshield glass

Front bumper

Hood

Headrest

Headlight

Spoiler bumper

Fog-light

Door hinge

Right-hand door

Right-hand mirror assembly

FRONT VIEW OF A RENAULT CLIO

Mechanical components

A TYPICAL MODERN CAR has several thousand individual mechanical components. These are assembled to form the car's various mechanical systems: engine and exhaust, transmission, steering, suspension, and brakes. To ensure that each system functions properly, components are manufactured to extremely fine tolerances—to within about one ten-thousandth of an inch in some cases.

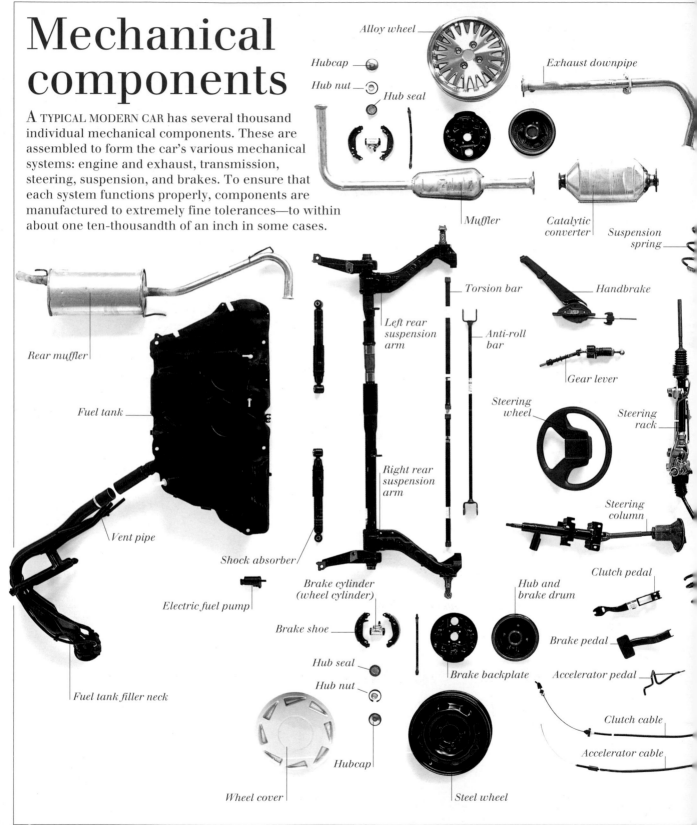

Alloy wheel

Hubcap

Hub nut

Hub seal

Exhaust downpipe

Muffler

Catalytic converter

Suspension spring

Torsion bar

Handbrake

Left rear suspension arm

Anti-roll bar

Gear lever

Steering wheel

Steering rack

Rear muffler

Fuel tank

Right rear suspension arm

Steering column

Vent pipe

Shock absorber

Brake cylinder (wheel cylinder)

Hub and brake drum

Clutch pedal

Electric fuel pump

Brake shoe

Brake pedal

Hub seal

Brake backplate

Accelerator pedal

Hub nut

Clutch cable

Fuel tank filler neck

Accelerator cable

Hubcap

Wheel cover

Steel wheel

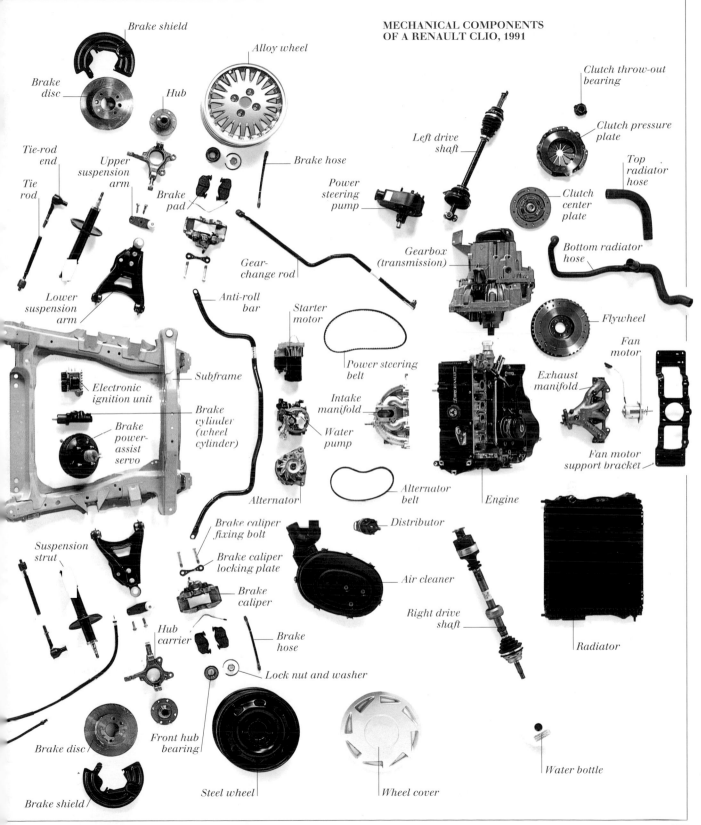

**MECHANICAL COMPONENTS
OF A RENAULT CLIO, 1991**

Brake shield

Alloy wheel

Clutch throw-out
bearing

Brake
disc

Hub

Clutch pressure
plate

Left drive
shaft

Top
radiator
hose

Tie-rod
end

Upper
suspension
arm

Brake hose

Tie
rod

Brake pad

Power
steering
pump

Clutch center
plate

Bottom radiator
hose

Gearbox
(transmission)

Gear-
change rod

Lower
suspension
arm

Anti-roll
bar

Starter
motor

Flywheel

Fan
motor

Power steering
belt

Exhaust
manifold

Subframe

Electronic
ignition unit

Brake
cylinder
(wheel
cylinder)

Intake
manifold

Water
pump

Fan motor
support bracket

Brake
power-
assist
servo

Alternator

Alternator
belt

Engine

Suspension
strut

Brake caliper
fixing bolt

Brake caliper
locking plate

Distributor

Air cleaner

Brake
caliper

Radiator

Hub
carrier

Brake
hose

Right drive
shaft

Lock nut and washer

Brake disc

Front hub
bearing

Brake shield

Steel wheel

Wheel cover

Water bottle

Car trim

A MODERN CAR HAS TWO TYPES OF TRIM, according to the materials used: hard (chrome and plastics) and soft (upholstered materials). Safety and comfort are priorities in the trim's design: seats help the occupants maintain a comfortable posture, rubber seals keep out dirt and moisture, and headlights light the way. Older cars had interior or leather paneling cut and fitted by craftsmen; modern cars use precisely molded plastics and seat fabrics cut by robot-controlled lasers to reduce costs and production time. Doors are now assembled off the production line so that complex wiring can be built in.

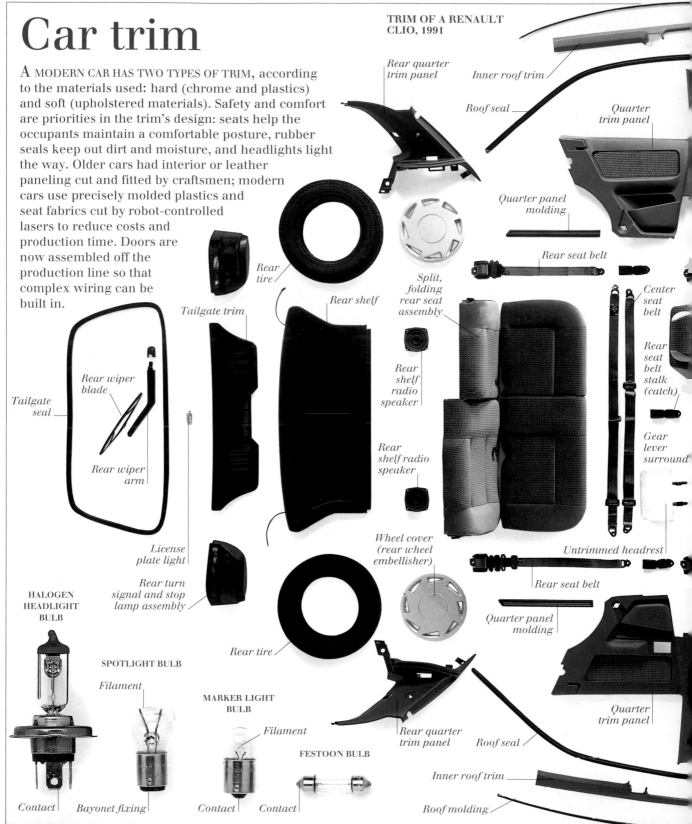

TRIM OF A RENAULT CLIO, 1991

Rear quarter trim panel

Inner roof trim

Roof seal

Quarter trim panel

Quarter panel molding

Rear seat belt

Split, folding rear seat assembly

Center seat belt

Rear seat belt stalk (catch)

Gear lever surround

Rear shelf radio speaker

Rear shelf radio speaker

Untrimmed headrest

Wheel cover (rear wheel embellisher)

Rear seat belt

Quarter panel molding

Quarter trim panel

Rear quarter trim panel

Roof seal

Inner roof trim

Roof molding

Rear tire

Rear shelf

Rear wiper blade

Tailgate trim

Tailgate seal

Rear wiper arm

License plate light

Rear turn signal and stop lamp assembly

Rear tire

HALOGEN HEADLIGHT BULB

SPOTLIGHT BULB

Filament

MARKER LIGHT BULB

Filament

FESTOON BULB

Contact

Bayonet fixing

Contact

Contact

Contact

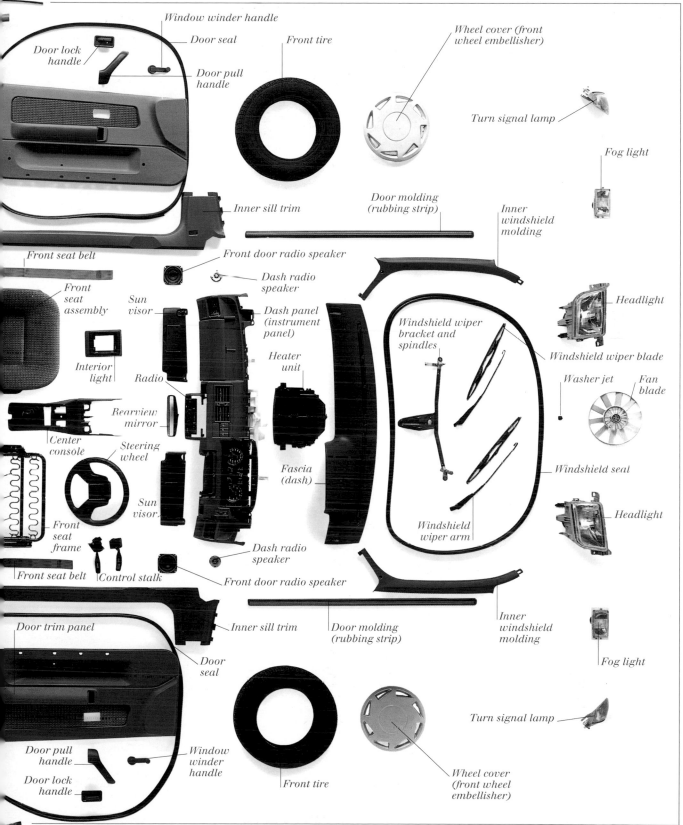

Window winder handle

Door seal

Front tire

Wheel cover (front wheel embellisher)

Door lock handle

Door pull handle

Turn signal lamp

Fog light

Inner sill trim

Door molding (rubbing strip)

Inner windshield molding

Front seat belt

Front door radio speaker

Dash radio speaker

Front seat assembly

Sun visor

Dash panel (instrument panel)

Windshield wiper bracket and spindles

Headlight

Windshield wiper blade

Heater unit

Interior light

Radio

Washer jet

Fan blade

Rearview mirror

Center console

Steering wheel

Fascia (dash)

Windshield seal

Sun visor

Front seat frame

Headlight

Windshield wiper arm

Front seat belt

Control stalk

Dash radio speaker

Front door radio speaker

Door trim panel

Inner sill trim

Door molding (rubbing strip)

Inner windshield molding

Door seal

Fog light

Door pull handle

Window winder handle

Turn signal lamp

Door lock handle

Front tire

Wheel cover (front wheel embellisher)

Hybrid car

THERE HAVE BEEN SEVERAL proposed alternatives
to conventional gas- or diesel-powered cars,
including cars that use solar or battery power. The
object is to lower harmful emissions and conserve
natural resources. One of the alternatives already
in production is the hybrid car. A hybrid vehicle uses
two or more fuels. Examples include diesel-electric
trains and mopeds. The latter combine the power
of a gasoline engine with pedal power. In a hybrid
car, gasoline consumption is reduced by the
provision of additional power by an electric motor
during acceleration. The motor is driven by power
from on-board batteries that are recharged when the
car is cruising or decelerating by an engine-driven
generator. Some hybrid cars transfer energy from the
wheels to a flywheel during braking. The flywheel
drives the generator, which recharges the batteries.

HONDA INSIGHT

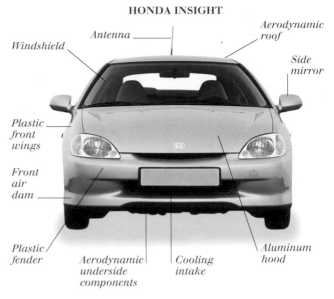

Antenna
Windshield
Aerodynamic roof
Side mirror
Plastic front wings
Front air dam
Plastic fender
Aerodynamic underside components
Cooling intake
Aluminum hood

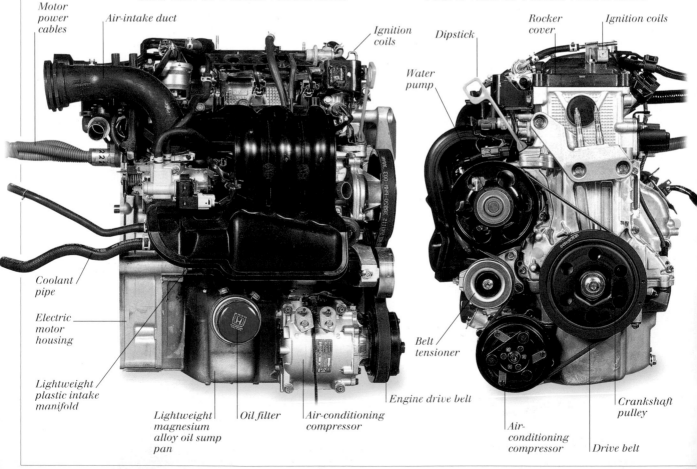

SIDE VIEW OF 1-LITER VTEC ENGINE

Motor power cables
Air-intake duct
Ignition coils
Coolant pipe
Electric motor housing
Lightweight plastic intake manifold
Lightweight magnesium alloy oil sump pan
Oil filter
Air-conditioning compressor
Engine drive belt

FRONT VIEW OF 1-LITER VTEC ENGINE

Dipstick
Rocker cover
Ignition coils
Water pump
Belt tensioner
Air-conditioning compressor
Crankshaft pulley
Drive belt

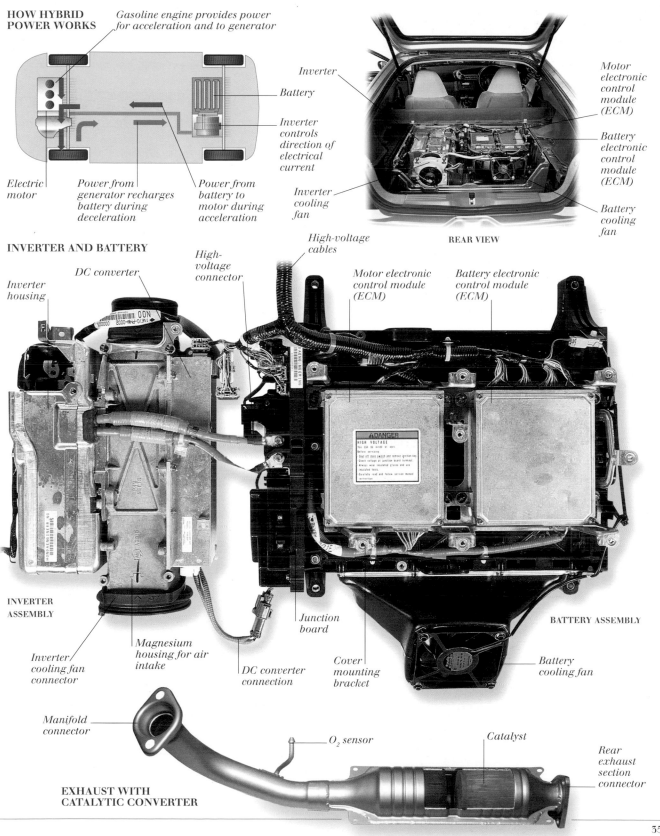

HOW HYBRID POWER WORKS

Gasoline engine provides power for acceleration and to generator

Battery

Inverter controls direction of electrical current

Electric motor

Power from generator recharges battery during deceleration

Power from battery to motor during acceleration

Inverter

Inverter cooling fan

Motor electronic control module (ECM)

Battery electronic control module (ECM)

Battery cooling fan

REAR VIEW

INVERTER AND BATTERY

High-voltage cables

DC converter

High-voltage connector

Inverter housing

Motor electronic control module (ECM)

Battery electronic control module (ECM)

⚠ DANGER
HIGH VOLTAGE

INVERTER ASSEMBLY

BATTERY ASSEMBLY

Inverter cooling fan connector

Magnesium housing for air intake

DC converter connection

Junction board

Cover mounting bracket

Battery cooling fan

EXHAUST WITH CATALYTIC CONVERTER

Manifold connector

O_2 sensor

Catalyst

Rear exhaust section connector

Racecars

Since the advent of driving, racecars have been a major focus of innovation in car design. Features that are now commonplace, such as disk brakes, turbochargers, and even seat belts, were used first on competition cars. Research into racecars has contributed to a new understanding of engine performance, aerodynamics, and tire adhesion, and has led to the development of ultralight materials such as carbon-fiber for car bodies. A modern McLaren Formula One car has a low, streamlined body and an open cockpit but, unlike its forerunner, it also has front and rear wings that push the wheels firmly onto the track, huge tires for extra grip, and electronic sensors that continually relay information to the pits about the car's performance.

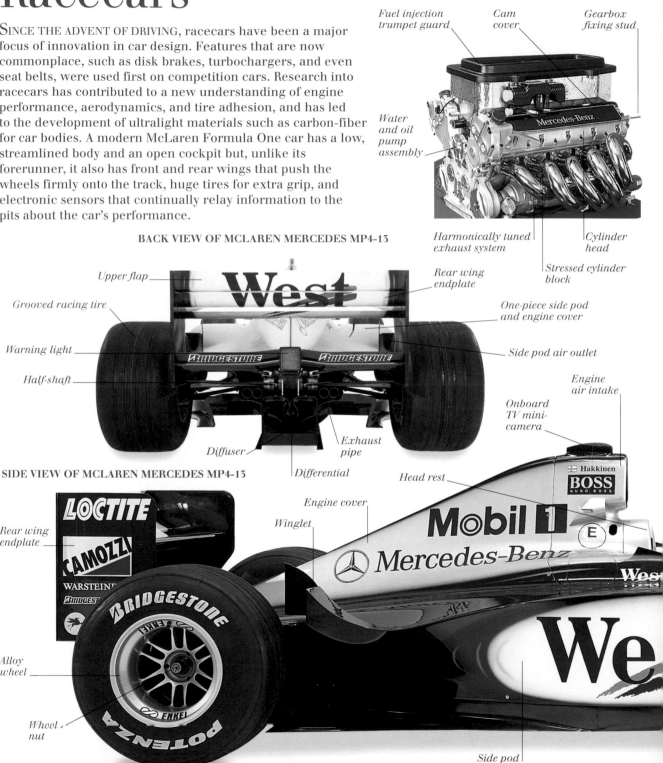

72° V10 ENGINE

Fuel injection trumpet guard

Cam cover

Gearbox fixing stud

Water and oil pump assembly

Mercedes-Benz

Harmonically tuned exhaust system

Cylinder head

Stressed cylinder block

BACK VIEW OF MCLAREN MERCEDES MP4-13

Upper flap

Grooved racing tire

Warning light

Half-shaft

Rear wing endplate

One-piece side pod and engine cover

Side pod air outlet

West

BRIDGESTONE

BRIDGESTONE

Diffuser

Exhaust pipe

Differential

SIDE VIEW OF MCLAREN MERCEDES MP4-13

Rear wing endplate

LOCTITE

CAMOZZI

WARSTEIN

BRIDGEST

Alloy wheel

Wheel nut

BRIDGESTONE

ENKEI

POTENZA

Winglet

Engine cover

Head rest

Onboard TV mini-camera

Engine air intake

Hakkinen

BOSS
HUGO BOSS

Mobil 1

E

Mercedes-Benz

West

We

Side pod

OVERHEAD VIEW OF MCLAREN MERCEDES MP4-13

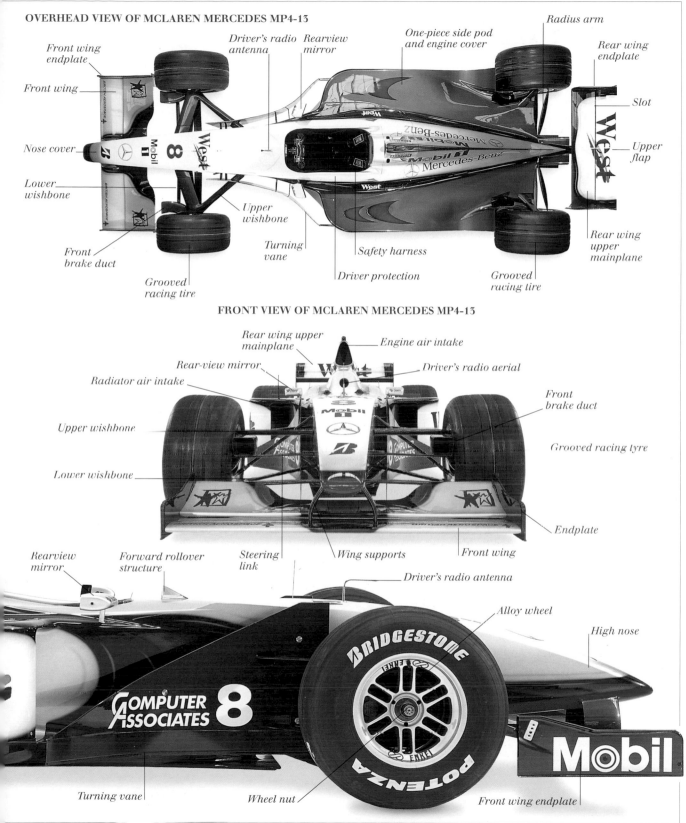

Front wing endplate

Driver's radio antenna

Rearview mirror

One-piece side pod and engine cover

Radius arm

Rear wing endplate

Front wing

Slot

Nose cover

Upper flap

Lower wishbone

Upper wishbone

Front brake duct

Turning vane

Safety harness

Rear wing upper mainplane

Grooved racing tire

Driver protection

Grooved racing tire

FRONT VIEW OF MCLAREN MERCEDES MP4-13

Rear wing upper mainplane

Engine air intake

Rear-view mirror

Driver's radio aerial

Radiator air intake

Front brake duct

Upper wishbone

Grooved racing tyre

Lower wishbone

Endplate

Steering link

Wing supports

Front wing

Rearview mirror

Forward rollover structure

Driver's radio antenna

Alloy wheel

High nose

COMPUTER ASSOCIATES 8

BRIDGESTONE

POTENZA

Mobil

Turning vane

Wheel nut

Front wing endplate

Bicycle anatomy

THE BICYCLE IS A TWO-WHEELED, lightweight machine, which is propelled by human power. It is efficient, cheap, easily manufactured, and one of the world's most popular forms of transportation. The first pedal-driven bicycle was built in Scotland in 1839. Since then the basic design—of a frame, wheels, brakes, handlebars, and a saddle—has been gradually improved, with the addition of a chain, gear system, and pneumatic tires (tires inflated with air). The recent invention of the mountain bike (all-terrain bike) has been an important development. With its strong, rugged frame, wide tires, and 21 gears, a mountain bike enables riders to reach rough and hilly areas that were previously inaccessible to cyclists.

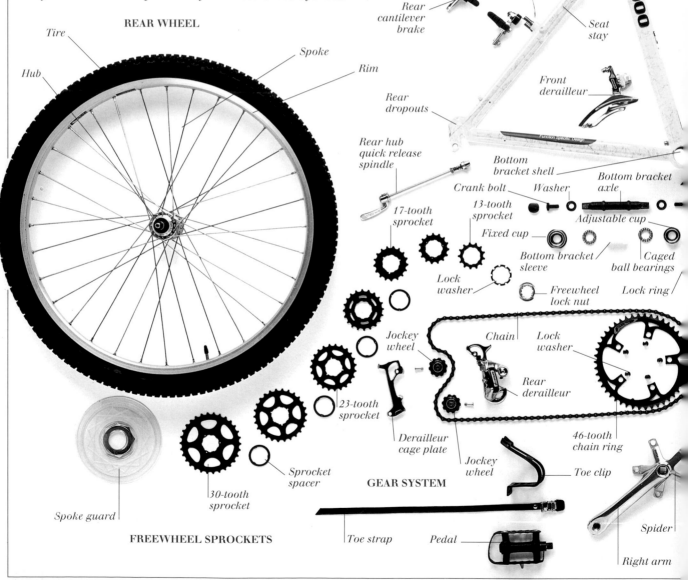

REAR WHEEL

Tire

Spoke

Hub

Rim

Saddle (seat)

Seat post

Cable guide

Seat post quick release bolt

Straddle wire

Seat tube

Rear cantilever brake

Seat stay

Front derailleur

Rear dropouts

Rear hub quick release spindle

Bottom bracket shell

Crank bolt

Washer

Bottom bracket axle

17-tooth sprocket

13-tooth sprocket

Adjustable cup

Fixed cup

Lock washer

Bottom bracket sleeve

Caged ball bearings

Lock ring

Freewheel lock nut

Jockey wheel

Chain

Lock washer

Rear derailleur

23-tooth sprocket

Derailleur cage plate

Jockey wheel

46-tooth chain ring

Sprocket spacer

GEAR SYSTEM

Toe clip

30-tooth sprocket

Spoke guard

Spider

Right arm

Toe strap

Pedal

FREEWHEEL SPROCKETS

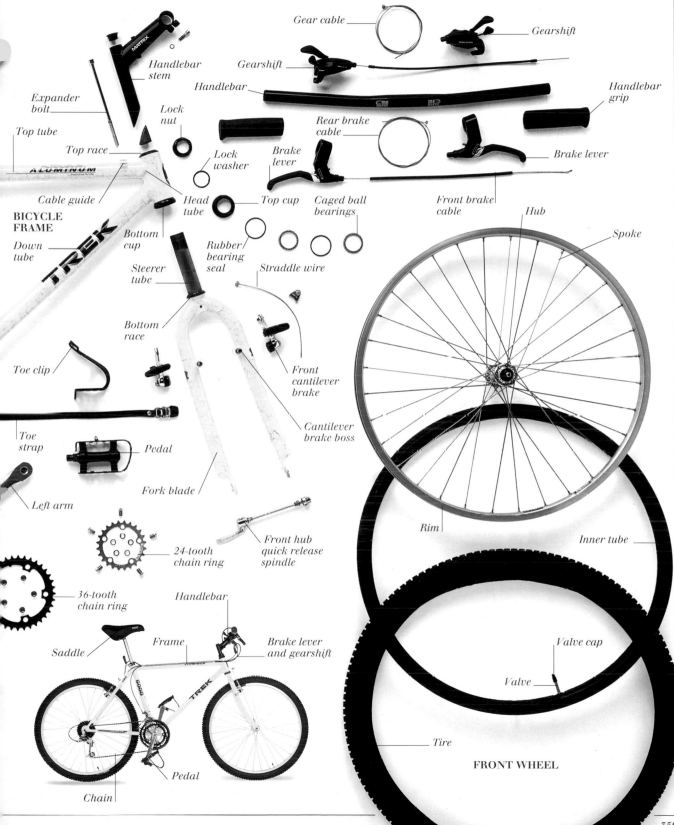

Gear cable

Gearshift

Gearshift

Handlebar
stem

Handlebar

Handlebar
grip

Expander
bolt

Lock
nut

Top tube

Rear brake
cable

Brake
lever

Top race

Lock
washer

Brake
lever

Cable guide

Head
tube

Top cup

Caged ball
bearings

Front brake
cable

Hub

Spoke

**BICYCLE
FRAME**

Down
tube

Bottom
cup

Rubber
bearing
seal

Steerer
tube

Straddle wire

Bottom
race

Toe clip

Front
cantilever
brake

Cantilever
brake boss

Toe
strap

Pedal

Fork blade

Rim

Inner tube

Left arm

Front hub
quick release
spindle

24-tooth
chain ring

36-tooth
chain ring

Handlebar

Valve cap

Saddle

Frame

Brake lever
and gearshift

Valve

Pedal

Tire

FRONT WHEEL

Chain

359

Bicycles

Aᴌᴛʜᴏᴜɢʜ ᴀʟʟ ʙɪᴄʏᴄʟᴇs are made up of the same basic components, they can vary greatly in design. A racing bike, such as the Eddy Merckx model, with its light frame and steep head- and seat-angles, is built for speed. Its design forces the rider to adopt the aero tuck, a crouched, aerodynamic position. While a touring bike resembles a racing bike in many respects, it is designed for comfort and stability on long-distance journeys. Touring bikes are characterized by more relaxed frame angles, heavy chain stays that support the rear panniers, and a long wheelbase (the distance between the wheel axles) for reliable handling. All-purpose bicycles, known as hybrids, combine the light weight and speed of sports bikes with the rugged durability of mountain bikes (see pp. 358-359). Bicycles that are not designed for conventional road use include time-trial bikes, which have a short head tube, sloping top tube, aero handlebars, and aerodynamic tubing. Most Human Powered Vehicles (HPVs) are recumbents—the rider has a recumbent position—which maximize power output and minimize drag (resistance). Essential to the safety of all riders are helmets, and both front and rear lights; locks protect against theft.

FRONT AND REAR LIGHTS

White front light

Red rear light

HELMET

Hard outer shell

Air vent

Polystyrene padding

Quick-release strap

EDDY MERCKX RACING BICYCLE

Saddle (seat)

Seat post

Cable guide

Saddle clamp

Seat-post bolt

Rear brake cable

Brake-block bolt

Brake block

Top tube (crossbar)

Steel frame

Seat tube

Down tube

Water-bottle cage

Front derailleur

Seat stay

Tire

Tire tread

Tire wall

Wheel rim

Freewheel sprocket

STEEL LOCK

Key

Hardened steel

Pick-proof lock

Rear derailleur

Pulley bolt

Tension pulley

Chain

Chain stay

Chain ring

Crank bolt

Crank

Spider

Pedal

Toe clip

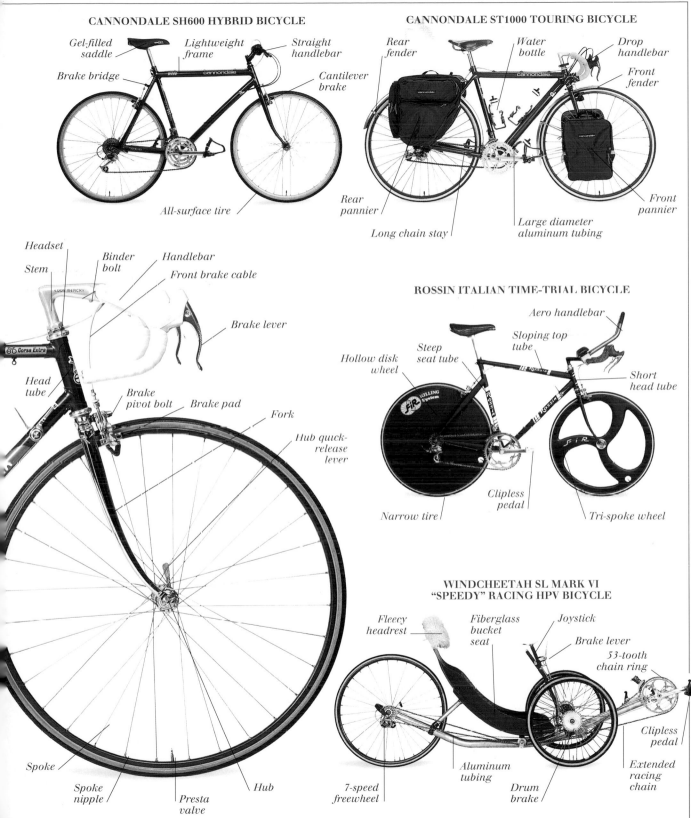

CANNONDALE SH600 HYBRID BICYCLE

Gel-filled saddle

Lightweight frame

Straight handlebar

Brake bridge

Cantilever brake

All-surface tire

CANNONDALE ST1000 TOURING BICYCLE

Rear fender

Water bottle

Drop handlebar

Front fender

Rear pannier

Front pannier

Long chain stay

Large diameter aluminum tubing

Headset

Binder bolt

Handlebar

Stem

Front brake cable

Brake lever

Head tube

Brake pivot bolt

Brake pad

Fork

Hub quick-release lever

Spoke

Spoke nipple

Presta valve

Hub

ROSSIN ITALIAN TIME-TRIAL BICYCLE

Aero handlebar

Steep seat tube

Sloping top tube

Hollow disk wheel

Short head tube

Clipless pedal

Narrow tire

Tri-spoke wheel

WINDCHEETAH SL MARK VI "SPEEDY" RACING HPV BICYCLE

Fleecy headrest

Fiberglass bucket seat

Joystick

Brake lever

53-tooth chain ring

Clipless pedal

7-speed freewheel

Aluminum tubing

Drum brake

Extended racing chain

The motorcycle

THE MOTORCYCLE HAS EVOLVED from a motorized cycle—a basic bicycle with an engine—into a sophisticated, high-performance machine. In 1901, the Werner brothers established the most viable location for the engine, positioning it low in the center of the chassis (see pp. 364-365): the new Werner became the basis for the modern motorcycle. Motorcycles are used for many purposes —for commuting, delivering messages, touring, and racing—and different machines have been developed to suit the demands of different types of riders. The Vespa scooter, for instance, which is small-wheeled, economical, and easy-to-ride, was designed to meet the needs of the commuter. Sidecars provided transportation for the family until the arrival of cheap cars caused their popularity to decline. Serious riders generally favor larger capacity machines that are capable of greater performance and offer more comfort. Four-cylinder machines have been common since the Honda CB750 appeared in 1969. Despite advances in motorcycle technology, many riders are attracted to the traditional look of motorcycles like the twin-cylinder Harley-Davidson. Harley-Davidson Glides exploit the style of the classic American V-twin engine, where the cylinders are placed in a V-formation.

1901 WERNER MOTORCYCLE

Vacuum-operated inlet valve

Fuel tank

Bicycle-type saddle

Electric ignition control

Pulley rim rear brake

Inlet-over-exhaust (IOE) engine

Alloy crankcase

Twisted rawhide drive belt

Cast iron cylinder barrel

1988 HARLEY-DAVIDSON FLHS ELECTRA GLIDE

1965 BMW R/60 WITH 1952 STEIB CHAIR

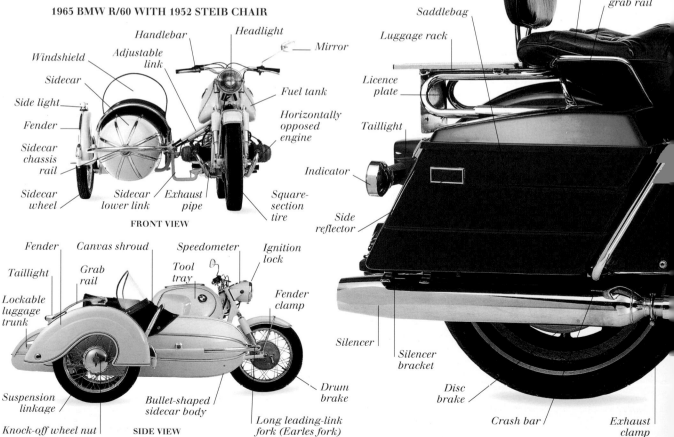

Backrest

Passenger seat

Passenger grab rail

Saddlebag

Luggage rack

Licence plate

Handlebar

Headlight

Adjustable link

Mirror

Windshield

Taillight

Sidecar

Fuel tank

Side light

Fender

Horizontally opposed engine

Sidecar chassis rail

Indicator

Sidecar wheel

Sidecar lower link

Exhaust pipe

Square-section tire

Side reflector

FRONT VIEW

Fender

Canvas shroud

Speedometer

Ignition lock

Taillight

Grab rail

Tool tray

Fender clamp

Lockable luggage trunk

Silencer

Silencer bracket

Suspension linkage

Bullet-shaped sidecar body

Drum brake

Disc brake

Knock-off wheel nut

SIDE VIEW

Long leading-link fork (Earles fork)

Crash bar

Exhaust clamp

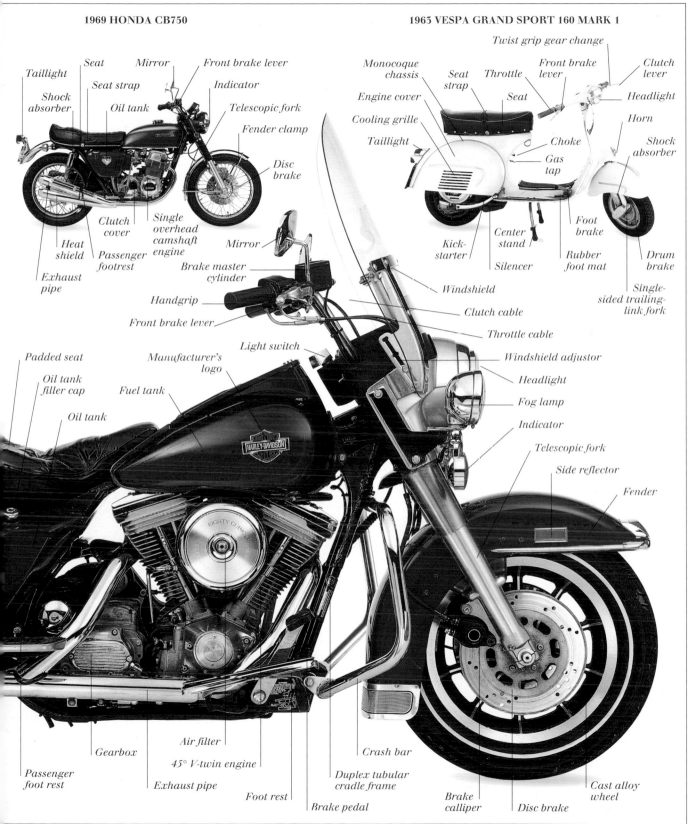

1969 HONDA CB750

Taillight

Shock absorber

Seat

Seat strap

Mirror

Oil tank

Front brake lever

Indicator

Telescopic fork

Fender clamp

Disc brake

Clutch cover

Single overhead camshaft engine

Heat shield

Passenger footrest

Exhaust pipe

Mirror

Brake master cylinder

Handgrip

Front brake lever

Padded seat

Oil tank filler cap

Oil tank

Manufacturer's logo

Fuel tank

Light switch

1963 VESPA GRAND SPORT 160 MARK 1

Twist grip gear change

Monocoque chassis

Engine cover

Cooling grille

Taillight

Seat strap

Throttle

Seat

Front brake lever

Clutch lever

Headlight

Horn

Shock absorber

Choke

Gas tap

Kick-starter

Center stand

Silencer

Foot brake

Rubber foot mat

Drum brake

Single-sided trailing-link fork

Windshield

Clutch cable

Throttle cable

Windshield adjustor

Headlight

Fog lamp

Indicator

Telescopic fork

Side reflector

Fender

Passenger foot rest

Gearbox

Air filter

45° V-twin engine

Exhaust pipe

Foot rest

Brake pedal

Duplex tubular cradle frame

Crash bar

Brake calliper

Disc brake

Cast alloy wheel

The motorcycle chassis

THE MOTORCYCLE CHASSIS is the main "body" of the motorcycle, to which the engine is attached. Consisting of the frame, wheels, suspension, and brakes, the chassis performs various functions. The frame, which is built from steel or alloy, keeps the wheels in line to maintain the handling of the motorcycle, and serves as a structure for mounting other components. The engine and gearbox unit is bolted into place, while items such as the seat, the fenders, and the fairing are more easily removable. Suspension cushions the rider from irregularities in the road surface. In most suspension systems, coil springs controlled by an oil damper separate the main mass of the motorcycle from the wheels. At the front, the spring and damper are usually incorporated in a telescopic fork; the rear employs a pivoted swing arm. The suspension also helps to retain maximum contact between the tires and the road, necessary to effective braking and steering. Drum brakes were common until the 1970s, but modern motorcycles use disc brakes, which are more powerful.

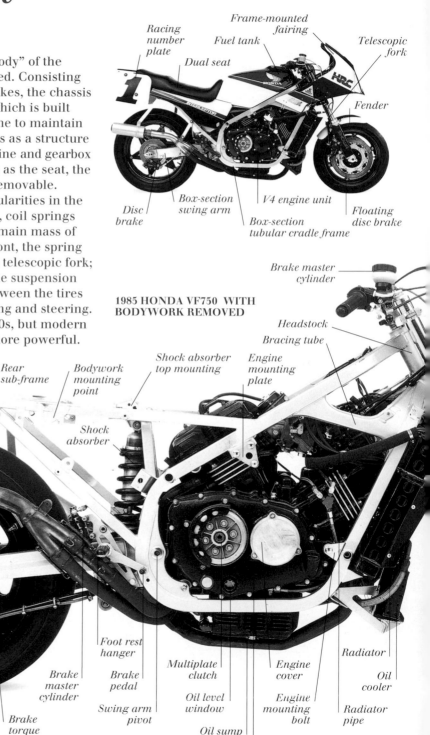

1985 HONDA VF750 WITH BODYWORK

Racing number plate
Frame-mounted fairing
Fuel tank
Dual seat
Telescopic fork
Fender
Disc brake
Box-section swing arm
V4 engine unit
Box-section tubular cradle frame
Floating disc brake

1985 HONDA VF750 WITH BODYWORK REMOVED

Brake master cylinder
Headstock
Bracing tube
Shock absorber top mounting
Engine mounting plate
Square-section steel tubing
Rear sub-frame
Bodywork mounting point
Shock absorber
Exhaust mounting strap
Exhaust pipe
Light alloy wheel
Axle adjustor
Disc brake
Disc brake calliper
Box-section swing arm
Brake torque arm
Brake master cylinder
Foot rest hanger
Brake pedal
Swing arm pivot
Multiplate clutch
Oil level window
Oil sump
Engine cover
Engine mounting bolt
V4 engine unit
Radiator
Oil cooler
Radiator pipe

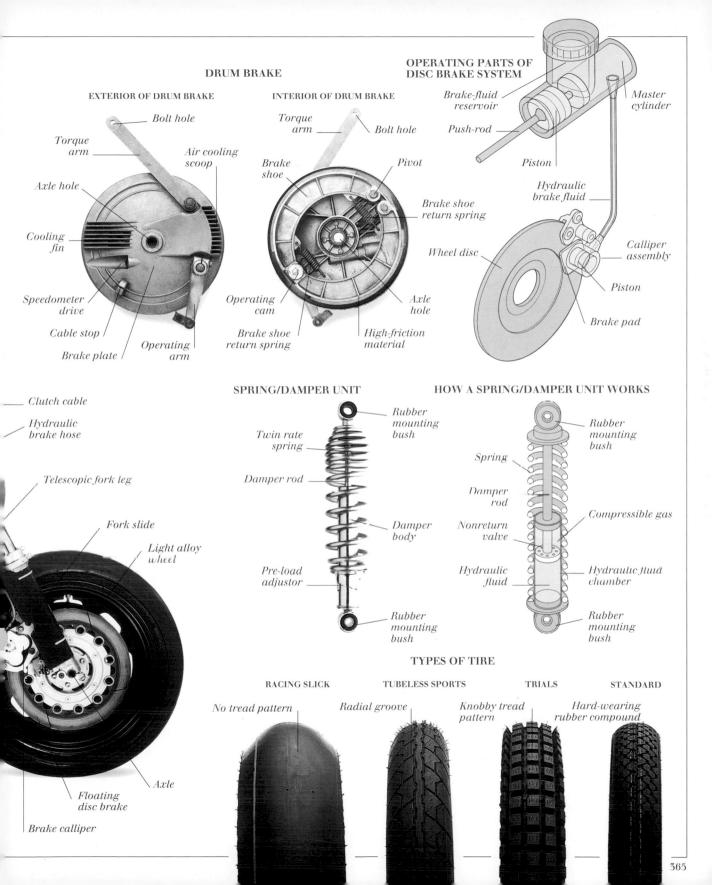

DRUM BRAKE

EXTERIOR OF DRUM BRAKE

Bolt hole

Torque arm

Air cooling scoop

Axle hole

Cooling fin

Speedometer drive

Cable stop

Brake plate

Operating arm

INTERIOR OF DRUM BRAKE

Torque arm

Bolt hole

Brake shoe

Pivot

Brake shoe return spring

Operating cam

Axle hole

Brake shoe return spring

High-friction material

OPERATING PARTS OF DISC BRAKE SYSTEM

Brake-fluid reservoir

Master cylinder

Push-rod

Piston

Hydraulic brake fluid

Wheel disc

Calliper assembly

Piston

Brake pad

Clutch cable

Hydraulic brake hose

Telescopic fork leg

Fork slide

Light alloy wheel

Axle

Floating disc brake

Brake calliper

SPRING/DAMPER UNIT

Rubber mounting bush

Twin rate spring

Damper rod

Damper body

Pre-load adjustor

Rubber mounting bush

HOW A SPRING/DAMPER UNIT WORKS

Rubber mounting bush

Spring

Damper rod

Compressible gas

Nonreturn valve

Hydraulic fluid

Hydraulic fluid chamber

Rubber mounting bush

TYPES OF TIRE

RACING SLICK

No tread pattern

TUBELESS SPORTS

Radial groove

TRIALS

Knobby tread pattern

STANDARD

Hard-wearing rubber compound

Motorcycle engines

MOTORCYCLE ENGINES must be lightweight and compact, and have a good power output. They have between one and six cylinders, can be cooled by air or water, and the capacity of the combustion chamber varies from 49cc (cubic centimeters) to 1500cc. Two types of internal combustion engine are common: the four-stroke, which is used in cars (see pp. 342-343), and the two-stroke. A basic two-stroke engine has only three moving parts—the crankshaft, the connecting rod, and the piston—but the power output is high. The engine fires every two strokes (rather than every four), giving a "power stroke" every revolution (see p. 343). Power is conveyed from the engine to the rear wheel by the transmission system. This usually consists of a clutch, a gearbox, and a final drive system. Clutches are multiplate devices, which run in oil. Gearboxes have five or six speeds and are operated by foot pedal. Shaft and belt drive systems are used in some cases, but chain drive to the rear wheel is most common.

EXTERIOR OF STANDARD TWO-STROKE ENGINE

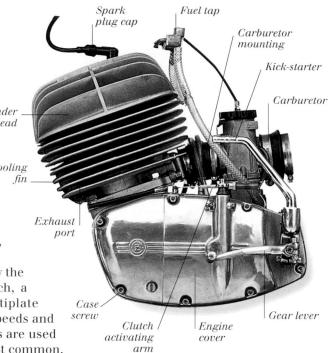

Spark plug cap
Fuel tap
Carburetor mounting
Kick-starter
Carburetor
Cylinder head
Cooling fin
Exhaust port
Case screw
Clutch activating arm
Engine cover
Gear lever

TRANSMISSION SYSTEM

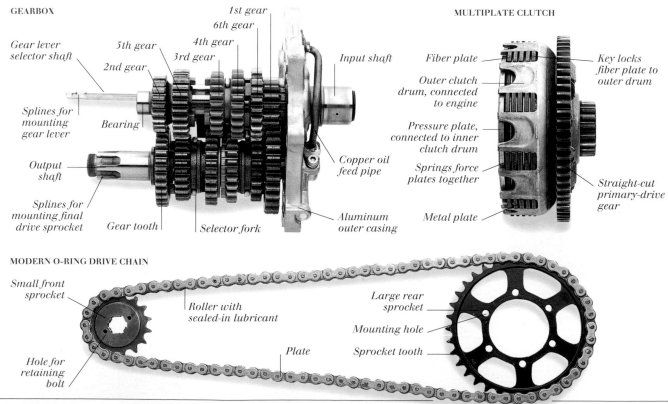

GEARBOX

Gear lever selector shaft
5th gear
2nd gear
4th gear
3rd gear
1st gear
6th gear
Input shaft
Splines for mounting gear lever
Bearing
Output shaft
Splines for mounting final drive sprocket
Gear tooth
Selector fork
Copper oil feed pipe
Aluminum outer casing

MULTIPLATE CLUTCH

Fiber plate
Outer clutch drum, connected to engine
Pressure plate, connected to inner clutch drum
Springs force plates together
Metal plate
Key locks fiber plate to outer drum
Straight-cut primary-drive gear

MODERN O-RING DRIVE CHAIN

Small front sprocket
Roller with sealed-in lubricant
Hole for retaining bolt
Plate
Large rear sprocket
Mounting hole
Sprocket tooth

**VELOCETTE OVERHEAD
VALVE (OHV) ENGINE**

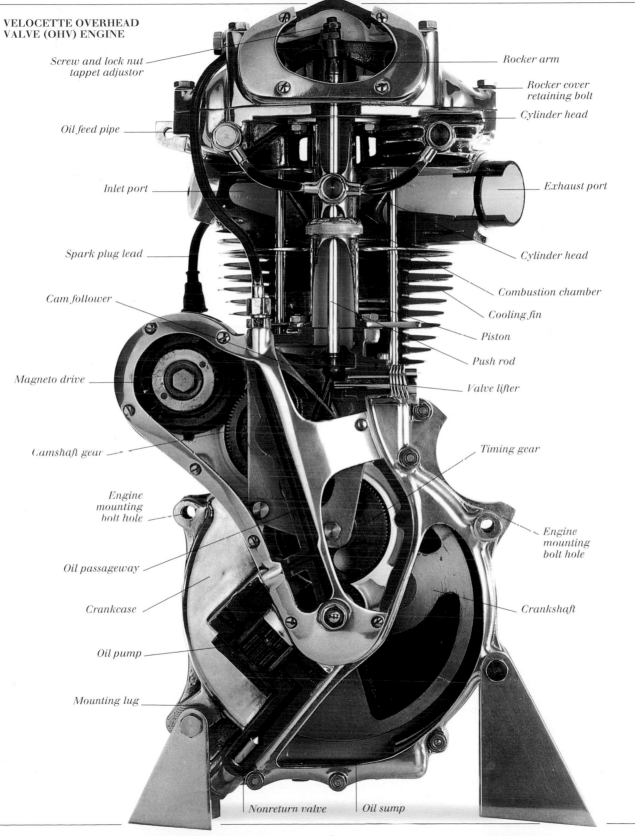

Screw and lock nut
tappet adjustor

Oil feed pipe

Inlet port

Spark plug lead

Cam follower

Magneto drive

Camshaft gear

Engine
mounting
bolt hole

Oil passageway

Crankcase

Oil pump

Mounting lug

Rocker arm

Rocker cover
retaining bolt

Cylinder head

Exhaust port

Cylinder head

Combustion chamber

Cooling fin

Piston

Push rod

Valve lifter

Timing gear

Engine
mounting
bolt hole

Crankshaft

Nonreturn valve

Oil sump

Competition motorcycles

THERE ARE MANY TYPES of motorcycle sports and in each, a special machine has evolved to perform to specific requirements. Races take place on roads or tracks or "off-road," in fields, dirt tracks, and even the desert. "Grand Prix" world championships in roadracing are contested by three classes: 125cc, 250cc two-strokes; the top class of 500cc two-strokes; and 900cc four-stroke machines. The latest racing sidecars have more in common with racing cars than motorcycles. The rider and passenger operate within an all-enclosing, aerodynamic fairing. The Suzuki RGV500 shown here, like other Grand Prix machines, carries advertising, which helps to cover the cost of developing motorcycle technology. In Speedway, which originated in the U.S. in 1902, motorcycles operate without brakes or a gearbox. Off-road competition motorcycles have less emphasis on high power output. In Motocross, for example, which is held on rough terrain, they must have high ground clearance, flexible long-travel suspension, and tires with a chunky tread pattern.

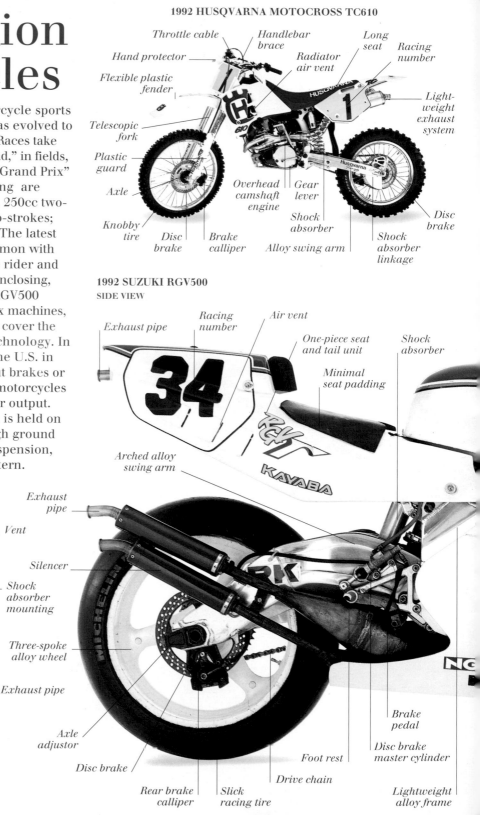

1992 HUSQVARNA MOTOCROSS TC610

Throttle cable • Hand protector • Flexible plastic fender • Telescopic fork • Plastic guard • Axle • Knobby tire • Disc brake • Brake calliper • Handlebar brace • Radiator air vent • Overhead camshaft engine • Gear lever • Shock absorber • Alloy swing arm • Long seat • Racing number • Light-weight exhaust system • Disc brake • Shock absorber linkage

1992 SUZUKI RGV500
SIDE VIEW

Exhaust pipe • Racing number • Air vent • One-piece seat and tail unit • Minimal seat padding • Shock absorber • Arched alloy swing arm

KAYABA

34

Exhaust pipe • Vent • Silencer • Shock absorber mounting • Three-spoke alloy wheel • Exhaust pipe

Exhaust pipe • Handlebar • Foot rest • Rear brake pedal • Drive chain • Wide, slick tire

REAR VIEW

MICHELIN

Axle adjustor • Disc brake • Rear brake calliper • Slick racing tire • Drive chain • Foot rest • Brake pedal • Disc brake master cylinder • Lightweight alloy frame

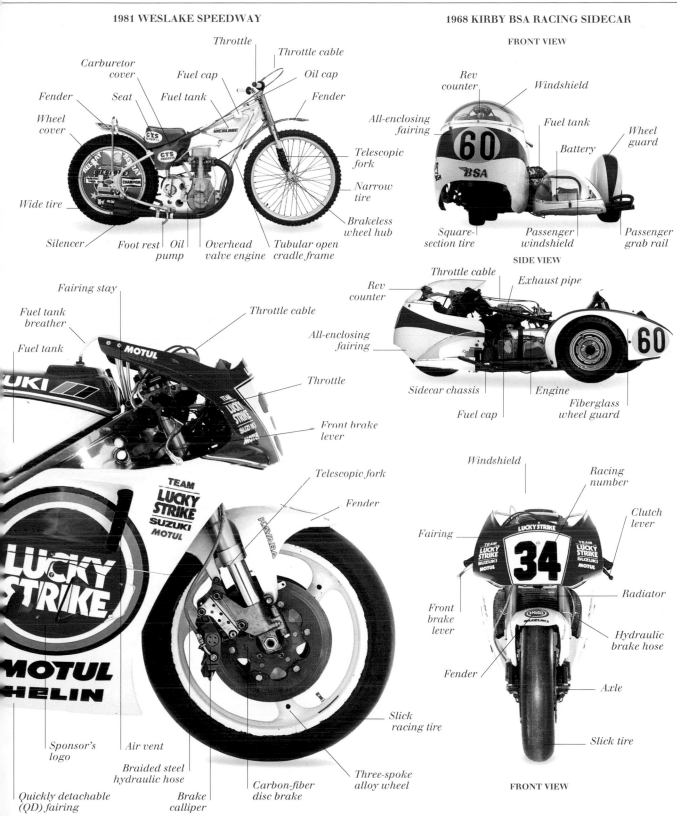

1981 WESLAKE SPEEDWAY

Throttle

Throttle cable

Carburetor cover

Fuel cap

Oil cap

Fender

Seat

Fuel tank

Fender

Wheel cover

Telescopic fork

Narrow tire

Wide tire

Brakeless wheel hub

Silencer

Foot rest

Oil pump

Overhead valve engine

Tubular open cradle frame

Fairing stay

Throttle cable

Fuel tank breather

Fuel tank

Throttle

Front brake lever

Telescopic fork

Fender

Sponsor's logo

Air vent

Braided steel hydraulic hose

Carbon-fiber disc brake

Three-spoke alloy wheel

Slick racing tire

Brake calliper

Quickly detachable (QD) fairing

1968 KIRBY BSA RACING SIDECAR

FRONT VIEW

Rev counter

Windshield

All-enclosing fairing

Fuel tank

Battery

Wheel guard

Square-section tire

Passenger windshield

Passenger grab rail

SIDE VIEW

Throttle cable

Exhaust pipe

Rev counter

All-enclosing fairing

Sidecar chassis

Engine

Fiberglass wheel guard

Fuel cap

Windshield

Racing number

Clutch lever

Fairing

Radiator

Front brake lever

Hydraulic brake hose

Fender

Axle

Slick tire

FRONT VIEW

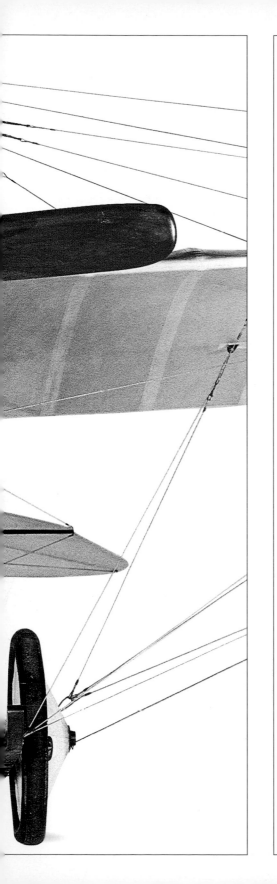

Sea and Air

Ships of Greece and Rome

ROMAN ANCHOR

IN THE EXPANSIVE EMPIRES OF GREECE AND ROME, powerful fleets were needed for battle, trade, and communication. Greek galleys were powered by a sail and many oars. A new armament, the embolos (ram), was fitted on to the galley bow. As ramming duels required fast and maneuverable boats, extra rows of oarsmen were added, culminating in the trireme. During the fifth and fourth centuries B.C., the trireme dominated the Mediterranean. It was powered by 170 oarsmen, each pulling one oar, and ranged on three levels, as the model opposite shows. The trireme also carried archers and soldiers for boarding enemy craft. Galleys were pulled out of the water when not in use, and were kept in dockyard ship-sheds. The merchant ships of the Greeks and Romans were mighty vessels, too. The full-bodied Roman corbita, for example, could hold up to 400 tons of cargo, such as spices, gems, silk, and animals. The construction of these boats was based on a stout hull with planking secured by mortice and tenon. Some of these ships made long trading voyages, sailing even as far as India. To make them easier to steer, corbitas set a foresail called an "artemon." It flew from a forward-leaning mast that was the forerunner of the long bowsprits carried by the great clipper ships of the 19th century.

Stock

Shank

Palm

Acutely angled arm

Ring

Crown

ATTIC VASE SHOWING A GREEK GALLEY

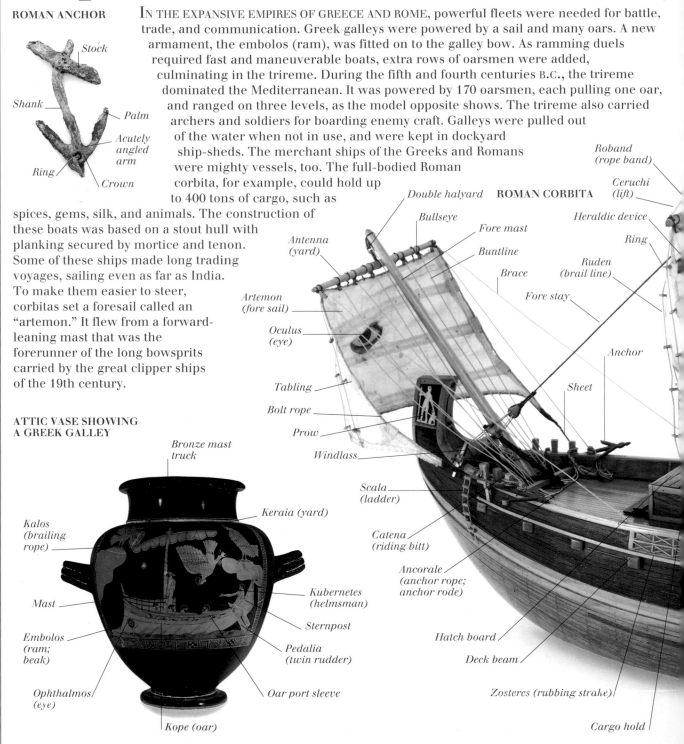

Roband (rope band)

Ceruchi (lift)

Double halyard   **ROMAN CORBITA**

Heraldic device

Bullseye   Fore mast

Ring

Antenna (yard)   Buntline

Ruden (brail line)

Brace

Fore stay

Artemon (fore sail)

Oculus (eye)

Anchor

Tabling

Sheet

Bolt rope

Prow

Windlass

Scala (ladder)

Catena (riding bitt)

Bronze mast truck

Keraia (yard)

Kalos (brailing rope)

Ancorale (anchor rope; anchor rode)

Kubernetes (helmsman)

Mast

Sternpost

Embolos (ram; beak)

Pedalia (twin rudder)

Hatch board

Deck beam

Ophthalmos (eye)

Oar port sleeve

Zosteres (rubbing strake)

Kope (oar)

Cargo hold

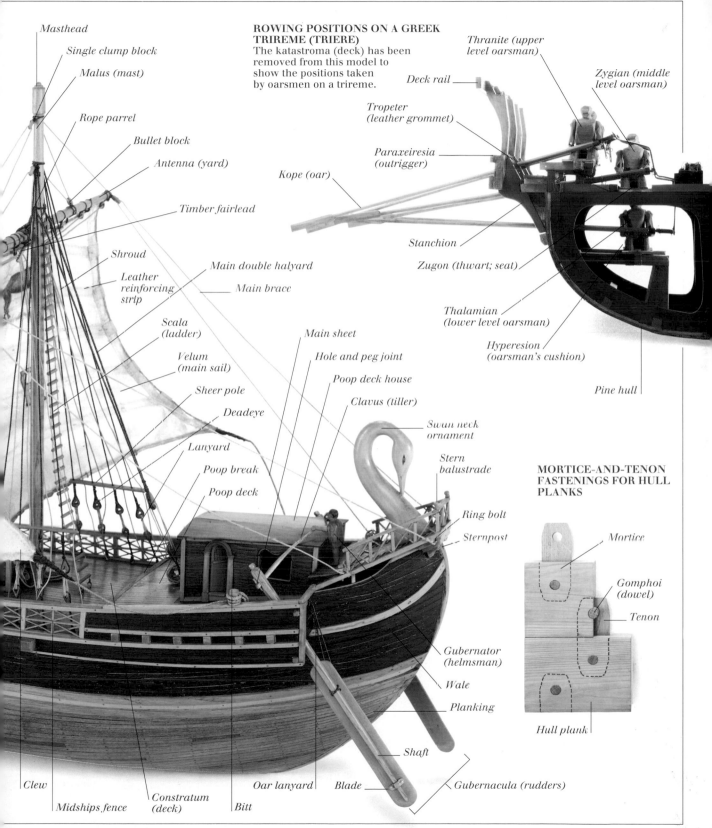

Masthead

Single clump block

Malus (mast)

Rope parrel

Bullet block

Antenna (yard)

Timber fairlead

Shroud

Leather reinforcing strip

Main double halyard

Main brace

Scala (ladder)

Velum (main sail)

Sheer pole

Deadeye

Lanyard

Poop break

Poop deck

ROWING POSITIONS ON A GREEK TRIREME (TRIERE)
The katastroma (deck) has been removed from this model to show the positions taken by oarsmen on a trireme.

Thranite (upper level oarsman)

Zygian (middle level oarsman)

Deck rail

Tropeter (leather grommet)

Paraxeiresia (outrigger)

Kope (oar)

Stanchion

Zugon (thwart; seat)

Thalamian (lower level oarsman)

Hyperesion (oarsman's cushion)

Pine hull

Main sheet

Hole and peg joint

Poop deck house

Clavus (tiller)

Swan neck ornament

Stern balustrade

Ring bolt

Sternpost

Gubernator (helmsman)

Wale

Planking

Shaft

Blade

Gubernacula (rudders)

MORTICE-AND-TENON FASTENINGS FOR HULL PLANKS

Mortice

Gomphoi (dowel)

Tenon

Hull plank

Clew

Midships fence

Constratum (deck)

Bitt

Oar lanyard

373

Viking ships

IN THE DARK AGES (roughly 500 A.D. to 1000 A.D.) the longships of Scandinavia were among the most feared sights for people of northern Europe. The Vikings launched raids from Scandinavia every summer in longships equipped with a single steering oar on the right, or "steerboard" side (hence, "starboard"). A longboat had one row of oars on each side and a single sail. The hull was clinker-built, with overlapping planks. Prowheads adorned fighting ships during war campaigns. The longship was also used for coastal travel. The karv below was probably built as transport for an important family, while the smaller faering was a rowing boat only. The fleet of William of Normandy that invaded England in 1066 owed much to the Viking boat building tradition, and has been depicted in the Bayeux Tapestry (right). Seals of port towns and royal courts through the ages provide a record of contemporary ship design. The seal opposite shows a European craft from somewhat later than the Viking period. Fighting platforms, or castles, and the addition of more masts and sails changed the character of the medieval ship. Note also that the steering oar has been replaced by a centered rudder.

BOAT BUILDERS' TOOLS

Shave
Broad axe
Sheer
Breast auger
Master shipwright
Stempost
Hood end
Keel
T-handle auger
Axe
Strake
Tree cut for planking

Zoomorphic head
Eye
Tooth

Roband
Leather diagonal reinforcement
Square sail of homespun yarn
Leech (leach)
Clew
Tye halyard
Foot

Braiding
Serpentine neck
Lozenge-shaped recess
Rectangular cross-band

Snake-tail ornament

VIKING KARV (COASTER)

Tiller
Sternpost
Boss (rudder pivot)

DRAGON PROWHEAD

Steering oar (side rudder)
Oar
Starboard (steerboard) side

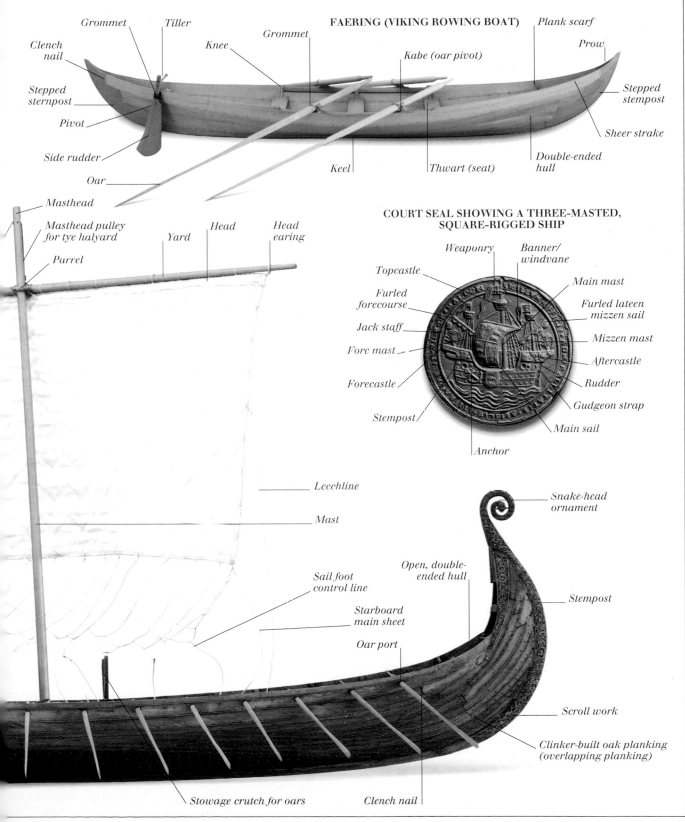

FAERING (VIKING ROWING BOAT)

Grommet

Tiller

Clench nail

Knee

Grommet

Kabe (oar pivot)

Plank scarf

Prow

Stepped sternpost

Pivot

Stepped stempost

Side rudder

Sheer strake

Oar

Keel

Thwart (seat)

Double-ended hull

Masthead

Masthead pulley for tye halyard

Yard

Head

Head earing

Parrel

COURT SEAL SHOWING A THREE-MASTED, SQUARE-RIGGED SHIP

Weaponry

Banner/ windvane

Topcastle

Main mast

Furled forecourse

Furled lateen mizzen sail

Jack staff

Mizzen mast

Fore mast

Aftercastle

Forecastle

Rudder

Stempost

Gudgeon strap

Main sail

Anchor

Leechline

Snake-head ornament

Mast

Sail foot control line

Open, double-ended hull

Stempost

Starboard main sheet

Oar port

Scroll work

Clinker-built oak planking (overlapping planking)

Stowage crutch for oars

Clench nail

Medieval warships and traders

FROM THE 16TH CENTURY, SHIPS WERE BUILT WITH A NEW FORM OF HULL, constructed with carvel (edge-to-edge) planking. Warships of the time, like King Henry VIII of England's Mary Rose, boasted awesome fire power. This ship carried both long-range bronze cannon, and short-range, anti personnel guns in iron. Elsewhere, ships took on a multiformity of shapes. Dhows transported slaves from East Africa to Arabia, their fore-and-aft rigged lateen sails allowing them to sail close to the wind around the lands of the Indian Ocean. The Chinese sailed to East Africa and Arabia in junks, trading goods that were carried in watertight compartments. New astronomical tools helped medieval sailors to find their way. Cross-staves and astrolabes were used to measure the altitude of the sun or stars. One of the cross-pieces was slid along the staff of the cross-stave—which was graduated in degrees of altitude—until its top aligned with the celestial body and its base with the horizon. The sighting rule of the astrolabe was simply lined up with a known body, and its altitude read from marks on the metal disk. Sundials used the shadow of the sun to show sailors the time of day.

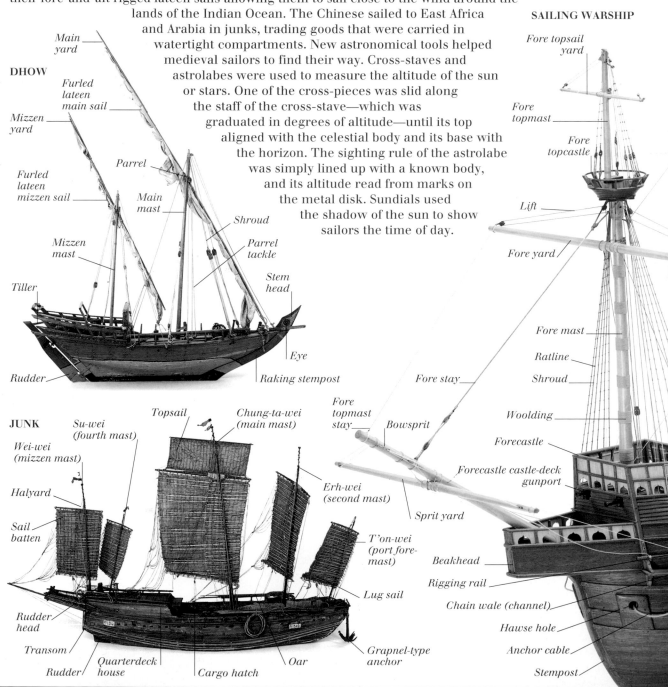

DHOW

Main yard
Furled lateen main sail
Mizzen yard
Parrel
Furled lateen mizzen sail
Main mast
Mizzen mast
Shroud
Parrel tackle
Tiller
Stem head
Rudder
Eye
Raking stempost

JUNK

Topsail
Su-wei (fourth mast)
Chung-ta-wei (main mast)
Wei-wei (mizzen mast)
Halyard
Sail batten
Erh-wei (second mast)
T'on-wei (port fore-mast)
Lug sail
Rudder head
Transom
Rudder
Quarterdeck house
Cargo hatch
Oar
Grapnel-type anchor

SAILING WARSHIP

Fore topsail yard
Fore topmast
Fore topcastle
Lift
Fore yard
Fore mast
Ratline
Shroud
Fore stay
Woolding
Fore topmast stay
Bowsprit
Forecastle
Forecastle castle-deck gunport
Sprit yard
Beakhead
Rigging rail
Chain wale (channel)
Hawse hole
Anchor cable
Stempost

Main topgallant mast

Main topgallant yard

Main topmast topcastle

Main top yard

Mizzen topmast

Main topmast stay

Mizzen top yard

Mizzen topcastle

Main topmast

Lift

Main topcastle

Bonaventure top yard

Lift

Bonaventure topmast

Main yard

Parrel

Tye

30 degree cross-piece

Brace

Jeer

Bonaventure topcastle

Main stay

Bonaventure yard

Mizzen mast

Bonaventure mast

Mizzen yard

Aftercastle

Main mast

Swifting tackle

Aftercastle castle-deck gunport

Outrigger

Upper deck gunport

Chain wale (channel)

Lid

Deadeye

Gangway

Gun carriage

Transom

Rudder

Sternpost

Keel

Blindage (removable archery screen)

Wale

Main deck gunport

Carvel planking

Port bower anchor

Alidade (sighting rule)

Bottom ballast

CROSS-STAVE (CROSS-STAFF)

90 degree cross-piece (transversary)

Clamp

Boxwood staff

60 degree cross-piece

Altitude scale in degrees and minutes

30 degree cross-piece

Ocular end

10 degree cross-piece (dutch shoe)

SUNDIAL

Style of the gnomon (edge)

Needle

Gnomon

Pivot

Hour line

Dial

Swivel suspension ring

Graduated ring

ASTROLABE

Scale of degrees

Pivot

Scribed arc decoration

The expansion of sail

By THE 18TH CENTURY, SAILING SHIPS had become fast and effective floating fortresses. The navies of the north European powers competed with each other by building heavily-armed fighting ships called "men-of-war." The distinctive round stern of the ship below, with its open gallery, balcony, and elaborate wood carving is typical of the period. Hulls around this time were semicircular in cross section, although many boat designers were soon to return to the V-shaped hulls used by the Vikings. Ships of the period carried more sail than ever before. A labyrinth of rigging supported the masts and yards from which the profusion of square sails were set. Ships grew higher as extra masts were fitted above the lower masts, and the bowsprit became longer, to allow the ship to carry staysails, spritsails, and jibs. Ships went into battle in single file, so that broadsides from the multiple decks of guns would have maximum effect. Ships were classified by rates, the rating of a vessel depending on how many guns it had. A first rate ship had more than 100 guns. The guns fired solid round shot, usually made of iron.

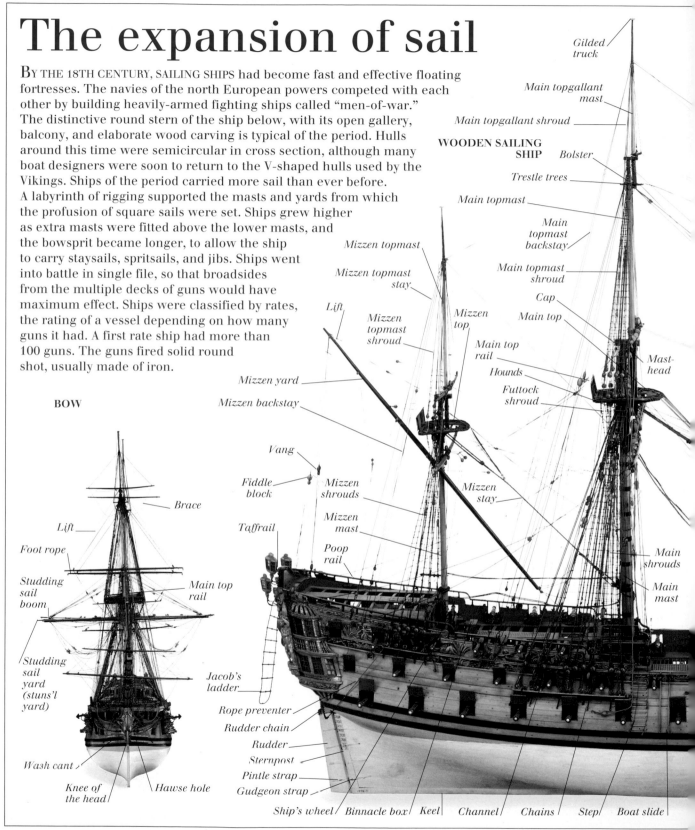

WOODEN SAILING SHIP

Gilded truck

Main topgallant mast

Main topgallant shroud

Bolster

Trestle trees

Main topmast

Main topmast backstay

Main topmast shroud

Cap

Main top

Main top rail

Mast-head

Hounds

Futtock shroud

Mizzen topmast

Mizzen topmast stay

Lift

Mizzen topmast shroud

Mizzen top

Mizzen yard

Mizzen backstay

Vang

Fiddle block

Mizzen shrouds

Mizzen stay

Mizzen mast

Taffrail

Poop rail

Main shrouds

Main mast

BOW

Brace

Lift

Foot rope

Studding sail boom

Main top rail

Studding sail yard (stuns'l yard)

Jacob's ladder

Rope preventer

Rudder chain

Rudder

Sternpost

Pintle strap

Gudgeon strap

Wash cant

Knee of the head

Hawse hole

Ship's wheel   Binnacle box   Keel   Channel   Chains   Step   Boat slide

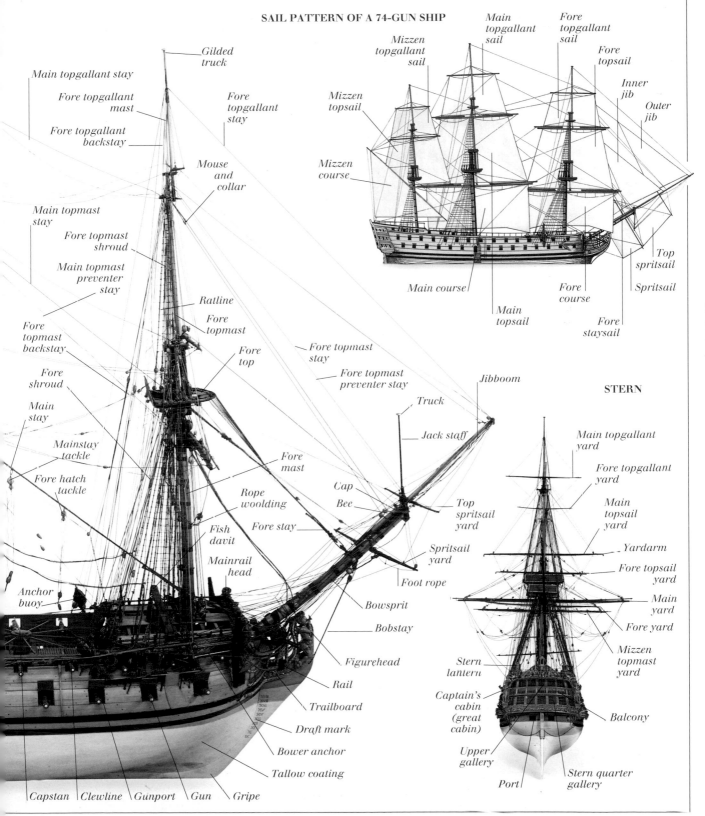

SAIL PATTERN OF A 74-GUN SHIP

Gilded truck

Main topgallant stay

Fore topgallant mast

Fore topgallant backstay

Fore topgallant stay

Mouse and collar

Main topmast stay

Fore topmast shroud

Main topmast preventer stay

Ratline

Fore topmast

Fore top

Fore topmast backstay

Fore shroud

Main stay

Mainstay tackle

Fore hatch tackle

Fore topmast stay

Fore topmast preventer stay

Fore mast

Rope woolding

Fore stay

Fish davit

Mainrail head

Anchor buoy

Capstan   *Clewline*   *Gunport*   *Gun*   *Gripe*

Tallow coating

Bower anchor

Draft mark

Trailboard

Rail

Figurehead

Bobstay

Bowsprit

Foot rope

Spritsail yard

Top spritsail yard

Bee

Cap

Jack staff

Truck

Jibboom

Mizzen topgallant sail

Main topgallant sail

Fore topgallant sail

Fore topgallant

Mizzen topsail

Inner jib

Outer jib

Mizzen course

Main course

Main topsail

Fore course

Fore staysail

Fore topsail

Top spritsail

Spritsail

STERN

Main topgallant yard

Fore topgallant yard

Main topsail yard

Yardarm

Fore topsail yard

Main yard

Fore yard

Mizzen topmast yard

Stern lantern

Balcony

Captain's cabin (great cabin)

Upper gallery

Port

Stern quarter gallery

A ship of the line

THE 74-GUN THIRD-RATER WAS A MAINSTAY of British and French battlefleets in the late 18th and early 19th centuries. (The biggest ships in the fledgling American navy of the time were 44-gun frigates.) The length of such a man-of-war was determined by the number of guns needed for each deck, allowing room for crews to man them. The gun deck of this vessel was about 170 ft (52 m) long. Her decks had to be strong to carry the weight of the guns. The deck planks have been removed in the model below to illustrate the number of beams needed to make the hull strong enough. Only timber with perfect grain was used. The upper deck was open at the waist, but forward and aft were officers' cabins. The forecastle (foc's'l) and quarterdeck carried light guns and provided platforms for handling the rigging and for reconnaissance. The ship's longboats, or launches, were carried on skids between the gangways.

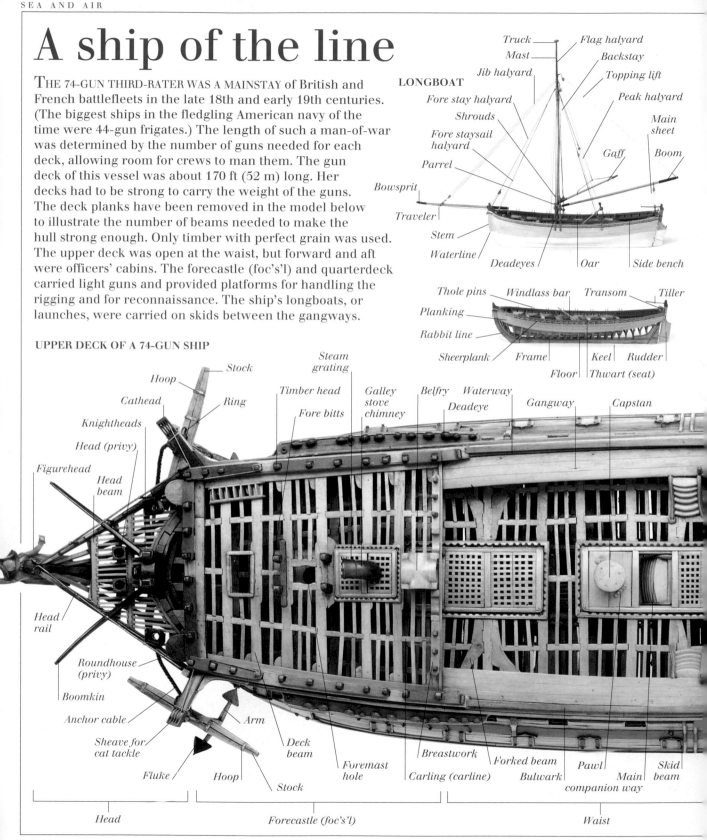

LONGBOAT

Truck — Flag halyard
Mast — Backstay
Jib halyard — Topping lift
Fore stay halyard — Peak halyard
Shrouds — Main sheet
Fore staysail halyard — Gaff — Boom
Parrel
Bowsprit
Traveler
Stem
Waterline — Deadeyes — Oar — Side bench

Thole pins — Windlass bar — Transom — Tiller
Planking
Rabbit line
Sheerplank — Frame — Keel — Rudder
Floor — Thwart (seat)

UPPER DECK OF A 74-GUN SHIP

Stock — Steam grating — Galley stove chimney — Belfry — Waterway — Gangway — Capstan
Hoop — Timber head — Deadeye
Cathead — Ring — Fore bits
Knightheads
Head (privy)
Figurehead
Head beam
Head rail
Roundhouse (privy)
Boomkin
Anchor cable — Arm
Sheave for cat tackle — Deck beam — Breastwork — Forked beam — Pawl — Skid beam
Fluke — Hoop — Stock — Foremast hole — Carling (carline) — Bulwark — Main companion way
Head — Forecastle (foc's'l) — Waist

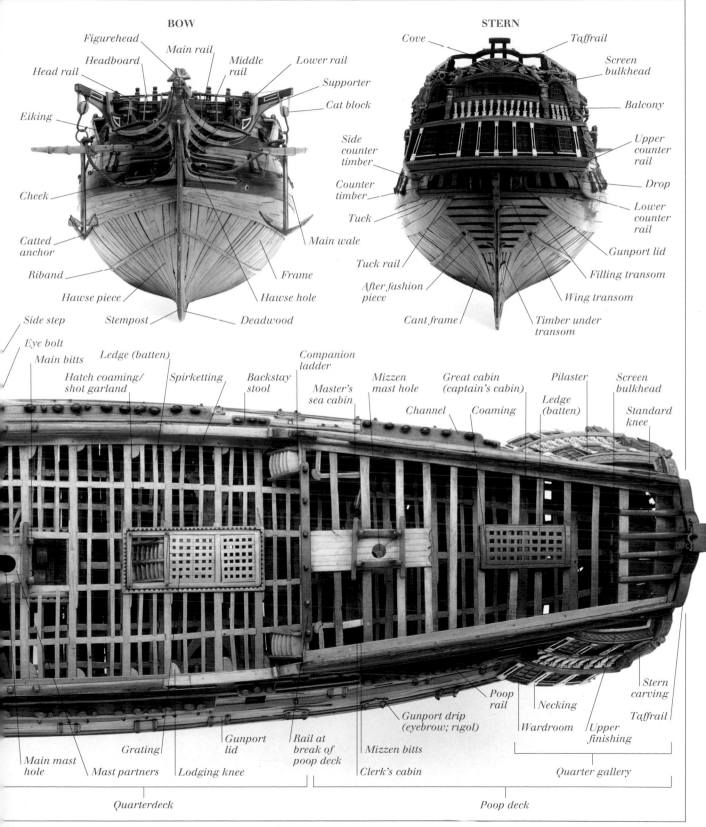

BOW

Figurehead

Main rail

Headboard

Middle rail

Lower rail

Head rail

Supporter

Eiking

Cat block

Cheek

Catted anchor

Riband

Main wale

Hawse piece

Frame

Side step

Hawse hole

Stempost

Deadwood

Eye bolt

STERN

Cove

Taffrail

Screen bulkhead

Balcony

Side counter timber

Upper counter rail

Counter timber

Drop

Tuck

Lower counter rail

Tuck rail

Gunport lid

After fashion piece

Filling transom

Cant frame

Wing transom

Timber under transom

Main bits

Ledge (batten)

Companion ladder

Mizzen mast hole

Great cabin (captain's cabin)

Pilaster

Screen bulkhead

Hatch coaming/ shot garland

Spirketting

Backstay stool

Master's sea cabin

Channel

Coaming

Ledge (batten)

Standard knee

Main mast hole

Mast partners

Grating

Lodging knee

Gunport lid

Rail at break of poop deck

Mizzen bits

Clerk's cabin

Poop rail

Gunport drip (eyebrow; rigol)

Wardroom

Necking

Upper finishing

Stern carving

Taffrail

Quarter gallery

Quarterdeck

Poop deck

Rigging

MOST SAILING SHIPS HAVE TWO TYPES OF RIGGING. Standing rigging—kept taut by turnbuckles or old-fashioned lanyards and deadeyes—refers to the ropes, wires, and chains that support the masts and yards (horizontal spars). Running rigging, which includes types of block and tackle, halyards, and sheets, is used to hoist, lower, or trim sails.

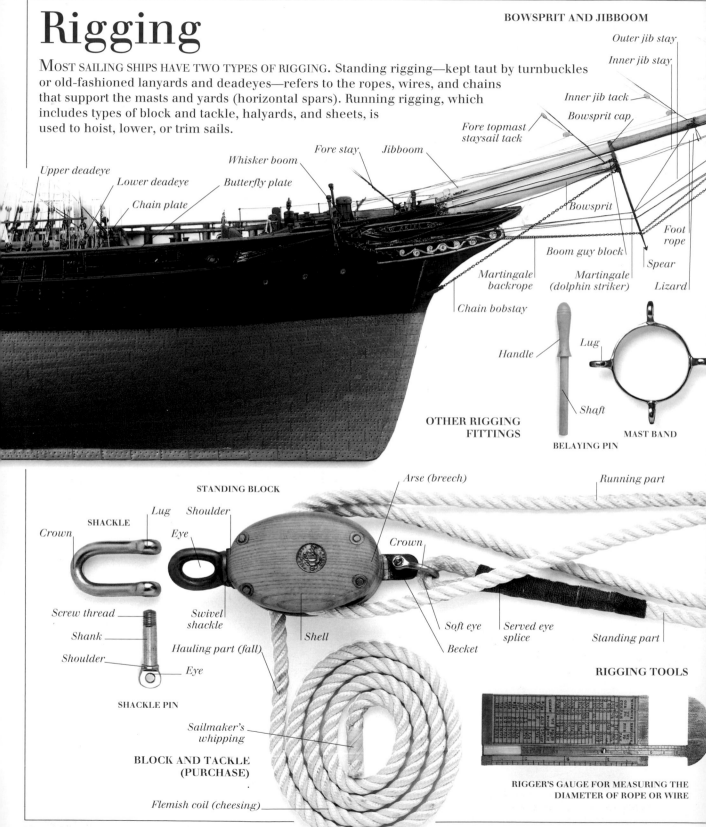

BOWSPRIT AND JIBBOOM

Outer jib stay

Inner jib stay

Inner jib tack

Bowsprit cap

Fore topmast staysail tack

Fore stay

Jibboom

Whisker boom

Upper deadeye

Lower deadeye

Butterfly plate

Chain plate

Bowsprit

Foot rope

Boom guy block

Martingale backrope

Martingale (dolphin striker)

Spear

Lizard

Chain bobstay

OTHER RIGGING FITTINGS

Handle

Lug

Shaft

Shaft

BELAYING PIN

MAST BAND

STANDING BLOCK

Arse (breech)

Running part

SHACKLE

Lug

Shoulder

Crown

Eye

Crown

Screw thread

Shank

Shoulder

Swivel shackle

Eye

Shell

Soft eye

Served eye splice

Standing part

Hauling part (fall)

Becket

SHACKLE PIN

Sailmaker's whipping

RIGGING TOOLS

BLOCK AND TACKLE (PURCHASE)

Flemish coil (cheesing)

RIGGER'S GAUGE FOR MEASURING THE DIAMETER OF ROPE OR WIRE

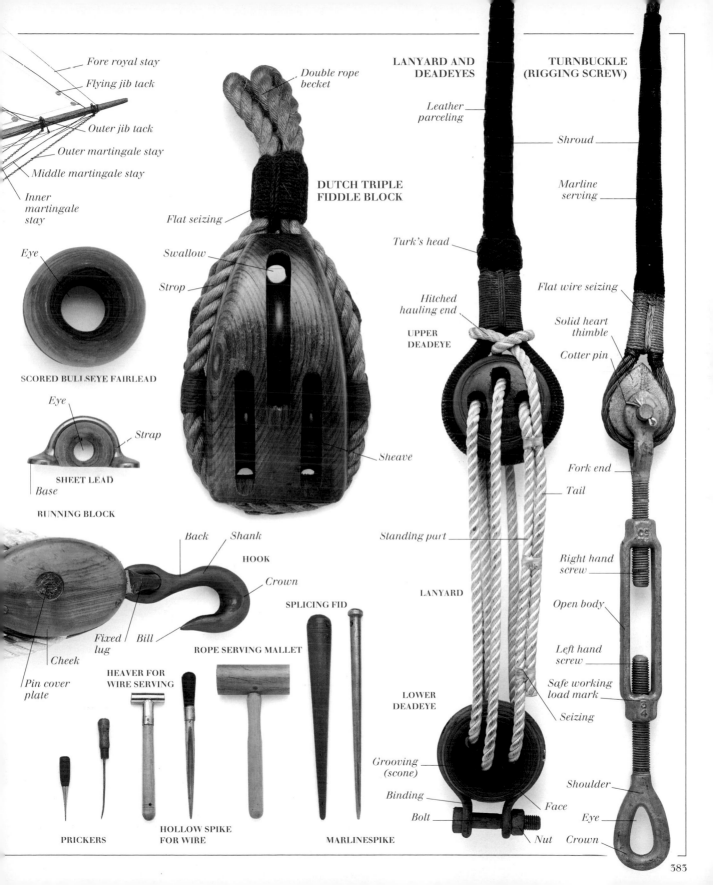

Fore royal stay

Flying jib tack

Outer jib tack

Outer martingale stay

Middle martingale stay

Inner martingale stay

Double rope becket

LANYARD AND DEADEYES

TURNBUCKLE (RIGGING SCREW)

Leather parceling

Shroud

DUTCH TRIPLE FIDDLE BLOCK

Marline serving

Eye

Flat seizing

Swallow

Strop

Turk's head

Flat wire seizing

Hitched hauling end

Solid heart thimble

SCORED BULLSEYE FAIRLEAD

UPPER DEADEYE

Cotter pin

Eye

Strap

Sheave

Fork end

Tail

SHEET LEAD

Base

RUNNING BLOCK

Standing part

Right hand screw

Back

Shank

HOOK

Crown

LANYARD

Open body

SPLICING FID

Left hand screw

Fixed lug

Bill

ROPE SERVING MALLET

Safe working load mark

Cheek

LOWER DEADEYE

Seizing

Pin cover plate

HEAVER FOR WIRE SERVING

Grooving (scone)

Shoulder

Binding

Face

PRICKERS

HOLLOW SPIKE FOR WIRE

MARLINESPIKE

Bolt

Nut

Eye

Crown

Sails

<small>THERE ARE TWO MAIN TYPES OF SAILS:</small> Old-fashioned square sails hang from yards at right angles
to the mast, and are powerful drivers with following winds; fore-and-aft sails are set parallel to the
length of the boat, with the luff (leading edge) of the sail attached to a mast or a stay. They are
more efficient for all-round sailing, and almost all modern sailboats are rigged this way. Some
fore-and-aft sails have a gaff at the head; Marconi-rig sails are pointed at the top (below). The bottom (foot)
of the sail is on a boom. Sails are made of strips of cloth sewn together. Cotton and flax are traditional sail
materials but synthetic fabrics are now more often used.

TOP OF A MARCONI SAIL

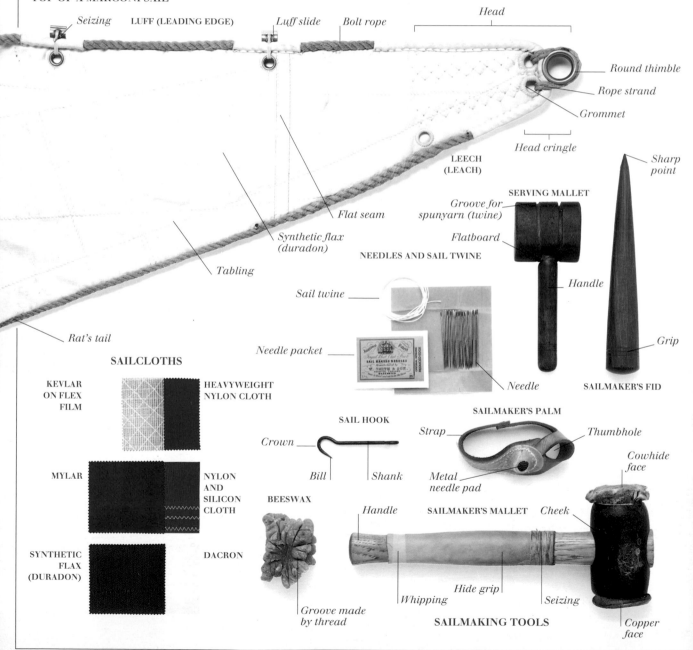

Seizing   LUFF (LEADING EDGE)   *Luff slide*   *Bolt rope*   *Head*

Round thimble

Rope strand

Grommet

Head cringle

LEECH
(LEACH)

*Sharp
point*

Flat seam

SERVING MALLET

*Groove for
spunyarn (twine)*

Flatboard

*Synthetic flax
(duradon)*

Handle

NEEDLES AND SAIL TWINE

Tabling

Sail twine

Grip

Rat's tail

Needle packet

Needle

SAILMAKER'S FID

SAILCLOTHS

KEVLAR
ON FLEX
FILM

HEAVYWEIGHT
NYLON CLOTH

SAILMAKER'S PALM

Strap   *Thumbhole*

SAIL HOOK

Crown

*Cowhide
face*

MYLAR

NYLON
AND
SILICON
CLOTH

Bill   *Shank*

*Metal
needle pad*

Handle   **SAILMAKER'S MALLET**   *Cheek*

BEESWAX

SYNTHETIC
FLAX
(DURADON)

DACRON

Whipping   *Hide grip*   *Seizing*

*Groove made
by thread*

SAILMAKING TOOLS

*Copper
face*

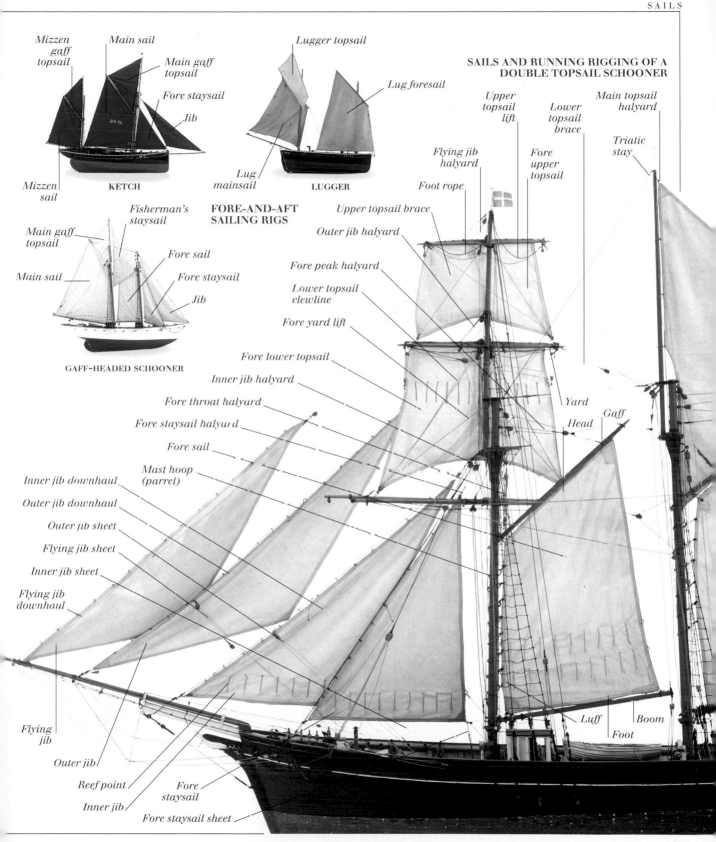

Mizzen gaff topsail

Main sail

Main gaff topsail

Fore staysail

Jib

Mizzen sail

KETCH

Lugger topsail

Lug foresail

SAILS AND RUNNING RIGGING OF A DOUBLE TOPSAIL SCHOONER

Upper topsail lift

Lower topsail brace

Main topsail halyard

Triatic stay

Flying jib halyard

Fore upper topsail

Lug mainsail

LUGGER

Foot rope

FORE-AND-AFT SAILING RIGS

Upper topsail brace

Fisherman's staysail

Outer jib halyard

Main gaff topsail

Fore sail

Fore peak halyard

Main sail

Fore staysail

Lower topsail clewline

Jib

Fore yard lift

Yard

GAFF-HEADED SCHOONER

Fore lower topsail

Head

Gaff

Inner jib halyard

Fore throat halyard

Fore staysail halyard

Fore sail

Mast hoop (parrel)

Inner jib downhaul

Outer jib downhaul

Outer jib sheet

Flying jib sheet

Inner jib sheet

Flying jib downhaul

Luff

Boom

Foot

Flying jib

Outer jib

Reef point

Fore staysail

Inner jib

Fore staysail sheet

Mooring and anchoring

IN MOST HARBORS AND PORTS, a ship can moor (tie up or "make fast") directly to a pier, wharf, or quay (pronounced "key"), using heavy hawsers and docking lines attached to bitts or bollards. Hawsers are tied to each other with knots called bends. In open water, however, ships that are not under way must drop an anchor, which attaches the ship securely to the seabed. The earliest anchors were simply heavy stones. Later, various anchor designs were developed for different uses. Most small vessels today use Danforth or plow anchors, which dig deeply into the sea bottom. A permanent mooring is an anchor set in the bottom to which a ship can tie up without using its own anchor. On old sailing ships, anchors were pulled up, or "weighed," by sailors pushing against bars that turned a capstan, which wound up the anchor cable. Now, most capstans are powered by electricity.

STONE ANCHOR (KILLICK)

Rope hole

TYPES OF ANCHOR

CLOSE-STOWING ANCHOR

CQR ANCHOR (PLOW ANCHOR)

BRITISH ADMIRALTY ANCHOR TYPE ACII

YACHTSMAN'S ANCHOR (KEDGE)

STOCKLESS ANCHOR

MUSHROOM ANCHOR (PERMANENT MOORING ANCHOR)

ANCHOR CHAIN

End link

Common link

Patent link

SHACKLE, SWIVELS, AND LINK

DANFORTH ANCHOR

Shank

Pea (bill)

Fluke (palm)

Stock

Tripping palm

Throat

Crown

Crown

Bolt

Lug

GALVANIZED "D" SHACKLE

MOORING SWIVEL

CHAIN SWIVEL

Screw thread

SCREW LINK

TWIN BOLLARDS (BITTS), WITH RAKED PILLARS AND A HAWSER (HEAVY ROPE)

Flat

Rim

Base

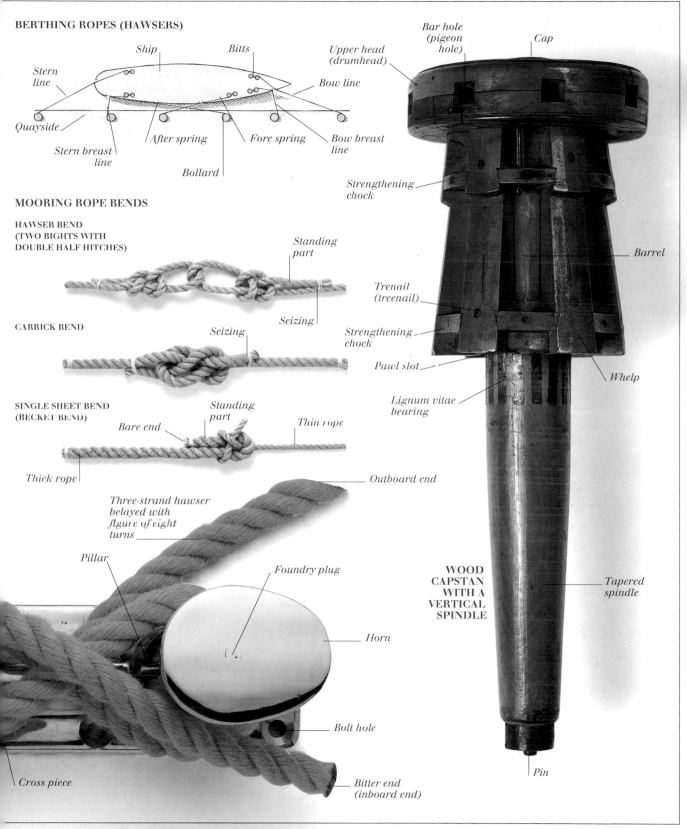

BERTHING ROPES (HAWSERS)

Ship

Bitts

Bar hole (pigeon hole)

Cap

Stern line

Upper head (drumhead)

Bow line

Quayside

Stern breast line

After spring

Fore spring

Bow breast line

Bollard

Bow breast line

Strengthening chock

MOORING ROPE BENDS

HAWSER BEND (TWO BIGHTS WITH DOUBLE HALF HITCHES)

Standing part

Seizing

Barrel

Trenail (treenail)

CARRICK BEND

Seizing

Seizing

Strengthening chock

Pawl slot

Lignum vitae bearing

Whelp

SINGLE SHEET BEND (BECKET BEND)

Bare end

Standing part

Thin rope

Thick rope

Outboard end

Three-strand hawser belayed with figure of eight turns

Pillar

Foundry plug

WOOD CAPSTAN WITH A VERTICAL SPINDLE

Tapered spindle

Horn

Bolt hole

Cross piece

Bitter end (inboard end)

Pin

Ropes and knots

ALL KINDS OF ROPES ARE USED AT SEA, from thin twines and yarn to thick hawsers. Synthetic fibers are much in use today. Nylon ropes stretch, and so are ideal for anchoring; polyester (frequently called by the trade name Dacron) has little stretch and is used for halyards and sheets. Different knots have different uses. Knots that join two ropes are often called bends; hitches join a rope to another object. Ropes, usually called "lines" on board ship, can also be joined by seizing (lashing them together side by side) or splicing (unraveling the ends and weaving them together).

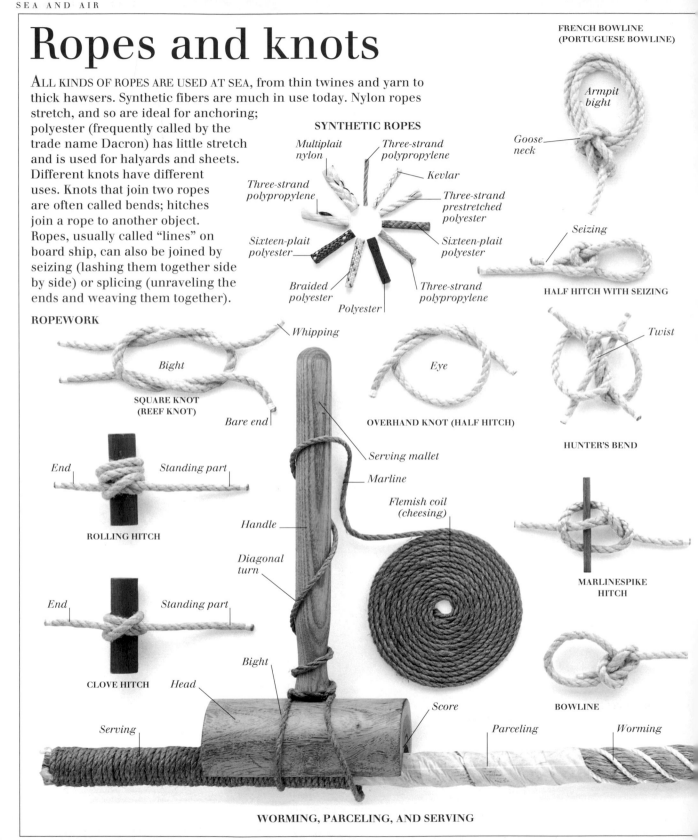

**FRENCH BOWLINE
(PORTUGUESE BOWLINE)**

Armpit bight

Goose neck

Seizing

HALF HITCH WITH SEIZING

SYNTHETIC ROPES

Multiplait nylon

Three-strand polypropylene

Kevlar

Three-strand polypropylene

Three-strand prestretched polyester

Sixteen-plait polyester

Sixteen-plait polyester

Braided polyester

Three-strand polypropylene

Polyester

ROPEWORK

Whipping

Bight

**SQUARE KNOT
(REEF KNOT)**

Bare end

Eye

OVERHAND KNOT (HALF HITCH)

Twist

HUNTER'S BEND

End   Standing part

ROLLING HITCH

Serving mallet

Marline

Flemish coil
(cheesing)

**MARLINESPIKE
HITCH**

End   Standing part

Handle

Diagonal turn

CLOVE HITCH

Head

Bight

BOWLINE

Serving

Score

Parceling

Worming

WORMING, PARCELING, AND SERVING

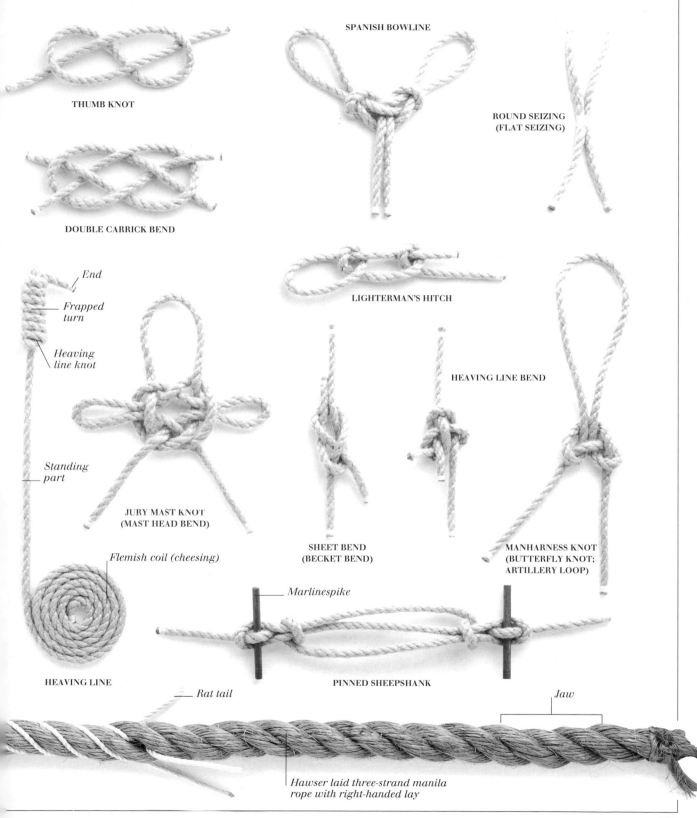

SPANISH BOWLINE

THUMB KNOT

**ROUND SEIZING
(FLAT SEIZING)**

DOUBLE CARRICK BEND

End

*Frapped
turn*

*Heaving
line knot*

LIGHTERMAN'S HITCH

HEAVING LINE BEND

*Standing
part*

**JURY MAST KNOT
(MAST HEAD BEND)**

**SHEET BEND
(BECKET BEND)**

**MANHARNESS KNOT
(BUTTERFLY KNOT;
ARTILLERY LOOP)**

Flemish coil (cheesing)

Marlinespike

HEAVING LINE

PINNED SHEEPSHANK

Rat tail

Jaw

*Hawser laid three-strand manila
rope with right-handed lay*

Paddle wheels and propellers

THE INVENTION OF THE STEAM ENGINE IN THE 18TH CENTURY made mechanically driven ships fitted with paddle wheels or propellers a viable alternative to sails. Paddle wheels have fixed or feathered floats, and the model shown below features both types. Feathered floats give more propulsive power than fixed floats because they are almost upright at all times in the water. Paddle wheels were superseded by the propeller on oceangoing vessels in the mid-19th century. Propellers are more efficient, work better in rough water, and are less vulnerable in collisions. The first propellers were two-bladed, but later three- and four-bladed versions are more powerful; the shape and pitch of the blades have also been refined over the years. At the beginning of the 18th century, tillers were replaced on many larger ships by the ship's wheel as a means of steering.

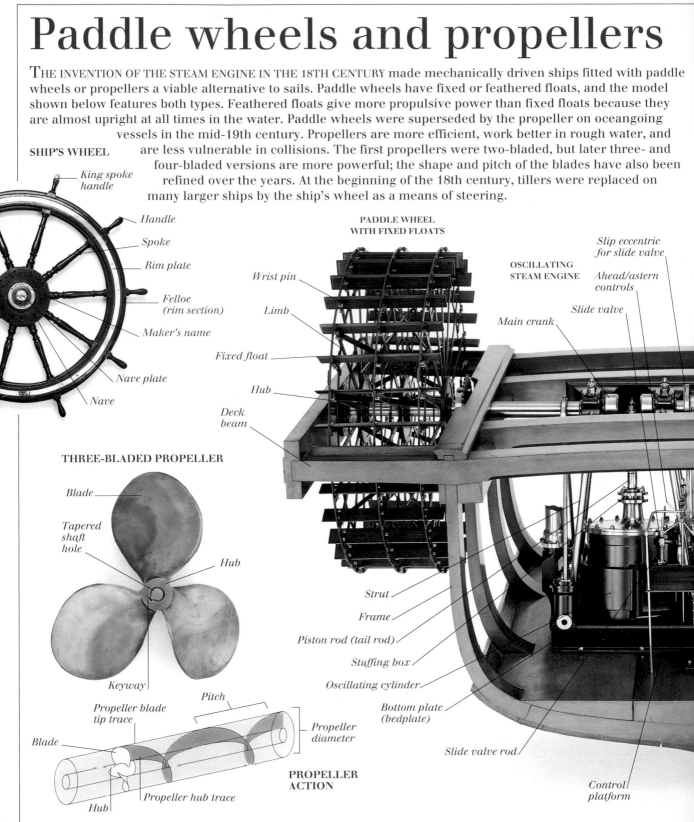

SHIP'S WHEEL

- King spoke handle
- Handle
- Spoke
- Rim plate
- Felloe (rim section)
- Maker's name
- Nave plate
- Nave

PADDLE WHEEL WITH FIXED FLOATS

- Wrist pin
- Limb
- Fixed float
- Hub
- Deck beam

OSCILLATING STEAM ENGINE

- Slip eccentric for slide valve
- Ahead/astern controls
- Slide valve
- Main crank

THREE-BLADED PROPELLER

- Blade
- Tapered shaft hole
- Hub
- Keyway

- Strut
- Frame
- Piston rod (tail rod)
- Stuffing box
- Oscillating cylinder
- Bottom plate (bedplate)
- Slide valve rod
- Control platform

- Propeller blade tip trace
- Pitch
- Blade
- Propeller diameter
- Hub
- Propeller hub trace

PROPELLER ACTION

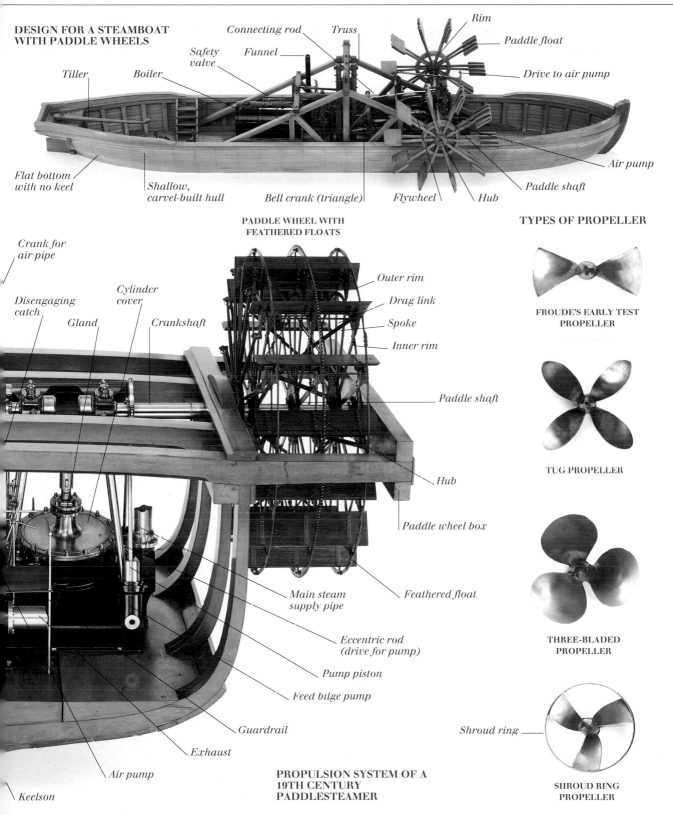

DESIGN FOR A STEAMBOAT WITH PADDLE WHEELS

Connecting rod

Truss

Rim

Safety valve

Funnel

Paddle float

Tiller

Boiler

Drive to air pump

Flat bottom with no keel

Shallow, carvel-built hull

Bell crank (triangle)

Flywheel

Hub

Air pump

Paddle shaft

PADDLE WHEEL WITH FEATHERED FLOATS

TYPES OF PROPELLER

Crank for air pipe

Disengaging catch

Cylinder cover

Gland

Crankshaft

Outer rim

Drag link

Spoke

Inner rim

Paddle shaft

Hub

FROUDE'S EARLY TEST PROPELLER

TUG PROPELLER

Paddle wheel box

Main steam supply pipe

Feathered float

Eccentric rod (drive for pump)

Pump piston

Feed bilge pump

Guardrail

Exhaust

Air pump

THREE-BLADED PROPELLER

Shroud ring

Keelson

PROPULSION SYSTEM OF A 19TH CENTURY PADDLESTEAMER

SHROUD RING PROPELLER

Anatomy of an iron ship

IRON PARTS WERE USED IN WOODEN SHIPS AS EARLY AS 1675, often in the same form as the wooden parts that they replaced. Eventually, as on the tea clipper Cutty Sark (below), iron standing rigging was found to be stronger than the traditional rope. The first "ironclads" were warships whose wooden hulls were protected by iron armor plates. Later ironclads actually had iron hulls. The model opposite is based on the British warship HMS Warrior, launched in 1860, the first battleship built entirely of iron. The plan of an iron paddlesteamer (bottom), built somewhat later, shows that the craft had the masts and bowsprit of a sailing ship; but it also boasted a steam propulsion plant amid ships that turned two side paddlewheels. Early iron plates were painstakingly riveted together (below), but by the 1940s, steel vessels were welded together, whole sections at a time. The Liberty ships built in America during World War II are prime examples of such "production-line" vessels.

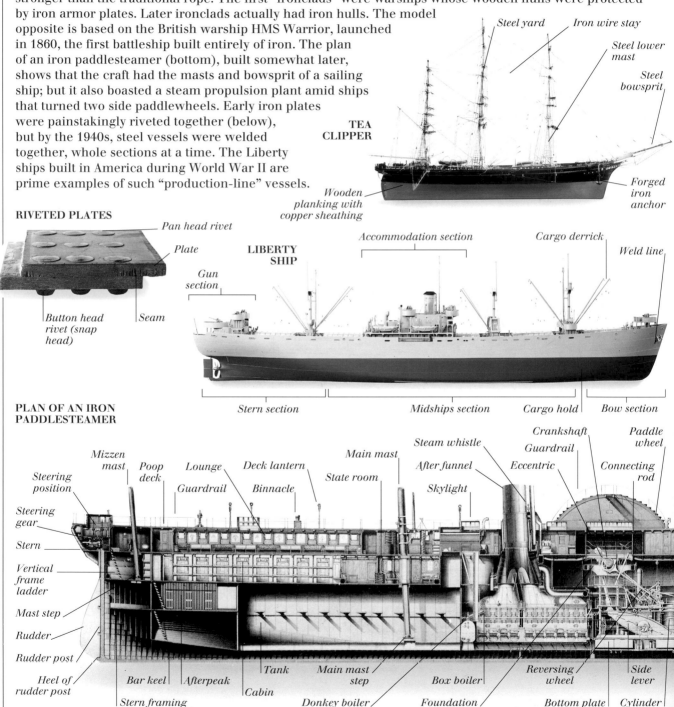

TEA CLIPPER

Steel yard
Iron wire stay
Steel lower mast
Steel bowsprit
Forged iron anchor
Wooden planking with copper sheathing

RIVETED PLATES

Pan head rivet
Plate
Button head rivet (snap head)
Seam

LIBERTY SHIP

Accommodation section
Cargo derrick
Weld line
Gun section
Stern section
Midships section
Cargo hold
Bow section

PLAN OF AN IRON PADDLESTEAMER

Steam whistle
Crankshaft
Paddle wheel
Main mast
After funnel
Guardrail
Eccentric
Connecting rod
Mizzen mast
Poop deck
Lounge
Deck lantern
State room
Skylight
Steering position
Guardrail
Binnacle
Steering gear
Stern
Vertical frame ladder
Mast step
Rudder
Rudder post
Heel of rudder post
Bar keel
Afterpeak
Tank
Main mast step
Box boiler
Reversing wheel
Side lever
Stern framing
Cabin
Donkey boiler
Foundation
Bottom plate
Cylinder

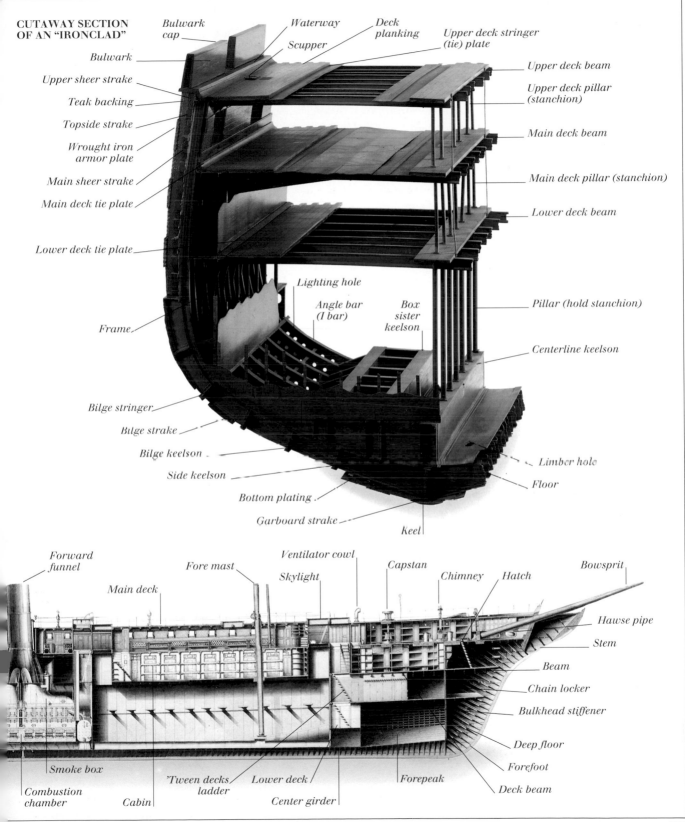

CUTAWAY SECTION OF AN "IRONCLAD"

Bulwark cap

Waterway

Deck planking

Upper deck stringer (tie) plate

Scupper

Bulwark

Upper deck beam

Upper sheer strake

Upper deck pillar (stanchion)

Teak backing

Topside strake

Main deck beam

Wrought iron armor plate

Main sheer strake

Main deck pillar (stanchion)

Main deck tie plate

Lower deck beam

Lower deck tie plate

Lighting hole

Angle bar (I bar)

Box sister keelson

Pillar (hold stanchion)

Frame

Centerline keelson

Bilge stringer

Bilge strake

Bilge keelson

Limber hole

Side keelson

Floor

Bottom plating

Garboard strake

Keel

Forward funnel

Ventilator cowl

Capstan

Bowsprit

Fore mast

Chimney

Hatch

Main deck

Skylight

Hawse pipe

Stem

Beam

Chain locker

Bulkhead stiffener

Deep floor

Smoke box

'Tween decks ladder

Lower deck

Forepeak

Forefoot

Combustion chamber

Cabin

Center girder

Deck beam

The battleship

IN THE EARLY YEARS OF THE 20TH CENTURY, sea warfare—attacking enemy vessels or defending a ship—was revolutionized by the introduction of Dreadnought-type battleships like the Brazilian vessel below. These new ships combined the latest advances in steam propulsion, gunnery, and armor plating. Their gun turrets, protected by armor up to 12 in (30 cm) thick, were designed to fire shells over great distances. The ship shown here, the Minas Geraes, was 500 ft (152 m) long. It was built at Elswick, England, and launched in 1908. Its chief armament was of 12 in (30 cm) guns (firing shells with a 12 in diameter). Other naval weapons developed in the 20th century include the torpedo—as portrayed on the upper cigarette card (right). This was a self-propelled underwater missile, often steered by gyro-control. Depth charges were designed in the First World War for use against submerged U-boats. They are canisters filled with explosives that are detonated by depth-sensitive pistols. The lower cigarette card shows depth charges being fired by a "thrower," fired from a torpedo tube, and rolled from the stern. Ship's shields were fitted to warships from the late 19th century onwards. The shield shown opposite depicts a traditional ship's cannon.

20TH CENTURY WEAPONRY

Torpedo tube

Sight

Warhead

TORPEDOES

DEPTH CHARGES

Side-thrown canister

Stern-rolled canister

Torpedo-fired canister

Boat handling derrick

BRAZILIAN BATTLESHIP

Gunnery spotting top

Rangefinder

Forward funnel

Light screen

Lifeboat

Compass

Purchase wire

Searchlight

Searchlight platform

Compass and rangefinder platform

Ship's wheel

Leading block

Tripod mast

Navigating bridge

Boat winch

Conning tower

Captain's shelter/ chart house

Arms of Brazil

Weather shutter for gun

"F" turret

Jack staff

12 in (30 cm) gun

Skylight

Stem (false ram bow)

Porthole

Belt armor

Forward accommodation ladder

Sighting hood

"A" turret

Turret barbette

Open gun mounting

4.7 in (12 cm) gun

Steam launch

Guest boat boom

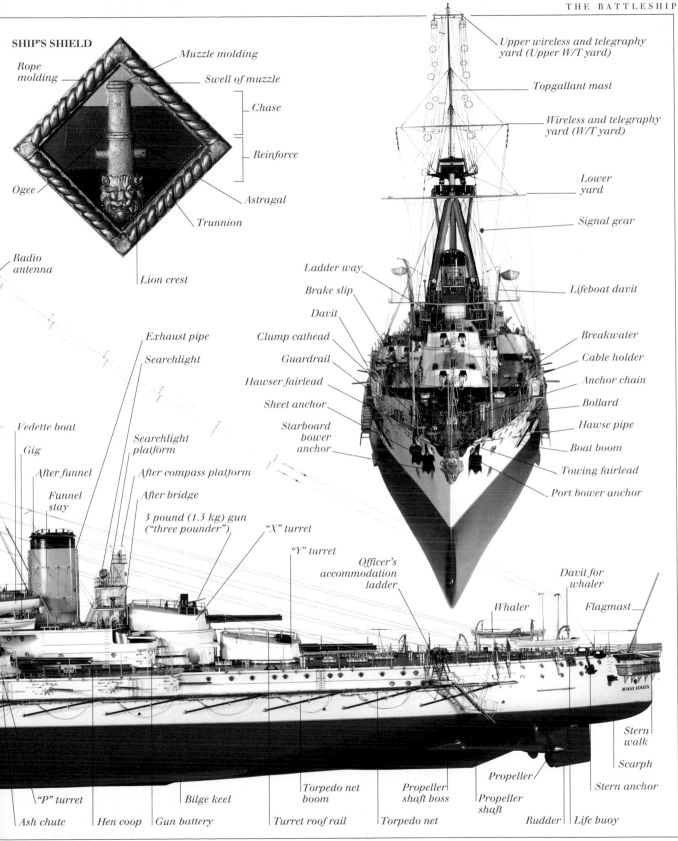

SHIP'S SHIELD

Rope molding

Muzzle molding

Swell of muzzle

Chase

Reinforce

Ogee

Astragal

Trunnion

Lion crest

Radio antenna

Upper wireless and telegraphy yard (Upper W/T yard)

Topgallant mast

Wireless and telegraphy yard (W/T yard)

Lower yard

Signal gear

Ladder way

Lifeboat davit

Brake slip

Davit

Breakwater

Clump cathead

Cable holder

Guardrail

Anchor chain

Hawser fairlead

Bollard

Sheet anchor

Hawse pipe

Starboard bower anchor

Boat boom

Towing fairlead

Port bower anchor

Exhaust pipe

Searchlight

Searchlight platform

After compass platform

After bridge

3 pound (1.3 kg) gun ("three pounder")

"X" turret

"Y" turret

Officer's accommodation ladder

Davit for whaler

Whaler

Flagmast

Vedette boat

Gig

After funnel

Funnel stay

MINAS GERAES

Stern walk

Scarph

Stern anchor

"P" turret

Ash chute

Hen coop

Gun battery

Torpedo net boom

Turret roof rail

Propeller shaft boss

Torpedo net

Propeller

Propeller shaft

Rudder

Life buoy

Frigates and submarines

FROM THE MID-19TH CENTURY, ARMORED SHIPS provided a new challenge to enemy craft. In response, huge revolving gun turrets were developed. These could shoot in any direction, were loaded quickly from the breech, and fired exploding shells. Today's fighting ships, like the Royal Navy frigate opposite, also carry missile launchers and helicopters. Submarines operate underwater, have great speed, and some can fire missiles while submerged. A nuclear sub can operate for several years without refueling.

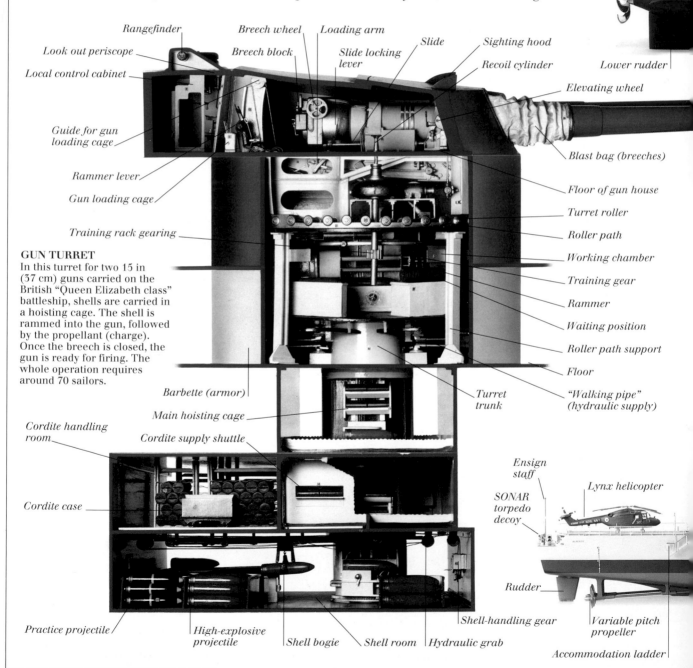

Stabilizer fin

Aft hydroplane

Propeller

Lower rudder

Rangefinder

Look out periscope

Local control cabinet

Breech wheel

Breech block

Loading arm

Slide locking lever

Slide

Sighting hood

Recoil cylinder

Elevating wheel

Guide for gun loading cage

Rammer lever

Gun loading cage

Training rack gearing

Blast bag (breeches)

Floor of gun house

Turret roller

Roller path

Working chamber

Training gear

Rammer

Waiting position

Roller path support

Floor

"Walking pipe" (hydraulic supply)

GUN TURRET
In this turret for two 15 in (37 cm) guns carried on the British "Queen Elizabeth class" battleship, shells are carried in a hoisting cage. The shell is rammed into the gun, followed by the propellant (charge). Once the breech is closed, the gun is ready for firing. The whole operation requires around 70 sailors.

Barbette (armor)

Main hoisting cage

Turret trunk

Cordite handling room

Cordite supply shuttle

Ensign staff

SONAR torpedo decoy

Lynx helicopter

Cordite case

Practice projectile

High-explosive projectile

Shell bogie

Shell room

Hydraulic grab

Shell-handling gear

Rudder

Variable pitch propeller

Accommodation ladder

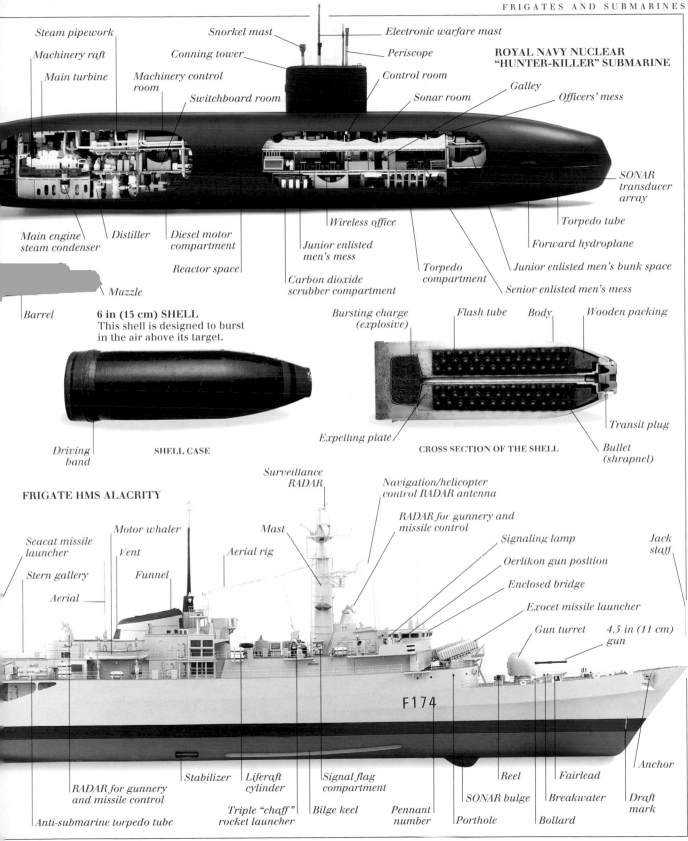

Steam pipework

Machinery raft

Main turbine

Machinery control room

Switchboard room

Snorkel mast

Conning tower

Electronic warfare mast

Periscope

Control room

Sonar room

Galley

Officers' mess

ROYAL NAVY NUCLEAR "HUNTER-KILLER" SUBMARINE

SONAR transducer array

Torpedo tube

Forward hydroplane

Junior enlisted men's bunk space

Senior enlisted men's mess

Main engine steam condenser

Distiller

Diesel motor compartment

Reactor space

Wireless office

Junior enlisted men's mess

Carbon dioxide scrubber compartment

Torpedo compartment

Muzzle

Barrel

6 in (15 cm) SHELL
This shell is designed to burst in the air above its target.

Bursting charge (explosive)

Flash tube

Body

Wooden packing

Transit plug

Driving band

SHELL CASE

Expelling plate

CROSS SECTION OF THE SHELL

Bullet (shrapnel)

FRIGATE HMS ALACRITY

Surveillance RADAR

Navigation/helicopter control RADAR antenna

RADAR for gunnery and missile control

Signaling lamp

Jack staff

Seacat missile launcher

Motor whaler

Mast

Oerlikon gun position

Vent

Aerial rig

Enclosed bridge

Stern gallery

Funnel

Exocet missile launcher

Aerial

Gun turret

4.5 in (11 cm) gun

F174

Anchor

RADAR for gunnery and missile control

Stabilizer

Liferaft cylinder

Signal flag compartment

Reel

Fairlead

Anti-submarine torpedo tube

Triple "chaff" rocket launcher

Bilge keel

Pennant number

SONAR bulge

Porthole

Breakwater

Bollard

Draft mark

Pioneers of flight

FLIGHT HAS FASCINATED MANKIND for centuries, and countless unsuccessful flying machines have been designed. The first successful flight was made by the French Montgolfier brothers in 1783, when they flew a balloon over Paris. The next major advance was the development of gliders, notably by the Englishman Sir George Cayley, who in 1845 designed the first glider to make a sustained flight, and by the German Otto Lilienthal, who became known as the world's first pilot because he managed to achieve controlled flights. However, powered flight did not become a practical possibility until the invention of lightweight, gas-driven internal-combustion engines at the end of the 19th century. Then, in 1903, the American brothers Orville and Wilbur Wright made the first powered flight in their Wright Flyer biplane, which used a four-cylinder, gas-driven engine. Aircraft design advanced rapidly, and in 1909 the Frenchman Louis Blériot made his pioneering flight across the English Channel (see pp. 400-401). The American Glenn Curtiss also achieved several "firsts" in his Model-D Pusher and its variants, most notably winning the world's first competition for airspeed at Reims in 1909.

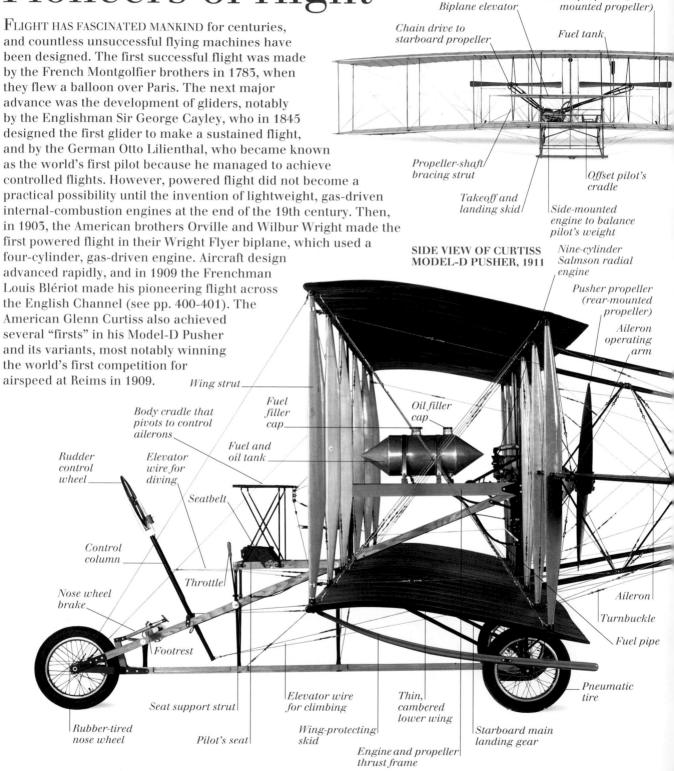

FRONT VIEW OF WRIGHT FLYER, 1903

Biplane elevator

Pusher propeller (rear-mounted propeller)

Chain drive to starboard propeller

Fuel tank

Propeller-shaft bracing strut

Takeoff and landing skid

Offset pilot's cradle

Side-mounted engine to balance pilot's weight

SIDE VIEW OF CURTISS MODEL-D PUSHER, 1911

Nine-cylinder Salmson radial engine

Pusher propeller (rear-mounted propeller)

Aileron operating arm

Wing strut

Body cradle that pivots to control ailerons

Fuel filler cap

Oil filler cap

Fuel and oil tank

Rudder control wheel

Elevator wire for diving

Seatbelt

Control column

Throttle

Nose wheel brake

Footrest

Aileron

Turnbuckle

Fuel pipe

Pneumatic tire

Rubber-tired nose wheel

Seat support strut

Pilot's seat

Elevator wire for climbing

Wing-protecting skid

Thin, cambered lower wing

Engine and propeller thrust frame

Starboard main landing gear

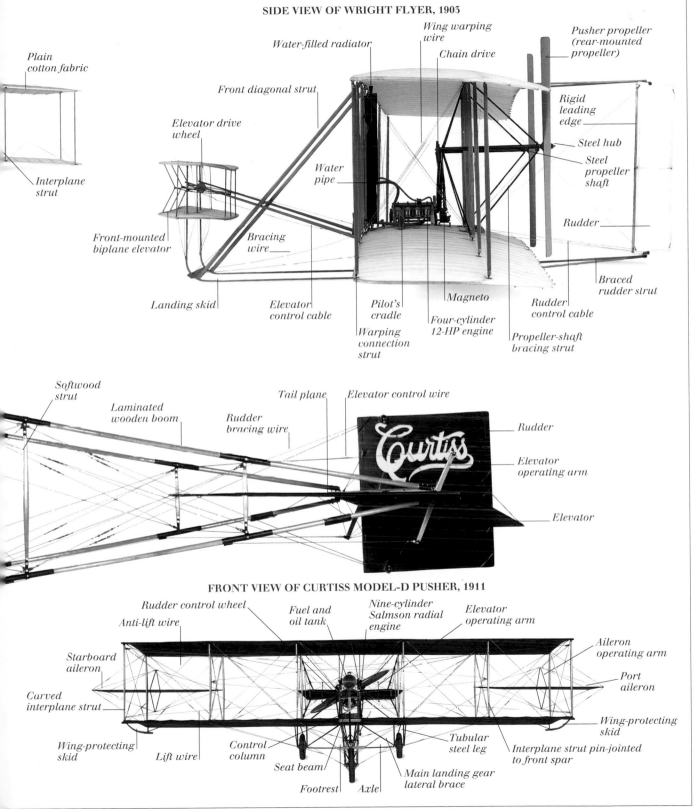

SIDE VIEW OF WRIGHT FLYER, 1903

Plain cotton fabric

Interplane strut

Water-filled radiator

Wing warping wire

Pusher propeller (rear-mounted propeller)

Front diagonal strut

Chain drive

Rigid leading edge

Elevator drive wheel

Steel hub

Steel propeller shaft

Water pipe

Front-mounted biplane elevator

Bracing wire

Rudder

Landing skid

Elevator control cable

Pilot's cradle

Magneto

Rudder control cable

Braced rudder strut

Warping connection strut

Four-cylinder 12-HP engine

Propeller-shaft bracing strut

Softwood strut

Tail plane

Elevator control wire

Laminated wooden boom

Rudder bracing wire

Rudder

Elevator operating arm

Elevator

FRONT VIEW OF CURTISS MODEL-D PUSHER, 1911

Rudder control wheel

Fuel and oil tank

Nine-cylinder Salmson radial engine

Elevator operating arm

Anti-lift wire

Aileron operating arm

Starboard aileron

Port aileron

Curved interplane strut

Wing-protecting skid

Wing-protecting skid

Lift wire

Control column

Tubular steel leg

Interplane strut pin-jointed to front spar

Seat beam

Main landing gear lateral brace

Footrest

Axle

Early monoplanes

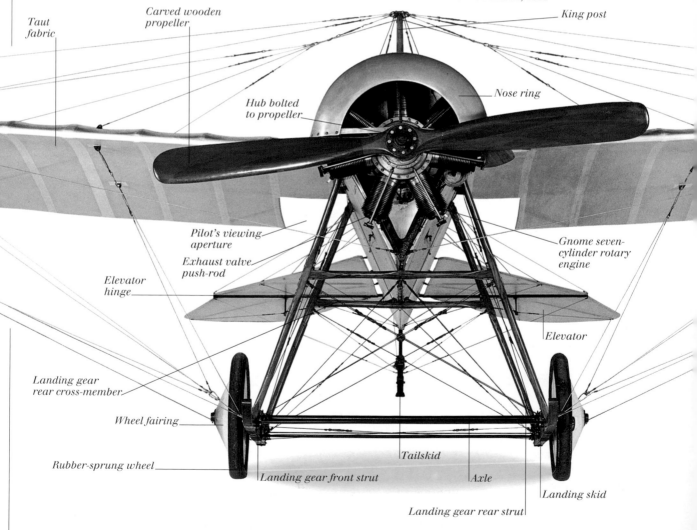

RUMPLER MONOPLANE, 1908

MONOPLANES HAVE ONE WING on each side of the fuselage. The principal disadvantage of this arrangement in early wooden-framed aircraft was that single wings were weak. They required strong wires to brace them to king posts above and below the fuselage. However, single wings also had advantages: they experienced less drag than multiple wings, allowing greater speed; they also made aircraft more maneuverable because single wings were easier to warp (twist) than double wings, and warping the wings was how pilots controlled the roll of early aircraft. By 1912, the French pilot Louis Blériot had used a monoplane to make the first flight across the English Channel, and the Briton Robert Blackburn and the Frenchman Armand Deperdussin had proved the greater speed of monoplanes. However, a spate of crashes caused by broken wings discouraged monoplane production, except in Germany, where all-metal monoplanes were developed in 1917. The wings of all-metal monoplanes did not need strengthening by struts or bracing wires, but despite this, such planes were not widely adopted until the 1930s.

FRONT VIEW OF BLACKBURN MONOPLANE, 1912

Taut fabric

Carved wooden propeller

King post

Hub bolted to propeller

Nose ring

Pilot's viewing aperture

Gnome seven-cylinder rotary engine

Exhaust valve push-rod

Elevator hinge

Elevator

Landing gear rear cross-member

Wheel fairing

Rubber-sprung wheel

Tailskid

Landing gear front strut

Axle

Landing skid

Landing gear rear strut

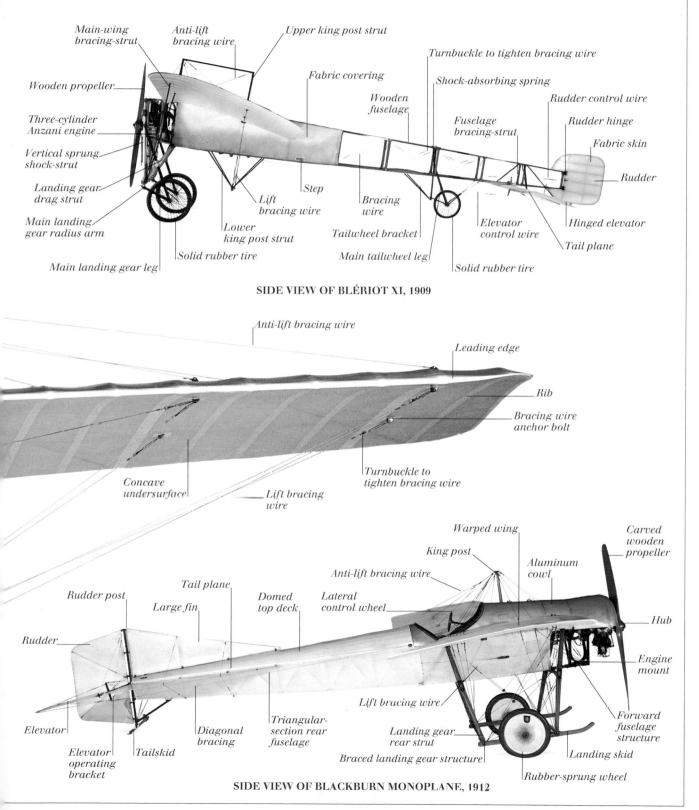

Main-wing bracing-strut

Anti-lift bracing wire

Upper king post strut

Turnbuckle to tighten bracing wire

Fabric covering

Shock-absorbing spring

Wooden propeller

Wooden fuselage

Rudder control wire

Rudder hinge

Three-cylinder Anzani engine

Fuselage bracing-strut

Fabric skin

Vertical sprung shock-strut

Rudder

Landing gear drag strut

Step

Rudder

Main landing gear radius arm

Lift bracing wire

Bracing wire

Elevator control wire

Hinged elevator

Lower king post strut

Tailwheel bracket

Tail plane

Main landing gear leg

Solid rubber tire

Main tailwheel leg

Solid rubber tire

SIDE VIEW OF BLÉRIOT XI, 1909

Anti-lift bracing wire

Leading edge

Rib

Bracing wire anchor bolt

Concave undersurface

Turnbuckle to tighten bracing wire

Lift bracing wire

Warped wing

Carved wooden propeller

King post

Aluminum cowl

Rudder post

Anti-lift bracing wire

Tail plane

Domed top deck

Lateral control wheel

Large fin

Hub

Rudder

Engine mount

Elevator

Lift bracing wire

Forward fuselage structure

Elevator operating bracket

Tailskid

Diagonal bracing

Triangular-section rear fuselage

Landing gear rear strut

Braced landing gear structure

Landing skid

Rubber-sprung wheel

SIDE VIEW OF BLACKBURN MONOPLANE, 1912

Biplanes and triplanes

BIPLANES DOMINATED AIRCRAFT DESIGN until the 1930s, largely because some early monoplanes (see pp. 400-401) were too fragile to withstand the stresses of flight. The struts between biplanes' wings made the wings strong compared with those of early monoplanes, although the greater surface area of biplanes' wings increased drag and reduced speed. Many aircraft designers also developed triplanes, which had a particular advantage over biplanes: more wings meant a shorter wingspan to achieve the same lifting power, and a shorter wingspan gave greater maneuverability. Triplanes were most successful as fighters during World War I, the German Fokker triplane being a notable example. However, the greater maneuverability of triplanes was no advantage for normal flying, so most manufacturers continued to make biplanes. Many other aircraft designs were attempted. Some were quadruplanes, with four pairs of wings. Some had tandem wings (two pairs of monoplane wings, one behind the other). One of the most bizarre designs was by the Englishman Horatio Phillips; it had 20 sets of narrow wings and looked rather like a Venetian blind.

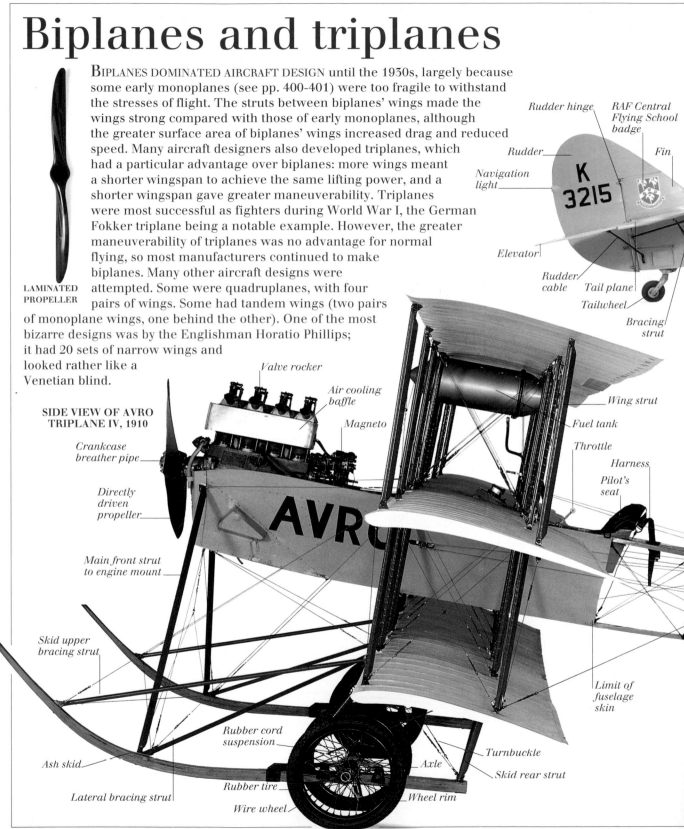

LAMINATED PROPELLER

Rudder hinge

RAF Central Flying School badge

Rudder

Fin

Navigation light

K 3215

Elevator

Rudder cable

Tail plane

Tailwheel

Bracing strut

Wing strut

SIDE VIEW OF AVRO TRIPLANE IV, 1910

Valve rocker

Air cooling baffle

Magneto

Fuel tank

Throttle

Crankcase breather pipe

Harness

Pilot's seat

Directly driven propeller

Main front strut to engine mount

Skid upper bracing strut

Limit of fuselage skin

Ash skid

Rubber cord suspension

Turnbuckle

Axle

Skid rear strut

Lateral bracing strut

Rubber tire

Wheel rim

Wire wheel

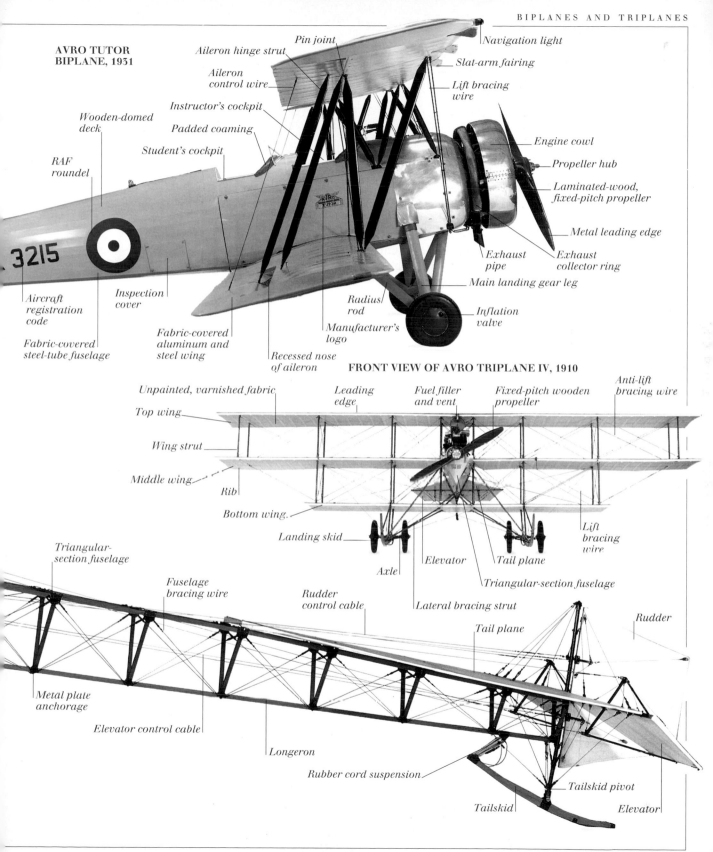

**AVRO TUTOR
BIPLANE, 1931**

Pin joint

Aileron hinge strut

Aileron
control wire

Navigation light

Slat-arm fairing

Lift bracing
wire

Instructor's cockpit

Wooden-domed
deck

Padded coaming

Student's cockpit

Engine cowl

Propeller hub

Laminated-wood,
fixed-pitch propeller

RAF
roundel

Metal leading edge

Exhaust
collector ring

Exhaust
pipe

Main landing gear leg

3215

Inflation
valve

Aircraft
registration
code

Inspection
cover

Radius
rod

Fabric-covered
steel-tube fuselage

Fabric-covered
aluminum and
steel wing

Manufacturer's
logo

Recessed nose
of aileron

FRONT VIEW OF AVRO TRIPLANE IV, 1910

Unpainted, varnished fabric

Leading
edge

Fuel filler
and vent

Fixed-pitch wooden
propeller

Anti-lift
bracing wire

Top wing

Wing strut

Middle wing

Rib

Bottom wing.

Landing skid

Axle

Elevator

Tail plane

Lift
bracing
wire

Triangular-section
fuselage

Fuselage
bracing wire

Rudder
control cable

Tail plane

Rudder

Triangular-section fuselage

Lateral bracing strut

Metal plate
anchorage

Elevator control cable

Longeron

Rubber cord suspension

Tailskid pivot

Tailskid

Elevator

World War I aircraft

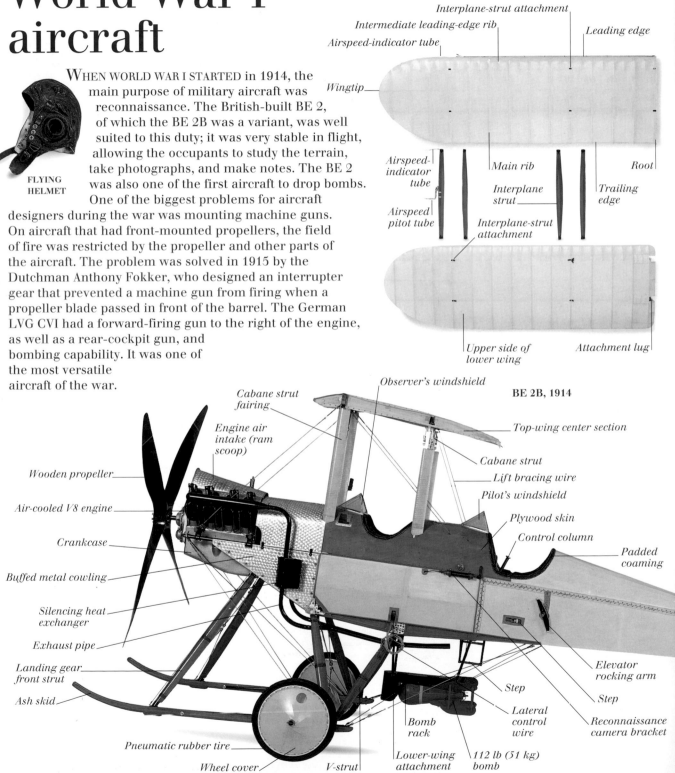

WHEN WORLD WAR I STARTED in 1914, the main purpose of military aircraft was reconnaissance. The British-built BE 2, of which the BE 2B was a variant, was well suited to this duty; it was very stable in flight, allowing the occupants to study the terrain, take photographs, and make notes. The BE 2 was also one of the first aircraft to drop bombs. One of the biggest problems for aircraft designers during the war was mounting machine guns. On aircraft that had front-mounted propellers, the field of fire was restricted by the propeller and other parts of the aircraft. The problem was solved in 1915 by the Dutchman Anthony Fokker, who designed an interrupter gear that prevented a machine gun from firing when a propeller blade passed in front of the barrel. The German LVG CVI had a forward-firing gun to the right of the engine, as well as a rear-cockpit gun, and bombing capability. It was one of the most versatile aircraft of the war.

FLYING HELMET

PORT WINGS FROM A BE 2B

Interplane-strut attachment

Intermediate leading-edge rib

Airspeed-indicator tube

Leading edge

Wingtip

Airspeed-indicator tube

Main rib

Root

Interplane strut

Trailing edge

Airspeed pitot tube

Interplane-strut attachment

Upper side of lower wing

Attachment lug

BE 2B, 1914

Observer's windshield

Cabane strut fairing

Engine air intake (ram scoop)

Top-wing center section

Cabane strut

Wooden propeller

Lift bracing wire

Air-cooled V8 engine

Pilot's windshield

Plywood skin

Crankcase

Control column

Padded coaming

Buffed metal cowling

Silencing heat exchanger

Exhaust pipe

Landing gear front strut

Elevator rocking arm

Ash skid

Step

Step

Lateral control wire

Reconnaissance camera bracket

Pneumatic rubber tire

Bomb rack

Wheel cover

V-strut

Lower-wing attachment

112 lb (51 kg) bomb

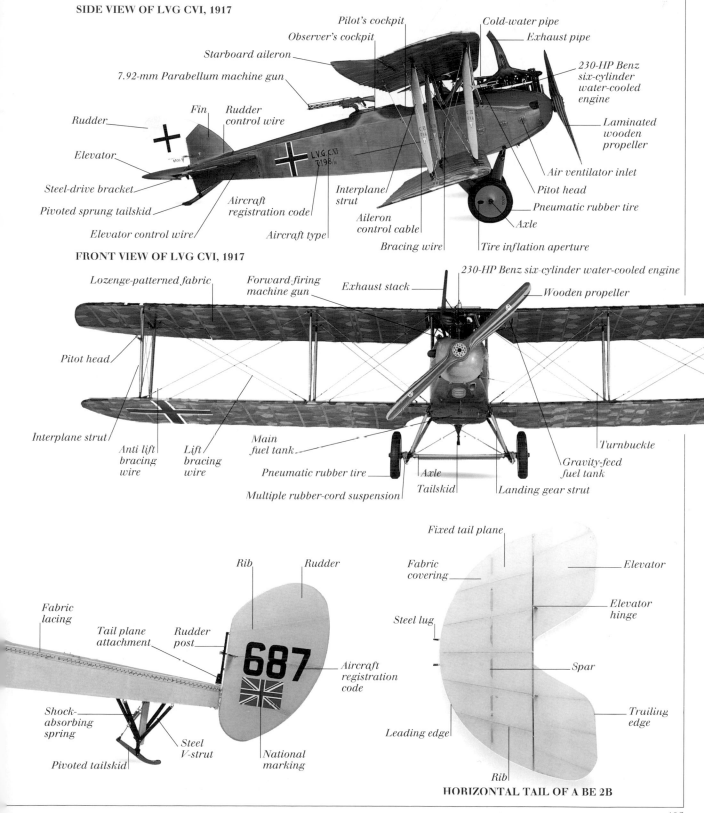

SIDE VIEW OF LVG CVI, 1917

Pilot's cockpit

Observer's cockpit

Cold-water pipe

Exhaust pipe

Starboard aileron

7.92-mm Parabellum machine gun

230-HP Benz
six-cylinder
water-cooled
engine

Rudder

Fin

Rudder
control wire

Laminated
wooden
propeller

Elevator

Steel-drive bracket

Pivoted sprung tailskid

Aircraft
registration code

Interplane
strut

Air ventilator inlet

Pitot head

Pneumatic rubber tire

Aileron
control cable

Axle

Elevator control wire

Aircraft type

Bracing wire

Tire inflation aperture

FRONT VIEW OF LVG CVI, 1917

Lozenge-patterned fabric

Forward-firing
machine gun

230-HP Benz six-cylinder water-cooled engine

Exhaust stack

Wooden propeller

Pitot head

Interplane strut

Anti lift
bracing
wire

Lift
bracing
wire

Main
fuel tank

Turnbuckle

Gravity-feed
fuel tank

Pneumatic rubber tire

Axle

Tailskid

Landing gear strut

Multiple rubber-cord suspension

Fixed tail plane

Rib

Rudder

Fabric
covering

Elevator

Fabric
lacing

Steel lug

Elevator
hinge

Tail plane
attachment

Rudder
post

Aircraft
registration
code

Spar

Shock-
absorbing
spring

Steel
V-strut

Leading edge

Trailing
edge

Pivoted tailskid

National
marking

Rib

HORIZONTAL TAIL OF A BE 2B

Early passenger aircraft

FRONT VIEW OF LOCKHEED ELECTRA, 1934

UNTIL THE 1930s, most passenger aircraft were biplanes, with two pairs of wings and a wooden or metal framework covered with fabric or, sometimes, plywood. Such aircraft were restricted to low speeds and low altitudes because of the drag on their wings. Many had an open cockpit, situated behind or in front of an enclosed—but unpressurized—cabin that carried a maximum of 10 people. The passengers usually sat in wicker chairs that were not bolted to the floor, and the journey could be bumpy when flying through turbulence. Warm clothing, and earplugs to reduce the effects of prolonged noise, were often required. During the 1930s, powerful, streamlined, all-metal monoplanes, such as the Lockheed Electra shown here, became widespread. By 1939, the advent of pressurized cabins allowed fast flights at high altitudes, where there is less turbulence. Flying boats were still necessary on many routes until 1945 because of inadequate runways and the frequency of emergency sea landings. World War II, however, resulted in enough good runways being built for land planes to become standard on all major airline routes.

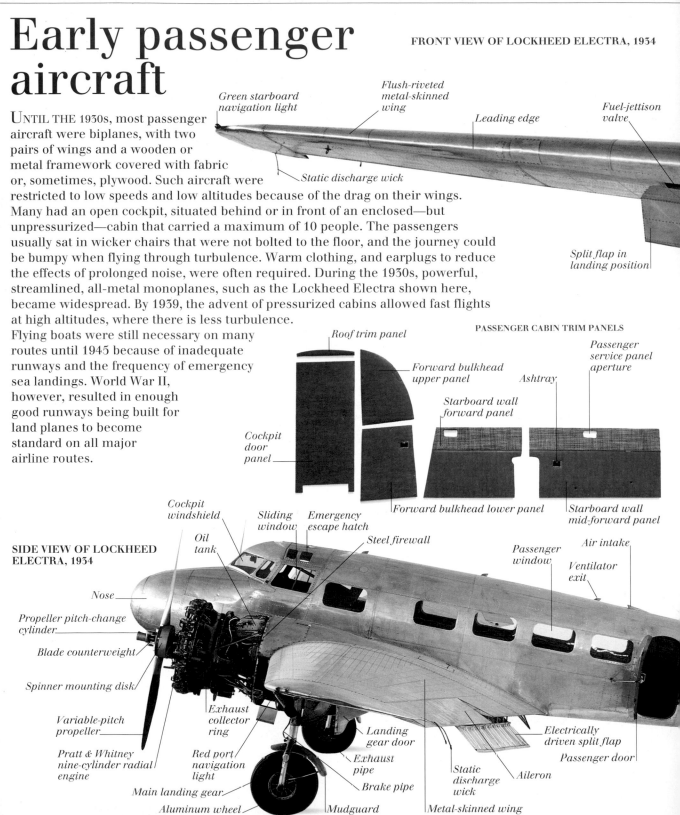

Green starboard navigation light

Flush-riveted metal-skinned wing

Leading edge

Fuel-jettison valve

Static discharge wick

Split flap in landing position

Roof trim panel

PASSENGER CABIN TRIM PANELS

Forward bulkhead upper panel

Passenger service panel aperture

Ashtray

Starboard wall forward panel

Cockpit door panel

Forward bulkhead lower panel

Starboard wall mid-forward panel

Cockpit windshield

Sliding window

Emergency escape hatch

Steel firewall

Air intake

Passenger window

Ventilator exit

Oil tank

SIDE VIEW OF LOCKHEED ELECTRA, 1934

Nose

Propeller pitch-change cylinder

Blade counterweight

Spinner mounting disk

Variable-pitch propeller

Pratt & Whitney nine-cylinder radial engine

Exhaust collector ring

Red port navigation light

Main landing gear

Aluminum wheel

Mudguard

Landing gear door

Exhaust pipe

Brake pipe

Static discharge wick

Aileron

Electrically driven split flap

Passenger door

Metal-skinned wing

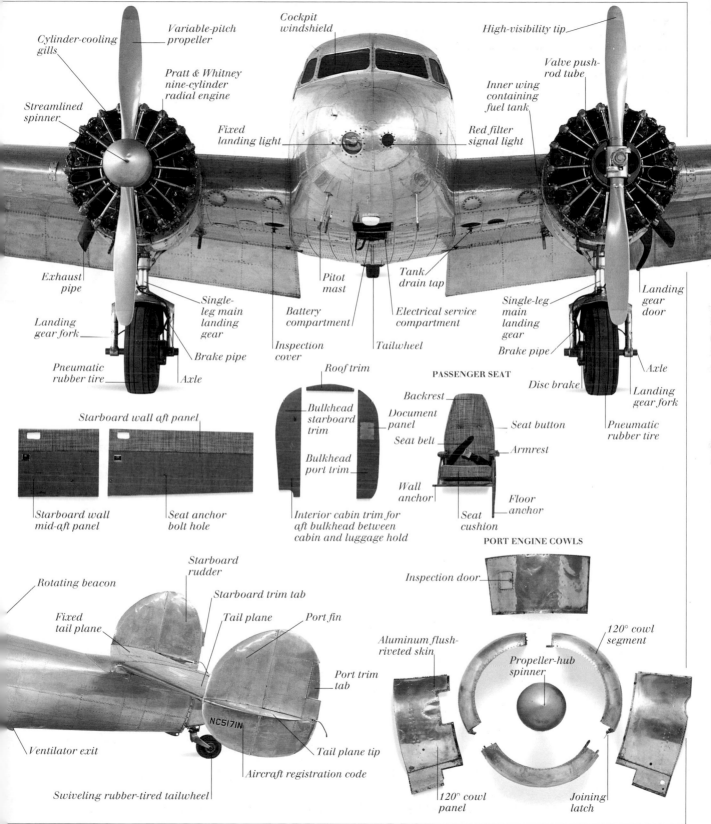

Cylinder-cooling gills

Variable-pitch propeller

Cockpit windshield

High-visibility tip

Streamlined spinner

Pratt & Whitney nine-cylinder radial engine

Valve push-rod tube

Inner wing containing fuel tank

Fixed landing light

Red filter signal light

Exhaust pipe

Single-leg main landing gear

Pitot mast

Tank drain tap

Single-leg main landing gear

Landing gear door

Landing gear fork

Battery compartment

Electrical service compartment

Brake pipe

Axle

Pneumatic rubber tire

Brake pipe

Axle

Inspection cover

Tailwheel

Disc brake

Landing gear fork

Roof trim

PASSENGER SEAT

Pneumatic rubber tire

Starboard wall aft panel

Bulkhead starboard trim

Backrest

Document panel

Seat button

Seat belt

Armrest

Bulkhead port trim

Starboard wall mid-aft panel

Seat anchor bolt hole

Interior cabin trim for aft bulkhead between cabin and luggage hold

Wall anchor

Seat cushion

Floor anchor

Seat anchor

PORT ENGINE COWLS

Inspection door

Rotating beacon

Starboard rudder

Starboard trim tab

Fixed tail plane

Tail plane

Port fin

Aluminum flush-riveted skin

120° cowl segment

Propeller-hub spinner

Port trim tab

Ventilator exit

NC517IN

Tail plane tip

Swiveling rubber-tired tailwheel

Aircraft registration code

120° cowl panel

Joining latch

World War II aircraft

When World War II began in 1939, air forces had already replaced most of their fabric-skinned biplanes with all-metal stressed-skin monoplanes. Aircraft played a far greater role in military operations during World War II than ever before. The wide range of aircraft duties and the introduction of radar tracking and guidance systems put pressure on designers to improve aircraft performance. The main areas of improvement were speed, range, and engine power. Bombers became larger and more powerful—converting from two to four engines—in order to carry a heavier bomb load; the U.S. B-17 Flying Fortress could carry up to 6 tons of bombs over a distance of about 2,000 miles (3,200 km). Some aircraft increased their range by using drop tanks (fuel tanks that were jettisoned when empty to reduce drag). Fighters needed speed and maneuverability: the Hawker Tempest shown here had a maximum speed of 435 mph (700 kph) and was one of the few Allied aircraft capable of catching the German jet-powered V1 "flying bomb." By 1944, Britain had introduced its first turbojet-powered aircraft, the Gloster Meteor fighter, and Germany had introduced the fastest fighter in the world, the turbojet-powered Me 262, which had a maximum speed of 540 mph (868 kph).

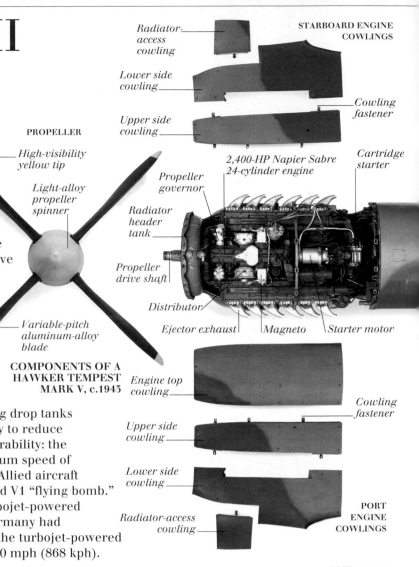

PROPELLER

High-visibility yellow tip

Light-alloy propeller spinner

Variable-pitch aluminum-alloy blade

COMPONENTS OF A HAWKER TEMPEST MARK V, c.1943

Radiator-access cowling

Lower side cowling

Upper side cowling

STARBOARD ENGINE COWLINGS

Cowling fastener

Cartridge starter

Propeller governor

Radiator header tank

Propeller drive shaft

2,400-HP Napier Sabre 24-cylinder engine

Distributor

Ejector exhaust

Magneto

Starter motor

Engine top cowling

Upper side cowling

Lower side cowling

Radiator-access cowling

Cowling fastener

PORT ENGINE COWLINGS

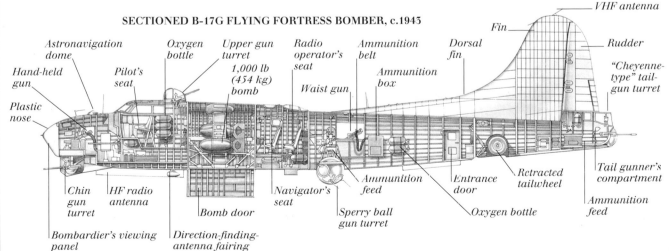

SECTIONED B-17G FLYING FORTRESS BOMBER, c.1943

Astronavigation dome

Hand-held gun

Plastic nose

Pilot's seat

Oxygen bottle

Upper gun turret

1,000 lb (454 kg) bomb

Radio operator's seat

Waist gun

Ammunition belt

Ammunition box

Dorsal fin

Fin

VHF antenna

Rudder

"Cheyenne-type" tail-gun turret

Chin gun turret

HF radio antenna

Bomb door

Direction-finding-antenna fairing

Navigator's seat

Ammunition feed

Sperry ball gun turret

Entrance door

Oxygen bottle

Retracted tailwheel

Tail gunner's compartment

Ammunition feed

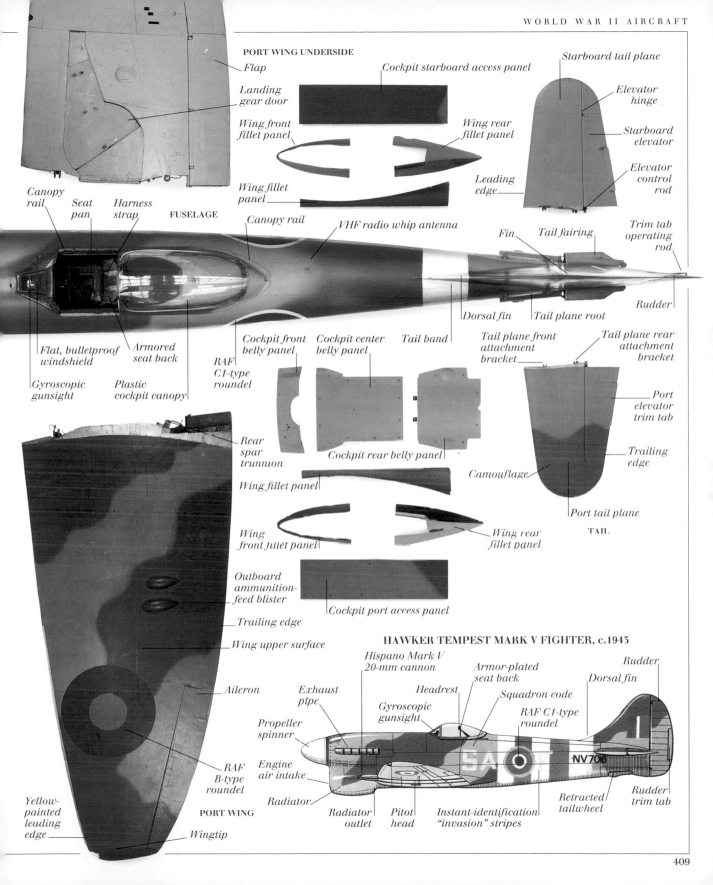

PORT WING UNDERSIDE

Flap

Cockpit starboard access panel

Starboard tail plane

Landing gear door

Elevator hinge

Wing front fillet panel

Wing rear fillet panel

Starboard elevator

Leading edge

Elevator control rod

Wing fillet panel

FUSELAGE

Canopy rail

Seat pan

Harness strap

Canopy rail

VHF radio whip antenna

Fin

Tail fairing

Trim tab operating rod

Dorsal fin

Tail plane root

Rudder

Flat, bulletproof windshield

Armored seat back

Tail band

Tail plane front attachment bracket

Tail plane rear attachment bracket

Gyroscopic gunsight

Plastic cockpit canopy

RAF C1-type roundel

Cockpit front belly panel

Cockpit center belly panel

Port elevator trim tab

Rear spar trunnion

Cockpit rear belly panel

Camouflage

Trailing edge

Wing fillet panel

Port tail plane

Wing front fillet panel

Wing rear fillet panel

TAIL

Outboard ammunition-feed blister

Cockpit port access panel

Trailing edge

Wing upper surface

HAWKER TEMPEST MARK V FIGHTER, c.1943

Hispano Mark V 20-mm cannon

Armor-plated seat back

Rudder

Aileron

Exhaust pipe

Headrest

Squadron code

Dorsal fin

Propeller spinner

Gyroscopic gunsight

RAF C1-type roundel

RAF B-type roundel

Engine air intake

Radiator

Yellow-painted leading edge

Radiator outlet

Pitot head

Instant-identification "invasion" stripes

Retracted tailwheel

Rudder trim tab

Wingtip

PORT WING

Modern piston aircraft engines

PISTON ENGINES today are used mainly to power the vast numbers of light aircraft and ultralights, as well as crop sprayers and crop dusters, small helicopters, and fire-bombers (which dump water on large fires). Virtually all heavier aircraft are now powered by jet engines. Modern piston aircraft engines work on the same basic principles as the engine used by the Wright brothers in the first powered flight in 1903. However, today's engines are more sophisticated than earlier engines. For example, modern aircraft engines may use a two-stroke or a four-stroke combustion cycle; they may have from one to nine air- or liquid-cooled cylinders, which may be arranged horizontally, in-line, in V formation, or radially; and they may drive the aircraft's propeller either directly or through a reduction gearbox. One of the more unconventional types of modern aircraft engine is the rotary engine shown here, which has a trilobate (three-sided) rotor spinning in a chamber shaped like a fat figure-eight.

MID WEST TWO-STROKE, THREE-CYLINDER ENGINE

MID WEST 75-HP TWO-STROKE, THREE-CYLINDER ENGINE

Spark plug
Coolant outlet
Cylinder head
Exhaust manifold
Piston
Cylinder barrel
Exhaust port
Cylinder liner
Upper crankcase

Reduction gearbox
Driven gear
Propeller drive flange
Torsional vibration damper
Sprag clutch
Gearbox mounting plate

Gearbox drive splines
Small end
Connecting rod (con-rod)
Big end
Counterweight
Crankshaft
Lower crankcase

Pump drive belt
Coolant pump
Generator rotor
Ignition trigger housing
Stator
Engine mounting plate

ROTOR AND HOUSINGS OF A MID WEST SINGLE-ROTOR ENGINE

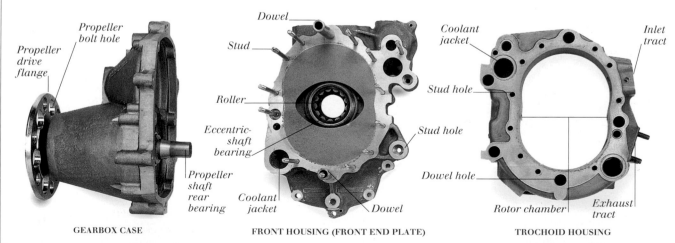

Propeller bolt hole
Propeller drive flange
Propeller shaft rear bearing

GEARBOX CASE

Dowel
Stud
Roller
Eccentric-shaft bearing
Coolant jacket
Dowel

FRONT HOUSING (FRONT END PLATE)

Coolant jacket
Inlet tract
Stud hole
Stud hole
Dowel hole
Rotor chamber
Exhaust tract

TROCHOID HOUSING

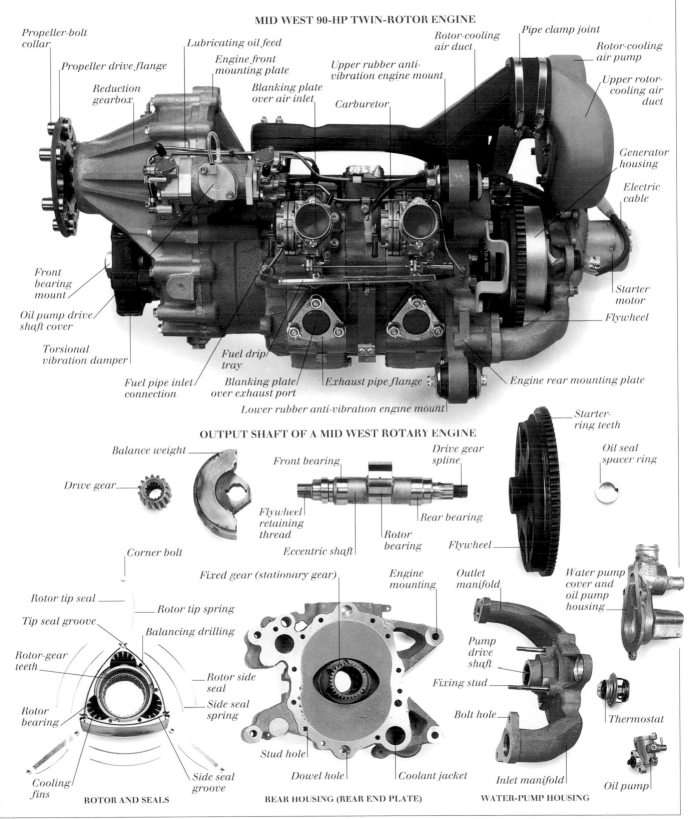

MID WEST 90-HP TWIN-ROTOR ENGINE

Propeller-bolt collar

Propeller drive flange

Reduction gearbox

Lubricating oil feed

Engine front mounting plate

Blanking plate over air inlet

Carburetor

Upper rubber anti-vibration engine mount

Rotor-cooling air duct

Pipe clamp joint

Rotor-cooling air pump

Upper rotor-cooling air duct

Generator housing

Electric cable

Starter motor

Flywheel

Front bearing mount

Oil pump drive shaft cover

Torsional vibration damper

Fuel pipe inlet connection

Fuel drip tray

Blanking plate over exhaust port

Exhaust pipe flange

Lower rubber anti-vibration engine mount

Engine rear mounting plate

OUTPUT SHAFT OF A MID WEST ROTARY ENGINE

Balance weight

Drive gear

Front bearing

Drive gear spline

Flywheel retaining thread

Eccentric shaft

Rotor bearing

Rear bearing

Flywheel

Starter-ring teeth

Oil seal spacer ring

Corner bolt

Rotor tip seal

Tip seal groove

Rotor-gear teeth

Rotor bearing

Cooling fins

Rotor tip spring

Balancing drilling

Rotor side seal

Side seal spring

Side seal groove

Fixed gear (stationary gear)

Engine mounting

Stud hole

Dowel hole

Coolant jacket

Outlet manifold

Pump drive shaft

Fixing stud

Bolt hole

Inlet manifold

Water pump cover and oil pump housing

Thermostat

Oil pump

ROTOR AND SEALS

REAR HOUSING (REAR END PLATE)

WATER-PUMP HOUSING

Modern jetliners 1

BAE 146 JETLINER

MODERN JETLINERS HAVE ENABLED ordinary people to travel to places where once only the wealthy could afford to go. Compared with the first jetliners (which were introduced in the 1940s), modern jetliners are much quieter, burn fuel more efficiently, and produce less air pollution. These advances are largely due to the replacement of turbojet engines with turbofan engines (see pp. 418-419). The greater power of turbofan engines at low speeds enables modern jetliners to carry more fuel and passengers than turbojet aircraft; a modern Boeing 747-400 (popularly known as a "jumbo jet") can fly 400 people for 8,500 miles (13,700 km) without needing to refuel. Jetliners fly at high altitudes, typically cruising at 26,000-36,000 ft (8,000-11,000 m), where they can use fuel efficiently and usually avoid bad weather. The pilot always controls the aircraft during takeoff and landing, but at other times the aircraft is usually controlled by an autopilot. Autopilots are complex onboard mechanisms that detect deviations from an aircraft's route and make appropriate adjustments to the flight controls. Flight decks are also equipped with radar that warns pilots of approaching hazards, such as mountain ranges, bad weather, and other aircraft.

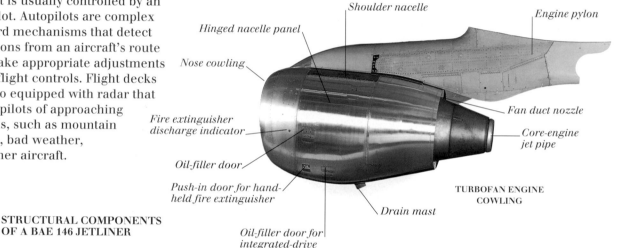

STRUCTURAL COMPONENTS OF A BAE 146 JETLINER

Shoulder nacelle

Engine pylon

Hinged nacelle panel

Nose cowling

Fan duct nozzle

Core-engine jet pipe

Fire extinguisher discharge indicator

Oil-filler door

Push-in door for hand-held fire extinguisher

Drain mast

TURBOFAN ENGINE COWLING

Oil-filler door for integrated-drive generator

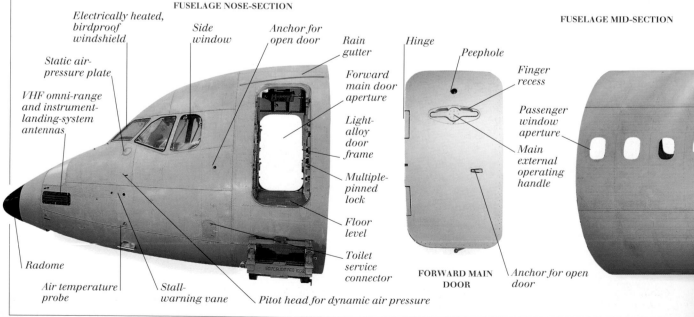

FUSELAGE NOSE-SECTION

FUSELAGE MID-SECTION

Electrically heated, birdproof windshield

Side window

Anchor for open door

Rain gutter

Hinge

Peephole

Finger recess

Static air-pressure plate

Forward main door aperture

Passenger window aperture

VHF omni-range and instrument-landing-system antennas

Light-alloy door frame

Main external operating handle

Multiple-pinned lock

Floor level

Radome

Toilet service connector

FORWARD MAIN DOOR

Anchor for open door

Air temperature probe

Stall-warning vane

Pitot head for dynamic air pressure

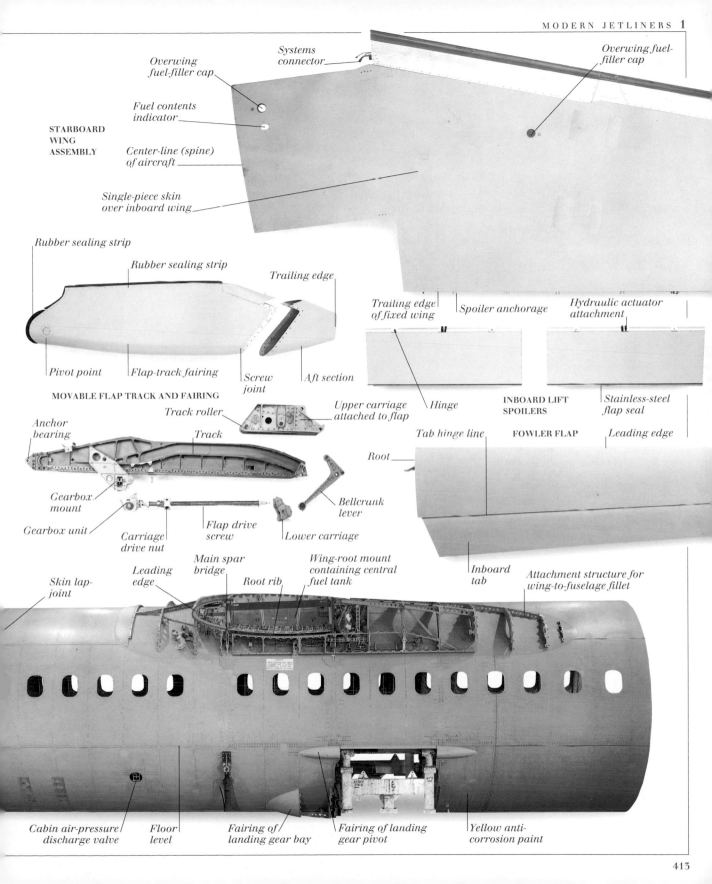

Overwing
fuel-filler cap

Systems
connector

Overwing fuel-
filler cap

Fuel contents
indicator

STARBOARD
WING
ASSEMBLY

Center-line (spine)
of aircraft

Single-piece skin
over inboard wing

Rubber sealing strip

Rubber sealing strip

Trailing edge

Trailing edge
of fixed wing

Spoiler anchorage

Hydraulic actuator
attachment

Pivot point

Flap-track fairing

Screw
joint

Aft section

Hinge

INBOARD LIFT
SPOILERS

Stainless-steel
flap seal

MOVABLE FLAP TRACK AND FAIRING

Track roller

Upper carriage
attached to flap

Tab hinge line

FOWLER FLAP

Leading edge

Anchor
bearing

Track

Root

Gearbox
mount

Gearbox unit

Carriage
drive nut

Flap drive
screw

Lower carriage

Bellcrank
lever

Skin lap-
joint

Leading
edge

Main spar
bridge

Root rib

Wing-root mount
containing central
fuel tank

Inboard
tab

Attachment structure for
wing-to-fuselage fillet

Cabin air-pressure
discharge valve

Floor
level

Fairing of
landing gear bay

Fairing of landing
gear pivot

Yellow anti-
corrosion paint

Modern jetliners 2

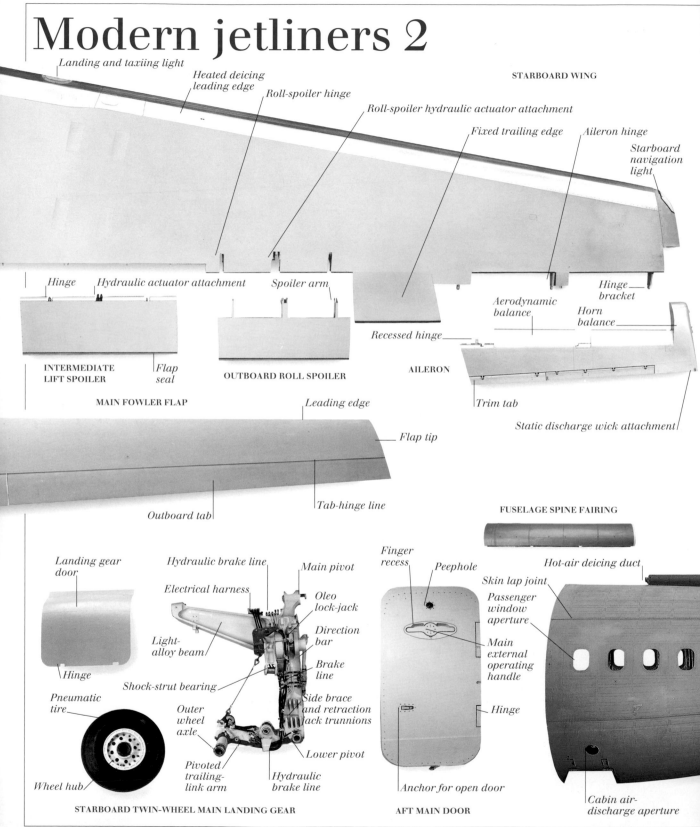

Landing and taxiing light

Heated deicing leading edge

Roll-spoiler hinge

Roll-spoiler hydraulic actuator attachment

STARBOARD WING

Fixed trailing edge

Aileron hinge

Starboard navigation light

Hinge

Hydraulic actuator attachment

Spoiler arm

Hinge bracket

Aerodynamic balance

Horn balance

Recessed hinge

INTERMEDIATE LIFT SPOILER

Flap seal

OUTBOARD ROLL SPOILER

AILERON

Trim tab

MAIN FOWLER FLAP

Static discharge wick attachment

Leading edge

Flap tip

Outboard tab

Tab-hinge line

FUSELAGE SPINE FAIRING

Landing gear door

Hydraulic brake line

Main pivot

Finger recess

Peephole

Hot-air deicing duct

Electrical harness

Oleo lock-jack

Skin lap joint

Passenger window aperture

Light-alloy beam

Direction bar

Brake line

Main external operating handle

Shock-strut bearing

Hinge

Pneumatic tire

Outer wheel axle

Side brace and retraction jack trunnions

Hinge

Pivoted trailing-link arm

Hydraulic brake line

Lower pivot

Wheel hub

Anchor for open door

Cabin air-discharge aperture

STARBOARD TWIN-WHEEL MAIN LANDING GEAR

AFT MAIN DOOR

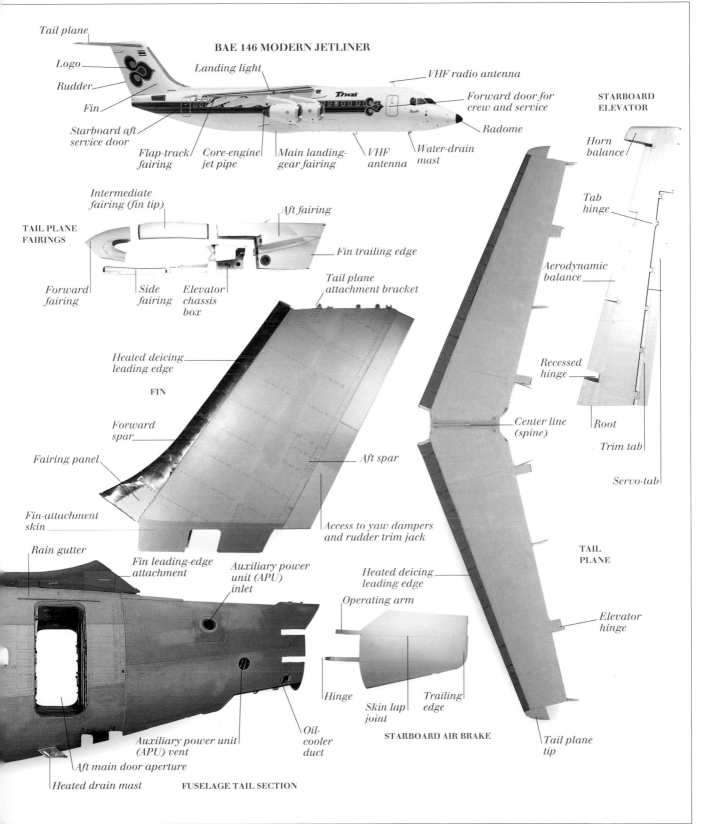

Tail plane

BAE 146 MODERN JETLINER

Logo

Landing light

Rudder

VHF radio antenna

Fin

Forward door for
crew and service

STARBOARD
ELEVATOR

Starboard aft
service door

Radome

Horn
balance

Flap-track
fairing

Core-engine
jet pipe

Main landing-
gear fairing

VHF
antenna

Water-drain
mast

Tab
hinge

Intermediate
fairing (fin tip)

Aft fairing

Aerodynamic
balance

TAIL PLANE
FAIRINGS

Fin trailing edge

Forward
fairing

Side
fairing

Elevator
chassis
box

Tail plane
attachment bracket

Recessed
hinge

Root

Heated deicing
leading edge

Center line
(spine)

Trim tab

FIN

Servo-tab

Forward
spar

Aft spar

Fairing panel

Fin-attachment
skin

Access to yaw dampers
and rudder trim jack

TAIL
PLANE

Rain gutter

Fin leading-edge
attachment

Auxiliary power
unit (APU)
inlet

Heated deicing
leading edge

Elevator
hinge

Operating arm

Auxiliary power unit
(APU) vent

Oil-
cooler
duct

Hinge

Skin lap
joint

Trailing
edge

Tail plane
tip

Aft main door aperture

Heated drain mast

FUSELAGE TAIL SECTION

STARBOARD AIR BRAKE

Supersonic jetliners

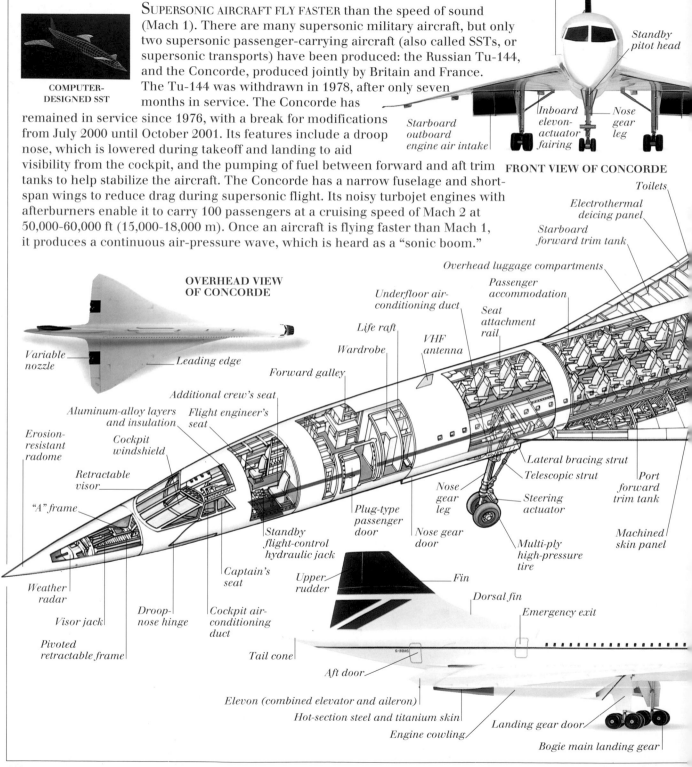

COMPUTER-DESIGNED SST

SUPERSONIC AIRCRAFT FLY FASTER than the speed of sound (Mach 1). There are many supersonic military aircraft, but only two supersonic passenger-carrying aircraft (also called SSTs, or supersonic transports) have been produced: the Russian Tu-144, and the Concorde, produced jointly by Britain and France. The Tu-144 was withdrawn in 1978, after only seven months in service. The Concorde has remained in service since 1976, with a break for modifications from July 2000 until October 2001. Its features include a droop nose, which is lowered during takeoff and landing to aid visibility from the cockpit, and the pumping of fuel between forward and aft trim tanks to help stabilize the aircraft. The Concorde has a narrow fuselage and short-span wings to reduce drag during supersonic flight. Its noisy turbojet engines with afterburners enable it to carry 100 passengers at a cruising speed of Mach 2 at 50,000-60,000 ft (15,000-18,000 m). Once an aircraft is flying faster than Mach 1, it produces a continuous air-pressure wave, which is heard as a "sonic boom."

Strake

Fin

Standby pitot head

Starboard outboard engine air intake

Inboard elevon-actuator fairing

Nose gear leg

FRONT VIEW OF CONCORDE

Toilets

Electrothermal deicing panel

Starboard forward trim tank

Overhead luggage compartments

Passenger accommodation

Seat attachment rail

OVERHEAD VIEW OF CONCORDE

Underfloor air-conditioning duct

Life raft

VHF antenna

Wardrobe

Forward galley

Variable nozzle

Leading edge

Additional crew's seat

Flight engineer's seat

Aluminum-alloy layers and insulation

Erosion-resistant radome

Cockpit windshield

Retractable visor

"A" frame

Plug-type passenger door

Lateral bracing strut

Telescopic strut

Port forward trim tank

Nose gear leg

Steering actuator

Machined skin panel

Weather radar

Standby flight-control hydraulic jack

Nose gear door

Multi-ply high-pressure tire

Captain's seat

Upper rudder

Fin

Visor jack

Dorsal fin

Emergency exit

Droop-nose hinge

Cockpit air-conditioning duct

Pivoted retractable frame

Tail cone

Aft door

Elevon (combined elevator and aileron)

Hot-section steel and titanium skin

Engine cowling

Landing gear door

Bogie main landing gear

G-BOAG

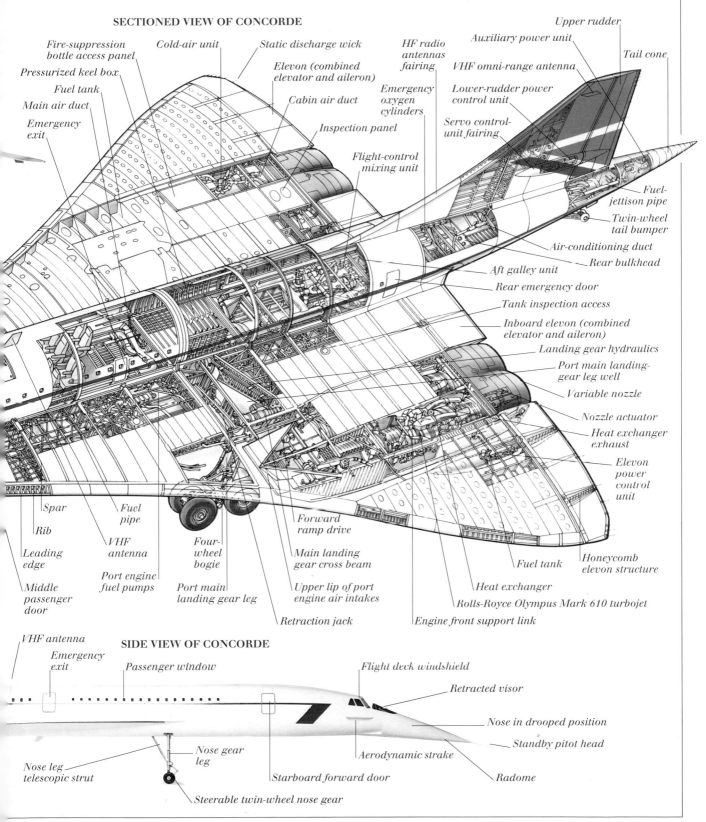

SECTIONED VIEW OF CONCORDE

Fire-suppression bottle access panel

Cold-air unit

Static discharge wick

Elevon (combined elevator and aileron)

HF radio antennas fairing

Auxiliary power unit

Upper rudder

Tail cone

VHF omni-range antenna

Pressurized keel box

Fuel tank

Main air duct

Emergency exit

Cabin air duct

Emergency oxygen cylinders

Lower-rudder power control unit

Inspection panel

Servo control-unit fairing

Flight-control mixing unit

Fuel-jettison pipe

Twin-wheel tail bumper

Air-conditioning duct

Rear bulkhead

Aft galley unit

Rear emergency door

Tank inspection access

Inboard elevon (combined elevator and aileron)

Landing gear hydraulics

Port main landing-gear leg well

Variable nozzle

Nozzle actuator

Heat exchanger exhaust

Elevon power control unit

Spar

Rib

Fuel pipe

VHF antenna

Four-wheel bogie

Forward ramp drive

Leading edge

Port engine fuel pumps

Port main landing gear leg

Main landing gear cross beam

Upper lip of port engine air intakes

Fuel tank

Honeycomb elevon structure

Middle passenger door

Retraction jack

Heat exchanger

Rolls-Royce Olympus Mark 610 turbojet

Engine front support link

SIDE VIEW OF CONCORDE

VHF antenna

Emergency exit

Passenger window

Flight deck windshield

Retracted visor

Nose in drooped position

Standby pitot head

Nose gear leg

Nose leg telescopic strut

Aerodynamic strake

Starboard forward door

Radome

Steerable twin-wheel nose gear

Jet engines

JET ENGINES ARE USED BY MOST MILITARY and heavy aircraft and by many helicopters. The simplest type of jet engine, or gas turbine, is the turbojet. It works by continuously burning a mixture of fuel and air in a combustion chamber to produce a jet of hot exhaust gas that is expelled through a nozzle to produce thrust. The hot gas also spins turbine blades which, in turn, spin the blades of an air compressor; the compressor forces air into the combustion chamber. Many of the fastest aircraft use turbojets, with additional booster units called afterburners, but their use is restricted by their high noise emission. Most jetliners use quieter turbofan jet engines. An enormous fan, driven by a low-pressure turbine, feeds some air into the compressor but feeds most of it through bypass ducts to join the exhaust jetstream in the tail cone. The bypass stream produces most of the thrust. Many smaller, propeller-driven aircraft use turboprop jet engines, in which the engine powers a propeller.

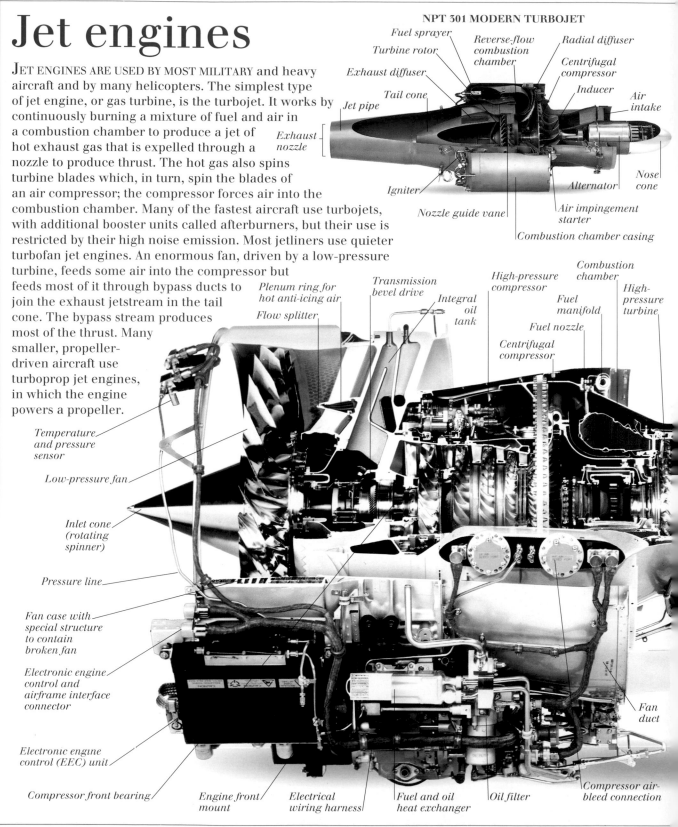

NPT 301 MODERN TURBOJET

Fuel sprayer
Turbine rotor
Reverse-flow combustion chamber
Radial diffuser
Exhaust diffuser
Centrifugal compressor
Tail cone
Inducer
Air intake
Jet pipe
Exhaust nozzle
Nose cone
Igniter
Alternator
Nozzle guide vane
Air impingement starter
Combustion chamber casing

Plenum ring for hot anti-icing air
Flow splitter
Transmission bevel drive
Integral oil tank
Combustion chamber
High-pressure compressor
High-pressure turbine
Fuel manifold
Fuel nozzle
Centrifugal compressor

Temperature and pressure sensor
Low-pressure fan
Inlet cone (rotating spinner)
Pressure line
Fan case with special structure to contain broken fan
Electronic engine control and airframe interface connector
Electronic engine control (EEC) unit
Compressor front bearing
Engine front mount
Electrical wiring harness
Fuel and oil heat exchanger
Oil filter
Fan duct
Compressor air-bleed connection

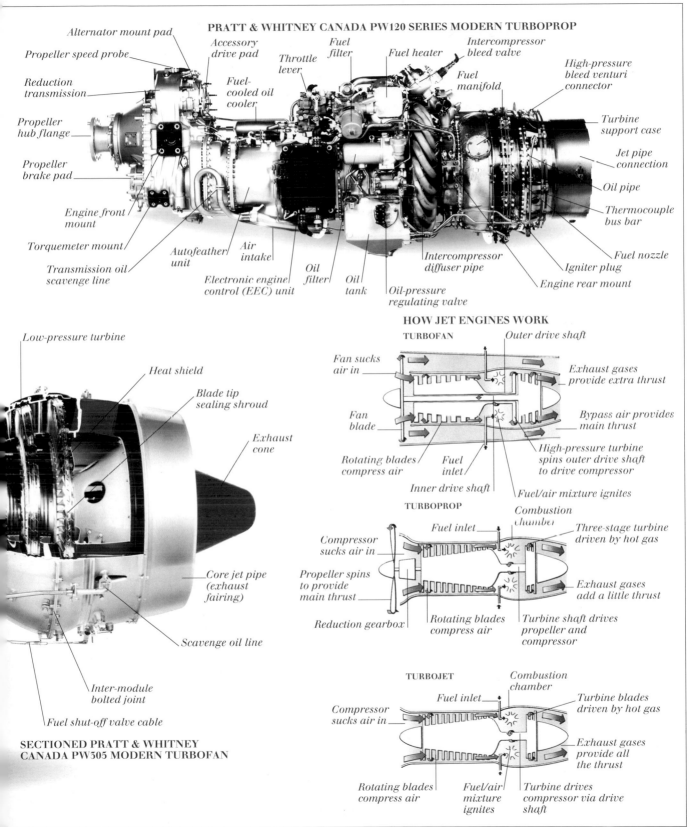

PRATT & WHITNEY CANADA PW120 SERIES MODERN TURBOPROP

Alternator mount pad
Propeller speed probe
Reduction transmission
Propeller hub flange
Propeller brake pad
Engine front mount
Torquemeter mount
Transmission oil scavenge line
Accessory drive pad
Throttle lever
Fuel-cooled oil cooler
Fuel filter
Fuel heater
Fuel manifold
Intercompressor bleed valve
High-pressure bleed venturi connector
Turbine support case
Jet pipe connection
Oil pipe
Thermocouple bus bar
Fuel nozzle
Igniter plug
Engine rear mount
Intercompressor diffuser pipe
Oil-pressure regulating valve
Oil tank
Oil filter
Electronic engine control (EEC) unit
Air intake
Autofeather unit

HOW JET ENGINES WORK

TURBOFAN

Fan sucks air in
Fan blade
Rotating blades compress air
Fuel inlet
Inner drive shaft
Outer drive shaft
Exhaust gases provide extra thrust
Bypass air provides main thrust
High-pressure turbine spins outer drive shaft to drive compressor
Fuel/air mixture ignites

TURBOPROP

Compressor sucks air in
Propeller spins to provide main thrust
Reduction gearbox
Rotating blades compress air
Fuel inlet
Combustion chamber
Three-stage turbine driven by hot gas
Exhaust gases add a little thrust
Turbine shaft drives propeller and compressor

TURBOJET

Compressor sucks air in
Rotating blades compress air
Fuel inlet
Fuel/air mixture ignites
Combustion chamber
Turbine blades driven by hot gas
Exhaust gases provide all the thrust
Turbine drives compressor via drive shaft

Low-pressure turbine
Heat shield
Blade tip sealing shroud
Exhaust cone
Core jet pipe (exhaust fairing)
Scavenge oil line
Inter-module bolted joint
Fuel shut-off valve cable

SECTIONED PRATT & WHITNEY CANADA PW305 MODERN TURBOFAN

Modern military aircraft

MODERN MILITARY AIRCRAFT ARE AMONG THE MOST SOPHISTICATED and expensive products of the 21st century. Fighters need computer-operated controls for maneuverability, powerful engines, and effective air-to-air weapons. Most modern fighters also have guided missiles, radar, and passive, infrared sensors. These developments enable today's fighters to engage in combat with adversaries who are outside visual range. Bombers carry a large weapon load and enough fuel for long-range flights. A few military aircraft, such as the Tornado and the F-14 Tomcat, have variable-sweep ("swing") wings. During takeoff and landing their wings are fully extended, but for high-speed flight and low-level attacks the wings are pivoted fully back. A recent development is the "stealth" bomber, which is designed to absorb or deflect enemy radar in order to remain undetected. Earlier bombers, such as the Tornado, use terrain-following radars to fly so close to the ground that they avoid enemy radar detection.

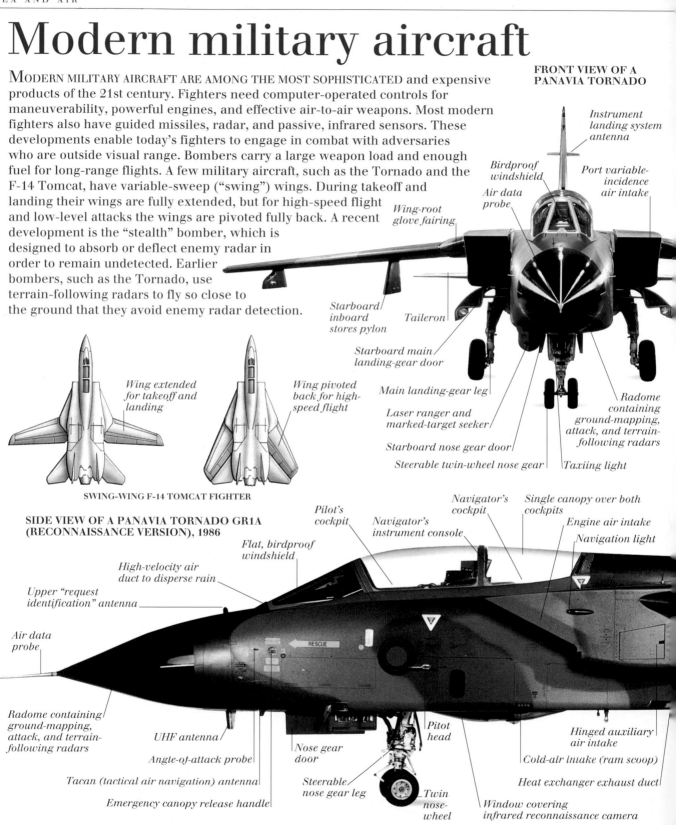

FRONT VIEW OF A PANAVIA TORNADO

Instrument landing system antenna

Birdproof windshield

Air data probe

Port variable-incidence air intake

Wing-root glove fairing

Starboard inboard stores pylon

Taileron

Starboard main landing-gear door

Main landing-gear leg

Laser ranger and marked-target seeker

Starboard nose gear door

Steerable twin-wheel nose gear

Radome containing ground-mapping, attack, and terrain-following radars

Taxiing light

Wing extended for takeoff and landing

Wing pivoted back for high-speed flight

SWING-WING F-14 TOMCAT FIGHTER

SIDE VIEW OF A PANAVIA TORNADO GR1A (RECONNAISSANCE VERSION), 1986

Pilot's cockpit

Navigator's instrument console

Navigator's cockpit

Single canopy over both cockpits

Engine air intake

Navigation light

Flat, birdproof windshield

High-velocity air duct to disperse rain

Upper "request identification" antenna

Air data probe

Radome containing ground-mapping, attack, and terrain-following radars

UHF antenna

Angle-of-attack probe

Tacan (tactical air navigation) antenna

Emergency canopy release handle

Nose gear door

Steerable nose gear leg

Pitot head

Twin nose-wheel

Window covering infrared reconnaissance camera

Hinged auxiliary air intake

Cold-air intake (ram scoop)

Heat exchanger exhaust duct

RESCUE

NORTHROP B-2 ("STEALTH" BOMBER), 1989

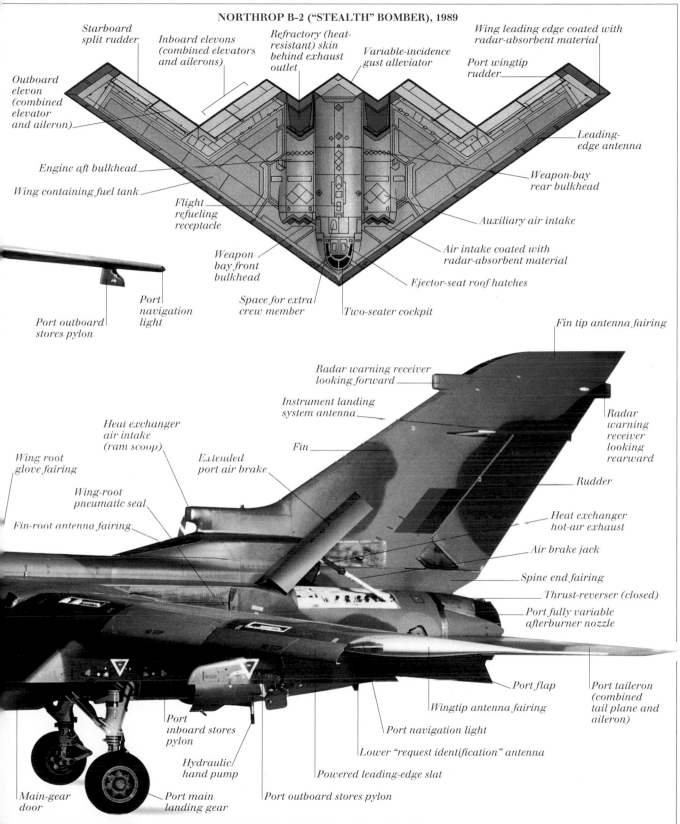

Starboard split rudder

Inboard elevons (combined elevators and ailerons)

Refractory (heat-resistant) skin behind exhaust outlet

Variable-incidence gust alleviator

Wing leading edge coated with radar-absorbent material

Port wingtip rudder

Outboard elevon (combined elevator and aileron)

Leading-edge antenna

Engine aft bulkhead

Wing containing fuel tank

Weapon-bay rear bulkhead

Flight refueling receptacle

Auxiliary air intake

Weapon bay front bulkhead

Air intake coated with radar-absorbent material

Ejector-seat roof hatches

Space for extra crew member

Two-seater cockpit

Port outboard stores pylon

Port navigation light

Fin tip antenna fairing

Radar warning receiver looking forward

Instrument landing system antenna

Radar warning receiver looking rearward

Fin

Wing root glove fairing

Heat exchanger air intake (ram scoop)

Extended port air brake

Wing-root pneumatic seal

Rudder

Fin-root antenna fairing

Heat exchanger hot-air exhaust

Air brake jack

Spine end fairing

Thrust-reverser (closed)

Port fully variable afterburner nozzle

Port flap

Port taileron (combined tail plane and aileron)

Wingtip antenna fairing

Port navigation light

Port inboard stores pylon

Hydraulic hand pump

Lower "request identification" antenna

Powered leading-edge slat

Main-gear door

Port main landing gear

Port outboard stores pylon

Helicopters

HELICOPTERS USE ROTATING BLADES for lift, propulsion, and steering. The first machine to achieve sustained, controlled flight using rotating blades was the autogiro built in the 1920s by Juan de la Cierva of Spain. His machine had unpowered blades above the fuselage that relied on the flow of air to rotate them and provide lift while the autogiro was driven forward by a conventional propeller. Then, in 1939, the Russian-born American Igor Sikorsky produced his VS-300, the forerunner of the modern helicopter. Its engine-driven blades provided lift, propulsion, and steering. It could take off vertically, hover, and fly in any direction, and had a tail rotor to prevent the helicopter body from spinning. The introduction of gas turbine jet engines to helicopters in 1955 produced quieter, safer, and more powerful machines. Because of their versatility in flight, helicopters are used today for many purposes, including crop spraying, traffic surveillance, and transporting crews to deep-sea oil rigs, as well as acting as gunships, air ambulances, and air taxis.

BELL 47G-3B1

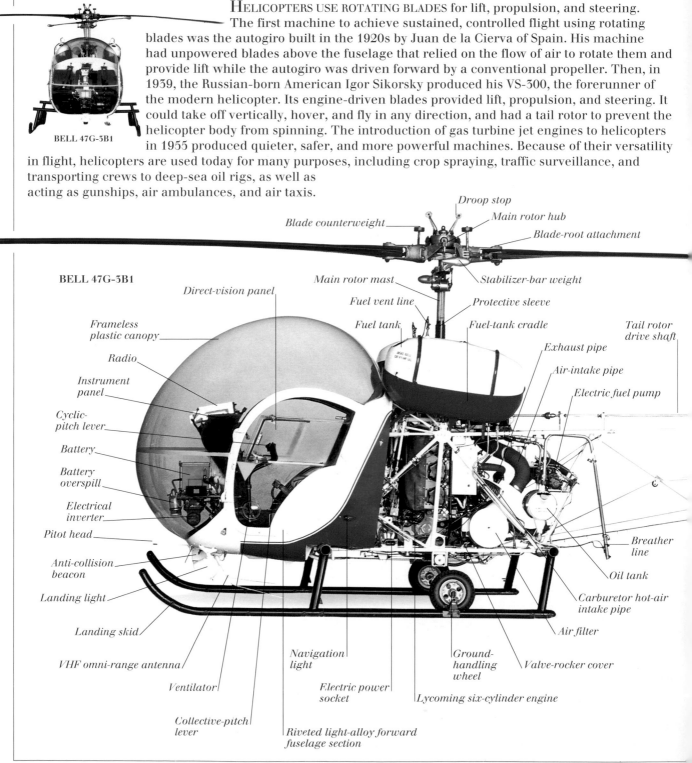

BELL 47G-3B1

Blade counterweight
Droop stop
Main rotor hub
Blade-root attachment

Direct-vision panel
Main rotor mast
Stabilizer-bar weight

Fuel vent line
Protective sleeve

Frameless plastic canopy
Fuel tank
Fuel-tank cradle
Tail rotor drive shaft

Radio
Exhaust pipe

Instrument panel
Air-intake pipe

Cyclic-pitch lever
Electric fuel pump

Battery

Battery overspill

Electrical inverter

Pitot head
Breather line

Anti-collision beacon
Oil tank

Landing light
Carburetor hot-air intake pipe

Landing skid
Air filter

VHF omni-range antenna
Navigation light
Ground-handling wheel
Valve-rocker cover

Ventilator
Electric power socket
Lycoming six-cylinder engine

Collective-pitch lever
Riveted light-alloy forward fuselage section

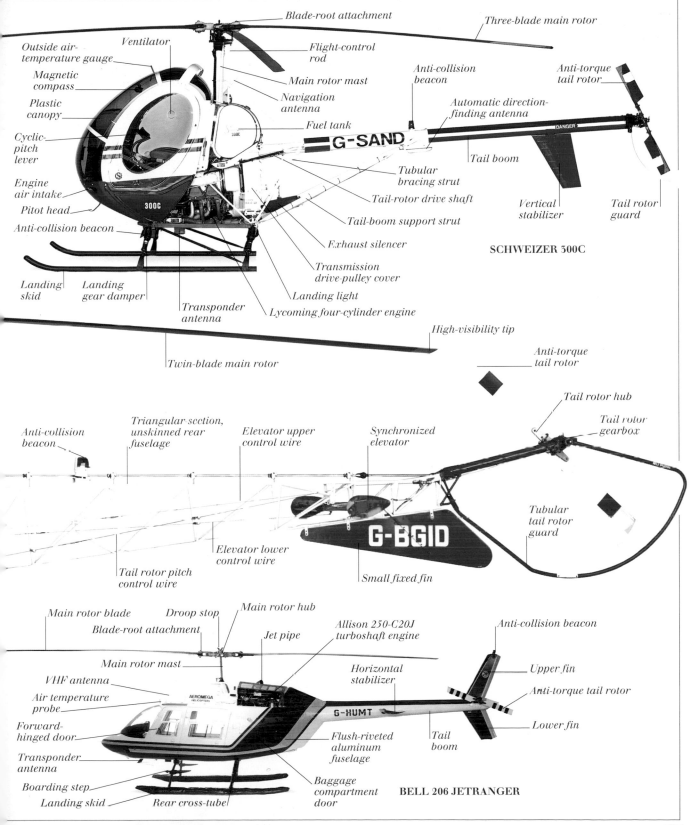

Blade-root attachment

Three-blade main rotor

Ventilator

Outside air-temperature gauge

Flight-control rod

Anti-collision beacon

Anti-torque tail rotor

Magnetic compass

Main rotor mast

Automatic direction-finding antenna

Navigation antenna

Plastic canopy

Fuel tank

Cyclic-pitch lever

G-SAND

Tail boom

Engine air intake

Tubular bracing strut

Vertical stabilizer

Tail rotor guard

Pitot head

Tail-rotor drive shaft

300C

Anti-collision beacon

Tail-boom support strut

Exhaust silencer

SCHWEIZER 300C

Transmission drive-pulley cover

Landing skid

Landing gear damper

Landing light

Transponder antenna

Lycoming four-cylinder engine

High-visibility tip

Twin-blade main rotor

Anti-torque tail rotor

Anti-collision beacon

Triangular section, unskinned rear fuselage

Elevator upper control wire

Synchronized elevator

Tail rotor hub

Tail rotor gearbox

Tubular tail rotor guard

G-BGID

Elevator lower control wire

Tail rotor pitch control wire

Small fixed fin

Main rotor blade

Droop stop

Main rotor hub

Blade-root attachment

Jet pipe

Allison 250-C20J turboshaft engine

Anti-collision beacon

Main rotor mast

VHF antenna

Horizontal stabilizer

Upper fin

Air temperature probe

Anti-torque tail rotor

Forward-hinged door

AEROMEGA

G-HUMT

Flush-riveted aluminum fuselage

Lower fin

Transponder antenna

Tail boom

Boarding step

Baggage compartment door

BELL 206 JETRANGER

Landing skid

Rear cross-tube

Light aircraft

LIGHT AIRCRAFT, SUCH AS THE ARV SUPER 2 shown here, are small, lightweight, and of simple construction. More than a million have been built since World War I, mainly for recreational use by private owners. Virtually all light aircraft have piston engines, most of which are air-cooled, although some are liquid-cooled. Open cockpits, almost universal in the 1920s, have now been replaced by enclosed cabins. The cabins of high-wing aircraft have one or two doors, while those of low-wing aircraft usually have a sliding or hinged canopy. Most modern light aircraft are made of aluminum alloy, although some are made of wood or of fiber-reinforced materials. Light aircraft today also usually have navigational instruments, an electrical system, cabin heating, wheel brakes, and a two-way radio.

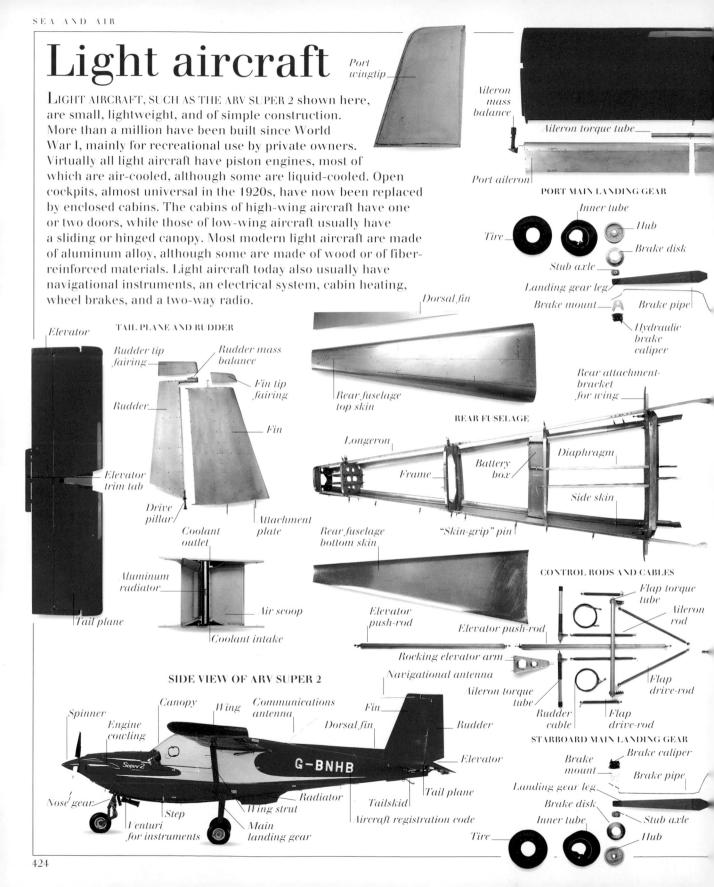

Port wingtip

Aileron mass balance

Aileron torque tube

Port aileron

PORT MAIN LANDING GEAR

Inner tube

Tire

Hub

Brake disk

Stub axle

Landing gear leg

Brake mount

Brake pipe

Hydraulic brake caliper

Dorsal fin

TAIL PLANE AND RUDDER

Elevator

Rudder tip fairing

Rudder mass balance

Fin tip fairing

Rudder

Fin

Rear fuselage top skin

Rear attachment-bracket for wing

REAR FUSELAGE

Longeron

Frame

Battery box

Diaphragm

Side skin

Elevator trim tab

Drive pillar

Attachment plate

"Skin-grip" pin

Coolant outlet

Aluminum radiator

Rear fuselage bottom skin

Air scoop

Coolant intake

Tail plane

CONTROL RODS AND CABLES

Flap torque tube

Aileron rod

Elevator push-rod

Elevator push-rod

Rocking elevator arm

Navigational antenna

Aileron torque tube

Rudder cable

Flap drive-rod

Flap drive-rod

SIDE VIEW OF ARV SUPER 2

Spinner

Canopy

Wing

Communications antenna

Fin

Dorsal fin

Rudder

Engine cowling

G-BNHB

Elevator

Radiator

Tail plane

Nose gear

Step

Wing strut

Tailskid

Aircraft registration code

Venturi for instruments

Main landing gear

STARBOARD MAIN LANDING GEAR

Brake caliper

Brake mount

Brake pipe

Landing gear leg

Brake disk

Inner tube

Stub axle

Tire

Hub

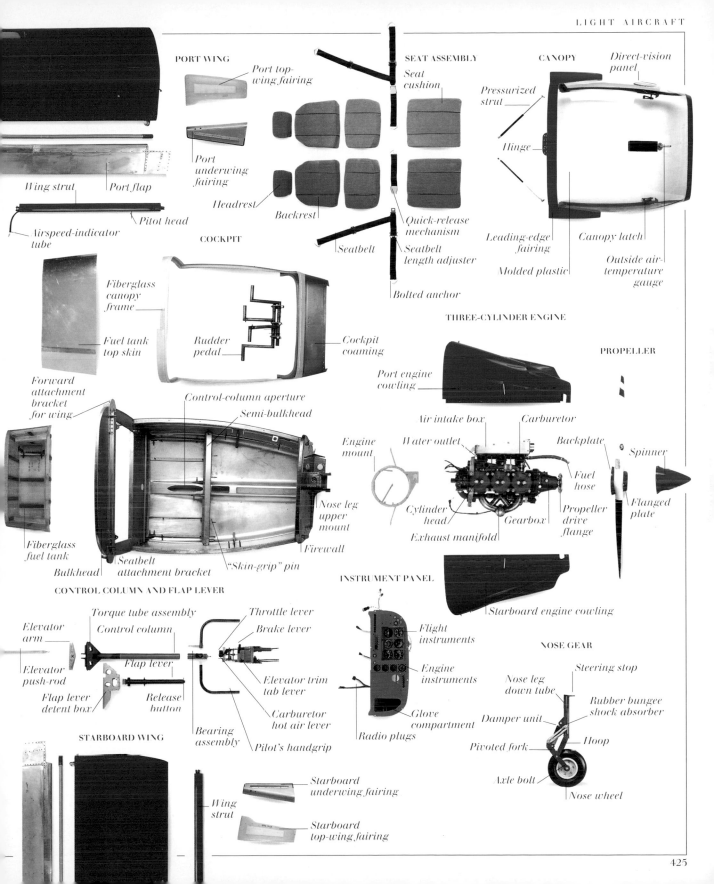

PORT WING

Port top-wing fairing

Port underwing fairing

Wing strut

Port flap

Pitot head

Airspeed-indicator tube

SEAT ASSEMBLY

Seat cushion

Headrest

Backrest

Seatbelt

Quick-release mechanism

Seatbelt length adjuster

Bolted anchor

CANOPY

Direct-vision panel

Pressurized strut

Hinge

Leading-edge fairing

Molded plastic

Canopy latch

Outside air-temperature gauge

COCKPIT

Fiberglass canopy frame

Fuel tank top skin

Forward attachment bracket for wing

Rudder pedal

Control-column aperture

Semi-bulkhead

Cockpit coaming

THREE-CYLINDER ENGINE

Port engine cowling

Air intake box

Water outlet

Carburetor

Backplate

Engine mount

Cylinder head

Exhaust manifold

Gearbox

Fuel hose

Propeller drive flange

Nose leg upper mount

Firewall

Fiberglass fuel tank

Bulkhead

Seatbelt attachment bracket

"Skin-grip" pin

PROPELLER

Spinner

Flanged plate

Starboard engine cowling

CONTROL COLUMN AND FLAP LEVER

Torque tube assembly

Throttle lever

Brake lever

Elevator arm

Control column

Flap lever

Elevator push-rod

Flap lever detent box

Release button

Bearing assembly

Elevator trim tab lever

Carburetor hot air lever

Pilot's handgrip

INSTRUMENT PANEL

Flight instruments

Engine instruments

Glove compartment

Radio plugs

NOSE GEAR

Steering stop

Nose leg down tube

Rubber bungee shock absorber

Damper unit

Pivoted fork

Hoop

Axle bolt

Nose wheel

STARBOARD WING

Wing strut

Starboard underwing fairing

Starboard top-wing fairing

Gliders, hang gliders, and ultralights

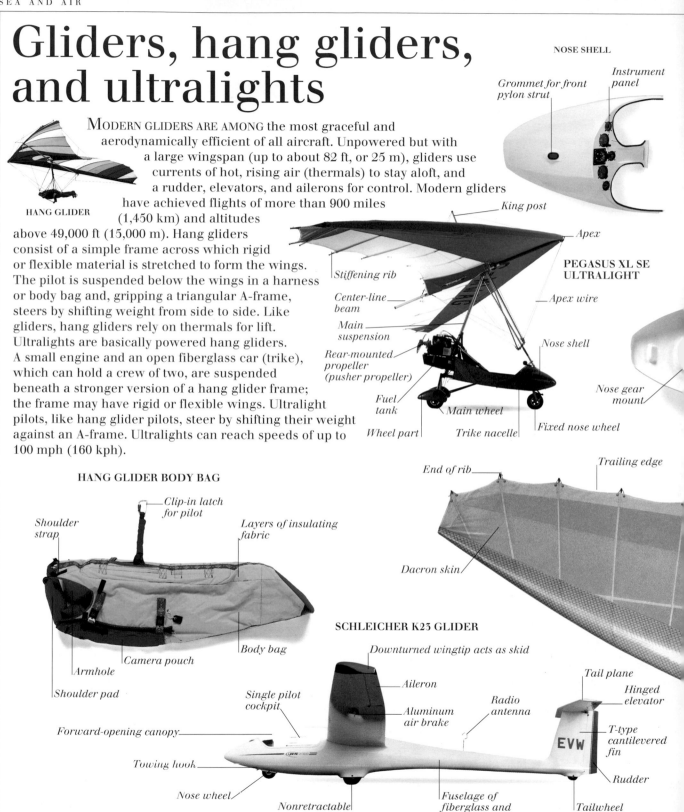

NOSE SHELL

Grommet for front pylon strut

Instrument panel

HANG GLIDER

MODERN GLIDERS ARE AMONG the most graceful and aerodynamically efficient of all aircraft. Unpowered but with a large wingspan (up to about 82 ft, or 25 m), gliders use currents of hot, rising air (thermals) to stay aloft, and a rudder, elevators, and ailerons for control. Modern gliders have achieved flights of more than 900 miles (1,450 km) and altitudes above 49,000 ft (15,000 m). Hang gliders consist of a simple frame across which rigid or flexible material is stretched to form the wings. The pilot is suspended below the wings in a harness or body bag and, gripping a triangular A-frame, steers by shifting weight from side to side. Like gliders, hang gliders rely on thermals for lift. Ultralights are basically powered hang gliders. A small engine and an open fiberglass car (trike), which can hold a crew of two, are suspended beneath a stronger version of a hang glider frame; the frame may have rigid or flexible wings. Ultralight pilots, like hang glider pilots, steer by shifting their weight against an A-frame. Ultralights can reach speeds of up to 100 mph (160 kph).

King post

Apex

PEGASUS XL SE ULTRALIGHT

Stiffening rib

Center-line beam

Main suspension

Rear-mounted propeller (pusher propeller)

Apex wire

Nose shell

Nose gear mount

Fuel tank

Wheel part

Main wheel

Trike nacelle

Fixed nose wheel

HANG GLIDER BODY BAG

Clip-in latch for pilot

Shoulder strap

Layers of insulating fabric

End of rib

Trailing edge

Dacron skin

SCHLEICHER K23 GLIDER

Camera pouch

Body bag

Armhole

Shoulder pad

Downturned wingtip acts as skid

Single pilot cockpit

Aileron

Tail plane

Hinged elevator

Forward-opening canopy

Aluminum air brake

Radio antenna

T-type cantilevered fin

Towing hook

EVW

Rudder

Nose wheel

Nonretractable main wheel

Fuselage of fiberglass and foam layers

Tailwheel

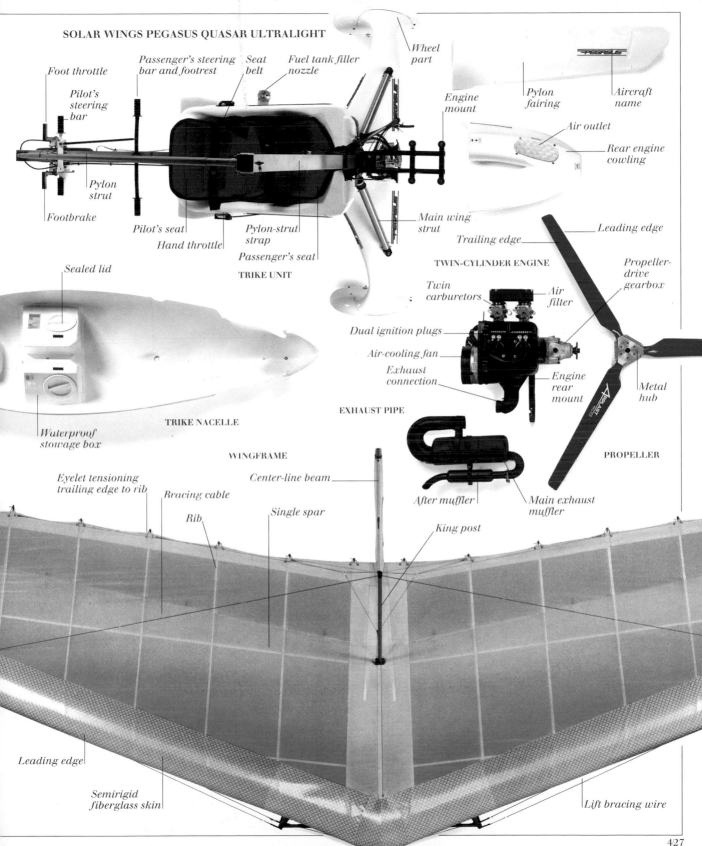

SOLAR WINGS PEGASUS QUASAR ULTRALIGHT

Foot throttle

Pilot's steering bar

Passenger's steering bar and footrest

Seat belt

Fuel tank filler nozzle

Wheel part

Engine mount

Pylon fairing

Aircraft name

Air outlet

Rear engine cowling

Pylon strut

Footbrake

Pilot's seat

Hand throttle

Pylon-strut strap

Passenger's seat

TRIKE UNIT

Main wing strut

Leading edge

Trailing edge

Propeller-drive gearbox

TWIN-CYLINDER ENGINE

Twin carburetors

Air filter

Dual ignition plugs

Air-cooling fan

Exhaust connection

Engine rear mount

Metal hub

Sealed lid

Waterproof stowage box

TRIKE NACELLE

EXHAUST PIPE

PROPELLER

WINGFRAME

Center-line beam

After muffler

Main exhaust muffler

Eyelet tensioning trailing edge to rib

Bracing cable

Rib

Single spar

King post

Leading edge

Semirigid fiberglass skin

Lift bracing wire

427

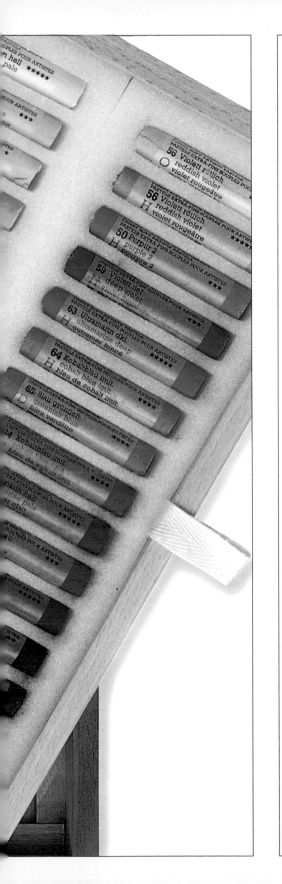

THE VISUAL ARTS

Drawing

DRAWINGS CAN BE FINISHED WORKS OF ART, or preparatory studies for paintings and other visual arts. They can be made using a wide variety of drawing instruments such as pencils, graphite sticks, chalks, charcoal, pens and inks, and silver wires. The most common drawing instrument is the graphite pencil. A graphite pencil consists of a thin rod of graphite mixed with clay, encased in wood. Charcoal is one of the oldest drawing instruments. It is produced by firing twigs of willow, vine, or other woods at high temperatures in airtight containers. Erasers can be used to rub out marks made by drawing materials such as graphite pencils or charcoal, or to achieve a particular effect—such as smudging. Fixative is often applied—using a mouth diffuser or aerosol spray fixative—to prevent smudging once a drawing is finished. Silver lines can be produced by drawing silver wire across specially prepared paper—a technique known as silverpoint. The lines are permanent and cannot be erased. In time the silver lines oxidize and turn brown.

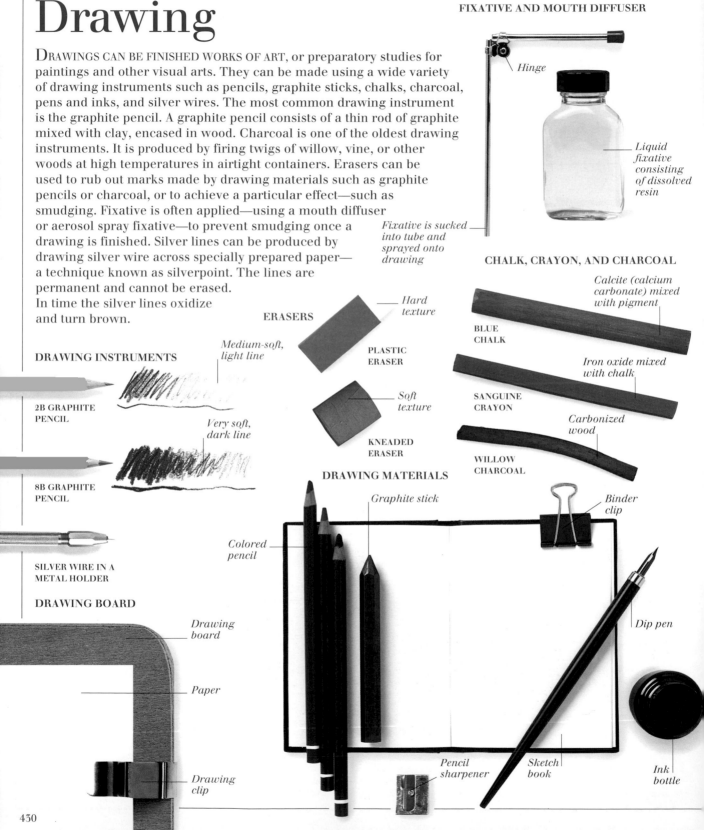

FIXATIVE AND MOUTH DIFFUSER

Hinge

Liquid fixative consisting of dissolved resin

Fixative is sucked into tube and sprayed onto drawing

CHALK, CRAYON, AND CHARCOAL

Calcite (calcium carbonate) mixed with pigment

BLUE CHALK

Iron oxide mixed with chalk

SANGUINE CRAYON

Carbonized wood

WILLOW CHARCOAL

ERASERS

Hard texture

PLASTIC ERASER

Medium-soft, light line

Soft texture

KNEADED ERASER

Very soft, dark line

DRAWING INSTRUMENTS

2B GRAPHITE PENCIL

8B GRAPHITE PENCIL

SILVER WIRE IN A METAL HOLDER

DRAWING BOARD

Drawing board

Paper

Drawing clip

DRAWING MATERIALS

Graphite stick

Colored pencil

Binder clip

Dip pen

Pencil sharpener

Sketch book

Ink bottle

Silver lines oxidize to a light brown color

Figures drawn in ink on top of lines

Line drawn in silverpoint using a ruler

Vanishing point located on head of man riding rearing horse

Lines of squared pavement slabs recede toward a single vanishing point

Complex perspective drawing done as a preparatory study for a painting

Paper prepared with size (glue) and pigment

EXAMPLE OF A SILVERPOINT DRAWING
The Adoration of the Magi, Leonardo da Vinci, 1481
Pen and ink over silverpoint on paper
6½ x 11½ in (16.5 x 29.2 cm)

Handmade, tinted paper

One of a series of drawings recording London during 1944–1945

Charcoal lines softened by rubbing and smudging

Broad charcoal mark

Charcoal gives strong, expressive lines

Lines rapidly drawn on site

EXAMPLE OF A CHARCOAL DRAWING
St. Paul's and the River, David Bomberg, 1945
Charcoal on paper
20 x 25⅛ in (50.8 x 65.8 cm)

Tempera

ILLUMINATED MANUSCRIPT

THE TERM TEMPERA is applied to any paint in which pigment is tempered (mixed) with a water-based binding medium—usually egg yolk. Egg tempera is applied to a smooth surface such as vellum (for illuminated manuscripts) or more commonly to hardwood panels prepared with gesso—a mixture of chalk and size (glue). Bristle brushes are used to apply the gesso. A layer of gesso grosso (coarse gesso) is followed by successive layers of gesso sotile (fine gesso) that are sanded between coats to provide a smooth, yet absorbent ground. The paint is applied with fine sable brushes in thin layers, using light brushstrokes. Tempera dries quickly to form a tough skin with a satin sheen. The luminous white surface of the gesso combined with the overlaid paint produces the brilliant crispness and rich colors particular to this medium. Egg tempera paintings are frequently gilded with gold. Leaves of finely beaten gold are applied to a bole (reddish-brown clay) base and polished by burnishing.

MATERIALS FOR GILDING

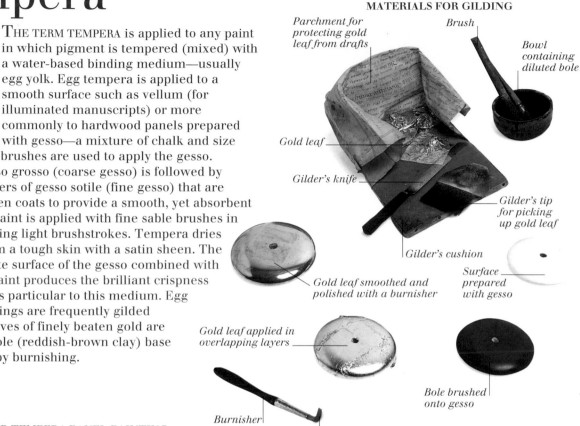

Parchment for protecting gold leaf from drafts

Brush

Bowl containing diluted bole

Gold leaf

Gilder's knife

Gilder's tip for picking up gold leaf

Gilder's cushion

Gold leaf smoothed and polished with a burnisher

Surface prepared with gesso

Gold leaf applied in overlapping layers

Bole brushed onto gesso

Burnisher

Agate tip

MATERIALS FOR TEMPERA PANEL PAINTING

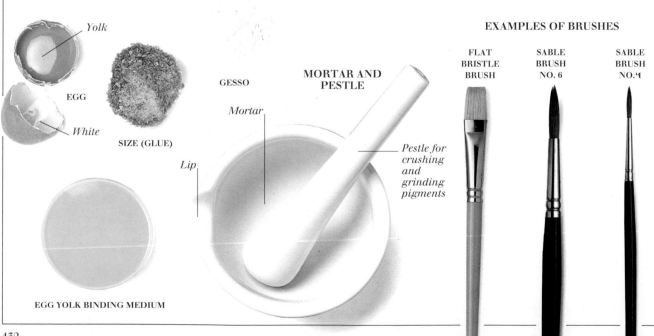

Yolk

EGG

White

SIZE (GLUE)

GESSO

Mortar

Lip

MORTAR AND PESTLE

Pestle for crushing and grinding pigments

EGG YOLK BINDING MEDIUM

EXAMPLES OF BRUSHES

FLAT BRISTLE BRUSH

SABLE BRUSH NO. 6

SABLE BRUSH NO. 4

EXAMPLE OF A TEMPERA PAINTING
Presentation in the Temple, Ambrogio Lorenzetti, 1342
Tempera on wood, 8 ft 5⅛ in x 5 ft 6⅛ in (257 x 168 cm)

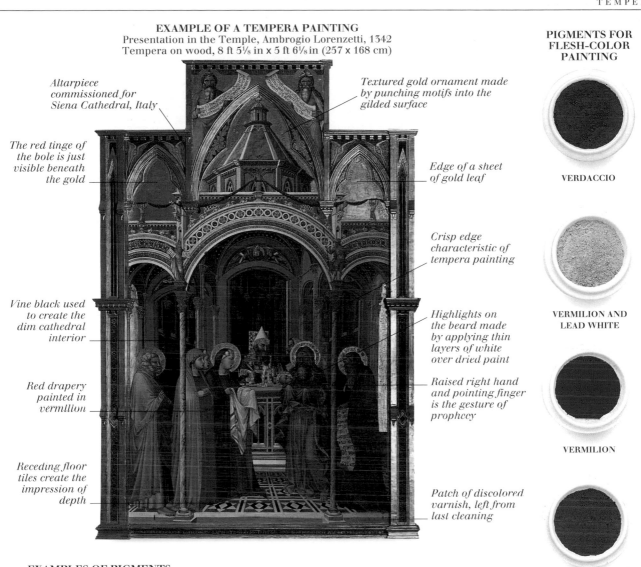

*Altarpiece
commissioned for
Siena Cathedral, Italy*

*Textured gold ornament made
by punching motifs into the
gilded surface*

*The red tinge of
the bole is just
visible beneath
the gold*

*Edge of a sheet
of gold leaf*

*Crisp edge
characteristic of
tempera painting*

*Vine black used
to create the
dim cathedral
interior*

*Highlights on
the beard made
by applying thin
layers of white
over dried paint*

*Red drapery
painted in
vermilion*

*Raised right hand
and pointing finger
is the gesture of
prophecy*

*Receding floor
tiles create the
impression of
depth*

*Patch of discolored
varnish, left from
last cleaning*

VERDACCIO

**VERMILION AND
LEAD WHITE**

VERMILION

**RED EARTH
(IRON OXIDE)**

EXAMPLES OF PIGMENTS

MALACHITE

**ULTRAMARINE
LAPIS LAZULI**

VINE BLACK

LEAD TIN YELLOW

*Warm flesh
tones achieved
by layering
vermilion and
white over an
undercoat of
verdaccio*

*Ultramarine
lapis lazuli, as
costly as gold,
was reserved for
significant
figures such as
the Virgin Mary*

*Patterned gold
halo glitters in
candlelight*

*Craquelure
(pattern of
cracks in
the paint)*

**DETAIL FROM "PRESENTATION
IN THE TEMPLE"**

Fresco

FRESCO IS A METHOD OF WALL PAINTING. In buon fresco (true fresco), pigments are mixed with water and applied to an intonaco (layer of fresh, damp lime-plaster). The intonaco absorbs and binds the pigments as it dries making the picture a permanent part of the wall surface. The intonaco is applied in sections called giornate (daily sections). The size of each giornata depends on the artist's estimate of how much can be painted before the plaster sets. The junctions between giornate are sometimes visible on a finished fresco. The range of colors used in buon fresco are limited to lime-resistant pigments such as earth colors (below). Slaked lime (burnt lime mixed with water), bianco di San Giovanni (slaked lime that has been partly exposed to air), and chalk can be used to produce fresco whites. In fresco secco (dry fresco), pigments are mixed with a binding medium and applied to dry plaster. The pigments are not completely absorbed into the plaster and may flake off over time.

CROSS-SECTION SHOWING FRESCO LAYERS

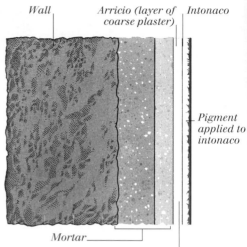

Wall

Arricio (layer of coarse plaster)

Intonaco

Pigment applied to intonaco

Mortar

Sinopia (design) drawn on surface of arricio

EXAMPLES OF EARTH COLOR PIGMENTS

EXAMPLES OF FRESCO BRUSHES

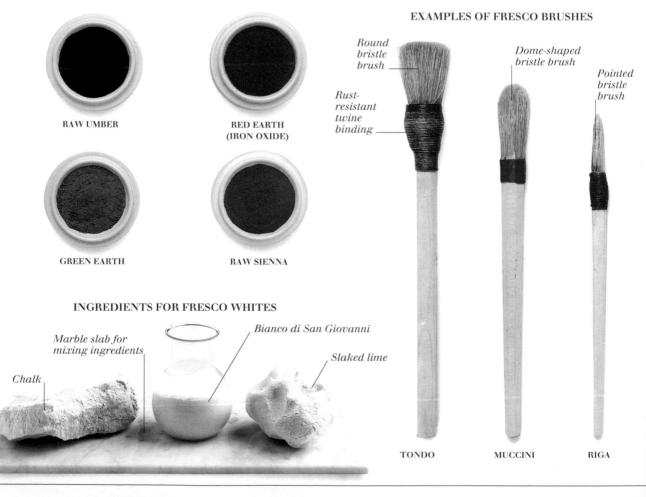

RAW UMBER

RED EARTH (IRON OXIDE)

GREEN EARTH

RAW SIENNA

INGREDIENTS FOR FRESCO WHITES

Marble slab for mixing ingredients

Bianco di San Giovanni

Slaked lime

Chalk

Round bristle brush

Rust-resistant twine binding

Dome-shaped bristle brush

Pointed bristle brush

TONDO

MUCCINI

RIGA

EXAMPLE OF A FRESCO
The Expulsion of the Merchants from the Temple, Giotto, c.1306
Fresco, 78 x 72 in (200 x 185 cm)

Temple acts as a backdrop for the action

Bianco di San Giovanni often used for fresco whites

Gold leaf applied to apostle's halo

Green earth pigment applied to robe

Child painted on top of apostle's robe

One of a series of frescoes in the Arena Chapel, Padua, Italy

Patches of azurite blue have turned green due to reaction with carbon dioxide

Hairline junction between giornate is visible

Red earth pigment applied in buon fresco has retained rich hue

Azurite blue applied in fresco secco has flaked off to reveal the plaster beneath

Dry, matt surface characteristic of buon fresco

Paint applied in buon fresco to child's face

White dove represents the Holy Ghost

Paint applied in fresco secco to child's body has flaked off

DETAIL FROM "THE EXPULSION"

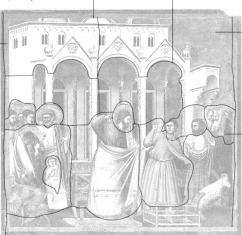

Artist has to finish giornata before plaster dries

Junction between giornate

A fresco was generally worked in zones from the top down

Area with little detail can be painted quickly, allowing a larger giornata to be completed

Highly detailed area takes a longer time to paint, restricting the size of the giornata

Sinopia (design) sketched in red earth

GIORNATE (DAILY SECTIONS) IN "THE EXPULSION"

Oils

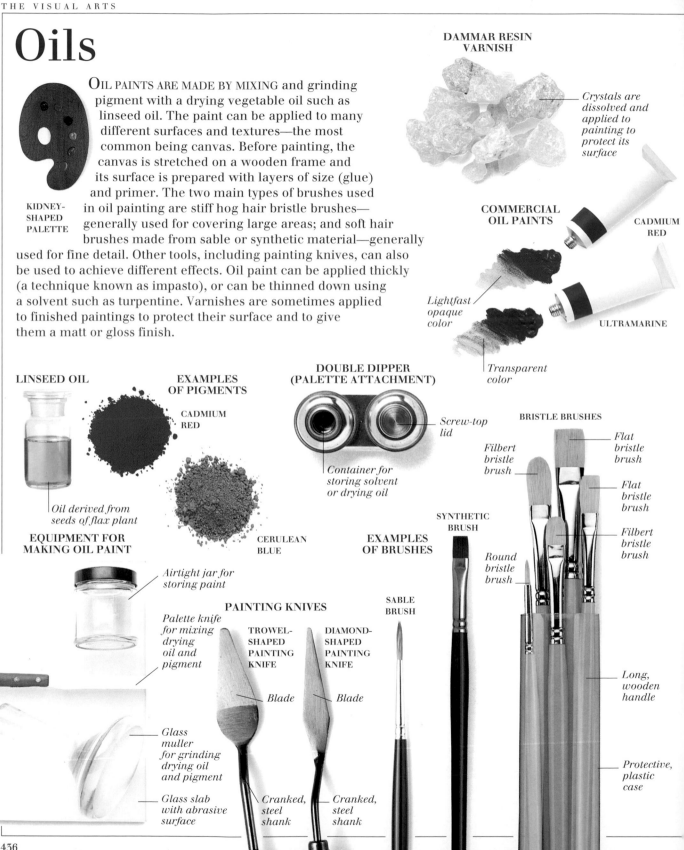

KIDNEY-SHAPED PALETTE

OIL PAINTS ARE MADE BY MIXING and grinding pigment with a drying vegetable oil such as linseed oil. The paint can be applied to many different surfaces and textures—the most common being canvas. Before painting, the canvas is stretched on a wooden frame and its surface is prepared with layers of size (glue) and primer. The two main types of brushes used in oil painting are stiff hog hair bristle brushes—generally used for covering large areas; and soft hair brushes made from sable or synthetic material—generally used for fine detail. Other tools, including painting knives, can also be used to achieve different effects. Oil paint can be applied thickly (a technique known as impasto), or can be thinned down using a solvent such as turpentine. Varnishes are sometimes applied to finished paintings to protect their surface and to give them a matt or gloss finish.

DAMMAR RESIN VARNISH

Crystals are dissolved and applied to painting to protect its surface

COMMERCIAL OIL PAINTS

CADMIUM RED

Lightfast opaque color

Transparent color

ULTRAMARINE

LINSEED OIL

Oil derived from seeds of flax plant

EXAMPLES OF PIGMENTS

CADMIUM RED

CERULEAN BLUE

DOUBLE DIPPER (PALETTE ATTACHMENT)

Screw-top lid

Container for storing solvent or drying oil

BRISTLE BRUSHES

Flat bristle brush

Filbert bristle brush

Flat bristle brush

Filbert bristle brush

SYNTHETIC BRUSH

Round bristle brush

EQUIPMENT FOR MAKING OIL PAINT

Airtight jar for storing paint

Palette knife for mixing drying oil and pigment

PAINTING KNIVES

TROWEL-SHAPED PAINTING KNIFE

DIAMOND-SHAPED PAINTING KNIFE

SABLE BRUSH

EXAMPLES OF BRUSHES

Blade

Blade

Glass muller for grinding drying oil and pigment

Glass slab with abrasive surface

Cranked, steel shank

Cranked, steel shank

Long, wooden handle

Protective, plastic case

EXAMPLE OF AN OIL PAINTING
Fritillarias, Vincent van Gogh, 1886
Oil on canvas, 29 x 24 in (73.5 x 60.5 cm)

Artist's signature scratched in wet paint with the end of the brush

Each leaf painted in a single, rapid stroke

Impasto (deep ridges of paint applied in thick strokes)

Strong directional brushstrokes on table draw attention to the vase

Background enlivened by dabs of white and green

Orange and blue (complementary colors) placed together to give maximum contrast and enhance one another to appear brighter

Features of vase highlighted by generous touches of yellow

STUDIO EASEL

Top sliding-block adjusts to canvas height

Canvas support

Height adjustment key

Angle adjustment key

Tripod

CANVAS STRETCHED ON WOODEN FRAME (VIEWED FROM THE BACK)

Staple

Canvas prepared with glue (size) and primer

Wooden frame

Unprimed canvas

EXAMPLES OF CANVASES

COTTON DUCK

FINE LINEN

COARSE LINEN

Watercolor

WATERCOLOR PAINT IS MADE OF GROUND PIGMENT mixed with a water-soluble binding medium, usually gum arabic. It is usually applied to paper using soft hair brushes such as sable, goat hair, squirrel, and synthetic brushes. Watercolors are often diluted and applied as overlaying washes (thin, transparent layers) to build up depth of color. Washes can be laid in a variety of ways to create a range of different effects. For example, a wet-in-wet wash can be achieved by laying a wash on top of another wet wash. The two washes blend together to give a fused effect. Sponges are used to modify washes by soaking up paint so that areas of pigment are lightened or removed from the paper. Watercolors can also be applied undiluted—a technique known as dry brush—to create a broken-color effect. Watercolors are generally transparent and allow light to reflect from the surface of the paper through the layers of paint to give a luminous effect. They can be thickened and made opaque by adding body color (Chinese white).

GUM ARABIC

Natural sap from acacia tree

NATURAL SPONGE

ANATOMY OF A SABLE BRUSH

Soft red sable hair

Toe (tip)

Wooden handle

SOFT HAIR BRUSHES

Hair trimmed and cemented into ferrule

ROUND SABLE BRUSH (NO. 6)

Round ferrule

Hair tied with clove hitch knot

ROUND SABLE BRUSH (NO. 1)

TUBES OF WATERCOLOR PAINT

SYNTHETIC WASH BRUSH

WINSOR GREEN

Winsor Green
Vert Winsor
Winsorgrun
Verde Winsor
Verde Winsor
0102 720 SL Series 1 A

Cadmium Yellow
Jaune de Cadmium
Kadmiumgelb
Amarillo de Cadmio
Giallo di cadmio
0102 108 SL Series 4 A

SQUIRREL MOP WASH BRUSH

PORTABLE BOX OF WATERCOLOR PAINTS

CADMIUM YELLOW

Painted color swatch

Chinese white

Pan of watercolor paint

Lid can be used for mixing colors

Chinese White
Blanc de Chine
Chinesischweiss
Blanco of China

LARGE GOAT HAKE WASH BRUSH

EXAMPLE OF A WATERCOLOR
Burning of the Houses of Parliament, Turner, 1834
Watercolor on paper, 11½ x 17½ in (29.2 x 44.5 cm)

Transparent washes laid on top of each other to create tonal depth

Highlight scratched out with a scalpel

Crowd painted with thin strokes laid over a pale wash

Transparent washes allow light to reflect off the surface of the paper to give a luminous effect

Paper shows through thin wash to give flames added highlight

Undiluted paint applied, then partly washed out, to create the impression of water

EXAMPLES OF WATERCOLOR PAPERS

SMOOTH-TEXTURED PAPER

MEDIUM-TEXTURED PAPER

ROUGH-TEXTURED PAPER

EXAMPLES OF WASHES

WASH OVER DRY BRUSH
Wash laid over paint applied with dry brush gives two-tone effect

GRADED WASH
Strong wash applied to tilted paper gives graded effect

DRY BRUSH
Undiluted paint dragged across surface of paper gives broken effect

WET-IN-WET
Two diluted washes left to run together to give fused effect

COLOR WHEEL OF WATERCOLOR PAINTS

Yellow (primary color)

Secondary colors made by mixing yellow and blue

Secondary colors made by mixing red and yellow

Blue (primary color)

Red (primary color)

Secondary colors made by mixing blue and red

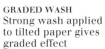
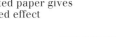

Pastels

PASTELS ARE STICKS OF PIGMENT made by mixing ground pigment with chalk and a binding medium, such as gum arabic. They vary in hardness depending on the proportion of the binding medium to the chalk. Soft pastel—the most common form of pastel—contains just enough binding medium to hold the pigment in stick form. Pastels can be applied directly to any support (surface) with sufficient tooth (texture). When a pastel is drawn over a textured surface, the pigment crumbles and lodges in the fibers of the support. Pastel marks have a particular soft, matt quality and are suitable for techniques such as blending, scumbling, and feathering. Blending is a technique of rubbing and fusing two or more colors on the support using fingers or various tools such as tortillons (paper stumps), soft hair brushes, kneaded erasers, and soft bread. Scumbling is a technique of building up layers of pastel colors. The side or blunted tip of a soft pastel is lightly drawn over an underpainted area so that patches of the color beneath show through. Feathering is a technique of applying parallel strokes of color with the point of a pastel, usually over an existing layer of pastel color. A thin spray of fixative can be applied— using a mouth diffuser (see pp. 430-431) or aerosol spray fixative—to a finished pastel painting, or in between layers of color, to prevent smudging.

EQUIPMENT FOR MAKING PASTELS

Glass muller

Chalk

Glass slab with abrasive surface *Gum arabic* *Ivory-black pigment* *Cobalt-blue pigment*

EXAMPLES OF SOFT PASTELS

COBALT-BLUE HALF PASTEL

VERMILION HALF PASTEL

OLIVE-GREEN FULL PASTEL

MAUVE FULL PASTEL

EQUIPMENT USED WITH PASTELS

BOXED PASTEL SET

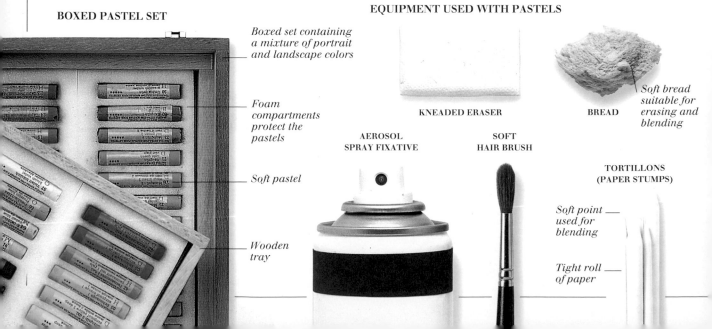

Boxed set containing a mixture of portrait and landscape colors

Foam compartments protect the pastels

Soft pastel

Wooden tray

KNEADED ERASER

AEROSOL SPRAY FIXATIVE

SOFT HAIR BRUSH

BREAD

Soft bread suitable for erasing and blending

TORTILLONS (PAPER STUMPS)

Soft point used for blending

Tight roll of paper

EXAMPLE OF A PASTEL PAINTING
Woman Drying her Neck, Edgar Degas, c.1898
Pastel on cardboard, 24½ x 25½ in (62.5 x 65.5 cm)

Pastels applied directly to support

Colors are blended together using fingers or tools such as tortillons

Built up layers of pastel

Rich color of fabric created by overlaying yellows and oranges

Broken colors, characteristic of scumbling technique

Toned color of paper visible beneath thinly applied pastels

Pure bright colors laid side by side produce strong contrasts

DETAIL FROM "WOMAN DRYING HER NECK"

Feathering technique used to produce skin tones

EXAMPLES OF TEXTURED PAPERS AND PASTEL BOARDS

WATERCOLOR PAPER (ROUGH TEXTURE)

GLASS PAPER

WATERCOLOR PAPER (MEDIUM TEXTURE)

INGRES PAPER

FLOCKED PASTEL BOARD

CANSON PAPER

EXAMPLES OF COLORED AND TINTED PAPERS

Acrylics

ACRYLIC PAINT IS MADE BY MIXING PIGMENT with a synthetic resin. It can be thinned with water but dries to become water insoluble. Acrylics are applied to many surfaces, such as paper and acrylic-primed board and canvas. A variety of brushes, painting knives, rollers, air-brushes, plastic scrapers, and other tools are used in acrylic painting. The versatility of acrylics makes them suitable for a wide range of techniques. They can be used opaquely or—by adding water—in a transparent, watercolor style. Acrylic mediums can be added to the paint to adjust its consistency for special effects such as glazing and impasto (ridges of paint applied in thick strokes) or to make it more matt or glossy. Acrylics are quick-drying, which allows layers of paint to be applied on top of each other almost immediately.

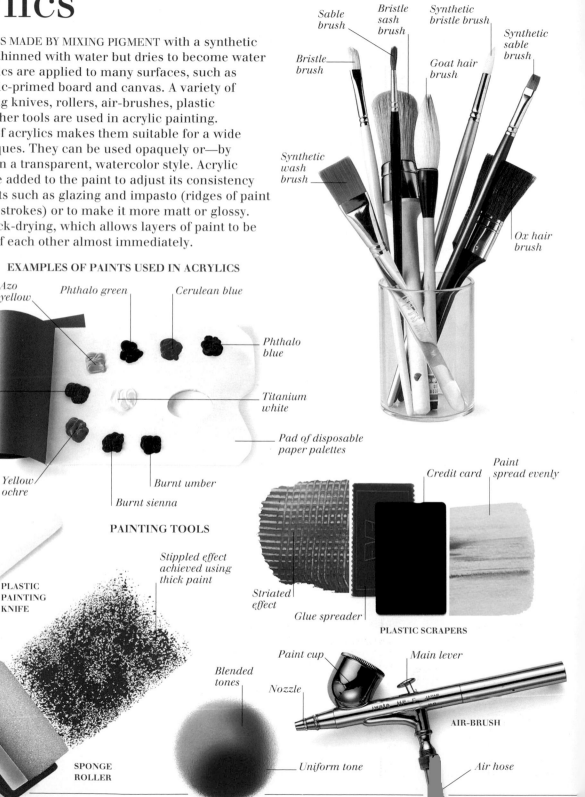

EXAMPLES OF BRUSHES

Sable brush

Bristle sash brush

Synthetic bristle brush

Synthetic sable brush

Bristle brush

Goat hair brush

Synthetic wash brush

Ox hair brush

EXAMPLES OF PAINTS USED IN ACRYLICS

Azo yellow

Phthalo green

Cerulean blue

Phthalo blue

Quinacridone red

Titanium white

Pad of disposable paper palettes

Yellow ochre

Burnt umber

Burnt sienna

PAINTING TOOLS

Flexible, plastic blade

Stippled effect achieved using thick paint

Credit card

Paint spread evenly

Striated effect

PLASTIC PAINTING KNIFE

Glue spreader

PLASTIC SCRAPERS

Paint cup

Main lever

Blended tones

Nozzle

AIR-BRUSH

Plastic handle

SPONGE ROLLER

Uniform tone

Air hose

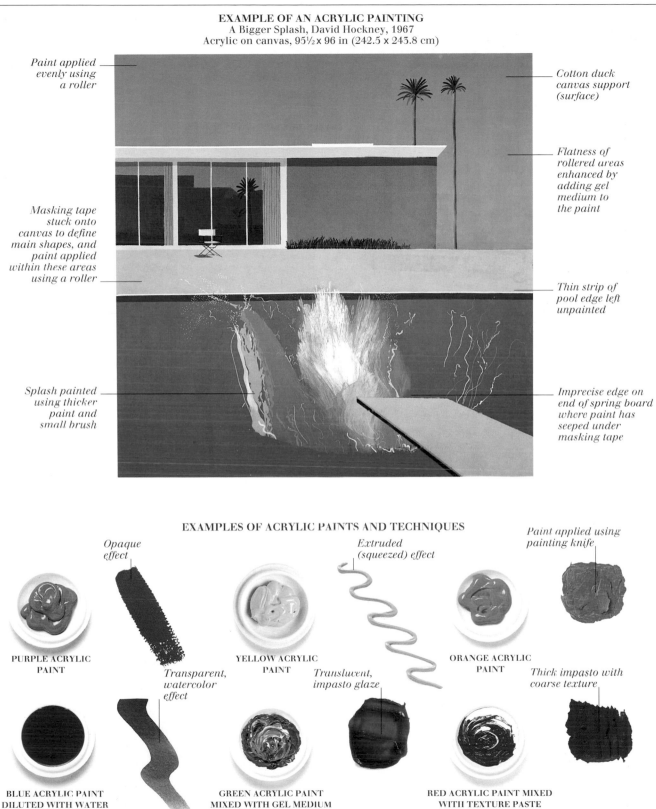

EXAMPLE OF AN ACRYLIC PAINTING
A Bigger Splash, David Hockney, 1967
Acrylic on canvas, 95½ x 96 in (242.5 x 243.8 cm)

Paint applied evenly using a roller

Cotton duck canvas support (surface)

Flatness of rollered areas enhanced by adding gel medium to the paint

Masking tape stuck onto canvas to define main shapes, and paint applied within these areas using a roller

Thin strip of pool edge left unpainted

Splash painted using thicker paint and small brush

Imprecise edge on end of spring board where paint has seeped under masking tape

EXAMPLES OF ACRYLIC PAINTS AND TECHNIQUES

Opaque effect

Extruded (squeezed) effect

Paint applied using painting knife

PURPLE ACRYLIC PAINT

YELLOW ACRYLIC PAINT

ORANGE ACRYLIC PAINT

Transparent, watercolor effect

Translucent, impasto glaze

Thick impasto with coarse texture

BLUE ACRYLIC PAINT DILUTED WITH WATER

GREEN ACRYLIC PAINT MIXED WITH GEL MEDIUM

RED ACRYLIC PAINT MIXED WITH TEXTURE PASTE

Calligraphy

CALLIGRAPHY IS BEAUTIFULLY FORMED LETTERING. The term applies to written text and illumination (the decoration of manuscripts using gold leaf and color). The essential materials needed to practice calligraphy are a writing tool, ink, and a writing surface. Quills are among the oldest writing tools. They are usually made from goose or turkey feathers, and are noted for their flexibility and ability to produce fine lines. A quill point, however, is not very durable and constant recutting and trimming is required. The most commonly used writing instrument in western calligraphy is a detachable, metal nib held in a penholder. The metal nib is very durable, and there are a wide range of different types. Particular types of nibs—such as copperplate, speedball, and round-hand nibs—are used for specific styles of lettering. Some nibs have integral ink reservoirs and others have reservoirs that are detachable. Brushes are also used for writing, and for filling in outlined letters and painting decoration. Other writing tools used in calligraphy are fountain pens, felt-tipped pens, rotring pens, and reed pens. Calligraphy inks may come in liquid form, or as a solid ink stick. Ink sticks are ground down in distilled water to form a liquid ink. The most common writing surfaces for calligraphy are good quality, smooth-surfaced papers. To achieve the best writing position, the calligrapher places the paper on a drawing board set at an angle.

EQUIPMENT USED IN BRUSH LETTERING

Brush rest

Wolf hair brush

Goat hair brush

BRUSHES AND BRUSH REST

Liquid ink made by grinding down ink stick in distilled water

Solid carbon ink stick

Ink stone

INK STICK AND STONE

Feather

PENS, NIBS, AND BRUSHES USED IN CALLIGRAPHY

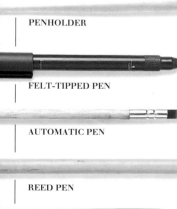

PENHOLDER

FELT-TIPPED PEN

AUTOMATIC PEN

REED PEN

SQUARE SABLE BRUSH

POINTED SABLE BRUSH

COPPERPLATE NIB

SPEEDBALL NIB

ROUND-HAND NIB AND DETACHABLE INK RESERVOIR

GOAT HAIR BRUSH

WOLF HAIR BRUSH

FOUNTAIN PEN AND INK

Feather stripped for better handling

Barrel

Bottle of permanent black ink

Barrel

Clip

Nib

Outer cap

Hand-cut point

GOOSE-FEATHER QUILL

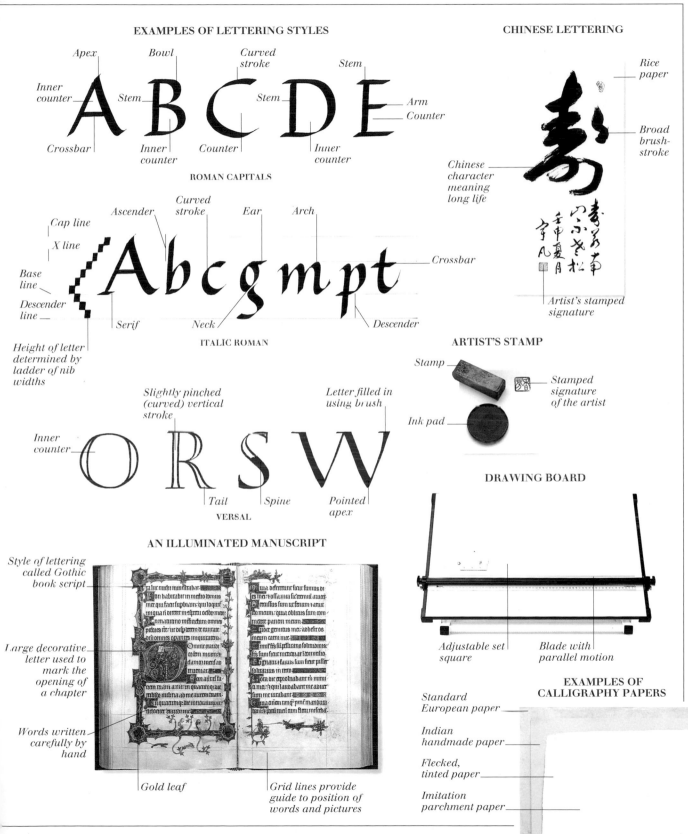

EXAMPLES OF LETTERING STYLES

Apex
Bowl
Curved stroke
Stem
Inner counter
Stem
Stem
Arm
Counter
Crossbar
Inner counter
Counter
Inner counter

ROMAN CAPITALS

Cap line
X line
Base line
Descender line
Ascender
Curved stroke
Ear
Arch
Crossbar
Serif
Neck
Descender
Height of letter determined by ladder of nib widths

ITALIC ROMAN

Slightly pinched (curved) vertical stroke
Letter filled in using brush
Inner counter
Tail
Spine
Pointed apex

VERSAL

AN ILLUMINATED MANUSCRIPT

Style of lettering called Gothic book script
Large decorative letter used to mark the opening of a chapter
Words written carefully by hand
Gold leaf
Grid lines provide guide to position of words and pictures

CHINESE LETTERING

Rice paper
Broad brush-stroke
Chinese character meaning long life
Artist's stamped signature

ARTIST'S STAMP

Stamp
Stamped signature of the artist
Ink pad

DRAWING BOARD

Adjustable set square
Blade with parallel motion

EXAMPLES OF CALLIGRAPHY PAPERS

Standard European paper
Indian handmade paper
Flecked, tinted paper
Imitation parchment paper

Printmaking 1

PRINTS ARE MADE BY FOUR BASIC printing processes – intaglio, lithographic, relief, and screen. In intaglio printing, lines are engraved or etched onto the surface of a metal plate. Lines are engraved using sharp metal tools. They are etched by corroding the metal plate with acid, using acid-resistant ground to protect the areas not to be etched. The plate is then inked and wiped, leaving the grooves filled with ink and the surface clean. Dampened paper is laid over the plate, and both paper and plate are passed through the rollers of an etching press. The pressure of the rollers forces the paper into the grooves, so that it takes up the ink, leaving an impression on the paper. Lithographic printing is based on the antipathy between grease and water. An image is drawn on a surface—usually a stone or metal plate—with a greasy medium, such as tusche (lihographic ink). The greasy drawing is fixed onto the plate by applying an acidic solution, such as gum arabic. The surface is then dampened and rolled with ink. The ink adheres only to the greasy areas and is repelled by the water. Paper is laid on the plate and pressure is applied by means of a press. In relief printing, the non-printing areas of a wood or linoleum block are cut away using gouges, knives, and other tools. The printing areas are left raised in relief and are rolled with ink. Paper is laid on the inked block and pressure is applied by means of a press or by burnishing (rubbing) the back of the paper. The most common forms of relief printing are woodcut, wood engraving, and linocut. In screen printing, the printing surface is a mesh stretched across a wooden frame. A stencil is applied to the mesh to seal the non-printing areas and ink is scraped through the mesh to produce an image.

THE FOUR MAIN PRINTING PROCESSES

Paper — Printed image
— Engraved or etched image
Metal plate — Inked area

INTAGLIO

Printed image —
Damp surface rejects ink —
Ink adheres to greasy image —
— Paper
— Image drawn on stone with greasy medium

LITHOGRAPHIC

Paper — Printed image
Raised figure —
Wood block — Inked surface

RELIEF

Ink forced through mesh —
— Wooden frame
— Stencil
— Printed image
Paper —

SCREEN

LEATHER INK DABBER

EQUIPMENT USED IN INTAGLIO PRINTING

ROCKER   SCRIBER   ROULETTE   SCRAPER   BURNISHER   CLAMP

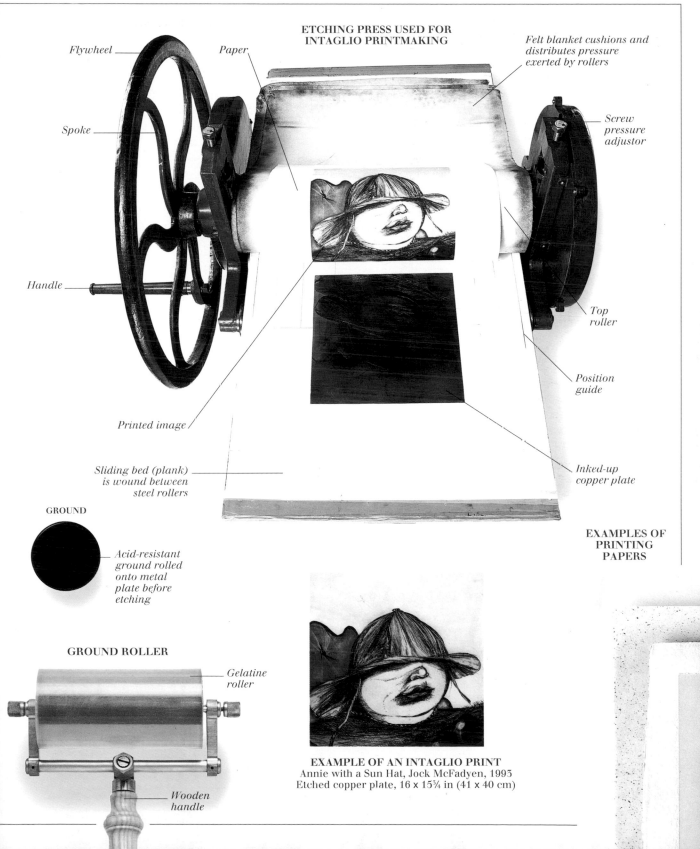

ETCHING PRESS USED FOR INTAGLIO PRINTMAKING

Flywheel

Paper

Felt blanket cushions and distributes pressure exerted by rollers

Screw pressure adjustor

Spoke

Handle

Top roller

Position guide

Printed image

Inked-up copper plate

Sliding bed (plank) is wound between steel rollers

GROUND

Acid-resistant ground rolled onto metal plate before etching

EXAMPLES OF PRINTING PAPERS

GROUND ROLLER

Gelatine roller

EXAMPLE OF AN INTAGLIO PRINT
Annie with a Sun Hat, Jock McFadyen, 1993
Etched copper plate, 16 x 15¾ in (41 x 40 cm)

Wooden handle

Printmaking 2

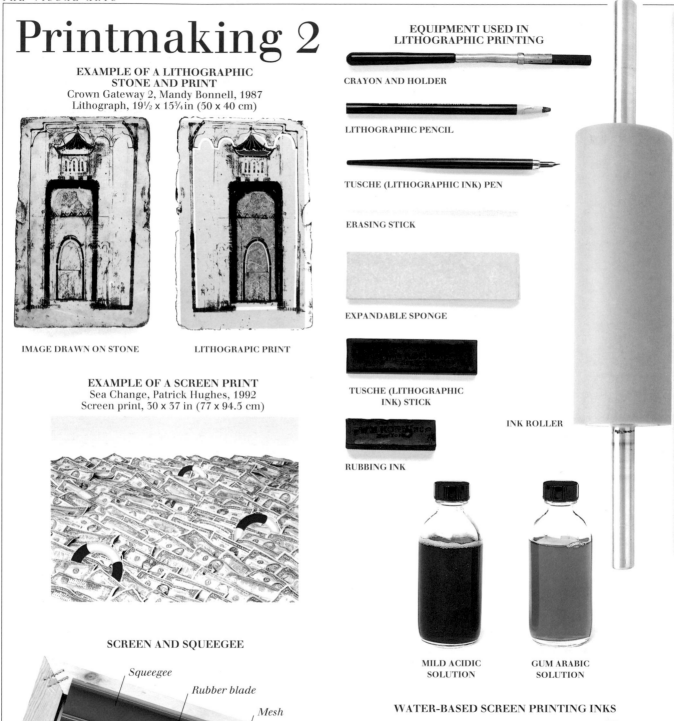

EXAMPLE OF A LITHOGRAPHIC STONE AND PRINT
Crown Gateway 2, Mandy Bonnell, 1987
Lithograph, 19½ x 15¾ in (50 x 40 cm)

IMAGE DRAWN ON STONE

LITHOGRAPIC PRINT

EXAMPLE OF A SCREEN PRINT
Sea Change, Patrick Hughes, 1992
Screen print, 30 x 37 in (77 x 94.5 cm)

SCREEN AND SQUEEGEE

Squeegee

Rubber blade

Mesh

Wooden frame

EQUIPMENT USED IN LITHOGRAPHIC PRINTING

CRAYON AND HOLDER

LITHOGRAPHIC PENCIL

TUSCHE (LITHOGRAPHIC INK) PEN

ERASING STICK

EXPANDABLE SPONGE

TUSCHE (LITHOGRAPHIC INK) STICK

INK ROLLER

RUBBING INK

MILD ACIDIC SOLUTION

GUM ARABIC SOLUTION

WATER-BASED SCREEN PRINTING INKS

BLUE ACRYLIC INK

RED ACRYLIC INK

BROWN TEXTILE INK

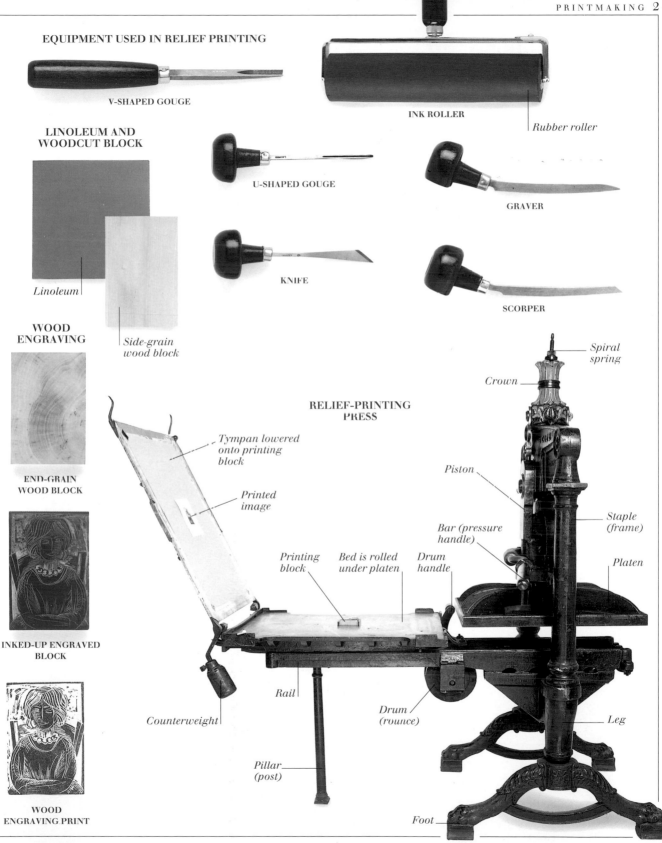

EQUIPMENT USED IN RELIEF PRINTING

V-SHAPED GOUGE

INK ROLLER

Rubber roller

LINOLEUM AND WOODCUT BLOCK

U-SHAPED GOUGE

GRAVER

Linoleum

KNIFE

SCORPER

Side-grain wood block

WOOD ENGRAVING

END-GRAIN WOOD BLOCK

INKED-UP ENGRAVED BLOCK

WOOD ENGRAVING PRINT

RELIEF-PRINTING PRESS

Tympan lowered onto printing block

Printed image

Spiral spring

Crown

Piston

Staple (frame)

Printing block

Bed is rolled under platen

Drum handle

Bar (pressure handle)

Platen

Rail

Counterweight

Drum (rounce)

Leg

Pillar (post)

Foot

Mosaic

MOSAIC IS THE ART OF MAKING patterns and pictures from tesserae (small, colored pieces of glass, marble, and other materials). Different materials are cut into tesserae using different tools. Smalti (glass enamel) and marble are cut into pieces using a hammer and a hardy (a pointed blade) embedded in a log. Vitreous glass is cut into pieces using a pair of pliers. Mosaics can be made using a direct or indirect method. In the direct method, the tesserae are laid directly into a bed of cement–based adhesive. In the indirect method, the design is drawn in reverse on paper or cloth. The tesserae are then stuck face down on the paper or cloth using water-soluble glue. Adhesive is spread with a trowel onto a solid surface—such as a wall—and the back of the mosaic is laid into the adhesive. Finally, the paper or cloth is soaked off to reveal the mosaic. Gaps between tesserae can be filled with grout. Grout is forced into gaps by dragging a grouting squeegee across the face of the mosaic. Mosaics are usually used to decorate walls and floors, but they can also be applied to smaller objects.

EQUIPMENT FOR BREAKING MARBLE

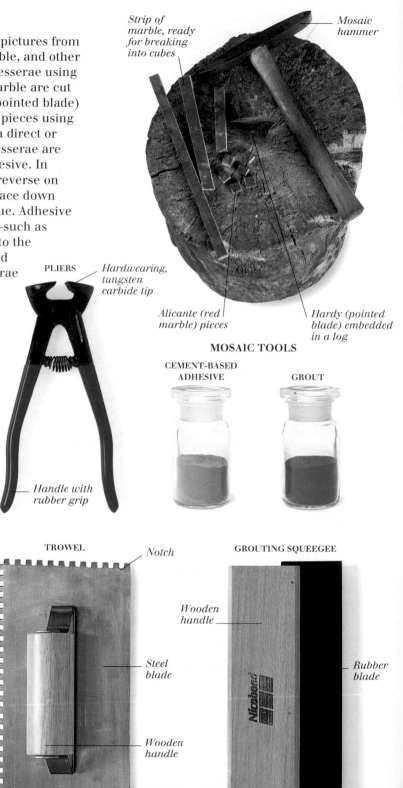

Strip of marble, ready for breaking into cubes

Mosaic hammer

PLIERS — *Hardwearing, tungsten carbide tip*

Alicante (red marble) pieces

Hardy (pointed blade) embedded in a log

MOSAIC TOOLS

CEMENT-BASED ADHESIVE

GROUT

Handle with rubber grip

SMALTI (GLASS ENAMEL)

EXAMPLE OF A MOSAIC (DIRECT METHOD)
Seascape, Tessa Hunkin, 1993
Smalti mosaic on board
31½ in (80 cm) diameter

RED SMALTI

Gold-leaf smalti

YELLOW SMALTI

BLUE SMALTI

TROWEL

Notch

Steel blade

Wooden handle

GROUTING SQUEEGEE

Wooden handle

Rubber blade

Nicoband

STAGES IN THE CREATION OF A MOSAIC (INDIRECT METHOD)

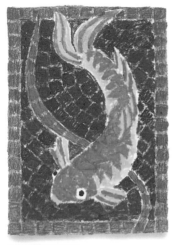

COLOR SKETCH
A color sketch is drawn
in oil pastel to give a clear
impression of how the finished
mosaic will look.

REVERSE IMAGE
Tesserae are glued face down
on reverse image on paper.
Mosaic is then attached to solid
surface and paper is removed.

MOSAIC POT

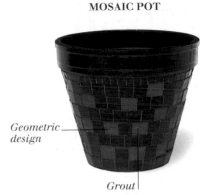

Geometric design

Grout

MOSAIC MOSQUE DESIGN

Floral design

Geometric border

VITREOUS GLASS

GREEN VITREOUS GLASS WITH GOLD LEAF

Plain finish

Ripple finish

RED VITREOUS GLASS

BLUE VITREOUS GLASS

SHEETS OF VITREOUS GLASS

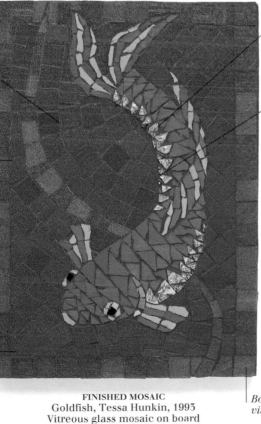

*Andamenti
(line along
which tesserae
are laid)*

*Grout fills
the gaps
between the
tesserae*

*Mosaic
mounted
on board*

*Vitreous
glass cut into
triangular
shape with
pliers*

*Gold tessera
with ripple
finish*

*Gold tessera
placed upside-
down*

FINISHED MOSAIC
Goldfish, Tessa Hunkin, 1993
Vitreous glass mosaic on board
14 x 10 in (35.5 x 25.5 cm)

*Border of square
vitreous glass*

Sculpture 1

THE TWO TRADITIONAL SCULPTURE METHODS are carving and modeling. A carved sculpture is made by cutting away the surplus from a block of hard material such as stone, marble, or wood. The tools used for carving vary according to the material being carved. Heavy steel points, claws, and chisels that are struck with a lump hammer are generally used for stone and marble. Sharp gouges and chisels that are struck with a wooden mallet are used for wood. Sculptures formed from hard materials are generally finished by filing with rasps, rifflers, and other abrasive implements. Modeling is a process by which shapes are built up, using malleable materials such as clay, plaster, and wax. The material is cut with wire-ended tools and modeled with the fingers or a variety of hardwood and metal implements. For large or intricate modeled sculptures an armature (frame), made from metal or wood, is used to provide internal support. Sculptures formed in soft materials may harden naturally or can be made more durable by firing in a kiln. Modeled sculptures are often first designed in wax or another material to be cast later in a metal (see pp. 454-455) such as bronze. The development of many new materials in the 20th century has enabled sculptors to experiment with new techniques such as construction (joining preformed pieces of material such as machine components, mirrors, and furniture) and kinetic (mobile) sculpture.

(see pp. 454-455)

EXAMPLES OF MARBLE-CARVING TOOLS

2½ lb (1.1 kg) iron head

Ash handle

LUMP HAMMER

CALLIPERS

Curved leg

Gap measures distance between two points on a sculpture

Wing nut

EXAMPLES OF WOOD-CARVING TOOLS

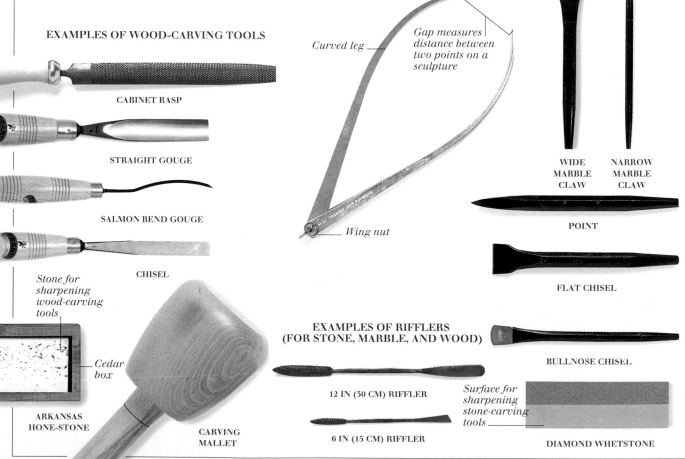

CABINET RASP

STRAIGHT GOUGE

SALMON BEND GOUGE

CHISEL

Stone for sharpening wood-carving tools

Cedar box

ARKANSAS HONE-STONE

CARVING MALLET

EXAMPLES OF RIFFLERS (FOR STONE, MARBLE, AND WOOD)

12 IN (30 CM) RIFFLER

6 IN (15 CM) RIFFLER

WIDE MARBLE CLAW

NARROW MARBLE CLAW

POINT

FLAT CHISEL

BULLNOSE CHISEL

Surface for sharpening stone-carving tools

DIAMOND WHETSTONE

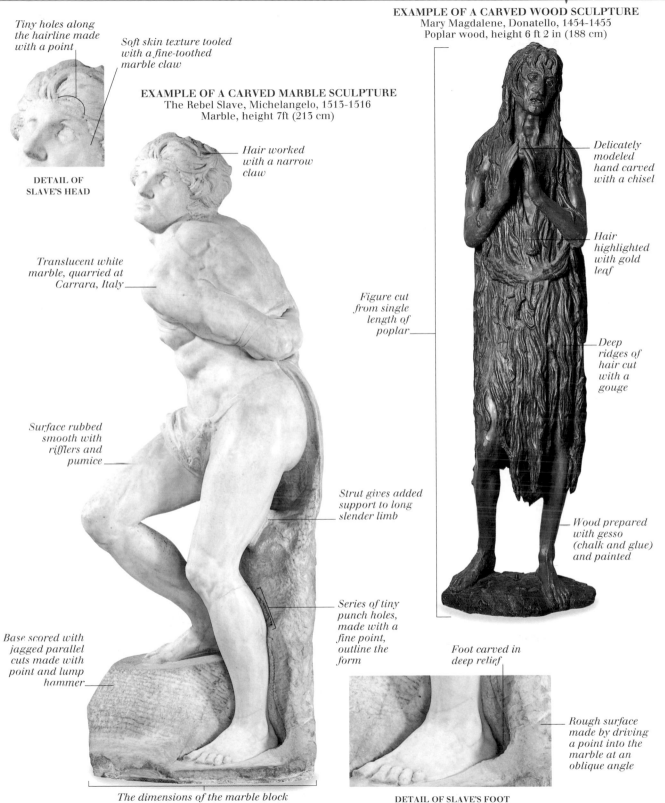

Tiny holes along
the hairline made
with a point

Soft skin texture tooled
with a fine-toothed
marble claw

**DETAIL OF
SLAVE'S HEAD**

EXAMPLE OF A CARVED WOOD SCULPTURE
Mary Magdalene, Donatello, 1454-1455
Poplar wood, height 6 ft 2 in (188 cm)

EXAMPLE OF A CARVED MARBLE SCULPTURE
The Rebel Slave, Michelangelo, 1513-1516
Marble, height 7ft (213 cm)

Hair worked
with a narrow
claw

Delicately
modeled
hand carved
with a chisel

Translucent white
marble, quarried at
Carrara, Italy

Hair
highlighted
with gold
leaf

Figure cut
from single
length of
poplar

Deep
ridges of
hair cut
with a
gouge

Surface rubbed
smooth with
rifflers and
pumice

Strut gives added
support to long
slender limb

Wood prepared
with gesso
(chalk and glue)
and painted

Series of tiny
punch holes,
made with a
fine point,
outline the
form

Base scored with
jagged parallel
cuts made with
point and lump
hammer

Foot carved in
deep relief

Rough surface
made by driving
a point into the
marble at an
oblique angle

The dimensions of the marble block
determine the size of the sculpture

DETAIL OF SLAVE'S FOOT

Sculpture 2

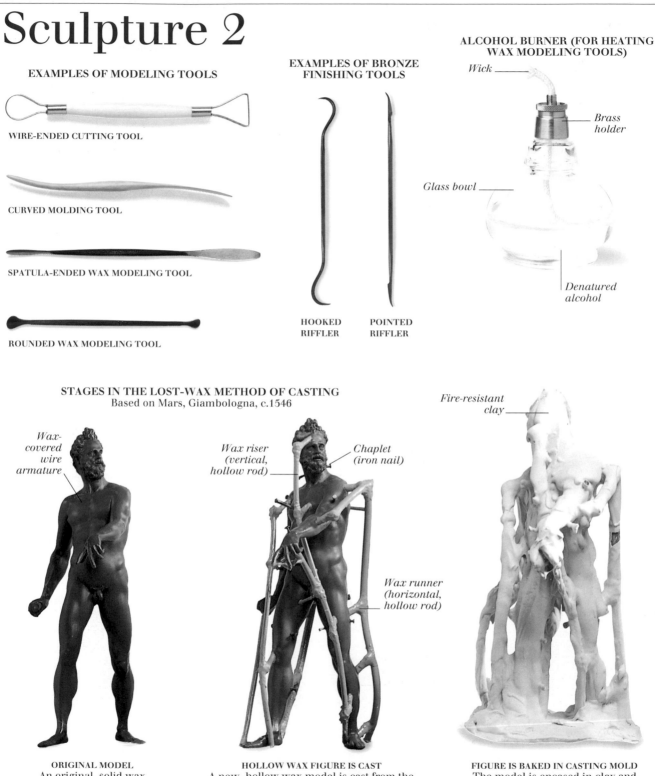

EXAMPLES OF MODELING TOOLS

WIRE-ENDED CUTTING TOOL

CURVED MOLDING TOOL

SPATULA-ENDED WAX MODELING TOOL

ROUNDED WAX MODELING TOOL

EXAMPLES OF BRONZE FINISHING TOOLS

HOOKED RIFFLER

POINTED RIFFLER

ALCOHOL BURNER (FOR HEATING WAX MODELING TOOLS)

Wick

Brass holder

Glass bowl

Denatured alcohol

STAGES IN THE LOST-WAX METHOD OF CASTING
Based on Mars, Giambologna, c.1546

Wax-covered wire armature

Wax riser (vertical, hollow rod)

Chaplet (iron nail)

Wax runner (horizontal, hollow rod)

Fire-resistant clay

ORIGINAL MODEL
An original, solid wax model is made and preserved so that numerous replicas can be cast.

HOLLOW WAX FIGURE IS CAST
A new, hollow wax model is cast from the original model. It is filled with a plaster core that is held in place with nails. Wax runners and risers are attached.

FIGURE IS BAKED IN CASTING MOLD
The model is encased in clay and baked. The wax melts away (through the channels made by the wax rods) and is replaced by molten bronze.

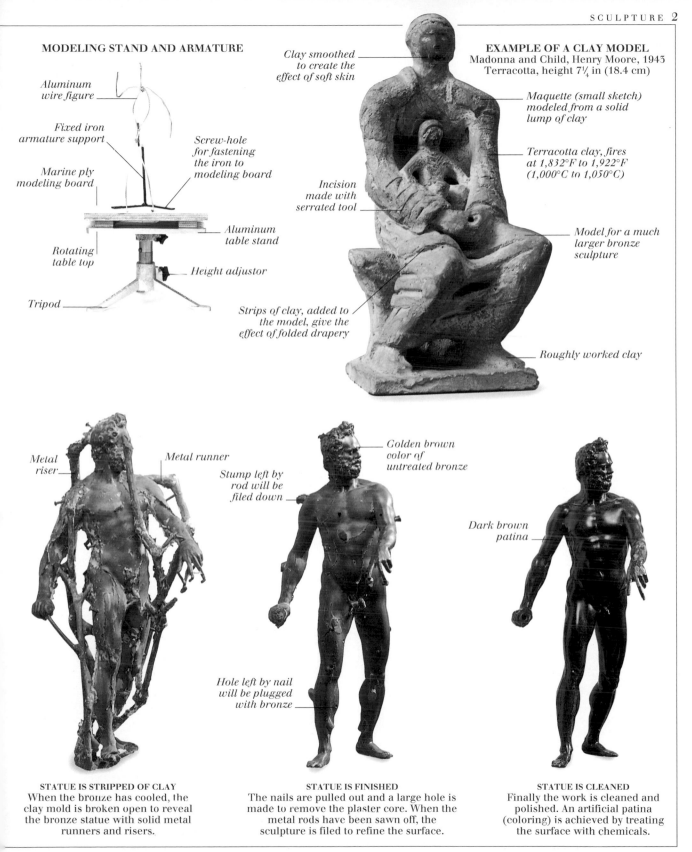

MODELING STAND AND ARMATURE

Aluminum wire figure

Fixed iron armature support

Marine ply modeling board

Screw-hole for fastening the iron to modeling board

Aluminum table stand

Rotating table top

Height adjustor

Tripod

Clay smoothed to create the effect of soft skin

Incision made with serrated tool

Strips of clay, added to the model, give the effect of folded drapery

EXAMPLE OF A CLAY MODEL
Madonna and Child, Henry Moore, 1943
Terracotta, height 7¼ in (18.4 cm)

Maquette (small sketch) modeled from a solid lump of clay

Terracotta clay, fires at 1,832°F to 1,922°F (1,000°C to 1,050°C)

Model for a much larger bronze sculpture

Roughly worked clay

Metal riser

Metal runner

Golden brown color of untreated bronze

Stump left by rod will be filed down

Dark brown patina

Hole left by nail will be plugged with bronze

STATUE IS STRIPPED OF CLAY
When the bronze has cooled, the clay mold is broken open to reveal the bronze statue with solid metal runners and risers.

STATUE IS FINISHED
The nails are pulled out and a large hole is made to remove the plaster core. When the metal rods have been sawn off, the sculpture is filed to refine the surface.

STATUE IS CLEANED
Finally the work is cleaned and polished. An artificial patina (coloring) is achieved by treating the surface with chemicals.

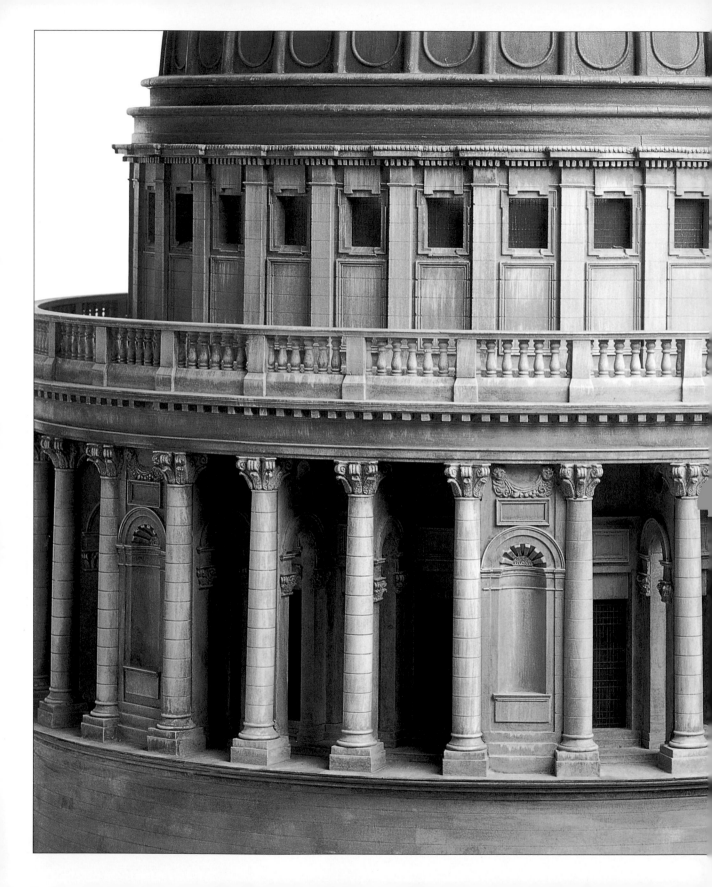

ARCHITECTURE

Ancient Egypt

THE CIVILIZATION OF THE ANCIENT EGYPTIANS (which lasted from about 3100 BC until it was finally absorbed into the Roman empire in 30 BC) is famous for its temples and tombs. Egyptian temples were often huge and geometric, like the Temple of Amon-Re (below and right). They were usually decorated with hieroglyphs (sacred characters used for picture writing) and painted reliefs depicting gods, Pharaohs (kings), and queens. Tombs were particularly important to the Egyptians, who believed that the dead were resurrected in the afterlife. The tombs were often decorated—for example, the surround of the false door opposite— in order to give comfort to the dead. The best-known ancient Egyptian tombs are the pyramids, which were designed to symbolize the rays of the sun. Many of the architectural forms used by the ancient Egyptians were later adopted by other civilizations. For example, columns and capitals were later used by the ancient Greeks (see pp. 460-461) and ancient Romans (see pp. 462-465).

Cornice decorated with cavetto molding

Campaniform (open papyrus) capital

Architrave

Papyrus-bud capital

Socle

Side aisle

Central nave

Side aisle

SIDE VIEW OF HYPOSTYLE HALL, TEMPLE OF AMON-RE, KARNAK, EGYPT, c.1290 BC

Horus, the sun-god

Architrave

Stone slab forming flat roof of side aisle

Kepresh crown with disc

Chons, the moon-god

Amon-Re, king of the gods

Hathor, the sky-goddess

Papyrus motif

Cartouche (oval border) containing the titles of the Pharaoh (king)

Socle

Aisle running north–south

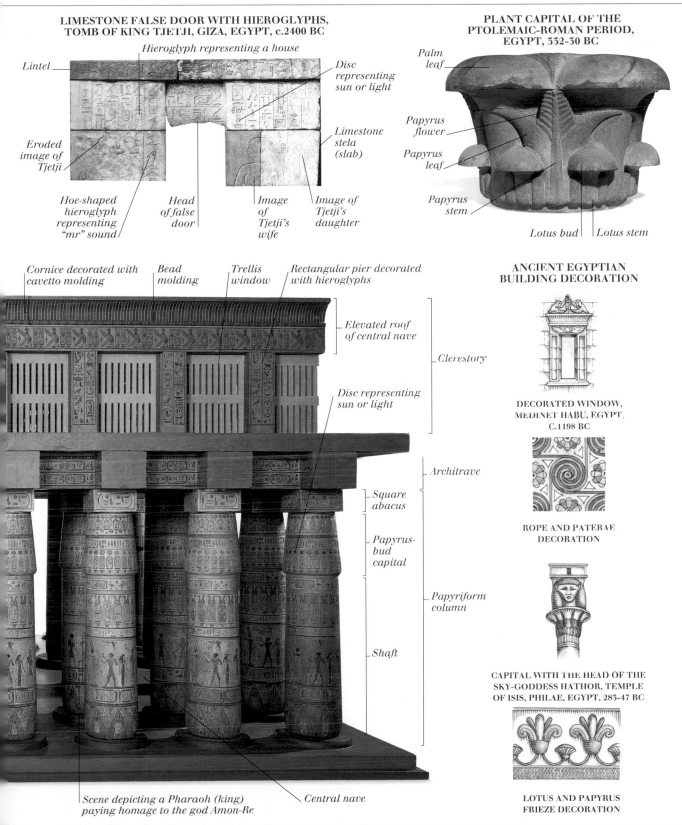

LIMESTONE FALSE DOOR WITH HIEROGLYPHS, TOMB OF KING TJETJI, GIZA, EGYPT, c.2400 BC

Hieroglyph representing a house

Lintel

Disc representing sun or light

Limestone stela (slab)

Eroded image of Tjetji

Hoe-shaped hieroglyph representing "mr" sound

Head of false door

Image of Tjetji's wife

Image of Tjetji's daughter

PLANT CAPITAL OF THE PTOLEMAIC-ROMAN PERIOD, EGYPT, 332-30 BC

Palm leaf

Papyrus flower

Papyrus leaf

Papyrus stem

Lotus bud   Lotus stem

Cornice decorated with cavetto molding

Bead molding

Trellis window

Rectangular pier decorated with hieroglyphs

Elevated roof of central nave

Clerestory

Disc representing sun or light

Architrave

Square abacus

Papyrus-bud capital

Papyriform column

Shaft

Scene depicting a Pharaoh (king) paying homage to the god Amon-Re

Central nave

ANCIENT EGYPTIAN BUILDING DECORATION

DECORATED WINDOW, MEDINET HABU, EGYPT, C.1198 BC

ROPE AND PATERAE DECORATION

CAPITAL WITH THE HEAD OF THE SKY-GODDESS HATHOR, TEMPLE OF ISIS, PHILAE, EGYPT, 285-47 BC

LOTUS AND PAPYRUS FRIEZE DECORATION

Ancient Greece

THE CLASSICAL TEMPLES OF ANCIENT GREECE were built according to the belief that certain forms and proportions were pleasing to the gods. There were three main ancient Greek architectural orders (styles), which can be distinguished by the decoration and proportions of their columns, capitals (column tops), and entablatures (structures resting on the capitals). The oldest is the Doric order, which dates from the seventh century BC and was used mainly on the Greek mainland and in the western colonies, such as Sicily and southern Italy. The Temple of Neptune, shown here, is a classic example of this order. It is hypaethral (roofless) and peripteral (surrounded by a single row of columns). About a century later, the more decorative Ionic order developed on the Aegean Islands. Features of this order include volutes (spiral scrolls) on capitals and acroteria (pediment ornaments). The Corinthian order was invented in Athens in the fifth century BC and is typically identified by an acanthus leaf on the capitals. This order was later widely used in ancient Roman architecture.

CAPITALS OF THE THREE ORDERS OF ANCIENT GREEK ARCHITECTURE

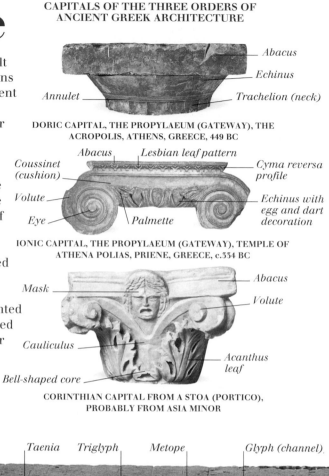

Abacus
Echinus
Annulet
Trachelion (neck)

DORIC CAPITAL, THE PROPYLAEUM (GATEWAY), THE ACROPOLIS, ATHENS, GREECE, 449 BC

Abacus *Lesbian leaf pattern*
Coussinet (cushion)
Cyma reversa profile
Volute
Echinus with egg and dart decoration
Eye *Palmette*

IONIC CAPITAL, THE PROPYLAEUM (GATEWAY), TEMPLE OF ATHENA POLIAS, PRIENE, GREECE, c.354 BC

Mask
Abacus
Volute
Cauliculus
Acanthus leaf
Bell-shaped core

CORINTHIAN CAPITAL FROM A STOA (PORTICO), PROBABLY FROM ASIA MINOR

TEMPLE OF NEPTUNE, PAESTUM, ITALY, c.460 BC

Raking cornice
Trachelion (neck) *Taenia* *Triglyph* *Metope* *Glyph (channel)*
Pediment
Doric entablature
Pteron (external colonnade)
Euthynteria *Drum* *Stylobate* *Column of the Doric order*

PLAN OF THE TEMPLE OF NEPTUNE, PAESTUM

Pronaos (vestibule)

Naos wall

Anta (pilaster terminating naos wall)

Naos (cella)

Peristyle

Opisthodomos (rear portico)

Pteron (external colonnade)

Hexastyle pteron (colonnade of six columns)

ANCIENT GREEK BUILDING DECORATION

Volute

FACADE, TREASURY OF ATREUS, MYCENAE, GREECE, 1550-1250 BC

Meander

FRETWORK, PARTHENON, ATHENS, GREECE, 447-436 BC

ACROTERION, TEMPLE OF APHAIA, AEGINA, GREECE, 490 BC

Griffon (gryphon)

Raking cornice

ANTEFIXA, TEMPLE OF APHAIA, AEGINA, GREECE, 490 BC

Palmette

Volute

Regula (short fillet beneath taenia)

Eaves

Cornice

Frieze

Architrave

Capital

Shaft

Crepidoma (stepped base)

Entasis (slight curve of a column)

Intercolumniation

Fluting

461

Ancient Rome 1

IN THE EARLY PERIOD OF THE ROMAN EMPIRE extensive use was made of ancient Greek architectural ideas, particularly those of the Corinthian order (see pp. 460-461). As a result, many early Roman buildings—such as the Temple of Vesta (opposite)—closely resemble ancient Greek buildings. A distinctive Roman style began to evolve in the first century AD. This style developed the interiors of buildings (the Greeks had concentrated on the exterior) by wing arches, vaults, and domes inside the buildings and by ornamenting internal walls; many of these features can be seen in the Pantheon. Exterior columns were often used for decorative rather than structural purposes, as in the Colosseum and the Porta Nigra (see pp. 464-465). Smaller buildings had timber frames with wattle-and-daub walls, as in the mill (see pp. 464-465). Roman architecture remained influential for many centuries, with some of its principles being used in the 11th century in Romanesque buildings (see pp. 468-469) and also in the 15th and 16th centuries in Renaissance buildings (see pp. 474-477).

ANCIENT ROMAN BUILDING DECORATION

FESTOON, TEMPLE OF VESTA, TIVOLI, ITALY, C.80 BC

RICHLY DECORATED ROMAN OVUM

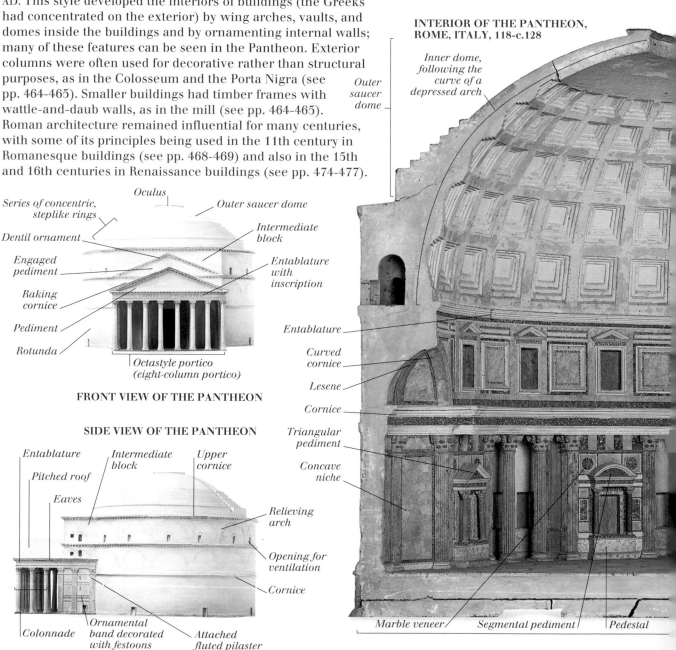

INTERIOR OF THE PANTHEON, ROME, ITALY, 118-c.128

- Inner dome, following the curve of a depressed arch
- Outer saucer dome
- Entablature
- Curved cornice
- Lesene
- Cornice
- Triangular pediment
- Concave niche
- Marble veneer
- Segmental pediment
- Pedestal

FRONT VIEW OF THE PANTHEON

- Series of concentric, steplike rings
- Oculus
- Outer saucer dome
- Intermediate block
- Dentil ornament
- Engaged pediment
- Entablature with inscription
- Raking cornice
- Pediment
- Rotunda
- Octastyle portico (eight-column portico)

SIDE VIEW OF THE PANTHEON

- Entablature
- Intermediate block
- Upper cornice
- Pitched roof
- Eaves
- Relieving arch
- Opening for ventilation
- Cornice
- Colonnade
- Ornamental band decorated with festoons
- Attached fluted pilaster

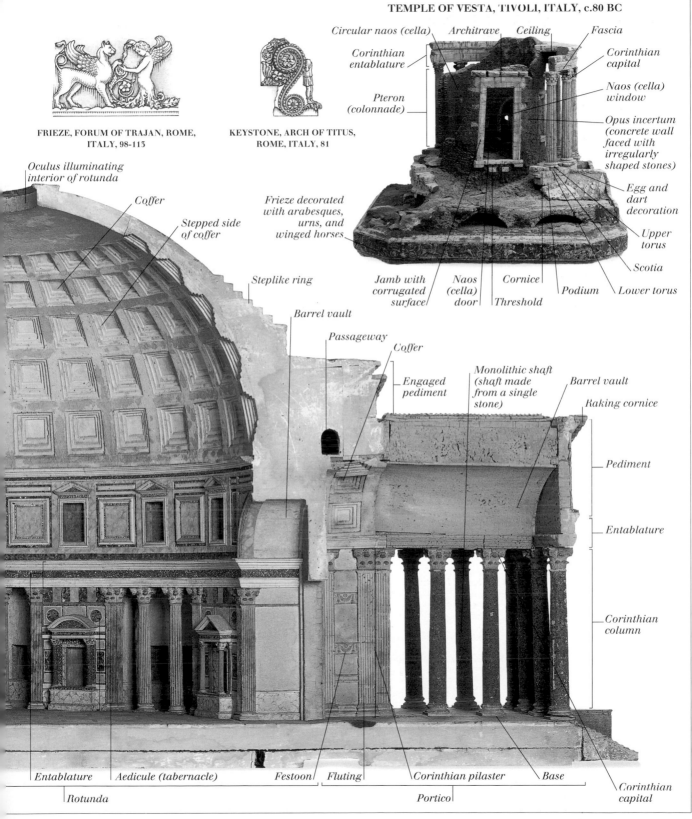

FRIEZE, FORUM OF TRAJAN, ROME, ITALY, 98-113

KEYSTONE, ARCH OF TITUS, ROME, ITALY, 81

TEMPLE OF VESTA, TIVOLI, ITALY, c.80 BC

Circular naos (cella)

Architrave

Ceiling

Fascia

Corinthian entablature

Corinthian capital

Pteron (colonnade)

Naos (cella) window

Opus incertum (concrete wall faced with irregularly shaped stones)

Egg and dart decoration

Upper torus

Scotia

Jamb with corrugated surface

Naos (cella) door

Cornice

Threshold

Podium

Lower torus

Oculus illuminating interior of rotunda

Coffer

Stepped side of coffer

Frieze decorated with arabesques, urns, and winged horses

Steplike ring

Barrel vault

Passageway

Coffer

Engaged pediment

Monolithic shaft (shaft made from a single stone)

Barrel vault

Raking cornice

Pediment

Entablature

Corinthian column

Entablature

Aedicule (tabernacle)

Festoon

Fluting

Corinthian pilaster

Base

Corinthian capital

Rotunda

Portico

Ancient Rome 2

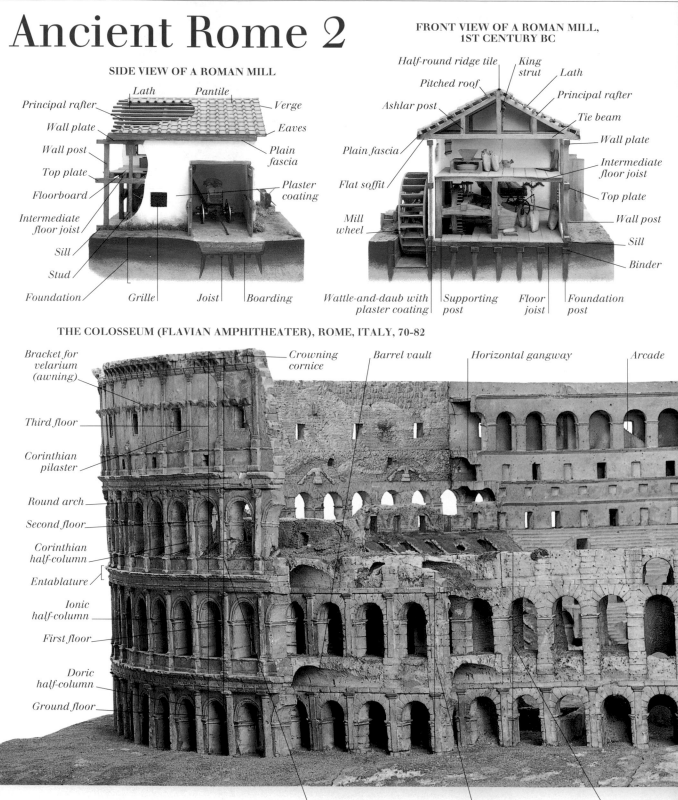

SIDE VIEW OF A ROMAN MILL

Lath · Pantile

Principal rafter · Verge

Wall plate · Eaves

Wall post · Plain fascia

Top plate

Floorboard · Plaster coating

Intermediate floor joist

Sill

Stud

Foundation · Grille · Joist · Boarding

FRONT VIEW OF A ROMAN MILL, 1ST CENTURY BC

Half-round ridge tile · King strut · Lath

Pitched roof · Principal rafter

Ashlar post · Tie beam

Plain fascia · Wall plate

Flat soffit · Intermediate floor joist

Top plate

Mill wheel · Wall post

Sill

Binder

Wattle-and-daub with plaster coating · Supporting post · Floor joist · Foundation post

THE COLOSSEUM (FLAVIAN AMPHITHEATER), ROME, ITALY, 70-82

Bracket for velarium (awning) · Crowning cornice · Barrel vault · Horizontal gangway · Arcade

Third floor

Corinthian pilaster

Round arch

Second floor

Corinthian half-column

Entablature

Ionic half-column

First floor

Doric half-column

Ground floor

External travertine shell · Intermediate shell · Inner shell

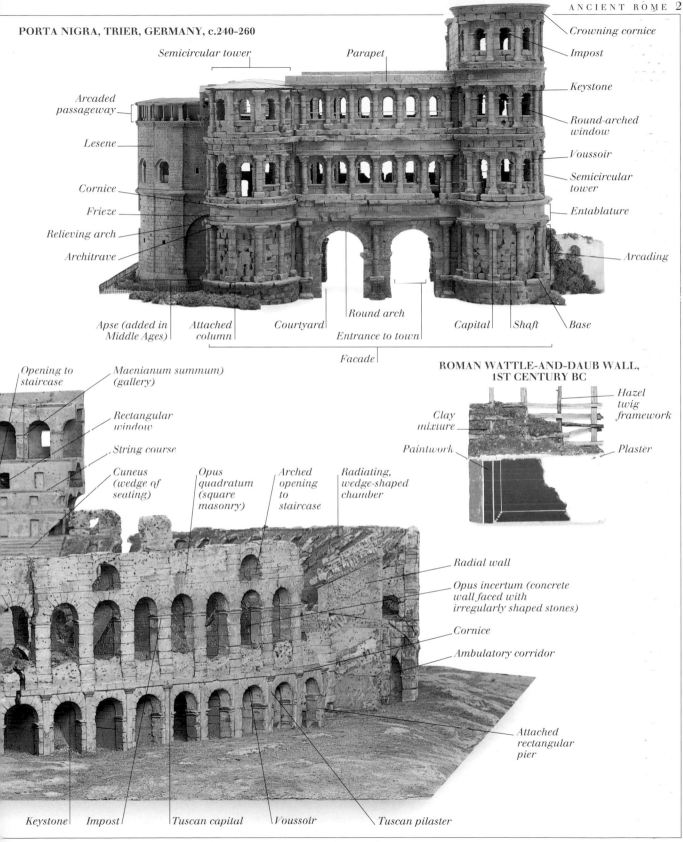

PORTA NIGRA, TRIER, GERMANY, c.240-260

Crowning cornice

Impost

Semicircular tower

Parapet

Keystone

Arcaded passageway

Round-arched window

Lesene

Voussoir

Semicircular tower

Cornice

Frieze

Entablature

Relieving arch

Architrave

Arcading

Apse (added in Middle Ages)

Attached column

Courtyard

Round arch

Entrance to town

Capital

Shaft

Base

Facade

ROMAN WATTLE-AND-DAUB WALL, 1ST CENTURY BC

Hazel twig framework

Clay mixture

Paintwork

Plaster

Opening to staircase

Maenianum summum) (gallery)

Rectangular window

String course

Cuneus (wedge of seating)

Opus quadratum (square masonry)

Arched opening to staircase

Radiating, wedge-shaped chamber

Radial wall

Opus incertum (concrete wall faced with irregularly shaped stones)

Cornice

Ambulatory corridor

Attached rectangular pier

Keystone

Impost

Tuscan capital

Voussoir

Tuscan pilaster

Medieval castles and houses

WARFARE WAS COMMON IN EUROPE in the Middle Ages, and many monarchs and nobles built castles as a form of defense. Typical medieval castles have outer walls surrounding a moat. Inside the moat is a bailey (courtyard), protected by a chemise (jacket wall). The innermost and strongest part of a medieval castle is the keep. There are two main types of keep: towers called donjons, such as the Tour de César and Coucy-le-Château in France, and rectangular keeps ("hall-keeps"), such as the Tower of London. Castles were often guarded by salients (projecting fortifications), like those of the Bastille. Medieval houses typically had timber cruck (tent-like) frames, wattle-and-daub walls, and pitched roofs, like those on medieval London Bridge (opposite).

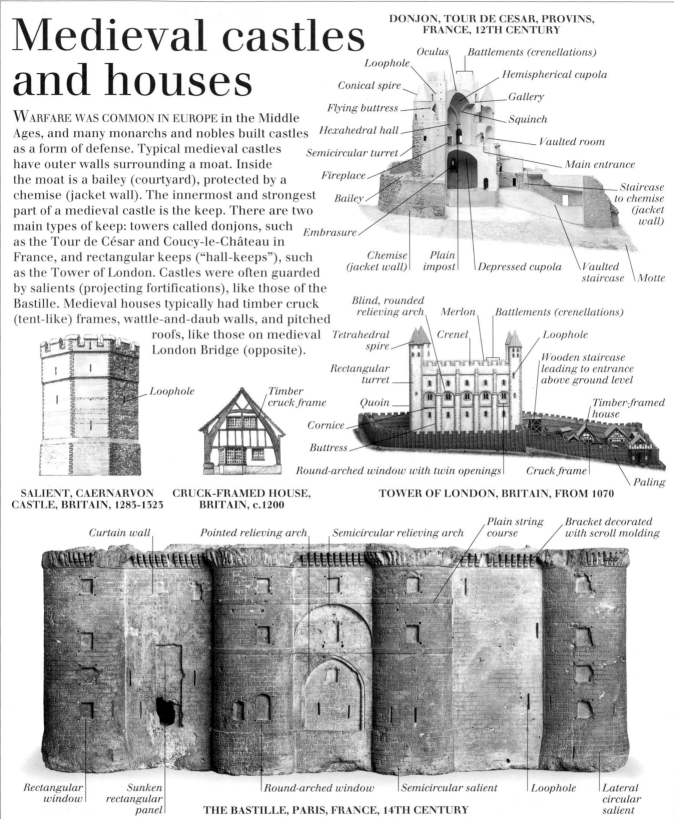

DONJON, TOUR DE CESAR, PROVINS, FRANCE, 12TH CENTURY

Oculus
Loophole
Battlements (crenellations)
Conical spire
Hemispherical cupola
Flying buttress
Gallery
Hexahedral hall
Squinch
Semicircular turret
Vaulted room
Fireplace
Main entrance
Bailey
Staircase to chemise (jacket wall)
Embrasure
Chemise (jacket wall)
Plain impost
Depressed cupola
Vaulted staircase
Motte

SALIENT, CAERNARVON CASTLE, BRITAIN, 1283-1323

Loophole

CRUCK-FRAMED HOUSE, BRITAIN, c.1200

Timber cruck frame

TOWER OF LONDON, BRITAIN, FROM 1070

Blind, rounded relieving arch
Merlon
Battlements (crenellations)
Tetrahedral spire
Crenel
Loophole
Rectangular turret
Wooden staircase leading to entrance above ground level
Quoin
Timber-framed house
Cornice
Buttress
Round-arched window with twin openings
Cruck frame
Paling

THE BASTILLE, PARIS, FRANCE, 14TH CENTURY

Curtain wall
Pointed relieving arch
Semicircular relieving arch
Plain string course
Bracket decorated with scroll molding
Rectangular window
Sunken rectangular panel
Round-arched window
Semicircular salient
Loophole
Lateral circular salient

MEDIEVAL LONDON BRIDGE, BRITAIN, 1176 (WITH 14TH-CENTURY BATTLEMENTED BUILDING, NONESUCH HOUSE, AND TWO-TOWERED GATE)

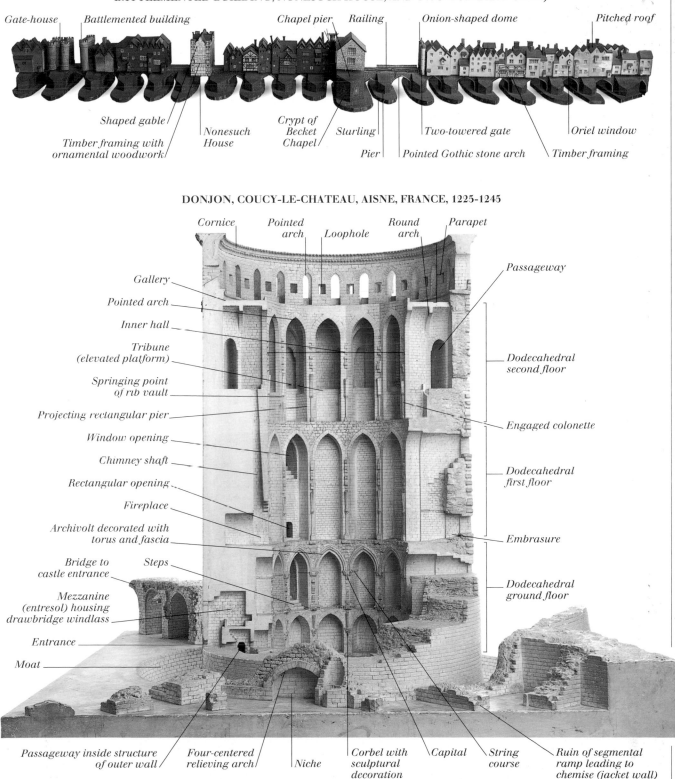

Gate-house

Battlemented building

Chapel pier

Railing

Onion-shaped dome

Pitched roof

Shaped gable

Nonesuch House

Crypt of Becket Chapel

Starling

Two-towered gate

Oriel window

Timber framing with ornamental woodwork

Pier

Pointed Gothic stone arch

Timber framing

DONJON, COUCY-LE-CHATEAU, AISNE, FRANCE, 1225-1245

Cornice

Pointed arch

Loophole

Round arch

Parapet

Passageway

Gallery

Pointed arch

Inner hall

Tribune (elevated platform)

Springing point of rib vault

Projecting rectangular pier

Window opening

Chimney shaft

Rectangular opening

Fireplace

Archivolt decorated with torus and fascia

Bridge to castle entrance

Steps

Mezzanine (entresol) housing drawbridge windlass

Entrance

Moat

Dodecahedral second floor

Engaged colonette

Dodecahedral first floor

Embrasure

Dodecahedral ground floor

Passageway inside structure of outer wall

Four-centered relieving arch

Niche

Corbel with sculptural decoration

Capital

String course

Ruin of segmental ramp leading to chemise (jacket wall)

Medieval churches

LARGE NUMBERS OF CHURCHES were built in Europe in the Middle Ages. European churches of this period typically have high vaults supported by massive piers and columns. In the 10th century, the Romanesque style developed. Romanesque architects adopted many Roman or early Christian architectural ideas, such as cross-shaped ground plans—like that of Angoulême Cathedral (opposite)—and the basilican system of a nave with a central vessel and side aisles. In the mid-12th century, flying buttresses and pointed vaults appeared. These features later became widely used in Gothic architecture (see pp. 470-471). Bagneux Church (opposite) has both styles: a Romanesque tower and a Gothic nave and choir.

ABBEY OF ST. FOI, CONQUES, FRANCE, c.1050-c.1130

- *Finial*
- *Octahedral spire*
- *Incline*
- *Circular staircase-turret*
- *Loophole*
- *Octahedral crossing tower*
- *Round-arched window*
- *Series of archivolts decorated with torus*
- *Series of jambs decorated with colonettes*

- *Pitched roof*
- *Barrel vault*
- *Lean-to roof*
- *Tribune (elevated platform)*
- *Semicircular transverse arch*
- *Transept*
- *Vaulting shaft*
- *Quadrant arch*
- *Attached half-column*
- *Colonette*
- *Round arcade arch*
- *Romanesque capital*
- *Round stilted arch*
- *Twin opening of gallery bays*
- *Arcade*
- *Compound pier*
- *Square central shaft*
- *Attached half-column*
- *Side aisle*
- *Main vessel*
- *Side aisle*

CHURCH ROOF BOSS, BRITAIN

ROMANESQUE CAPITALS

"THE FLIGHT INTO EGYPT" CAPITAL, CATHEDRAL OF ST. LAZARE, AUTUN, FRANCE, 1120-1150

"CHRIST IN MAJESTY" CAPITAL, BASILICA OF ST. MADELEINE, VEZELAY, FRANCE, 1120-1140

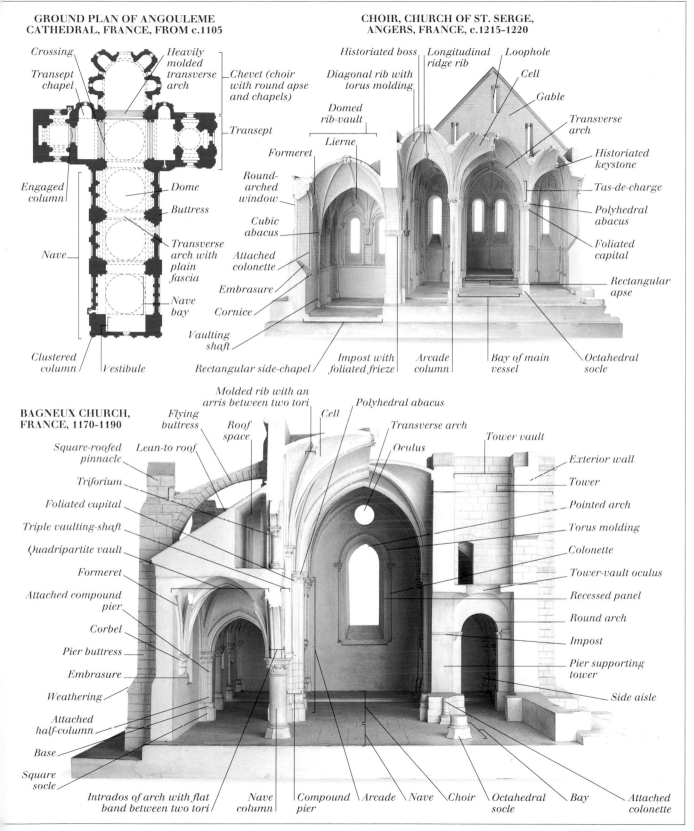

GROUND PLAN OF ANGOULEME CATHEDRAL, FRANCE, FROM c.1105

Crossing

Transept chapel

Heavily molded transverse arch

Chevet (choir with round apse and chapels)

Transept

Engaged column

Dome

Buttress

Nave

Transverse arch with plain fascia

Attached colonette

Embrasure

Cornice

Nave bay

Vaulting shaft

Clustered column

Vestibule

Rectangular side-chapel

CHOIR, CHURCH OF ST. SERGE, ANGERS, FRANCE, c.1215-1220

Historiated boss

Longitudinal ridge rib

Loophole

Cell

Gable

Transverse arch

Historiated keystone

Tas-de-charge

Polyhedral abacus

Foliated capital

Rectangular apse

Octahedral socle

Bay of main vessel

Arcade column

Impost with foliated frieze

Diagonal rib with torus molding

Domed rib-vault

Lierne

Formeret

Round-arched window

Cubic abacus

BAGNEUX CHURCH, FRANCE, 1170-1190

Molded rib with an arris between two tori

Flying buttress

Roof space

Cell

Polyhedral abacus

Transverse arch

Oculus

Tower vault

Exterior wall

Tower

Pointed arch

Torus molding

Colonette

Tower-vault oculus

Recessed panel

Round arch

Impost

Pier supporting tower

Side aisle

Square-roofed pinnacle

Lean-to roof

Roof space

Triforium

Foliated capital

Triple vaulting-shaft

Quadripartite vault

Formeret

Attached compound pier

Corbel

Pier buttress

Embrasure

Weathering

Attached half-column

Base

Square socle

Intrados of arch with flat band between two tori

Nave column

Compound pier

Arcade

Nave

Choir

Octahedral socle

Bay

Attached colonette

Gothic 1

GOTHIC STAINED GLASS WITH FOLIATED SCROLL MOTIF, ON WOODEN FORM

GOTHIC BUILDINGS are characterized by rib vaults, pointed or lancet arches, flying buttresses, decorative tracery and gables, and stained-glass windows. Typical Gothic buildings include the Cathedrals of Salisbury and old St. Paul's in England, and Notre Dame de Paris in France (see pp. 472-473). The Gothic style developed out of Romanesque architecture in France (see pp. 468-469) in the mid-12th century and then spread throughout Europe. The decorative elements of Gothic architecture became highly developed in buildings of the English Decorated style (late 13th-14th century) and the French Flamboyant style (15th-16th century). These styles are exemplified by the tower of Salisbury Cathedral and by the staircase in the Church of St. Maclou (see pp. 472-473), respectively. In both of these styles, embellishments such as ballflowers and curvilinear (flowing) tracery were used liberally. The English Perpendicular style (late 14th-15th century), which followed the Decorated style, emphasized the vertical and horizontal elements of a building. A notable feature of this style is the hammer-beam roof.

GROUND PLAN OF SALISBURY CATHEDRAL

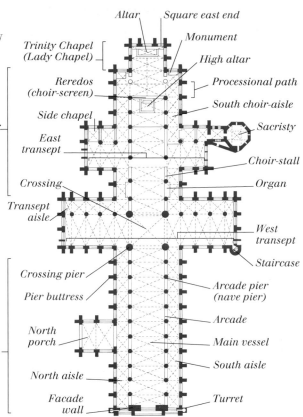

Altar
Square east end
Trinity Chapel (Lady Chapel)
Monument
High altar
Reredos (choir-screen)
Processional path
Side chapel
South choir-aisle
Choir
Sacristy
East transept
Choir-stall
Crossing
Organ
Transept aisle
West transept
Crossing pier
Staircase
Pier buttress
Arcade pier (nave pier)
Arcade
North porch
Main vessel
Nave
South aisle
North aisle
Facade wall
Turret

GOTHIC TORUS WITH BALLFLOWERS

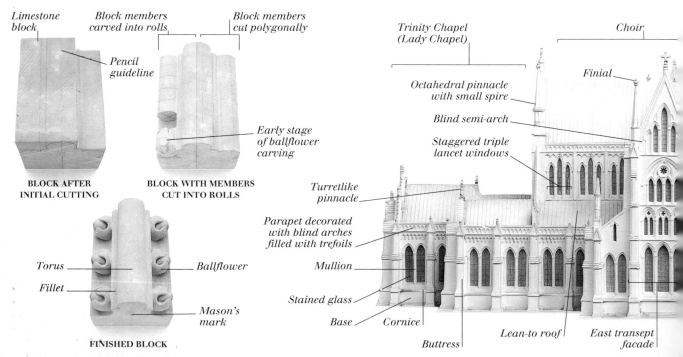

Limestone block
Block members carved into rolls
Block members cut polygonally
Pencil guideline
Early stage of ballflower carving

BLOCK AFTER INITIAL CUTTING

BLOCK WITH MEMBERS CUT INTO ROLLS

Torus
Ballflower
Fillet
Mason's mark

FINISHED BLOCK

Trinity Chapel (Lady Chapel)
Choir
Octahedral pinnacle with small spire
Finial
Blind semi-arch
Staggered triple lancet windows
Turretlike pinnacle
Parapet decorated with blind arches filled with trefoils
Mullion
Stained glass
Base
Cornice
Lean-to roof
East transept facade
Buttress

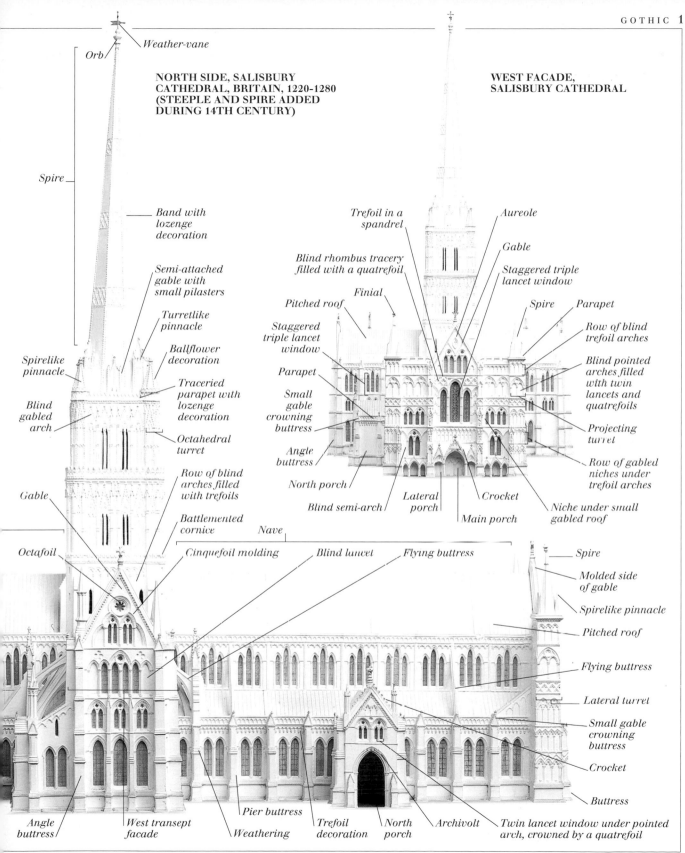

NORTH SIDE, SALISBURY CATHEDRAL, BRITAIN, 1220-1280 (STEEPLE AND SPIRE ADDED DURING 14TH CENTURY)

WEST FACADE, SALISBURY CATHEDRAL

Weather-vane

Orb

Spire

Band with lozenge decoration

Semi-attached gable with small pilasters

Turretlike pinnacle

Ballflower decoration

Traceried parapet with lozenge decoration

Octahedral turret

Spirelike pinnacle

Blind gabled arch

Gable

Row of blind arches filled with trefoils

Battlemented cornice

Octafoil

Cinquefoil molding

Nave

Blind lancet

Flying buttress

Trefoil in a spandrel

Aureole

Gable

Blind rhombus tracery filled with a quatrefoil

Staggered triple lancet window

Finial

Pitched roof

Spire

Parapet

Staggered triple lancet window

Row of blind trefoil arches

Parapet

Small gable crowning buttress

Blind pointed arches filled with twin lancets and quatrefoils

Angle buttress

Projecting turret

North porch

Blind semi-arch

Lateral porch

Crocket

Row of gabled niches under trefoil arches

Main porch

Niche under small gabled roof

Spire

Molded side of gable

Spirelike pinnacle

Pitched roof

Flying buttress

Lateral turret

Small gable crowning buttress

Crocket

Buttress

Angle buttress

West transept facade

Weathering

Pier buttress

Trefoil decoration

North porch

Archivolt

Twin lancet window under pointed arch, crowned by a quatrefoil

Gothic 2

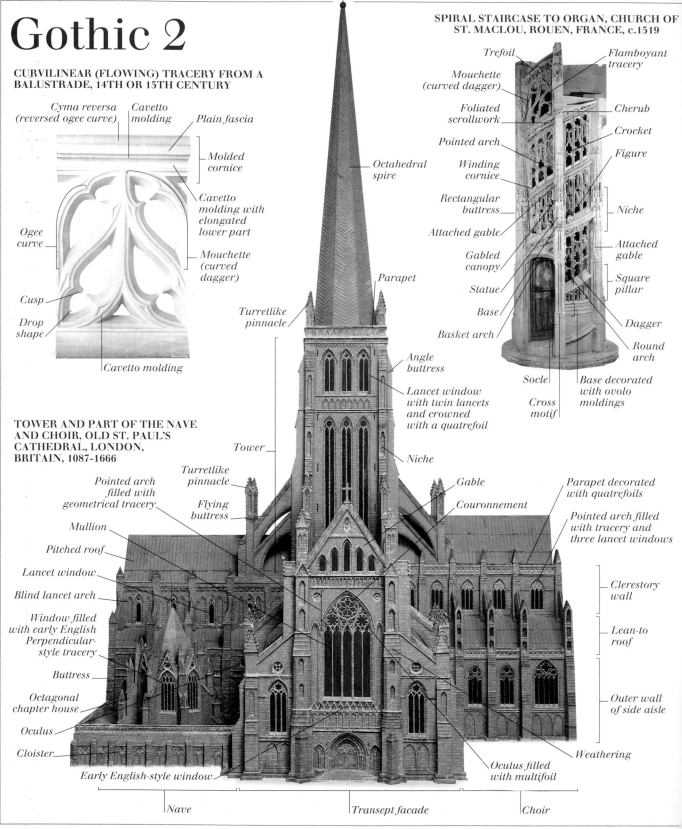

CURVILINEAR (FLOWING) TRACERY FROM A BALUSTRADE, 14TH OR 15TH CENTURY

Cyma reversa (reversed ogee curve)

Cavetto molding

Plain fascia

Molded cornice

Cavetto molding with elongated lower part

Ogee curve

Mouchette (curved dagger)

Cusp

Drop shape

Cavetto molding

SPIRAL STAIRCASE TO ORGAN, CHURCH OF ST. MACLOU, ROUEN, FRANCE, c.1519

Trefoil

Mouchette (curved dagger)

Foliated scrollwork

Pointed arch

Winding cornice

Rectangular buttress

Attached gable

Gabled canopy

Statue

Base

Basket arch

Flamboyant tracery

Cherub

Crocket

Figure

Niche

Attached gable

Square pillar

Dagger

Round arch

Socle

Cross motif

Base decorated with ovolo moldings

Octahedral spire

Parapet

Turretlike pinnacle

Angle buttress

Lancet window with twin lancets and crowned with a quatrefoil

Niche

TOWER AND PART OF THE NAVE AND CHOIR, OLD ST. PAUL'S CATHEDRAL, LONDON, BRITAIN, 1087-1666

Tower

Turretlike pinnacle

Pointed arch filled with geometrical tracery

Flying buttress

Mullion

Pitched roof

Lancet window

Blind lancet arch

Window filled with early English Perpendicular-style tracery

Buttress

Octagonal chapter house

Oculus

Cloister

Gable

Couronnement

Parapet decorated with quatrefoils

Pointed arch filled with tracery and three lancet windows

Clerestory wall

Lean-to roof

Outer wall of side aisle

Weathering

Oculus filled with multifoil

Early English-style window

Nave

Transept facade

Choir

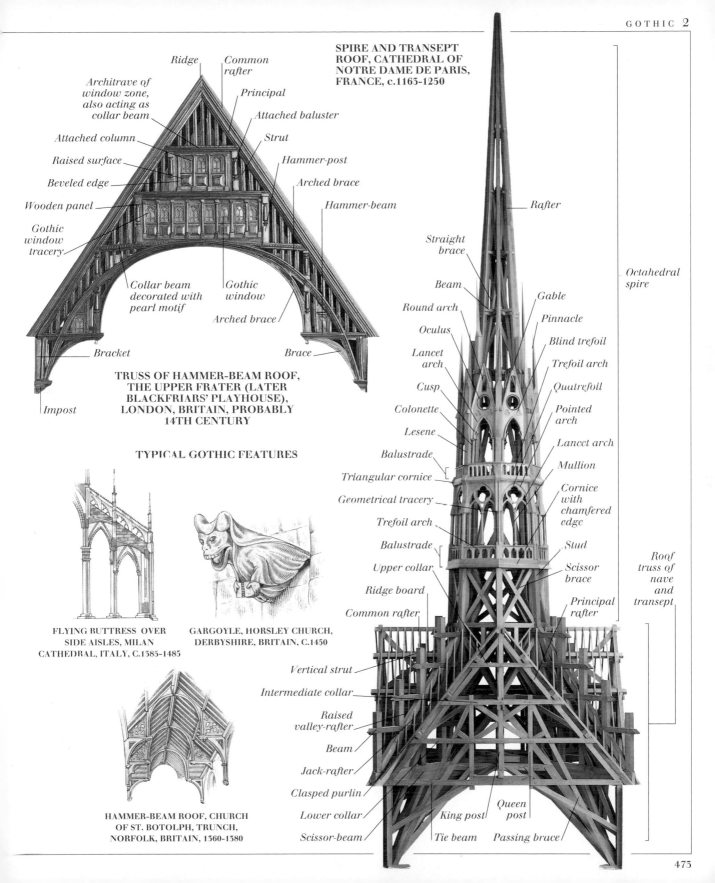

SPIRE AND TRANSEPT ROOF, CATHEDRAL OF NOTRE DAME DE PARIS, FRANCE, c.1163-1250

Ridge

Common rafter

Architrave of window zone, also acting as collar beam

Principal

Attached baluster

Strut

Attached column

Hammer-post

Raised surface

Arched brace

Beveled edge

Hammer-beam

Wooden panel

Gothic window tracery

Collar beam decorated with pearl motif

Gothic window

Arched brace

Bracket

Brace

Impost

Rafter

Straight brace

Beam

Gable

Round arch

Pinnacle

Oculus

Blind trefoil

Lancet arch

Trefoil arch

Cusp

Quatrefoil

Colonette

Pointed arch

Lesene

Lancet arch

Balustrade

Mullion

Triangular cornice

Cornice with chamfered edge

Geometrical tracery

Trefoil arch

Stud

Balustrade

Scissor brace

Upper collar

Ridge board

Principal rafter

Common rafter

Vertical strut

Intermediate collar

Raised valley-rafter

Beam

Jack-rafter

Clasped purlin

Lower collar

Queen post

King post

Scissor-beam

Tie beam

Passing brace

Octahedral spire

Roof truss of nave and transept

TRUSS OF HAMMER-BEAM ROOF, THE UPPER FRATER (LATER BLACKFRIARS' PLAYHOUSE), LONDON, BRITAIN, PROBABLY 14TH CENTURY

TYPICAL GOTHIC FEATURES

FLYING BUTTRESS OVER SIDE AISLES, MILAN CATHEDRAL, ITALY, C.1385-1485

GARGOYLE, HORSLEY CHURCH, DERBYSHIRE, BRITAIN, C.1450

HAMMER-BEAM ROOF, CHURCH OF ST. BOTOLPH, TRUNCH, NORFOLK, BRITAIN, 1360-1380

Renaissance 1

THE RENAISSANCE was a period in European history—lasting roughly from the 14th century to the mid-17th century—during which the arts and sciences underwent great changes. In architecture, these changes were marked by a return to the classical forms and proportions of ancient Roman buildings. The Renaissance originated in Italy, and the buildings most characteristic of its style can be found there, such as the Palazzo Strozzi shown here. Mannerism is a branch of the Renaissance style that distorts the classical forms; an example is the Laurentian Library staircase. As the Renaissance style spread to other European countries, many of its features were incorporated into the local architecture. For example, the Château de Montal in France (see pp. 476-477) incorporates aedicules (tabernacles).

FACADE ON TO PIAZZA, PALAZZO STROZZI

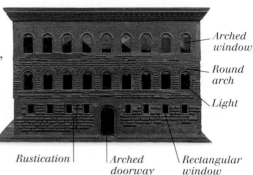

Crowning cornice

Arched window

Round arch

Light

Rustication

Arched doorway

Rectangular window

SIDE VIEW OF PALAZZO STROZZI, FLORENCE, ITALY, 1489 (BY G. DA SANGALLO, B. DA MAIANO, AND CRONACA)

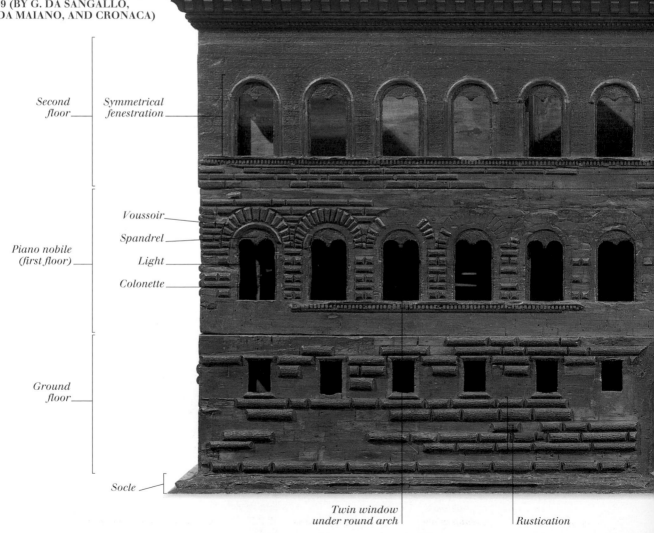

Second floor

Symmetrical fenestration

Piano nobile (first floor)

Voussoir

Spandrel

Light

Colonette

Ground floor

Socle

Twin window under round arch

Rustication

DETAILS FROM ITALIAN RENAISSANCE BUILDINGS

PANEL FROM DRUM OF DOME,
FLORENCE CATHEDRAL, 1420-1436

COFFERING IN DOME,
PAZZI CHAPEL,
FLORENCE, 1429-1461

STAIRCASE,
LAURENTIAN LIBRARY,
FLORENCE, 1559

PORTICO, VILLA ROTUNDA,
VICENZA, 1567-1569

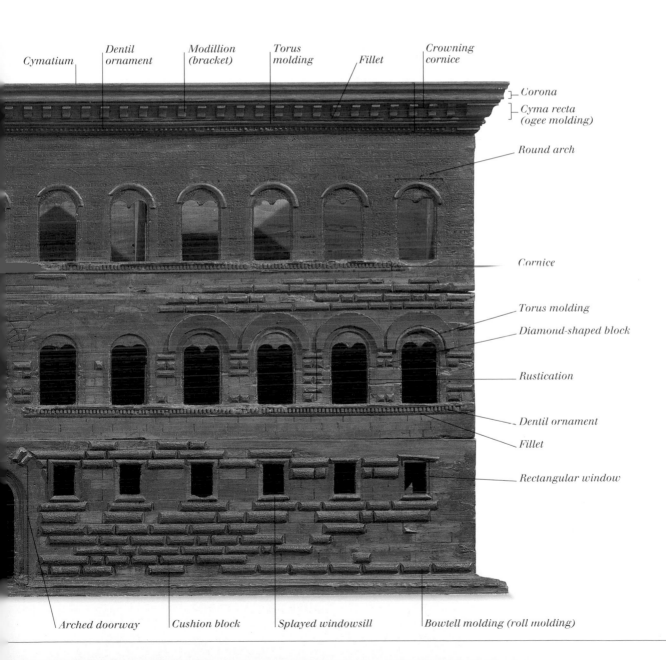

Cymatium

Dentil ornament

Modillion (bracket)

Torus molding

Fillet

Crowning cornice

Corona

Cyma recta (ogee molding)

Round arch

Cornice

Torus molding

Diamond-shaped block

Rustication

Dentil ornament

Fillet

Rectangular window

Arched doorway

Cushion block

Splayed windowsill

Bowtell molding (roll molding)

Renaissance 2

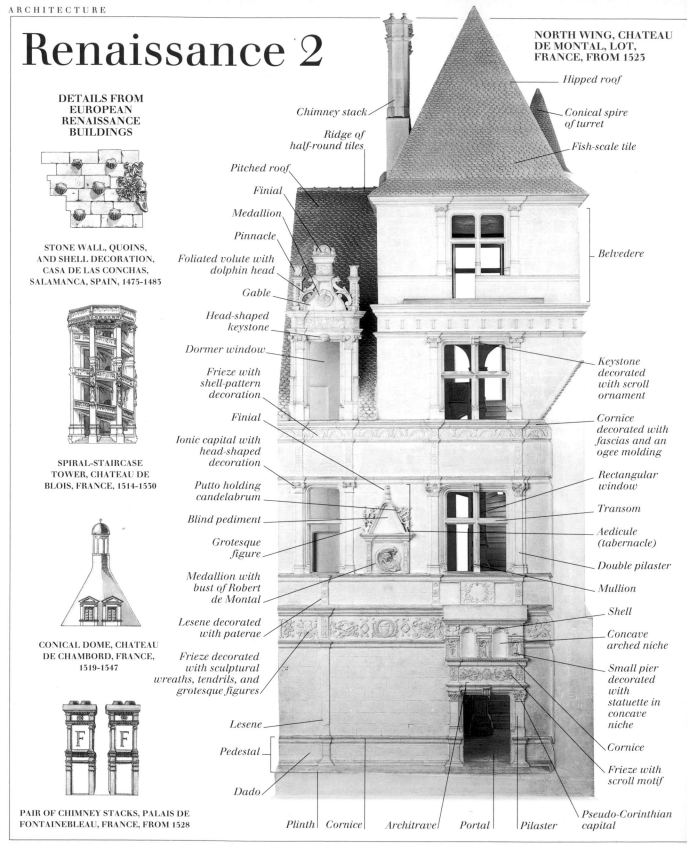

DETAILS FROM EUROPEAN RENAISSANCE BUILDINGS

STONE WALL, QUOINS, AND SHELL DECORATION, CASA DE LAS CONCHAS, SALAMANCA, SPAIN, 1475-1483

SPIRAL-STAIRCASE TOWER, CHATEAU DE BLOIS, FRANCE, 1514-1530

CONICAL DOME, CHATEAU DE CHAMBORD, FRANCE, 1519-1547

PAIR OF CHIMNEY STACKS, PALAIS DE FONTAINEBLEAU, FRANCE, FROM 1528

NORTH WING, CHATEAU DE MONTAL, LOT, FRANCE, FROM 1523

Chimney stack

Ridge of half-round tiles

Pitched roof

Finial

Medallion

Pinnacle

Foliated volute with dolphin head

Gable

Head-shaped keystone

Dormer window

Frieze with shell-pattern decoration

Finial

Ionic capital with head-shaped decoration

Putto holding candelabrum

Blind pediment

Grotesque figure

Medallion with bust of Robert de Montal

Lesene decorated with paterae

Frieze decorated with sculptural wreaths, tendrils, and grotesque figures

Lesene

Pedestal

Dado

Plinth   Cornice   Architrave   Portal   Pilaster

Hipped roof

Conical spire of turret

Fish-scale tile

Belvedere

Keystone decorated with scroll ornament

Cornice decorated with fascias and an ogee molding

Rectangular window

Transom

Aedicule (tabernacle)

Double pilaster

Mullion

Shell

Concave arched niche

Small pier decorated with statuette in concave niche

Cornice

Frieze with scroll motif

Pseudo-Corinthian capital

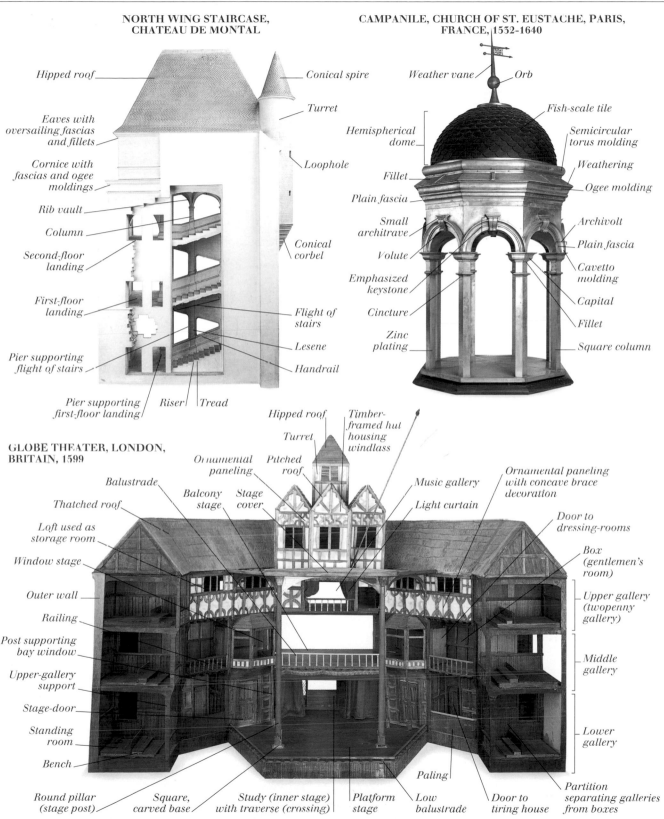

**NORTH WING STAIRCASE,
CHATEAU DE MONTAL**

Hipped roof

Eaves with
oversailing fascias
and fillets

Cornice with
fascias and ogee
moldings

Rib vault

Column

Second-floor
landing

First-floor
landing

Pier supporting
flight of stairs

Pier supporting
first-floor landing

Riser

Tread

Conical spire

Turret

Loophole

Conical
corbel

Flight of
stairs

Lesene

Handrail

**CAMPANILE, CHURCH OF ST. EUSTACHE, PARIS,
FRANCE, 1532-1640**

Weather vane

Orb

Hemispherical
dome

Fillet

Plain fascia

Small
architrave

Volute

Emphasized
keystone

Cincture

Zinc
plating

Fish-scale tile

Semicircular
torus molding

Weathering

Ogee molding

Archivolt

Plain fascia

Cavetto
molding

Capital

Fillet

Square column

**GLOBE THEATER, LONDON,
BRITAIN, 1599**

Balustrade

Thatched roof

Loft used as
storage room

Window stage

Outer wall

Railing

Post supporting
bay window

Upper-gallery
support

Stage-door

Standing
room

Bench

Round pillar
(stage post)

Square,
carved base

Study (inner stage)
with traverse (crossing)

Balcony
stage

Ornamental
paneling

Stage
cover

Hipped roof

Turret

Pitched
roof

Timber-
framed hut
housing
windlass

Music gallery

Light curtain

Ornamental paneling
with concave brace
decoration

Door to
dressing-rooms

Box
(gentlemen's
room)

Upper gallery
(twopenny
gallery)

Middle
gallery

Lower
gallery

Platform
stage

Low
balustrade

Paling

Door to
tiring house

Partition
separating galleries
from boxes

477

Baroque and neoclassical 1

THE BAROQUE STYLE EVOLVED IN THE EARLY 17TH CENTURY in Rome. It is characterized by curved outlines and ostentatious decoration, as can be seen in the Italian church details (right). The baroque style was particularly widely favored in Italy, Spain, and Germany. It was also adopted in Britain and France, but with adaptations. The British architects Sir Christopher Wren and Nicholas Hawksmoor, for example, used baroque features—such as the concave walls of St. Paul's Cathedral and the curved buttresses of the Church of St. George in the East (see pp. 480-481)—but they did so with restraint. Similarly, the curved buttresses and volutes of the Parisian Church of St. Paul-St. Louis are relatively plain. In the second half of the 17th century, a distinct classical style (known as neoclassicism) developed in northern Europe as a reaction to the excesses of baroque. Typical of this new style were churches such as the Madeleine (a proposed facade is shown below), as well as secular buildings such as the Cirque Napoleon (opposite) and the buildings of the British architect Sir John Soane (see pp. 482-483). In early 18th century France, an extremely lavish form of baroque developed, known as rococo. The balcony from Nantes (see pp. 482-483) with its twisted ironwork and head-shaped corbels is typical of this style.

SCROLLED BUTTRESS, CHURCH OF ST. MARIA DELLA SALUTE, VENICE, 1651-1682

STATUE OF THE ECSTASY OF ST. THERESA, CHURCH OF ST. MARIA DELLA VITTORIA, ROME, 1645-1652

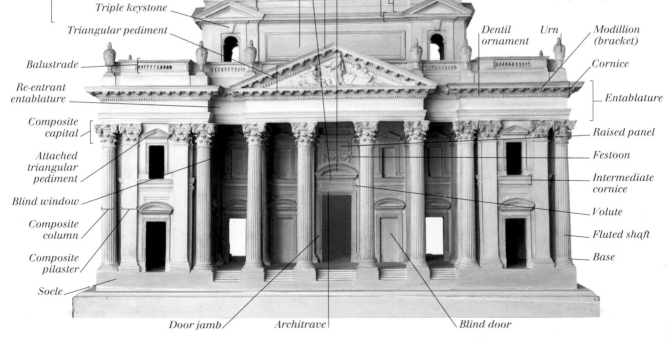

Attic story
Round-arched window
Twin pilaster
Coved dome
Triple keystone
Triangular pediment
Balustrade
Re-entrant entablature
Composite capital
Attached triangular pediment
Blind window
Composite column
Composite pilaster
Socle

Raking cornice
Panel
Frieze
Attached segmental pediment
Lantern
Parapet
Cornice
Finial

Dentil ornament
Urn
Modillion (bracket)
Cornice
Entablature
Raised panel
Festoon
Intermediate cornice
Volute
Fluted shaft
Base

Door jamb
Architrave
Blind door

PROPOSED FACADE, THE MADELEINE (NEOCLASSICAL), PARIS, FRANCE, 1764 (BY P. CONTANT D'IVRY)

CIRQUE NAPOLEON (NEOCLASSICAL), PARIS, FRANCE, 1852 (BY J.I. HITTORFF)

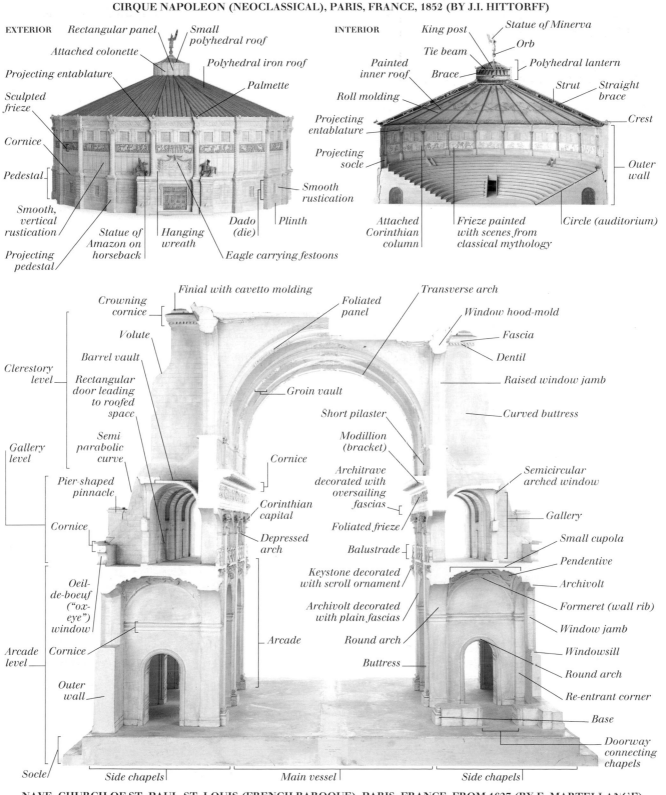

EXTERIOR

Rectangular panel
Small polyhedral roof
Attached colonette
Polyhedral iron roof
Projecting entablature
Palmette
Sculpted frieze
Cornice
Pedestal
Smooth, vertical rustication
Statue of Amazon on horseback
Hanging wreath
Eagle carrying festoons
Smooth rustication
Dado (die)
Plinth
Projecting pedestal

INTERIOR

Statue of Minerva
King post
Orb
Tie beam
Painted inner roof
Brace
Polyhedral lantern
Roll molding
Strut
Straight brace
Projecting entablature
Crest
Projecting socle
Outer wall
Attached Corinthian column
Frieze painted with scenes from classical mythology
Circle (auditorium)

Finial with cavetto molding
Transverse arch
Crowning cornice
Foliated panel
Window hood-mold
Volute
Fascia
Barrel vault
Dentil
Rectangular door leading to roofed space
Clerestory level
Groin vault
Raised window jamb
Semi parabolic curve
Short pilaster
Curved buttress
Gallery level
Modillion (bracket)
Pier-shaped pinnacle
Architrave decorated with oversailing fascias
Semicircular arched window
Cornice
Corinthian capital
Gallery
Cornice
Foliated frieze
Small cupola
Depressed arch
Balustrade
Pendentive
Oeil-de-boeuf ("ox-eye") window
Keystone decorated with scroll ornament
Archivolt
Cornice
Archivolt decorated with plain fascias
Formeret (wall rib)
Arcade
Window jamb
Arcade level
Round arch
Windowsill
Outer wall
Buttress
Round arch
Re-entrant corner
Base
Doorway connecting chapels
Socle
Side chapels
Main vessel
Side chapels

NAVE, CHURCH OF ST. PAUL-ST. LOUIS (FRENCH BAROQUE), PARIS, FRANCE, FROM 1627 (BY E. MARTELLANGE)

Baroque and neoclassical 2

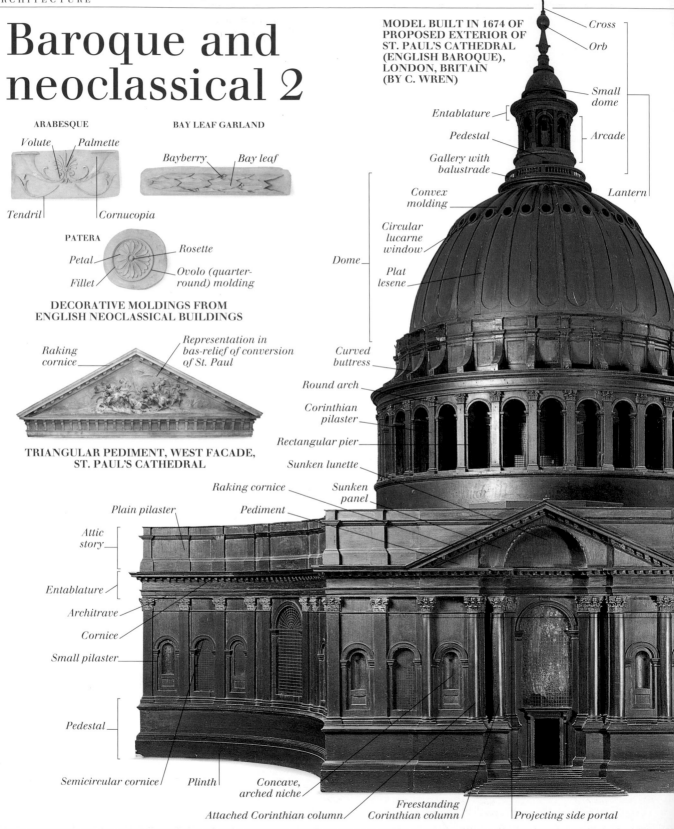

ARABESQUE

Volute
Palmette
Tendril
Cornucopia

BAY LEAF GARLAND

Bayberry
Bay leaf

PATERA

Petal
Rosette
Fillet
Ovolo (quarter-round) molding

DECORATIVE MOLDINGS FROM ENGLISH NEOCLASSICAL BUILDINGS

Raking cornice
Representation in bas-relief of conversion of St. Paul

TRIANGULAR PEDIMENT, WEST FACADE, ST. PAUL'S CATHEDRAL

Plain pilaster
Attic story
Entablature
Architrave
Cornice
Small pilaster
Pedestal
Semicircular cornice
Plinth
Concave, arched niche
Attached Corinthian column
Freestanding Corinthian column
Projecting side portal

MODEL BUILT IN 1674 OF PROPOSED EXTERIOR OF ST. PAUL'S CATHEDRAL (ENGLISH BAROQUE), LONDON, BRITAIN (BY C. WREN)

Cross
Orb
Small dome
Entablature
Pedestal
Arcade
Gallery with balustrade
Lantern
Convex molding
Circular lucarne window
Dome
Plat lesene
Curved buttress
Round arch
Corinthian pilaster
Rectangular pier
Sunken lunette
Sunken panel
Raking cornice
Pediment

CHURCH OF ST. GEORGE IN THE EAST (ENGLISH BAROQUE), LONDON, BRITAIN, 1714-1734 (BY N. HAWKSMOOR)

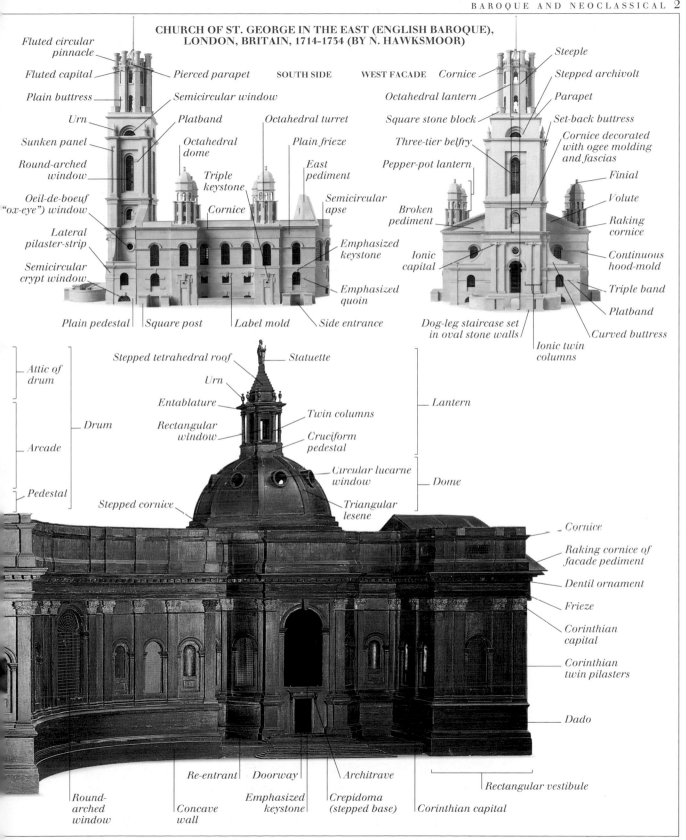

SOUTH SIDE

Fluted circular pinnacle

Fluted capital

Plain buttress

Urn

Sunken panel

Round-arched window

Oeil-de-boeuf ("ox-eye") window

Lateral pilaster-strip

Semicircular crypt window

Pierced parapet

Semicircular window

Platband

Octahedral dome

Triple keystone

Cornice

Octahedral turret

Plain frieze

East pediment

Semicircular apse

Emphasized keystone

Emphasized quoin

Plain pedestal

Square post

Label mold

Side entrance

WEST FACADE

Steeple

Cornice

Octahedral lantern

Square stone block

Three-tier belfry

Pepper-pot lantern

Broken pediment

Ionic capital

Stepped archivolt

Parapet

Cornice decorated with ogee molding and fascias

Finial

Volute

Raking cornice

Continuous hood-mold

Triple band

Platband

Curved buttress

Dog-leg staircase set in oval stone walls

Ionic twin columns

Attic of drum

Drum

Arcade

Pedestal

Stepped tetrahedral roof

Urn

Entablature

Rectangular window

Stepped cornice

Statuette

Twin columns

Cruciform pedestal

Circular lucarne window

Triangular lesene

Lantern

Dome

Cornice

Raking cornice of facade pediment

Dentil ornament

Frieze

Corinthian capital

Corinthian twin pilasters

Dado

Round-arched window

Concave wall

Re-entrant

Doorway

Emphasized keystone

Architrave

Crepidoma (stepped base)

Corinthian capital

Rectangular vestibule

Baroque and neoclassical 3

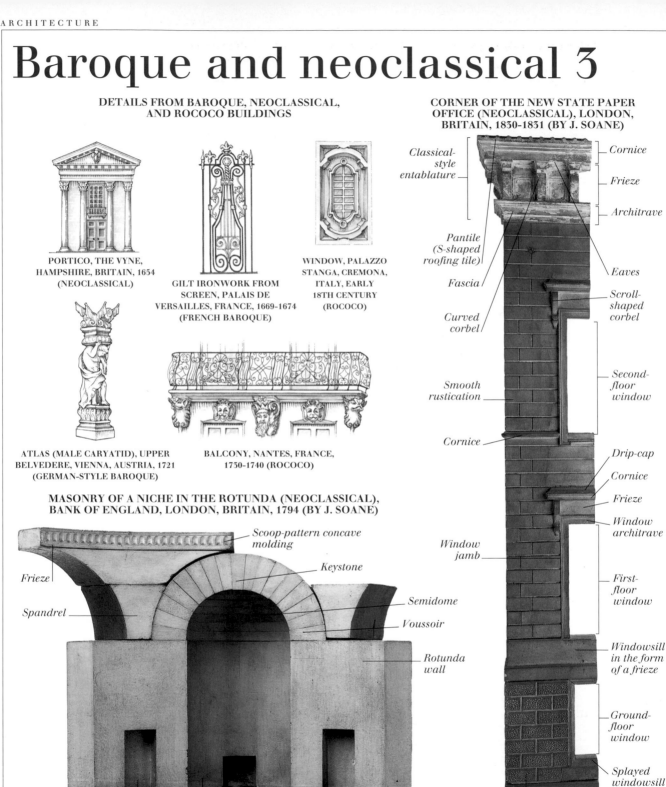

DETAILS FROM BAROQUE, NEOCLASSICAL, AND ROCOCO BUILDINGS

PORTICO, THE VYNE, HAMPSHIRE, BRITAIN, 1654 (NEOCLASSICAL)

GILT IRONWORK FROM SCREEN, PALAIS DE VERSAILLES, FRANCE, 1669-1674 (FRENCH BAROQUE)

WINDOW, PALAZZO STANGA, CREMONA, ITALY, EARLY 18TH CENTURY (ROCOCO)

ATLAS (MALE CARYATID), UPPER BELVEDERE, VIENNA, AUSTRIA, 1721 (GERMAN-STYLE BAROQUE)

BALCONY, NANTES, FRANCE, 1730-1740 (ROCOCO)

MASONRY OF A NICHE IN THE ROTUNDA (NEOCLASSICAL), BANK OF ENGLAND, LONDON, BRITAIN, 1794 (BY J. SOANE)

Scoop-pattern concave molding

Keystone

Frieze

Semidome

Spandrel

Voussoir

Rotunda wall

Window jamb

Flat, rectangular niche

Rounded niche

Flat, square niche

CORNER OF THE NEW STATE PAPER OFFICE (NEOCLASSICAL), LONDON, BRITAIN, 1830-1831 (BY J. SOANE)

Classical-style entablature

Cornice

Frieze

Architrave

Pantile (S-shaped roofing tile)

Fascia

Eaves

Scroll-shaped corbel

Curved corbel

Smooth rustication

Second-floor window

Cornice

Drip-cap

Cornice

Frieze

Window architrave

First-floor window

Windowsill in the form of a frieze

Ground-floor window

Splayed windowsill

Vermiculated rustication

TYRINGHAM HOUSE (NEOCLASSICAL), BUCKINGHAMSHIRE, BRITAIN, 1793-1797 (BY J. SOANE)

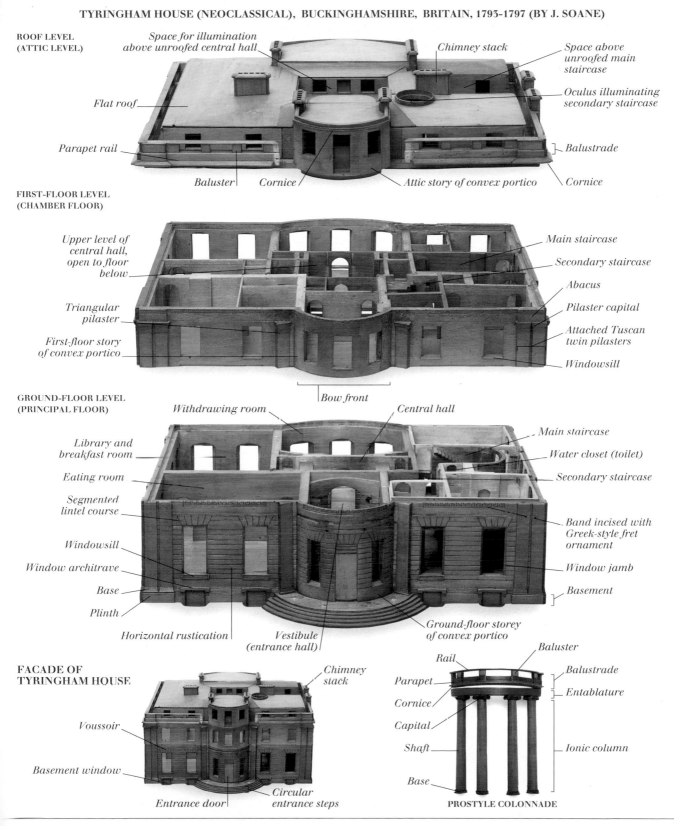

ROOF LEVEL (ATTIC LEVEL)

Space for illumination above unroofed central hall

Chimney stack

Space above unroofed main staircase

Oculus illuminating secondary staircase

Flat roof

Parapet rail

Balustrade

Baluster

Cornice

Attic story of convex portico

Cornice

FIRST-FLOOR LEVEL (CHAMBER FLOOR)

Upper level of central hall, open to floor below

Main staircase

Secondary staircase

Abacus

Triangular pilaster

Pilaster capital

First-floor story of convex portico

Attached Tuscan twin pilasters

Windowsill

Bow front

GROUND-FLOOR LEVEL (PRINCIPAL FLOOR)

Withdrawing room

Central hall

Library and breakfast room

Main staircase

Water closet (toilet)

Eating room

Secondary staircase

Segmented lintel course

Windowsill

Band incised with Greek-style fret ornament

Window architrave

Base

Window jamb

Plinth

Basement

Horizontal rustication

Vestibule (entrance hall)

Ground-floor storey of convex portico

FACADE OF TYRINGHAM HOUSE

Chimney stack

Baluster

Rail

Balustrade

Parapet

Voussoir

Cornice

Entablature

Capital

Basement window

Shaft

Ionic column

Entrance door

Circular entrance steps

Base

PROSTYLE COLONNADE

Arches and vaults

ARCHES ARE CURVED STRUCTURES used to bridge spans and to support the weight of upper parts of buildings, such as domes, as in St. Paul's Cathedral (below) and the historical temple (opposite). The voussoirs (wedge-shaped blocks) that form an arch (right) support each other and convert the downward force of the weight of the building into an outward force. This outward force is in turn transferred to buttresses, piers, or abutments. A vault is an arched roof or ceiling. There are four main types of vault (opposite). A barrel vault is a single vault, semicircular in cross-section; a groin vault consists of two barrel vaults intersecting at right angles; a rib vault is a groin vault reinforced by ribs; and a fan vault is a rib vault in which the ribs radiate from the springing point (where the arch begins) like a fan.

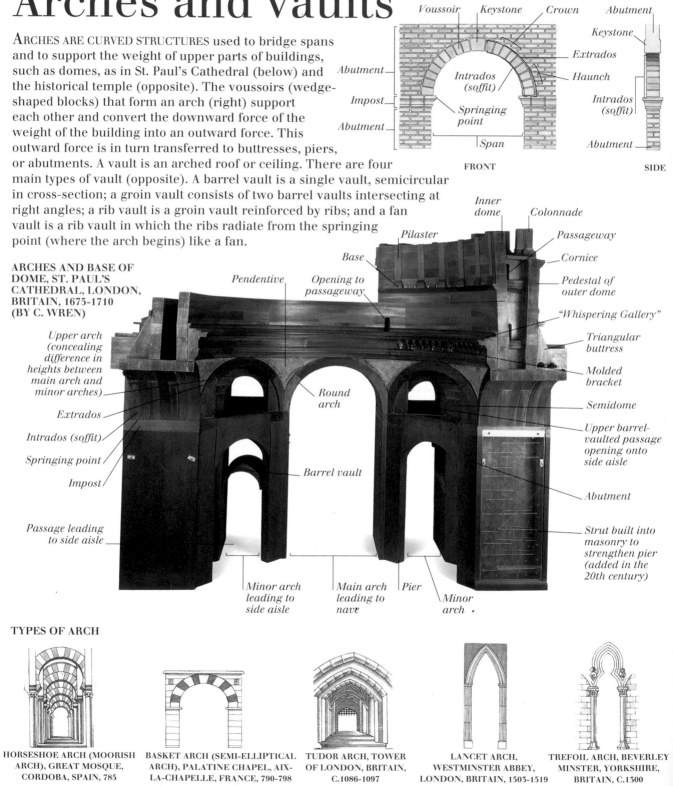

PARTS OF AN ARCH

Voussoir · Keystone · Crown · Abutment

Keystone

Abutment

Extrados

Intrados (soffit)

Impost

Haunch

Intrados (soffit)

Abutment

Springing point

Abutment

Span

FRONT

SIDE

ARCHES AND BASE OF DOME, ST. PAUL'S CATHEDRAL, LONDON, BRITAIN, 1675-1710 (BY C. WREN)

Inner dome

Colonnade

Passageway

Cornice

Pilaster

Base

Pedestal of outer dome

Pendentive

Opening to passageway

"Whispering Gallery"

Triangular buttress

Molded bracket

Semidome

Upper arch (concealing difference in heights between main arch and minor arches)

Extrados

Intrados (soffit)

Springing point

Impost

Round arch

Barrel vault

Upper barrel-vaulted passage opening onto side aisle

Abutment

Passage leading to side aisle

Minor arch leading to side aisle

Main arch leading to nave

Pier

Minor arch

Strut built into masonry to strengthen pier (added in the 20th century)

TYPES OF ARCH

HORSESHOE ARCH (MOORISH ARCH), GREAT MOSQUE, CORDOBA, SPAIN, 785

BASKET ARCH (SEMI-ELLIPTICAL ARCH), PALATINE CHAPEL, AIX-LA-CHAPELLE, FRANCE, 790-798

TUDOR ARCH, TOWER OF LONDON, BRITAIN, C.1086-1097

LANCET ARCH, WESTMINSTER ABBEY, LONDON, BRITAIN, 1503-1519

TREFOIL ARCH, BEVERLEY MINSTER, YORKSHIRE, BRITAIN, C.1300

TYPES OF VAULT

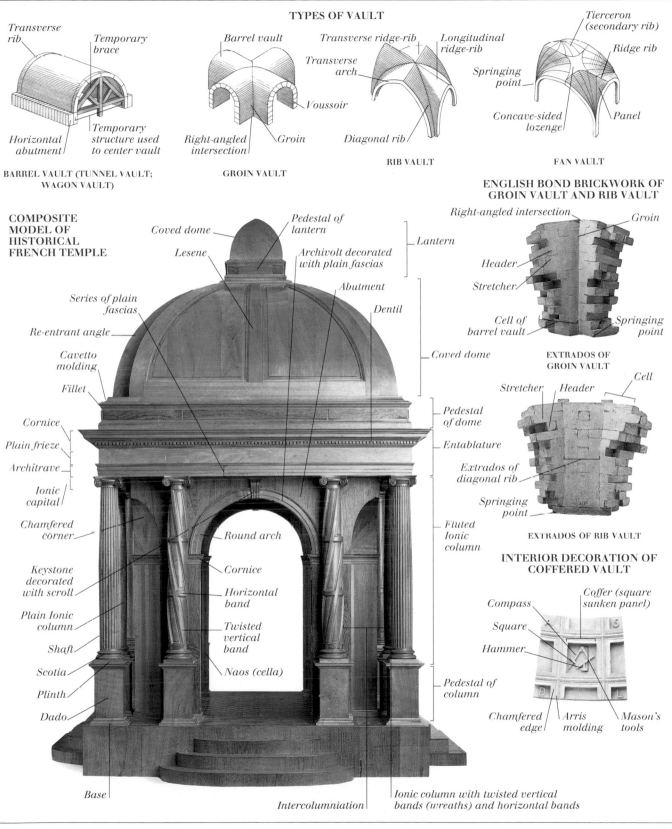

Transverse rib

Temporary brace

Horizontal abutment

Temporary structure used to center vault

BARREL VAULT (TUNNEL VAULT; WAGON VAULT)

Barrel vault

Right-angled intersection

Voussoir

Groin

GROIN VAULT

Transverse ridge-rib

Longitudinal ridge-rib

Transverse arch

Diagonal rib

RIB VAULT

Tierceron (secondary rib)

Ridge rib

Springing point

Concave-sided lozenge

Panel

FAN VAULT

COMPOSITE MODEL OF HISTORICAL FRENCH TEMPLE

Coved dome

Pedestal of lantern

Lesene

Archivolt decorated with plain fascias

Lantern

Abutment

Dentil

Coved dome

Series of plain fascias

Re-entrant angle

Cavetto molding

Fillet

Cornice

Plain frieze

Architrave

Ionic capital

Chamfered corner

Keystone decorated with scroll

Plain Ionic column

Shaft

Scotia

Plinth

Dado

Round arch

Cornice

Horizontal band

Twisted vertical band

Naos (cella)

Pedestal of dome

Entablature

Fluted Ionic column

Pedestal of column

Base

Intercolumniation

Ionic column with twisted vertical bands (wreaths) and horizontal bands

ENGLISH BOND BRICKWORK OF GROIN VAULT AND RIB VAULT

Right-angled intersection

Groin

Header

Stretcher

Cell of barrel vault

Springing point

EXTRADOS OF GROIN VAULT

Stretcher

Header

Cell

Extrados of diagonal rib

Springing point

EXTRADOS OF RIB VAULT

INTERIOR DECORATION OF COFFERED VAULT

Compass

Coffer (square sunken panel)

Square

Hammer

Chamfered edge

Arris molding

Mason's tools

Domes

A DOME IS A CONVEX ROOF. Domes are categorized according to the shapes of both the base and the section through the center of the dome. The base may be circular, square, or polygonal (many-sided), depending on the plan of the drum (the walls on which the dome rests). The section of a dome may be the same shape as any arch (see pp. 484-485). Various types of dome are illustrated here: a hemispherical dome, which has a circular base and a semicircular section; a saucer dome, which has a circular base and a segmental (less than a semicircle) section; a polyhedral dome, which is a dome on a polygonal base whose sides meet at the top of the dome; and an onion dome, which has a circular or polygonal base and an ogee-shaped section. Many domes have a lantern (a turret with windows) to provide light inside.

LANTERN AND UPPER DOME TIMBERING, ST. PAUL'S CATHEDRAL

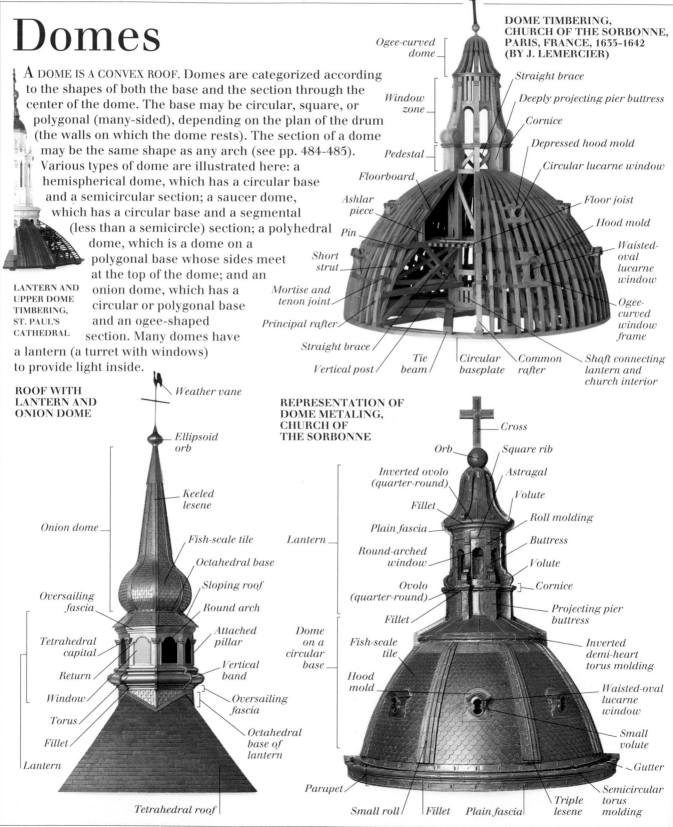

DOME TIMBERING, CHURCH OF THE SORBONNE, PARIS, FRANCE, 1635-1642 (BY J. LEMERCIER)

Ogee-curved dome

Straight brace

Deeply projecting pier buttress

Window zone

Cornice

Depressed hood mold

Pedestal

Circular lucarne window

Floorboard

Ashlar piece

Hood mold

Pin

Waisted-oval lucarne window

Short strut

Ogee-curved window frame

Mortise and tenon joint

Principal rafter

Straight brace

Shaft connecting lantern and church interior

Vertical post

Tie beam

Circular baseplate

Common rafter

ROOF WITH LANTERN AND ONION DOME

Weather vane

Ellipsoid orb

Keeled lesene

Onion dome

Fish-scale tile

Octahedral base

Oversailing fascia

Sloping roof

Round arch

Tetrahedral capital

Attached pillar

Return

Vertical band

Window

Oversailing fascia

Torus

Octahedral base of lantern

Fillet

Lantern

Tetrahedral roof

REPRESENTATION OF DOME METALING, CHURCH OF THE SORBONNE

Cross

Orb

Square rib

Inverted ovolo (quarter-round)

Astragal

Fillet

Volute

Plain fascia

Roll molding

Round-arched window

Buttress

Lantern

Volute

Ovolo (quarter-round)

Cornice

Fillet

Projecting pier buttress

Dome on a circular base

Fish-scale tile

Inverted demi-heart torus molding

Hood mold

Waisted-oval lucarne window

Small volute

Gutter

Parapet

Semicircular torus molding

Small roll

Fillet

Plain fascia

Triple lesene

TYPES OF DOME

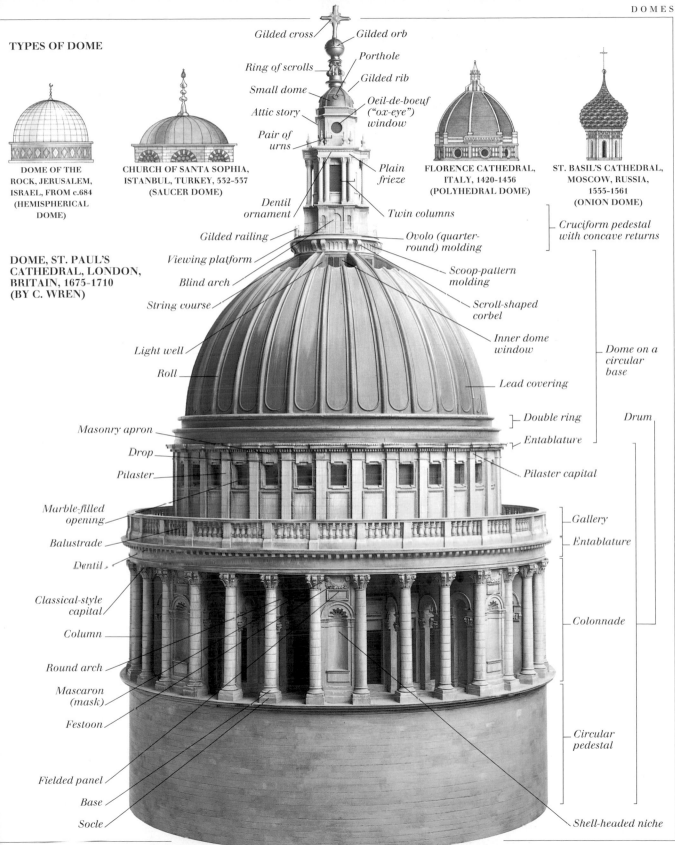

DOME OF THE
ROCK, JERUSALEM,
ISRAEL, FROM c.684
(HEMISPHERICAL
DOME)

CHURCH OF SANTA SOPHIA,
ISTANBUL, TURKEY, 532-537
(SAUCER DOME)

FLORENCE CATHEDRAL,
ITALY, 1420-1436
(POLYHEDRAL DOME)

ST. BASIL'S CATHEDRAL,
MOSCOW, RUSSIA,
1555-1561
(ONION DOME)

**DOME, ST. PAUL'S
CATHEDRAL, LONDON,
BRITAIN, 1675-1710
(BY C. WREN)**

Gilded cross
Gilded orb
Porthole
Ring of scrolls
Gilded rib
Small dome
Attic story
Oeil-de-boeuf
("ox-eye")
window
Pair of
urns
Plain
frieze
Twin columns
Dentil
ornament
Ovolo (quarter-
round) molding
Gilded railing
Viewing platform
Scoop-pattern
molding
Blind arch
Scroll-shaped
corbel
String course
Inner dome
window
Light well
Roll
Lead covering
Double ring
Masonry apron
Entablature
Drop
Pilaster
Pilaster capital
Marble-filled
opening
Gallery
Balustrade
Entablature
Dentil
Classical-style
capital
Colonnade
Column
Round arch
Mascaron
(mask)
Festoon
Circular
pedestal
Fielded panel
Base
Socle
Shell-headed niche

Cruciform pedestal
with concave returns
Dome on a
circular
base
Drum

487

Islamic buildings

OPUS SECTILE MOSAIC DESIGN

THE ISLAMIC RELIGION was founded by the prophet Mohammed, who was born in Mecca (in present-day Saudi Arabia) about 570 AD. During the next three centuries, Islam spread from Arabia to North Africa and Spain, as well as into India and much of the rest of Asia. The worldwide influence of Islam remains strong today. Common characteristics of Islamic buildings include ogee arches and roofs, onion domes, and walls decorated with carved stone, paintings, inlays, or mosaics. The most important type of Islamic building is the mosque—the place of worship—which generally has a minaret (tower) from which the muezzin (official crier) calls Muslims to prayer. Most mosques have a mihrab (decorative niche) that indicates the direction of Mecca. As figurative art is not allowed in Islam, buildings are ornamented with geometric and arabesque motifs and inscriptions (frequently Koranic verses).

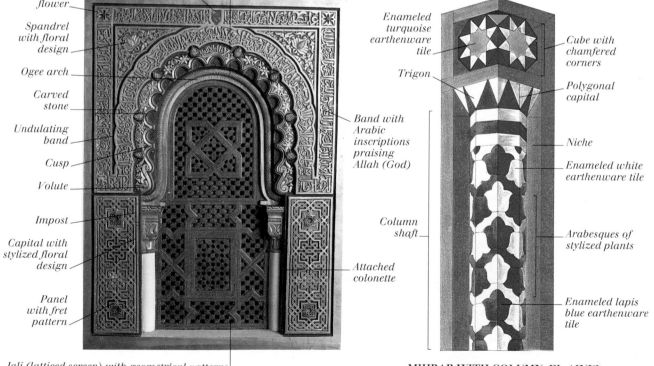

- Budlike onion dome
- Depressed arch surrounding mihrab
- Painted roof pavilion
- Turkish crescent finial
- Lotus flower pendentive
- Crest
- Arabic inscription
- Painted minaret with censer (incense burner)
- Spandrel
- Series of recessed arches
- Semidome
- Arched niche within a niche
- Mural resembling tomb
- Polyhedral niche
- Recessed colonettes

MIHRAB, JAMI MASJID (PRINCIPAL OR CONGREGATIONAL MOSQUE), BIJAPUR, INDIA, c.1636

- Tablet flower
- Shield
- Herringbone pattern
- Spandrel with floral design
- Ogee arch
- Carved stone
- Undulating band
- Cusp
- Volute
- Impost
- Capital with stylized floral design
- Panel with fret pattern
- Band with Arabic inscriptions praising Allah (God)
- Attached colonette

Jali (latticed screen) with geometrical patterns

ARCH, THE ALHAMBRA, GRANADA, SPAIN, 1333-1354

- Enameled turquoise earthenware tile
- Cube with chamfered corners
- Trigon
- Polygonal capital
- Niche
- Enameled white earthenware tile
- Column shaft
- Arabesques of stylized plants
- Enameled lapis blue earthenware tile

MIHRAB WITH COLUMN, EL-AINYI MOSQUE, CAIRO, EGYPT, 15TII CENTURY

EXAMPLES OF ISLAMIC MOSAICS, EGYPT AND SYRIA

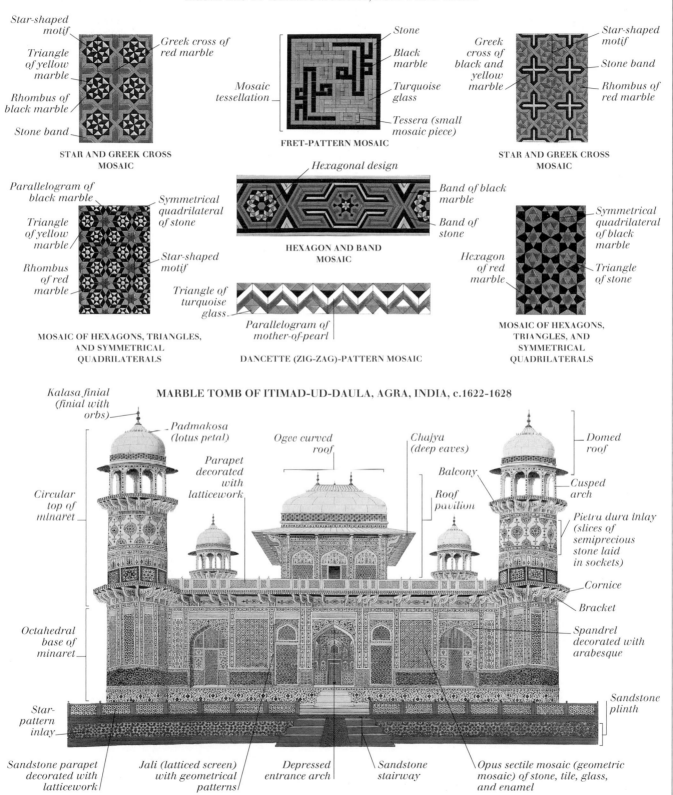

Star-shaped motif

Triangle of yellow marble

Greek cross of red marble

Rhombus of black marble

Stone band

STAR AND GREEK CROSS MOSAIC

Stone

Black marble

Mosaic tessellation

Turquoise glass

Tessera (small mosaic piece)

FRET-PATTERN MOSAIC

Star-shaped motif

Greek cross of black and yellow marble

Stone band

Rhombus of red marble

STAR AND GREEK CROSS MOSAIC

Parallelogram of black marble

Triangle of yellow marble

Symmetrical quadrilateral of stone

Star-shaped motif

Rhombus of red marble

MOSAIC OF HEXAGONS, TRIANGLES, AND SYMMETRICAL QUADRILATERALS

Hexagonal design

Band of black marble

Band of stone

HEXAGON AND BAND MOSAIC

Triangle of turquoise glass

Parallelogram of mother-of-pearl

DANCETTE (ZIG-ZAG)-PATTERN MOSAIC

Symmetrical quadrilateral of black marble

Hexagon of red marble

Triangle of stone

MOSAIC OF HEXAGONS, TRIANGLES, AND SYMMETRICAL QUADRILATERALS

MARBLE TOMB OF ITIMAD-UD-DAULA, AGRA, INDIA, c.1622-1628

Kalasa finial (finial with orbs)

Padmakosa (lotus petal)

Ogee curved roof

Chajya (deep eaves)

Domed roof

Parapet decorated with latticework

Balcony

Circular top of minaret

Roof pavilion

Cusped arch

Pietra dura inlay (slices of semiprecious stone laid in sockets)

Cornice

Bracket

Octahedral base of minaret

Spandrel decorated with arabesque

Star-pattern inlay

Sandstone plinth

Sandstone parapet decorated with latticework

Jali (latticed screen) with geometrical patterns

Depressed entrance arch

Sandstone stairway

Opus sectile mosaic (geometric mosaic) of stone, tile, glass, and enamel

South and east Asia

THE TRADITIONAL ARCHITECTURE of south and east Asia has been profoundly influenced by the spread from India of Buddhism and Hinduism. This influence is shown by both the abundance and by the architectural styles of temples and shrines in the region. Many early Hindu temples consist of rooms carved from solid rock faces. However, freestanding structures began to be built in southern India from about the eighth century AD. Many were built in the Dravidian style, like the Temple of Virupaksha (opposite), with its characteristic antarala (terraced tower), perforated windows, and numerous arches, pilasters, and carvings. The earliest Buddhist religious monuments were Indian stupas, which consisted of a single hemispherical dome surmounted by a chattravali (shaft) and surrounded by railings with ornate gates. Later Indian stupas and those built elsewhere were sometimes modified. For example, in Sri Lanka, the dome became bell-shaped, and was called a dagoba. Buddhist pagodas, such as the Burmese example (right), are multistoried temples, each story having a projecting roof. The form of these buildings probably derived from the yasti (pointed spire) of the stupa. Another feature of many traditional Asian buildings is their imaginative roof forms, such as gambrel (mansard) roofs, and roofs with angle rafters (below).

SEVEN-STORIED PAGODA IN BURMESE STYLE, c.9TH–10TH CENTURY

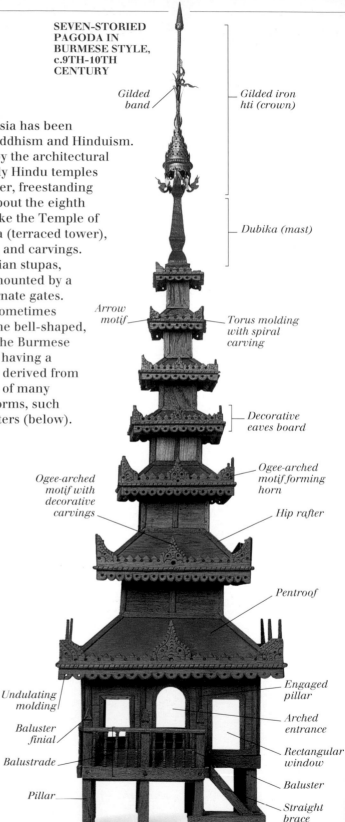

Gilded band

Gilded iron hti (crown)

Dubika (mast)

Arrow motif

Torus molding with spiral carving

Decorative eaves board

Ogee-arched motif with decorative carvings

Ogee-arched motif forming horn

Hip rafter

Pentroof

Undulating molding

Engaged pillar

Baluster finial

Arched entrance

Balustrade

Rectangular window

Pillar

Baluster

Straight brace

DETAILS FROM EAST ASIAN BUILDINGS

KASUGA-STYLE ROOF WITH SUMIGI (ANGLE RAFTERS), KASUGADO SHRINE OF ENJOJI, NARA, JAPAN, 12TH–14TH CENTURY

TERRACES, TEMPLE OF HEAVEN, BEIJING, CHINA, 15TH CENTURY

GAMBREL (MANSARD) ROOF WITH UPSWEPT EAVES AND UNDULATING GABLES, HIMEJI CASTLE, HIMEJI, JAPAN, 1608–1609

CORNER CAPITAL WITH ROOF BEAMS, POPCHU-SA TEMPLE, POPCHU-SA, SOUTH KOREA, 17TH CENTURY

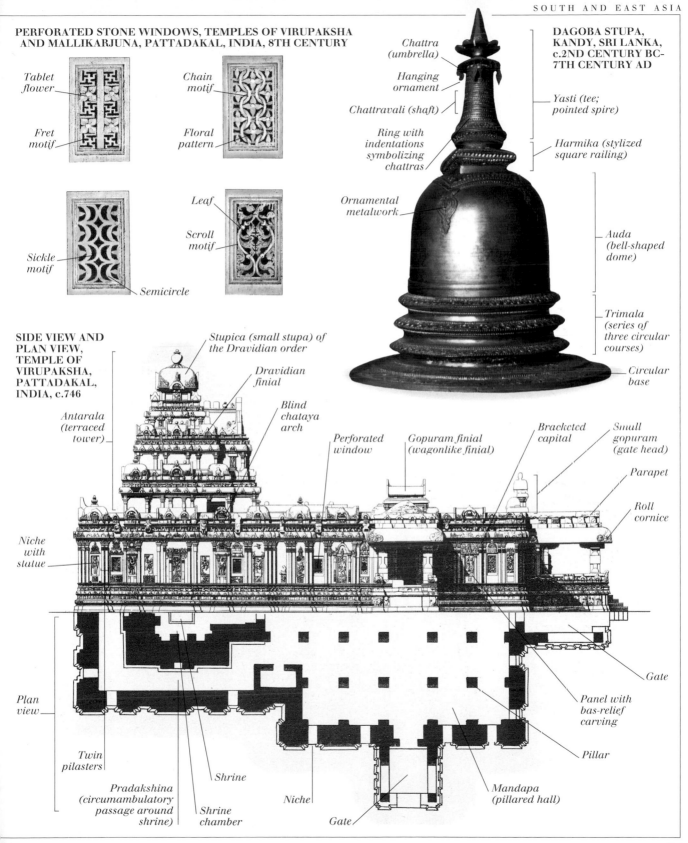

PERFORATED STONE WINDOWS, TEMPLES OF VIRUPAKSHA AND MALLIKARJUNA, PATTADAKAL, INDIA, 8TH CENTURY

Tablet flower

Fret motif

Chain motif

Floral pattern

Leaf

Scroll motif

Sickle motif

Semicircle

DAGOBA STUPA, KANDY, SRI LANKA, c.2ND CENTURY BC– 7TH CENTURY AD

Chattra (umbrella)

Hanging ornament

Chattravali (shaft)

Ring with indentations symbolizing chattras

Ornamental metalwork

Yasti (tee; pointed spire)

Harmika (stylized square railing)

Auda (bell-shaped dome)

Trimala (series of three circular courses)

Circular base

SIDE VIEW AND PLAN VIEW, TEMPLE OF VIRUPAKSHA, PATTADAKAL, INDIA, c.746

Stupica (small stupa) of the Dravidian order

Dravidian finial

Blind chataya arch

Perforated window

Gopuram finial (wagonlike finial)

Bracketed capital

Small gopuram (gate head)

Parapet

Roll cornice

Antarala (terraced tower)

Niche with statue

Gate

Panel with bas-relief carving

Pillar

Plan view

Twin pilasters

Pradakshina (circumambulatory passage around shrine)

Shrine

Shrine chamber

Niche

Gate

Mandapa (pillared hall)

The 19th century

BUILDINGS OF THE 19TH CENTURY are characterized by the use of new materials and by a great diversity of architectural styles. From the end of the 18th century, iron and steel became widely used as alternatives to wood for the framework of buildings, as in the flax-spinning mill shown here. Built in Britain in 1796, this mill exemplifies an architectural style that became common throughout the industrialized world for more than a century. The Industrial Revolution also brought mass production of building parts—a development that enabled the British architect Sir Joseph Paxton to erect London's Crystal Palace (a building made entirely of iron and glass) in only nine months, ready for the Great Exhibition of 1851. The 19th century saw a widespread revival of older architectural styles. For example, in the United States and Germany, Neo-Greek architecture was fashionable; in Britain and France, Neo-Baroque, Neo-Byzantine, and Neo-Gothic styles (as seen in the Palace of Westminster and Tower Bridge, London) were dominant.

SECTION THROUGH A FLAX-SPINNING MILL

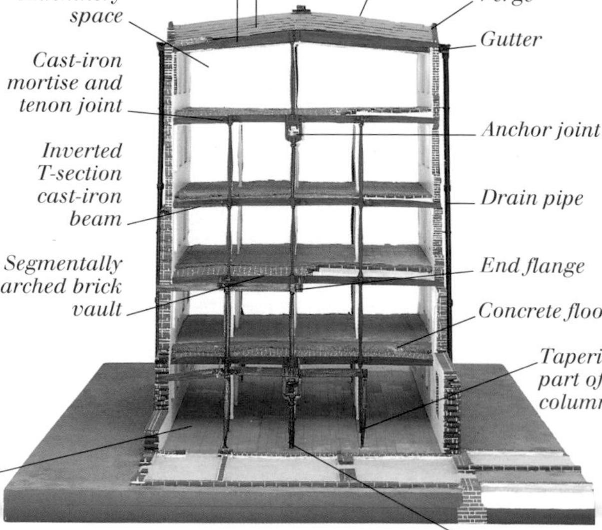

Cast-iron wall plate
Pitched roof
Ridge
Verge
Machinery space
Gutter
Cast-iron mortise and tenon joint
Anchor joint
Inverted T-section cast-iron beam
Drain pipe
Segmentally arched brick vault
End flange
Concrete floor
Tapering part of column
Paved ground floor
Strengthened central column

FLAX-SPINNING MILL, SHREWSBURY, BRITAIN, 1796 (BY C. BAGE)

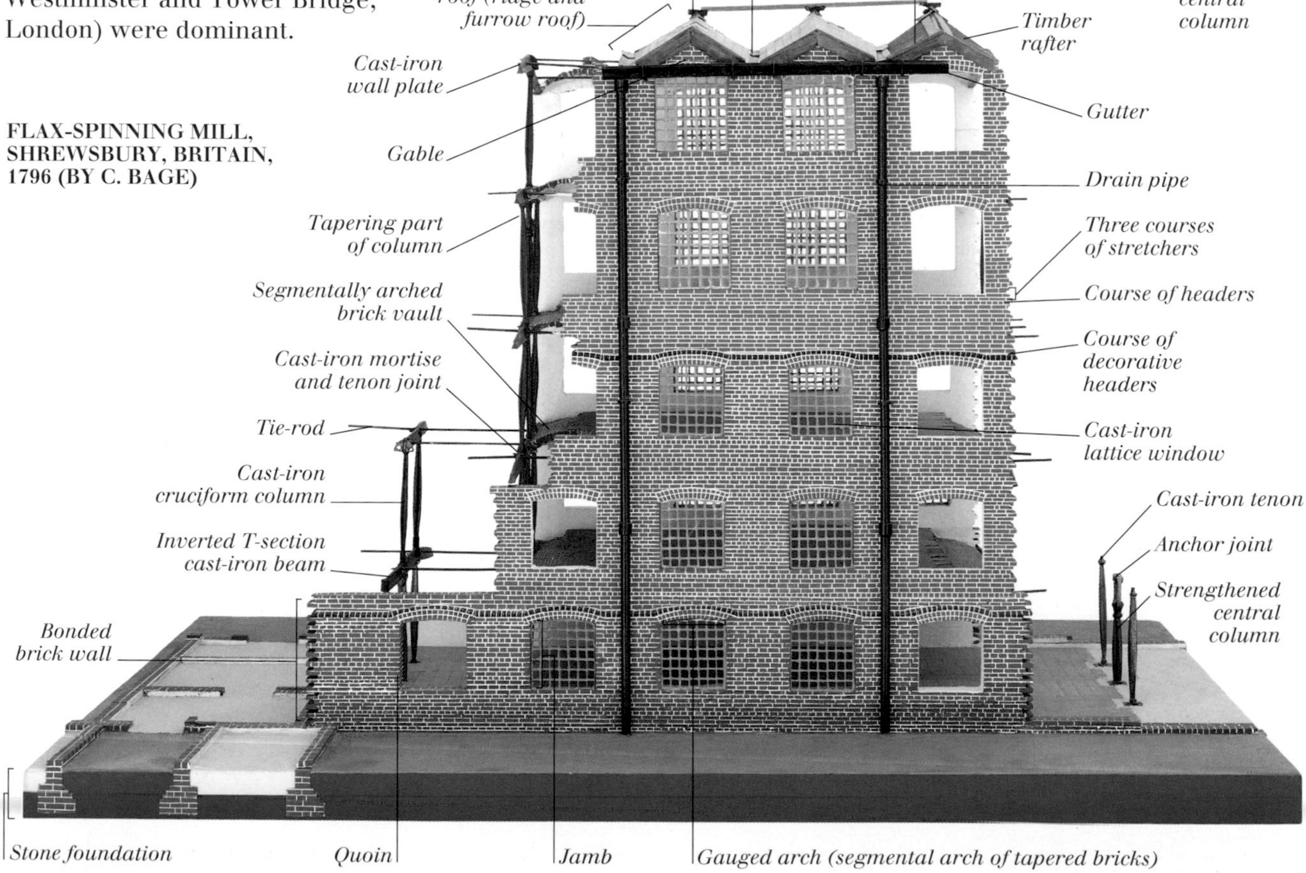

Multi-gabled roof (ridge and furrow roof)
Ridge
Furrow
Verge
Timber rafter
Cast-iron wall plate
Gutter
Gable
Drain pipe
Tapering part of column
Three courses of stretchers
Segmentally arched brick vault
Course of headers
Cast-iron mortise and tenon joint
Course of decorative headers
Tie-rod
Cast-iron cruciform column
Cast-iron lattice window
Inverted T-section cast-iron beam
Cast-iron tenon
Anchor joint
Strengthened central column
Bonded brick wall
Stone foundation
Quoin
Jamb
Gauged arch (segmental arch of tapered bricks)

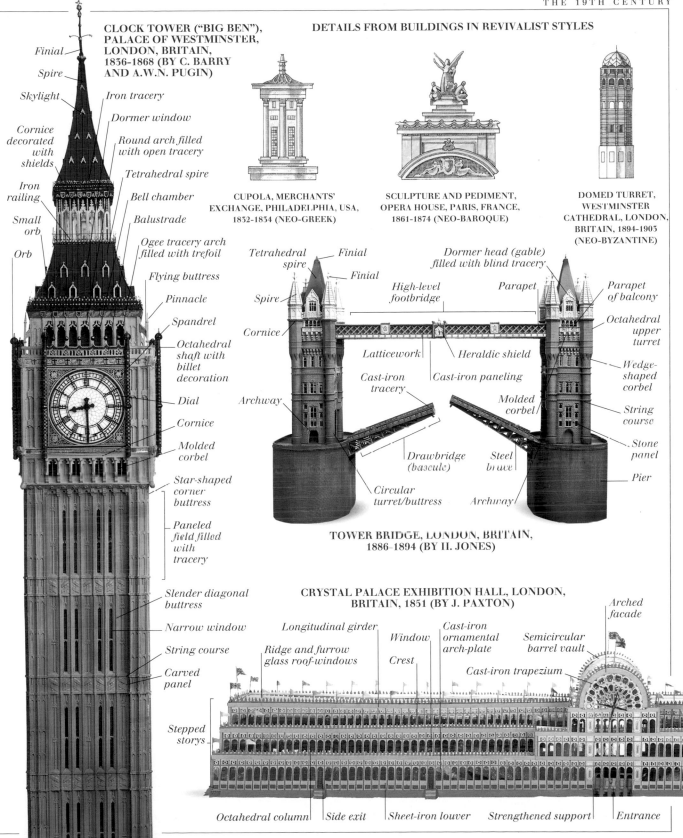

CLOCK TOWER ("BIG BEN"), PALACE OF WESTMINSTER, LONDON, BRITAIN, 1836–1868 (BY C. BARRY AND A.W.N. PUGIN)

Finial
Spire
Skylight
Cornice decorated with shields
Iron railing
Small orb
Orb
Iron tracery
Dormer window
Round arch filled with open tracery
Tetrahedral spire
Bell chamber
Balustrade
Ogee tracery arch filled with trefoil
Flying buttress
Pinnacle
Spandrel
Octahedral shaft with billet decoration
Dial
Cornice
Molded corbel
Star-shaped corner buttress
Paneled field filled with tracery
Slender diagonal buttress
Narrow window
String course
Carved panel
Stepped storys
Octahedral column
Side exit

DETAILS FROM BUILDINGS IN REVIVALIST STYLES

CUPOLA, MERCHANTS' EXCHANGE, PHILADELPHIA, USA, 1832–1834 (NEO-GREEK)

SCULPTURE AND PEDIMENT, OPERA HOUSE, PARIS, FRANCE, 1861–1874 (NEO-BAROQUE)

DOMED TURRET, WESTMINSTER CATHEDRAL, LONDON, BRITAIN, 1894–1903 (NEO-BYZANTINE)

TOWER BRIDGE, LONDON, BRITAIN, 1886–1894 (BY H. JONES)

Tetrahedral spire
Finial
Finial
Spire
Cornice
High-level footbridge
Parapet
Parapet of balcony
Dormer head (gable) filled with blind tracery
Octahedral upper turret
Wedge-shaped corbel
String course
Molded corbel
Stone panel
Pier
Archway
Latticework
Heraldic shield
Cast-iron paneling
Cast-iron tracery
Drawbridge (bascule)
Steel brace
Circular turret/buttress
Archway

CRYSTAL PALACE EXHIBITION HALL, LONDON, BRITAIN, 1851 (BY J. PAXTON)

Longitudinal girder
Window
Cast-iron ornamental arch-plate
Crest
Ridge and furrow glass roof-windows
Arched facade
Semicircular barrel vault
Cast-iron trapezium
Sheet-iron louver
Strengthened support
Entrance

The early 20th century

EMPIRE STATE
BUILDING, NEW
YORK, USA, 1929-1931
(BY R. H. SHREVE,
T. LAMB, AND
A. L. HARMON)

ARCHITECTURE OF THE EARLY 20TH CENTURY is notable for radical new types of steel and glass buildings—particularly skyscrapers—and the widespread use of steel-reinforced concrete. The steel-framed skyscraper was pioneered in Chicago in the 1880s but did not become widespread until the first decades of the 20th century. As construction techniques were refined, skyscrapers became higher and higher. For example, the Empire State Building (right) of 1929-1931 has 102 storys. Many buildings of this period were constructed from lightweight concrete slabs that could be supported by cantilever beams or by pilotis (stilts), as in the Villa Savoye (below). The early 20th century also produced a great variety of architectural styles, some of which are illustrated opposite. Despite their diversity, the styles of this period generally had one thing in common: they were completely new, with few links to past architectural styles. This originality is in marked contrast to 19th-century architecture (see pp. 492-493), much of which was revivalist.

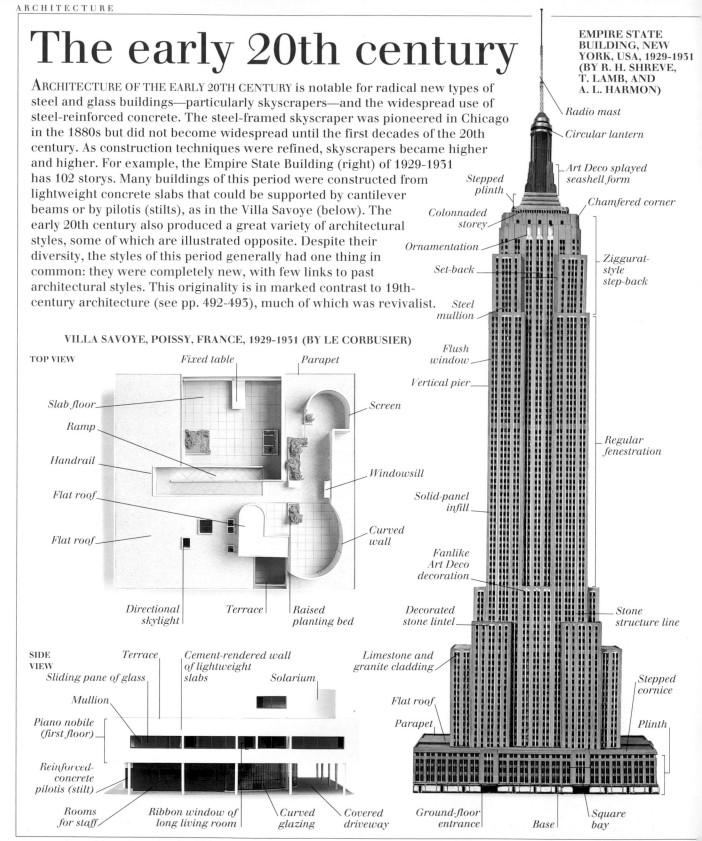

VILLA SAVOYE, POISSY, FRANCE, 1929-1931 (BY LE CORBUSIER)

TOP VIEW

Fixed table

Parapet

Slab floor

Ramp

Screen

Handrail

Windowsill

Flat roof

Curved wall

Flat roof

Directional skylight

Terrace

Raised planting bed

SIDE VIEW

Terrace

Cement-rendered wall of lightweight slabs

Solarium

Sliding pane of glass

Mullion

Piano nobile (first floor)

Reinforced-concrete pilotis (stilt)

Rooms for staff

Ribbon window of long living room

Curved glazing

Covered driveway

Radio mast

Circular lantern

Art Deco splayed seashell form

Stepped plinth

Chamfered corner

Colonnaded storey

Ornamentation

Ziggurat-style step-back

Set-back

Steel mullion

Flush window

Vertical pier

Regular fenestration

Solid-panel infill

Fanlike Art Deco decoration

Decorated stone lintel

Stone structure line

Limestone and granite cladding

Flat roof

Stepped cornice

Parapet

Plinth

Ground-floor entrance

Base

Square bay

MIDWAY GARDENS, CHICAGO, USA, 1914 (BY F. L. WRIGHT)

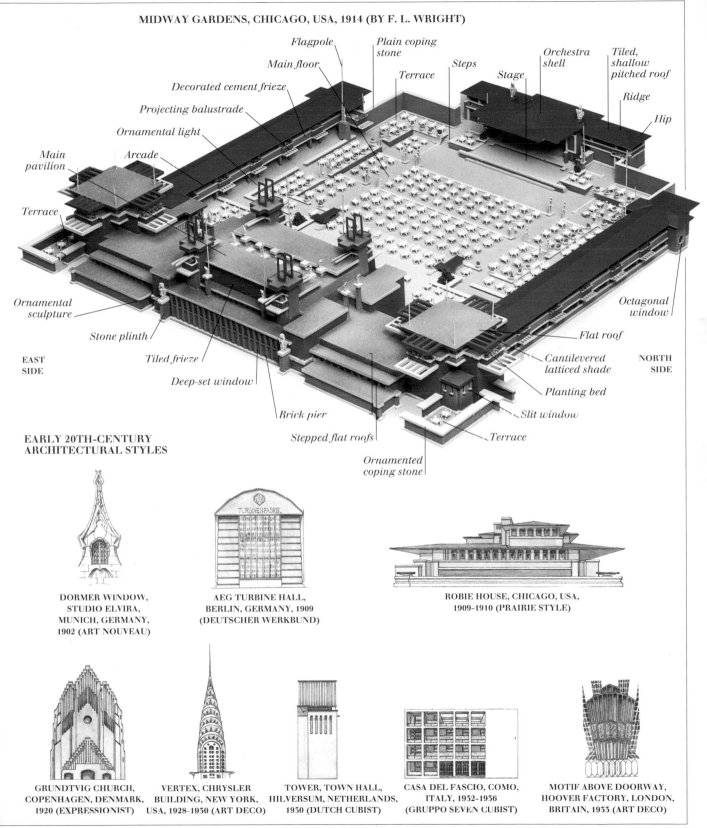

Flagpole

Plain coping stone

Main floor

Terrace

Steps

Stage

Orchestra shell

Tiled, shallow pitched roof

Decorated cement frieze

Ridge

Projecting balustrade

Hip

Ornamental light

Arcade

Main pavilion

Terrace

Ornamental sculpture

Stone plinth

Octagonal window

EAST SIDE

NORTH SIDE

Tiled frieze

Flat roof

Cantilevered latticed shade

Deep-set window

Planting bed

Brick pier

Slit window

Stepped flat roofs

Terrace

Ornamented coping stone

EARLY 20TH-CENTURY ARCHITECTURAL STYLES

DORMER WINDOW, STUDIO ELVIRA, MUNICH, GERMANY, 1902 (ART NOUVEAU)

AEG TURBINE HALL, BERLIN, GERMANY, 1909 (DEUTSCHER WERKBUND)

ROBIE HOUSE, CHICAGO, USA, 1909–1910 (PRAIRIE STYLE)

GRUNDTVIG CHURCH, COPENHAGEN, DENMARK, 1920 (EXPRESSIONIST)

VERTEX, CHRYSLER BUILDING, NEW YORK, USA, 1928–1930 (ART DECO)

TOWER, TOWN HALL, HILVERSUM, NETHERLANDS, 1930 (DUTCH CUBIST)

CASA DEL FASCIO, COMO, ITALY, 1932–1936 (GRUPPO SEVEN CUBIST)

MOTIF ABOVE DOORWAY, HOOVER FACTORY, LONDON, BRITAIN, 1933 (ART DECO)

Modern buildings 1

KAWANA HOUSE, JAPAN, FROM 1987 (BY N. FOSTER)

ARCHITECTURE SINCE ABOUT THE 1950s is generally known as modern architecture. One of its main influences has been functionalism—a belief that a building's function should be apparent in its design. Both the Centre Georges Pompidou (below and opposite) and the Hong Kong and Shanghai Bank (see pp. 498-499) are functionalist buildings. On each, elements of engineering and the building's services are clearly visible on the outside. In the 1980s, some architects rejected functionalism in favor of postmodernism, in which historical styles—particularly neoclassicism—were revived, using modern building materials and techniques. In many modern buildings, walls are made of glass or concrete hung from a frame, as in the Kawana House (right); this type of wall construction is known as curtain walling. Other modern construction techniques include the intricate interlocking of concrete vaults—as in the Sydney Opera House (see pp. 498-499)—and the use of high-tension beams to create complex roof shapes, such as the paraboloid roof of the Church of St. Pierre de Libreville (see pp. 498-499).

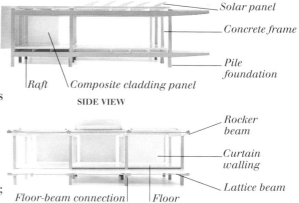

Solar panel
Concrete frame
Pile foundation
Raft
Composite cladding panel
SIDE VIEW

Rocker beam
Curtain walling
Lattice beam
Floor-beam connection
Floor
FRONT VIEW

SERVICES FACADE, CENTRE GEORGES POMPIDOU, PARIS, FRANCE, 1977 (BY R. PIANO AND R. ROGERS)

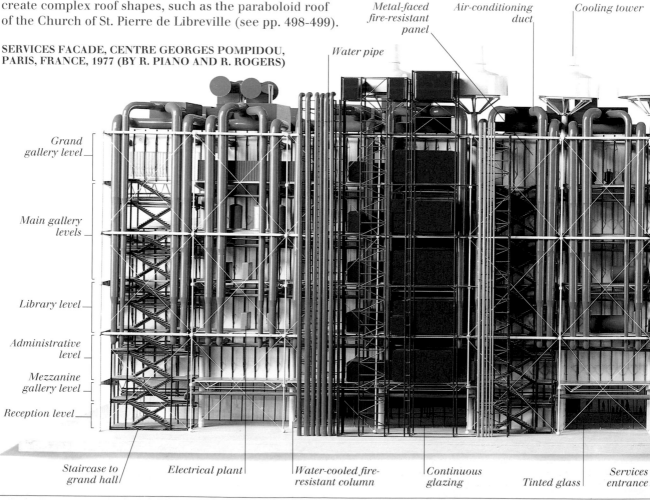

Water pipe
Metal-faced fire-resistant panel
Air-conditioning duct
Cooling tower

Grand gallery level
Main gallery levels
Library level
Administrative level
Mezzanine gallery level
Reception level

Staircase to grand hall
Electrical plant
Water-cooled fire-resistant column
Continuous glazing
Tinted glass
Services entrance

PRINCIPAL FACADE, CENTRE GEORGES POMPIDOU

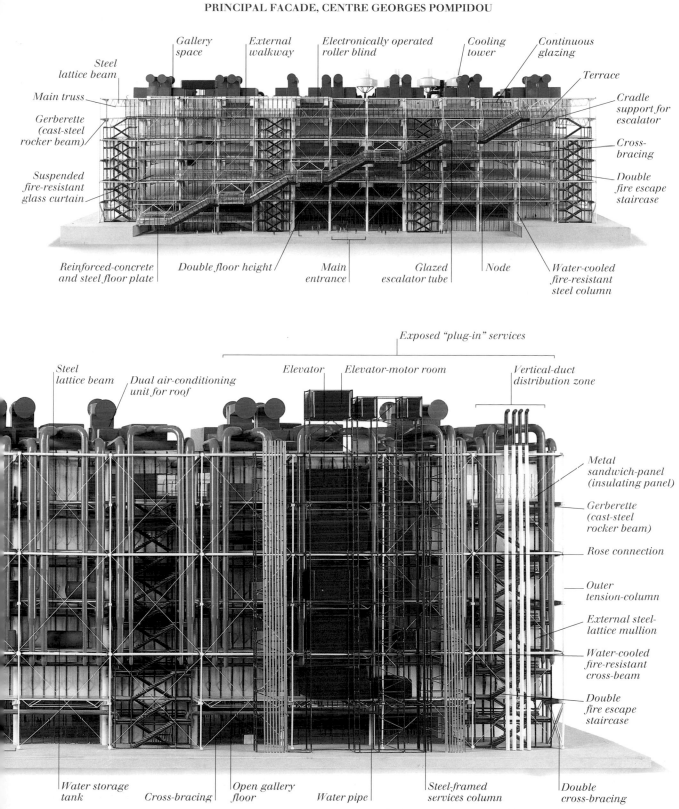

Gallery space

External walkway

Electronically operated roller blind

Cooling tower

Continuous glazing

Steel lattice beam

Terrace

Main truss

Cradle support for escalator

Gerberette (cast-steel rocker beam)

Cross-bracing

Suspended fire-resistant glass curtain

Double fire escape staircase

Reinforced-concrete and steel floor plate

Double floor height

Main entrance

Glazed escalator tube

Node

Water-cooled fire-resistant steel column

Exposed "plug-in" services

Steel lattice beam

Dual air-conditioning unit for roof

Elevator

Elevator-motor room

Vertical-duct distribution zone

Metal sandwich-panel (insulating panel)

Gerberette (cast-steel rocker beam)

Rose connection

Outer tension-column

External steel-lattice mullion

Water-cooled fire-resistant cross-beam

Double fire escape staircase

Water storage tank

Cross-bracing

Open gallery floor

Water pipe

Steel-framed services column

Double cross-bracing

Modern buildings 2

HONG KONG AND SHANGHAI BANK, HONG KONG, 1981-1985 (BY N. FOSTER)

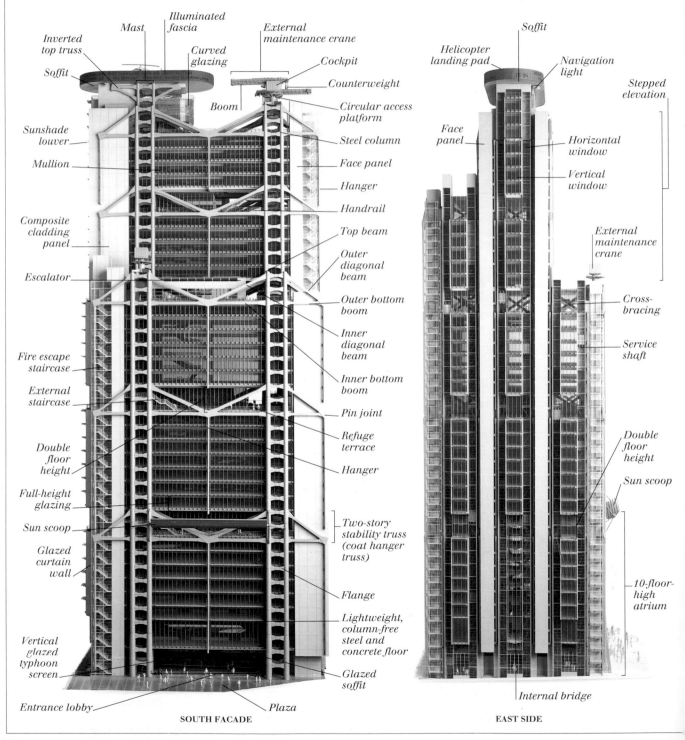

Mast

Illuminated fascia

Inverted top truss

Soffit

Curved glazing

External maintenance crane

Cockpit

Counterweight

Boom

Circular access platform

Steel column

Sunshade louver

Face panel

Mullion

Hanger

Handrail

Composite cladding panel

Top beam

Outer diagonal beam

Escalator

Outer bottom boom

Inner diagonal beam

Fire escape staircase

Inner bottom boom

External staircase

Pin joint

Refuge terrace

Double floor height

Hanger

Full-height glazing

Sun scoop

Two-story stability truss (coat hanger truss)

Glazed curtain wall

Flange

Vertical glazed typhoon screen

Lightweight, column-free steel and concrete floor

Entrance lobby

Glazed soffit

Plaza

SOUTH FACADE

Soffit

Helicopter landing pad

Navigation light

Stepped elevation

Face panel

Horizontal window

Vertical window

External maintenance crane

Cross-bracing

Service shaft

Double floor height

Sun scoop

10-floor-high atrium

Internal bridge

EAST SIDE

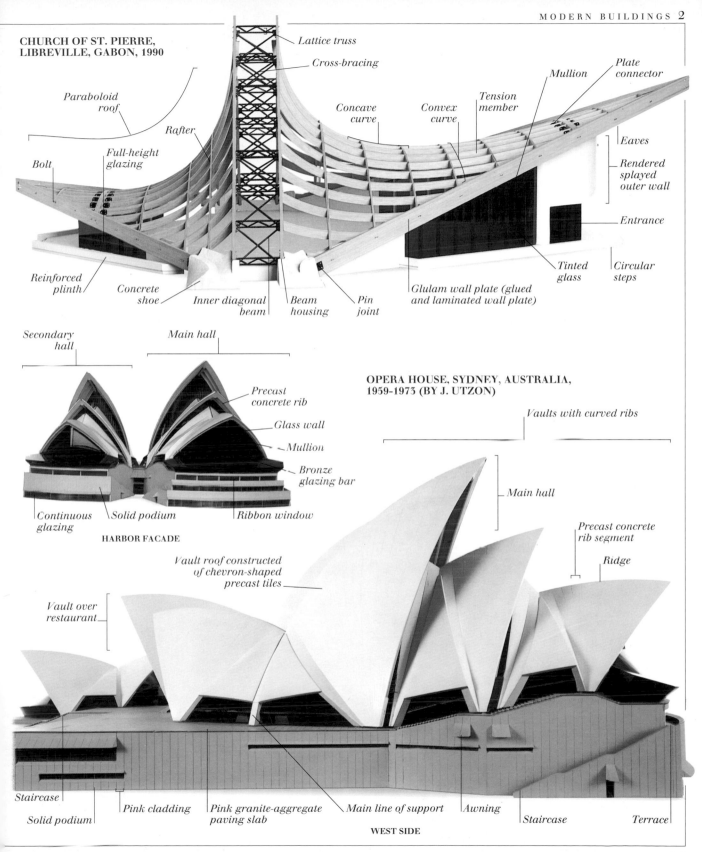

CHURCH OF ST. PIERRE, LIBREVILLE, GABON, 1990

Lattice truss

Cross-bracing

Mullion

Plate connector

Paraboloid roof

Rafter

Concave curve

Convex curve

Tension member

Eaves

Rendered splayed outer wall

Full-height glazing

Bolt

Entrance

Reinforced plinth

Concrete shoe

Inner diagonal beam

Beam housing

Pin joint

Glulam wall plate (glued and laminated wall plate)

Tinted glass

Circular steps

Secondary hall

Main hall

OPERA HOUSE, SYDNEY, AUSTRALIA, 1959-1973 (BY J. UTZON)

Vaults with curved ribs

Precast concrete rib

Glass wall

Mullion

Bronze glazing bar

Main hall

Precast concrete rib segment

Ridge

Continuous glazing

Solid podium

Ribbon window

HARBOR FACADE

Vault roof constructed of chevron-shaped precast tiles

Vault over restaurant

Staircase

Solid podium

Pink cladding

Pink granite-aggregate paving slab

Main line of support

Awning

Staircase

Terrace

WEST SIDE

Music

Musical notation

MUSICAL NOTATION IS ANY METHOD by which sounds are written down so that they can be read and performed by others. The present-day conventional system of notation uses a five-line stave (staff)—divided by vertical lines into sections known as bars—on which notes, rests, clefs, key signatures, time signatures, accidentals, and other symbols are written. A note indicates the duration of a sound and, according to its position on the stave, its pitch. Notes can be arranged on the stave in order of pitch to form a scale. A silence in the music is indicated by a rest. The clef, which is placed at the begininng of a stave, fixes the pitch. The key signature, which is placed after the clef, indicates the key. The time signature, placed after the key signature, shows the number of beats in a bar. Accidentals are used to indicate the raising or lowering of the pitch of a note.

ELEMENTS OF MUSICAL NOTATION

CLEFS

Treble (or G) clef

Alto (or C) clef

Bass (or F) clef

NOTES

Breve Minim Quaver

Semibreve Crotchet Semiquaver

RESTS

Breve rest Minim rest Quaver rest

Semibreve rest Crotchet rest Semiquaver rest

SCALE

C D E F G A B C

ACCIDENTALS

Sharp Natural Double sharp

Flat Double flat Key signature

TIME SIGNATURES

Six-eight time

3/4

6/8

Stave (staff)

Three-four time

Moderately fast and quiet

Tie (bind)

Repeat the previous bar

Treble clef

Bass clef

Four-four time (common time)

Key signature

Alto clef

Treble voice

Alto voice

Tenor voice

Bass voice

Organ part for right hand

Organ part for left hand

Organ pedal line

Instruments of the orchestra written in Italian

Bar line

Bass clef

Bar

Crotchet

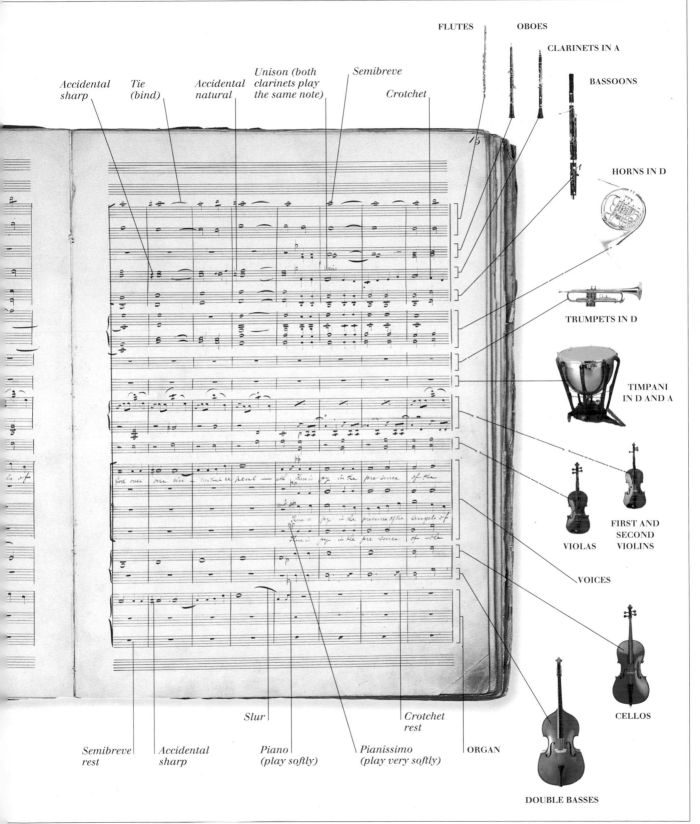

FLUTES

OBOES

CLARINETS IN A

BASSOONS

Accidental sharp

Tie (bind)

Accidental natural

Unison (both clarinets play the same note)

Semibreve

Crotchet

HORNS IN D

TRUMPETS IN D

TIMPANI IN D AND A

FIRST AND SECOND VIOLINS

VIOLAS

VOICES

CELLOS

Semibreve rest

Accidental sharp

Slur

Piano (play softly)

Pianissimo (play very softly)

Crotchet rest

ORGAN

DOUBLE BASSES

Orchestras

AN ORCHESTRA IS A GROUP of musicians that plays music written for a specific combination of instruments. The number and type of instruments included in the orchestra depends on the style of music being played. The modern orchestra (also known as a symphony orchestra) is made up of four sections of instruments—stringed, woodwind, brass, and percussion. The stringed section consists of violins, violas, cellos (violoncellos), double basses, and sometimes a harp (see pp. 510-511). The main instruments of the woodwind section are flutes, oboes, clarinets, and bassoons—the piccolo, cor anglais, bass clarinet, saxophone, and double bassoon (contrabassoon) can also be included if the music requires them (see pp. 508-509). The brass section usually consists of horns, trumpets, trombones, and the tuba (see pp. 506-507). The main instruments of the percussion section are the timpani (see pp. 518-519). The snare drum, bass drum, cymbals, tambourine, triangle, tubular bells, xylophone, vibraphone, gong (tam-tam), castanets, and maracas can also be included in the percussion section (see pp. 516-517). The musicians are usually arranged in a semi-circle—strings spread along the front, woodwind and brass in the center, and percussion at the back. A conductor stands in front of the musicians and controls the tempo (speed) of the music and the overall balance of the sound, ensuring that no instruments are too loud or too soft in relation to the others.

XYLOPHONE

VIBRAPHONE

TAM-TAM (GONG)

TUBULAR BELLS

CASTANETS

TAMBOURINE

MARACAS

TRIANGLE

TRUMPETS

HORNS

CLARINETS

BASS CLARINET

SAXOPHONE

PICCOLO

HARP

SECOND VIOLINS

FIRST VIOLINS

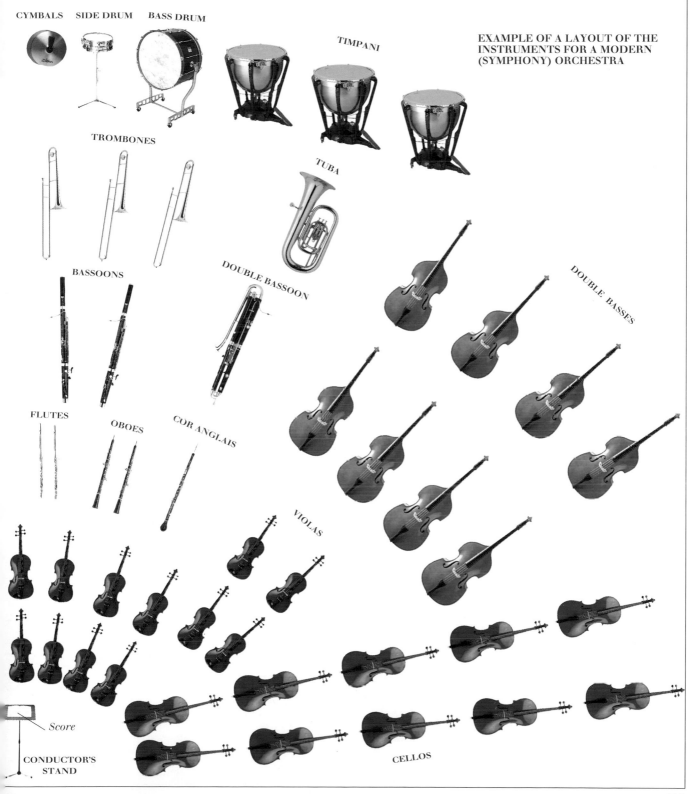

CYMBALS SIDE DRUM BASS DRUM

TIMPANI

**EXAMPLE OF A LAYOUT OF THE
INSTRUMENTS FOR A MODERN
(SYMPHONY) ORCHESTRA**

TROMBONES

TUBA

BASSOONS

DOUBLE BASSOON

DOUBLE BASSES

FLUTES

OBOES

COR ANGLAIS

VIOLAS

Score

CONDUCTOR'S
STAND

CELLOS

Brass instruments

BUGLE

BRASS INSTRUMENTS ARE WIND INSTRUMENTS that are made of metal, usually brass. Although they appear in many different shapes and sizes, all brass instruments have a mouthpiece, a length of hollow tube, and a flared bell. The mouthpiece of a brass instrument may be cup-shaped, as in the cornet, or cone-shaped, as in the horn. The tube may be wide or narrow, mainly conical, as in the horn and tuba, or mainly cylindrical, as in the trumpet and trombone. The sound of a brass instrument is made by the player's lips vibrating against the mouthpiece, so that the air vibrates in the tube. By changing lip tension, the player can vary the vibrations and produce notes of different pitches. The range of notes produced by a brass instrument can be extended by means of a valve system. Most brass instruments, such as the trumpet, have piston valves that divert the air in the instrument along an extra piece of tubing (known as a valve slide) when pressed down. The total length of the tube is increased and the pitch of the note produced is lowered. Instead of valves, the trombone has a movable slide that can be pushed away from or drawn toward the player. The sound of a brass instrument can also be changed by inserting a mute into the bell of the instrument.

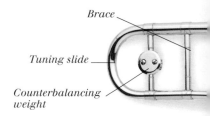

Brace

Tuning slide

Counterbalancing weight

SIMPLIFIED DIAGRAM SHOWING HOW A PISTON VALVE SYSTEM WORKS

Piston valves at rest

Air bypasses piston valves

PISTON VALVES AT REST

First piston valve pressed down

Second and third piston valves at rest

Air diverted through first valve slide

PISTON VALVE PRESSED DOWN

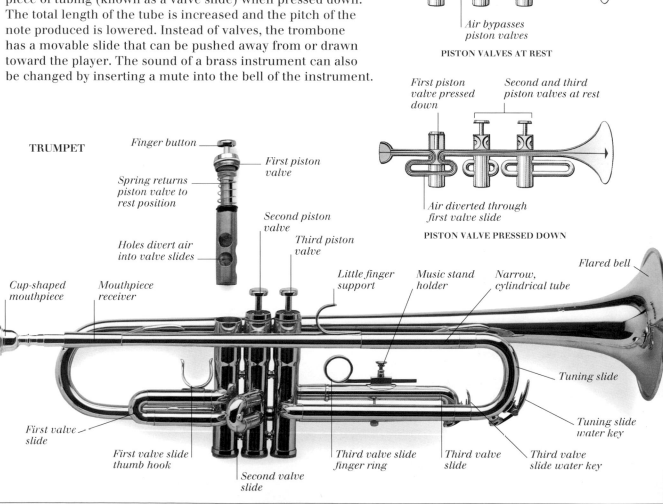

TRUMPET

Finger button

First piston valve

Spring returns piston valve to rest position

Second piston valve

Third piston valve

Holes divert air into valve slides

Little finger support

Music stand holder

Narrow, cylindrical tube

Flared bell

Cup-shaped mouthpiece

Mouthpiece receiver

Tuning slide

First valve slide

First valve slide thumb hook

Second valve slide

Third valve slide finger ring

Third valve slide

Tuning slide water key

Third valve slide water key

SECTIONS OF A TROMBONE

EXAMPLES OF MUTES

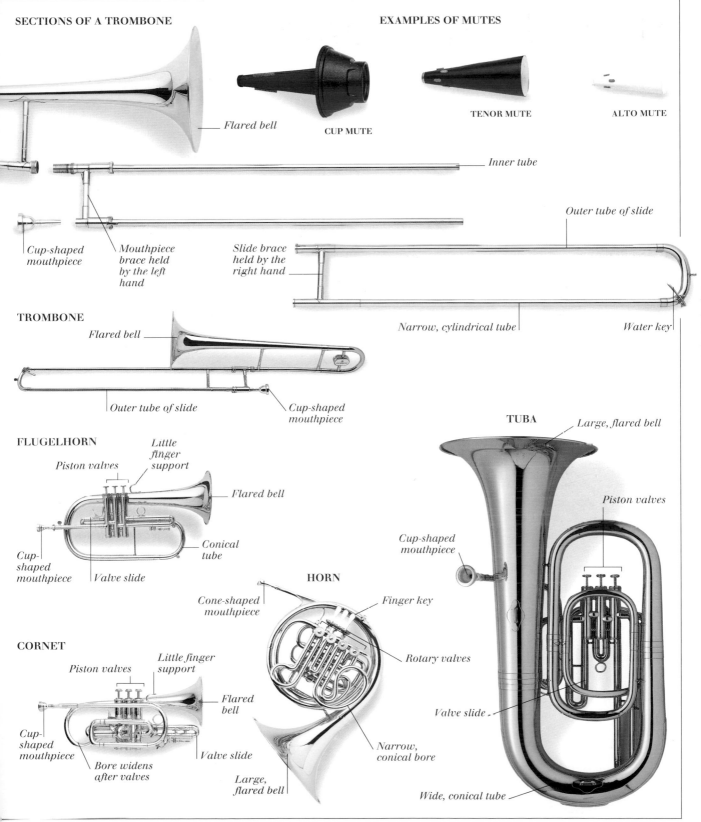

Flared bell

CUP MUTE

TENOR MUTE

ALTO MUTE

Inner tube

Outer tube of slide

Cup-shaped
mouthpiece

Mouthpiece
brace held
by the left
hand

Slide brace
held by the
right hand

Narrow, cylindrical tube

Water key

TROMBONE

Flared bell

Outer tube of slide

Cup-shaped
mouthpiece

FLUGELHORN

Little
finger
support

Piston valves

Flared bell

Cup-
shaped
mouthpiece

Valve slide

Conical
tube

HORN

Cone-shaped
mouthpiece

Finger key

Rotary valves

Narrow,
conical bore

Large,
flared bell

TUBA

Large, flared bell

Piston valves

Cup-shaped
mouthpiece

Valve slide

Wide, conical tube

CORNET

Little finger
support

Piston valves

Flared
bell

Cup-
shaped
mouthpiece

Bore widens
after valves

Valve slide

Woodwind instruments

WOODWIND INSTRUMENTS ARE wind instruments that are generally made of wood, although some are made of metal or plastic. The sound of a woodwind instrument is produced by the vibration of air in a hollow tube. The air is made to vibrate by blowing across a blow hole—as in the flute and piccolo—or by blowing through a single reed—as in the clarinet and saxophone—or a double reed—as in the bassoon, cor anglais, and oboe. The pitch of a woodwind instrument can be changed by opening or closing holes cut into the tube of the instrument.

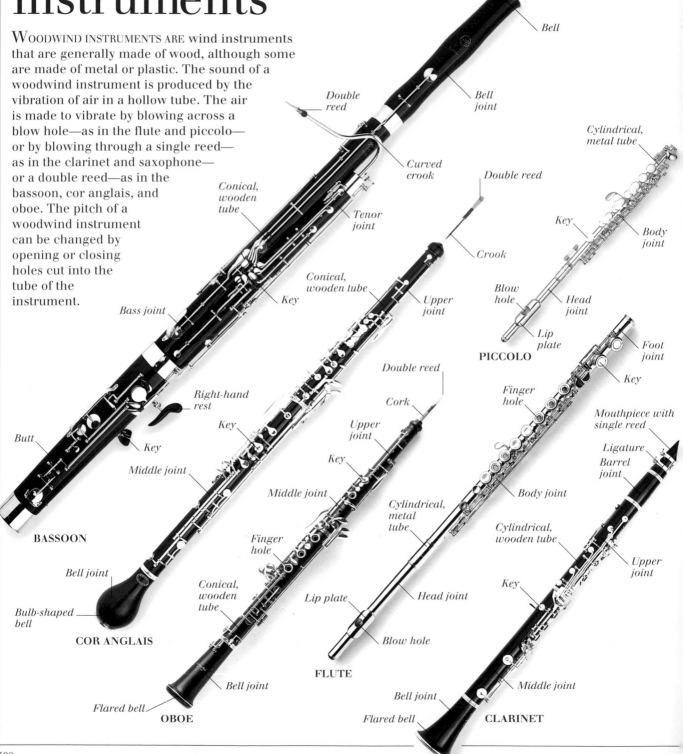

Bell

Double reed

Bell joint

Cylindrical, metal tube

Curved crook

Double reed

Key

Body joint

Conical, wooden tube

Tenor joint

Crook

Blow hole

Head joint

Conical, wooden tube

Upper joint

Lip plate

PICCOLO

Key

Bass joint

Double reed

Foot joint

Cork

Key

Right-hand rest

Upper joint

Finger hole

Key

Mouthpiece with single reed

Butt

Key

Key

Middle joint

Ligature

Barrel joint

Middle joint

Cylindrical, metal tube

Body joint

BASSOON

Finger hole

Cylindrical, wooden tube

Bell joint

Conical, wooden tube

Lip plate

Head joint

Key

Upper joint

Bulb-shaped bell

Blow hole

COR ANGLAIS

Bell joint

FLUTE

Middle joint

Flared bell

OBOE

Bell joint

Flared bell

CLARINET

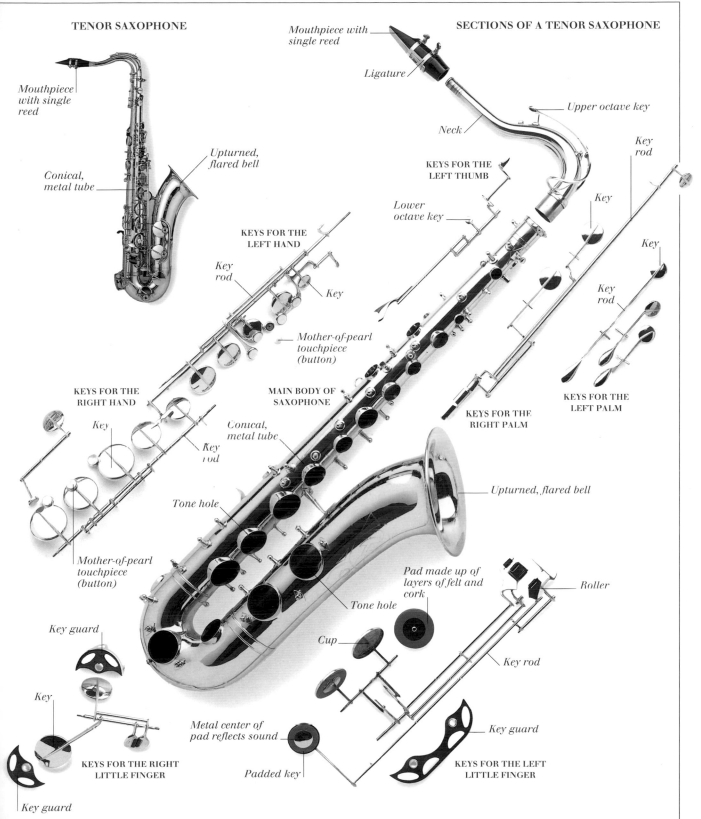

TENOR SAXOPHONE

Mouthpiece with single reed

Conical, metal tube

Upturned, flared bell

SECTIONS OF A TENOR SAXOPHONE

Mouthpiece with single reed

Ligature

Upper octave key

Neck

Key rod

KEYS FOR THE LEFT THUMB

Lower octave key

Key

KEYS FOR THE LEFT HAND

Key rod

Key

Mother-of-pearl touchpiece (button)

Key

Key rod

KEYS FOR THE LEFT PALM

KEYS FOR THE RIGHT HAND

Key

Key rod

MAIN BODY OF SAXOPHONE

Conical, metal tube

Tone hole

Mother-of-pearl touchpiece (button)

KEYS FOR THE RIGHT PALM

Upturned, flared bell

Tone hole

Pad made up of layers of felt and cork

Roller

Cup

Key rod

Key guard

Key

Metal center of pad reflects sound

KEYS FOR THE RIGHT LITTLE FINGER

Padded key

Key guard

KEYS FOR THE LEFT LITTLE FINGER

Key guard

Stringed instruments

STRINGED INSTRUMENTS PRODUCE SOUND by the vibration of stretched strings. This may be done by drawing a bow across the strings, as in the violin; or by plucking the strings, as in the harp and guitar (see pp. 512-513). The four modern members of the bowed string family are the violin, viola, cello (violoncello), and double bass. Each consists of a hollow, wooden body, a long neck, and four strings. The bow is a wooden stick with horsehair stretched across its length. The vibrations made by drawing the bow across the strings are transmitted to the hollow body, and this itself vibrates, amplifying and enriching the sound produced. The harp consists of a set of strings of different lengths stretched across a wooden frame. The strings are plucked by the player's thumbs and fingers—except the little finger of each hand—which produces vibrations that are amplified by the harp's sound board. The pitch of the note produced by any stringed instrument depends on the length, weight, and tension of the string. A shorter, lighter, or tighter string gives a higher note.

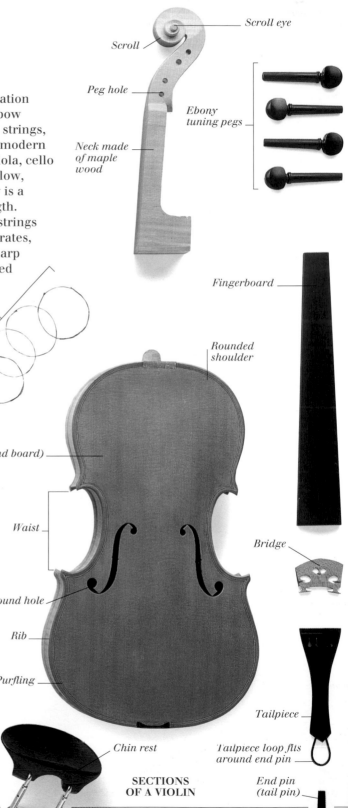

Scroll eye

Scroll

Peg hole

Ebony tuning pegs

Neck made of maple wood

Strings

Fingerboard

Rounded shoulder

Belly (sound board)

Waist

Sound hole

Rib

Purfling

Chin rest

Bridge

Tailpiece

Tailpiece loop fits around end pin

End pin (tail pin)

SECTIONS OF A VIOLIN

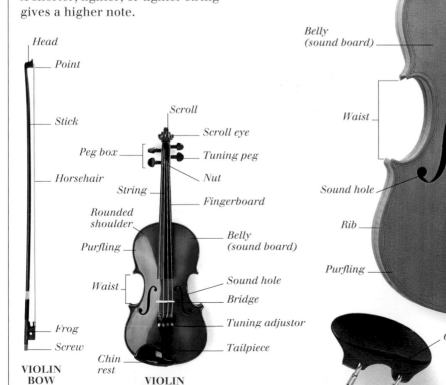

Head

Point

Stick

Scroll

Scroll eye

Peg box

Tuning peg

Horsehair

Nut

String

Fingerboard

Rounded shoulder

Belly (sound board)

Purfling

Waist

Sound hole

Bridge

Tuning adjustor

Frog

Tailpiece

Screw

Chin rest

VIOLIN BOW

VIOLIN

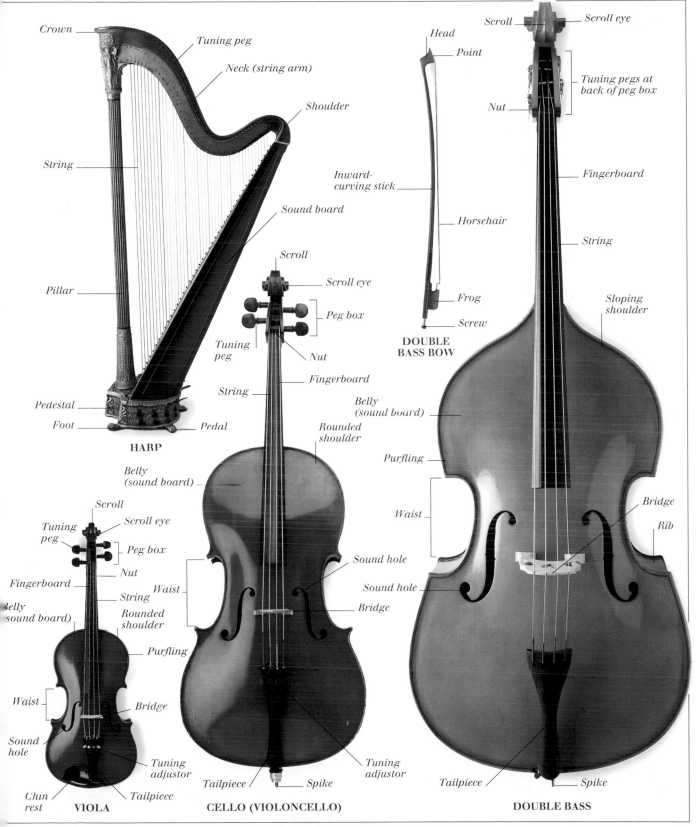

HARP

Crown

Tuning peg

Neck (string arm)

Shoulder

String

Sound board

Pillar

Pedestal

Foot

Pedal

DOUBLE BASS BOW

Head

Point

Inward-curving stick

Horsehair

Frog

Screw

VIOLA

Scroll

Tuning peg

Scroll eye

Peg box

Nut

Fingerboard

Belly (sound board)

String

Rounded shoulder

Purfling

Waist

Bridge

Sound hole

Chin rest

Tuning adjustor

Tailpiece

CELLO (VIOLONCELLO)

Scroll

Scroll eye

Peg box

Tuning peg

Nut

Fingerboard

String

Belly (sound board)

Rounded shoulder

Waist

Sound hole

Bridge

Tailpiece

Spike

Tuning adjustor

DOUBLE BASS

Scroll

Scroll eye

Tuning pegs at back of peg box

Nut

Fingerboard

String

Sloping shoulder

Belly (sound board)

Purfling

Waist

Bridge

Rib

Sound hole

Sound hole

Tailpiece

Spike

Guitars

THE GUITAR IS A PLUCKED stringed instrument (see pp. 510-511). There are two types of guitar—acoustic and electric. Acoustic guitars have hollow bodies and six or twelve strings. Plucking or strumming the strings produces vibrations that are amplified by their hollow bodies. Electric guitars usually have solid bodies and six strings. Pick-ups placed under the strings convert vibrations into electronic signals that are magnified by an amplifier, and sent to a loudspeaker where they are converted into sounds (see pp. 520-521). Electric bass guitars are very similar in structure to electric guitars, and produce sound in the same way, but have four heavier-gage strings and play lower pitched notes.

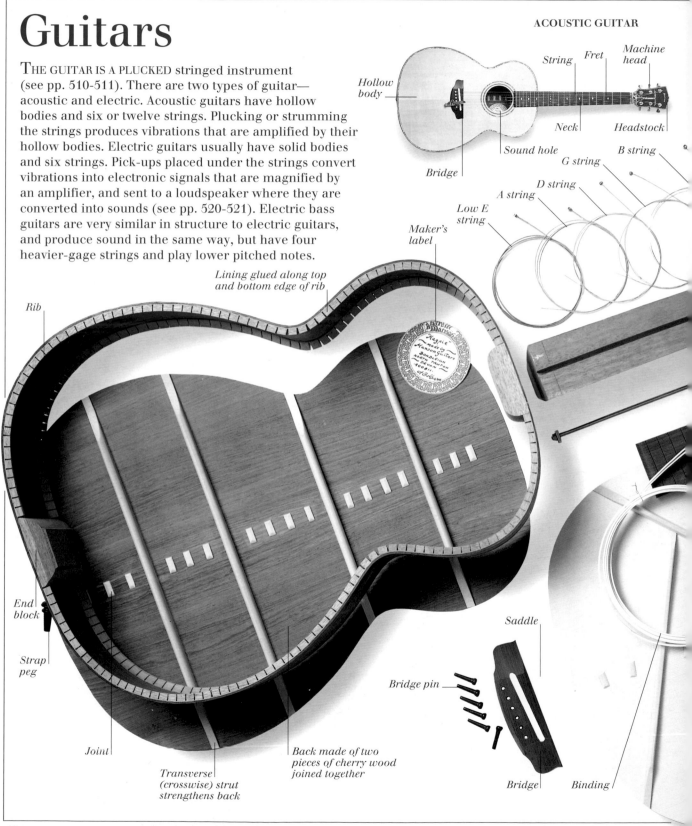

ACOUSTIC GUITAR

Hollow body

String

Fret

Machine head

Neck

Headstock

Sound hole

Bridge

B string

G string

D string

A string

Low E string

Maker's label

Lining glued along top and bottom edge of rib

Rib

End block

Strap peg

Joint

Transverse (crosswise) strut strengthens back

Back made of two pieces of cherry wood joined together

Saddle

Bridge pin

Bridge

Binding

COMPONENTS OF AN ACOUSTIC GUITAR

EXAMPLES OF ACOUSTIC GUITARS

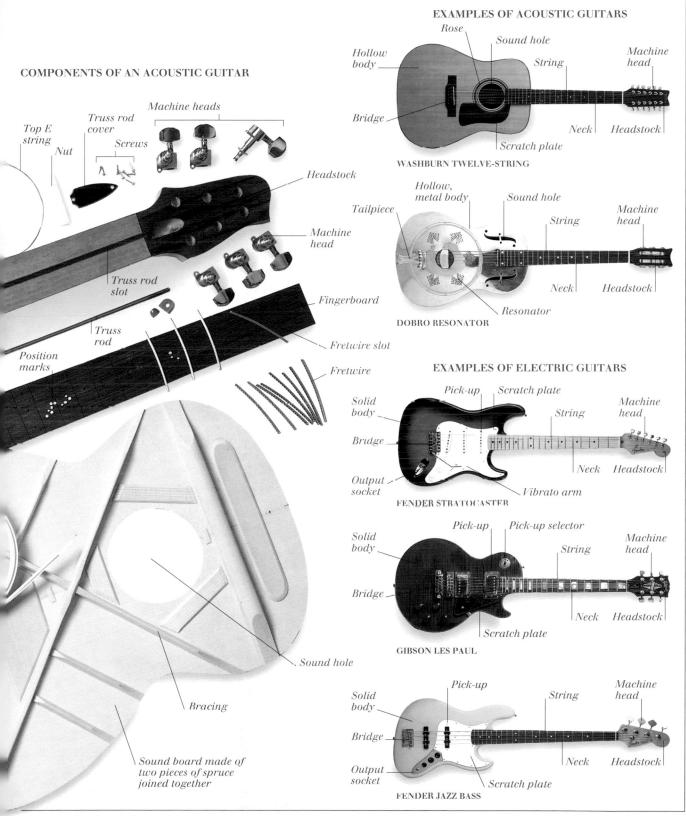

Machine heads

Truss rod cover

Screws

Top E string

Nut

Headstock

Machine head

Truss rod slot

Fingerboard

Truss rod

Fretwire slot

Position marks

Fretwire

Sound hole

Bracing

Sound board made of two pieces of spruce joined together

Rose

Hollow body

Sound hole

String

Machine head

Bridge

Neck

Headstock

Scratch plate

WASHBURN TWELVE-STRING

Hollow, metal body

Sound hole

Machine head

Tailpiece

String

Neck

Headstock

Resonator

DOBRO RESONATOR

EXAMPLES OF ELECTRIC GUITARS

Pick-up

Scratch plate

Solid body

String

Machine head

Bridge

Neck

Headstock

Output socket

Vibrato arm

FENDER STRATOCASTER

Pick-up

Pick-up selector

Solid body

String

Machine head

Bridge

Neck

Headstock

Scratch plate

GIBSON LES PAUL

Pick-up

Machine head

Solid body

String

Bridge

Neck

Headstock

Output socket

Scratch plate

FENDER JAZZ BASS

Keyboard instruments

KEYBOARD INSTRUMENTS are instruments that are sounded by means of a keyboard. The organ and piano are two of the principal members of the keyboard family. The organ consists of pipes which are operated by one or more keyboards and foot pedals. The pipes are lined up in rows (known as ranks or registers) on top of a wind chest. The sound of the organ is made when air is admitted into a pipe by pressing a key or pedal. The piano consists of wire strings stretched over a metal frame, and a keyboard and pedals that operate hammers and dampers. The piano frame is either vertical—as in the upright piano—or horizontal—as in the grand piano. When a key is at rest, a damper lies against the string to keep it from vibrating. When a key is pressed down, the damper moves away from the string as the hammer strikes it, causing the string to vibrate and sound a note.

ORGAN PIPE

UPRIGHT PIANO

Muffler felt
Pressure bar
Tuning pin
Pin block
Hammer
Hammer rail
88–note keyboard
Wooden case
Keybed
Sound board
Metal frame
String
Hitch pin
Treble bridge
Bass bridge
Una corda (soft) pedal
Sostenuto pedal
Damper (sustaining) pedal

ORGAN CONSOLE

Pipe
Pedal stop
Music stand
Swell stop
Choir stop
Swell manual (keyboard)
Great stop
Great manual (keyboard)
Thumb piston
Choir manual (keyboard)
Toe piston
Pedal board
Foot pedal
Swell pedal

UPRIGHT PIANO ACTION

KEY AT REST

String
Hammer
Damper lies against string, and keeps it from vibrating
Hammer rest
Back check
Damper lever
Action lever
Jack
Capstan screw
Key released

KEY PRESSED DOWN

String
Hammer strikes string
Damper moves away from string, allowing it to vibrate
Hammer rest
Back check
Damper lever
Action lever
Capstan screw
Jack
Key pressed down

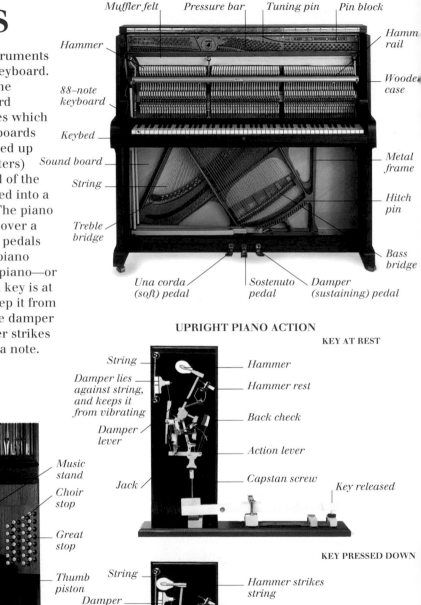

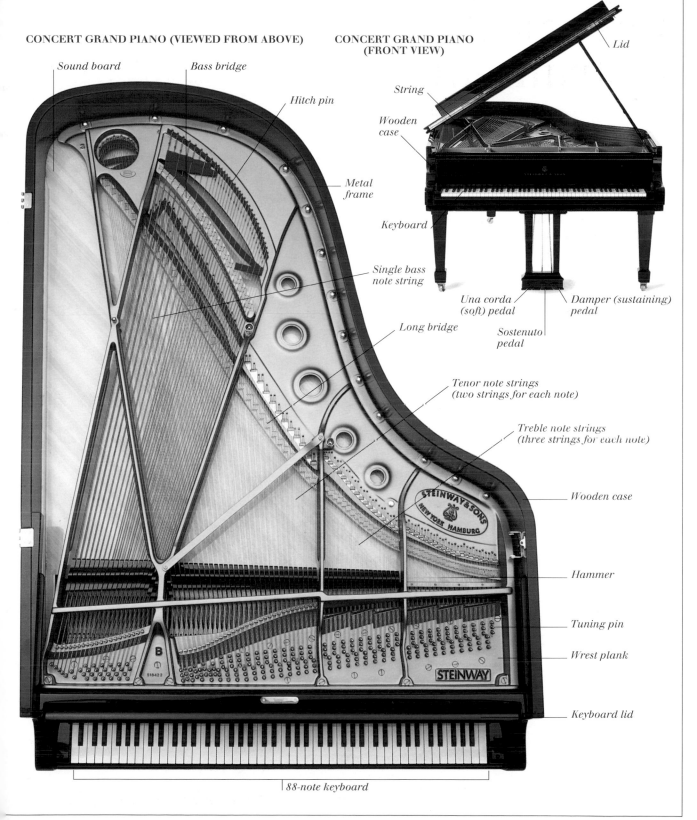

CONCERT GRAND PIANO (VIEWED FROM ABOVE)

CONCERT GRAND PIANO (FRONT VIEW)

Sound board

Bass bridge

Hitch pin

Metal frame

Single bass note string

Long bridge

Lid

String

Wooden case

Keyboard

Una corda (soft) pedal

Sostenuto pedal

Damper (sustaining) pedal

Tenor note strings (two strings for each note)

Treble note strings (three strings for each note)

Wooden case

Hammer

Tuning pin

Wrest plank

Keyboard lid

88-note keyboard

STEINWAY & SONS NEW YORK HAMBURG

STEINWAY

B

518422

Percussion instruments

TEMPLE BLOCKS

PERCUSSION INSTRUMENTS are a large group of instruments that produce sound by being struck, shaken, scraped, or clashed together. Some percussion instruments—such as the gong (tam-tam), cymbals, and maracas—do not have a definite pitch and are used for rhythm and impact, and the distinctive timber (color) of their sound. Other percussion instruments— such as the xylophone, vibraphone, and tubular bells—are tuned to a definite pitch and can play melody, harmony, and rhythms. The xylophone and vibraphone each have two rows of bars that are arranged in a similar way to the black and white keys of a piano. Metal tubes are suspended below the bars to amplify the sound. The vibraphone has electrically operated fans that rotate in the tubes and produce a vibrato (wavering pitch) effect.

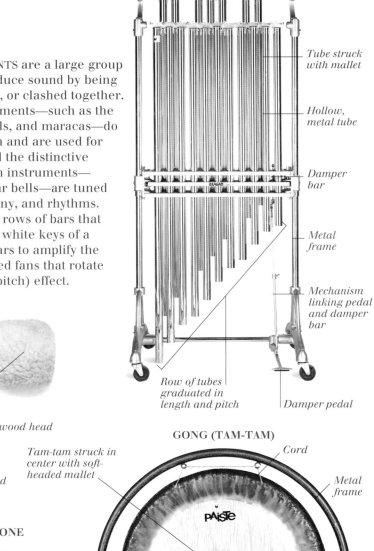

TUBULAR BELLS

Tube struck with mallet

Hollow, metal tube

Damper bar

Metal frame

Mechanism linking pedal and damper bar

Row of tubes graduated in length and pitch

Damper pedal

EXAMPLES OF MALLETS

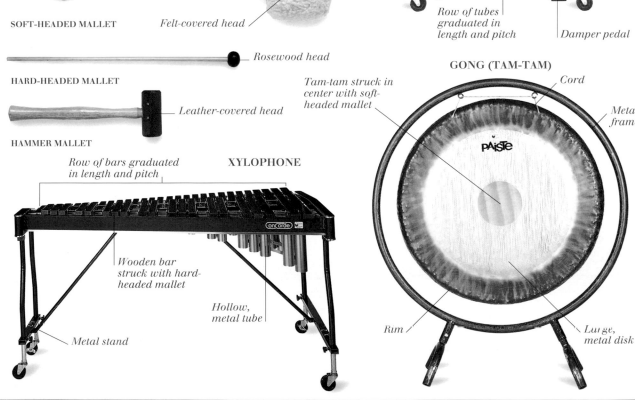

SOFT-HEADED MALLET

Felt-covered head

HARD-HEADED MALLET

Rosewood head

HAMMER MALLET

Leather-covered head

XYLOPHONE

Row of bars graduated in length and pitch

Wooden bar struck with hard-headed mallet

Hollow, metal tube

Metal stand

GONG (TAM-TAM)

Tam-tam struck in center with soft-headed mallet

Cord

Metal frame

Rim

Large, metal disk

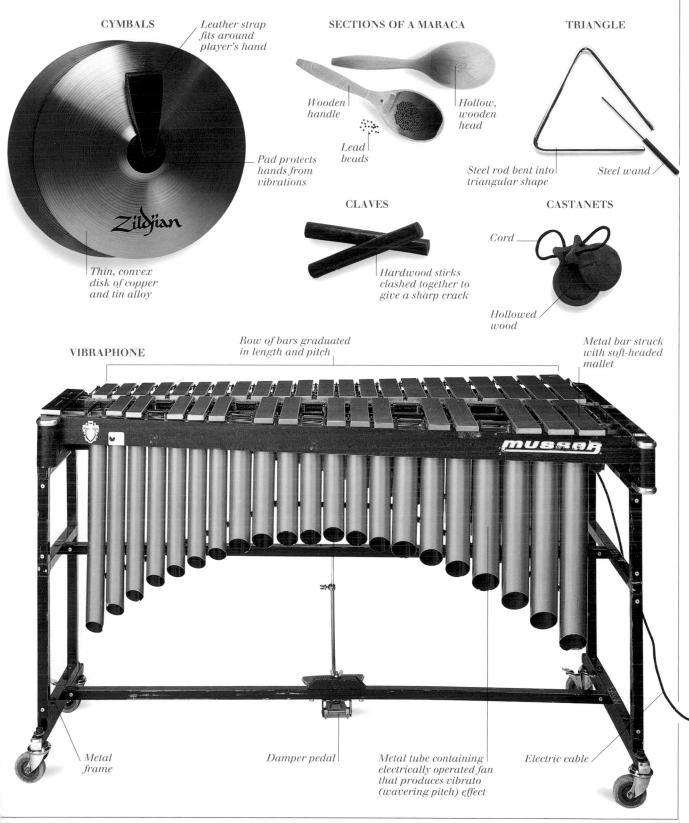

CYMBALS

Leather strap fits around player's hand

Pad protects hands from vibrations

Thin, convex disk of copper and tin alloy

SECTIONS OF A MARACA

Wooden handle

Lead beads

Hollow, wooden head

TRIANGLE

Steel rod bent into triangular shape

Steel wand

CLAVES

Hardwood sticks clashed together to give a sharp crack

CASTANETS

Cord

Hollowed wood

VIBRAPHONE

Row of bars graduated in length and pitch

Metal bar struck with soft-headed mallet

Metal frame

Damper pedal

Metal tube containing electrically operated fan that produces vibrato (wavering pitch) effect

Electric cable

Drums

TAMBOURINE

A DRUM IS A percussion instrument that consists of a drumhead, made of skin or plastic, stretched over one or both ends of a hollow vessel (the body shell). Drums are played in most parts of the world and are made in a number of different shapes and sizes. They can be divided into three groups according to the shape of the body shell: frame drums (e.g., tambourines), bowl-shaped drums (e.g., timpani), and tubular drums (e.g., congas). Drums are usually sounded by striking the drumhead with the hands or with mallets, such as a hard-headed stick. The drumhead vibrates, and its vibrations are amplified by the hollow body shell. The snare drum has wires—known as snares—stretched across the lower drumhead; the snares vibrate against the lower drumhead when the drum is played. Most drums, such as congas, do not have a definite pitch and can play only rhythms (see pp. 516-517). Other drums, such as timpani, have a definite pitch and can play melody, harmony, and rhythms. They can be tuned by adjusting the tension of the drumhead. Different types of drum can be combined together with other percussion instruments to form a drum kit. The basic components of the drum kit are bass drum, tom-toms, floor tom (tenor drum), snare drum, and cymbals.

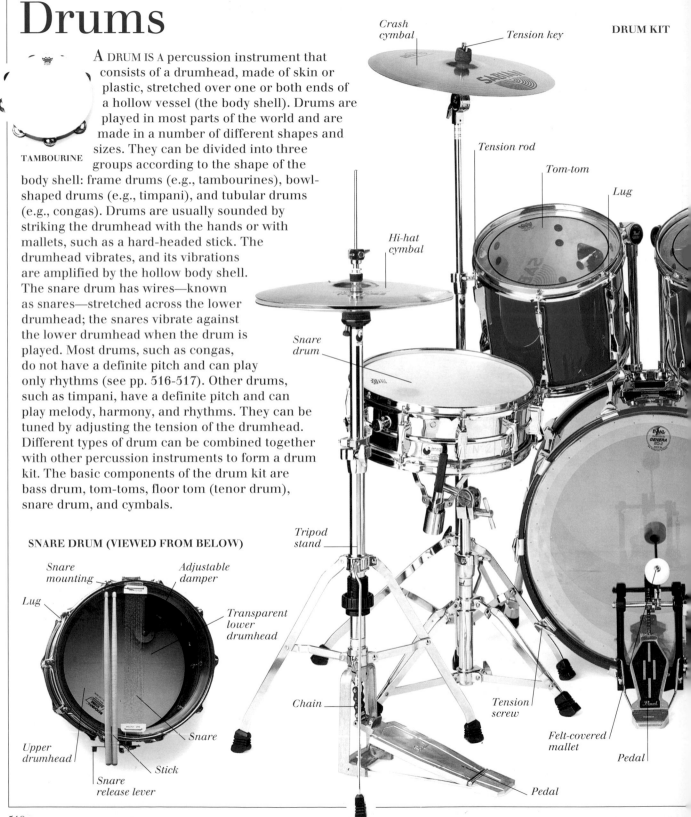

Crash cymbal

Tension key

DRUM KIT

Tension rod

Tom-tom

Lug

Hi-hat cymbal

Snare drum

Tripod stand

Chain

Tension screw

Felt-covered mallet

Pedal

Pedal

SNARE DRUM (VIEWED FROM BELOW)

Snare mounting

Adjustable damper

Lug

Transparent lower drumhead

Upper drumhead

Snare

Stick

Snare release lever

EXAMPLES OF STICKS

Acorn

HARD-HEADED STICK

Taper

SOFT-HEADED STICK

Felt-covered head

WIRE BRUSH

Wire bristles

Ride cymbal

Tension key

Tom-tom

Height adjustment key

Tension rod

Lug

Floor tom (tenor drum)

Tension rod

Lug

Wooden body shell

Height adjustment key

Leg

Bass drum

Rubber foot

CONGAS

Metal hoop

Drumhead

Tension rod

Wooden body shell

Tripod stand

Leg

TIMPANUM (KETTLE DRUM)

Drumhead

Tension rod

Metal hoop

Tuning gauge

Copper body shell

Strut

Crown

Tension rod

Tuning pedal

Castor

519

Electronic instruments

ELECTRONIC INSTRUMENTS generate electronic signals that are magnified by an amplifier and sent to a loudspeaker, where they are converted into sounds. Synthesizers, and other electronic instruments, simulate the characteristic sounds of conventional instruments, and also create entirely new sounds. Most electronic instruments are keyboard instruments, but electronic wind and percussion instruments are also popular. A digital sampler records and stores sounds from musical instruments or other sources. When the sound is played back, the pitch of the original sound can be altered. A keyboard can be connected to the sampler so that a tune can be played using the sampled sounds. With a MIDI (Musical Instrument Digital Interface) system, a computer can be linked with other electronic instruments, such as keyboards and electronic drums, to make sounds together or in sequence. It is also possible, using music software, to compose and play music on a home computer.

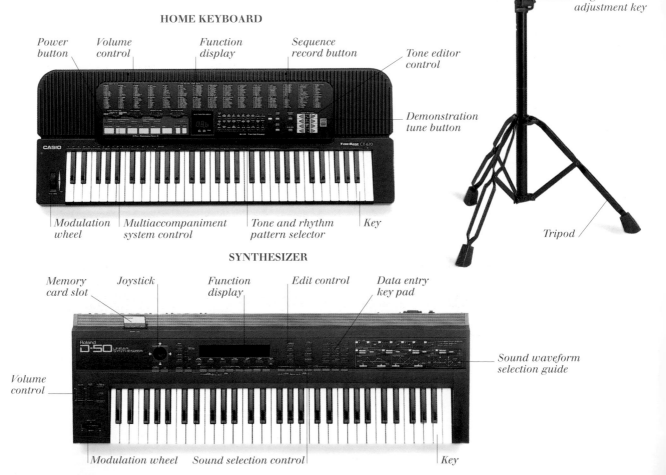

Drum pad

Height adjustment key

Tripod

HOME KEYBOARD

Power button

Volume control

Function display

Sequence record button

Tone editor control

Demonstration tune button

Modulation wheel

Multiaccompaniment system control

Tone and rhythm pattern selector

Key

SYNTHESIZER

Memory card slot

Joystick

Function display

Edit control

Data entry key pad

Sound waveform selection guide

Volume control

Modulation wheel

Sound selection control

Key

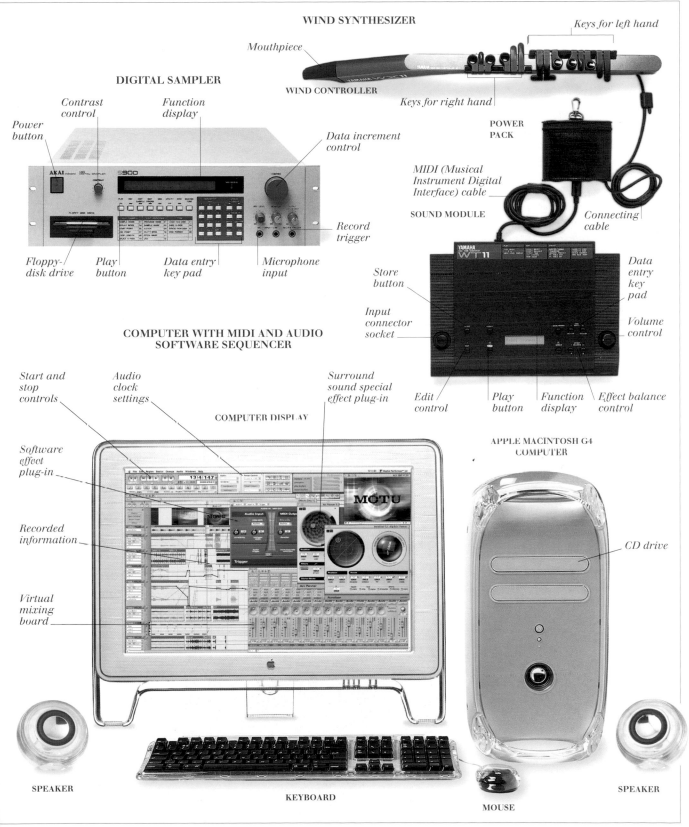

WIND SYNTHESIZER

Keys for left hand

Mouthpiece

DIGITAL SAMPLER

WIND CONTROLLER

Keys for right hand

Contrast control

Function display

Power button

Data increment control

POWER PACK

MIDI (Musical Instrument Digital Interface) cable

Connecting cable

SOUND MODULE

Record trigger

Floppy-disk drive

Play button

Data entry key pad

Microphone input

Store button

Data entry key pad

Input connector socket

Volume control

COMPUTER WITH MIDI AND AUDIO SOFTWARE SEQUENCER

Start and stop controls

Audio clock settings

Surround sound special effect plug-in

Edit control

Play button

Function display

Effect balance control

COMPUTER DISPLAY

Software effect plug-in

APPLE MACINTOSH G4 COMPUTER

Recorded information

CD drive

Virtual mixing board

SPEAKER

KEYBOARD

MOUSE

SPEAKER

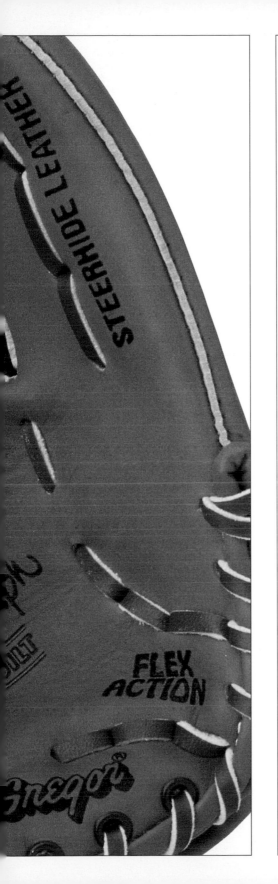

SPORTS

Soccer

GAMES INVOLVING KICKING A BALL have a long history and were recorded in China as early as 300 BC; in medieval Europe, street football was banned as a menace to the public; only in 1863 were the rules established, specifically banning carrying the ball for all players except the goalkeeper, and separating rugby from soccer. Soccer, also known as association football, is a team sport in which players attempt to score goals by passing and dribbling the ball down the field past opposing defenders, and kicking or heading the ball into the goal net, outwitting the defending goalkeeper or "goalie." Each team consists of ten outfield players (defenders, midfielders, and strikers) and a goalkeeper. Players from the opposing team may challenge the player in possession of the ball, but an illegal or foul tackle results in a penalty if a foul occurs inside the penalty area or a free kick if outside the penalty area. The round ball used in soccer is more easily controlled than the oval balls used in American, Canadian, and Australian rules football and in rugby. The result is a more "open" or flowing game which is played and watched by millions of people worldwide.

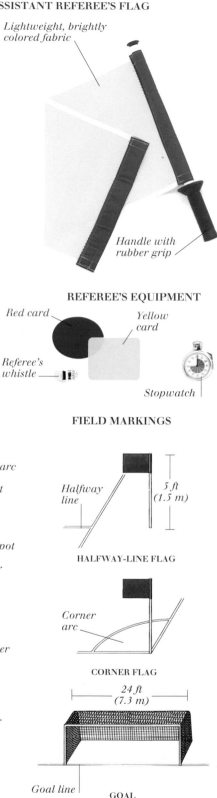

ASSISTANT REFEREE'S FLAG

Lightweight, brightly colored fabric

Handle with rubber grip

REFEREE'S EQUIPMENT

Red card

Yellow card

Referee's whistle

Stopwatch

FIELD MARKINGS

Halfway line

5 ft (1.5 m)

HALFWAY-LINE FLAG

Corner arc

CORNER FLAG

24 ft (7.3 m)

Goal line

GOAL

SOCCER FIELD

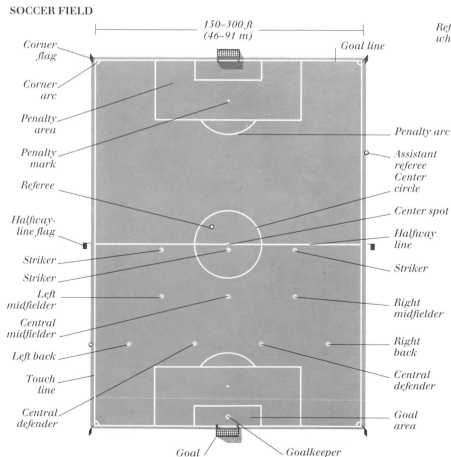

150–300 ft (46–91 m)

Goal line

Corner flag

Corner arc

Penalty area

Penalty mark

Referee

Halfway-line flag

Striker

Striker

Left midfielder

Central midfielder

Left back

Touch line

Central defender

Penalty arc

Assistant referee Center circle

Center spot

Halfway line

Striker

Right midfielder

Right back

Central defender

Goal area

Goal

Goalkeeper

GOALKEEPER

Goalkeeper's shirt

Glove

Shin guard

Shorts

Sock

Soccer shoe

SOCCER UNIFORM

Open-neck collar

Lightweight, man-made fabric team shirt

Team logo

Manufacturer's logo

Ribbed welt

Sponsor's logo

Manufacturer's name

Edge cut to fit perfectly

lotto

Motta

MAKING A SOCCER BALL

Hole punched in panel for stitching

Ball size number

Mitre

MULTIPLEX

Waxed thread

Mitre

MULTIPLEX

5

8½–9 in (22–23 cm)

Needle

Bladder valve

Bladder made from latex rubber

Long cotton sock

Club crest

Team shorts

Laminated panel

Panels sewn together with ball inside out

Synthetic shoelace

Interchangeable nylon stud

SOCCER SHOE

525

Football

IN AMERICAN AND CANADIAN FOOTBALL, the object of the game is to get the ball across the opponent's goal line, either by passing or carrying it across (a touchdown), or by kicking it between their goalposts (a field goal). An American football team has 11 players on the field at a time, although up to 40 players can appear for each side in a single game. The agile offense tries to score points, and the heavy hitting defense holds back the opposition. When in possession of the ball, a team has four chances (downs), to move it at least ten yards up the field to make a first down. The opposition gains possession if they fail, or by tackling and intercepting the ball. Canadian football is played on a larger field, with 12 men on each side. A team has only three chances, instead of four, to achieve a first down. Otherwise, the game is very similar to American football. Helmets, face masks, and layers of body padding are worn by the players for protection.

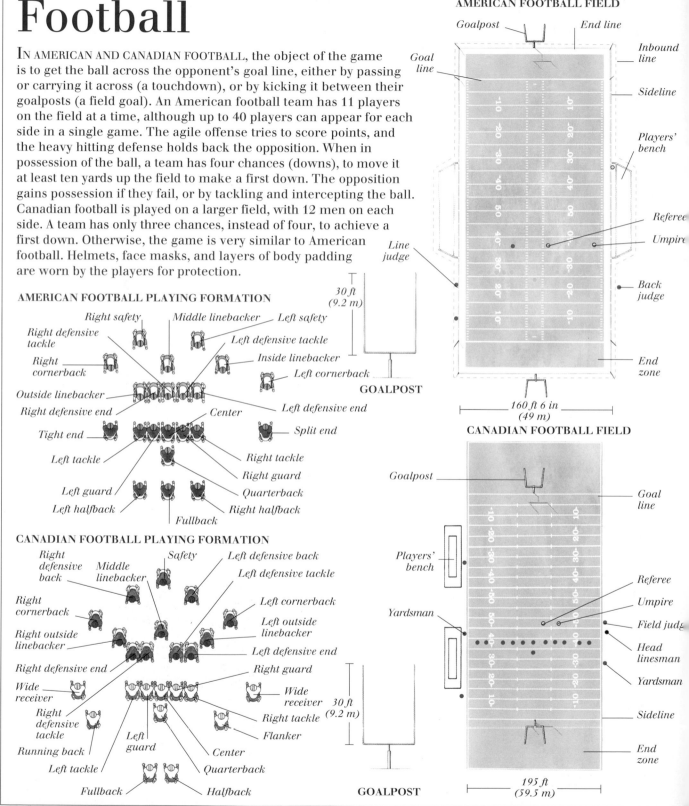

AMERICAN FOOTBALL FIELD

Goalpost
End line
Goal line
Inbound line
Sideline
Players' bench
Referee
Umpire
Back judge
End zone

Line judge

30 ft (9.2 m)

GOALPOST

160 ft 6 in (49 m)

AMERICAN FOOTBALL PLAYING FORMATION

Right safety
Middle linebacker
Left safety
Right defensive tackle
Left defensive tackle
Right cornerback
Inside linebacker
Left cornerback
Outside linebacker
Right defensive end
Center
Left defensive end
Tight end
Split end
Left tackle
Right tackle
Right guard
Left guard
Quarterback
Left halfback
Right halfback
Fullback

CANADIAN FOOTBALL PLAYING FORMATION

Right defensive back
Middle linebacker
Safety
Left defensive back
Left defensive tackle
Right cornerback
Left cornerback
Left outside linebacker
Right outside linebacker
Left defensive end
Right defensive end
Right guard
Wide receiver
Wide receiver
Right defensive tackle
Right tackle
Flanker
Running back
Left guard
Center
Left tackle
Quarterback
Fullback
Halfback

30 ft (9.2 m)

GOALPOST

CANADIAN FOOTBALL FIELD

Goalpost
Goal line
Players' bench
Referee
Umpire
Field judge
Yardsman
Head linesman
Yardsman
Sideline
End zone

195 ft (59.5 m)

PLAYER

Team logo

Helmet

Wrist pad

Player's number

Thigh pad

Pants

Tie to shoulder pads

Studded shoe

PROTECTIVE EQUIPMENT

11 in (28 cm)

Painted white ring

Lace

Brown pebbled leather

FOOTBALL

HELMET

Non-breakable plastic

Rubber-coated plastic

Shock absorber

SHOULDER PAD

Chest protector weight up to 5 lb 8 oz (2.5 kg)

BIKE

AIR·LITE

BLUE LASER 40-42

RIB PADS

Strap ties onto shoulder pad

UPPER ARM PAD

BIKE

BIKE

Tail bone pad

Foam-sponge filling

BIKE AL60

HIP PAD

BIKE AL60

ELBOW PAD

Rigid plastic covering

BIKE AL62

BIKE AL62

THIGH PAD

FINGERLESS GLOVE

Screw-in stud

PONY

PONY

Fold-over leather tongue

FOOTWEAR

PANTS

KNEE PAD

REFEREE'S SIGNALS

TIME OUT

TOUCHDOWN OR FIELD GOAL

PERSONAL FOUL

OFFSIDE OR ENCROACHMENT

HOLDING

ILLEGAL MOTION

FIRST DOWN

PASS INTERFERENCE

Australian rules and Gaelic football

VARIETIES OF FOOTBALL have developed all over the world and Australian rules football is considered to be one of the roughest versions, allowing full body tackles although participants wear no protective padding. Two teams of 18 players play on a large, oval pitch. Players can kick or punch the ball, which is shaped like a rugby ball, but cannot throw it. Running with the ball is permitted, as long as the ball touches the ground at least once every ten meters. The full backs defend two sets of posts. Teams try to score goals (six points) between the inner posts or behinds (one point) inside the outer posts. Each game has four quarters of 25 minutes, and the team with the most points at the end of the allotted time is the winner. In Gaelic football, an Irish version of soccer (see pp. 524–525), a size 5 association football is used. Each team can have 15 players on the field at a time. Players are allowed to catch, fist, and kick the ball, or dribble it using their hands or feet, but cannot throw it. Teams are awarded three points for getting the ball into the net, and one point for getting it through the posts above the crossbar. Gaelic football is rarely played outside of Ireland.

START OF PLAY

Field umpire

Center circle

SCORING

GOAL
(6 POINTS)

BEHIND
(1 POINT)

AUSTRALIAN RULES FOOTBALL FIELD

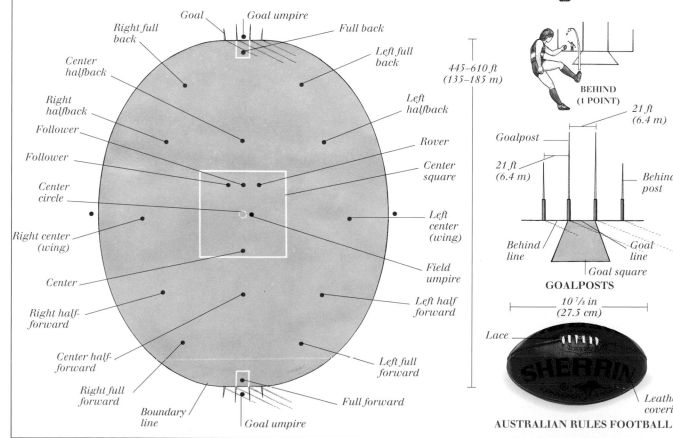

Goal

Goal umpire

Right full back

Full back

Center halfback

Left full back

Right halfback

Left halfback

Follower

Rover

Follower

Center square

Center circle

Left center (wing)

Right center (wing)

Field umpire

Center

Left half forward

Right half-forward

Center half-forward

Left full forward

Right full forward

Full forward

Boundary line

Goal umpire

445–610 ft
(135–185 m)

21 ft
(6.4 m)

Goalpost

21 ft
(6.4 m)

Behind post

Behind line

Goal line

Goal square

GOALPOSTS

10 7/8 in
(27.5 cm)

Lace

Leather covering

AUSTRALIAN RULES FOOTBALL

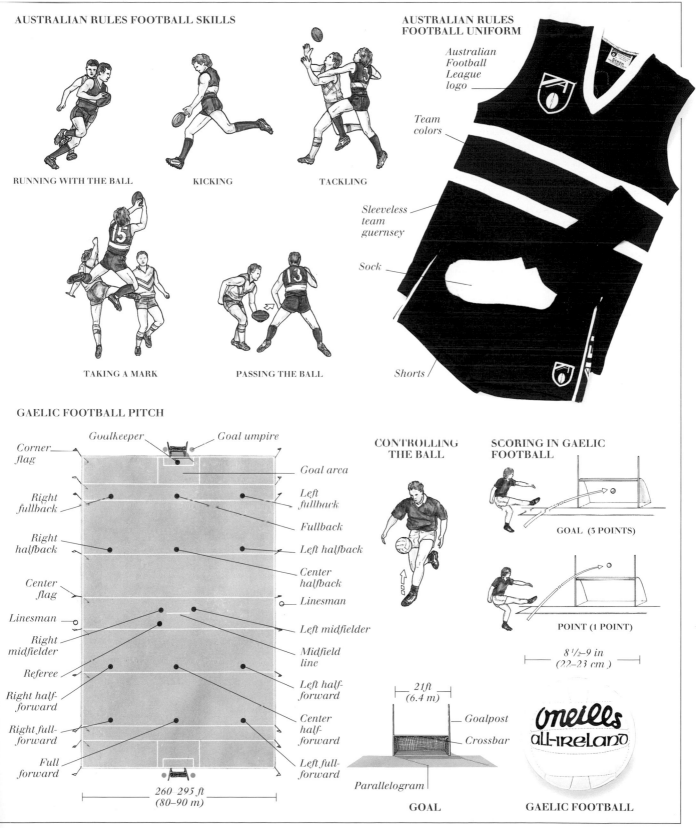

AUSTRALIAN RULES FOOTBALL SKILLS

RUNNING WITH THE BALL

KICKING

TACKLING

TAKING A MARK

PASSING THE BALL

AUSTRALIAN RULES FOOTBALL UNIFORM

Australian Football League logo

Team colors

Sleeveless team guernsey

Sock

Shorts

GAELIC FOOTBALL PITCH

Goalkeeper

Goal umpire

Corner flag

Goal area

Right fullback

Left fullback

Fullback

Right halfback

Left halfback

Center halfback

Center flag

Linesman

Linesman

Left midfielder

Right midfielder

Midfield line

Referee

Right half-forward

Left half-forward

Right full-forward

Center half-forward

Full forward

Left full-forward

260 295 ft
(80–90 m)

CONTROLLING THE BALL

SCORING IN GAELIC FOOTBALL

GOAL (3 POINTS)

POINT (1 POINT)

8 1/2–9 in
(22–23 cm)

21ft
(6.4 m)

Goalpost

Crossbar

Parallelogram

GOAL

oneills
all-ireland

GAELIC FOOTBALL

Rugby

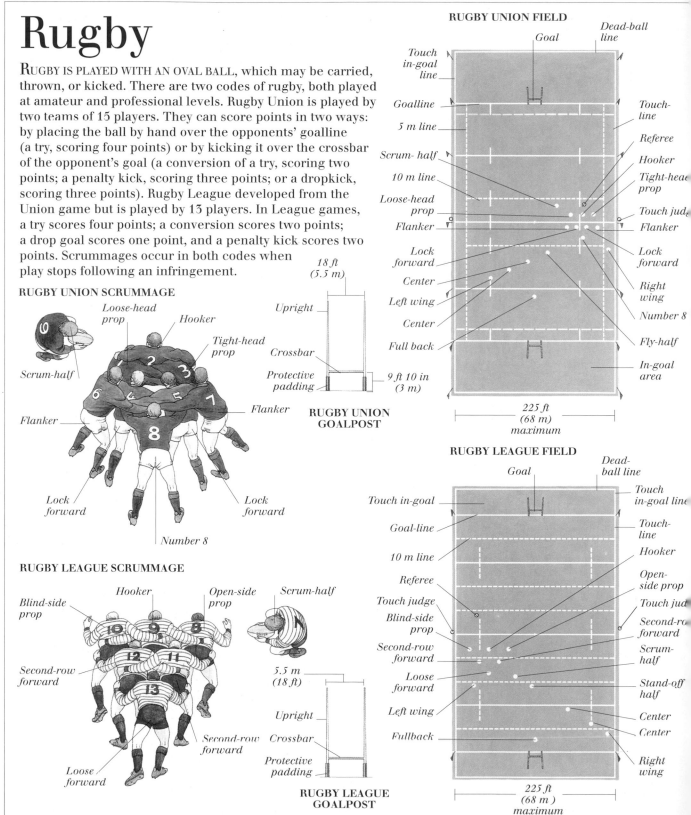

RUGBY IS PLAYED WITH AN OVAL BALL, which may be carried, thrown, or kicked. There are two codes of rugby, both played at amateur and professional levels. Rugby Union is played by two teams of 15 players. They can score points in two ways: by placing the ball by hand over the opponents' goalline (a try, scoring four points) or by kicking it over the crossbar of the opponent's goal (a conversion of a try, scoring two points; a penalty kick, scoring three points; or a dropkick, scoring three points). Rugby League developed from the Union game but is played by 13 players. In League games, a try scores four points; a conversion scores two points; a drop goal scores one point, and a penalty kick scores two points. Scrummages occur in both codes when play stops following an infringement.

RUGBY UNION FIELD

Touch in-goal line
Goalline
5 m line
Scrum-half
10 m line
Loose-head prop
Flanker
Lock forward
Center
Left wing
Center
Full back

Goal
Dead-ball line
Touch-line
Referee
Hooker
Tight-head prop
Touch judge
Flanker
Lock forward
Right wing
Number 8
Fly-half
In-goal area

225 ft (68 m) maximum

RUGBY UNION SCRUMMAGE

Loose-head prop
Hooker
Tight-head prop
Scrum-half
Flanker
Flanker
Lock forward
Lock forward
Number 8

18 ft (5.5 m)
Upright
Crossbar
Protective padding
9 ft 10 in (3 m)

RUGBY UNION GOALPOST

RUGBY LEAGUE FIELD

Goal
Dead-ball line
Touch in-goal
Goal-line
10 m line
Referee
Touch judge
Blind-side prop
Second-row forward
Loose forward
Left wing
Fullback

Touch in-goal line
Touch-line
Hooker
Open-side prop
Touch judge
Second-row forward
Scrum-half
Stand-off half
Center
Center
Right wing

225 ft (68 m) maximum

RUGBY LEAGUE SCRUMMAGE

Hooker
Open-side prop
Scrum-half
Blind-side prop
Second-row forward
Second-row forward
Loose forward

5.5 m (18 ft)
Upright
Crossbar
Protective padding

RUGBY LEAGUE GOALPOST

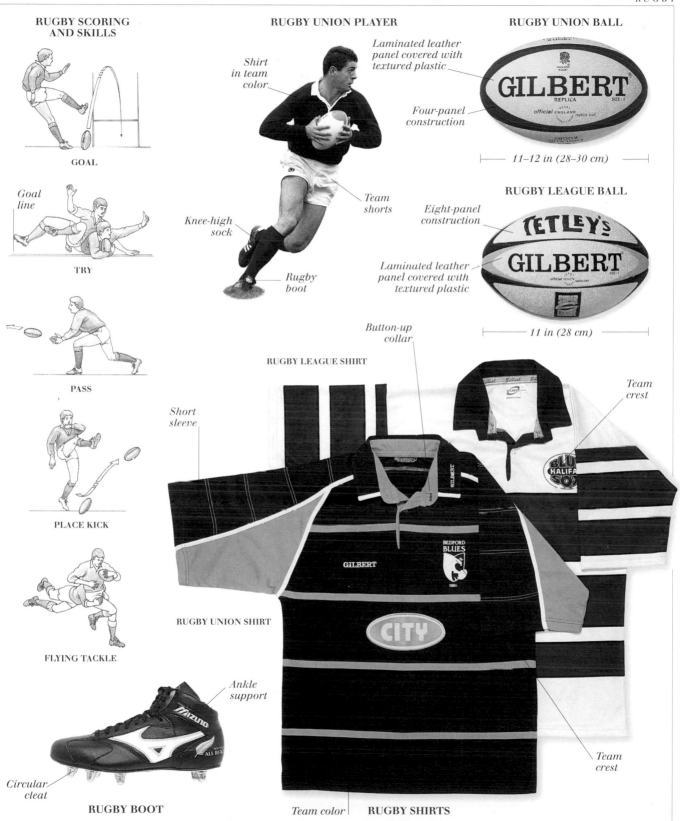

RUGBY SCORING AND SKILLS

GOAL

Goal line

TRY

PASS

PLACE KICK

FLYING TACKLE

RUGBY UNION PLAYER

Shirt in team color

Knee-high sock

Team shorts

Rugby boot

RUGBY UNION BALL

Laminated leather panel covered with textured plastic

Four-panel construction

GILBERT
REPLICA
SIZE: 5
official ENGLAND replica ball

11–12 in (28–30 cm)

RUGBY LEAGUE BALL

Eight-panel construction

Laminated leather panel covered with textured plastic

TETLEY'S
GILBERT
official TETLEY'S replica ball

11 in (28 cm)

Button-up collar

Team crest

RUGBY LEAGUE SHIRT

Short sleeve

GILBERT

BEDFORD BLUES 1886

CITY

Team crest

RUGBY UNION SHIRT

Ankle support

RUGBY BOOT

Circular cleat

MIZUNO
ALL BLACK

Team color | **RUGBY SHIRTS**

Basketball

BASKETBALL IS A BALL GAME for two teams of five players, originally devised in 1890 by James Naismath for the Y.M.C.A. in Springfield, Massachusetts. The object of the game is to take possession of the ball and score points by throwing the ball into the opposing team's basket. A player moves the ball up and down the court by bouncing it along the ground or "dribbling"; the ball may be passed between players by throwing, bouncing, or rolling. Players may not run with or kick the ball, although pivoting on one foot is allowed. The game begins with the referee throwing the ball into the air and a player from each team jumping up to try and "tip" the ball to a teammate. The length of the game and the number of periods played varies at different levels. There are amateur, professional, and international rules. No game ends in a draw. As many extra periods as necessary are played to break the tie. In addition to the five players on court, each team has up to seven substitutes, but players may only leave the court with the permission of the referee. Basketball is a noncontact sport and fouls on other players are penalized by a throw-in awarded against the offending team; a free throw at the basket is awarded when a player is fouled in the act of shooting. Basketball is a fast-moving game, requiring both physical and mental coordination. Skillful tactical play matters more than simple physical strength and the agility of the players makes the game an excellent spectator sport.

BASKETBALL SKILLS

CHEST PASS

DRIBBLE

OVERHEAD PASS

LAY-UP SHOT

JUMP SHOT

LONG PASS

INTERNATIONAL BASKETBALL COURT

Backboard
End-line
Restraining circle
Player's bench
Referee
Timekeeper
Clock operator
Scorer
Referee
Right forward
Three-point line
Basket
Semi-circle
Right guard
Left guard
Center
Centerline
Left forward
Center circle
Free-throw line
Sideline

49 ft 3 in (15 m)

BASKET AND BACKBOARD

Backboard
Metal rim
Cord net

6 ft
(1.8 m)

BASKET AND BACKBOARD STRUCTURE

10 ft
(3.05 m)

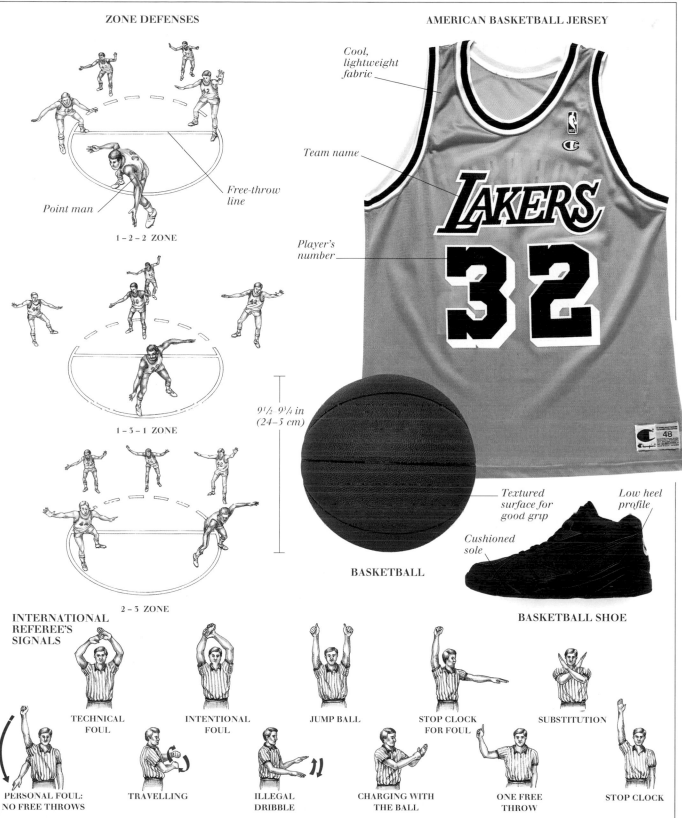

ZONE DEFENSES

Point man

Free-throw line

1 – 2 – 2 ZONE

1 – 3 – 1 ZONE

2 – 3 ZONE

AMERICAN BASKETBALL JERSEY

Cool, lightweight fabric

Team name

Player's number

LAKERS

32

9½ – 9¾ in (24–5 cm)

Textured surface for good grip

BASKETBALL

Low heel profile

Cushioned sole

BASKETBALL SHOE

INTERNATIONAL REFEREE'S SIGNALS

TECHNICAL FOUL

INTENTIONAL FOUL

JUMP BALL

STOP CLOCK FOR FOUL

SUBSTITUTION

PERSONAL FOUL: NO FREE THROWS

TRAVELLING

ILLEGAL DRIBBLE

CHARGING WITH THE BALL

ONE FREE THROW

STOP CLOCK

Volleyball, netball, and handball

VOLLEYBALL, NETBALL, AND HANDBALL are fast-moving team sports played with balls, usually on courts with a hard surface. In volleyball, the object of the game is to hit the ball over a net strung across the center of the court so that it touches the ground on the opponent's side. The team of six players can take three hits to direct the ball over the net, although the same player cannot hit the ball twice in a row. Players can hit the ball with their arms, hands or any other part of their upper body. Teams score points only while serving. The first team to score 15 points, with a two-point margin over their opponent, wins the game. Netball is similar to basketball (see pp. 532–533), but is played on a slightly larger court with seven players instead of five. A team moves the ball toward the goal by throwing, passing, and catching it with the aim of throwing the ball through the opponents' goal net. Players are confined by their playing position to specific areas of the court. Team handball is one of the world's fastest games. Each side has seven players. A team moves the ball by dribbling, passing, or bouncing it as they run. Players may stop, catch, throw, bounce, or strike the ball with any part of the body above the knees. Each team tries to score goals by directing the ball past the opposition's goalkeeper into the net, which is similar to a soccer goal net (see pp. 524–525).

VOLLEYBALL SHOTS

OVERHAND SERVE   SPIKE (SMASH)

UNDERHAND SERVE   FOREARM PASS (DIG)

VOLLEYBALL KIT

Team colors
Ribbed cuff
Cotton-knit jersey
Leather covering
Elastic waist
Elastic knit fabric
Shorts
Injected molded padding

VOLLEYBALL COURT

End line, Linesman, Clear space, Attack zone, Attack line, Umpire, Center forward, Right forward, Center back, Linesman, Service area, Server, Linesman, Sideline, Players' bench, Referee, Scorer, Net, Left forward, Back zone, Left back, Linesman

29 ft 6 in (9 m)

8 in (21 cm)

VOLLEYBALL

VOLLEYBALL NET

Tape, Net, Antenna, Post
Men's: 8 ft (2.4 m)
Women's: 7 ft 4 in (2.2 m)

KNEE PADS

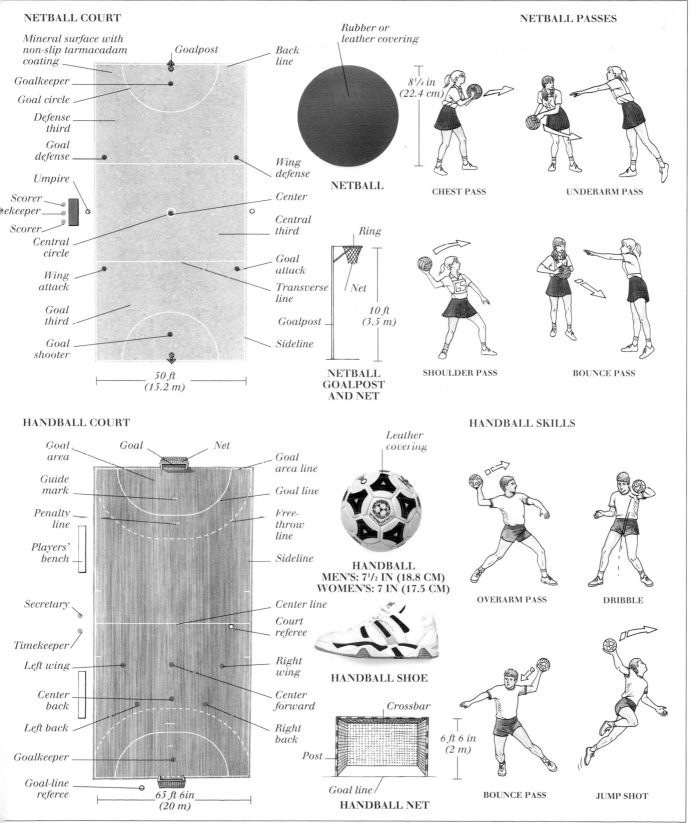

NETBALL COURT

Mineral surface with non-slip tarmacadam coating

Goalpost

Back line

Goalkeeper

Goal circle

Defense third

Goal defense

Wing defense

Umpire

Scorer ekeeper

Center

Scorer

Central third

Central circle

Goal attack

Wing attack

Transverse line

Goal third

Goalpost

Goal shooter

Sideline

50 ft (15.2 m)

NETBALL PASSES

Rubber or leather covering

8³/₄ in (22.4 cm)

NETBALL

CHEST PASS

UNDERARM PASS

Ring

Net

10 ft (3.5 m)

Goalpost

NETBALL GOALPOST AND NET

SHOULDER PASS

BOUNCE PASS

HANDBALL COURT

Goal area

Goal

Net

Goal area line

Guide mark

Goal line

Penalty line

Free-throw line

Players' bench

Sideline

Secretary

Center line

Court referee

Timekeeper

Left wing

Right wing

Center back

Center forward

Left back

Right back

Goalkeeper

Goal-line referee

65 ft 6in (20 m)

HANDBALL SKILLS

Leather covering

HANDBALL
MEN'S: 7¹/₂ IN (18.8 CM)
WOMEN'S: 7 IN (17.5 CM)

OVERARM PASS

DRIBBLE

HANDBALL SHOE

Crossbar

6 ft 6 in (2 m)

Post

Goal line

HANDBALL NET

BOUNCE PASS

JUMP SHOT

Baseball

BASEBALL IS A BALL GAME for two teams of nine players.
The batter hits the ball thrown by the opposing team's pitcher,
into the area between the foul lines. He then runs round all four
fixed bases in order to score a run, touching or "tagging" each base
in turn. The pitcher must throw the ball at a height between the
batter's armpits and knees, a height which is called the strike zone.
A ball pitched in this area that crosses over the home plate is called
a "strike" and the batter has three strikes in which to try to hit the
ball (otherwise he has "struck out"). The fielding team tries to get
the batting team out by catching the ball before it bounces, tagging
a player of the batting team who is running between bases with
the ball, or by tagging a base before the player has reached it.
Members of the batting team may stop safely at a base as long
as it is not occupied by another member of their team. When
the batter runs to first base, his teammate at first base must run
onto second – this is called a force play. A game consists of nine
innings and each team will bat once during an inning. When
three members of the batting team are out, the teams swap
roles. The team with the most runs wins the game.

BATTER'S HELMET

Plastic shell

Peak

Foam padding

CATCHER'S MASK

Wire coated in strong nylon

Plastic-coated foam padding

BASEBALL FIELD

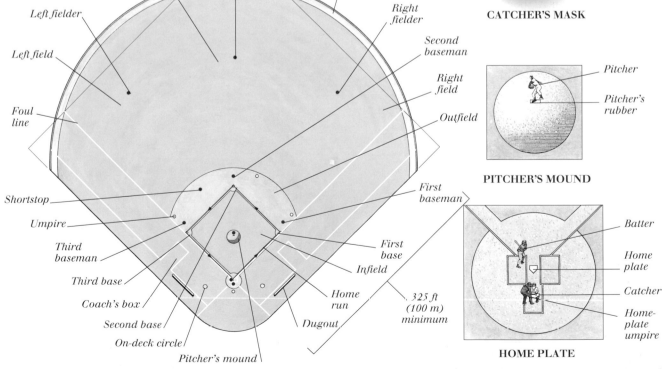

Center fielder

Center field

Warning track

Left fielder

Right fielder

Left field

Second baseman

Right field

Foul line

Outfield

Shortstop

First baseman

Umpire

First base

Third baseman

Infield

Third base

Coach's box

Home run

Second base

Dugout

On-deck circle

Pitcher's mound

PITCHER'S MOUND

Pitcher

Pitcher's rubber

HOME PLATE

Batter

Home plate

Catcher

Home-plate umpire

325 ft (100 m) minimum

MAKING A BASEBALL

Wool yarn

Rubber inner casing

Horsehide strip

Cork center

Cotton thread outer casing

Wool strand

Red outer stitching

BASEBALL EQUIPMENT

Webbed pocket

Fingers laced together

Strap

Thumb

Palm

Leather stitching

Heel

FIELDER'S GLOVE AND BALL

Metal heel plate

AMERICAN BASEBALL SHOE

Metal toe plate

THE PITCHING SEQUENCE

THE WINDUP 1

THE WINDUP 2

THE WINDUP 3

THE WINDUP 4

THE RELEASE

THE FOLLOW-THROUGH

UMPIRING SIGNALS

BALL

INFIELD

STRIKE

FAIR BALL

RUNNER IS SAFE

FOUL TIP

Batter's helmet

Bat

Batting glove

Team shirt

Undershirt

Pants

Spiked shoe

BATTER

Hitting area

Crest

3 ft 6 in (1.1 m) maximum

Handle

Knob

BAT

Cricket

CRICKET IS A BALL GAME PLAYED by two teams of eleven players on a pitch with two sets of three stumps (wickets). The bowler bowls the ball down the pitch to the batsman of the opposing team, who must defend the wicket in front of which he stands. The object of the game is to score as many runs as possible. Runs can be scored individually by running the length of the playing strip, or by hitting a ball which lands outside the boundary (six), or which lands inside the boundary but bounces or rolls outside (four); the opposing team will bowl and field, attempting to dismiss the batsmen. A batsman can be dismissed in one of several ways: by the bowler hitting the wicket with the ball ("bowled"); by a fielder catching the ball hit by the batsman before it touches the ground ("caught"); by the wicket-keeper or another fielder breaking the wicket while the batsman is attempting a run and is therefore out of his ground ("stumped" or "run out"); by the batsman breaking the wicket with his own bat or body ("hit wicket"); by a part of the batsman's body being hit by a ball that would otherwise have hit the wicket ("leg before wicket" ["lbw"]). A match consists of one or two innings and each innings ends when the tenth batsman of the batting team is out, when a certain number of overs (a series of six balls bowled) have been played, or when the captain of the batting team "declares" ending the innings voluntarily.

FORWARD DEFENSIVE STROKE   BACKWARD DEFENSIVE STROKE

ON-DRIVE   OFF-DRIVE

PULL   HOOK

POSSIBLE FIELD POSITIONS FOR AN AWAY SWING BOWLER TO A RIGHT-HANDED BATSMAN (IN RED) AND OTHER FIELD POSITIONS

CRICKET PITCH

Wicket-keeper

Batsman

Wicket

Bowling crease

66 ft (20 m)

Long on   *Long off*

Umpire   *Bowler*

Boundary line   *Non-striking batsman*

Deep mid-wicket

Mid-on   *Extra cover*

Silly mid-on   *Mid-off*

Forward short leg   *Silly mid-off*

Square leg   *Cover*

Deep square leg   *Point*

Square-leg umpire   *Gulley*

Batsman   *Third man*

Long leg   *Second slip*

Leg slip   *Bowler*   *Return crease*

Wicket-keeper   *First slip*

Fine leg   *Sight screen*   *Umpire*   *Non-striking batsman*

SQUARE CUT   LEG GLANCE

CRICKET BALL AND WICKET

Leather skin   *Seam*

BALL

Bail

WICKET

Stump

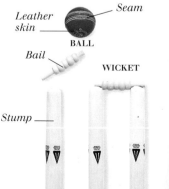

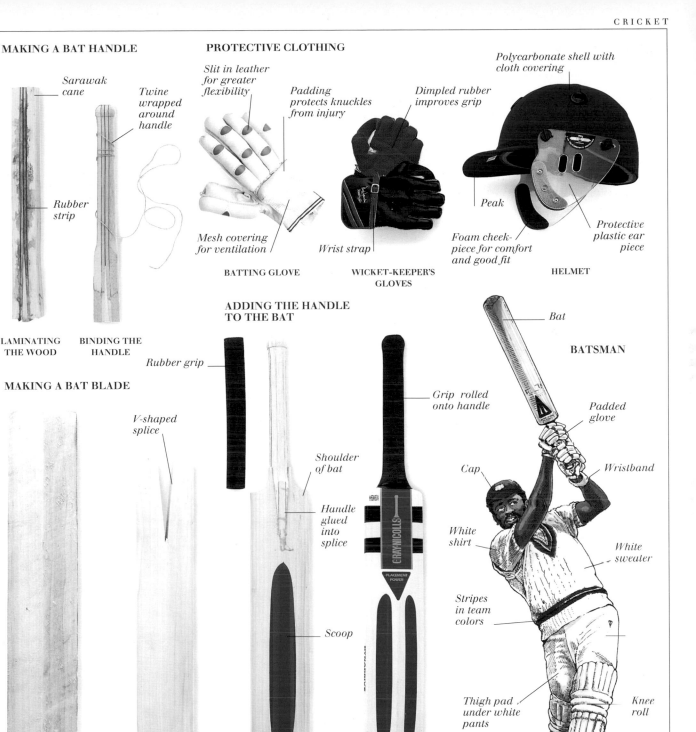

MAKING A BAT HANDLE

Sarawak cane

Twine wrapped around handle

Rubber strip

LAMINATING THE WOOD

BINDING THE HANDLE

MAKING A BAT BLADE

V-shaped splice

Kiln-dried willow

SEASONING THE TIMBER

Blade planed by hand

CUTTING THE SPLICE

ADDING THE HANDLE TO THE BAT

Rubber grip

Shoulder of bat

Handle glued into splice

Scoop

Toe of the bat shaped

FITTING THE HANDLE

PROTECTIVE CLOTHING

Slit in leather for greater flexibility

Padding protects knuckles from injury

Dimpled rubber improves grip

Polycarbonate shell with cloth covering

Mesh covering for ventilation

BATTING GLOVE

Wrist strap

WICKET-KEEPER'S GLOVES

Peak

Foam cheek-piece for comfort and good fit

Protective plastic ear piece

HELMET

Grip rolled onto handle

Bat

BATSMAN

Padded glove

Cap

Wristband

White shirt

White sweater

Stripes in team colors

Thigh pad under white pants

Knee roll

Cricket shoe

Leg pad

Sanded and polished bat

FINISHING TOUCHES

Dimpled rubber sole

Field hockey, lacrosse, and hurling

ALL OVER THE WORLD, TEAM GAMES have evolved which require that a ball be struck or carried, and tossed at the end of a stick. Early forms of these games include hurling, shinty, bandy, and pelota. Field hockey is played by men and women: two teams of eleven players try to gain and keep possession of the ball and score goals by using the hockey stick to propel the ball into their opponents' goal net. Skills such as passing, pushing, or hitting the ball by slapping or lifting it in a flicking movement, and shooting at the goal are crucial. Field hockey is played indoors and outdoors on grass or synthetic fields. Lacrosse is played internationally as a 12-a-side game for women and as 10-a-side game for men. The women's field has no absolute boundaries but the men's has clearly defined sidelines and end lines. The ball is kept in play by being carried, thrown or batted with the crosse, and rolled or kicked in any direction. In men's and women's lacrosse, play can continue behind the marked goal areas. Similar skills are required in hurling – a Gaelic field game played on the same pitch as Gaelic football (see pp. 528–529), using the same goalposts and net. In hurling, the ball may be struck with or carried on the hurley and, when off the ground, may be struck with the hand or kicked. Goals (three points) are scored when the ball passes between the posts and under the crossbar; one point is scored when the ball passes between the posts and over the crossbar.

GOALKEEPER'S EQUIPMENT

Hard shell

Air vent

Face mask

HELMET

Strap

Rigid palm

Padded wrist

GAUNTLET

FIELD HOCKEY STICK AND BALL

STICK

Handle — *Tape* — *Steam-bent ash head* — *Blade*

Slazenger FLEXI

— 3 ft (91 cm) —

Stitched seam

2¾–3 in (7–7.5 cm)

BALL

FIELD HOCKEY FIELD

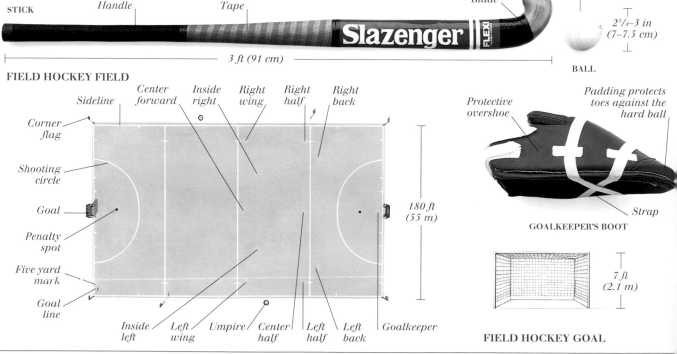

Sideline — *Center forward* — *Inside right* — *Right wing* — *Right half* — *Right back*

Corner flag

Shooting circle

Goal

Penalty spot

Five yard mark

Goal line

Inside left — *Left wing* — *Umpire* — *Center half* — *Left half* — *Left back* — *Goalkeeper*

180 ft (55 m)

Protective overshoe — *Padding protects toes against the hard ball*

Strap

GOALKEEPER'S BOOT

7 ft (2.1 m)

FIELD HOCKEY GOAL

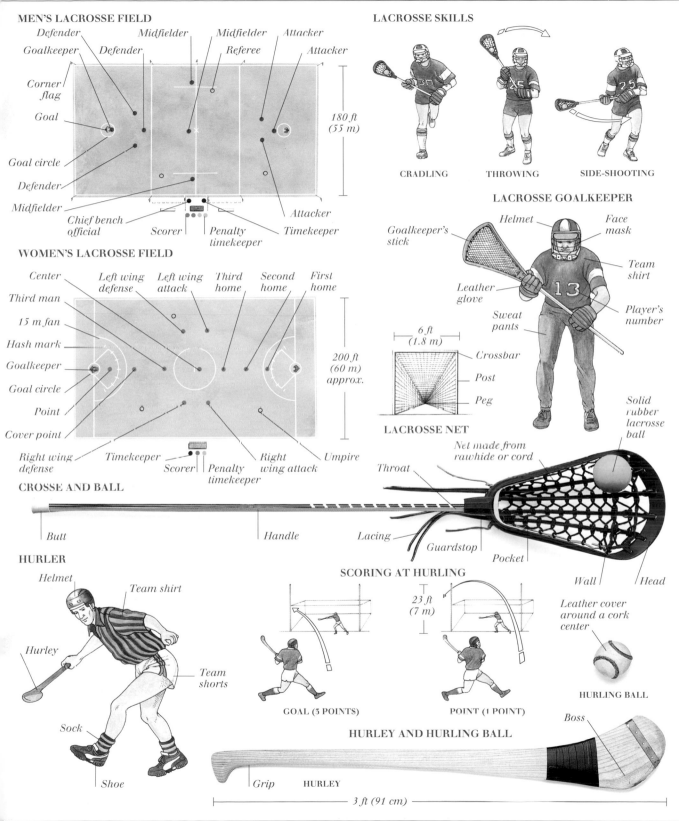

MEN'S LACROSSE FIELD

Defender
Goalkeeper
Defender
Midfielder
Midfielder
Referee
Attacker
Attacker
Corner flag
Goal
Goal circle
Defender
Midfielder
Chief bench official
Scorer
Penalty timekeeper
Timekeeper
Attacker

180 ft (55 m)

WOMEN'S LACROSSE FIELD

Center
Third man
15 m fan
Hash mark
Goalkeeper
Goal circle
Point
Cover point
Right wing defense
Left wing defense
Left wing attack
Third home
Second home
First home
Timekeeper
Scorer
Penalty timekeeper
Right wing attack
Umpire

200 ft (60 m) approx.

CROSSE AND BALL

Butt
Handle
Lacing
Guardstop
Throat
Pocket
Wall
Head

HURLER

Helmet
Team shirt
Hurley
Team shorts
Sock
Shoe

SCORING AT HURLING

23 ft (7 m)

GOAL (3 POINTS)
POINT (1 POINT)

HURLEY AND HURLING BALL

Grip
HURLEY
3 ft (91 cm)
Boss

LACROSSE SKILLS

CRADLING
THROWING
SIDE-SHOOTING

LACROSSE GOALKEEPER

Goalkeeper's stick
Helmet
Face mask
Leather glove
Team shirt
Sweat pants
Player's number
Solid rubber lacrosse ball

6 ft (1.8 m)
Crossbar
Post
Peg

LACROSSE NET

Net made from rawhide or cord

Leather cover around a cork center

HURLING BALL

Track and field

**FIELD EVENT
EQUIPMENT**

THE SPORTS that make up athletics are divided into two main groups: track events – which include sprinting, middle, and long distance running, relay running, hurdling, and walking – and field events which require jumping and throwing skills. Contests designed to test the speed, strength, agility, and stamina of athletes were held by the ancient Greeks over 4,000 years ago. However, the abolition of the Olympic Games in 393 AD meant that track and field events were neglected until the revival of large-scale competitions in the mid-nineteenth century. Modern stadiums offer areas reserved for the long jump, triple jump, and pole vault usually situated outside the running track. The javelin, shot, hammer, and discus are thrown within the track area. Most athletes specialize in one or two events but, in the heptathlon, women compete in seven events, held over two days: 200 m and 800 m races, 100 m hurdles, javelin, shot put, high jump, and long jump. In the decathlon, men compete in ten events over two days: 100 m, 400 m, and 1,500 m races, 110 m hurdles, javelin, discus, shot put, pole vault, high jump, and long jump.

Steel wire
Head
Body
Swivel
Metal rim
Center weight

DISCUS
MEN'S: 4 LB 7 OZ (2 KG)
WOMEN'S: 2 LB 3 OZ (1 KG)

**HAMMER
16 LB (7 KG)**

Hammer handle

Rubber coating
Shot pellet filling

5 in (12.7 cm)
4 in (10 cm)

**MEN'S SHOT
16 LB (7 KG)**
**WOMEN'S SHOT
8 LB 12 OZ (4 KG)**

JAVELIN
Cord grip
Shaft
Tip

Men: 8 ft 6 in (2.6 m)
Women: 7 ft 6 in (2.3 m)

TRACK AND FIELD

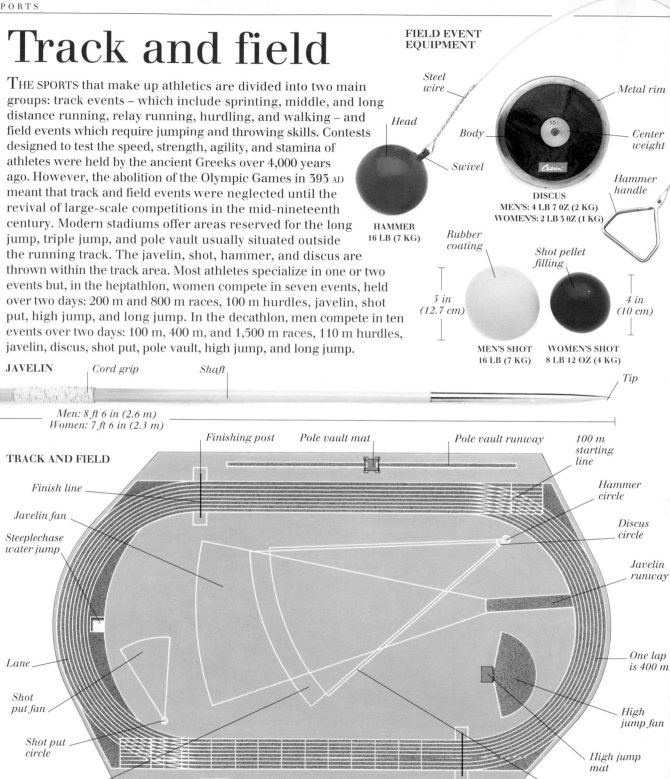

Finishing post
Pole vault mat
Pole vault runway
100 m starting line
Finish line
Hammer circle
Javelin fan
Discus circle
Steeplechase water jump
Javelin runway
Lane
One lap is 400 m
Shot put fan
High jump fan
Shot put circle
High jump mat
Discus fan
Hammer fan
Triple jump takeoff board
Triple jump takeoff line
Indicator board
Triple jump runway
Long jump takeoff board
Landing area

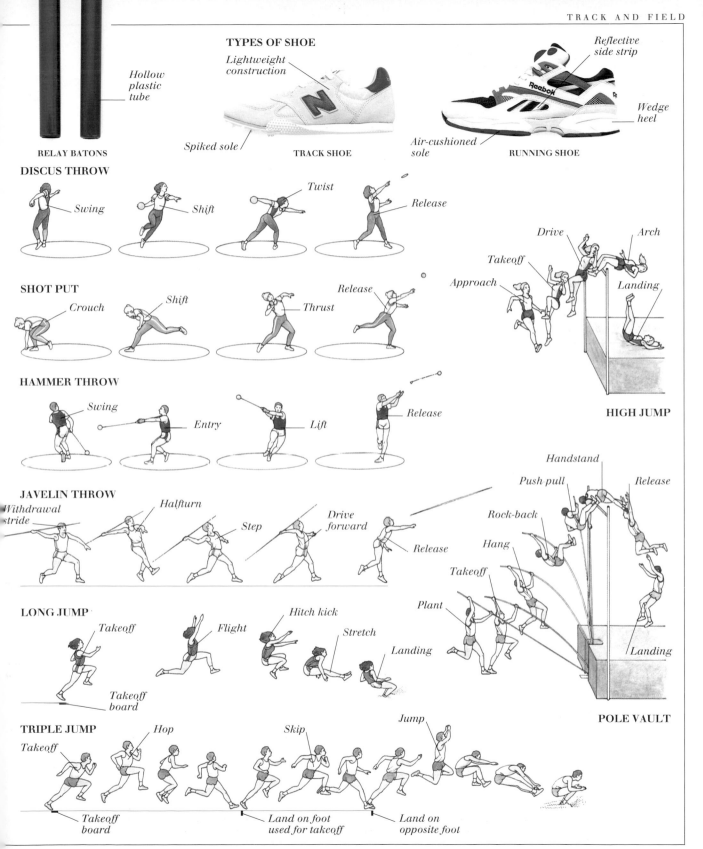

RELAY BATONS

Hollow plastic tube

TYPES OF SHOE

Lightweight construction

Spiked sole

TRACK SHOE

Reflective side strip

Wedge heel

Air-cushioned sole

RUNNING SHOE

DISCUS THROW

Swing — Shift — Twist — Release

SHOT PUT

Crouch — Shift — Thrust — Release

HAMMER THROW

Swing — Entry — Lift — Release

JAVELIN THROW

Withdrawal stride — Halfturn — Step — Drive forward — Release

LONG JUMP

Takeoff — Flight — Hitch kick — Stretch — Landing

Takeoff board

TRIPLE JUMP

Takeoff — Hop — Skip — Jump

Takeoff board — Land on foot used for takeoff — Land on opposite foot

HIGH JUMP

Approach — Takeoff — Drive — Arch — Landing

POLE VAULT

Plant — Takeoff — Hang — Rock-back — Push pull — Handstand — Release — Landing

Racket sports

PROTECTIVE EYEWEAR

THE OBJECT OF ALL RACKET SPORTS is to make shots the opponent cannot return. Games are played by two players (singles) or four players (doubles). Racket shape and size is tailored to each sport, but all rackets are constructed of wood, plastic, aluminum, or high-performance materials such as fiberglass and carbon graphite. Racket strings are usually synthetic, although natural gut is still used. Tennis is played on a court divided by a low net. Opposing players serve alternate games. At least six games must be won to gain a set, and two or sometimes three sets are needed to win a match. Tennis courts may be concrete, grass, clay, or synthetic, each surface requiring a different style of play. Badminton is an indoor sport that is played with light, flexible rackets and a birdie on a court with a high net. Players can score points only on their serve. The first to reach 15 points (11 points for women's singles) wins the game. Two games are needed to win a match. Squash and racketball are both played in enclosed courts. One player hits the ball against the front wall, and the other tries to return it before it bounces on the floor more than once. Squash rackets have smaller, rounder heads and stiffer frames than badminton rackets. International courts are wider than those in the U.S., where a much harder ball is used. Squash games are played to nine points (international) or 15 points (U.S.). In racketball, players use a ball that is larger and bouncier than a squash ball. The racketball racket is thick and sturdy, with a large head, short handle, and a strap that loops around the wrist. Points can be won only when serving, and the first player to reach 21 points wins.

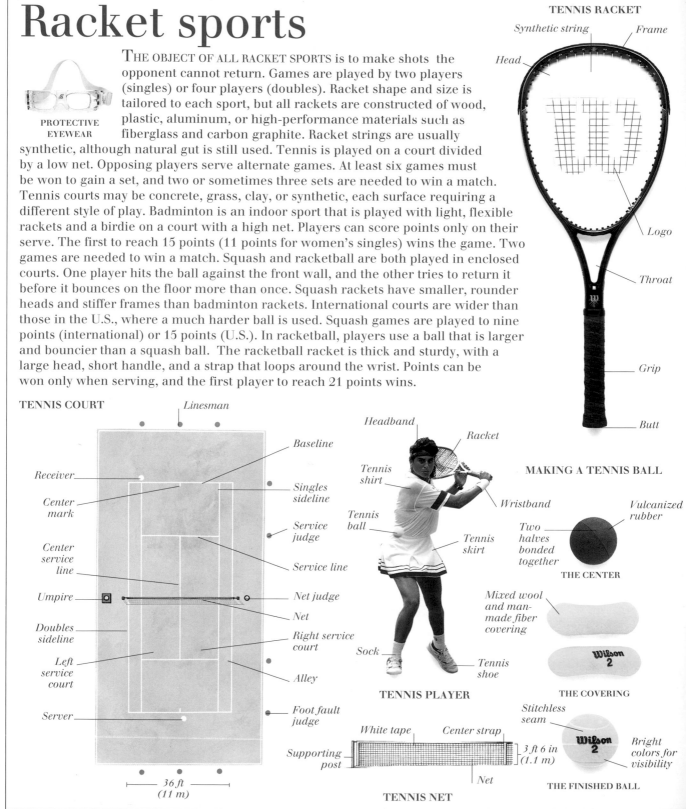

TENNIS RACKET

Synthetic string

Frame

Head

Logo

Throat

Grip

Butt

TENNIS COURT

Linesman

Receiver

Baseline

Center mark

Singles sideline

Center service line

Service judge

Service line

Umpire

Net judge

Net

Doubles sideline

Right service court

Left service court

Alley

Server

Foot fault judge

36 ft (11 m)

TENNIS PLAYER

Headband

Racket

Tennis shirt

Tennis ball

Wristband

Tennis skirt

Tennis shoe

Sock

MAKING A TENNIS BALL

Vulcanized rubber

Two halves bonded together

THE CENTER

Mixed wool and man-made fiber covering

THE COVERING

Stitchless seam

Bright colors for visibility

THE FINISHED BALL

TENNIS NET

White tape

Center strap

Supporting post

3 ft 6 in (1.1 m)

Net

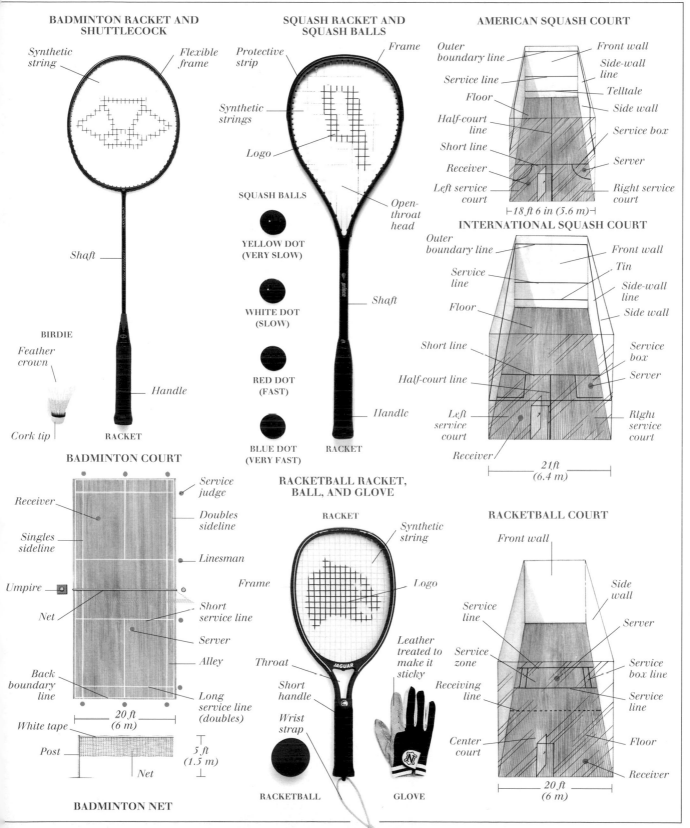

BADMINTON RACKET AND SHUTTLECOCK

Synthetic string

Flexible frame

Shaft

BIRDIE

Feather crown

Handle

Cork tip

RACKET

SQUASH RACKET AND SQUASH BALLS

Protective strip

Frame

Synthetic strings

Logo

SQUASH BALLS

YELLOW DOT (VERY SLOW)

WHITE DOT (SLOW)

RED DOT (FAST)

BLUE DOT (VERY FAST)

Open-throat head

Shaft

Handle

RACKET

AMERICAN SQUASH COURT

Outer boundary line

Front wall

Service line

Side-wall line

Floor

Telltale

Half-court line

Side wall

Short line

Service box

Receiver

Server

Left service court

Right service court

⊢18 ft 6 in (5.6 m)⊣

INTERNATIONAL SQUASH COURT

Outer boundary line

Front wall

Service line

Tin

Floor

Side-wall line

Side wall

Short line

Service box

Half-court line

Server

Left service court

Right service court

Receiver

21 ft (6.4 m)

BADMINTON COURT

Receiver

Service judge

Doubles sideline

Singles sideline

Linesman

Umpire

Short service line

Net

Server

Alley

Back boundary line

Long service line (doubles)

20 ft (6 m)

White tape

Post

5 ft (1.5 m)

Net

BADMINTON NET

RACKETBALL RACKET, BALL, AND GLOVE

RACKET

Synthetic string

Logo

Frame

Throat

Short handle

Leather treated to make it sticky

Wrist strap

RACKETBALL

GLOVE

RACKETBALL COURT

Front wall

Side wall

Service line

Server

Service zone

Service box line

Receiving line

Service line

Center court

Floor

Receiver

20 ft (6 m)

545

Golf

Dimpled surface

Wound yarn

Liquid

Balata cover

Membrane to contain liquid

GOLF BALL AND TEE

THE GAME OF GOLF was first played in Scotland some 400 years ago. Players are required to hit a ball, using a wooden or iron club, from a smooth level point or teeing ground, down the fairway, and onto a putting green where the target hole is located. The fairway is a strip of clear land along which there are natural hazards – such as ponds and streams, man-made hazards – such as bunkers (sand pits), and rough (areas of uncut grass). Championship golf courses have 18 holes. The object of the game is to hit the ball into each hole in turn, and to complete the "round" using as few strokes as possible. Players may compete individually or in teams, playing the course together in groups of two, three, or four. The two basic forms of competition are match play and stroke play. In match play, the side winning the majority of holes over a certain number of rounds wins the match. In stroke play, the winner is the player who finishes a certain number of rounds having made the fewest strokes.

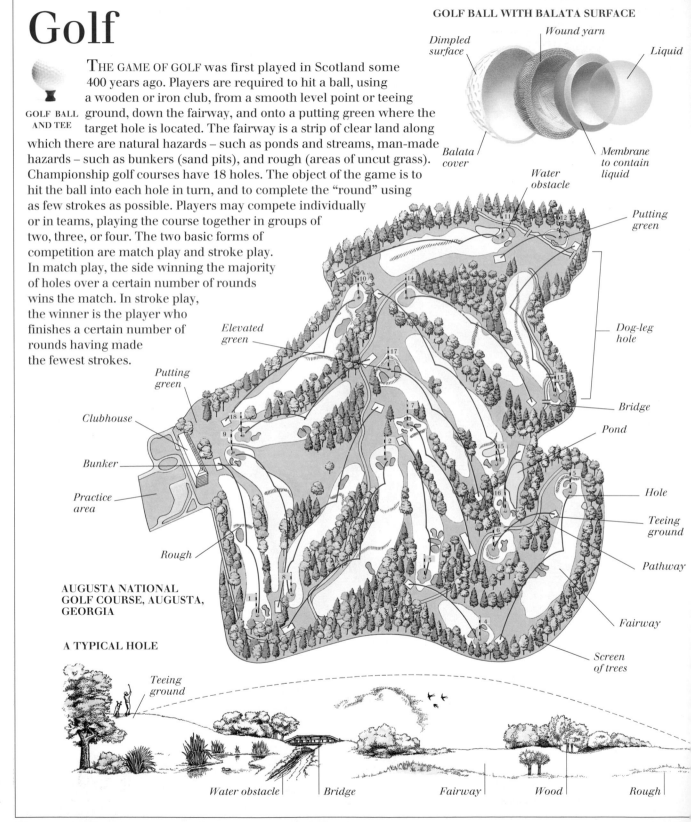

Water obstacle

Putting green

Dog-leg hole

Elevated green

Bridge

Putting green

Pond

Clubhouse

Bunker

Hole

Practice area

Teeing ground

Pathway

Rough

AUGUSTA NATIONAL GOLF COURSE, AUGUSTA, GEORGIA

Fairway

Screen of trees

A TYPICAL HOLE

Teeing ground

Water obstacle   *Bridge*   *Fairway*   *Wood*   *Rough*

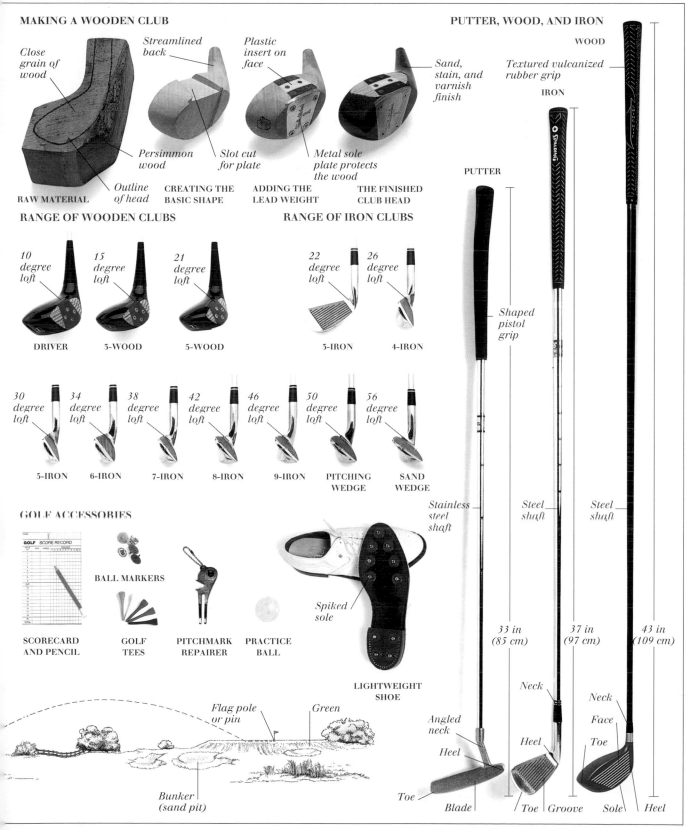

MAKING A WOODEN CLUB

Close grain of wood

Streamlined back

Plastic insert on face

Sand, stain, and varnish finish

Persimmon wood

Slot cut for plate

Metal sole plate protects the wood

Outline of head

RAW MATERIAL

CREATING THE BASIC SHAPE

ADDING THE LEAD WEIGHT

THE FINISHED CLUB HEAD

RANGE OF WOODEN CLUBS

10 degree loft

15 degree loft

21 degree loft

DRIVER

3-WOOD

5-WOOD

30 degree loft

34 degree loft

38 degree loft

42 degree loft

46 degree loft

50 degree loft

56 degree loft

5-IRON

6-IRON

7-IRON

8-IRON

9-IRON

PITCHING WEDGE

SAND WEDGE

RANGE OF IRON CLUBS

22 degree loft

26 degree loft

3-IRON

4-IRON

GOLF ACCESSORIES

BALL MARKERS

SCORECARD AND PENCIL

GOLF TEES

PITCHMARK REPAIRER

PRACTICE BALL

Spiked sole

LIGHTWEIGHT SHOE

Flag pole or pin

Green

Bunker (sand pit)

PUTTER, WOOD, AND IRON

WOOD

Textured vulcanized rubber grip

IRON

PUTTER

Shaped pistol grip

Stainless steel shaft

Steel shaft

Steel shaft

33 in (85 cm)

37 in (97 cm)

43 in (109 cm)

Neck

Neck

Angled neck

Face

Heel

Toe

Heel

Toe

Blade

Toe

Groove

Sole

Heel

547

Archery and shooting

TARGET SHOOTING AND ARCHERY EVOLVED as practice for hunting and battle skills. Modern bows, although designed according to the principles of early hunting bows, use laminates, fiberglass, dacron, and carbon, and are equipped with sights and stabilizers. Competitors in target archery shoot over distances of 100 ft (30 m), 165 ft (50 m), 230 ft (70 m), and 300 ft (90 m) for men, and 100 ft (30 m), 165 ft (50 m), 200 ft (60 m), and 230 ft (70 m) for women. The closer the shot is to the center of the target, the higher the score. The individual scores are added up, and the archer with the highest total wins the competition. Crossbows are used in match competitions over 33 ft (10 m), and 100 ft (30 m). Rifle shooting is divided into three categories: smallbore, bigbore, and air rifle. Contests take place over a variety of distances and further subdivisions are based on the type of shooting position used; prone, kneeling, or standing. The Olympic biathlon combines cross-country skiing and rifle shooting over a course of approximately $12\frac{1}{2}$ miles (20 km). Additional magazines of ammunition are carried in the butt of the rifles. Bigbore rifles fitted with a telescopic sight can be used for hunting and running game target shooting. Pistol shooting events, using rapid-fire pistols, target pistols, and air pistols, take place over 33 ft (10 m), 82 ft (25 m), and 165 ft (50 m) distances. In rapid-fire pistol shooting, a total of 60 shots are fired from a distance of 82 ft (25 m).

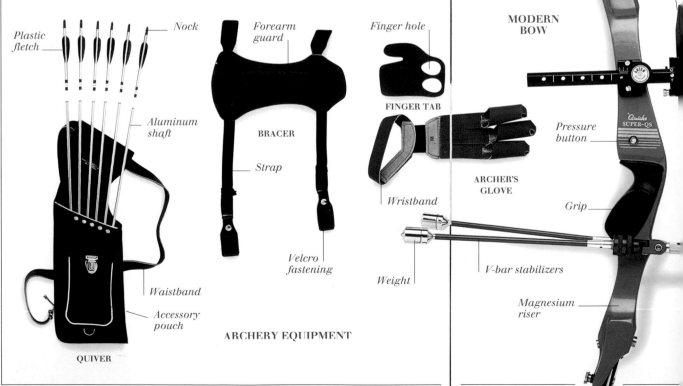

CROSSBOW AND BOLT

Laminated fiberglass bow

Bolt

Bolt rest

Stirrup held between feet when drawing bow

Sight

$1\frac{3}{4}$ in (45 mm)

CROSSBOW TARGET

Hardwood laminate limb

Dacron string

Sight

MODERN BOW

Plastic fletch

Nock

Forearm guard

Finger hole

Aluminum shaft

FINGER TAB

BRACER

Strap

Pressure button

ARCHER'S GLOVE

Wristband

Grip

Velcro fastening

Weight

V-bar stabilizers

Waistband

Accessory pouch

Magnesium riser

ARCHERY EQUIPMENT

QUIVER

SMALLBORE BIATHLON RIFLE

Rifle sight without magnifying lens

Fore sight

Barrel

Trigger

Trigger guard

0.22 in (5.6 m) caliber bullet

Magazine

Extra magazine stored in rifle butt

6 in (155 m)

SMALLBORE FREE RIFLE TARGET FOR 165 FT (50 M) RANGE

BIGBORE HUNTING RIFLE

Bolt handle

Bolt

Telescopic sight

Open sight

Open sight

0.3 in (7.62 mm) calibre bullet

Sling fixing point

39 in (1 m)

BIGBORE RIFLE TARGET FOR 1000 FT (300 M) RANGE

AIR PISTOL

Cocking lever and barrel

Wooden grip shaped to fit the hand

Piston

6 in (155 mm)

AIR-PISTOL TARGET FOR 33 FT (10 M) RANGE

TARGET PISTOL

Back sight

Fore sight

Hammer

Firing pin

Sight pin

Sight ring attachment

Magazine

0.35 in (9 mm) calibre bullet

7³/₄ in (197 mm)

PISTOL TARGET FOR 60 FT (18 M) RANGE

Trigger

Air-pistol pellet

FIELD ARROW

Nock

Metal tip

Feathering

Wooden shaft

Straw butt

White inner 2 points

Aluminum longrod stabilizer

Blue outer 5 points

Yellow inner 10 points (bull's-eye)

ARCHERY TARGET

Ice hockey

ICE HOCKEY IS PLAYED by two teams of six players on an ice rink, with a goal net at each end. The object of this fast, and often dangerous, game is to hit a frozen rubber puck into the opposing team's net with an ice hockey stick. The game begins when the referee drops the puck between the sticks of two players from opposing teams, who face off. The rink is divided into three areas: defending, neutral, and attacking zones. Players may move with the puck and pass it to one another along the ice, but the puck should not travel more than two zones across the rink markings. A goal is scored when the puck entirely crosses the goal-line between the posts and under the crossbar of the goal. A team may field up to 20 players although only six players are allowed on the ice at one time; substitutions occur frequently. Each game consists of three periods of 20 minutes, divided by breaks of 15 minutes.

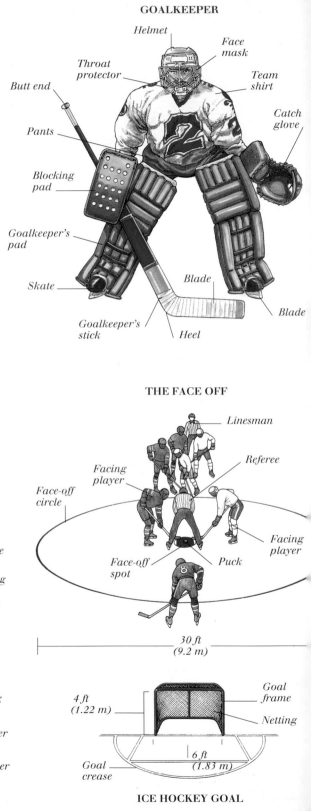

GOALKEEPER

Helmet
Face mask
Throat protector
Team shirt
Butt end
Pants
Catch glove
Blocking pad
Goalkeeper's pad
Blade
Skate
Blade
Goalkeeper's stick
Heel

ICE HOCKEY RINK

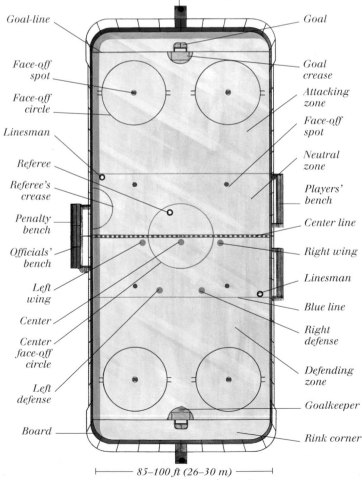

Goal judge
Goal-line
Goal
Face-off spot
Goal crease
Face-off circle
Attacking zone
Linesman
Face-off spot
Referee
Neutral zone
Referee's crease
Players' bench
Penalty bench
Center line
Officials' bench
Right wing
Left wing
Linesman
Center
Blue line
Center face-off circle
Right defense
Left defense
Defending zone
Board
Goalkeeper
Rink corner

85–100 ft (26–30 m)

THE FACE OFF

Linesman
Facing player
Referee
Face-off circle
Face-off spot
Puck
Facing player

30 ft (9.2 m)

4 ft (1.22 m)
Goal frame
Netting
Goal crease
6 ft (1.83 m)

ICE HOCKEY GOAL

550

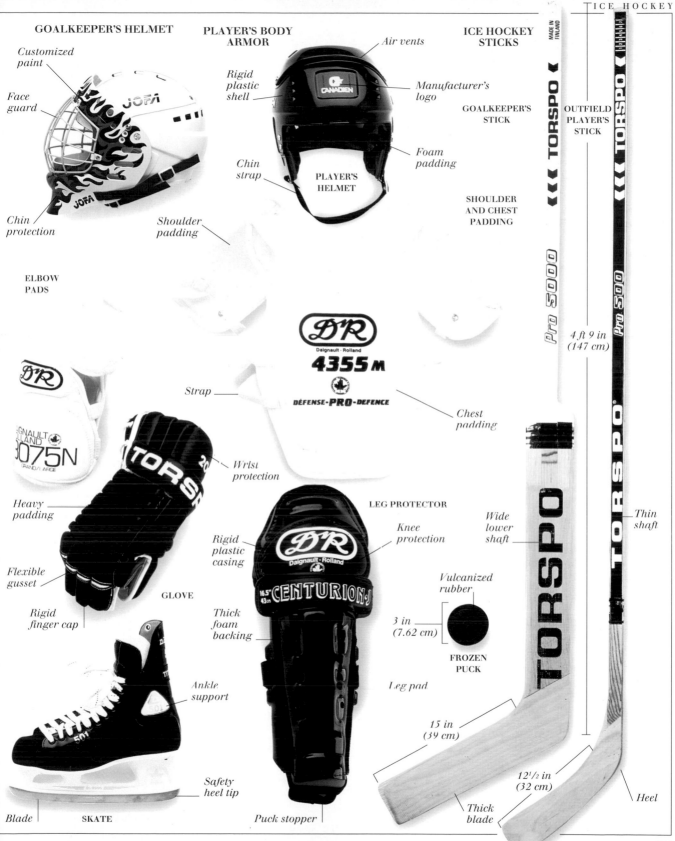

GOALKEEPER'S HELMET

Customized paint

Face guard

Chin protection

PLAYER'S BODY ARMOR

Rigid plastic shell

Chin strap

Air vents

Manufacturer's logo

Foam padding

PLAYER'S HELMET

Shoulder padding

ICE HOCKEY STICKS

GOALKEEPER'S STICK

SHOULDER AND CHEST PADDING

OUTFIELD PLAYER'S STICK

MADE IN FINLAND

TORSPO

TORSPO

Pro 5000

Pro 5000

4 ft 9 in (147 cm)

ELBOW PADS

Strap

DR
Daignault · Rolland
4355 M
DÉFENSE · **PRO** · DEFENCE

Chest padding

DR

AIGNAULT OLLAND

3075N
GRAND/LARGE

TORSPO

Heavy padding

Flexible gusset

Rigid finger cap

GLOVE

Wrist protection

LEG PROTECTOR

Rigid plastic casing

Thick foam backing

DR
Daignault · Rolland

16.5" 43cm **CENTURION·J**

Knee protection

Wide lower shaft

TORSPO

TORSPO

Thin shaft

Vulcanized rubber

3 in (7.62 cm)

FROZEN PUCK

Ankle support

Leg pad

Safety heel tip

15 in (39 cm)

12 1/2 in (32 cm)

Blade   SKATE

Puck stopper

Thick blade

Heel

551

Alpine skiing

COMPETITIVE ALPINE SKIING is divided into four disciplines: downhill, slalom, giant slalom, and super-giant slalom (Super-G). Each one tests different skills. In downhill skiing, competitors race down a slope marked out by control flags, known as "gates," and are timed on a single run only. Competitors wear crash helmets, one-piece Lycra suits, and long skis with flattened tips to minimize air resistance. Slalom and giant slalom skiers negotiate a twisting course requiring balance, agility, and quick reactions. Courses are defined by pairs of gates. Racers must pass through each pair of gates to complete the course successfully. Competitors are timed on two runs over different courses, and the skier who completes the courses in the shortest time wins. The equipment and protective guards used by slalom skiers are shown opposite. In Super-G races, competitors ski a single run that combines the technical challenge of slalom with the speed of downhill. The course requires skiers to complete medium-to-long radius turns at high speed, and contain up to two jumps. Clothing is the same as for downhill, but slightly shorter skis are used.

DOWNHILL SKIER

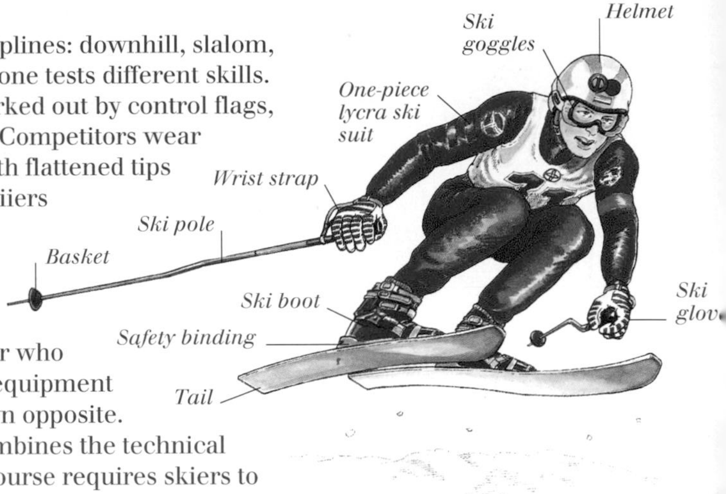

Helmet

Ski goggles

One-piece lycra ski suit

Wrist strap

Ski pole

Basket

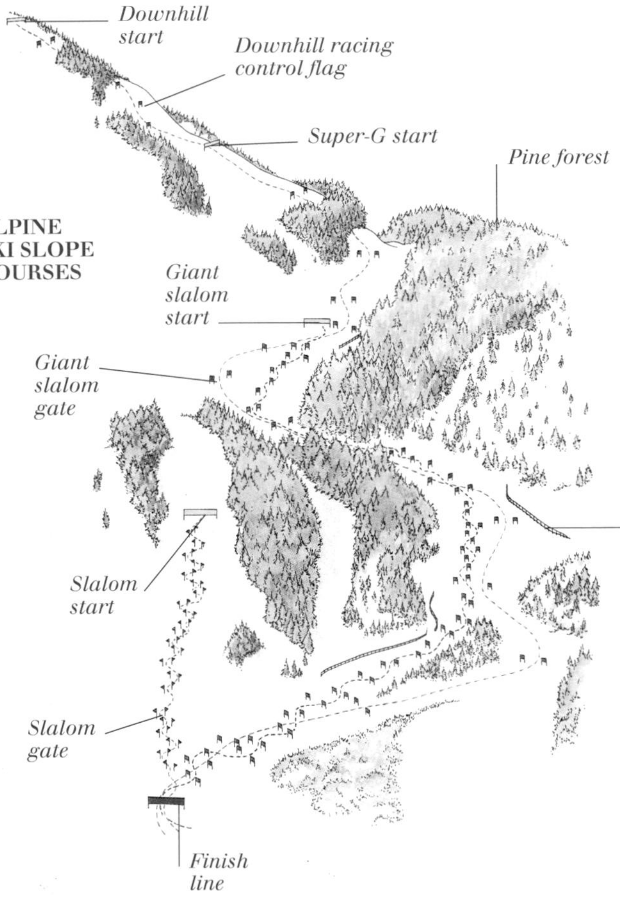

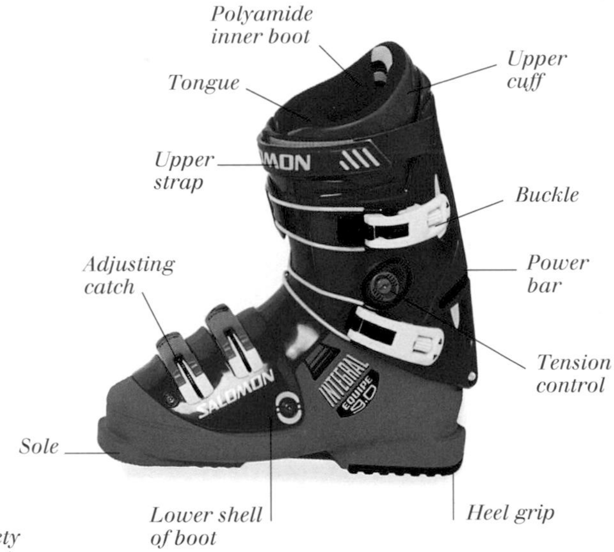

Ski boot

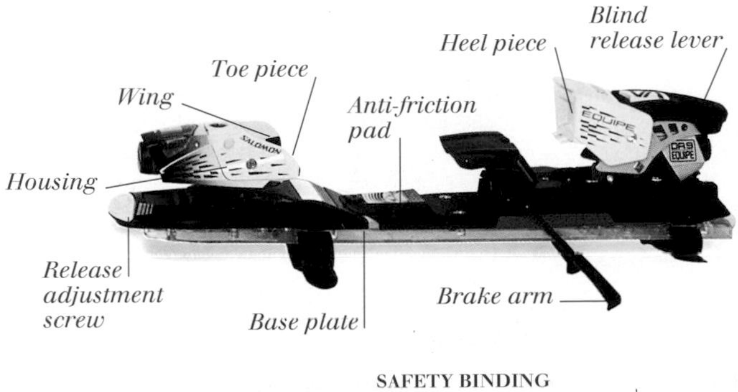

Safety binding

Tail

Ski glove

ALPINE SKI SLOPE COURSES

Downhill start

Downhill racing control flag

Super-G start

Pine forest

Giant slalom start

Giant slalom gate

Slalom start

Slalom gate

Safety barrier

Finish line

SKI BOOT

Polyamide inner boot

Tongue

Upper cuff

Upper strap

Buckle

Adjusting catch

Power bar

Tension control

Sole

Lower shell of boot

Heel grip

SAFETY BINDING

Blind release lever

Heel piece

Toe piece

Wing

Anti-friction pad

Housing

Release adjustment screw

Base plate

Brake arm

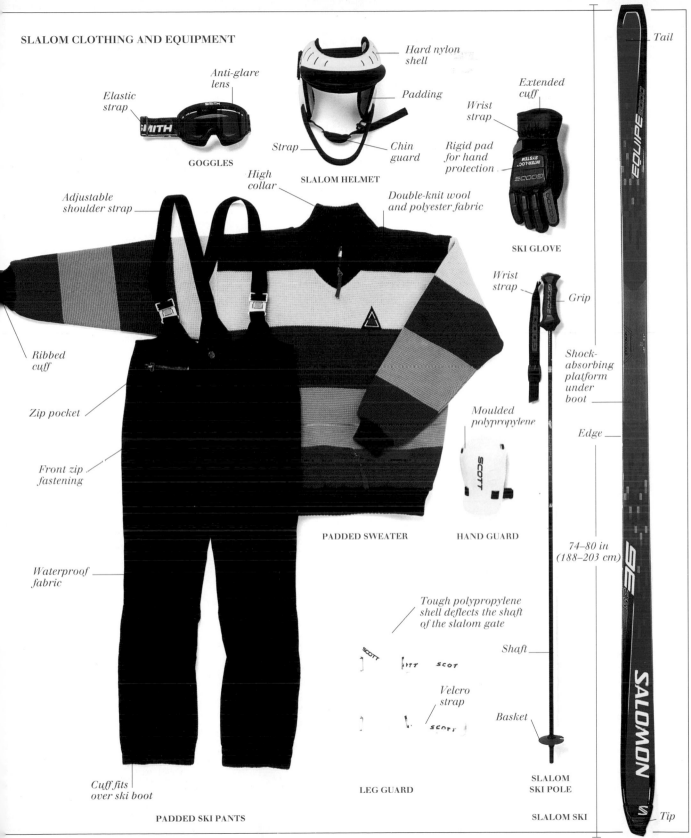

SLALOM CLOTHING AND EQUIPMENT

Anti-glare lens

Elastic strap

GOGGLES

Hard nylon shell

Padding

Strap

Chin guard

SLALOM HELMET

Extended cuff

Wrist strap

Rigid pad for hand protection

SKI GLOVE

High collar

Double-knit wool and polyester fabric

Adjustable shoulder strap

Ribbed cuff

Zip pocket

Front zip fastening

Waterproof fabric

Cuff fits over ski boot

PADDED SKI PANTS

PADDED SWEATER

Moulded polypropylene

HAND GUARD

Tough polypropylene shell deflects the shaft of the slalom gate

Velcro strap

LEG GUARD

Wrist strap

Grip

Shock-absorbing platform under boot

Shaft

Basket

SLALOM SKI POLE

Tail

Edge

74–80 in (188–203 cm)

Tip

SLALOM SKI

553

Equestrian sports

EQUESTRIAN SPORTS HAVE TAKEN place throughout the world for centuries: events involving mounted horses were recorded in the Olympic Games of 642 BC. Show jumping, however, is a much more recent innovation, and the first competitions were held at the beginning of the 1900s. In this sport, horse and rider must negotiate a course of variable, unfixed obstacles, making as few mistakes as possible. Show-jumping fences consist of wooden stands, known as standards or wings, that support planks or poles. Parts of the fence are designed to collapse on impact, preventing injury to the horse and rider. Judges penalize competitors for errors, such as knocking down obstacles, refusing jumps, or deviating from the course. Depending on the type of competition, the rider with the fewest faults, most points, or fastest time wins. There are two basic forms of horse racing – flat races and races with jumps, such as steeplechase or hurdle races. Thoroughbred horses are used in this sport, because they have great strength and stamina and can achieve speeds of up to 40 mph (65 kph). Jockeys wear silks – caps and jackets designed in distinctive colors and patterns which help identify the horses. In harness racing, the horse is driven from a light, two-wheeled carriage called a sulky. Horses are trained to trot and to pace, and different races are held for each of these types of gait. In pacing races, the horses wear hobbles to prevent them from breaking into a trot or gallop. Breeds such as the Standard-bred and the French Trotter have been developed especially for this sport.

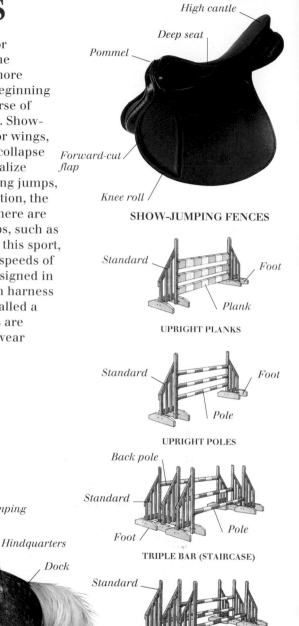

SHOW-JUMPING SADDLE

High cantle

Deep seat

Pommel

Forward-cut flap

Knee roll

SHOW-JUMPING FENCES

Standard · Foot · Plank

UPRIGHT PLANKS

Standard · Foot · Pole

UPRIGHT POLES

Back pole · Standard · Foot · Pole

TRIPLE BAR (STAIRCASE)

Standard · Pole · Foot

HOG'S-BACK

Pillar · Wooden block painted to resemble a brick

WALL

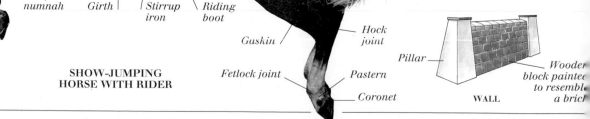

Hard hat

Riding jacket

Browband

Throat-latch

Rein

Jodhpurs

Cheek-piece

Show-jumping saddle

Hindquarters

Dock

Running martingale

Noseband

Brushing boot

Sheepskin numnah

Girth

Stirrup iron

Riding boot

Gaskin

Hock joint

Hoof

Fetlock joint

Pastern

Coronet

SHOW-JUMPING HORSE WITH RIDER

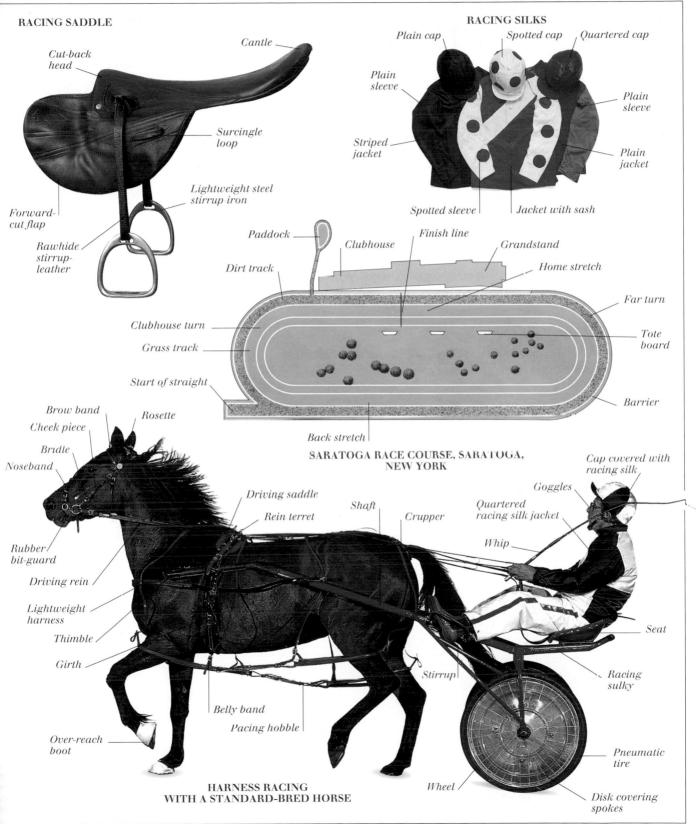

RACING SADDLE

Cut-back head

Cantle

Surcingle loop

Lightweight steel stirrup iron

Forward-cut flap

Rawhide stirrup-leather

RACING SILKS

Plain cap

Spotted cap

Quartered cap

Plain sleeve

Plain sleeve

Striped jacket

Plain jacket

Spotted sleeve

Jacket with sash

Paddock

Clubhouse

Finish line

Grandstand

Home stretch

Dirt track

Far turn

Clubhouse turn

Tote board

Grass track

Start of straight

Barrier

Back stretch

SARATOGA RACE COURSE, SARATOGA, NEW YORK

Brow band

Rosette

Cheek piece

Bridle

Noseband

Driving saddle

Rein terret

Shaft

Crupper

Cap covered with racing silk

Goggles

Quartered racing silk jacket

Whip

Rubber bit-guard

Driving rein

Lightweight harness

Thimble

Girth

Seat

Belly band

Pacing hobble

Stirrup

Racing sulky

Over-reach boot

Pneumatic tire

Wheel

Disk covering spokes

HARNESS RACING WITH A STANDARD-BRED HORSE

Judo and fencing

COMBAT SPORTS ARE BASED ON THE SKILLS used in fighting. In these sports, the competitors may be unarmed – as in judo and boxing – or armed – as in fencing and kendo. Judo is a system of unarmed combat developed in the East. Translated from the Japanese the name means "the gentle way." Students learn how to turn an opponent's force to their own advantage. The usual uniform is loose white pants and a jacket, fastened with a cloth belt. The color of belt indicates the student's level of expertise, from white-belted novices to the expert black belts. Competitions take place on a mat or "shiaijo," 30 or 33 ft (9 or 10 m) square in size, bounded by "danger" and "safety" areas to prevent injury. Competitors try to throw, pin, or master their opponent by applying pressure to the arm joints or neck. Judo matches are strictly monitored, and competitors receive points for superior technique, not for injuring their opponent. Fencing is a combat sport using swords, which takes place on a narrow piste or strip 46 ft (14 m) long. Competitors try to hit specific target areas on their opponent with their sword or foil while avoiding being touched themselves. The winner is the one who scores the greatest number of hits. Fencers wear uniforms made from strong white material, which affords maximum protection while allowing freedom of movement, steel mesh masks with padded bibs to protect the fencer's neck, and a long white glove on their sword hand. Fencing foils do not have sharpened blades, and their tips end in a blunt button to prevent injuries. Three types of swords are used – foils, épées, and sabres. Official foil and épée competitions always use an electric scoring system. The sword tips are connected to lights by a long wire that passes underneath each fencer's jacket. A bulb flashes when a hit is made.

JUDO HOLDS AND THROWS

SIDE FOUR QUARTER HOLD

SINGLE WING

BODY DROP

ONE ARM SHOULDER THROW

SHOULDER WHEEL

SWEEPING LOW THROW

STOMACH THROW

KNEE WHEEL

JUDO MAT

52 ft 6 in (16 m)

Judge

Scorer

Holding timekeeper

Timekeeper

Danger area

Contestant

JUDO KIT

Drawstring

Contestant

Referee

Contest area

Safety area

Cotton pants

Black belt

Heavy-duty cotton jacket

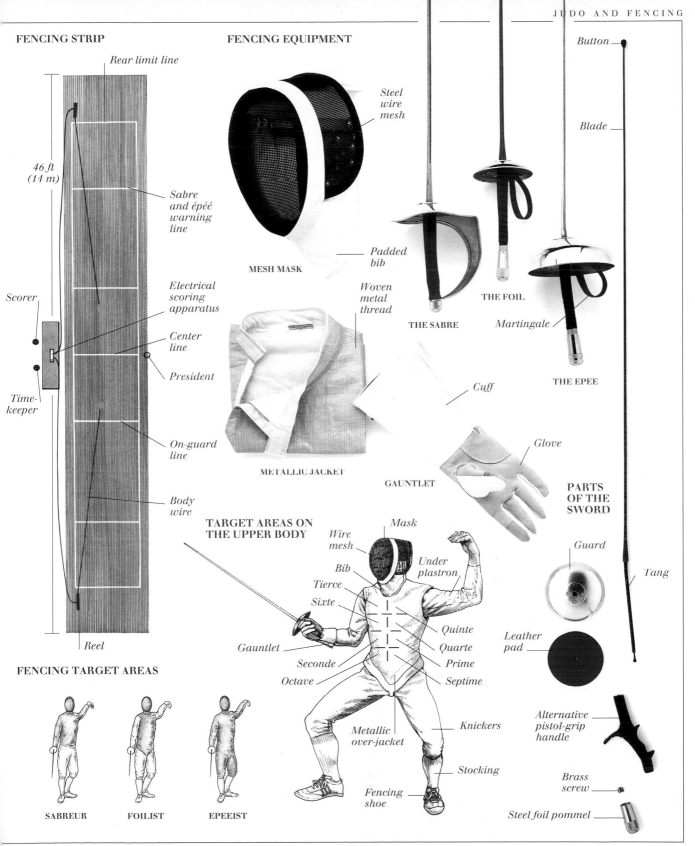

FENCING STRIP

Rear limit line

46 ft (14 m)

Scorer

Time-keeper

Sabre and épéé warning line

Electrical scoring apparatus

Center line

President

On-guard line

Body wire

Reel

FENCING TARGET AREAS

SABREUR

FOILIST

EPEEIST

FENCING EQUIPMENT

Steel wire mesh

MESH MASK

Padded bib

Woven metal thread

Cuff

METALLIC JACKET

GAUNTLET

Glove

THE SABRE

THE FOIL

Martingale

THE EPEE

Button

Blade

TARGET AREAS ON THE UPPER BODY

Mask

Wire mesh

Bib

Tierce

Sixte

Gauntlet

Seconde

Octave

Under plastron

Quinte

Quarte

Prime

Septime

Metallic over-jacket

Knickers

Stocking

Fencing shoe

PARTS OF THE SWORD

Guard

Tang

Leather pad

Alternative pistol-grip handle

Brass screw

Steel foil pommel

557

Swimming and diving

SWIMMING GOGGLES

SWIMMING WAS INCLUDED in the first modern Olympic Games in 1896 and diving events were added in 1904. Swimming is both an individual and a team sport and races take place over a predetermined distance in one of the four major categories of stroke – freestyle (usually front crawl), butterfly, breaststroke, and backstroke. Competition pools are clearly marked for racing and anti-turbulence lane lines are used to separate the swimmers and help keep the water calm. The first team or individual to finish the race is the winner. Competitive diving is divided into men's and women's springboard and platform (highboard) events. There are six official groups of dives: forward dives, backward dives, armstand dives, twist dives, reverse dives, and inward dives. Competitors perform a set number of dives and after each one a panel of judges awards marks according to the quality of execution and the degree of difficulty.

STYLES OF DIVES

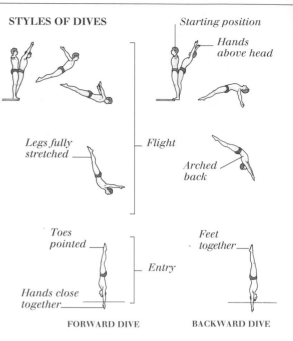

Starting position

Hands above head

Legs fully stretched — Flight — Arched back

Toes pointed — Entry — Feet together

Hands close together

FORWARD DIVE   **BACKWARD DIVE**

SWIMWEAR

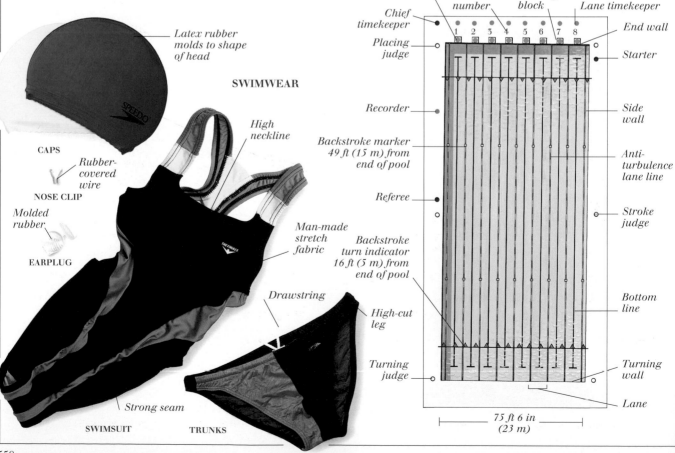

Latex rubber molds to shape of head

CAPS

Rubber-covered wire

NOSE CLIP

Molded rubber

EARPLUG

High neckline

Man-made stretch fabric

Drawstring

High-cut leg

Strong seam

SWIMSUIT   **TRUNKS**

SWIMMING POOL

Swimmer
Lane number
Starting block
Chief timekeeper
Lane timekeeper
Placing judge
End wall
Starter

1 2 3 4 5 6 7 8

Recorder
Side wall

Backstroke marker 49 ft (15 m) from end of pool
Anti-turbulence lane line

Referee
Stroke judge

Backstroke turn indicator 16 ft (5 m) from end of pool
Bottom line

Turning judge
Turning wall

Lane

75 ft 6 in (23 m)

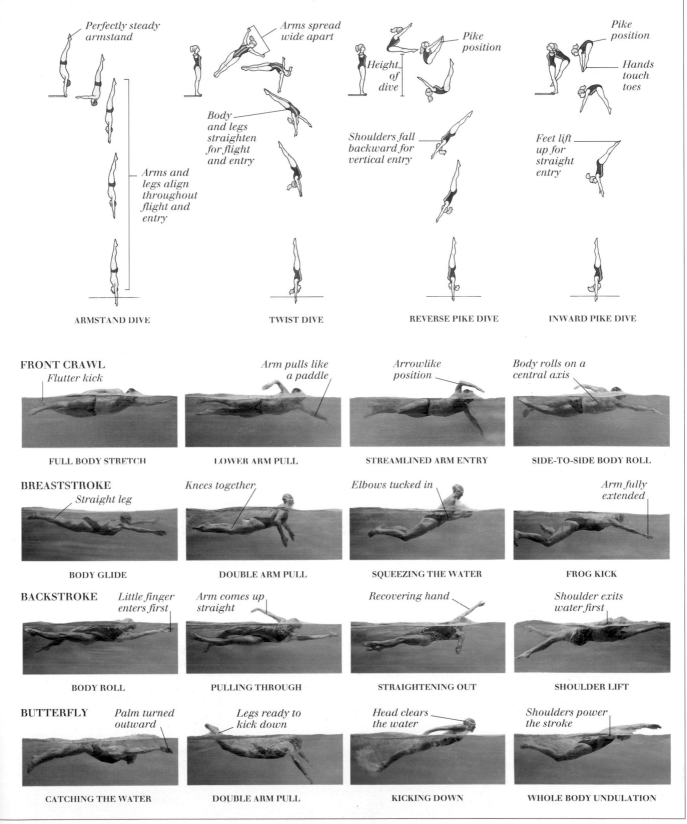

ARMSTAND DIVE

Perfectly steady armstand

Arms and legs align throughout flight and entry

TWIST DIVE

Arms spread wide apart

Body and legs straighten for flight and entry

REVERSE PIKE DIVE

Pike position

Height of dive

Shoulders fall backward for vertical entry

INWARD PIKE DIVE

Pike position

Hands touch toes

Feet lift up for straight entry

FRONT CRAWL
Flutter kick

FULL BODY STRETCH

Arm pulls like a paddle

LOWER ARM PULL

Arrowlike position

STREAMLINED ARM ENTRY

Body rolls on a central axis

SIDE-TO-SIDE BODY ROLL

BREASTSTROKE
Straight leg

BODY GLIDE

Knees together

DOUBLE ARM PULL

Elbows tucked in

SQUEEZING THE WATER

Arm fully extended

FROG KICK

BACKSTROKE
Little finger enters first

BODY ROLL

Arm comes up straight

PULLING THROUGH

Recovering hand

STRAIGHTENING OUT

Shoulder exits water first

SHOULDER LIFT

BUTTERFLY
Palm turned outward

CATCHING THE WATER

Legs ready to kick down

DOUBLE ARM PULL

Head clears the water

KICKING DOWN

Shoulders power the stroke

WHOLE BODY UNDULATION

Kayaking, rowing, and sailing

WATERBORNE SPORTS are as varied as the crafts used. There are two disciplines in rowing; sweep rowing, in which each rower has one oar, and sculling, in which rowers use two oars. There are a number of different Olympic and competitive rowing events for both men and women. The number of rowers and weight classes vary. Some rowing events use a coxswain; a steersman who does not row but directs the crew. Kayaks are used in straight sprint and slalom races. Slalom races take place over a course consisting of 20 to 25 gates, including at least six upstream gates. In yacht racing, competitors must complete prescribed courses, organized by the race committees, in the shortest possible time, using sail power only. Olympic events include classes for keel boats, dinghies, catamarans, and windsurfers.

SAILING GEAR

Personal flotation device

Sleeveless long johns

Long-sleeved jacket

Neoprene material

Belt

GLOVE

Bootlace

Ribbed top

Non-slip sole

BOOT

ONE-PERSON KAYAK AND PADDLE

Blade

Rim

Shaft

Nose cone

Right rail

Cockpit

Back strap

Stern

High density polythene

Grab loop

Bow

Left rail

Seat

Cockpit rim

SINGLE SCULL AND OARS (WITH CLOTH DECKING REMOVED)

Neck

Collar

Shaft

Port-side oar

Spoon

Blade

Colors

Oarlock

Gate

Grip

Starboard oar

Button

Loom

Stretcher

Water shoot

Rigger

Sycamore beam

Keel

Stern deck

Spruce beam

Diagonal frame

Aluminum beam

Bung

Aft shoulder

Shoe

Keelson

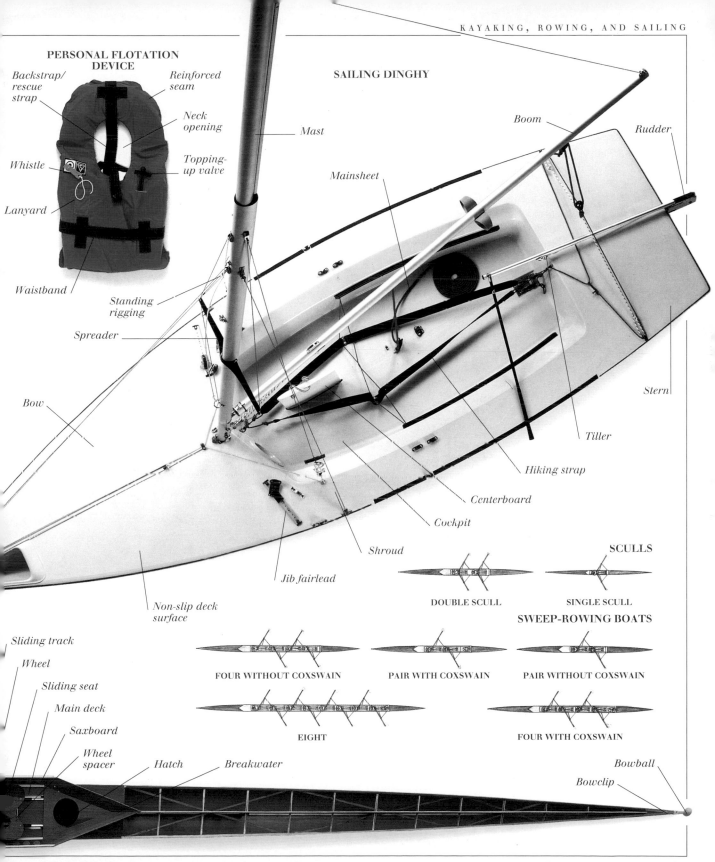

PERSONAL FLOTATION DEVICE

Backstrap/rescue strap

Reinforced seam

Neck opening

Whistle

Topping-up valve

Lanyard

Waistband

Standing rigging

Spreader

Bow

SAILING DINGHY

Mast

Mainsheet

Boom

Rudder

Stern

Tiller

Hiking strap

Centerboard

Cockpit

Shroud

Jib fairlead

Non-slip deck surface

SCULLS

DOUBLE SCULL

SINGLE SCULL

SWEEP-ROWING BOATS

FOUR WITHOUT COXSWAIN

PAIR WITH COXSWAIN

PAIR WITHOUT COXSWAIN

EIGHT

FOUR WITH COXSWAIN

Sliding track

Wheel

Sliding seat

Main deck

Saxboard

Wheel spacer

Hatch

Breakwater

Bowball

Bowclip

Angling

ANGLING MEANS FISHING WITH A ROD, reel, line, and lure. There are several different types of angling: freshwater coarse angling, for members of the carp family and pike; freshwater game angling, for salmon and trout; and sea angling, for sea fish such as flatfish, bass, and mackerel. Anglers use a variety of methods of catching fish. These include bait fishing, in which bait (food to allure the fish) is placed on a hook and cast into the water; fly fishing, in which a natural or artificial fly is used to lure the fish; and spinning, in which a lure that looks like a small fish revolves as it is pulled through the water. The angler uses the rod, reel, and line to cast the lure over the water. The reel controls the line as it spills off the spool and as it is wound back. Weights may be fixed to the line so that it will sink. Swivels are attached to prevent the line from twisting. When a fish bites, the hook must become embedded in its mouth and remain there while the catch is reeled in.

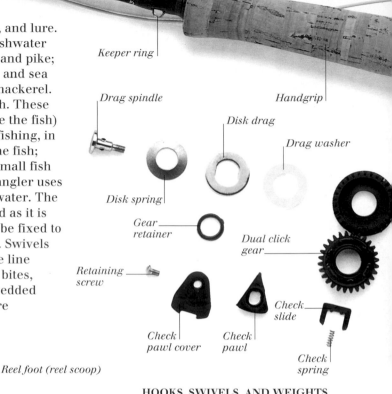

Keeper ring

Drag spindle

Handgrip

Disk drag

Drag washer

Disk spring

Gear retainer

Dual click gear

Retaining screw

Check slide

Check pawl cover

Check pawl

Check spring

REELS

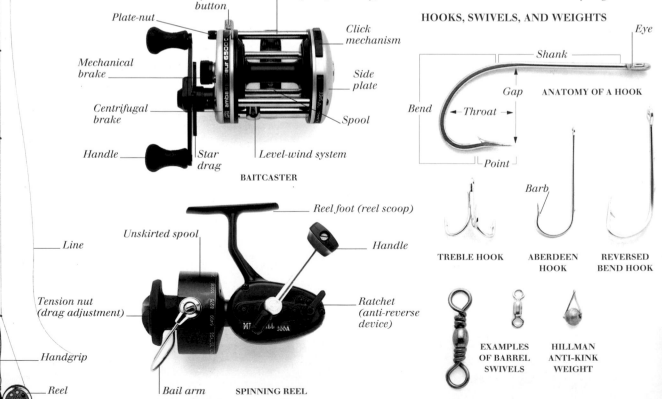

Spool-release button

Reel foot (reel scoop)

Plate-nut

Click mechanism

Mechanical brake

Side plate

Centrifugal brake

Spool

Handle

Star drag

Level-wind system

BAITCASTER

Line

Reel foot (reel scoop)

Unskirted spool

Handle

Tension nut (drag adjustment)

Ratchet (anti-reverse device)

Handgrip

Reel

Bail arm

SPINNING REEL

HOOKS, SWIVELS, AND WEIGHTS

Eye

Shank

Gap

ANATOMY OF A HOOK

Bend

Throat

Point

Barb

TREBLE HOOK

ABERDEEN HOOK

REVERSED BEND HOOK

EXAMPLES OF BARREL SWIVELS

HILLMAN ANTI-KINK WEIGHT

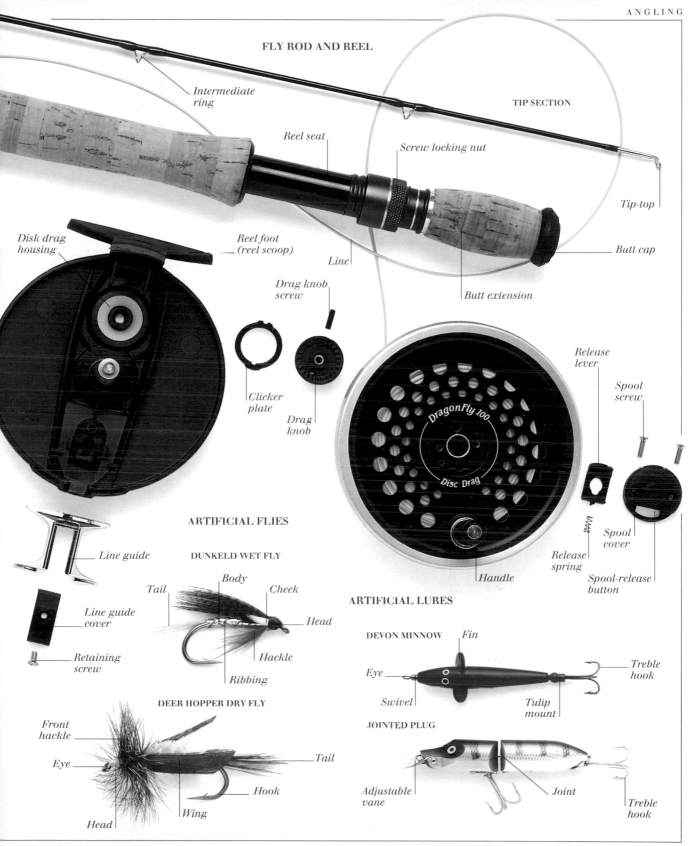

FLY ROD AND REEL

Intermediate ring

TIP SECTION

Reel seat

Screw locking nut

Tip-top

Disk drag housing

Reel foot (reel scoop)

Butt cap

Line

Drag knob screw

Butt extension

Clicker plate

Release lever

Spool screw

Drag knob

ARTIFICIAL FLIES

DragonFly 100

Disc Drag

Line guide

DUNKELD WET FLY

Spool cover

Body

Release spring

Spool-release button

Tail

Cheek

Handle

Line guide cover

Head

ARTIFICIAL LURES

Retaining screw

Hackle

Ribbing

DEVON MINNOW

Fin

Eye

Treble hook

DEER HOPPER DRY FLY

Swivel

Tulip mount

Front hackle

JOINTED PLUG

Eye

Tail

Hook

Adjustable vane

Joint

Wing

Treble hook

Head

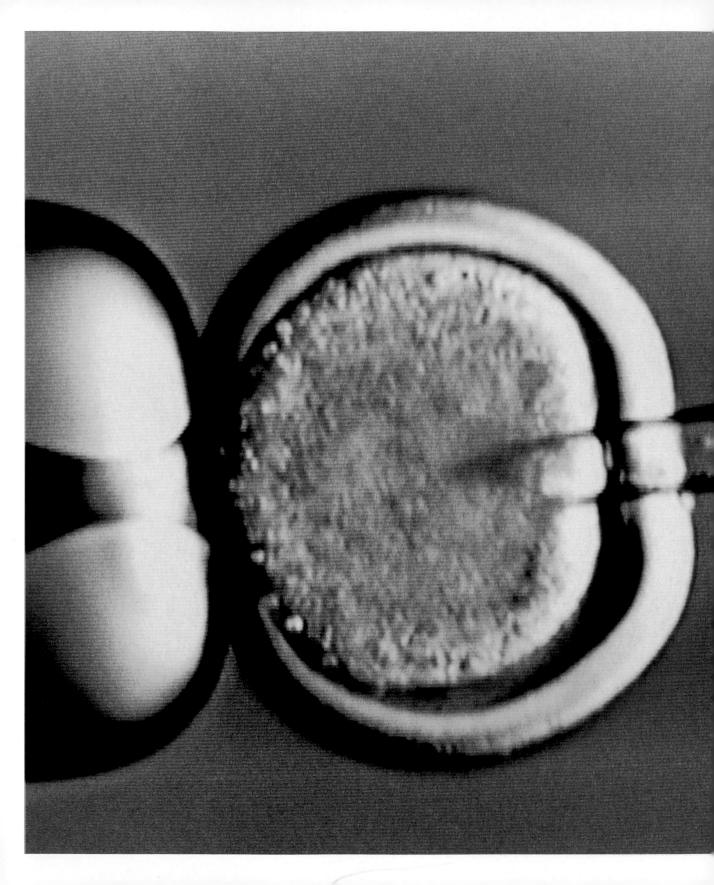

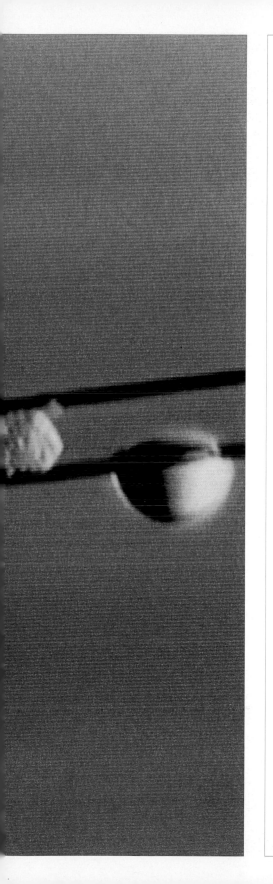

THE MODERN WORLD

Personal computer

PERSONAL COMPUTERS (PCs) fall into two main types: IBM-compatible PCs, known simply as PCs, and Apple Macintosh PCs, known as "Macs." They differ in the way files and programs, and the user's access to them, are organized, and programs must be tailored for each type. However, in most other respects PCs and Macs have much in common. Both contain microchips, or integrated circuits, that store and process data. The "brain" of any PC is a chip known as the central processing unit (CPU), which performs mathematical operations in order to run program instructions and receive, store, and output data. The most powerful CPUs today perform over a billion calculations a second. Data can be input via CDs and other storage media, as well as via modems. Highly portable laptop PCs are also in widespread use. Most PCs are able to communicate with many other devices, from video cameras (see pp. 582–83) to personal data assistants (see pp. 568–69).

APPLE POWER MAC G4 1GHz DUAL PROCESSOR

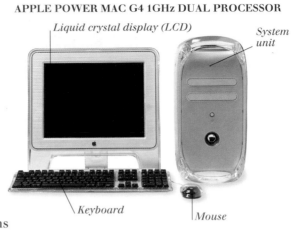

Liquid crystal display (LCD)

System unit

Keyboard

Mouse

REAR VIEW OF SYSTEM UNIT

FRONT VIEW OF SYSTEM UNIT

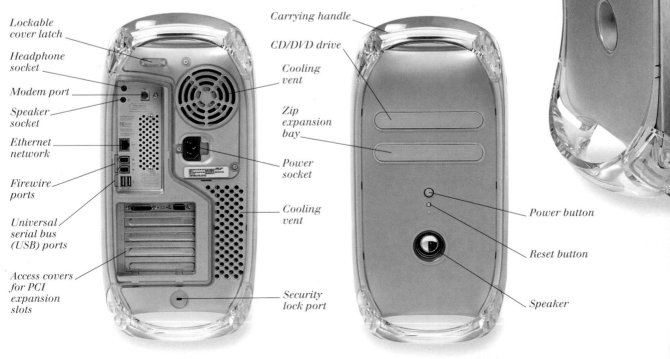

Lockable cover latch

Headphone socket

Modem port

Speaker socket

Ethernet network

Firewire ports

Universal serial bus (USB) ports

Access covers for PCI expansion slots

Carrying handle

CD/DVD drive

Cooling vent

Zip expansion bay

Power socket

Cooling vent

Security lock port

Power button

Reset button

Speaker

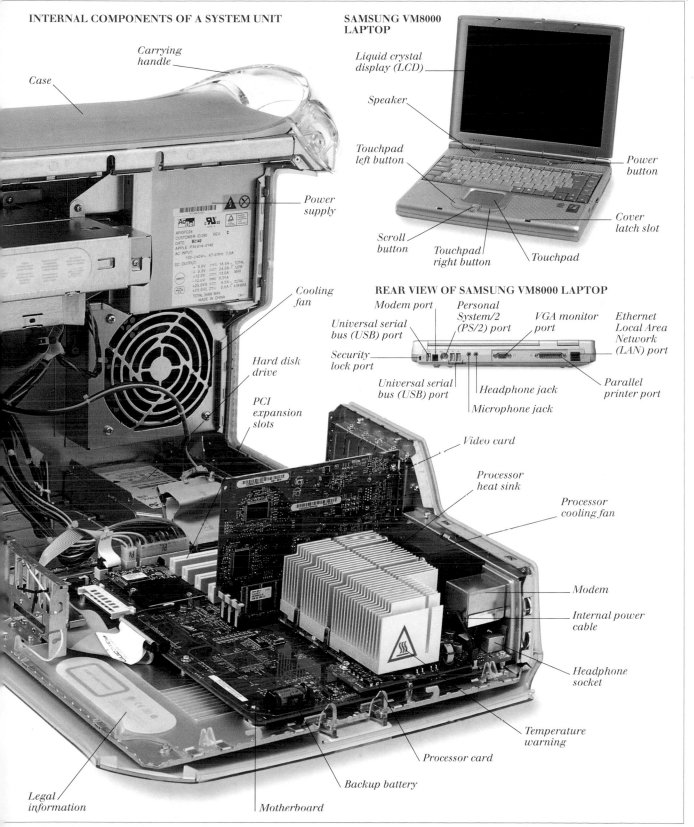

INTERNAL COMPONENTS OF A SYSTEM UNIT

Carrying handle

Case

Power supply

Cooling fan

Hard disk drive

PCI expansion slots

Legal information

Motherboard

Backup battery

Processor card

SAMSUNG VM8000 LAPTOP

Liquid crystal display (LCD)

Speaker

Touchpad left button

Power button

Scroll button

Touchpad right button

Touchpad

Cover latch slot

REAR VIEW OF SAMSUNG VM8000 LAPTOP

Modem port

Personal System/2 (PS/2) port

VGA monitor port

Ethernet Local Area Network (LAN) port

Universal serial bus (USB) port

Security lock port

Universal serial bus (USB) port

Headphone jack

Microphone jack

Parallel printer port

Video card

Processor heat sink

Processor cooling fan

Modem

Internal power cable

Headphone socket

Temperature warning

Handheld computer

PERSONAL DIGITAL ASSISTANTS (PDAs), or handheld
computers, are one of the many small electronic
devices that began to be developed during the last
years of the 20th century. There are two main types
of PDA: those with integral keyboards and those
without. PDAs with keyboards are larger and heavier
than their keyboardless counterparts, which can be
easily held in one hand. The latter employ a
combination of touch-screen technology and
handwriting-recognition programs to receive
instructions and data. In order to write data into the
PDA screen with a stylus, users must usually learn to
use a special alphabet that the computer understands.
PDAs are not intended to replace personal computers
(PCs) – there is a high risk of losing data if the
batteries are not recharged or replaced before they
go flat. The contents of a PDA's memory needs to be
regularly backed up onto a PC. In addition to their
basic programs, such as address book, calendar, and
note pad, PDAs are increasingly absorbing the
functions of other small electronic devices,
such as MP3 players (see pp. 586–587),
Global Positioning System (GPS) receivers
(see pp. 590–591), and mobile phones (see
pp. 588–589). Some can also access email
and the internet.

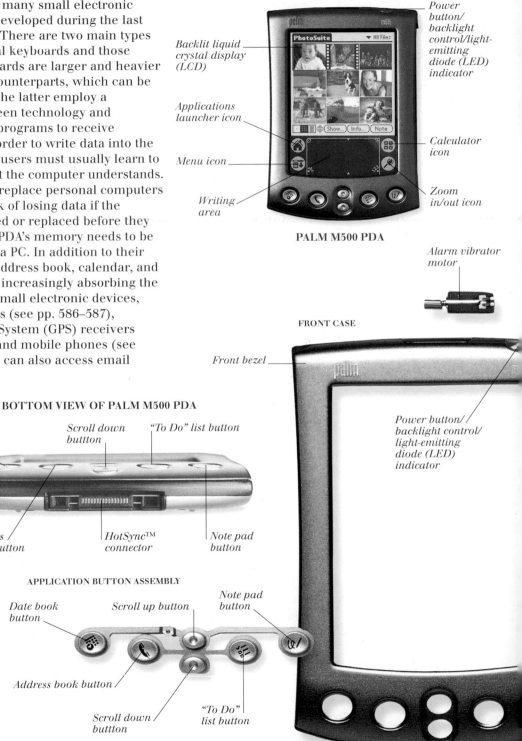

Backlit liquid crystal display (LCD)

Applications launcher icon

Menu icon

Writing area

Power button/ backlight control/light-emitting diode (LED) indicator

Calculator icon

Zoom in/out icon

PALM M500 PDA

Alarm vibrator motor

FRONT CASE

Front bezel

Power button/ backlight control/ light-emitting diode (LED) indicator

BOTTOM VIEW OF PALM M500 PDA

Date book button

Scroll down buttton

"To Do" list button

Front case

Rear case

Address book button

HotSync™ connector

Note pad button

APPLICATION BUTTON ASSEMBLY

Date book button

Scroll up button

Note pad button

Writing tip

STYLUS

Address book button

Scroll down buttton

"To Do" list button

EXAMPLES OF SOFTWARE

COMPONENTS OF A PALM M500 PDA

REAR CASE

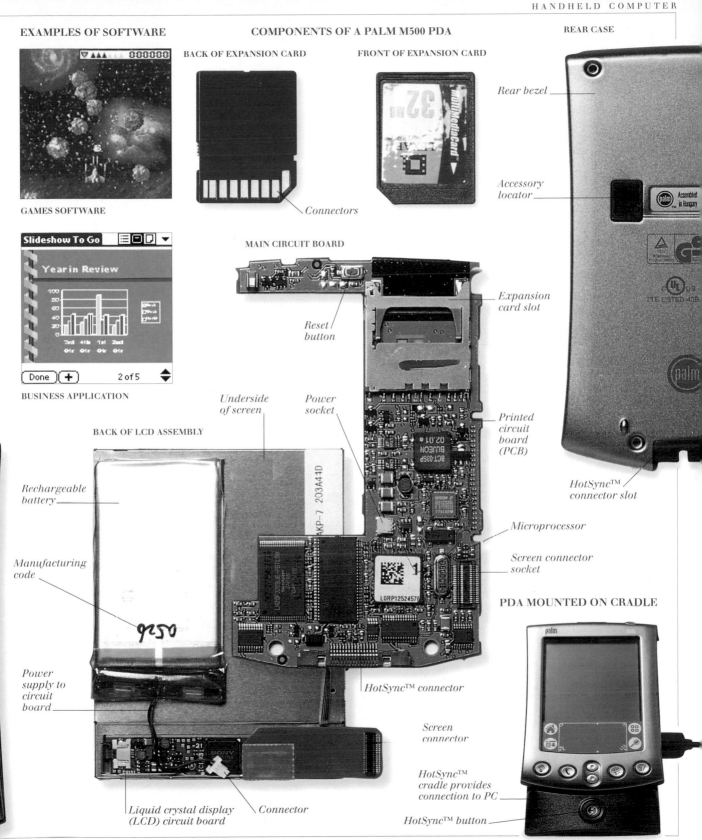

GAMES SOFTWARE

BACK OF EXPANSION CARD

FRONT OF EXPANSION CARD

Connectors

Rear bezel

Accessory
locator

Slideshow To Go

Year in Review

Done   +   2 of 5

BUSINESS APPLICATION

MAIN CIRCUIT BOARD

*Reset
button*

*Expansion
card slot*

*Printed
circuit
board
(PCB)*

*HotSync™
connector slot*

BACK OF LCD ASSEMBLY

*Underside
of screen*

*Power
socket*

*Rechargeable
battery*

*Manufacturing
code*

Microprocessor

*Screen connector
socket*

PDA MOUNTED ON CRADLE

*Power
supply to
circuit
board*

HotSync™ connector

*Screen
connector*

*HotSync™
cradle provides
connection to PC*

*Liquid crystal display
(LCD) circuit board*

Connector

HotSync™ button

Flatbed scanner

SCANNERS CONVERT physical images into electronic form, allowing them to be sent over the internet, displayed on a website, stored on a computer, and manipulated using specialized software. Scanners work by detecting and analyzing light reflected from an opaque image, such as a photographic print. Some can also scan photographic transparencies by analyzing light that has passed through the image. Flatbed scanners contain a unit, called the scan head, that contains a lamp, mirrors, a lens, and an array of CCDs (Charge-Coupled Devices). The carriage passes beneath the image; the lamp shines light onto or through the original; the mirrors reflect the light onto the lens, which focuses it onto the CCD array. Each CCD detects the brightness of light from a particular pixel (picture element) along a horizontal strip and converts this data into an electric signal. For color images, the light is usually passed through red, green, and blue filters and then directed to the CCD array so that it can be broken down into its component colors. This information is then converted to digital form. The quality of the image depends on its resolution, measured in dpi (Dots Per Inch).

HOW A FLATBED SCANNER WORKS

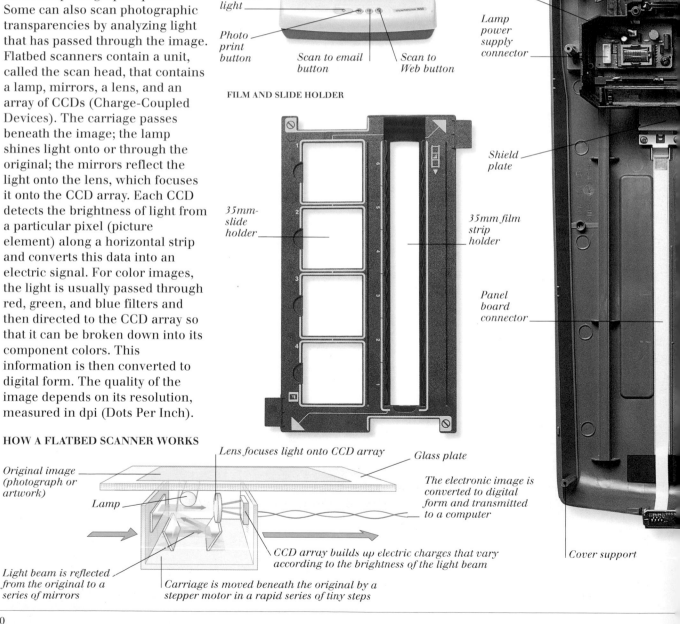

EPSON PERFECTION 1650 SCANNER

Integrated transparency unit (TPU)

Glass plate

Start button and indicator light

Photo print button

Scan to email button

Scan to Web button

Power supply cable

Reflective document mat

Direct current (DC) inlet

TPU connector port

Lock

Inverter board

Lamp power supply connector

FILM AND SLIDE HOLDER

35mm-slide holder

35mm film strip holder

Shield plate

Panel board connector

Lens focuses light onto CCD array

Glass plate

Original image (photograph or artwork)

The electronic image is converted to digital form and transmitted to a computer

Lamp

CCD array builds up electric charges that vary according to the brightness of the light beam

Light beam is reflected from the original to a series of mirrors

Carriage is moved beneath the original by a stepper motor in a rapid series of tiny steps

Cover support

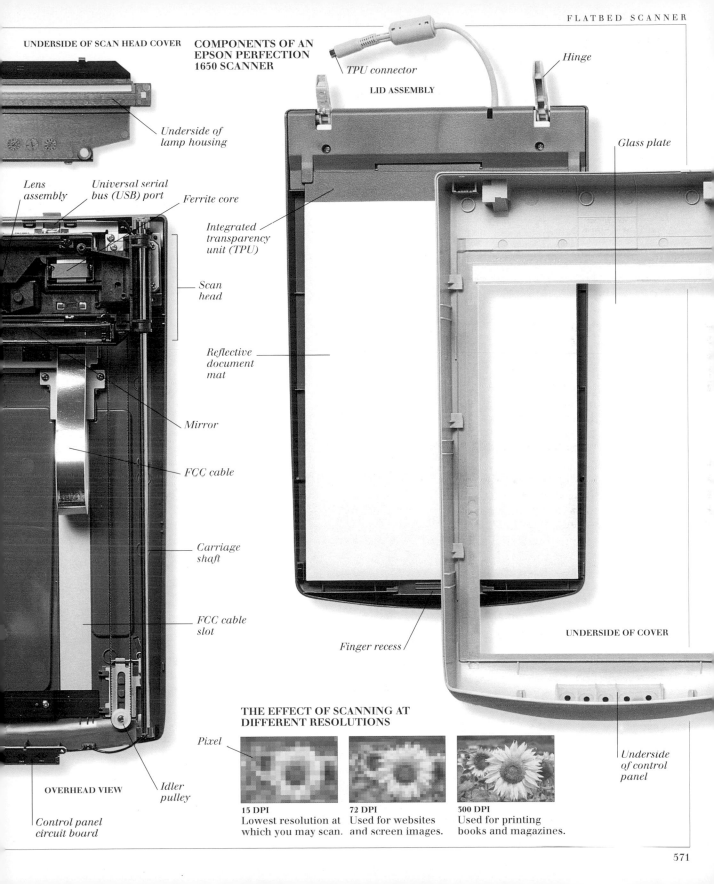

UNDERSIDE OF SCAN HEAD COVER

COMPONENTS OF AN EPSON PERFECTION 1650 SCANNER

TPU connector

Hinge

LID ASSEMBLY

Underside of lamp housing

Glass plate

Lens assembly

Universal serial bus (USB) port

Ferrite core

Integrated transparency unit (TPU)

Scan head

Reflective document mat

Mirror

FCC cable

Carriage shaft

FCC cable slot

UNDERSIDE OF COVER

Finger recess

Underside of control panel

OVERHEAD VIEW

Idler pulley

Control panel circuit board

THE EFFECT OF SCANNING AT DIFFERENT RESOLUTIONS

Pixel

15 DPI
Lowest resolution at which you may scan.

72 DPI
Used for websites and screen images.

300 DPI
Used for printing books and magazines.

571

Fax machine

FAX (FACSIMILE) MACHINES TRANSMIT and receive images of documents over the telephone network. Like a scanner (see pp. 570–571, a fax machine scans the original document in a series of horizontal strips, each composed of many pixels (picture elements). A page fed into the machine passes over a lamp whose light is reflected off the page on to an array of about 1,800 tiny CCDs (Charge-Coupled Devices). Each CCD detects the brightness of light reflected from a pixel in the current horizontal strip of the page and produces a corresponding electric signal. The signals are processed and transmitted to another fax machine, which reproduces the pixellated image as a series of black dots interspersed with unprinted, white areas.

COMPONENTS OF BROTHER T-78 FAX MACHINE

UNDERSIDE OF CONTROL PANEL CASING

Document pressure bar assembly

BROTHER T-78 FAX MACHINE

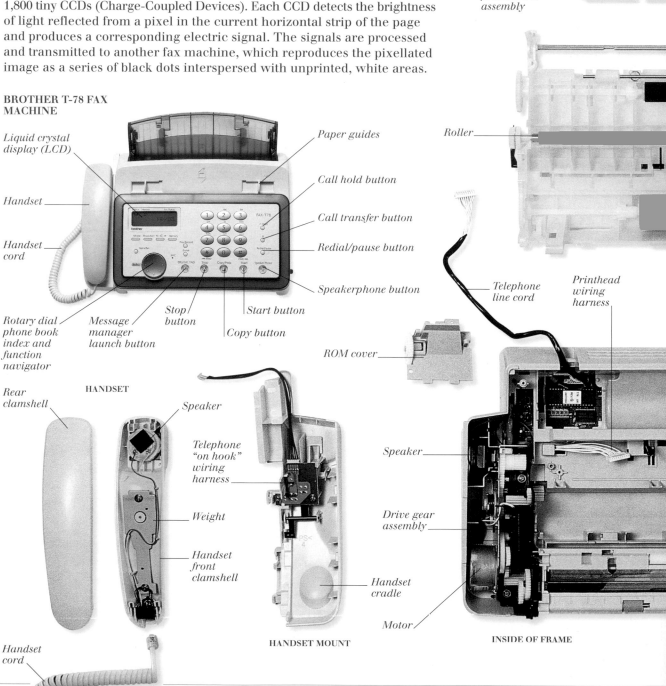

Liquid crystal display (LCD)

Paper guides

Handset

Call hold button

Handset cord

Call transfer button

Redial/pause button

Roller

Speakerphone button

Rotary dial phone book index and function navigator

Message manager launch button

Stop button

Start button

Copy button

Telephone line cord

Printhead wiring harness

ROM cover

Rear clamshell

HANDSET

Speaker

Telephone "on hook" wiring harness

Speaker

Weight

Drive gear assembly

Handset front clamshell

Handset cradle

Motor

Handset cord

HANDSET MOUNT

INSIDE OF FRAME

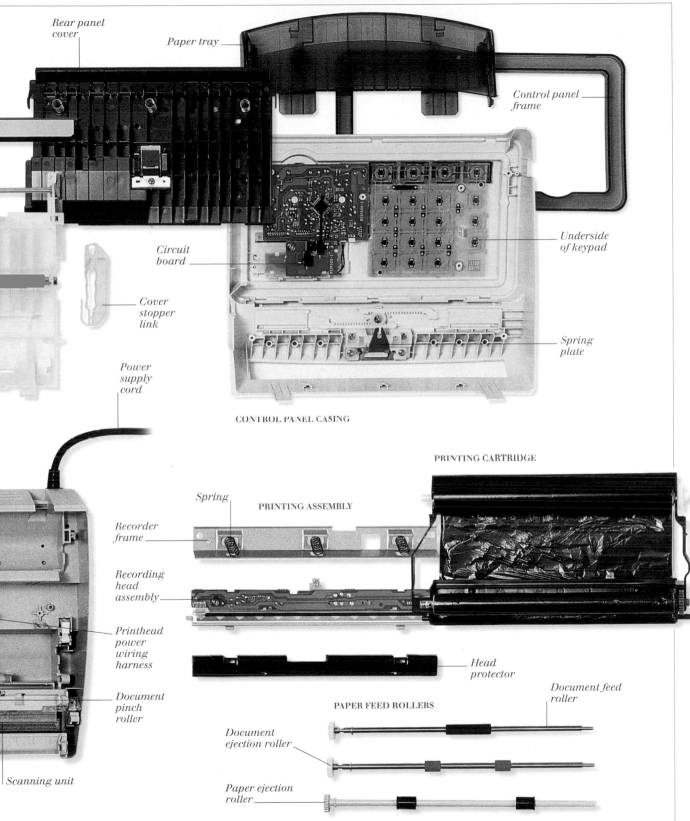

Rear panel cover

Paper tray

Control panel frame

Circuit board

Underside of keypad

Cover stopper link

Spring plate

Power supply cord

CONTROL PANEL CASING

PRINTING CARTRIDGE

Spring

PRINTING ASSEMBLY

Recorder frame

Recording head assembly

Printhead power wiring harness

Head protector

Document pinch roller

Document feed roller

PAPER FEED ROLLERS

Document ejection roller

Paper ejection roller

Scanning unit

Inkjet printer

INKJET PRINTERS EXPEL ink droplets from hundreds of tiny jets, or nozzles, onto a medium, such as paper, to print an image. Each droplet corresponds to a single pixel (picture element). Black-and-white printers use only black ink, while color printers overprint combinations of the printing colors (cyan, yellow, magenta, and black) to create a full color range. The printhead containing the nozzles moves sideways across the paper, creating a line of pixels, before the paper moves slightly forward so the next line can be printed. Two basic methods are used to eject ink: thermal, in which ink is heated to form an expanding bubble that expels a droplet from the nozzle, and piezoelectric, in which an electric current expands a crystal causing it to push out the ink droplet. The printer shown here can print digital photographs directly from a memory card.

EPSON STYLUS PHOTO 895 COLOR INKJET PRINTER

Printer cover
Carriage drive belt
Color ink-cartridge clamp
Settings display
Black ink-cartridge clamp
Settings control panel
Power button
Output tray
PC card adapter
Output tray extension
Ink-cartridge replacement button
Roll paper manipulation button
Maintenance button

OVERHEAD VIEW WITH OUTER CASING REMOVED

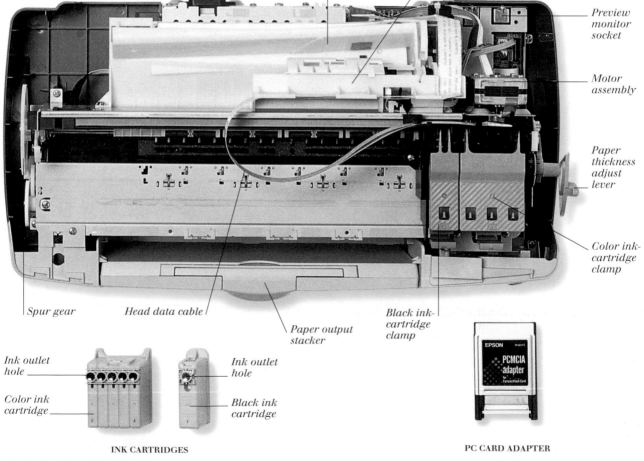

Paper hopper
Head data cable support
Preview monitor socket
Motor assembly
Paper thickness adjust lever
Color ink-cartridge clamp
Spur gear
Head data cable
Paper output stacker
Black ink-cartridge clamp

Ink outlet hole
Ink outlet hole
Color ink cartridge
Black ink cartridge

INK CARTRIDGES

EPSON Insert ▲
PCMCIA adapter
for CompactFlash Card

PC CARD ADAPTER

PAPER FEED COMPONENTS

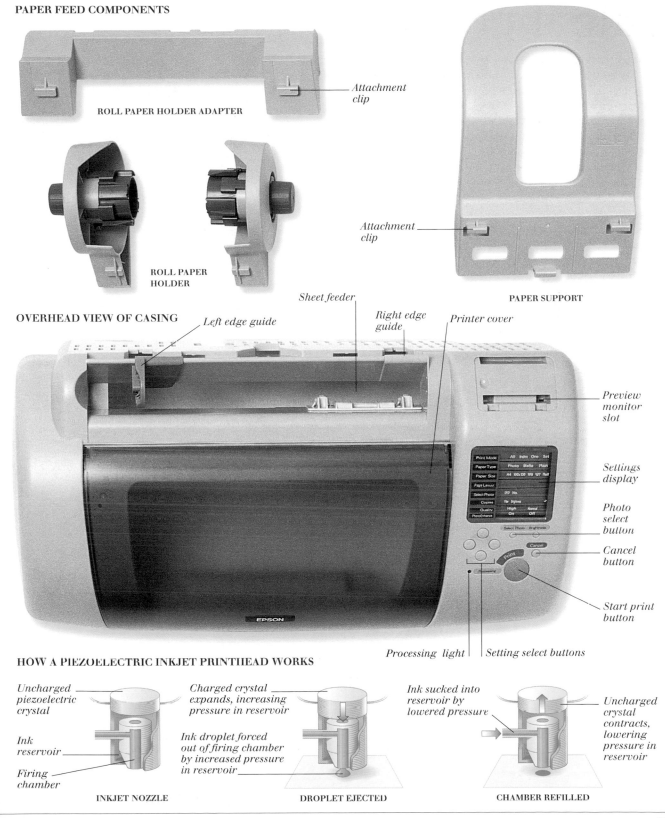

Attachment clip

ROLL PAPER HOLDER ADAPTER

ROLL PAPER HOLDER

Attachment clip

PAPER SUPPORT

Sheet feeder

Right edge guide

Printer cover

OVERHEAD VIEW OF CASING

Left edge guide

Preview monitor slot

Settings display

Photo select button

Cancel button

Start print button

Processing light

Setting select buttons

EPSON

HOW A PIEZOELECTRIC INKJET PRINTHEAD WORKS

Uncharged piezoelectric crystal

Ink reservoir

Firing chamber

Charged crystal expands, increasing pressure in reservoir

Ink droplet forced out of firing chamber by increased pressure in reservoir

Ink sucked into reservoir by lowered pressure

Uncharged crystal contracts, lowering pressure in reservoir

INKJET NOZZLE

DROPLET EJECTED

CHAMBER REFILLED

The internet

THE INTERNET CONSISTS OF TENS of thousands of computer networks linked together to form one huge, global network, allowing any computer on one network to communicate with any computer on another. The two main services used on the internet are email and the World Wide Web. Email allows text messages to be sent—along with attached computer files, images, or video clips, for example— to other computers on the internet. The web consists of billions of pages made up of digital files that are stored on computers across the world and can be viewed using a Web browser. The web also provides interactive access to various services, such as banking and shopping.

Recipient's ISP receives message and stores it until retrieved by the recipient

Sender's internet service provider (ISP) directs message into the internet

Server guides message to its intended destination

Telephone line

HOW EMAIL WORKS

EMAIL SENDER

Screen displays email program

Modem encodes and sends message via the telephone line

E-MAIL ADDRESS

User name   *Domain name*

anna@merlin.provider.co.uk

Separator   *Country code*

EMAIL PROGRAM

Reply icon   *Reply all icon*   *Forward icon*   *Print icon*   *Send/receive icon*   *Find icon*

File menu   *New mail icon*   *View selector panel*   *Inbox icon*   *Outbox icon*   *Sent items icon*   *Deleted items icon*   *Drafts icon*

Toolbar   *Addresses icon*   *Delete icon*   *Message list*   *Preview panel*

Inbox - Outlook Express - Main Identity

File   Edit   View   Tools   Message   Help

New Mail   Reply   Reply All   Forward   Print   Delete   Send/Recv   Addresses   Find

Views: Show All Messages

Inbox   Main Identity

Folders
Outlook Express
 Local Folders
  Inbox
  Outbox
  Sent Items
  Deleted Items
  Drafts
 msnnews.msn.com
 netnews.msn.com

! 0 ? From   Subject
Microsoft Outlook Express   Welcome to Outlook Express 5

Contacts ▼
rebecca
richard
tim
siblings

From: Microsoft Outlook Express Team   To: New Outlook Express User
Subject: Welcome to Outlook Express 5

Outlook Express The solution for all your messaging needs

Featuring
• E-mail and Newsgroups
• Multiple accounts and Identities
• HTML message support
• Address Book and directory services
• Offline synchronization

msn Hotmail™
Tired of sharing your email account with others in your household? Get a free Hotmail account! Then read your mail from any place on earth.

1 message(s), 0 unread   Working Offline

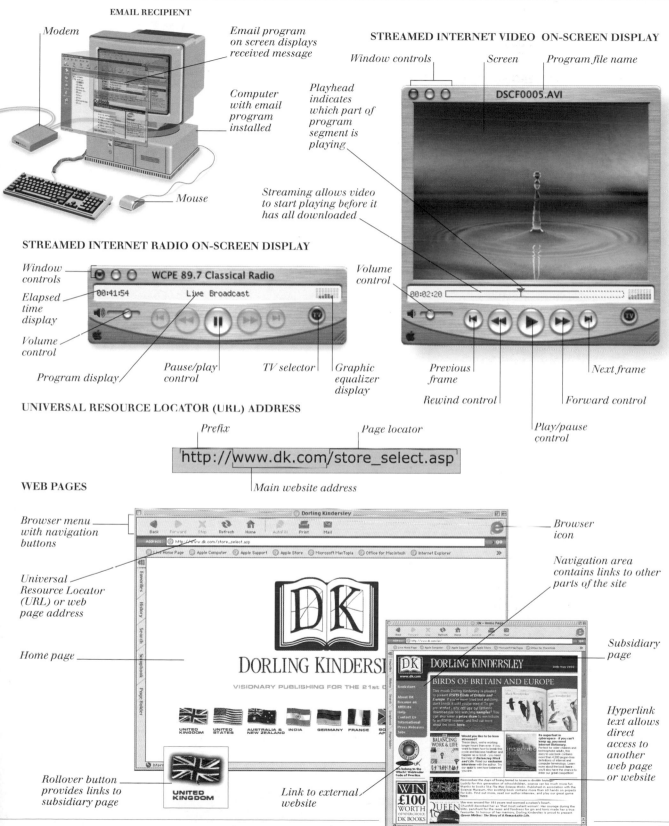

EMAIL RECIPIENT

Modem

Email program on screen displays received message

Computer with email program installed

Mouse

STREAMED INTERNET VIDEO ON-SCREEN DISPLAY

Window controls

Screen

Program file name

DSCF0005.AVI

Playhead indicates which part of program segment is playing

Streaming allows video to start playing before it has all downloaded

00:02:20

Volume control

Previous frame

Next frame

Rewind control

Forward control

Play/pause control

STREAMED INTERNET RADIO ON-SCREEN DISPLAY

Window controls

WCPE 89.7 Classical Radio

Elapsed time display

00:41:54

Live Broadcast

Volume control

Program display

Pause/play control

TV selector

Graphic equalizer display

UNIVERSAL RESOURCE LOCATOR (URL) ADDRESS

Prefix

Page locator

http://www.dk.com/store_select.asp

Main website address

WEB PAGES

Browser menu with navigation buttons

Browser icon

Universal Resource Locator (URL) or web page address

Navigation area contains links to other parts of the site

Home page

Subsidiary page

DORLING KINDERSLEY

VISIONARY PUBLISHING FOR THE 21st C

UNITED KINGDOM
UNITED STATES
AUSTRALIA & NEW ZEALAND
INDIA
GERMANY
FRANCE

BIRDS OF BRITAIN AND EUROPE

Hyperlink text allows direct access to another web page or website

Rollover button provides links to subsidiary page

UNITED KINGDOM

Link to external website

Electronic games

VIDEO GAMES HAVE BEEN around since the early 1970s. They are played on PCs, arcade machines, home consoles, and portable handheld players. All these types of players have certain components in common. They need devices such as joysticks and control pads with buttons for controlling on-screen movement and action. The game itself is stored in the form of digital information on CD, DVD or microchip—which may be integral or stored in a removable cartridge—or on an internal hard disk. A central processing unit (CPU) (see pp. 566-567) is needed to process commands from the player, while specialized graphics chips are used to process the complex mapping and texturing functions that make modern games appear so realistic.

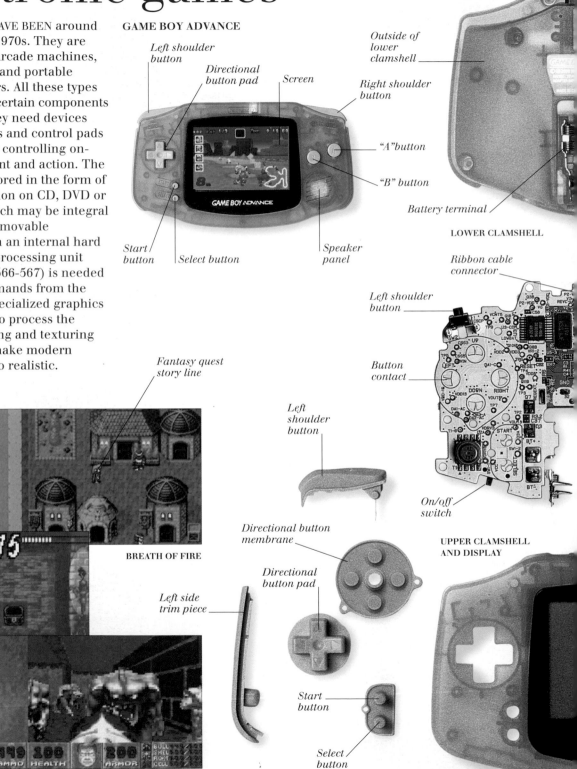

GAME BOY ADVANCE

Left shoulder button

Directional button pad

Screen

Start button

Select button

Speaker panel

Outside of lower clamshell

Right shoulder button

"A" button

"B" button

Battery terminal

LOWER CLAMSHELL

Ribbon cable connector

Left shoulder button

Button contact

On/off switch

UPPER CLAMSHELL AND DISPLAY

GAME BOY ADVANCE GAMES

High-resolution color graphics

Fantasy quest story line

BREATH OF FIRE

Left shoulder button

Directional button membrane

Directional button pad

Left side trim piece

Start button

Select button

WARIO LAND 4

Score panel

DOOM

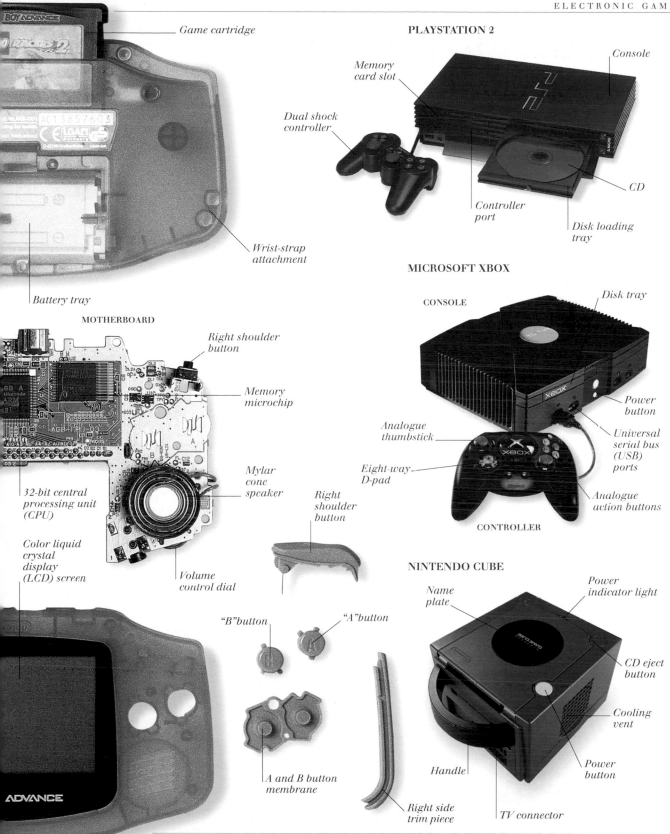

Game cartridge

PLAYSTATION 2

Memory card slot

Console

Dual shock controller

Controller port

CD

Disk loading tray

Wrist-strap attachment

Battery tray

MOTHERBOARD

Right shoulder button

Memory microchip

MICROSOFT XBOX

Disk tray

CONSOLE

Power button

Analogue thumbstick

Universal serial bus (USB) ports

Eight-way D-pad

Analogue action buttons

CONTROLLER

32-bit central processing unit (CPU)

Mylar cone speaker

Right shoulder button

Color liquid crystal display (LCD) screen

Volume control dial

NINTENDO CUBE

Power indicator light

Name plate

"B"button

"A"button

CD eject button

Cooling vent

"A" and B button membrane

Handle

Power button

Right side trim piece

TV connector

ADVANCE

Digital camera

FOR MORE THAN 200 YEARS, CAMERAS recorded pictures as chemical changes in silver-containing substances, on a strip of flexible, celluloid film. The digital camera records pictures in electronic form. At its heart is a specialized integrated circuit known as a charge-coupled device (CCD). This has millions of microunits known as pixels. It works in the opposite way to a miniature computer or TV screen. Instead of electric signals making pixels shine, when light hits a pixel it generates a tiny electrical signal, according to the light's color and brightness. The signals from the CCD's millions of pixels are analogue: they vary continuously in a wavelike fashion. They are converted by a microchip to digital codes of numbers, represented as on-off electronic pulses. The digital signals are processed and fed both to the in-camera memory chip, which holds a temporary version, and the memory stick, which can be removed to download its contents into a computer or television. The rest of the camera is similar to the traditional design.

FRONT VIEW OF SONY CYBER-SHOT DSC-P1 DIGITAL CAMERA

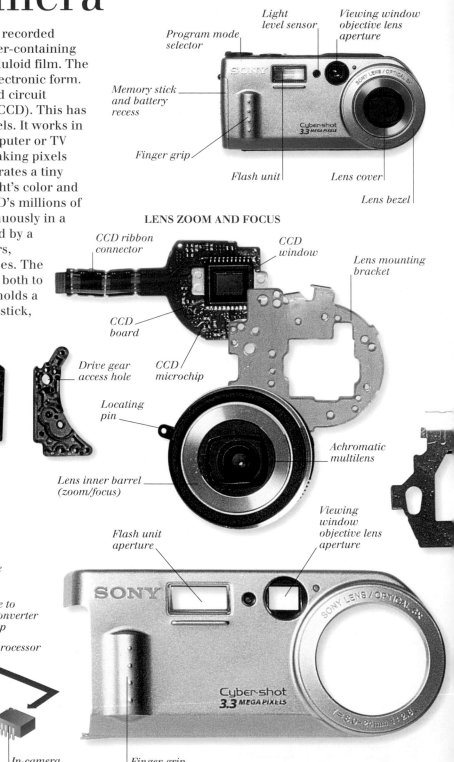

Light level sensor

Viewing window objective lens aperture

Program mode selector

Memory stick and battery recess

Finger grip

Flash unit

Lens cover

Lens bezel

LENS ZOOM AND FOCUS

CCD ribbon connector

CCD window

Lens mounting bracket

CCD board

CCD microchip

Drive gear access hole

Locating pin

Achromatic multilens

Lens inner barrel (zoom/focus)

Flash unit aperture

Viewing window objective lens aperture

Zoom motor

Drive pin

HOW A DIGITAL CAMERA WORKS

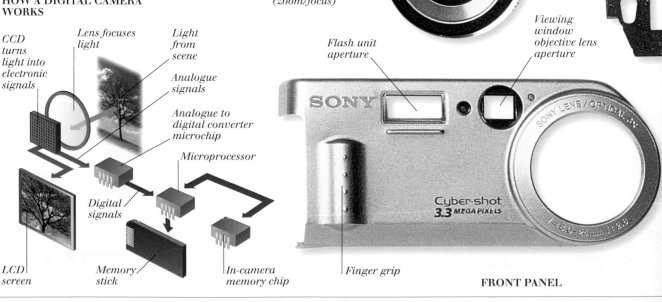

CCD turns light into electronic signals

Lens focuses light

Light from scene

Analogue signals

Analogue to digital converter microchip

Microprocessor

Digital signals

LCD screen

Memory stick

In-camera memory chip

Finger grip

FRONT PANEL

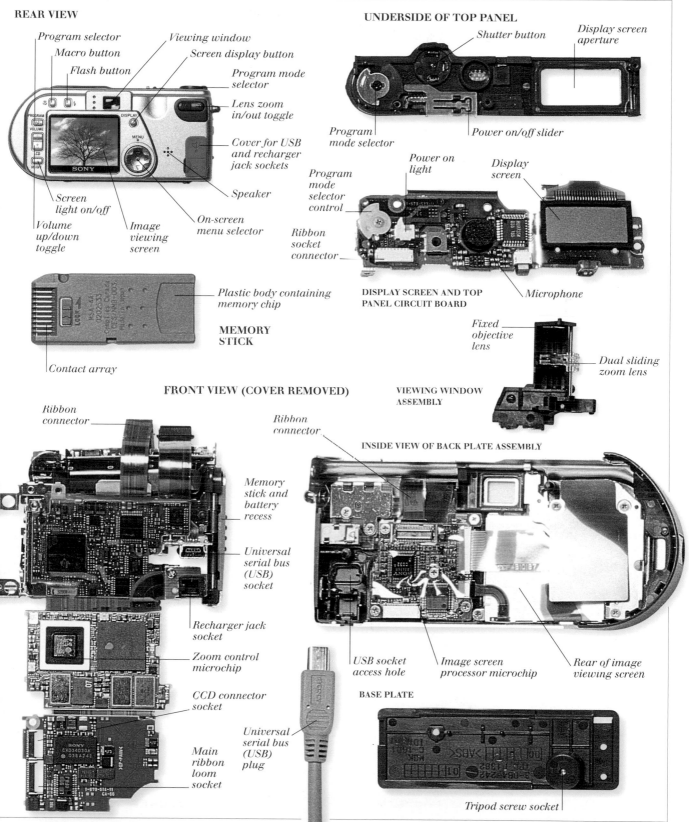

REAR VIEW

Program selector

Macro button

Flash button

Viewing window

Screen display button

Program mode selector

Lens zoom in/out toggle

Cover for USB and recharger jack sockets

Speaker

On-screen menu selector

Image viewing screen

Volume up/down toggle

Screen light on/off

UNDERSIDE OF TOP PANEL

Shutter button

Display screen aperture

Program mode selector

Power on/off slider

Power on light

Display screen

Program mode selector control

Ribbon socket connector

Microphone

DISPLAY SCREEN AND TOP PANEL CIRCUIT BOARD

Plastic body containing memory chip

MEMORY STICK

Contact array

Fixed objective lens

Dual sliding zoom lens

VIEWING WINDOW ASSEMBLY

FRONT VIEW (COVER REMOVED)

Ribbon connector

Ribbon connector

Memory stick and battery recess

Universal serial bus (USB) socket

Recharger jack socket

Zoom control microchip

CCD connector socket

Main ribbon loom socket

Universal serial bus (USB) plug

INSIDE VIEW OF BACK PLATE ASSEMBLY

USB socket access hole

Image screen processor microchip

Rear of image viewing screen

BASE PLATE

Tripod screw socket

581

Digital video camera

A VIDEO CAMERA, OR CAMCORDER, records a scene as
a sequence of 25 still images per second, along with
sound. It comprises a camera to capture light from
the scene, a viewfinder through which the scene may
be viewed, a screen on which the recorded scene
may be viewed, charge-coupled devices (CCDs) to
convert the visual data into an electric signal, and
a means of storing the signal. Digital video cameras
convert the signal into digital form—a series of
separate measurements of the initial analogue
(continuously varying) signal. They record the digital
signal on tape, hard disk, or DVD. Digital recordings
can be copied accurately, whereas analogue
recordings tend to "fade" with each copy.

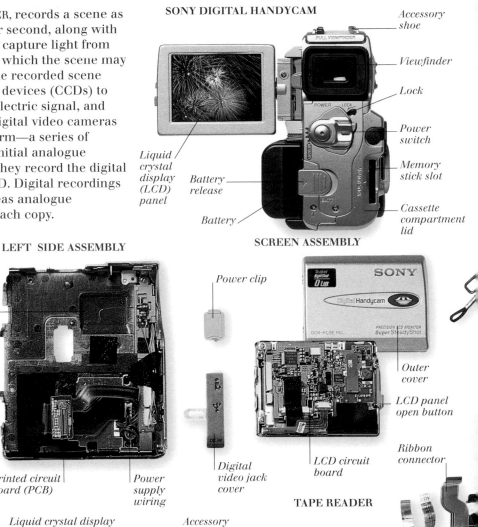

SONY DIGITAL HANDYCAM

Accessory shoe

Viewfinder

Lock

Power switch

Memory stick slot

Cassette compartment lid

Liquid crystal display (LCD) panel

Battery release

Battery

SCREEN ASSEMBLY

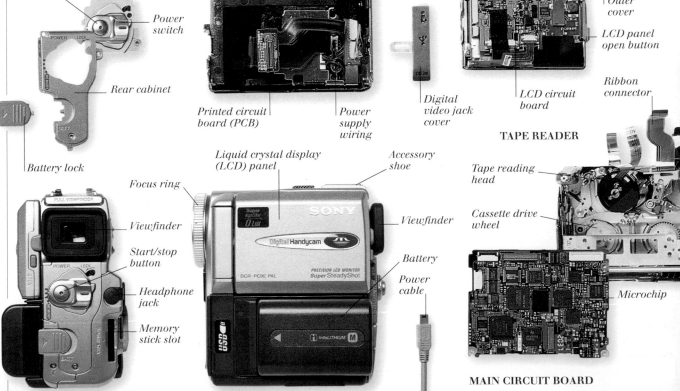

REAR ASSEMBLY

Ribbon connector

LEFT SIDE ASSEMBLY

Underside of touch panel

Power clip

Start/stop button

Power switch

Rear cabinet

Battery lock

Printed circuit board (PCB)

Power supply wiring

Digital video jack cover

Outer cover

LCD panel open button

LCD circuit board

Ribbon connector

TAPE READER

Focus ring

Liquid crystal display (LCD) panel

Accessory shoe

Tape reading head

Cassette drive wheel

Viewfinder

Start/stop button

Viewfinder

Headphone jack

Battery

Power cable

Microchip

Memory stick slot

MAIN CIRCUIT BOARD

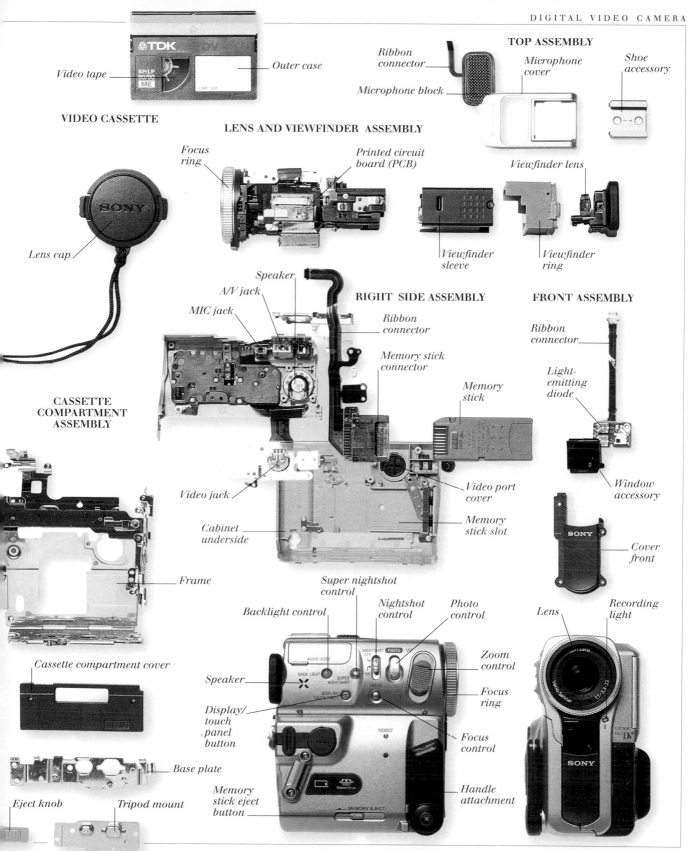

VIDEO CASSETTE

Video tape

Outer case

TOP ASSEMBLY

Ribbon connector

Microphone block

Microphone cover

Shoe accessory

LENS AND VIEWFINDER ASSEMBLY

Focus ring

Printed circuit board (PCB)

Viewfinder lens

Viewfinder sleeve

Viewfinder ring

Lens cap

RIGHT SIDE ASSEMBLY

Speaker

A/V jack

MIC jack

Ribbon connector

Memory stick connector

Memory stick

FRONT ASSEMBLY

Ribbon connector

Light-emitting diode

Window accessory

CASSETTE COMPARTMENT ASSEMBLY

Video jack

Cabinet underside

Video port cover

Memory stick slot

Cover front

Frame

Super nightshot control

Backlight control

Nightshot control

Photo control

Lens

Recording light

Speaker

Zoom control

Focus ring

Cassette compartment cover

Display/touch panel button

Focus control

Base plate

Eject knob

Tripod mount

Memory stick eject button

Handle attachment

583

Home theater

HOME THEATER REPLICATES a real movie theater with visuals from a plasma wide-screen, and acoustics from strategically placed loudspeakers that give the viewer/listener the sense of being surrounded by sound. The source for sound and vision is a DVD (Digital Versatile Disc). Its player uses standard CD (Compact Disc) digital technology, but with a higher density of laser-read microscopic pits—more than 20 billion such pits in multilevel spiral tracks that, stretched out, would extend for about 25 miles. It is hard for the human ear to discern the direction of low-pitched sounds, so these emanate from a central bass speaker, often built into or below the screen unit. The direction of high-pitched sounds, like people screaming and tires squealing, is easier to detect. Mid- and high-frequency speakers are positioned around the viewer, so these sounds fit the location of the action. Plasma screens use fluorescent tube ("strip-light") technology. Tiny three-cell pixels, each about one millimeter across, contain red, green and blue phosphor chemicals and a gas mix. Where electric pulses coincide for a split second in the crisscross matrix of wire electrodes, the gas energizes and emits ultraviolet light, which in turn makes the phosphor glow.

SPEAKER UNITS

Small cabinet for discrete mounting on stand or shelf

Large, heavy cabinet emphasizes deep-pitched sounds

Bass ports emit vibrating air of low-frequency sound waves

Acoustically transparent covering allows all sounds to pass through

TWEETER (MID AND HIGH NOTES)　　WOOFER (DEEP NOTES)

HOW SURROUND SOUND WORKS

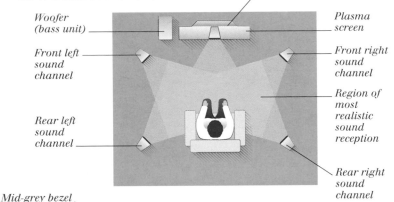

DVD player under screen

Woofer (bass unit)

Plasma screen

Front left sound channel

Front right sound channel

Region of most realistic sound reception

Rear left sound channel

Rear right sound channel

WIDE-SCREEN PLASMA DISPLAY

Mid-grey bezel

Antishock swivel base

16:9 (width:height) screen proportions fit human field of vision

HOW A PLASMA SCREEN WORKS

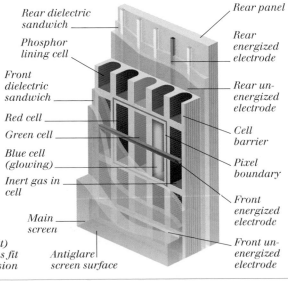

Rear dielectric sandwich

Rear panel

Phosphor lining cell

Rear energized electrode

Front dielectric sandwich

Rear un-energized electrode

Red cell

Green cell

Cell barrier

Blue cell (glowing)

Pixel boundary

Inert gas in cell

Main screen

Front energized electrode

Antiglare screen surface

Front un-energized electrode

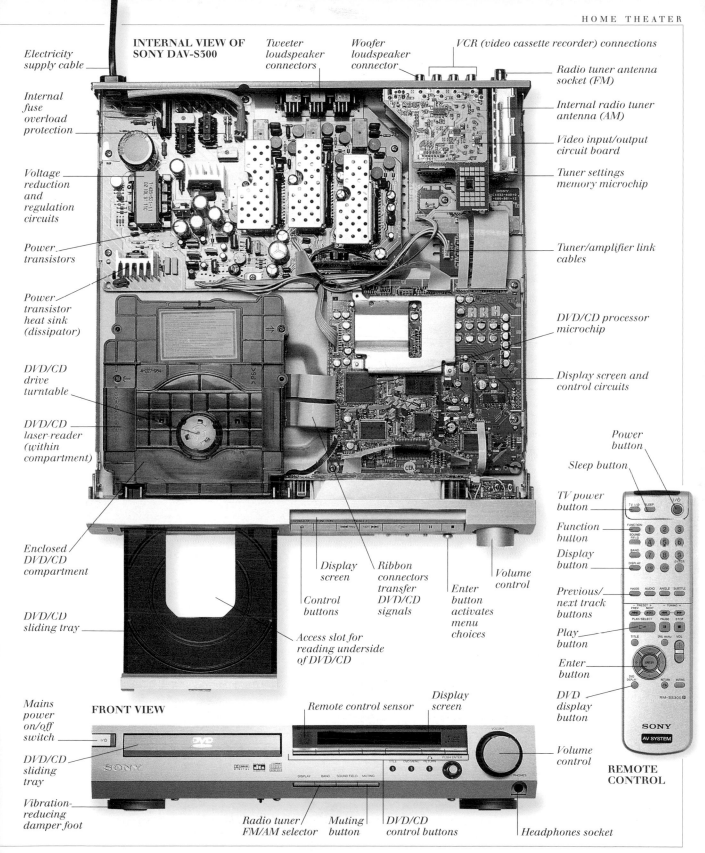

INTERNAL VIEW OF SONY DAV-S300

Electricity supply cable

Internal fuse overload protection

Voltage reduction and regulation circuits

Power transistors

Power transistor heat sink (dissipator)

DVD/CD drive turntable

DVD/CD laser-reader (within compartment)

Enclosed DVD/CD compartment

DVD/CD sliding tray

Tweeter loudspeaker connectors

Woofer loudspeaker connector

VCR (video cassette recorder) connections

Radio tuner antenna socket (FM)

Internal radio tuner antenna (AM)

Video input/output circuit board

Tuner settings memory microchip

Tuner/amplifier link cables

DVD/CD processor microchip

Display screen and control circuits

Display screen

Ribbon connectors transfer DVD/CD signals

Control buttons

Enter button activates menu choices

Volume control

Access slot for reading underside of DVD/CD

FRONT VIEW

Mains power on/off switch

DVD/CD sliding tray

Vibration-reducing damper foot

Radio tuner FM/AM selector

Muting button

Remote control sensor

Display screen

DVD/CD control buttons

Volume control

Headphones socket

Power button

Sleep button

TV power button

Function button

Display button

Previous/next track buttons

Play button

Enter button

DVD display button

Volume control

REMOTE CONTROL

585

Personal music

THE FIRST SOURCE OF SOUND and music small and light enough to carry, and functioning without external electricity, was the transistor radio of the 1950s. In the 1970s, the magnetic audio cassette tape allowed recorded music to be played via portable tape players such as Sony's *Walkman*. Also, new metal alloys permitted the tiny but high-power magnets needed for lightweight earphones. In the mid 1980s optical CDs (compact discs) brought recorded sound into the digital era. Sony's MD or minidisc introduced rerecordable CDs combining magnetic and optical technology. From the mid 1990s music could be stored in all-electronic digital form in a memory "chip," usually in the file format called MP3. These files can be sent to and from computers and via the internet.

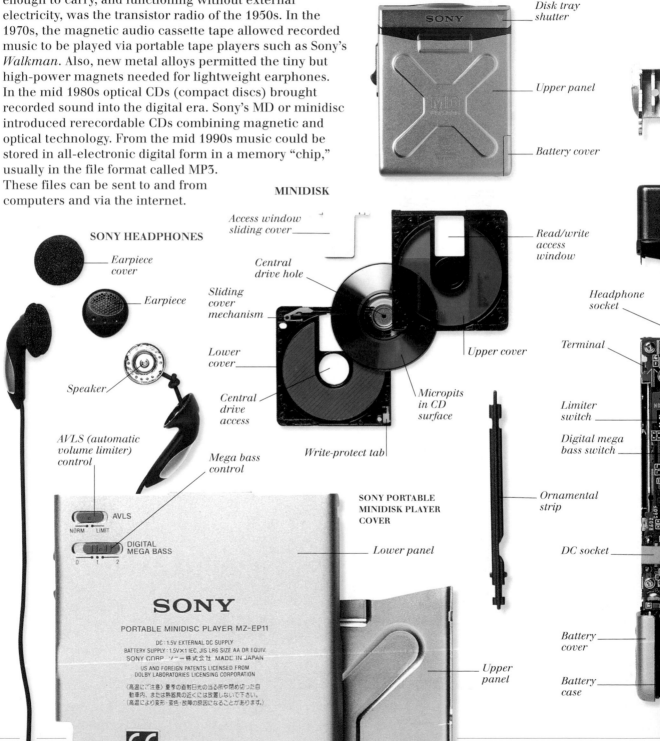

SONY PORTABLE MINIDISK PLAYER MZ-EP11

Disk tray shutter

Upper panel

Battery cover

MINIDISK

Access window sliding cover

Read/write access window

Central drive hole

Headphone socket

Sliding cover mechanism

SONY HEADPHONES

Earpiece cover

Earpiece

Speaker

Lower cover

Upper cover

Terminal

Micropits in CD surface

Limiter switch

Central drive access

Digital mega bass switch

AVLS (automatic volume limiter) control

Mega bass control

Write-protect tab

Ornamental strip

AVLS

NORM   LIMIT

DIGITAL MEGA BASS

0   1   2

SONY PORTABLE MINIDISK PLAYER COVER

Lower panel

DC socket

SONY

PORTABLE MINIDISC PLAYER MZ-EP11

DC : 1.5V EXTERNAL DC SUPPLY
BATTERY SUPPLY: 1.5V×1 IEC, JIS LR6 SIZE AA OR EQUIV.
SONY CORP. ソニー株式会社 MADE IN JAPAN
US AND FOREIGN PATENTS LICENSED FROM
DOLBY LABORATORIES LICENSING CORPORATION

〈高温にご注意〉夏季の直射日光の当る所や閉め切った自
動車内、または熱器具の近くには放置しないで下さい。
〈高温により変形・変色・故障の原因となることがあります。〉

Upper panel

Battery cover

Battery case

CE

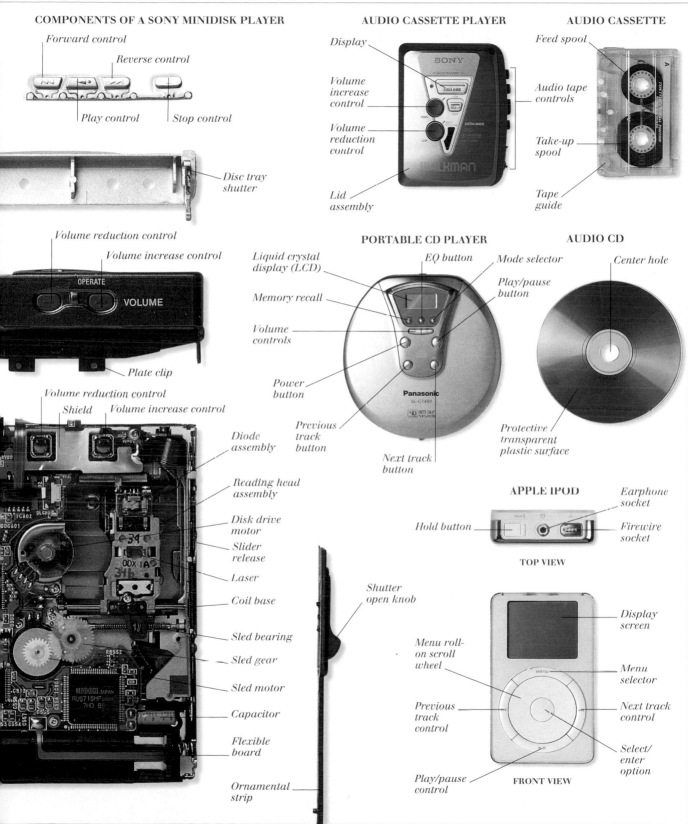

COMPONENTS OF A SONY MINIDISK PLAYER

Forward control

Reverse control

Play control

Stop control

Disc tray shutter

Volume reduction control

Volume increase control

OPERATE

VOLUME

Plate clip

Volume reduction control

Shield

Volume increase control

Diode assembly

Reading head assembly

Disk drive motor

Slider release

Laser

Coil base

Sled bearing

Sled gear

Sled motor

Capacitor

Flexible board

Ornamental strip

Shutter open knob

AUDIO CASSETTE PLAYER

Display

Volume increase control

Volume reduction control

Lid assembly

SONY

MEGA BASS

HIGH

LOW

WALKMAN

AUDIO CASSETTE

Feed spool

Audio tape controls

Take-up spool

Tape guide

PORTABLE CD PLAYER

Liquid crystal display (LCD)

EQ button

Mode selector

Play/pause button

Memory recall

Volume controls

Power button

Previous track button

Next track button

Panasonic

SL-CT480

40 ANTI-SKIP SYSTEM

AUDIO CD

Center hole

Protective transparent plastic surface

APPLE IPOD

Earphone socket

Hold button

Firewire socket

TOP VIEW

Display screen

Menu roll-on scroll wheel

menu

Menu selector

Previous track control

Next track control

Play/pause control

Select/ enter option

FRONT VIEW

Cell phone

UP TO THE EARLY 1990S THE CELL PHONE was a rare luxury, but since the late 1990s, it has outsold almost every other electrical gadget—as a professional tool, domestic convenience, and even a fashion accessory. The typical cell phone has also shrunk in size, due to improvements in rechargeable batteries, which now store more electricity for longer in a smaller package, and to smaller, more efficient electronics that use less electricity. A cell phone is basically a low-power radio receiver-transmitter, plus a tiny microphone to convert sounds into electrical signals, and a small speaker that does the reverse. A liquid crystal display (LCD) shows numbers, letters, and symbols. Newer models have a larger screen for more complex images in color, and some incorporate other functions such as internet access, radio, and an audio player. When the cell phone is activated, it sends out a radio pulse that is answered by nearby mast transmitter-receivers. The phone locks onto the clearest signal and uses this while within range (the range of each transmitter is known as a cell). The phone continuously monitors signal strength and switches to an alternative transmitter when necessary.

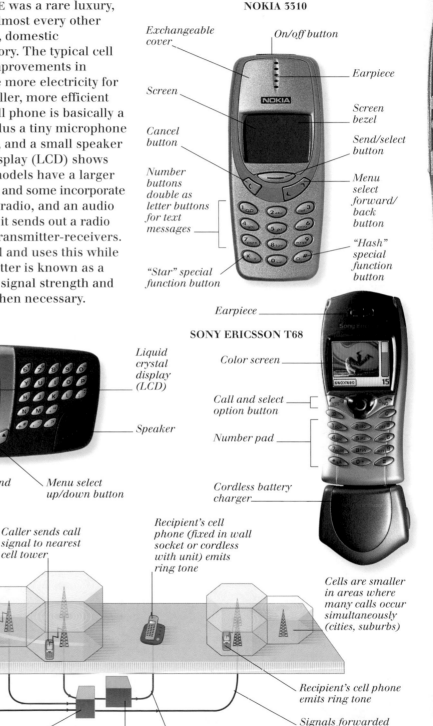

NOKIA 3310

Exchangeable cover

On/off button

Screen

Earpiece

Screen bezel

Cancel button

Send/select button

Number buttons double as letter buttons for text messages

Menu select forward/back button

"Star" special function button

"Hash" special function button

NOKIA 5510

Upper number pad

Letter keys

Special function buttons

Liquid crystal display (LCD)

Speaker

Screen surround

Power button

Call-send button

Menu select up/down button

SONY ERICSSON T68

Earpiece

Color screen

Call and select option button

Number pad

Cordless battery charger

HOW A CELL PHONE WORKS

Phone locks onto signals from local mast within home cell

Phone out of signal range – no reception

Activated phone auto-switches to signals from next cell as it moves across cell boundary

Caller sends call signal to nearest cell tower

Recipient's cell phone (fixed in wall socket or cordless with unit) emits ring tone

Cells are smaller in areas where many calls occur simultaneously (cities, suburbs)

Landlines (or tower-to-tower links) carry phone signals to local exchange

Local mobile phone network exchange

Main telephone network exchange

Signals forwarded to non-cell phone

Recipient's cell phone emits ring tone

Signals forwarded to relevant cell for transmission

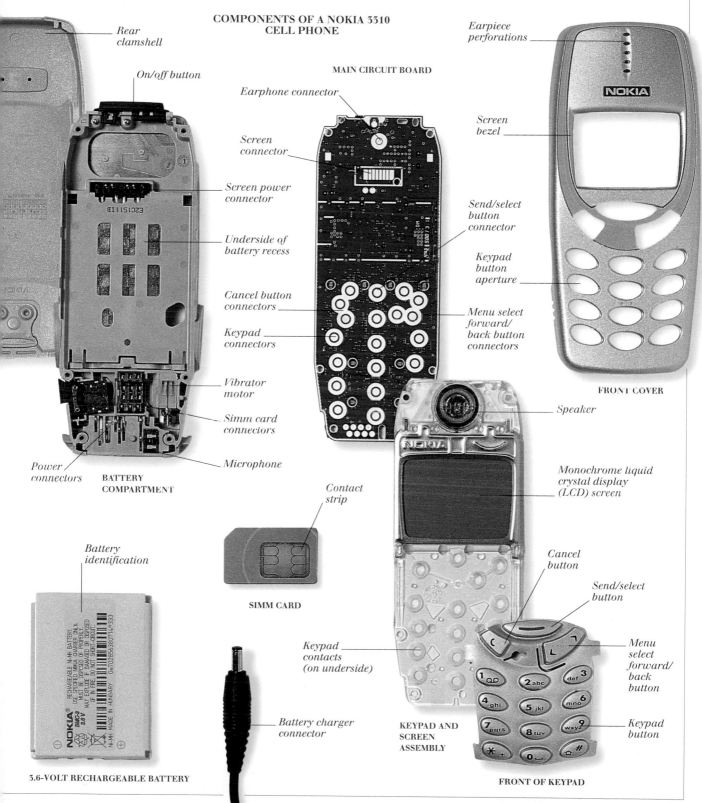

COMPONENTS OF A NOKIA 3310 CELL PHONE

Rear clamshell

On/off button

MAIN CIRCUIT BOARD

Earphone connector

Screen connector

Screen power connector

Underside of battery recess

Cancel button connectors

Keypad connectors

Vibrator motor

Simm card connectors

Power connectors

BATTERY COMPARTMENT

Microphone

Earpiece perforations

Screen bezel

Send/select button connector

Keypad button aperture

Menu select forward/ back button connectors

FRONT COVER

Speaker

Monochrome liquid crystal display (LCD) screen

Cancel button

Send/select button

Menu select forward/ back button

Keypad button

Battery identification

Contact strip

SIMM CARD

Keypad contacts (on underside)

Battery charger connector

KEYPAD AND SCREEN ASSEMBLY

FRONT OF KEYPAD

3.6-VOLT RECHARGEABLE BATTERY

Global positioning system

THE GLOBAL POSITIONING SYSTEM (GPS) is a network of 24 navigation satellites orbiting the Earth that people can use to pinpoint their position. The satellites orbit at a height of 12,500 miles (20,000 kilometers). A GPS receiver picks up signals from any of these satellites that are above the horizon. It uses information in each signal to work out how far away it is from the satellite. It can calculate its position on the Earth's surface when it has information from at least three satellites. A basic GPS receiver shows the latitude and longitude of its position on its screen. A more advanced receiver shows the position on a digital map. Some receivers display extra information, such the distance that has been traveled and the average speed of the vehicle in which the receiver is installed.

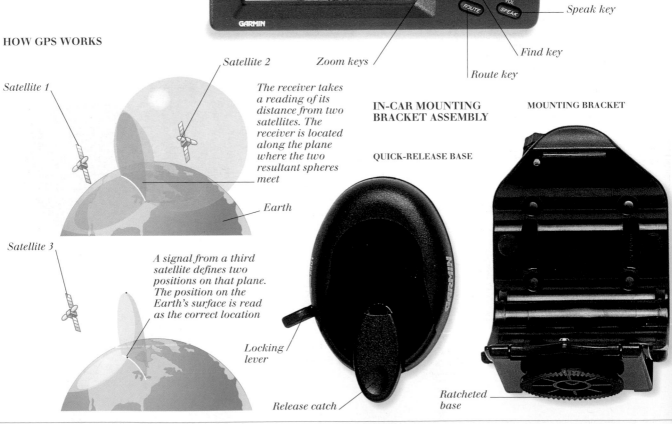

Cigarette lighter adapter and speaker cable

Antenna

GARMIN STREET PILOT III GPS

Page key

On/off and screen control button

Enter key

Quit key

Rocker pad

Menu key

Speak key

Liquid crystal display (LCD) screen

Find key

Route key

Zoom keys

StreetPilot III GPS

ColorMap

Point of Interest

Mountbatten Exhibition N 50°59.220'
2.2%   282°   W001°29.705'

GARMIN

HOW GPS WORKS

Satellite 1

Satellite 2

The receiver takes a reading of its distance from two satellites. The receiver is located along the plane where the two resultant spheres meet

Earth

Satellite 3

A signal from a third satellite defines two positions on that plane. The position on the Earth's surface is read as the correct location

IN-CAR MOUNTING BRACKET ASSEMBLY

MOUNTING BRACKET

QUICK-RELEASE BASE

Locking lever

Release catch

Ratcheted base

GARMIN GPS V

Speaker plug

Power plug

Adjustable antenna

Power backlight key

Rocker keypad

Liquid crystal display (LCD) screen

COMPONENTS OF A GARMIN STREET PILOT III GPS

Data plug

Antenna

Memory battery

Data plug socket

Main printed circuit board (PCB)

Rear case

USB PROGRAMMER ASSEMBLY

Shielded receiver

Data cartridge

Universal serial bus (USB) programmer

Front case

Liquid crystal display (LCD) assembly

Underside of control pad

SPARE FUSES

Vacuum cleaner

IN A CONVENTIONAL VACUUM CLEANER, an electric motor spins a fan that sucks in air carrying dust and debris. The air is forced through tiny pores in a dust bag, trapping most particles. In the 1990s, James Dyson's dual cyclone "bagless" design did away with the dust bag—and the reduced airflow caused by clogging of its pores. An electrically-driven fan creates a partial vacuum within the machine. Air is forced at more than 60 miles per hour past a rotating brush that loosens dirt. The airflow passes along the wand and hose to the outer part of a cylinder-shaped bin. As the air whirls around at 180 miles per hour (like a miniature hurricane or cyclone), centrifugal force flings larger particles outward, to fall to the bin's base. The air then passes through perforations into the cone-shaped, narrower inner bin, where a second cyclone spins even faster, almost 600 miles per hour, flinging off even smaller particles. The now almost-clean air exits via two microporous filters.

Wand handle and brushbar controls

Upper wand

Lower wand

Motorized brushbar floor tool

DYSON DC05 MOTORHEAD

CYCLONE ASSEMBLY

Air intake from hose

Air exit to bin/cyclone cover

Hose electricity connector

Inner cyclone cone

Hose slider

WASHABLE PRE-MOTOR FILTER

Microporous filter

Bin upper seal seating

Perforated shroud

Bin handle clip

Hose slider seating

Hose electricity supply

Post-motor micropore filter

Central retaining screw

Filter rim casing

DUST COLLECTION BIN

Inner bin fin

Bin upper seal

Bin base

Bin lower seal

Bin handle

Inner bin dust collection area

Polycarbonate plastic bin body

Bin cover retaining clip

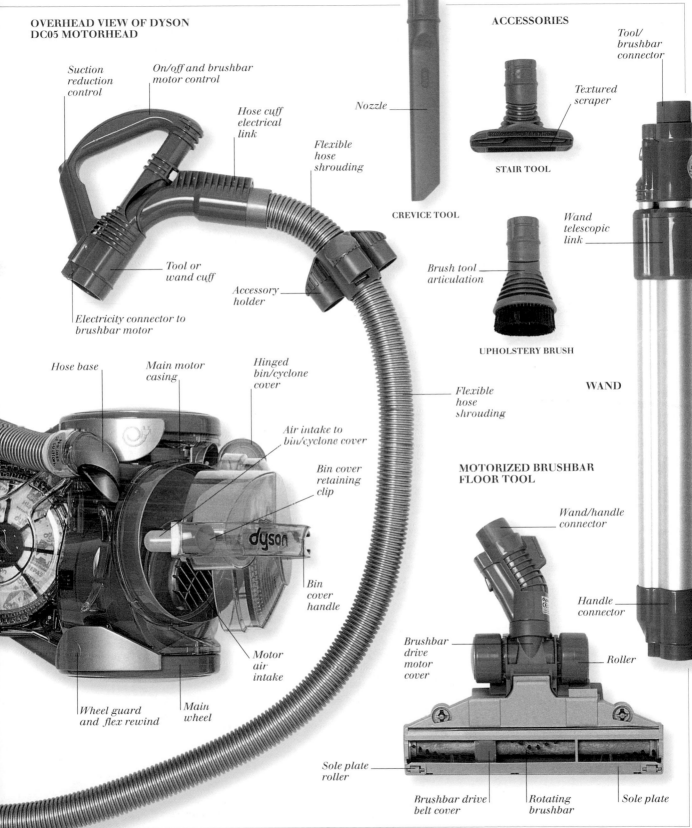

OVERHEAD VIEW OF DYSON DC05 MOTORHEAD

Suction reduction control

On/off and brushbar motor control

Hose cuff electrical link

Flexible hose shrouding

Tool or wand cuff

Accessory holder

Electricity connector to brushbar motor

Hose base

Main motor casing

Hinged bin/cyclone cover

Air intake to bin/cyclone cover

Bin cover retaining clip

dyson

Bin cover handle

Motor air intake

Wheel guard and flex rewind

Main wheel

ACCESSORIES

Nozzle

CREVICE TOOL

Textured scraper

STAIR TOOL

Tool/ brushbar connector

Wand telescopic link

WAND

Brush tool articulation

UPHOLSTERY BRUSH

Flexible hose shrouding

MOTORIZED BRUSHBAR FLOOR TOOL

Wand/handle connector

Handle connector

Roller

Brushbar drive motor cover

Sole plate roller

Brushbar drive belt cover

Rotating brushbar

Sole plate

Iron and washer-dryer

IN THE DAYS BEFORE WASHING MACHINES, laundry was done by hand—washed in a barrel, squeezed in a roller-mangle, hung on a line, and smoothed with an iron heated on the hob or stove. In the 1880s electrically heated irons were one of the first home electrical appliances. Today's iron still applies heat, sometimes moistened with steam, to dampen and flatten garment fibres. Machines with electric heaters and motors took the strain out of washing from the 1910s. Up to the 1960s, three machines were needed to wash, spin, and dry. Now clothes are swirled in a rotating ribbed tub of hot water, then spun fast to throw off most of the water, before slowly tumbling in electrically heated air to dry—all in one appliance.

FRONT VIEW OF A MIELE WASHER-DRYER

Detergent tray

Control panels

Door

Filter access flap

COMPONENTS OF A STEAM IRON

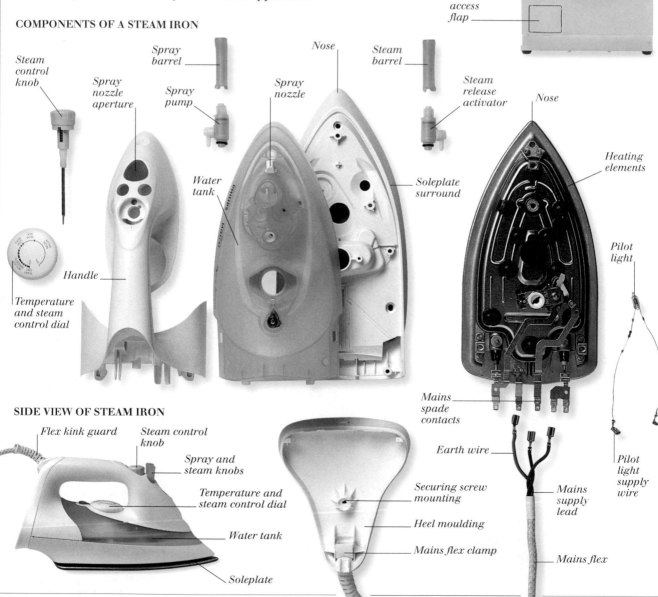

Steam control knob

Spray barrel

Spray nozzle aperture

Spray pump

Spray nozzle

Nose

Steam barrel

Steam release activator

Nose

Heating elements

Water tank

Soleplate surround

Handle

Temperature and steam control dial

Pilot light

Mains spade contacts

Earth wire

Pilot light supply wire

SIDE VIEW OF STEAM IRON

Flex kink guard

Steam control knob

Spray and steam knobs

Temperature and steam control dial

Water tank

Securing screw mounting

Heel moulding

Mains flex clamp

Mains supply lead

Soleplate

Mains flex

COMPONENTS OF A MIELE WASHER-DRYER

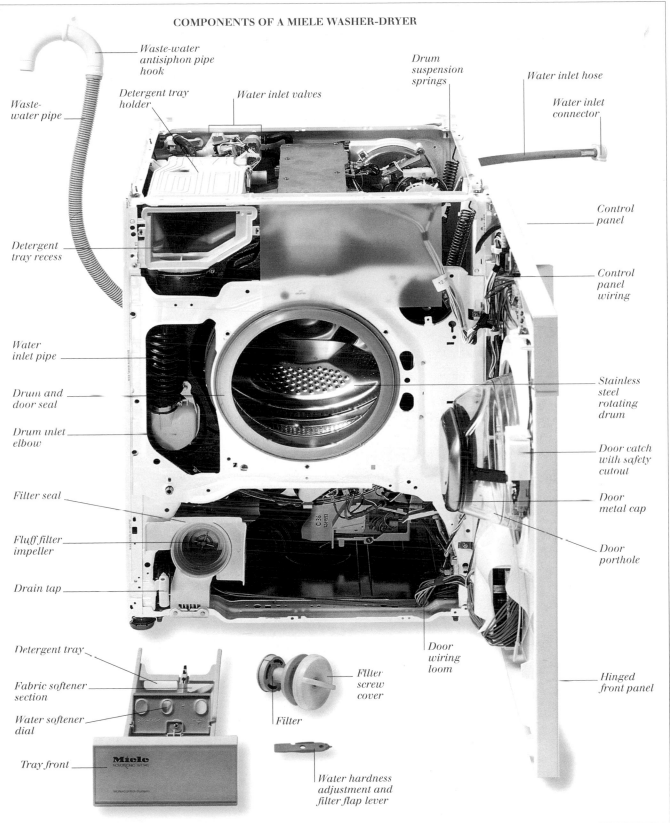

Waste-water antisiphon pipe hook

Detergent tray holder

Water inlet valves

Drum suspension springs

Water inlet hose

Water inlet connector

Waste-water pipe

Detergent tray recess

Control panel

Control panel wiring

Water inlet pipe

Drum and door seal

Drum inlet elbow

Stainless steel rotating drum

Filter seal

Fluff filter impeller

Drain tap

Door catch with safety cutout

Door metal cap

Door porthole

Detergent tray

Fabric softener section

Water softener dial

Tray front

Filter screw cover

Filter

Door wiring loom

Hinged front panel

Water hardness adjustment and filter flap lever

Miele

Microwave combination oven

CONVENTIONAL OVENS use electrically warmed elements or a flame to heat food. In a microwave oven heat energy is created by electromagnetic waves produced by a magnetron and led by waveguides into the oven compartment. These microwaves cannot pass through the compartment's metal casing, being reflected within and spread evenly by a fan. But they do pass through most types of plastic, ceramics, and glass. Therefore platters or containers made from these materials are suitable for use in microwave ovens. A combination oven also has conventional heating elements, to grill and "brown" in the traditional fashion, either alone or in conjunction with microwaves.

MICROWAVE COMBINATION OVEN

Turntable rotator

Door lock

Display screen

Metal cook/grill tray (non-microwave)

Control panel

Rollers

Glass cooking turntable

Metal turntable cover (non-microwave)

Metal grill/griddle (non-microwave)

Under-turntable roller ring (non-microwave)

HOW MICROWAVES HEAT FOOD

Oxygen atom

Hydrogen atom

Each water molecule in food has two hydrogen atoms and one oxygen atom

Water molecules spin with energy from microwaves

Microwaves make water molecules vibrate

Friction from spinning molecules creates heat

SIDE VIEW OF MICROWAVE COMBINATION OVEN

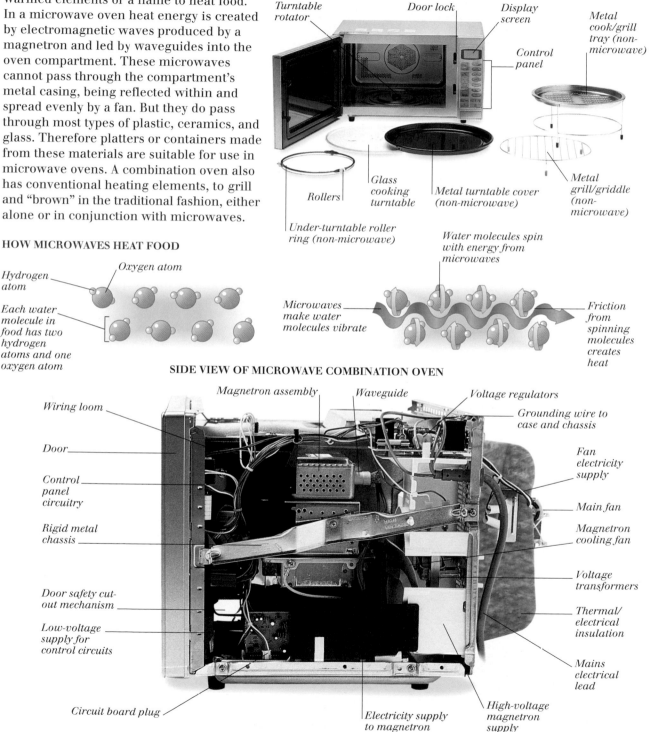

Wiring loom

Magnetron assembly

Waveguide

Voltage regulators

Grounding wire to case and chassis

Door

Control panel circuitry

Rigid metal chassis

Door safety cut-out mechanism

Low-voltage supply for control circuits

Fan electricity supply

Main fan

Magnetron cooling fan

Voltage transformers

Thermal/electrical insulation

Mains electrical lead

Circuit board plug

Electricity supply to magnetron

High-voltage magnetron supply

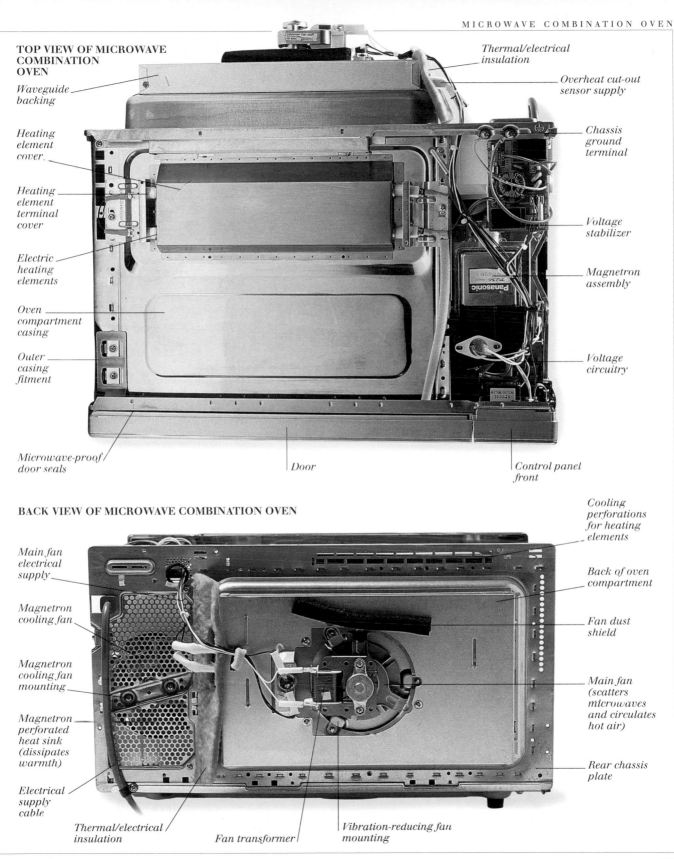

TOP VIEW OF MICROWAVE COMBINATION OVEN

Thermal/electrical insulation

Waveguide backing

Overheat cut-out sensor supply

Heating element cover

Chassis ground terminal

Heating element terminal cover

Electric heating elements

Voltage stabilizer

Oven compartment casing

Magnetron assembly

Outer casing fitment

Voltage circuitry

Microwave-proof door seals

Door

Control panel front

BACK VIEW OF MICROWAVE COMBINATION OVEN

Cooling perforations for heating elements

Main fan electrical supply

Back of oven compartment

Magnetron cooling fan

Fan dust shield

Magnetron cooling fan mounting

Magnetron perforated heat sink (dissipates warmth)

Main fan (scatters microwaves and circulates hot air)

Electrical supply cable

Rear chassis plate

Thermal/electrical insulation

Fan transformer

Vibration-reducing fan mounting

Toaster

MOST ELECTRIC TOASTERS not only grill slices of bread, they also pop them up when ready. While the slices rest on a spring-loaded rack, electric heating elements toast the bread. At the same time, a bimetallic strip heats and expands. One of the two metals in this strip expands more quickly than the other, causing the strip to curve. As it bends, it completes an electrical circuit and activates an electromagnet. The magnet attracts a catch, releasing the spring that holds the rack down in the toaster. The elements switch off, and the toasted slices pop up.

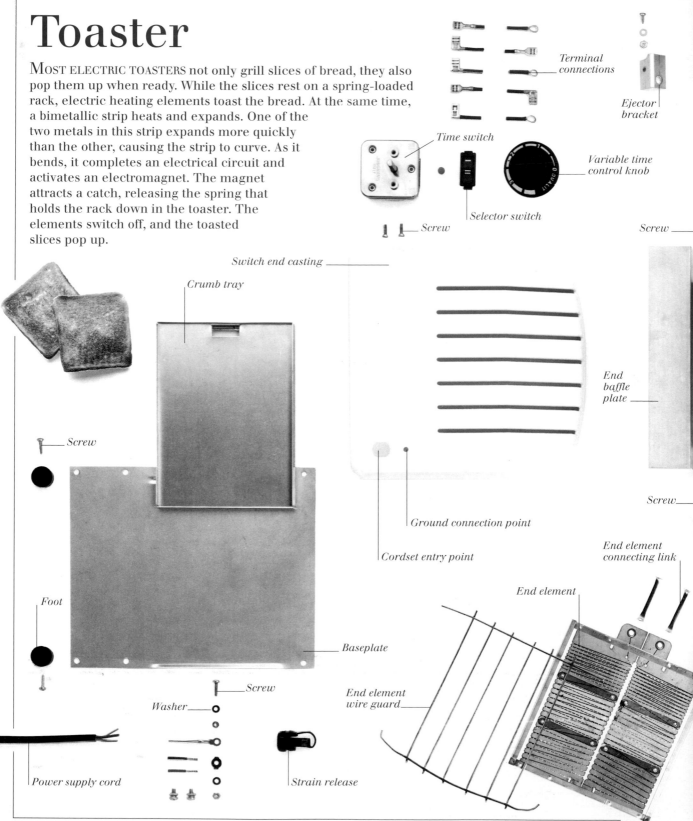

Terminal connections

Ejector bracket

Time switch

Variable time control knob

Selector switch

Screw

Screw

Switch end casting

Crumb tray

End baffle plate

Screw

Screw

Ground connection point

Cordset entry point

End element connecting link

End element

Foot

Baseplate

Power supply cord

Washer

Screw

Strain release

End element wire guard

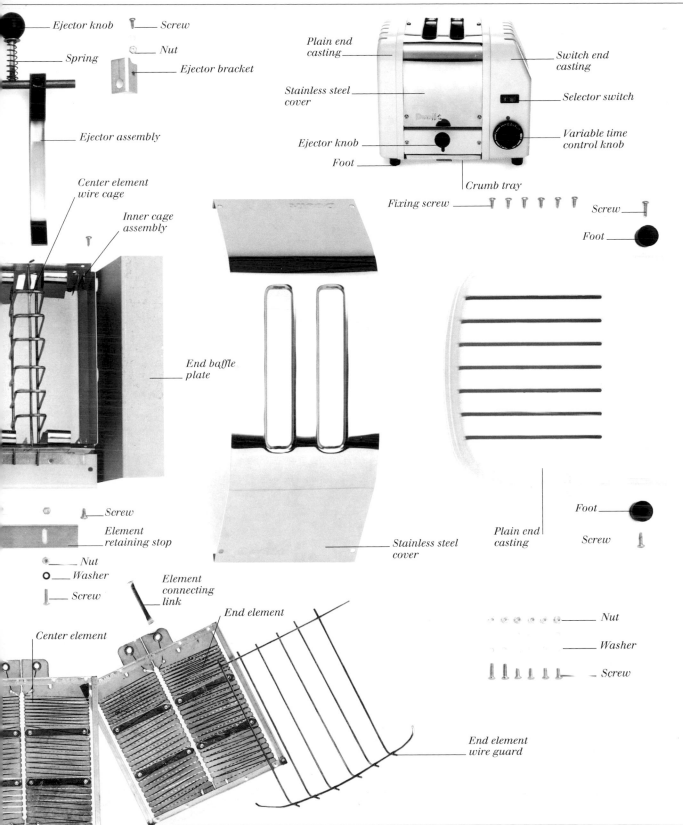

Ejector knob

Screw

Spring

Nut

Ejector bracket

Ejector assembly

Plain end casting

Switch end casting

Stainless steel cover

Selector switch

Ejector knob

Variable time control knob

Foot

Crumb tray

Fixing screw

Screw

Foot

Center element wire cage

Inner cage assembly

End baffle plate

Screw

Element retaining stop

Stainless steel cover

Plain end casting

Foot

Screw

Nut

Washer

Screw

Nut

Washer

Screw

Element connecting link

End element

Center element

End element wire guard

Drills

THE ELECTRICALLY POWERED MOTOR OF A POWER DRILL, cooled by a fan, turns a shaft at high speed. The shaft connects, in turn, to a system of gears that rotates a chuck even faster. Clamped by the chuck, a sharp bit cuts out the hole, and at the same time the bit's screw-shaped grooves channel the waste out of the hole. For drilling hard materials, many power drills have a hammer mechanism: when this is operated a ratchet in the gearcase causes the chuck and bit to pound in and out as they drill. A hand drill, although slower and less forceful than a power drill, is easier to control. For cutting wide holes, carpenters often prefer a brace-and-bit. This acts like a lever: the bowed handle of the brace moves a larger distance than the bit, turning the bit with extra force.

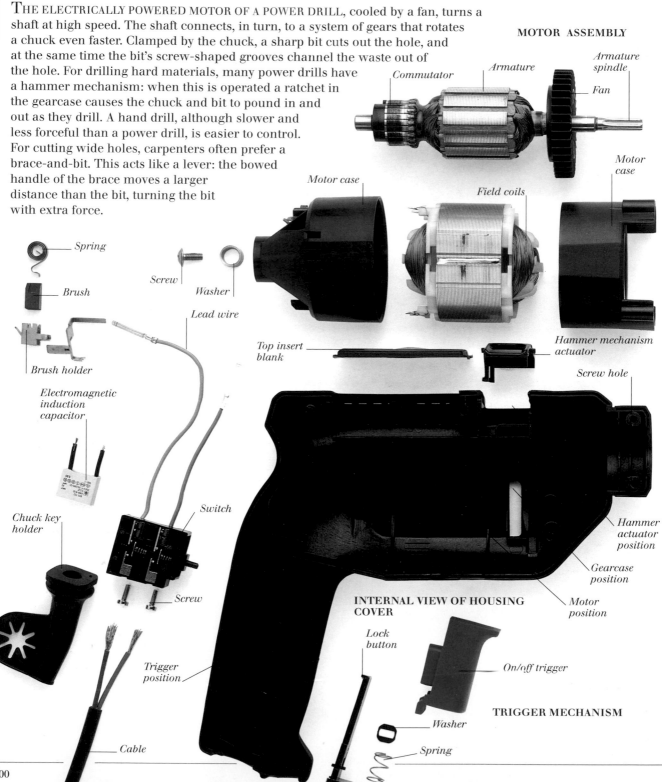

MOTOR ASSEMBLY

Commutator

Armature

Armature spindle

Fan

Motor case

Field coils

Motor case

Spring

Brush

Screw

Washer

Lead wire

Brush holder

Electromagnetic induction capacitor

Top insert blank

Hammer mechanism actuator

Screw hole

Chuck key holder

Switch

Screw

Hammer actuator position

Gearcase position

Motor position

INTERNAL VIEW OF HOUSING COVER

Trigger position

Lock button

On/off trigger

TRIGGER MECHANISM

Washer

Cable

Spring

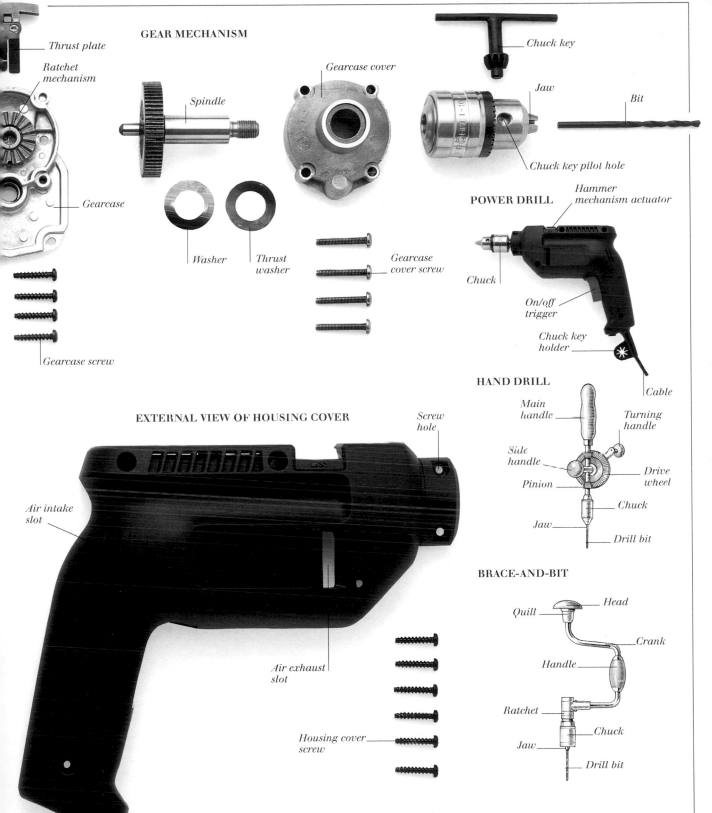

GEAR MECHANISM

Thrust plate

Ratchet mechanism

Spindle

Gearcase cover

Chuck key

Jaw

Bit

Gearcase

Chuck key pilot hole

Washer

Thrust washer

Gearcase cover screw

Gearcase screw

POWER DRILL

Hammer mechanism actuator

Chuck

On/off trigger

Chuck key holder

Cable

HAND DRILL

Main handle

Turning handle

Side handle

Drive wheel

Pinion

Chuck

Jaw

Drill bit

EXTERNAL VIEW OF HOUSING COVER

Screw hole

Air intake slot

Air exhaust slot

Housing cover screw

BRACE-AND-BIT

Head

Quill

Crank

Handle

Ratchet

Chuck

Jaw

Drill bit

House of the future

HOUSES IN THE FUTURE are likely to be more environmentally friendly and energy-efficient than older dwellings, by making better use of materials and intelligent control systems. The Integer house was designed by Cole Thompson Associates, Bree Day Partnership, and Paul Hodgkins Associates, and built in conjunction with the Building Research Establishment in the UK. One of its key features is a large sun room that warms one side of the house. Extensive use is made of recycled, natural, and renewable materials and energy. The walls are made from timber and insulated with fiber from recycled newspaper; wastewater from the bathrooms is saved and used to flush the toilets; and a wind turbine and solar panels contribute some of the electricity requirements. Many elements were prefabricated off-site for ease of construction. The Integer house uses only half the energy and a third less water than a traditionally built house.

WALL CONSTRUCTION

Cellulose fiber insulation

Vertical batten

Plasterboard

Vertical batten

Red cedar boarding

Noggin

Baseboard

Breather paper

Floating floor

Cables and ducting

Wooden boarding

SIDE AND REAR VIEW OF THE INTEGER HOUSE

Single-glazed sun room

Gutter collects rainwater for use in the yard

Composter for recycling kitchen waste

FRONT VIEW OF THE INTEGER HOUSE

Turfed roof helps to regulate temperature

Passive stack vents from bathroom

Automatic louvers cool sun room

Small windows reduce heat loss

Red cedar walls that do not require painting or staining

Intelligent electronic door-lock

Hatch for home deliveries

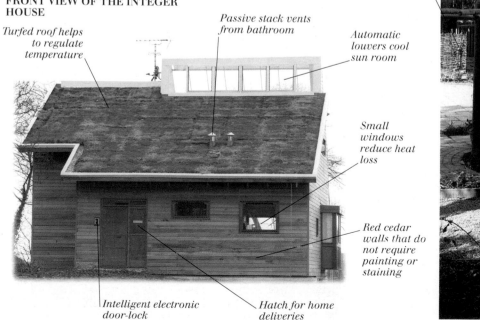

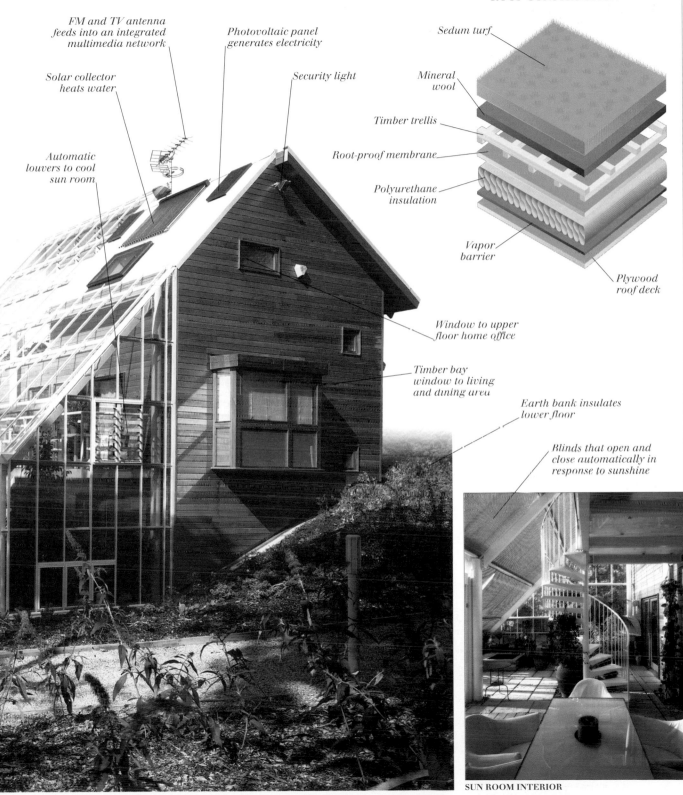

ROOF CONSTRUCTION

Sedum turf

Mineral wool

Timber trellis

Root-proof membrane

Polyurethane insulation

Vapor barrier

Plywood roof deck

FM and TV antenna feeds into an integrated multimedia network

Photovoltaic panel generates electricity

Solar collector heats water

Security light

Automatic louvers to cool sun room

Window to upper floor home office

Timber bay window to living and dining area

Earth bank insulates lower floor

Blinds that open and close automatically in response to sunshine

SUN ROOM INTERIOR

603

Renewable energy

RENEWABLE ENERGY COMES from sources that do not become depleted as we use the energy. When a fossil fuel such as coal is burned, it is gone forever, but a renewable source remains available no matter how much is used. The tides, waves, flowing water, sunlight, and the wind are all renewable sources of energy. Wind and water energy are captured by a device called a turbine. The turbine spins and drives an electricity generator. Energy from sunlight, or solar energy, is changed into electricity in two main ways. One uses mirrors to concentrate solar energy and magnify its heating effect which is used to change water into steam to drive turbines. Photovoltaic cells change sunlight directly into electricity. A cell is made from two layers of silicon. One gives out electrons (negative particles) and the other receives them. Sunlight knocks electrons out of atoms where the two layers meet, separating them from the positive particles. The electrons are attracted to one layer of the cell, the positive particles to the other layer. Electrons are naturally attracted to the positive particles, but to come together again, the electrons must flow out of the cell, through an external electric circuit, or load, and back to the other side of the cell, creating a charge. The cell supplies electric current for as long as light keeps falling on it.

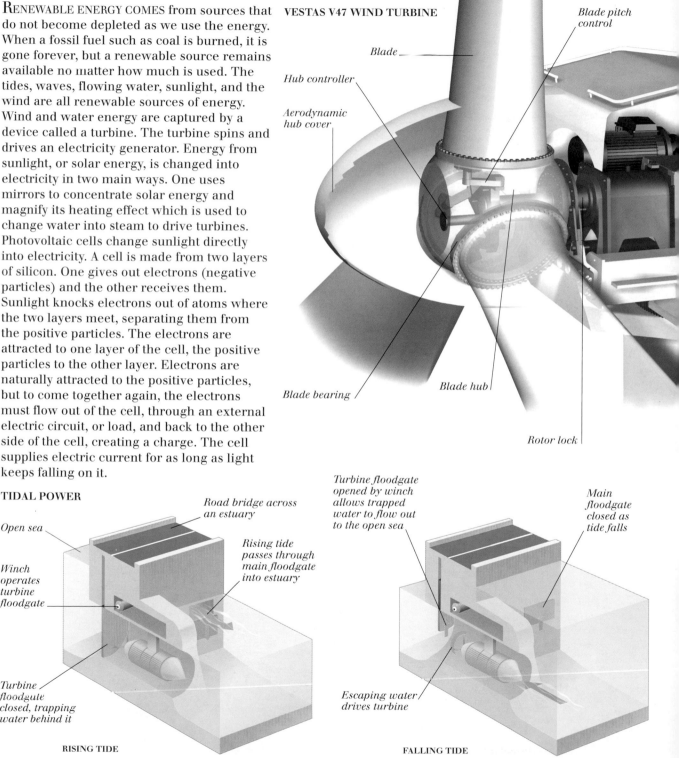

VESTAS V47 WIND TURBINE

Blade pitch control

Blade

Hub controller

Aerodynamic hub cover

Blade bearing

Blade hub

Rotor lock

TIDAL POWER

Road bridge across an estuary

Open sea

Rising tide passes through main floodgate into estuary

Winch operates turbine floodgate

Turbine floodgate closed, trapping water behind it

RISING TIDE

Turbine floodgate opened by winch allows trapped water to flow out to the open sea

Main floodgate closed as tide falls

Escaping water drives turbine

FALLING TIDE

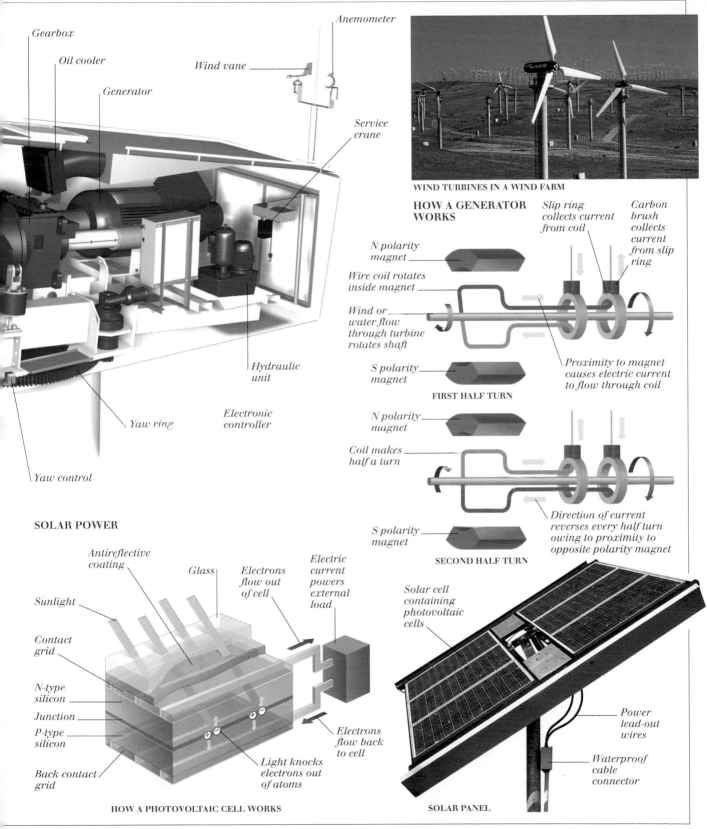

Gearbox

Oil cooler

Generator

Wind vane

Anemometer

Service crane

Hydraulic unit

Electronic controller

Yaw ring

Yaw control

WIND TURBINES IN A WIND FARM

HOW A GENERATOR WORKS

Slip ring collects current from coil

Carbon brush collects current from slip ring

N polarity magnet

Wire coil rotates inside magnet

Wind or water flow through turbine rotates shaft

S polarity magnet

Proximity to magnet causes electric current to flow through coil

FIRST HALF TURN

N polarity magnet

Coil makes half a turn

S polarity magnet

Direction of current reverses every half turn owing to proximity to opposite polarity magnet

SECOND HALF TURN

SOLAR POWER

Antireflective coating

Glass

Electrons flow out of cell

Electric current powers external load

Sunlight

Contact grid

N-type silicon

Junction

P-type silicon

Back contact grid

Light knocks electrons out of atoms

Electrons flow back to cell

Solar cell containing photovoltaic cells

Power lead-out wires

Waterproof cable connector

HOW A PHOTOVOLTAIC CELL WORKS

SOLAR PANEL

Cloning technology

IN A LIVING CELL THE GENETIC MATERIAL DNA (deoxyribonucleic acid) contains thousands of units called genes that carry instructions for development, growth, and repair of the living creature. During normal reproduction, half the mother's genetic material contained in an egg cell joins with half the genetic material from the father carried in a sperm cell, to form a unique new genome (set of genes) for a new life. During the early stages of embryo development, the fertilized egg divides into stem cells, which have the potential to become specialized into the hundreds of cell types in a body. Through therapeutic cloning, stem cells can be produced in a laboratory. It is hoped that in the future this technology can be used to grow new tissue that can be transplanted back into the donor to treat illness, without the tissue being rejected. Rejection is when the body recognizes a transplanted part as "foreign" because it has different genes, and tries to destroy it. In another form of cloning, performed experimentally using animals, genetic material from a donor animal has been inserted into an egg from another animal that has been emptied of its own genetic material, to produce an animal genetically identical to the donor.

NORMAL REPRODUCTION

Spare cells from egg development

Nucleus with mother's genetic material

Egg cell membrane

Egg cell

Polar body (spare genetic material) forms as part of final egg cell division

THERAPEUTIC CLONING

Nucleus with mother's genetic material

Egg cell with polar body

Zona pellucida (outer casing of egg cell)

Fragments of DNA stain as dark "bar code" bands

"Plug" of zona removed

Gentle suction through micro-needle

GEL IMAGE SHOWING DNA PROFILE

Suction through micro-pipette holds egg steady

Micro-needle inserted through egg cell membrane

Zona plug discarded

Polar body removed

Discarded parts no longer needed

Egg cell provides conditions for multiplication

Egg genetic material in nucleus removed

Zona (casing)

Egg cell

Egg cell nucleus containing genetic material

"Enucleated" egg cell (lacks nucleus with genetic material)

Stem cells (unspecialized or undifferentiated cells) collected from donor

Donor genetic material introduced into egg cell

GENETIC MATERIAL REMOVED FROM EGG

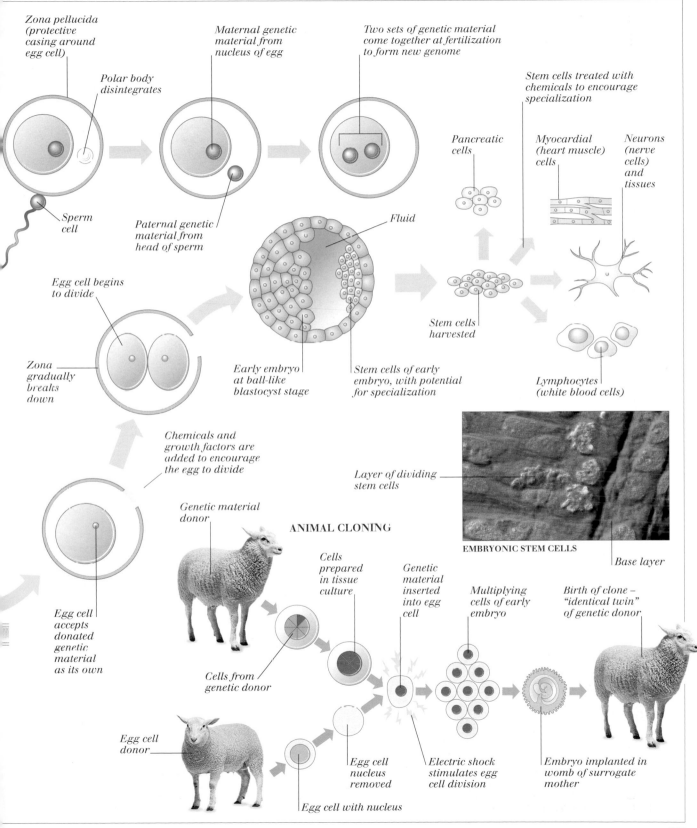

Zona pellucida (protective casing around egg cell)

Polar body disintegrates

Maternal genetic material from nucleus of egg

Two sets of genetic material come together at fertilization to form new genome

Stem cells treated with chemicals to encourage specialization

Pancreatic cells

Myocardial (heart muscle) cells

Neurons (nerve cells) and tissues

Sperm cell

Paternal genetic material from head of sperm

Fluid

Egg cell begins to divide

Stem cells harvested

Zona gradually breaks down

Early embryo at ball-like blastocyst stage

Stem cells of early embryo, with potential for specialization

Lymphocytes (white blood cells)

Chemicals and growth factors are added to encourage the egg to divide

Layer of dividing stem cells

Genetic material donor

ANIMAL CLONING

EMBRYONIC STEM CELLS

Base layer

Egg cell accepts donated genetic material as its own

Cells prepared in tissue culture

Genetic material inserted into egg cell

Multiplying cells of early embryo

Birth of clone – "identical twin" of genetic donor

Cells from genetic donor

Egg cell donor

Egg cell nucleus removed

Electric shock stimulates egg cell division

Embryo implanted in womb of surrogate mother

Egg cell with nucleus

Robots

ROBOTS ARE MACHINES THAT CAN carry out a variety of tasks on their own, with little or no human control. Most robots are mechanical arms used to build things in factories. The end of the robot's arm can be equipped with different tools for gripping, drilling, cutting, welding, and painting. Robot toys have become popular, too. They incorporate sensors that respond to sounds and sometimes touch. Some of them can even understand spoken words. The Aibo robot dog can understand 75 voice commands. Scientists are also trying to create more advanced humanlike robots that can see, hear, learn, and make their own decisions. Cog, a robot that has been progressively developed at the Massachusetts Institute of Technology since the 1990s, is one of these "humanoid" robots.

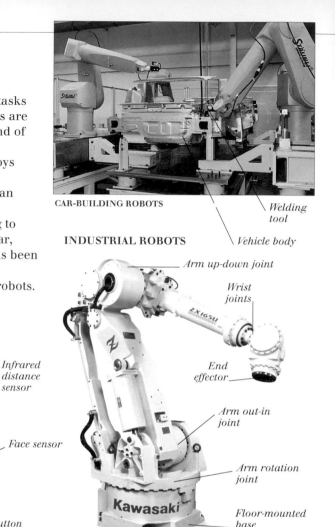

CAR-BUILDING ROBOTS

Welding tool

INDUSTRIAL ROBOTS

Vehicle body

Arm up-down joint

Wrist joints

End effector

Arm out-in joint

Arm rotation joint

Kawasaki

Floor-mounted base

KAWASAKI INDUSRIAL ROBOT

SONY AIBO ROBOT DOG

Head sensor

Retractable headlight

Stereo microphone

Infrared distance sensor

Back sensor

Tail sensors

Face sensor

Taillight

Back indicator

Face light

Pause button

Chest light

Foot pad

ELEMENTS OF ROBOT ACTION

CENTRAL PROCESSING UNIT (CPU)

Information from sensors

Information from sensors interpreted by CPU to modify actions

Preprogrammed instructions

SENSORS

| LIGHT |
| SOUND |
| TOUCH |
| PROXIMITY |
| SMELL |
| TASTE |

MECHANICAL ACTIONS

COG HUMANOID ROBOT

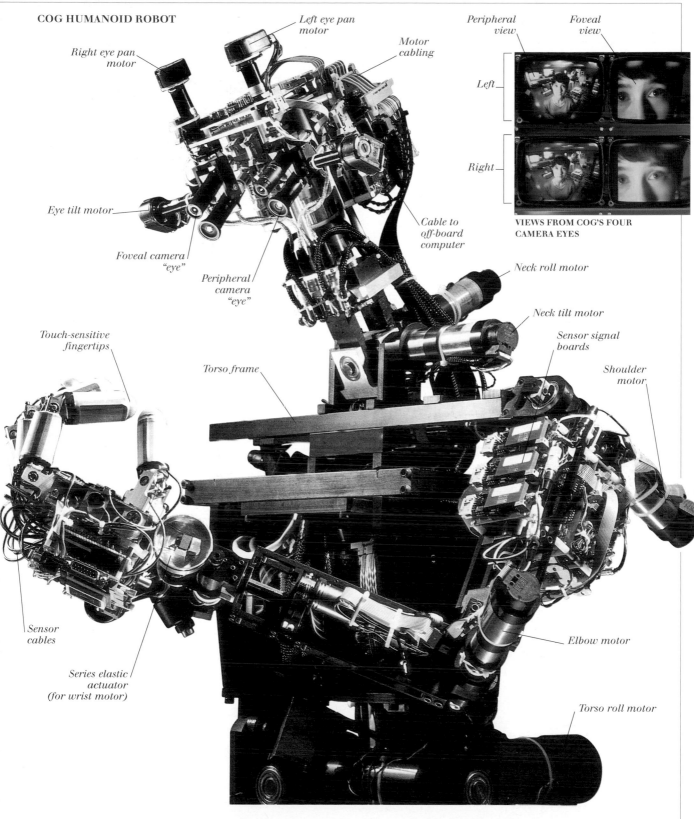

Right eye pan motor

Left eye pan motor

Motor cabling

Eye tilt motor

Foveal camera "eye"

Peripheral camera "eye"

Cable to off-board computer

Peripheral view

Foveal view

Left

Right

VIEWS FROM COG'S FOUR CAMERA EYES

Neck roll motor

Neck tilt motor

Sensor signal boards

Shoulder motor

Touch-sensitive fingertips

Torso frame

Sensor cables

Elbow motor

Series elastic actuator (for wrist motor)

Torso roll motor

High-performance microscopes

OPTICAL MICROSCOPES FORM a magnified image by using lenses to bend light. Some optical microscopes used in industry and research are designed for observing particular materials, such as living cells. They produce magnifications of up to about 1,000. Electron microscopes produce magnifications of as much as 1.5 million. Their images are formed by means of electrons focused by magnetic lenses. There are two main types: scanning electron microscopes (SEMs) scan electrons back and forth across the surface of a specimen; transmission electron microscopes (TEMs) transmit electrons through a thin slice of the specimen.

FEI TECNAI G² TRANSMISSION ELECTRON MICROSCOPE

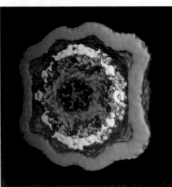

TEM IMAGE OF A VIRUS

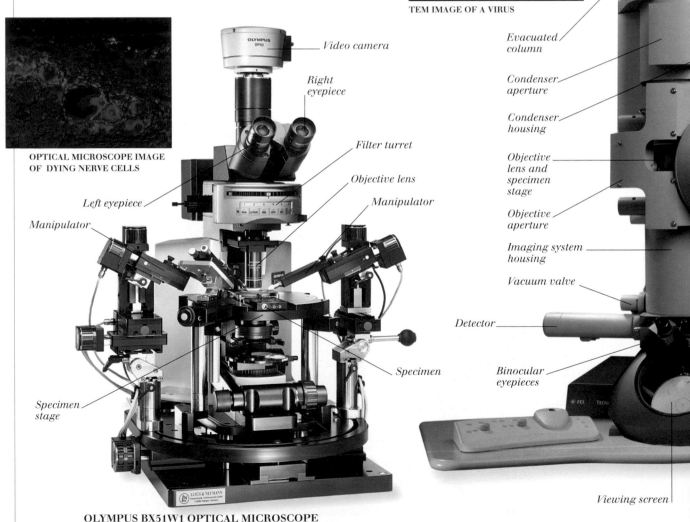

OPTICAL MICROSCOPE IMAGE OF DYING NERVE CELLS

Video camera

Right eyepiece

Filter turret

Objective lens

Left eyepiece

Manipulator

Manipulator

Manipulator

Specimen

Specimen stage

OLYMPUS BX51W1 OPTICAL MICROSCOPE

Electron gun housing

Evacuated column

Condenser aperture

Condenser housing

Objective lens and specimen stage

Objective aperture

Imaging system housing

Vacuum valve

Detector

Binocular eyepieces

Viewing screen

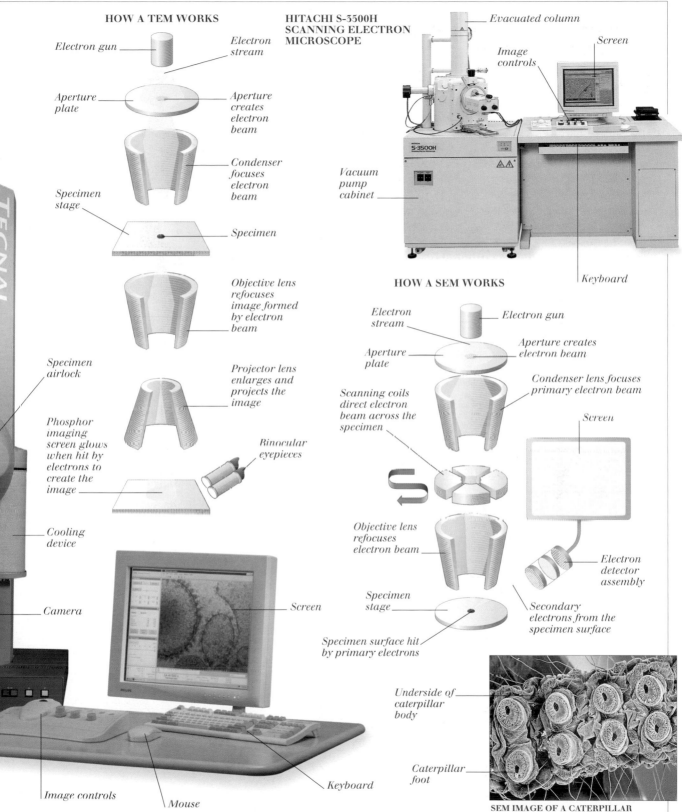

HOW A TEM WORKS

Electron gun

Electron stream

Aperture plate

Aperture creates electron beam

Condenser focuses electron beam

Specimen stage

Specimen

Objective lens refocuses image formed by electron beam

Projector lens enlarges and projects the image

Specimen airlock

Phosphor imaging screen glows when hit by electrons to create the image

Binocular eyepieces

Cooling device

Camera

Screen

Image controls

Mouse

Keyboard

HITACHI S-3500H SCANNING ELECTRON MICROSCOPE

Evacuated column

Screen

Image controls

Vacuum pump cabinet

Keyboard

HOW A SEM WORKS

Electron stream

Electron gun

Aperture plate

Aperture creates electron beam

Scanning coils direct electron beam across the specimen

Condenser lens focuses primary electron beam

Screen

Objective lens refocuses electron beam

Electron detector assembly

Specimen stage

Secondary electrons from the specimen surface

Specimen surface hit by primary electrons

Underside of caterpillar body

Caterpillar foot

SEM IMAGE OF A CATERPILLAR

611

Space telescope

SPACE TELESCOPES ORBIT THE EARTH hundreds of miles above the ground, their instruments collecting light from stars and galaxies. Telescopes in space have a clearer view than those on Earth, because they are unaffected by the Earth's atmosphere, which absorbs or distorts much of this radiation. There are a variety of types of space telescopes designed to observe different types of light. The Hubble Space Telescope observes infrared, ultraviolet, and visible light. It can detect objects that are 100 times fainter than those any telescopes on Earth can see. When this 242-ton (11,000-kilogram), 50-foot (13-meter) long telescope was launched by the Space Shuttle in 1990, it was found that its primary mirror was faulty and its images were blurred. Astronauts installed extra optics to correct the problem in 1993.

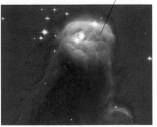

IMAGES TAKEN FROM HUBBLE

Pillar of gas

CONE NEBULA

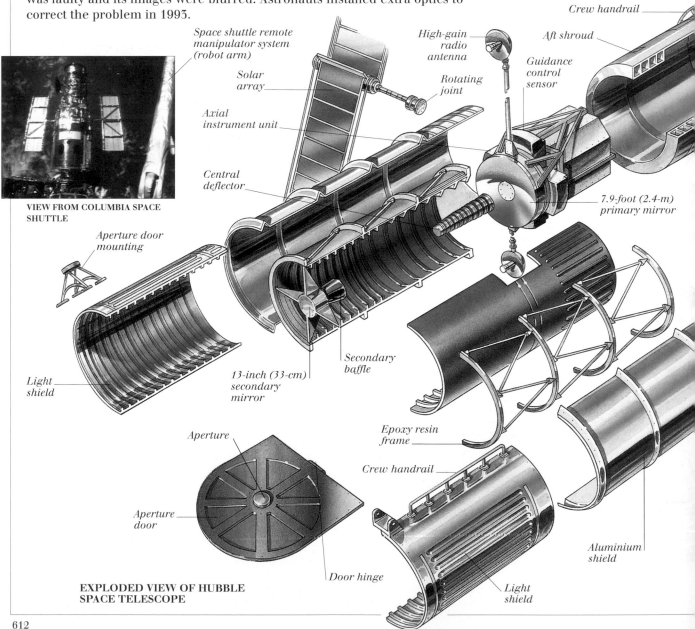

VIEW FROM COLUMBIA SPACE SHUTTLE

Space shuttle remote manipulator system (robot arm)

Solar array

Axial instrument unit

Central deflector

High-gain radio antenna

Rotating joint

Crew handrail

Aft shroud

Guidance control sensor

7.9-foot (2.4-m) primary mirror

Aperture door mounting

Light shield

13-inch (33-cm) secondary mirror

Secondary baffle

Epoxy resin frame

Crew handrail

Aperture

Aperture door

Door hinge

Aluminium shield

Light shield

EXPLODED VIEW OF HUBBLE SPACE TELESCOPE

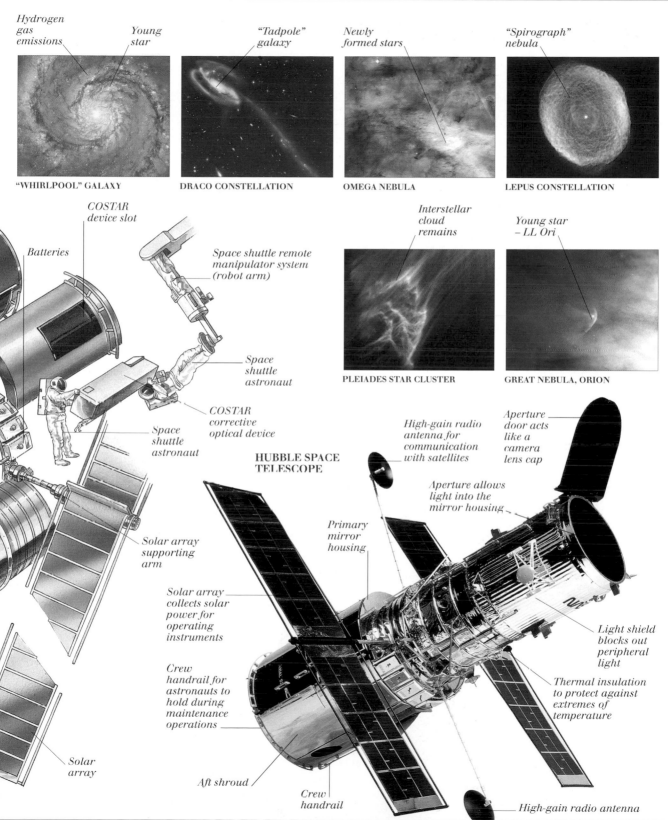

Hydrogen gas emissions

Young star

"WHIRLPOOL" GALAXY

"Tadpole" galaxy

DRACO CONSTELLATION

Newly formed stars

OMEGA NEBULA

"Spirograph" nebula

LEPUS CONSTELLATION

COSTAR device slot

Batteries

Space shuttle remote manipulator system (robot arm)

Space shuttle astronaut

Space shuttle astronaut

COSTAR corrective optical device

Interstellar cloud remains

PLEIADES STAR CLUSTER

Young star – LL Ori

GREAT NEBULA, ORION

HUBBLE SPACE TELESCOPE

High-gain radio antenna for communication with satellites

Aperture door acts like a camera lens cap

Aperture allows light into the mirror housing

Primary mirror housing

Solar array supporting arm

Solar array collects solar power for operating instruments

Light shield blocks out peripheral light

Crew handrail for astronauts to hold during maintenance operations

Thermal insulation to protect against extremes of temperature

Solar array

Aft shroud

Crew handrail

High-gain radio antenna

Probing the Universe

SPACE PROBES HAVE VISITED every planet in the Solar System except Pluto. They take close-up photographs and gather information that cannot be collected from Earth-based equipment. Some probes fly past or go into orbit around planets or moons. Others are designed to land. Two Voyager space probes flew past most of the outer planets in the 1970s and 1980s. Two Viking spacecraft landed on Mars in 1976. The Magellan spacecraft orbited Venus from 1989 and mapped its surface. The Pathfinder spacecraft landed on Mars in 1997 and released a rover vehicle to explore the surface. The Cassini space probe with a mini probe called Huygens is due to arrive at Saturn in 2004. Huygens will be dropped onto Titan, one of Saturn's moons.

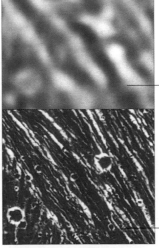

High-gain antenna

Fields and particles intruments

Ganymede photographed by Voyager

Huygens mini probe

Propulsion module

Heat shield

THE LAUNCH OF THE CASSINI SPACE PROBE ON OCTOBER 10, 1997

JUPITER AND ITS MOON IO PHOTOGRAPHED BY CASSINI

A MAP OF JUPITER'S VAST MAGNETIC FIELD PRODUCED BY CASSINI'S INSTRUMENTS

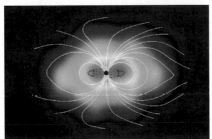

Ganymede photographed by Cassini

IMPROVING CLARITY
Cassini provides clearer images than earlier probes as shown by these views of Ganymede, a moon of Jupiter.

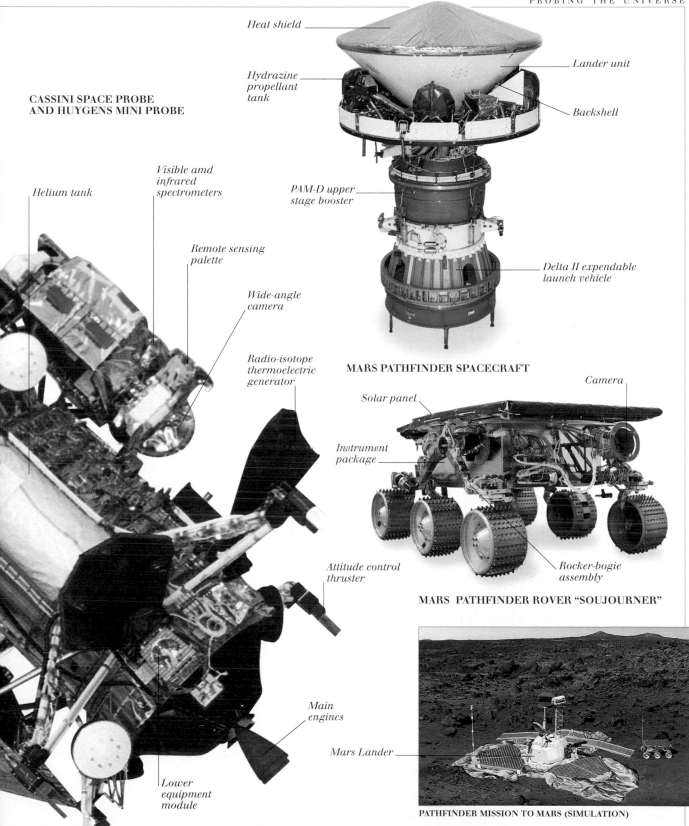

**CASSINI SPACE PROBE
AND HUYGENS MINI PROBE**

Heat shield

Lander unit

Hydrazine
propellant
tank

Backshell

Helium tank

Visible amd
infrared
spectrometers

Remote sensing
palette

PAM-D upper
stage booster

Wide-angle
camera

Delta II expendable
launch vehicle

Radio-isotope
thermoelectric
generator

MARS PATHFINDER SPACECRAFT

Camera

Solar panel

Instrument
package

Attitude control
thruster

Rocker-bogie
assembly

MARS PATHFINDER ROVER "SOUJOURNER"

Main
engines

Mars Lander

Lower
equipment
module

PATHFINDER MISSION TO MARS (SIMULATION)

Political map of the world

This map depicts the political boundaries of the world's nations. There are currently 193 independent countries in the world – a marked increase from the 82 that existed in 1950. With the trend toward greater fragmentation, this figure is likely to increase. There are also some 60 overseas dependencies still in existence, with various forms of local administration, but all belonging to a sovereign state. The largest country in the world is the Russian Federation, which covers 6,592,800 sq. mi. (17,075,400 sq. km), while the smallest is the Vatican City, covering 0.17 sq. mi. (0.44 sq. km). Under the Antarctic Treaty of 1959, no countries are permitted to have territorial claims in Antarctica.

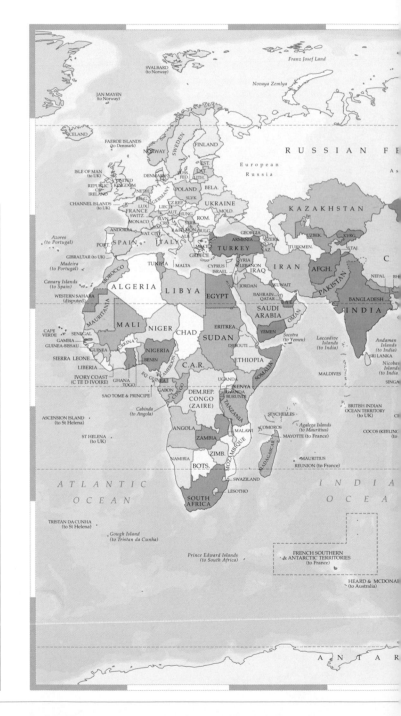

ABBREVIATIONS	
AFGH.	Afghanistan
ALB.	Albania
AUT.	Austria
AZ. OR AZERB.	Azerbaijan
B. & H.	Bosnia & Herzegovina
BELG.	Belgium
BELO.	Belorussia
BOTS.	Botswana
BULG.	Bulgaria
CAMB.	Cambodia
C.A.R.	Central African Republic
CRO.	Croatia
CZ. REP.	Czech Republic
DOM. REP.	Dominican Republic
EST.	Estonia
HUNG.	Hungary
KYRG.	Kyrgyzstan
LAT.	Latvia
LIECH.	Liechtenstein
LITH.	Lithuania
LUX.	Luxemburg
MACED.	Macedonia
MOLD.	Moldavia
NETH.	Netherlands
NETH. ANT.	Netherlands Antilles
PORT.	Portugal
ROM.	Romania
RUSS. FED.	Russian Federation
SERB. & MON.	Serbia & Montenegro
SLVK.	Slovakia
SLVN.	Slovenia
S.M.	San Marino
SWITZ.	Switzerland
TAJ.	Tajikistan
THAI.	Thailand
TURKMEN.	Turkmenistan
U.A.E.	United Arab Emirates
UZBEK.	Uzbekistan
VAT. CITY	Vatican City
ZIMB.	Zimbabwe

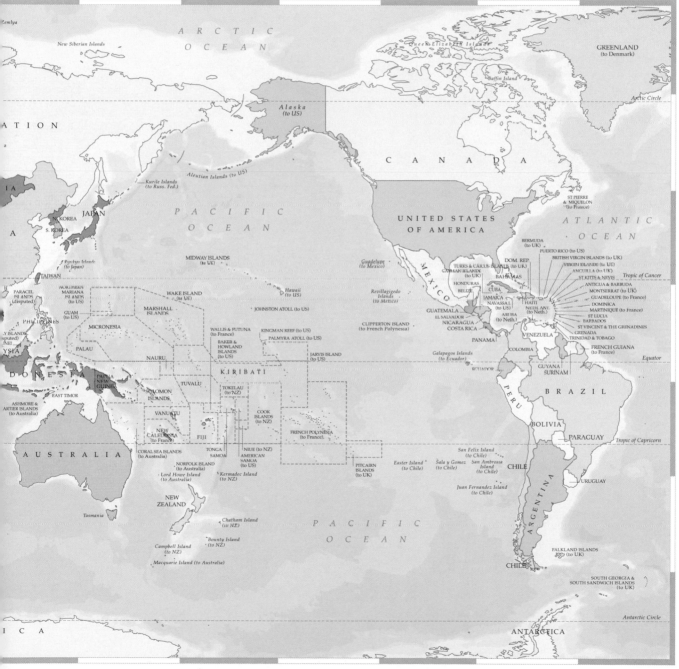

KEY

CONTINENTS

Europe

Africa

Asia

Australasia & Oceania

North & Central America

South America

Antarctica

LABEL STYLES

Eg. MEXICO — Independent state

Eg. FAEROE ISLANDS — Self-governing territory
(to Denmark) (parent state)

Eg. ANDAMAN ISLANDS — Non self-governing territory
(part of India) (parent state)

ARCTIC OCEAN

New Siberian Islands

Zemlya

Queen Elizabeth Islands

GREENLAND
(to Denmark)

Baffin Island

Arctic Circle

Alaska
(to US)

CANADA

ATION

a

Aleutian Islands (to US)

Kurile Islands
(to Russ. Fed.)

ST PIERRE
& MIQUELON
(to France)

IA

N.KOREA
S. KOREA

JAPAN

PACIFIC
OCEAN

UNITED STATES
OF AMERICA

ATLANTIC
OCEAN

BERMUDA
(to UK)

A

Ryukyu Islands
(to Japan)

MIDWAY ISLANDS
(to US)

Guadelupe
(to Mexico)

PUERTO RICO (to US)

TAIWAN

BRITISH VIRGIN ISLANDS (to UK)

VIRGIN ISLANDS (to UK)

Tropic of Cancer

ANGUILLA (to UK)

DOM. REP.

TURKS & CAICOS ISLANDS
(to UK)

ST KITTS & NEVIS

PARACEL
ISLANDS
(disputed)

NORTHERN
MARIANA
ISLANDS
(to US)

WAKE ISLAND
(to US)

Hawaii
(to US)

Revillagigedo
Islands
(to Mexico)

MEXICO

CAYMAN ISLANDS
(to UK)

BAHAMAS

ANTIGUA & BARBUDA

MONTSERRAT (to UK)

HONDURAS

BELIZE

CUBA

GUADELOUPE (to France)

GUAM
(to US)

MARSHALL
ISLANDS

JOHNSTON ATOLL (to US)

DOMINICA

MARTINIQUE (to France)

PHILIPPINES

MICRONESIA

NAVASSA I.
(to US)

JAMAICA

HAITI

NETH. ANT.
(to Neth.)

ST LUCIA

BARBADOS

Y ISLANDS
(disputed)
NEI

WALLIS & FUTUNA
(to France)

KINGMAN REEF (to US)

GUATEMALA

EL SALVADOR
NICARAGUA
COSTA RICA

ARUBA
(to Neth.)

ST VINCENT & THE GRENADINES

GRENADA

TRINIDAD & TOBAGO

YSIA

PALAU

BAKER &
HOWLAND
ISLANDS
(to US)

PALMYRA ATOLL (to US)

CLIPPERTON ISLAND
(to French Polynesia)

PANAMA

VENEZUELA

FRENCH GUIANA
(to France)

NAURU

JARVIS ISLAND
(to US)

COLOMBIA

Galapagos Islands
(to Ecuador)

Equator

DONESIA

KIRIBATI

ECUADOR

GUYANA

SURINAM

EAST TIMOR

PAPUA
NEW
GUINEA

TUVALU

TOKELAU
(to NZ)

PERU

BRAZIL

ASHMORE &
ARTIER ISLANDS
(to Australia)

SOLOMON
ISLANDS

VANUATU

COOK
ISLANDS
(to NZ)

FRENCH POLYNESIA
(to France)

BOLIVIA

NEW
CALEDONIA
(to France)

FIJI

TONGA

NIUE (to NZ)

PARAGUAY

Tropic of Capricorn

AUSTRALIA

CORAL SEA ISLANDS
(to Australia)

SAMOA

AMERICAN
SAMOA
(to US)

San Felix Island
(to Chile)

Easter Island
(to Chile)

Šala y Gomez
(to Chile)

San Ambrosia
Island
(to Chile)

CHILE

NORFOLK ISLAND
(to Australia)

Lord Howe Island
(to Australia)

Kermadec Island
(to NZ)

PITCAIRN
ISLANDS
(to UK)

Juan Fernandez Island
(to Chile)

URUGUAY

Tasmania

NEW
ZEALAND

Chatham Island
(to NZ)

PACIFIC
OCEAN

ARGENTINA

Campbell Island
(to NZ)

Bounty Island
(to NZ)

FALKLAND ISLANDS
(to UK)

Macquarie Island (to Australia)

CHILE

SOUTH GEORGIA &
SOUTH SANDWICH ISLANDS
(to UK)

Antarctic Circle

ICA

ANTARCTICA

Time zones

The world is divided into 24 time zones, measured in relation to 12 noon Greenwich Mean Time (GMT), on the Greenwich Meridian (0º). Time advances by one hour for every 15º longitude east of Greenwich (and goes back one hour for every 15° west), but the system is adjusted in line with administrative boundaries. Numbers on the map show the number of hours that must be added to, or subtracted from GMT to calculate the time in each zone. Thus, the eastern US (–5) is 5 hours behind GMT.

TYPES OF CALENDAR

GREGORIAN
The 365-day Gregorian calendar was introduced by Pope Gregory XIII in 1582 and is now in use throughout most of the Western world. Every four years (leap year) an extra day is added. Below are the names of the months (and number of days).

January (31)	July (31)
February (28, 29 in leap years)	August (31)
March (31)	September (30)
April (30)	October (31)
May (31)	November
June (30)	December (31)

JEWISH
The Jewish calendar is a lunar calendar adapted to the solar year. It normally has 12 months but in leap years, which occur seven times in every cycle of 19 years, there are 13 months. The years are calculated from the Creation (which is placed at 3761 BC); the months are Nisan, Iyyar, Sivan, Thammuz, Ab, Elul, Tishri, Hesvan, Kislev, Tebet, Sebat, and Adar, with an intercalary month (First Adar) being added in leap years.

MUSLIM
The Muslim calendar is based on a year of 12 months, each month beginning roughly at the time of the new moon. The months are Muharram, Safar, Rabi'I, Rabi'II, Jumada I, Jumada II, Rajab, Sha'ban, Ramadan, Shawwal, Dhu l-Qa'dah, and Dhu l-Hijja.

CHINESE
The Chinese calendar is a lunar calendar, with a year consisting of 12 months. Intercalary months are added to keep the calendar in step with the solar year of 365 days. Months are referred to by a number within a year, but also by animal names that, from ancient times, have been attached to years and hours of the day.

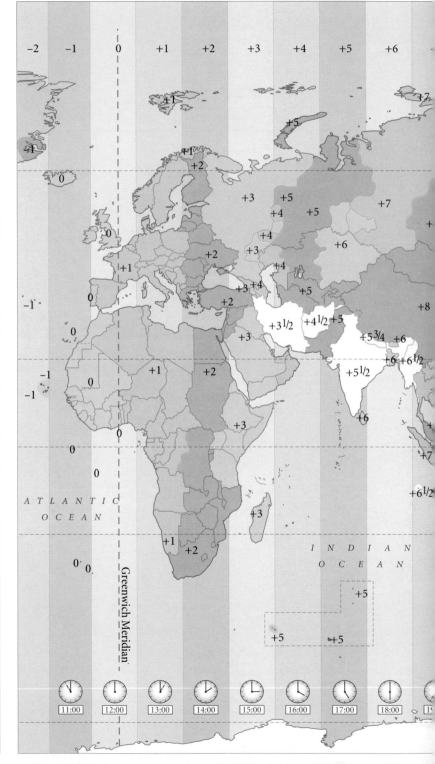

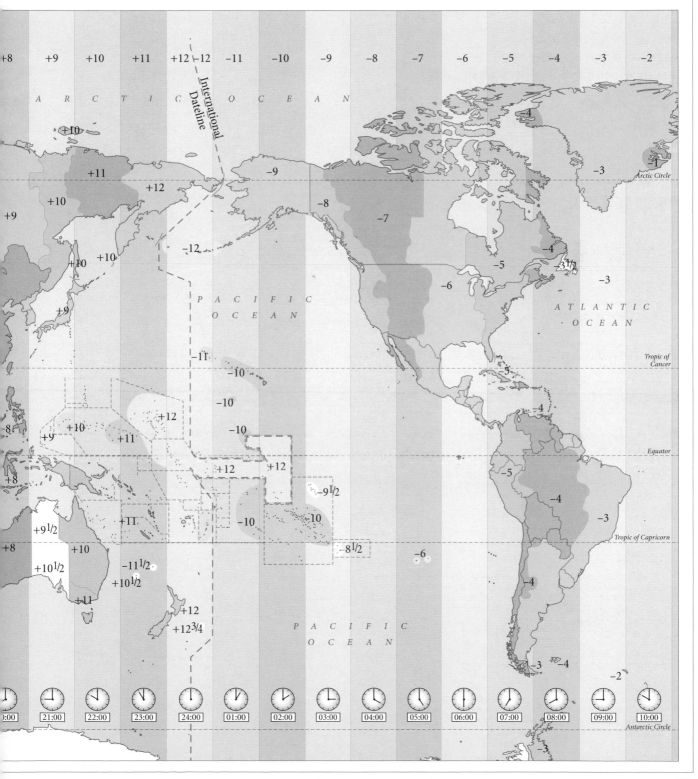

Useful data

UNITS OF MEASUREMENT

METRIC UNIT	EQUIVALENT
Length	
1 centimeter (cm)	10 millimeters (mm)
1 meter (m)	100 centimeters
1 kilometre (km)	1,000 metres
Mass	
1 kilogram (kg)	1,000 grams (g)
1 tonne (t)	1,000 kilograms
Area	
1 square centimeter (cm²)	100 square millimetres (mm²)
1 square meter (m²)	10,000 square centimeters
1 hectare	10,000 square meters
1 square kilometer (km²)	1,000,000 square meters
Volume	
1 cubic centimeter (cc)	1 milliliter (ml)
1 liter (l)	1,000 milliliters
1 cubic meter (m³)	1,000 liters
Capacity (liquid and dry measures)	
1 centiliter (cl)	10 milliliters (ml)
1 deciliter (dl)	10 centiliters
1 liter (l)	10 deciliters
1 decaliter (dal)	10 liters
1 hectoliter (hi)	10 decaliters
1 kiloliter (kl)	10 hectoliters

IMPERIAL UNIT	EQUIVALENT
Length	
1 foot (ft)	12 inches (in)
1 yard (yd)	3 feet
1 rod (rd)	5.5 yards
1 mile (mi)	1,760 yards
Mass	
1 dram (dr)	27.344 grains (gr)
1 ounce (oz)	16 drams
1 pound (lb)	16 ounces
1 hundredweight (cwt) (long)	112 pounds
1 hundredweight (cwt) (short)	100 pounds
1 ton (long)	2,240 pounds
1 ton (short)	2,000 pounds
Area	
1 square foot (ft²) (in²)	144 square inches
9 square feet	1 square yard (yd²)
1 acre	4,840 square yards
1 square mile	640 acres
Volume	
1 cubic foot	1,728 cubic inches
1 cubic yard	27 cubic feet
Capacity (liquid and dry measures)	
1 fluidram (fl dr)	60 minims (min)
1 fluid ounce (fl oz)	8 fluidrams
1 gill (gi)	5 fluid ounces
1 pint (pt)	4 gills
1 quart (qt)	2 pints
1 gallon (gal)	4 quarts
1 peck (pk)	2 gallons
1 bushel (bu)	4 pecks

NUMBER SYSTEMS

ROMAN	ARABIC
I	1
II	2
III	3
IV	4
V	5
VI	6
VII	7
VIII	8
IX	9
X	10
XI	11
XII	12
XIII	13
XIV	14
XV	15
XX	20
XXI	21
XXX	30
XL	40
L	50
LX	60
LXX	70
LXXX	80
XC	90
C	100
CI	101
CC	200
CCC	300
CD	400
D	500
DC	600
DCC	700
DCCC	800
CM	900
M	1,000
MM	2,000

METRIC - IMPERIAL CONVERSIONS

TO CONVERT	INTO	MULTIPLY BY
Length		
Centimeters	inches	0.3937
Meters	feet	3.2810
Kilometers	miles	0.6214
Meters	yards	1.0940
Mass		
Grams	ounces	0.0352
Kilograms	pounds	2.2050
Tonnes	long tons	0.9843
Tonnes	short tons	1.1025
Area		
Square centimeters	square inches	0.1550
Square meters	square feet	10.7600
Hectares	acres	2.4710
Square kilometers	square miles	0.3861
Square meters	square yards	1.1960
Volume		
Cubic centimeters	cubic inches	0.0610
Cubic meters	cubic feet	35.3100
Capacity		
Liters	pints	2.1134
Liters	gallons	0.2642

IMPERIAL - METRIC CONVERSIONS

TO CONVERT	INTO	MULTIPLY BY
Length		
Inches	centimeters	2.5400
Feet	meters	0.3048
Miles	kilomecentimeters	1.6090
Yards	meters	0.9144
Mass		
Ounces	grams	28.3500
Pounds	kilograms	0.4536
Long tons	tonnes	1.0160
Short tons	tonnes	0.9070
Area		
Square inches	square centimeters	6.4520
Square feet	square meters	0.0929
Acres	hectares	0.4047
Square miles	square kilometers	2.5900
Square yards	square meters	0.8361
Volume		
Cubic inches	cubic centimeters	16.3900
Cubic feet	cubic metrers	0.0283
Capacity		
Pints	litres	0.4732
Gallons	litres	4.4049

RULES OF ALGEBRA

EXPRESSION	COMMENTS	EXPRESSION BECOMES
a + a	Simple addition	2a
a + b = c + d	Subtract b from either side	a = c + d − b
ab = cd	Divide both sides by b	a = cd ÷ b
(a + b) (c + d)	Multiply terms in parentheses	ac + ad + bc + bd
$a^2 + ab$	Use parentheses	a(a + b)
$(a + b)^2$	Expand terms in parentheses	$a^2 + 2ab + b^2$
$a^2 − b^2$	Difference of two squares	(a + b)(a − b)
1/a + 1/b	Find common denominator	(a + b)/ab
a/b ÷ c/d	Dividing by a fraction is the same as multiplying by its reciprocal	a/b × d/c

POWERS OF TEN USED WITH SCIENTIFIC UNITS

FACTOR	NAME	PREFIX	SYMBOL
10^{18}	quintillion	exa-	E
10^{15}	quadrillion	peta-	P
10^{12}	trillion	tera-	T
10^9	billion	giga-	G
10^6	million	mega-	M
10^3	thousand	kilo-	k
10^2	hundred	hecto-	h
10^1	ten	deca-	da
10^{-1}	one tenth	deci-	d
10^{-2}	one hundredth	centi-	c
10^{-3}	one thousandth	milli-	m
10^{-6}	one millionth	micro-	μ
10^{-9}	one billionth	nano-	n
10^{-12}	one trillionth	pico-	p
10^{-15}	one quadrillionth	femto-	f
10^{-18}	one quintillionth	atto-	a

Note: The American system of numeration for denominations above one million is used in this book. In this system, each of the denominations above one billion (1,000 millions) is 1,000 times the preceding one.

BIOLOGY SYMBOLS

SYMBOL	MEANING
○	female individual (used in inheritance charts)
□	male individual (used in inheritance charts)
♀	female
♂	male
x	crossed with; hybrid
+	wild type
F_1	offspring of the first generation
F_2	offspring of the second generation

TEMPERATURE SCALES

To convert from Fahrenheit to Celsius: C = (F − 32) × 5 ÷ 9
To convert from Celsius (C) to Fahrenheit (F): F = (C × 9 ÷ 5) + 32
To convert from Celsius to Kelvin (K): K = C + 273
To convert from Kelvin to Celsius: C = K − 273

Fahrenheit	-4	14	32	50	68	86	104	122	140	158	176	194	212
Celsius	-20	-10	0	10	20	30	40	50	60	70	80	90	100
Kelvin	253	263	273	283	293	303	313	323	333	343	353	363	373

PHYSICS SYMBOLS

SYMBOL	MEANING
α	alpha particle
β	beta ray
γ	gamma ray; photon
ε	electromotive force
η	efficiency; viscosity
λ	wavelength
μ	micro-; permeability
ν	frequency; neutrino
ρ	density; resistivity
σ	conductivity
c	velocity of light
e	electronic charge

SCIENTIFIC NOTATION

NUMBER	NUMBER BETWEEN 1 AND 10	POWER OF TEN	SCIENTIFIC NOTATION
10	1	10^1	1.5×10^1
150	1.5	10^2 (= 100)	1.5×10^2
274,000,000	2.74	10^8 (= 100,000,000)	2.74×10^8
0.0023	2.3	10^{-3} (= 0.001)	2.3×10^{-3}

MATHEMATICAL SYMBOLS

SYMBOL	EXPLANATION
+	addition
−	subtraction
×	multiplication
÷	division
=	equals
≠	does not equal
>	greater than
<	less than
≥	greater than or equal to
≤	less than or equal to
∞	infinity
%	percent
π	pi (3.1416)
°	degree
≈	is approximately equal to
∠	angle
∥	parallel to
Σ	summation
u,u	vectors
f(x)	function
!	factorial
√	square root
$\mathscr{E}$	universal set
A ∩ B	intersection
A ∪ B	unison
A ⊂ B	subset
∅	null set

CHEMISTRY SYMBOLS

SYMBOL	MEANING
+	plus; together with
−	single bond
•	single bond; single unpaired electron; two separate parts or compounds regarded as loosely joined
=	double bond
≡	triple bond
R	group
X	halogen atom
Z	atomic number

TRIGONOMETRY

Angle A (degrees)	sin A	cos A	tan A
0	0	1	0
30	1/2	$\sqrt{3}/2$	$1/\sqrt{3}$
45	$1/\sqrt{2}$	$1/\sqrt{2}$	1
60	$\sqrt{3}/2$	1/2	$\sqrt{3}$
90	1	0	∞

Shapes: Plane

Two-dimensional shapes are termed plane (or flat) shapes. Plane shapes constructed with straight sides, as illustrated here, are called polygons. They are categorized according to the number of sides they have – for example, three-sided polygons are known as triangles. A polygon that has sides of equal length and internal angles of equal size, such as a square, are said to be regular.

AREAS AND PERIMETERS

The formulae for calculating the areas and perimeters of simple plane shapes were devised by Classical Greek mathematicians.

SCALENE TRIANGLE
A triangle (three-sided polygon) with no equal sides or angles.

ISOSCELES TRIANGLE
A triangle with only two sides and two angles equal.

RIGHT-ANGLED TRIANGLE
A triangle with one angle as a right angle (90°).

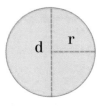

CIRCLE
r = radius
d = diameter = $2 \times r$

Circumference = $2 \times \pi \times r$
Area = $\pi \times r^2$
($\pi = 3.1416$)

EQUILATERAL TRIANGLE
A regular triangle. All angles are 60°.

SQUARE
A regular quadrilateral. All angles are 90°.

RHOMBUS
A quadrilateral with all sides equal and two pairs of equal angles.

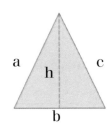

TRIANGLE
Height = h
Sides = a, b, c

Perimeter = $a + b + c$
Area = $\frac{1}{2} \times b \times h$

RECTANGLE
A quadrilateral with four right angles and opposite sides of equal length.

PARALLELOGRAM
A quadrilateral with two pairs of parallel sides.

TRAPEZIUM
A quadrilateral with one pair of parallel sides.

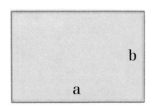

RECTANGLE
Sides = a, b

Perimeter = $2 \times (a + b)$
Area = $a \times b$

PENTAGON
A five-sided polygon. A regular pentagon is shown above.

HEXAGON
A six-sided polygon. A regular hexagon is shown above.

OCTAGON
An eight-sided polygon. A regular octagon is shown above.

Shapes: Solid

Three-dimensional shapes are known as solid shapes, and include spheres, cubes, and pyramids. A solid shape with a polygon at each face is called a polyhedron.

Volume refers to the amount of space that a solid object occupies. Its surface area is the sum of the area of each of its faces.

CYLINDER
Surface area =
$2 \times \pi \times r \times h + 2\pi r^2$
Volume $= \pi \times r^2 \times h$

Height = h
Radius = r

TETRAHEDRON
A four-sided polyhedron. A regular tetrahedron is shown.

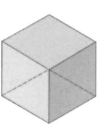

CUBE
A regular hexahedron. All sides are equal and all angles are 90°.

OCTAHEDRON
A polyhedron with eight sides.

PRISM
A polyhedron of constant cross-sections in planes perpendicular to its longitudinal axis.

PYRAMID
A polygonal base and triangular sides that meet at a point.

TORUS
A doughnut-like, ring shape.

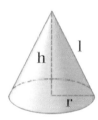

CONE
Surface area =
$\pi \times r \times l + \pi r^2$
Volume $= \frac{1}{3} \times \pi \times r^2 \times l$

Height = h
Radius = r
Side = l

SPHERE
A round shape, as in a ball or an orange.

HEMISPHERE
Formed when a sphere is cut exactly in half.

SPHEROID
An egg-shaped solid object whose cross-section is a circle or an ellipse.

CONE
An elliptical or circular base with sides tapering to a single point.

RIGHT CYLINDER
A tube-shaped, solid figure. A right cylinder has parallel faces.

HELIX
A twisted curve. The distance moved in one revolution is its pitch.

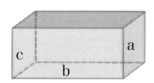

RECTANGULAR BLOCK
Surface area =
$2 (a \times b + b \times c + a \times c)$
Volume $= a \times b \times c$

Sides = a, b, c

Index

Alternator
  Diesel train 326
  Ford V6 12-valve engine 344
  Jaguar V12 engine 345
  NPT 301 turbojet 418
  Renault Clio 351
Alternator belt 351
Altitude scale 377
Alto clef 502
Altocumulus cloud 302
Alto mute 507
Altostratus cloud 302
Alto voice 502
Aludra 21
Alula 191
Aluminum 311
  Earth's composition 39
  Earth's crust 58
Aluminum alloy backing 346
Aluminum arrow shaft 548
Aluminum beam 560
Aluminum cowl 401
Aluminum flush-riveted skin 407
Aluminum gearbox casing 366
Aluminum racket 544
Aluminum shield 612
Aluminum wheel 406
Aluminum wire figure 455
Alveolar artery and vein 247
Alveolar bone 247
Alveoli 254-255
Amaryllis 155
Amateur rules 552
Amazon Basin 39
Amazonis Planitia 43
Amazon River 264
Ambiens muscle
  Albertosaurus 84
  Iguanodon 97
Ambulacral groove 79, 175
Ambulatory corridor 465
Ameldental junction 247
American alligator 186
American beaver 197
American black bear 195
American squash court 545
American squash game 544
Americium 311
Ammonia
  Jupiter's atmosphere 45
  Saturn's atmosphere 47
  Structure of Neptune 51
  Structure of Uranus 49
Ammonite 278-279
Ammonite shell 267
Ammonium dichromate 312
Ammonium hydrosulfide
  Jupiter's atmosphere 45
  Saturn's atmosphere 47
Ammophila arenaria 113
Ammunition 548-549
Ammunition box 408
Amnion 192-193, 260
Amniotic egg 80
Amniotic fluid 192, 260
Amniotic sac 260
Amoebocyte 166
Amphibia 182
Amphibian 80-81, 182-183
  Earth's evolution 56
  Fossil 278
  Fossil record 279
  Primitive 68-69, 78
Amphibole 275
Amphitheatre 464-465
Amplification
  Drums 518
  Electronic instruments 520

Guitar 512
Stringed instruments 510
  Vibraphone 516
  Xylophone 516
Amplifier 520
Amps 316
Ampulla
  Ear 242-243
  Fallopian tube 258-259
  Sea urchin 175
  Starfish 174
Ampullar nerve 242
Anal canal 249
Anal clasper 169
Anal fin
  Bony fish 180-181
  Lamprey 178
Anal fin ray 180
Anal flap 200
Analogue action buttons 579
Analogue thumb stick 579
Anal sphincter muscle 249
Anchisaurus 88-89
Anchor
  74-gun ship 380
  BAe-146 components 412, 414
  Battleship 394-395
  Frigate 397
  Junk 376
  Roman corbita 372
  Square-rigged ship 375
  Tea clipper 392
  Types 386
  Wooden sailing ship 379
Anchor bearing 413
Anchor buoy 379
Anchor cable
  74-gun ship 380
  Sailing warship 376
Anchor chain 386, 395
Anchoring 386-387
Anchor-joint 492
Anchor rode 372
Anchor rope 372-373
Ancient Egyptian building 458-459
Ancient Greek building 460-461, 462
Ancient Greeks 542
Ancient Roman building 462-465, 474
Ancillary drive belt 347
Ancillary drive pulley 345
Ancorale 372
Andamenti 451
Andes
  Cretaceous period 73
  Earth's external features 39
  Jurassic period 71
  Quaternary period 77
  Satellite map 264
  Tertiary period 75
  Triassic period 69
Androecium 140-141, 143
Andromeda 19, 20
Andromeda Galaxy 14, 19
Antares 18, 21
Antefixa 461
Antelope 198
Antenna
  Battleship 395
  Crab 172
  Crayfish 173
  Frigate 397
  Global positioning system 590, 591
  Honda Insight 354
  Insects 168-169
  Malacostraca 172
  Roman corbita 372-373
  Shrimp 172
  Volleyball net 534
Antennule 173
Anterior antebrachial muscle 86
Anterior aorta 170
Anterior arch 222

Angular process 194
Angular unconformity 276
Anhydrous copper sulfate 313
Animal cloning 607
Animal life
  Electromagnetic radiation 314
  Primitive 78
Animal remains
  Fossils 278
  Sedimentary rocks 276
Animal stances 82
Animals 56, 67, 78
Anions 308
Ankle
  Anchisaurus 89
  Corythosaurus 98
  Edmontonia 95
  Herrerasaurus 86
  Human 211
  Iguanodon 96
  Pachycephalosaurus 100
  Psittacosaurus 103
  Stegoceras 101
  Stegosaurus 92
  Triceratops 102
  Tyrannosaurus 84
Ankle joint
  Brachiosaurus 90
  Diplodocus 90
  Euoplocephalus 94
  Human 219
  Parasaurolophus 98
  Plateosaurus 88
  Stegoceras 101
  Struthiomimus 87
  Triceratops 102
  Tyrannosaurus 84
Ankylosaurs 83, 92, 94-95
Anne's Spot 47
Annual growth ring 125
Annuals 128
Annular river drainage 288
Annular tendon 241
Annulet 460
Annulus
  Fern 121
  Mushroom 115
Annulus of trunk 201
Ant 168
Anta 461
Antarala 490-491
Antarctica
  Cretaceous period 72-73
  Earth's physical features 264-265
  Jurassic period 70
  Late Carboniferous period 66
  Quaternary period 76-77
  Tertiary period 74-75
  Triassic period 68
Antarctic Circle
  Satellite map 265
  Surface currents 297
Antarctic circumpolar current 296
Antares 18, 21
Antefixa 461
Antelope 198
Antenna
  Battleship 395
  Crab 172
  Crayfish 173
  Frigate 397
  Global positioning system 590, 591
  Honda Insight 354
  Insects 168-169
  Malacostraca 172
  Roman corbita 372-373
  Shrimp 172
  Volleyball net 534
Antennule 173
Anterior antebrachial muscle 86
Anterior aorta 170
Anterior arch 222

Anterior brachial muscle
  Brachiosaurus 91
  Gallimimus 86
Anterior branch of spinal nerve 223
Anterior chamber 241
Anterior chamber of cloaca 185
Anterior crural muscle
  Brachiosaurus 90
  Gallimimus 86
Anterior dorsal fin
  Bony fish 181
  Dogfish 179
  Lamprey 178
Anterior fontanelle 220
Anterior horn 223
Anterior median fissure 223, 238
Anterior median vein 253
Anterior nasal spine 220-221
Anterior petal 141
Anterior root 238
Anterior semicircular canal 243
Anterior sepal 141
Anterior tentacle 177
Anterior tibial artery 253
Anterior tibial muscle
  Albertosaurus 84
  Iguanodon 97
Anterior tubercle 222
Anterior wing of shell 176
Antheridium 117
  Fern 121
  Moss 119
Antherozoids 116-117
  Fern 121
  Moss 119
Anthers 140-143, 145
  Dicotyledons 126-127
  Fertilization 146-147
  Pollination process 144-145
Anthozoa 166
Anthracite coal 280
Anthropoids 202
Anthriscus sp. 135
Anthurium andreanum 143
Antibodies 253
Anticlinal fold 60
Anticline 60-61, 62
Anticline trap 280-281
Anticlinorium 61
Anti-collision beacon 422-423
Anti-corrosion paint 413
Anticyclonic storm system
  Cloud features of Neptune 50
  Structure of Saturn 47
Anti-friction pad 552
Anti-glare lens 553
Anti-glare screen surface 584
Antihelix 242
Anti-lift bracing wire
  Avro triplane 403
  Blackburn monoplane 401
  Blériot XI monoplane 401
  LVG CVI fighter 405
Anti-lift wire 399
Antimacassar 329
Antimony 311
Antipodal cell 147
Anti-reflective coating 605
Anti-reverse drive 562
Anti-roll bar
  Renault Clio 350-351
  Volkswagen Beetle 340
Antishock swivel base 584
Anti-submarine torpedo tube 397
Anti-surge baffle 344

Anti-torque tail rotor 423
Antitragus 242
Anti-vibration engine mount 411
Antler hammer 109
Antler harpoon 109
Antlia 18, 21
Antoniadi 41
Antorbital fenestra
  Baryonyx 83
  Camarasaurus 91
  Diplodocus 90
  Plateosaurus 88
Anura 182
Anus
  Barnacle 173
  Bony fish 181
  Butterfly 169
  Cow 198
  Crayfish 173
  Dolphin 205
  Domestic cat 195
  Elephant 200
  Human 249, 258, 261
  Octopus 176
  Rabbit 196
  Sea urchin 175
  Snail 177
  Spider 170
  Starfish 174
  Tortoise 187
Anvil 242
Aorta
  Anterior 170
  Bony fish 181
  Dogfish 179
  Dolphin 205
  Dorsal 179, 181, 182
  Human 215, 250-251, 252, 255, 256-257
  Posterior 170
  Spider 170
  Ventral 179
Apatite 271
Ape 108, 202-203
Aperture 610, 612, 613
Aperture door 612, 613
Aperture door mounting 612
Aperture plate 611
Apex
  Beetle wing 168
  Butterfly wing 169
  Calligraphy characters 445
  Clubmoss shoot 120
  Fern frond 121
  Fern pinnule 121
  Horsetail shoot 120
  Leaf 136-137, 154-155
  Lung 255
  Moss 119
  Pegasus XL SE microlight 426
  Pine shoot 125
  Snail shell 177
  Tongue 244-245
Apex seal 347
Apex wire 426
Aphelion 30-31
Aphrodite Terra 36-37
Apical bud
  Bulb 155
  Pine shoot 125
Apical foramen 247
Apical meristem 134
Apical notch
  Seaweed 116
  Thalloid liverwort 118
Apollo 41
Apomixis 146
Apophysis 119
Apothecium 114
Appalachian mountains
  Late Cretaceous period 67
  Mountain building 62
  Quaternary period 77
  Satellite map 264
  Tertiary period 75

Triassic period 69
Apparent magnitude 22
Appendix
  Chimpanzee 202
  Human 249
  Rabbit 196
Appendix orifice 249
Apple 148-149
Apple Ipod 587
Apple Macintosh G4 computer 521
Apple Macintosh PCs 566
Apple Power Mac G4 1GHz dual processor 567
Approach 543
Apse 465, 469, 481
Aquarius 19, 20
Aquatic mammals 104
Aqueduct 236
Aqueous humour 241
Aquiclude 292
Aquifer 292
Aquiferous system 166
Aquila 19, 20
Ara 20
Ara ararauna 190
Arabesque
  Islamic building 488-489
  Neoclassical molding 480
Arabia
  Cretaceous period 72
  Jurassic period 70
Arabian Desert 265
Arabic number system 620
Arachnids 170-171
Arachnoid granulation 237
Arachnoid mater 237, 240
Aral Sea 265
Araneae 170
Araucaria araucana 68
Arcade
  Ancient Roman building 464-465
  Baroque church 479-481
  Gothic building 470-471
  Medieval church 468-469
  Twentieth-century building 495
Arcadia Planitia 43
Arch 484-485
  Ancient Roman building 462, 464-465
  Asian building 490-491
  Baroque church 479, 480
  Calligraphy characters 445
  Cathedral dome 487
  Coastline features 295
  French temple 484-485
  Gothic church 470-473
  High jump 543
  Islamic building 488-489
  Medieval building 466-469
  Nineteenth-century building 492-493
  Renaissance building 474-475
Archaeopteryx 57, 84, 85
Arched brace 473
Arched doorway 474, 475
Arched roof 493
Archegoniophore 118
Archegonium
  Fern 121
  Liverwort 118
  Moss 119
  Scots pine 122
Archery 548-549
Archery screen 377
Archimedes 40
Architrave
  Ancient Egyptian temple 458-459

648

668

Acknowledgments

Dorling Kindersley would like to thank (in order of sections):

**The Universe
(consultant editors – Sue Becklake, Gevorkyan Tatyana Alekseyevna):**
John Becklake; the Memorial Museum of Cosmonautics, Moscow; The Cosmos Pavilion, Moscow; The United States Space and Rocket Centre, Alabama; Broadhurst, Clarkson and Fuller Ltd; Susannah Massey

**Prehistoric Earth
(consultant editors – William Lindsay, Martyn Bramwell, Dr Ralph E. Molnar, David Lambert):**
Dr Monty Reid, Andrew Neuman, and the staff of the Royal Tyrrell Museum of Palaeontology, Drumheller, Alberta; Dr Angela Milner and the staff of the Department of Palaeontology, the Natural History Museum, London; Professor W. Ziegler and the staff, in particular Michael Loderstaedt, of the Naturmuseum Senckenburg, Frankfurt; Dr Alexander Liebau, Axel Hunghrebüller, Reiner Schoch, and the staff of the Institut und Museum für Geologie und Paläontologie der Universität, Tübingen; Rupert Wild of the Institut für Paläontologie, Staatliches Museum für Naturkunde, Stuttgart; Dr Scheiber of the Stadtmuseum, Nördlingen; Professor Dr Dietrich Herm of Staatssammlung für Paläontologie und Historische Geologie, München; Dr Michael Keith-Lucas of the Department of Botany, University of Reading; Richard Walker; American Museum of Natural History, New York

**Plants
(consultant editor – Richard Walker):**
Diana Miller; Lawrie Springate; Karen Sidwell; Chris Thody; Michelle End; Susan Barnes and Chris Jones of the EMU Unit of the Natural History Museum, London; Jenny Evans of Kew Gardens, London; Kate Biggs of the Royal Horticultural Society Gardens, Wisley, Surrey; Spike Walker of Microworld Services; Neil Fletcher; John Bryant of Bedgebury Pinetum, Kent; Dean Franklin

**Animals
(consultant editor – Richard Walker):**
David Manning's Animal Ark; Intellectual Animals; Howletts Zoo, Canterbury; John Dunlop; Alexander O'Donnell; Sue Evans of the Royal Veterinary College, London; Dr Geoff Potts and Fred Frettsome of the Marine Biological Association of the United Kingdom, Plymouth; Jeremy Adams of the Booth Museum of Natural History, Brighton; Derek Telling of the Department of Anatomy, University of Bristol; the Natural History Museum, London; Andy Highfield of the Tortoise Trust; Brian Harris of the Aquarium, London Zoo; the Invertebrate Department, London Zoo; Dr Harold McClure of the Yerkes Regional Primate Research Center, Emory University, Atlanta, Georgia; Nielson Lausen of the Harvard Medical School, New England Regional Primates Research

Centre, Southborough, Massachusetts; Dr Paul Hopwood of the Department of Veterinary Anatomy, University of Sydney; Dean Franklin

**The Human Body
(consultant editors – Dr Frances Williams, Dr Fiona Payne, Richard Cummins FRCS):**
Derek Edwards and Dr Martin Collins, British School of Osteopathy; Dr M.C.E. Hutchinson of the Department of Anatomy, United Medical and Dental Schools of Guy's and St Thomas' Hospitals, London. Models – Barry O'Rorke (Bodyline Agency) and Pauline Swaine (MOT Model Agency)

**Geology, Geography, and Meteorology
(consultant editor – Martyn Bramwell):**
Dr John Nudds of the Manchester Museum, Manchester; Dr Alan Wooley and Dr Andrew Clark of the Natural History Museum, London; Graham Bartlett of the National Meteorological Library and Archive, Bracknell; Tony Drake of BP Exploration, Uxbridge; Jane Davies of the Royal Society of Chemistry, Cambridge; Dr Tony Waltham of Nottingham Trent University, Nottingham; staff of the Smithsonian Institute, Washington; staff of the United States Geological Survey, Washington; staff of the National Geographic Society, Washington; staff of Edward Lawrence Associates (Export Ltd), Midhurst; John Farndon; David Lambert

**Rail and Road
Rail (consultant editor – John Coiley)**
Michael Ashworth of the London Transport Museum

Road (consultant editors – David Burgess-Wise, Hugo Wilson)
The National Motor Museum, Beaulieu; Alf Newell of Renault UK Ltd; David Suter of Cheltenham Cutaway Exhibits Ltd; Francesca Riccini of the Science Museum, London. Signore Amadelli of the Museo dell' Automobile Carlo Biscaretti di Ruffia; Paul Bolton of the Mazda MCL Group; Duncan Bradford of Reg Mills Wire Wheels; John and Leslie Brewster of Autocavan; David Burgess-Wise; Trevor Cass of Garrett Turbo Service; John Corbett of The Patrick Collection; Gary Crumpler of Williams Grand Prix Engineering Ltd; Mollie Easterbrooke and Duncan Gough of Overland Ltd; Arthur Fairley of the Vauxhall Motor Company; Paul Foulkes-Halbard of Filching Manor Motor Museum; Frank Gilbert of I. Wilkinson and Son Ltd; Paolo Gratton of Gratton Museum; Colvin Gunn of Gunn and Son; Judy Hogg of Ecurie Bertelli; Milton Holman of Dream Cars; Ian Matthews of IMAT Electronics; Eric Neal of Jaguar Cars Ltd; Paul Niblett, Keith Davidson, Mark Reumel, and David Woolf of Michelin Tyre plc; Doug Nye; Kevin O'Keefe of O'Keefe Cars; Seat UK; Ian Whitley, Raj Johal and Andy Faiers of the Honda Institute; Roger Smith; Jim Stirling of Ironbridge Gorge Museum, Staffordshire; Jon Taylor; Doug Thompson; Martyn Watkins of Ford Motor Company Ltd, John Cattermole, Customer Services Manager at London Northern Buses; F. W. Evans Cycles Ltd; Trek UK Ltd (Bicycle); Sam Grimmer; Colin Uttley

**Physics and Chemistry
(consultant editor – Jack Challoner)**

**Sea and Air
Sea (consultant editors – Geoff Hales and Harvey B. Loomis):**
David Spence, Gillian Hutchinson, David Topliss, Simon Stephens, Robert Baldwin, Jonathan Betts, all of the National Maritime Museum, London; Ian Friel; Simon Turnage of Captain O.M. Watts of London Ltd; Davey and Company Ltd, Great Dunmow; Avon Inflatables Ltd, Llanelli; Musto Ltd, Benfleet; Peter Martin of Spencer Rigging Ltd, Southampton; Peter Rowson of Ratseys Sailmakers, Southampton; Swiftech Ltd, Wallingford; Colin Scattergood of the Barrow Boat Company Ltd, Colchester; Professor J.S. Morrison of the Trireme Trust, Cambridge; The Cutty Sark Maritime Trust; Adrian Daniels of Kelvin Hughes Marine Instruments, London; Arthur Credland of Hull City Council Museums and Art Galleries; The Hull Maritime Society; Gerald Clark; Peter Fitzgerald of the Science Museum, London; Alec Michael of HMB Subwork Ltd, Great Yarmouth, and Ray Ward of the OSEL Group, Great Yarmouth; Richard Bird of UWI, Weybridge; Walker Marine Instruments, Birmingham; The International Sailing Craft Association; The Exeter Maritime Museum; Jane Wilson of the Trinity Lighthouse Company, London; The Imperial War Museum Collections; Thorn Security Ltd; Michael Bach

Air (consultant editor – Bill Gunston):
Aeromega Helicopters, Stapleford; Aero Shopping, London; Avionics Mobile Services Ltd, Watford; Roy Barber and John Chapman of the RAF Museum, Hendon; Mitch Barnes Aviation, London; Mike Beach; British Caledonian Flight Training Ltd; Fred Coates of Helitech (Luton) Ltd; Michael Cuttell and CSE Aviation Ltd, Oxford; Dowty Aerospace Landing Gear, Gloucester; Guy Hartcup of the Airship Association; Anthony Hooley, Chris Walsh, and David Cord of British Aerospace Regional Aircraft Ltd; Ken Huntley of Mid-West Aero Engines Ltd; Imperial War Museum, Duxford; The London Gliding Club, Dunstable; Musée des Ballons, Calvados; Noel Penny Turbines Ltd; Andy Pavey of Aviation Scotland Ltd; Tony Pavey of Thermal Aircraft Developments, London; the Commanding Officer and personnel of RAF St Athan; the Commanding Officer and personnel of RAF Wittering; The Science Museum, London; Ross Sharp of the Science Museum, Wroughton; The Shuttleworth Collection; Skysport Engineering; Mike Smith; Solar Wings Ltd, Marlborough; Julian Temple of Brooklands Museum Trust Ltd; Kelvin Wilson of Flying Start

**Architecture
(consultant editor – Alexandra Kennedy):**
Stephen Cutler for advice and text; Gavin Morgan of the Museum of London, London; Chris Zeuner of the Weald and Downland Museum, Singleton, Sussex; Alan Hills and James Putnam of the British Museum, London; Dr Simon Penn and Michael Thomas of the Avoncroft Museum of Buildings, Bromsgrove,

Worcestershire; Christina Scull of Sir John Soane's Museum, London; Paul Kennedy and John Williamson of the London Door Company, London; Lou Davis of The Original Box Sash Window Company, Windsor; Goddard and Gibbs Studios Ltd, London, for access to stained glass windows; The Royal Courts of Justice, Strand, London; Charles Brooking and Peter Dalton for access to the doors and windows in the Charles Brooking Collection, University of Greenwich, Dartford, Kent; Clare O'Brien of the Shakespeare Globe Trust, Shakespeare's Globe Museum, Bear Gardens, Southwark, London; Ken Teague of the Horniman Museum, London; Canon Haliburton, Mike Payton, Ken Stones, and Anthony Webb of St Paul's Cathedral, London; Roy Spring of Salisbury Cathedral; Reverend Gillean Craig of the Church of St George in the East, London; the Science Museum, London; Dr Neil Bingham; Lin Kennedy of Historic Royal Palaces; Katy Harris of Sir Norman Foster and Partners; Production Design, Thames Television plc, London; Dominique Reynier of Le Centre Georges Pompidou, Paris; Denis Roche of Le Musée National des Monuments Français, Paris; Franck Gioria and students of Les Compagnons du Devoir, Paris, for access to construction models; Frank Folliot of Le Musée Carnavalet, Paris; Dr Martina Harms of Hessische Landesmuseums, Darmstadt; Jefferson Chapman of the University of Tennessee, Knoxville, for access to the model of the Hypostyle Hall, Temple of Amon-Re; staff of the Palazzo Strozzi, Florence; staff of the Sydney Opera House, Sydney; staff of the Empire State Building, New York, Nick Jackson; Ann Terrell

The Visual Arts
(consultant editor – Pip Seymour):

Rosemary Simmons; Michael Taylor of Paupers Press, London; Tessa Hunkin and Emma Biggs of Mosaic Workshop, London; John Tiranti, Jonathan Lyons of Alec Tiranti Ltd, London; Chris Hough; Dr Ashok Roy; Satwinder Sehmi of Alphabet Soup, London; Phillip Poole of Cornelissens, London; George Weil and Sons Ltd, London; The National Gallery, London; Chris Webster of the Tate Gallery, London; China Art Cultural Centre, London; London Graphic Centre, London; A.P. Fitzpatrick, London; Flowers Graphics, London; Intaglio Printmaker, London; Falkiner Papers, London; Edgar Udny and Co, London; John Green

Music
(consultant editor – Susan Sturrock):

Boosey and Hawkes Music Publishers Ltd, London, for permission to reproduce extract from The Prodigal Son by Arthur Sullivan; The Bass and Drum Cellar, London; Empire Drums and Percussion, London; Argents (part of World of Music), London; Bill Lewington Ltd, London; Frobenius organ at Kingston Parish Church, Surrey; Yamaha-Kemble Music (UK) Ltd, Tilbrook, Milton Keynes; Yamaha Atelier, London; Akai (UK) Ltd, Hounslow, Middlesex; Casio Electronics Co. Ltd, London; Roland (UK) Ltd, Fleet, Hampshire; Richard Schulman; Andy Brown of Musictrack

Sports
The Sports Council Information Centre, London; The British Olympic Games Committee; Brian Crennell of Black's Leisure Group (First Sport); Lillywhites of Piccadilly, London; Mitre Sports International Ltd, Huddersfield; David Bloomfield of the Football Association; Denver Athletics Ltd, Norfolk; Greg Everest and Keith Birley of the British League of Australian Rules Football; Peter McNally of the Gaelic Athletic Association; Jeremy Garman of James Gilbert Ltd.; Rex King of the Rugby Football Union, Twickenham; Neil Tunnicliffe and John Huxley of the Rugby Football League, Leeds; Wayne Patterson of the Basketball Hall of Fame, Springfield, Connecticut; Brian Coleman of the English Basketball Association; All American Imports, Northampton; George Bulman of the English Volleyball Association; Julie Longdon of Mizuno Mallory (UK) Ltd; Juliet Stanford of the All-England Netball Association; Jeff Rowland of the British Handball Association; Cally Melin of Adidas UK Ltd; Patrick Donnely of the Baseball Hall of Fame, Cooperstown, New York; Ian Lepage and Stephen Barlow of the Hockey Association, Milton Keynes; Alison Taylor and Anita Mason of the All England Women's Lacrosse Association, Birmingham; David Shuttleworth of the English Lacrosse Union; Les Barnett and Jock Bentley of the British Athletic Federation Ltd, Birmingham; Mike Gilks of the Badminton Association of England; Gurinder Purewall for advice on archery; Chris McCartney of the US Archery Association; Geoff Doe of the National Smallbore Rifle Association, Bisley, Surrey, for information and reference material on shooting; Fagan Sports Goods Distributors, Surrey; Konrad Bartelski for advice on skiing; The British Ski Federation, Edinburgh; Mike Barnett of Snow and Rock of London; Sally Spurway of Mast-Co. Ltd, Reading; Sarah Morgan for advice on equestrian sports; Steve Brown and the New York Racing Association Inc, New York; Danrho of London; Alan Skipp and James Chambers of the Amateur Fencing Association, London; Carla Richards of the US Fencing Association; Hamilton Bland and John Dryer of the Amateur Swimming Association, Loughborough; Cotswold Camping Ltd, London; Tim Spalton of Glyn Locke (Racing Shells) Ltd, Chalgrove; Terry Friel of the US Rowing Association; House of Hardy; Leeda Fishing Tackle

The Modern World
John Lewis, Brent Cross, for the loan of products for photography; Apple Computers UK; Palm Inc.; Epson UK; Naynesh Mistry of Brother UK; Nintendo; Sony UK; Nokia Mobile Phones Ltd; Sony Ericsson; Tony Broad of Garmin Europe; Dualit Ltd; Black and Decker Ltd; James Honour of the Buildings Research Establishment; Craig Anders of Cole Thompson Associates; Vestas Wind Systems; Bryan Adams of MIT; Dr Julian Heath of Microscopy and Analysis; Fei UK Ltd; Steve Parker; Ian Graham

PHOTOGRAPHY:
M. Alexander; Peter Anderson; Colin Bowling; Charles Brooks; Jane Burton; Peter Chadwick; Simon Clay; Gordon Clayton; John Coiley; Andy Crawford; Geoff Dann; Philip Dowell; John Downs; Mike Dunning; Torla Evans; David Exton; Paul Forrester; Robert and Anthony Fretwell of Fretwell Photography Ltd.; Philip Gatward; Steve Gorton; Anna Hodgson; Gary Kevin; J. Heseltine; Cyril Laubscher; John Lepine; Lynton Gardiner (American Museum of Natural History, New York); Steve Gorton; Michelangelo Gratton; Judith Harrington; Peter Hayman; Anna Hodgson; Colin Keates; Gary Kevin; Dave King; Bob Langrish; Brian D.Morgan; Nick Nicholls; Nick Parfitt; Tim Parmenter and Colin Keates (Natural History Museum, London); Tim Ridley; Dave Rudkin; Philippe Sebert; James Stevenson; Clive Streeter; Harry Taylor; Matthew Ward; Jerry Young

PHOTOGRAPHIC ASSISTANCE:
Kevin Zak; Gary Ombler

ILLUSTRATORS:
Julian Baum; Rick Blakeley; Kuo Kang Chen; Karen Cochrane; Simone End; Ian Fleming; Roy Flooks; Mark Franklin; David Gardner; Will Giles; Mick Gillah; David Hopkins; Selwyn Hutchinson, Mei Lim, Linden Artists; Nick Loates; Chris Lyon; Kathleen McDougall; Coral Mula; Sandra Pond; Dave Pugh; Colin Rose; Graham Rosewarne; John Temperton, Halli Verrinder; John Woodcock; Chris Woolmer

MODEL MAKERS:
Roby Braun; David Donkin; Morrison Frederick; Gordon Models; John Holmes; Graham High and Jeremy Hunt of Centaur Studios; Richard Kemp; Kelvin Thatcher; Paul Wilkinson

ADDITIONAL DESIGN ASSISTANCE:
Stefan Morris; Ulysses Santos; Suchada Smith

ADDITIONAL EDITORIAL ASSISTANCE:
Helen Castle; Colette Connolly; Camela Decaire; Nick Harris; Andrea Horth; Stewart McEwen; Damien Moore; Melanie Tham

INDEX: Kay Wright; Lynn Bresler

Picture credits:

Action Plus 530tc; Anglo Australian Telescope Board 11cl, 11cra, 11cbl, 12tr, 12bc, 13tl, 13bl, 14tl, 16b, 17tc, 17bl, 22tl/D.Malin 16tl, 26tr, 27tl; Apple Computer Inc. 521b; Austin Brown and the Aviation Picture Library 426tl; Baptistery, Florence/Alison Harris 453r; Biophoto Associates 217ca, 217cra, 228cbc, 228cbc 230tr; BRE Imaging 602bl, 602r, 603tr, 603br; Paul Brierley 311bra; British Aerospace/Anthony Hooley 412tl, 415tl; British Aerospace (Commercial Aircraft) Ltd 416tl; By prmission of the British Library 432tl, 445bl; British Museum 459tl, 459tr, 460tr, 460tc, 460tb, 489b; BP Exploration 299; Duncan Brown 25tl; Frank Lloyd Wright, American, 1867-1959, Model of Midway Gardens, 1914, executed by Richard Tickner, mixed media, 1987, 41.9 x 81.3 x 76.2, 1989.48. view 1. Photography courtesy of the Art Intitute of Chicago 495t; J.A. Coiley 331cr; Bruce Coleman Ltd/Andy Price 272tl; Courtesy of the Board of Trustees of the Victoria and Albert Museum, London 454-455b; Dyson 592tr; European Passenger Services 329tl; ESA /PLV 11bl; Fei Co. 610tc, 610r; French Railways 329c; Garmin Europe 590c; Geoscience Features 311cla; Robert Harding Picture Library 62tl; Hitachi High-Technologies Co. Ltd 611tr; Michael Holford/British Museum 372bl, Michael Holford 374tr; Honda 354tr, 355b; Hutchison Picture Library 60cl; The Image Bank/Edward Bower 306tr; Jet Propulsion Laboratory 11cbr; 30bc; 31bc; 31bcr; 38tl; 42crb; 44cb; 44cbr; 44bc; 44br; 46tl; 46cr; 46cb; 46bc; 46br; 50tl; 50cra; 50cl; 50c; 50cr; 50br; KeyMed Ltd 248bl, 249bl, 249bcl; Department of Prints and Drawings, Uffizi, Florence/Philip Gatward 431tc/Uffizi, Florence/Philip Gatward 433tl; Robin Kerrod/Spacecharts 615br; Dr D.N. Landon (Institute of Neurology) 228bl,br; Life Science Images/Ron Boardman 244bl, 244br; The Lund Observatory 15bc; Microsoft Coporation 579cr; Brian Morrison 329tl, 329tr; © The Henry Moore Foundation 455tr; Musée d'Orsay, Paris/Philippe Sebert 437tc, 441tc;

Musée du Louvre, Paris/Philippe Sebert 453tl, 453l, 453br; Musictrack/MOTU Digital performer 521bcl; NASA/AUI 13tr; NASA/JPL 11 cbr, 11br, 30tl, 30bl, 30br, 30bc, 31bc, 31bcr, 31bl, 34cr, 38tl, 40tl, 40cr, 42cr, 44tl, 44cb, 44cbr, 44bc, 44br, 44cr, 46crb, 46tl, 46cr, 46cb, 46bc, 46br, 48tl, 48cra, 48bca, 48bc, 48br, 50tl, 50bc, 50bc, 50cbr, 50br, 50cr, 52cr, 612cr, 612tr, 613tl, 613tcl, 613tcr, 613tr, 613c, 613cr, 614cl, 614cbl, 614bl, 614c, 614r, 615tr, 615cr; National Maritime Museum 373br, 392-393b; National Medical Slide Bank 217cr; Nature Photographers/Paul Sterry 286tl; Newage International 317bl; Nintendo Co. Ltd 579br; Nintendo Magazine 578tc,578cl, 578cbl,578bl; Olympus 610cl, 610bl; Oxford Scientific Films/Breck P. Kent 166tl; Planet Earth 274tr; Quadrant 326tr; Margaret Robinson 332tl; Giotto The Expulsion of the Merchants from the Temple Scala 435tc, 435bl, 435br; Science Photo Library 10bl, 13tr, 28tr, 214bcr, 214bl, 236tr/Michael Abbey 225tc/Agema Infrared Systems 318tl/AGFA 220tl/Alex Barte 605tr/David Becker 607cr/Biophoto Associates: 217crb/Dr Jeremy Burgess/Science Photo Library 132tr; Dr Jeremy Burgess 235bcl/CNRI 214tl, 214cl, 214c, 214cr, 214bl, 214clb, 214crb, 214blc, 214br, 217cb, 235bcr, 238tl, 249bcr, 253tr, 253cra, 256tl; Science Photo library /Earth Satellite Corporation 288cl, 293br/Dr Brian Eyden 228cbr/Professor C. Ferlaud 245bl/Vaughan Fleming 311tl/Simon Fraser/U.S. Dept.of Energy 214bcl, 266tl/Eric Grave 217br/Hale Observatories 32br/Max Planck Institute for Radio Astronomy 15tl/Jan Hinsch 225tc/Jodrell Bank 11 tr, 13c /Manfred Kage 217c, 235br, 237br/Dr William C. Keel 13br/Keith Kent 564c/James King-Holmes 316tl, 606bl/Russ Lappa 310bra/John Mead 605br/Astrid & Hans-Freider Michler 217tr/Dennis Milon 52bl/NASA 11cla, 12tl, 15tr, 30c, 31br, 32tl, 35tl, 36tl, 36cl, 36cr, 36bc, 42br, 42tr, 44tl 52tl, 291tr, 300tl/National Optical Astro Observatory 52tr/NIBSC 253crb/Novosti Press Agency 42bc/Sam Ogden 609c, 609tr/Omikron 244bc/David Parker 63bl, 304-305, 308br/Alfred Pasieka 606cr/Philippe Plailly 308tl/Quest

611br/Roussel-UCLAF/CNRI 217tc/Rev Ronald Royer 32cr/Royal Observatory, Edinburgh/D Malin 11tl, 11cr,12c, 16cl, 16cr, 17br/David Scharf 235bl/Dr Kaus Schiller 248bcl, 248bcr, 248br/Secchi-Lecaque/Roussel-UCLAF/CNRI 253br/H. Sochurek 214cb/Stammers/Thompson 230tl/Sheila Terry 234tl/US Department of Energy 310bc/U.S Geological Survey/Science Photo Library 8-9, 30bcr, 42tl, 42bl/Tom Van Sant/Geosphere Project, Santa Monica/Science Photo Library 273tr, 281tr, 296tr, 297tl/Dr Christopher B. Williams/(Saint Marks Hospital) 249br; Oxford Scientific Films/Animals Animals/Breck P. Kent 167tl; Palm 568tc, 568cl,569tl,569tcl,569tc; Pratt & Whitney Canada 418-419b, 419t; Science Museum 306bl,306bcl. 306 bcr, 324t, 326-327b, 330tr, 331ct, 331 cb; Sony Corporation 579tr, 608bl; Sony Ericsson 588cr; Sporting Pictures 524tl, 544cr; Tony Stone Worldwide 280tl; David Bomberg St Pauls and River 1945/Dinora Davies-Rees/Tate Gallery 431bc; David Hockney A Bigger Splash 1967/ © David Hockney/Tate Gallery 443tc; J.M.W. Turner The Burning of the Houses of Parliament Tate Gallery 439tc; Vision 26tr, 27c; Jerry Young 306tl; Dr Robert Youngson 241cr; courtesy of Vestas Wind Systems 604t; Zefa 217bc/Janicek 276tl/H. Sochurek 210tl, 250tl, 254tl,/ G. Steenmans 292tl;

Jacket:
Indianapolis Motor Speedway Foundation front cover bc; NASA background to 2001 on spine, front cover, front inside flap

(t=top, b=bottom, a=above, l-left, r=right, c=centre)

Every effort has been made to trace the copyright holders. Dorling Kindersley apologises for any unintentional omissions and would be pleased, in any such cases, to add an acknowledgment in future editions.

Some pages in this book previously appeared in the *Visual Dictionary* series published by Dorling Kindersley. Contributors to this series include:

Project Art Editors: Duncan Brown, Ross George, Nicola Liddiard, Andrew Nash, Clare Shedden, Bryn Walls

Designers: Lesley Betts, Paul Calver, Simone End, Ellen Woodward

Additional design assistance: Sandra Archer, Christina Betts, Alexandra Brown, Nick Jackson, Susan Knight

Project Editors: Fiona Courtney-Thompson, Paul Docherty, Tim Fraser, Stephanie Jackson, Mary Lindsay

Editorial Assistant: Emily Hill

Additional editorial assistance: Susan Bosanko, Edward Bunting, Candace Burch, Deirdre Clark, Jeanette Cossar, Danièle Guitton, Jacqui Hand, David Harding, Nicholas Jackson, Edwina Johnson, David Lambert, Gail Lawther, David Learmount, Paul Jackson, Christine Murdock, Bob Ogden, Cathy Rubinstein, Louise Tucker, Dr Robert Youngson

Picture Researchers: Vere Dodds, Danièle Guitton, Anna Lord, Catherine O'Rourke, Christine Rista, Sandra Schneider, Vanessa Smith, Clive Webster

Series Editor: Martyn Page

Series Art Editor: Paul Wilkinson

Managing Art Editors: Philip Gilderdale, Steve Knowlden

Art Director: Chez Picthall

Managing Editor: Ruth Midgley

Production: Jayne Simpson